MORIARTY'S POLICE LAW

An Arrangement of Law and Regulations for the Use of Police Officers

First Edition	*February 1929*
Second Edition	*April 1931*
Third Edition	*November 1933*
Fourth Edition	*July 1935*
Fifth Edition	*May 1937*
Sixth Edition	*May 1939*
War Edition (Seventh)	*March 1941*
War Edition (Eighth)	*February 1945*
Ninth Edition	*January 1948*
Tenth Edition	*January 1950*
Eleventh Edition	*September 1951*
Twelfth Edition	*August 1953*
Thirteenth Edition	*August 1954*
Fourteenth Edition	*February 1957*
Fifteenth Edition	*May 1959*
Sixteenth Edition	*June 1961*
Seventeenth Edition	*May 1963*
Eighteenth Edition	*April 1965*
Nineteenth Edition	*March 1968*
Twentieth Edition	*June 1970*
Twenty-first Edition	*June 1972*
Twenty-second Edition	*July 1974*
Twenty-third Edition	*September 1976*

MORIARTY'S POLICE LAW

An Arrangement of Law and Regulations for the Use of Police Officers

TWENTY-THIRD EDITION

BY THE LATE

Sir WILLIAM J. WILLIAMS

K.C.V.O., O.B.E., Q.P.M., D.L., B.Sc., LL.B.
formerly Chief Constable of the Gwynedd Constabulary

LONDON
BUTTERWORTHS
1976

ENGLAND: BUTTERWORTH & CO. (PUBLISHERS) LTD.
LONDON: 88 KINGSWAY, WC2B 6AB

AUSTRALIA: BUTTERWORTHS PTY. LTD.
SYDNEY: 586 PACIFIC HIGHWAY, CHATSWOOD, NSW 2067
ALSO AT MELBOURNE, BRISBANE, ADELAIDE AND PERTH

CANADA: BUTTERWORTH & CO. (CANADA) LTD.
TORONTO: 2265 MIDLAND AVENUE, SCARBOROUGH, M1P 4S1

NEW ZEALAND: BUTTERWORTHS OF NEW ZEALAND LTD.
WELLINGTON: 26/28 WARING TAYLOR STREET, 1

SOUTH AFRICA: BUTTERWORTH & CO. (SOUTH AFRICA) (PTY.) LTD.
DURBAN: 152/154 GALE STREET

U.S.A.: BUTTERWORTH & CO. (PUBLISHERS) INC.
BOSTON: 19 CUMMINGS PARK, WOBURN, MASS. 01801

ISBN 0 406 84607 3

PREFACE TO TWENTY-THIRD EDITION

In presenting the Twenty-third Edition of Moriarty's Police Law, once again I wish to draw attention to what I have reiterated on many occasions, namely the difficulty created by the modern method of bringing Acts of Parliament into operation by the "appointed day" procedure. Certain recent Acts of Parliament are marred by poor drafting, circumlocution and obscurity. It is high time Sir Ernest Gower's book *Plain English* became compulsory study for Parliamentary Draftsmen and the Civil Service.

Since the last edition, the following Acts, in addition to many regulations, have been noted:

Hallmarking Act 1973
Slaughterhouses Act 1974
Biological Weapons Act 1974
Rabies Act 1974
Consumer Credit Act 1974
Merchant Shipping Act 1974
Road Traffic Act 1974
Trade Union and Labour Relations Act 1974
Rehabilitation of Offenders Act 1974
Prevention of Terrorism Act 1974
Nursing Homes Act 1975
Diseases of Animals Act 1975
Salmon and Freshwater Fisheries Act 1975
Safety of Sports Grounds Act 1975
Public Service Vehicles (Arrest of Offenders) Act 1975
Lotteries Act 1975
Guard Dogs Act 1975.

Once again I am grateful to various people who have written to me and as I have been in ill-health for the last few months, I have relied heavily on the great assistance I have received from

Ex-Chief Superintendent Islwyn Jones of the North Wales Police.

W. J. Williams

Caernarvon
February, 1976

SIR WILLIAM WILLIAMS

Just seven weeks after writing his Preface to this edition, Sir William died. Despite failing health he was determined to complete his revision of *Moriarty* for the Twenty-third Edition. Such was his regard and affection for the book that nothing would deter him from finishing the task which he had set himself and started.

Sir William joined the Birmingham City Police in 1926 with a science degree and subsequently graduated in law. He became Chief Constable of Caernarvonshire in 1946 and from 1950 to 1970 he was Chief Constable of the Gwynedd Constabulary. In 1969 he was created a K.C.V.O. for his work in connection with the Investiture of the Prince of Wales.

Sir William was born into the Police Service, his father being a member of the former Merioneth Constabulary, and throughout his life was devoted to the Service. It was a source of considerable delight to him that he was given the opportunity to carry on the work of Mr. Moriarty.

Islwyn Jones

June, 1976

PREFACE TO FIFTEENTH EDITION

For the first time this is a new Edition of Police Law without a preface by the author, Mr. Cecil Charles Hudson Moriarty, C.B.E., LL.D.

After distinguishing himself at Trinity College, Dublin, Mr. Moriarty joined the Royal Irish Constabulary in 1902. In 1918 he was appointed Assistant Chief Constable of Birmingham, becoming Chief Constable in 1935. In 1941 he retired from the police service but continued to take an active part in the revision of the police books he had written until he was taken ill shortly before his death in April, 1958.

The first edition of Police Law appeared in 1929 and was described by the late Sir Charles Rafter in his foreword as a book which went a long way in providing in a comprehensive form the knowledge which a constable finds difficult to obtain. During the following 30 years, Fourteen Editions and Seventeen Impressions of Police Law have been published. This proves that Mr. Moriarty in writing what has become the standard text-book of the policeman has ensured for himself the gratitude and esteem of generations of policemen.

Those who had the privilege of serving with Mr. Moriarty can testify to his gifts for hard work, clear thinking and his exceptional ability to condense abstruse legal phraseology into lucid and simple language.

Much of the revision necessary for the present edition had been approved by Mr. Moriarty before he was taken ill at the beginning of 1958, and the revision has been completed upon the lines which he himself laid down.

W. J. WILLIAMS

CAERNARVON
January, 1959

PREFACE TO FIRST EDITION

The author has compiled this book with the view of assisting police officers in attaining a working knowledge of the law that they have to enforce.

The law dealing with each offence and with its kindred offences has been brought together under appropriate headings, and the chapters have been arranged in an order suitable for instructional purposes.

Legal principles and the more serious crimes are but briefly dealt with, and students would do well to study the law thereon as given in such standard text-books as Harris's Criminal Law and Archbold's Criminal Pleading, Evidence and Practice.

More prominence is given to the many Acts of Parliament and Statutory Orders and Regulations which should be known by the police, and which, of course, are to be found in Stone's Justices' Manual.

Particulars are given of the powers and duties entrusted to the police by law, and the book should prove useful in Police Training Schools, as in it a recruit may study Police Law and thus be able to follow his instructors when dealing with the steps to be taken for its practical enforcement.

It should also be useful to police officers desirous of refreshing their knowledge of Police Law, either preparatory to sitting for an examination, or with the object of becoming more proficient in their professional duties.

The author takes this opportunity of expressing his thanks to Mr. A. E. Field, of the Birmingham Prosecuting Solicitor's Staff, and to Superintendent B. D. Pinkerton, formerly Police Instructor in the Birmingham City Police Training School, for their assistance in revising the proofs.

C. C. H. MORIARTY

BIRMINGHAM
January, 1929

TABLE OF CONTENTS

	PAGE
PREFACE TO TWENTY-THIRD EDITION	v
PREFACE TO FIFTEENTH EDITION	vii
PREFACE TO FIRST EDITION	viii
ABBREVIATIONS	xviii
FOREWORD BY THE LATE SIR CHARLES HAUGHTON RAFTER, K.B.E., CHIEF CONSTABLE OF THE BIRMINGHAM CITY POLICE FORCE	xix

PART I. LEGAL PRINCIPLES, PROCEDURE AND EVIDENCE

CHAPTER 1. CRIME . . . 3
Law. Crime. Proof of Criminal Intent. Motive. Crime and Offence. Classification of Crime. Indictable Offences. Punishment for Crime. Excuses for Crime. Exemptions from Liability for Crime. Remission of Penalty.

CHAPTER 2. CRIMINALS . . . 12
Criminals. Incitement to Crime. Attempt to Commit Crime. Accomplice. Accessories to a Crime. Assisting Offenders. Concealing Offences or Giving False Information. Extradition. Convicted Persons.

CHAPTER 3. ARREST . . . 17
Arrest without Warrant at Common Law and by Statute. Arrest with Warrant. Re-Arrest.

CHAPTER 4. COURTS OF JUSTICE . . . 29
Courts of Justice. Justices of the Peace. Proceedings before Justices. Trial by Jury. Progress of a Case. Open Court. Speeches in Court.

PAGE

CHAPTER 5. PROCEDURE 44
Information. Affidavit. Summons. Subpoena. Indictment. Venue. Accused or Defendant. Finger-Prints. Warrants. Commitment. Detention by Police. Recognizance. Bail. Bail by Police. Remand. Acquittal. Appeal. Case Stated. Certiorari and Mandamus. Habeas Corpus. Limitation of Proceedings. Costs in Criminal Cases. Director of Public Prosecutions. Justices' Clerks Rules 1970.

CHAPTER 6. RECORD OF EVIDENCE 70
Judges' Rules. Notes on the Judges' Rules. Administrative Directions on Interrogation and the Taking of Statements. Admissions and Confessions. Dying Declaration. Deposition. Taking of Depositions of Persons dangerously ill.

CHAPTER 7. EVIDENCE 81
Evidence. Oath or Affirmation. Number of Witnesses. Corroborative Evidence. Evidence for the Prosecution. Accused Persons and their Husbands or Wives. Competency of Witnesses. Witnesses out of Court. Interference with Witnesses. Nature of Evidence. Parol or Oral Evidence. Proof by Written Statement. Proof by Formal Admission. Documentary Evidence. Evidence by Certificate. Hearsay Evidence. Opinion. Handwriting. Extent of Evidence. Circumstantial Evidence. Presumptions. Privilege. Leading Questions. Refreshing Memory. Hostile Witness. Unwilling Witness. Onus or Burden of Proof. Examination-in-chief. Cross-examination. Re-examination. Recalling a Witness. Rebutting Evidence. Notice of Alibi. Character after Conviction. Previous Convictions. The Perfect Witness.

PART II. OFFENCES AGAINST PERSONS

CHAPTER 8. ASSAULT 105
Assault. Statutory Assaults. Assaulting, Obstructing or Resisting the Police. Powers of Arrest. Wounding and other

PAGE

Serious Assaults. Threats and Menaces. Blackmail. Hijacking Act 1971. Protection of Aircraft Act 1973.

CHAPTER 9. HOMICIDE 112
Homicide. Murder. Manslaughter. Suicide. Legal Consequences of Homicide and kindred Offences. Genocide Act 1969. Search Warrant: 1861 Act.

CHAPTER 10. OFFENCES AGAINST FEMALES 117
Sexual Offences. Rape and Similar Offences. Indecent Assault. Incest. Procuration. Abduction of Females. Prostitution. Harbouring Prostitutes. Brothels. Arrest and Search Warrant.

CHAPTER 11. INDECENCY 127
Indecent Conduct, by Language, by Exhibitions and by Exposure. Indecent Publications and Advertisements. Unnatural Crimes. Sexual Offences Act 1967. Indecency with Children Act 1960.

CHAPTER 12. CHILDREN AND PERSONS UNDER 21 . . . 135
Abortion. Child Destruction. Infanticide. Concealment of Birth. Abandoning Child. Children and Young Persons. Child Protection. Cruelty. Arrest, Search Warrant and Procedure. Smoking. Care. Education. Employment. Entertainment. Dangerous Performances. Powers of Entry. Restriction on Persons under 18 going Abroad for Employment. Treatment of Youthful Offenders. Remand Centres. Detention Centres. Attendance Centres. Community Service. Harmful Publications. Tattooing of Minors Act 1969. Ages fixed by Law.

PART III. OFFENCES IN CONNECTION WITH PROPERTY

CHAPTER 13. BURGLARY 163
Burglary. Aggravated Burglary.

CHAPTER 14. THEFT 164
Basic Definition. Robbery. Removal of Articles from Places open to the Public,

PAGE

Taking Motor Vehicles, etc. Abstracting Electricity. Thefts from Mails outside England and Wales. Obtaining Property by Deception. Obtaining Pecuniary Advantage by Deception. False Accounting. Liability of Company Officers. False Statements by Company Directors. Suppression of Documents. Handling Stolen Goods. Advertising Rewards. Scope of Offences relating to Stolen Goods. Going Equipped for Stealing. Interpretation. Taking or Killing Deer. Taking or Destroying Fish. Bankruptcy Offences. Compensation Orders.

CHAPTER 15. CRIMINAL DAMAGE 176
Destroying or Damaging Property. Threats. Possession of Articles with Intent. Search Warrant.

CHAPTER 16. COINAGE 179
Arrest, Seizure and Evidence. Counterfeit Currency (Convention) Act 1935.

CHAPTER 17. FORGERY 183
Forgery. Principal Forgery Offences. Paper Money Offences.

CHAPTER 18. PROPERTY 187
Property in General. Treasure Trove. Police (Property) Act 1897. Restitution of Stolen Property. Public Stores. Wrecks.

CHAPTER 19. POACHING 195
Poaching Offences. Game Laws. Deer Act 1963. Fishery Laws. Trespass.

PART IV. OFFENCES AFFECTING THE COMMUNITY IN GENERAL

CHAPTER 20. OFFENCES AGAINST THE STATE AND RELIGION 205
Treason. Sedition. Drilling. Biological Weapons. Prevention of Terrorism (Temporary Provisions) Act 1974. Official Secrets Acts. Unauthorised Disclosure of Spent Convictions. Piracy. Foreign Enlistment Act 1870. Blasphemy. Disturbing Public Worship. Bigamy.

PAGE

CHAPTER 21. PUBLIC JUSTICE OFFENCES 216
Contempt of Court. Escape. Prison Breach. Rescue. Pound Breach. Perjury. Bribery. Extortion. Misconduct by Public Officers. Election Offences. Obstructing Public Justice.

CHAPTER 22. PUBLIC ORDER 225
Breach of the Peace and Sureties. Sureties of the Peace and for Good Behaviour. Affray. Unlawful Assembly. Riot. Riot Damage. Forcible Entry and Detainer. Labour Disputes. Intimidation. Breaking Contract of Service. Public Order Act 1936. Rent Act 1965. Administration of Justice Act 1970 (Harassment of Debtors). Meetings. Emergency Powers.

CHAPTER 23. CONSPIRACY AND DEFAMATION 237
Conspiracy. Libel. Slander.

PART V. TRAFFIC LAW

CHAPTER 24. TRAFFIC 243
Highways, Streets and Roads. Obstruction. Highway Act 1835, s. 72. Town Police Clauses Act 1847, s. 28. Highways Act 1959. Highways Act 1971. Impounding Animals. Regulation of Traffic. Road Traffic Acts, etc. Police Powers: Road Traffic Act 1972 and Theft Act 1968.

CHAPTER 25. ROAD VEHICLES 336
Vehicles. Pedal Cycles. Hackney Carriages and Stage Coaches. Public Service Vehicles. Goods Vehicles. Drivers' Hours. Mechanically Propelled Vehicles. Registration and Licensing of Vehicles. Exhibition of Licences and Registration Marks. Vehicles exempt from Licence Duty. Trade Licences. Hackney Carriages. Foreign-owned Motor Vehicles. Road Traffic (Foreign Vehicles) Act 1972. Construction and Use of Motor Vehicles and Trailers.

PAGE

CHAPTER 26. COMMUNICATIONS 376
Post Office. Telegraphs. Wireless. Railways. Merchant Shipping Acts. Air Navigation. Smuggling.

PART VI. OTHER STATUTORY OFFENCES AND REGULATIONS

CHAPTER 27. VAGRANCY AND CHARITY 389
Vagrancy Acts. Fraudulent Mediums. Charities. Street Collections. War Charities Act 1940. House to House Collections Act 1939 and Regulations 1947. Common Lodging-houses.

CHAPTER 28. PREVENTION OF CRIME. 399
Penalties. Discharge of Offenders. Probation of Offenders. Borstal Institution. Persistent Offenders. Loiterers and Suspected Persons. Prisons. Restriction of Offensive Weapons.

CHAPTER 29. PERSONS 410
Aliens. Immigration Act 1971. Husband and Wife. Landlord and Tenant. Clergyman. Constables. Lawyers, etc. Doctors. Dentists. Veterinary Surgeons. Farriers. Pharmaceutical Chemists. Opticians. Nurses. Midwives. Master and Servant. Architects. Personation.

CHAPTER 30. HER MAJESTY'S FORCES 420
Interference with Military. False Characters. False Discharges. Deserters and Absentees. Property of H.M. Forces. Pensioners. Uniforms. Decorations. Billeting. Requisitioning of Vehicles. Incitement to Disaffection Act 1934.

CHAPTER 31. DEALERS 426
Scrap Metal Dealers. Pedlars. Hawkers. Game Dealers. Police Prosecutions. Domestic Servants' Registries. Dealers in Securities. Mock Auctions Act 1961. Protection of Depositors Act 1963. Ministry of Social Security Act 1966.

PAGE

CHAPTER 32. TRADE 436
Business Names. Printing and Publishing. Trade Marks. Trade Description. Hall-marks. Weights and Measures. Food and Drugs. Shops. Trading Representations (Disabled Persons) Act 1958. Trading Stamps Act 1964. Consumer Credit Act 1974.

CHAPTER 33. EXPLOSIVES 446
Explosives Offences. Petroleum. Petroleum Spirit Conveyance. Regulations. Tank Wagons and Tank Trailers. Carbide of Calcium. Acetylene. Celluloid and Cinematograph Film. Carbon Disulphide. Gas Cylinders' Conveyance.

CHAPTER 34. FIREARMS 458
Firearms Act 1968. Firearm Certificate. Shotgun Certificate. Firearms Dealers. Conversion of Weapons. Prohibitions and Exemptions. Criminal Use of Firearms. Possession of Firearms by Minors. Supplying Firearms to Minors, Person Drunk or Insane. Grant, Renewal, Variation and Revocation of Firearm Certificates. Police Register. Gun Barrel Proof Acts 1868 and 1950.

CHAPTER 35. ANIMALS 479
Diseases of Animals. Cruelty to Animals. Prevention of Unnecessary Pain. Operations on Animals. Injured Animals. Performing Animals. Horses. Dogs. Birds. Destructive Imported Animals Act 1932. Slaughter of Animals. Riding Establishments. Pet Animals. Animal Boarding Establishments. Conservation of Seals Act 1970. Animals Act 1971. Badgers Act 1973.

CHAPTER 36. BETTING AND GAMING 503
Betting, Gaming and Lotteries Act 1963. Betting. Lotteries and Prize Competitions. Amusements with Prizes. Gaming Act 1968.

PAGE

CHAPTER 37. PUBLIC ENTERTAINMENTS 529
Theatres. Sunday Theatre Act 1972. Theatrical Employers Registration Act 1925. Cinematograph Acts. Music, Singing and Dancing. Billiards. Ingress and Egress. Sunday Entertainments Act 1932. Hypnotism Act 1952. Safety of Sports Grounds.

CHAPTER 38. LIQUOR LICENSING LAWS 542
Licensed Premises and Intoxicating Liquor. Justices' Licences. Excise Licences and Law. Occasional Licence. Hotel. Restaurants and Guest Houses. Billiards. Sale of Tobacco. Billeting. Music, etc. Licensing Justices. Grant of Licences. Renewal of Licences. Transfer of Licences. Removal of Licence. Appeal. Register of Licences. Disqualified Persons and Premises. Permitted Hours. Extended Hours. Seasonal Licences. Exemption Order. Compulsory Closing. The Licensed Premises. Conduct of Licensed Premises. Sale of Intoxicants. Offences, not of Drunkenness, by non-licensed Persons. Prosecution. Police Powers of Entry. Drunkenness. Clubs. Seamen's Canteens. Late Night Refreshment Houses. Licensing, New Towns. Methylated Spirits.

CHAPTER 39. PUBLIC HEALTH 572
Public Health Acts. Poisons. Misuse of Drugs Act 1971. Mental Health. Nursing Homes. Births, Deaths and Marriages. Burials. Fires. Coroners and Inquests. Fumigation. Unauthorised Dumping. Poisonous Waste. Abatement of Litter. Noise Abatement.

APPENDIX I. Speed Limits for Motor Vehicles . . 589

APPENDIX II. Regulations as to the Construction and Use of Motor Vehicles and Trailers . 599

APPENDIX III. Regulations as to the Prosecution of Offences 668

APPENDIX IV. Prosecution and Punishment of Road Traffic Offences 671

	PAGE
APPENDIX V. Principal Arrestable Offences	697
APPENDIX VI. The Justices' Clerks Rules 1970	701
TABLE OF STATUTES	703
TABLE OF CASES	737
TABLE OF ORDERS, REGULATIONS AND RULES	743
INDEX	749

ABBREVIATIONS

B.G. & L. Act = Betting, Gaming and Lotteries Act.
C.A. Act = Criminal Appeal Act.
C.J. Act = Criminal Justice Act.
C.J.A. Act = Criminal Justice Administration Act.
C.L. Act = Criminal Law Act.
C.P. (A. of W.) Act = Criminal Procedure (Attendance of Witnesses) Act.
C. & Y.P. Act = Children and Young Persons Act.
D.P.P. = Director of Public Prosecutions.
h.g.v. = Heavy goods vehicle.
L.G. Act = Local Government Act.
M.C. Act = Magistrates' Courts Act.
M.C. Rules = Magistrates' Courts Rules.
M.V. (C. & U.) Regs. = Motor Vehicle (Construction and Use) Regulations.
O.A.P. Act = Offences Against the Person Act.
P. of C.C. Act = Powers of Criminal Courts Act.
P.S.V. = Public Service Vehicle.
R. & R.T. Act = Road and Rail Traffic Act.
R.S. Act = Road Safety Act.
R.T. Act = Road Traffic Act.
R.T. (D.I.) Act = Road Traffic (Driving Instruction) Act.
R.T.L. Act = Road Transport Lighting Act.
R.T.L. (A.) Act = Road Transport Lighting (Amendment) Act.
R.T.R. Act = Road Traffic Regulation Act.
R.T. & R.I. Act = Road Traffic and Roads Improvement Act.
R.V.L. Regs. = Road Vehicles Lighting Regulations.
T. Act = Transport Act.
T.P.C. Act = Town Police Clauses Act.

FOREWORD TO FIRST EDITION

BY THE LATE SIR CHARLES HAUGHTON RAFTER, K.B.E.
CHIEF CONSTABLE OF THE BIRMINGHAM CITY POLICE FORCE

IN writing these remarks I feel impelled to make a few observations upon the police themselves.

After a long and varied experience of them and of the way in which they perform their various duties I must give unqualified testimony to my admiration and respect for the Police Forces of this country. Their fairness to and consideration for prisoners —as for any one in distress—their tact, their courtesy, the many little acts of kindness that they do so quietly and unostentatiously from day to day, their great services to the public, have so endeared them to me that I am proud to reckon myself one of their number.

Only one closely associated with them can realise the immense knowledge possessed by the police of the intimate private lives and affairs of so many people. Yet never a hint of these matters is ever made public. The police force is, indeed, a silent service. What social mischief would ensue, were it otherwise, it is impossible to imagine. The public are justified in the confidence they place in their integrity and discretion.

In the course of his daily duties the constable must encounter many matters of much difficulty upon which he must decide on the instant—matters calling for tact, judgment, knowledge of the law and of his duties, and for decision of character.

To anyone responsible for the administration of a great police force one experience which recurs from time to time must make him think. It is the occasion of a great criminal trial, or perhaps a great criminal appeal. Ranged on each side are the best legal brains and the best legal knowledge in the country, and, on the Bench, some of our most learned and most distinguished Judges.

Many conferences have been held, and great time and large fees have been spent in obtaining the best legal advice, and in putting the case forward in its best legal aspect, both by the prosecution and the defence. The Court—both bench and bar—is piled up with legal reference books. Case after case is quoted and debated. There is much discussion of the "Judges' Rules".

In the midst of all this there is a solitary police constable. He is the principal witness for the prosecution. He is in charge of the case. Naturally the question arises, "What's it all about?" It is the conduct or the action of the constable that is being discussed.

Quite away from any help or legal advice, alone and unassisted by books of reference, he has arrested a man for murder who is now on trial or appealing against his conviction. The great question now is whether the constable has acted legally—in making the arrest, in cautioning his prisoner, in taking a voluntary statement from him which he now denies or alleges to have been extorted, in the method by which the prisoner has been identified, and in many other points which counsel, at their leisure, after consulting their clients and their books, most ingeniously devise. Clearly the constable is on his trial as well as the accused.

As he goes on his daily tour of duty he knows not what is in store for him, or what emergency he may encounter. It behoves him to adopt the Boy Scouts' motto and "Be Prepared" for any eventuality that may arise. He will have no time to consult musty reference books. The law and his knowledge of duty must be in his head, upon which he can alone rely to do the right thing at the right time; so that he may emerge unscathed from the ordeal of legal criticism that he must encounter later on.

The constable suffers from many disabilities, not the least of which is the paucity of those books from which he may make himself master of his powers and duties.

Of these powers and duties, that of arrest with all its concomitants is the greatest, as well as his greatest responsibility.

The Common Law with regard to arrests is very complicated, depending as it does on abstruse definitions of various crimes, and their division into felonies, misdemeanours, and minor offences, or petty misdemeanours, the power of arrest varying in each case.

In felonies and misdemeanours the power of arrest comes from the Common Law and Statutes; in case of minor offences the police can only arrest where the statute creating the offence gives that power.

In felonies and misdemeanours also the powers of arrest vary in accordance with a variety of circumstances. The Common

Law of arrest is interpreted, or amended also from time to time by an immense number of judgments in what is called "Case Law". These legal decisions are intended to make the law clear for the guidance of the Courts and for lawyers.

There is no concise and easily understood direction for the guidance of constables. The main books of reference also are inaccessible to the ordinary constable.

At a meeting of the Chief Constables' Association on May 30, 1918, in an address I said:

"Consider that most important subject, the powers and duties of constables in making arrests. I do not know any book published for the use of the English police forces which gives full and adequate instruction on this subject. The best instruction for police that I know is in the Irish Constables' Guide, by the late Sir Andrew Reed, K.C.B., Inspector-General of the Royal Irish Constabulary.

In order to compile a complete and exhaustive instruction on this point one has to consult many books. In none of the ordinary law books available by the police can one find the subject treated as a whole. For example, in Stone's Justices. Manual it is dealt with in scraps in over fifty different places' In Archbold's Pleading, Evidence and Practice in Criminal Cases, in about twenty. The reason of this is that these books are not written for police purposes. The most comprehensive statement of the law on this subject, and the standard authority, is Burn's Justice of the Peace (now out of print); but, to complete it, one has to consult many others, including not only those above referred to, but Blackstone's Commentaries, Russell on Crimes, and other standard works

These books are not wi.thin reach of the ordinary police constable. How, then, is he to know the law, and his powers and duty under it, if this instruction is not collected from its various sources and put before him in the form of a comprehensive book?"

These being my views on the subject of police instruction, I congratulate Mr. Moriarty on his meticulously careful preparation of this book of "Police Law", which goes a long way in providing in a comprehensive form that knowledge which the constable finds it difficult to obtain.

The book shows much evidence of careful research and co-ordination. I think it will supply a long-felt want to many members of the Police Service.

C. H. Rafter

Birmingham
December, 1928

PART I – LEGAL PRINCIPLES, PROCEDURE AND EVIDENCE

CHAPTER 1

CRIME

	Page		Page
Law	3	Indictable Offences . .	7
Crime	5	Punishment for Crime .	8
Proof of Criminal Intent .	5	Excuses for Crime . .	8
Motive	5	Exemptions from Liability for Crime . . .	10
Crime and Offence . .	6	Remission of Penalty .	11
Classification of Crime .	6		

Law – A law is defined by the great lawyer Blackstone as a rule of action prescribed or dictated by some superior which an inferior is bound to obey. It also has been defined as a rule of action to which men are bound to make their conduct conform.

The word "law" implies obedience. When the laws of nature, of a country, of sport are referred to, it means those rules which people, citizens, sportsmen should obey.

The word law also implies penalty or sanction—namely, that if a law is broken some punishment ought to fall on the breaker, so as to prevent a repetition of the breach and to deter others from doing likewise.

The law of a country means the rules of conduct under which the people of that country live, and without which no person could hope to live peaceably and in safety as regards himself and his belongings. These rules either have gradually come into existence by the general agreement of the people or have been prescribed by those responsible for the government of the country.

Obedience to law must be enforced and the duty of enforcing the laws is assigned to the police, who are responsible to the State and to the people for the proper performance of their duty.

The law of England is composed of two kinds of laws, viz.:

(1) The Common Law, which is made up of those general customs which have been regarded as laws in the land from time immemorial. By general agreement endorsed by the practice of the courts certain rules of conduct have by custom become laws—and these laws are known as the common law. Breaches of these laws are termed common law offences—for example: affray and conspiracy.

It is now much easier and speedier to create laws by written statute or order of the ruling authority, but it is still possible to deal with an act tending to the prejudice of the community, not especially provided for by the law, by bringing the offender before a judge and jury, who, by convicting him, will thus create another common law offence.

(2) The Statute Law, which includes all the laws made by direct order of the State and set out in Acts of Parliament or Statutes, which are ordinances made by the supreme power in this country, which is Parliament, consisting of the Sovereign, the House of Lords, and the House of Commons.

Such a law, in the form of a **Bill,** is usually proposed in the House of Commons. It is there discussed and if necessary amended, and if then approved it has to pass in the same manner through the House of Lords before it is presented to the Sovereign for assent.

When a Bill has received the Royal Assent it becomes a **Statute** or **Act of Parliament,** and is known by a short name or title indicating its purport, and it may also be referred to by its chapter or number in the year of the reign of the Sovereign during whose reign it was passed.

Thus a Statute passed in the year 1933 dealing with the prevention of cruelty to children and other matters is known as the Children & Young Persons Act 1933 and as 23 Geo. 5, c. 12. Usually several Statutes are enacted during each year of a Sovereign's reign, so they are numbered in the order of their passing as chapters in the complete law made during that year. Also each Statute or Act is subdivided into parts or sections to facilitate reference to the particular points dealt with.

Thus 23 Geo. 5, c. 12, s. 7, means the 7th section of the 12th Act of Parliament passed in the 23rd year of the reign of King George the Fifth—viz. 1933. However, by the Acts of Parliament Numbering and Citation Act 1962, the chapter numbers of Acts of Parliament passed in 1963 and after are assigned by reference to the *calendar* year in which they are passed, as opposed to the *regnal* year (or year of the sovereign's reign) mentioned above. Thus the first Act to receive the Royal Assent after January 1, 1963, was cited as "1963, c. 1" and the Betting, Gaming and Lotteries Act 1963 as "1963, c. 2". Statutes may empower the making of Regulations or Statutory Orders or Rules all now termed "Statutory Instruments" (see Statutory Instruments Act 1946) which also have the force of law.

Many offences which were originally common law offences have been dealt with by Act of Parliament; hence an offence may be both a common law offence and a statutory offence.

Crime – Stephen's Criminal Law defines a crime as an act of disobedience of the law forbidden under pain of punishment. Punishment in this criminal sense may be death or loss of liberty or (and) money penalty. There is however another kind of disobedience of law called a "civil injury", which is a wrongful act injuring some person or persons but which does not disturb the community in general. Eminent lawyers have framed definitions of the word "crime", designed to show the difference between a crime and a civil injury, but the difficulty is that both are breaches of law, and for some wrongful acts (such as assault) both civil and criminal remedies are available.

Generally speaking, a crime affects the interest of the community at large, while the effect of a civil injury is usually restricted to the injured person or persons. The criminal law is intended to secure public peace and order. The object of criminal proceedings is punishment, and the offender is punished as a warning to persons in general not to commit crime, but in civil proceedings the persons whose rights have been interfered with take action to obtain for themselves compensation or damages.

The practical test as to whether a particular act is a crime is whether it is punishable by the criminal law; therefore any conduct punishable by the criminal law is a crime.

A crime consists of some wrongful act or conduct together with some guilty or blameable condition of mind. The criminal law does not punish illegal thoughts; it waits until an unlawful thought is evidenced by some action or by neglect to take action. If an act, which by law should have been done, is not done, it is called an omission.

The guilty or blameable state of mind which is necessary to constitute a crime is known as **mens rea,** or the offender's mind. When a person of his own free will does an act he is said to do it wilfully. If an act is not freely willed by the doer, it is said to be involuntary.

Proof of Criminal Intent – A court or jury, in determining whether a person has committed an offence

(a) shall not be bound in law to infer that he intended or foresaw a result of his actions by reason only of its being a natural and probable consequence of those actions; but

(b) shall decide whether he did intend or foresee that result by reference to all the evidence, drawing such inferences from the evidence as appear proper in the circumstances (C.J. Act 1967, s. 8).

Motive – The motive for a crime is the condition of mind which leads the criminal to commit the crime; his reason for his conduct. "Motive" is not intention, for a person's intention is connected with the results or consequences of the act he intends to do. Thus a man may intend to go to an inn, his motive being to get a drink. In robbery the motive is usually need of money, and the intention will be to take money from the attacked person.

Motive, from the police point of view, is of the greatest importance. If the motive of a criminal be known, it will throw much light on the case and materially assist in the elucidation of the facts.

Crime and Offence – The word "crime" is applied generally to any illegal act or conduct which entails criminal punishment, but it is usually applied in a narrower sense to an act which is punishable on indictment—that is, on a written charge put before a judge and jury, and therefore called indictable. See "Indictment", Chap. 5. The word "offence" also means an illegal action and, in a broad sense, may be applied to any illegal act or conduct which entails criminal punishment, but it usually refers to an act which is punishable on summary conviction by the magistrates. The C.L. Act 1967 introduced a new term "arrestable offence". "Arrestable offence" means (a) an offence for which the sentence is fixed by law or for which a person (not previously convicted) may be sentenced by statute to 5 years' imprisonment and (b) attempts to commit such an offence.

The expression "criminal offence" is sometimes used and has the same meaning as "crime" or "offence", that is any illegal act or omission liable by law to punishment such as imprisonment or fine.

Thus "crimes" usually mean indictable offences or the more serious illegal and punishable acts, and "offences" usually indicate those minor illegal acts which are punishable by the magistrates in their courts.

For the purposes of the Magistrates' Courts Act 1952, the Act gives special meanings to "summary offences" and "indictable offences" (s. 125). See "A Magistrates' Court", Chap. 4.

Classification of Crime – Crimes may be arranged in two groups, viz.:

(1) Indictable Offences, which are the more serious breaches of the criminal law and for which an indictment lies which is a charge triable by a judge and jury.

(2) Summary Offences, which are less serious and are triable by justices without a jury and are termed non-indictable.

However, this arrangement is merely a general classification. Many indictable offences may now, by Statute, be dealt with by justices without a jury. For instance the Magistrates' Courts Act 1952, s. 19, allows a court of justices to deal summarily with a person of 17 or upwards for any of the indictable offences mentioned in Sched. 1 to the Act if he consents to such a trial. A person accused of an indictable offence must be present at his trial.

Also under s. 25 of the same Act, a person aged 17 years or more charged before a summary court with a summary offence (which is not assault or offences under ss. 30, 31 of the Sexual Offences Act 1956, or s. 32 of the said Act if the immoral purpose is other than the commission of a homosexual act, or s. 5 of the Sexual Offences Act 1967) for which he is liable on conviction to imprisonment for more than 3 months, has the right, if present in person, to claim trial by jury, and should be told so before the charge is gone into. See "Progress of a Case", Chap. 4.

If the law declares a particular offence to be punishable on conviction on indictment or on summary conviction, the offence should be regarded as an indictable offence. See *R.* v. *Fussell* (1951).

Any offence which could be tried on indictment may be regarded as indictable. See *Hastings and Folkestone Glassworks, Ltd.* v. *Kalsan* (1948).

The Director of Public Prosecutions should be informed of every prosecution of an indictable offence and of a summary offence which has been wholly withdrawn or was not proceeded with within a reasonable time. See Appendix III.

Indictable Offences – At one time the more serious indictable offences (e.g. treason, murder, rape and arson) were called felonies, whereas the less serious (e.g. assault, bribery, perjury and incest) were classified as misdemeanours.

By the C.L. Act 1967 all distinctions between felony and misdemeanour have been abolished, and on all matters on which a distinction had previously been made between them, the law and practice in relation to all offences shall be that which previously was applicable in relation to a misdemeanour (s. 1).

Any breach of the criminal law is a misdemeanour, meaning wrong doing, but it is not usual to describe the minor summary offences as misdemeanours.

The description **offence** is usually restricted to those minor breaches of the law which may be dealt with summarily by magistrates without a jury. They have been created by Statutes which give the magistrates power to deal with them.

It is of the utmost importance that a police officer should know whether any particular breach of the law is an "arrestable offence" or not. (For list see Appendix V.) He has no power to arrest without warrant in a case of misdemeanour unless (1) it is an "arrestable offence", or (2) a breach of the peace is committed in his presence, or (3) some statute has specially given him the power to arrest without warrant for that particular offence. As regards a summary offence he has no power to arrest without warrant unless the Statute which has created the offence has expressly given him such power of arrest. See "Arrest", Chap. 3.

Punishment for Crime – In early days such punishments included death by various painful methods, torture, loss of property, incarceration and fine, but as time went on most of these penalties fell into disuse. The Criminal Justice Act 1948, abolished penal servitude, imprisonment with hard labour or in a particular division of the prison (s. 1) and whipping by sentence of a court (s. 2). The C.J. Act 1967, s. 65, abolished corporal punishment in prisons.

The law now allows the following punishments. Sentence to death on conviction of treason, piracy with violence, and certain naval and military offences.

Imprisonment can be imposed for many crimes and offences, but not on an offender under 17 and on an offender under 21 only where no other method of dealing with him is appropriate (P. of C.C. Act 1973, s. 19). Instead of imprisonment an offender who is suffering from mental illness, psychopathic disorder, subnormality or severe subnormality can be sent to a hospital or placed under guardianship (Mental Health Act 1959, s. 60).

There is no limit to the imprisonment which can be inflicted for a common law offence (*R.* v. *Morris* (1950)).

Binding over to keep the peace and (or) to be of good behaviour is a precautionary measure.

Under the P. of C.C. Act 1973 a convicted offender may be put on probation with additional requirements (s. 2), or he may be discharged either absolutely or conditionally that he commits no offence during a period (s. 7).

P. of C.C. Act 1973, s. 22, provides for "suspended sentences". See also "Penalties", Chap. 28.

Excuses for Crime – The law presumes that every person is sane and accountable for his actions, but it is open to an offender, when charged with an offence, to prove that he is not responsible in law for his illegal act because he had no intention or wish to do wrong, or to prove that he was justified in doing what he did. These defences or excuses are as follows:

(1) Insanity. The accused may be an idiot or totally deranged in his mind or insane on some subject or subjects, and his insanity may be permanent or temporary. A person of unsound mind may be arrested and charged with an offence; evidence may be given to prove he is insane and the decision rests with the court.

(2) Drunkenness as a rule is not an excuse for crime, except when it is involuntary—that is, contrived deliberately by other persons.

A person in a state of intoxication is *prima facie* liable for his acts, but he may plead his condition in mitigation of punishment. In a case where a particular intent is essential to make his conduct a crime, if he can prove that owing to his condition he had no such criminal intent, he may be acquitted.

If fraudulently made drunk by another an offender would not be accountable for his actions while under that influence.

(3) Ignorance or Mistake. Ignorance of the law will not justify any breach of the law, even when committed by a foreigner. Aliens in our country are subject to our laws. An honest and reasonable mistake of fact may excuse a crime if the intention of the person committing the crime was not unlawful. However, the excuse of ignorance or mistake will not be of avail in the case of acts forbidden absolutely by law—for instance, the sale of intoxicants to a drunken person.

(4) Accident may be an excuse for an offence committed in the performance of a lawful act which is being done with proper caution.

(5) Compulsion. This excuse is also known as **coercion** or **duress** and would probably hold good in the case of a person compelled by direct physical compulsion to commit an offence. The compulsion of necessity will not justify the commission of a crime. Even threats to property or of future injury to the person will not excuse crime.

(6) Married women. The common law presumed that a crime, other than murder, committed by a wife in the presence of her husband, was committed under his coercion and therefore excused her from punishment. However, this presumption was abolished by the Criminal Justice Act 1925, s. 47, which also directs that when a wife is charged with any offence except treason or murder, it shall be a good defence if she can prove that the offence was committed in the presence of, and under the coercion of, her husband.

Husband and wife may not alone be found guilty of conspiracy, being for some purposes considered in law as one person and therefore as having but one will.

(7) Justification. An act which ordinarily would be criminal may be authorised by law, as in the case of justifiable homicide, in which no guilt or fault attaches to the slayer, in his act.

An assault may be justified as committed in defence of person or property, or as committed in the process of reasonably correcting a child or scholar. Justification may be advanced as a defence in any prosecution, but its effect will depend on the facts of the case.

Exemptions from Liability for Crime – The following are more or less exempt from punishment for offences which they may commit:

(1) The Sovereign. The maxim is that the Sovereign can do no wrong, and the Sovereign is beyond the reach of the law.

(2) Foreign Sovereigns and Ambassadors from foreign countries while resident in this country, do not come under the jurisdiction of the English courts. If they commit offences they may be requested by the State to leave the country. Diplomatic privileges have been extended to staffs and representatives of members of certain international organisations (as, for example, the United Nations) and to Commonwealth High Commissioners and their official and domestic staffs.

(3) A Corporation or Company composed of several persons obviously cannot be dealt with for crime as a human person, as it cannot be hanged or imprisoned; but it can be prosecuted, as a corporation, for all offences which may be punished by a fine.

Magistrates' Courts Act 1952, s. 36, and Sched. 2, gives the procedure to be followed in the prosecution of a corporation for an indictable offence. If a crime is committed by the order of a corporation those concerned may be prosecuted individually and personally punished.

On the trial by a magistrates' court of an information against a corporation, a representative may on behalf of the corporation enter a plea of guilty or not guilty (C.J. Act 1967, s. 29 (1)).

(4) Infants under the age of ten years are not punishable for any offence, as the law holds that under that age no child can be guilty of any offence (C. & Y.P. Act 1933, s. 50, as amended by C. & Y.P. Act 1963, s. 16). A child under ten, therefore, should not be arrested or charged with any offence, but if needing care or control such a child may be taken to a place of safety and brought before a court. See Chap. 12.

Children between the ages of ten and fourteen years are regarded as so wanting in discretion that they must not be punished for an offence unless it is proved that they knew quite well that they were doing wrong.

Offenders between ten and fourteen may therefore be arrested and tried for an offence, but may not be found guilty unless there is clear proof of their guilty knowledge.

A boy under fourteen years cannot commit rape or any offence of carnal knowledge.

Persons of fourteen years and upwards are considered to be of sufficient discretion to be liable for their illegal acts.

Offenders, therefore, of and above fourteen years of age may be arrested, tried, and found guilty of any offence against the criminal law.

Remission of Penalty – The Crown has the right to remit punishment, by granting a pardon either with or without conditions, or by commuting the sentence.

By the Remission of Penalties Act 1859, the Crown may remit in whole or in part any sum of money which under any Act may be imposed as a penalty or forfeiture on a convicted offender, although such money may be in whole or in part payable to some party other than the Crown.

The Sovereign may extend the Royal mercy to any person who may be imprisoned for non-payment of any sum of money so imposed, although it may be in whole or in part payable to some party other than the Crown.

Prison Act 1952, s. 25, allows remission of part of a sentence of imprisonment on the ground of industry and good conduct.

CHAPTER 2

CRIMINALS

	Page		Page
Criminals	12	Assisting Offenders . .	14
Incitement to Crime .	12	Concealing Offences or Giving False Information .	14
Attempt to Commit Crime	13	Extradition	15
Accomplice	13	Convicted Persons . .	15
Accessories to a Crime .	13		

Criminals – Strictly speaking a person who has committed a crime is a criminal, but the term is usually confined to a person who has been convicted of a crime. Although he may not have caused the commission of the intended crime, a person who incites another, conspires with another, or himself attempts to commit a crime is a criminal. Such intended crimes are called inchoate crimes to indicate—e.g. in the case of an attempt—that the intended crime has been begun but has not been completed. A person may also become a criminal by being unlawfully connected with a crime that has already been committed.

Incitement to Crime – The inciting or urging some other person to commit a crime is a misdemeanour at common law. The offence is committed even though the other person does not commit the suggested crime.

Incitement to Mutiny Act 1797, s. 1. It is an offence to incite any member of Her Majesty's Forces on sea or land to mutiny. See also "Sedition", Chap. 20, and "Incitement to Disaffection", Chap. 30.

Official Secrets Act 1920, s. 7. It is an offence to incite another to commit a breach of the Official Secrets Acts.

Offences against the Person Act 1861, s. 4. Incitement to murder any other person is an offence.

Incitement of a woman to cause her own miscarriage is an offence under s. 58 of this Act.

Post Office Act 1953, s. 68. It is an offence to incite any person to commit any offence indictable under this Act.

An attempt to incite to the commission of a crime is an offence, as is a conspiracy to incite a person to commit crime.

When the incitement has caused the commission of the offence, the inciter is liable as a principal.

Magistrates' Courts Act 1952, s. 19, permits that an adult (17 or over) if he consents may be dealt with summarily for any offence of inciting to commit a summary offence and for the offence of inciting to commit any indictable offence which may be dealt with summarily as given in Sched. 1 to the Act.

Attempt to Commit Crime – An attempt to commit a crime is any act done with intent to commit that crime and forming part of a series of acts which if not interrupted would result in the actual commission of the crime. An intention to commit an offence is not sufficient, as criminal liability does not commence until the offender takes some step towards the commission of a crime. Preparation for an intended crime will not amount to an "attempt"; for example, buying a box of matches will not be "attempted arson".

The intent must be shown by some overt or open act connected with the commission of the intended crime.

Under the Magistrates' Courts Act 1952, s. 19, and Sched. 1, any attempt by an adult to commit any indictable offence which may be dealt with summarily, may be so dealt with by consent of the accused.

Accomplice – When two or more persons are concerned in the commission of an offence, each one is an accomplice of the other or others. An accomplice may give evidence on behalf of the prosecution, or, as it is sometimes called, give "Queen's Evidence", against his partners in the offence. Such evidence is usually given in the hope of escaping punishment and should be accepted with great caution. Naturally an accomplice will be able to give the facts of the crime, but his evidence will require corroboration. See "Corroborative Evidence", Chap. 7.

In practice a prisoner ought not to be convicted on the sole evidence of an accomplice, as other independent evidence implicating the prisoner will be required before the court is satisfied (*R.* v. *Baskerville* (1916)).

If an "accomplice" witness refuses to give evidence, it will be for the court to decide whether the witness is in peril of prosecution (see "Privilege", Chap. 7), and whether he should or should not give evidence.

Accessories to a Crime – There are no "accessories" in treasons and summary offences, as all concerned are treated as principals.

The Accessories and Abettors Act 1861 directs that any person who aids, abets, counsels, or procures the commission of any offence is liable to be punished as a principal (s. 8).

The Magistrates' Courts Act 1952, s. 35, enacts that a person who aids, abets, counsels or procures the commission by another person of a summary offence shall be guilty of the like offence and may be tried (whether or not he is charged as a principal) either by a court having jurisdiction to try that other person or by a court having by virtue of his own offence jurisdiction to try him. The words "aid, abet, counsel, or procure" may be used to describe the offence (*Gough* v. *Rees* (1929)). If the abettor and principal are indicted together as principals, the abettor may be convicted, although the principal is acquitted (*R.* v. *Burton* (1875)). It should be proved that the aider knew the facts of the offence committed (*Thomas* v. *Lindop* (1950)).

M.C. Act 1952, s. 19, and Sched. 1, allows an adult if he consents to be dealt with summarily for aiding, abetting, counselling or procuring the commission of any indictable offence which may be dealt with summarily.

Assisting Offenders – By the C.L. Act 1967—Where a person has committed an "arrestable offence", any other person who, knowing or believing him to be guilty of the offence or of some other arrestable offence, does without lawful authority or reasonable excuse any act with intent to impede his apprehension or prosecution shall be guilty of an offence. The consent of the D.P.P. is necessary for proceedings, but this does not prevent the arrest or the issue of a warrant for the arrest of a person for such an offence, or the remand in custody or on bail of a person charged with such an offence. The offence is extraditable (s. 4).

Concealing Offences or Giving False Information – By the C.L. Act 1967—Where a person has committed an arrestable offence, any other person who, knowing or believing that the offence or some other arrestable offence has been committed, and that he has information which might be of material assistance in securing the prosecution or conviction of an offender for it, accepts or agrees to accept for not disclosing that information any consideration other than the making good or loss of injury caused by the offence, or the making of reasonable compensation for that loss or injury, commits an offence (s. 5 (1)).

A person who causes any wasteful employment of the police by knowingly making to any person a false report tending to show than an offence has been committed, or to give rise to apprehension for the safety of any persons or property, or tending to show that he has information material to any police enquiry, commits an offence (s. 5 (2)).

No proceedings shall be instituted for offences under the above two paragraphs except by or with the consent of the D.P.P. (s. 5 (3)).

The compounding of an offence other than treason shall not be an offence otherwise than under this section (s. 5 (5)).

(*This section replaces the old offences of compounding an offence and misprision of felony. It also provides a means of prosecuting for what used to be termed "public mischief".)*

Extradition – Extradition is the process by which a person who has committed a crime in this country and has fled abroad, or vice versa, is arrested and taken for trial to the country in which he had committed the crime.

The procedure as regards extradition to and from foreign countries is governed by the Extradition Acts and by the treaties in force with foreign countries, and extradition is possible only in the case of a person charged with any of the crimes mentioned in the treaty concerned.

The Fugitive Offenders Act 1967 provides for the return from the U.K. to other Commonwealth countries and U.K. dependencies of persons accused or convicted of offences in those countries and dependencies.

Cases under these Acts must be reported to the Director of Public Prosecutions. See Appendix III.

Criminal Justice Act 1948, s. 31, directs that any British subject employed under H.M. Government in the United Kingdom in the service of the Crown who commits, in a foreign country, in the course of his employment, any offence which would be indictable if committed in England is subject to the same punishment as if the offence had been committed in England.

Convicted Persons – When a person is convicted of a crime or summary offence a record of the conviction is made by the court which has convicted him.

Evidence Act 1851, s. 13, allows the production in evidence, in any proceedings whatever, of a copy of the record of the trial and conviction, or acquittal, of a person charged with an indictable offence, provided it is certified by the officer having custody of the records of the court of trial. This is subject to the provisions of the Rehabilitation of Offenders Act 1974, under which a conviction may, after the appropriate rehabilitation period, become "spent" and therefore inadmissible in evidence in any judicial proceedings. The rehabilitation period varies according to the sentence imposed. For adult offenders, a conviction leading to a fine is spent after five years; a sentence of imprisonment of less than six months is spent after seven years; and a sentence of imprisonment of between six and thirty months is spent after ten years. Sentences in excess of thirty months are excluded from rehabilitation.

A conviction leading only to discharge or a period of probation is, whether spent or not, deemed not to be a conviction for the purposes of later proceedings (P. of C.C. Act 1973, s. 13).

Where admissible a previous conviction may be proved by producing a record or extract of such conviction signed by the Clerk of the court of conviction, and giving proof of the identity of the person with the person shown by the extract to have been convicted (Prevention of Crimes Act 1871, s. 18). The accused person should be present to be identified.

A summary conviction may be proved by producing a copy of the minute or memorandum of the conviction entered in the court register, purporting to be signed by the Clerk of the court by whom the register is kept, and by proving the identity of the person (Criminal Justice Administration Act 1914, s. 28 (1)).

In any criminal proceedings a previous conviction may be proved against any person by finger-prints. A certificate from the Metropolitan Police that finger-prints are those of a person previously convicted, giving the conviction, with a certificate from the prison or remand centre in which the person was detained, that finger-prints are those of this person, together with a certificate from the Metropolitan Police that both these sets of finger-prints are finger-prints of the same person, shall be evidence of the fact (Criminal Justice Act 1948, s. 39). "Finger-prints" includes "palm-prints" (C.J. Act 1967, s. 33).

If a person admits the previous conviction, evidence of identity will not be necessary, but as a rule it is advisable to produce the record of the conviction.

An offender shall not be liable to be punished twice for the same offence (Interpretation Act 1889, s. 33). If again charged with the identical offence or on the same acts or omissions on which he was previously convicted, he can effectively plead "Autrefois Convict".

Outstanding charges (previous offences not detected) which an accused admits after conviction for a later similar offence and asks should be taken into consideration before sentence, may be taken into consideration by the court, but any such previous offence which the court would not have had jurisdiction to try should be excluded (*R.* v. *Warn* (1937)).

However, where a person is convicted of an offence and other offences of his are taken into consideration before sentence, such taking into consideration does not amount to conviction on them (*R.* v. *Neal* (1949)).

When the court announces conviction there is a conviction even if no sentence is pronounced and the case cannot be re-tried. (*R.* v. *Sheridan* (1937) and *R.* v. *Campbell, Ex parte Hoy* (1953)).

A magistrates' court has no power to alter its sentence once it is pronounced even though it has not been recorded in the register (*R.* v. *Essex Justices, Ex parte Final* (1962)).

CHAPTER 3

ARREST

	Page
Arrest	17
Arrest without Warrant at Common Law . .	18
Arrest without Warrant by Statute . . .	19
Arrest with Warrant .	27
Re-arrest . . .	28

Arrest is the taking or apprehending of a person and restraining him from his liberty. Arrest in a criminal sense is the apprehension or restraining of a person in order that he or she shall be forthcoming to answer an alleged or suspected offence.

The person making an arrest should give to his prisoner the reason for the arrest at the time of the arrest, though in law this requirement does not exist if the circumstances are such that the person arrested must know the general nature of the alleged offence for which he is detained (*Christie* v. *Leachinsky* (1947)). In this case the House of Lords on final appeal in 1947 declared that when a police officer arrests without warrant on reasonable suspicion he must normally inform his prisoner of the true ground of arrest. Precise or technical language need not be used but the prisoner should be told in substance the reason why he is being detained. If this is not done the officer may be liable for false imprisonment unless the prisoner has made it impossible to so inform him by running away or assaulting the officer, or unless the circumstances of the crime are so apparent that the prisoner must know the nature of the crime for which he is detained. A person may use reasonable force in the prevention of crime, or in effecting or assisting in the lawful arrest of offenders or suspected offenders, or of persons unlawfully at large.

On arrest there is a right to search the prisoner for any article material to a criminal charge and the seizure of articles in possession or control of a person arrested is excused if later they are evidence of a crime committed by someone (*Elias* v. *Pasmore* (1934)).

For procedure after arrest, see "Bail by Police", Chap. 5.

An arrest may be either without or with a warrant or written authority (see "Warrants", Chap. 5). Every police officer has certain powers of arrest either without warrant or with warrant. These powers are as follows:

1. Arrest without Warrant at Common Law – A constable's power of arrest without warrant under the common law may be classified according to the evidence available of the offence.

(1) On his own View. A constable may and should arrest any person whom he sees committing any treason or inflicting any dangerous wound.

It is also his duty to interfere in the case of any riot, assault, or other breach of the peace, and to stop or prevent the same by arresting the persons he sees actually engaged therein.

A constable may arrest any person whom he sees threatening to commit treason or any breach of the peace, but if the threat is merely an idle one and there is no breach of the peace, an arrest would not be advisable.

He may arrest any person who assaults or obstructs him in the discharge of his duty.

He cannot at common law, arrest without warrant for an ordinary assault not committed in his presence, nor ought he arrest without warrant after an affray is over and is not likely to be renewed.

He cannot arrest without warrant on a charge of misdemeanour unless express power to do so is given by statute. He can, at common law, arrest without warrant when a breach of the peace is committed in his presence or when he has reasonable ground for believing it is about to be committed or renewed in his presence.

In *North* v. *Pullen* (1961), it was held that a constable has power to arrest any person who in his presence commits a misdemeanour or breach of the peace, if the arrest is effected at the time when, or immediately after, the offence is committed, or while there is a danger of its renewal.

(2) On his own Suspicion. A constable who has reasonable cause to suspect that treason has been committed by any person or that a dangerous wound has been given by any person may arrest such person. If it should afterwards appear that no such offence has been committed the arrest will be justified provided it was made on reasonable grounds of suspicion.

If it is established that the person so arrested is not concerned in a crime, he should be released.

(3) On the Charge of a Third Person. When a person requests a constable to take another person into custody, alleging such other person is guilty of treason, or an arrestable offence, or inflicting a grievous wound, the constable should, if the charge is reasonable, and made by a person deserving of credence, arrest the person so charged.

If the charge prove unfounded the person making it and not the constable will be responsible.

In such a case the constable, if he does not act, may render himself liable to punishment, but before taking action he should consider the repute of the person making the charge and also of the person accused, as well as the seriousness of the offence charged.

If no definite charge is made, but the information is merely given to the constable, leaving him to act or not act upon it as he may think right, the constable should make inquiry into the allegation and act very cautiously. If the offence alleged is a misdemeanour he has no power to arrest unless he procures a magistrates' warrant.

2. Arrest without Warrant by Statute – Many Acts of Parliament contain provisions empowering a constable to arrest without warrant in specified cases. See the following alphabetical list:

Aliens Order 1953, art. 28. Any person who acts in contravention of this Order, of is reasonably suspected of having so acted may be arrested without warrant by any constable. See Chap. 29 for fuller description of this power.

Animals. Diseases of Animals Act 1950, s. 71. A constable may stop and detain any person seen or found committing, or reasonably suspected of being engaged in committing, an offence against the Act (or orders or regulations made thereunder), and may arrest such person without warrant if his name and address are unknown and he fails to give them to the satisfaction of the constable. A constable may also without warrant arrest any person who obstructs or impedes him in the execution of his duty under the Act or the orders or regulations made thereunder. See Chap. 35.

Animals. Protection of Animals Acts 1911 to 1960. Section 12 of the 1911 Act provides that any constable may arrest without warrant any person who he has reason to believe is guilty of an offence under these Acts which is punishable by imprisonment without the option of a fine (cruelty to an animal), whether upon his own view thereof or upon the complaint and information of any other person who shall declare his name and place of abode to the constable. See Chap. 35.

Army Act 1955, s. 186. On reasonable suspicion a deserter or absentee without leave may be arrested without a warrant. See Chap. 30.

Army Act 1955, s. 195 (3). A person who has in his possession, etc., without proper excuse any Army property, documents, etc. may be arrested without warrant. See Chap. 30.

Betting and Gaming. Betting, Gaming and Lotteries Act 1963. Any constable may take into custody without warrant any person found committing an offence under this section (which deals with street betting) and may seize and detain any article liable to be forfeited thereunder (s. 8). A constable may arrest without warrant anyone whom he finds in a street or public place and whom he suspects ,with reasonable cause, to be taking part in gaming (Gaming Act 1968, s. 5). See Chap. 36.

Children and Young Persons Act 1933, s. 13. For the commission of any offence given in Sched. 1 to the Act (cruelty, injury, etc., as given in Chap. 12) a constable may arrest without warrant any person he sees committing same if he does not know and cannot ascertain the offender's name and residence, or any person who has committed or who he has reason to believe has committed same if he believes such person will abscond, or if he does not know and cannot ascertain such person's name and address.

Children and Young Persons Act 1963, s. 10. If a person has in pursuance of s. 9 of this Act—which deals with the temporary committal of persons ordered to be sent to approved schools—been committed by an approved school order to custody in any place other than a prison, remand home, remand centre or special reception centre, or to the custody of a fit person and he escapes, or is without lawful authority taken from that custody, he may be arrested without warrant in any part of the U.K., Channel Islands or the Isle of Man.

Coinage Offences Act 1936, s. 11. Any person found committing any offence against this Act other than one against s. 8 (medals) may be arrested without warrant by any person. See Chap. 16.

Conservation of Seals Act 1970, s. 4. A constable may stop any person he suspects with reasonable cause of committing an offence under the Act, and without warrant arrest that person if he fails to give his name and address to the constable's satisfaction.

Criminal Damage Act 1971. All offences under this Act are "arrestable offences". See Chap. 15.

Criminal Justice Act 1948, s. 66. Any person required or authorised by the Act to be taken to any place or to be kept in custody, shall, while being so taken or kept, be deemed to be in legal custody and a constable while taking or keeping such person shall have all the powers, authorities, protection and privileges of a constable as well beyond his constablewick as within it. See Chap. 21.

Criminal Justice Act 1961, s. 35. Any person required or authorised by or under this Act to be taken to any place, or to be kept in custody, shall, while being so taken or kept, be deemed to be in legal custody, and a constable while taking or keeping such person shall have all the powers, authorities, protection and privileges which a constable has within the area for which he acts as constable. See Chap. 21.

Criminal Justice Act 1967, s. 23. (1) A constable may arrest without warrant any person who has been admitted to bail (a) if the constable has reasonable grounds for believing that that person is likely to break the condition that he will appear at the time and place required or any other condition on which he was admitted to bail, or has reasonable cause to suspect that that person is breaking or has broken any such other condition; or (b) on being notified in writing by any surety for that person that the surety believes that that person is likely to break the first mentioned condition and for that reason the surety wishes to be relieved of his obligations as a surety.

(2) A person arrested under the foregoing subsection (a) shall, except where he was so arrested within the period of 24 hours immediately preceding an occasion on which he is required by virtue of a condition of his bail to appear before any court, be brought as soon as practicable and in any event within 24 hours after his arrest before a justice of the peace acting for the petty sessions area in which he was arrested; and (b) in the said excepted case shall be brought before the court before which he is required to appear as aforesaid.

(3) A justice of the peace before whom a person is brought under the last foregoing subsection may, if of the opinion that that person has broken or is likely to break any condition on which he was admitted to bail, remand him in custody or commit him to custody, as the case may require, or alternatively release him on his original recognizance or on a new recognizance, with or without sureties, and if not of that opinion shall release him on his original recognizance.

Criminal Law Act 1967. The powers of summary arrest conferred by the following subsections shall apply to offences for which the sentence is fixed by law or for which a person (not previously convicted) may under or by virtue of any enactment be sentenced to imprisonment for a term of 5 years, and to attempts to commit any such offence; and in this Act, including any amendment made by this Act in any other enactment, "arrestable offence" means any such offence or attempt (s. 2 (1)).

Any person may arrest without warrant anyone who is, or whom he, with reasonable cause, suspects to be, in the act of committing an arrestable offence (s. 2 (2)).

Where an arrestable offence has been committed, any person may arrest without warrant anyone who is, or whom he, with reasonable cause, suspects to be, guilty of the offence (s. 2 (3)).

Where a constable, with reasonable cause, suspects that an arrestable offence has been committed, he may arrest without warrant anyone whom he, with reasonable cause, suspects to be guilty of the offence (s. 2 (4)).

A constable may arrest without warrant any person who is, or whom he, with reasonable cause, suspects to be, about to commit an arrestable offence (s. 2 (5)).

For the purpose of arresting a person under any power conferred by this section a constable may enter (if need be, by force) and search any place where that person is or where the constable, with reasonable cause, suspects him to be (s. 2 (6)).

This section shall not affect the operation of any enactment restricting the institution of proceedings for an offence, nor prejudice any power of arrest conferred by law apart from this section (s. 2 (7)).

Deer Act 1963, s. 5. A constable may arrest without warrant any person he suspects with reasonable cause of committing any offence against the Act.

Drilling. Unlawful Drilling Act 1819, s. 1. Any meeting for the purpose of its members being drilled without lawful authority may be dispersed by any constable and those present may be arrested. See Chap. 20.

Ecclesiastical Courts Jurisdiction Act 1860, ss. 2 and 3. Any person molesting, etc., any authorised preacher or clergyman celebrating Divine Service, etc., or "brawling" in a place of religious worship or churchyard may be arrested by a constable or churchwarden. See Chaps. 20 and 29.

Explosives Act 1875, s. 78. Any person found committing any act which is an offence under this Act or the bye-laws or rules made under it, and which tends to cause explosion or fire, in or about any factory, magazine, store, railway, canal, harbour, wharf, carriage, ship or boat, may be arrested without warrant by a constable. See Chap. 33.

Firearms Act 1968, s. 50. A constable making a search of premises under the authority of a warrant under s. 46 may arrest without warrant any person found on the premises whom he has reason to believe to be guilty of an offence relevant for the purposes of that section. A constable may arrest without warrant any person whom he has reasonable cause to suspect to be committing an offence under ss. 19 (carrying firearm in a public place), 20 (trespassing with firearm), 21 (possession of firearms by persons previously convicted of crime), or 47 (2) (failing to hand over firearm or ammunition when required to do so by a constable), and for the purpose of exercising this power may enter any place. A constable may also arrest without warrant a person who refuses to declare his name and address when required to do so under s. 48 (2), or whom he in such a case suspects of giving a false name and address or of intending to abscond.

Game Laws (Amendment) Act 1960, s. 1. A police constable may arrest a person found on any land committing an offence under ss. 1 or 9 of the Night Poaching Act 1828 (which refer to persons trespassing in pursuit of game by night). The powers exercisable under s. 31 of the Game Act 1831 (which provides that occupiers of land may require any person found in pursuit of game in the daytime to quit the land and give his name and address, and if he fails to do so, may arrest him) shall also be exercisable by a police constable. See Chap. 19.

Highways Act 1959, s. 121. If a person, without lawful authority or excuse, in any way wilfully obstructs the free passage along a highway he shall be guilty of an offence, and a constable may arrest without warrant any person whom he sees committing the offence. See Chap. 24.

Immigration Act 1971. A constable or immigration officer may arrest without warrant anyone who has, or whom he, with reasonable cause, suspects to have, committed or attempted to commit offences against the section (viz. illegal entry and similar offences) (s. 24) or any person guilty of assisting illegal entry (s. 25).

Indecent Advertisements Act 1889, s. 6. Any constable may arrest without warrant any person whom he shall find committing any offence against this Act. See Chap. 11.

Licensing Act 1872, s. 12. Any person who in any public place is drunk and disorderly, or drunk in charge of any carriage, horse, steam engine or cattle, or who (anywhere) is drunk in possession of loaded firearms may be arrested. See Chap. 38.

Licensing Act 1902, ss. 1 and 2. Any person found in a public place or licensed premises, drunk and incapable, or drunk while in charge of a child apparently under the age of seven years may be arrested. See Chap. 38.

Licensing Act 1964, s. 187. A constable executing a search warrant for intoxicants in unlicensed premises, when he has seized or removed liquor, may demand the name and address of any person found on the premises and if his answers are not satisfactory, he may arrest him without warrant. See Chap. 38.

Malicious Damage Act 1861. Maliciously obstructing railways (s. 35), damaging ships by false signals (s. 47) and malicious damage to buoys (s. 48) are "arrestable offences".

Mental Health Act 1959, s. 136. A constable may arrest a person suffering from mental disorder and in immediate need of care or control, whom he finds in a public place, and take him to a place of safety.

Misuse of Drugs Act 1971, s. 24. A constable may arrest without warrant a person who has committed, or whom the constable, with reasonable cause, suspects to have committed, an offence under the Act, if: (a) he, with reasonable cause, believes that that person will abscond unless arrested; or (b) the name and address of that person are unknown to, and cannot be ascertained by him; or (c) he is not satisfied that a name and address furnished by that person as his name and address are true. This section shall not prejudice any power of arrest conferred by law apart from this section.

Municipal Corporations Act 1882, s. 193. A county borough constable may, while on duty, arrest any idle and disorderly person whom he finds disturbing the public peace. See Chap. 28.

Official Secrets Act 1911, s. 6. Any person who is found committing an offence under this Act, or who is reasonably suspected of having committed or having attempted to commit or being about to commit such an offence, may be arrested without warrant. See Chap. 20.

Pedlars Act 1871, s. 18. Any person acting as a pedlar, who refuses to produce to a constable his pedlar's certificate or who has none, or who refuses inspection of his pack, may be arrested without warrant by the constable. See Chap. 31.

Poaching. Night Poaching Act 1828, s. 2. The owners or occupiers of the land, their gamekeepers and assistants, may arrest any persons found offending against the Act and deliver them to a constable. This power is extended to police constables by the Game Laws (Amendment) Act 1960. See Chap. 19.

Prevention of Crime Act 1953. The power of arrest for without authority or reasonable excuse having an "offensive weapon" in a public place is set out in Chap. 28.

Prevention of Offences Act 1851, s. 11. Any person found committing (that is in the act of committing) any indictable offence in the night may be arrested without warrant by any person.

Prevention of Terrorism (Temporary Provisions) Act 1974. A constable may arrest without warrant a person whom he reasonably suspects to be: (a) a person guilty of an offence under s. 1 or s. 3; (b) a person concerned in the commission, preparation, or instigation of acts of terrorism; (c) a person subject to an exclusion order (s. 7 (1)). A constable may arrest without warrant a person whom he reasonably suspects to be a person guilty of an offence of displaying of support in public for a proscribed organisation (s. 2). See Chap. 20.

Prison Act 1952, s. 49 (and C.J. Act 1961, s. 30). Any person sentenced to imprisonment or borstal training, or ordered to be detained in a detention centre or committed to a prison or remand centre, who is unlawfully at large in the United Kingdom, Channel Islands or Isle of Man, may be arrested by a constable without warrant and taken to the place where he is to be detained. Section 8: Every prison officer while acting as such shall have all the powers, authority, protection and privileges of a constable. See Chap. 28.

Public Health Act 1925, s. 74 (2). Any person riding or driving so as to endanger the life or limb of any person or to the common danger of the passengers in any street outside the Metropolitan Police District may be arrested without warrant by any constable who witnesses the occurrence. This section may be applied by Order to any rural district. Metropolitan Police Act 1839, s. 54, gives the same power in that district. See Chap. 24.

Public Order Act 1936, s. 7. A constable may without warrant arrest any person reasonably suspected by him to be committing an offence under s. 1 (political uniforms), s. 4 (offensive weapons) or s. 5 (offensive conduct) of the Act. By s. 6 he may also arrest without warrant for an offence under the added subsection to s. 1 of the Public Meeting Act 1908 (disorderly conduct). See Chap. 22.

Public Service Vehicles (Arrest of Offenders) Act 1975. A constable may without warrant arrest a person whom he has reasonable cause to suspect of contravening or failing to comply with a provision of regulations made under s. 147 of R.T. Act 1960 (which relates to the conduct of passengers in P.S.V.s). See Chap. 24.

Representation of the People Act 1949. Power of arrest for disorderly conduct at a political meeting is given by s. 84 of this Act. Schedule 2 gives power of arrest for misconduct or alleged personation in a polling station. See "Election Offences", Chap. 21.

Road Traffic Act 1972. A constable in uniform may arrest without warrant any person driving or attempting to drive a motor vehicle on a road whom he has reasonable cause to suspect of being disqualified (s. 100).

A constable may arrest without warrant:

(a) a person who, when driving or attempting to drive, or when in charge of a motor vehicle on a road or other public place, is unfit to drive through drink or drugs; (s. 5)

(b) a person who, when riding a cycle on a road or other public place, is unfit to ride through drink or drugs (s.19);

(c) the driver of a motor vehicle who within his view commits an offence of dangerous or careless driving on a road, unless the driver either gives his name and address or produces his licence (s. 164);

(d) the rider of a cycle who within his view commits an offence of dangerous or careless cycling on a road, unless the rider gives his name and address (s. 164). See Chap. 24.

Sexual Offences Act 1956. A constable may arrest without warrant in a case of procuration (s. 40), and anyone may arrest without warrant a man soliciting in a public place (s. 41). See Chap. 10.

Sexual Offences Act 1967, s. 5. Anyone may arrest without warrant a person found living on earnings of male prostitution.

Street Offences Act 1959, s. 1. A constable may arrest without warrant anyone he finds in a street or public place and suspects, with reasonable cause, to be a common prostitute loitering or soliciting in such street or public place for the purpose of prostitution. See Chap. 10.

Theft Act 1968. With the exceptions given below all offences under this Act and attempts to commit them are "arrestable offences". Any person may arrest without warrant anyone who is, or whom he, with reasonable cause, suspects to be going equipped for stealing etc. (s. 25), or taking or killing deer (Sched. 1, para. 1), or taking or destroying fish at night (Sched. 1, para. 2). (There is no power of arrest for the following offences under the Act: taking a pedal cycle without authority (s. 12 (5)) and advertising rewards for the return of goods stolen or lost (s. 23)).

Town Gardens Protection Act 1863. A constable may apprehend any person damaging, etc., any grounds in a city or borough set apart for the use of the inhabitants. See Chap. 15.

Town Police Clauses Act 1847, s. 28. Any constable may arrest without warrant any person who within his view in any street (in an urban district where the Act is in force) commits any offence under s. 28 of the Act (various nuisances to the obstruction, annoyance, or danger of the residents or passengers). See Chap. 24.

Vagrancy Act 1824, s. 6, and Penal Servitude Act 1891, s. 7. Any person may arrest without warrant any suspected person or reputed thief loitering in any street, etc., with intent to commit an offence against the Acts. See Chap. 28.

Vagrancy Act 1824, s. 6. Any person found offending against the Act may be arrested without a warrant by any person and conveyed before a justice or delivered to a constable who is liable to a penalty if he refuses to take him into custody.

However, by Criminal Justice Act 1948, s. 68, a fortune teller, palmist, etc., can be so arrested only by a constable and not even by him unless he believes the offender will abscond or if he is not satisfied as to the identity or residence of the offender. See Chap. 27.

Note.—Fuller information regarding the various powers of arrest is given in the appropriate succeeding chapters.

Where a person is arrested without a warrant for an offence and retained in custody he should be brought before a magistrates' court as soon as practicable (M.C. Act 1952, s. 38 (4)). After arrest without warrant the prisoner should be taken as soon as reasonably practicable (see *John Lewis and Co.* v. *Tims* (1952)) before a justice or to a police station (where the officer in charge has power to grant bail (see "Bail by Police", Chap. 5)). He should not be taken to the scene of the crime. If after such an arrest the officer becomes satisfied that the prisoner is not guilty of the crime he should release him.

UNNECESSARY ARRESTS – The main object of an arrest is that the person should be made amenable to the law, and a constable should be most careful to avoid unnecessary arrests. Arrests should not be made for minor offences when the offenders may be made amenable by summons. A constable has great powers of arrest, but he should exercise these powers with intelligence and discretion.

3. Arrest with Warrant – A warrant to arrest is a written authority signed by a justice directing the arrest of an offender so that he may be dealt with according to law.

A warrant to arrest should give the offence charged, the authority under which the arrest is to be made, the person or persons who are to execute it and the person who is to be arrested. It may contain a direction admitting the prisoner to bail. See "Warrants" and "Bail by Police", Chap. 5.

In cases in which immediate arrest is not necessary it is wiser to obtain a justice's warrant authorising the arrest of the offender.

No action may be brought against a constable who has acted under a justice's warrant until demand in writing for perusal and copy of the warrant has been made and refused or neglected for 6 days after such demand. If action is brought (and it must be brought within 6 months), on production and proof of the warrant, the jury must find for the constable notwithstanding any defect of jurisdiction in the justice (Constables Protection Act 1750).

4. Re-arrest – If a person is arrested without warrant on a particular ground and later only a charge based on another ground is to be proceeded with, it seems that according to the case of *Christie* v. *Leachinsky* (1947) the prisoner should be discharged and re-arrested on the new charge.

CHAPTER 4

COURTS OF JUSTICE

	Page		Page
Courts of Justice . .	29	Progress of a Case . .	38
Justices of the Peace .	32	Open Court . . .	41
Proceedings before Justices	33	Speeches in Court . .	42
Trial by Jury . .	36		

Courts of Justice – There are several courts before which criminal offences may come, as follows:

1. The High Court of Parliament, or **the House of Lords.** This court is composed of the Lords of Appeal in Ordinary, who are lawyers of eminence holding peerages and members of the House of Lords, and they will deal with points of law of general public importance brought before them on appeal from any decision of the Supreme Court.

2. The Supreme Court which consists of (a) the Court of Appeal, (b) the High Court and (c) the Crown Court.

(a) **The Court of Appeal,** which consists of the Master of the Rolls and the Lords Justices of Appeal. The Court of Appeal consists of two divisions, (a) the civil division and (b) the criminal division. Judges of the Queen's Bench Division of the High Court may sit at sittings of the criminal division of the Court of Appeal. See "Appeal", Chap. 5.

(b) **The High Court** (Queen's Bench Division). The Queen's Bench Division, which consists of the Lord Chief Justice, who is president, and other judges. One judge, sitting and acting as a Judge of the High Court, has all the jurisdiction and powers of the High Court. Judges of the Queen's Bench Division sit in London and can deal with criminal cases and cases brought before the court by an order of certiorari or habeas corpus, or on a case stated, etc.

(c) **The Crown Court,** which was established by the Courts Act 1971. This court replaces the former courts of Assize and Quarter Sessions, which were abolished by the Act. The Crown Court is a superior court of record, and its jurisdiction and powers shall be exercised by any judge of the High Court, or any

Circuit Judge or Recorder. In certain circumstances justices of the peace will sit with such a judge or Recorder.

3. A Magistrates' Court. The M.C. Act 1952 (supplemented by the Magistrates' Courts Rules 1968 and 1975) defines a "magistrates' court" as meaning any justice or justices of the peace acting under any enactment (including public and local Acts and orders and regulations made under them (s. 126)) or by virtue of their commission or under the common law (s. 124).

The Justices of the Peace Act 1949, s. 44, also defines a "magistrates' court" as a court of summary jurisdiction or examining justices and includes a single examining justice.

Such a court acts in a petty sessional court-house for a petty sessions area of a county and the justices may appoint another place (or places) as an occasional court-house (M.C. Act 1952, s. 123).

At least two justices are necessary in a magistrates' court to try an information summarily or hear a complaint unless a single justice is allowed to do so by law in any particular case (M.C. Act 1952, s. 98), or the court is composed of a stipendiary (legally qualified) magistrate, who may sit alone (M.C. Act 1952, s. 121).

A magistrates' court to try summarily an indictable offence or hear a complaint must sit in a petty sessional court-house, but can try a non-indictable offence and impose imprisonment when sitting in an occasional court-house or a petty sessional court-house (s. 98).

Such courts are open to the public unless otherwise provided by law (s. 98). A court of a single justice or a court sitting in an occasional court-house cannot order more than 14 days imprisonment or £1 fine (s. 98).

One justice sitting alone may deal with simple drunkenness (C.J.A. Act 1914, s. 38), and any other offences definitely so allowed by some statutes.

A magistrates' court can deal with summary offences, that is offences which by Statute can be disposed of then and there, and can, if it thinks fit and is so allowed by statute, deal with many indictable offences under circumstances laid down by statutes. It can also send an accused person to be dealt with by a higher court.

Under the 1952 Act, s. 2, such a court for a county can try all summary offences committed within its county. It has jurisdiction, when the magistrates are sitting as examining justices (see later), over any offence committed by a person who is before the court whether or not the offence was committed within the county. Under C.J. Act 1967, s. 28, a magistrates' court for any area by which a person is tried for an offence shall have jurisdiction to try him for any summary offence for which he could be tried by a magistrates' court for any other area.

Where the magistrates are sitting as examining justices they can try summarily any indictable offence which they have power to try under ss. 18 or 19 of the Act (s. 2).

As far as this Act is concerned "summary offence" means an offence which if committed by an adult (17 years or over) is triable by a magistrates' court (whether or not it is also triable on indictment) except the indictable offences which may be tried summarily with the consent of the accused under s. 19 of the Act (see "Progress of a Case", later) and libel published in a newspaper (s. 125).

In this 1952 Act "indictable offence" means an offence which if committed by an adult is triable on indictment (whether or not it is also triable by a magistrates' court) except an offence otherwise triable only by a magistrates' court but which under s. 25 of the Act (right to claim trial by jury) or any other Act is required to be tried on indictment by the accused or the prosecutor (s. 25).

A Juvenile Court under the Children & Young Persons Act 1933 is a Court of Summary Jurisdiction (s. 45). It is composed of specially qualified justices (C. & Y.P. Act 1963, Sched. 2) and deals with charges against and applications relating to children and young persons (s. 46). See the Magistrates' Courts (C. and Y.P.) Rules 1970.

The provisions of the M.C. Act 1952 relating to the constitution, place of sitting and procedure of magistrates' courts have effect as regards juvenile courts subject to any special rules regarding such courts (s. 130).

It should deal with persons under 17 (who are not jointly charged with adults), and in certain circumstances it may deal with persons over 17 (s. 46 and s. 48 as amended by C.J. Act 1948, Sched. 9; and C. & Y.P. Act 1963, Sched. 3). It sits apart (different room or time) from other courts, and is not an open court (s. 47 as amended by C. & Y.P. Act 1963, s. 17). See "Open Court" later and "Treatment of Youthful Offenders", Chap. 12.

It should consist of not more than three justices, including one man, and one woman. A stipendiary magistrate may sit alone (Juvenile Courts (Constitution) Rules 1954).

A Domestic Proceedings Court is somewhat similar to a juvenile court. It deals with guardianship of infants, separation and maintenance matters, family allowances and marriage under 21 and is not an open court. Newspaper reports of such proceedings are restricted to prescribed particulars and any contravention requires the consent of the Attorney-General before prosecution (M.C. Act 1952, ss. 56 to 62).

The Coroner's Court deals with inquiries (inquests) as to the cause of the sudden or violent or unnatural death of any person, and also inquires into cases of treasure trove (valuables found concealed in the earth). The Coroner is in sole charge of this court and may have the assistance of a jury. See "Coroners and Inquests", Chap. 39.

Justices of the Peace – A justice is a magistrate appointed by the Crown and commissioned to keep the peace, to receive complaints of offences, to deal with offences determinable in a summary way, and to commit offenders for trial by jury.

Justices are appointed for a "Commission Area" (Administration of Justice Act 1973, s. 1). A commission area means any county, any London commission area and the City of London. They receive no salary but may get travelling and lodging allowances. Before a justice may act he must take the judicial oath and the oath of allegiance. His appointment is for life or until deprived of the Commission of the Peace but he may be placed on the supplemental list owing to age or for other reasons.

A Stipendiary Magistrate is a barrister or solicitor appointed to act as a paid magistrate. He is a justice of the peace and can do alone any act which by law requires two or more justices (M.C. Act 1952, s. 121).

The ordinary sittings or sessions in court of the justices are termed magistrates' courts and take place in an open court-house. These are courts of Summary Jurisdiction.

A single justice sitting alone in a court-house may deal with a few summary offences (such as drunkenness) when the power to do so has been specially given by the Act of Parliament creating the offence.

A single justice may receive informations and complaints, issue summonses and warrants, and under s. 4, M.C. Act 1952, he can as an examining justice hold the preliminary inquiries into indictable offences which are known as "taking depositions", and discharge the prisoner or send him for trial on indictment.

"Examining justices" means the justices before whom a charge is made against a person for an indictable offence and the term includes a single examining justice (C.J. Act 1925, s. 49 (2)).

A justice who is a member of a local authority must not act in a court dealing with any proceedings by or against the local authority. (Justices of the Peace Act 1949, s. 3).

A single justice has power, even when not sitting in a court, to bind over persons who quarrel or commit a breach of the peace in his presence and to deal with some statutory offences.

However, this power is seldom exercised, and a justice as a rule does not act judicially unless as a justice in a court.

Justices were originally appointed for the conservation of the peace, but their jurisdiction and powers have been greatly extended by Acts of Parliament. They now have power to deal summarily with many offences, including a number of those indictable offences regarding which they formerly could hold only a preliminary inquiry to ascertain whether the case was one which ought to be sent for trial by a jury (see s. 19, M.C. Act 1952, for list of such offences which is given later).

Proceedings before Justices – The proceedings of magistrates' courts and examining justices are now regulated by the M.C. Acts 1952 and 1957, C.J. Act 1967 and M.C. Rules 1968 and 1975 and s. 46 (1A), C. & Y.P. Act 1933, as added by Sched. 5 (para. 4) C. & Y.P. Act 1969. (References in brackets are to the 1952 Act, unless otherwise stated.)

MAGISTRATES' COURTS – On the summary trial of an information the court shall, if the accused appears, tell him the charge and ask him whether he pleads guilty or not. After hearing the evidence and the parties, the court shall convict the accused or dismiss the information. If accused pleads guilty the court may convict him without hearing evidence (s. 13). The M.C. Act 1957, as supplemented by the M.C. Rules 1968, introduced a procedure for magistrates' courts, other than Juvenile Courts, which allows defendants, in certain circumstances, to plead guilty without appearing in court, and also provided for the easier proof of previous convictions in the defendant's absence.

In cases which appear appropriate, it rests with the prosecution to initiate the new procedure, by serving with the summons a notice outlining the procedure and another notice giving a "Statement of Facts", which will be read to the court. (A copy of the "Statement of Facts" must be sent to the Clerk of the magistrates' court. M.C. Rules 1968, r. 61.) (This procedure may be applied by courts in England and Wales in respect of accused persons who are in Scotland (C.J. (Scotland) Act 1963, s. 40). The summons must be backed by a court in Scotland, but the notice and statement of facts do not require backing.) At the hearing the prosecution will not be allowed to add to the "Statement of Facts". After conviction, the court may take into account any previous convictions if satisfied that the defendant has had 7 days' notice served upon him, in the prescribed manner, that the convictions would be brought to the notice of the court. This procedure may not be used for an offence triable on indictment, nor for an offence punishable by more than 3 months' imprisonment (M.C. Act 1957, s. 1). The court may at any time adjourn the trial (M.C. Act 1952, s. 14). See "Remand", Chap. 5.

If the prosecutor appears but the accused does not, the court, on proof of summons, may proceed in his absence or adjourn the hearing. If the conditions of this section and of s. 4, M.C. Act 1957, are satisfied the court may issue a warrant to arrest him and bring him before the court (s. 15). A warrant of arrest under the aforementioned section shall not be issued unless (a) the offence is punishable with imprisonment, and (b) the court, having convicted the defendant, proposes to impose a disqualification on him (C.J. Act 1967, s. 24 (2)).

If the accused appears but the prosecutor does not, the court may dismiss the case or if evidence had been previously received proceed in the absence of the prosecutor or adjourn the trial (s. 16).

If both prosecutor and accused do not appear the court may dismiss the case or proceed in their absence if evidence had been received on a previous occasion (s. 17).

Subject to any law allowing unsworn evidence, evidence given before a court shall be on oath (s. 78). A party to any proceedings before a magistrates' court may be represented by counsel or solicitor and an absent party so represented shall be deemed not to be absent except in cases where law or recognizance require his presence (s. 99).

A magistrates' court shall not impose imprisonment for less than 5 days and shall not order imprisonment on any person under 17 (s. 107). A magistrates' court, unless it is of opinion that no other method of dealing with him is appropriate, shall not pass sentence of imprisonment on an offender under 21 (C.J. Act 1948, s. 17). Their power to order imprisonment is dealt with in s. 108 and to order detention in ss. 109 to 111.

A court by or before which a person is convicted of an offence, in addition to dealing with him in any other way, may make a "compensation order" requiring him to pay compensation for any personal injury, loss or damage resulting from that offence or any other offence which is taken into consideration by the court in determining sentence (P. of C.C. Act 1973, s. 35).

Justices sitting in a magistrates' court may, when necessary, act as examining justices.

EXAMINING JUSTICES – The functions of examining justices may be discharged by a single justice. Evidence shall be given in the presence of the accused and the defence may question any witness (s. 4) but examining justices may allow evidence to be given before them in the absence of the accused if (a) they consider that by reason of his disorderly conduct before them it is not practicable for the evidence to be given in his presence; or (b) he cannot be present for reasons of health but is represented by counsel or a solicitor and has consented to the evidence being given in his absence (C.J. Act 1972, s. 45).

A witness's evidence shall be taken down in writing and his deposition shall be authenticated by the justice. The accused can give evidence and call witnesses to give evidence and his counsel or solicitor shall be heard on his behalf (M.C. Rules 1968, r. 4).

The justices shall issue a witness order in respect of each witness examined, other than the accused and a witness as to character only, requiring him to attend and give evidence at the court of trial. See "Deposition", Chap. 6. The witness order is to be conditional if it appears to the court, after taking into account any representation made by the accused or the prosecutor, that the attendance of the witness at the trial is unnecessary. See M.C. Rules 1968, r. 5.

The justices may at any time adjourn the hearing and remand the accused (s. 6), see "Remand", Chap. 5. Any statement by accused in answer to the charge should be taken down in writing and signed by one of the justices (M.C. Rules 1968, r. 5) and may be given in evidence at his trial without further proof (C.J. Act 1925, s. 12, as amended by Sched. 5, M.C. Act 1952).

If satisfied that there is sufficient evidence to put the accused on trial for any indictable offence, the justices shall commit him in custody or on bail for trial by jury. If not so satisfied, if he is in custody for no other cause, they shall discharge him (s. 7).

In any proceedings before a magistrates' court enquiring into a sexual offence (any offence, or attempt to commit such an offence, under the Sexual Offences Act 1956, or the Indecency with Children Act 1960) as examining justices, (1) a child shall not be called as a prosecution witness, but (2) any statement made in writing by or taken in writing from the child shall be admissible in evidence of any matter of which his oral testimony would be admissible, except (a) where at or before the time when such a statement is tendered in evidence the defence objects or (b) where the prosecution requires the attendance of the child for the purpose of establishing the identity of any person or (c) where the court is satisfied that it has not been possible to obtain from the child such a statement or (d) where the enquiry into the offence takes place after the court has discontinued to try it summarily and the child has given evidence in the summary trial. Where the proceedings have begun as committal proceedings and a statement from the child has been put in, but the proceedings changed to a summary trial the child must be called as a witness if his evidence is necessary for the summary trial (s. 27, C. & Y.P. Act 1963).

Before a statement made in writing by or taken in writing from a child is received in evidence under the above s. 27, the court shall cause the effect to be explained to the accused in ordinary language and, if the defence does not object, shall inform him that he may ask questions about the circumstances in which the statement was made or taken.

Examining justices may, if satisfied that all the evidence (whether for the prosecution or defence) consists of written statements, with or without exhibits, commit the defendant for trial without consideration of the contents, unless (a) a defendant is not represented by counsel or solicitor; (b) the court is requested to consider a submission that the statements disclose insufficient evidence (C.J. Act 1967, s. 1).

In committal proceedings, a written statement by any person shall, if the conditions set out below are satisfied, be admissible as evidence to the like extent as oral evidence to the like effect by that person. The conditions are: (a) the statement purports to be signed by the person who made it; (b) the statement contains a declaration by that person that it is true and that he made it knowing that, if it were tendered in evidence, he would be liable to prosecution if he wilfully stated in it anything which he knew to be false or did not believe to be true; (c) before the statement is tendered in evidence, a copy of it is given by or on behalf of the tenderer to each of the other parties to the proceedings; (d) none of the other parties, before the statement is tendered at the proceedings, objects to it being tendered; (e) the statement of a person under 21 must show his age [if the person is under 14, the declaration under condition (b) above should be to the effect that he understands the importance of telling the truth. C. & Y.P. Act 1969, Sched. 5, para. 55—when in force]; (f) if it is made by a person who cannot read, it shall be read to him before he signs it and must be accompanied by a declaration by the reader that it was so read; and (g) if it refers to any other document as an exhibit, the copy given to any other party to the proceedings under (c) above shall be accompanied by a copy of that document or such information that would enable the party to inspect it or a copy of it.

Although a written statement may be admissible under this section, the court may require the person who made it to attend in person.

Any document or object referred to as an exhibit and identified in a written statement tendered in evidence under this section shall be treated as if it had been produced as an exhibit and identified in court by the maker of the statement.

A person whose written statement is tendered in evidence in committal proceedings under this section shall be treated for the purposes of s. 1 of C.P. (A. of W.) Act 1965 (witness orders) as a witness who has been examined by the court (C.J. Act 1967, s. 2).

If any person in a written statement tendered in evidence in criminal proceedings by virtue of s. 2 above wilfully makes a statement material in those proceedings which he knows to be false or does not believe to be true he commits an offence. The Perjury Act 1911 shall have effect as if this section were contained in that Act (C.J. Act 1967, s. 89).

The reporting of committal proceedings is restricted to prescribed particulars, and any contravention requires the consent of the Attorney-General before prosecution (C.J. Act 1967, s. 3).

Notice of the result of committal proceedings must be displayed in the public part of a court-house (C.J. Act 1967, s. 4).

It is the duty of examining justices to sit in open court except in special circumstances (C.J. Act 1967, s. 6).

Trial by Jury – For criminal law purposes a jury is a body of persons called together to give a decision on a criminal matter.

It is the right of every adult to be tried for any serious crime by a jury of his fellow citizens and it is the duty of his fellow citizens to attend for the purpose when summoned to do so. Men and women over 18 years of age may serve on a jury. Persons over 65 or engaged in various professions and occupations are exempted from jury service. Others who may not serve include: the mentally ill; persons who have not been resident in the U.K. for at least 5 years; persons who have ever been sentenced to more than 5 years' imprisonment; and persons who have in the past 10 years served any part of a sentence of 3 months or more.

Persons summoned to attend as jurors who do not attend may be fined by the court.

There are two stages in a criminal trial by jury.

1. Preferring the Indictment. Before a criminal charge can be tried at the Crown Court a written accusation of the crime, which is termed a bill of indictment, must be presented to the Court and approved by the proper authority.

If a person has been committed for trial for an indictable offence (that is for trial by jury), or if a judge of the High Court has consented to or directed such a trial, or if an order under s. 9 of the Perjury Act 1911 has been made directing prosecution for perjury, a bill of indictment charging the accused with the crime, may be preferred by any person before a court in which he may lawfully be indicted for that crime. The Indictments (Procedure) Rules 1933 regulate the manner in which a judge may direct a voluntary bill of indictment where the accused has not been committed for trial by Justices. See Administration of Justice (Misc. Provisions) Act 1933, s. 2.

Thus, where a person is sent for trial by the justices or by a Judge, etc., and a bill of indictment against him is framed and handed in (by the prosecution), and is duly signed by the Clerk of the Court, the case is ready for trial by a jury.

2. Trial by Jury. A "panel" or list of persons summoned to attend at the Crown Court as persons qualified and liable to serve as jurors is prepared and is in readiness in court. A jury consists of 12 persons, the first 12 names called at random from the list by the Clerk of the Court. When the 12 jurors take their place in the jury box they are sworn to well and truly try the case and to give a true verdict according to the evidence.

The indictment against the prisoner is read, and the case proceeds. If a juror dies or has to be discharged through illness, but the number is not reduced below nine, the trial may proceed and a verdict reached. However, on a trial for murder or for any offence punishable by death, this will not apply unless both sides assent in writing. On the death or discharge of a member of the jury in the course of a criminal trial, the court may discharge the jury if it sees fit to do so (Juries Act 1974, s. 16).

The duty of the jury is to listen to the evidence and to give their verdict whether the prisoner is innocent or guilty.

Before the 12 jurors are called to come to the jury box, the prisoner should be informed that he has a right to challenge (or object to) any or all of them before they are sworn.

The Crown or the prisoner may challenge the array, that is the whole panel or list of jurors, or may challenge the polls, that is individual jurors, and cause or good reason for every such objection must be shown.

A person charged on indictment may challenge peremptorily not more than 7 jurors without cause, and any juror or jurors for cause (Juries Act 1974, s. 12). The Crown has the right of calling on jurors to "stand by", that is, not to enter the jury box when called, but to remain in their places in the court as they are not wanted on that particular jury.

The verdict of the jury in criminal proceedings need not be unanimous if (a) in a case where there are not less than eleven jurors, ten of them agree; and (b) where there are ten jurors, nine of them agree (Juries Act 1974, s. 17). The jury must not have any communication with the outside public, and a juror must not disclose what has occurred in the jury room.

The common law offence of embracery consists in attempting by any corrupt means to illegally influence jurors or incline them to favour one party in the case. It is also a common law offence to personate a juryman.

Progress of a Case – As shown in Chap. 1, offences may be arranged in two groups, viz. indictable offences and summary offences, which are termed non-indictable. How a case may be dealt with will depend whether the offence is indictable or non-indictable.

(1) PROCEDURE IN AN INDICTABLE OFFENCE CASE – The alleged offender is either arrested and brought before a summary court or examining justices or comes on summons before a summary court. If the case is dealt with as indictable to go before a higher court, the evidence is given and recorded in writing in the form of depositions (see Chap. 6) and the justices or court can discharge him or commit him (in custody or on bail) for trial at the Crown Court.

At such a court an indictment is preferred, the witnesses give evidence (against him and for him) and a jury decides whether he is guilty or not guilty. If guilty, the judge of the court pronounces sentence. If convicted, the offender may appeal to the criminal division of the Court of Appeal and may have a further appeal to the House of Lords. See "Appeal", Chap. 5.

Persons of 17 and over charged before summary courts with certain indictable offences may consent to be dealt with summarily (M.C. Act 1952, s. 19).

These indictable offences are given in Sched. 1 to this 1952 Act as amended and include offences under:

(1) Criminal Damage Act 1971, ss. 1 (1) or 1 (1) and (3), or 2 or 3; (2) Offences against the Person Act 1861, ss. 20, 27, 47, 60; (3) Telegraph Act 1868, s. 20; (4) Stamp Duties Management Act 1891, s. 13; (5) Post Office Act 1953, ss. 53, 55 to 58; (6) Perjury Act 1911, s. 5, *re* statutory declarations; (7) Forgery Act 1913, ss. 2 (2) (*a*), 7 (*a*) where value of money or property does not exceed £100 (C.J. Act 1967, s. 27, extends the jurisdiction of a magistrates' court by adding the forgery of receipts under s. 2 (2) (*a*) and of documents in general under s. 4, and the uttering of any document the forgery of which is triable summarily under M.C. Act 1952, s. 19 (This new jurisdiction is subject to no financial limitation); (8) Any indictable offence under the Theft Act 1968 except (a) robbery, aggravated burglary, blackmail and assault with intent to rob; and (b) burglary comprising the commission of, or an intention to commit, an offence which is not included in this Schedule; and (c) burglary in a dwelling if entry to the dwelling or the part of it in which the burglary was committed, or to any building or part of a building containing the dwelling, was obtained by force or deception or by the use of any tool, key or appliance, or if any person in the dwelling was subjected to violence or the threat of violence; and (d) handling stolen goods from an offence not committed in the United Kingdom; (9) Criminal Justice Act 1925, s. 36; (10) Agricultural Credits Act 1928, s. 11; (11) Coinage Offences Act 1936, ss. 4, 5, 7 and 8; (12) Indecent assault on male or female; (13) Offences *re* national insurance stamps; (14) Aiding, abetting, counselling or procuring the commission of any of the preceding offences, attempting to commit any such offence, and attempting to commit any offence which is both an indictable offence and a summary offence; (15) Any incitement to commit a summary offence or to commit any offence mentioned in paras. 1 to 18 of the Schedule; (16) C.L. Act 1967, s. 4 (5); (17) Sexual Offences Act 1967, s. 4.

Note.—A person of 17 or upwards who is before a summary court charged with an offence (not an assault or an offence under ss. 30 or 31 of the Sexual Offences Act 1956 or s. 32 of the said Act if the immoral purpose is other than the commission of a homosexual act, or s. 5 of the Sexual Offences Act 1967) punishable with imprisonment exceeding 3 months, has the right to claim trial by jury and if he does the case will be dealt with as indictable (M.C. Act 1952, s. 25).

(2) PROCEDURE IN OFFENCES PUNISHABLE SUMMARILY OR ON INDICTMENT – The Magistrates' Courts Act 1952, s. 18 (as amended by C. & Y.P. Act 1969, s. 6 (2)), deals with such cases as follows:

Where an information charges a person with such an offence the summary court shall, if the accused is 17 or over, proceed as if the case was indictable unless the court having jurisdiction to try the case summarily, determines to do so on the application of the prosecution made before any evidence is offered (sub-ss. (1) and (2)).

Where the magistrates under sub-s. (1) have begun to try such a case summarily, they may, at any time before the conclusion of the evidence for the prosecution, discontinue the summary trial and proceed to inquire into the case as examining justices (sub-s. (5)). But, except as thus provided in s. 18 (5) (or s. 13, C.J.A. Act 1962), a summary court, having begun to try an indictable case summarily, cannot afterwards deal with it as indictable (s. 24). Where the magistrates, under sub-s. (1), have begun to inquire into the case as examining justices then, at any time during the inquiry, on representations made by either party in the presence of the accused, they may proceed to try the case summarily but if the Director of Public Prosecutions is prosecuting his consent is necessary (sub-s. (3)). If such a summary trial is agreed on, any evidence (except a written statement which is admissible as evidence in committal proceedings under C.J. Act 1967, s. 2) already given before the examining justices shall be deemed to have been given to the court for the purposes of the summary trial (s. 23, see Examining Justices *ante*—for evidence of children in committal proceedings for sexual offences), but unless accused pleads guilty the court shall recall such previous witnesses for cross-examination except any not required for such purpose by the prosecutor or accused (M.C. Rules 1968, r. 19).

This s. 18 does not affect any right given by law enabling the accused or the prosecutor to claim that a summary offence shall be tried by a jury (sub-s. (6)).

A person of 17 or more charged with any of the indictable offences given in Sched. 1 (see above) may be dealt with summarily. This can be done at any time during the inquiry, after representations made in the presence of the accused by either party, if the court considers it expedient and the accused consents. If the Director of Public Prosecutions is the prosecutor his consent is necessary as is the consent of the prosecutor in a case affecting the property or affairs of the Crown or of a public body (M.C. Act 1952, s. 19).

The accused should be told of his right to be tried by a jury and should be asked whether he wishes, instead of being tried summarily, to be tried by a jury, and should be told (as directed by s. 19) that if convicted summarily, the court, on hearing his character and antecedents, may commit him under s. 29, M.C. Act 1952 in custody or on bail to the Crown Court for heavier punishment in accordance with s. 42 of P. of C.C. Act 1973. See "Previous Convictions", Chap. 7.

Where, under s. 19 (5) of M.C. Act 1952 a magistrates' court has ceased to inquire into an information summarily, the court may, at any time before the conclusion of the evidence for the prosecution, discontinue the summary trial and resume the inquiry as examining justices (C.J.A. Act 1962, s. 13).

(3) PROCEDURE IN A SUMMARY OFFENCE CASE – The offender comes before a magistrates' court usually on summons but sometimes on arrest with or without warrant. The evidence is heard and the justices give their decision. A person thus convicted may appeal to the Crown Court, or may take a special case stated on a point of law to the Queen's Bench Division. The decision of the Crown Court on any question of fact is final, but that court may state a special case on a point of law for the opinion of the Queen's Bench Division. See "Case Stated", Chap. 5.

If a person of 17 or more is charged with a summary offence (which is not an assault nor an offence under ss. 30, 31, or 32 of the Sexual Offences Act 1956 or s. 32 of the said Act if the immoral purpose is other than the commission of a homosexual act, or s. 5 of the Sexual Offences Act 1967) which is punishable by more than 3 months imprisonment or if a previous conviction of a like offence would justify like imprisonment, and if he appears in court in person and before he pleads to the charge, he should be informed by the court that he has the right to claim trial by jury. (M.C. Act 1952, s. 25). If his right to so claim is based on the fact that he was previously convicted of a like offence, the court should make enquiry to verify the fact of his previous conviction (M.C. Rules 1968, r. 21). Proper proof of such conviction seems advisable.

Where the prosecutor is entitled to claim trial by jury he must make his claim before the accused pleads to the charge.

If either party, being so entitled, makes such claim, the case has to be treated as indictable.

Where an accused of 17 or over is charged with a summary offence for which he may claim trial by jury and which is also triable on indictment, if the court, having begun to inquire into it as an indictable offence then proceeds under s. 18 of the Act (see above) to deal with it summarily, the court shall, before asking the accused if he wishes to be tried by a jury, explain to him that if tried summarily and convicted he may be committed to the Crown Court (under s. 29) if his character and antecedents call for greater punishment than the summary court can inflict (M.C. Act 1952, s. 25).

Open Court – The general rule regarding the trial of an offence, whether indictable or summary, is that the trial should take place in open public court—that is, in a room or place to which the public generally may have access so far as the same may conveniently contain them. See M.C. Act 1952, s. 98 (4).

All evidence in a case must be given in court in the presence of the accused or his advocate (*R.* v. *Bodmin Justices, Ex parte McEwen* (1947)).

This "open court" rule applies to the taking of evidence by examining justices in indictable cases which are not being dealt with summarily, but it does not apply to applications for summonses or warrants, and such preliminary steps preceding actual trial may be taken privately.

Also it has been established by decided cases that a court has an inherent power to exclude the public from a trial if it is necessary for the administration of justice, but such power should be exercised only for good reason. See 92 J.P.N. 79.

No person other than court officials, persons concerned in the case, and press representatives, is allowed to attend in a Juvenile Court, except by leave of the court (C. & Y.P. Act 1933, s. 47); and the same rule applies to Domestic Proceedings Courts (M.C. Act 1952, s. 57).

The only persons prohibited by law from being present as spectators in court are children under 14 years of age, not being infants in arms. If a child is present in court he shall be removed unless he is the accused or during such times as his presence is required as a witness or otherwise for the purposes of justice, but the prohibition does not apply to messengers, clerks, etc. required to attend at a court for purposes connected with their employment (C. & Y.P. Act 1933, s. 36).

When a child or young person is to give evidence in relation to an offence or conduct contrary to decency or morality, the court may order the court to be cleared and all persons who are not officers of the court or connected with the case or pressmen shall be excluded from the court (C. & Y.P. Act 1933, s. 37).

In any proceedings under the Official Secrets Acts, the court on the application of the prosecution, may exclude the public during the hearing of the case (s. 8 (4), Official Secrets Act 1920).

A court has power to order the removal of persons who disturb the proceedings. See also "Contempt of Court", Chap. 21.

A court has power to order witnesses out of court. See "Witnesses out of Court", Chap. 7. A witness who has given evidence should remain in court until permitted to leave.

Speeches in Court – Under the Magistrates' Courts Act 1952, s. 13, on the summary trial of an information, the court will hear the parties in the case who, by s. 99, may be represented by counsel or solicitor.

On the summary trial of an information, where the accused does not plead guilty, the prosecutor shall call the evidence for the prosecution, and before doing so may address the court. At the conclusion of the evidence for the prosecution, the accused may address the court, whether or not he afterwards makes an unsworn statement or calls evidence. At the conclusion of the evidence, if any, for the defence, the prosecutor may call evidence to rebut that evidence. At the conclusion of the evidence for the defence and any unsworn statement which the accused may make and the evidence, if any, in rebuttal, the accused may address the court if he has not already done so. Either party may, with the leave of the court, address the court a second time, but where the court grants leave to one party it shall not refuse leave to the other. Where both parties address the court twice the prosecutor shall address the court for the second time before the accused does so. (M.C. Rules 1968, r. 13).

M.C. Rules 1968, r. 14, prescribes the procedure on the hearing of a complaint (civil proceedings) except where the court makes an order under s. 45 of the Act (civil debt, etc.) with the consent of the defendant without hearing evidence.

The "prosecutor" could be the person who, under M.C. rule 1, laid the information or his counsel or solicitor or other person authorised in that behalf. See also "Lawyers", Chap. 29.

In cases of arrest without warrant the charge sheet would appear to be the "information" and "prosecutor" apparently would include the person who signs the charge sheet as well as the police officer who made the arrest.

M.C. rule 4 deals with the proceedings in a magistrates' court preliminary to the trial of an offence on indictment.

CHAPTER 5

PROCEDURE

	Page
Information	44
Affidavit	45
Summons	45
Subpœna	49
Indictment	50
Venue	50
Accused or Defendant	50
Finger-Prints	51
Warrants	51
Commitment	57
Detention by Police	58
Recognizance	58
Bail	59
Bail by Police	61
Remand	62
Acquittal	63
Appeal	64
Case Stated	65
Certiorari and Mandamus	66
Habeas Corpus	67
Limitation of Proceedings	67
Costs in Criminal Cases	68
Director of Public Prosecutions	69
Justices' Clerks Rules 1970	69

Information – An information is a charge made before a justice (one justice is sufficient) to the effect that some person has or is suspected of having committed an offence (M.C. Act 1952, s. 1). (It is the preliminary step towards obtaining a summons or warrant. The accused person need not be present and, as a rule, is not present). An information need not be in writing or on oath unless some law directs it to be in writing or on oath and it can be made by the prosecutor or by his counsel or solicitor or other person authorised in that behalf (M.C. Rules 1968, r. 1). The laying of an information, other than one on oath, may be made before a Justices' Clerk (see Appendix VI).

When a warrant to arrest is required the information should be written and on oath. A written sworn information is advisable in cases of indictable offences (M.C. Act 1952, s. 1).

It should give the name, address, and occupation of the person charged and a brief outline of the offence or act alleged together with the time and place where it was committed. The offence should be described in ordinary language and reasonable information of the charge should be given. If the offence is one created by law there should be a reference to the law, giving the section. This applies to every information, summons, warrant or other document made for or in connection with any proceedings before a magistrates' court for any offence (M.C. Rules 1968, r. 83).

An information should not charge more than one offence but two or more informations can be set out in one document (M.C. Rules 1968, r. 12). Several offenders may be included in the same information provided it refers to the same act or offence committed at the same place and time.

A justice in his discretion on an information may grant a summons or warrant (M.C. Act 1952, s. 1). Where any law gives power to a magistrates' court to deal with an offence or issue a summons or warrant against a person suspected of an offence on complaint of any person, for references to a complaint there shall be substituted references to an information (M.C. Act 1952, s. 42).

Except as otherwise expressly provided by any enactment a magistrates' court shall not try an information unless the information was laid within 6 months from the time when the offence was committed but this does not restrict summary trial of an indictable offence which may be tried summarily with the consent of the accused but not otherwise (M.C. Act 1952, s. 104).

No objection to defects in an information shall be allowed (M.C. Act 1952, s. 100, but see under "Summons" later).

An informant in summary cases may conduct his case, examine and cross-examine witnesses and if necessary give evidence (*Duncan* v. *Toms* (1887)).

Affidavit – An affidavit is a written statement upon oath taken before any person duly authorised to administer the oath. An affidavit may be made before a justice or a Commissioner or other person empowered by law to administer an oath.

The knowingly and wilfully making of a false statement in an affidavit is punishable under the Perjury Act 1911, and the forgery of an affidavit with intent to defraud or deceive is an offence under the Forgery Act 1913.

The service of a summons may be proved by affidavit.

Summons – A summons is a written order directing the person named therein to appear at a given time in the court named with reference to a matter set out therein. A summons shall be signed by the justice issuing it or state his name and be authenticated by the signature of the Clerk of a magistrates' court (M.C. Rules 1968, r. 81). A summons may also be issued by a Justices' Clerk (see Appendix VI).

A summons should state shortly the matter of the information or complaint. If an offence is charged the offence should be described in ordinary language, and if the offence is one created by Statute or Regulation, etc., the section creating it should be given (M.C. Rules 1968, r. 83). Where two or more informations (or complaints) are laid against the same person or persons a single summons may be issued against that person or each of those persons in respect of all the informations, provided that the matter of each information (or complaint) shall be separately stated in the summons. Any such summons shall be treated as if it were a separate summons in respect of each information (or complaint). See M.C. Rules 1968, r. 81.

Proceedings by summons is the usual method of making persons amenable for offences, and the issue of a summons rests in the discretion of the justice to whom application is made.

Under the M.C. Act 1952, s. 1, a justice on information before him that a person has or is suspected to have committed an offence, may issue a summons requiring him to appear before a magistrates' court in his county. The issue of the summons is subject to the conditions laid down in the section and depends on the place of the offence and the whereabouts of the person (ss. 1 and 3).

If law requires the information to be laid before two or more justices one justice may issue the summons (or warrant) (M.C. Act 1952, s. 1). A summons remains valid even if the justice who issued it has died or ceased to be a justice (M.C. Act 1952, s. 101).

Although a summons for an indictable offence has been issued a warrant to arrest may afterwards be issued at any time (M.C. Act 1952, s. 1).

Where a summons has been issued under the above section and a magistrates' court has begun to try the information, then if (a) the defendant, at any time during or after the trial makes a statutory declaration that he did not know of the summons or the proceedings until a date specified in the declaration, being a date after the court has begun to try the information and (b) within 14 days of that date the declaration is served on the Clerk of the justices, without prejudice to the validity of the information, the summons and all subsequent proceedings shall be void (C.J. Act 1967, s. 24 (3)). (Where the Clerk of a magistrates' court receives such a statutory declaration, he shall (a) note the receipt of the declaration, and (b) inform the prosecutor and, if the prosecutor is not a constable, the chief officer of police (M.C. Rules 1968, r. 18)). Where any proceedings have become void by virtue of the above, the information shall not be tried again by any of the same justices (C.J. Act 1967, s. 24 (6)).

Witness summonses direct persons to appear before a court and give evidence or produce documents or things.

Where a justice is satisfied that any person in England or Wales is likely to give material evidence or produce any document or thing as material evidence at any inquiry or trial or hearing by a magistrates' court for his area and that person will not voluntarily attend the court and give evidence etc., he shall issue a summons directing the person to attend and give evidence etc.

If a justice is satisfied by evidence on oath as above and it is probable such person will not attend on summons, he may, instead of summons, issue a warrant to arrest him and bring him before the court (but this cannot be done for the hearing of a complaint). If such person does not attend on summons without just excuse, the court, on evidence on oath, may issue a warrant to arrest him and bring him before the court.

If such a witness, in court, refuses without just excuse to be sworn or give evidence or produce any document or thing, the court may commit him in custody for up to 7 days or until he sooner complies (M.C. Act 1952, s. 77). An application for a witness summons or warrant under the foregoing s. 77 may be made either by the applicant in person or by his counsel or solicitor; and an application for a witness summons only (not a warrant) may be made by sending it in writing to the Clerk of the magistrates' court for submission to a magistrate (M.C. Rules 1968, r. 88). Conduct money should be paid or tendered with a witness summons.

As regards civil jurisdiction and procedure, the issue of summons on complaint and the hearing of and dealing with complaints are dealt with in ss. 43 to 55 of the M.C. Act 1952.

Under s. 43 a justice acting for a petty sessions area, when complaint is made to him upon which the local summary court has power to make an order against any person, may issue a summons requiring that person to appear before such court.

Under s. 100 of the M.C. Act 1952, no objection shall be allowed to any information or complaint or to any summons, or warrant to procure the presence of a defendant, for any defect in substance or form or any variance between it and the evidence at the hearing, but if the court considers that any variance between a summons or warrant and the evidence at the hearing has misled the defendant, it shall, on the application of the defendant, adjourn the hearing.

Service of a summons issued by a justice of the peace on a person other than a corporation may be effected:

(a) by delivering it to the person to whom it is directed; or
(b) by leaving it for him with some person at his last known or usual place of abode; or
(c) by sending it by post in a registered letter or by recorded delivery service addressed to him at his last known or usual place of abode (M.C. Rules 1968, r. 82 (1)).

If the person summoned fails to appear, service of a summons in manner authorised by sub-paragraph (b) or (c) of the preceding paragraph shall not be treated as proved unless it is proved that the summons came to his knowledge; and for that purpose any letter or other communication purporting to be written by him or on his behalf in such terms as reasonably to justify the inference that the summons came to his knowledge shall be admissible as evidence of that fact:

Provided that this paragraph shall not apply to any summons in respect of a summary offence which is not also an indictable offence (M.C. Rules 1968, r. 82 (2)).

Service for the purposes of the Act of a summons or other document issued by a justice of the peace on a corporation may be effected by delivering it at, or sending it by post to, the registered office of the corporation, if that office is in England and Wales, or, if there is no registered office in England and Wales, any place in England and Wales where the corporation trades or conducts its business (M.C. Rules 1968, r. 82 (3)).

Any summons or other document served in manner authorised by the preceding provisions of this rule shall, for the purposes of any enactment other than the Act or these Rules requiring a summons or other document to be served in any particular manner, be deemed to have been as effectively served as if it had been served in that manner; and nothing in this rule shall render invalid the service of a summons or other document in that manner (M.C. Rules 1968, r. 82 (4)).

Sub-paragraph (c) of paragraph (1) of this rule shall not authorise the service by post of:

(a) a summons requiring the attendance of any person to give evidence or produce a document or thing; or
(b) a summons issued under any enactment relating to the liability of members of the naval, military or air forces of the Crown for the maintenance of their wives and children, whether legitimate or illegitimate;

or authorise a summons to be served outside England and Wales (M.C. Rules 1968, r. 82 (5)).

Where this rule or any other of these Rules provides that a summons or other document may be sent by post to a person's last known or usual place of abode that rule shall have effect as if it provided also for the summons or other document to be sent in the manner specified in the rule to an address given by that person for that purpose (M.C. Rules 1968, r. 82 (6)).

This rule shall not apply to a judgment summons (M.C. Rules 1968, r. 82 (7)).

If service by post is not effective and therefore the summons has not been served within the prescribed time after the commission of the offence, on proof of due posting, a second summons may be issued (M.C. Act 1952, s. 37).

A summons for an indictable offence should be served by a constable and for a summary offence by a constable or other person to whom it shall be delivered.

The person who has served a summons should endorse his copy with the time, place and manner of service and may have to attend court to prove the service.

A summons should be served a reasonable time previous to the hearing of the case and it must be personally served when so directed by the Statute, etc., under which proceedings are taken.

Process (including summons, warrants, etc.) issued by a summary court in England may be executed in Scotland and (by Order 1928) the Isle of Man if duly endorsed by a justice of the district in which it is to be executed. See Summary Jurisdiction (Process) Act 1881, C.J. Act 1972, s. 51, and P. of C.C. Act 1973, s. 53.

The service on any person of a summons or document required or authorised to be served in any proceedings before a magistrates' court and the handwriting or seal of a justice or other person on any summons, warrant or document issued or made in any such proceedings may be proved in any legal proceedings by a solemn declaration made under this rule. The service of any document which should be served and the proper preparation and posting of a letter containing such a document may be proved in a summary court and at the Crown Court in appeal cases by a certificate signed by the person who effected the service or posted or registered the letter (M.C. Rules 1968, r. 55). Service by registered post has been extended to include service by recorded delivery (M.C. Rules 1968, r. 92).

Any statement false in a material particular in any solemn declaration certificate or other writing made to be used as evidence of the service of any document or the handwriting or seal of any person is punishable summarily (M.C. Act 1952, s. 82).

For the purpose of any criminal proceedings before the Crown Court a witness summons, viz. a summons requiring the person to whom it is directed to attend before the court and give evidence or produce any document or thing specified in the summons, may be issued out of that court or the High Court. The court which has issued a witness summons is empowered to direct that the summons shall be of no effect if satisfied by the person to whom the summons was issued that he cannot give material evidence or produce the document or thing required (C.P. (A. of W.) Act 1965, s. 2).

Section 4 of the C.P. (A. of W.) Act 1965 makes further provision for securing the attendance at a court of trial of a witness who is thought unlikely to comply with a witness order or witness summons to which he is subject or who has failed to comply with such an order or summons. A new power is given under this Act to a High Court judge by which he may issue a warrant for the arrest of a witness where he is satisfied that the witness is unlikely to appear. This power was already possessed by magistrates under s. 77 of the M.C. Act 1952.

Subpœna – A subpœna is a writ or order commanding attendance in court on a certain day named therein under a penalty (*pœna*). A witness summons has much the same effect.

Subpœnas may be issued by the Crown Court.

A person served with a subpœna may also be given a reasonable sum of money, sufficient to enable him to get to the court.

Subpœnas may be used to secure the attendance of witnesses. A subpœna may merely direct a witness to attend and give evidence (a subpœna *ad testificandum*), or it may direct him to attend, give evidence, and produce named documents in evidence (a subpœna *duces tecum*).

By the C.P. (A. of W.) Act **1965**, s. 8—No subpœna *ad testificandum* or subpœna *duces tecum* shall issue in respect of any proceedings for the purpose of which a witness summons may be issued under s. 2 of this Act, or in respect of any proceedings for the purpose of which a summons may be issued under s. 77 of the M.C. Act 1952.

Indictment – An indictment is a written or printed accusation setting out the crime for which a person is to be tried by the Crown Court.

Hence the term "indictable offence" which is applied to all offences which may be tried at the Crown Court.

More than one person may be charged with the crime in an indictment, as in the case of conspiracy.

Several crimes may be charged in an indictment, and each will be described in a separate paragraph, called a "count", but no one count should charge more than one offence. Each count should be put to the prisoner separately and he must be asked to plead to each count (*R.* v. *Boyle* (1954)).

Before a prisoner can be tried for a crime at the Crown Court, this written accusation, then called a "bill of indictment", must be given to the Clerk of the Court and it must be signed by him. Otherwise the case cannot be heard by the court and jury. When so signed the "bill" becomes an "indictment". See "Trial by Jury", Chap. 4.

Venue – The venue is the place of trial.

A magistrates' court may try all summary offences committed within its county. It has jurisdiction as examining justices over any offence committed by a person who appears or is brought before the court whether or not the offence was committed within its county, and in such cases it has jurisdiction to try summarily indictable offences where it has power to do so under ss. 18 (3) and 19 of the Act (M.C. Act 1952, s. 2).

The jurisdiction of a summary court extends to offences committed on boundaries and on journeys begun in one jurisdiction and completed in another (M.C. Act 1952, s. 3).

Accused or Defendant – An "accused" is a person charged on information with an offence, summary or indictable and liable to be tried by a court (see M.C. Act 1952, s. 1).

If he is arrested and appears before a court in custody he is "the prisoner". At the Crown Court he must take his place in the dock or place for prisoners and face the judge and jury being thus the prisoner at the bar of the court.

A "defendant" is a person ordered by legal process to appear before a court to defend what he has done or left undone.

A defendant is called to a magistrates' court by summons issued (on complaint) by a justice of the petty sessions area, who can do so when such court has power to make an order against any person upon such complaint (see M.C. Act 1952, s. 43).

When his case is to be tried the accused's name is called. The charge against him is read and he is asked whether he is or is not guilty.

The burden of proving any excuse, exemption, etc., rests on the accused (M.C. Act 1952, s. 81).

The trial will then proceed, unless an adjournment is allowed by the court (M.C. Act 1952, ss. 13, 14). See "Proceedings before Justices", Chap. 4 and "Remand", later.

Where a complaint is to be heard the court shall state the complaint to the defendant and hear evidence and make an order or dismiss the complaint or may adjourn the hearing (M.C. Act 1952, ss. 45, 46).

Finger-Prints – Where any person not less than 14 years of age who has been taken into custody or summoned is charged with an offence before a magistrates' court the court may, on the application of a police officer not below the rank of inspector, order that his finger-prints or palm-prints shall be taken by a constable. These may be taken by any reasonable force necessary, either at the court or at any place to which the person may be committed or remanded in custody. If the person is acquitted or discharged by the examining justices, the finger-prints and all copies and records thereof shall be destroyed (M.C. Act 1952, s. 40, as amended by C.J. Act 1967, s. 33). See also "Convicted Persons", Chap. 2.

Note.—The direction above as to destruction if prisoner is acquitted or discharged applies only to finger-prints or palm-prints taken under this s. 40.

Warrants – A warrant is a written authority, signed by a justice, directing the person or persons to whom it is addressed, to arrest an offender to be dealt with according to law, to take a person to prison, to search premises, to levy distress for the non-payment of a legal penalty, etc. (Warrants of commitment or of distress may be signed by justices' Clerks: M.C. Rules 1968, r. 93.)

Before a warrant to arrest may be granted it is necessary that a written sworn information should be made and the warrant may be issued by one justice notwithstanding any law requiring the information to be laid before two or more justices (M.C. Act 1952, s. 1). Such a warrant shall not be issued unless (a) the offence to which the warrant relates is an indictable offence or is punishable with imprisonment, or (b) the address of the defendant is not sufficiently established for a summons to be served on him (C.J. Act 1967, s. 24 (1)). The known circumstances of the case should be placed before the justice, as he has the responsibility for the issue of the warrant. When a warrant to arrest is required in a case depending on the evidence of a witness, it will sometimes be advisable to have a sworn information from the witness stating what he can prove, in support of the application for warrant.

On application for a warrant to arrest for an indictable offence the justice may issue a summons and afterwards issue a warrant at any time. A justice has jurisdiction to issue a warrant to arrest for an offence similar to that allowing him to issue a summons for the offence (M.C. Act 1952, s. 1). See "Summons", above.

A warrant should contain a statement of the offence with which the accused is charged, and this should be set out in ordinary language. If the offence is one created by or under any written law, there should be a reference to the section of the Statute or Regulation etc. (M.C. Rules 1968, r. 83).

The doing of the act directed in the warrant is called the execution of the warrant. The direction of a warrant should be strictly observed, otherwise the person executing it may not be justified in his acts. When a constable receives a warrant for execution he should read it over carefully, to see what it orders him to do and to see that the particulars in it are correct. If a mistake is found in a warrant it must not be altered, but the warrant should be returned without delay to the Clerk to the justices.

A warrant remains valid even if the justice who issued it dies or ceases to hold office (M.C. Act 1952, s. 101).

A warrant of arrest, commitment, distress or search issued by a justice may be executed anywhere in England and Wales by any person to whom it is directed or by any constable acting within his police area (M.C. Act 1952, s. 102, and General Rate Act 1967, s. 99). A warrant to arrest for an offence or a search warrant may be issued and executed on Sunday as on any other day (M.C. Act 1952, s. 102). Such power of execution by any constable in any place does not extend to warrants issued elsewhere than in England or Wales (Criminal Justice Act 1925, s. 49 (3)).

A warrant to arrest a person charged with an offence or an accused person or witness who after due process has not appeared in court or a commitment warrant, where the person has gone to the Isle of Man, Channel Islands or Northern Ireland, or *vice versa*, may be executed in the place where the person is if it is backed (endorsed) by a local magistrate who can do so if the warrant is accompanied by a sworn statement verifying the handwriting (signature) of the justice who has issued the warrant

(Indictable Offences Act 1848, s. 13, and M.C. Act 1952, s. 103). Such a warrant issued in Scotland may be executed in England and Wales and *vice versa,* whether or not it has been backed (endorsed) by a local magistrate (C.J. (Scotland) Act 1963, s. 39).

A warrant issued in the Republic of Ireland may be executed in the United Kingdom provided it has been endorsed (backed) by a magistrate in the United Kingdom. (Backing of Warrants (Republic of Ireland) Act 1965). See also The Magistrates' Courts (Backing of Warrants) Rules 1965. This procedure is complementary to the arrangements for the endorsement and execution in the Irish Republic of warrants issued in the United Kingdom, the Channel Islands and the Isle of Man, legalised by the Irish Extradition Act 1965.

When a constable executing a warrant has it in his possession if asked he should show it and read it to the person concerned but should not allow it out of his possession.

All warrants executed or returned unexecuted should be endorsed by the constable concerned with the date, time and manner of execution, or with the reason for failure to execute or with date of attempt to execute, together with his signature and the date.

WARRANT TO ARREST – Every warrant to arrest should give the offence charged, the authority under which the arrest is made, the person or persons who are to execute it, and the person to be arrested. These warrants direct that the person arrested should be taken forthwith before a court or before a magistrate where the court is situate.

A warrant of arrest issued by a justice remains in force until it is executed or withdrawn.

A warrant to arrest for an offence may be executed by a constable although it is not in his possession at the time, but on demand of the prisoner it shall be shown to him as soon as practicable (M.C. Act 1952, s. 102). In the execution of a warrant for an "arrestable offence" a constable may enter (if need be, by force) and search any place where the person to be arrested is, or where the constable with reasonable cause suspects him to be (C.L. Act 1967, s. 2 (6)). However, the breaking open of outer doors is so dangerous a proceeding that a constable should not resort to it except on reasonable grounds of suspicion and in extreme cases when an immediate arrest is necessary.

WARRANT TO REMAND OR TO COMMIT – This warrant directs that a person be taken to a specified place of detention, where he is to be detained as set forth in the warrant. When the constable delivers such a person at the place, he should hand in the warrant with him and obtain a receipt for the person, which subsequently should be handed in at his police station.

WARRANT TO COMMIT TO PRISON IN DEFAULT – Such a warrant directs that the person be arrested and taken to H.M. Prison unless he pays the amount shown on the warrant.

The person should be asked for the amount. If he pays it a receipt should be given him and the warrant should be endorsed with the date and manner of execution.

The constable holding such a warrant of commitment may receive part payment of the amount and shall note such payment on the warrant. Such a payment will reduce the period of imprisonment (M.C. Act 1952, s. 67, M.C. Rules 1968, r. 45 and General Rate Act 1967, s. 102). If the person cannot or will not pay, he must be arrested and lodged in prison. If the person is arrested after the prison has closed or cannot be brought to the prison before 10 p.m., he may be lodged in the nearest police station until he can be received into prison.

DISTRESS WARRANT – When default is made by a person in paying a sum adjudged to be paid by a conviction or order of a magistrates' court, the court may issue a warrant of distress for levying the sum, or issue a commitment warrant if the distress does not cover the sum or instead of a distress warrant (M.C. Act 1952, s. 64). Under M.C. Rules 1968, r. 44, a distress warrant shall be issued to the police or "authorised person" or any other person named in the warrant requiring them to levy the said sum by distress and sale of the goods belonging to the said person.

The warrant when it is directed to the police may be executed by any person under the direction of a constable. It will authorise the taking of any money as well as any goods of the person and require the person charged with the execution to pay the sum to be levied to the Clerk of the Court.

The wearing apparel or bedding of any person and his family or the tools and implements of his trade up to the value of £50 must not be seized. The distress seized shall be sold within such period specified in the warrant not earlier than the sixth day after the making of the distress or if no period is specified within the period beginning on the sixth day and ending on the fourteenth day after the making of the distress. However the distress may be sold, with the written consent of the person before the beginning of the said period. The distress shall be sold by public auction or in such manner as the person may in writing allow.

There shall be no sale if the sum and the charges of taking and keeping are paid. If household goods are seized they shall not, without the person's written consent, be removed from the house until the day of sale.

A conspicuous mark shall be affixed on the articles impounded. The constable charged with the execution of the warrant shall cause the distress to be sold and may deduct out of the proceeds all costs and charges incurred and return to the owner any balance, retaining the sum payable with the proper costs and charges.

The constable executing the warrant shall as soon as practicable send a written account of the costs and charges incurred to the Clerk of the Court.

If the person pays the sum to the constable or authorised person or produces a receipt for same from the Clerk of the Court and also pays the costs and charges incurred, the constable or authorised person shall not execute the warrant or shall cease to execute as the case may be (M.C. Rules 1968, r. 44). Any constable holding a warrant of distress or commitment in default of payment may receive a part payment (M.C. Rules 1968, r. 45).

Any person who interferes with the mark or removes the marked goods is liable to fine up to £5, and if any person charged with the execution of a distress warrant wilfully retains or exacts excess charges or makes any improper charge he is liable to similar fine on summary conviction (M.C. Act 1952, s. 66).

If there are no goods or no sufficient goods the constable should notify the Clerk of the Court. The warrant should not be executed between sunset and sunrise. Premises should not be broken into and excessive distraint should be avoided.

It is also the duty of the police to execute distress warrants for rates (General Rate Act 1967, s. 99).

The court may order a person adjudged to pay a sum by conviction (or on an affiliation order) to be searched and any money so found or found on him when arrested or in prison, in default of payment or want of sufficient distress to satisfy such sums, may be applied towards payment of the sum adjudged, unless the court is satisfied that such money does not belong to him or that the loss of it would be more injurious to his family than his detention (M.C. Act 1952, s. 68).

SEARCH WARRANT – A warrant to search usually authorises the person to whom it is addressed and his assistants to enter, by force if necessary, the place or premises named, to search every place and thing inside, to seize and take away any articles mentioned in the warrant, and to arrest the persons named in the warrant or the persons in whose possession the articles named are found. A search warrant remains in force until executed or when any limitation of time ends. It is usually "executed" when a search has been made, whether the articles named are found or not, but some search warrants authorise entry at any time or times.

A search warrant may be granted and executed on Sunday (M.C. Act 1952, s. 102). The officer should have the warrant in his possession and produce it to be read if required.

Any special directions in a search warrant must be strictly observed. A search warrant may be granted at common law on sworn complaint alleging suspicion that theft has been committed. It authorises search in any house, etc., in the daytime, and arrest of any person found in possession of the stolen goods.

Reasonable ground of suspicion is necessary before a search warrant is granted, as a justice will not issue a warrant on bare surmise. A search warrant is really a warrant to search for evidence of a crime which is believed to have been committed.

A search warrant may be executed anywhere in England and Wales by the person to whom it is directed or by any constable within his area (M.C. Act 1952, s. 102).

Search warrants may be granted on sworn informations under over 50 Acts of Parliament and in each case the directions given in the Act must be observed. For example:

Theft Act 1968.	For stolen goods.
Coinage Offences Act 1936.	For counterfeit coin, implements, etc.
Forgery Act 1913.	For forged papers, etc.
Explosives Act 1875.	For explosives.
Children and Young Persons Act 1933.	For recovery of children or young persons cruelly treated.
Betting, Gaming and Lotteries Act 1963.	For betting on premises.
Obscene Publications Acts 1959 and 1964.	For obscene articles.
Sexual Offences Act 1956.	For men living on earnings of prostitution and for women detained for immoral purposes.
Licensing Act 1964.	For intoxicating liquor or registered or unregistered clubs.
Offences against the Person Act 1861.	For instruments, etc., for committing an indictable offence under the Act.
Criminal Damage Act 1971.	For things intended for use in committing offences of criminal damage.
Gaming Act 1968.	For gaming on premises.

and other Acts such as the Official Secrets Act 1911, Petroleum (Consolidation) Act 1928, Cruelty to Animals Act 1876, Customs and Excise Act 1952.

Under s. 26 of the Theft Act 1968, a search warrant to search and seize any stolen goods may be granted by a justice; but no such warrant shall be addressed to a person other than a constable except where there is express statutory authority. Also under the same section an authority to a constable to search any premises for stolen goods may be given in writing by a police officer not below the rank of superintendent (a) if the person in occupation of the premises has been convicted within the preceding 5 years of handling stolen goods or of any offence involving dishonesty and punishable with imprisonment; or (b) if a person who has been convicted within the preceding 5 years of handling stolen goods has within the preceding 12 months been in occupation of the premises.

Where a person is authorised to search premises for stolen goods, he may enter and search the premises, and may seize any goods he believes to be stolen goods. (This gives statutory authority for the law laid down in *Chic Fashions* (*West Wales*), *Ltd.* v. *Jones* (1968).) Property which has come into the possession of the police under this section shall be subject to the Police (Property) Act 1897, which enables a magistrates' court to decide claims to property in the possession of the police.

Under s. 73 of the Explosives Act 1875, on reasonable ground for believing that an offence has been or is being committed with respect to an explosive, and if the case is one of emergency and delay in obtaining a warrant would be likely to endanger life, a superintendent of police or other officer of equal or superior rank, may give a written order to enter at any time, if needs be by force, any place, and examine the same and search for explosives therein and take samples of any explosives or ingredients thereof found therein.

Under s. 9 of the Official Secrets Act 1911, in a case of great emergency, when in the interest of the State immediate action is necessary, a superintendent of police may by written order empower any constable to enter, at any time, any place named in the warrant, by force if necessary, and to search such place and every person found therein, and to seize anything which is evidence of an offence under the Official Secrets Act.

Commitment – Commitment or committal in the legal sense means sending a person to prison or detention or for trial or sentence.

A warrant of commitment shall state the offence or other ground on which the person is committed. It is directed to a person named in the warrant or to the police or authorised person of the area to arrest him and convey him to the place mentioned and to the keeper of the place of detention to keep him in his custody in accordance with the directions in the warrant. The arresting officer shall deliver him with the warrant and get the keeper's receipt for the person (M.C. Rules 1968, r. 80).

A person by order of a court or by the warrant of a justice may be committed to prison. When a person has been convicted summarily and sentenced to imprisonment a commitment warrant is made out and on this warrant he is taken to prison to serve his sentence.

A warrant is not necessary in the case of a prisoner sentenced at the Crown Court.

A committal or commitment to prison warrant may be issued in the case of non-payment of money. See "Warrants".

After the preliminary hearing (or examination) by a justice or justices a person accused of an indictable offence may be committed for trial by a judge, etc., and jury in a higher court. Such "committal for trial" means committed to prison but it also includes a person admitted to bail on recognizance to appear and stand his trial (Interpretation Act 1889, s. 27).

Any commitment by a justice to any form of detention shall be by a warrant of commitment (M.C. Rules 1968, r. 77).

Detention by Police – Under the M.C. Act 1952, a magistrates' court may order the detention of persons in police premises as follows:

Detention up to 4 days in police cells, etc., certified for the purpose by the Secretary of State instead of any imprisonment which the court has power to impose (s. 109). This must be by warrant of commitment (M.C. Rules 1968, r. 77).

Detention up to 8 p.m. of the day on which the order is made, in a police station or court-house where the court has power to commit to prison a person convicted of an offence, but the order must not deprive the offender of a reasonable opportunity of returning to his abode on that day (s. 110).

Detention by warrant in a police station when the court has power to commit a person to prison in default of payment of a sum adjudged to be paid by a summary conviction.

This warrant, unless the sum is sooner paid, shall authorise any police constable to arrest the defaulter and take him to a police station where the officer in charge shall detain him until 8 a.m. of the day following that on which he is arrested, or if he is arrested between midnight and 8 a.m., until 8 a.m. of the day on which he was arrested. Provided that the officer may release him at any time within 4 hours before 8 a.m. if the officer thinks it is expedient to do so in order to enable him to go to his work or for any other reason appearing to the officer to be sufficient (s. 111).

If imprisonment for default of payment or sufficient distress is reduced by part payment to less than 5 days, the person may be committed either to prison or to a certified place (under s. 109 above) (M.C. Rules 1968, r. 45). If a magistrates' court has power to remand a person in custody, if the remand does not exceed 3 days, it may commit him to the custody of a constable (M.C. Act 1952, s. 105). This must be by warrant of commitment (M.C. Rules 1968, r. 77).

Recognizance – A recognizance is an obligation of bond under which a person acknowledges that he owes the Crown a certain sum of money if the condition or conditions specified in the recognizance are not carried out.

A person may be ordered to enter into a recognizance with or without sureties.

The recognizances of sureties may be taken separately and before or after the recognizance of the principal (C.J.A. Act 1914, s. 24).

If sureties are required, the person who enters into the recognizance (the principal) and the sureties are liable to pay the amounts specified if the condition prescribed is not fulfilled.

Recognizances may be required for several purposes, such as to keep the peace or to be of good behaviour, to prosecute a particular person, to pursue an appeal, to appear and give evidence, to surrender to a court or when placed on probation.

If a surety makes complaint in writing and on oath to a justice for any county that his principal has broken or is about to break the conditions of his recognizance to keep the peace or be of good behaviour, the justice if the principal is in such area or the recognizance was entered before a magistrates' court of such area, may issue a warrant to arrest the principal and bring him before a magistrates' court. If such complaint is not on oath the justice may issue a summons (M.C. Act 1952, s. 92).

If a recognizance to keep the peace or be of good behaviour or to appear before a magistrates' court or to do anything connected with a proceeding before the court appears to be forfeited, the court may declare it forfeited and adjudge the persons bound to pay the amounts or parts of them. However, if the recognizance was to keep the peace or be of good behaviour, the court shall not declare it forfeited except by order made on complaint (M.C. Act 1952, s. 96). See Chap. 22.

Breach of recognizance is not an offence so there is no appeal against the forfeiting of a recognizance (*R.* v. *Durham Justices, Ex parte Laurent* (1944)).

A magistrates' court may fix the amounts of any recognizance which later may be taken by any justice or the Clerk of any summary court or any police officer not below the rank of inspector or the officer in charge of any police station or the governor or keeper of the prison or place in which the person is detained.

A certificate from the Clerk of the Court giving particulars of the recognizance should be produced to any such person before he takes the recognizance and the recognizance should be sent to the Clerk of the Court (M.C. Act 1952, s. 95; M.C. Rules 1968, r. 72).

Bail – Bail is a recognizance or bond taken by a duly authorised person to ensure the appearance of an accused person at an appointed place and time to answer to the charge made against him. See also "Recognizance", above.

It is based on the principle that an accused person should not be kept unnecessarily in custody, so whenever it is possible and can with safety be done, an untried prisoner should be released on bail.

Bail may be granted by a court, by a justice, and in some cases, as provided by statute, by the officer in charge of a police station.

A person charged with treason shall not be admitted to bail except by order of a judge of the High Court or the Secretary of State (M.C. Act 1952, s. 8).

The object of bail being to secure the attendance of an accused person at the trial, the following points should be considered before bail is allowed:

(1) The probability of accused's appearance at the trial.
(2) The nature and gravity of the charge.
(3) The nature and weight of evidence in support of the charge.
(4) The sufficiency of the sureties, if sureties are required.

Section 18 of C.J. Act 1967 imposes restrictions on refusal of bail. The general rule is that when a court adjourns the trial and remands the prisoner, it shall remand him on bail. However, the rule shall not require a magistrates' court to remand or commit a person on bail (a) where he is charged with an offence punishable by that court with imprisonment for a term of not less than 6 months and it appears to the court that he has been previously sentenced to imprisonment or borstal training; (b) where it appears to the court that, having been released on bail on any occasion, he has failed to comply with the conditions of any recognizance entered into by him on that occasion; (c) where he is charged with an offence alleged to have been committed while he was released on bail; (d) where it appears to the court that it is necessary to detain him to establish his identity or address; (e) where it appears to the court that he has no fixed abode or that he is ordinarily resident outside the United Kingdom; (f) where the act or any of the acts constituting the offence with which he is charged consisted of an assault on or threat of violence to another person, or of having or possessing a firearm, an imitation firearm, an explosive or an offensive weapon, or of indecent conduct with or towards a person under the age of 16 years; (g) where it appears to the court that unless he is remanded or committed in custody he is likely to commit an offence; or (h) where it appears to the court necessary for his own protection to refuse to remand or commit him on bail.

A prisoner may be released on his own recognizance, or one or more sureties may be required in addition to his own bond. Such sureties are termed his bails or bailsmen, and they are responsible, in the amounts fixed, for the prisoner's attendance in court.

The amount of bail is discretionary and will depend on the nature of the charge and the quality of the prisoner. It is illegal to require excessive bail. Usually two householders are accepted as bails, provided the justice or police officer is satisfied of their ability to answer the sums in which they are bound. Bail can be found after a court has risen. See "Recognizance", above.

A bail recognizance may be conditioned for the appearance of the person at every hearing during the course of the proceedings, (M.C. Act 1952, s. 105). This is termed "continuous bail".

If a person charged with or convicted of an offence is released on bail to appear before a summary court and fails to appear, the court may issue a warrant for his arrest (M.C. Act 1952, s. 97).

A person bailed to appear is by law in the custody of his sureties, and they may arrest him either with or without warrant if they fear his escape, and bring him before a magistrate, thereby clearing themselves of their obligation.

If a person on bail fails to appear before the court the recognizance may be forfeited or estreated, and he and his sureties may be adjudged to pay the amounts in which they were bound (M.C. Act 1952, s. 96 and see "Recognizance", above).

The officer in charge of a police station has power to admit to bail prisoners arrested without warrant, and he must, unless there are grave reasons to the contrary, admit to bail prisoners under 17 years of age.

For police powers of arrest of persons granted bail, see C.J. Act 1967, s. 23. Chap. 3, *ante*.

Bail by Police – Certain statutes authorise the police to admit prisoners to bail as follows:

(1) Persons Arrested without Warrant. When a person is arrested without warrant and brought to a police station a police officer not below the rank of inspector or the officer in charge of the station may, and if it will not be practicable to bring him before a summary court within 24 hours of the arrest, will inquire into the case and, unless the offence appears to be a serious one, release him on his entering into a recognizance with or without sureties, for a reasonable amount, to appear before a summary court at a named time and place (this does not affect prisoners under 17 for which see later).

If the inquiry into the case cannot be completed forthwith the officer may release the prisoner on recognizance with or without sureties for a reasonable amount, to appear at the police station at a fixed time unless he receives written notice that his attendance is not required. If the prisoner appears to be under 17, the recognizance conditioned for his appearance at the police station may be taken from his parent or guardian with or without sureties.

If such a prisoner is kept in custody he shall be brought before a summary court as soon as practicable (M.C. Act 1952, s. 38).

(2) Persons Arrested without Warrant for Offences against Children and Young Persons. A person so arrested and brought to a police station shall be released on bail, with or without sureties to attend the hearing of the charge unless his release would tend to defeat the ends of justice or to cause injury or danger to the child or young person against whom the offence is alleged to have been committed (C. & Y.P. Act 1933, s. 13). See "Cruelty to Children and Young Persons", Chap. 12.

(3) Prisoners under 17 years of Age. When a person apparently under 17 is arrested with or without warrant and cannot be brought forthwith before a summary court, his case should be inquired into by the police and he may be released on bail but see "Treatment of Youthful Offenders", Chap. 12, and see above as regards a recognizance to appear at a police station.

(4) Persons Arrested on Warrant. If the warrant to arrest has been endorsed by the justice issuing it with his consent to the prisoner, when arrested, being released on bail, the prisoner, when brought to a police station, should be released on bail in accordance with the directions in the endorsement (M.C. Act 1952, s. 93).

(5) Persons Arrested without Warrant in County Boroughs. Any idle or disorderly person found disturbing the public peace may be arrested by a county borough constable and brought to a police station. Such a prisoner may, if it is thought fit, be released on bail to appear before a justice (Municipal Corporations Act 1882, s. 193).

Remand – Remand is the process of adjourning the hearing of the case against a person and taking precautions to ensure his presence at a future hearing.

A remand is therefore an adjournment under which the court puts back the person in custody or upon recognizance.

The M.C. Act 1952 deals with remand as follows:

A magistrates' court may, before inquiring into an offence as examining justices or at any time during the inquiry adjourn the hearing and, if it does so, shall remand the accused (s. 6).

The court may at any time adjourn the trial of an information. The court, after convicting the accused and before sentence, may adjourn the case (up to 3 weeks at a time if in custody, or 4 weeks if on bail (C.J. Act 1967, s. 30)) for inquiries to be made or to decide the best method of dealing with it.

On adjourning a trial the court may remand the accused and shall do so if the accused is 17 or over and the offence is an indictable one or an indictable offence being tried summarily (s. 14).

If, on the trial by a magistrates' court of an offence punishable on summary conviction with imprisonment, the court is satisfied that the accused did the act or made the omission charged but considers inquiry should be made into his mental or physical condition it shall adjourn the case (up to 3 weeks if in custody, or 4 weeks if on bail (C.J. Act 1967, s. 30)) so that the accused may be medically examined and remand him for that purpose as laid down in the section (s. 26 as amended by Sched. 7 of the Mental Health Act 1959).

A court may at any time adjourn the hearing of a complaint and remand the defendant (ss. 46, 47). A court, at common law, may adjourn for a reasonable time on reasonable grounds.

Where an accused has been convicted by a magistrates' court and the trial has been adjourned before sentence is given, he may be sentenced by a later court provided that if the later court is not composed of the same justices it must inquire into the facts and circumstances of the case before sentencing him (s. 98).

Where a magistrates' court has power to remand any person it may commit him to custody (prison or other detention, s. 126) or remand him on bail usually for 8 clear days but it may be for longer periods as provided in the section, and if the remand in custody is for not more than 3 days it may commit him to the custody of a constable (s. 105). This must be by warrant of commitment (M.C. Rules 1968, r. 77).

Section 106 deals with further remands and also allows a court to further remand a person remanded to appear or be brought to court but unable to do so by reason of illness or accident, or to enlarge the recognizance of a person on bail in his absence.

"Clear days" means complete intervening days, excluding the day of remand and the day of appearing in court.

For remand of persons under 21, see "Treatment of Youthful Offenders", Chap. 12.

A summary court may adjourn the hearing of an information or complaint and fix a time for its resumption or, if it does not remand the accused or the defendant, it may leave the resumption to be decided later by the court (viz. adjournment *sine die*) (M.C. Act 1952, ss. 14 and 46).

Acquittal – When a person has been tried by a judge and jury for an indictable offence and the jury return a general verdict of "Not Guilty", the prisoner is thereby acquitted or freed from the accusation and must be at once discharged, unless there is some other charge against him.

If his discharge was the result of some defect in the proceedings (e.g. the indictment was not sufficient so that he had not been in danger upon it), he may be detained and prosecuted afresh.

It is a rule at common law that a man may not be put twice in peril for the same offence. If a person is legally acquitted of an offence, he should not again be prosecuted for that offence.

If such a person is again prosecuted for the same offence he may, when asked to plead or reply to the charge against him, make the special plea of **autrefois acquit,** that is, that he had previously been acquitted of the same offence. If he effectively makes out this plea he will be discharged.

The fact that a person accused of an indictable offence has been discharged by the court does not prevent his re-arrest, subsequent prosecution and conviction, if he had not been in danger of conviction on the first occasion.

If a person accused of an indictable offence is discharged by the examining justices under s. 7 of the M.C. Act 1952, he can again be brought before them if more evidence is forthcoming.

If a case has been tried on its merits and dismissed, the dismissal is a bar to subsequent proceedings for the same offence as the defendant was in danger and was acquitted.

Where on summary trial, under the provisions of the Act, of an offence which otherwise would have been punishable on indictment only, the court dismisses the information, this is equal to acquittal on indictment (M.C. Act 1952, s. 22).

If the justices dismiss a charge of assault under ss. 42 or 43 after a hearing upon the merits, they shall, if requested, give the defendant a certificate of dismissal which is a release from all further proceedings, civil or criminal, for the same cause (Offences against the Person Act 1861, ss. 44 and 45).

Appeal – Under the Magistrates' Courts Act 1952, and Rules, a person convicted by a magistrates' court may appeal to the Crown Court:

(1) if he pleaded guilty—against the sentence;
(2) if he did not plead guilty—against the conviction or sentence;
(3) if sentenced for the offence in respect of which he was *previously* put on probation or conditionally discharged—against the sentence.

In such cases "sentence" includes any order made on conviction by a summary court except:

(a) a probation order or an order for conditional discharge (see Chap. 28);
(b) an order for payment of costs;
(c) an order for the destruction of an animal under s. 2, Protection of Animals Act 1911; or
(d) an order made under any enactment which allows the court no discretion as to its making or terms (s. 83).

If the appellant is in custody, the summary court may release him on recognizance to appear at the hearing of the appeal, except in the case of committal to the Crown Court, under s. 28 (Borstal) or s. 29 (for sentence on conviction for indictable offence (s. 89)).

There is an appeal to the Crown Court against an order binding over to be of good behaviour under the Justices of the Peace Act

1361, 34 Edward III. See "Surety for Good Behaviour", Chap. 22.

There is no right of appeal to the Crown Court against the dismissal of a case except in bastardy cases (M.C. Act 1952, s. 83) and excise cases (Customs and Excise Act 1952, s. 283) but application may be made for case stated (see later).

A person convicted of an offence on indictment may appeal to the Court of Appeal against his conviction (a) on any ground which involves a question of law alone; and (b) with the leave of the Court of Appeal, on any ground which involves a question of fact alone, or a question of mixed law and fact, or on any other ground which appears to the Court of Appeal to be a sufficient ground of appeal; but if the judge of the court of trial grants a certificate that the case is fit for appeal on a ground which involves a question of fact, or a question of mixed law and fact, an appeal lies under this section without the leave of the Court of Appeal (C.A. Act 1968, s. 1).

Under s. 10 of the C.A. Act 1968 there are provisions relating to the rights of appeal against sentence when a person is dealt with by the Crown Court for an offence of which he was not convicted on indictment.

An appeal lies to the House of Lords, at the instance of the defendant or the prosecutor, from any decision of the Court of Appeal on an appeal to that court under Part I (Appeal to Court of Appeal in Criminal Cases).

The appeal lies only with the leave of the Court of Appeal or the House of Lords; and leave shall not be granted unless it is certified by the Court of Appeal that a point of law of general public importance is involved in the decision and it appears to the Court of Appeal or the House of Lords (as the case may be) that the point is one which ought to be considered by that House (C.A. Act 1968, s. 33). See *R.* v. *Rumping* (1962), where the Court of Criminal Appeal dismissed Rumping's appeal against his conviction for murder, but certified that a point of law of general public importance was involved, viz. the question whether a letter written by Rumping to his wife, which was never delivered to her, was admissible in evidence. The court held that the point was not one which ought to be considered by the House of Lords and refused leave to appeal to that House. However, the House of Lords consented to hear the appeal, which was again dismissed.

The criminal division of the Court of Appeal may order new trials in cases of fresh evidence (Criminal Appeal Act 1968, s. 7).

Case stated – Under the M.C. Act 1952, ss. 87–90, any person who was a party to any proceeding before a magistrates' court or is aggrieved by the conviction, order, determination or other proceeding of the court, may question it on the ground that it is wrong in law or is in excess of jurisdiction by applying within

14 days to the court to state a case for the opinion of the High Court on the question of law or jurisdiction involved.

He cannot do so if it is a decision against which he has a right to appeal to the High Court or which, since 1879, is by law final (s. 87).

If the justices consider the application is frivolous they may refuse to state a case and certify accordingly, and the High Court may make an order of mandamus requiring them to state a case.

The justices shall not refuse the Attorney-General's application to state a case. If the application to state a case is in respect of a decision any right of the applicant to appeal to the Crown Court shall cease (s. 87).

The justices need not state a case until the applicant has entered into a recognizance, with or without sureties, to prosecute the matter without delay and submit to the judgment of the High Court and pay any costs awarded (s. 90). If the applicant is in custody the summary court may release him on recognizance, with or without sureties, to appear before the magistrates' court within 10 days after the judgment of the High Court, unless the decision has been reversed, but a person committed in custody under ss. 28 or 29 cannot be so released (s. 89).

The procedure to be followed in relation to applications to a magistrates' court for a case to be stated is contained in M.C. Rules 1968 (rr. 65 to 68) as amended by the M.C. (Amendment) (No. 2) Rules 1975.

The High Court has power to release the applicant on recognizance. In exercising this power the High Court may direct that a recognizance shall be entered into or other security given before the Crown Court, or a summary court, or a justice or by a police officer not below the rank of inspector, or a prison governor or the keeper of a place of detention (C.J. Act 1948, s. 37 as amended by Courts Act 1971, Sched. 8).

The Queen's Bench Division will hear and determine the question and except as provided by the Administration of Justice Act 1960, its decision shall be final (Summary Jurisdiction Act 1857, s. 6).

At one time it was considered that licensing justices had no power to state a case, but in *Jeffrey* v. *Evans* (1964) the divisional court held that they could. This decision was approved by the Court of Appeal in *R.* v. *East Riding Quarter Sessions, Ex parte Newton and others* (1967).

Certiorari and Mandamus – Certiorari is the name of an order of the Queen's Bench Division directing that the proceedings are to be removed from an inferior court and taken to the Queen's Bench Division to be there examined and if necessary quashed.

This order may be granted on proof that there has been some defect in the proceedings or excess of jurisdiction or that some difficult point of law is likely to arise on the trial, or that a fair and impartial trial cannot be had in the court below, or that a conviction has been obtained fraudulently, etc., etc.

Evidence for and against the granting of the order will be heard and if the Queen's Bench Division thinks fit, the order of certiorari will be issued so that the case may be examined. The High Court has power to vary sentence on certiorari (Administration of Justice Act 1960, s. 16).

If a justice (or justices) does not perform any duty laid upon him, application by affidavit may be made to the Queen's Bench Division asking for leave to apply for an order of mandamus. If leave is granted the application is made after notice has been served on all persons directly affected, and the court, if satisfied, may grant an order of mandamus, i.e. an order requiring the justice or justices to perform the duty.

Habeas Corpus – This is the name given to a writ or order of the Queen's Bench Division, addressed to the person who holds another in custody, directing him to produce the body (corpus) of the prisoner and show the cause of his detention.

It came into existence as a remedy against illegal detention or undue detention without trial. A prisoner should be tried as soon as possible and must not be kept unduly in prison untried.

A writ of habeas corpus may now be used to investigate any alleged illegal action of justices regarding an untried prisoner. It may also be used to bring a prisoner, who is in custody on one charge, before another court to answer another charge. However, when the attendance of a person under legal detention is required at any place in the interests of justice or for any public inquiry or where such a person requires treatment in hospital, etc., the Secretary of State may direct him to be taken there (Prison Act 1952, s. 22 and C.J. Act 1961, s. 29).

The procedure on application for habeas corpus and appeal in habeas corpus proceedings are dealt with by the Administration of Justice Act 1960 (ss. 14 and 15).

Limitation of Proceedings – The general principle is that there should be no delay in taking proceedings (that is, laying the information) after the discovery of the offender. In many cases a definite time limit is fixed by statute and after the prescribed period has elapsed no proceedings may be taken.

INDICTABLE OFFENCES – There is, at common law, no limit of time within which a prosecution for an offence must be commenced. No matter how long previous an indictable offence has been committed, proceedings may be taken against the offender unless some Act of Parliament or legal rule prevents such action by fixing a time limit to proceedings in the case of the particular offence. In the majority of indictable offences there is no such time limit.

SUMMARY OFFENCES – Under s. 104, M.C. Act 1952, except as otherwise expressly provided by any enactment a magistrates' court shall not try an information or hear a complaint unless same was made within 6 months from the time when the offence was committed or the matter of complaint arose. But this section does not restrict any power to try summarily an indictable offence under s. 19 of this Act, or under any enactment under which an indictable offence may be tried summarily with the consent of the accused nor would it apply to a continuing offence.

Costs in Criminal Cases – Where a person is prosecuted or tried on indictment before the Crown Court, the court may: (a) order the payment out of central funds of the costs of the prosecution; (b) if the accused is acquitted, order the payment out of central funds of the costs of the defence (Costs in Criminal Cases Act 1973, s. 3 (1)). Where an appeal is brought to the Crown Court against a conviction by a magistrates' court of an indictable offence, or against the sentence imposed on such a conviction, the court may: (a) order the payment out of central funds of the costs of the prosecution; (b) if the appeal is against a conviction, and the conviction is set aside, order the payment of the costs of the defence (Costs in Criminal Cases Act 1973, s. 3 (2)). The above costs shall be reasonably sufficient (a) to compensate the prosecutor or the accused for expenses properly incurred, and (b) to compensate any witness for the prosecution, or the defence, for the expense, trouble or loss of time properly incurred in or incidental to his attendance (Costs in Criminal Cases Act 1973, s. 3 (3)).

A Crown Court before which any person is prosecuted (a) may, if the accused is convicted, order him to pay the whole or any part of the costs incurred in or about the prosecution and conviction, including any proceedings before the examining justices; (b) may, if the accused is acquitted order the prosecutor to pay the whole or any part of the costs incurred in or about the defence, including any proceedings before the examining justices (Costs in Criminal Cases Act 1973, s. 4 (1)).

Magistrates dealing summarily with an indictable offence or inquiring as examining justices may order payment of the costs of the prosecution. If they dismiss such a case they may order payment of the costs of the defence or compensation to any witness (Costs in Criminal Cases Act 1973, s. 1).

On summary trial of an information a magistrates' court may order payment of costs on conviction to be paid by accused to the prosecution but on dismissal of the case may order the costs to be paid by the prosecution to the accused. Only actual costs may be ordered; if an amount in excess is ordered it would be a penalty (*R.* v. *Highgate Justices* (1954)).

If examining justices determine not to commit the accused for trial considering that the evidence was not sufficient and that the charge was not made in good faith they may order the prosecution to pay the costs of the defence, but if the amount of such costs exceeds £25 the prosecutor may appeal to the Crown Court (Costs in Criminal Cases Act 1973, s. 2).

Director of Public Prosecutions – The Director is the head of a legal department in London. He is appointed under the Prosecution of Offences Act 1908, and it is his duty, under the superintendence of the Attorney-General, to carry on such criminal proceedings and to give such advice and assistance to Chief Officers of Police, Clerks to Justices and other persons concerned in criminal proceedings as may be prescribed by regulations or as directed in any special case by the Attorney-General. Such regulations provide for the Director taking action in cases of importance or difficulty or which by statute require his action. He can undertake at any stage the conduct of any criminal proceedings (s. 3). The Regulations of 1946 are given in Appendix III at the end of the book.

The Justices' Clerks Rules 1970 state that the things specified in the Schedule to the Rules, being things authorised to be done by, to or before a single justice of the peace for a petty sessions area, may be done by, to or before the Justices' Clerk for that area. For Schedule, see Appendix VI.

CHAPTER 6

RECORD OF EVIDENCE

	Page
Judges' Rules . . .	70
Notes on the Judges' Rules	73
Administrative Directions on Interrogation and the Taking of Statements .	74
Admissions and Confessions	76
Dying Declaration . .	77
Deposition	78
Taking of Depositions of Persons dangerously ill .	79

Judges' Rules – The origin of the Judges' Rules is probably to be found in a letter dated October 26, 1906, which the then Lord Chief Justice, Lord Alverstone, wrote to the Chief Constable of Birmingham in answer to a request for advice in consequence of the fact that on the same circuit one judge had censured a member of his force for having cautioned a prisoner, whilst another judge had censured a constable for having omitted to do so. The first four of the present Rules were formulated and approved by the judges of the King's Bench Division in 1912; the remaining five in 1918. They have been much criticised, *inter alia* for alleged lack of clarity and of efficacy for the protection of persons who are questioned by police officers; on the other hand it has been maintained that their application unduly hampers the detection and punishment of crime. A Committee of judges has devoted considerable time and attention to producing, after consideration of representative views, a new set of Rules which has been approved by a meeting of all the Queen's Bench Judges. These replaced the old Rules in January, 1964 and are set out below:

I. When a police officer is trying to discover whether, or by whom, an offence has been committed he is entitled to question any person, whether suspected or not, from whom he thinks that useful information may be obtained. This is so whether or not the person in question has been taken into custody so long as he has not been charged with the offence or informed that he may be prosecuted for it.

II. As soon as a police officer has evidence which would afford reasonable grounds for suspecting that a person has committed an offence, he shall caution that person or cause him to be cautioned before putting to him any questions, or further questions, relating to that offence.

The caution shall be in the following terms:

> "You are not obliged to say anything unless you wish to do so but what you say may be put into writing and given in evidence."

When after being cautioned a person is being questioned, or elects to make a statement, a record shall be kept of the time and place at which any such questioning or statement began and ended and of the persons present.

III—(a) Where a person is charged with or informed that he may be prosecuted for an offence he shall be cautioned in the following terms:

> "Do you wish to say anything? You are not obliged to say anything unless you wish to do so but whatever you say will be taken down in writing and may be given in evidence."

(b) It is only in exceptional cases that questions relating to the offence should be put to the accused person after he has been charged or informed that he may be prosecuted. Such questions may be put where they are necessary for the purpose of preventing or minimising harm or loss to some other person or to the public or for clearing up an ambiguity in a previous answer or statement.

Before any such questions are put the accused should be cautioned in these terms:

> "I wish to put some questions to you about the offence with which you have been charged (*or* about the offence for which you may be prosecuted). You are not obliged to answer any of these questions, but if you do the questions and answers will be taken down in writing and may be given in evidence."

Any questions put and answers given relating to the offence must be contemporaneously recorded in full and the record signed by that person or if he refuses by the interrogating officer.

(c) When such a person is being questioned, or elects to make a statement, a record shall be kept of the time and place at which any questioning or statement began and ended and of the persons present.

IV. All written statements made after caution shall be taken in the following manner:

(a) If a person says that he wants to make a statement he shall be told that it is intended to make a written record of what he says. He shall always be asked whether he wishes to write down himself what he wants to say; if he says that he cannot write or that he would like someone to write it for him, a police officer may offer to write the statement for him. If he accepts the offer the police officer shall, before starting, ask the person making the statement to sign, or make his mark to, the following:

> "I, ..., wish to make a statement. I want someone to write down what I say. I have been told that I need not say anything unless I wish to do so and that whatever I say may be given in evidence."

(b) Any person writing his own statement shall be allowed to do so without any prompting as distinct from indicating to him what matters are material.

(c) The person making the statement, if he is going to write it himself, shall be asked to write out and sign before writing what he wants to say, the following:

> "I make this statement of my own free will. I have been told that I need not say anything unless I wish to do so and that whatever I say may be given in evidence."

(d) Whenever a police officer writes the statement, he shall take down the exact words spoken by the person making the statement, without putting any questions other than such as may be needed to make the statement coherent, intelligible and relevant to the material matters: he shall not prompt him.

(e) When the writing of a statement by a police officer is finished the person making it shall be asked to read it and to make any corrections, alterations or additions he wishes. When he has finished reading it he shall be asked to write and sign or make his mark on the following Certificate at the end of the statement:

> "I have read the above statement and I have been told that I can correct, alter or add anything I wish. This statement is true. I have made it of my own free will."

(f) If the person who has made a statement refuses to read it or to write the above mentioned Certificate at the end of it or to sign it, the senior police officer present shall record on the statement itself and in the presence of the person making it, what has happened. If the person making the statement cannot read, or refuses to read it, the officer who has taken it down shall read it over to him and ask him whether he would like to correct, alter or add anything and to put his signature or make his mark at the end. The police officer shall then certify on the statement itself what he has done.

V. If at any time after a person has been charged with, or has been informed that he may be prosecuted for an offence a police officer wishes to bring to the notice of that person any written statement made by another person who in respect of the same offence has also been charged or informed that he may be prosecuted, he shall hand to that person a true copy of such written statement, but nothing shall be said or done to invite any reply or comment. If that person says that he would like to make a statement in reply, or starts to say something, he shall at once be cautioned or further cautioned as prescribed by Rule III (a).

VI. Persons other than police officers charged with the duty of investigating offences or charging offenders shall, so far as may be practicable, comply with these Rules.

Notes on the Judges' Rules – These Rules do not affect the principles

(a) that citizens have a duty to help a police officer to discover and apprehend offenders;
(b) that police officers, otherwise than by arrest, cannot compel any person against his will to come to or remain in any police station;
(c) that every person at any stage of an investigation should be able to communicate and to consult privately with a solicitor. This is so even if he is in custody provided that in such a case no unreasonable delay or hindrance is caused to the processes of investigation or the administration of justice by his doing so;
(d) that when a police officer who is making enquiries of any person about an offence has enough evidence to prefer a charge against that person for the offence, he should without delay cause that person to be charged or informed that he may be prosecuted for the offence;
(e) that it is a fundamental condition of the admissibility in evidence against any person, equally of any oral answer given by that person to a question put by a police officer and of any statement made by that person, that it shall have been voluntary, in the sense that it has not been obtained from him by fear of prejudice or hope of advantage, exercised or held out by a person in authority, or by oppression.

The principle set out in paragraph (e) above is overriding and applicable in all cases. Within that principle the above Rules are put forward as a guide to police officers conducting investigations. Non-conformity with these Rules may render answers and statements liable to be excluded from evidence in subsequent criminal proceedings.

Administrative Directions on Interrogation and the Taking of Statements

1. PROCEDURE GENERALLY – (a) When possible statements of persons under caution should be written on the forms provided for the purpose. Police officers' notebooks should be used for taking statements only when no forms are available.

(b) When a person is being questioned or elects to make a statement, a record should be kept of the time or times at which during the questioning or making of a statement there were intervals or refreshment was taken. The nature of the refreshment should be noted. In no circumstances should alcoholic drink be given.

(c) In writing down a statement, the words used should not be translated into "official" vocabulary; this may give a misleading impression of the genuineness of the statement.

(d) Care should be taken to avoid any suggestion that the person's answers can only be used in evidence against him, as this may prevent an innocent person making a statement which might help to clear him of the charge.

2. RECORD OF INTERROGATION – Rule II and Rule III (c) demand that a record should be kept of the following matters:

(a) when, after being cautioned in accordance with Rule II, the person is being questioned or elects to make a statement—of the time and place at which any such questioning began and ended and of the persons present;
(b) when, after being cautioned in accordance with Rule III (a) or (b) a person is being questioned or elects to make a statement—of the time and place at which any questioning and statement began and ended and of the persons present.

In addition to the records required by these Rules full records of the following matters should additionally be kept:

(a) of the time or times at which cautions were taken, and
(b) of the time when a charge was made and/or the person was arrested, and
(c) of the matters referred to in paragraph 1 (b) above.

If two or more police officers are present when the questions are being put or the statement made, the records made should be countersigned by the other officers present.

3. COMFORT AND REFRESHMENT – Reasonable arrangements should be made for the comfort and refreshment of persons being questioned. Whenever practicable both the person being questioned or making a statement and the officers asking the questions or taking the statement should be seated.

4. INTERROGATION OF CHILDREN AND YOUNG PERSONS – As far as practicable children (i.e. all under 17 years of age) (whether

suspected of crime or not) should only be interviewed in the presence of a parent or guardian, or, in their absence, some person who is not a police officer and is of the same sex as the child. A child or young person should not be arrested, nor even interviewed, at school if such action can possibly be avoided. Where it is found essential to conduct the interview at school, this should be done only with the consent, and in the presence, of the head teacher, or his nominee.

5. INTERROGATION OF FOREIGNERS – In the case of a foreigner making a statement in his native language:

(a) The interpreter should take down the statement in the language in which it is made.
(b) An official English translation should be make in due course and be proved as an exhibit with the original statement.
(c) The foreigner should sign the statement at (a).

Apart from the question of apparent unfairness, to obtain the signature of a suspect to an English translation of what he said in a foreign language can have little or no value as evidence if the suspect disputes the accuracy of this record of his statement.

6. SUPPLY TO ACCUSED PERSONS OF WRITTEN STATEMENT OF CHARGES – (a) The following procedure should be adopted whenever a charge is preferred against a person arrested without warrant for any offence:

As soon as a charge has been accepted by the appropriate police officer the accused person should be given a written notice containing a copy of the entry in the charge sheet or book giving particulars of the offence with which he is charged. So far as possible the particulars of the charge should be stated in simple language so that the accused person may understand it, but they should also show clearly the precise offence in law with which he is charged. Where the offence charged is a statutory one, it should be sufficient for the latter purpose to quote the section of the statute which created the offence.

The written notice should include some statement on the lines of the caution given orally to the accused person in accordance with the Judges' Rules after a charge has been preferred. It is suggested that the form of notice should begin with the following words:

"You are charged with the offence(s) shown below. You are not obliged to say anything unless you wish to do so, but whatever you say will be taken down in writing and may be given in evidence."

(b) Once the accused person has appeared before the court it is not necessary to serve him with a written notice of any further charges which may be preferred. If, however, the police decide, before he has appeared before a court, to modify the charge or to prefer further charges, it is desirable that the person concerned should be formally charged with the further offence and given a written copy of the charge as soon as it is possible to do so having regard to the particular circumstances of the case. If the accused person has then been released on bail, it may not always be practicable or reasonable to prefer the new charge at once, and in cases where he is due to surrender to his bail within 48 hours or in other cases of difficulty it will be sufficient for him to be formally charged with the further offence and served with a written notice of the charge after he has surrendered to his bail and before he appears before the court.

7. FACILITIES FOR DEFENCE – (a) A person in custody should be allowed to speak on the telephone to his solicitor or to his friends provided that no hindrance is reasonably likely to be caused to the processes of investigation or the administration of justice by his doing so.

He should be supplied on request with writing materials and his letters should be sent by post or otherwise with the least possible delay. Additionally, telegrams should be sent at once, at his own expense.

(b) Persons in custody should not only be informed orally of the rights and facilities available to them, but in addition notices describing them should be displayed at convenient and conspicuous places at police stations and the attention of persons in custody should be drawn to these notices.

Admissions and Confessions – A person summoned to a magistrates' court may in certain cases write pleading guilty and not attend (see "Proceedings before Justices", Chap. 4). An admission made by a party in a case or made on his behalf is a disclosure of or an agreement with some fact which more or less tells against his case. An admission may be made in words or in writing or by mere silent conduct. If a statement is made in the presence of someone who would naturally contradict it if not true, but who nevertheless remains silent, he impliedly admits its truth unless he can show good cause for his silence.

A confession is a statement made by a person charged with a crime admitting that he committed the crime. A confession is an admission, but an admission may not amount to a confession of guilt.

All admissions and confessions in criminal cases, to be admissible in evidence, must be free and voluntary. It is the duty of the prosecution to prove that any confession produced in evidence has been given voluntarily.

If there has been any inducement or constraint from any person in authority over the accused, his resulting confession will not be admitted in evidence as it cannot be regarded as free and voluntary.

A police officer is a person in authority over a prisoner and he must be most careful in his conduct towards the prisoner so that he may be able to prove affirmatively that he held out no inducement or threat towards a prisoner who has made a confession or admission of any kind. An inducement or threat held out to a prisoner by a person not in authority over him does not prevent the giving in evidence of a resulting confession.

Any statement, admission, or confession, freely made without inducement or threat, to a police officer by a prisoner, is admissible in evidence.

No person should be compelled to incriminate himself and the Judges' Rules regarding statements from prisoners must be carefully observed. A prisoner's replies to questions may not, *prima facie*, be regarded as free and voluntary. The circumstances of the case must be taken into account and a police officer should not question his prisoner unless he can show good reason for doing so; for example, a person who gives himself up for a crime may be asked questions necessary to elicit the facts.

Where a statement or complaint or charge is made in the presence of a person accusing him of a crime, his behaviour on the occasion may be given in evidence so that the jury may decide whether or not, at that time, he accepted or admitted the statement made against him.

Such a statement or charge is not evidence of the acts alleged therein, but the conduct of the accused when the statement was made may be equivalent to an admission of its correctness. However, a prisoner, when cautioned, may reply that he does not wish to say anything or he may remain silent.

Although a confession may not, for some reason, be admissible in evidence, yet anything discovered in consequence of what was stated in the confession will be admitted in evidence. Thus the finding of stolen goods as the result of an inadmissible confession may be proved.

Dying Declaration – A dying declaration is a statement made by an injured and dying person as to the facts and circumstances which caused his injuries. It should give in the actual words of the injured person what has happened to him; it should contain his opinion that he is dying and has no hope of recovery; it need not be on oath; it may be signed by the injured person if he is able to sign it; the person charged with causing the injuries need not be present, though he may be; and the person taking it should sign and date it and get it signed also by all the persons (if any) who have heard it being made by the injured person.

Any person may take a dying declaration.

The injured person should not be sworn, as it is considered

that a person in such a serious position will feel bound to speak the truth.

There is no particular form of dying declaration, and if questions are put to the injured person the questions as well as the answers should be written down and will form part of the declaration.

If the person accused of causing the injuries be present, the injured person should be given the opportunity of identifying him, and everything said by both parties should be written down.

Dying declarations are admissible in evidence in cases where the death of the deceased person is the subject of the charge, that is, in trials for murder or manslaughter.

Before a judge will receive a dying declaration in evidence he must be satisfied:

(1) That at the time it was made the declarant was in actual danger of death.

(2) That he then realised his condition and had no hope of recovery.

(3) That he died and that the cause of death was the subject of the dying declaration.

However, if the accused person is available, and if it is at all possible, a magistrate should be procured so that a deposition may be taken in the presence and hearing of the accused.

Deposition - A deposition is a statement made on oath before a justice, taken down in writing in the presence and hearing of the accused, and read over to the deponent or person making it, and by the justice. It must be stated in the deposition that it was taken in the presence and hearing of the accused and he must be given an opportunity of cross-examining the deponent. It ought to be signed by the deponent.

When examining justices are inquiring into an offence the evidence of each witness shall be taken down in writing in the form of a deposition and read over to the accused (M.C. Rules 1968, r. 4).

A deposition is a record of the evidence which a witness can give in a case and it should state in the words of the witness what the witness can testify. It is written down by the Magistrates' Clerk and remains in his custody until it is required at the court where the trial of the accused person is to take place.

A person who thus makes a deposition in a case which is sent forward for trial by a jury may have to attend to give evidence. The justices shall issue a witness order in respect of each witness examined requiring him to attend at the court of trial. The witness order is to be conditional if it appears to the court, after taking into account any representation made by the accused or the prosecutor, that the attendance of the witness at the trial is unnecessary. C.P. (A of W.) Act 1965.

If a witness is dead or insane or too ill to travel, or kept away by the defence, or is a person in respect of whom a conditional witness order has been made, his deposition may be read in evidence if the conditions of the section are satisfied (C.J. Act 1925, s. 13 as amended by C.P. (A. of W.) Act 1965, s. 2. This section applies to any written statement tendered in evidence at committal proceedings under C.J. Act 1967, s. 2.).

Taking of Depositions of Persons dangerously ill – Where a person is able and willing to give material information relating to an indictable offence or to anyone accused of an indictable offence, if a justice is satisfied by medical evidence that such person is dangerously ill and unlikely to recover and it is not practicable for examining justices to take his evidence in the normal manner, the justice may take in writing the deposition of the sick person on oath. Such a deposition may be given in evidence before examining justices and on the trial of the offender subject to the conditions laid down in s. 6 of the Criminal Law Amendment Act 1867 (M.C. Act 1952, s. 41).

Where a justice of the peace takes the deposition of a person under s. 41, M.C. Act, and the deposition relates to an offence with which a person has been charged, the justice shall give the person, whether prosecutor or accused, against whom it is proposed to use it reasonable notice of the intention to take the deposition, and shall give that person or his counsel or solicitor full opportunity of cross-examining the deponent. The justice shall sign the deposition and add to it a statement of his reason for taking it, the day when, and the place where, it was taken and the names of any persons present when it was taken (M.C. Rules 1968, r. 29).

The conditions prescribed by s. 6 of the C.L. Amendment Act 1867 are that before being given in evidence the following must be complied with:

(a) proof that the deponent is dead or that there is no reasonable probability that he will ever be able to travel or to give evidence;
(b) the deposition purports to be signed by the justice by or before whom it purports to have been taken;
(c) proof that reasonable notice (in writing) of the intention to take such deposition had been given to the person against whom it was proposed to be read in evidence and that such person or his lawyer had, if present, full opportunity of cross-examining the deponent. Section 7 of this Act provides for the attendance of the accused when he is in custody at the time.

As regards a deposition taken from an injured child or young person, see "Arrest, Search Warrant and Procedure", Chap. 12.

The above will apply in the case of a person seriously injured by another where his story should be placed on legal record as soon as possible. It also applies in the case of a necessary witness in an indictable case who is dangerously ill.

In such cases a statement should be taken from the person, his doctor should be interviewed and the facts laid before the Clerk to the justice so that he and a justice should come and take the deposition.

If the injured person thinks he is going to die, and there is no hope of his recovery, his "dying declaration" should be taken, in case it is not possible to take his deposition as above.

See "Dying Declaration", above.

CHAPTER 7

EVIDENCE

	Page		Page
Evidence	81	Handwriting	92
Oath or Affirmation	82	Extent of Evidence	93
Number of Witnesses	83	Circumstantial Evidence	95
Corroborative Evidence	83	Presumptions	95
Evidence for the Prosecution	83	Privilege	95
Accused Persons and their Husbands or Wives	83	Leading Questions	96
Competency of Witnesses	85	Refreshing Memory	97
Witnesses out of Court	85	Hostile Witness	97
Interference with Witnesses	86	Unwilling Witness	97
Nature of Evidence	86	The Onus or Burden of Proof	97
Parol or Oral Evidence	87	Examination-in-chief	98
Proof by Written Statement	87	Cross-examination	98
Proof by Formal Admission	88	Re-examination	99
Documentary Evidence	89	Recalling a Witness	99
Evidence by Certificate	89	Rebutting Evidence	99
Hearsay Evidence	91	Notice of Alibi	100
Opinion	92	Character after Conviction	100
		Previous Convictions	101
		The Perfect Witness	102

Evidence – The word evidence means that which makes evident or manifest or which supplies proof. In law the term "evidence" is used to indicate the means by which any fact or point in issue or question may be proved or disproved in a manner complying with the legal rules governing the subject.

A court holds a judicial inquiry to ascertain whether a person is or is not guilty of some offence. The burden or task or proving that the accused is guilty rests on the prosecutor or person who asserts that he is guilty, as the law presumes a man to be innocent until the contrary is proved (*Woolmington* v. *Director of Public Prosecutions* (1935)). See "Onus of Proof", later.

The prosecutor, therefore, has to produce evidence, viz, a witness or witnesses who on oath relate the facts of the case and (or) produce any things necessary for that purpose. The accused person on his part may also tender witnesses to exonerate him from the charge and to prove that he had previously borne a good character. This tendering of evidence and the nature of the evidence so given are subject to legal rules, the rules of evidence. The object of these rules in criminal cases is to elicit the truth without causing undue prejudice to the prisoner.

To prove a particular fact the evidence must be **competent,** that is, it must be fit and appropriate proof of the fact alleged, and it should be **satisfactory,** that is, it must be sufficient to satisfy the court beyond reasonable doubt. Facts are proved by persons testifying to their existence or occurrence, and the **credibility of a witness** depends on his knowledge of the facts, his impartiality, and his truthfulness.

When a witness comes before the court to give evidence he is sworn to tell the truth, the whole truth, and nothing but the truth. Under the guidance of the party by whom he is called he gives his evidence and this is called his **examination in chief.** When this is finished he may be questioned or **cross-examined** by the opposing party, and when this is concluded, he may be **re-examined** by the side which has produced him to give evidence. Later he may be **recalled** by the court to answer further questions.

Oath or Affirmation – At common law the evidence of a witness was not admissible unless he had been sworn to tell the truth. Evidence given before a magistrates' court shall be given on oath except where unsworn evidence is authorised by law (M.C. Act 1952, s. 78). The Oaths Act 1909 prescribes the present form of oath: "I swear by Almighty God that the evidence I shall give, shall be the truth, the whole truth, and nothing but the truth." Instead of "I swear by Almighty God that" the words "I promise before Almighty God" should be used by any person in a Juvenile Court and by a child or young person before any other court (C. & Y.P. Act 1963, s. 28). If a witness objects to being sworn on the grounds that the taking of an oath is contrary to his religious belief or that he has no religious belief, he may make a solemn affirmation, declaring that the evidence he is about to give is the truth (Oaths Act 1888). An affirmation instead of an oath may be made when it is not reasonably practicable without inconvenience or delay to administer an oath in the manner appropriate to a person's religious beliefs (Oaths Act 1961). Christians are sworn on the New Testament, with their hats off. Jews are sworn on the Old Testament, with their hats on. Mahommedans are sworn on the Koran. The general rule is that a witness may claim to be sworn in the manner prescribed by his religion or national law, and the oath should be such as the witness considers binding on his conscience, but if a witness objects to being sworn his solemn affirmation will be accepted. A child of tender years need not be sworn in offence cases (C. & Y.P. Act 1933, s. 38). See "Children", Chap. 12.

Number of Witnesses – The general rule is that the evidence of one witness may be sufficient to convict an accused person. However, at least two witnesses are required in the cases of personation at an election, and blasphemy.

In certain other cases as given below, corroboration of the evidence of only one witness is necessary before conviction.

Corroborative Evidence means other independent evidence tending to support the truthfulness and accuracy of evidence already given. Corroboration of the evidence of one witness by other evidence connecting the accused with the offence is required by law in cases of perjury, procuration, of the unsworn evidence of children of tender years, and a motorist cannot be convicted for exceeding a speed limit merely on the opinion of one witness as to the rate of speed. See also Chap. 10 as to corroboration in sexual offence cases.

Also in practice, the evidence of the injured party in sexual cases (*R.* v. *Freebody* (1935)) and the evidence of an accomplice (*R.* v. *Baskerville* (1916)) should be corroborated, but the jury after warning by the judge may convict without corroboration.

Evidence for the Prosecution may be given by the prosecutor and any witnesses he may produce, but the wife of the accused cannot be required to give evidence for the prosecution except in the cases given below.

The husband or wife of the prosecutor is a competent witness for the prosecution or for the defence.

A confession of guilt which is proved to have been freely and voluntarily made by the defendant to anyone, may be given in evidence. See "Admissions and Confessions", Chap. 6.

Accused Persons and their Husbands or Wives are entitled to give evidence on oath for the defence. An accused person can make a statement without being sworn. The accused is not a compellable witness, and should be told by the court that he has a right to give evidence on his own behalf. He should not be called as a witness except on his own application. If he does not give evidence, his failure to do so must not be commented on by the prosecution.

An accused person who does give sworn evidence may be asked any question in cross-examination (even if the answer would incriminate him) as to the offence charged against him, but he may not be questioned as to any other offence he may have committed or as to his bad character, unless (1) he has given evidence of his good character or the defence has questioned the prosecution witnesses with a view to establish the good character of the accused or the defence has attacked the character of the prosecutor or of the witnesses for the prosecution (see *R.* v. *Clark* (1955)), or unless (2) the fact that he has committed such other offence is admissible in evidence against him (see "Extent of Evidence"), or unless (3) he has given evidence against another person charged with the same offence (Criminal Evidence Act 1898, s. 1). With these exceptions he may be asked any relevant question.

(*Stirland* v. *Director of Public Prosecutions* (1944), gives rules regarding the cross-examination as to his credit of an accused person who has given evidence.)

In the following cases the wife or husband of the accused may be called as a witness for the prosecution or for the defence and without the consent of the accused.

(1) By statute, in cases of rape, indecent assault, procuration, incest, bigamy, cruelty to children, indecent conduct towards young children, etc., as given by s. 4 and the Schedule to the Criminal Evidence Act 1898 and in later Acts. In cases under these statutes the husband or wife is competent to give evidence if willing to do so but is not compellable (*Leach* v. *R.* (1912)).

(2) At common law, where the one is charged with personal injury to the other, or the husband with forcible abduction followed by marriage, or perhaps in cases of treason. In such cases the husband or wife is a competent witness and is also a compellable witness, viz. can be ordered to give evidence (*R.* v. *Lapworth* (1931)).

The Theft Act 1968 shall apply in relation to the parties to a marriage, and to property belonging to the wife or husband, as it would apply if they were not married (s. 30 (1)).

Subject to sub-s. (4) below, a person shall have the same right to prosecute that person's wife or husband for any offence (whether under this Act or otherwise) as if they were not married, and the person prosecuting shall be competent to give evidence for the prosecution at every stage of the proceedings (s. 30 (2)).

Where a person is charged in proceedings not brought by that person's wife or husband with having committed any offence with reference to that person's wife or husband or to property belonging to the wife or husband, the wife or husband shall be competent to give evidence at every stage of the proceedings, whether for the defence or the prosecution.

Provided that (a) the wife or husband (unless compellable at common law) shall not be compellable either to give evidence or, in giving evidence, to disclose any communication made to her or him during the marriage by the accused: and (b) her or his failure to give evidence shall not be made the subject of any comment by the prosecution (s. 30 (3)).

Proceedings shall not be instituted against a person for any offence of stealing or doing unlawful damage to property which at the time of the offence belongs to that person's wife or husband, or for any attempt, incitement or conspiracy to commit such an offence, unless the proceedings are instituted by or with the consent of the Director of Public Prosecutions. Provided that (a) this subsection shall not apply to proceedings against a person for an offence (i) if that person is charged with committing the offence jointly with the wife or husband, or (ii) if by virtue of any judicial decree or order that person and the wife or husband are at the time of the offence under no obligation to cohabit; and (b) this subsection shall not prevent the arrest, or the issue of a warrant for the arrest, of a person for an offence, or the remand in custody or on bail of a person charged with an offence, where the arrest (if without a warrant) is made, or the warrant of arrest issues on an information laid, by a person other than the wife or husband (s. 30 (4)).

In any proceedings for an offence under the Ministry of Social Security Act 1966 the wife or husband of the accused shall be competent to give evidence, whether for or against the accused, but shall not be compellable either to give evidence, or in giving evidence, to disclose any communication made to her or to him by the accused during the marriage (s. 33 (6)).

Competency of Witnesses – The question whether a person is competent or fit to give evidence is one to be determined by the court. The general rule is that all persons are competent to give evidence in all cases. A court may decide that a witness is not competent to give evidence because of want of discretion, as in the case of persons incapable of understanding the nature of an oath or of giving a rational answer to a sensible question. For example, an idiot, a lunatic, a drunken person. A child of tender years, who does not understand the nature of an oath, may give evidence in offence cases if the court is satisfied that such child has sufficient intelligence and understands the duty of speaking the truth, but for a conviction there must be corroboration of such evidence (C. & Y.P. Act 1933, s. 38). The husband or wife of the accused is not a competent witness for the prosecution, except in certain cases. See preceding paragraphs as to "Accused Persons and their Husbands or Wives".

The Evidence Act 1843 provides that no persons shall be excluded from giving evidence on account of incapacity from crime or interest. Accordingly persons who have been convicted of crime, or who stand to gain or lose by the result of the trial, cannot be prevented on those grounds from giving evidence.

Witnesses out of Court – At any period during a trial, the court, at the request of either party, will usually order such witnesses of the opposite party as have not been examined to leave the court until they are called in to give evidence (see s. 57, M.C. Act 1952). This is done so that each witness may be examined out of the hearing of other witnesses who are to be examined after him, the object being that the evidence of each witness should not be influenced by what he has heard previous witnesses testifying. Should a witness remain in court after such order, the court has no right to reject his evidence on this ground, but may punish him for contempt of court.

Interference with Witnesses – It is an offence against the administration of justice, to dissuade, hinder, or prevent from attending court any witness duly summoned or bound over by recognizance. It is also an offence to attempt in any way to keep witnesses away. Any interference with witnesses renders those concerned liable to committal for contempt of court (see Chap. 21). A witness duly subpœnaed or summoned, or bound over by recognizance, is privileged from arrest on civil process whilst attending court and for a reasonable time before and after the trial.

Where it becomes necessary to call as a witness a person under legal detention, application should be made to the Secretary of State for an order for him to be brought to the court. See "Habeas Corpus", Chap. 5.

Nature of Evidence – Evidence may be given in the following manner:

(1) A relation of a fact or facts by a witness. Such verbal evidence is termed **parol or oral evidence.**

(2) A written statement by any person shall, if certain conditions apply, be admissible as evidence in any criminal proceedings.

(3) A document being produced and the contents read to the Court. This is termed **documentary evidence.**

(4) An article connected with the circumstances of the case being produced by a witness (who usually gives parol evidence accounting for it). This may be called **real evidence.**

The rule is that the best evidence the nature of the case will admit should be produced at the trial, as its absence will tell against the party neglecting to produce it.

The best evidence is termed **primary evidence,** or evidence at first hand, and such evidence is also called **direct** or **positive evidence,** meaning that the evidence of any fact alleged to have been seen, heard, or perceived by the senses must be the evidence of a person who says he saw, heard, felt, etc., that fact. Primary or direct evidence of a document or thing is the production of the original document or actual thing. If primary evidence of a fact is not available, then the next best evidence of that fact, which is termed **secondary evidence,** may be offered. Thus secondary evidence of a person, document, or thing would be the production of a deposition or statement, a copy of the document, or a mode, of the thing. But before secondary evidence of a fact may be given it will be necessary to prove that primary evidence is not available; for example, if a party wishes to put in evidence a particular document he should produce the original document (primary evidence), but if he can prove that the original document is destroyed, lost, cannot be moved, or in possession of the opposite party, he will be permitted to prove it by the secondary evidence of a true copy or of verbal evidence of its contents, but in the last case only if notice to produce it has been given to the party in whose possession it is or is supposed to be.

Parol or Oral Evidence given by a witness is admissible:

(1) When it is the best evidence (primary evidence) of the fact which it is sought to establish.

(2) As secondary evidence of the contents of a document which cannot be produced in court.

Oral evidence of a fact should be confined to direct evidence of that fact as within the personal knowledge of the witness, who should only relate facts which happened in his presence or within reach of his senses. To this rule there are some exceptions, such as hearsay evidence and the opinion or belief of a witness, which are dealt with in later paragraphs.

A confession of guilt by the accused or an admission that part of the evidence for the prosecution is correct, made by the accused or by some authorised person on his behalf, may be proved by the direct evidence of some person who has heard the confession or admission. As such evidence amounts to proof of a statement made by a person not called as a witness in the case, it is hearsay evidence to a certain extent, but as it comes, or is alleged to come, from the defendant or with his authority, confessions and admissions are not here included as hearsay but are dealt with separately in Chap. 6.

Proof by Written Statement – In any criminal proceedings other than committal proceedings, a written statement by any person shall, if the conditions set out below are satisfied, be admissible as evidence to the like extent as oral evidence to the like effect by that person. The conditions are (a) the statement purports to be signed by the person who made it; (b) the statement contains a declaration by that person that it is true and that he made it knowing that, if it were tendered in evidence, he would be liable to prosecution if he wilfully stated in it anything which he knew to be false or did not believe to be true; (c) before the hearing at which the statement is tendered in evidence, a copy of it is served, by or on behalf of the party proposing to tender it, on each of the other parties to the proceedings; (d) none of the other parties or their solicitors, within 7 days from the service of the copy of the statement, serves a notice on the party so proposing objecting to the statement being tendered in evidence under this section (provided that the conditions mentioned in paragraphs (c) and (d) above shall not apply if the parties agree before or during the hearing that the statement shall be so tendered); (e) the statement of a person under the age of 21 must show his age [if the person is under 14, the declaration under condition "b" above should be to the effect that he understands the importance of telling the truth (C. & Y.P. Act 1969, Sched. 5, para. 55—when in force)]; (f) if it is made by a person who cannot read it, it shall be read to him before he signs it and shall be accompanied by a declaration by the reader that it was so read; and (g) if it refers to any other document as an exhibit, the copy served on any other party to the proceedings under paragraph (c) above shall be accompanied by a copy of that document or such information that would enable the party on whom it is served to inspect it or a copy of it.

Notwithstanding that a written statement made by any person may be admissible as evidence by virtue of this section (a), the party by whom or on whose behalf a copy of the statement was served may call that person to give evidence; and (b) the court may, of its own motion or on the application of any party to the proceedings, require that person to attend before the court and give evidence.

Any document or object referred to as an exhibit and identified in a written statement tendered in evidence under this section shall be treated as if it had been produced as an exhibit and identified in court by the maker of the statement.

A document required by this section to be served on any person may be served (a) by delivering it to him or to his solicitor; or (b) by addressing it to him and leaving it as his usual or last known place of abode or place of business or by addressing it to his solicitor and leaving it at his office; or (c) by sending it in a registered letter or by the recorded delivery service addressed to him at his usual or last known place of abode or place of business or addressed to his solicitor at his office; or (d) in the case of a body corporate, by delivering it to the secretary or clerk of the body at its registered or principal office or sending it in a registered letter or by the recorded delivery service addressed to the secretary or clerk of that body at that office (C.J. Act 1967, s. 9).

If any person in a written statement tendered in evidence in criminal proceedings by virtue of s. 9 above wilfully makes a statement material in those proceedings which he knows to be false or does not believe to be true, he commits an offence. The Perjury Act 1911 shall have effect as if this section were contained in that Act (C.J. Act 1967, s. 89).

Proof by Formal Admission – Any fact of which oral evidence may be given in any criminal proceedings may be admitted for the purpose on those proceedings by or on behalf of the prosecutor or defendant, and the admission by any party of any such fact shall as against that party be conclusive evidence in those proceedings of the fact admitted.

Such an admission (a) may be made before or at the proceedings; (b) if made otherwise than in court, shall be in writing; (c) if made in writing by an individual, shall purport to be signed by the person making it and, if so made by a body corporate, shall purport to be signed by an officer of the body corporate; (d) if made on behalf of a defendant who is an individual, shall be made by his counsel or solicitor; (e) if made at any stage before the trial by a defendant who is an individual, must be approved by his counsel or solicitor (whether at the time it was made or subsequently) before or at the proceedings in question.

An admission under this section for the purpose of proceedings relating to any matter shall be treated as an admission for the purpose of any subsequent criminal proceedings relating to that matter (including any appeal or retrial), and may with the leave of the court be withdrawn in the proceedings for the purpose of which it is made or any subsequent criminal proceedings relating to the same matter (C.J. Act 1967, s. 10).

Documentary Evidence – Normally, a document produced before a court has to be proved by a witness. A document 20 or more years old and produced from proper custody is admissible in evidence without further proof (Evidence Act 1938, s. 4).

If any instrument (except a will) in any proceedings requires attestation, it may, instead of being proved by an attesting witness, be proved in the manner in which it might be proved if no attesting witness were alive (Evidence Act 1938, s. 3).

Evidence by Certificate – The Criminal Justice Act 1948, s. 41 (1), provides that in any criminal proceedings a certificate by a constable or person having qualifications as prescribed (by rules made by the Secretary of State) certifying that the plan or drawing exhibited is correctly made to scale by him, of the place or object specified, shall be evidence of the relative position of the things shown in the plan or drawing.

The Theft Act 1968, s. 27 (4), provides that in any proceedings for the theft of anything in the course of transmission (whether by post or otherwise) or for handling stolen goods from such a theft, a statutory declaration by any person that he sent, received or failed to receive any such articles, or that such articles when he sent or received them were in a particular state or condition shall be admissible as evidence of the facts stated in the declaration.

The Road Traffic Act 1972, s. 181, provides that in any proceedings to which that section is applied by Column 7 of Part 1 of Sched. 4 to the Act, or which is punishable by virtue of s.178 thereof, or for an offence against any other enactment relating to the use of vehicles on roads a certificate in the prescribed form, purporting to be signed by a constable and certifying that a person specified in the certificate stated to the constable that a particular motor vehicle—

(a) was being driven or used by or belonged to, that person on a particular occasion; or
(b) on a particular occasion was used by or belonged to a firm in which that person also stated that he was at the time of the statement a partner; or
(c) on a particular occasion was used by or belonged to a corporation of which that person also stated that he was at the time of the statement a director, officer or employee,

shall be admissible as evidence for the purpose of determining by whom the vehicle was being driven or used, or to whom it belonged on that occasion.

However such a certificate shall not be admissible in evidence unless oral evidence to the like effect would have been admissible and unless a copy has been served on the accused person not less than 7 days before the hearing or trial, or if the accused, not later than 3 days before the hearing or trial, serves notice on the prosecutor requiring the attendance at the trial of the person who signed the certificate. Evidence by Certificate Rules 1961 and 1962, prescribe what is necessary, including the use of the recorded delivery service.

The R.T. Act 1972, s. 10 (1), provides for the admissibility of a certificate by an authorised analyst as to the proportion of alcohol in a specimen of blood or urine taken from or provided by a person charged with unfitness to drive a motor vehicle. See Chap. 24.

The Diplomatic Privileges Act 1964, s. 4, provides that if in any proceedings any question arises whether or not any person is entitled to any privilege or immunity under this Act, a certificate issued by or under the authority of the Secretary of State stating any fact relating to the question shall be conclusive evidence of that fact.

A certificate from the Clerk of a magistrates' court giving the court register or any extract from it shall be admissible in evidence in any legal proceedings (M.C. Rules 1968, r. 56).

Evidence by certificate from the police can also be produced in some other cases. See "Summons", Chap. 5 and "Deserters and Absentees", Chap. 30.

The R.T. Act 1972, s. 182, provides that a statement in certain documents duly authenticated and purporting to be part of the records maintained by the Secretary of State in connection with vehicle and driving licenses shall be admissible in civil or criminal proceedings as evidence of any fact stated therein, to the same extent as oral evidence of that fact would be admissible. (S. 182 (2A) provides for the admissibility of a statement specifying an alleged previous conviction in proceedings for an offence involving obligatory or discretionary disqualification, provided a notice is served on the accused not less than 7 days before the statement is produced in court.) The Vehicles and Driving Licences Records (Evidence) Regs. 1970 prescribe the matters in respect of which evidence may be given in this manner. The matters concerned include documents relating to the licensing of drivers, the licensing and registration of mechanically propelled vehicles and the examination of goods vehicles in connection with the determination of plated weights, etc.

Hearsay Evidence is evidence of a fact not actually perceived by a witness with his own senses, but proved by him to have been stated by another person (not the accused). Such evidence is not admissible unless what was said had been said in the presence and hearing of the accused. Hearsay is not admitted in evidence because what the other person said was not upon oath, and because the accused had no opportunity of contradicting or cross-examining him. There are some exceptions to this rule, and hearsay evidence may be admissible in certain cases, such as:

(1) Dying declarations of persons whose death is the subject of the charge and whose declarations deal with the cause of death. See "Dying Declaration", Chap. 6.

(2) Rape, indecent assault on females and males and other similar offences. In such cases the fact that a complaint was made by the injured person to some other person as soon as reasonably possible after the act alleged and the particulars of the complaint may be given in evidence by that other person not as proof or corroboration of the act alleged, but as evidence of the conduct of the injured person and of the fact that the act was not consented to (*R.* v. ***Lillyman*** (1896); and *R.* v. *Osborne* (1905). See also *R.* v. ***Camelleri*** (1922), and *R.* v. *Cummings* (1948).

(3) Written records or statements made by deceased persons in the regular course of duty or business. For example, police reports, entries in official note-books, etc.

(4) Statements made by a person as to his bodily or mental feelings, if such feelings are material in the case. Thus in a poisoning case, the deceased's words as to his symptoms and feelings before death would be very material as part of the transaction on which the charge is made.

(5) When the hearsay comes in as part of the *res gestae* or things done or incidents relevant to the matter in issue, viz. where it is one of the facts which actually make up the occurrence or transaction on which the charge is based. For example, in a case of manslaughter a statement made by the deceased immediately after he had been knocked down as to the cause of his injuries was admitted in evidence. However, it is extremely difficult to put in evidence hearsay as part of the matter which is the subject of the inquiry.

(6) The Criminal Evidence Act 1965 enabled certain trade or business records to be admissible in evidence in criminal proceedings. A statement contained in a document will, on production of the document, be admissible in any criminal proceedings as evidence of a fact, provided: (1) that direct oral evidence of the fact would be admissible; and (2) that the document is a record relating to any trade or business and was compiled, in the course of that trade or business, from information supplied by persons who had personal knowledge of the facts recorded; and (3) the person who supplied the information recorded (a) is dead, or beyond the seas, or unfit by reason of his bodily or mental condition to attend as a witness, or (b) cannot with reasonable diligence be identified or found, or (c) cannot reasonably be expected to have any recollection of the matters dealt with in the information he supplied.

Opinion – The rule is that a witness is permitted to give direct or primary evidence, and is not allowed to testify as to matters which he cannot himself prove. However, in some cases a witness may be allowed to give his opinion or belief regarding a fact in issue; for instance:

(1) In matters of science or trade, an expert or skilled person may be asked the probable result or consequence of certain facts which have already been proved by evidence. For example, the opinion of a doctor as to whether a wound was or was not self-inflicted, or as to whether a man has died from the results of a wound or from natural causes. The opinion of an expert on the facts as proved is admissible in evidence.

(2) In a question of the genuineness of handwriting, the opinion of an expert is admissible.

(3) When there is a dispute as to the identity of a particular person or thing, the belief of a person in a position to judge will be admitted.

(4) As to the good character of the accused, that is, his general reputation.

(5) The opinion of experts as to the literary, artistic, scientific or other merits of an article which is alleged to be obscene but which the defence claims is justified as being for the public good, may be admitted in any proceedings under the Obscene Publications Acts 1959 and 1964.

Handwriting – The handwriting of a person may be proved by:

(1) The evidence of the writer himself.

(2) A witness who actually saw the paper or signature written.

(3) A witness who has a knowledge of the person's writing, by having seen him write on other occasions.

(4) A witness who has seen in the ordinary course of business documents presumably written or signed by the person.

(5) Comparison of the disputed writing with any writing proved to be genuine, made by witnesses acquainted with the handwriting or by skilled witnesses who are experts in handwriting.

The opinion of such a witness as in (3), (4) or (5), that the handwriting is or is not the handwriting of the person, is admissible.

Extent of Evidence – Any matter which may lawfully be deposed to and which may contribute, however slightly, to the clearing up of any question in dispute in a court may be tendered in evidence, if accepted by the court as admissible.

Evidence may be given of any fact arising in or out of the case (facts in issue), and of any fact **relevant** to any fact in issue (that is, related to or connected with such fact in issue), subject to the decision of the court as to whether the evidence offered is too remote to be material in the case, as the introduction of matter having no bearing on the case would unduly prolong the trial and confuse the issue.

The general rule is that the evidence in a case should be confined to evidence proving or disproving the matter in dispute.

The following facts would be regarded as relevant in a prosecution:

(1) Facts showing a motive for the offence, preparation for its commission, and conduct after its commission.

(2) The conduct of the person against whom the offence was committed.

(3) Facts connected with the facts of the case, as being explanatory or introductory, fixing times or places, showing the relation of the parties concerned, establishing identity of persons or things, proving the genuineness of documents, or leading up to other facts which may be relevant.

The general rule given above would render inadmissible any evidence of things done or said by the accused in connection with other matters, which might have been similar to, but yet were not connected with the case under trial. Accordingly evidence that the accused had a bad character or had committed other offences would be excluded by this rule. However, in some cases the fact that the accused had said or done other things may assist the court by throwing some light on the offence for which he is being tried. Accordingly evidence of other similar but unconnected transactions may be admissible in the following cases:

(1) To prove intention or guilty knowledge on the part of the accused. In general a man is not held criminally responsible for his act unless he did it with some criminal intention.

This intention or "malice" as a rule is displayed by the nature of the act committed, as the law presumes that a man intends the probable or natural results of his actions. Such proof of intention rebuts any suggestion or defence of accident or mistake. The question of intention or design is relevant in cases of murder, arson, rape, indecent exposure, forgery, coinage offences, conspiracy, embezzlement, false pretences, larceny, etc.

Under the Theft Act 1968, s. 27 (3), where a person is being proceeded against for handling stolen goods (but only on such a charge), then at any stage of the proceedings, if evidence has been given of his having or arranging to have in his possession the goods the subject of the charge, or of his undertaking or assisting in, or arranging to undertake or assist in, their retention, removal, disposal or realisation, the following evidence shall be admissible for the purpose of proving that he knew or believed the goods to be stolen goods—(a) evidence that he has had in his possession, or has undertaken or assisted in the retention, removal, disposal or realisation of, stolen goods from any theft taking place not earlier than 12 months before the offence charged; and (b) (provided that 7 days' notice in writing has been given to him of the intention to prove the conviction) evidence that he has within the 5 years preceding the date of the offence charged been convicted of theft or of handling stolen goods.

Where a suspected person or reputed thief is charged with frequenting or loitering with intent to commit an arrestable offence, evidence of his known character (including previous convictions) may be given as part of the evidence against him as it is a fact in issue. (Vagrancy Act 1824, s. 4, supplemented by Prevention of Crimes Act 1871, s. 15, and Penal Servitude Act 1891, s. 7).

See also "Loiterers and Suspected Persons", Chap. 28. For the special cases of a "persistent offender", see Chap. 28, and of a spy, see "Official Secrets Acts", Chap. 20.

(2) To prove system or course of conduct on the part of the accused, viz. that the act with which he is charged formed part of a number of similar acts in each of which he was concerned. This applies in arson, false pretences, poisoning and other cases.

(3) To prove character. An accused may call witnesses to prove that he has previously borne a good character (that is, a good reputation), and then the prosecution is at liberty to prove his previous convictions (if any), and to give evidence of bad character so as to rebut his evidence of good character.

(4) The accused may give in evidence anything which might justify or excuse his act. For example, he might in sexual cases, produce evidence of the prosecutor's bad character because her character to some extent is in question, as she may have consented to the act.

Circumstantial evidence (see below) may be regarded also as an exception to the rule, as it does not directly or positively prove or disprove the matter in issue, although the facts it indirectly proves may be directly connected with the issue.

Circumstantial Evidence means evidence, not of the actual fact to be proved, but of other facts from which that fact may be presumed with more or less certainty.

When there is a question of the past or present existence of a fact, direct evidence of that fact is the best evidence, but direct evidence of other relevant facts may enable the court or jury to infer the past or present existence of the fact in question.

Circumstantial evidence may clearly establish guilt or innocence, and in any event it will usefully supplement direct evidence.

Presumptive Evidence is the same as circumstantial evidence. When on the proof of some fact the existence of another fact may naturally be inferred, the fact thus inferred is said to be presumed—that is, taken for granted until the contrary is proved. These **presumptions of fact** stand good until proved incorrect. For example, if a man was stabbed in a field and the accused was seen standing beside him with a bloodstained pitchfork in his hands, these facts would raise a presumption that the accused had stabbed him.

Presumptions of Law are certain directions that certain things are to be taken for granted. These directions are either conclusive, viz. they cannot be contradicted, or disputable, viz. they can be proved incorrect.

Conclusive Presumptions cannot be challenged: for example, a child under 10 is incapable of committing a crime; a male under 14 cannot commit rape.

Disputable Presumptions can be overcome: for example, an accused person is presumed innocent; every person is presumed sane until the contrary is proved.

Circumstantial evidence indirectly establishes a fact by proving by direct or positive evidence certain facts from which the existence of the fact to be established may be reasonably inferred or presumed. Therefore, circumstantial evidence may be regarded as indirect evidence in its relation to the whole matter in issue.

Privilege is the right claimed by witnesses to decline to give evidence on certain matters. The general rule is that every person should testify as to what he knows, and it is for the court to decide, subject to the practice as given below, whether any particular evidence need not be given on the ground that it is privileged.

(1) Husband and wife. The Evidence Amendment Act 1853

and the Criminal Evidence Act 1898, s. 1, enact that a husband cannot be compelled to disclose any communication made to him by his wife during their marriage, and that likewise a wife need not disclose anything told her by her husband during marriage.

(2) A witness is not bound to answer any question which might, in the opinion of the court, expose him to the risk of any punishment, penalty, or forfeiture, but this does not apply to an accused giving evidence on his own behalf. (See "Accused Persons and their Husbands or Wives," in this chapter.)

(3) Lawyer and client. Communications between a lawyer and his client for the purpose of the case are confidential and privileged.

(4) Priest and confessions. In practice a clergyman may not be required to give evidence of a confession made to him in his capacity as a priest, but he cannot claim privilege as of right.

(5) Public policy. If it would be contrary to the public interest or injurious to the public service to disclose a particular fact, the witness may claim privilege on the ground of public policy. The court will then not compel the witness to disclose it. Official documents (with some exceptions) are privileged if their disclosure would be contrary to the public interest, and the witness, whenever necessary, should claim privilege and ask the court for a direction on the matter. A police officer should not disclose the name of an informant unless ordered by the judge to do so and the disclosure is material or is necessary in the interest of the accused.

Communications between a doctor and his patient, no matter how confidential, are not privileged.

Leading Questions are questions which are so framed as to suggest to the witness the answer desired or which contain the answer desired. Generally speaking, they are questions which can be answered by "Yes" or "No".

The rule is that leading questions on material points must not be asked by the side which produces the witness, but for convenience a party is allowed to put leading questions to his witness in the following cases:

(1) On all matters which are merely introductory and which do not form material part of the case.

(2) For the purpose of identifying persons or things.

(3) When a witness is called to contradict something to which another witness has sworn.

(4) Where a witness appears hostile to the party who has called him, provided the court gives permission.

Where a witness's memory is defective or where the matter in question is complicated, questions of such a nature as to lead the mind of the witness to the subject of the matter under inquiry may be allowed.

Refreshing Memory – A witness in the witness-box is allowed to refresh his memory by referring to any entry in a book or paper made by himself or by someone in his presence, or seen and examined by him shortly after the occurrence of the fact to which the entry relates, provided that he can swear to the fact from his recollection.

Such entry must be produced and shown to the opposing side if so required, and the witness may be questioned on it. A witness cannot use a copy of an entry to refresh his memory, unless the copy was made by himself or in his presence and he knew it to be correct.

Hostile Witness – When a witness shows himself adverse or opposed to the side which has called him he may be regarded as a "hostile witness". However, the fact that a witness's evidence is unfavourable to his side does not necessarily render him a hostile witness. It is for the court to decide whether a witness should be treated as a "hostile witness".

If the court gives permission, the side that has called a hostile witness may:

(1) Put leading questions to him;

(2) Cross-examine him;

(3) Contradict him by other evidence;

(4) Prove that he has made at other times a statement inconsistent with his present testimony, provided that before such proof is given, the circumstances of this previous statement must be mentioned to the witness and he must be asked whether he has or has not made such statement (Criminal Procedure Act 1865, s. 3).

Unwilling Witness – If a person attending or brought before a magistrates' court refuses without just excuse to be sworn or give evidence or to produce any document or thing, the court may commit him in custody for up to 7 days or until he sooner gives evidence or produce the document or thing (M.C. Act 1952, s. 77).

The Onus or Burden of Proof of any fact rests on the person who alleges it, therefore the task of proving an alleged offence rests on the prosecution, who have to satisfy the court (and jury if there is one) beyond all reasonable doubt that the evidence proves the defendant guilty of the offence charged (*Woolmington* v. *Director of Public Prosecutions* (1935)). However, when the necessary facts are proved, the burden of proof is shifted to the accused, who has to prove his innocence or be convicted. In some cases Acts of Parliament place the burden of proof on the accused; for example, the person found in possession of coining implements or counterfeit coins must prove a lawful excuse, and in a customs case the accused has to prove that the duties have been paid or the goods were lawfully imported.

A Court should take **judicial notice**—that is, admit in evidence, without proof—certain facts of general knowledge, such as the laws of the country, the extent of the realm, the course of nature, etc.

In a criminal case all facts alleged should be proved and the accused's admissions will not enable the prosecution to dispense with proof though his confession may be proved against him.

Examination-in-chief – This is the examination of a witness by the party who produces him, and it is also called his direct **examination,** of which the two main rules are:

(1) The witness should be allowed to relate his story, and any questions asked should relate solely to the matter immediately in issue. No question should be asked if the probable answer would not have a tendency to prove the offence or the defence or other matter being tried. Questions must be relevant—that is, they should be such as are likely to elicit evidence of facts on which the court may decide the guilt or innocence of the defendant.

(2) Leading questions on material points must not be asked. The few exceptions to this rule have been given above.

If an irrelevant or leading question is put, the opposing side may at once object, and if necessary appeal to the court.

Cross-examination – When the direct examination has finished the witness may be questioned or cross-examined by the other side. If the witness has told the whole truth, cross-examination of his evidence will render his story stronger and will impress the court still more. In such a case cross-examination may be confined to questions attacking his credibility, by questioning his means of knowledge, his impartiality, or his character.

If the witness is not telling the truth, then he may be questioned as to his facts, as well as to his credibility, and the truth can later be proved by other witnesses.

In cross-examination a witness may be asked leading questions. In fact great latitude is allowed in cross-examination, though the rule is that questions should be relevant to the issue or calculated to bring out the witness's title to credit (or discredit).

Questions irrelevant to the issue may be put for the purpose of challenging his character or testing his credit, but the answers of the witness to such questions must be taken and cannot be contradicted by independent evidence except in the case where he denies that he has been previously convicted, as if so the conviction may be proved by production of certificate of conviction with proof of identity (Criminal Procedure Act 1865, s. 6; Prevention of Crimes Act 1871, s. 18).

If the questions put relate to relevant facts, the answers of the witness may be contradicted by independent evidence.

A witness can claim the right to refuse to answer certain questions, questions where the answers might expose him to any criminal charge, etc., as given more fully under the heading of "Privilege". He can appeal to the court, which will decide whether he ought or ought not to answer such questions.

A witness can be cross-examined as to previous statements made by him in writing or reduced into writing relative to the case at trial, without such writing being shown to him.

If a witness, on cross-examination as to a former statement (written or verbal) made by him relative to the case and inconsistent with his present testimony, does not admit he made that statement, proof may be given that he did in fact make it, provided that he is first given the circumstances of the disputed statement and asked whether or not he did make it (Criminal Procedure Act 1865, s. 4).

Accused persons giving evidence on their own behalf may be cross-examined subject to the restrictions given under "Accused persons and their husbands or wives".

Re-examination – After a witness has been cross-examined the party who called him has a right to re-examine him upon any new facts which may have arisen out of the cross-examination, and may also ask questions necessary in order to explain any part of his cross-examination. He has no right to go further than this, and may not introduce matter new in itself and not necessary to explain any part of the cross-examination.

Recalling a Witness – The court may at any time recall a witness and ask him any questions. If something has been left out in the direct examination and cannot be brought in in re-examination because it was not referred to in the cross-examination, it is usual to ask the court to make the inquiry of the witness, and the request is usually granted. If a witness for the prosecution is thus recalled, the accused is allowed to cross-examine him on the new evidence given.

When the magistrates begin to inquire into an indictable offence as examining justices and later proceed to deal summarily with the accused then, unless the accused pleads guilty, they shall recall for cross-examination any witnesses who have given evidence except any not required by the accused or prosecutor (M.C. Rules 1968, r. 19).

Rebutting Evidence – When the defence has produced evidence introducing new matter which the prosecution has not dealt with, the court in its discretion may allow the prosecution to give evidence in reply to rebut or contradict it. When such rebutting evidence is given the defence is entitled to comment on it.

Thus evidence may be called to rebut or contradict an alibi. The Latin word "alibi" means "elsewhere," and **an alibi** is an effort to prove that the accused was elsewhere at the time of the alleged offence, and therefore could not have committed it. The prosecution also may call evidence to rebut evidence of good character given by the defence.

Notice of Alibi – On a trial on indictment the defendant shall not without the leave of the court adduce evidence in support of an alibi unless, before the end of the prescribed period, he gives notice of particulars of the alibi.

On any such trial the defendant shall not without the leave of the court call any other person to give such evidence unless (a) the notice includes the name and address of the witness or, if the name or address is not known to the defendant at the time he gives the notice, any information in his possession which might be of material assistance in finding the witness; (b) if the name or the address is not included in that notice, the court is satisfied that the defendant, before giving the notice, took and thereafter continued to take all reasonable steps to secure that the name or address would be ascertained; (c) if the name or the address is not included in that notice, but the defendant subsequently discovers the name or address or receives other information which might be of material assistance in finding the witness, he forthwith gives notice of the name, address or other information, as the case may be; and (d) if the defendant is notified by or on behalf of the prosecutor that the witness has not been traced by the name or at the address given, he forthwith gives notice of any such information which is then in his possession, or, on subsequently receiving any such information, forthwith gives notice of it.

Any evidence tendered to disprove an alibi may, subject to any directions by the court as to the time it is to be given, be given before or after evidence is given in support of the alibi.

"Evidence in support of an alibi" means evidence tending to show that by reason of the presence of the defendant at a particular place or in a particular area at a particular time he was not, or was unlikely to have been, at the place where the offence is alleged to have been committed at the time of its alleged commission.

"The prescribed period" means the period of 7 days (not including Sunday, Christmas Day, Good Friday, bank holiday, or a day for public thanksgiving or mourning) from the end of the proceedings before the examining justices (C.J. Act 1967, s. 11).

Character after Conviction – When an accused person has been found guilty it is customary for the court to inquire as to his previous character. It is the duty of the police to exercise the most scrupulous care in presenting to any court the record of an accused person. Such evidence of character will consist of the record of any previous convictions which are not "spent" or otherwise inadmissible (see Chap. 2), the result of any inquiries that may have been made, and what the officer testifying can depose to of his own personal knowledge. Nothing should be omitted that is in favour of the prisoner, and nothing should be said to his prejudice which the officer is not able to substantiate.

Previous Convictions – The admissibility of evidence of previous convictions is now governed by the Rehabilitation of Offenders Act 1974, the effects of which are that after a "rehabilitation period", certain convictions may become "spent" and thereafter are effectively deemed not to exist. The Act is retrospective, i.e. it applies to convictions which occurred before it came into force, and further details are given in "Convicted Persons", Chap. 2.

For proof of an admissible conviction strictly there should be documentary evidence from the convicting court and oral evidence of the identity of the person with the person referred to in such documentary evidence or the evidence of finger-prints as mentioned under "Convicted Persons" in Chap. 2. Such strict proof is necessary if a previous conviction is used for any purpose before the conviction of an accused person unless the accused admits it. After conviction, any previous convictions as given in the accused's official record, other than those which are spent, may be mentioned as part of his antecedents and character (*R.* v. *Van Pelz* (1943)).

The general rule is that information as to previous convictions, etc., should not be told to the court until after conviction but—

(1) If an adult (17 or over) is tried summarily for an indictable offence and convicted, information as to his character and antecedents should then be given to the court, including previous convictions if any. If the court considers that greater punishment should be inflicted than the court can inflict, the court can commit the accused in custody or on bail to the Crown Court for sentence (M.C. Act 1952, s. 29). If a second summary conviction would entail an increased penalty the first one should be properly proved. See "Convicted Persons", Chap. 2. See s. 3, M.C. Act 1957 as to proof of a previous summary conviction when a magistrates' court convicts a person of a summary offence, and M.C. Rules 1968 as to notice of it and service of summons.

(2) When considering bail the court may consider any previous convictions of the accused (*R.* v. *Fletcher*, (1949)).

The judges of the High Court in January, 1955, issued a statement as to the antecedent history of accused and convicted persons to the following effect:

1. Details of previous convictions should, on request be supplied by the police to the defending lawyer so that the defence may be properly conducted as regards accused's character.
2. A prisoner's previous convictions will be given on the Confidential Calendar supplied to the judge by the Governor of the prison. The police need not supply them to the court before conviction but should give to the Governor any information he may require.
3. A police officer, for evidence, should prepare a statement containing a list of previous convictions with particulars of the accused's antecedents and circumstances.

   The prosecution should have this statement. If accused is convicted, the police officer should be sworn and the statement given to the court and to the defence.

   If it is to be said that the accused associates with bad characters the officer saying so must be able to speak of this from his own knowledge.

In any proceedings for an offence committed or alleged to have been committed by a person of or over the age of 21, any offence of which he was found guilty while under the age of 14 shall be disregarded for the purpose of any evidence about his previous convictions and no question is to be put to him about such an offence (C. & Y.P. Act 1963, s. 16).

The Perfect Witness – He should relate in ordinary language the story he can tell of his own knowledge as to what he has seen, heard, etc. He should confine himself to facts, avoiding inferences and opinions or beliefs. He should tell his story in the natural order and sequence of events as they occurred. He should speak from memory, expressing himself clearly and accurately. He should not produce his notebook as a matter of course and read out all his evidence therefrom. If he finds it necessary to refresh his memory he may be allowed to consult his notes. When asked a question, he should listen carefully to the question, make sure that he understands it, and give an intelligent and proper answer to the best of his ability. He should only answer the questions put to him, and then, in as few words as possible, promptly and frankly. He should never lose his temper under cross-examination, and should always reply politely and quietly to offensive questions.

He should not show partisanship or prejudice, and ought to give his evidence fairly and impartially, giving all the evidence in favour of the accused in addition to the evidence against him. If he does not know something asked he should say so. He is sworn to tell the whole truth, and nothing but the truth.

PART II – OFFENCES AGAINST PERSONS

CHAPTER 8

ASSAULT

	Page
Assault	105
Statutory Assaults . .	106
Assaulting, Obstructing or Resisting the Police .	107
Powers of Arrest . .	108
Wounding and other Serious Assaults . .	108
Threats and Menaces .	109
Blackmail . . .	109
Hijacking Act 1971 . .	110
Protection of Aircraft Act 1973	110

Assault – An assault is any act which intentionally—or possibly recklessly—causes another person to apprehend immediate and unlawful personal violence (*Fagan* v. *Metropolitan Police Commissioner* (1969)). To constitute the offence, some deliberate act must have been performed; a mere omission to act cannot amount to an assault. It is a common law offence.

To constitute an assault it is not necessary that the other party should be touched or receive any injury. Some act accompanied by such circumstances as indicate an intention of using actual violence against the person of another will amount to an assault, provided that the attacker has the means of carrying out his intention.

A battery is the actual application of unlawful force to another, and any hostile touching, no matter how slight, is a battery.

A battery usually includes an assault, but this is not necessarily so. A person attacked from behind, for example, may have no opportunity to apprehend immediate and unlawful violence.

In practice the word "assault" is used to cover both the assault and the battery.

It is not necessary that the injury should be effected directly by the hand of the assailant, as, for example, there may be an assault by setting a dog at another person.

The intention is material, as an accidental injury does not amount to an "assault" in law. Where the act is done with the consent of the other party, it is not an "assault" unless such consent has been obtained through fraud or is the result of ignorance, or unless the act is attended with a breach of the peace or is in some way injurious to the public or unless there was such a degree of violence that bodily harm is a probable consequence. As regards consent, see *R.* v. *Donovan* (1934).

Thus a prize fight or a duel is unlawful, even though there is consent on both sides, as amounting to a breach of the peace. A challenge to fight or to fight a duel is also unlawful, being an offence likely to cause a breach of the peace. However a prize fight properly conducted under rules indicating that the object is to win by skill, and not through exhaustion or injuries caused, is not illegal.

A parent or teacher or other person in lawful control or charge may administer reasonable and moderate chastisement to a child or young person (Children and Young Persons Act 1933, s. 1).

In some cases an assault may be justified at law, as in the case of a constable arresting his prisoner or of a person using necessary violence in self-defence or in defence of his wife (husband), parents, property, etc. However, in such cases the force used must be only so great as is necessary for effecting the object.

Insulting or provocative words do not make an assault and do not justify an assault.

Statutory Assaults – Assaults can be dealt with summarily or on indictment, according to their nature, as follows:

Offences against the Person Act 1861.

S. 42: To unlawfully assault or beat any other person. This offence can be dealt with summarily when the information is made by the injured party or by someone on his behalf.

S. 43: An assault or battery of an aggravated nature upon any boy whose age does not exceed 14 years or upon any female, on the information of the party aggrieved or otherwise, can be punished summarily.

"Aggravated" here means made worse in respect of violence, but not in respect of indecency (*R.* v. *Baker* (1883)).

If a person charged under ss. 42 or 43 is convicted or acquitted with certificate of dismissal (s. 44), he is by s. 45 of the Act released from all other proceedings for the same cause. Therefore any future action to recover compensation cannot be taken against him.

The consent of a person under 16 years of age to an indecent assault affords no defence to the charge as such a person cannot in law consent to it. See Sexual Offences Act 1956, s. 15.

A charge of indecent assault on any person can be dealt with summarily provided the accused consents to be so dealt with (Magistrates' Courts Act 1952, s. 19 and Sched. 1, as amended by C.J.A. Act 1962). See also "Unnatural Crimes," Chap. 11.

S. 47: To assault any person, thereby occasioning actual bodily harm.

S. 20: To maliciously wound or inflict grievous bodily harm upon any person with or without any instrument.

These two offences (ss. 20 and 47) can be dealt with summarily if the accused consents (M.C. Act 1952, s. 19 and Sched. 1).

S. 38: To assault any person with intent to resist or prevent a lawful arrest (as amended by C.L. Act 1967).

In many other cases statutes provide penalties for assaults with intent to commit various offences. These assaults are mentioned with the offences with which they are connected. The right given to a defendant to claim trial by jury where the offence is punishable by more than 3 months imprisonment does not apply to an assault. (M.C. Act 1952, s. 25).

Offences against the Person Act 1861, s. 46, provides that if a summary court finds that the assault is one that should be dealt with on indictment, the court should abstain from any adjudication thereon. It also declares that the justices are not authorised to hear and determine any assault arising out of any question of the title to land or of any bankruptcy, insolvency, or execution under the process of any court of justice. This is termed "ouster of jurisdiction".

Assaulting, Obstructing or Resisting the Police – Any person who assaults a constable in the execution of his duty, or a person assisting a constable in the execution of his duty, shall be guilty of an offence and liable: (a) on summary conviction to imprisonment for a term not exceeding 6 months or in the case of a second or subsequent offence 9 months, or to a fine not exceeding £100, or to both; (b) on conviction on indictment to imprisonment for a term not exceeding 2 years or to a fine or to both (s. 25 (1) of the M.C. Act 1952 as amended by the Police Act 1964, s. 51, confers no right to trial by jury in the case of an "assault" and this includes an assault on a policeman in the execution of his duty (*R.* v. *Woolwich Justices, Ex parte Toohey* (1965)). The Firearms Act 1968, s. 17 (2) (additional penalty for possession of firearms when committing certain offences) shall apply to these offences. A person who resists or wilfully obstructs a constable in the execution of his duty or a person assisting a constable in the execution of his duty shall be guilty of an offence and liable on summary conviction to imprisonment for a term not exceeding one month or to a fine not exceeding £20, or to both (Police Act 1964, s. 51).

Offences against the Person Act 1861, s. 38.—It is an offence to assault any person with intent to resist or prevent the lawful apprehension or detainer of himself or of any other person for any offence.

An attempted rescue of a prisoner may be dealt with summarily as assaulting, obstructing or resisting the police.

A police officer has power to direct a motorist to disobey traffic regulations if such a direction is reasonably necessary for the preservation of life or property, and an officer giving such a direction is acting in the execution of his duty (*Johnson* v. *Phillips* (1975)).

Powers of Arrest – A constable may arrest when an assault is committed in his presence. However, he should exercise this power with discretion, the main points to consider being the seriousness of any injury sustained and the likelihood of a repetition of the offence. In ordinary assaults the parties as a rule may be left to proceed by summons. A constable may also arrest a person who, in his view, threatens to commit an assault, except where the threat appears to be an empty one and there has been no breach of the peace.

A constable should arrest in cases where dangerous injuries have been inflicted, or are likely to be inflicted should the parties not be separated, or where the peace has been disturbed and the removal of the offender is necessary for its preservation.

If an interval has elapsed after the commission of a common assault, the constable should not arrest, except in the case of continued pursuit to arrest the person who has committed the assault.

Wounding and other Serious Assaults – The Offences against the Person Act 1861 provides severe punishment for these serious attacks on the person, which in some cases just fall short of homicide.

Wounding – S. 18: Maliciously wounding or causing grievous bodily harm to any person with intent to do him grievous bodily harm, or with intent to prevent or resist the lawful apprehension of any person.

To constitute a "wounding" the skin must be broken. To "maim" is to injure any part of the body so as to render the person less capable of fighting. Grievous bodily harm means really serious bodily harm.

S. 20: Maliciously wounding or inflicting any grievous bodily harm upon any person, either with or without any weapon or instrument. This can be dealt with summarily with accused's consent (M.C. Act 1952, s. 19 and Sched. 1).

Choking – S. 21: Attempting to choke, suffocate, or strangle any person, or attempting to render any person insensible or incapable of resistance by any means calculated to choke, suffocate or strangle, with intent to commit an indictable offence. This crime is usually committed by robbers who choke their victims into unconsciousness so as to take their property.

Drugging – S. 22: Unlawfully administering or attempting to cause to be taken, any chloroform or other stupefying drug or thing with intent to enable the committing of an indictable offence. See also "Procuration", Chap. 10.

Poisoning – S. 23: Maliciously administering any poison or other destructive or noxious thing so as thereby to endanger human life or cause grievous bodily harm.

S. 24: Maliciously administering any poison or other destructive or noxious thing with intent to injure, aggrieve or annoy.

Burning, etc. – S. 29: Maliciously and with intent to burn, maim, disfigure, disable or cause grievous bodily harm, sending, placing, throwing or otherwise applying any corrosive fluid or any destructive or explosive substance, whether any bodily harm be effected or not. For the causing of grievous bodily harm by the unlawful use of explosives, see "Explosives", Chap. 33.

Threats and Menaces – As it is possible that a person who has been threatened in any way may take such action as might lead to a breach of the peace, any person who makes any threats either verbally or by action or in writing is liable to be bound over to keep the peace and (or) be of good behaviour.

See "Breach of the Peace and Sureties", Chap. 22.

Threatening letters and certain threats and menaces affecting person, property or reputation are dealt with by statute as follows:

Offences against the Person Act 1861, s. 16. It is an offence maliciously to send, deliver or utter or directly or indirectly cause to be received knowing the contents thereof, any letter or writing threatening to kill or murder any person.

Criminal Damage Act 1971, s. 2. A person who without lawful excuse makes to another a threat, intending that that other would fear it would be carried out, (a) to destroy or damage any property belonging to that other, or a third person; or (b) to destroy or damage his own property in a way which he knows is likely to endanger the life of that other or a third person, commits an offence.

Theft Act 1968, s. 21. A person is guilty of **blackmail** if with a view to gain for himself or another or with intent to cause loss to another, he makes any unwarranted demand with menaces. Such a demand is unwarranted unless the person making it does so in the belief (a) that he has reasonable grounds for making the demand, and (b) that the use of the menaces is a proper means of reinforcing it.

The nature of the act or omission demanded is immaterial and it is also immaterial whether the menaces relate to action to be taken by the person making the demand. The offence is not triable summarily.

For definitions of "gain" and "loss" see s. 34 (2) (a) under "Interpretation", Chap. 14.

Sexual Offences Act 1956, s. 2. It is an offence by threats or intimidation to procure or attempt to procure any woman or girl to have any unlawful sexual intercourse in any part of the world. See also "Procuration", Chap. 10.

For threats, etc., in labour disputes, see "Intimidation", Chap. 22.

Hijacking Act 1971. A person on board an aircraft in flight who unlawfully, by the use of force or by threats of any kind, seizes the aircraft or exercises control of it commits the offence of hijacking, but subject to sub-s. (2) below (s. 1 (1)).

If (a) the aircraft is used in military, customs or police service; or (b) both the place of take off and the place of landing are in the territory of the state in which the aircraft is registered, sub-s. (1) above shall not apply unless (i) the person seizing or exercising control of the aircraft is such a person as is mentioned in sub-s. (3) below; or (ii) his act is committed in the United Kingdom; or (iii) the aircraft is registered in the United Kingdom or is used in the military or customs service of the U.K., or in the service of any police force in the U.K. (s. 1 (2)).

The persons referred to in sub-s. (2) (i) above, are (a) a citizen of the U.K. and colonies; (b) a British subject by virtue of the British Nationality Act 1948, s. 2; (c) a British subject without citizenship by virtue of ss. 13 and 16 of that Act; (d) a British subject by virtue of the British Nationality Act 1965; and (e) a British protected person within the meaning of the British Nationality Act 1948 (s. 1 (3)). A person who (a) commits the offence of hijacking; or (b) in the U.K. induces or assists the commission elsewhere of an act which would be the offence of hijacking but for sub-s. (2) above, is liable to life imprisonment (s. 1 (4)).

Without prejudice to the Tokyo Convention Act 1967, s. 1 (which makes provision for offences on board British-controlled aircraft—see Chap. 26), where a person does on board any aircraft and while outside the U.K. any act which, if done in the U.K., would constitute the offence of murder, attempted murder, manslaughter, culpable homicide or assault or an offence under ss. 18, 20, 21, 22, 23, 28 or 29 of the O.A.P. Act 1861, or s. 2 of the Explosives Substances Act 1883, his act shall constitute the offence if it is done in connection with the offence of hijacking committed or attempted by him on board that aircraft (s. 2).

Proceedings for an offence under this act shall not be instituted except by or with the consent of the Attorney-General (s. 5 (1)). But this shall not prevent the arrest, or the issue of a warrant for the arrest, of any person in respect of any offence under this Act, or the remanding in custody or on bail of any person charged with any such offence (s. 5 (1A) as added by Protection of Aircraft Act 1973, s. 6 (2)).

Protection of Aircraft Act 1973. It is an offence to destroy an aircraft in service, or so to damage it as to render it incapable of flight, or as to be likely to endanger its safety in flight, or to commit on board an aircraft in flight any act of violence which is likely to endanger the safety of the aircraft (s. 1(1)), or unlawfully and intentionally to place, or cause to be placed, on an aircraft in service any device or substance which is likely so to damage it as to render it incapable of flight or as to be likely to endanger its safety in flight (s. 1 (2)).

It is an offence to destroy, damage or interfere with the operation of property used for the provision of air navigation facilities, or to intentionally communicate false, misleading or deceptive information, where the communciation of the information endangers, or is likely to endanger the safety of an aircraft in flight (s. 2).

The institution of proceedings under the above sections requires the consent of the Attorney-General, but this does not prevent the arrest of an alleged offender without such consent being obtained.

It is an offence to bring into an aircraft, or an aerodrome, or an air navigation installation, a firearm or any article having the appearance of being a firearm, or any explosive or other dangerous weapon, without lawful authority or reasonable cause (s. 16).

Where a constable has reasonable cause to suspect that a person about to embark on an aircraft, or a person on board such an aircraft, intends to commit, in relation to the aircraft, an offence under sections 1–6 of this Act, or under the Hijacking Act 1971, the constable may prohibit him from travelling on board the aircraft and may arrest him without warrant and detain him for so long as may be necessary for that purpose (s. 19 (1)).

For the protection of aircraft, aerodrome and Air Navigation Installations against acts of violence the Secretary of State is given power by s. 10 to give a direction in writing to the manager of any aerodrome requiring him to use his best endeavours to secure that searches specified in the direction be carried out. When such a direction is for the time being in force, a constable if he has reasonable cause to suspect that an article to which s. 16 of this Act applies is in, or may be brought into, any part of the aerodrome, he may without a warrant search any part of the aerodrome or any aircraft, vehicle, goods or other moveable property of any description which, or person who, is for the time being in any part of the aerodrome, and for that purpose (a) may enter any building or works in an aerodrome, or enter upon any land in the aerodrome, if need be by force, and (b) may stop any aircraft, vehicle, goods, property or person and detain it or him for so long as may be necessary for that purpose (s. 19 (2)).

CHAPTER 9

HOMICIDE

	Page		Page
Homicide . . .	112	Legal Consequences of Homicide and kindred Offences . . .	115
Murder	113	Genocide Act 1969 . .	115
Manslaughter . . .	114	Search Warrants: 1861 Act	116
Suicide	114		

Homicide – This is the killing of a human being by a human being. Every case of "causing death" should be regarded as a possible murder unless there is evidence to show that it is not murder.

In all cases of homicide the prosecution should call as witnesses all persons present at the killing to give a full account of the circumstances. If there is evidence to indicate murder the accused, if he can, should produce evidence to prove that his action was justifiable or excusable or that it did not amount to an offence.

Homicide may be justifiable—that is, not deserving of any blame—under the following circumstances:

(1) Where a criminal is executed in accordance with his sentence.

(2) Where an officer of the law whilst performing his duty has of necessity to kill a person who is resisting or preventing him in the execution of his duty.

(3) Where it is committed to prevent a forcible and atrocious crime, such as murder or rape.

Homicide also may be excusable—that is, excused by law but not quite free from blame—as in the following cases:

(1) Where a person kills another by misadventure or accident, without any intention of harm, whilst doing a lawful act in a proper manner.

(2) Where a person, in defending himself or his wife or family from attack, unavoidably in the course of the struggle kills another.

If homicide cannot be justified or excused it is criminal. There are three forms of criminal homicide, viz.:

(1) Murder, which is defined as where a person of sound memory and discretion unlawfully killeth any reasonable creature in being with malice aforethought either express or implied, the death following within a year and a day.

(2) Manslaughter, which is defined as the unlawful killing of another without any malice either express or implied.

(3) Infanticide, which is the offence committed by a woman when by any wilful act or omission she causes the death of her newly born child, her mind being then unbalanced. See "Infanticide" and "Child Destruction", Chap. 12.

Murder – Only persons of sound memory and discretion are liable to conviction for murder; children under 10 and the insane are not so liable. A person who is abnormal, suffering from diminished responsibility, shall not be convicted of murder but may be convicted of manslaughter (Homicide Act 1957, s. 2). The killing must have been unlawful and without justification or excuse. It may be done by direct act or by wicked negligence. The person killed must have been a reasonable creature in being, so to constitute infanticide the child should have been born alive. See also "Abortion", "Child Destruction", and "Infanticide", Chap. 12.

The killing must have been with malice aforethought—that is, some evil intent beforehand to do harm without just cause or excuse.

Malice is express when a person with deliberate design kills another. Such clear intent may be proved by the circumstances of the killing, by previous threats, by lying in wait, etc., etc.

Malice may be implied or presumed from the circumstances attending the homicide.

In a prosecution for murder, in addition to proving the homicide, it is necessary to prove that death resulted from a voluntary act on the part of the accused and also malice either express or implied on the part of the accused. The accused is entitled to show by evidence and/or by examination of the evidence against him that the homicide was either unintentional or provoked. The prosecution must prove the prisoner's guilt beyond reasonable doubt (*Woolmington* v. *Director of Public Prosecutions* (1935)).

The deceased must have died of the injury given him by the accused, and within a year and a day after he had received it. If he died after that time the law presumes his death occurred from some other cause.

Circumstantial evidence may be sufficient to establish the guilt of the killer, but it must be very strong to justify conviction in cases where the body of the killed person has not been found. See "Circumstantial Evidence", Chap. 7.

Manslaughter – The absence of malice will reduce murder to manslaughter. Manslaughter may be voluntary—that is, where a person in a sudden fight kills another—or it may be involuntary —that is, where a person who is doing some unlawful act accidentally kills another, or where a person, by culpably neglecting his duty, accidentally causes the death of another. Also the existence of provocation may reduce murder to manslaughter. but the provocation must have been great and such as would deprive a reasonable person of his self-control (see *Mancini* v. *Director of Public Prosecutions* (1942)). In such case the sufficiency of the provocation shall be left to the determination of the jury (Homicide Act 1957, s. 3).

If a person, by his neglect or default, unintentionally causes the death of another, he may be convicted of manslaughter. It will be no defence to plead that the person killed contributed to his own death by his negligence.

Neglect or ill-treatment of helpless persons (such as children, sick, aged, or lunatic persons) which results in death, may be murder if premeditated, or manslaughter if there has been gross and culpable negligence.

A person can be convicted of manslaughter arising out of the driving of a motor vehicle. Proof of a very high degree of negligence is necessary to establish a charge of manslaughter, but the law of manslaughter has not been altered by the introduction of motor vehicles on the road (*Andrews* v. *Director of Public Prosecutions* (1937)).

Manslaughter in connection with the driving of a motor vehicle can be dealt with as reckless or dangerous driving. See "Dangerous Driving", Chap. 24.

Suicide – Suicide is where a person kills himself, and a "suicide pact" means a common agreement between two or more persons having for its object the death of all of them, whether or not each is to take his own life, but nothing done by a person who enters into a suicide pact is to be treated as done by him in pursuance of the pact unless it is done while he has the settled intention of dying in pursuance of the pact.

It is manslaughter, and not murder, for a person acting in pursuance of a suicide pact between him and another to kill the other or be a party to the other being killed by a third person.

Where it is shown that a person charged with the murder of another, killed the other or was a party to his being killed, it is a defence to prove that the person charged was acting in pursuance of a suicide pact between him and the other (Homicide Act 1957, s. 4).

Under the Suicide Act 1961 suicide ceased to be a crime (s. 1) therefore the attempt to commit suicide is no longer a crime, but a person may still be criminally liable for complicity in another's suicide.

A person who aids, abets, counsels or procures the suicide of another, or an attempt by another to commit suicide, commits a serious offence (s. 2 (1)).

If on the trial for murder or manslaughter it is proved that the accused aided, abetted, counselled or procured the suicide of the person in question, he may be found guilty of that offence (s. 2 (2)).

Proceedings must be by or with the consent of the D.P.P. However, where the victim is a child or young person it will be lawful, before the D.P.P. has been consulted, to exercise the powers conferred by ss. 13 and 40 of the C. & Y.P. Act 1933 to arrest the offender and to remove the victim to a place of safety (s. 2 (4)).

Legal Consequences of Homicide and kindred Offences – Murder (Abolition of Death Penalty) Act 1965.

The death penalty for murder is abolished and replaced by life imprisonment. The court may recommend a minimum period of imprisonment (s. 1).

Offences against the Person Act 1861:

S. 1: Murder. Persons under eighteen when they commit the crime shall not be sentenced to death or life imprisonment but shall be sentenced to be detained during Her Majesty's pleasure (C. & Y.P. Act 1933 s. 53, as amended by s. 1 (5) of Murder (Abolition of Death Penalty) Act 1965).

Imprisonment for life instead of sentence of death on conviction of murder shall be pronounced in the case of an expectant mother (Sentence of Death (Expectant Mothers) Act 1931).

S. 4: Conspiracy to murder any person anywhere, or inciting or proposing to murder any person anywhere, is an offence punishable by imprisonment for 10 years.

S. 5: Manslaughter is a crime punishable by imprisonment for life, or by fine. Infanticide is punishable as manslaughter (Infanticide Act 1938). Child destruction (Chap. 12) is punishable by imprisonment for life.

S. 9: Murder or manslaughter by a British subject abroad may be dealt with in England.

S. 16: Sending, uttering, etc., a letter or writing threatening to murder any person is an arrestable offence. See "Threats and Menaces", Chap. 8.

All these serious offences must be tried at the Crown Court.

Genocide Act 1969 – Genocide means any of the following acts committed with intent to destroy, in whole or in part, a national, ethnical, racial or religious group, as such (a) killing members of the group; (b) causing serious bodily or mental harm to members of the group; (c) deliberately inflicting on the group conditions of life calculated to bring about its physical destruction in whole or in part; (d) imposing measures intended to prevent births within the group, (e) forcibly transferring children of the group to another group.

A person commits an offence of genocide if he commits any act falling within the above definition. A person guilty of an offence of genocide shall on conviction on indictment (a) if the offence consists of the killing of any person, be sentenced to imprisonment for life; (b) in any other case, be liable to imprisonment for a term not exceeding 14 years. Proceedings shall not be instituted except by consent of the Attorney–General (s. 1). The Extradition (Genocide) Order 1970 applies the Extradition Acts 1870 to 1935, as amended by the Genocide Act 1969, to the offence of genocide in the case of those states with which the U.K. has Extradition Treaties and which are also parties to the Genocide Convention.

Search Warrants: 1861 Act – S. 64 of the Offences against the Person Act 1861, makes it an offence knowingly to have in possession or make any gunpowder, explosive substance or any dangerous or noxious thing or any machine, engine, instrument or thing, with intent by means thereof to commit, or for the purpose of enabling any other person to commit, any of the indictable offences in this Act mentioned, and s. 65 empowers a justice, on reasonable cause on oath, to issue a warrant to search any house or place where the same is suspected to be for such purpose as hereinbefore mentioned.

CHAPTER 10

OFFENCES AGAINST FEMALES

	Page
Sexual Offences	117
Rape and Similar Offences	119
Indecent Assault	120
Incest	120
Procuration	121
Abduction of Females	122
Prostitution	123
Harbouring Prostitutes	124
Brothels	125
Arrest and Search Warrant	126

Sexual Offences – In a case in which a man is charged with a sexual offence against a female the words of Sir Matthew Hale relative to rape should be remembered: "It is an accusation easy to be made and hard to be proved, but harder to be defended by the party accused though innocent." The first consideration is the credibility of the female's story. The question of consent and corroboration available must then be considered.

The following circumstances will support her evidence: good reputation, reporting the occurrence without delay, marks of violence on her person, signs of struggle at the scene, and any other evidence corroborating her statement.

The following will weaken her testimony: bad reputation, concealment of the occurrence for any unreasonable length of time, making no outcry in a place where she might have been heard, and no corroboration of her story.

In general, the evidence of one witness in sexual cases should be corroborated in some material particular by other evidence implicating the accused, otherwise it will be the evidence of the female alone against that of the man. The fact that she made a complaint is admissible in evidence. See "Hearsay Evidence", Chap. 7.

In a case of alleged rape the injured female should without delay, if she consents, be examined by a doctor. If she is under 16 her parents' consent should be obtained. This examination cannot be made without her consent, but her refusal to undergo such an examination will naturally descredit her story.

The Sexual Offences Act 1956 consolidates the statute law relating to sexual crimes, abduction, procuration and prostitution of females and kindred offences.

The mode of trial and penalties for offences under this Act are dealt with in Part II of Sched. 2.

"Sexual intercourse" whether natural or unnatural shall be deemed complete upon proof of penetration only (s. 44). In the Act "man" without the addition of "boy" or vice versa does not prevent any provision of the Act applying to any person to whom it would have applied if both words were used, and similarly with the words "woman" and "girl" (s. 46).

Under s. 40 a constable may arrest a person without a warrant if he has reasonable cause to suspect him of having committed or of attempting to commit an offence under s. 22 (procuring a woman to be a prostitute) or s. 23 (procuring a girl under 21 to have unlawful sexual intercourse).

Under s. 41 anyone may arrest without a warrant a person found committing an offence under s. 32 (man soliciting in a public place for immoral purposes).

Section 42 allows a justice, on sworn information that there is reasonable cause to suspect that a house or part of it is used by a woman for prostitution and that a man residing or frequenting the house is living wholly or in part on her earnings, to issue a warrant authorising a constable to enter and search the house and to arrest the man.

The C. & Y.P. Act 1933, s. 40, allows the issue of a warrant to search for and remove a child or young person. In addition s. 43 of the Sexual Offences Act 1956 empowers a justice to issue a warrant to search for and remove a woman detained for immoral purposes and so detained against her will or if she is under 16 or is a defective (see s. 45) or is under 18 and is so detained against the will of her parent or guardian.

Section 39 directs that the wife or husband of the accused shall be competent to give evidence on a charge of any offence under this 1956 Act for the defence or the prosecution (except in so far as it is excluded in the case of s. 12 (buggery), s. 15 (indecent assault on a man) and s. 16 (assault with intent to commit buggery)). Provided that:

(a) the wife or husband shall not be compellable to give evidence or to disclose in evidence any communication made to him or her during the marriage by the accused, and

(b) the failure of the wife or husband of the accused to give evidence shall not be commented on by the prosecution.

This s. 39 shall not affect s. 1 of the Criminal Evidence Act 1898 or any case where the wife or the husband of the accused may at common law be called as a witness without the consent of the accused.

For the provisions of the Indecency with Children Act 1960, see Chap. 11, and for evidence of children in committal proceedings for sexual offences, see "Proceedings before Justices", Chap. 4.

Rape and Similar Offences – Sexual Offences Act 1956, s. 1. It is an arrestable offence for a man to rape a woman and it will be rape where a man induces a married woman to have sexual intercourse with him by impersonating her husband.

Rape is the unlawful carnal knowledge of a female by force or fraud against her will. By ss. 2, 3, 4 it is an offence to procure a woman to have unlawful sexual intercourse in any part of the world

(a) by threats or intimidation (s. 2);
(b) by false pretences or false representations (s. 3);
(c) by applying or administering to or causing to be taken by, a woman any drug, matter or thing with intent to stupefy or overpower her so as thereby to enable any man to do so (s. 4)

There cannot be a conviction of any of these offences on the evidence of one witness only unless the witness is corroborated in some material particular by evidence implicating the accused.

Carnal knowledge means penetration to any degree, and to constitute rape there must be proof of penetration. It is no excuse if the woman consented through fear or fraud or that she was a prostitute. The consent of the woman is a good defence, but such consent must have been freely given and not induced by fraud, threats, etc. Belief, whether reasonable or unreasonable, that there is consent is also a defence (*D.P.P.* v. *Morgan* (1975)), although it should be noted that at the date of going to press a Sexual Offences (Amendment) Bill was before Parliament to reverse this rule. If the woman is of weak intellect and incapable of giving a true consent the accused may be convicted of rape.

A boy under the age of 14 cannot be convicted of rape as it is presumed that he is physically incapable of the act. Generally speaking a husband cannot be convicted of rape upon his wife (but a charge of assault may be made), but he can be so convicted if husband and wife have been legally separated (*R.* v. *Clarke* (1949)). A boy under 14 can be convicted of indecent assault.

Sexual Offences Act 1956, s. 5—It is an arrestable offence for a man to have unlawful sexual intercourse with a girl under 13.

Section 6. It is an offence for a man to have unlawful sexual intercourse with a girl under 16. Proceedings for this offence may not be commenced more than 12 months after commission of the offence (Sched. 2).

However the man will not be guilty of this offence if:

(a) the girl is his "wife" (an invalid marriage as she is under age) or

(b) the man is under 24, has not been previously charged with a like offence and has reasonable cause for his belief that the girl is 16 or over.

Section 7. It is an offence for a man to have unlawful sexual intercourse with a woman who is a defective. But he will not be guilty of this offence if he does not know and has no reason to suspect her to be a defective (as amended by the Mental Health Act 1959, s. 127).

Section 9. It is an offence for a person to procure a woman who is a defective to have unlawful sexual intercourse in any part of the world. But he will not be guilty of this offence if he does not know and has no reason to suspect her to be a defective.

Section 45. "Defective" means a person suffering from severe subnormality within the meaning of the Mental Health Act 1959.

It is an offence for a man who is employed in, or is the manager of a hospital or mental nursing home to have unlawful sexual intercourse on the premises with a woman who is a patient receiving treatment for mental disorder, or for a man to have unlawful sexual intercourse with a mentally disordered woman who is in his custody or care, or subject to his guardianship. But a man will not be guilty of this offence if he does not know and has no reason to suspect her to be a mentally disordered patient (Mental Health Act 1959, s. 128). This shall have effect as if any reference therein to having unlawful sexual intercourse with a woman included a reference to committing buggery or an act of gross indecency with another man (Sexual Offences Act 1967, s. 1).

Any offence of rape and carnal knowledge of mental defectives or of girls under 13 must be reported to the Director of Public Prosecutions (see Appendix III).

Indecent Assault – Sexual Offences Act 1956, s. 14. It is an offence for a person to make an indecent assault on a woman. A girl under 16 cannot in law give any consent to such an assault. (See also s. 28 (later) for indecent assault on a girl under 16). However where marriage is invalid (the wife being under 16) the husband will not be guilty of this offence if he has reasonable cause to believe her to be his wife.

A woman who is a defective cannot in law consent to such an assault but the person who so assaults her will be guilty of this offence only if he knew or had reason to suspect her to be a defective.

A constable has power to arrest without warrant for indecent assaults on young persons (C. & Y.P. Act 1933, s. 13).

Indecent assault on any person (male or female) may be dealt with summarily if the court is satisfied and the accused consents (M.C. Act 1952, s. 19 and Sched. 1 and C.J.A. Act 1962). Certain indecent assaults should be reported to the Director of Public Prosecutions (see Appendix III).

Incest – Sexual Offences Act 1956, s. 10. It is an offence for a man to have sexual intercourse with a woman whom he knows to be his grand-daughter, daughter, sister or mother.

"Sister" in this section includes half-sister and the relation above in this section applies although not traced through lawful wedlock.

Section 11. It is an offence for a woman aged 16 or over to permit a man whom she knows to be her grandfather, father, brother or son to have sexual intercourse with her by her consent. "Brother" in this section includes half-brother and the relationship above in this section applies although not traced through lawful wedlock.

Under s. 38 of the Act, on a man being convicted of incest or attempted incest against a girl under 18 the court may, by order, divest him of all authority over her, etc. (as amended by Family Law Reform Act 1969, Sched. 1).

Procuration – Procuration is the obtaining of females for immoral purposes. The practice is often referred to as the white slave traffic, particularly in connection with the procuring of girls to go abroad for immoral purposes.

There is considerable risk in females accepting employment abroad unless there is sufficient evidence as to the *bona fide* character of the engagement. The real object of the employer or agent may be concealed under the pretext of engaging the victim for some theatrical or other employment.

Any case of suspicion should be reported to the Commissioner of Metropolitan Police, who is the central authority for this country under the International Agreement of 1904, arrived at to try to put an end to this white slave traffic. Also, both at home and abroad, friendless or unprotected girls are liable to fall into the hands of unscrupulous persons.

Sexual Offences Act 1956, s. 22. It is an offence for a person to procure:

(a) a woman to become in any part of the world a common prostitute: or

(b) a woman to leave the United Kingdom intending her to become an inmate of or frequent a brothel elsewhere: or

(c) a woman to leave her usual place of abode in the United Kingdom, intending her to become an inmate of or frequent a brothel in any part of the world for the purposes of prostitution.

Conviction of any of the above offences cannot take place on the evidence of one witness only unless the witness is corroborated in some material particular by evidence implicating the accused.

Section 23. It is an offence for a person to procure a girl under 21 to have unlawful sexual intercourse in any part of the world with a third person.

In such an offence, to ensure conviction, the evidence of only one witness must be corroborated materially by evidence implicating the accused.

Section 24. It is an offence for a person to detain a woman against her will on any premises with the intention that she shall have unlawful sexual intercourse with men or a particular man or to detain a woman against her will in a brothel. This section states that withholding her clothes or any of her property or threatening legal proceedings if she takes away clothes provided for her by him or on his directions shall be deemed to be such detention.

Also the woman shall not be liable to any legal proceedings for taking or having any clothes she needed to enable her to leave such premises or brothel.

Sections 25, 26 and 27 declare that where a person who is the owner or occupier of any premises or who has or acts or assists in the management or control of any premises, induces or knowingly suffers a female (see below) to resort or be on those premises for the purpose of having unlawful sexual connection with men or a particular man, such person commits crime as follows:

(a) it is an arrestable offence if the female is a girl under 13 (s. 25).

(b) it is an offence if the female is a girl under 16 (s. 26).

(c) it is an offence if the female is a defective (see s. 45) but if such person did not know and had no reason to suspect her to be a defective he will not be guilty of this offence (s. 27).

Abduction of Females – Sexual Offences Act 1956, s. 17. It is an arrestable offence for a person to take away or detain a woman against her will with the intention that she shall marry or have unlawful sexual intercourse with that or any other person if she is so taken away or detained either by force or for the sake of her property or expectations of property (being any interest in property the property of a person to whom she is a next of kin).

Section 19. It is an offence for a person to take an unmarried girl under 18 out of the possession of her parent or guardian (person who has lawful care or charge of her) against his will, if she is so taken with the intention that she shall have unlawful sexual intercourse with men or a particular man. ("Unlawful" means "illicit", i.e. outside the bond of marriage: *R.* v. *Chapman* (1958).) However, belief on reasonable cause that the girl is 18 or over will avoid this offence.

C. & Y.P. Act 1933, s. 40, provides for a warrant to search for and remove such a girl in cases of necessity.

Sexual Offences Act 1956, s. 20. It is an offence for a person acting without lawful authority to take an unmarried girl under 16 out of the possession of her parent or guardian (lawful) against his will.

Section 21. It is an offence for a person to take a woman who is a defective out of the possession of her parent or guardian (lawful) against his will if she is taken with the intention that she shall have unlawful sexual intercourse with men or with a particular man.

However a person is not guilty of this offence if he does not know and has no reason to suspect her to be a defective.

Prostitution – Sexual Offences Act 1956, s. 28. It is an offence for a person to cause or encourage the prostitution of, or the commission of unlawful sexual intercourse with, or of an indecent assault on, a girl under 16 for whom he is responsible.

This section states that a person shall be deemed to have caused or encouraged this offence if he knowingly allowed her to consort with or to enter or continue in the employment of any prostitute or person of known immoral character.

Under the section the parent or legal guardian and any person who has actual possession or control or custody or charge or care of such girl are so responsible for her as regards this section. "Parent" and "legal guardian" are explained in this section.

Section 29. It is an offence for a person to cause or encourage the prostitution in any part of the world of a woman who is a defective, unless he does not know and has no reason to suspect her to be a defective.

Section 30. It is an offence for a man knowingly to live wholly or in part on the earnings of prostitution.

Under this section, a man, unless he proves the contrary, will be presumed to commit this offence, if he lives with or is habitually in the company of a prostitute, or exercises control, direction or influence over a prostitute's movements in a way which shows he is aiding, abetting or compelling her prostitution with others.

Section 31. It is an offence for a woman for purposes of gain to exercise control, direction or influence over a prostitute's movements in a way which shows she is aiding, abetting or compelling her prostitution.

The power of arrest for offences under ss. 30, 31 previously given by s. 41 of the Act has been withdrawn by the C.L. Act 1967, Sched. 3.

Section 32. It is an offence for a man persistently to solicit or importune in a public place for immoral purposes. Proceedings must be within 12 months where the immoral purpose is the commission of a homosexual act.

Section 36. It is an offence for the tenant or occupier of any premises knowingly to permit the whole or part of the premises to be used for the purposes of habitual prostitution.

Note—Offences under ss. 30, 31, 32 may be dealt with summarily or on indictment. Offences under s. 36 may be dealt with summarily (see Sched. 2).

A common prostitute is a female who for reward offers her body commonly for sexual connection or for acts of lewdness. Lewd conduct by a *virgo intacta* without sexual intercourse may amount to prostitution (*R.* v. *De Munck* (1918)). It is immaterial whether the lewdness consists in passive or active indecent conduct on the part of the woman, and will include such acts as masturbation by her of male clients (*R.* v. *Webb* (1963)).

Vagrancy Act 1824, s. 3. Every common prostitute wandering in the public streets or public highway or in any place of public resort and behaving in a riotous or indecent manner may be arrested by any person when found so offending and summarily punished as an idle and disorderly person. See "Vagrancy Acts", Chap. 27.

Street Offences Act 1959. It shall be an offence for a common prostitute to loiter or solicit in a street or public place for the purpose of prostitution (s. 1 (1)).

A constable may arrest without warrant anyone he finds in a street or public place and suspects, with reasonable cause, to be committing an offence under this section (s. 1 (3)).

For the purpose of this section, "street" includes any bridge, road, lane, footway, subway, square, court, alley or passage, whether a thoroughfare or not, which is for the time being open to the public, and the doorways and entrances of premises abutting on a street (as herein before defined) and any ground adjoining and open to a street, shall be treated as forming part of the street (s. 1 (4)).

It is desirable that every practicable step should be taken to divert from prostitution women, and particularly girls, who are taking to that way of life. Accordingly, it has become acknowledged police practice not to charge a woman under this section unless (a) she has already been convicted of a similar offence under this Act or similar repealed provision, or (b) she has been cautioned by the police on at least two occasions and the cautions have been formally recorded.

The Act provides that where a woman has been cautioned by a constable she may, within 14 days, apply to a magistrates' court for an order that the caution shall not be entered on the register of cautions or, if entered, shall be expunged. The court is required to make such an order unless it is satisfied that on the occasion in question the woman was loitering or soliciting (s. 2).

It is an offence for a man or woman to knowingly live wholly or in part on the earnings of prostitution of another man. A person accused of an offence under this section cannot claim to be tried on indictment under s. 25, M.C. Act 1952. Anyone may arrest without a warrant a person found committing an offence under this section (Sexual Offences Act 1967, s. 5).

Harbouring Prostitutes – Town Police Clauses Act 1847, s.

35. It is an offence for any person keeping any house, shop, room, or other place of public resort in any urban district (where the Act is in force) for the sale or consumption of refreshments of any kind knowingly to suffer common prostitutes or reputed thieves to assemble and continue there.

Late Night Refreshment Houses Act 1969, s. 9. It is an offence for a person licensed to keep a refreshment house under the Act knowingly to suffer prostitutes, etc., to assemble or continue on his premises.

Licensing Act 1964, s. 175. The holder of a justices' licence (and the holder of an occasional licence (s. 179)) shall not knowingly permit his premises to be the habitual resort or place of meeting of reputed prostitutes. He may only allow such to remain in his premises to obtain reasonable refreshment for such time as is necessary for the purpose.

Licensing Act 1964, s. 100. If the licence is a restaurant, residential, or residential and restaurant licence or a licence under the Late Night Refreshment Houses Act 1969, the holder is liable to disqualification for holding such licences if he is convicted of permitting the premises to be the resort of prostitutes. The premises may also be disqualified.

Brothels – A common brothel is a house or room used by persons of opposite sexes for the purpose of prostitution.

Keeping a brothel is an offence at common law, being a common nuisance as endangering the public peace and corrupting both sexes.

Sexual Offences Act 1956, s. 33. It is an offence for a person to keep a brothel or to manage or act or assist in the management of a brothel.

Section 34. It is an offence for the lessee or landlord of any premises to let the whole or part of the premises with the knowledge that it is to be used, in whole or in part, as a brothel, or, where the whole or part of the premises is used as a brothel, to be wilfully a party to that use continuing.

Section 35. It is an offence for the tenant or occupier or person in charge of any premises to permit the whole or part of the premises to be used as a brothel. The rest of this section and Sched. 1 to the Act deal with the rights and duties of the landlord or lessor of such premises.

Offences under the above three sections may be dealt with summarily as directed in Sched. 2 to the Act.

Premises shall be treated for purposes of ss. 33 to 35 of the 1956 Act as a brothel if people resort to it for the purpose of lewd homosexual practices in circumstances in which resort thereto for lewd heterosexual practices would have led to its being treated as a brothel for the purposes of those sections (Sexual Offences Act 1967, s. 6).

Licensing Act 1964, s. 176. The holder of a justices' licence (or of an occasional licence (s. 179)) shall not permit his premises to be a brothel. On conviction for this offence, whether under this section or otherwise his licence shall be forfeited and by s. 9 of this Act he is disqualified for holding a justices' licence. Under s. 100 of the Licensing Act 1964 if the licence is a restaurant, residential, or residential and restaurant licence or a licence under the Late Night Refreshment Houses Act 1969, the holder is liable to disqualification as well as forfeiture of the licence, and the premises may be disqualified.

A licensee was held guilty of this offence although no evidence of a previous case of like kind on the premises was given, and although he was absent from the premises at the time (*R.* v. *Holland, Lincolnshire Justices* (1882)).

Children and Young Persons Act 1933, s. 3. It is an offence punishable on indictment or on summary conviction for any person having the custody, charge or care of any child or young person aged 4 or upwards and under 16 to allow such child or young person to reside in or frequent a brothel.

Arrest and Search Warrant - As will be seen later under "Arrest, Search Warrant and Procedure" in Chap. 12, the C. & Y.P. Act 1933, ss. 13, 40, gives constables certain powers of arrest without warrant and allows justices to issue search warrants in cases where children or young persons are subjected to any of the offences mentioned in Sched. 1 to the Act, which now includes many offences under the Sexual Offences Act 1956 and the Indecency with Children Act 1960.

Also ss. 40, 41 of this 1956 Act give further powers of arrest without warrant for certain offences (see above).

CHAPTER 11

INDECENCY

	Page
Indecent Conduct . .	127
Indecent Language . .	127
Indecent Exhibitions .	128
Indecent Exposure . .	128
Indecent Publications and Advertisements . .	128
Unnatural Crimes . .	132
Sexual Offences Act 1967	133
Indecency with Children Act 1960 . . .	134

Indecent Conduct – Offences against decency may be committed by language and behaviour, by the giving of some display or exhibition, by exposure of the person, or by making public any indecent matter. For indecent assault see "Assault", Chap. 8.

Indecent Language – "Indecent" may be defined as unbecoming, not decent, contrary to propriety, or offensive to modesty.

"Obscene", which is an adjective of similar but somewhat stronger meaning, conveys the idea of something disgusting, filthy, repulsive, or offensive to chastity or delicacy.

"Profane" indicates something unclean, polluted, disrespectful, irreverent, impious, or blasphemous.

Town Police Clauses Act 1847, s. 28. It is a summary offence for any person to use any profane or obscene language or to sing any profane or obscene song or ballad in any street in any urban district (including any place to which the public have a right of access, also any place of public resort and any unfenced ground adjoining any street in any urban district) where this section is in force by Order (Public Health Acts Amendment Act 1907, s. 81), to the annoyance of the residents or passengers, and the offender may be arrested without warrant.

Byelaws. In many districts it is an offence, by byelaw, to make use of any indecent language, gesture or conduct.

For indecent behaviour of prostitutes, see "Prostitution", Chap. 10.

Indecent Exhibitions – Any indecent performance or exhibition is a common nuisance and is indictable as an offence at common law.

Vagrancy Act 1824, s. 4. Any person wilfully exposing to view in any street, highway or public place any indecent exhibition may be arrested without warrant and convicted as a rogue and vagabond (s. 6).

Town Police Clauses Act 1847, s. 28. It is a summary offence to exhibit to public view any profane, indecent or obscene representation in any street in any urban district (where the Act is in force), to the annoyance of residents or passengers, and the offenders may be arrested without warrant.

Byelaws. In many districts byelaws and regulations deal with indecent shows and entertainments.

Indecent Exposure – It is a public nuisance and therefore indictable as an offence at common law publicly to expose the naked person.

Such an exposure will be public at common law if made in a place where it is seen by other persons.

Vagrancy Act 1824, s. 4. It is a summary offence for any person wilfully, openly, lewdly and obscenely to expose his person with intent to insult any female, and the offender may be arrested without warrant and convicted as a rogue and a vagabond. "Person" refers to the penis, not other parts of the body (*Evans* v. *Ewels* (1972)).

If possible a female who has been so insulted should be called as a witness, but if such female cannot be traced or is not available to give evidence, accused may be convicted of this offence on other evidence proving that he systematically exposed himself with an apparent intent to insult females.

Town Police Clauses Act 1847, s. 28. It is a summary offence wilfully and indecently to expose the person in any street in any urban district (where the Act is in force), to the annoyance of residents or passengers, and the offender may be arrested without warrant.

For indecent assault on a female, see "Indecent Assault", Chap. 10, and for indecent assault on a male and gross indecency between males, see "Statutory Assaults", Chap. 8, and "Unnatural Crimes" (later).

A public bath or bathing place will be a public and open place as regards offences against decency (Public Health Act 1936, s. 224).

Indecent Publications and Advertisements. – Any publication, sale, exhibition to public view, or circulation through the post, of anything of an indecent or obscene nature is an offence.

Vagrancy Acts 1824, s. 4, and 1838, s. 2. Every person

wilfully exposing to view in any street, highway or public place, or in the window or other part of any shop or building situate in any street, highway or public place, any obscene print, picture, or other indecent exhibitions, may be arrested without warrant and convicted as a rogue and a vagabond.

Town Police Clauses Act 1847, s. 28. It is an offence for any person publicly to offer for sale or distribution or to exhibit to public view any profane, indecent or obscene book, paper, print, drawing, painting or representation, in any street in any urban district (where the Act is in force) (for extent of "street" see "Indecent Language"), to the annoyance of the residents or passengers, and the offender may be arrested without warrant.

Indecent Advertisements Act 1889. It is a summary offence to do any of the following acts in connection with any picture or printed or written matter of an indecent or obscene nature:

(1) To affix to or inscribe same on any building, wall, hoarding, gate, fence, post, tree or other thing whatsoever, so as to be visible to any person in any street, public highway or footpath.

(2) To affix or inscribe same on any public urinal.

(3) To deliver, attempt to deliver or exhibit same to any inhabitant or person in any street, highway or footpath.

(4) To throw down same into the area of any house.

(5) to exhibit same to public view in the window of any house or shop (s. 3).

It is also an offence to give or deliver to any other person any such indecent pictures or writings with intent that same should be so affixed, inscribed, delivered or exhibited (s. 4).

Any advertisement relating to syphilis, nervous debility or other infirmity arising from or relating to sexual intercourse will be deemed indecent matter within the meaning of this Act, if it is attached to anything so as to be visible to any person in any public highway or footpath or put up in any public urinal or delivered or attempted to be delivered to any person in any public highway or footpath, except where such an advertisement is published for any local or public authority or for a person publishing them with the sanction of the Secretary of State (s. 5 as amended by s. 1 of the Indecent Advertisements (Amendment) Act 1970).

Any constable may arrest without warrant any person whom he finds committing any offence against this Act.

Venereal Disease Act 1917. It is an offence (which may be dealt with summarily) for any person to advertise in any manner any treatment for venereal disease.

However, this prohibition does not apply to advertisements, recommendations, etc., published by any local or public authority.

Obscene Publications Acts 1959 and 1964. For the purposes of these Acts:

(1) An article is obscene if its effect or the effect of any one of its items is, if taken as a whole, such as to tend to deprave and corrupt persons who are likely to read, see or hear the matter contained or embodied in it.

(2) "Article" means any description of article containing or embodying matter to be read or looked at or both, any sound record, and any film or other record of a picture or pictures.

(3) A person publishes an article who:

(a) distributes, circulates, sells, lets on hire, gives, or lends it, or who offers it for sale or for letting on hire; or

(b) in the case of an article containing or embodying matter to be looked at or a record, shows, plays or projects it. (This paragraph does not apply to a public cinematograph exhibition or to television or sound broadcasting). (1959 Act, s. 1).

Any person who, whether for gain or not, publishes an obscene article or who has an obscene article for publication for gain (whether gain to himself or gain to another) is liable to be punished summarily or on indictment. This offence supersedes the common law offence. Summary proceedings may be brought at any time within 12 months of the commission of the offence, and a prosecution on indictment shall not be commenced more than 2 years after the commission of the offence.

It is a defence if the accused proves that he had not examined the article and had no reasonable cause to suspect that it was obscene. A person shall be deemed to have an article for publication for gain if with a view to such publication he has the article in his ownership possession or control (1959 Act, s. 2 and 1964 Act, s. 1).

A justice may grant a search warrant (only on an information laid by or on behalf of the D.P.P. or by a constable (C.J. Act 1967, s. 25)) if he is satisfied by information on oath that there is reasonable ground for suspecting that, in any premises or on any stall or vehicle, obscene articles are, or are from time to time, kept for publication for gain. Such search warrant authorises a constable to enter and search the premises, stall or vehicle, within 14 days from the date of the warrant, and to seize and remove not only obscene articles but also documents which relate to a trade or business carried on at the premises (or stall or vehicle) being searched.

Any obscene articles seized shall be brought before a magistrate who may issue a summons to the occupier of the premises or the user of the stall or vehicle, to show cause why the articles should not be forfeited.

In addition to the person summoned, any other person being the owner, author, or maker of any of the articles, or any other person through whose hands they had passed before being seized, shall be entitled to appear to show cause why they should not be forfeited (1959 Act, s. 3). Where articles are seized under s. 3 of the 1959 Act and a person is convicted under s. 2 of that Act of having them for publication for gain the court shall order the forfeiture of those articles. References to publication for gain shall apply to any publication with a view to gain whether the gain is to accrue by way of consideration for the publication or in any other way (1964 Act, s. 1).

A person shall not be convicted of publishing an obscene article, and an order for forfeiture shall not be made, if it is proved that publication of the article is justified as being for the public good on the ground that it is in the interests of science, literature, art, or learning or of other objects of general concern. The opinion of experts as to the literary, artistic, scientific or other merits of an article may be admitted in any proceedings under this Act, either to establish or negative the said ground (1959 Act, s. 4). The 1959 Act as amended by the 1964 Act shall apply to negatives as well as to material produced from the negatives (1964 Act, s. 2).

Customs Consolidation Act 1876, s. 42. The importation into this country of any indecent or obscene prints, paintings, photographs, books, etc., or any indecent or obscene articles, is prohibited and such articles may be forfeited.

Judicial Proceedings (Regulation of Reports) Act 1926. It is a summary offence to print or publish in relation to any judicial proceedings any indecent matter or details the publication of which would be calculated to injure public morals, or any particulars of divorce or marriage judicial proceedings, other than the names, etc., of the parties and witnesses, a concise statement of the charges and defences, the law points raised, and the summing up, finding and judgment of the court. Prosecution under the Act requires the sanction of the Attorney-General.

This prohibition does not apply to printing for the use of courts or to books of law reports or to publications intended for circulation among the legal and medical professions.

Children and Young Persons Act 1933. In any proceedings in any court, the court may direct that press reports shall not identify any child or young person concerned (s. 39). The press shall not, in their reports, identify any child or young person concerned in any proceedings in a Juvenile Court unless the court or the Secretary of State so permit (s. 49). See "Treatment of Youthful Offenders", Chap. 12.

Post Office Act 1953, s. 11. It is an offence to enclose any indecent or obscene print, painting, photograph, book or card or any indecent or obscene article in any postal packet, or to have on any postal packet or on the cover thereof any words, marks or designs of an indecent, obscene or grossly offensive character. An offender may be dealt with summarily or on indictment. See Prosecution of Offences Regulations 1946 (Appendix III) for cases of indecent or obscene matter which are to be reported to the Director of Public Prosecutions.

Unnatural Crimes – Sexual Offences Act 1956, s. 12. It is an arrestable offence for a person to commit buggery with another person or with an animal. (But see amendments under Sexual Offences Act 1967, *post.*)

See s. 39 (in Chap. 10) as regards the evidence, and this also affects ss. 15 and 16 which follow here.

This s. 39 does not apply in the case of this section except on a charge of the offence with a person under 17. And a person shall be presumed to be under 17 unless the contrary is proved if it is so stated in the charge of indictment and the person appears to the court to have been so at the time of the offence.

Section 13. It is an offence for a man to commit an act of gross indecency with another man, whether in public or private, or to be a party to the commission by a man of an act of gross indecency with another man, or to procure the commission by a man of an act of gross indecency with another man. (Proceedings must be taken within 12 months.) The word "with" in the above section does not mean "with the consent of" but has the looser meaning of "against" or "directed towards" (*R.* v. *Hall* (1963)). Sexual Offences Act 1967, s. 4 (3), provides that a man shall not be guilty of procuring an act of gross indecency between another man and himself if the act is no longer an offence.

Section 16. It is an offence for a person to assault another person with intent to commit buggery.

However s. 39 of this Act (see above) as to the evidence of the husband or wife of the accused does not apply as regards this section except on a charge of an assault (apparently this assault) on a person under 17 (who by this section shall be presumed to be under 17, unless the contrary is proved (see under s. 12 above)).

Section 15. It is an offence to make an indecent assault on a man.

A boy under 16 cannot in law give any consent which prevents an act being such an assault.

A defective cannot in law consent to such an act but a person is only to be treated as guilty of an indecent assault on a defective by reason of that incapacity to consent if such person knew or had reason to suspect him to be a defective.

However, s. 39 of this Act (evidence of wife or husband) as noted in Chap. 10 does not apply as regards this section except on a charge of indecent assault on a boy under 17 (or apparently under 17 unless the contrary is proved).

This offence could be dealt with summarily (see Sched. 2).

Section 32. It is an offence for a man persistently to solicit or importune in a public place for immoral purposes.

This can be prosecuted on indictment or summarily (see Sched. 2). Proceedings must be taken within 12 months if the immoral purpose is the commission of a homosexual act.

Proceedings for an offence of buggery by a man with another man not amounting to an assault on that other man and not being an offence by a man with a boy under the age of 16 must be taken within 12 months (Sexual Offences Act 1967, s. 7 (2) (*c*)).

Sexual Offences Act 1967 – Notwithstanding any statutory or common law provision, but subject to the provisions of s. 2, a homosexual act in private shall not be an offence provided that the parties consent thereto and have attained the age of 21 years (s. 1 (1)).

An act which would otherwise be treated for the purposes of this Act as being done in private shall not be so treated if done (a) when more than two persons take part or are present; or (b) in a lavatory to which the public have or are permitted to have access, whether on payment or otherwise (s. 1 (2)).

A man who is suffering from severe subnormality within the meaning of the Mental Health Act 1959 cannot in law give any consent which, by virtue of s. 1 above, would prevent a homosexual act from being an offence, but a person shall not be convicted, on account of the incapacity of such a man to consent, of an offence consisting of such an act if he proves that he did not know and had no reason to suspect that man to be suffering from severe subnormality (s. 1 (3)).

In any proceedings where it is charged that a homosexual act is an offence the prosecutor shall have the burden of proving that the act was done otherwise than in private or otherwise than with the consent of the parties or that any of the parties had not attained the age of 21 years (s. 1 (6)).

For the purpose of this section a man shall be treated as doing a homosexual act if, and only if, he commits buggery with another man or commits an act of gross indecency with another man or is a party to the commission by a man of such an act (s. 1 (7)).

Section 2 relates to homosexual acts on merchant ships. Acts of buggery or gross indecency, or being a party to acts of gross indecency which would otherwise cease to be offences under s. 1 shall remain offences if committed on board a U.K. merchant ship by a man who is a member of the crew of that ship with another man who is the member of a crew of a U.K. merchant ship (s. 2 (1)).

A man who procures another man to commit with a third man an act of buggery (which by reason of s. 1 above is not an offence) commits an offence (s. 4 (1)).

It is an offence for a man or woman to knowingly live wholly or in part on the earnings of prostitution of another man. A person accused of an offence under this section cannot claim to be tried on indictment under s. 25 of the M.C. Act 1952. Anyone may arrest without a warrant a person found committing an offence under this section (s. 5).

No proceedings shall be instituted except by or with the consent of the Director of Public Prosecutions against any man for the offence of buggery with, or gross indecency with, another man, for attempting to commit either offence, or for aiding, abetting, counselling, procuring or commanding its commission where either of those men was at the time of its commission under the age of 21:

Provided that this section shall not prevent the arrest, or the issue of a warrant for the arrest, of a person for any such offence, or the remand in custody or on bail of a person charged with any such offence (s. 8). This section does not apply to proceedings under the Indecency with children Act 1960, (C.J. Act 1972, s. 48).

Indecency with Children Act 1960 – It is an offence for any person to commit an act of gross indecency with or towards a child under the age of 14, or to incite a child under that age to such an act with him or another (s. 1 (1)).

On a charge of such an offence the wife or husband of an accused person is competent to give evidence at all stages of the proceedings, whether for the defence or for the prosecution, and whether the accused is charged solely or jointly with another person: but the wife or husband cannot be compelled either to give evidence, or, in giving evidence, to disclose any communication made to her or him during the marriage by the accused; and the failure of the wife or husband of the accused to give evidence shall not be made the subject of any comment by the prosecution.

The foregoing paragraph does not affect s. 1 of the Criminal Evidence Act 1898, or any case where the wife or husband of the accused can be called as a witness at common law without the consent of the accused (s. 2).

CHAPTER 12

CHILDREN AND PERSONS UNDER 21

	Page
Abortion	135
Child Destruction	136
Infanticide	137
Concealment of Birth	137
Abandoning Child	137
Children and Young Persons	137
Child Protection	138
Cruelty to Children and Young Persons	140
Arrest, Search Warrant and Procedure	142
Smoking by Juveniles	144
Care of Juveniles	144
Education	145
Employment of Juveniles	145
Entertainment by Children	147
Dangerous Performances by Juveniles	147
Powers of Entry (Employment)	148
Restrictions on Persons under 18 going abroad	148
Treatment of Youthful Offenders	148
Remand Centres	151
Detention Centres	151
Attendance Centres	152
Community Service	153
Harmful Publications	153
Tattooing of Minors Act 1969	153
Ages fixed by Law	153

Abortion – Abortion may be defined as the unlawful taking or administering of poison or other noxious thing or the unlawful use of any means whatsoever with intent to procure miscarriage.

Offences Against the Person Act 1861 deals with this crime and with the three classes of persons who may be involved.

(1) The Woman. It is an offence for any woman being with child and with intent to procure her own miscarriage, unlawfully to take any poison or other noxious thing or use any instrument or other means whatsoever (s. 58).

(2) The Person Administering, etc. It is an offence for any person, with intent to procure the miscarriage of any woman whether she be or be not with child, unlawfully to administer to her or cause to be taken by her any poison or other noxious thing or use any instrument or other means whatsoever (s. 58).

(3) The Person Supplying the Means. It is an offence for any person unlawfully to supply or procure any poison or other noxious thing or any instrument or thing whatsoever, knowing that the same is intended to be unlawfully used or employed with intent to procure the miscarriage of any woman whether she be or be not with child (s. 59). "Procure" in this section means to get possession from another person of something which the defendant has not already got and does not cover the case of a person who already has an instrument in a cupboard or elsewhere and produces it for the purpose of sterilising it or some other purpose (*R.* v. *Mills* (1963)).

By the Abortion Act 1967, a person shall not be guilty of an offence under the law relating to abortion, when a pregnancy is terminated by a registered medical practitioner if two registered medical practitioners are of the opinion, formed in good faith, (a) that the continuance of the pregnancy would involve risk to the life of the pregnant woman or of injury to the physical or mental health of the pregnant woman or any existing children of her family, greater than if the pregnancy were terminated, or (b) that there is a substantial risk that if a child were born it would suffer from such physical or mental abnormalities as to be seriously handicapped.

Any treatment for the termination of pregnancy must be carried out in an approved hospital, but in cases where termination is immediately necessary to save the life of or prevent grave permanent injury to the physical or mental health of the woman, termination may be carried out in any place and without the opinion of a second practitioner (s. 1).

Nothing in the Act shall affect the provisions of the Infant Life (Preservation) Act 1929. For the purposes of the law relating to abortion, anything done with intent to procure the miscarriage of a woman is unlawfully done unless authorised by s. 1 of the Act (s. 5).

Publishing any advertisement of any article in terms calculated to lead to its use for abortion is a summary offence under ss. 9 and 10 of the Pharmacy and Medicines Act 1941, and the consent of the Attorney-General is required for a prosecution.

Any offence of abortion must be reported to the Director of Public Prosecutions. See Appendix III.

Child Destruction – This offence is committed where a person, with intent to destroy the life of a child capable of being born alive, by any wilful act causes the child to die before it has an existence independent of its mother. Provided that a person shall not be found guilty of this offence unless it is proved that such act was not done to preserve the life of the mother. Evidence of pregnancy for 28 weeks or more shall be *prima facie* proof that the child was capable of being born alive.

If tried for murder, manslaughter, infanticide or abortion, the accused may be convicted of child destruction. If tried for child destruction there may be a conviction for abortion (Infant

Life (Preservation) Act 1929 as amended by C.L. Act 1967, Sched. 3).

Infanticide – Under the Infanticide Act 1938, where a woman by any wilful act or omission causes the death of her child under the age of 12 months, but at the time of the act or omission the balance of her mind was disturbed by reason of her not having fully recovered from the effect of giving birth to the child or the effect of lactation, she shall be guilty of infanticide which is punishable as manslaughter.

If a woman is tried for the murder of her child under the age of 12 months the jury may return a verdict of murder or of infanticide.

On the indictment for the murder of a child the jury may return a verdict of manslaughter or of not guilty by reason of insanity (which verdict may be given on an indictment for infanticide).

Concealment of Birth – This is an offence and is committed by every person who, when a child has been born (alive or dead), endeavours to conceal the birth by any secret disposition of the dead body of the child.

As evidence is required to prove that a child has been born, the mother should be examined as soon as possible by a doctor, but only if she consents, for if she does not consent such an examination would amount to an assault upon her. The dead body of the child should be found and identified. The body should be examined by a doctor to ascertain whether the child was born alive, and, if so, by what means it died. Denial of the birth of the child is not sufficient, as there must have been some act of secret disposal of the body. Any "secret disposition" is sufficient, and every person who uses any such endeavours to conceal the birth is liable, and where another person may be liable it is immaterial whether there be any evidence against the mother or not. An arrest for this offence should not be made without a warrant.

This offence may be dealt with summarily with the consent of the accused (C.J.A. Act 1962, Sched. 3).

Abandoning Child – It is an arrestable offence unlawfully to abandon or expose any child under the age of 2 years whereby its life is endangered or its health is or is likely to be permanently injured (Offences Against the Person Act 1861, s. 27). This offence may be dealt with summarily with the consent of the accused (C.J.A. Act 1962, Sched. 3).

Children and Young Persons – The main statutes dealing with children and young persons and persons under 21 are the Children and Young Persons Acts 1933, 1952, 1963 and 1969, the Education Act 1944, the Criminal Justice Act 1948, the Children Acts 1948 and 1958, and the Indecency with Children Act 1960.

The Children and Young Persons Act 1933, is the principal Act.

In criminal law, a "child" means a person under the age of 14 years. A "young person" means a person who has attained the age of 14 years and is under the age of 17 years (1933 Act, s. 107). An "adult" is a person who is of the age of 17 years or upwards for the purposes of summary trial of indictable offences (M.C. Act 1952, s. 19). The age of majority is 18 (Family Law Reform Act 1969, s. 1).

"Place of Safety" means a community home provided by a local authority or a controlled community home, any police station, or any hospital, surgery or any other suitable place the occupier of which is willing temporarily to receive an infant, child or young person (1933 Act, s. 107 as amended by 1969 Act, Sched. 5 (12)).

"Street" includes any highway and any public bridge, road, lane, footway, square, court, alley or passage, whether a thoroughfare or not (1933 Act, s. 107).

"Public Place" includes any public park, garden, sea beach or railway station and any ground to which the public for the time being have or are permitted to have access whether on payment or otherwise (1933 Act, s. 107).

"Guardian" includes any person who, in the opinion of the court, has for the time being the charge of or control over the child or young person (1933 Act, s. 107 and M.C. Act 1952, s. 126).

Where the age of any person at any time is material for the purposes of the Act, his age at the material time shall be deemed to be that which appears to the court, after considering any available evidence, to have been his age at that time (M.C. Act 1952, s. 126). By the Administration of Justice Act 1970, s. 50 (as amended by C.J. Act 1972, Sched. 6), the provisions of s. 126 of the M.C. Act 1952 shall have effect as if they included ss. 18, 24 (1) and (2), and 33 of C.J. Act 1967.

The procedure in courts with respect to juveniles is regulated by the Magistrates' Courts (C. & Y.P.) Rules 1970.

Child Protection – The Children Act 1958, as amended by the Act of 1969, makes provision for the protection of children living away from their parents. Part I (ss. 1–17) deals with the supervision of "foster" children by local authorities.

It is the duty of local authorities to ensure the well-being of "foster" children (s. 1). A "foster" child is one below the upper limit of compulsory school age whose care and maintenance are undertaken by a person who is not a relative or guardian of his, but not one whose well-being is already the responsibility of some competent authority (s. 2).

Persons maintaining "foster" children must notify the local authority and provide particulars such as name, age, place of birth, etc. (s. 3). The local authority has power to inspect premises, impose conditions or prohibit the keeping of "foster" children (s. 4). Any person aggrieved by any requirement imposed under s. 4 may appeal to a juvenile court (s. 5). Certain disqualifications for keeping "foster" children are detailed in s. 6. A juvenile court may order the removal of a child from unsuitable surroundings (s. 7).

Under s. 40 of C. & Y.P. Act 1933, a warrant authorising the search for a child may be issued on suspicion that unnecessary suffering is being caused to a child. Any refusal to allow the visiting of a "foster" child gives reasonable ground for such a suspicion (1958 Act, s. 8).

Failure to make any of the notifications required or making a false or misleading notice; refusing to allow the visiting of any "foster" child by a duly authorised officer; failure to comply with any requirements imposed by a local authority; maintaining a "foster" child in contravention of s. 6 or refusing to comply with an order for the removal of any "foster" child; or obstructing any person in the execution of such an order, shall be summary offences (s. 14).

Under the Nurseries and Child-Minders Regulation Act 1948, as amended by the Health Services and Public Health Act 1968, s. 60, any person who for reward receives in his home a child under 5 of whom he is not a relative, to be looked after for the day, for a part or parts thereof of a duration, or an aggregate duration of 2 hours or longer, or for longer period not exceeding 6 days, commits a summary offence unless registered with the local social services authority (ss. 1 and 4). The local health authority may register fit persons and fit premises and impose requirements (s. 2). It will issue certificates of registration (s. 3) and may cancel same for cause (s. 5). It will authorise inspection of premises and children, and a justice may issue a warrant authorising entry (s. 7). The local social services authority may prosecute offences under the Act (s. 11). The Act does not apply to hospitals, schools and approved nursery schools and institutions (s. 8).

The Children Act 1948 makes further provisions for the welfare of certain juveniles up to the age of 18. It is the duty of the local authority for the definition of local authority see s. 38) to take into their care a child under 17 who has no parents or guardian or who is abandoned or lost or whose parents or guardian are prevented from properly maintaining him and who requires their intervention. If it does so it should be responsible until he is 18. However, the care of such child may later be taken over by a parent or guardian or relative or friend (s. 1). If it takes over care of such a child, the local authority may, by resolution, assume parental rights (until he is 18, s. 4), if his parents are dead and he has no guardian or if his parents or guardian have abandoned him or are incapable or unfit and consent or if a juvenile court so order if no consent is given (s. 2). See also C & Y.P. Act 1963, s. 48.

It will be a summary offence without lawful authority to take away, to induce, assist, etc., such a child to run away or to harbour such a runaway (s. 3, as amended by C. & Y.P. Act 1963, Sched. 3). The parent of a child who is in the care of the local authority shall keep the authority informed of his address; if he does not he commits a summary offence (s. 10). The local authority may board out a child in their care or maintain him in a community home or in a voluntary home (ss. 13 and 19 as substituted by ss. 49 and 50 of C. & Y.P. Act 1969). Every local authority shall establish a children's committee to carry out their functions under these 1933, 1948, 1963 and 1969 Acts, and also regarding the adoption of children, unless exempted by the Secretary of State (ss. 39, 40). A local authority shall appoint a children's officer and provide an adequate staff (s. 41). A local authority shall make provision in community homes for children removed to a "place of safety" (s. 51 as amended by Sched. 5, C. & Y.P. Act 1969).

"Child" in the Children Act 1948, means generally a person under 18 and any person who has attained that age and is the subject of a care order, "guardian" means a person so appointed by deed or will or by a court, "parent" of an illegitimate child means his mother and a person who has adopted a child is his "parent" under the Act (s. 59, as amended by C. & Y.P. Act 1969, Sched. 5).

Cruelty to Children and Young Persons – Part I of the Children and Young Persons Act 1933, deals with cruelty to juveniles and with certain other similar offences.

The offences under Part I are as follows:

(1) CRUELTY – That is, any person who has attained the age of 16 years who has the custody, charge or care of *any person under sixteen,* wilfully assaulting, ill-treating, neglecting, abandoning or exposing such juvenile or causing or procuring same to be done, in a manner likely to cause him unnecessary suffering or injury to health.

It is an offence punishable on indictment or summarily.

Failure to provide adequate food, clothing, medical aid or lodging for such juvenile or failure to take steps to get same provided under the National Assistance Act 1948, will be deemed to be "neglect" likely to cause injury to health under this section, on the part of the person legally liable to maintain such juvenile.

If the death of an infant under 3 was caused by suffocation (not due to disease or foreign body in the throat) while in bed with a person of 16 or over, who had gone to bed under the influence of drink, that person will be deemed to have neglected the infant in a manner likely to cause injury to health (s. 1).

If actual suffering or injury or its likelihood is prevented by the action of another person or if the juvenile dies, the responsible person may be convicted under this section.

If it is proved that the person convicted was in any way interested in any money accruable or payable on the death of the juvenile and knew it, the punishment may be heavier.

Nothing in this section shall affect the right of any parent, teacher or other person in lawful control or charge to administer punishment to a child or young person (s. 1).

Assaults on children and young persons may also be dealt with as assaults. See Chap. 8, "Statutory Assaults".

(2) BROTHELS – Any person having the custody, charge or care of a person of the age of 4 and under 16, allowing such juvenile to reside in or frequent a brothel. An offence punishable summarily (s. 3). See Chap. 10, "Brothels".

(3) BEGGING – Any person causing or procuring or when having the custody, charge or care of such juvenile, allowing a person under 16 to be in any street, premises or place for the purpose of begging or getting alms in any manner. Summary offence (s. 4).

If a person singing, etc., in a public place has with him a child lent or hired to him, the child shall be deemed to be there for the getting of alms (s. 4).

(4) INTOXICANTS – It is a summary offence for any person to give or cause to be given to any child under 5 any intoxicating liquor, except on doctor's orders or in case of sickness or other urgent causes (s. 5).

(5) TOBACCO OR CIGARETTE PAPERS – Sale to persons under 16 is a summary offence (s. 7). See "Smoking by Juveniles", later.

(6) SCRAP METAL – Dealers must not purchase scrap metal from persons under 16 (s. 5, Scrap Metal Dealers Act 1964). See Chap. 31, "Dealers in Scrap Metal".

(7) VAGRANTS AND CHILDREN – It is a summary offence for a person habitually to wander from place to place and take with him any child of 5 or more or any young person still liable to compulsory schooling, unless he can prove that the child or young person is not, by so "wandering" prevented from receiving efficient full-time education. (Proceedings for this offence shall not be instituted except by a local authority. (C. & Y.P. Act 1969, Sched. 5, para. 2).) Any constable, on reasonable grounds of suspicion, may arrest without warrant such person.

(8) UNPROTECTED FIRE – Where any person of 16 or over who has the custody, charge or care of any child under 12, allows such child to be in any room containing an open

fire grate or any heating appliance liable to cause injury by contact not sufficiently protected to guard against the risk, without taking reasonable precautions against the risk of the child being burnt or scalded and by reason thereof the child is killed or suffers serious injury. Summary offence (s. 11 and s. 8 of the C. & Y.P. (Amendment) Act 1952).

See also the Heating Appliances (Fireguards) Act 1952.

(9) ENTERTAINMENTS – Failing to provide for the safety of children at entertainments is a summary offence (s. 12). See Chap. 37, "Ingress and Egress".

As regards juveniles and licensed premises see Licensing Act 1964, ss. 168, 169 and 170: Chap. 38.

(10) Under s. 56 of the Offences against the Person Act 1861, it is an arrestable offence to unlawfully, by force or fraud, lead or take away or decoy or entice away or detain any child under 14, with intent to deprive the parent or lawful custodian of the possession of such child, or with intent to steal any article on such child, or with any such intent to receive or harbour any such child knowing it has been so abducted, except where the abductor has claimed a right to the possession of such child or is the mother or has claimed to be the father of such illegitimate child.

CUSTODY, CHARGE OR CARE OF A CHILD OR YOUNG PERSON:

The parent or legal guardian or person legally liable to maintain him is presumed to have the custody of him, and desertion by the father does not in itself end his custody.

A person to whose charge he is committed by any person who has the custody of him, is presumed to have charge of him.

A person having actual possession or control of him is presumed to have care of him (s. 17).

Arrest, Search Warrant and Procedure – Any constable may arrest without warrant:

(1) Any person who within his view commits any of the offences in the Sched. 1 to the Act, if he does not know and cannot ascertain his name and residence.

(2) Any person who has committed, or whom he has reason to believe to have committed, any of the offences in the Sched. 1 to the Act, if he has reasonable ground for believing such person will abscond or if he does not know and cannot ascertain his name and address (s. 13).

SCHED. 1 TO ACT OF 1933 AS AMENDED – This schedule mentions the following offences where committed against children or young persons:

Murder, manslaughter, infanticide. (The reference to the murder or manslaughter of a child or young person applies also to aiding, abetting, counselling or procuring the suicide of a child or young person (Suicide Act 1961).)

Offences against the Person Act 1861: s. 27 (abandoning or exposing a child under 2); s. 56 (kidnapping child under 14); s. 5 (manslaughter); s. 42 (assault); s. 43 (aggravated assault on boy under 14 or female).

Children and Young Persons Act 1933, s. 1 (cruelty to juvenile under 16); s. 3 (allowing juvenile of 4 and under 16 to be in a brothel); s. 4 (causing or allowing juvenile under 16 to be used for begging); s. 11 and s. 8, 1952 Act (exposing child under 12 to risk of burning); s. 23 (causing or allowing juvenile under 16 to take part in performances endangering life or limb).

Sexual Offences Act 1956, offences under ss. 2 to 7, 10 to 16, 19, 20, 22 to 26, and 28, and any attempt to commit offences under ss. 2, 5, 6, 7, 10, 11, 12, 22, 23. Section 99 (2) of the C. & Y.P. Act 1933, shall apply where necessary.

Offences against the Indecency with Children Act 1960.

Any other offence involving bodily injury.

After such an arrest without warrant the prisoner shall be released on bail at the police station, unless his release would tend to defeat the ends of justice or cause danger to the juvenile concerned (s. 13). See Chap. 5, "Bail by Police".

SEARCH WARRANT – A justice may issue a warrant authorising any constable named therein to enter, if need be by force, any place specified in the warrant, and either to search for and remove to a place of safety any child or young person if it is found that he has been or is being assaulted, ill-treated or neglected or the subject of any Sched. 1 offence, or to remove a juvenile to a place of safety. The juvenile need not be named and the warrant may direct the arrest of any person accused. The person laying the information may accompany the constable unless the justice otherwise directs and the justice may direct the attendance of a doctor (s. 40).

PROCEDURE – The same information or summons may charge any of the above Sched. 1 offences in respect to two or more juveniles. The same information or summons may also charge a person as having the care, custody or charge, and charge him with the offences of assault, neglect, abandonment or exposure together or separately. The dates of the acts making up a continuous offence need not be specified (s. 14).

The wife or husband of the accused is a competent witness for the prosecution or the defence without the consent of the accused but is not compellable to give evidence (s. 15).

The unsworn evidence of a child of tender years in offence cases may be received if the court is satisfied that the child has sufficient intelligence and understands the duty of speaking the truth, but such evidence must be corroborated (s. 38).

In the case of any Sched. 1 offence, the presence of the juvenile at the hearing of the case may be dispensed with if the court does not consider it essential (s. 41).

In a Sched. 1 offence case, if the attendance of the injured juvenile would involve serious danger to his life or health, and a doctor gives evidence to that effect, a justice may take the juvenile's deposition and send it to the court (s. 42). Such a deposition is admissible in evidence, on medical evidence of the juvenile's condition, provided that notice of the intention to take it had been served on the accused and that he or his lawyer had (or might have had if he had chosen to be present) an opportunity of cross-examining the juvenile on his deposition (s. 43).

Smoking by Juveniles – Section 7 of the Children and Young Persons Act 1933, deals with persons under the age of 16 years smoking tobacco (which includes cigarettes).

It is a summary offence to sell to anyone apparently under the age of 16 years, any tobacco or cigarette papers, whether for his own use or not.

However, sale of tobacco other than cigarettes shall not be an offence if seller had no reason to believe that the tobacco was for the use of the juvenile buyer.

It is the duty of a constable and of a park-keeper in uniform to seize tobacco or cigarette papers in the possession of any person apparently under the age of 16 whom he finds smoking in any street or public place (including any ground to which the public have access, whether on payment or otherwise, s. 107).

It is not an offence to sell to, and there is no power of seizure in the case of:

(1) Boy messengers in uniform in the course of their employment;

(2) Persons employed by tobacconists for the purpose of their business.

On proof that any automatic machine for the sale of tobacco kept on any premises is being extensively used by persons apparently under 16, a magistrates' court may order the owner of the machine or the occupier of the place where the machine is kept to take specified precautions to prevent the practice or if necessary to remove the machine.

Care of Juveniles – The C. & Y.P. Act 1969, has replaced former legislation dealing with the care and control of juveniles through court proceedings. Care proceedings may be brought in a juvenile court by any local authority, constable or authorised person (the N.S.P.C.C.) who reasonably believes that there are grounds for making an order under the section in respect of a child or young person (s. 1 (1)). The court may make an order provided it is satisfied, firstly, that one of six conditions applies, viz., that the child or young person (a) is neglected or ill-treated; (b) another child or young person who is or was a member of the household to which he belongs has been neglected or ill-treated; (c) is exposed to moral danger; (d) is beyond the control of his parent or guardian; (e) is not going to school; or (f) is guilty of an offence, excluding homicide. Secondly, the juvenile court may make an order under the section only, if in addition to one of the conditions mentioned being satisfied, it is also of opinion that the child is in need of care or control which he is unlikely to receive unless such an order is made (s. 1 (2)). The order which a court may make under this section in respect of a child or young person is: (a) an order requiring the parent or guardian to take proper care and exercise proper control over him; or (b) a supervision order; or (c) a care order; or (d) a hospital order; or (e) a guardianship order (s. 1 (3)).

No child or young person shall be brought before a juvenile court by his parent or guardian on the ground that he is unable to control him. However, the parent may report the circumstances to the Local Authority and the Authority could take action under s. 1 of 1969 Act (s. 3 (1) of 1963 Act).

Education – The Education Act 1944 made several alterations in the law affecting children. Compulsory school age is now between 5 years and 16 years (s. 35 as amended by the Raising of the School Leaving Age Order 1972). The parent or guardian or person having the actual custody is bound to cause such person to receive efficient full-time education (s. 36). For non-attendance at school the local Education Authority may serve a school attendance order (s. 37). The parent will be guilty of an offence if his "child" does not attend school regularly (s. 39). School attendance may be enforced by fine and/or imprisonment and the court may direct that the "child" be brought before a juvenile court which may deal with him under s. 1 of the C. & Y.P. Act 1969, as needing care, or control (s. 40). "Child" here means a person not over compulsory school age (s. 114).

Employment of Juveniles – C. & Y.P. Act 1933, Part II (ss. 18–30) deals with the employment of children and young persons. Section 18 imposes restrictions on the employment of children, and s. 30 directs that any person assisting in any trade or occupation carried on for profit shall be deemed to be employed although he receives no reward for his labour.

For the purposes of byelaws made by the local authority under Part II of this 1933 Act the expression "child" shall have the same meaning as it has for the purposes of the said Part II (Education Act 1944, s. 120 (5)). Also for the purposes of any enactment relating to the employment of children and young persons any person not over compulsory school age shall be deemed to be a child within the meaning of that enactment (Education Act 1944, s. 58).

However, a chorister taking part in religious services or practices, whether paid or not, shall not be deemed to be employed (s. 30).

By s. 18 (as amended by 1963 Act, s. 34 and Sched. 3) the general restrictions are as follows:

(1) No child shall be employed until his age is 13 years. However, byelaws may allow the parent or guardian to employ a child in light agricultural or horticultural work.

(2) No child shall be employed before the close of his day's school hours. However, byelaws may allow a child to be employed for one hour before his day's school hour.

(3) No child shall be employed before 7 a.m. or after 7 p.m. nor for more than 2 hours on any of his school days.

(4) No child shall be employed on any Sunday for more than 2 hours.

(5) No child shall be employed to lift, carry, or move anything so heavy as to be likely to cause injury to him.

Nothing in this section, or in any byelaw made under this section, shall prevent a child from taking part in a performance: (a) under the authority of a licence granted under this Part of this Act; or (b) in a case where by virtue of s. 37 (3) of the C. & Y.P. Act 1963 no licence under that section is required for him to take part in the performance.

STREET TRADING – No person under 17 shall engage or be employed in street trading, but byelaws may allow persons of 14 up to 17 to be so employed by their parents. A local authority may make byelaws regulating or prohibiting street trading by persons under 18. A person under 18 is prohibited from engaging in or being employed in street trading on Sunday, except where the trading is of a description to which s. 58 of the Shops Act 1950 applies (s. 20 as amended by 1963 Act, s. 35). A person under 18 who engages in street trading in contravention of above, is liable to fine on summary conviction (s. 21).

"Street trading" includes hawking of newspapers, matches, flowers and other articles, playing, singing or performing for profit, shoe-blacking and other like occupations carried on in streets or public places (s. 30).

If a person is employed in contravention of any of the above restrictions, his employer (unless he proves he used all due diligence to observe the law) and any person (other than the employee) to whose act or default the contravention is attributable, are liable to fine on summary conviction (s. 21). For the right of entry to make enquiries see "Powers of Entry (Employment)", later.

Entertainment by Children – A child under the upper limit of compulsory school age may not take part in (a) any performance in connection with which a charge is made (whether for admission or otherwise); (b) any performance in licensed premises within the meaning of the Licensing Act 1964, or in premises in respect of which a club is registered under the Licensing Act 1964; (c) any broadcast performance; (d) any performance recorded (by whatever means) with a view to its use in a broadcast or in a film intended for public exhibition; and a child shall be treated for the purposes of this section as taking part in a performance if he takes the place of a performer in any rehearsal or in any preparation for the recording of the performance, unless (1) a licence has been granted by the local authority for the area in which he lives or, if he does not live in Great Britain, in which the applicant for the licence lives or has his place of business, or (2) he takes part in performances on not more than 4 days in any period of 6 months, or performances for which a licence is not required (C. & Y.P. Act 1963, s. 37).

The restrictions and conditions subject to which licences may be granted and the hours of work, rest and meals for children taking part in unlicensed performances are laid down in the Children (Performances) Regulations 1968.

For right of entry to make enquiries, see "Powers of Entry (Employment)", later.

Dangerous Performances by Juveniles – C. & Y.P. Act 1933, Part II.

(1) No person under 16 shall take part in any performance to which s. 37 of 1963 Act applies, and in which his life or limbs are endangered. Causing or procuring or being the parent or guardian allowing him to do so is a summary offence which may be prosecuted only by or with the authority of the Chief Officer of Police (s. 23);

(2) No person under 12 shall be trained to take part in performances of a dangerous nature (including acrobatic and contortionist work, s. 30) and

(3) No person under 16 shall be trained to take part in such performances except on licence (s. 24).

Causing or procuring or being the parent or guardian allowing any such training except on licence is a summary offence punishable by fine (s. 24).

A local authority may grant a licence for a person of 12 and under 16 years to be so trained. The licence shall specify the place or places where such person is to be trained and conditions for his protection may be included (s. 24 as amended by s. 41 of 1963 Act).

For the right of entry to make enquiries, see "Powers of Entry (Employment)", later.

Powers of Entry (Employment) – C. & Y.P. Act 1933, s. 28. On reasonable cause to believe that the provisions of Part II as to employment, entertainments and dangerous performances or of any byelaw made thereunder, are being contravened with respect to any person, the local authority or any constable may obtain from a justice a written order giving power to enter at any reasonable time within 48 hours of the making of the order, any place in or in connection with which such person is or is believed to be employed, trained, etc., and to make enquiries therein with respect to such person. The provisions of the above s. 28 have now been extended by s. 43 of the 1963 Act which provides that any authorised officer of the local authority or any constable may: (a) at any time enter any place used as a broadcasting studio or film studio or used for the recording of a performance with a view to its use in a broadcast or in a film intended for public exhibition and make inquiries therein as to any children taking part in performances to which s. 37 of the C. & Y.P. Act 1963 applies; (b) at any time during the currency of a licence granted under the said s. 37 or under the provisions of this Part of this Act relating to training for dangerous performances enter any place (whether or not it is such a place as is mentioned in paragraph (a) of this subsection) where the person to whom the licence relates is authorised by the licence to take part in a performance or to be trained, and may make inquiries therein with respect to that person. It is a summary offence to obstruct such constable or officer or to refuse to answer or answer falsely any enquiry thus authorised.

Restrictions on Persons under 18 going abroad for the purpose of Performing for Profit – (1) No person having the custody, charge or care of any person under the age of 18 years shall allow him, nor shall any person cause or procure any person under that age, to go abroad for the purpose of singing, playing, performing, or being exhibited, for profit, unless a licence has been granted in respect of him under this section: Provided that this subsection shall not apply in any case where it is proved that the person under the age of 18 years was only temporarily resident within the U.K. (C. & Y.P. Act 1933, s. 25 as amended by the C. & Y.P. Act 1963, Sched. 3).

Contravention of the above is a summary offence, and if a person procured any such juvenile to go abroad by false pretence or false representation he is liable on indictment to 2 years' imprisonment (s. 26 as amended by C. & Y.P. Act 1963, Sched. 3).

Treatment of Youthful Offenders – Where a person is arrested without warrant and cannot be brought immediately before a magistrates' court, then if either (a) he appears to be a child and his arrest is for homicide; or (b) he appears to be a young person and his arrest is for any offence, the police officer in charge of the police station to which he is brought shall forthwith enquire into the case, and shall release him unless: (1) the officer considers that he ought in his own interests to be further detained; or (2) the officer has reason to believe that he has committed homicide or another grave crime or that his release would defeat the ends of justice or that if he were released he would fail to appear to answer to any charge which might be made (C. & Y.P. Act 1969, s. 29 (1)).

See also the powers under M.C. Act 1952, s. 38, Chap. 5.

Where a child or young person is arrested on warrant, he shall not be released unless he or his parent or guardian enters into a recognizance for such amount as the officer aforesaid considers will secure his attendance at the hearing of the charge. The recognizance may be conditioned for the attendance of the parent or guardian at the hearing in addition to the person charged (1969 Act, s. 29 (2)). This subsection applies also to a person arrested without a warrant if the officer has decided that an information should be laid in respect of an offence alleged to have been committed by him (C.J. Act 1972, s. 43).

An officer who enquires into a case in pursuance of s. 1 above, and does not release the person to whom the enquiry relates shall, unless the officer certifies that it is impracticable to do so, or that he is of so unruly a character as to make it inappropriate to do so, make arrangements for him to be taken into the care of a local authority; and a certificate made under this subsection shall be produced to the court (1969 Act, s. 29 (3)).

A person detained by virtue of the above sub-s. (3) shall be brought before a magistrates' court within 72 hours from the time of his arrest, unless within that period a police officer not below the rank of inspector certifies to a magistrates' court that by reason of illness or accident he cannot be brought before the court within that period (1969 Act, s. 29 (5)).

Where a court (or justice) remands or commits for trial or sentence a person not under 17, but under 21 charged with or convicted of an offence and not released on bail, it may commit him to a remand centre (if available) or to prison. (C. & Y.P. Act 1969, Sched. 5, para. 24.)

Where a person (15–21) is committed, in custody, by a magistrates' court for sentence of Borstal training, he should be sent to a suitable available remand centre and if not, to prison (M.C. Act 1952, s. 28 as amended).

If not less than 14, a person arrested or summoned for an offence may have his finger-prints and palm-prints taken by order of a magistrates' court (M.C. Act 1952, s. 40, as amended by C.J. Act 1967, s. 33). See "Finger-Prints", Chap. 5.

If a child or young person is arrested at least one parent or guardian should be informed by the person who arrested him. Where a child or young person is for any reason brought before a court, his parent or guardian may be required to attend the court during any stages of the proceedings unless the court is satisfied that it would be unreasonable (1933 Act, s. 34, as substituted by 1963 Act, s. 25 and amended by the 1969 Act, Sched. 5, para. 3). His attendance may be enforced by summons or warrant (Magistrates' Courts (C. & Y.P.) Rules 1970).

While detained in a police station or being conveyed to or from a court or while waiting before or after attendance at court, a juvenile shall be prevented from associating with an adult (not being a relative) charged with any offence other than the offence with which the juvenile is jointly charged. If a girl, she shall be under the care of a woman (1933 Act, s. 31).

In the case of any proceedings the court may direct that no newspaper report, sound or television broadcast shall give the picture, name, address or school or any particulars calculated to identify any child or young person concerned in the proceedings either as accused, prosecutor or witness. Breach of any such direction of the court is punishable summarily by fine (1933 Act, s. 39 as amended by C. & Y.P. Act 1963, s. 57 and Sched. 5).

Unless the court or the Secretary of State by order permit, no newspaper report, sound or television broadcast of any proceedings in a juvenile court or on appeal from a juvenile court shall give the picture, name, address, school or any particulars calculated to identify any child or young person concerned in the proceedings as accused, prosecutor or witness. Any contravention is punishable summarily by fine (1933 Act, s. 49 as amended by C. & Y.P. Act 1963, s. 57).

Further limitations on publication of particulars of children and young persons are imposed by C. & Y.P. Act 1969, s. 10.

Charges against children and young persons (and also applications for orders or licences relating to them) shall be heard by juvenile courts. However, this does not apply to a joint charge against a person under 17 and a person of 17 or over, nor does it apply when a person under 17 is charged and another person of 17 or upwards is charged with aiding, abetting, causing, procuring, allowing or permitting that offence, and a magistrates' court may continue dealing with a case even though it transpires in the course of the proceedings that the person concerned is a person under 17 (1933 Act, s. 46).

If a notification that the accused desires to plead guilty without appearing before the court is received by the Clerk of a Court in pursuance of s. 1, M.C. Act 1957, and the court has no reason to believe that the accused is a child or young person then, if he is a child or young person he shall be deemed to have attained the age of 17 for the purposes of this section in its application to the proceedings in question (s. 46 (1A), C. & Y.P. Act 1933, as added by C. & Y.P. Act 1969, Sched. 5, para. 4).

A magistrates' court which is not a juvenile court may hear an information against a child or young person if he is charged (a) with aiding, abetting, causing, procuring, allowing or permitting an offence with which a person who has attained the age of 17 is charged at the same time, or (b) with an offence arising out of circumstances which are the same as or connected with those giving rise to an offence with which a person who has attained the age of 17 is charged at the same time (C. & Y.P. Act 1963, s. 18).

A juvenile court may deal with a charge against a person believed to be a child or young person although it is discovered that the person is not a juvenile (1933 Act, s. 48 (1)).

Any justice or justices may entertain an application for bail or remand and hear the evidence, no matter what the age of the defendant is (1933 Act, s. 46 (2)).

If a juvenile is remanded by a juvenile court for information to be obtained concerning him, the remand may be for periods not exceeding 21 days and another juvenile court may subsequently deal with him (1933 Act, s. 48 (3)).

Any court by or before which a child or young person is found guilty of an offence other than homicide, may, and if it is not a juvenile court shall, unless undesirable to do so, remit the case to a juvenile court to deal with the offender (1933 Act, s. 56).

The Magistrates' Courts (C. & Y.P.) Rules 1970 deal with the procedure in court respecting juvenile offenders and juveniles in need of care, or control. See Stone's Justices' Manual.

Remand Centres – A remand centre is a place for the detention of persons not less than 14, but under 21, who are remanded or committed in custody for trial or sentence. They should have facilities for the observation of a prisoner's physical or mental condition (Prison Act 1952, s. 43). A person of 15 to 21 committed in custody to the Crown Court with a view to Borstal training should go to a suitable available remand centre (M.C. Act 1952, s. 28).

Detention Centres – A detention centre is a place in which persons not less than 14 but under 21 may be detained for short periods under suitable discipline (Prison Act 1952, s. 43).

Where a court has power, or would have but for the statutory restrictions upon the imprisonment of young offenders, to pass sentence of imprisonment on an offender under 21 but not less than 14, the court may order him to be detained in a detention centre. A detention order is generally for a term of 3 months, but a person of 17 or over may be sent to a detention centre for a term of 3 to 6 months, in certain special circumstances, by the Crown Court (C.J. Act 1961, s. 4).

A person detained in a detention centre in pursuance of an order under C.J. Act 1961, s. 4, shall, after his release and until the expiration of the period of 12 months from the date of his release, be under the supervision of such society or person as may be specified in a notice to be given to him by the Secretary of

State on his release, and shall, while under that supervision, comply with such requirements as may be specified:

Provided that the Secretary of State may at any time modify or cancel any of the requirements or order that a person who is under supervision shall cease to be under supervision.

If before the expiration of the period of 12 months the Secretary of State is satisfied that a person under supervision has failed to comply with any requirement for the time being specified in the notice given to him, he may by order recall him to a detention centre; and he shall be liable to be detained in the detention centre until the expiration of a period equivalent to that part of his term which was unexpired on the date of his release from the detention centre, or until the expiration of the period of 14 days from the date of his being taken into custody under the order, whichever is the later, and, if at large, shall be deemed to be unlawfully at large:

Provided that (a) a person shall not be recalled more than once by virtue of the same order under the C.J. Act 1961, s. 4, and (b) an order shall, at the expiration of the said period of 12 months, cease to have effect unless the person to whom it relates is then in custody thereunder.

The Secretary of State may at any time release a person who is detained in a detention centre under an order of recall (C.J. Act 1961, s. 13 and Sched. 1).

An order for the recall of an offender will be sent by the Secretary of State to the Chief Officer of Police.

These centres will be available gradually to be regulated by the Detention Centre Rules 1952 and 1968. See Chap. 21 (Prison Breach) for offence of harbouring escapee.

Attendance Centres – An attendance centre is a place at which offenders under 21 may be ordered to attend at specified times to be given under supervision appropriate occupation and instruction. The Secretary of State may make arrangements for such places with any local or police authority (C.J. Act 1948, s. 48). If a magistrates' court has or would have had but for the statutory restrictions, power to impose imprisonment on a person under 21, or to deal with such a person for breach of a probation order, the court may order him to attend at a reasonably accessible attendance centre for not less than 12 hours, except where he is under 14 years and the court is of opinion that 12 hours would be excessive, and not more than 24 hours where the court is of opinion that 12 hours is inadequate. Such an order may not be made in the case of certain previous offenders mentioned in the section. If the person fails to attend or contravenes the rules, he may be brought on summons or warrant before a magistrates' court and be dealt with for the original offence (C.J. Act 1948, s. 19). The Attendance Centre Rules 1958 deal with discipline, rules, records, etc. (C.J. Act 1948, s. 52).

Community Service – The P. of C.C. Act 1973 (ss. 14–17) provide a method of dealing with offenders by means of deprivation of leisure time for a constructive purpose. The courts are empowered to order offenders to carry out up to 240 hours unpaid work of service to the Community in their spare time. Community service schemes are administered by the Probation and After Care services.

Harmful Publications – The C. & Y.P. (Harmful Publications) Act 1955 makes it a summary offence to print, publish, sell or let on hire or have for the purpose of sale or letting on hire any book, magazine, etc., consisting wholly or mainly of stories told in pictures portraying the commission of crimes or acts of violence or cruelty or repulsive or horrible incidents in such a way as would tend to corrupt a child or young person (under 17) into whose hands it might fall or be likely to fall. Prosecution can be only by or with the consent of the Attorney-General. A search warrant under the Act may be obtained. Importation of such works, their printing plates and films is prohibited.

Tattooing of Minors Act 1969 – This Act makes it an offence to tattoo a person under 18 except when performed for medical reasons by a qualified medical practitioner or by a person working under his direction. (Reasonable cause to believe that the person tattooed was over 18 is a defence) (s. 1). "Tattoo" means the insertion into the skin of any colouring material designed to leave a permanent mark (s. 3).

Ages fixed by Law.

Under 1	Death of such infant caused by mother may be infanticide (Infanticide Act 1938).
Under 2	Abandoning or exposing such child so as to endanger life or health (Offences against the Person Act 1861, s. 27).
Under 3	Suffocation of such child in bed caused by drunkenness of person over 16 (C. & Y.P. Act 1933, s. 1).
Under 5	Intoxicants must not be given to such child unless for a good reason (C. & Y.P. Act 1933, s. 5).
	Minding for reward such children from more than one household needs registration (Nurseries and Child-Minders Act 1948, ss. 1, 4).
Over 5	Education compulsory (Education Act 1944, s. 35).
Over 5 *to* 15	Person habitually wandering from place to place with such child and unable to prove that child gets efficient education (C. & Y.P. Act 1933, s. 10).
Under 7	Drunk in charge of such child in public place or licensed premises (Licensing Act 1902, s. 2).

Under 10 Not criminally responsible for his acts (C. & Y.P. Act 1933, s. 50 as substituted by 1963 Act, s. 16).

Under 12 Such child must not be trained in dangerous performances (C. & Y.P. Act 1933, s. 24).

Exposing child under 12 to risk of burning or scalding in a room (C. & Y.P. Acts 1933, s. 11 and 1952, s. 8).

Selling an animal as a pet to such child (Pet Animals Act 1951, s. 3).

Over 12 A local authority may grant a licence for such child to be trained in performances of a dangerous nature (by a court) (C. & Y.P. Act 1933, s. 24).

Under 13 Defilement of a girl under 13 (Sexual Offences Act 1956, s. 5).

Occupier, etc., of premises inducing or suffering her to be there for that purpose (Sexual Offences Act 1956, s. 25).

Gunpowder must not be sold to such child (Explosives Act 1875, s. 31).

No child shall be employed until his age is 13 (Children Act 1972).

Under 14 Such person is a "child" (C. & Y.P. Act 1933, s. 107) and if over 10 is in law responsible for offences (except rape). If proved to have sufficient capacity to know what he or she is doing, should be dealt with by a juvenile court (1933 Act, s. 46). "Child" of tender years who does not understand the nature of an oath may give unsworn evidence in offence cases if of sufficient intelligence and understands the duty of speaking the truth (C. & Y.P. Act 1933, s. 38). Such a child shall not be called as a witness for the prosecution in sexual cases except in certain cases (C. & Y.P. Act 1963, s. 27).

Air guns: must not accept as a gift any air weapon or ammunition for an air weapon. Must not have in his possession, unless under supervision of a person 21 years or over. If on premises must not fire any missile beyond those premises. Exceptions for members of rifle clubs, etc., and use at shooting galleries (Firearms Act 1968).

Court: must not be in a court unless as defendant or witness or a child in arms (1933 Act, s. 36).

Firearm or ammunition (except 24 in. shotgun or air gun, etc.)—must not be lent or given to him (Firearms Act 1968, s. 24 (2)).

Gross indecency with or towards a child or inciting a child to such an act (Indecency with Children Act 1960).

Under 14– *contd.* Kidnapping or knowingly harbouring such child when stolen. (Offences against the Person Act 1861, s. 56.)

Licensed premises: must not be in the bar during permitted hours unless resident or merely passing through or in railway refreshment rooms (Licensing Act 1964, s. 168).

Rags dealer: must not give child any article whatsoever (Public Health Act 1936, s. 154). Article includes animal, fish, bird or living thing (Public Health Act 1961, s. 42).

Rape: such a boy cannot be convicted of rape or carnal knowledge, but may be for indecent assault.

Over 14 Is a "young person" up to 17 (C. & Y.P. Act 1933, s. 107) and is responsible criminally for acts. If in custody or summoned for an offence a summary court may order his finger-prints and palm-prints to be taken by the police (Magistrates' Courts Act 1952, s. 40 as amended by C.J. Act 1967, s. 33).

May be sent to a detention centre (C.J. Act 1961, s. 4).

Under 15 Such a person shall not be admitted to, or be permitted to remain in, a knacker's yard during slaughtering or cutting up the carcase of any animal (Slaughter of Animals (Prevention of Cruelty) Regs. 1958, r. 23).

Education is compulsory. A person under 15 who does not comply with a school attendance order may be sent to an approved school or to care of fit person or be placed under supervision, and the parent or guardian is punishable. Employment of such person is limited under s. 18 of C. & Y.P. Act 1933 and any byelaws made thereunder (Education Act 1944, ss. 35, 40, 44, 58, and Sched. 8).

Any person who for reward, receives a "foster child" of compulsory school age must notify the local authority, also any change of residence or its death or removal (Children Act 1958, s. 3).

The law protects such children under compulsory school age who are maintained for reward apart from their parents (Children Act 1948, s. 5).

Shot gun: must not have assembled shot gun in his possession unless under supervision of person of 21 or over, or gun is covered with securely fastened gun cover so that it cannot be fired (Firearms Act 1968 (s. 22 (3)) and no person

Under 15–*contd.* shall give him a shot gun or ammunition (s. 24 (3)).

Over 15 A child of 15 in the care of the local authority may be placed in a community home until he is 21 (Children Act 1948, s. 19, as amended by C. & Y.P. Act 1969, s. 50).

Borstal Institution: may be sent there if over 15 and under 21 (C.J. Act 1961, s. 1).

Under 16 Abduction of such girl (Sexual Offences Act 1956, s. 20).

Alien: need not register until aged 16 (Aliens Order 1953, arts. 14, 19).

Begging: causing or procuring or allowing such person to be in any place for alms (C. & Y.P. Act 1933, s. 4).

Brothel: if aged 4 and under 16 must not be allowed by person having charge to reside in or frequent a brothel (C. & Y.P. Act 1933, s. 3).

Tobacco or cigarette papers must not be sold to such person unless to a boy messenger in uniform or an employee in the trade, for others (C. & Y.P. Act 1933, s. 7).

Cruelty: to such person by person over 16 (C. & Y.P. Act 1933, s. 1).

Dangerous performances: shall not take part in any performance to which s. 37 of C. & Y.P. Act 1963, applies and in which life or limbs are endangered (s. 23).

Defilement of girl under 16 (Sexual Offences Act 1956, s. 6).

Occupier, etc., of premises inducing or knowingly suffering her to be there for that purpose (Sexual Offences Act 1956, s. 26).

Indecent assault on person under 16: consent no defence (Sexual Offences Act 1956, ss. 14, 15).

Liqueur chocolates must not be sold to such person (Licensing Act 1964, s. 167).

Marriage of person under 16 is void (Marriage Act 1949, s. 2).

Motor vehicle: Such person must not drive a motor vehicle on a road (Road Traffic Act 1972, s. 4).

Scrap metal must not be purchased by dealers from such person (Scrap Metal Dealers Act 1964, s. 5).

Seduction, prostitution, unlawful carnal knowledge or indecent assault on such girl must not be caused or encouraged by person having charge of her (Sexual Offences Act 1956, s. 28).

Smoking by such person in public place entails

Under 16– *contd.* seizure of the tobacco and cigarette papers (C. & Y.P. Act 1933, s. 7).

Over 16 Alien: must register if under restriction on the length of his stay (Aliens Orders 1953 and 1960).

Incest: female of 16 or over who consents to incest against herself (Sexual Offences Act 1956, s. 11).

Motor cycle or invalid carriage and certain descriptions of agricultural tractor only may be driven on a road by such person (Road Traffic Act 1972, s. 4).

Licensed premises:—Such person (16–18) may have beer, porter, perry or cider with a meal (Licensing Act 1964, s. 169).

Under 17 If over 14 such person is a "young person" (C. & Y.P. Act 1933, s. 107), and is responsible in law for his or her offences. Unless charged with homicide must be dealt with by a juvenile court except when jointly charged with a person of 17 or over, or where another, over 17, is charged with aiding, etc., the offence (s. 46). A magistrates' court,other than a juvenile court may hear charges against a person of or over 17 when a person under 17 is charged with aiding and abetting, or where a person under 17 and a person of 17 or over are charged with offences arising out of circumstances that are the same or connected (C. & Y.P. Act 1963, s. 18). Can be dealt with summarily by consent for any indictable offence except homicide. Any time must not exceed £50 (C.J. Act 1961, s. 8).

Street trading by such person is prohibited, except when allowed by byelaw for young person employed by parent (C. & Y.P. Act 1933, s. 20).

Air guns: must not have in his possession in any public place, except air gun or air rifle covered with a securely fastened gun cover, so that it cannot be fired (Firearms Act 1968, s. 22 (5)). (Exceptions for members of rifle clubs and use at shooting galleries.) (Firearms Act 1968, s. 23 (2).)

Care, or control: when such is required court may deal with him (C. & Y.P. Act 1969).

Firearm or ammunition: must not purchase or hire and same must not be sold or hired to such person (Firearms Act 1968, s. 22 (1)).

Pedlar's certificate must not be issued to such person (Pedlars Acts 1871 and 1881).

At police stations, courts etc.: must not be allowed to associate with adult prisoners except

Under 17– *contd.* relatives or persons jointly charged. A girl must be under care of a woman (C. & Y.P. Act 1933, s. 31).

Cannot be sent to prison (P. of C.C. Act 1973, s. 19).

The local authority shall provide for such a juvenile who is abandoned, lost, etc., and keep him in its care until he is 18 (Children Act 1948, s. 1).

Must not be in sole charge of an aircraft in motion (Air Navigation Order 1974, art. 20 and Sched. 9).

Over 17 Such person is of "full age" (Family Law Reform Act 1969, s. 1).

Motor cars (and certain descriptions of road rollers) may be driven on a road by a duly licensed person (Road Traffic Act 1972, s. 4).

A magistrates' court which convicts him of an indictable offence may commit him, in custody or on bail, to the Crown Court for heavier sentence (Magistrates' Courts Act 1952, s. 29).

Where a court (or justice) remands or commits for trial or sentence a person over 17 but under 21, not on bail, it may commit him to a remand centre (if available) or to prison (C. & Y.P. Act 1969, Sched. 5 (24)).

Under 18 Such a person is a "minor" (Family Law Reform Act 1969, s. 12).

Abduction of such unmarried girl with unlawful and carnal intent (Sexual Offences Act 1956, s. 19).

Betting with such person and his employment for betting, is prohibited (Betting, Gaming and Lotteries Act 1963, s. 21).

Betting circulars shall not be sent to such person (Betting, Gaming and Lotteries Act 1963, s. 22 as amended by Family Law Reform Act 1969, Sched. 1).

Employment of such persons over 15 and under 18 may be regulated by byelaws (C. & Y.P. Act 1933, ss. 19, 20; Education Act 1944, Sched. 8).

Employment abroad to sing, etc., for profit is prohibited unless over 14 and with licence (C. & Y.P. Act 1933, s. 25).

Gaming: No person under 18 shall take part in gaming in public houses and hotels (Gaming Act 1968, s. 7).

Licensed premises: intoxicants must not be supplied for consumption by him on the premises except beer, porter, cider or perry with a meal to a person of 16–18 (Licensing Act 1964, s. 169).

Under 18– *contd.* Public Service vehicle: must not be licensed as a conductor (Road Traffic Act 1960, s. 144).

The protection provisions of the Children Act 1948, may continue to apply until such a lost, abandoned child is 18 (s. 1) and the local authority may assume parental rights (s. 2).

Such a person remains a "child" as far as the Children Act 1948 is concerned (s. 59), and within Part I of the Children Act 1958 (s. 17).

"Tattooing" such a person is an offence (Tattooing of Minors Act 1969).

Over 18 Licence to keep a riding establishment may be granted under the Riding Establishments Act 1964.

May marry without consent of parent or guardian (Family Law Reform Act 1969, s. 2).

May vote at a parliamentary or local government election (Representation of the People Act 1969).

Under 21 Borstal Institution may be ordered if over 15 and under 21 (C. J. Act 1948, s. 20).

When committed or remanded in custody by a magistrates' court for Borstal training he should be sent to an available remand centre, and if not, to prison (Magistrates' Courts Act 1952, s. 28).

Motors: locomotives, tractors and heavy motor cars must not be driven on a road by such person except tractors used primarily for work on land in connection with agriculture and certain descriptions of road rollers (Road Traffic Act 1972, s. 4).

Procuration of such a girl for unlawful carnal connection (Sexual Offences Act 1956, s. 23).

Public service vehicle: must not be licensed as a driver (Road Traffic Act 1960, s. 144).

No court or justice shall impose imprisonment on him unless no other method of dealing with him is appropriate (P. of C.C. Act 1973, s. 19 (2)).

He can be ordered to attend at an attendance centre instead of imprisonment or for breach of a probation order (C.J. Act 1948, s. 19 as amended).

If remanded or committed in custody and 17 or over he should be sent to a remand centre (if available) or to prison (C. & Y.P. Act 1969, Sched. 5, para. 24).

Of or over 21 Except in certain cases, minimum age for driving a motor car constructed to draw a partially superimposed trailer and driven with such a trailer attached if the unladen weight of the

Of or over 21 motor car exceeds 2 tons increased from 17 to
–contd. 21 (M.V. (Minimum Age for driving) Regs. 1963).
Consenting males may take part in homosexual acts in private (Sexual Offences Act 1967, s. 1).

Under 24 In the case of a man under 24 his reasonable belief that the girl was 16 or over, will be a defence on the first occasion on which he is charged with the defilement of a girl under 16 (Sexual Offences Act 1956, s. 6).

Note.—The above ages refer to males and females unless otherwise indicated. After January 1, 1970, the time at which a person attains a particular age expressed in years shall be the commencement of the relevant anniversary of the date of his birth (Family Law Reform Act 1969, s. 9).

PART III – OFFENCES IN CONNECTION WITH PROPERTY

CHAPTER 13

BURGLARY

	Page		Page
Burglary	163	Aggravated Burglary .	163

Burglary – Under the Theft Act 1968, a person is guilty of burglary if (a) he enters any building or part of a building as a trespasser and with intent to commit any of the following offences—stealing anything in the building or part of a building in question; inflicting on any person therein any grievous bodily harm or raping any women therein; and doing unlawful damage to the building or anything therein, or (b) having entered any building or part of a building as a trespasser he steals or attempts to steal anything in the building or that part of it or inflicts or attempts to inflict on any person therein any grievous bodily harm.

References to a "building" shall apply also to an inhabited vehicle or vessel, and shall apply to any such vehicle or vessel at times when the person having a habitation in it is not there as well as at times when he is (s. 9). The offence is triable summarily with the accused's consent only in certain circumstances. (See M.C. Act 1952, Sched. 1. para (8). Chap. 4 (s. 29 (2)).

Aggravated Burglary – A person is guilty of aggravated burglary if he commits any burglary and at the time he has with him any firearm or imitation firearm, any weapon of offence, or any explosive (s. 10). The offence is not triable summarily (s. 29 (2)).

"Firearm" includes an airgun or air pistol, and "imitation firearm" means anything which has the appearance of being a firearm, whether capable of being discharged or not.

"Weapon of offence" means any article made or adapted for use for causing injury to or incapacitating a person, or intended by the person having it with him for such use.

"Explosive" means any article manufactured for the purpose of producing a practical effect by explosion, or intended by the person having it with him for that purpose.

CHAPTER 14

THEFT

	Page
Basic Definition of Theft	164
Robbery	167
Removal of Articles from Places open to the Public	167
Taking Motor Vehicle or other Conveyance without Authority	167
Abstracting Electricity	168
Extension to Thefts from Mails outside England and Wales and Robbery etc., on such a Theft	168
Obtaining Property by Deception	168
Obtaining Pecuniary Advantage by Deception	169
False Accounting	169
Liability of Company Officers for certain Offences by Company	170
False statements by Company Directors etc.	170
Suppression, etc., of Documents	170
Handling Stolen Goods	171
Advertising Rewards for Return of Goods Stolen or Lost	171
Scope of Offences Relating to Stolen Goods	172
Going Equipped for Stealing, Etc.	172
Interpretation	173
Taking or Killing Deer	173
Taking or Destroying Fish	173
Bankruptcy Offences	174
Compensation Orders	174

Basic Definition of Theft – A person is guilty of theft if he dishonestly appropriates property belonging to another with the intention of permanently depriving the other of it (Theft Act 1968, s. 1 (1)). It is immaterial whether the appropriation is made with a view to gain, or is made for the thief's own benefit (s. 1 (2)). The offence is triable summarily with accused's consent (s. 29 (2)).

The definitions in ss. 2–6 below shall have effect as regards the interpretation and operation of this section (and, except as otherwise provided by this Act, shall apply only for the purposes of this section) (s. 1 (3)).

"Dishonestly" – A person's appropriation of property belonging to another is not to be regarded as dishonest if he appropriates the property in the belief (a) that he has in law the right to deprive the other of it, on behalf of himself or of a third person; or (b) that he would have the other's consent if the other knew of the appropriation and the circumstances of it; or (c) (except where the property came to him as trustee or personal representative) that the person to whom the property belongs cannot be discovered by taking reasonable steps (s. 2 (1)). A person's appropriation of property belonging to another may be dishonest notwithstanding that he is willing to pay for the property (s. 2 (2)).

"Appropriates" – Any assumption by a person of the rights of an owner amounts to an appropriation, and this includes, where he has come by the property (innocently or not) without stealing it, any later assumption of a right to it by keeping or dealing with it as owner (s. 3 (1)). Where property or a right or interest in property is or purports to be transferred for value to a person acting in good faith, no later assumption by him of rights which he believed himself to be acquiring shall, by reason of any defect in the transferor's title, amount to theft of the property (s. 3 (2)).

"Property" – "Property" includes money and all other property, real or personal, including things in action and other intangible property (s. 4 (1)). (This definition applies generally for the purposes of the Act (s. 34 (1).)

A person cannot steal land, or things forming part of land and severed from it by him or by his directions, except in the following cases, (a) when he is a trustee or personal representative, or is authorised by power of attorney, or as liquidator of a company, or otherwise, to sell or dispose of land belonging to another, and he appropriates the land or anything forming part of it by dealing with it in breach of the confidence reposed in him; or (b) when he is not in possession of the land and appropriates anything forming part of the land by severing it or causing it to be severed, or after it has been severed; or (c) when, being in possession of the land under a tenancy he appropriates the whole or part of any fixture or structure let to be used with the land.

For purposes of this subsection "land" does not include incorporeal hereditaments; "tenancy" means a tenancy for years or any less period and includes an agreement for such a tenancy, but a person who after the end of a tenancy remains in possession as statutory tenant or otherwise is to be treated as having possession under the tenancy, and "let" shall be construed accordingly (s. 4 (2)).

A person who picks mushrooms growing wild on any land, or who picks flowers, fruit or foliage from a plant growing wild on any land, does not (although not in possession of the land) steal what he picks, unless he does it for reward or for sale or other commercial purpose.

For purpose of this subsection "mushroom" includes any fungus, and "plant" includes any shrub or tree (s. 4 (3)).

Wild creatures, tamed or untamed, shall be regarded as

property; but a person cannot steal a wild creature not tamed nor ordinarily kept in captivity, or the carcase of any such creature, unless either it has been reduced into possession by or on behalf of another person and possession of it has not since been lost or abandoned, or another person is in course of reducing it into possession (s. 4 (4)).

"Belonging to Another" – Property shall be regarded as belonging to any person having possession or control of it, or having in it any proprietary right or interest (not being an equitable interest arising only from an agreement to transfer or grant an interest (s. 5 (1)). (This subsection applies generally for the purposes of the Act (s. 34 (1).)

Where property is subject to a trust, the persons to whom it belongs shall be regarded as including any person having a right to enforce the trust and an intention to defeat the trust shall be regarded accordingly as an intention to deprive of the property any person having that right (s. 5 (2)).

Where a person receives property from or on account of another, and is under an obligation to the other to retain and deal with that property or its proceeds in a particular way, the property or proceeds shall be regarded (as against him) as belonging to the other (s. 5 (3)).

Where a person gets property by another's mistake, and is under an obligation to make restoration (in whole or in part) of the property or its proceeds or of the value thereof, then to the extent of that obligation the property or proceeds shall be regarded (as against him) as belonging to the person entitled to restoration, and an intention not to make restoration shall be regarded accordingly as an intention to deprive that person of the property or proceeds (s. 5 (4)).

Property of a corporation sole shall be regarded as belonging to the corporation notwithstanding a vacancy in the corporation (s. 5 (5)).

With the Intention of Permanently Depriving the other of it – A person appropriating property belonging to another without meaning the other permanently to lose the thing itself is nevertheless to be regarded as having the intention of permanently depriving the other of it if his intention is to treat the thing as his own to dispose of regardless of the other's rights; and a borrowing or lending of it may amount to so treating it if, but only if, the borrowing or lending is for a period and in circumstances making it equivalent to an outright taking or disposal (s. 6 (1)).

Without prejudice to the generality of subsection (1) above, where a person, having possession or control (lawfully or not) of property belonging to another, parts with the property under a condition as to its return which he may not be able to perform, this (if done for purposes of his own and without the other's authority) amounts to treating the property as his own to dispose of regardless of the other's rights (s. 6 (2)).

(This section shall apply for the purposes of s. 15 (obtaining property by deception), with the necessary adaptation of the reference to appropriating (s. 15).)

Robbery – A person is guilty of robbery if he steals, and immediately before or at the time of doing so, and in order to do so, he uses force on any person or puts or seeks to put any person in fear of being then and there subjected to force (s. 8). The offence is not triable summarily.

Removal of Articles from Places open to the Public – Subject to subsections (2) and (3) below, where the public have access to a building in order to view the building or part of it, or collection or part of a collection housed in it, any person who without lawful authority removes from the building or its grounds the whole or part of any article displayed or kept for display to the public in the building or that part of it or in its grounds commits an offence. "Collection" includes a collection got together for a temporary purpose, but references in this section to a collection do not apply to a collection made or exhibited for the purpose of effecting sales or other commercial dealings (s. 11 (1)).

It is immaterial for purposes of subsection (1) above, that the public's access to a building is limited to a particular period or particular occasion; but where anything removed from a building or its grounds is there otherwise than as forming part of, or being on loan for exhibition with, a collection intended for permanent exhibition to the public, the person removing it does not thereby commit an offence under this section unless he removes it on a day when the public have access to the building as mentioned in subsection (1) above (s. 11 (2)).

A person does not commit an offence under this section if he believes that he has lawful authority for the removal of the thing in question or that he would have it if the person entitled to give it knew of the removal and the circumstances of it (s. 11 (3)).

The offence is triable summarily with the accused's consent (s. 29 (2)).

Taking Motor Vehicle or other Conveyance without Authority – Subject to subsections (5) and (6) below, a person shall be guilty of an offence if, without having the consent of the owner or other lawful authority, he takes any conveyance for his own or another's use or, knowing that any conveyance has been taken without such authority, drives it or allows himself to be carried in or on it (s. 12 (1)). The offence is triable summarily with accused's consent (s. 29 (2)).

Offences under subsection (1) above and attempts to commit them shall be deemed for all purposes to be arrestable offences within the meaning of section 2 of the Criminal Law Act 1967 (s. 12 (3)).

Subsection (1) above shall not apply in relation to pedal cycles; but, subject to subsection (6) below, a person who, without having the consent of the owner or other lawful authority, takes a pedal cycle for his own or another's use, or rides a pedal cycle knowing it to have been taken without such authority, shall on summary conviction be liable to a fine (s. 12 (5)).

A person does not commit an offence under this section by anything done in the belief that he has lawful authority to do it or that he would have the owner's consent if the owner knew of his doing it and the circumstances of it (s. 12 (6)).

For purposes of this section—(a) "conveyance" means any conveyance constructed or adapted for the carriage of a person or persons whether by land, water or air, except that it does not include a conveyance constructed or adapted for use only under the control of a person not carried in or on it and "drive" shall be construed accordingly; and (b) "owner", in relation to a conveyance which is the subject of a hiring agreement or hire-purchase agreement, means the person in possession of the conveyance under that agreement (s. 12 (7)).

Abstracting of Electricity – A person who dishonestly uses without due authority, or dishonestly causes to be wasted or diverted, any electricity commits an offence (s. 13). The offence is triable summarily with accused's consent (s. 29 (2)).

Extension to Thefts from Mails outside England and Wales and Robbery, etc., on such a Theft – Where a person (a) steals or attempts to steal any mail bag or postal packet in the course of transmission as such between places in different jurisdictions in the British postal area, or any of the contents of such a mail bag or postal packet; or (b) in stealing or with intent to steal any such mail bag or postal packet or any of its contents, commits any robbery, attempted robbery or assault with intent to rob; then, notwithstanding that he does so outside England and Wales, he shall be guilty of committing or attempting to commit the offence against this Act as if he had done so in England or Wales, and he shall accordingly be liable to be prosecuted, tried and punished in England and Wales without proof that the offence was committed there. The reference to different jurisdictions in the British postal area is to be construed as referring to the several jurisdictions of England and Wales, of Scotland, of Northern Ireland, of the Isle of Man and of the Channel Islands. "Mail bag" includes any article serving the purpose of a mail bag (s. 14).

Obtaining Property by Deception – A person who by any deception dishonestly obtains property belonging to another, with the intention of permanently depriving the other of it, commits an offence (s. 15 (1)). The offence is triable summarily with the accused's consent (s. 29 (2)).

For purposes of this section a person is to be treated as obtaining property if he obtains ownership, possession or control of it, and "obtain" includes obtaining for another or enabling another to obtain or to retain (s. 15 (2)).

Section 6 above ("with the intention of permanently depriving the other of it") shall apply for purposes of this section, with the necessary adaption of the reference to appropriating, as it applies for purposes of section 1 (s. 15 (3)).

For purposes of this section "deception" means any deception (whether deliberate or reckless) by words or conduct as to fact or as to law, including a deception as to the present intentions of the person using the deception or any other person (s. 15 (4)).

Obtaining Pecuniary Advantage by Deception – A person who by deception dishonestly obtains for himself or another any pecuniary advantage commits an offence (s. 16 (1)). The offence is triable summarily with the accused's consent (s. 29 (2)).

The cases in which a pecuniary advantage within the meaning of this section is to be regarded as obtained for a person are cases where—(a) any debt or charge for which he makes himself liable or is or may become liable (including one not legally enforceable) is reduced or in whole or in part evaded or deferred; or (b) he is allowed to borrow by way of overdraft, or to take out any policy of insurance or annuity contract, or obtains an improvement of the terms on which he is allowed to do so; or (c) he is given the opportunity to earn remuneration or greater remuneration in an office or employment, or to win money by betting (s. 16 (2)).

For purposes of this section "deception" has the same meaning as in section 15 (s. 16 (3)).

False Accounting – Where a person dishonestly, with a view to gain for himself or another or with intent to cause loss to another, (a) destroys, defaces, conceals or falsifies any account or any record or document made or required for any accounting purpose; or (b) in furnishing information for any purpose produces or makes use of any account, or any such record or document as aforesaid, which to his knowledge is or may be misleading, false or deceptive in a material particular: he commits an offence (s. 17 (1)). The offence is triable summarily with accused's consent (s. 2 (2)).

For purposes of this section a person who makes or concurs in making in an account or other document an entry which is or may be misleading, false or deceptive in a material particular, or who omits or concurs in omitting a material particular from an account or other document, is to be treated as falsifying the account or document (s. 17 (2)).

Liability of Company Officers for certain Offences by Company – Where an offence committed by a body corporate under ss. 15, 16 or 17 of this Act is proved to have been committed with the consent or connivance of any director, manager, secretary or other similar officer of the body corporate, or any person who was purporting to act in any such capacity, he as well as the body corporate shall be guilty of that offence, and shall be liable to be proceeded against and punished accordingly (s. 18 (1)).

Where the affairs of a body corporate are managed by its members, this section shall apply in relation to the acts and defaults of a member in connection with his functions of management as if he were a director of the body corporate (s. 18 (2)).

False Statements by Company Directors etc. – Where an officer of a body corporate or unincorporated association (or person purporting to act as such), with intent to deceive members or creditors of the body corporate or association about its affairs, publishes or concurs in publishing a written statement or account which to his knowledge is or may be misleading, false or deceptive in a material particular, he commits an offence (s. 19 (1)). The offence is triable summarily with accused's consent (s. 29 (2)).

For purposes of this section a person who has entered into a security for the benefit of a body corporate or association is to be treated as a creditor of it (s. 19 (2)).

Where the affairs of a body corporate or association are managed by its members, this section shall apply to any statement which a member publishes or concurs in publishing in connection with his functions of management as if he were an officer of the body corporate or association (s. 19 (3)).

Suppression, etc., of Documents – A person who dishonestly, with a view to gain for himself or another or with intent to cause loss to another, destroys, defaces or conceals any valuable security, any will or other testamentary document or any original document of or belonging to, or filed or deposited in, any court of justice or any government department commits an offence (s. 20 (1)).

A person who dishonestly, with a view to gain for himself or another or with intent to cause loss to another, by any deception procures the execution of a valuable security commits an offence; and this subsection shall apply in relation to the making, acceptance, indorsement, alteration, cancellation or destruction in whole or in part of a valuable security, and in relation to the signing or sealing of any paper or other material in order that it may be made or converted into, or used or dealt with as, a valuable security, as if that were the execution of a valuable security (s. 20 (2)).

For purposes of this section "deception" has the same meaning as in section 15 of this Act, and "valuable security" means any document creating, transferring, surrendering or releasing any right to, in or over property, or authorising the payment of money or delivery of any property, or evidencing the creation, transfer, surrender or release of any such right, or the payment of money or delivery of any property, or the satisfaction of any obligation (s. 20 (3)).

These offences are triable summarily with accused's consent (s. 29 (2)). For definitions of "gain" and "loss" see s. 34 (2) (a) under "Interpretation", *post*.

Handling Stolen Goods – A person handles stolen goods if (otherwise than in the course of the stealing) knowing or believing them to be stolen goods he dishonestly receives the goods, or dishonestly undertakes or assists in their retention, removal, disposal or realisation by or for the benefit of another person, or if he arranges to do so (s. 22). The offence is triable summarily with the accused's consent unless the stolen goods are from an offence not committed in the United Kingdom (s. 29 (2)).

Goods obtained by deception (s. 15 (1)) or blackmail (s. 21) are regarded as stolen goods (s. 24 (4)). "Goods", except in so far as the context otherwise requires, includes money and every other description of property except land, and includes things severed from the land by stealing (s. 32 (2) (b)). (Land is not included in the definition of "goods"; therefore it seems that the offence of handling stolen goods does not apply to land or the proceeds of stolen land.)

Any number of persons may be charged in one indictment, with reference to the same theft, with having at different times or at the same time handled all or any of the stolen goods, and the persons so charged may be tried together (s. 27 (1)). On the trial of two or more persons indicted for jointly handling any stolen goods the jury may find any of the accused guilty if the jury are satisfied that he handled all or any of the stolen goods, whether or not he did so jointly with the other accused or any of them (s. 27 (2)).

In a prosecution for handling stolen goods, special evidence of guilty knowledge may be given. See "Extent of Evidence", Chap. 7.

For "Restitution of Stolen Property", see Chap. 18.

On the conviction of a pawnbroker for handling stolen goods the court may forfeit his licence. See Chap. 31.

Advertising Rewards for Return of Goods Stolen or Lost – Where any public advertisement of a reward for the return of any goods which have been stolen or lost uses any words to the effect that no questions will be asked, or that the person producing the goods will be safe from apprehension or inquiry, or that any money paid for the purchase of the goods or advanced by way of loan on them will be repaid, the person advertising the reward and any person who prints or publishes the advertisement commits an offence (s. 23).

Scope of Offences Relating to Stolen Goods – The provisions of the Act relating to goods which have been stolen shall apply whether the stealing occurred in England or Wales or elsewhere, and whether it occurred before or after the commencement of the Act, provided that the stealing (if not an offence under the Act) amounted to an offence where and at the time when the goods were stolen; and references to stolen goods shall be construed accordingly (s. 24 (1)).

For purposes of those provisions references to stolen goods shall include, in addition to the goods originally stolen and parts of them (whether in their original state or not), (a) any other goods which directly or indirectly represent or have at any time represented the stolen goods in the hands of the thief as being the proceeds of any disposal or realisation of the whole or part of the goods stolen or of goods so representing the stolen goods; and (b) any other goods which directly or indirectly represent or have at any time represented the stolen goods in the hands of a handler of the stolen goods or any part of them as being the proceeds of any disposal or realisation of the whole or part of the stolen goods handled by him or of goods so representing them (s. 24 (2)).

But no goods shall be regarded as having continued to be stolen goods after they have been restored to the person from whom they were stolen or to other lawful possession or custody, or after that person and any other person claiming through him have otherwise ceased as regards those goods to have any right to restitution in respect of the theft (s. 24 (3)).

For purposes of the provisions of the Act relating to goods which have been stolen (including subsections (1) to (3) above) goods obtained in England or Wales or elsewhere either by blackmail or in the circumstances described in section 15 (1) of the Act shall be regarded as stolen (s. 24 (4)).

Going Equipped for Stealing, etc. – A person shall be guilty of an offence if, when not at his place of abode, he has with him any article for use in the course of or in connection with any burglary, theft or cheat (s. 25 (1)).

Where a person is charged with an offence under this section, proof that he had with him any article made or adapted for use in committing a burglary, theft or cheat shall be evidence that he had it with him for such use (s. 25 (3)).

Any person may arrest without warrant anyone who is, or

whom he, with reasonable cause, suspects to be, committing an offence under this section (s. 25 (4)).

For purposes of this section an offence under section 12 (1) of taking a conveyance shall be treated as theft, and "cheat" means an offence under section 15 (s. 25 (5)).

The offence is triable summarily with the accused's consent (s. 29 (2)).

Interpretation – Sections 4 (1) (part of the definition of "property") and 5 (1) (part of the definition of "belonging to another") of this Act shall apply generally for purposes of this Act as they apply for purposes of section 1 (s. 34 (1)).

For purposes of this Act (a) "gain" and "loss" are to be construed as extending only to gain or loss in money or other property, but as extending to any such gain or loss whether temporary or permanent; and (i) "gain" includes a gain by keeping what one has, as well as a gain by getting what one has not; and (ii) "loss" includes a loss by not getting what one might get, as well as a loss by parting with what one has; (b) "goods", except in so far as the context otherwise requires, includes money and every other description of property except land, and includes things severed from the land by stealing (s. 34 (2)).

Taking or Killing Deer – A person who unlawfully takes or kills, or attempts to take or kill, any deer in inclosed land where deer are usually kept commits an offence (Sched. 1, para. 1 (1)).

Any person may arrest without warrant anyone who is, or whom he, with reasonable cause, suspects to be, committing an offence under this paragraph (Sched. 1, para. 1 (2)).

Taking or Destroying Fish – Subject to sub-paragraph (2) below, a person who unlawfully takes or destroys, or attempts to take or destroy, any fish in water which is private property or in which there is any private right of fishery commits an offence (Sched. 1, para. 2 (1)).

Sub-paragraph (1) above shall not apply to taking or destroying fish by angling in the daytime (that is to say, in the period beginning one hour before sunrise and ending one hour after sunset); but a person who by angling in the daytime unlawfully takes or destroys, or attempts to take or destroy, any fish in water which is private property or in which there is any private right of fishery commits an offence (Sched. 1, para. 2 (2)).

The court by which a person is convicted of an offence under this paragraph may order the forfeiture of anything which, at the time of the offence, he had with him for use for taking or destroying fish (Sched. 1, para. 2 (3)).

Any person may arrest without warrant anyone who is, or whom he, with reasonable cause, suspects to be, committing an offence under sub-paragraph (1) above, and may seize from any person who is, or whom he, with reasonable cause, suspects to be, committing any offence under this paragraph anything which on that person's conviction of the offence would be liable to be forfeited under sub-paragraph (3) above (Sched. 1, para. 2 (4)).

Bankruptcy Offences – The Bankruptcy Act 1914 creates many offences against the criminal law, and the following are some that may be committed by bankrupts:

(1) Fraudulently removing property to the value of £10 or upwards (s. 154 (4));
(2) Concealing, destroying, falsifying, etc., books and documents (s. 154 (9));
(3) Obtaining credit to the extent of £10 or upwards from any person without informing him that he is an undischarged bankrupt (s. 155); obtaining cash with an order for services never rendered or for goods never delivered is not "obtaining credit" (*Fisher* v. *Raven* (1963)).
(4) An undischarged bankrupt engaging in business under another name and not disclosing to all persons with whom he does business the name under which he was adjudicated bankrupt (s. 155);
(5) Concealing, disposing or removing property with intent to defraud creditors (s. 156). See also Debtors Act 1869 which deals with persons defrauding their creditors by transferring or removing their property.

Quitting England and taking with him, or attempting or making preparation to quit England and take with him, any part of his property to the amount of £20 or upwards which ought by law to be divided amongst his creditors is an offence (s. 159).

Certain of these offences can only be prosecuted on order of the court and by s. 164 summary proceedings shall not be taken after one year after first discovery of the offence nor after 3 years from the date of the offence. See Stone, title "Bankrupt and Fraudulent Debtors".

Compensation Orders – A court by or before which a person is convicted of an offence, in addition to dealing with him in any other way, may make a "compensation order" requiring him to pay compensation for any personal injury, loss or damage resulting from that offence or any other offence which is taken into consideration by the court in determining sentence (P. of C.C. Act 1973, s. 35 (1)).

In the case of an offence under the Theft Act 1968, where the property in question is recovered, any damage to the property occurring while it was out of the owner's possession shall be treated for the purposes of s. 35 (1) above, as having resulted from the offence, however and by whomsoever the damage was caused (s. 35 (2)).

No compensation order shall be made in respect of loss suffered by the dependants of a person in consequence of his death, and no such order shall be made in respect of injury, loss or damage due to an accident arising out of the presence of a motor vehicle on a road, except such damage as is treated by s. 35 (2) above as resulting from an offence under the Theft Act (s. 35 (3)).

The compensation to be paid under a compensation order made by a Magistrates' Court in respect of any offences of which the court has convicted the offender shall not exceed £400 (s. 35 (5)).

CHAPTER 15

CRIMINAL DAMAGE

	Page		Page
Destroying or Damaging Property	176	Possession of articles with Intent	177
Threats	176	Search Warrant	177

The Criminal Damage Act 1971 re-states and modernises the law with regard to the offence of destroying or damaging another's property, and the serious offence of destroying or damaging any property intending to endanger the life of another or being reckless in that regard. It has abolished the common law offence of arson. All offences under this Act are "arrestable offences".

Destroying or Damaging Property – A person who without lawful excuse destroys or damages any property belonging to another intending to destroy or damage such property or being reckless as to whether any such property would be destroyed or damaged shall be guilty of an offence (s. 1 (1)).

A person who without lawful excuse destroys any property, whether belonging to himself or another: (a) intending to destroy or damage any property or being reckless as to whether any property would be destroyed or damaged; and (b) intending by the destruction or damage to endanger the life of another or being reckless as to whether the life of another would be thereby endangered, shall be guilty of an offence (s. 1 (2)).

An offence committed under this section by destroying or damaging property by fire shall be charged as arson (s. 1 (3)).

Threats to Destroy or Damage Property – A person who without lawful excuse makes to another a threat, intending that that other would fear it would be carried out: (a) to destroy or damage any property belonging to that other or a third person; or (b) to destroy or damage his own property in a way which he knows is likely to endanger the life of that other or a third person, shall be guilty of an offence (s. 2).

Possessing anything with Intent to Destroy or Damage Property - A person who has anything in his custody or under his control intending without lawful excuse to use it or cause or permit another to use it: (a) to destroy or damage any property belonging to some other person; or (b) to destroy or damage his own or the user's property in a way which he knows is likely to endanger the life of some other person, shall be guilty of an offence (s. 3).

WITHOUT LAWFUL EXCUSE - Section 5 applies to any offence under s. 1 (1) above and any offence under ss. 2 or 3 above other than one involving a threat by the person charged to destroy or damage property in a way which he knows is likely to endanger the life of another or involving an intent by the person charged to use or cause or permit the use of something in his custody or under his control so to destroy or damage property (s. 5 (1)).

A person charged with an offence to which this section applies shall, whether or not he would be treated for the purposes of this Act as having a lawful excuse apart from this subsection, be treated for those purposes as having a lawful excuse: (a) if at the time of the act or acts alleged to constitute the offence he believed that the person or persons whom he believed to be entitled to consent to the destruction of or damage to the property in question has so consented, or would have so consented to it if he or they had known of the destruction or damage and its circumstances; or (b) if he destroyed or damaged or threatened to destroy or damage the property in question or, in the case of a charge of an offence under s. 3 above, intended to use or cause or permit the use of something to destroy or damage it, in order to protect property belonging to himself or another or a right or interest in property which was or which he believed to be vested in himself or another, and at the time of the act or acts alleged to constitute the offence, he believed: (1) that the property, right or interest was in immediate need of protection; (2) that the means of protection adopted or proposed to be adopted were or would be reasonable having regard to all the circumstances (s. 5 (2)). It is immaterial whether a belief is justified or not if it is honestly held (s. 5 (3)). For the purposes of s. 5 (2) above, a right or interest in property includes any right or privilege in or over land, whether created by grant, licence or otherwise (s. 5 (4)). This section shall not be construed as casting doubt on any defence recognised by law as a defence to criminal charges (s. 5 (5)).

Search Warrant - For things intended for use in committing offences of criminal damage: If it is made to appear by information on oath before a justice of the peace that there is reasonable cause to believe that any person has in his custody or under his control or on his premises anything which there is reasonable cause to believe has been used or is intended for use without lawful excuse: (a) to destroy or damage property belonging to another; or (b) to destroy or damage any property in a way likely to endanger the life of another, the justice may grant a warrant authorising any constable to search for and seize that thing (s. 6 (1)).

A constable who is authorised under this section to search premises for anything may enter (if need be by force) and search the premises accordingly and may seize anything which he believes to have been used or to be intended to be used as aforesaid (s. 6 (2)).

The Police (Property) Act 1897 (disposal of property in the possession of the police) shall apply to property which has come into the possession of the police under the section as it applies to property which has come into the possession of the police in the circumstances mentioned in that Act (s. 6 (3)).

Evidence in connection with offence under the Act: A person shall not be excused, by reason that to do so may incriminate that person or the wife or husband of that person of an offence under the Act: (a) from answering any question put to that person in proceedings for the recovery or administration of any property, for the execution of any trust or for an account of any property or dealings with property; or (b) from complying with any order made in any such proceedings; but no statement or admission made by a person in answering a question put or complying with an order made as aforesaid shall, in proceedings for an offence under this Act, be admissible in evidence against that person or (unless they married after the making of the statement or admission) against the wife or husband of that person (s. 9).

In this Act, "property" means property of a tangible nature, whether real or personal, including money, and: (a) including wild creatures which have been tamed or are ordinarily kept in captivity, and any other wild creatures or their carcasses if, but only if, they have been reduced into possession which has not been lost or abandoned, or are in the course of being reduced into possession; but (b) not including mushrooms growing wild on any land or flowers, fruit or foliage of a plant growing wild on any land. "Mushroom" includes any fungus, "plant" includes any shrub or tree (s. 10 (1)).

Property shall be treated for the purposes of this Act as belonging to any person: (a) having the custody or control of it; (b) having in it any proprietary right or interest (not being an equitable interest arising only from an agreement to transfer an interest); or (c) having a charge on it (s. 10 (2)).

Where property is subject to a trust, the persons to whom it belongs shall be so treated as including any person having a right to enforce the trust (s. 10 (3)).

CHAPTER 16

COINAGE

	Page		Page
Arrest, Seizure and Evidence	181	Counterfeit Currency (Convention) Act 1935 .	182

Counterfeiting the Sovereign's money was regarded as a most heinous crime, and in 1351 the Statute of Treasons made it high treason. It is an offence under the Coinage Offences Act 1936.

"Current coin" means any coin which has been coined in any of Her Majesty's mints, or is lawfully current, by proclamation or otherwise, in any part of Her Majesty's Dominions or is lawfully current in any foreign country (1936 Act, s. 17.)

"Counterfeit coin" means coin which is not current coin but is falsely made resembling any current coin, and includes any current coin which has been gilt, silvered or altered in any manner so as to resemble any current coin of a higher denomination (s. 17).

"Uttering coin" means the passing off or putting into circulation of coin.

"Uttering" includes "tendering" and "passing off". If a coin is offered in payment but refused by the person to whom it was tendered it is an "uttering". The offence is charged as "tendering, uttering or putting off".

"Impairing coin" means the clipping, diminishing or lightening of current gold or silver coin with intent to pass it off when so diminished as current coin.

Current gold or silver coin suspected to have been diminished otherwise than by reasonable wearing may be bent, cut, broken or defaced by any person to whom it is tendered, the loss to fall on the person tendering if it proves to be impaired of counterfeit (s. 14).

The offences may be grouped in four classes:

(1) MAKING OR ALTERING

Falsely making or counterfeiting any coin resembling any current coin (s. 1).

Casing over or colouring any coin resembling any current gold or silver coin, or gilding, silvering, colouring, altering, filing or preparing in any way any coin or piece of metal with intent to make it resemble or pass for current gold or silver coin (s. 2).

Impairing, diminishing or lightening any current gold or silver coin with intent that it might then pass as current coin (s. 3).

Defacing any current coin by stamping thereon any names or words. Coin so defaced is not legal tender (s. 4).

Without lawful authority or excuse, knowingly making, mending, buying, selling or having in possession any coining tools or instruments (s. 9).

Without lawful authority or excuse, knowingly conveying coining tools, coins, or metal out of any of Her Majesty's mints (s. 10).

Without lawful authority or excuse, making, selling or having in possession for sale, any medal, cast, coin, or other like thing made wholly or partially of metal and either resembling current gold or silver coin or having a device resembling a device on such current coin or being so made that it can, by colouring, etc., be made to resemble such current coin (s. 8). There is no power of arrest without warrant for this offence (s. 11).

No piece of gold, silver, copper or bronze, or of any metal or mixed metal, of any value whatever, shall be made or issued except by or with the authority of the Mint, as a coin or a token for money, or as purporting that the holder thereof is entitled to demand any value denoted thereon (Coinage Act 1971, s. 9 (1)). It is a summary offence to contravene the provisions of this section (s. 9 (2)).

It is an offence, except under the authority of a Treasury licence, for any person to melt down, or break up any metal coin which is for the time being current in the U.K., or which, having been current there, has at any time after May 16, 1969 ceased to be so (Coinage Act 1971, s. 10 (1)).

(2) DEALING IN COUNTERFEIT COIN

Without lawful authority or excuse, buying, selling or trafficking in any counterfeit coin (complete or incomplete) at a lower rate or value than the same purports to be (s. 6).

Without lawful authority or excuse, knowingly importing into this country any counterfeit gold or silver coin (s. 7).

Without lawful authority or excuse, knowingly exporting counterfeit coin (s. 7).

Selling any coin, medal, etc., resembling current gold or silver coin (s. 8). See above under "Making or Altering".

(3) UTTERING

Knowingly uttering any false or counterfeit current coin (s. 5).

Knowingly uttering any counterfeit current gold or silver coin and having in possession at the time any other such coin, or on the same day or within 10 days knowingly uttering any other such coin (s. 5).

Uttering counterfeit current gold or silver coin of the realm, or knowingly having 3 or more such coins in possession, having been previously convicted of a similar offence or of any offence which used to be a felony under the Act (s. 5).

With intent to defraud, uttering as current gold or silver coin, any coin, medal, etc., resembling current coin but being of less value (s. 5).

Uttering any current coin of the realm defaced by having words, etc., stamped on it. Summary offence, but the consent of the Attorney-General is required for a prosecution (s. 4, and see under "Making", above).

The uttering is complete even if the counterfeit is not complete (s. 5).

(4) POSSESSION

Knowingly having in possession three or more counterfeit current gold or silver coins with intent to utter same (s. 5).

Knowingly having in possession three or more counterfeit current copper coins with intent to utter same (s. 5).

Unlawfully and knowingly having in possession any clippings, filings, dust, etc., obtained by impairing or diminishing any current gold or silver coin (s. 3). As regards possession of coinage tools, see "Making", above.

Having in possession for sale any coin, medal, etc., resembling current gold or silver coin (s. 8). See under "Making", above.

Note.—References to silver coin in the Coinage Offences Act 1936 shall include references to coin of cupro-nickel (Coinage Act 1971, s. 12 (1)).

Arrest, Seizure and Evidence – Any person may arrest anyone found committing any offence against the Act, except the offence under s. 8, regarding medals, etc. (s. 11).

Counterfeit coin, coining instruments, or any filings, dust, etc., produced by sweating gold or silver coin, found in any place or in possession of anyone without lawful excuse, may be seized by any person and brought before a Justice. On reasonable cause of suspicion a justice may issue a warrant to search premises by day or by night, and seize counterfeit coin, instruments, etc. (s. 11).

Persons found uttering counterfeit coins may be arrested without warrant. All the counterfeit coins should be secured and marked so that they may afterwards be identified.

Counterfeiting may be proved by circumstantial evidence, such as finding coining instruments and pieces of finished or partly finished counterfeit coin on defendant's premises. The offence is complete even though the counterfeiting may not have been quite finished (s. 1).

Any credible witness may prove coin counterfeit (s. 13).

Where "lawful authority or excuse" is put forward as a defence such must be proved by the accused (ss. 6–10).

"Possession" under the Act includes not only the personal possession or custody of the article, but also the knowingly having it in the possession of any other person or in some building or place (s. 17).

Intent may be proved by evidence sufficient to allow the jury to infer it; for example, accused attempted to pass the coin, or had similar coins in his possession. Guilty knowledge may be proved by evidence that accused had previously uttered counterfeit coin or had other counterfeit coins in his possession at the time.

Any offence against the Coinage Offences Act 1936 must be reported to the Director of Public Prosecutions. See Appendix III.

Counterfeit Currency (Convention) Act 1935 – This Act declares that currency notes issued by the Government of any country outside the United Kingdom and legal tender in that country, are deemed to be bank-notes within the Forgery Act 1913 and this Act (s. 1).

Section 2 of the Revenue Act 1889 which prohibits the importation of imitation coin, shall apply also to imitation foreign coin (s. 3). See also the Customs and Excise Act 1952.

Attempts to commit offences in connection with counterfeit currency are extraditable (s. 4).

CHAPTER 17

FORGERY

	Page		Page
Forgery	183	Offences as regards Paper Money . . .	185
Principal Forgery Offences	184		

Forgery – Forgery is the making of a false document (or writing) in order that it may be used as genuine or the counterfeiting of certain specified seals and dies, and forgery with intent to defraud or deceive is punishable. This definition is given in s. 1 of the Forgery Act 1913 which consolidated and amended the law relating to forgery.

At common law forgery was the fraudulent making or alteration of a writing to the prejudice of another man's right.

A document is false within the meaning of the Act:

(1) If the whole or any material part thereof purports to be made by or on behalf of a person who did not make it or authorise its making, or

(2) If, though properly authorised, the time or place of making or the identifying mark is falsely stated therein, or

(3) If any unauthorised material alteration has been made in it, or

(4) If it purports to be made by or for a fictitious or deceased person, or

(5) If it has been made with the intention that it should pass as having been made by some person other than the maker or authoriser (s. 1).

Under s. 35, C.J. Act 1925 a document false in any way and made to be used as genuine is a forged document.

The uttering of a forged document, etc., is committed when a person, knowing the same to be forged and with intent to defraud or deceive, uses, offers, publishes, delivers, disposes of, tenders or exposes for payment, sale or exchange, exchanges, tenders in evidence or puts it off in any way (s. 6).

In a prosecution for forgery the intent should be shown. The intent to defraud applies particularly to documents of a private nature, such as deeds, wills, etc., and the intent to deceive mainly concerns documents of an official nature, such as birth certificates, court records, etc. To deceive is to induce a person to believe a thing is true which is false, and to defraud is to induce by deceit a person to act to his injury. It is not necessary to prove intent to defraud or deceive any particular person (s. 17). Such intent generally is sufficient.

Under section 16 of the Forgery Act 1913 a search warrant can issue, on reasonable cause to believe that any person has in his custody or possession, without lawful authority or excuse, any banknote, or implement or materials for the forgery of a banknote, or any forged document, seal or die or any implements, etc., used or intended to be used for the forgery of any document. This warrant authorises search and seizure.

While the principal statute is the Forgery Act 1913 other statutes created forgery offences; for instance, the Forgery Act 1861, the Stamp Duties Management Act 1891, the Post Office Act 1953, and the Customs and Excise Act 1952. The main offences under these Acts will now be given, followed by the offences relating to paper money.

Principal Forgery Offences

(1) Forgery, with intent to defraud, of many specified valuable documents, such as wills, probates, bank-notes, deeds, bonds, valuable securities, insurance policies, etc. (1913 Act, s. 2). Some of these offences if accused consents may be dealt with summarily. (M.C. Act, 1952 s. 19, and Sched. 1, and C.J. Act 1967, s. 27.)

(2) Forgery, with intent to defraud or deceive, of certain documents, mostly of an official nature, such as records of births, baptisms, marriages, deaths or burials, marriage licences, documents of any court of justice, etc. (1913 Act, s. 3).

Any offence against these two sections (2 and 3) must be reported to the Director of Public Prosecutions. See Appendix III.

(3) Forgery, with intent to defraud, of any document (1913 Act, s. 4). This offence is triable summarily with consent of accused (C.J. Act 1967, s. 27).

(4) Forgery, with intent to defraud or deceive, of any public document (1913 Act, s. 4). This offence is triable summarily with consent of accused (C.J. Act 1967, s. 27).

(5) Forgery with intent to defraud or deceive, of certain seals and dies, such as the Great Seal, or a seal of any court of justice (1913 Act, s. 5).

(6) Uttering, knowingly and with intent, any forged document, seal or die (1913 Act, s. 6).

(7) With intent to defraud, demanding, receiving or obtaining or endeavouring to obtain any money or other property on forged instruments (1913 Act, s. 7). May be dealt with summarily if the value does not exceed £100 and accused consents (M.C. Act 1952, s. 19, and Sched. 1).

(8) Without lawful authority or excuse, having in possession any forged stamp, die or label, as specified (1913 Act, s. 8). This does not include any die used for marking of gold or silver wares (Hallmarking Act 1973, Sched. 7).

(9) Altering a money order, including a postal order, with intent to defraud, or knowingly offering or uttering any such altered money order (Post Office Act 1953, s. 23 as amended by the 1969 Act, Sched. 4).

(10) An officer of any court knowingly uttering any false copy or certificate of any record, or any person knowingly delivering any false process or order of court to any person or professing to act under any such false process (Forgery Act 1861, s. 28).

(11) Acknowledging any recognisance or other instrument before any court or authorised person, in the name of any other person, without lawful authority or excuse (Forgery Act 1861, s. 34).

(12) Destroying, injuring, falsifying, etc., any official records of births, baptisms, marriages, deaths or burials (Forgery Act 1861, ss. 36 and 37).

(13) Fraudulently printing, altering, obliterating, mutilating, or "faking" in any way, any stamp (impressed or adhesive indicating any duty or fee, s. 27), or selling or using any fraudulently made stamp or knowingly and without lawful excuse having a fraudulently made stamp in possession (Stamp Duties Management Act 1891, s. 13). Offences under this section may be dealt with summarily with the accused's consent (M.C. Act 1952, s. 19 and Sched. 1).

(14) Forgery of any trade mark. See "Trade Marks", Chap. 32.

(15) Forgery of any passport or the knowingly making of a false statement for the purpose of procuring a passport (Criminal Justice Act 1925, s. 36). This offence may be punished summarily with consent of accused (M.C. Act 1952, s. 19 and Sched. 1). See "Aliens", Chap. 29.

(16) Forgery or deceitful use of documents, etc. (Road Traffic Act 1960, s. 233). This section applies to permits issued under the Transport Act 1968, s. 30. See also R.T. Act 1972, s. 169.

(17) Forgery of a motor index mark or licence or registration document is a summary offence (Vehicles (Excise) Act 1971, s. 26).

(18) Forgery, with intent to deceive, of documents required or authorised for the purposes of the Mental Health Act 1959.

Offences as regards Paper Money

(1) Forgery, with intent to defraud, of any bank-note (defined in s. 18 of the Act) or valuable security (such as a currency note) (1913 Act, s. 2).

(2) Uttering, knowingly and with intent, any forged bank-note or valuable security (1913 Act, s. 6).

(3) Without lawful authority or excuse, knowingly purchasing, receiving or having in possession any forged bank-note (1913 Act, s. 8).

(4) Without lawful authority or excuse, making, using or knowingly having in possession, any paper intended to resemble and pass as special paper used for bank-notes, Treasury bills or London County bills or as revenue paper, or the instruments for making or dealing with such paper (1913 Act, s. 9).

(5) Without lawful authority or excuse, engraving or making on any material any words or devices resembling those on bank-notes or stock or dividend certificates, or having such engraved material in possession, or having in possession any paper upon which such words or devices have been printed (1913 Act, s. 9).

(6) Making, using or uttering for any purpose whatsoever any document purporting to be, or in any way resembling, or so nearly resembling as to be calculated to deceive, any currency or bank-note. Summary offence. Such documents and their plates, etc., may be ordered to be destroyed. Any person whose name appears on such a document is *prima facie* liable and he must give the name and address of the printer to the police (Criminal Justice Act 1925, s. 38).

(7) The Currency and Bank-Notes Acts 1928 and 1954 allow the Bank of England to issue bank-notes of such denominations as the Treasury may approve, and such bank-notes shall be current and legal tender.

If any person prints, stamps or impresses on any bank-note, any words, letters or figures, he will commit a summary offence (1928 Act, s. 12).

Under the Counterfeit Currency (Convention) Act 1935 currency notes of other countries which are legal tender are deemed to be bank-notes within the Forgery Act 1913 (s. 1), and any forged bank-note or plant for forging same which is seized shall by order of the court or justice be delivered to the Secretary of State or to any person authorised by him (s. 2). (The Commissioner of Police of the Metropolis has been so authorised.) Attempts to forge same are extraditable (s. 4).

CHAPTER 18

PROPERTY

	Page		Page
Property in General .	187	Public Stores . . .	193
Treasure Trove . .	187	Wrecks	193
Police (Property) Act 1897	188		
Restitution of Stolen Property	190		

Property in General – The word "property" has several meanings, but in police circles it is used to signify money, things or goods which come into the possession of the police, such as stolen property, lost property, prisoners' property, etc.

In legal textbooks the word "property" is also used to indicate the exclusive right of possessing, enjoying and disposing of a thing; in other words, to mean the title or right of ownership that an owner possesses with respect to a thing which is his property.

What the expression "property" in the Theft Act 1968 includes is given fully in s. 4 of the Act. See "Property", Chap. 14.

The owner, therefore, is said to have property in a thing which he owns. Thus the word "property" may in one sense mean an article, thing, house, or estate, and it may be used in another sense to indicate the owner's rights over that article, thing, house, or estate.

The great majority of crimes are committed in respect of property, especially as regards its possession.

Treasure Trove – Treasure trove (or treasure found) is where any gold or silver, in coin, plate or bullion is found hidden in a house or in the earth or other private place.

If the owner is unknown the treasure belongs to the Crown. The finding should be reported to the coroner, who may hold an inquest to determine whether articles of gold or silver so found are treasure trove or not. See "Courts of Justice", Chap. 4.

Concealing the discovery of any treasure trove is an offence, being an offence at common law, and the offence may be committed by a person who receives the treasure trove knowing it is treasure trove from the finder who was ignorant of its nature.

Police (Property) Act 1897 – The Police (Property) Act 1897 deals with the disposal of property which has come into police possession in connection with criminal matters.

On application either by the police or by a claimant of such property or where the owner cannot be ascertained a magistrates' court may make an order disposing, as it thinks right, of any property which has come into the possession of the police:

(1) In connection with their investigation of a suspected offence (C.J. Act 1972, s. 58), or

(2) Under s. 26 (4) of the Theft Act 1968 (property which has come into the possession of the police under this section), or

(3) Under s. 66 of the Metropolitan Police Act 1839 (seizure of suspected stolen property), or s. 48 of the City of London Police Act 1839.

Within 6 months after such an order a person may take legal proceedings for recovery of the property against the possessor under the order (s. 1).

Regulations of September 1975, which came into operation on November 1, 1975, apply to:

(1) . . . property in the possession of the police to which the Police (Property) Act 1897 applies and in respect of which—

- (a) in the case of property in the possession of the police by virtue of section 43 of the Powers of Criminal Courts Act 1973, no application by a claimant has been made within six months of the making of the order under that section or no such application has succeeded;
- (b) in any other case the owner has not been ascertained and no order of a competent court has been made.

(2) Subject to the following provisions of this Regulation, property to which this Regulation applies (other than money) shall be sold.

(3) If the Chief Officer of Police is satisfied that the nature of the property is such that it is not in the public interest that it should be sold, it shall be destroyed or otherwise disposed of in accordance with his directions.

(4) Subject to s. 2 (3) of the Police (Property) Act 1897 (which provides for the sale of property which is perishable or the custody of which involves unreasonable expense or inconvenience) property which is in the possession of the police by virtue of section 43 of the Powers of Criminal Courts Act 1973 shall not be disposed of until the expiration of six months from the date on which the order in respect of the property was made under that section on the conviction of an offender or, if an application by a claimant of the property

has been made within that period or the offender has appealed against the conviction or sentence, until that application or appeal has been determined; and any other property shall not be disposed of until it has remained in the possession of the police for a year.

(5) The proceeds of all sales under this Regulation and any money to which this Regulation applies shall be paid to the Police Authority and shall be kept in a separate account to be called the Police Property Act Fund (hereinafter referred to as "the Fund").

(6) The Fund, or any part thereof, may be invested as the Police Authority think fit and the income derived from the investments shall be added to and become part of the Fund.

(7) The moneys, including income from investments, standing to the credit of the Fund shall be applicable:

(*a*) to defray expenses incurred in the conveyance, storage and safe custody of the property and in connection with its sale and otherwise in executing these Regulations;

(*b*) to pay reasonable compensation, the amount of which shall be fixed by the Police Authority, to persons by whom property has been delivered to the police;

(*c*) to make payments of such amounts as the Police Authority may determine for such charitable purposes as they may select.

(8) The Chief Officer of Police may, at the request of the Police Authority, exercise the powers and perform the duties of the Police Authority under the foregoing paragraphs of this Regulation.

(9) The Fund shall be audited by an auditor nominated for that purpose by the Police Authority (S.I. 1975 No. 1474, Reg. 4).

Where any property has been taken from a person charged before a magistrates' court with any offence, the police shall report same to the court and the court considering that it or part of it may be returned to the accused consistently with the interests of justice and the safe custody of the accused, may direct that it or part of it shall be returned to the accused or to such other person as he may require (M.C. Act 1952, s. 39).

Where a person is convicted of an offence punishable on indictment with not less than two years' imprisonment and the court by or before which he is convicted is satisfied that any property which was in his possession or under his control at the time of his apprehension—

(a) has been used for the purpose of committing, or facilitating the commission of, any offence; or

(b) was intended by him to be used for that purpose,

the court may make an order under this section in respect of that property (P. of C.C. Act 1973, s. 43 (1)).

References in this section to facilitating the commission of an offence include references to the taking of any steps after it has been committed for the purpose of disposing of any property to which it relates or of avoiding apprehension or detection (s. 43 (2)).

An order under this section shall operate to deprive the offender of his rights, if any, in the property to which it relates, and the property shall (if not already in their possession) be taken into the possession of the police (s. 43 (3)).

The Police (Property) Act 1897 shall apply, with the following modifications, to property which is in the possession of the police by virtue of this section—

(a) no application shall be made under s. 1 (1) of that Act by any claimant of the property after the expiration of six months from the date on which the order in respect of the property was made under this section; and
(b) no such application shall succeed unless the claimant satisfies the court either that he had not consented to the offender having possession of the property or that he did not know, and had no reason to suspect, that the property was likely to be used for the purpose mentioned in sub-s. (1) of this section (s. 43 (4)).

In relation to such property as aforesaid, the power to make regulations under s. 2 (1) of the said Act of 1897 (disposal of property in cases where the owner of the property has not been ascertained and no order of a competent court has been made with respect thereto) shall include power to make regulations for disposal in cases where no application by a claimant of the property has been made within the period specified in sub-s. (4) (a) of this section or no such application has succeeded (s. 43 (5)).

Restitution of Stolen Property – When property is stolen, the thief deprives the owner of all the benefits of his ownership, but he does not deprive the owner of his ownership. The article itself is gone, but the owner still retains his property in the article: that is, his legal right of ownership over the article.

Where goods have been stolen, and either a person is convicted of any offence with reference to the theft (whether or not the stealing is the gist of his offence) or a person is convicted of any other offence but such an offence as aforesaid is taken into consideration in determining his sentence, the court by or before which the offender is convicted may on the conviction exercise any of the following powers—

(a) the court may order anyone having possession or control of the goods to restore them to any person entitled to recover them from him; or

(b) on the application of a person entitled to recover from the person convicted any other goods directly or indirectly representing the first-mentioned goods (as being the proceeds of any disposal or realisation of the whole or part of them or of goods so representing them), the court may order those other goods to be delivered or transferred to the applicant; or

(c) the court may order that a sum not exceeding the value of the first-mentioned goods shall be paid, out of any money of the person convicted which was taken out of his possession on his apprehension, to any person who, if those goods were in the possession of the person convicted, would be entitled to recover them from him (s. 28 (1)).

Where under sub-s. (1) above the court has power on a person's conviction to make an order against him both under paragraph (b) and under para. (c) with reference to the stealing of the same goods, the court may make orders under both paragraphs provided that the person in whose favour the orders are made does not thereby recover more than the value of those goods (s. 28 (2)).

Where under sub-s. (1) above the court on a person's conviction makes an order under para. (a) for the restoration of any goods, and it appears to the court that the person convicted has sold the goods to a person acting in good faith, or has borrowed money on the security of them from a person so acting, the court may order that there shall be paid to the purchaser or lender, out of any money of the person convicted which was taken out of his possession on his apprehension, a sum not exceeding the amount paid for the purchase by the purchaser or, as the case may be, the amount owed to the lender in respect of the loan" (s. 28 (3)).

The court shall not exercise the powers conferred by this section unless in the opinion of the court the relevant facts sufficiently appear from evidence given at the trial or the available documents, together with admissions made by or on behalf of any person in connection with any proposed exercise of the powers; and for this purpose "the available documents" means any written statements or admissions which were made for use, and would have been admissible, as evidence at the trial, the depositions taken at any committal proceedings and any written statements or admissions used as evidence in those proceedings (s. 28 (4)).

Any order under this section shall be treated as an order for the restitution of property within the meaning of ss. 30 and 42 of the Criminal Appeal Act 1968 (which provide for the suspension of a restitution order pending an appeal to the criminal division of the Court of Appeal or the House of Lords) (s. 28 (5)).

The powers conferred by—

(a) sub-s. (1) (c) of the said s. 28 (payment to owner of stolen goods out of money taken from the offender on his apprehension); and

(b) sub-s. (3) of that section (payment to purchaser of, and lender on the security of, stolen goods out of money so taken),

shall be exercisable without any application being made in that behalf or on the application of any person appearing to the court to be interested in the property concerned (C.J. Act 1972, s.6 (2)).

The powers conferred by the said s. 28 shall be exercisable not only where a person is convicted of an offence with reference to the theft of the goods in question but also where, on the conviction of a person of any other offence, the court takes an offence with reference to the theft of those goods into consideration in determining sentence (s. 6 (3)).

Where an order is made under the said s. 28 against any person in respect of an offence taken into consideration in determining his sentence—

(a) the order shall cease to have effect if he successfully appeals against his conviction of the offence or, if more than one, all the offences, of which he was convicted in the proceedings in which the order was made;

(b) he may appeal against the order as if it were part of the sentence imposed in respect of the offence or, if more than one, any of the offences, of which he was so convicted (s. 6 (4)).

Any order under the said s. 28 made by a magistrates' court shall be suspended—

(a) in any case until the expiration of the period for the time being prescribed by law for the giving of notice of appeal against a decision of a magistrate's court;

(b) where notice of appeal is given within the period so prescribed, until the determination of the appeal;

but this subsection shall not apply where the order is made under s. 28 (1) (a) or (b) and the court so directs, being of the opinion that the title to the goods to be restored or, as the case may be, delivered or transferred under the order is not in dispute (s. 6 (5)).

A magistrates' court has also power to make an order under the Police (Property) Act 1897, restoring to the owner any stolen property which has come into the possession of the police under the circumstances given in the Act. This covers cases in which a thief has been acquitted, or a person has been charged on summons or warrant but not arrested, or in which all the stolen property has not been included in the charge, or in which stolen property has been recovered as mentioned in the Act.

The general rule as regards any sale or transfer of property is that the purchaser, even if he acts *bona fide* and pays the fair value, acquires no better right to the ownership of the property than what the seller or giver had.

A court by or before which a person is convicted of an offence, in dealing with him in any other way, may make a "compensation order" requiring him to pay compensation for any personal injury, loss or damage resulting from that offence or any other offence which is taken into consideration by the court in determining sentence (P. of C.C. Act 1973, s. 35).

Public Stores – The Public Stores Act 1875 applies to all stores under the care or control of any public department or office or of any person in the service of Her Majesty, and such stores are known as Her Majesty's Stores.

Certain marks (such as the broad arrow, a crown, Her Majesty's arms, coloured threads in the materials, etc., as described in the Act) are appropriate for distinguishing public stores. It is an offence to apply these marks to any stores without lawful authority, and it is an offence to obliterate such marks with intent to conceal Her Majesty's property in any such stores (ss. 4 and 5).

Any person charged with having in possession any of Her Majesty's stores reasonably suspected of being stolen or unlawfully obtained, and who does not account satisfactorily to the court how he came by the same, will be deemed guilty of an offence and may be punished summarily (s. 7).

If such stores are found in the possession of:

(1) A person in Her Majesty's service, or
(2) A person in the service of a public department, or
(3) A dealer in scrap metals, or
(4) A pawnbroker,

and he is taken or summoned before a magistrates' court, and the court is satisfied such stores are or were Her Majesty's property, if such person does not satisfy the court that he came lawfully by such stores, he will be liable to conviction and fine up to £5 (s. 9).

For the purposes of this Act stores shall be deemed to be in the possession of any person if he knowingly has them in the possession of any other person or in any premises, field or place, open or enclosed, whether occupied by himself or not, and whether for the use or benefit of himself or of another (s. 10).

A constable, if authorised in writing by a department, may stop, search and detain any vehicle or person reasonably suspected of conveying any such stores stolen or unlawfully obtained (s. 6). See also "Property of H.M. Forces", Chap. 30.

Wrecks – The Minister of Transport has the general superintendence of all matters relating to shipwrecks, and may appoint any person to be a receiver of wreck and look after wrecked property in accordance with the Merchant Shipping Act 1894.

In addition to the shipwrecked vessel, "wreck" will include goods cast into the sea while the ship is in danger and which sink (jetsam), goods which float on the surface (flotsam) and goods at the bottom of the sea and tied to a buoy (lagan).

A receiver of wreck has power to requisition all necessary assistance for the preservation of shipwrecked persons, vessels, cargo, etc. He must be notified by the finder of all wreck found, and all wreck found which is not taken by the owner must be delivered to him. It is an offence to take wreck or to keep possession of wreck, or to refuse to deliver wreck to the reciever, who may take such wreck by force if necessary. The receiver may obtain a search warrant to search for and seize concealed wreck. The receiver has full power to protect wreck; he may arrest persons plundering or interfering with same, and may use force to suppress any interference or obstruction.

The Merchant Shipping Act 1894 also makes it an offence to interfere with lighthouses or their lights, lightships, buoys or beacons, or to exhibit any light or fire in such a manner as to be mistaken for a light from a lighthouse, after notice to screen or extinguish such light.

The Malicious Damage Act 1861, ss. 47 and 48, makes it an offence to exhibit false lights or signals with intent to bring any vessel into danger or to do anything tending to the loss or destruction of any vessel, or to remove or conceal buoys and other sea marks.

The Offences against the Person Act 1861, s. 17, makes it an offence to prevent or impede any person in his endeavour to save life at a shipwreck, and s. 37 makes it an offence to assault any person, lawfully authorised, who is carrying out his duty in connection with a wreck.

The Protection of Wrecks Act 1973 givee the Secretary of State power by order to designate as a "restricted area" the area round the site of a vessel lying wrecked on or on the sea bed, and on account of the historical, archaeological or artistic importance of the vessel it ought to be protected. It will be an offence to tamper with the wreck, or carry out diving or salvage operations in contravention of the terms of the licence issued by the Secretary of State.

CHAPTER 19

POACHING

	Page		Page
Poaching Offences . .	194	Fishery Laws . . .	199
Game Laws . . .	197	Trespass . . .	200
Deer Act 1963 . .	198		

Poaching Offences – Poaching is the offence committed by a person who pursues, kills, or takes certain game birds and animals on land where he has no right to go. It amounts to trespass on land accompanied by taking or attempting to take certain property.

Poaching Prevention Act 1862 as amended by the Game Laws (Amendment) Act 1960: Under these Acts "game" includes hares, rabbits, woodcocks, snipe, also pheasants, partridges, grouse, black or moor game and their eggs.

Any constable, in any highway, street or public place, may search any person whom he may have good cause to suspect of coming from any land where he shall have been unlawfully in pursuit of game and having in his possession any game unlawfully obtained or any gun, part of a gun, cartridges and other ammunition, nets, traps, snares and other devices of a kind used for the killing or taking of game.

Such constable may also stop and search any conveyance in or upon which he shall have good cause to suspect that any such game or article or thing is being carried by any such person.

Should any such game, article or thing be found, he may seize and detain same. He has no power to arrest, or to seize dogs or ferrets.

If a constable makes such a seizure he should summon the person and the court, if satisfied that the accused had obtained such game by unlawfully going on any land or had used such article or thing for unlawfully killing or taking game or had been accessory thereto, may fine him and may forfeit such game, gun, etc. In the event of a conviction not being recorded, the game or other thing seized, or its value, should be restored to the person from whom it was seized.

Night Poaching Acts 1828 and 1844 as amended by the

Game Laws (Amendment) Act 1960: Under these Acts "game" includes hares, pheasants, partridges, grouse, heath or moor game, black game, bustards, woodcocks and snipes.

Unlawfully taking or destroying any game or rabbits by night in any land (open or enclosed) or public road, highway or path, is a summary offence (1828 Act, s. 1, and 1844 Act).

By night unlawfully entering or being on any land, whether open or enclosed, with any gun, net, engine or other instrument for the purpose of taking or destroying game is a summary offence (1828 Act, s. 1).

Offenders, as above described, who assault or offer violence with any offensive weapon to owners or occupiers of land, their gamekeepers, servants or their assistants, commit an offence (1828 Act, s. 2).

Three or more persons together unlawfully by night entering or being on any land, open or enclosed, to take or destroy game or rabbits, any of such persons being armed with any offensive weapon, commit an offence (1828 Act, s. 9).

Under these Acts the "night" commences at the expiration of the first hour after sunset and ends at the beginning of the first hour before sunrise (1828 Act, s. 12).

Owners, occupiers, gamekeepers and their assistants may arrest any such offenders caught in the act or in pursuit, and deliver them to any peace officer (1828 Act, s. 2).

Game Act 1831: Under this Act "game" includes hares, pheasants, partridges, grouse, heath or moor game and black game.

The following are summary offences:

Trespassing in search or pursuit of game or of woodcocks, snipe or rabbits, on any land:

(1) in the daytime (s. 30);

(2) and not giving real name and address, or wilfully continuing or returning upon the land when required to quit and give name and address by the owner or occupier or other authorised person, or any police officer (Game Laws (Amendment) Act 1960) who in such latter case may arrest the offender and bring him before a justice (s. 31);

(3) in the day-time in company with 4 or more persons, any of such persons having a gun and any of such persons using violence or threat to prevent any other person approaching them for the purpose of requiring them to quit or to tell their names (s. 32).

The daytime in this Act commences at the beginning of the last hour before sunrise and ends at the expiration of the first hour after sunset (s. 34).

Any prosecution should be commenced within 3 months of the offence (s. 41).

The Act does not apply to persons hunting or coursing with hounds or greyhounds (s. 35).

Game Laws (Amendment) Act 1960: this Act gives constables additional powers to arrest, enter land, search offenders and to seize articles from poachers.

A police constable may arrest a person found on any land committing an offence under ss. 1 or 9 of the 1828 Act (s. 1).

If he reasonably suspects that a person is committing such an offence or an offence under s. 30 of the Game Act 1831 a constable may enter on the land for the purpose of making the arrest. The power of entry does not apply to land occupied by or under the management of the Ministry of Defence or the United Kingdom Atomic Energy Authority (s. 2).

Where a person is arrested under s. 1 of this Act or s. 2 of the 1828 Act or s. 31 of the Game Act 1831, à police constable by or in whose presence he was arrested may search him, seize and detain any game or rabbits or any gun, part of a gun, etc. found in his possession, and the court may order their forfeiture whether or not the offence concerned that game, rabbit or gun, etc. If no conviction takes place, the game or other thing seized, or its value, shall be restored to the person from whom it was seized (s. 4).

For the purposes of this s. 4, "game", includes hares, pheasants, partridges, grouse, heath or moor game, black game, bustards, woodcocks and snipes.

Game Laws – Several statutes, such as the Game Act 1831, the Game Licences Act 1860, the Ground Game Act 1880, the Ground Game (Amendment) Act 1906, and Game Act 1970, deal with matters affecting game birds and animals.

The unlawful pursuit and taking of game is dealt with under "Poaching Offences".

If authorised by the local authority a constable may prosecute an offence under the excise Acts relating to any duty of excise in respect of licences for dealing in game, killing game and guns (Finance Act 1961, s. 11).

Game is defined as including hares, pheasants, partridges, grouse, heath or moor game and black game (Game Act 1831, s. 2).

A person must not take, kill or pursue or use any dog, gun or other instrument for the purpose of taking, killing or pursuing any game or woodcock, snipe, or coney or deer, without a game certificate (s. 23 of the Game Act 1831, as amended by the Game Licences Act 1860, which in s. 5 gives the cases where the possession of a game certificate is not necessary).

However the Ministry of Agriculture, Fisheries and Food may require in writing any person to kill, take or destroy on specified land rabbits, hares, deer, foxes, etc. Non-compliance will be a summary offence (Agriculture Act 1947, ss. 98 and 100, and Pests Act 1954, s. 2).

Under the Game Act 1831, s. 3, it is unlawful to take or kill game on Sunday or Christmas Day, and also during the close seasons, which are:

Pheasants, between February 1 and October 1.
Partridges, between February 1 and September 1.
Grouse, between December 10 and August 12.
Black game, between December 10 and August 20.

Other birds are in general now protected throughout the year. See "Birds", Chap. 35.

Hares: It is illegal to sell or expose native hares for sale during the months of March, April, May, June and July (Hares Preservation Act 1892).

Deer Act 1963 – No person shall take or wilfully kill certain specified deer during the prescribed close seasons (s. 1 and Sched. 1). These are:

Stags and Buck	May 1–July 31 inclusive
Hinds and Doe	March 1–October 31 inclusive

Provision is made for certain exceptions.

Any person who takes or wilfully kills any deer between the first hour after sunset and the last hour before sunrise commits an offence (s. 2).

If any person (a) sets in position any trap, snare or poisoned or stupefying bait; or (b) uses for killing or taking any deer any such article, or any net; or (c) uses for injuring or killing or taking any deer (i) specified firearms or ammunition; (ii) any arrow, spear or similar missile; (iii) any missile, whether discharged from a firearm or otherwise, carrying or containing any poison, stupefying drug or muscle-relaxing agent, he commits an offence.

If any person, unless he has the written authority of the occupier of enclosed land where deer are kept, (a) discharges any firearm or projects any missile, from any mechanically propelled vehicle at any deer; or (b) uses any mechanically propelled vehicle for the purpose of driving deer, he commits an offence (s. 3 and Sched. 2).

Any person who attempts to commit an offence against this Act is guilty of an offence. Any person who, for the purpose of committing an offence against this Act, has in his possession any prohibited article or any firearm or ammunition commits an offence (s. 4).

A constable may arrest without warrant any person he suspects with reasonable cause of committing any offence against this Act (s. 5).

The court has power to forfeit any deer or weapons (s. 6).

A constable may seize any deer, firearm, ammunition or prohibited article which is liable to be forfeited under s. 6 above.

A constable may sell any deer seized under this section and the net proceeds of the sale shall be liable to forfeiture (s. 7).

Fishery Laws – The law provides for the preservation or conservation of fish in the rivers and waters of the country and for the protection of the rights of owners of fisheries.

The regulation and control of fishing for salmon, trout, freshwater fish and eels has been vested in Water Authorities, who may appoint water bailiffs and make byelaws fixing the close seasons for fish and for many other purposes.

The Salmon and Freshwater Fisheries Act 1975 provides:

Water Authorities may grant licences to fish for salmon or trout (s. 25).

It is an offence to fish for or take salmon or trout otherwise than by means of an instrument which the fisherman is duly licensed to use for that purpose (s. 27).

Any constable, water bailiff, member of a Water Authority, or person producing his licence under this Act may require any person found fishing to produce his licence and give his name and address. Failure to comply is an offence but if within 7 days after its production was required, the person produces his licence at the office of the water authority, he shall not be convicted of the offence (s. 35).

The following acts in connection with salmon, trout or freshwater fish are summary offences under the Act:

S. 1: To use any firearm, otter lath or jack, wire or snare; a crossline or setline; a spear, gaff, stroke-haul, snatch or other like instrument; of a light, or to have same in possession under circumstances showing the intent to use same for that purpose, or to throw missiles into water for that purpose.

S. 2 (1): To use fish roe for the purpose of fishing, or to buy, sell or have salmon or trout roe for that purpose.

S. 2 (2): To knowingly take any such fish which is unclean or immature or to have in possession any such unclean or immature fish.

S. 2 (4): To wilfully disturb any spawn or spawning fish.

S. 3: To use nets in a certain manner or to use nets with meshes smaller than the dimensions prescribed.

S. 4: To cause or knowingly permit any poisonous substances to flow or be put into any waters containing fish.

S. 5: To use in or near any waters any explosive substance, any poison or other noxious substance, or any electrical device, with intent to take or destroy fish: or without lawful excuse, destroy or damage any dam, flood-gate or sluice with intent to take or destroy fish.

S. 6: To use fixed nets or other fixed engines unless duly authorised.

Ss. 19 and 20: To fish for or take or obstruct any salmon or trout during the close seasons, or during the weekly close time (usually 6 a.m. Saturday to 6 a.m. Monday) except with rod and line.

S. 22: To buy, sell or have in possession for sale any salmon between August 31 and February 1, or any trout between August 31 and March 1, except salmon or trout other than rainbow trout caught abroad, or preserved abroad, or preserved within this country between February 1 (or March 1, as regards trout) and August 31.

This Act of 1975 contains many other provisions for the protection of fish. It gives power of entry, search and seizure of fish and instruments, to duly appointed water bailiffs, who are deemed to be constables for the enforcement of the Act (s. 36), and persons resisting or obstructing them are guilty of an offence against the Act (s. 31).

Any person who during the night is found illegally taking fish or at or near waters with intent illegally to take fish or having in his possession any prohibited instrument, may be arrested without warrant by any water bailiff and his assistants and delivered to the police (s. 34).

The Theft Act 1968, s. 32, and Sched. 1, deal with the offences of unlawfully taking or destroying of fish. See Chap. 14.

Sea Fish (Conservation) Act 1967. No person shall in Great Britain sell, expose or offer for sale, or have in possession for sale, any sea fish of a size smaller than that prescribed by Order (s. 1). The market authority (in their market), any officer of police and certain fishery officials, in order to enforce the section, may, at all reasonable times, board any fishing boat or enter any premises used for any business for the treatment, storage or sale of sea-fish, search for and examine any sea-fish and seize any sea-fish kept in contravention of the section (s. 16).

"Sea fish" means fish (fresh or cured) of any kind found in the sea and includes shell fish (s. 22).

The Immature Sea Fish Order 1968 gives the following minimum sizes in centimetres: cod (30), haddock (27), hake (30), plaice (25), witches (28), lemon soles (25), soles (24), turbot (30), brill (30), megrims (25), whiting (25), and dabs (15).

Trespass – The word "trespass" is used to describe the act of entering or being upon land or premises without any right to be thereon.

Civil action in the County Court may be taken against a trespasser, but the mere fact of a person trespassing does not make him liable under the criminal law.

A trespasser who refuses to leave on request may by his conduct tend to provoke a breach of the peace and thereby become liable to arrest and prosecution. See Chap. 22.

Trespassing in pursuit of game is dealt with under "Poaching". For trespass on railway premises, see "Railways", Chap. 26.

A trespasser on premises may be removed, but he should first be requested to depart, and no more force than is necessary to remove him should be used. A person is entitled to protect himself and property against trespassers, but he will be liable criminally if he uses unnecessary violence.

Persons found in any premises or enclosed area for any unlawful purpose may be arrested and dealt with under s. 4, Vagrancy Act 1824. See "Loiterers, etc.", Chap. 28.

Under s. 31 of the Offences against the Person Act 1861 it is an offence to set any spring-gun, man-trap or other engine calculated to destroy human life or inflict grievous bodily harm upon a trespasser or other person coming into contact therewith, or for the occupier to knowingly permit any such engine to remain so set, provided that this section does not make it illegal to set traps to destroy vermin or to set spring guns or other engines from sunset to sunrise in a dwelling-house for the protection thereof.

As regards commons and waste lands, the public have rights of access for air and exercise subject to any regulations affecting such land.

It is a summary offence without lawful authority to draw or drive upon such land any carriage, cart, caravan or other vehicle or to camp or light any fire thereon or to fail to observe any conditions lawfully prescribed (Law of Property Act 1925, s. 193).

See also Road Traffic Act 1972, s. 36, as to the summary offence of driving a motor vehicle on land not part of a road ("Road Traffic Acts, etc.").

PART IV – OFFENCES AFFECTING THE COMMUNITY IN GENERAL

CHAPTER 20

OFFENCES AGAINST THE STATE AND RELIGION

	Page
Treason	205
Sedition	206
Drilling	206
Biological weapons . .	207
Prevention of Terrorism (Temporary Provisions) Act 1974 . . .	207
Official Secrets Acts .	209
Piracy	213
Foreign Enlistment Act 1870	214
Blasphemy . . .	214
Disturbing Public Worship	214
Bigamy	214

Treason – Treason means treachery. It is a betraying or breach of faith and in law denotes the grave crime of treachery towards the Sovereign as head of the State or any betraying of the State itself. Blackstone terms it the highest civil crime which any man can possibly commit.

The Treason Acts declare certain offences to be treason: for example, compassing the death of the Sovereign, levying war against the Sovereign, adhering to the Sovereign's enemies.

Treason is a most serious crime, being directed against the security of the State, and is punishable on conviction by death. All persons concerned in any treason are regarded as principals.

Any knowledge and concealment of treason, even without any assent to it, is termed misprision of treason, and is an offence at common law. The procedure in treason cases is to be the same as in murder cases (C.L. Act 1967, s. 12).

A person charged with treason shall not be admitted to bail except by order of a judge of the High Court or the Secretary of State (M.C. Act 1952, s. 8).

Many acts directed against the safety or interests of the State are also punishable under the Official Secrets Acts. See "Official Secrets Acts".

Treason Felony Act 1848: Under this statute the following acts of treason may be prosecuted and dealt with as offences which are punishable with imprisonment for life.

(1) Compassing to deprive or depose the Sovereign from the style, honour and name of the Crown of the United Kingdom or of any other of her Dominions.

(2) Levying war against the Sovereign within the United Kingdom in order by force or constraint to compel her to change her measures or counsels, or to intimidate or overawe Parliament.

(3) Stirring up any foreigner with force to invade the United Kingdom or any other part of the Sovereign's dominions.

See also "Incitement to Disaffection", Chap. 30.

Every case of treason must be reported to the Director of Public Prosecutions. See Appendix III.

Sedition - Sedition is a general term covering attempts to excite discontent or disaffection, disorder or tumult, or to subvert the Government, constitution or laws of the country.

Sedition, being against the safety of the State, is an offence at common law.

Sedition consists of acts, writings or conduct which do not amount to treason, but which must be punished in the interests of the State, for if unchecked, sedition leads to disorder, and possibly to revolution.

It is a crime against society nearly allied to that of treason.

The offence of sedition is usually committed by writing or speaking words which may pervert the minds of the people and cause general disaffection or public disorder.

It will be for a jury to decide whether such writings or words are seditious.

A writing of a seditious nature is known as a seditious libel (see "Libel", Chap. 23), and the writer cannot plead the truth of his libel as an excuse for his publishing it.

A speaker at a meeting who has used seditious words may be indicted for his seditious speech, and the circumstances of the meeting itself may render the meeting an unlawful assembly.

Seditious conduct may be dealt with as conduct likely to lead to a breach of the peace, and those concerned may be bound over by the court. See "Breach of the Peace and Sureties", Chap. 22.

An alien may be punished on indictment or summarily for any attempt to cause sedition or disaffection or to promote industrial unrest (Aliens Restriction (Amendment) Act 1919, s. 3).

See Stone, under title "Sedition".

Any offence of sedition and seditious libel must be reported to the Director of Public Prosecutions. See Appendix III.

Drilling - Under the Unlawful Drilling Act 1819, all meetings of persons for the purpose of training or drilling to the use of arms or for practising military movements without lawful authority are prohibited. Every person present at such meeting for the purpose of drilling and training others or who trains or drills others or assists therein, and every person present for the purpose of being drilled or trained or who is drilled or trained thereat is guilty of an offence.

Any such unlawful meeting may be dispersed by any justice or by any constable and his assistants, and those present may be arrested and detained.

Under the Firearms Act 1920, s. 16, a Secretary of State or any officer deputed by him for the purpose has power to authorise meetings and assemblies for the purpose of training or drilling as above mentioned. See also "Public Order Act 1936", Chap. 22.

Biological Weapons Act 1974 – No person shall develop, produce, stockpile, acquire or retain, (a) any biological agent or toxin of a type and in a quantity that has no justification for prophylactic, protective or other peaceful purposes, or (b) any weapon, equipment or means of delivery designed to use biological agents or toxins for hostile purposes or in armed conflict. Any person who contravenes this section is liable to imprisonment for life (s. 1).

Proceedings must have the consent of the Attorney General, but this does not prevent the issue of a warrant or the remanding in custody or on bail of a person charged with an offence under the Act (s. 2).

If a justice of the peace is satisfied by information on oath that there is reasonable ground for suspecting that an offence under s. 1 has been, or is about to be, committed, he may grant a search warrant authorising a constable named therein, (a) to enter, at any time within 1 month from the date of the warrant any premises or place named therein, if necessary by force, and to search the premises or place and every person found therein; (b) to inspect any document found in the premises or place or in the possession of any person found therein and to take copies of, or seize or detain any such documents; (c) to inspect, seize and detain any equipment so found; and (d) to inspect, sample, seize and detain any substance so found (s. 4 (1)).

A warrant issued under sub-s. (1), authorising a constable to take steps mentioned in that subsection may also authorise any person named in the warrant to accompany the constable and assist him in taking any of those steps (s. 4 (2)).

Prevention of Terrorism (Temporary Provisions) Act 1974 – Any person commits an offence who (a) belongs or professes to belong to a proscribed organisation, (b) solicits or invites financial or other support for a proscribed organisation, or knowingly makes or receives any contribution in money or otherwise to the resources of a proscribed organisation, or (c) arranges or assists in the arrangement or management of, or addresses, any meeting of 3 or more persons (whether or not it is a meeting to which the public are admitted) knowing that the meeting is to support, or further the activities of a proscribed organisation, or is to be addressed by a person belonging or professing to belong to a proscribed organisation (s. 1 (1)).

The only organisation so far proscribed is the Irish Republican Army.

Any person who in a public place (a) wears any item of dress, or (b) wears, carries or displays any article, in such a way or in such circumstances as to arouse reasonable apprehension that he is a member or supporter of a proscribed organisation, commits an offence. A constable may arrest without a warrant a person whom he reasonably suspects to be a person guilty of an offence under this section. "Public place" includes any highway and any other premises or place to which at the material time the public have, or are permitted to have, access whether on payment or otherwise (s. 2). (See *Moran* v. *D.P.P.*, Chap. 22.)

The Secretary of State is empowered to make orders to exclude from the U.K. or Gt. Britain (in the case of persons who have a connection with Northern Ireland) persons concerned in terrorism.

If (a) a person subject to an exclusion order fails to comply with the order, or (b) a person is knowingly concerned in securing or facilitating the entry into Gt. Britain of a person subject to an exclusion order, or (c) a person knowingly harbours a person subject to an exclusion order, he will commit an offence (s. 3 (8)).

A constable may arrest without warrant a person whom he reasonably suspects to be (a) a person guilty of an offence under s. 1 or 3, (b) a person concerned in the commission, preparation, or instigation of acts of terrorism; (c) a person subject to an exclusion order (s. 7 (1)).

A person arrested under this section shall not be detained, in right of the arrest, for more than 48 hours, but the Secretary of State may extend the period for a further 5 days (s. 7 (2)).

Proceedings for any offence under ss. 1, 2, or 3 shall not be instituted except by or with the consent of the Attorney General. This shall not prevent the issue or execution of a warrant of arrest or the remanding of any person charged with an offence (Sched. 3, para. 4).

If a justice of the peace is satisfied that there is reasonable ground for suspecting that (a) evidence of the commission of an offence under section 1 or 3 of this Act, or (b) evidence sufficient to justify the making of an order under section 1 of this Act or an exclusion order is to be found at any premises or place, he may grant a search warrant authorising entry to the premises or place.

An application for a warrant shall be made by a member of a police force of a rank not lower than the rank of an inspector, and he shall give his information to the justice on oath.

The warrant shall authorise the applicant, and any other member of any police force, to enter the premises or place, if necessary by force, and to search the premises or place and every person found therein and to seize anything found on the premises or place. or on any such person, which any member of a police force acting under the warrant has reasonable grounds for suspecting to be evidence.

If a member of a police force of a rank not lower than the rank of superintendent has reasonable grounds for believing that the case is one of great emergency and that in the interests of the State immediate action is necessary, he may by a written order signed by him give to any member of a police force the authority which may be given by a search warrant under this paragraph.

Where any authority is so given, particulars of the case shall be notified as soon as may be to the Secretary of State.

No woman shall, in pursuance of a warrant or order given under this paragraph, be searched except by a woman. (Sched. 3, para. 5.)

In any circumstances in which a constable has power under section 7 of this Act to arrest a person, he may also, for the purpose of ascertaining whether he has in his possession any document or other article which may constitute evidence that he is a person liable to arrest, stop that person, and search him.

Where a constable has arrested a person under the said section, for any reason other than for the commission of a criminal offence, he or any other constable, may search him for the purpose of ascertaining whether he has in his possession any document or other article which may constitute evidence that he is a person liable to arrest.

No woman shall be searched except by a woman. (Sched. 3, para. 7.)

The Prevention of Terrorism (Supplemental Temporary Provisions) Order 1974, S.I. 1975 – This order contains provisions for supplementing the Act. A constable is an examining officer under the Act (art. 3). An examining officer is empowered to examine any person arriving in or seeking to leave Gt. Britain to determine whether he appears to be a person concerned in the commission, preparation or instigation of acts of terrorism or subject to an exclusion or is a person who there are reasonable grounds for suspecting has committed an offence under s. 3 (8) (art. 4).

Any person examined under art. 4 is required to produce such information or documents as may be required by the examining officer (art. 5).

Articles found during the search of persons examined and their baggage and ships or aircraft or any vehicle searched may be detained for specified purposes (art. 6).

Persons disembarking from or embarking on a ship or aircraft coming from or going to the Republic of Ireland, Northern Ireland, Channel Islands or Isle of Man are required to have landing or embarkation cards (art. 7).

Official Secrets Acts – The Official Secrets Act 1911, amended and supplemented by the Official Secrets Acts 1920 and 1939, deals with spying and other practices prejudicial to the safety or interests of the State.

In the interests of the State, certain premises and localities are declared to be "prohibited places", and the Acts aim at preventing spying on such places.

A "prohibited place" includes any work of defence, camp, ship, aircraft, telegraph station, munition factory, etc., belonging to or occupied by the Crown; any place were munitions of war or documents relating thereto are made or kept on behalf of the Crown; and any railway, road, canal, work of public character or place declared to be a prohibited place by order of the Secretary of State (1911 Act, s. 3).

For any purpose prejudicial to the safety or interests of the State, to approach, inspect or enter any prohibited place, or to make any sketch, model or note likely to be of any use to an enemy (including a potential enemy: *R.* v. *Parrott* (1913)), or to obtain, record, or communicate to any other person any secret official code or password or any document or information which might be useful to an enemy. This applies to sabotage as well as spying (*Chandler* v. *D.P.P.* (1962)). The prosecution may give evidence of the accused's character (1911 Act, s. 1).

For any person in possession of information of a secret official nature, or relating to a prohibited place, or obtained in contravention of the Act, or entrusted in confidence to him by a person holding office under Her Majesty, or procured by virtue of his office under Her Majesty, to communicate same to any unauthorised person, or to use same in any manner prejudicial to the safety or interests of the State, or to unauthorisedly retain same, or to unreasonably endanger the safety of same (1911 Act, s. 2).

For the purposes of s. 2 of the Official Secrets Act 1911, membership of, or any office or employment under the Post Office shall be deemed to be an office under Her Majesty, and a contract with the Post Office shall be deemed to be a contract with Her Majesty; and any telegraph, telephone, wireless or signal station or office belonging to, or occupied by, the Post Office shall be a prohibited place (Post Office Act 1969, Sched. 4).

A constable is a person who holds office under Her Majesty (*Lewis* v. *Cattle* (1938)). He is a public servant and an officer of the Crown (*Fisher* v. *Oldham Corporation* (1930)).

To communicate any information relating to munitions of war to any foreign power, or in any other manner prejudicial to the safety or interests of the State (1911 Act, s. 2, and 1920 Act).

To knowingly receive any document, information, etc., communicated to him in contravention of the Act (1911 Act, s. 2).

To knowingly harbour any person about to commit or who has committed an offence under the Act, or to wilfully omit or refuse to disclose to a superintendent of police any information he may have regarding such person (1911 Act, s. 7, and 1920 Act).

For the purpose of gaining admission to a prohibited place or for any other purpose prejudicial to the safety or interests of the State, to use, without lawful authority, any official uniform or to make any false declaration or application, or to forge any pass or other official document, or to personate any official, or to use or have without authority any genuine or counterfeit official die, seal or stamp (1920 Act, s. 1).

Without lawful authority, to retain for any purpose prejudicial to the safety or interests of the State, any official document, or to fail to comply with any direction respecting same (1920 Act, s. 1).

Without lawful authority, to communicate to any other person any official information issued for one's own use alone, or to have in possession official information issued for the use of some person other than himself (1920 Act, s. 1).

On obtaining possession of any official document by finding or otherwise, to neglect or fail to restore it to the person for whose use it was issued, or to a police constable (1920 Act, s. 1).

To interfere in any way with a police officer or any member of Her Majesty's Forces engaged on guard or other duty in relation to any prohibited place (1920 Act, s. 3).

To fail to give on demand to a chief officer of police duly so authorised by a Secretary of State, or so acting in a case of great emergency, any information in one's power relating to an offence or suspected offence under s. 1 of the 1911 Act, or to fail to attend at such reasonable time and place as may be specified to furnish such information (Official Secrets Act 1939).

Any attempt, aid, incitement, etc., to an offence under the Acts will be as punishable as the offence concerned (1920 Act, s. 7).

A Secretary of State, by warrant, may require any person who owns or controls any cable or wireless telegraphic apparatus to produce any or all telegrams received or sent by him. Failure to do so is punishable summarily (1920 Act, s. 4).

Every person who carries on the business of receiving for reward, letters, telegrams or other postal packets for delivery or forwarding to the persons for whom they are intended (known as an "accommodation address", must be registered with the Chief Officer of Police of the district, and must keep a book in which he must record:

(1) The name and address of every person for whom any postal packet is received or who has requested that postal packets received may be sent to him;

(2) Any instructions as to the sending of postal packets;

(3) The place of sending, the date of posting (as per post-mark) and the date of receipt of every postal packet received, also the name of sender if given thereon, and the registration particulars if it is registered;

(4) The date of delivery and name and address of the person to whom any postal packet is delivered;

(5) If a postal packet is forwarded, the date and name and address of person to whom it is forwarded.

He must not deliver a letter to any person until that person has signed a receipt for same in this book, nor must he give the letter to any other person or send it on to any other address, unless he has received written instructions to that effect signed by the addressee.

This book and all postal packets and instructions regarding same must be kept at all reasonable times open to inspection by any police constable. Any contravention of the above rules or false information given or false entry made is an offence and is punishable summarily (1920 Act, s. 5).

POWER OF ARREST – Any person found committing, or reasonably suspected of having committed or having attempted to commit or being about to commit an offence under the Act, may be arrested without warrant (1911 Act, s. 6).

POWER OF SEARCH – On reasonable grounds a justice may grant a search warrant authorising any constable named therein to enter at any time any premises or place named, and to search same and every person found therein, and to seize any document or thing found in connection with which there is reasonable ground for suspecting that an offence under the Act has been or is about to be committed.

In a case of great emergency necessitating immediate action in the interests of the State, a superintendent of police can, by a written order, give any constable the like authority as may be given by a justice's search warrant (1911 Act, s. 9). See Chap. 5.

PROSECUTION – Any person charged with any offence under these Acts may be arrested, or a warrant for his arrest may be issued and executed, and such person may be remanded in custody or on bail, but no further proceedings or prosecution may be taken without the consent of the Attorney-General (1911 Act, s. 8).

Any offence under these Acts must be reported to the Director of Public Prosecutions. See Appendix III.

During trial the court may be cleared. See "Open Court", Chap. 4.

Unauthorised disclosure of spent convictions – Any person who, in the course of his official duties has, or at any time has had custody of or access to any official record, or the information contained therein shall be guilty of an offence, if knowing or having reasonable cause to suspect that any specified information he has obtained in the course of those duties is specified information, he discloses it otherwise than in the course of those duties to another person (Rehabilitation of Offenders Act 1974, s. 9 (2)).

Any person who obtains any specified information from any official record by means of any fraud, dishonesty or bribe shall be guilty of an offence (s. 9 (4)).

The Secretary of State may by order make provision for excepting the disclosure of specified information derived from an official record, from the provisions of s. 9 (2) (s. 9 (5)).

Proceedings for an offence under s. 9 (2) shall not be instituted except by or on behalf of the D.P.P. (s. 9 (8)).

Piracy – This is robbery on the sea, and is the taking of a ship or any of its contents on the high seas from the control of those lawfully entitled, and taking it away without any authority. It is an offence at common law and under the Piracy Acts, and if accompanied by violence it is punishable with death and therefore every such case must be reported to the Director of Public Prosecutions. See Appendix III.

By the Tokyo Convention Act 1967, s. 4, for the purposes of any proceedings before a court in the U.K. in respect of piracy, the provisions set out in the Schedule to the Act (given below) shall be treated as constituting part of the law of nations; and any such court having jurisdiction in respect of piracy committed on the high seas shall have jurisdiction in respect of piracy committed by or against an aircraft wherever that piracy is committed.

The Schedule referred to above contains the following provisions of Geneva Convention on the High Seas to be treated as part of the law of nations:

Art. 15: Piracy consists of any of the following acts:

(1) Any illegal acts of violence, detention or any act of depredation, committed for private ends by the crew or the passengers of a private ship or a private aircraft, and directed:

(a) On the high seas, against another ship or aircraft, or against persons or property on board such ship or aircraft;

(b) Against a ship, aircraft, persons or property in a place outside the jurisdiction of any State;

(2) Any act of voluntary participation in the operation of a ship or of an aircraft with knowledge of facts making it a pirate ship or aircraft;

(3) Any act of inciting or of intentionally facilitating an act described in sub-paragraph (1) or sub-paragraph (2) of this article.

Art. 16: The acts of piracy, as defined in article 15, committed by a warship, government ship or government aircraft whose crew has mutinied and taken control of the ship or aircraft are assimilated to acts committed by a private ship.

Art. 17: A ship or aircraft is considered a pirate ship or aircraft if it is intended by the persons in dominant control to be used for the purpose of committing one of the acts referred to in article 15. The same applies if the ship or aircraft has been used to commit any such act, so long as it remains under the control of the persons guilty of that act.

Foreign Enlistment Act 1870 – This statute is intended to prevent British subjects from assisting any foreign State at war with a friendly State. It is an offence for any British subject, without licence, to enlist in the service of, or to recruit for, or to leave this country with intent to enlist in the service of, or to convey illegally enlisted persons to, any foreign State at war with another State at peace with this country. It is also an offence to build, equip or despatch a vessel knowing same is to be employed in the service of such a State, or to prepare, without licence, any military or naval expedition against any friendly State.

Blasphemy – This is the use of language (spoken or written) having a tendency to vilify the Christian religion or the Bible. The offence lies in the attacking of Christianity in an indecent manner, with intent to bring religion into contempt, corrupt public morals and shock or insult believers. It is an offence at common law. See Stone, under title "Blasphemy".

Disturbing Public Worship – Riotous, violent or indecent behaviour (known as "brawling") in any place of religious worship at any time or in any churchyard or burial ground is a summary offence, and the offender may be arrested by a constable or churchwarden (Ecclesiastical Courts Jurisdiction Act 1860, ss. 2 and 3). See also "Clergymen", Chap. 29, and Stone, under title "Church".

Bigamy – Bigamy is the crime committed by a person who being legally married goes through a lawful form of marriage with another person during the life of the former husband or wife.

This second "marriage" is void, and the crime lies in the profanation of the solemn ceremony of marriage, such profanation being regarded as an outrage on public decency. Bigamy is an offence which is triable at the Crown Court.

Offences against the Person Act 1861, s. 57: Whosoever being married shall marry any other person during the life of the former husband or wife, whether the second marriage shall have taken place in England or Ireland or elsewhere, shall be guilty of an arrestable offence.

This section does not apply (and no offence is committed) in the case of a second marriage contracted:

(1) Outside England and Ireland by a person who is not a subject of Her Majesty's, or

(2) By a person divorced (decree having been made absolute) from his or her wife or husband, or

(3) By a person whose former marriage has been declared void by a court of competent jurisdiction, or

(4) By a person whose husband or wife has been continuously absent for seven years then last past and was not known by such person to be living within that time.

Having regard to the above description, it will be necessary that the prosecution should prove the following in a case of bigamy:

(1) The first marriage and that it was a valid marriage This is usually proved by a certified copy of the marriag. register. An admission of the marriage by the accused is not sufficient. It must be proved that the marriage was a valid or binding marriage, and if after this has been proved, the accused asserts that it was not valid (if it is invalid the second marriage is not bigamous) the onus of proof that it is invalid rests on him.

(2) The identity of the parties, viz. that they are the persons mentioned in the marriage certificates produced. The best proof will be the evidence of persons present at the marriages.

(3) The second marriage ceremony.

This can usually be proved by a certified copy of the marriage register. It must be proved that this second ceremony was a lawful ceremony of marriage. It is immaterial whether the ceremony took place in England or abroad so long as it is legal according to the law of the place where celebrated. It is no defence to show that this second marriage was invalid or void by law.

(4) That the first husband or wife was alive when the second marriage took place.

This can be proved by the production of the first husband or wife, or by evidence that he or she was alive at the time.

(5) If the first husband or wife had been absent for seven years then past, the prosecution should prove that the accused **knew** he or she was alive at the time. If this cannot be proved the accused may be acquitted under s. 57 as above.

However, *bona fide* belief on reasonable grounds that the wife (or husband) is dead even within 7 years is a good defence (*R.* v. *Tolson* (1889)). An honest belief based on reasonable grounds that the previous marriage was invalid is a good defence (*R.* v. *King* (1963)).

The second "husband" or "wife" can give evidence, as he or she is not legally the husband or wife of the accused. The real husband or wife of the accused may be called as a witness for the prosecution or for the defence and without the consent of the accused, but he or she cannot be compelled to give evidence (Criminal Justice Administration Act 1914, s. 28 (3)).

CHAPTER 21

PUBLIC JUSTICE OFFENCES

	Page
Contempt of Court	216
Escape	217
Prison Breach	217
Rescue	218
Pound Breach	218
Perjury	218
False statements in company documents	220
False written statements tendered in evidence	220
Bribery	221
Extortion	222
Misconduct by Public Officers	222
Election Offences	222
Personation	222
Bribery	223
Treating	223
Undue influence	223
Obstructing Public Justice	224

Contempt of Court – Contempt of court is of two kinds, civil or criminal. Civil contempt consists of disobeying an order of a court in civil proceedings. Criminal contempt is an offence at common law and may be committed by disorderly behaviour in court, by a defendant insulting the judge, by a witness remaining in court after the witnesses have been ordered to leave, by obstructing or interfering with the course of justice or lawful process of the courts, by intimidation of the jurors, parties or witnesses and by publication of comments or information likely to prejudice the hearing of a case.

Administration of Justice Act 1960, s. 11. A person shall not be guilty of contempt of court by publishing any matter calculated to interfere with the course of justice in connection with any proceedings pending or imminent at the time of publication if at that time (having taken all reasonable care) he did not know and had no reason to suspect that the proceedings were pending or imminent. A person shall not be guilty of contempt of court by distributing such a publication if at the time of distribution (having taken all reasonable care) he did not know that it contained such matter and had no reason to suspect that it was likely to do so. The proof of any fact tending to establish a defence afforded by the above to any person in proceedings for contempt of court shall lie upon that person.

Criminal Justice Act 1925, s. 41. It is a summary offence to take any photograph in any court of justice or to make any sketch in any court for publication of a judge, registrar, justice or coroner, a juror, a witness, or a party to any proceedings before the court, or to publish any such photograph or sketch. This protection covers the persons named while in or entering or leaving a court-room or the premises in which a court is held.

For press reports as to juvenile courts, etc., see "Treatment of Youthful Offenders", Chap. 12.

Justices have no power to commit persons summarily for contempt, but higher courts may deal summarily with such cases. Proceedings may be taken by indictment triable at the Crown Court or by criminal information in the Queen's Bench Division.

A magistrates' court may order a person to find sureties for his good behaviour if his conduct in court is disrespectful or unmannerly, obstructive or insulting, or likely to lead to a breach of the peace. If such person fails to give the required surety he may be committed to prison in default of giving surety.

Usually justices will direct such an offender to be removed from the court.

Any person who without just excuse disobeys a witness order or witness summons requiring him to attend before any court shall be guilty of contempt of that court and may be punished summarily by that court as if his contempt had been committed in the face of that court (C.P. (A. of W.) Act 1965, s. 3).

Escape – It is an offence at common law for a prisoner, whether innocent or guilty, to escape with or without the use of force from lawful custody on a criminal charge.

If a prisoner makes a voluntary escape by consent or connivance of his custodian, the custodian will be guilty of an offence.

Any constable or other person who has a prisoner lawfully in his custody and who negligently suffers him to go at large commits a misdemeanour at common law.

Every person is bound to hold a lawful prisoner and to deliver him up to the proper authority. If a prisoner escapes and is not briskly pursued and taken again before he has been lost sight of, the escape will be considered a "negligent" escape.

Criminal Justice Acts 1948 and 1961, ss. 66 and 35 respectively, state that any person required or authorised by or under the Acts to be taken to any place or to be kept in custody, shall, while being so taken or kept, be deemed to be in legal custody, and s. 49, Prison Act 1952 authorises arrest without warrant of certain persons unlawfully at large. See Chap. 3.

Prison Breach is escape by force from a lawful imprisonment by means of some actual breaking of the prison or place of custody. Under s. 39 of the Prison Act 1952 it is an offence for any person to aid a prisoner in escaping or attempting to escape from any prison. An unsuccessful attempt to break out of prison or any conspiracy to effect prison breach is an offence at common law.

It is an offence to knowingly harbour a person who has escaped from a prison, borstal institution, detention centre, remand centre; or who, having been sentenced in any part of the United Kingdom, Channel Islands or Isle of Man to imprisonment, corrective training, preventive detention, borstal training or detention in a detention centre is unlawfully at large. Assisting any such person with intent to prevent, hinder or interfere with his being taken into custody is also an offence (C.J. Act 1961, s. 22). This has been extended to apply to escapees from Naval, Military and Air Force Establishments by S.I. 1962, no. 1242 and S.I. 1961, nos. 2395 and 2397.

Rescue – Rescue is the forcible liberation of a prisoner from lawful custody.

For attempted rescue and assaulting the police, see "Assault", Chap. 8, and as regards the prisoner, see "Escape".

The forcible rescue of goods which have been lawfully seized under legal process is an offence at common law.

Under the County Courts Act 1959 the rescue or attempted rescue of goods seized under process of a County Court is a summary offence and a court bailiff may arrest the offender and bring him before the judge (s. 127) and an assault on an officer of the court acting in the execution of his duty is also a summary offence and a court bailiff may arrest the offender and bring him before the judge (s. 30).

Pound Breach, or the forcible rescue of cattle by breach of the pound in which they had been lawfully placed, is an offence at common law.

To release or attempt to rescue or release any cattle impounded under the Highways Act before the same shall have been legally discharged, or to damage the pound, is a summary offence (Highways Act 1959, s. 135; Town Police Clauses Act 1847, s. 26).

Under the Pound Breach Act 1843 it is a summary offence to release or attempt to release any cattle or other beasts lawfully seized for the purpose of being impounded or on the way to or from the pound, or to in any way damage the pound. See "Impounding Animals", Chap. 24.

Perjury – Perjury is an offence at common law and also by statute. It was made an offence because the taking of a wilful false oath in a court of law is an abuse of public justice. The law relating to perjury and kindred offences was consolidated by the Perjury Act 1911 as follows:

(1) PERJURY – Perjury is the crime committed by a person lawfully sworn as a witness or interpreter in a judicial proceeding who wilfully makes a statement material in that proceeding

which he knows to be false or does not believe to be true (1911 Act, s. 1).

"Lawfully sworn" includes affirmation and declaration as well as any oath administered without objection by the person sworn (1911 Act, s. 15).

"Judicial proceeding" includes a proceeding before any court, tribunal or person having by law power to hear, receive and examine evidence on oath.

"Material statement" is one such as might affect the decision of the court, tribunal or person, and the judge at the trial will decide whether the statement is or is not material (1911 Act, s. 1).

It must be clear that the perjury was deliberate and wilful, not merely carelessness or mistake.

(2) FALSE STATEMENTS ON OATH NOT IN JUDICIAL PROCEEDINGS – If a person is authorised or required by law to make any statement on oath for any purpose and is lawfully sworn otherwise than in a judicial proceeding, and he wilfully makes a statement which is material for that purpose and which he knows to be false or does not believe to be true he commits an offence.

If a person wilfully uses any false affidavit for the purposes of the Bills of Sale Act 1878, he commits an offence (1911 Act, s. 2).

(3) FALSE STATEMENTS – It is an offence to wilfully and falsely make statements:

(a) As to marriage, such as false oaths, declarations, notices, certificates, particulars required, representations, etc. (1911 Act, s. 3).

Such offences may be dealt with summarily within 12 months (Criminal Justice Act 1925, s. 28).

(b) As to births or deaths, such as false particulars, certificates, declarations, etc. (1911 Act, s. 4), and such offences may be dealt with summarily and within 12 months (Criminal Justice Act 1925, s. 28).

(c) To obtain registration on, or a certificate of registration from, any register kept by law of persons qualified by law to practise any vocation or calling (1911 Act, s. 6).

(For example, medical, dental, pharmaceutical, etc., registers.)

It is a summary offence for any person to make any statement or representation which he knows to be false, (a) for the purpose of obtaining benefit or any other payment under the Ministry of Social Security Act 1966, or (b) for the purpose of avoiding any liability under the Act (s. 29).

(4) FALSE DECLARATIONS NOT ON OATH – It is an offence to knowingly and wilfully make otherwise than on oath a statement false in a material particular in:

(a) A statutory declaration, or

(b) Any account, certificate, report or other document authorised or required by any Act of Parliament, or

(c) Any oral declaration or answer required under any Act of Parliament (1911 Act, s. 5). False statements in statutory declarations may be punished summarily on consent of accused to trial (M.C. Act 1952, s. 19 and Sched. 1).

(5) SUBORNATION OF PERJURY – This is the common law offence of procuring another to commit perjury. It is an offence to aid, abet, counsel, procure, incite or attempt to procure another person to commit an offence against the Act (1911 Act, s. 7).

Corroboration is necessary to ensure a conviction for any offence against this Act, as the evidence of one witness alone as to the falsity of the statement will not be regarded as sufficient (1911 Act, s. 13). One witness together with proof of other material and relevant facts substantially confirming his testimony will meet the requirements as without corroboration it would be merely one oath against another. See "Corroboration", Chap. 7.

A judge or person presiding over a court, or a justice sitting in special sessions, if of opinion that a witness in the proceedings before him has been guilty of perjury, may order the prosecution of that witness for such perjury, and may commit him for trial (1911 Act, s. 9).

FALSE STATEMENTS IN COMPANY DOCUMENTS – It is an offence for any person to knowingly and wilfully make a statement, false in any material particular, in any balance sheet, report or other document required for the purposes of several sections of the Act, as specified in Sched. 15, and the offence may be dealt with summarily (Companies Act 1948, s. 438).

False statements in declarations, certificates or writings made to be used as evidence of the service of any document or the handwriting or seal of any person is punishable summarily. (M.C. Act 1952, s. 82).

The Redundancy Payments Act 1965 creates an obligation to make redundancy payments to employees who have been dismissed by reason of redundancy. The Act specifies that making a statement in providing any information required by a notice under the Act, which is false in a material particular, shall be an offence.

FALSE WRITTEN STATEMENTS TENDERED IN EVIDENCE – If any person in a written statement tendered in evidence in criminal proceedings by virtue of ss. 2 or 9 of the C.J. Act 1967 wilfully makes a statement material in those proceedings which he knows to be false or does not believe to be true, he commits an offence. The Perjury Act 1911 shall have effect as if this section were contained in that Act (C.J. Act 1967, s. 89).

Bribery is the offering to or the receiving by any person of any undue reward in order to incline him to do or to reward him for doing a thing contrary to the rules of honesty and integrity.

At common law the bribery of any person who has a duty to do anything in which the public are interested, particularly the administration of justice, is an offence, and statute law also makes certain forms of bribery an offence.

In the offence of bribery the giver and the receiver are equally guilty, and an unsuccessful attempt to bribe is also an offence.

Public Bodies Corrupt Practices Act 1889, s. 1, makes it an offence for any person to corruptly solicit, receive or agree to receive for himself or for any other person, or to promise, give or offer to any person, any gift, loan, reward or advantage whatever, as an inducement to or reward for or otherwise on account of, any member, officer or servant of a public body (such as a county, city or town council, board, etc.) doing or forbearing to do anything in respect of any matter or transaction whatsoever, actual or proposed, in which said public body is concerned. Thus any bribery and corruption in connection with the members and servants of public bodies is a misdemeanour by statute, but by s. 4 no prosecution under the Act may be instituted without the consent of the Attorney-General.

Prevention of Corruption Act 1906: This statute deals with the corruption of and by any agent or person employed by or acting for another, and makes the following offences triable on indictment or summarily:

(1) For any agent to corruptly accept, obtain or agree to accept, or to attempt to obtain from any person for himself or for any other person, any gift or consideration, as an inducement or reward for doing or not doing any act in relation to his principal's affairs or business, or for showing or not showing favour or disfavour to any person in relation to his principal's affairs or business;

(2) For any person to corruptly offer, give or agree to give any gift or consideration to any agent for like reason;

(3) For any person to knowingly give to any agent, or for any agent to knowingly use with intent to deceive his principal, any receipt, account or document which is false or incorrect in any material particular and which to his knowledge is intended to mislead the principal.

A person serving under the Crown or under any corporation, borough, county or district council is an agent under this Act. So also is a police constable.

The consent of the Attorney-General is necessary before a prosecution may be instituted, the information must be on oath.

Prevention of Corruption Act 1916 declares that when money or other consideration is paid, given to or received by a person in the employment of the Crown or of a public body, by or from a person holding or seeking to obtain a contract from the Crown or public body, such money or consideration shall be deemed to have been given or received corruptly unless the contrary is proved.

This statute extends the expression "public body" (1889 Act, s. 1) to include local and public authorities of all descriptions, and states that a person serving under any such body is an agent within the meaning of the Prevention of Corruption Act 1906.

Any offence of bribery and corruption of or by a public official must be reported to the Director of Public Prosecutions. See Appendix III.

As regards bribery and other corrupt practices at elections, see "Election Offences", below.

Licensing Act 1964, s. 178. It is a summary offence for any holder of a justices' licence to bribe or attempt to bribe any constable (see "Conduct of Licensed Premises", Chap. 38). Bribery of an officer of customs and excise is a serious offence and the offender may be detained (Customs and Excise Act 1952, s. 9).

Extortion – It is an offence at common law for any public officer to extort or unlawfully take, by virtue of his official position, any money or thing of value that is not due to him or more than is due, or before it is due.

Misconduct by Public Officers – Generally speaking, any misconduct by an officer of justice, either by wrong-doing or by culpable neglect, is a common law offence.

For stealing or embezzlement by a public officer, see Chap. 14.

Police Act 1964, s. 53. Any person who causes, or attempts to cause, or does any act calculated to cause, disaffection amongst the members of any police force, or induces or attempts to induce, or does any act calculated to induce, any member of a police force to withhold his services or to commit breaches of discipline, commits an offence. This section applies to Special Constables.

The Crown Proceedings Act 1947 gives the right to sue the Crown (authorised departments or the Attorney-General, s. 17) by civil proceedings in accordance with the provisions of the Act.

Election Offences – The Representation of the People Acts 1949 and 1969 deal with parliamentary and local government elections. The franchise is the right to vote and in polling (voting) votes are given by secret ballot.

PERSONATION – This is the voting as some other person living or dead or fictitious, and application for or the marking of a ballot paper shall be deemed to be voting. It is a corrupt practice (s. 47). It is an offence, and aiding, abetting, counselling or procuring it is also an offence. Two witnesses are necessary to prove it (s. 146).

OTHER VOTING OFFENCES – These are dealt with in ss. 48, 49 and are illegal practices and any tampering with, destruction, stealing of, etc., of ballot papers or nomination papers are offences (s. 52). Breaches of the secrecy of voting will be summary offences (s. 53).

BRIBERY – That is directly or indirectly using any consideration of value to induce a voter to vote or refrain from voting is a corrupt practice (s. 99).

TREATING – This is the providing or accepting any meat, drink, entertainment or provision for corruptly influencing any person to vote or refrain from voting and is a corrupt practice (s. 100).

UNDUE INFLUENCE – This is the using or threatening to use any force, restraint or threats against any person to make him vote or refrain from voting or impeding or preventing the free exercise of the franchise. It is a corrupt practice (s. 101). A corrupt practice is punishable on indictment or summarily (s. 146). An illegal practice is punishable summarily (s. 147). It will be the duty of the Director of Public Prosecutions to inquire into any allegations of corrupt or illegal practices and to institute such prosecutions as he may consider necessary (s. 159).

It will be an illegal practice for any person to act or incite others to act in a disorderly manner for the purpose of preventing the transaction of the business at a political meeting held between the dates of the issue of and the return to a writ for a parliamentary election in the constituency or at a meeting in the electoral area for a local government election held on or within three weeks before the day of election.

If any constable reasonably suspects any person of committing this offence, he may, if so requested by the chairman of the meeting, require that person to give him his name and address. If such person refuses or fails to do so or gives a false name and address, he will be liable to summary conviction. If he refuses his name and address or if the constable reasonably suspects him of giving a false name and address, the constable may without warrant arrest him (s. 84). No member of a police force shall in any manner try to persuade any person to give or not to give his vote in any constituency or electoral area wholly or partly within the police area (s. 87).

SECOND SCHEDULE TO THE ACT – A constable shall not be admitted to vote in person elsewhere than at his own polling station, except on production and surrender of a certificate as to his employment signed by the prescribed officer of police or by the returning officer (para. 33).

If a person misconducts himself in a polling station or fails to obey the presiding officer he may be removed by order of the presiding officer by a constable and such person, if charged with the commission of an offence in the polling station, may be dealt with as a person arrested by a constable, without a warrant, for an offence (para. 34).

If a person applies in a polling station for a ballot paper and the candidate or his election or polling agent declares to the presiding officer that he has reasonable cause to believe that such person has committed personation and undertakes to substantiate the charge in a court of law, the presiding officer may order a constable to arrest him and he shall be dealt with as a person arrested without warrant for an offence (para. 37). The Act was followed by the Representation of the People Regs. 1950, 1954.

Obstructing Public Justice – Any conspiracy to obstruct, prevent, pervert or defeat the course of public justice or falsely to accuse of any crime is an offence.

It is not necessary that proceedings should have already commenced at the time when the conspiracy to conceal or to prevent proceedings takes place. Public justice requires that every crime should be suitably dealt with (*R.* v. *Sharpe and Stringer* (1938)).

Note.—Any offence of conspiracy to pervert or defeat the course of justice must be reported to the Director of Public Prosecutions. See Appendix III.

CHAPTER 22

PUBLIC ORDER

	Page
Breach of the Peace and Sureties	225
Surety of the Peace	226
Surety for Good Behaviour	226
Affray	227
Unlawful Assembly	227
Riot	228
Riot Damage	228
Forcible Entry and Detainer	228
Labour Disputes	229
Intimidation	230
Breaking Contract of Service	230
Public Order Act 1936	230
Rent Act 1965	233
Administration of Justice Act 1970	234
Meetings	235
Emergency Powers	235

Breach of the Peace and Sureties – The "Queen's Peace" or shortly "the peace" is the normal state of society, and any interruption of that peace and good order which ought to prevail in a civilised country is a breach of the peace. Breaches of the peace may be serious, affecting large numbers of people, such as riots; they may involve comparatively few persons, such as affrays; and they may consist of acts of violence confined to 2 or more persons, such as assaults.

For offensive conduct in a public place or at a public meeting which is likely to cause a breach of the peace, a constable can arrest without warrant. See "Public Order Act 1936", later.

The justices are empowered to take measures to prevent any apprehended or likely breach of the peace, and may, on evidence produced before them, order a person to enter into a recognizance and find sureties either to keep the peace or to be of good behaviour.

The process is termed "binding over" to keep the peace or to be of good behaviour. Upon complaint by any person a magistrates' court may hear the complainant and defendant and their witnesses and may make an order adjudging the defendant to enter into a recognizance, with or without sureties, to keep the peace or to be of good behaviour towards the complainant. If he fails to comply with the order the court may commit him to custody for up to 6 months or until he sooner complies with the order (M.C. Act 1952, s. 91).

For breach of such an order, forfeiture of the recognizances may be ordered. See "Recognizance", Chap. 5.

Where a magistrates' court has committed a person to custody in default of finding sureties ordered on complaint of another person, the committed person or his representative by complaint against that other person, may apply to the court which, on fresh evidence, may reduce the amount of any surety or dispense with them or otherwise deal with the case as it thinks just (M.C. Act 1952, s. 94, and Rules).

Before binding over a person, the court should hear evidence from both sides. Even if no application that a person be bound over is made, the court may, if it thinks fit, bind over that person.

Binding over is a precautionary measure, to be adopted when there is reasonable ground to anticipate some present or future danger. It is not a conviction or a punishment. It should not be ordered for some act that is past and is not likely to be repeated, but it may be added to a punishment for a definite offence, as, in a case of assault, allowed by C.J. Act 1925, s. 39.

Surety of the Peace – Persons engaged in committing a breach of the peace may be arrested by a constable and ordered by the justices to give surety of the peace. If a person has just cause to fear that another will do him or his family some bodily harm or damage his property, he may demand the surety of the peace against him.

Threats of violence or threats to injure or procure others to injure the complainant will justify binding over to keep the peace.

An applicant should satisfy the court that he is actually under fear and that he has cause to be so.

If the parties are before the court on another charge, the court, if satisfied that there is a fear of future danger, may exercise their power of binding over.

Surety for Good Behaviour – This surety is more comprehensive than the surety of the peace, as it includes the surety of the peace, and a person who is bound over to be of good behaviour is also bound to the peace.

All disturbers of the peace may be bound over to be of good behaviour, and it need not be proved or even suggested that any person is put in fear. The Justices of the Peace Act 1361 authorises justices to take security of their good behaviour from "all them that be not of good fame". When a person is bound over to keep the peace or be of good behaviour he can appeal to the Crown Court. (Magistrates Courts (Appeals from Binding Over Orders) Act 1956.)

Generally speaking, the court can bind over to be of good behaviour for any act of misbehaviour, but justices may not exercise this power for rash, unmannerly or quarrelsome words, unless they tend to a breach of the peace or to scandalise the Government.

This power to bind over to be of good behaviour is limited only by the discretion of the court. It is not confined to breach of the peace. It is preventive justice to prevent a person doing something against the law. See *R.* v. *Sandbach, Ex parte Williams* (1935).

Affray – An affray is the offence committed by 2 or more people fighting together to the terror of the Queen's subjects, and it is not a necessary ingredient of the offence that it should occur in a public place (*Button and Swain* v. *Director of Public Prosecutions* (1966)). It is at common law an offence.

An affray differs from a riot in that an affray is not premeditated and in that it requires 3 or more persons to constitute a riot, whereas 2 persons can make an affray.

If 2 persons fight in a street or public place, but not to the terror of the people, it is not an affray, but such conduct may be dealt with as an assault or breach of the peace.

A constable should quell an affray which happens in his presence. He may arrest the offenders without warrant and bring them before a justice, who may commit them for trial or bind them over to keep the peace. See Chap. 3.

Unlawful Assembly – An assembly of persons is unlawful at common law when it is composed of 3 or more persons who have met together to carry into effect some illegal purpose or who have met in such numbers or under such circumstances as to endanger the public peace or cause alarm and apprehension to Her Majesty's subjects. An unlawful assembly, therefore, would be any gathering of 3 or more persons for any unlawful purpose or with intent to carry out any common purpose in such a manner as is likely to endanger the peace, as shown by the large numbers assembled or by the circumstances of the assembly.

Any meeting of numbers of people with such circumstances of terror as cannot but endanger the peace and cause alarm among the Queen's subjects is an unlawful assembly.

All persons who join an unlawful assembly and all who give support to it are liable to prosecution for misdemeanour at common law. It does not matter whether the object of the meeting be lawful or unlawful, for, if the circumstances accompanying it (e.g. great numbers, etc.) are, in the opinion of firm and rational men, likely to endanger the peace, the meeting will be an unlawful assembly.

It is the duty of the police to disperse and put an end to an unlawful assembly, arresting the ringleaders and persons who offer resistance either on the spot if it is possible and advisable, or subsequently by warrant. As an alternative, proceedings may subsequently be taken against individuals by summons for any assaults, obstruction, etc., that may have taken place. An unchecked unlawful assembly may end in a riot.

Riot – A riot is a tumultuous disturbance of the peace by 3 persons or more, assembling together of their own authority, with an intent mutually to assist one another against anyone who shall oppose them in the execution of some enterprise of a private nature, and afterwards actually executing the same in a violent and turbulent manner, to the terror of the people, whether the act intended were of itself lawful or unlawful (Archbold).

The assembly becomes a riot when those assembled begin to execute their enterprise by a breach of the peace to the terror of the public.

If a number of people meet together and suddenly quarrel and fight amongst themselves it is an affray (see "Affray"), not a riot; but if they divide into parties and the parties fight together, each party with a common purpose, it is a riot.

Riot is an offence at common law, and all persons encouraging, promoting or taking part are liable.

A riot is where 3 or more assemble with a common purpose to do an unlawful act and make some advances towards doing it. A rout is the step just previous to a riot. Rout is an offence at common law.

It is the duty of the police to suppress a riot, using force if necessary, and they have authority to call on all other subjects of the Queen to assist them in so doing. It is the duty of every citizen to assist in suppressing a riot.

It is an offence at common law for a person to refuse to assist a constable in the execution of his duty when duly called on to do so and the person is capable of so doing and has no lawful excuse for refusing.

Any two justices may order all licensed premises to remain closed during any time they may appoint, in or near the place where any riot or tumult happens or is expected to happen (Licensing Act 1964, s. 188).

Riot Damage – Under the Riot (Damages) Act 1886 (as amended by the Police Act 1964), a person whose house or premises has been damaged or the property therein injured, stolen or destroyed by rioters may claim compensation from the Police Authority in accordance with the Secretary of State's Regulations dated October 1, 1921, which also apply in the case of rioters plundering a wreck.

Forcible Entry and Detainer – Forcible entry is the taking possession of lands or buildings by force and without the authority of the law. It is an offence by statute and at common law.

The offence lies in the use of violence, such as threats, force, large numbers of people, etc., and the fact that the offender had a right to enter the premises will not justify such use of violence.

Proceedings are by indictment, and charges of assault, etc., may also be made, if the circumstances justify same.

An entry without force may be a trespass. See Chap. 19.

Forcible detainer is the continuing to hold possession by force of lands or buildings which have been entered wrongfully.

This is a similar offence and will be committed by a person who, without any right to the property, forcibly keeps possession.

However, a trespasser may be removed from premises by the rightful owner provided that no more force is used than is necessary for his removal and that his goods are removed with proper care.

Labour Disputes – Any combination of workmen for the purpose of securing a rise in wages or an alteration in their conditions of employment was at one time illegal. In 1825 the laws against such combinations were repealed, and in 1871 trade unions were made lawful.

In 1875, s. 3 of the Conspiracy and Protection of Property Act exempted trade unions from liability to the law as regards conspiracy (see "Conspiracy") by enacting that an agreement or combination by 2 or more persons to do or procure to be done any act in contemplation or furtherance of an industrial dispute should not be indictable as a conspiracy, if such act, when committed by one person, would not be punishable as a crime.

However, this section does not exempt from punishment any person guilty of a conspiracy for which a punishment is directed by any Act of Parliament, and it does not affect the law relating to riot, unlawful assembly, breach of the peace, or sedition, or any offence against the State or the Sovereign.

By virtue of the Police Act 1964, s. 47, a member of a police force shall not be a member of a trade union, or of any association having for its objects, or one of its objects, to control or influence the pay, pensions or conditions of service of any police force, provided that where a person was a member of a trade union before becoming a member of a police force, he may with the consent of the chief officer of police, continue to be a member of that union during the time of his service in the police force. This applies to police cadets but does not apply to membership of the Police Federations.

PEACEFUL PICKETING. It shall be lawful for one or more persons in contemplation of a trade dispute to attend at or near, (a) a place where another person works or carries on business; or (b) any other place where another person happens to be, not being a place where he resides, for the purpose only of peacefully obtaining or communicating information or peacefully persuading any person to work or abstain from working (Trade Union and Labour Relations Act 1974, s. 15). For the meaning of "trade dispute" see s. 29 of the Act.

Intimidation – Conspiracy and Protection of Property Act 1875, s. 7. Every person commits a summary offence, but may claim trial by jury on indictment who, with a view to compel any other person to abstain from doing or to do any act which such other person has a legal right to do or abstain from doing, wrongfully and without legal authority:

(1) uses violence to or intimidates such other person or his wife or children or injures his property, or

(2) persistently follows such other person about from place to place, or

(3) hides any tools, clothing or other property owned or used by such other person, or deprives him of or hinders him in the use thereof, or

(4) follows such other person with 2 or more other persons in a disorderly manner in or through any street or road, or

(5) watches or besets the house or place where such other person resides or works or carries on business or happens to be, or the approach to such house or place.

Breaking Contract of Service – Conspiracy and Protection of Property Act 1875, ss. 4 and 5. It is a summary offence for any person employed in the supply of gas or water to wilfully and maliciously break his contract of service knowing that the consequences will be to deprive the inhabitants of their supply of gas or water, and for any person to wilfully and maliciously break a contract of service or hiring knowing that the probable consequences will be to endanger life or property.

See Stone, under title "Labour Laws".

Public Order Act 1936 – This Act deals with political uniforms, private quasi-military associations, processions, offensive conduct and public meetings.

Under the Act, "meeting" means a meeting held for the purpose of discussion of matters of public interest or for the expression of views thereon. "Public meeting" includes any meeting in a public place and any meeting which the public or any section thereof are permitted to attend, whether on payment or otherwise.

"Public procession" means a procession in a public place.

"Public place" includes any highway and any other premises or place to which at the material time the public have or are permitted to have access, whether on payment or otherwise (s. 9 as substituted by C.J. Act 1972, s. 33).

POLITICAL UNIFORMS. Section 1 – It will be a summary offence for any person to wear uniform signifying his association with any political organisation or with the promotion of any political object, in any public place or at any public meeting, unless such wearing has been permitted on special occasion by the Chief Officer of Police, by order made with the consent of the Secretary of State (s. 1). Men wearing dark glasses, black berets, and dark clothing escorting the coffin of a fellow supporter of the Irish Republican Movement were held to be wearing a uniform signifying association with a political party (*Moran* v. *D.P.P.* (1974), *The Times*, December 12th). A constable may arrest without warrant any person reasonably suspected to be committing this offence (s. 7). A court may remand in custody for eight days only or on bail, but no further proceedings shall be taken without the consent of the Attorney-General (s. 1).

QUASI-MILITARY ORGANISATIONS. Section 2 – It will be an offence (punishable summarily or on indictment: s. 7) for any person to take part in the control or management or in the organising or training of any association of persons whose members or adherents are:

(1) organised or trained or equipped for the purpose of enabling them to be employed in usurping the functions of the police or armed forces of the Crown, or

(2) organised and trained or organised and equipped either for the purpose of enabling them to be employed for the use or display of physical force in promoting any political object or in such manner as to arouse reasonable apprehension that they are organised and either trained or equipped for that purpose.

A prosecution shall not be instituted without the consent of the Attorney-General.

The High Court, on application by the Attorney-General, has power to deal with the property of any such association. A judge of the High Court may grant a search warrant to enter any place or premises within one month and search the place or premises and persons therein (women to be searched by a woman) and seize anything found which is reasonably suspected to be evidence of this offence.

Proof of things done or words written, spoken or published, by any person taking part in the control or management or in organising, etc., shall be admissible as evidence of the purposes for which or the manner in which members, etc., of the association were organised or trained or equipped.

This s. 2 shall not prohibit the employment, arrangements for or instruction in their duties of a reasonable number of persons as stewards to assist in preserving order at any public meeting held upon private premises (s. 2), that is premises to which the public have access (on payment or otherwise) only by permission of the owner, occupier or lessee of the premises (s. 9). Nor does it prohibit their being furnished with badges or other distinguishing signs (s. 2).

PROCESSIONS. Section 3 – If the Chief Officer of Police, having regard to the time or place and the circumstances and to the route taken or proposed to be taken by any public procession, has reasonable ground for apprehending that the procession may occasion serious public disorder, he may give directions imposing upon the organisers or the processionists such conditions as may appear to him necessary for preserving public order, including prescribing the route and prohibiting entry of any public place specified.

Provided no conditions restricting display of flags, banners or emblems shall be imposed except such as are reasonably necessary to prevent risk of a breach of the peace.

If he considers that under existing circumstances in a borough or urban district the above powers will not be sufficient to prevent serious public disorder arising from the holding of public processions in any part of the area, the Chief Officer of Police shall apply to the Council of the Borough or District for an order prohibiting for a specified period (not exceeding three months) all public processions or any specified class of public procession, and the Council, with the consent of the Secretary of State, may make such an order. The Commissioners of the City of London and of the Metropolis have the same power, as above given to Councils, in their police areas.

Any person who knowingly fails to comply with any directions or conditions so prescribed under the section, or who organises or assists in organising any public procession held or intended to be held in contravention of such an order or incites any person to take part in same, will commit a summary offence.

Arranging the route, etc., of an unlawful procession amounts to organising it (*Flockhart* v. *Robertson* (1950)).

OFFENSIVE WEAPONS. Section 4 – It will be a summary offence for any person while present at any public meeting or on the occasion of any public procession, to have with him any offensive weapon, otherwise than in pursuance of lawful authority. A person shall not be deemed to be acting in pursuance of lawful authority unless he is acting in his capacity as a servant of the Crown or of either House of Parliament or of any local authority or as a member of a recognised corps (viz. rifle club, miniature rifle club or cadet corps duly approved: s. 9) or as a member of a fire brigade or as a constable. A constable may without warrant arrest any person reasonably suspected to be committing this offence (s. 7). See also under "Robbery", Chap. 14.

OFFENSIVE CONDUCT. Section 5 (as substituted by s. 7 of the Race Relations Act 1965) – It will be a summary offence for any person in any public place or at any public meeting (a) to use threatening, abusive or insulting words or behaviour, or (b) to distribute or display any writing, sign or visible representation which is threatening, abusive or insulting with intent to provoke a breach of the peace or whereby a breach of the peace is likely to be occasioned. A speaker at a public place or public meeting must take his audience as he finds them, and if the words used to a particular audience or part of it (even a part intent on obstructing the speaker) are likely to provoke a breach of the peace, then the speaker is guilty of an offence under the section (*Jordan* v. *Burgoyne* (1963)). This section is intended not only to preserve public order where many people are involved, but also to preserve public order in a public place; and is not limited to conduct at political meetings (*Holman* v. *Ward* (1964)). A constable may without warrant arrest any person reasonably suspected to be committing this offence (s. 7).

PUBLIC MEETINGS. Public Meeting Act 1908, s. 1, as amended by the Public Order Act 1963 makes it an offence, punishable summarily or on indictment, for any person at a lawful public meeting to act in a disorderly manner for the purpose of preventing the transaction of the business for which the meeting was called together. Inciting another to commit the offence will be a like offence. See also "Offensive Conduct" above, and "Election Offences", Chap. 21.

The following has been added to this Act by s. 6 of the Public Order Act. If a constable reasonably suspects any person of committing the above offence he may if requested to do so by the chairman of the meeting require that person to give his name and address. If such person refuses or fails to do so or gives a false name and address, he will commit a summary offence. If such person refuses or fails to give his name and address or if the constable reasonably suspects him of giving a false name and address, the constable may without warrant arrest him.

INCITEMENT TO RACIAL HATRED. It is an offence for a person, with intent, to stir up hatred against any section of the public in Great Britain distinguished by colour, race, or ethnic or national origins, (a) to publish or distribute written matter which is threatening, abusive, or insulting, or (b) to use in any public place or at any public meeting words which are threatening, abusive or insulting, being matter or words likely to stir up hatred against that section on grounds of colour, race, or ethnic or national origins (Race Relations Act 1965, s. 6). No prosecution for such an offence shall be instituted except with the consent of the Attorney-General.

Rent Act 1965 – Protection against harassment and eviction without due process of law.

S. 30 (1) If any person unlawfully deprives the residential occupier of any premises of his occupation of the premises or any part thereof or attempts to do so he shall be guilty of an offence unless he proves that he believed, and had reasonable cause to believe, that the residential occupier had ceased to reside in the premises.

(2) If any person with intent to cause the residential occupier of any premises:

(a) to give up the occupation of the premises or any part thereof; or

(b) to refrain from exercising any right or pursuing any remedy in respect of the premises or part thereof;

does acts calculated to interfere with the peace or comfort of the residential occupier or members of his household, or persistently withdraws or withholds services reasonably required for the occupation of the premises as a residence, he shall be guilty of an offence.

The general effect of s. 30 (1), read with s. 32 (which prohibits eviction without due process of law), is that eviction is an offence except where a court order for possession has been obtained. The effect of s. 30 (2) is to create the new offence of "harassment".

(Normally the local housing authority, not the police, will institute proceedings for alleged offences under s. 30, but the police should report to the local housing authority any breaches of this law which are brought to their notice).

Administration of Justice Act 1970 – Unlawful harassment of debtors: A person commits an offence if, with the object of coercing another person to pay money claimed from the other as a debt due under a contract he (a) harasses the other with demands for payment which, in respect of their frequency or the manner or occasion of making any such demand, or of any threat or publicity by which any demand is accompanied, are calculated to subject him or members of his family or household to alarm, distress or humiliation; (b) falsely represents, in relation to the money claimed, that criminal proceedings lie for failure to pay it; (c) falsely represents himself to be authorised in some official capacity to claim or enforce payment; or (d) utters a document falsely represented by him to have some official character or purporting to have some official character which he knows it has not (s. 40 (1)). A person may be guilty of an offence by virtue of sub-s. (1) (a) above if he concerts with others in the taking of such action as is described in that paragraph, notwithstanding that his own course of conduct does not by itself amount to harassment (s. 40 (2)). Subsection (1) (a) above does not apply to anything done by a person which is reasonable (and otherwise permissible in law) for the purpose: (a) of securing the discharge of an obligation due, or believed to be due, to himself or to persons for whom he acts, or protecting himself or them from future loss; or (b) of the enforcement of any liability by legal process (s. 40 (3)).

Meetings – There is no right to hold meetings in any public place, as such places are for people to pass along. Every unauthorised obstruction of the highway is illegal as being either an offence by some statute or byelaw or indictable as a common nuisance. Sreets are for passage, and passage is superior to everything else, and nothing short of absolute necessity will justify a person in obstructing a highway. An obstruction is committed even if only part of the highway is obstructed. However, meetings may be permissible in certain public places in accordance with local custom, but usually not as of right.

When a meeting is held in a private place, those present, whether there by payment, by ticket, or free, are there by permission of the persons responsible for the meeting, and if requested to leave they should leave the premises. (See below as regards the police.)

A person who does not leave on such request becomes a trespasser and may be put out by reasonably necessary force. If such a trespasser uses violence to those removing him he commits a breach of the peace. The chairman of such a meeting has authority to regulate the proceedings. He may call on a disorderly person to keep quiet or else leave the meeting, and if such request is disobeyed he may direct the removal of such person. The stewards or agents of the promoters of the meeting may then use reasonably necessary force to eject the disturber, and if he resists and uses violence he will be liable for having committed a breach of the peace. See "Arrest", Chap. 3.

It has been held that the police are entitled to enter and remain on private premises (in this case it was a meeting in a hired hall and the public were invited to attend without charge for admission) when there are reasonable grounds for believing that an offence or a breach of the peace is likely to be committed thereon. A constable in the execution of his duty has a right to enter and remain on private premises when he has reasonable ground for believing that an offence is imminent or is likely to be committed (*Thomas* v. *Sawkins* (1935)).

As regards meetings in streets it has been held that as it is the duty of the police to prevent an apprehended breach of the peace and accordingly to prohibit and prevent a meeting which would likely result in a disturbance if held, a person attempting to hold the meeting and refusing to desist was rightly convicted of obstructing a police inspector in the execution of his duty (*Duncan* v. *Jones* (1936)).

Emergency Powers – The Emergency Powers Act 1920, as amended by the Emergency Powers Act 1964, empowers the

Sovereign to issue proclamations of emergency. This can be done if it appears that there have occurred, or are about to occur, events of such a nature as to be calculated, by interfering with the supply and distribution of food, water, fuel or light or with the means of locomotion, to deprive the community of the essentials of life.

No such proclamation shall be in force for more than one month without prejudice to the issue of another proclamation at or before the end of that period.

Regulations may be made for securing the essentials of life and should be laid before Parliament for approval of their continuance.

CHAPTER 23

CONSPIRACY AND DEFAMATION

	Page		Page
Conspiracy . . .	237	Slander	238
Libel	238		

Conspiracy – Conspiracy is the crime committed when 2 or more persons combine together to execute some act for the purpose of injuring some other person or the public. It is an offence at common law. An indictment will lie for conspiracy to commit an offence which itself is triable summarily only (*R.* v. *Blamires Transport Services, Ltd.* (1963)).

The essence of the crime is the agreement of 2 or more persons to do some unlawful act or to do some lawful act by unlawful means, and it is not necessary that any act should have been done in pursuance of the agreement. Conspiracy involves the element of *mens rea,* in that the prosecution must prove not only an agreement between the alleged conspirators to carry out an unlawful purpose, as signified by words or other means of communication between them, but also an intention in the mind of any alleged conspirator to carry out the unlawful purpose (*R.* v. *Thomson* (1966)). It is an offence of confederacy or combination. Unless a third person is charged with them, husband and wife cannot be jointly charged with the crime as the law regards them to be one. All the accused need not be brought to trial together; one person may be prosecuted for conspiracy with others known or unknown. Everything said, written or done by any one of the conspirators in furtherance of their common purpose will be evidence against the other conspirators.

There may be a conspiracy to defraud any person or persons, to injure an individual by some wrongful act or by blackmailing him, to commit some offence or some public mischief, etc.

It may be possible to deal with an act of fraud which does not come within the definition of false pretences as a conspiracy.

For conspiracy to murder, see Chap. 9.

See also "Labour Disputes" and "Intimidation", Chap. 22, and "Obstructing Public Justice", Chap. 21.

Libel – The offence termed libel consists in making public in some way a defamatory document concerning some person, class of persons, or system so as to tend to lower him, them or it in the estimation of right-thinking members of society generally. Libel is an offence when it is likely to cause a breach of the peace by exciting feelings of revenge, stirring up hatred against persons, or tending to disturb the peace and good order of the country.

The mere writing of a libel is not an offence, but the offence is committed when the libel is published, viz. communicated to some other person or persons by means of writing, printing, pictures, etc.

In criminal proceedings, communication of the libel to the injured person is sufficient, as it may provoke him to a breach of the peace, and the truth of the libel will not be a good defence unless accused can prove that the publication of it was for the public benefit.

Criminal proceedings for libel are as a rule not undertaken unless some public interest is concerned, something affecting the State and the general administration and interest of the country.

Any offence of libel *re* persons occupying judicial or public offices must be reported to the Director of Public Prosecutions. See Appendix III.

Libel Act 1843, ss. 4 and 5. It is an offence to maliciously publish any defamatory libel, and the punishment is greater should it be charged and proved that it was published, knowing it to be false.

If the intention of publication is to excite disaffection against the Sovereign, the Government, the administration of justice, or to incite to crime, disaffection, etc., the libel becomes a seditious libel. See "Sedition", Chap. 20.

If the writing blasphemes God or turns the Christian religion into contempt or ridicule, etc., the person responsible may be indicted for blasphemous libel.

A libel may be dealt with as an obscene libel, if the matter therein is obscene and likely to deprave and corrupt those into whose hands it might fall. See Appendix III.

As regards the privilege extended to fair and accurate newspaper reports of proceedings in courts or at public meetings and meetings of public bodies, and to departmental and police publications, see the Law of Libel Amendment Act 1888. See also C.J. Act 1967, s. 5.

The Newspaper Libel and Registration Act 1881, deals with summary court proceedings in respect of libels published in newspapers.

Slander is the utterance in words of defamatory matter, viz. matter which directly or indirectly tends to lower any person or persons in the estimation of right-thinking members of society.

It is thus a kind of verbal libel and redress may be obtained by civil action for damages.

Slander may be indictable if the words are seditious, blasphemous or obscene, or tend to provoke a breach of the peace.

The law as to libel, slander and other malicious falsehoods has been amended by the Defamation Act 1952.

PART V–TRAFFIC LAW

CHAPTER 24

TRAFFIC

	Page
Highways, Streets and Roads	243
Obstruction	244
Highway Act 1835, s. 72 .	245
Town Police Clauses Act 1847, s. 28 . . .	245
Highways Act 1959 .	247
Highways Act 1971 .	249
Impounding animals .	250
Regulation of Traffic .	250
Road Traffic Acts, etc. .	252
Chronically Sick and Disabled Persons Act 1970	293
Police Powers . .	334

Highways, Streets and Roads – "Highway" means a strip of land over which every member of the public may lawfully pass. The public have only the right to pass along the highway. A *cul-de-sac* or way closed at one end so that there is no thoroughfare may be a highway.

Highways are common to the public, and "highway", in the full sense, is a public road over which all the subjects of the realm have a right to pass and repass (Stephen's Commentaries).

"Street" for the purposes of the Public Health Act 1875 (see s. 4), includes any highway, road, lane, footway, square, court, alley, or passage, whether a thoroughfare or not; and the term is usually applied to a road with houses in a town or urban district; it has a similar meaning in the Public Health Act 1936.

A highway or street includes any footways or footpaths at the sides, and offences in relation to "highways" or "streets" may be committed on the footway as well as in the carriage-way. However, there are several distinct offences confined to footways and they will be indicated separately.

The Road Traffic Act 1972 states that a "road", for the purposes of the Act, means any highway and any other road to which the public has access and includes bridges over which a road passes (s. 196).

This includes the private forecourt of a hotel to which the public have access habitually without let or hindrance (*Bugge* v. *Taylor* (1941)). But see also *Thomas* v. *Dando* (1951) where the forecourt was not habitually used by the public. A road includes the footway as well as the carriageway (*Bryant* v. *Marx* (1932)), and generally includes its footpath (or pavement) which would include its grass verge.

Public highways and streets are maintained by the Local Authorities. The police deal with highway and street offences which affect the public and report to Local Authorities any interference with the highways and streets.

Generally speaking, any wrongful act or omission upon or near a highway which interferes with the public right to freely, safely and conveniently pass along the highway may be held to be a nuisance at common law, and therefore indictable and punishable.

A person who has sustained damage by reason of a nuisance may sue for damages and (or) an injunction to end the nuisance.

Obstruction – Members of the public have a right to pass along any public highway, and any interference with that right amounts to obstruction. Only absolute necessity will justify any obstruction of the highway.

Any unauthorised obstruction of the highway is a nuisance and indictable as a misdemeanour at common law. Several statutes provide penalties for various forms of obstruction, but if any particular form of obstruction is not expressly penalised by statute, the offender may be indicted for the nuisance. For example, a shopkeeper whose display in his windows collected large crowds, thereby obstructing the highway, has been convicted on indictment for nuisance.

Obstruction may be caused by:

(1) Persons—who in any way wilfully obstruct the free passage of any highway or footway.

(2) Things—which by their presence on the highway or footway interfere with the public right to pass along. The persons responsible are liable.

(3) Vehicles—for which the driver or person in charge is liable. The law cases as to obstruction were reviewed in *Gill* v. *Carson* (1917), and the test is the unreasonable use of the highway. In *Solomon* v. *Durbridge* (1956) it was held that a motor car could become an unnecessary obstruction of the highway if it was left at a particular place for too long.

The several obstruction offences are given in subsequent sections, under "Highways Acts", "Town Police Clauses Act", "Regulation of Traffic", also see "Obstruction", Appendix II.

In addition to the statutes dealing with obstruction on the highways generally throughout the country, and with obstruction in the streets of cities, towns or urban districts, many localities have local byelaws and regulations dealing with particular forms of obstruction, such as jostling on the footpaths.

The statute law under which road obstruction is usually dealt with is:

(1) Highway Act 1835, s. 78, obstruction in any way of the free passage of the highway.

(2) Town Police Clauses Act 1847, s. 28 (where it applies). Wilful obstruction of the street by vehicle or animal, to the obstruction, annoyance or danger of the residents or passengers.

(3) Construction and Use Regs., reg. 95 and Tracklaying Vehicles Regs., reg. 67. Unnecessary obstruction of the road by a motor vehicle or its trailer. See "Obstruction", Appendix II.

(4) Highways Act 1959, s. 121. Wilful obstruction in any way of the free passage along a highway. In the case of *Seekings* v. *Clarke* (1961), a shopkeeper was convicted of an offence under this section by placing articles for sale on the pavement in front of his shop. A constable may arrest without warrant any person whom he sees committing this offence.

Highway Act 1835, s. 72 – The following acts are summary offences:

Tethering any horse, ass, sheep, mule, swine or cattle on any highway so as to suffer or permit the tethered animal to be thereon.

Wilfully riding upon any footpath or causeway by the side of any road made or set apart for the use or accommodation of foot passengers. "Footpath" means a way over which the public have a right of way on foot only (R.T. Act 1972, s. 196).

Wilfully leading or driving any horse, ass, sheep, mule, swine, cattle or carriage of any description (including bicycles and other similar machines (Local Government Act 1888, s. 85)) or any truck or sledge upon any such footpath or causeway.

Under s. 78 it is a summary offence for any person by negligence or misbehaviour to prevent, hinder or interrupt the free passage of any person, wagon, cart or other carriage, or horses, mules or other beasts of burden on any highway.

Town Police Clauses Act 1847, s. 28 (where it applies), declares that the following acts are offences when they are committed in any street (which includes any road, square, court, alley and thoroughfare, or public passage (s. 3), and means a place to which the public have a right of access, including the footpaths), in a town or urban district to the obstruction, annoyance or danger of the residents or passengers:

Exposing for show, hire or sale (except in a market or fair) any horse or other animal.

Exhibiting in a caravan or otherwise any show or public entertainment.

Shoeing, bleeding or farrying any horse or animal (except in case of accident).

Cleaning, exercising, training, breaking or turning loose any horse or animal.

Making or repairing any part of any carriage (except necessary repairs after accidents).

Slaughtering or dressing any cattle or any part thereof (except in cases of accident).

Placing any line, cord or pole across any street or hanging or placing any clothes thereon.

Wantonly discharging any firearm or throwing or discharging any stone or other missile.

Making any bonfire or throwing or setting fire to any firework.

Wilfully and wantonly disturbing any inhabitant by pulling or ringing any door bell or knocking at any door.

Wilfully or unlawfully extinguishing the light of any lamp.

Flying any kite or making or using any slide upon ice or snow.

Cleaning or preparing any cask or tub, or cutting, etc., any timber or stone, or slaking, sifting or screening lime.

Throwing or laying down any stones, coal, timber or other material (except building materials so enclosed as to prevent mischief to passengers).

Beating or shaking any carpet, rug or mat (except doormats before 8 a.m.).

Fixing or placing any flower-pot, box or other heavy article in any upper window without sufficiently guarding same against being blown down.

Throwing from any roof or any part of a building any slate, brick, rubbish or other thing (except snow so as not to fall on passengers).

Ordering or permitting any person in his service to stand on the sill of a window so as to carry out any operation on the outside (unless such window is in the basement storey).

Leaving open any vault or cellar or underground entrance without a sufficient fence or handrail, or leaving the covering of same defective.

Insufficiently fencing any area, pit or sewer left open, or leaving same without a sufficient light after sunset.

Throwing or laying any dirt, litter or ashes or any rubbish on any street.

Causing any offensive matter to run from any premises into any street.

Keeping swine (or pigsty) in or near any street so as to be a common nuisance.

(It is not an offence to lay sand or other materials in time of frost to prevent accidents, or to lay litter, etc., to prevent the freezing of pipes or to prevent noise in case of sickness, but same must be removed when the occasion for them ceases.)

The following offences are confined to footways:

Wilfully causing any obstruction in any public footpath by means of any cart, carriage, sledge, truck, barrow, animal or other means (viz. of the same kind).

Leading or driving any horse or other animal or drawing or driving any cart, carriage, sledge, truck, or barrow upon any footway of any street.

Fastening any horse or other animal so that it stands across or upon any footway.

Placing or leaving any furniture, goods, wares or merchandise or any cask, tub, basket, pail, or bucket, or placing or using any standing place, stool, bench, stall, or show-board on the footway.

Placing any blind, shade, covering, awning or other projection over or along any such footway unless 8 feet in height at least in every part from the ground.

Placing, hanging up or otherwise exposing to sale any goods, wares, merchandise, matter or thing whatsoever, so that the same project into or over any footway or beyond the line of any house, shop or building at which the same are so exposed, so as to obstruct or incommode the passage of any person over or along such footway.

Rolling or carrying any cask, tub, hoop, or wheel, or any ladder, plank, pole, timber, or log of wood upon any footway, except for the purpose of loading or unloading any cart or carriage or for the purpose of crossing the footway.

All these acts in contravention of s. 28 are offences in urban districts when committed to the obstruction, annoyance or danger of the residents or passengers.

This s. 28 of the Town Police Clauses Act 1847 creates a number of offences in connection with streets and allows a constable to arrest any person whom he sees committing any of these offences. The police can prosecute (lay the information) for offences under this s. 28 because they have the power of arrest for them. For other offences under this 1847 Act and the Public Health Acts, proceedings may be taken by an aggrieved person, by a local authority or with the consent of the Attorney-General (*Sheffield Corporation* v. *Kitson* (1929)). This section applies only in towns and urban districts (s. 171, Public Health Act 1875), and in those rural districts to which it has been extended by special order under s. 276 of the Public Health Act 1875, and s. 13, Public Health Act 1936 (which sections are now repealed by the Local Government Act 1972).

Highways Act 1959 – The Highways Act 1959 consolidated the statute law relating to highways, streets and bridges. It has since been amended by the Highways (Miscellaneous Provisions) Act 1961.

DAMAGE TO HIGHWAYS, ETC. – It will be an offence if a person without lawful authority or excuse, (a) deposits anything whatsoever on a highway so as to damage the highway; or (b) paints or otherwise inscribes, or affixes on the surface of a highway, or upon any tree, structure or works on or in a highway, any picture, letter, sign or other mark; or (c) lights any fire, discharges any firearm or firework, within 50 feet from the centre of a highway, and in consequence thereof the highway is damaged; or (d) pulls down, damages or obliterates a traffic sign placed on or near a highway, or a milestone or direction post (not being a traffic sign); provided that it shall be a defence to show that the traffic sign, milestone or post was not lawfully placed (s. 117 and Highway (Misc. Prov.) Act 1961, s. 7).

DEPOSITING THINGS, OR PITCHING BOOTHS, ETC., ON HIGHWAYS – It will be an offence, if without lawful authority or excuse, (a) a person deposits on a made-up carriageway, or on any highway which consists of or comprises a made-up carriageway within 15 feet from the centre of that carriageway, any dung, compost or other material for dressing land, or any rubbish; or (b) a person deposits any thing whatsoever on a highway to the interruption of any user of the highway; or (c) a hawker or other itinerant trader or a gipsy pitches a booth, stall or stand, or encamps, on a highway (s. 127).

"Made-up carriageway" means a carriageway, or a part thereof, which has been metalled or in any other way provided with a surface suitable for the passage of vehicles (s. 295).

DANGER OR ANNOYANCE – It will be an offence (a) if a person without lawful authority or excuse, deposits any thing whatsoever on a highway in consequence whereof a user of the highway is injured or endangered; (b) if a person, without lawful authority or excuse, lights any fire or discharges any firearm or firework, within 50 feet of the centre of a highway, which consists of or comprises a carriageway, and in consequence thereof a user of the highway is injured, interrupted or endangered; (c) if a person plays at football or any other game on a highway to the annoyance of a user thereof; (d) if a person, without lawful authority or excuse, allows any filth, dirt, lime or other offensive matter or thing to run or flow on to a highway from any adjoining premises (s. 140).

"Carriageway" means a way constituting or comprised in a highway, being a way (other than a cycle track) over which the public have a right of way for the passage of vehicles (s. 295).

PLACING A ROPE, ETC., ACROSS THE HIGHWAY – It will be an offence if a person who for any purpose places any rope, wire or other apparatus across a highway in such a manner as to be likely to cause danger to persons using the highway, unless he proves that he had taken all necessary means to give adequate warning of the danger (s. 141).

POWER TO REQUIRE REMOVAL OF BARBED WIRE – Barbed wire on a fence adjoining the highway and likely to be injurious to persons or animals on the highway is a nuisance and the appropriate authority may serve notice on the occupier requiring him to abate it. If he does not obey a summary court may order him to do so (s. 143).

REGULATION OF DEPOSIT OF BUILDING MATERIALS AND MAKING OF EXCAVATIONS IN STREETS – A person may, with the consent of the highway authority, temporarily deposit building materials, rubbish or other things in a street or make a temporary excavation. He shall properly fence the obstruction or excavation, and during the hours of darkness have it lighted (s. 146).

RESTRICTION ON PLACING RAILS, BEAMS, ETC., OVER HIGHWAYS – No person shall fix or place any overhead beam, rail, pipe, cable, wire or other similar apparatus over, along or across a highway without the consent of the highway authority, who may attach conditions to the consent. A person contravening these provisions or the terms or conditions of the consent, will be guilty of an offence (s. 152).

OBSTRUCTION OF PERSONS EXECUTING THE ACT – A person who wilfully obstructs any person acting in the execution of this Act or of a byelaw or order made thereunder shall, in any case for which no other provision is made by this Act, be guilty of an offence and shall be liable in respect thereof to a fine not exceeding £5, and, if the offence in respect of which he was convicted is continued after conviction, he shall be guilty of a further offence and shall be liable in respect thereof to a fine not exceeding £5 for each day on which the offence is so continued (s. 262).

RESTRICTION ON INSTITUTION OF PROCEEDINGS – Proceedings for offences against ss. 146, 152 and 262 shall not, without the written consent of the Attorney-General, be taken by any person other than a person aggrieved or a highway authority or a council (s. 271).

Highways Act 1971 – Control of builders' skips – A "builder's skip" means a container designed to be carried on a road vehicle and to be placed on a highway or other land for the storage of builders' materials or for the removal and disposal of builders' rubble, waste, household and other rubbish or earth (s. 31 (11)). A builder's skip shall not be deposited on a highway without the permission of the highway authority (s. 31 (1)). Contravention is an offence (s. 31 (3)). Where a skip is lawfully deposited on the highway it must be properly lighted during the hours of darkness, and be clearly and indelibly marked with the owner's name and telephone number or address (s. 31 (4)). When a builder's skip is deposited on the highway, the highway authority or a constable in uniform may require the owner to remove or reposition it. Failure to comply with the requirement is an offence. The highway authority or a constable in uniform may themselves remove or reposition skips. If they do so, the owner (if known) should be notified (s. 32).

Impounding Animals - Cattle and animals of the like kind constitute a nuisance and a danger to the public when straying on the highway, and when so found may be taken by any person to the pound or place set apart for that purpose. Cattle may be on the highway only for the purpose of passing and repassing.

If any horse, cattle, sheep, goats or swine are at any time found straying or lying on or at the side of a highway, the keeper (i.e. the person having possession of the animal) shall be guilty of an offence; this shall not apply in relation to a part of the highway passing over any common, waste or unenclosed ground. The keeper shall be liable to pay the expense of removing any animal to his own premises or to the common pound or such other place provided for the purpose and the pound fees. It will be an offence if a person, without lawful authority or excuse, releases any animal from the pound, or on the way to or from the pound, or damages the pound (Highways Act 1959, s. 135, as amended by Highways Act 1971, s. 33).

Town Police Clauses Act 1847, ss. 24 and 25, declares that any cattle, including horses, asses, mules, sheep, goats and swine, found at large in any street in any urban district without any person having the charge thereof, may be impounded by any constable or resident, and detained there until a penalty not exceeding £2 is paid, together with the expenses of impounding and feeding such cattle. If same be not paid within 3 days, the cattle may be sold, after 7 days' notice to the owner if known or 7 days after advertisement in a local newspaper.

Protection of Animals Act 1911, s. 7, enacts that any person who impounds any animal is bound to supply it with sufficient food and water, and that if an animal is left in a pound without sufficient food or water for 6 successive hours or longer, any person may enter the pound and supply same. The cost of food and water supplied to an impounded animal may be recovered summarily from the owner. See "Cruelty to Animals", Chap. 35.

Regulation of Traffic - The police in the pursuance of their duty to maintain order have a general power to regulate traffic so that every person may freely and safely pass and repass on the highway.

Every constable in uniform engaged for the time being in the regulation of traffic has power to regulate traffic (R.T. Act 1972, s. 22). If a traffic survey is carried out on or in the vicinity of a road, a constable may give traffic directions for the purposes of the survey, although he may not require an unwilling person to furnish survey information, nor cause unreasonable delay to such a person (R.T. Act 1972, s. 22A). The powers of a constable set out in R.T. Act 1972, s. 22, may be exercised by a traffic warden (S.I. 1970, No. 1958). A constable who is for the time being engaged in the regulation of traffic in a road, or any person acting under his authority may, on or in the vicinity of the road, light and use a flare for the purpose of regulating the traffic. "Flare" means a firework or other device designed to produce a light by a process of combustion (R.T. Act 1974, s. 18). Several statutes prescribe rules which must be obeyed by the drivers of vehicles. Breaches of these rules are summary offences, as will be seen by the following extracts from the Acts in question.

HIGHWAY ACT 1835, s. 78: The following acts are offences punishable by fine or imprisonment in default.

Driver of any wagon, cart or other carriage of any kind riding upon same or upon any horse drawing same, on the highway, and not having another person on foot or on horseback to guide the same. (Carts and carriages driven with reins and conducted by some person holding the reins of all the horses drawing the same are excepted).

Driver of any carriage whatsoever on the highway quitting the same and going on the other side of the highway fence, or being negligently or wilfully at such distance from such carriage or in such a situation that he cannot have the direction and government of the horses or cattle drawing the same.

Driver of any carriage whatsoever leaving any cart or carriage on the highway so as to obstruct the passage thereof.

Driver of any wagon, cart or other carriage whatsoever or of any horses, mules or other beasts of burden, meeting any other carriage or beasts of burden, and not keeping his carriage or beasts on the left or near side of the road.

Any person in any manner wilfully preventing any other person from passing him or any wagon, cart or other carriage or beasts of burden under his care upon such highway, or by negligence or misbehaviour preventing, hindering or interrupting the free passage of any person, carriage or beast of burden on any highway, or not keeping his carriage or beast of burden on the left or near side of the road for the purpose of allowing such passage.

TOWN POLICE CLAUSES ACT 1847, s. 28: The following acts are offences when committed in any street in any urban district to the obstruction, annoyance or danger of the inhabitants or passengers:

Having the care of any wagon, cart or carriage and riding on the shafts, or without having reins and holding the same riding on such carriage or on any animal drawing the same, or being at such a distance as not to have due control over every animal drawing the same.

Meeting another carriage and not keeping his carriage to the left or near side. Passing another carriage and not keeping his carriage on the right or off side (except in cases of actual necessity or some sufficient reason for deviation).

Wilfully preventing, by obstructing the street, any person or carriage from passing him or any carriage under his care.

Causing any public carriage, sledge, truck or barrow, with or without horses, or any beast of burden, to stand longer than is necessary for loading or unloading goods, or for taking up or setting down passengers (except vehicles and beasts of burden standing for hire in any place appointed for that purpose by the Local Authority).

By means of any cart, carriage, sledge, truck or barrow or any animal, wilfully interrupting any public crossing, or wilfully causing any obstruction in any public footpath, or other thoroughfare.

Causing any tree, timber, or iron beam to be drawn on any carriage without having sufficient means of safely guiding the same.

Under ss. 21 and 22 of this Act the Local Authority, to prevent obstruction, may make orders for the route of vehicles, horses and persons.

Road Traffic Acts, etc. – The Road Traffic Act 1972, consolidated, with corrections and improvements, most previous enactments relating to road traffic. The Act is arranged in 7 Parts, as follows: Part I: Principal Road Safety Provisions. Part II: Construction and use of vehicles and equipment. Part III: Licensing of drivers of vehicles. Part IV: Licensing of drivers of heavy goods vehicles. Part V: Driving instruction. Part VI: Third-party liabilities. Part VII: Miscellaneous and general.

CAUSING DEATH BY DANGEROUS DRIVING – A person who causes the death of another person by the driving of a motor vehicle on a road recklessly, or at a speed or in a manner which is dangerous to the public, having regard to all the circumstances of the case, including the nature, condition and use of the road, and the amount of traffic which is actually at the time, or which might reasonably be expected to be, on the road, commits an offence. Section 20 of the Coroners (Amendment) Act 1926 (see Chap. 39) applies to this offence (s. 1).

DANGEROUS DRIVING – Any person driving a motor vehicle on a road recklessly, or at a speed or in a manner which is dangerous to the public, having regard to all the circumstances of the case, including the nature, condition and use of the road, and the amount of traffic which is actually at the time, or which might reasonably be expected to be on the road, commits an offence, (s. 2). On trial on indictment for causing death by dangerous driving, the jury may find an accused guilty of dangerous driving (R.T. Act 1972, Sched. 4, Part I; Part IV, para. 5).

For power of arrest, see s. 164. The offender must be warned of intended prosecution (see s. 179) unless there has been an accident (s. 179 (3A), added by R.T. Act 1974, Sched. 6). The section does not apply to tramcars (see s. 198).

In a case of driving at a speed dangerous to the public, it is not necessary to prove actual danger; potential danger must be considered (*Kingman* v. *Seager* (1938) and *Bracegirdle* v. *Oxley* (1947)).

Several other statutes deal with the driving of vehicles on the highway, prescribing punishment for certain acts which cause or may cause injury to person or property:

Highway Act 1835, s. 78: The driver of any carriage whatsoever on any part of any highway, by negligence or wilful misbehaviour, causing any hurt or damage to any person, horse, cattle or goods conveyed in any carriage passing or being upon such highway.

(Bicycles, tricycles and other similar machines are carriages within the meaning of the Highway Acts (Local Government Act 1888, s. 85)).

Any person riding any horse or beast or driving any sort of carriage, riding or driving the same furiously so as to endanger the life or limb of any passenger.

Town Police Clauses Act 1847, s. 28: Any person in any street (where the Act applies) to the obstruction, annoyance or danger of the residents or passengers, riding or driving furiously any horse or carriage, or driving furiously any cattle. Any constable witnessing the offence may arrest without warrant and convey the offender before a justice. A bicycle is a carriage (*Taylor* v. *Goodwin* (1879)).

Offences against the Person Act 1861, s. 35: Any person, having the charge of any carriage or vehicle, by wanton or furious driving or racing or other wilful misconduct or by wilful neglect, doing or causing to be done any bodily harm to any person.

Public Health Act 1925, s. 74 (2): Any person riding or driving so as to endanger the life or limb of any person or to the common danger of the passengers in any street, not being a street within the Metropolitan Police District (wherein the Metropolitan Police Act 1839 gives similar powers), may be arrested without warrant by any constable who witnesses the occurrence, and may be fined.

CARELESS DRIVING – Any person driving a motor vehicle on a road without due care and attention or without reasonable consideration for other persons using the road commits an offence (1972 Act, s. 3). For power of arrest, see s. 164. The offender must be warned of intended prosecution (s. 179) unless there has been an accident (s. 179 (3A), added by R.T. Act 1974, Sched. 6). The section does not apply to tramcars (s. 198).

There are two separate offences in this section and it is a question of fact for the justices.

Inexperience of a learner is no excuse. There is only one standard of careful driving (*McCrone* v. *Riding* (1938)). A driver who allows himself to be overtaken by sleep while driving is at least guilty of the offence of driving without due care and attention (*Kay* v. *Butterworth* (1945)).

If a magistrates' court considers a charge of reckless or dangerous driving (s. 2) is not proved, then during the hearing, or immediately thereafter, the court may direct or allow a charge of careless or inconsiderate driving (s. 3) to be preferred forthwith, and may proceed with the charge provided the accused is given an opportunity of answering it or may adjourn the hearing if it considers that the accused is prejudiced in his defence to the new charge (Sched. 4, Part I, col. 7; Part IV, para. 1).

DRIVING UNDER AGE – A person shall not drive on a road a motor vehicle of a class specified in the first column of the following Table if he is under the age specified in relation thereto in the second column of that Table (s. 4 (1)).

Class of motor vehicle	*Age*
1. Motor cycle or invalid carriage . . .	16
2. Motor car	17
3. Tractor used primarily for work on land in connection with agriculture . . .	17
4. Heavy locomotive, light locomotive, motor tractor or heavy motor car, but not including such a tractor as is mentioned in para. 3	21

Regulations may provide that in relation to motor cycles or, if it is so prescribed by the regulations, in relation to motor cycles of a class so prescribed, the foregoing Table shall have effect as if it specified such minimum age as may be so prescribed, not being less than (a) 16 years, in the case of motor cycles other than those of the class specified in the following paragraph; (b) 15 years, in the case of motor cycles whereof the cylinder capacity of the engine does not exceed 50 cubic centimetres, being cycles equipped with pedals by means whereof they are capable of being propelled; but a person shall not be prohibited by virtue of regulations having effect by virtue of this subsection from driving motor cycles of any class if at any time before the coming into force of the regulations he has held or was entitled (on making the requisite application and declaration and on payment of the appropriate fee) to the grant of a licence, other than a provisional licence, authorising him to drive that class of motor cycle or if at the time of the coming into force of the regulation he holds a provisional licence (s. 4 (2)).

Regulations may provide—

(a) that except in the case of a person who fulfils the conditions specified for the purpose of para. (d) below the age under which a person may not drive on a road a motor car constructed as mentioned in s. 190 (9) of this Act shall, if the motor car is of a class specified in the regulations, and is driven with a trailer attached to it in the manner mentioned in that subsection, be 21 instead of 17;

(b) that the age under which a person may not drive on a road a tractor used primarily for work on land in connection with agriculture shall, if the tractor is of a class specified in the regulations and is driven in circumstances so specified, be 16 instead of 17;

(c) that the age under which a person may not drive on a road a road roller falling within para. 4 of the Table set out in sub-s. (1) above shall, if the roller is of a class specified in the regulations and is driven in circumstances so specified, be 17 instead of 21;

(d) that, in the case of a person who fulfils such conditions as may be specified in the regs. with respect to his training and employment (including membership of a training scheme approved by the Secretary of State), the age under which he may not drive a vehicle falling within para. 4 of the table in sub-s. (1) other than a road roller, shall, if the vehicle is of a class specified in the regs. be 18 instead of 21.

but—

(i) a person shall not be prohibited by virtue of regulations under para. (a) above from driving a motor car of any class if at any time before the coming into force of the regulations he has held, or was entitled (on making the requisite application and declaration and on payment of the appropriate fee) to the grant of, a licence, other than a provisional licence, authorising him to drive that class of motor car; and

(ii) a person under the age of 17 who has not passed the prescribed test of competence to drive such a tractor as is mentioned in para. (b) above shall not be authorised by regulations made under that paragraph to drive such a tractor on a road except while taking, proceeding to or returning from such a test (s. 4 (3)).

A person who drives, or causes or permits a person to drive, a motor vehicle in contravention of the provisions of this section shall be guilty of an offence (s. 4 (4)).

The Motor Vehicles (Minimum Age for Driving) Regs. 1963

and 1975 provide that except in a case where reg. 5 below applies the minimum age for driving a motor car constructed to draw a partially superimposed trailer and driven with such a trailer attached, if the unladen weight of the motor car exceeds 2 tons (i.e. certain vehicles known as articulated vehicles) is increased from 17 to 21 (reg. 2); the minimum age for driving certain descriptions of agricultural tractor when driven in certain circumstances is reduced from 17 to 16 (reg. 3); the minimum age for driving certain descriptions of road roller is reduced from 21 to 17 (reg. 4) and reduced from 21 to 18 the age at which a person may drive a HGV in a case where he is participating in the training scheme which has been established by the national joint training committee for young HGV drivers in the Road Goods Transport Industry (reg. 5).

DRIVING, OR BEING IN CHARGE, WHEN UNDER THE INFLUENCE OF DRINK OR DRUGS – It is an offence, punishable on indictment or summarily, to drive or attempt to drive a motor vehicle on a road or other public place, when unfit to drive through drink or drugs (s. 5 (1)).

It is also an offence, punishable on indictment or summarily, to be in charge of a motor vehicle on a road or other public place when unfit to drive through drink or drugs (5 (2)). The person shall be deemed not to have been in charge of the vehicle if he proves that at the time there was no likelihood of his driving the vehicle (5 (3)). For the purposes of this section a person shall be taken to be unfit to drive if his ability to drive properly is for the time being impaired (s. 5 (4)). A constable may arrest without warrant a person committing an offence under this section (s. 5 (5)).

DRIVING OR BEING IN CHARGE, WITH BLOOD ALCOHOL CONCENTRATION ABOVE THE PRESCRIBED LIMIT – If a person drives or attempts to drive a motor vehicle on a road or other public place, having consumed alcohol in such a quantity that the proportion thereof in his blood, as ascertained from a laboratory test for which he subsequently provides a specimen under s. 9 of this Act, exceeds the prescribed limit at the time he provides the specimen, he shall be guilty of an offence (s. 6 (1)).

Without prejudice to sub-s. (1) above, if a person is in charge of a motor vehicle on a road or other public place having consumed alcohol as aforesaid, he shall be guilty of an offence (s. 6 (2)). A person shall not be convicted under this section of being in charge of a motor vehicle if he proves that at the material time the circumstances were such that there was no likelihood of his driving it so long as there was any probability of his having alcohol in his blood in a proportion exceeding the prescribed limit (s. 6 (3)).

In determining for the purposes of sub-s. (3) above the

likelihood of a person's driving a motor vehicle when he is injured or the vehicle is damaged, the jury, in the case of proceedings on indictment, may be directed to disregard, and the court in any other case may disregard, the fact that he had been injured or that the vehicle had been damaged (s. 6 (4)).

EVIDENCE ON CHARGE OF UNFITNESS TO DRIVE – In any proceedings for an offence under s. 5 of this Act, the court shall, subject to s. 10 (5) thereof, have regard to any evidence which may be given of the proportion or quantity of alcohol or of any drug which was contained in the blood or present in the body of the accused, as ascertained by analysis of a specimen of blood taken from him with his consent by a medical practitioner, or of urine provided by him, at any material time; and if it is proved that the accused, when so requested by a constable at any such time, refused to consent to the taking of or to provide a specimen for analysis, his refusal may, unless reasonable cause therefor is shown, be treated as supporting any evidence given on behalf of the prosecution, or as rebutting any evidence given on behalf of the defence, with respect to his condition at that time (s. 7 (1)).

A person shall not be treated for the purposes of sub-s. (1) above as refusing to provide a specimen unless— (a) he is first requested to provide a specimen of blood, but refuses to do so; (b) he is then requested to provide two specimens of urine within one hour of the request, but fails to provide them within the hour or refuses at any time within the hour to provide them; and (c) he is again requested to provide a specimen of blood, but refuses to do so (s. 7 (2)).

The first specimen of urine provided in pursuance of a request under sub-s. (2) (b) above shall be disregarded for the purposes of sub-s. (1) above (s. 7 (3)).

BREATH TESTS – A constable in uniform may require any person driving or attempting to drive a motor vehicle on a road or other public place to provide a specimen of breath for a breath test there or nearby, if the constable has reasonable cause (a) to suspect him of having alcohol in his body, or (b) to suspect him of having committed a traffic offence while the vehicle was in motion; but no requirement may be made by virtue of paragraph (b) above unless it is made as soon as reasonably practicable after the commission of the traffic offence (s. 8 (1)).

Driving or attempting to drive. Whether a person is "driving or attempting to drive" is a question of degree and fact in each case. Where a person remains in the driving seat after stopping the vehicle the test is whether what he is doing is connected with his driving. A person may be required to give a specimen even though he has ceased driving or attempting to drive, provided that the requirement follows the observed driving or attempted driving so closely as to form a continuous sequence (*Sakhuja* v. *Allen* (1973)). But a person is no longer "driving" some minutes after he has locked and left his car (*R.* v. *Bove* (1970)), nor even when actually locking the car (*R.* v. *Garforth* (1970)). A person is not driving if he no longer has possession of the car keys because they have been taken from him (*Cruickshank* v. *Devlin* (1974)) or because he has given them up (*Harman* v. *Wardrop* (1971)), although where a constable takes possession of them this may depend on the circumstances (*R.* v. *Cooper* (1974)). Pushing a car is not driving (*R.* v. *MacDonagh* (1974)), nor is guiding the vehicle while walking beside it (*Ames* v. *McLeod* (1969)).

On a road. A requirement for a specimen may be made off the road provided that it follows sufficiently closely on the driving that it forms part of a continuous chain of action. A motorist will not be permitted to avoid a breath test merely by driving a few feet off a highway when it could otherwise be properly required (*R.* v. *E.J.M. Jones* (1970)).

If an accident occurs owing to the presence of a motor vehicle on a road or other public place, a constable in uniform may require any person who he has reasonable cause to believe was driving or attempting to drive the vehicle at the time of the accident to provide a specimen of breath for a breath test (a) except while that person is at a hospital as a patient, either at or near the place where the requirement is made or, if the constable thinks fit, at a police station specified by the constable; (b) in the said excepted case, at the hospital; but a person shall not be required to provide such a specimen while at a hospital as a patient if the medical practitioner in immediate charge of his case is not first notified of the proposal to make the requirement or objects to the provision of a specimen on the ground that its provision or the requirement to provide it would be prejudicial to the proper care or treatment of the patient (s. 8 (2)).

A person who, without reasonable excuse, fails to provide a specimen of breath for a breath test under sub-s. (1) or (2) above shall be guilty of an offence (s. 8 (3)).

If it appears to a constable in consequence of a breath test carried out by him on any person under sub-s. (1) or (2) above that the device by means of which the test is carried out indicates that the proportion of alcohol in that person's blood exceeds the prescribed limit, the constable may arrest that person without warrant except while that person is at a hospital as a patient (s. 8 (4)).

If a person required by a constable under sub-s. (1) or (2) above to provide a specimen of breath for a breath test fails to do so and the constable has reasonable cause to suspect him of having alcohol in his body, the constable may arrest him without warrant except while he is at a hospital as a patient (s. 8 (5)).

Subsections (4) and (5) above shall not be construed as prejudicing the provisions of s. 5 (5) of this Act (s. 8 (6)).

A person arrested under this section, or under the said s. 5 (5), shall, while at a police station, be given an opportunity to provide a specimen of breath for a breath test there (s. 8 (7)).

In this section "traffic offence" means an offence under any provision of this Act except Part V thereof or under any provision of Part III of the Road Traffic Act 1960 or the Road Traffic Regulation Act 1967 (s. 8 (8)).

LABORATORY TESTS – A person who has been arrested under s. 5 (5) or 8 of this Act may, while at a police station, be required by a constable to provide a specimen for a laboratory test (which may be a specimen of blood or of urine), if he has previously been given an opportunity to provide a specimen of breath for a breath test at that station under sub-s. (7) of the said s. 8, and either (a) it appears to a constable in consequence of the breath test that the device by means of which the test is carried out indicates that the proportion of alcohol in his blood exceeds the prescribed limit, or (b) when given the opportunity to provide that specimen, he fails to do so (s. 9 (1).

A person while at a hospital as a patient may be required by a constable to provide at the hospital a specimen for a laboratory test (a) if it appears to a constable in consequence of a breath test carried out on that person under s. 8 (2) of this Act that the device by means of which the test is carried out indicates that the proportion of alcohol in his blood exceeds the prescribed limit, or (b) if that person has been required, whether at the hospital or elsewhere, to provide a specimen of breath for a breath test, but fails to do so and a constable has reasonable cause to suspect him of having alcohol in his body; but a person shall not be required to provide a specimen for a laboratory test under this subsection if the medical practitioner in immediate charge of his case is not first notified of the proposal to make the requirement or objects to the provision of a specimen on the ground that its provision, the requirement to provide it or a warning under sub-s. (7) below would be prejudicial to the proper care or treatment of the patient (s. 9 (2)).

A person who, without reasonable excuse, fails to provide a specimen for a laboratory test in pursuance of a requirement imposed under this section shall be guilty of an offence (s. 9 (3)).

Nothing in the foregoing provisions of this section shall affect the provisions of s. 7 (1) of this Act (s. 9 (4)).

A person shall not be treated for the purposes of sub-s. (3) above as failing to provide a specimen unless (a) he is first requested to provide a specimen of blood, but refuses to do so; (b) he is then requested to provide two specimens of urine within one hour of the request, but fails to provide them within the hour or refuses at any time within the hour to provide them; and (c) he is again requested to provide a specimen of blood, but refuses to do so (s. 9 (5)).

The first specimen of urine provided in pursuance of a request under sub-s. (5) (b) above shall be disregarded for the purposes of s. 6 of this Act (s. 9 (6)).

A constable shall on requiring any person under this section to provide a specimen for a laboratory test warn him that failure to provide a specimen of blood or urine may make him liable to imprisonment, a fine and disqualification, and, if the constable fails to do so, the court before which that person is charged with an offence under s. 6 of this Act or this section may direct an acquittal or dismiss the charge, as the case may require.

In this subsection "disqualification" means disqualification for holding or obtaining a licence to drive a motor vehicle granted under Part III of this Act (s. 9 (7)).

EVIDENCE IN PROCEEDINGS FOR AN OFFENCE UNDER S. 5 OR 6 – For the purposes of any proceedings for an offence under s. 5 or 6 of this Act, a certificate purporting to be signed by an authorised analyst, and certifying (a) the proportion of alcohol or any drug found in a specimen identified by the certificate, and (b) for the purposes only of proceedings for an offence under the said s. 5, in the case of a specimen of urine, the proportion of alcohol or of that drug in the blood which corresponds to the proportion found in the specimen, shall, subject to sub-s. (3) below, be evidence of the matters so certified and of the qualification of the analyst (s. 10 (1)).

For the purposes of any proceedings for an offence under the said s. 5 or 6, a certificate purporting to be signed by a medical practitioner that he took a specimen of blood from a person with his consent shall, subject to sub-s. (3) below, be evidence of the matters so certified and of the qualification of the medical practitioner (s. 10 (2)).

Subsections (1) and (2) above shall not apply to a certificate tendered on behalf of the prosecution unless a copy has been served on the accused not less than 7 days before the hearing or trial, nor if the accused, not less than 3 days before the hearing or trial, or within such further time as the court may in special circumstances allow, has served notice on the prosecutor requiring the attendance at the hearing or trial of the person by whom the certificate was signed.

A copy of a certificate required by this subsection to be served on the accused or of a notice required by this subsection to be served on the prosecutor may either be personally served on the accused or the prosecutor (as the case may be) or sent to him by registered post or the recorded delivery service (s. 10 (3)).

In any proceedings in Scotland for an offence under the said s. 5 or 6, a certificate complying with sub-s. (1) or (2) above and, where the person by whom such a certificate was signed is called as a witness, the evidence of that person, shall be sufficient evidence of the facts stated in the certificate (s. 10 (4)).

Where, in proceedings for an offence under the said s. 5 or 6 the accused, at the time a specimen of blood or urine was taken from or provided by him, asked to be supplied with such a specimen, evidence of the proportion of alcohol or any drug found in the specimen shall not be admissible on behalf of the prosecution unless (a) the specimen is either one of two taken or provided on the same occasion or is part of a single specimen which was divided into two parts at the time it was taken or provided, and (b) the other specimen or part was supplied to the accused (s. 10 (5)).

A constable requesting any person to consent to the taking of or to provide a specimen of blood or urine for analysis shall offer to supply to him, in a suitable container, part of the specimen or, in the case of a specimen of blood which it is not practicable to divide, another specimen which he may consent to have taken (s. 10 (6)).

In this section "authorised analyst" means any person possessing the qualifications prescribed by regulations made under s. 89 of the Food and Drugs Act 1955, or s. 27 of the Food and Drugs (Scotland) Act 1956, as qualifying persons for appointment as public analysts under those Acts, and any other person authorised by the Secretary of State to make analyses for the purposes of this section (s. 10 (7)).

DETENTION OF PERSONS WHILE AFFECTED BY ALCOHOL – Any person required to provide a specimen for a laboratory test under s. 9 (1) of this Act may thereafter be detained at the police station until he provides a specimen of breath for a breath test and it appears to a constable that the device by means of which the test is carried out indicates that the proportion of alcohol in that person's blood does not exceed the prescribed limit (s. 11).

INTERPRETATION – In ss. 6 to 11 of this Act, except so far as the context otherwise requires—"breath test" means a test for the purpose of obtaining an indication of the proportion of alcohol in a person's blood carried out by means of a device of a type approved for the purpose of such a test by the Secretary of State, on a specimen of breath provided by that person; "fail", in relation to providing a specimen, includes refuse and "failure" shall be construed accordingly; "hospital" means an institution which provides medical or surgical treatment for in-patients or out-patients; "laboratory test" means the analysis of a specimen provided for the purpose; "the prescribed limit" means 80 milligrammes of alcohol in 100 millilitres of blood or such other proportion as may be prescribed by regulations made by the Secretary of State (s. 12 (1)).

A person shall be treated for the purposes of ss. 6 and 9 of this Act as providing a specimen of blood if, but only if, he consents to the specimen being taken by a medical practitioner and it is so taken and shall be treated for those purposes as providing it at the time it is so taken (s. 12 (2)).

References in ss. 8, 9 and 11 of this Act to providing a specimen of breath for a breath test are references to providing a specimen thereof in sufficient quantity to enable that test to be carried out (s. 12 (3)).

For the purposes of s. 6 and s. 12, 107 milligrammes of alcohol in 100 millilitres of urine shall be treated as equivalent to 80 milligrammes of alcohol in 100 millilitres of blood, and the power conferred by s. 12 (1) above to prescribe some other proportion of alcohol in the blood shall include power to prescribe a proportion of alcohol in urine which is to be treated as equivalent to the prescribed proportion of alcohol in the blood (s. 12 (4)).

A person liable to be charged with an offence under s. 5, 6 or 9 of this Act shall not be liable to be charged under s. 12 of the Licensing Act 1872, with the offence of being drunk while in charge, on a highway or other public place, of a carriage (s. 13).

MOTOR RACING ON HIGHWAYS – A person who promotes or takes part in a race or trial of speed between motor vehicles on a public highway commits an offence (R.T. Act 1972, s. 14).

REGULATION OF MOTORING EVENTS ON PUBLIC HIGHWAYS – A person who promotes or takes part in a competition or trial (other than a race or trial of speed) involving the use of motor vehicles on a public highway commits an offence unless the competition or trial is authorised and is conducted in accordance with any conditions imposed by or under Regulations (R.T. Act 1972, s. 15).

The Motor Vehicles (Competitions and Trials) Regs. 1969 regulate the holding of competitions or trials (other than races or trials of speed) involving the use of motor vehicles on a public highway.

RESTRICTION ON CARRIAGE OF PERSONS ON MOTOR CYCLES – It is not lawful for more than one person in addition to the driver to be carried on any two-wheeled motor cycle, or for such one person to be carried otherwise than sitting astride the cycle on a proper seat securely fixed to the cycle behind the driver's seat (R.T. Act 1972, s. 16).

RECKLESS AND DANGEROUS CYCLING – Any person riding a cycle, not being a motor vehicle, on a road (including a bridleway) recklessly, or at a speed or in a manner which is dangerous to the public, having regard to all the circumstances of the case, including the nature, condition and use of the road, and the amount of traffic which is actually at the time, or which might reasonably be expected to be on the road, commits an offence (R.T. Act 1972, s. 17). For power of arrest, see s. 164. The offender must be warned of intended prosecution (s. 179), unless there has been an accident (s. 179 (3A), added by R.T. Act 1974, Sched. 6).

CARELESS AND INCONSIDERATE CYCLING – Any person riding a cycle, not being a motor vehicle, on a road (including a bridleway) without due care and attention, or without reasonable consideration for other persons using the road, commits an offence (s. 18).

For power of arrest, see s. 164. The offender must be warned of intended prosecution (s. 179), unless there has been an accident (s. 179 (3A), added by R.T. Act 1974, Sched. 6).

If a magistrates' court considers the charge of dangerous or reckless cycling (s. 17) is not proved, then during the hearing, or immediately thereafter, the court may direct or allow a charge of careless cycling (s. 18) to be preferred forthwith and may proceed with the charge provided the accused is given an opportunity of answering it or may adjourn the hearing if it considers that the accused is prejudiced in his defence to the new charge (Sched. 4, Part I; Part IV, para. 4).

CYCLING WHEN UNDER THE INFLUENCE OF DRINK – It is a summary offence to ride a cycle, not being a motor vehicle, on a road (including a bridleway) or other public place when unfit to ride through drink or drugs (s. 19). An offender may be arrested without warrant by a constable.

A person liable to be charged with this offence shall not be liable to be charged under s. 12 of the Licensing Act 1872, with the offence of being drunk while in charge of a carriage.

"Unfit to ride through drink or drugs" means, as regards a person riding a cycle, under the influence of drink or a drug to such an extent as to be incapable of having proper control of it (s. 19).

REGULATION OF CYCLE RACING ON HIGHWAYS – A person who promotes or takes part in a race or trial of speed on a public highway (which includes a bridleway but not a footpath) between cycles, not being motor vehicles, shall, unless the race or trial is authorised, and is conducted in accordance with any conditions imposed, by or under regulations, commits a summary offence (s. 20).

The Cycle Racing on Highways Regulations 1960 and 1963 provide for the authorisation of such races or trials of speed on public highways. Certain powers are given to Chief Officers of Police under the Regulations.

RESTRICTION ON CARRIAGE OF PERSONS ON BICYCLES – It is not lawful for more than one person to be carried on a road (including a bridleway) on a pedal bicycle unless it is constructed or adapted for the carriage of more than one person. "Person carried" includes the rider. If this section is contravened each person carried commits an offence (s. 21).

DRIVERS TO COMPLY WITH TRAFFIC DIRECTIONS – It is an offence for any person driving or propelling any vehicle (a) to neglect or refuse to stop the vehicle or to make it proceed in or keep to a particular line of traffic when directed to do so by a police constable, for the time being engaged in the regulation of traffic on a road, in the execution of his duty; (b) to fail to conform to the indication given by any traffic sign lawfully placed on or near any road and being lawfully authorised (s. 22). The offender must be warned of intended prosecution (see s. 179) unless there has been an accident (s. 179 (3A), added by R.T. Act 1974, Sched. 6). R.T. Act 1974, s. 6 inserts a new section 22A in the R.T. Act 1972, giving a constable the power to direct traffic for the purpose of a traffic survey.

A traffic sign on or near a road shall be deemed to be of the prescribed size, colour and type or of another authorised character and to be lawfully there unless the contrary is proved (s. 22). Therefore the onus is placed on a defendant to prove the sign is not legal if he so alleges.

PEDESTRIANS TO COMPLY WITH DIRECTIONS OF CONSTABLES – A person on foot who proceeds across or along the carriageway in contravention of a direction to stop given by a constable in uniform regulating traffic in the road, commits an offence (s. 23). A constable may require such a person to give his name and address and failure to do so is an offence (s. 165).

LEAVING VEHICLES IN DANGEROUS POSITIONS – It is an offence for a person in charge of a vehicle to cause or permit the vehicle, or a trailer drawn thereby, to remain at rest on a road in such a position or in such condition or in such circumstances as to be likely to cause danger to other persons using the road (s. 24). The offender must be warned of intended prosecution (see s. 179), unless there has been an accident (s. 179 (3A), added by R.T. Act 1974, Sched. 6).

ACCIDENTS – If in any case, owing to the presence of a motor vehicle on a road, an accident occurs whereby personal injury is caused to a person other than the driver of that motor vehicle or damage is caused to a vehicle other than that motor vehicle or a trailer drawn thereby or to an animal other than an animal in or on that motor vehicle or a trailer drawn thereby, or to any other property constructed on, fixed to, growing in or otherwise forming part of the land on which the road in question is situated or land adjacent thereto the driver of the motor vehicle shall stop and, if required so to do by any person having reasonable grounds for so requiring, give his name and address, and also the name and address of the owner and the identification marks of the vehicle (s. 25).

If for any reason he does not so give his name and address to any such person, such driver shall report the accident at a police station or to a police constable as soon as reasonably practicable and in any case within 24 hours of the accident. Failure to comply with this section is an offence. "Animal" here means any horse, cattle, ass, mule, sheep, pig, goat or dog (s. 25).

A bicycle is a vehicle (*Ellis* v *Nott-Bower* (1896)).

This liability to report extends to every case where the driver has not in fact given his name and address, for example, no one asked for it or no one was present at the time (*Peek* v. *Towle* (1945)).

Refusal, on reasonable requirement, to give name and address is an offence not excused by subsequent report to the police (*Dawson* v. *Winter* (1932) and *North* v. *Gerrish* (1959)).

If the driver gives his name and address (or drivers exchange names and addresses) as required, there is no duty to report to the police (*Adair* v. *Fleming* (1932) and *Green* v. *Dunn* (1953)).

A driver did not know he had collided with a stationary car and did not report. He was convicted but the K.B.D. quashed the conviction (*Harding* v. *Price* (1948)).

This section imposes a duty, so failure to report where the driver was unaware of the act was not an offence.

If an accident arises out of the presence of a motor vehicle (tramcars excepted) on a road, the Secretary of State may direct inquiry into the cause and any person authorised by him has power to inspect any vehicle concerned and to enter premises for the purpose. It will be an offence to obstruct him. The Secretary of State may also direct a public inquiry to be held. Any report by or to the Secretary of State as a result of an inquiry under this section shall not be used in evidence by or on behalf of any person by or against whom legal proceedings are instituted in consequence of the accident (s. 26).

TAMPERING WITH MOTOR VEHICLES – If, while a motor vehicle is on a road or on a parking place provided by a local authority, a person otherwise than with lawful authority or reasonable cause gets on to the vehicle or tampers with the brake or other part of its mechanism, he commits an offence (s. 29). This may be action preparatory to stealing or likely to cause damage.

HOLDING ON TO A VEHICLE WHILE IN MOTION – If a person otherwise than with lawful authority or reasonable cause takes or retains hold of, or gets on to, a motor vehicle or trailer while in motion on a road, for the purpose of being carried, he commits an offence. If a person takes or retains hold of a motor vehicle or trailer while in motion on a road for the purpose of being drawn he commits an offence (s. 30).

(It is now an absolute offence to hold on to a vehicle for the purpose of being drawn and it will no longer be a defence to show that the accused did so with lawful authority or excuse.)

CONTROL OF DOGS ON ROADS – A local authority may by order made after consultation with the police, "designate" a road. Then any person who causes or permits a dog to be on a designated road without the dog being held on a lead will commit a summary offence. This shall not apply to dogs for driving sheep or cattle or sporting dogs under proper control (s. 31).

WEARING OF PROTECTIVE HEADGEAR – The Secretary of State may make regulations requiring persons driving or riding (otherwise than in side-cars) on motor cycles to wear protective headgear. Any person driving or riding in contravention of the regulations will commit an offence (s. 32).

PROTECTIVE HELMETS FOR MOTOR CYCLISTS – The Motor Cycles (Wearing of Helmets) Regs. 1973 require persons travelling on roads on motor cycles (except in a side-car) to wear protective headgear of a specific description. However this does not apply to mowing machines nor to motor bicycles when propelled by pedestrians. The protective headgear for this purpose means headgear which (a) is either (1) a helmet complying with British Standard 2001, or B.S. 1869, or B.S. 2495, or (2) a helmet which could reasonably be expected to afford protection to motor cyclists from injury in the event of an accident similar to or greater than that provided by one of those specified in (1) above, and (b) is securely fastened to the head of the wearer by means of straps or other fastening provided for that purpose. The Secretary of State may make regulations prescribing types of helmets for affording protection to persons on or in motor cycles, from injury in the event of accident (s. 33). It is an offence to sell any helmet as one affording such protection if the helmet sold is not of a type prescribed by the Motor Cycles (Protective Helmets) Regs. 1974. Supplementary provisions in connection with proceedings for offences under this section are contained in Sched. 1 of the Act (s. 33).

PERSONS TO ATTEND TO LOCOMOTIVES AND TRAILERS – Two persons shall be employed in driving or attending a heavy or light locomotive on a highway, and if it draws a trailer or trailers, one or more persons in addition to the two aforesaid shall be employed for attending to the trailer or trailers at the rate of one such additional person for each trailer in excess of one. This does not apply to a road roller while rolling a road. If a motor vehicle other than a locomotive draws a trailer or trailers on a highway one person in addition to the driver must be carried to attend to the trailer or trailers. As regards "attendants", the term "trailer" does not include a vehicle used solely for carrying water for the motor vehicle or any agricultural vehicle not made to carry a load. Any person causing or permitting a breach of this section commits an offence (s. 34).

RESTRICTIONS ON USE OF MOTOR VEHICLES OFF ROADWAY – No person shall promote or take part in a trial of any description between motor vehicles on a footpath or bridleway unless the trial has been authorised by the local authority with the consent of the owner and the occupier of the land over which the footpath or bridleway runs (s. 35).

The driving of a motor vehicle, without lawful authority, on to or upon any common land, moorland, or other land (not being part of a road) or on any road being a footpath or bridleway, is an offence except when done for the purpose of saving life, extinguishing fire or other like emergency, or on land within 15 yds. of a road for the purpose only of parking the vehicle. However, this section does not affect the rights of the public over commons and waste lands, or any byelaws as to lands or the law of trespass, and it does not confer any right to park a vehicle on any land (s. 36).

Prohibition of parking of heavy commercial vehicles on verges and footways. A person who parks a heavy commercial vehicle (a goods vehicle of unladen weight exceeding 3 tons) wholly or partly (a) on the verge of a road, or (b) on any land between 2 carriageways and which is not a footway, or (c) on a footway shall commit an offence. A person shall not be convicted if he satisfies the court (a) that the vehicle was parked with permission given by a constable in uniform, or (b) it was parked for the purpose of saving life, extinguishing fire, or meeting any other like emergency, or (c) it was parked for the purpose of loading or unloading which could not have been satisfactorily performed otherwise, and the vehicle was not left unattended (s. 36A).

[Similar provisions respecting vehicles other than heavy commercial vehicles have been introduced by s. 36B, R.T. Act 1972 (added by s. 7 of R.T. Act 1974, which was not in force at the date of going to press).]

The Traffic Signs (Temporary Obstructions) Regs. 1966 and 1975, prescribe traffic signs which may be placed by anyone on the carriageway, footway, verge or any other part of any road to warn traffic of a temporary obstruction on the carriageway. The sign is a triangle with a red border each side of the triangle being about 20 ins. long or between 450 and 550 mms. long. The sign must be placed at least 50 yds. from the obstruction and in a position from which it will warn traffic on the same side of the carriageway as the obstruction.

HIGHWAY CODE – Section 37 of the R.T. Act 1972 states that "The Highway Code" introduced under s. 45 of the R.T. Act 1930 (and revised under s. 74 of R.T. Act 1960) shall continue to have effect. The Secretary of State is responsible for preparing the code which comprises directions for the guidance of persons using roads. It may be revised from time to time, subject to the approval of Parliament.

This code is printed and available to the public.

Failure by a person to observe any provision of this code shall not of itself render him liable to criminal proceedings, but such a failure may in any civil or criminal proceedings be relied upon as tending to establish or to negative any liability which is in question in such proceedings.

The code contains advice and directions to all users of the highway, to drivers of motor vehicles, to motor cyclists, to drivers of horse-drawn vehicles, to persons in charge of animals, to pedal cyclists, and to pedestrians. It gives the various traffic signs and signals and the law's demands upon road users together with some hints on driving and cycling.

POWERS TO MAKE REGULATIONS AS TO CONSTRUCTION AND USE OF VEHICLES AND EQUIPMENT – The Secretary of State may, by statutory instrument, make regulations generally as to the use of motor vehicles and trailers on roads, their construction and equipment (including lighting equipment and reflectors—added by s. 9, R.T. Act 1974) and the conditions under which they may be so used. It will be an offence for any person to use or cause or permit to be used on a road, any motor vehicle or trailer which does not comply with the Regulations (s. 40). Regulations regarding lighting equipment and reflectors, may require (a) that lamps may be kept lit at specified times and circumstances, and (b) may extend to vehicles of any description. However, any regulations which vary the rules as to construction or weight must exempt therefrom for at least 5 years any vehicles registered before the expiration of one year from the making of the regulations (s. 41), and the Secretary of State has power to authorise the use on roads of special types of motor vehicles (s. 42). For Regulations, see Appendix II.

TESTS OF SATISFACTORY CONDITION OF VEHICLES OTHER THAN GOODS VEHICLES TO WHICH S. 45 APPLIES – The Secretary of State may make regulations for the purpose of ascertaining whether the prescribed statutory requirements relating to the construction and condition of motor vehicles are complied with. If the conditions are satisfied then a "test certificate" may be issued. The examinations of vehicles shall be carried out by "Authorised Examiners". If a test certificate is refused the person aggrieved may appeal to the Secretary of State who can cause a further examination to be made (s. 43). Under this section the Motor Vehicles (Tests) Regulations 1968 to 1975 were made. These Regulations apply to motor vehicles (not being track-laying vehicles) which are heavy motor cars, motor cars and motor cycles, except that they do not apply to (a) a goods vehicle over 30 cwt. in weight unladen; (b) a public service vehicle adapted to carry 8 or more passengers; (c) an articulated vehicle or a vehicle constructed or adapted for the purpose of forming part of an articulated vehicle; (d) a works truck; or (e) a pedestrian controlled vehicle.

PRESCRIBED STATUTORY REQUIREMENTS FOR EXAMINATIONS – Every motor vehicle to which the Motor Vehicles (Tests) Regs. apply which is submitted for examination, shall be examined for the purpose of ascertaining whether the statutory requirements specified in Sched. 2 are complied with. Motor vehicles submitted for examination while being used on roads in connection with the examination by, or under the direction of, a person empowered to carry out the examination are exempted from certain provisions of the Motor Vehicles (Construction and Use) Regs. 1973.

The statutory requirements which are prescribed for the purposes of an examination of a motor vehicle are as follows: those contained in the provisions of the M.V. (C. & U.) Regs. 1973, which relate (1) to the braking system or systems; (2) to the steering gear; (3) to the lighting equipment and reflectors; (4) to condition and maintenance of tyres; and (5) to the fitting of seat belts (Sched. 2).

OBLIGATORY TEST CERTIFICATES FOR VEHICLES OTHER THAN GOODS VEHICLES TO WHICH S. 45 APPLIES – Section 44, R.T. Act 1972 prohibits (subject to exceptions) the use on a road of motor vehicles registered for not less than 3 years unless a test certificate has been issued under s. 43 within the last 12 months, or such shorter period as may be prescribed. Exemptions are given in the Motor Vehicles (Tests) (Exemptions) Regs. 1969, 1971 and 1974.

TESTS OF SATISFACTORY CONDITION OF CERTAIN CLASSES OF GOODS VEHICLES AND DETERMINATION OF PLATED WEIGHTS AND OTHER PARTICULARS THEREFOR – The Secretary of State may make Regs. for the examination of goods vehicles, either for the purpose of determining the plated particulars to be marked on them or for the purpose of ascertaining whether they comply with prescribed construction and use requirements. Any person aggrieved by a determination may appeal to the Area Mechanical Engineer and if aggrieved by his determination may appeal to the Secretary of State (s. 44). See the Goods Vehicles (Plating and Testing) Regs. 1971 to 1975.

OBLIGATORY TEST CERTIFICATES FOR GOODS VEHICLES TO WHICH S. 45 APPLIES – If any person uses on a road or causes or permits to be so used, a goods vehicle of a class required by Regs. under s. 45 to have been submitted for examination (1) for plating and at that time no plating certificate was in force, or (2) for a goods vehicle test and at that time there was no test certificate in force, he shall be guilty of an offence.

Exemption from liability may be granted (s. 46).

TESTING OF CONDITION OF VEHICLES ON ROADS – Section 53, R.T. Act 1972, provides that an authorised examiner may test a motor vehicle on a road to see that the legal requirements as to brakes, silencers, steering gear, tyres, lighting equipment and reflectors and as to the prevention or reduction of noise, smoke, fumes or vapour are complied with. Only a constable may stop it for such test. Such an examiner has to produce his authority, if so required. Any constable or any other person can be authorised so to act by a chief officer. The driver may elect to have such test deferred to a time and place as arranged under Sched. 3 of the Act provided that if there has been an accident a constable may require a test forthwith.

UNROADWORTHY VEHICLES – The sale, supply or offer to sell or supply or to expose for sale a motor vehicle or trailer for delivery in such a condition that its use on a road in such condition would be unlawful as not complying with the regulation under s. 40 as respects brakes, steering gear or tyres, or as respects the construction, weight or equipment of vehicles, or as respects the maintenance of vehicles, their parts and accessories in such a condition that no danger is or is likely to be caused, or in such a condition, as respects lighting equipment or reflectors, or the maintenance thereof, that it is not capable of being used on a road during the hours of darkness without contravening the regs. regarding the lights on vehicles, shall be an offence. It is also an offence to alter a motor vehicle or trailer so as to render its condition such that its use on a road would be unlawful. However, a person shall not be convicted of an offence under this section in respect of sale, supply, offer, exposure for sale or alteration if he proves that it was done for export from Great Britain or with reasonable cause to believe that the vehicle would not be used on a road in Great Britain or would not be so used until put into lawful condition (s. 60).

It is an offence either to fit a vehicle (or to get others to fit it) with any part which is unsuitable for that vehicle in that its presence would make it illegal to use the vehicle on a road, or to sell or supply, or offer for sale or supply, or to get others to sell or supply, or offer for sale or supply, any part if the vendor knows that part will be fitted to a vehicle for which it is unsuitable (s. 60A added by s. 12 of R.T. Act 1974).

Lights on Vehicles – The use of lights on vehicles at night is regulated by the Road Traffic Act 1972, ss. 68–80. These sections will be repealed when R.T. Act 1974, s. 24 (3) and Sched. 7 are fully in force, and replaced by regs. made under s. 9. These repeals had not taken effect at the date of going to press.

The Act regulates the lighting of vehicles (including vehicle machines and implements) used "during the hours of darkness" on any public highway and any other road to which the public has access but do not apply to tramcars or vehicles used on railway lines (s. 198). Provisions as to the position, etc., of the lamps and reflectors to be carried are contained in the Road Vehicles Lighting Regs. 1971 and 1973 and the Road Vehicles Lighting (Standing Vehicles) (Exemption) (General) Regs. 1975.

OBLIGATORY FRONT AND REAR LAMPS AND HEADLAMPS – Every vehicle on a road shall, without prejudice to the requirements of sub-s. (2) below, during the hours of darkness carry (a) two lamps, each showing to the front a white light visible from a reasonable distance; and (b) two lamps, each showing to the rear a red light visible from a reasonable distance (s. 68 (1)).

Subject as aforesaid, every vehicle on a road, being a vehicle of any such class as may be prescribed, shall carry such lamps or lamp designed to illuminate the road as may be prescribed in relation to vehicles of that class (s. 68 (2)).

Regulations under sub-s. (2) above may make different provision in relation to vehicles of different classes or in relation to vehicles of any class when used in different circumstances (s. 68 (3)).

The lamps carried by a vehicle in pursuance of this section shall be kept lit (a) in the case of a lamp carried in pursuance of sub-s. (1) above, while the vehicle is on a road during the hours of darkness; (b) in the case of a lamp carried in pursuance of sub-s. (2) above, in such circumstances when the vehicle is in motion on a road during the hours of darkness as may be prescribed (s. 68 (4)).

The lamps carried by a vehicle in pursuance of sub-s. (1) and (2) above shall comply with such conditions as may be prescribed and shall, while the vehicle is on a road during the hours of darkness, be attached to the vehicle in such position and manner as may be prescribed (s. 68 (5)).

The lamps carried by a vehicle in pursuance of sub-s (1) above shall, while the vehicle is on a road during the hours of darkness, be kept properly trimmed and in a clean and efficient condition (s. 68 (6)).

It shall be the duty of any person who causes or permits a vehicle to be on any road during the hours of darkness to provide the vehicle with lamps in accordance with the requirements of this and the following sections of this Part of this Act and of any regulations made under those sections (other than s. 79) (s. 68 (7)).

In this and the following sections of this Part of this Act, "vehicle", unless the context otherwise requires, means a vehicle of any description and includes a machine or implement of any kind drawn or propelled along roads whether by animal or mechanical power (s. 68 (8)).

OBLIGATORY REFLECTORS – Subject to the following provisions of this Part of this Act, every vehicle on a road shall during the hours of darkness carry attached to it two unobscured and efficient red reflectors each facing to the rear (s. 69 (1)).

It shall be the duty of any person who causes or permits a vehicle to be on any road during the hours of darkness to provide the vehicle with reflectors in accordance with the requirements of this section and any regulations made for the purposes thereof under the following provisions of this Part of this Act (s. 69 (2)).

RESTRICTIONS ON THE NATURE OF THE LAMPS TO BE CARRIED – No vehicle shall, subject to the provisions of s. 79 of this Act and of any regulations made under s. 78 (5) thereof, show (a) a red light to the front, or (b) any light to the rear, other than a red light or a white light for the purpose of reversing (s. 70 (1)).

Paragraph (b) of sub-s. (1) above shall not prevent a vehicle from carrying a lamp showing a light to the rear for the purposes of (a) the internal illumination of the vehicle, or (b) (subject to sub-s. (3) below) illuminating a number plate, taxi meter, or any device for giving signals to overtaking traffic, or (c) in the case of a public passenger vehicle, illuminating boards, plates or devices indicating the route or destination of the vehicle; and the said para. (b) shall not prevent a bicycle or tricycle from carrying amber coloured reflectors which are attached to or incorporated in or form part of the pedals of the bicycle or tricycle notwithstanding that any such reflectors show a light to the rear (s. 70 (2)).

Subsection (2) (b) above shall not authorise a vehicle of any class to carry a lamp showing a light to the rear for the purpose of illuminating any device for giving signals to overtaking traffic other than a device of a type required or authorised to be carried on a vehicle of that class by virtue of s. 40 of this Act (s. 70 (3)).

RESTRICTION ON MOVEMENT OF LAMPS – Unless otherwise provided by the Secretary of State by regulation, and subject to sub-s. (2) below, no light shown by a vehicle, other than a dipping headlight, shall be moved by swivelling, deflecting or otherwise while the vehicle is in motion (s. 71 (1)).

Subsection (1) above shall not apply to amber coloured reflectors which are attached to or incorporated in or form part of the pedals of a bicycle or tricycle (s. 71 (2)).

MULTI-PURPOSE LAMPS AND COMBINED LAMPS AND REFLECTORS – Subject to sub-s. (2) below, nothing in ss. 68 to 78 of this Act shall require a vehicle to carry separate lamps for different purposes, if it carries a lamp satisfying all the requirements which would be applicable to separate lamps carried by it for those purposes (s. 72 (1)).

Subsection (1) above shall not apply in relation to any requirement to carry a headlamp under s. 68 (2) of this Act, but regulations may authorise the combination in a single unit of such a lamp and a lamp required to be carried by s. 68 (1) (a) of this Act (s. 72 (2)).

Where a vehicle's tail lamp is so constructed that, when not showing a light, it is an efficient red reflector facing to the rear and complying with any regulations made for the purposes of s. 69 of this Act and for the purposes of this subsection which apply to the vehicle, it shall be treated for those purposes as being such a reflector when it is, as well as when it is not, showing a light (s. 72 (3)).

REGULATION OF POSITION, CHARACTER, USE, ETC. OF LAMPS AND REFLECTORS – The Secretary of State may by regulations prescribe the conditions to be complied with by any of the following lamps carried by a vehicle, namely (a) any lamp showing a light to the front; (b) any lamp showing a white light to the rear for the purpose of reversing; and (c) any lamp carried in pursuance of any of the provisions of s. 68 to 78 of this Act or of any regulations made thereunder and showing a red light to the rear; and, without prejudice to the foregoing, the conditions subject to which the lamps described in paras. (a) and (b) above may be used (s. 73 (1)).

Regulations under sub-s. (1) above may make different provision in relation to vehicles of different classes or in relation to vehicles of the same class in different circumstances (s. 73 (2)).

The conditions which may be prescribed by regulations under sub-s. (1) above as conditions to be complied with by any lamp shall include conditions with respect to (a) position and manner of attachment to the vehicle; (b) power, intensity, colour and angle of projection of light; (c) height, width and range of illumination of beam; (d) provision for obscuration or deflection of light or beam; and such regulations may provide for the method by which the height, width or range of illumination of a beam is to be ascertained (s. 73 (3)).

Regulations under sub-s. (1) above may make special provision, in relation to any class of vehicle, as to the position in which a lamp carried for the purposes both of para. (a) and of para. (b) of s. 68 (1) of this Act is to be attached; and in a case for which special provision is so made the reference in s. 72 (1) of this Act to the requirements which would be applicable to separate lamps shall not include the requirements of any regulations as to the position of a separate lamp carried for the purposes of the said para. (a) or (b) (s. 73 (4)).

The Secretary of State may by regulations prescribe the conditions to be complied with by any reflector carried in pursuance of any of the provisions of ss. 69 to 78 of this Act or of any regulations made thereunder, and the position and manner in which it is to be attached; and any regulations made under this subsection may make different provision in relation to vehicles of different classes or in relation to vehicles of the same class in different circumstances (s. 73 (5)).

BICYCLES, TRICYCLES AND INVALID CARRIAGES – In the application of ss. 68 to 73 of this Act (except so far as those sections relate to any headlamps required to be carried under s. 68 (2) thereof) to bicycles, tricycles and invalid carriages the following modifications shall apply:

(a) in the case of a bicycle not having a side-car attached thereto, whether propelled by mechanical power or not, or of a tricycle not propelled by mechanical power, or of an invalid carriage, only a single lamp showing a white light light to the front instead of two such lamps need be carried;

(b) in the case of a bicycle or tricycle not propelled by mechanical power, or of a bicycle propelled by mechanical power and not having a side-car attached thereto—

(i) only a single lamp showing a red light to the rear instead of two such lamps, and

(ii) only a single red reflector instead of two such reflectors,

need be carried;

(c) in the case of a bicycle not having a side-car attached thereto, whether propelled by mechanical power or not, or of a tricycle not propelled by mechanical power, no lamp need be carried if the bicycle or tricycle is being wheeled by a person on foot as near as possible to the near or left hand edge of the carriageway;

(d) in the case of a bicycle or tricycle not propelled by mechanical power, no light required by the said ss. 68 to 73 need be shown, if the bicycle or tricycle is stationary owing to the exigencies of the traffic or in order to comply with any traffic signal or direction, and the bicycle or tricycle is as near as possible to the near or left hand edge of the carriageway:

Provided that the provisions of paragraph (d) above shall have effect only until such day as the Secretary of State may by order made by statutory instrument appoint (s. 74).

HORSE-DRAWN AGRICULTURAL VEHICLES – In the application of ss. 68 to 73 of this Act (except so far as those sections relate to any headlamps required to be carried under s. 68 (2) thereof to vehicles drawn by horses or other animals the following modifications shall apply:

(a) any vehicle engaged for the time being in carrying agricultural produce of an inflammable nature in the course of the internal operations of a farm shall be exempted from carrying lamps;

(b) without prejudice to para. (a) above, in the case of an agricultural implement or of any vehicle used for the time being by a person engaged in agriculture for the conveyance of his agricultural produce or articles required by him for use in agriculture—

(i) only one lamp showing a light to the front need be carried, and that lamp shall be attached to the off or right hand side of the vehicle, and

(ii) subject to the provisions of s. 76 of this Act, a lamp showing a red light to the rear need not be carried (s. 75 (1)).

In this section "agriculture" includes the use of land as meadow land or pasture land, or orchard land or for market gardens or allotments, but does not include the use of land as woodlands, and "agricultural" shall be construed accordingly (s. 75 (2)).

VEHICLES CARRYING OVERHANGING OR PROJECTING LOADS – Without prejudice to ss. 68 to 75 of this Act, where a vehicle on a road during the hours of darkness carries a load overhanging laterally on any side more than 12 ins. from the centre of the outermost of the lamps showing a white light to the front on that side, the vehicle shall carry, in substitution for or in addition to that lamp, a lamp showing to the front a white light visible from a reasonable distance and in such a position that no part of the load overhangs laterally more than 12 ins. beyond a vertical line through the centre of the substituted or additional lamp (s. 76 (1)).

Subject to sub-s. (3) below, where a vehicle on a road during the hours of darkness carries a load projecting to the rear more than 3½ ft. behind its tail lamp, the vehicle shall carry a rear lamp in such a position that no part of the load projects to the rear more than 3½ ft. behind that rear lamp.

In this section "rear lamp" means a lamp showing to the rear a red light visible from a reasonable distance (s. 76 (2)).

The Secretary of State may by regulations direct that in relation to vehicles of any prescribed class sub-s. (2) above shall have effect with the substitution, for references to 3½ ft., of references to such longer distance, not being more than 6 ft., as may be prescribed in respect of vehicles of that class (s. 76 (3)).

The Secretary of State may by regulations provide that, subject to any prescribed exceptions, where a vehicle on a road during the hours of darkness carries a load overhanging laterally by more than the prescribed distance (measured from such point as may be specified in the regulations), the vehicle shall carry a rear lamp in the prescribed position to indicate the overhang; and any such regulations may apply to a vehicle otherwise exempted from carrying a rear lamp by s. 77 of this Act (s. 76 (4))

Every rear lamp carried in pursuance of this section or regulations made under it shall comply with the prescribed conditions and shall, subject to sub-s. (6) below, be carried in addition to the tail lamp (s. 76 (5)).

The Secretary of State may by regulations exempt a vehicle carrying a rear lamp in pursuance of this section from carrying a tail lamp or from carrying two tail lamps (s. 76 (6)).

Nothing in s. 75 (1) (b) of this Act shall exempt any implement or vehicle to which that paragraph applies from complying with sub-ss. (2) to (5) above or any regulations made under them, but in relation to any such implement or vehicle a reference to the red reflectors required by s 69 (1) of this Act shall be substituted for the reference in sub-s. (2) above to the tail lamp (s. 76 (7)).

VEHICLES TOWING AND BEING TOWED – In the application of ss. 68 to 76 of this Act (except so far as those sections relate to any headlamps required to be carried under s. 68 (2) thereof in the case of a vehicle drawing one or more vehicles the following modifications shall, subject to the following provisions of this section, apply: (a) lamps showing lights to the front need not be carried on any vehicle being drawn; (b) lamps showing red lights to the rear need not be carried on any of the vehicles except the rearmost vehicle; (c) reflectors facing to the rear need not be carried on any of the vehicles except the rearmost vehicle or a vehicle more than 5 ft. from the vehicle behind it (s. 77 (1)).

If the distance between any two of the vehicles exceeds 5 ft., then as respects any light to be shown to the rear the foremost of the two vehicles, and as respects any light to be shown to the front the rearmost of the two vehicles, shall be required to carry the same lamps as if the one were not drawing the other (s. 77 (2)).

If a vehicle being drawn or any load carried thereon projects laterally on any side more than 12 ins. beyond the outermost of the lamps showing a white light to the front on that side carried by the vehicle by which it is being drawn or by any preceding vehicle which is also being drawn by the same vehicle, the first-mentioned vehicle shall carry on the side on which the vehicle or its load so projects a lamp showing to the front a white light visible from a reasonable distance in such a position that no part of the vehicle or its load projects laterally more than 12 ins. beyond a vertical line through the centre of the lamp required to be carried by this subsection (s. 77 (3)).

This section shall have effect subject to the provisions of any regulations made under s. 76 (4) of this Act in the case of any vehicles to which those regulations apply (s. 77 (4)).

For the purposes of this section, the distance between two vehicles shall be measured between the nearest points of those vehicles, disregarding the drawbar and any fitting for its attachment (s. 77 (5)).

POWERS OF EXEMPTION AND VARIATION OF REQUIREMENTS – The Secretary of State may by regulations exempt either wholly or partly from any of the requirements of ss. 68 to 77 of this Act—

(a) vehicles while carrying inflammable or explosive goods of a nature specified in the regulations, or when in a place where inflammable or explosive material of a nature so specified is handled or stored, if an application is made for the purpose by any body which in the opinion of the Secretary of State is a body proper to make such an application;
(b) any vehicles used for naval, military or air force purposes;
(c) vehicles standing or parked on any road with respect to which a speed limit on the driving of mechanically propelled vehicles is in force by virtue of any enactment, or on any road verge or in any parking place or any stand for hackney carriages;
(d) vehicles drawn or propelled by hand (s. 78 (1)).

The Secretary of State may by regulations add to or vary the requirements of the said ss. 68 to 77, and require or permit distinctive lamps to be carried displaying lights of such colour and used under such conditions as may be prescribed, in the case of (a) vehicles used as public passenger vehicles or any class thereof or as hackney carriages; (b) vehicles used for naval, military, air force or police purposes, or as ambulances, or for any other special purposes mentioned in the regulations; and where distinctive lamps are so required or permitted, prohibit similar lamps being carried by any other vehicles (s. 78 (2)).

The Secretary of State may by regulations increase, in relation to vehicles of any class specified in the regulations, the number of tail lamps required by s. 68 (1) (b) of this Act (s. 78 (3)).

Regulations made under sub-s. (3) above may make different provision in relation to vehicles of different classes or in relation to vehicles of any class when used in different circumstances; and any such regulations may modify the provisions of s. 74 of this Act so far as it relates to the tail lamps of vehicles to which the regulations apply (s. 78 (4)).

The Secretary of State may, notwithstanding anything in s. 70 of this Act, by regulations make provision (a) requiring or authorising a light of a prescribed colour to be shown by the prescribed means to the rear of a vehicle of any prescribed class; and (b) where any such light is required or authorised by the regulations to be so shown by means of reflecting or fluorescent material, provision imposing conditions with respect to the material, its position and dimensions (s. 78 (5)).

Without prejudice to the powers conferred by the foregoing provisions of this section, the Secretary of State may by regulations exempt, either wholly or partly, from the requirements of s. 69 of this Act, vehicles of any particular class (s. 78 (6)).

Regulations under any of the provisions of ss. 68 to 77 of this Act or this section granting exemptions from any of the requirements thereof (a) may grant exemptions from any such requirement in such cases as may be specified in the regulations and subject to such conditions as may be specified in or under the regulations; and (b) may make different provisions as respects different areas, as respects different classes of vehicles or as respects the same class of vehicles in different circumstances (s. 78 (7)).

POWER TO IMPOSE ADDITIONAL REQUIREMENTS FOR VEHICLES OVER PRESCRIBED LENGTH AND TRAILERS – The Secretary of State may by regulations provide that, subject to any exemptions prescribed by the regulations—

(a) where the length of a vehicle, or the overall length of two or more vehicles of which one is drawing the other or others, inclusive of any load on the vehicle or vehicles, exceeds a length so prescribed, the vehicle or vehicles shall when on a road during the hours of darkness carry such lamps or reflectors each showing a light, or as the case may be facing, to the side as may be so prescribed;

(b) a vehicle constructed or adapted so as to be drawn by another vehicle shall when on a road during the hours of darkness carry such lamps each showing a light to the front or the side, or both, as may be prescribed;

and any such regulations may prescribe the conditions with which lamps or reflectors carried on a vehicle in pursuance of the regulations must comply and the position and manner in which they are to be attached, and may make different provision in respect of vehicles of different classes or in respect of vehicles of the same class in different circumstances (s. 79 (1)).

Any lamps or reflectors required to be carried by virtue of this section shall be carried in addition to, and not instead of, those required to be carried by or by virtue of the provisions of ss. 68 to 78 of this Act, and accordingly any such lamps or reflectors shall for the purposes of those provisions, and in particular s. 70 of this Act, be treated as not showing a light to the front or to the rear (s. 79 (2)).

OFFENCES – If any person causes or permits any vehicle to be on any road in contravention of any of the provisions of ss. 68 to 79 of this Act or of regulations made thereunder or otherwise fails to comply with any of those provisions he shall be guilty of an offence:

Provided that it shall be a defence for a person driving or being in charge of a vehicle who is charged with an offence under this subsection to prove to the satisfaction of the court that the offence arose through the negligence or default of some other person whose duty it was to provide the vehicle with any lamp or reflector (s. 81 (1)).

If any person sells, or offers or exposes for sale, any appliance adapted for use as a reflector or tail lamp to be carried on a vehicle in accordance with the provisions of this Act or of any regulations made thereunder, not being an appliance which complies with the conditions prescribed under ss. 68 to 79 of this Act for a class of vehicles for which the appliance is adapted, he shall be guilty of an offence (s. 81 (2)). [This will be amended by s. 9 (3), R.T. Act 1974, when in force.]

INTERPRETATION – "Hours of darkness" means the time between half-an-hour after sunset and half-an-hour before sunrise; "tail lamp" means, in relation to a vehicle, any lamp carried attached to the vehicle for the purpose of showing a red light to the rear in accordance with s. 68 (1) (b) of this Act or regulations under any of ss. 68 to 79 thereof (s. 82).

Road Vehicles Lighting Regulations 1971.

Front Lamps – By virtue of the Road Vehicles Lighting Regs. 1971 –

(a) An obligatory front lamp shall be so fixed that its centre is not higher than 5 ft. from the ground. This does not apply to large passenger vehicles or snow ploughs. (On horse-drawn vehicles it may not exceed 5 ft. 9 ins. from the ground, and on land, agricultural and industrial tractors, agricultural implements and engineering plant, not more than 6 ft. 3 ins. (reg. 4).)

Except in the case of a snow plough or aerodrome fire tender or aerodrome runway sweeper or a land tractor, an agricultural tractor, an industrial tractor, an agricultural implement or engineering plant, every electric light (over 7 watts) or acetylene lamp showing light to the front must be fixed not more than 3 ft 6 ins. from the ground and except in the case of a lamp used only in fog or falling snow, not less than 2 ft. from the ground. Provided that this will not apply to a vehicle registered before January 1, 1952, a vehicle for combative purposes or for engineering operations in combat areas or a vehicle supplied to the Forces before January 1, 1956 (regs. 8, 9).

(b) An obligatory front lamp shall be fixed so that no part of the vehicle or its equipment (except mirror and indicator: reg. 3) extends more than 12 ins. beyond the centre of the lamp on the side that the lamp is placed. This does not apply to motor or pedal bicycles or to tower wagons (reg. 4).

(c) On horse-drawn vehicles, such a front lamp shall not be behind the axle if only one axle, and it shall not be more than 18 ins. behind the front axle in the case of a vehicle having more than one axle (reg. 4).

(d) If there is only one obligatory front lamp, it shall be

fixed on the off-side of the vehicle except in the case of a solo motor or pedal bicycle (reg. 6).

(e) If two obligatory front lamps are carried, they shall be fixed on opposite sides of the vehicle, and, except in the case of a bicycle with side-car, they shall be fixed at the same height from the ground (reg. 5).

Any dual-purpose lamp (showing white light to the front and red light to the rear) on a side-car, tractor, hand or horse-drawn vehicle should be not more than 16 ins. from the side of the vehicle (reg. 7).

Anti-Dazzle – Unless allowed by regulation, no light from a vehicle other than a dipping headlight, shall be moved by swivelling, deflecting or otherwise while the vehicle is in motion—but in the case of a bicycle or tricycle, amber coloured reflectors attached to or incorporated in or forming part of the pedals are permissible (R.T. Act 1972, s. 71). Under the Road Vehicles Lighting Regs. 1971, no front lamp (electric or acetylene) shall be used on any vehicle other than a pedal bicycle or tricycle unless it is so made, fitted and kept, that the beam of light from it:

(1) is permanently deflected downwards so that it cannot dazzle a person standing more than 25 ft. distant, whose eye level is not less than 3 ft. 6 ins. high; or

(2) can be deflected downwards or both downwards and to the left so that it cannot dazzle such a person, or

(3) can be extinguished by a device which leaves a non-dazzling beam of light (as under (1)), or

(4) can be extinguished by a device which at the same time either deflects the light from another lamp downwards or both downwards and to the left so that it cannot dazzle (see (1) above), or brings into or leaves in operation a non-dazzling light from lamps other than the obligatory front lamps. Provided that a lamp will not comply with (1) unless its centre is not less than 2 ft. from the ground unless it is used only in fog or falling snow (reg. 9).

The above does not apply to any direction indicator or lamp with an electric bulb or bulbs not exceeding 7 watts in power and having frosted glass or other light-diffusing material nor to a lamp carried on a 4-wheeled pedal cycle, and flashing blue or amber lights carried by certain vehicles, e.g. ambulances, and road clearance vehicles (reg. 9).

It applies to electric light lamps and acetylene light lamps on vehicles (reg. 9).

The light from not more than two front lamps (other than the obligatory front lamps) may be deflected to either side by the movements of the front wheels provided such lamps are not more than 3 ft. 6 ins. from the ground (reg. 10).

Every electric light bulb in a front lamp in a motor vehicle shall have the rated wattage marked in a readily legible manner (reg. 11).

No bulb or bulbs over 7 watts power in a front lamp shall be kept lighted while the vehicle is stationary in a road. However, this shall not apply during an enforced stoppage of the vehicle; to a large passenger vehicle stopping to set down or pick up passengers; to interior lighting of vehicles; to break-down vehicles or tower-wagons in use at their special work; to direction indicators; to blue lights on ambulance or vehicles used for police, fire brigade or fire salvage purposes, and an amber light on a road clearance vehicle; to searchlights or special lamps used for naval, military, air force, police or fire brigade purposes or to searchlights or special lamps on vehicles used for repairs to sewers, gas, electricity or water mains whilst repairs are being made (reg. 13).

Headlamps – The Road Vehicles (Lighting) Regs. 1971 contain requirements as to the use of headlamps on vehicles moving at night.

INTERPRETATION – In these Regulations, except where the context otherwise requires, the following expressions have the meanings hereby assigned to them respectively,

"dipped beam" means a beam of light emitted by a headlamp, being a beam which is deflected downwards or both downwards and to the left to such an extent that it is at all times incapable of dazzling any person who is on the same horizontal plane as the vehicle at a greater distance than 25 ft. from the lamp whose eye-level is not less than 3 ft. 6 ins. above that plane;

"obligatory headlamp" means any headlamp required to be carried by a vehicle by reg. 15 or 16 of these Regulations;

"obligatory front lamp" means a lamp showing to the front a white light which is required to be carried under s. 1 of the Act and these Regs. (reg. 3).

Except as provided by para. (2) of this regulation, Part III of these Regulations apply to every motor vehicle—(a) which is a wheeled vehicle; (b) the obligatory front lamp or lamps of which are electrically operated; and (c) which is on a road (reg. 14 (1)).

Part III of these regulations do not apply—(a) to a vehicle first used before January 1, 1931; or (b) to a vehicle controlled by a pedestrian; or (c) to an agricultural implement, a land locomotive, a land tractor, a works truck or a road roller; or (d) to a vehicle which is so constructed as to be incapable of exceeding a speed of 6 m.p.h. on the level; or (e) to a vehicle brought temporarily into G.B. by a person resident outside the U.K., provided it complies in every respect with the requirements as to lighting equipment and reflectors contained in the Geneva Convention on Road Traffic 1949; or (f) to a vehicle manufactured in G.B. which has been purchased by a person who is temporarily in G.B. and is or is about to be resident abroad, provided certain conditions are complied with; or (ff) to a vehicle manufactured in Great Britain which has been zero rated for VAT purposes; or (g) to a vehicle used for naval, military or air force purposes; or (h) to a vehicle in the service of a visiting force; or (i) to an electrically propelled goods vehicle which is so constructed as to be incapable of exceeding a speed of 15 m.p.h. on the level; or (j) until January 1, 1974 to an electrically propelled goods vehicle which has 2 or 3 wheels, which is first used before January 1, 1972 and which is so constructed as to be capable of exceeding a speed of 15 m.p.h. on the level (reg. 14 (2)).

HEADLAMPS TO BE CARRIED BY VEHICLES WITH TWO WHEELS AND SOME VEHICLES WITH THREE WHEELS – This regulation applies to a motor vehicle to which these Regulations apply and which (a) has 2 wheels; or (b) has 3 wheels and is first used before January 1, 1972; or (c) has three wheels, is first used on or after January 1, 1972, and except in the case of a motor bicycle with a side-car attached thereto has an unladen weight of not more than 400 kilogrammes and an overall width of not more than 1.30 metres (R.V.L., reg. 15 (1)).

Every vehicle to which this regulation applies shall carry—

(a) one headlamp in the vertical plane passing through the longitudinal axis of the vehicle (disregarding, for the purpose of ascertaining such axis, any side-car attached thereto) which either:

(i) in the case of a moped with or without a side-car attached thereto and first used before January 1, 1972 or in the case of any vehicle which is so constructed as to be incapable of exceeding a speed of 25 m.p.h. on the level, can only emit a dipped beam; or

(ii) in the case of any vehicle, is wired to a device the operation of which at the will of the driver can cause to be emitted from it either a main beam or a dipped beam; or

(b) a matched pair of headlamps, both headlamps in the pair being wired to a device the operation of which at the will of the driver can cause to be emitted from them at the same time either:

(i) in the case of any vehicle which is so constructed as to be incapable of exceeding a speed of 25 m.p.h. on the level, only dipped beams; or

(ii) in the case of any vehicle, either main beams or dipped beams (reg. 15 (2)).

Every beam emitted by any lamp required to be carried by this regulation shall be derived from the filament or filaments of an electric bulb or bulbs, or from the filament or filaments of a sealed beam lamp, the rating of such filament or at least one of such filaments not being less than:

(a) 10 watts in the case of a main or dipped beam emitted by a lamp carried by a moped with or without a side-car attached thereto which was first used before January 1, 1972, and which is so constructed as to be incapable of exceeding a speed of 25 m.p.h. on the level;

(b) 15 watts in the case of a main or dipped beam emitted by a lamp carried by:

(i) a moped with or without a side-car attached thereto which is first used on or after January 1, 1972, and which is so constructed as to be incapable of exceeding a speed of 25 m.p.h. on the level; or

(ii) a moped with or without a side-car attached thereto which is first used before January 1, 1972 and which is so constructed as to be capable of exceeding a speed of 25 m.p.h. on the level; or

(iii) a motor bicycle (not being a moped) with or without a side-car attached thereto, which was first used before January 1, 1972, and whereof the cylinder capacity of the engine is not more than 250 cubic centimetres;

(c) 18 watts in the case of a main or dipped beam emitted by a lamp carried by:

(i) a moped with or without a side-car attached thereto which is first used on or after January 1, 1972 and which is so constructed as to be capable of exceeding a speed of 25 m.p.h. on the level; or

(ii) a motor bicycle (not being a moped) with or without a side-car attached thereto, which is first used on or after January 1, 1972, and whereof the cylinder capacity of the engine is not more than 250 cubic centimetres;

(d) 24 watts in the case of a dipped beam emitted by a lamp carried by any other vehicle; and

(e) 30 watts in the case of a main beam emitted by a lamp carried by any other vehicle (reg. 15 (3)).

Where any vehicle carries a matched pair of headlamps in accordance with the requirements of this regulation, each of the lamps in the pair shall, except in the case of lamps carried by a vehicle which is engineering plant, an industrial tractor or a motor cycle with or without a side-car attached thereto, be so positioned on one side of the vehicle that no part of its illuminated area is less than 300 mm from any part of the illuminated area of the other lamp in the pair (reg. 15 (4)).

HEADLAMPS TO BE CARRIED BY SOME VEHICLES WITH THREE WHEELS AND BY VEHICLES WITH FOUR OR MORE WHEELS – This regulation applies to a motor vehicle to which Part III of these

Regulations apply and which (a) has 3 wheels, is not a motor bicycle with a side-car attached thereto, is first used on or after January 1, 1972 and has an unladen weight of more than 400 kilogrammes or an overall width of more than 1·30 metres; or (b) has 4 or more wheels (R.V.L., reg. 16 (1)).

Every vehicle to which this regulation applies shall carry:

(a) a matched pair of headlamps, both headlamps in the pair being wired to a device the operation of which at the will of the driver can cause to be emitted from them at the same time either:

- (i) in the case of any vehicle which is so constructed as to be incapable of exceeding a speed of 25 m.p.h. on the level, only dipped beams; or
- (ii) in the case of any vehicle, either main beams or dipped beams; or:

(b) two or more matched pairs of headlamps, the headlamps being arranged so that:

- (i) they form two groups of headlamps, one on each side of the vertical plane passing through the longitudinal axis of the vehicle;
- (ii) the headlamps in one of the matched pairs, which are at least as far away from the vertical plane passing through the longitudinal axis of the vehicle as any other headlamps in another matched pair of headlamps, can each emit a dipped beam without at the same time emitting a main beam, and so that every other headlamp can emit a main beam; and
- (iii) all the headlamps in both groups are wired to a device the operation of which at the will of the driver can at the same time extinguish every main beam emitted by every headlamp in both groups, and cause either to be emitted or to continue to be emitted the dipped beams from the two headlamps in the matched pair which are at least as far away from the vertical plane passing through the longitudinal axis of the vehicle as any other headlamps in another matched pair of headlamps:

Provided that in the case of a public service vehicle first used before October 1, 1969 it shall be a sufficient compliance with the requirements of this paragraph if the vehicle carries a matched pair of headlamps one of which can emit a dipped beam, without either lamp at the same time emitting a main beam (reg. 16 (2)).

Every main or dipped beam emitted by any lamp required to be carried by this regulation shall be derived from the filament or filaments of an electric bulb or bulbs or from the filament or filaments of a sealed beam lamp the rating of such filament or at least one of such filaments not being less than 30 watts (reg. 16 (3)).

Every headlamp which emits a dipped beam carried by a vehicle in accordance with the requirements of this regulation shall, except in the case of a lamp carried by a vehicle which is engineering plant or an industrial tractor, be so positioned on one side of the vehicle that:

(a) no part of its illuminated area is, in the case of a vehicle first used before October 1, 1969, less than 350 millimetres, or, in the case of a vehicle first used on or after that date, less than 600 millimetres, from any part of the illuminated area of any such lamp on the other side; and

(b) in the case of a vehicle first used on or after January 1, 1972 the outermost part of the illuminated area of the lamp is not more than 400 millimetres from the outermost part of the vehicle on the side on which the lamp is placed (reg. 16 (4)).

SINGLE UNITS FOR SIDE AND HEADLAMPS – In the case of a vehicle which carries one obligatory side lamp and one obligatory headlamp, such lamps may be combined so as to form a single unit (reg. 17 (1)).

In the case of a motor bicycle with a side-car attached thereto, being a vehicle which carries two obligatory side lamps and one obligatory headlamp, one of the obligatory side lamps may be combined with the obligatory headlamp so as to form a single unit (reg. 17 (2)).

In the case of a vehicle which carries two obligatory side lamps they may be combined:

(a) in the case of a vehicle which has only two obligatory headlamps, with such lamps, or

(b) with the two obligatory headlamps in the matched pair which are at least as far away from the vertical plane passing through the longitudinal axis of the vehicle as any other obligatory headlamps in another matched pair of obligatory headlamps

so as to form two single units each comprising an obligatory headlamp and an obligatory side lamp (reg. 17 (3)).

REQUIREMENTS FOR EVERY OBLIGATORY HEADLAMP – Every obligatory headlamp carried by any vehicle shall comply with the following conditions, namely: (1) it shall be securely fixed to the vehicle; (2) it shall be so constructed and maintained that the direction of the beam of light emitted therefrom can be adjusted whilst the vehicle is stationary so that the lamp when lit emits the type of beam which it is required to be capable of emitting by these Regulations; and (3) it shall be kept in a clean and efficient condition (R.V.L., reg. 18).

REQUIREMENTS FOR EVERY MATCHED PAIR OF OBLIGATORY HEADLAMPS – Every matched pair of obligatory headlamps carried on any vehicle to which Part III of the Regs. applies shall comply with the following conditions: (1) both lamps in the pair shall, except in the case of lamps carried by a P.S.V. first used before October 1, 1969, have the same area and shape when illuminated; (2) both lamps, except in the case of lamps carried by a P.S.V. first used before October 1, 1969, have their wiring arranged so that: (a) if they can emit either main beams or dipped beams, the beams which they can emit can only be switched on or off together; (b) if they can emit both main and dipped beams, the dipped beams can only be switched on or off together and the main beams can only be switched on or off together; (c) if they can emit supplementary main beams, such beams can only be switched on or off together with the main beams emitted by another pair of obligatory headlamps; and (3) both lamps in the pair shall, when lit, emit beams of the same colour light (R.V.L., reg. 19).

Every main or dipped beam emitted by any headlamp or fog lamp carried on any vehicle to which these Regulations apply shall be a beam of white or yellow light (reg. 20).

REQUIREMENTS AS TO USE OF HEADLAMPS – This regulation applies to every motor vehicle to which Part III of these Regulations applies and which has 4 or more wheels (R.V.L.,reg. 21 (1)).

This regulation applies to every length of road, except that it does not apply to a length of road (a) on which there is provided a system of street lighting furnished by means of lamps placed not more than 200 yds. apart, and (b) while such lamps are lit (reg. 21 (2)).

When any motor vehicle to which these Regulations apply is in motion during the hours of darkness on a length of road to which this regulation applies a matched pair of obligatory headlamps carried by the vehicle shall be kept lit:

Provided that this paragraph shall not apply (i) in conditions of fog or whilst snow is falling to a vehicle which carries two permitted lamps, if both such permitted lamps are kept lit; (ii) to a public service vehicle first used before October 1, 1969, if one obligatory headlamp carried by the vehicle is kept lit, or, in conditions of fog or whilst snow is falling, and if the vehicle carries a fog lamp, if that lamp is kept lit; (iii) to a vehicle being drawn by another vehicle; or (iv) to a vehicle while being used to propel in front thereof a snow plough (reg. 21 (3)).

In this regulation "two permitted lamps" means two fog lamps or one fog lamp and one headlamp (not being an obligatory headlamp), being lamps which comply with the following conditions, namely:

(a) the two lamps shall be fixed one on each side of the vertical plane passing through the longitudinal axis of the vehicle;

(b) the centres of both lamps shall be at the same height above the ground;

(c) the distances between the centre of each lamp and the vertical plane passing through the longitudinal axis of the vehicle shall be the same; and

(d) each lamp shall be so positioned that:

(i) in the case of a vehicle first used before January 1, 1971, no part of the illuminated area of one lamp is less than 350 millimetres from any part of the illuminated area of the other lamp; and

(ii) in the case of a vehicle first used on or after January 1, 1971, the outermost part of the illuminated area of either lamp is not more than 400 millimetres from the outermost part of the vehicle on the side on which the lamp is placed (reg. 21 (4)).

Two or three wheeled motor vehicles fitted either with an obligatory headlamp or a matched pair of obligatory headlamps in motion during the hours of darkness on unlit roads are, in general, required to have lit such headlamp or headlamps (reg. 22).

Breaches of the above Regulations constitute offences punishable under the R.T. Act 1972, s. 81.

The Road Vehicles (Use of Lights during Daytime) Regs. 1975 provide that where a vehicle, which carries the obligatory lamps, is used on a road during daytime hours, those lamps shall be kept lit while the vehicle is in motion during any period when poor visibility conditions prevail on that road. "Poor visibility conditions" mean such conditions adversely affecting visibility (whether consisting of or including fog, smoke, heavy rain or spray, snow, dense cloud or any similar condition) as seriously reduce the visibility of the driver (after the appropriate use by him of any windscreen wiper and washer) to see other vehicles or persons on the road, or the ability of other users of the road to see the vehicle.

Rear Lamps – The area of such lamp shall be a 2 in. diameter or equivalent area if not circular when on vehicles except in the case of motor cycles, sidecars, bicycles, tricycles, 4-wheeled pedal cycles, agricultural implements, trailer pumps, hand-propelled and horse-drawn vehicles when the diameter may be 1½ ins. or equivalent area if not round. An exception is allowed for a lamp on a motor vehicle or trailer made in Italy if the lamp bears a marking approved by the Italian Ministry of Transport, viz. "IGM" and "LP". In the case of motor cycles and sidecars the electric bulbs must not be less than 5 watts. When two rear lamps are carried they must look alike and be so wired that if one goes out the other remains alight and this reg. shall not apply to existing large passenger vehicles (R.V.L., reg. 24).

Obligatory red rear lamps should be fixed on a vehicle in accordance with Sched. 1 to the 1971 Regs. (reg. 23). On a vehicle (a) constructed or adapted to carry goods or burden, and (b) carrying a load projecting to the rear in such manner that the rear lights would not be visible from a reasonable distance, the lamps shall be attached to the load in the prescribed positions (reg. 62).

Reversing White Lights – A vehicle may carry one or two reversing lights showing a white light to the rear only for the purposes of reversing (1972 Act, s. 70).

Any such light shall be electric (not exceeding 24 watts) non-dazzling and switched on either automatically by use of the reverse gear or by a switch operated by the driver. In vehicles manufactured after July 1, 1954, this switch must serve no other purpose and there must be a device to show that the light is on. Only when the vehicle is reversing shall the reversing white light be shown (R.V.L., regs. 26–29).

Red Reflectors – The 1972 Act, s. 69, directs that every vehicle on any road during the hours of darkness must carry two unobscured and efficient red reflectors. Reflector in this section means one facing to the rear. A person who causes or permits a vehicle to be on a road must provide same. Bicycles, tricycles and solo motor cycles need have only one. Every red reflector carried on a vehicle shall be so fixed to the vehicle that the reflecting area of the reflector is in a vertical position and facing squarely to the rear, and must be kept clean and plainly visible from the rear (R.V.L., reg. 31).

On a vehicle (a) constructed or adapted to carry goods or burden, and (b) carrying a load projecting to the rear in such manner that the reflectors would be obscured the reflectors shall be attached to the load in the prescribed positions (reg. 62).

PROJECTING OR OVERHANGING LOADS – If a load on a vehicle projects to the rear more than 3½ ft. behind its tail lamp or any red reflector, a separate red rear lamp must be carried so that no part of the load projects to the rear more than 3½ ft. behind that rear lamp. Such a "projecting" lamp may be in addition to or in substitution for any lamp showing red to the rear or any reflector (s. 76). In relation to: (a) a vehicle carrying a fire escape; and (b) a mechanically propelled vehicle being a land tractor or an agricultural tractor on which is mounted an agricultural implement, instead of 3½ ft. the distance shall be 6 ft. (R.V.L. Regs. 1971, reg. 36).

If a load overhangs laterally by more than 12 ins. measured—(a) from the outermost part of the vehicle on the same side as that on which the load overhangs; or (b) if the vehicle is drawing one or more vehicles, from the outermost part of the rearmost vehicle on the same side as that on which the load overhangs, the vehicle shall carry a rear lamp in the "relevant position" to indicate the overhang (reg. 37 (1)).

"Relevant position" means a position on any side on which the load overhangs laterally, which is as near as practicable to the outer edge of the load and which is such that no part of the load projects outwards more than 12 ins. beyond a vertical line through the nearest part of the illuminated area of the rear lamp (reg. 37 (2)).

This regulation applies to a towed vehicle which need not carry red rear lights by virtue of s. 77 of R.T. Act 1972, but it does not apply to any vehicle carrying loose agricultural produce not baled or crated but shall apply to a vehicle fitted with a movable platform being a vehicle used to facilitate overhead working, as if none of the special equipment were a load (reg. 37 (3 and 4)).

Rear lamps marking projecting loads must at night be kept properly trimmed, lighted and in a clean and efficient condition (reg. 38).

Lights on Long Vehicles and Trailers – The R.V.L. Regs. 1971 (Part VIII) provide for the carriage at night by certain long vehicles or combinations of vehicles and by trailers of additional lamps which are called "front corner marker lamps" and "side marker lamps" and are designed, as their names imply, to show up the vehicles and their loads at night. The chief provisions are: combinations of a towing vehicle and a trailer or trailers carrying a supported load which inclusive of load exceed 40 ft. but do not exceed 60 ft. in length, must carry "side marker lamps" (reg. 43); trailers must carry "front corner marker lamps" (for exceptions see reg. 47). If they are over 30 ft. in length "side marker lamps" must be carried (reg. 45; "front corner" and "side marker" lamps must comply with the conditions laid down in regs. 48 and 49.

Additional Reflectors on Long Vehicles and Trailers – The R.V.L. Regs. 1971 (Part IX) provide for side facing reflectors on certain motor vehicles and trailers. A "side facing reflector" means a reflector which—(a) is not an obligatory reflector, (b) is amber in colour and (c) is marked with an approval mark.

During the hours of darkness these vehicles shall carry two side facing reflectors on each side of the vehicle (regs. 50–56).

VEHICLES OF HOME FORCES AND VISITING FORCES – R.V.L. Regs. 1971 (regs. 57–60) deal with vehicles used for Naval, Military, or Air Force purposes, and vehicles of the visiting forces.

Vehicles used on manœuvres, and vehicles used in training, on special occasions when notice within 48 hours is given to the police, are exempt from all the requirements as to lighting. Searchlights may be used on such vehicles.

Where from 6 to 12 such vehicles are proceeding in convoy on tactical or driving exercises after notice to the police, white lights on front vehicle, faint underneath white lights on the middle vehicles and red rear light on last vehicle are allowable.

Vehicles constructed or adapted for combative purposes should have red rear lamps and red reflectors not more than 5 ft. 6 ins. from the ground.

Vehicles of a visiting force should comply with the rules regarding vehicles from abroad, which follow.

VEHICLES DRAWN OR PROPELLED BY HAND (SUCH AS HAND-CARTS, WHEELBARROWS, PERAMBULATORS, ETC) – Under the R.V. Lighting Regs. 1971.

(a) If such vehicle and any load is not more than 2½ ft. wide, 6 ft. long and 4½ ft. high, it need not carry any lamps provided it is kept as nearas possible to the edge of the carriageway during the hours of darkness.

(b) If such vehicle and any load exceeds any or all of the preceding measurements but is not more than 4 ft. wide, it need show only one obligatory front light and a red rear lamp or a red rear reflector.

(c) If such vehicle and any load exceeds 4 ft. in width it must carry two lamps showing white light to the front. It must also have a red rear reflector or a red rear lamp.

(d) Any red rear reflector or red rear lamp referred to in paras. (b) and (c) above, must be fixed on the off-side within at least 16 ins. from the side, and no more than 3 ft. 6 ins. or less than 15 ins. from the ground.

(e) If the vehicle carries a load extending more than 3½ ft. behind its tail light, a red rear lamp must also be carried so that no part of the load projects more than 3½ ft. beyond it (reg. 61).

VEHICLES FROM ABROAD – Mechanically propelled vehicles brought temporarily into G.B. by a person resident outside the United Kingdom need not comply with the above regulations provided they comply with the requirements of the Annex to the Geneva Convention on Road Traffic, September 19, 1949 (reg. 63).

DISTINCTIVE LAMPS ON CERTAIN VEHICLES – An ambulance, police, fire brigade, fire salvage, foresty commission vehicles used for fighting fires, bomb disposal, nuclear accident or incident involving radioactivity, blood transfusion, coastguard and N.C.B. rescue vehicles may carry a lamp displaying a blue light. Road clearance vehicles, break-down vehicles, vehicles used for the purposes of testing, maintaining, improving, cleansing or watering roads, and vehicles used for the purposes of inspecting, cleansing, maintaining, adjusting, renewing or installing any apparatus which is in, on, under or over a road and vehicles used for or in connection with any purpose for which they are authorised by an order under R.T. Act 1972, s. 42 (1) (see Appendix II Special Types of Motor Vehicles) may use a lamp displaying an amber light. Road clearance vehicles may carry amber reflecting surfaces facing to the rear of the vehicle (R.V.L. Regs. 1971, r. 64 and r. 66).

Break-down vehicles may carry one or more lamps showing a white light for the purposes of illuminating the scene of an accident or break-down but it must not dazzle the driver of a vehicle, although it is permissible to move it by swivelling, etc. (1971, reg. 65). There are also special provisions with respect to vehicles which are fitted with platforms which may be moved by extensible booms for the purpose of facilitating overhead working (1971, reg. 67).

Direction Indicator – This means a device fitted to a motor vehicle or trailer for the purpose of intimating the intention of the driver to change the direction of the vehicle to the right or to the left (reg. 3). Subject to certain exceptions, motor vehicles and trailers are required to be fitted with direction indicators complying with the specified conditions contained in Sched. 5 which provide, *inter alia,* that the colour of a direction indicator shall (a) if it shows to the front and rear, be amber, (b) if it shows only to the front, be amber or white, and (c) if it shows only to the rear, be amber or red. The light shall be diffused by frosted glass or other adequate means (regs. 69, 70). With certain exemptions, motor vehicles first used and trailers manufactured on or after July 1, 1973, must be fitted with direction indicators marked with an approval mark (reg. 71). All direction indicators when in use on roads must be properly maintained (reg. 76). Direction indicators may be used by the simultaneous illumination of all the indicators as a hazard warning (a) when a motor vehicle is stationary on a road due to a break-down of the vehicle, or any other vehicle, a road accident or any other emergency, for the purpose of warning other road users of a temporary obstruction on the carriageway of a road or (b) if the motor vehicle is a public service vehicle (whether stationary or in motion) for the purpose of summoning assistance for the driver, conductor or an inspector (reg. 77).

Stop Lamp – This means a lamp fitted to a motor vehicle or to a trailer drawn by a motor vehicle for the purpose of warning other road users, when the lamp is lit, that the brakes of the motor vehicle or in the case of a trailer, the brakes of the drawing vehicle or the combination of vehicles, are being applied (reg. 3). Subject to certain exceptions, motor vehicles and trailers are required to be fitted with stop lamps complying with the specified conditions contained in Sched. 6, which provide, *inter alia*, that every stop lamp shall show a steady red light (regs. 72 and 73). With certain exemptions, motor vehicles first used and trailers manufactured on or after July 1, 1973, must be fitted with stop lamps marked with approval marks (reg. 73). All stop lamps when in use on roads must be properly maintained (reg. 76).

Rear Markings – The Motor Vehicles (Rear Markings) Regs. 1970 and 1972 prescribe that motor vehicles exceeding 3 tons unladen weight and trailers exceeding 1 ton unladen weight, unless excepted, must be fitted with rear markings which are illuminated by the use of red fluorescent material and yellow reflex reflecting material conforming in size, colour and type with Part I of the Schedule to the Regs. Among others, the following are "excepted vehicles": a passenger vehicle, land tractor, land locomotive, agricultural trailer, industrial tractor, works truck, engineering plant, fire fighting vehicles, home forces vehicles, and vehicles used as tar boilers or asphalt mixers. Unless "excepted", motor vehicles more than 13 metres long and trailers forming part of a combination of vehicles more than 13 metres long must have rear markings embodying the words "long vehicle."

Every rear marking must be maintained in a clean and efficient condition while the vehicle is on a road.

The Motor Vehicles (Rear Markings) Regs. 1975 permit the display at the rear of certain vehicles engaged in the international carriage of dangerous goods by road of plates designed to reflect lights to the rear of the vehicle and specify the size, colour and type of such plates and the position in which they are to be fixed.

Lighting of Rear Identification or Registration Mark – Whenever during the hours of darkness a mechanically propelled vehicle, not being a works truck, first registered before October 1, 1938, is upon a public road, a lamp shall be kept burning thereon so contrived as to illuminate by means of reflection, or otherwise, and render easily distinguishable every letter and figure of the registration mark on the back of the vehicle or on the back of the rearmost vehicle attached to the vehicle (Reg. & Lic. Regs. 1971, reg. 20 and Sched. 3).

On every mechanically propelled vehicle registered for the first time on or after October 1, 1938, not being a works truck or an agricultural machine, this illuminated rear registration mark must be easily legible in the absence of fog by an observer, not more than 60 ft., directly behind (50 ft., behind in the case of a bicycle, an invalid vehicle, or pedestrian controlled vehicle), provided that this does not apply where the police authorise vehicles without lights on adequately lighted parking places or hackney carriage stands (Reg. & Lic. Regs. 1971, reg. 19).

Unless a registration mark is so designed and constructed that it may be illuminated from behind by means of translucency it shall be formed of white, silver or light grey letters and figures on a black surface. If it is so designed and constructed to be illuminated from behind as aforesaid the letters and figures must, when so illuminated during the hours of darkness, appear white against a black background (Reg. & Lic. Regs. 1971, reg. 17 and Sched. 2).

Parking Lights – This subject is dealt with by Road Vehicles Lighting (Standing Vehicles) (Exemption) (General) Regs. 1975. The Regs. apply to passenger vehicles, goods vehicles of which the unladen weight does not exceed 30 cwts., invalid carriages and motor cycles and pedal cycles with or without side-cars but do not apply to vehicles needing special lamps (see R.T. Act 1972, s. 76) or with trailers (reg. 3).

"Passenger Vehicle" here means motor vehicle (not cycle or invalid carriage) made solely for passengers and their effects and adapted to carry not more than 7 persons and the driver.

"Goods Vehicle" here means motor vehicle constructed or adapted for the carriage of goods or burden of any description (reg. 2).

A vehicle to which reg. 3 applies shall when standing or parked on a road on which a speed limit of 30 m.p.h. or less is in force, be exempted from showing the required lights (a) if it is lawfully standing or parked in a recognised parking place, or (b) if it is standing or parked on a road which is not a one-way street, the vehicle is parked with its left or nearside as close as may be and parallel to the edge of the carriageway. If the road is a one-way street the vehicle must be left with its nearside as close as may be and parallel to the left hand edge of the carriageway or its right or offside as close as may be and parallel to the right hand edge of the carriageway. No part of the vehicle must be within 15 yards of a road junction.

Chronically Sick and Disabled Persons Act 1970 – Section 20 exempts from certain statutory restrictions invalid carriages complying with the requirements of the Use of Invalid Carriages on Highways Regs. 1970. Invalid carriages complying with these Regs. may be driven on footways and may be treated as not being motor vehicles for the purposes of the R.T.R. Act 1967, and R.T. Act 1972, and are exempted from the provisions of ss. 68 to 81 of the 1972 Act.

"Footway" means a footway, footpath or bridleway within the meaning of the Highways Act 1959. "Invalid Carriage" is a vehicle, whether mechanically propelled or not, constructed or adapted for use for the carriage of one person, being a person suffering from some physical defect or disability. The requirements of the Regs. prescribe—(a) that an invalid carriage shall be used by an invalid or by another person in connection with its maintenance or repair; and (b) other matters relating to the maximum unladen weight (250 lb), speed (4 m.p.h.) brakes and lighting. Section 21 provides for a scheme to enable disabled drivers and disabled passengers and their vehicles to be identified by means of a special badge.

Driving Licences – It shall be an offence for a person to drive on a road a motor vehicle of any class if he is not the holder of a licence authorising him to drive a motor vehicle of that class (R.T. Act, s. 84 (1)).

It shall be an offence for a person to employ a person to drive on a road a motor vehicle of any class if the person employed is not the holder of a licence authorising him to drive a motor vehicle of that class (s. 84 (2)).

Notwithstanding the foregoing provisions of this section, a person may, without holding a licence, act as steersman of a motor vehicle, being a vehicle on which a speed limit of 5 m.p.h. or less is imposed by or under s. 78 of the Road Traffic Regulation Act 1967, under the orders of another person engaged in the driving of the vehicle who is licensed in that behalf in accordance with the requirements of this Part of this Act and Part IV of this Act, and a person may employ another person who is not the holder of a licence so to act (s. 84 (3)).

Notwithstanding the foregoing provisions of this section, a person may at any time drive or employ another person to drive a vehicle of any class if—

(a) the driver has held and is entitled to obtain a licence to drive vehicles of that class; and
(b) an application by the driver for the grant of such a licence for a period which includes that time has been received by the Secretary of State or such a licence granted to him has been revoked or surrendered in pursuance of s. 89 of this Act; and
(c) any conditions which by virtue of s. 88 (2) or (4) of this Act apply to the driving under the authority of the licence of vehicles of that class are complied with;

but the benefit of the foregoing provisions of this subsection shall not extend beyond the date when a licence is granted in pursuance of the application mentioned in para. (b) above or, as the case may be, in pursuance of sub-s. (4) of the said s. 89 in consequence of the revocation or surrender so mentioned nor (in a case where a licence is not in fact so granted) beyond the expiration of the period of one year or such shorter period as may be prescribed beginning on the date of the application or, as the case may be, the revocation or surrender mentioned in para. (b) above (s. 84 (4)).

Regulations may provide that a person who becomes resident in Great Britain shall, during the prescribed period after he becomes so resident, be treated for the purposes of sub-ss. (1) and (2) above as the holder of a licence authorising him to drive motor vehicles of the prescribed classes if he satisfies the prescribed conditions and is the holder of a permit of the prescribed description authorising him to drive vehicles under the law of a country outside the United Kingdom; and the regulations may provide for the application of any enactment relating to licences or licence holders, with or without modifications, in relation to any such permit and its holder respectively (s. 84 (5)).

PHYSICAL FITNESS OF DRIVERS – An application for the grant of a licence shall include a declaration by the applicant, in such form as the Secretary of State may require, stating whether he is suffering or has at any time (or, if a period is prescribed for the purposes of this subsection, has during that period) suffered (a) from any prescribed disability or from any other disability likely to cause the driving of a vehicle by him in pursuance of the licence to be a source of danger to the public (such prescribed or other disability being hereafter in this section referred to as a "relevant disability" or (b) from any other disability which at the time of the application is not of such a kind that it is a relevant disability but which, by virtue of the intermittent or progressive nature of the disability or otherwise, may become a relevant disability in course of time (such disability being hereafter in this section referred to as a "prospective disability") (s. 87 (1)).

If it appears from the declaration aforesaid, or if on inquiry the Secretary of State is satisfied from other information, that the applicant is suffering from a relevant disability, then, subject to the following provisions of this section, the Secretary of State shall refuse to grant the licence (s. 87 (2)).

The Secretary of State shall not by virtue of sub-s. (2) above refuse to grant a licence—

(a) on account of any relevant disability which is prescribed for the purposes of this paragraph, if the applicant has at any time passed a relevant test and it does not appear to the Secretary of State that the disability has arisen or become more acute since that time or was, for whatever reason, not disclosed to the Secretary of State at that time;

(b) on account of any relevant disability which is prescribed for the purposes of this paragraph, if the applicant satisfies such conditions as may be prescribed with a view to authorising the grant of a licence to a person in whose case the disability is appropriately controlled;

(c) on account of any relevant disability which is prescribed for the purposes of this paragraph, if the application is for a provisional licence (s. 87 (3)). See also M.V. (D.L.) (A.) No. 2 Regs. 1975.

If as the result of a test of competence to drive the Secretary of State is satisfied that the person who took the test is suffering from a disability such that there is likely to be danger to the public (a) if he drives any vehicle, or (b) if he drives a vehicle other than a vehicle of a particular construction or design, the Secretary of State shall serve notice in writing to that effect on that person and shall include in the notice a description of the disability; and where a notice is served in pursuance of this subsection, then—

(i) if the notice is in pursuance of para. (a) of this subsection and the disability is not prescribed under sub-s. (1) above it shall be deemed to be so prescribed in relation to the person aforesaid and if the disability is prescribed for the purposes of sub-s. 3 (c) above, it shall be deemed not to be so prescribed in relation to him; and
(ii) if the notice is in pursuance of para. (b) of this subsection, any licence granted to that person shall be limited to vehicles of the particular construction or design specified in the notice (s. 87 (4)).

If the Secretary of State is at any time satisfied on inquiry—(a) that the licence holder is suffering from a relevant disability, and (b) that the Secretary of State would be required by virtue of sub-s. (2) or (4) (ii) above to refuse an application for the licence made by him at that time, the Secretary of State may serve notice in writing on the licence holder revoking the licence with effect from such date as may be specified in the notice, not being earlier than the date of service of the notice; and it shall be the duty of a person whose licence is revoked under this subsection to deliver up the licence to the Secretary of State forthwith after the revocation (s. 87 (5)).

In this section—"disability" includes disease; and "relevant test", in relation to an application for a licence, means any such test of competence as is mentioned in s. 85 of this Act or a test as to fitness or ability in pursuance of s .100 of the Road Traffic Act 1960 as originally enacted, being a test authorising the grant of a licence in respect of vehicles of the classes to which the application relates; and for the purposes of sub-s. (3) (a) above a person to whom a licence was granted after the making of a declaration under para. (c) of the proviso to s. 5 (2) of the Road Traffic Act 1930 (which contained transitional provisions with respect to certain disabilities) shall be treated as having passed, at the time of the declaration, a relevant test in respect of vehicles of the classes to which the licence related (s. 87 (6)).

Section 87 (A) deals with the obligation of licence holders to notify the Secretary of State of the onset or deterioration of a relevant or prospective disability.

DURATION OF LICENCES – A licence shall, unless previously revoked or surrendered, remain in force—

(a) except in a case falling within para. (aa), (b) or (c) of this subsection for the period ending on the 70th anniversary of the applicant's date of birth or for a period of 3 years whichever is the longer;

(aa) except in a case falling within para. (b) or (c) of this subsection if the Secretary of State so determines in the case of a licence to be granted to a person appearing to him to be suffering from a relevant or prospective disability within the meaning of s. 87 for such period of not more than 3 years and not less than 1 year;

(b) in the case of a licence granted in exchange for a subsisting licence and in pursuance of an application requesting a licence for the period authorised by this paragraph, for a period equal to the remainder of that for which the subsisting licence was granted; and

(c) in the case of a provisional licence, for such a period as may be prescribed, or, if the Secretary of State so determines in the case of a licence to be granted to such a person as is referred to in para. (aa) for such shorter period of not less than 1 year;

and any such period shall begin with the date on which the licence in question is expressed to come into force (s. 89 (1)).

APPEAL AGAINST REFUSAL OR REVOCATION OF LICENCE – A person who is refused a driving licence or whose licence is revoked for physical unfitness may appeal to a magistrates' court for the area in which he resides (R.T. Act 1972, s. 90).

DRIVING WITH UNCORRECTED DEFECTIVE EYESIGHT – If a person drives a motor vehicle on a road while his eyesight is such (whether through a defect which cannot be or one which is not for the time being sufficiently corrected) that he cannot comply with any requirement as to eyesight prescribed under Part III of R.T. Act 1972, for the purposes of tests of competence to drive, he shall be guilty of an offence.

A constable having reason to suspect that a person driving a motor vehicle may be guilty of the above offence may require him to submit to a test for the purpose of ascertaining whether, using no other means of correction than he used at the time of driving, he can comply with the said requirements as to eyesight. Refusal to submit to the test is an offence (R.T. Act 1972, s. 91).

DISQUALIFICATION AND ENDORSEMENT OF LICENCES – Where a person is convicted of an offence—

(a) under a provision of this Act specified in column 1 of Part I of Sched. 4 to this Act (see Appendix IV) in relation to which there appears in column 5 of that Part the word "obligatory" or the word "obligatory" qualified by conditions or circumstances relating to the offence; and
(b) where the said word "obligatory" is so qualified, the conditions or circumstances are satisfied or obtain in the case of the offence of which he is convicted;

or where a person is convicted of the offence specified in Part II of that Schedule (any such offence being in this Part of this Act referred to as an "offence involving obligatory disqualification") the court shall order him to be disqualified for such period not less than 12 months as the court thinks fit unless the court for special reasons thinks fit to order him to be disqualified for a shorter period or not to order him to be disqualified (s. 93 (1)).

Where a person is convicted of an offence—

(a) under a provision of this Act specified in column 1 of Part I of Sched. 4 to this Act in relation to which there appears in column 5 of that Part the word "discretionary" or the word "discretionary" qualified by conditions or circumstances relating to the offence; and
(b) where the said word "discretionary" is so qualified, the conditions or circumstances are satisfied or obtain in the case of the offence of which he is convicted;

or where a person is convicted of an offence specified in Part III of that Schedule (any such offence being in this Part of this Act referred to as an "offence involving discretionary disqualification"), the court may order him to be disqualified for such period as the court thinks fit (s. 93 (2)).

Where a person convicted of an offence involving obligatory or discretionary disqualification has within the 3 years immediately preceding the commission of the offence been convicted on not less than two occasions of any such offence and particulars of the convictions have been ordered to be endorsed in accordance with s. 101 of this Act, the court shall order him to be disqualified for such period not less than 6 months as the court thinks fit, unless the court is satisfied, having regard to all the circumstances, that there are grounds for mitigating the normal consequences of the conviction and thinks fit to order him to be disqualified for a shorter period or not to order him to be disqualified (s. 93 (3)).

Where a person convicted of an offence under any of the following provisions of this Act, namely s. 5 (1), 6 (1) or 9 (3) (where the latter is an offence involving obligatory disqualification), has within the 10 years immediately preceding the commission of the offence been convicted of any such offence, sub-s.

(1) above shall apply in relation to him with the substitution of 3 years for 12 months (s. 93 (4)).

The period of any disqualification imposed under sub-s. (3) above shall be in addition to any other period of disqualification imposed (whether previously or on the same occasion) under this section or s. 5 of the Road Traffic Act 1962 or under the Road Traffic Act 1960 or an enactment repealed by that Act or under the Motor Car Act 1903 (s. 93 (5)).

The foregoing provisions of this section shall apply in relation to a conviction of an offence committed by aiding, abetting, counselling or procuring, or inciting to the commission of an offence involving obligatory disqualification as if the offence were an offence involving discretionary disqualification (s. 93 (6)).

Where a person is convicted of an offence involving obligatory or discretionary disqualification the court may, whether or not he has previously passed the test of competence to drive prescribed under this Act, and whether or not the court makes an order under the foregoing provisions of this section, order him to be disqualified until he has, since the date of the order, passed that test; and a disqualification by virtue of an order under this subsection shall be deemed to have expired on production to the Secretary of State of evidence, in such form as may be prescribed by regulations under s. 107 of this Act, that the person disqualified has, since the order was made, passed that test (s. 93 (7)).

APPEAL AGAINST DISQUALIFICATION – A person disqualified by an order of a court for holding or obtaining a licence may appeal against the order in the same manner as against a conviction. The disqualification may be suspended pending the appeal (R.T. Act 1972, s. 94).

REMOVAL OF DISQUALIFICATION – A person who by an order of a court is disqualified for holding or obtaining a driving licence may apply to such court to remove the disqualification. The court may, having regard to the character of the person and his conduct subsequent to the order, the nature of the offence, and any other circumstances of the case, either remove the disqualification or refuse the application.

An application shall not be made for:

(a) 2 years if disqualification is for less than 4 years.
(b) One half of the period of the disqualification if it is for less than 10 years, but not less than 4 years.
(c) 5 years in any other case (R.T. Act 1972, s. 95).

After a refusal to remove the disqualification, a further application shall not be made for 3 months.

The procedure for applying for the removal is prescribed by M.C. Rules 1968 (r. 84). Application to a magistrates' court is by complaint. A summons should be served on the police to show cause why the application should not be granted.

DISQUALIFICATION OF PERSONS UNDER AGE – A person who under s. 4 is prohibited by reason of his age from driving a motor vehicle or a motor vehicle of any class is disqualified for holding or obtaining a licence other than a licence authorising him to drive such motor vehicles (if any) as he is not by s. 4 forbidden to drive (s. 96).

DISQUALIFICATION TO PREVENT DUPLICATION – A person is disqualified for obtaining a licence to drive a motor vehicle of any class so long as he is the holder of another licence authorising him to drive a motor vehicle of that class whether the licence is suspended or not (s. 97).

EFFECT OF DISQUALIFICATION – A licence shall be treated as being revoked with effect from the beginning of the period of disqualification which for the purposes of a licence suspended pending an appeal means the day on which the licence ceases to be suspended (R.T. Act 1974, Sched. 3). A licence obtained by any person disqualified shall be of no effect (s. 98).

OFFENCE OF OBTAINING LICENCE, OR DRIVING, WHILE DISQUALIFIED – If a person disqualified for holding or obtaining a licence (a) obtains a licence while he is so disqualified, or (b) while he is so disqualified drives on a road a motor vehicle, or if the disqualification is limited to the driving of a motor vehicle of a particular class, a motor vehicle of that class, he shall be guilty of an offence (s. 99).

ARREST OF PERSONS DRIVING WHILE DISQUALIFIED – A constable in uniform may arrest without warrant any person driving or attempting to drive a motor vehicle on a road whom he has reasonable cause to suspect of being disqualified (s. 100).

DRIVING DISQUALIFICATION WHERE VEHICLE USED FOR PURPOSES OF CRIME – Where a person is convicted before the Crown Court of an offence punishable on indictment with not less than 2 years' imprisonment or, having been convicted by a magistrates' court of such an offence, is committed to the Crown Court for sentence under s. 29 of the Magistrates' Courts Act 1952, the Crown Court, if satisfied that a motor vehicle was used (by that person or by anyone else) for the purpose of committing, or facilitating the commission of, the offence, may order that person to be disqualified, for such period as the court thinks fit, for holding or obtaining a licence to drive a motor vehicle granted under Part III of the Road Traffic Act 1972 (P. of C.C. Act 1973, s. 44).

A court which makes an order under this section disqualifying a person for holding or obtaining any such licence as is mentioned in sub-s. (1) of this section shall require him to produce any such licence held by him; and if he does not produce the licence as required he shall be guilty of an offence under s. 101 (4) of the Road Traffic Act 1972 (failure to produce licence for endorsement (P. of C.C. Act 1973, s. 44 (3)).

ENDORSEMENT OF LICENCES – Subject to sub-s. (2) below, where a person is convicted of an offence—

(a) under a provision of this Act specified in column 1 of Part I of Sched. 4 (see Appendix IV) to this Act in relation to which there appears in column 6 of that Part the word "obligatory" or the word "obligatory" qualified by conditions relating to the offence; and
(b) where the said word "obligatory" is so qualified, the conditions are satisfied in the case of the offence of which he is convicted;

or where a person is convicted of an offence specified in Part II or Part III of that Schedule (any such offence being in this section referred to as an "offence involving obligatory endorsement"), the court shall order that particulars of the conviction, and, if the court orders him to be disqualified, particulars of the disqualification, shall be endorsed on any licence held by him; and particulars of any conviction or disqualification so endorsed may be produced as prima facie evidence of the conviction or disqualification (s. 101 (1)).

If the court does not order the said person to be disqualified, the court need not order particulars of the conviction to be endorsed as aforesaid if for special reasons it thinks fit not to do so (s. 101 (2)).

An order that the particulars of a conviction or of a disqualification to which the convicted person has become subject are to be endorsed on any licence held by him shall, whether he is at the time the holder of a licence or not, operate as an order that any licence he may then hold or may subsequently obtain shall be so endorsed until he becomes entitled under sub-s. (7) below to have a licence issued to him free from the particulars (s. 101 (3)).

A person who is prosecuted for an offence involving obligatory endorsement and who is the holder of a licence, shall either (a) cause it to be delivered to the clerk of the court not later than the day before the date appointed for the hearing, or (b) post it, at such a time that in the ordinary course of post it would be delivered not later than that day, in a letter duly addressed to the clerk and either registered or sent by the recorded delivery service, or (c) have it with him at the hearing; and if he is convicted of the offence the court shall before making any order under sub-s. (1) require the licence to be produced to it; and if the offender has not posted the licence or caused it to be delivered as aforesaid and does not produce it as required then, unless he satisfies the court that he has applied for a new licence and has not received it, he shall be guilty of an offence and the licence shall be suspended from the time when its production was required until it is produced to the court and shall, while suspended, be of no effect (s. 101 (4)).

On the issue of a new licence to a person any particulars ordered to be endorsed on any licence held by him shall be entered on the licence unless he has become entitled under sub-s. (7) below to have a licence issued to him free from those particulars (s. 101 (5)).

If a person whose licence has been ordered to be endorsed with any particulars and who has not previously become entitled under sub-s. (7) below to have a licence issued to him free from those particulars applies for or obtains a licence without giving particulars of the order, he shall be guilty of an offence and any licence so obtained shall be of no effect (s. 101 (6)).

Where an order has been made in respect of a person under this section or any previous enactment requiring any licence held by him to be endorsed with any particulars, he shall be entitled, either on applying for the grant of a licence in pursuance of s. 88 (1) (a) of this Act and satisfying the other requirements of that subsection, or subject to the payment of the prescribed fee and the surrender of any subsisting licence on an application at any time to have issued to him a new licence free from the particulars, if the application is made not less than 4 years after the date of the conviction in consequence of which the order was made or, if it was a conviction of an offence under any of the following provisions of this Act, namely s. 5 (1), 6 (1) or 9 (3) (where the latter was an offence involving obligatory disqualification), not less than 11 years after that conviction (s. 101 (7)).

INFORMATION AS TO DATE OF BIRTH AND SEX – If on convicting a person of an offence involving obligatory or discretionary disqualification or of such other offence as may be prescribed, the court does not know his date of birth, the court shall order him to state that date in writing (R.T. Act 1972, s. 104 (1) (as amended by R.T. Act 1974, Sched. 3)).

It shall be the duty of a person giving a notification to the clerk of a court in pursuance of s. 1 (2) of the M.C. Act 1957 (which relates to pleas of guilty in the absence of the accused) in respect of an offence mentioned in sub-s. (1) of this section to include in the notification a statement of the date of birth and the sex of the accused; and in a case where the foregoing provisions of this subsection are not complied with the court shall, if on convicting the accused it does not know his date of birth or sex, order him to furnish that information in writing to the court (s. 104 (2) (as amended by R.T. Act 1974, Sched. 3)).

A person who knowingly fails to comply with an order under sub-s. (1) or sub-s. (2) of this section shall be guilty of an offence (s. 104 (4)).

Where in accordance with this section a person has stated his date of birth to a court or in such a notification as aforesaid, the Secretary of State may serve on that person a notice in writing requiring him to furnish the Secretary of State—(a) with such evidence in that person's possession or obtainable by him as the Secretary of State may specify for the purpose of verifying that date; and (b) if his name differs from his name at the time of his birth, with a statement in writing specifying his name at that time; and a person who knowingly fails to comply with a notice under this subsection shall be guilty of an offence (s. 104 (5)).

In any case where a court exercises its power under s. 93 or 101 of this Act not to order any disqualification or endorsement or to order disqualification for a shorter period than would otherwise be required, it shall state the grounds for doing so in open court and, if it is a magistrates' court shall cause them to be entered in the register of its proceedings (s. 105 (1)).

A "special reason" is one which is special to the facts which constitute the offence. A circumstance peculiar to the offender is not a special reason (*R.* v. *Crossan* (1939); *Whittall* v. *Kirby* (1946); *Knowler* v. *Rennison* (1947); *Jowett-Shooter* v. *Franklin* (1949); *Lines* v. *Hersom* (1951); and *R.* v. *Wickins* (1958)).

Where a court orders particulars to be endorsed on a licence held by a person, or where by an order of a court a person is disqualified, the court shall send notice of the order to the Secretary of State and, in a case where a person is so disqualified, shall also on the production of the licence for the purpose of endorsement (or its production to comply with s. 24 (3) of the C.J. Act 1972 or s. 44 (3) of the P. of C.C. Act 1973 in the case of disqualification under s. 24 or s. 44 as the case may be) retain the licence and forward it to the Secretary of State, who may dispose of it as he thinks fit (s. 105 (2) as amended by R.T. Act 1974, Sched. 3).

NORTHERN IRELAND DRIVERS' LICENCES – The holder of a driving licence (in force) granted in Northern Ireland may drive in Great Britain, under the terms of his licence. Such a driver is bound to produce his licence for examination, and if he is disqualified by a conviction or order of a court he must give his licence to the court for transmission to the Secretary of State, to whom also a court shall send particulars of any conviction of any such driver which it considers ought to be endorsed on his licence (R.T. Act 1972, s. 111).

MOTOR VEHICLES (DRIVING LICENCES) REGS. 1971 – The holder of a provisional driving licence shall not drive or ride a motor vehicle—(a) otherwise than under the supervision of a qualified driver who is present with him in or on the vehicle, except (1) when he is undergoing a test or a test of competence to drive heavy goods vehicles; or (2) is driving a vehicle (not a motor car) constructed to carry only one person and not adapted to carry more than one person; or (3) is driving an electrically propelled goods vehicle, not exceeding 16 cwts, constructed or adapted to carry only one person; or (4) is driving a road roller not exceeding 3 tons; or (5) is riding a motor bicycle, with or without a side-car.

(b) unless the prescribed letter "L", in red on white ground is clearly displayed on the front and rear of the vehicle;

(c) while it is being used to draw a trailer, except when driving an agricultural tractor, or articulated vehicle;

(d) which is a motor bicycle without side-car while carrying on it a person who is not a qualified driver, unless he is riding a motor-assisted pedal cycle of the tandem type (reg. 6).

A provisional licence authorises only the driving of motor vehicles of a class or description included in group K (mowing machine or vehicle controlled by a pedestrian) in any case where the applicant is unable to read in good daylight (with the aid of glasses if worn) a registration mark at a distance of 75 ft. if the letters are 3½ ins. high, or 67 ft. if the letters are 3⅛ ins. high (reg. 7).

A full licence which authorised its holder to drive certain classes and descriptions of motor vehicles shall not authorise its holder to drive motor vehicles of all other classes and descriptions subject to the same conditions as if he were authorised by a provisional licence to drive the last mentioned vehicles if it is a licence which (a) is limited to vehicles of a particular construction or design pursuant to R.T. Act 1972, s. 87, or (b) authorises its holder to drive vehicles in group K only (reg. 8).

Every person to whom a driving licence is granted shall forthwith sign it in ink with his usual signature (reg. 9). Failure to comply is an offence (R.T. Act 1972, Sched. 4, Part I).

If he suffers from epilepsy; mental disorder or severe subnormality; sudden attacks of disabling giddiness or fainting; or is unable to satisfy the eyesight test, he cannot obtain a driving licence and is not entitled to claim a driving test. The eyesight standard is prescribed as ability to read in good daylight (with glasses if worn) a series of letters and figures coloured white on a black background which comply as respects size, shape and arrangement with the relevant requirements relating to registration marks of motor vehicles, at a distance of 75 ft. in the case of letters and figures 3½ ins. high, and a distance of 67 ft. in the case of letters and figures 3⅛ ins. high. In the case of a mowing machine or a pedestrian controlled vehicle, the reading distance is 45 ft. in the case of symbols 3½ ins. high, or 40 ft. in the case of symbols 3⅛ ins. high.

An applicant suffering from epilepsy shall satisfy the conditions: (a) he shall have been free from any epileptic attack whilst awake for at least 3 years; (b) in the case of an applicant who has had such attacks whilst asleep during that period he shall have been subject to such attacks whilst asleep but not whilst awake since before the beginning of that period; (c) the driving of a vehicle by him is not likely to be a source of danger to the public (reg. 20; see also M.V. (D.L.) (Amendment) (No. 2) Regs. 1975)).

Provision is made allowing a person who has recently become resident in Great Britain to drive for 3 months after becoming resident if he holds a valid foreign domestic driving licence, an international driving permit or a British Forces (Germany) driving licence. The holder must also satisfy the condition that he is not disqualified for holding or obtaining a licence in Great Britain (reg. 21).

For other driving licences see "Public Service Vehicles" and "Goods Vehicles", Chap. 25.

Compulsory Insurance or Security against Third Party Risks – It shall not be lawful for a person to use, or to cause or permit any other person to use, a motor vehicle on a road unless there is in force in relation to the use of the vehicle by that person or that other person such a policy of insurance, or such a security in respect of third-party risks as complies with R.T. Act 1972, Part VI. This does not apply to invalid carriages.

A person charged with this offence shall not be convicted if he proves that the vehicle did not belong to him and was not in his possession under a contract of hiring or of loan, that he was using the vehicle in the course of his employment and that he neither knew, nor had reason to believe that there was not in force in relation to the vehicle a policy of insurance or security (s. 143).

The above does not apply to a vehicle owned by a person who has deposited and keeps deposited the sum of fifteen thousand pounds as laid down in the section, nor does it apply (a) to a vehicle owned by a local authority at a time when the vehicle is being driven under the owner's control, nor (b) to a vehicle owned by a police authority at a time when it is being driven under the owner's control, or to a vehicle at a time when it is being driven for police purposes by or under the direction of a police constable, or by a person employed by a police authority, nor (c) to a vehicle driven for salvage purposes under the Merchant Shipping Act 1894, nor (d) to the use of a vehicle for the purpose of its being furnished in pursuance of a direction under s. 166 (2) (*b*) of the Army Act 1955 or the corresponding provision of the Air Force Act 1955, nor (e) to a vehicle owned by the London Transport Executive (s. 144).

POLICIES OF INSURANCE, ETC. – A policy of insurance must satisfy the following conditions:—It must be issued by an authorised insurer (R.T. Act 1974, s. 20 adds the requirement that the insurer must be a member of the Motor Insurers' Bureau). It must insure such person, persons or classes of person as may be specified in the policy in respect of any liability which may be incurred by him or them in respect of the death of or bodily injury to any person caused by, or arising out of, the use of the vehicle on a road, and it must also insure him or them in respect of any liability which may be incurred by him or them under the provisions relating to payment for emergency treatment. However, it shall not be required to cover liability in respect of the death arising out of and in the course of his employment, of a person in the employment of a person insured by the policy or of bodily injury sustained by such a person arising out of and in the course of his employment, or any contractual liability (s. 145).

A "security" is an undertaking to make good, up to at least £5,000 (£25,000 in case of public service vehicles) any liability (third-party risks) required to be covered by a policy of insurance. The requirements in respect of such a "security" are contained in s. 146.

A policy of insurance shall be of no effect, unless and until there is delivered by the insurer to the "insured" a "certificate of insurance" in the prescribed form. (Policy of insurance includes a covering note). A security shall be of no effect unless and until there is delivered by the person giving the security to the "secured" a "certificate of security" in the prescribed form. The holder of a certificate of insurance, shall within 7 days, surrender it to the insurer if the policy is cancelled by consent or by virtue of any provision in the policy. If the certificate is lost or destroyed he shall make a statutory declaration to that effect. These provisions of the Act apply also to a certificate of security. Failure to comply with these provisions is an offence (s. 147).

Certain restrictions on the scope of a policy covering third-party risks, limiting the age or mental or physical condition of drivers, the condition of the vehicle, the number of persons carried, the goods carried etc., shall be of no effect as regards the liabilities for third-party injuries which must be covered under s. 145. The insurer in such case remains liable but he may recover from the insured person any money he has paid (s. 148).

Where a person uses a motor vehicle in circumstances such that under s. 143 there is required to be in force in relation to his use of it such a policy of insurance or security as is mentioned in sub-s. (1) of that section, then, if any other person is carried in or upon the vehicle while the user is so using it, any antecedent agreement or understanding between them (whether intended to be legally binding or not) shall be of no effect so far as it purports or might be held: (a) to negative or restrict any such liability of the user in respect of persons carried in or upon the vehicle as is required by s. 145 to be covered by a policy of insurance; or (b) to impose any conditions with respect to the enforcement of any such liability of the user; and the fact that a person has willingly accepted as his the risk of negligence on the part of the user shall not be treated as negativing any such liability of the user.

A person carried includes a person entering or getting on to, or alighting from the vehicle (s. 148).

It will be the duty of a person against whom a claim is made in respect of any liability for death or bodily injury arising out of the use of a motor vehicle on a road to give particulars of his insurance to the person making the claim. To fail to do so, or to give false information is an offence (s. 151).

If any payment is made by an insurer in respect to death or bodily injury arising out of the use of a motor vehicle and the person has received treatment at a hospital the insurer shall pay the reasonable hospital expenses up to £200 per in-patient and £20 per out-patient (s. 154).

If bodily or fatal injury to a person is caused by or arises out of the use of a motor vehicle on a road and emergency medical or surgical treatment or examination is immediately required and effected by a doctor or hospital, the person who was using the vehicle at the time is responsible for payment for same at the rate of £1·25 per person so treated, and mileage in excess of two miles at 2½p. per mile (s. 155).

A claim for payment for such emergency treatment may be made orally at the time or in writing (personal delivery or registered letter) within 7 days to a person who was using the vehicle and the amount will be recoverable as a simple contract debt. The police shall on request furnish such claimant with any information available as to the vehicle and its driver (s. 156).

THE MOTOR VEHICLES (THIRD PARTY RISKS) REGS. 1972 deal with these certificates and prescribes the particulars which must be inscribed thereon. The driver of a motor vehicle may have, according to the nature of the "insurance";

(1) A certificate of motor insurance (Form A or Form B). This will be signed by the insuring person or company and will give the name of the policy holder, the effective date of commencement and date of expiry, the persons or classes of persons entitled to drive, the limitations as to use, and either the identification mark of the vehicle or the description of vehicle insured (reg. 5).

A covering note may precede issue of certificate of insurance.

(2) A certificate of security (Form D). This will be signed by the authorised person, and will give the name of the holder of security, the effective date of commencement and date of expiry, and the conditions to which security is subject (reg. 5).

(3) A certificate of deposit (Form E). This will give the identification mark of the vehicle, will certify the owner has deposited the £15,000, and will be signed by the owner of the vehicle (reg. 7).

(4) A certificate of ownership by a specified body or police authority (Form F). This will give the identification mark of

the vehicle and will be signed by someone on behalf of the authority (reg. 7).

(5) An International Motor Insurance Card. See "Foreign-Owned Motor Vehicles", Chap. 25.

If the holder of a policy or security is entitled to drive any motor vehicle other than that specified in it, he may have a further certificate of insurance or security (reg. 5).

A person applying for a vehicle licence under the Vehicles (Excise) Act 1971 must produce any necessary certificate of insurance or security (or evidence that the vehicle is properly insured or is exempt from insurance). But this does not apply to persons who let motor vehicles on hire as regards any such vehicle intended to be used solely for such purpose and driven by the hirer or persons under his control (reg. 9).

Insuring companies, specified bodies and persons depositing £15,000, must keep a record of the certificates they issue and of the vehicles concerned, and are bound to furnish particulars to the police on request (reg. 10).

Any contravention of these Regulations is an offence (reg. 14).

The Motor Vehicles (Compulsory Insurance) Regs. 1973 and 1974 make certain amendments to the Road Traffic Act 1972 resulting in the compulsory motor vehicle insurance cover required by Part VI of that Act being extended to include liabilities arising out of the use of a motor vehicle or trailer which are compulsorily insurable in the territories of the member States of the European Community.

Note.—The Motor Insurers' Bureau may pay compensation to a person injured by a non-insured vehicle. Any insurance office will supply information on this matter.

Power of Police to Stop Vehicles – A person driving a motor vehicle on a road, and a person riding a cycle, not being a motor vehicle, on a road shall stop the same on being so required by a police constable in uniform, and if he fails to do so he commits an offence (R.T. Act 1972, s. 159).

(For police powers to regulate traffic: see s. 22).

WEIGHING OF MOTOR VEHICLES – A person authorised by a highway authority or a constable authorised on behalf of a highway authority by a police authority or a chief officer of police, on production of his authority, may require the person in charge to allow a motor vehicle or its trailer to proceed to a weigh-bridge to be weighed. Refusal or neglect to comply or obstructing such an authorised person or constable is an offence. However, such person or constable should not require such vehicle to be unloaded for the purpose of weighing it unladen. When so weighed, a certificate of the weight must be given to the person in charge of the vehicle. If the weight proves to be within the legal limit and the vehicle has had to travel more than a mile to the weigh-bridge, the highway authority shall pay for loss occasioned. A certifying officer or examiner or any of the Secretary of State's officers authorised by him in that behalf may at any time, on production of his authority, exercise with respect to the weighing of goods vehicles all such powers as are exercisable by a police constable in respect of the weighing of motor vehicles (s. 160). The section contains powers to make regs. governing the standards and methods of weighing vehicles for the enforcement of C. & U. Regs. on vehicle loading, and to deal with incidental matters.

POWER OF POLICE TO REQUIRE PRODUCTION OF DRIVING LICENCES – Any such person as follows, that is to say (a) a person driving a motor vehicle on a road, or (b) a person whom a police constable has reasonable cause to believe to have been the driver of a motor vehicle at a time when an accident occurred owing to its presence on a road, or (c) a person whom a police constable has reasonable cause to believe to have committed an offence in relation to the use of a motor vehicle on a road, or (d) a person who supervises the holder of a provisional driving licence while the holder is driving a motor vehicle on a road, or whom a police constable has reasonable cause to believe was supervising the holder of such a licence while driving at a time when an accident occurred owing to the presence of the vehicle on a road or at a time when an offence is suspected of having been committed by the said holder in relation to the use of a vehicle on a road, shall on being so required by a police constable, produce his licence for examination so as to enable the constable to ascertain the name and address of the holder of the licence, the date of issue and the authority by which it was issued, and shall in prescribed circumstances, on being so required by the constable, state his date of birth.

Where a driving licence has been revoked by the Secretary of State under R.T. Act 1972, s. 87 or s. 89, and the holder has failed to return it to the Secretary of State, a police constable may require him to produce it, and then seize it and deliver it to the Secretary of State.

A constable, on reasonable belief that a driving licence was obtained by false statement, may require the holder to produce it, or state his date of birth. Failure to do so is an offence; however, if the holder produces the licence in person at a specified police station within 5 days, he shall not be convicted of the offence in respect of a failure to produce his licence (s. 161).

The circumstances in which a person mentioned above shall, on being requested by a police constable, state his date of birth are as follows: (1) where that person fails to produce forthwith for examination his licence; (2) where, on being so required, he produces a licence (a) which was granted by a local authority;

(b) which the constable has reason to suspect (i) was not granted to that person, or (ii) was granted to that person in error, or (iii) contains an alteration made with intent to deceive (M.V. (Driving Licences) Regs. 1971, reg. 22).

POLICE POWERS TO OBTAIN NAMES AND ADDRESSES, ETC. – Any such person as follows, that is to say—(a) a person driving on a road a motor vehicle (other than an invalid carriage); (b) a person whom a police constable has reasonable cause to believe to have been the driver of a motor vehicle (other than an invalid carriage), at a time when an accident occurred owing to its presence on a road; or (c) a person whom a police constable has reasonable cause to believe to have committed an offence in relation to the use on a road of a motor vehicle (other than an invalid carriage) shall, on being so required by a police constable, give his name and address, and the name and address of the owner of the vehicle, and produce for examination—(1) the certificate of insurance or security, or such other evidence that the vehicle was not being driven in contravention of s. 143 as may be prescribed by regulations (see Motor Vehicles (Third Party Risks) Regs. 1972), and (2) a test certificate required under s. 44 and (3) in relation to a goods vehicle the use of which on a road without a plating certificate or a goods vehicle test certificate, is an offence under s. 46 (1) or (2), any such certificate issued in respect of that vehicle or any trailers drawn by it. Failure to do so is an offence. However, if the "certificate" is produced within 5 days following at a police station specified by him at the time of such demand, he shall not be convicted of the offence by reason only of failure to produce his "certificate".

A person who supervises the holder of a provisional licence while the holder is driving a motor vehicle (other than an invalid carriage) on a road, or whom a police constable has reasonable cause to believe was supervising the holder of such a licence while driving at a time when an accident occurred owing to the presence of the vehicle on a road, or at a time when an offence is suspected of having been committed by the said holder in relation to the use of the vehicle on a road, shall, on being so required by a police constable, give his name and address, and the name and address of the owner of the vehicle. Failure to do so is an offence (s. 162). "Owner" in relation to a vehicle which is the subject of a hiring agreement includes each party to the agreement (s. 162).

This section applies to vehicles and persons in the public service of the Crown in so far as the production of test certificates and the giving of names and addresses are concerned (R.T. Act 1972, s. 188).

POWERS OF CERTIFYING OFFICERS AND EXAMINERS RE GOODS VEHICLES – A certifying officer or an examiner may at any time, on production if so required of his authority, exercise in the case of goods vehicles all such powers as are exercisable by a police constable under ss. 161 (1) or 162 (s. 163).

FAILURE TO GIVE NAME AND ADDRESS, AND POWER OF ARREST IN CASES OF DANGEROUS OR CARELESS DRIVING OR CYCLING – Any such person as the following, namely—(a) the driver of a motor vehicle who is alleged to have committed an offence of dangerous (s. 2) or careless (s. 3) driving or (b) the rider of a cycle who is alleged to have committed an offence of dangerous (s. 17) or careless (s. 18) cycling; who refuses, on being so required by any person having reasonable ground for so requiring, to give his name or address, or gives a false name or address, commits an offence.

A police constable may—(a) arrest without warrant the driver of a motor vehicle who within his view commits an offence of dangerous (s. 2) or careless (s. 3) driving, unless the driver either gives his name and address or produces his licence for examination; (b) arrest without warrant the rider of a cycle who within his view commits an offence of dangerous (s. 17) or careless (s. 18) cycling, unless the rider gives his name and address (s. 164).

DRIVER TO PRODUCE INSURANCE CERTIFICATE OR REPORT "INJURY" ACCIDENTS – If in any case where, owing to the presence on a road of a motor vehicle (other than an invalid carriage), an accident occurs involving personal injury to another person, the driver of the vehicle does not at the time produce to a police constable or some person who, having reasonable grounds for so doing, has required its production, such a certificate of insurance or security, the driver shall as soon as possible, and in any case within 24 hours, report the accident at a police station or to a police constable and produce his "certificate". Failure to do so is an offence; however, he shall not be convicted by reason only of a failure to produce his "certificate" if within 5 days after the accident the certificate or other evidence is produced at a police station specified by him at the time the accident was reported (s. 166). Where owing to the presence on a road of a motor vehicle specified in an insurance card (that is, an International Motor Insurance Card) an accident occurs involving personal injury to a person other than the driver of the vehicle, and by reason of ss. 162 or 166 of the Act, the insurance card, together with a duplicate page, is produced to a police constable or at a police station, that police constable or a police constable at that station may detach the duplicate page from the card and arrange for its retention for the purposes of recording or producing insurance particulars relating to the accident (M.V. (International Motor Insurance Card) Regs. 1971, reg. 6 (3)).

The owner of a motor vehicle is bound to give such information as he may be required by or on behalf of a chief officer of police to give for the purpose of determining whether the use of the vehicle was or was not properly insured on any occasion when the driver was bound, under this section, to produce his certificate. Failure to do so is an offence. "Owner" in relation to a vehicle which is the subject of a hiring agreement includes each party to the agreement (s. 167).

INFORMATION TO BE GIVEN AS TO IDENTITY OF DRIVERS – This section applies (*a*) to any offence under the foregoing provisions of this Act except an offence under Part V thereof or under s. 15, 32, 45 (7), 50 (5), 53 (4), 55 (5), 56 (3), 91 or 119, and (*b*) to offences against any other enactment relating to the use of vehicles on roads (s. 168 (1)).

Where the driver of a vehicle is alleged to be guilty of an offence to which this section applies (*a*) the person keeping the vehicle shall give such information as to the identity of the driver as he may be required to give by or on behalf of a chief officer of police or in the case of an offence under s. 36A or s. 36B by or on behalf of a local authority, and (*b*) any other person shall if required as aforesaid give any information which it is in his power to give and may lead to the identification of the driver. In this subsection references to the driver of a vehicle include references to the person riding a cycle, not being a motor vehicle (s. 168 (2) as amended).

A person who fails to comply with the requirement of sub-s. (2) (a) above shall be guilty of an offence unless he shows to the satisfaction of the court that he did not know and could not with reasonable diligence have ascertained who the driver of the vehicle, or, as the case may be, the rider of the cycle, was; and a person who fails to comply with the requirement of sub-s. (2) (b) above shall be guilty of an offence (s. 168 (3)).

See also R.T. Act 1960, s. 232, and R.T.R. Act 1967, s. 85 as amended.

Forgery of Documents – A person shall be guilty of an offence who, with intent to deceive (*a*) forges, or alters, or uses or lends to, or allows to be used by, any other person, a document or other thing to which this section applies, or (*b*) makes or has in his possession any document or other thing so closely resembling a document or other thing to which this section applies as to be calculated to deceive (s. 169 (1)).

This section applies to the following documents and other things, namely—

(a) any licence under any Part of this Act;

(b) any test certificate, goods vehicle test certificate, plating certificate, certificate of conformity or Minister's approval certificate;

(c) any plate containing plated particulars or containing other particulars required to be marked on a goods vehicle by s. 47 of this Act or regulations thereunder;

(d) any records required to be kept by virtue of s. 59 of this Act;

(e) any document which, in pursuance of s. 85 (2) or 119 (1) of this Act, is issued as evidence of the result of a test of competence to drive;

(f) any badge or certificate prescribed by regulations under s. 135 of this Act;

(g) any certificate of insurance or certificate of security under Part VI of this Act;

(gg) any document produced as evidence of insurance in pursuance of Reg. 6 of Motor Vehicles (Compulsory Insurance) (No. 2) Regs. 1973;

(h) any document issued under regulations made by the Secretary of State in pursuance of his power under para. (i) of s. 162 (1) of this Act to prescribe evidence which may be produced in lieu of a certificate of insurance or a certificate of security (s. 169 (2));

(i) any international road haulage permit.

In this section "plated particulars", "certificate of conformity" and "Minister's approval certificate" have the same meanings as they respectively have for the purposes of Part II of this Act; and in the application of this section to England and Wales "forges" means forges within the meaning of the Forgery Act 1913 (s. 169 (3)).

See also R.T. Act 1960, s. 233, as amended.

Forgery, etc., of a parking meter ticket or authorisation is an offence under the R.T.R. Act 1967, s. 86, as amended.

A person who knowingly makes a false statement for the purpose of procuring the grant or issue to himself or any other person of any such authorisation, commits an offence (s. 86 (3), R.T.R. Act 1967, added by Transport Act 1968, s. 127 (10)).

If any person authorised in that behalf by or under a designation order, has reasonable cause to believe that a document or article carried on a vehicle, or by the driver or person in charge thereof is a document or article in relation to which an offence has been committed under s. 86 (1), he may detain that document or article, and may for that purpose require the driver or person in charge of the vehicle to deliver up the document or article. Failure to do so is an offence (s. 86 (4), R.T.R. Act 1967, added by Transport Act 1968, s. 127 (10)).

FALSE STATEMENTS AND WITHHOLDING INFORMATION – A person shall be guilty of an offence who knowingly makes a false statement for the purpose (a) of obtaining the grant of a licence under the Act to himself or any other person, or (b) of preventing the grant of any such licence, or (c) of procuring the imposition of a condition or limitation in relation to any such licence, or (d) of securing entry or retention in the register of approved driving instructors, or (e) of obtaining the grant of an international road haulage permit to himself or any other person. A person shall be guilty of an offence who makes a false statement or withholds any material information for the purpose of obtaining the issue of a certificate of insurance or security or any document in lieu thereof (s. 170).

A person shall be guilty of an offence who fails without reasonable excuse to notify the Secretary of State of the onset or deterioration of a relevant or prospective disability, as required by s. 87A (1) but proceedings for this offence require the approval of the Secretary of State (s. 170 (5A), to be added by R.T. Act 1974, s. 13 (2) when brought into force).

ISSUE OF FALSE DOCUMENTS – If a person issues any certificate of insurance or security or a test certificate (which includes a certificate of conformity) which is to his knowledge false in a material particular, he commits an offence (s. 171).

USING GOODS VEHICLE WITH UNAUTHORISED WEIGHTS, ETC – If there is fixed to a goods vehicle a plate containing plated weights any description determined for that vehicle by virtue of s. 45 of this Act or specified in a certificate therefor under s. 47 (5), (6), (8) or (11) of this Act, the vehicle shall not, while it is used on a road, be marked with any other weights, except other plated weights, other weights required or authorised to be marked on the vehicle by regulations under s. 40 of this Act or weights so authorised for the purposes of this section by regulations made by the Secretary of State and marked in the prescribed manner; and in the event of a contravention of or failure to comply with this section the owner of the vehicle shall be guilty of an offence (s. 172).

POWER TO SEIZE ARTICLES WITH RESPECT TO OFFENCES – If a constable has reasonable cause to believe that a document produced to him in pursuance of s. 137 of this Act, or in pursuance of any of the foregoing provisions of this Part of this Act, is a document in relation to which an offence has been committed under s. 169, 170 or 171 of this Act or under s. 86 of the Road Traffic Regulation Act 1967, he may seize the document; and when a document is seized under this subsection, the person from whom it was taken shall, unless the document has been previously returned to him or he has been previously charged with an offence under any of those sections, be summoned before a magistrates' court to account for his possession of the said document and the court shall make such order respecting the disposal of the said document and award such costs as the justice of the case may require (s. 173 (1)).

If a constable, a certifying officer appointed under Part III of the Road Traffic Act 1960 or an examiner appointed under s. 56 of this Act has reasonable cause to believe that a document or plate carried on a motor vehicle or by the driver thereof is a document or plate in relation to which an offence has been committed under s. 169, 170 or 171 of this Act in so far as they apply—

(a) to documents evidencing the appointment of examiners for the purposes of s. 56 to 58 of this Act, or
(b) to goods vehicle test certificates, plating certificates, certificates of conformity or Minister's approval certificates, or
(c) to plates containing plated particulars or containing other particulars required to be marked on goods vehicles by s. 47 of this Act or regulations made thereunder, or
(d) to records required to be kept by virtue of s. 59 of this Act, or
(e) to international road haulage permits,

he may seize the document or plate; and when a document or plate is seized under this subsection, either the driver or owner of the vehicle shall, if the document or plate is still detained and neither of them has previously been charged with an offence in relation thereto under s. 169, 170 or 171 of this Act, be summoned before a magistrates' court to account for his possession of, or the presence on the vehicle of, the said document or plate and the court shall make such order respecting the disposal of the said document or plate and award such costs as the justice of the case may require.

For the purposes of this subsection the power to seize includes power to detach from a vehicle (s. 173 (2)).

In sub-s. (2) above "plated particulars", "certificate of conformity" and "Minister's approval certificate" have the same meanings as they respectively have for the purposes of Part II of this Act (s. 173 (3)).

PERSONATION OF "AUTHORISED EXAMINERS" – If a person with intent to deceive falsely represents himself to be, or to be employed by, a person authorised by the Secretary of State under s. 43 of the Act as an "authorised examiner" (to test the fitness of vehicles) he shall commit an offence (s. 174).

BREACH OF REGULATIONS – Section 239 of the 1960 Act provides that a person who acts in contravention of, or fails to comply with, any regulations made by the Secretary of State under the Act shall be guilty of an offence.

Prosecution and Punishment of Offences – Part I of Sched. 4 to this Act (see Appendix IV) shall have effect with respect to the prosecution and punishment of the offences against the provisions of this Act specified in column 1 of that Part of that Schedule or regulations made thereunder (of which the general nature is indicated in column 2 thereof) (s. 177 (1)).

In relation to any such offence—

(a) column 3 of that Part of that Schedule shows whether the offence is punishable on summary conviction or on indictment or either in one way or the other;
(b) column 4 of that Part of that Schedule shows the maximum punishment by way of fine or imprisonment which

may be imposed on a person convicted of the offence in the way specified in relation thereto in column 3 (that is to say, summarily or on indictment), any reference in column 4 to a period of years or months being construed as a reference to a term of imprisonment of that duration;

(c) column 5 of that Part of that Schedule shows in relation to which offences the court is required by s. 93 (1) or empowered by s. 93 (2) of this Act to order the person convicted to be disqualified for holding or obtaining a licence to drive a motor vehicle under Part III of this Act (whether or not the court is also required to disqualify him for an additional period by s. 93 (3) of this Act), any reference in column 5 to obligatory disqualification importing such a requirement and any reference therein to discretionary disqualification importing such a power;

(d) column 6 of that Part of that Schedule shows in relation to which offences the court is required by s. 101 (1) of this Act to order that particulars of the conviction, and, if the court orders him to be disqualified, particulars of the disqualification, are to be endorsed on any licence held by him; and

(e) column 7 of that Part of that Schedule applies to such of the offences against provisions of this Act specified in column 1 as are indicated by entries against those offences in column 7 the additional provisions of this Act (relating to the prosecution and trial of such offences) specified in those entries (s. 177 (2)).

Parts II and III of that Schedule show offences which are not offences under this Act and are not punishable thereunder but on conviction of which the court is required by s. 93 (1), or, as the case may be, empowered by s. 93 (2) of this Act to order the person convicted to be disqualified for holding or obtaining a licence to drive a motor vehicle under Part III of the Act, and in either case, required by s. 101 (1) of this Act to order that particulars of the conviction, and, if the court orders him to be disqualified, particulars of the disqualification, are to be endorsed on any licence held by him (s. 177 (3)).

The provisions contained in Part IV of that Schedule (being provisions as to alternative verdicts, as to charges which may be preferred when a person is not convicted of an offence charged and as to the conviction of persons of certain offences despite the absence of a warning of prosecution of those offences) shall have effect in relation to such of the offences against provisions of this Act specified in Column 1 of Part I of that Schedule as are indicated by entries against those offences in column 7 of that Part (s. 177 (4)).

Part V of that Schedule shall have effect for the interpretation of that Schedule (s. 177 (5)).

Any reference in that Schedule to a section by its number only is a reference to a section of this Act (s. 177 (6)).

RESTRICTION ON PROSECUTIONS FOR CERTAIN OFFENCES – This section applies to (a) any offence under this Act to which it is applied by column 7 of Part I of Sched. 4 to this Act; and (b) any offence under s. 77 (7) of the Road Traffic Regulation Act 1967 or punishable by virtue of s. 78A of that Act (s. 179 (1)).

Subject to the following provisions of this section and to the provisions of para. 5, 6 and 7 of Part IV of the said Schedule 4, where a person is prosecuted for an offence to which this section applies he shall not be convicted unless either–

(a) he was warned at the time the offence was committed that the question of prosecuting him for some one or other of the offences to which this section applies would be taken into consideration; or
(b) within fourteen days of the commission of the offence a summons for the offence was served on him; or
(c) within the said fourteen days a notice of the intended prosecution specifying the nature of the alleged offence and the time and place where it is alleged to have been committed, was—
   (i) in the case of an offence against s. 17 or 18 of this Act, served on him,
   (ii) in the case of any other offence, served on him or on the person, if any, registered as the keeper of the vehicle at the time of the commission of the offence;

and the notice shall be deemed for the purposes of paragraph (c) above to have been served on any person if it was sent by registered post or recorded delivery service addressed to him at his last known address, notwithstanding that the notice was returned as undelivered or was for any other reason not received by him (s. 179 (2)).

The requirement of sub-s. (2) above shall in every case be deemed to have been complied with unless and until the contrary is proved (s. 179 (3)).

The requirement of sub-s. (2) above shall not apply in relation to an offence if at the time of the offence, or immediately thereafter, an accident occurs owing to the presence on a road of the vehicle in respect of which the offence was committed (s. 179 (3A), added by R.T. Act 1974).

Failure to comply with the requirement of sub-s. (2) above shall not be a bar to the conviction of the accused in a case where the court is satisfied—

(a) that neither the name and address of the accused nor the name and address of the registered keeper, if any, could with reasonable diligence have been ascertained in time for a summons or, as the case may be, a complaint to be served or for a notice to be served or sent in compliance with the said requirement; or

(b) that the accused by his own conduct contributed to the failure (s. 179 (4)).

On trial on indictment for manslaughter or causing death by dangerous driving of a motor vehicle, the jury may find the accused guilty of reckless or dangerous driving.

If a person is charged with dangerous driving and the requirements regarding notice of intended prosecution in respect of that offence had been complied with but the court is of opinion that the offence is not proved, he may be convicted of careless driving notwithstanding that the intention to prosecute him for this offence was not conveyed to him within 14 days.

A similar provision applies to a conviction for careless cycling (R.T. Act 1972, Sched. 4, Part IV).

TIME FOR COMMENCING PROCEEDINGS FOR CERTAIN OFFENCES – Summary proceedings for an offence under this Act to which this section is applied by column 7 of Part I of Sched. 4 may be brought within 6 months from the date on which evidence sufficient in the opinion of the prosecutor to warrant the proceedings came to his knowledge; but no such proceedings shall be brought by virtue of this section more than 3 years after the commission of the offence. For the purposes of this section a certificate signed by or on behalf of the prosecutor and stating the date on which such evidence as aforesaid came to his knowledge shall be conclusive evidence of that fact; and a certificate stating that matter and purporting to be so signed shall be deemed to be so signed unless the contrary is proved (R.T. Act 1972, s. 180).

EVIDENCE BY CERTIFICATE – In any proceedings for an offence to which R.T. Act 1972, s. 181, is applied by column 7 of Part I of Sched. 4, or which is punishable by virtue of s. 178 thereof, or for an offence against any other enactment relating to the use of vehicles on roads; evidence by certificate in the prescribed form is admissible (s. 181); see Chap. 7.

ADMISSIBILITY OF RECORDS AS EVIDENCE – A statement contained in a document purporting to be (a) a part of the records maintained by the Secretary of State in connection with any functions exercisable by him by virtue of Part III of this Act or a part of any other records maintained by the Secretary of State with respect to vehicles; or (b) a copy of a document forming part of those records; or (c) a note of any information contained in those records, and to be authenticated by a person authorised in that behalf by the Secretary of State shall be admissible in any proceedings as evidence of any fact stated therein to the same extent as oral evidence of that fact is admissible in those proceedings (s. 182 (1)).

In sub-s. (1) above "document" and "statement" have the same meanings as in s. 10 (1) of the Civil Evidence Act 1968, and the reference to a copy of a document shall be construed in accordance with s. 10 (2) of that Act; but nothing in this subsection shall be construed as limiting to civil proceedings the references to proceedings in sub-s. (1) above (s. 182 (2)).

In any case where (a) any such statement as is referred to in sub-s. (1) above is produced to a magistrates' court in any proceedings for an offence involving obligatory or discretionary disqualification, and (b) the statement specifies an alleged previous conviction of an accused person of any such offence, and (c) it is proved to the satisfaction of the court that not less than 7 days before the statement is so produced a notice was served on the accused, in such form and manner as may be so prescribed, specifying the previous conviction and stating that it is proposed to bring it to the notice of the court, and (d) the accused is not present in court, the court may take account of the previous conviction as if the accused had appeared and admitted it (s. 182 (2A), to be added by R.T. Act 1974, s. 13 (3) when in force).

Nothing in the foregoing provisions of this section shall enable evidence to be given with respect to any other matter than a matter of the prescribed description (s. 182 (3)).

PROOF, IN SUMMARY PROCEEDINGS, OF IDENTITY OF DRIVER OF VEHICLE – Where on the summary trial in England or Wales of an information for an offence under this Act to which this section is applied by column 7 of Part I of Sched. 4 to this Act or which is punishable by virtue of s. 178 thereof or for an offence against any other enactment relating to the use of vehicles on roads—

(a) it is proved to the satisfaction of the court, on oath or in manner prescribed by rules made under s. 15 of the Justices of the Peace Act 1949, that a requirement under s. 168 (2) of this Act to give information as to the identity of the driver of a particular vehicle on the particular occasion to which the information relates has been served on the accused by post; and
(b) a statement in writing is produced to the court purporting to be signed by the accused that the accused was the driver of that vehicle on that occasion,

the court may accept that statement as evidence that the accused was the driver of that vehicle on that oocasion (s. 183).

Application to the Crown – Subject to the provisions of this section—

(a) Part I (ss. 1–39) of this Act,
(b) Part II (ss. 40–83) except ss. 56, 57, 58, 59 and 61,
(c) Part III (ss. 84–111), except s. 100,
(d) Part IV (ss. 112–125), and in
(e) Part VII (ss. 159, 160, 161, 164, 165, 174, 175 and 179)

shall apply to vehicles and persons in the public service of the Crown (s. 188 (1)).

Section 162 of this Act, in so far as it provides for the production of test certificates and the giving of names and addresses, shall apply to a person in connection with a vehicle to which s. 44 of this Act applies notwithstanding that he or the driver is or was at any material time in the public service of the Crown; and sub-s. (1) of the said s. 162, in so far as it provides for the production of any certificate mentioned in para. (iii) thereof, shall apply to a person in connection with a goods vehicle so mentioned notwithstanding that he or the driver is or was at any material time in the public service of the Crown (s. 188 (2)).

Section 4 of this Act (in so far as it imposes restrictions on persons under 21 years of age with respect to the driving of heavy locomotives, light locomotives, motor tractors, heavy motor cars or motor cars) shall not apply in the case of motor vehicles owned by the Secretary of State for Defence and used for naval, military or air force purposes, or in the case of vehicles so used while being driven by persons for the time being subject to the orders of a member of the armed forces of the Crown (s. 188 (3)).

Sections 45 to 51 and s. 62 of this Act shall apply to vehicles in the public service of the Crown only if they are registered or liable to be registered under the Vehicles (Excise) Act 1971, and to trailers in the public service of the Crown only while drawn by vehicles (whether or not in the public service of the Crown) which are required to be so registered; and shall so apply subject to the following modifications:

(a) examinations of such vehicles in pursuance of regulations under s. 45 or 50 (1) (a) of this Act may be made by or under the direction of examiners authorised by the Secretary of State for the purpose instead of by or under the directions of examiners appointed under s. 56 of this Act or of certifying officers or P.S.V. examiners appointed under Part III of the Road Traffic Act 1960;

(b) s. 45 (3) of this Act shall not apply to the determination of an examiner so authorised on any such examination, but any person aggrieved by such a determination may appeal to the Secretary of State and on the appeal the Secretary of State shall cause the vehicle to be re-examined by an officer appointed by him for the purpose and may make such determination on the basis of the re-examination as he thinks fit (s. 188 (4)).

Neither sub-s. (2) nor sub-s. (4) of s. 88 of this Act in so far as it prevents such a licence as is there mentioned from authorising a person to drive motor cycles whereof the cylinder capacity of the engine exceeds 250 cubic centimetres shall apply in the case of motor cycles owned by the Secretary of State for Defence and used for naval, military or air force purposes, or in the case of motor cycles so used while being ridden by persons for the time being subject to the orders of a member of the armed forces of the Crown (s. 188 (6)).

The function of issuing licences under Part IV of this Act to persons subject to the Naval Discipline Act 1957, to military law or to air force law to drive goods vehicles in the public service of the Crown and of revoking and suspending such licences shall be exercised by the prescribed licensing authority; and references in that Part to the licensing authority shall be construed accordingly (s. 188 (7)).

For the purpose of proceedings for an offence under this Act (except an offence under s. 81) in connection with a vehicle in the public service of the Crown, being proceedings against a person other than the driver or rider of the vehicle, the person nominated in that behalf by the department in whose service the vehicle is used shall be deemed to be the person actually responsible unless it is shown to the satisfaction of the court that the driver or rider only was responsible (s. 188 (8)).

For the purposes of s. 68 to 81 of this Act in their application to vehicles in the public service of the Crown, the person whom the department in whose service any such vehicle is used names as the person actually responsible shall be deemed to be the person who causes or permits the vehicle to be on the road (s. 188 (9)).

APPLICATION OF SS. 6 TO 11 OF THE ACT TO PERSONS SUBJECT TO SERVICE DISCIPLINE – The application of ss. 6 to 11 (driving with blood alcohol concentration above the prescribed limit, etc.) to persons subject to service discipline is regulated by this section (s. 189).

Interpretation: Classes or Descriptions of Motor Vehicles – "Motor vehicle" means a mechanically propelled vehicle intended or adapted for use on roads, and "trailer" means a vehicle drawn by a motor vehicle.

Provided that a side-car attached to a motor cycle shall, if it complies with such conditions as may be specified in regulations made by the Secretary of State, be regarded as forming part of the vehicle to which it was attached and not as being a trailer.

"Motorcar" means a mechanically propelled vehicle, not being a motor cycle or an invalid carriage, which is constructed itself to carry a load or passengers and the weight of which unladen (a) if it is constructed solely for the carriage of passengers and their effects, is adapted to carry not more than 7 passengers, exclusive of the driver, and is fitted with tyres of such type as may be specified in regulations made by the Secretary of State, does not exceed 3 tons; (b) if it is constructed or adapted for use for the conveyance of goods or burden of any description, does not exceed 3 tons, or 3½ tons if the vehicle carries a container or containers for holding for the purpose of its propulsion any fuel which is wholly gaseous at 60 degrees Fahr. under pressure of 30 ins. of mercury or plant and materials for producing such fuel; (c) does not exceed 2½ tons in a case falling within neither of the foregoing.

"Heavy motor car" means a mechanically propelled vehicle, not being a motor car, which is constructed itself to carry a load or passengers and the weight of which unladen exceeds 2½ tons.

"Motor cycle" means a mechanically propelled vehicle, not being an invalid carriage, with less than 4 wheels and the weight of which unladen does not exceed 8 cwts.

"Invalid carriage" means a mechanically propelled vehicle the weight of which unladen does not exceed 5 cwts and which is specially designed and constructed, and not merely adapted, for the use of a person suffering from some physical defect or disability and is used solely by such a person. The Motor Vehicles (Driving Licences) Regs. 1971 (reg. 23) varies the maximum weight of invalid carriages from 5 cwt. to 8 cwt. for the purposes of all regulations which relate to the minimum age of driving motor vehicles and the licensing of drivers thereof.

"Motor tractor" means a mechanically propelled vehicle which is not constructed itself to carry a load, other than the following articles, that is to say, water, fuel, accumulators and other equipment used for the purpose of propulsion, loose tools and loose equipment, and the weight of which unladen does not exceed 7¼ tons.

"Light locomotive" means a mechanically propelled vehicle which is not constructed itself to carry a load, other than any of the articles aforesaid, and the weight of which unladen does not exceed 11½ tons but does exceed 7¼ tons.

"Heavy locomotive" means a mechanically propelled vehicle which is not constructed itself to carry a load, other than any of the articles aforesaid, and the weight of which unladen exceeds 11½ tons.

In a case where a motor vehicle is so constructed that a trailer may by partial superimposition be attached to the vehicle in such a manner as to cause a substantial part of the weight of the trailer to be borne by the vehicle, that vehicle shall be deemed to be a vehicle itself constructed to carry a load.

In the case of a motor vehicle fitted with a crane, dynamo, welding plant or other special appliance or apparatus which is a permanent or essentially permanent fixture, the appliance or apparatus shall not be deemed to constitute a load or goods or burden of any description, but shall be deemed to form part of the vehicle (s. 190 and R.T.R. Act 1967, s. 99).

ARTICULATED VEHICLES – A vehicle so constructed that it can be divided into two parts both of which are vehicles and one of which is a motor vehicle shall (when not so divided) be treated for the purposes of this Act as that motor vehicle with the other part attached as a trailer (s. 191).

HOVER VEHICLES – For the purposes of this Act a hovercraft within the meaning of the Hovercraft Act 1968 (in this section referred to as a hover vehicle) (a) shall be a motor vehicle, whether or not it is adapted or intended for use on roads; but (b) shall be treated, subject to sub-s. (2) below, as not being a vehicle of any of the classes defined in sub-s. (2) to ((8) of s. 190 of this Act (s. 192 (1)).

The Secretary of State may by regulations provide (a) that any provision of this Act which would otherwise apply to hover vehicles shall not apply to them or shall apply to them subject to such modifications as may be specified in the regulations; or (b) that any such provision which would not otherwise apply to hover vehicles shall apply to them, subject to such modifications (if any) as may be specified in the regulations (s. 192 (2)).

For the purposes of the Hovercraft Act 1968 (under which enactments and instruments relating, amongst other things, to motor vehicles may, if passed before the commencement of that Act, be applied to hovercraft) any enactment contained in or instrument made under this Act shall be treated as included among the enactments and instruments which can be so applied (s. 192 (3)).

CERTAIN VEHICLES NOT TO BE TREATED AS MOTOR VEHICLES – For the purposes of the R.T. Act 1972, (a) a mechanically propelled vehicle for cutting grass which is controlled by a pedestrian and is not capable of being used or adapted for any other purpose, and (b) any other mechanically propelled vehicle controlled by a pedestrian which may be specified by Regulations shall be treated as not being a motor vehicle. "Controlled by a pedestrian" means that the vehicle either (a) is constructed or adapted for use only under such control, or (b) is made or adapted for use either under such control or under the control of a person carried on it but it is not for the time being in use under, or proceeding under, the control of a person carried on it (s. 193) Section 103 of the R.T.R. Act 1967 contains similar provisions.

WEIGHT OF MOTOR VEHICLES – The weight unladen of a vehicle or trailer means the weight of the vehicle or trailer inclusive of the body and all parts (the heavier being taken where alternative bodies or parts are used) which are necessary to or ordinarily used with the vehicle or trailer when working on a road but exclusive of the weight of water, fuel or accumulators used for its propulsion, and of loose tools and loose equipment (s. 194).

CARRIAGES – A motor vehicle or trailer shall be deemed to be a carriage within the meaning of any Act of Parliament, rule regulation or byelaw, and if used as a carriage of any particular class shall be deemed to be a carriage of that class (s. 195).

DEFINITIONS – "Bridleway" means a way over which the public have the following, but no other rights of way, that is to say, a right of way on foot and a right of way on horseback or leading a horse, with or without a right to drive animals of any description along the way.

"Carriage of goods" includes the haulage of goods.

"Cycle" means a bicycle, tricycle or cycle having four or more wheels, not being in any case a motor vehicle.

Except for the purposes of s. 1 (and s. 42 of R.T.R. Act 1967), "Driver," where a separate person acts as steersman of a motor vehicle, includes that person as well as any other person engaged in the driving of the vehicle, and "drive" shall be construed accordingly.

A person steering a towed broken down motor vehicle is not a driver (*Wallace* v. *Major* (1946)).

A person who steers a motor vehicle down a slope without the engine running is a "driver" (*Saycell* v. *Bool* (1948)).

"Footpath" means a way over which the public have a right of way on foot only.

"Owner", in relation to a vehicle which is the subject of a hiring or hire-purchase agreement, means the person in possession of the vehicle under that agreement.

"Road", means any highway and any other road to which the public has access, and includes bridges over which a road passes. The road includes the footway as well as the carriageway (*Bryant* v. *Marx* (1932)).

"Tramcar" includes any carriage used on any road by virtue of an order made under the Light Railways Act 1896.

"Trolley Vehicle" means a mechanically propelled vehicle adapted for use upon roads without rails and moved by power transmitted thereto from some external source (s. 196).

TRAMCARS AND TROLLEY VEHICLES – Part VI of Transport Act 1968 shall not apply to tramcars or trolley vehicles: ss. 4, 14, 29, 30 and 36 of the 1972 Act shall not apply to tramcars or trolley vehicles, and ss. 2, 3, 5 (1), and 26 shall not apply to tramcars.

Sections 34, 40, 44, 52 and 60 and any orders or regulations made under them shall not apply to tramcars or trolley vehicles.

Sections 68 to 81 shall not apply to tramcars.

Sections 84 to 111 shall not apply to tramcars, and s. 111 shall not apply to trolley vehicles.

Sections 143 to 158 shall not apply to tramcars or trolley vehicles.

Sections 159, 160, 162, 164, 166, 167, 175, 179, 194 and 195 shall not apply to tramcars or trolley vehicles, and s. 161 shall not apply to tramcars.

NUISANCE – Nothing in the Road Traffic Acts 1960 and 1972 shall authorise a person to use on a road a vehicle so constructed or used as to cause a public or private nuisance or affect the liability whether under statute or common law of the driver or owner so using such a vehicle (s. 269 (1960 Act) and s. 207 (1972 Act)). There is a similar provision in s. 112 of the R.T.R. Act 1967 with respect to that Act.

Traffic Regulation outside London Traffic Area – Sections 1, 5, 9 and 10, R.T.R. Act 1967, and s. 126, Transport Act 1968 authorise the Minister of Transport to make orders regulating traffic on trunk roads, and local authorities to make similar regulations regarding other roads. The procedure to be followed in making these orders is governed by the Traffic Regulation Orders (Procedure) (England and Wales) Regs. 1961. Driving a vehicle, or causing or permitting a vehicle to be driven in contravention of the order is an offence (s. 1). See also the Heavy Commercial Vehicles (Controls and Regulations) Act 1973.

TRAFFIC REGULATION IN LONDON TRAFFIC AREA – Sections 6–11 R.T.R. Act 1967 and s. 126, Transport Act 1968 contain provisions for facilitating and improving the regulation of traffic in and near London.

TRAFFIC REGULATION IN SPECIAL CASES – A highway authority, to obviate danger to the public or serious damage to the highway, may by notice restrict or prohibit temporarily the use of a road by vehicles or foot passengers. It may also, on occasion of works being executed or proposed to be executed on or near a road or by reason of the likelihood of danger to the public or of serious damage to the highway, prohibit or restrict traffic or foot passengers by order. Notices of such a notice or order must be posted on the road giving the alternative route for traffic (R.T.R. Act 1967, s. 12 and Sched. 3, and s. 126, Transport Act 1968).

A local authority outside the London Traffic Area, with the Minister's approval, may make orders as to the use of highways by public service vehicle (s. 15, as amended by Transport Act 1968, s. 128).

The Minister may by order prohibit or restrict the driving of vehicles on all roads (except special roads) specified in the order if he is satisfied that it is desirable that such an order should be made. To drive a vehicle, or cause or permit a vehicle to be driven, in contravention of such an order is an offence (s. 16).

A bridge authority, by proper notice in proper position at each end of a bridge over which a road passes, may prohibit the use of the bridge by any vehicle of which (a) the weight exceeds a maximum weight specified in the notice, not being less than 5 tons; or (b) (i) the weight exceeds a maximum weight so specified, not being less than 5 tons or (ii) any axle weight exceeds a maximum axle weight so specified, not being less than 3 tons, either absolutely or when travelling at more than a specified speed. It will be an offence to contravene such notice unless the bridge authority has given a permit to do so. If in any proceedings for this offence the prosecutor satisfies the court that there are reasonable grounds for believing that the weight of the vehicle exceeded the maximum weights specified in the notice, or that any axle weight of the vehicle exceeded the maximum axle weight so specified, the onus of proving that the weight or weights did not exceed the maximum shall lie on the defendant (s. 17). (This section will come into operation when the Minister makes an Order).

A highway or a bridge authority may grant a permit as regards its roads or bridges allowing a trailer drawn by a locomotive to carry weights (as specified) in excess of what is prescribed by regulation (s. 18).

DRIVING OVER MENAI BRIDGE – Driving over Menai Bridge except in accordance with any regulations is an offence. The Minister has made the Menai Suspension Bridge (Traffic Regulation) Order 1955, which forbids overtaking on either of the dual carriageways except bicycles by bicycles (s. 19).

REMOVAL OF PARKED VEHICLES, ETC. – Section 20, R.T.R. Act 1967, as amended by the Removal and Disposal of Vehicles (Alteration of Enactments) Order 1967, and the Transport Act 1968, gives the Minister powers to make regulations for the removal of vehicles illegally, obstructively or dangerously parked, abandoned or broken down, and s. 53, R.T.R. Act 1967 (as amended by the above-mentioned regulation and Act) gives a competent authority power to dispose of abandoned vehicles. The Removal and Disposal of Vehicles Regulations 1968, provide that where a vehicle (a) has broken down, or been permitted to remain at rest, on a road in such a position or in such condition or in such circumstances as to cause obstruction to other persons using the road or as to be likely to cause danger to such other persons, or (b) has been permitted to remain at rest or has broken down and remained at rest on a road in contravention of any relevant law, a constable may require the owner, driver or other person in control or in charge to remove it as directed. Failure to comply will amount to an offence under s. 87, R.T.R. Act 1967 (reg. 3). Where a vehicle (a) is one to which reg. 3 applies, or (b) having broken down on a road or on land in the open air, appears to have been abandoned without lawful authority, or (c) has been permitted to remain at rest on a road in such a position, condition, or circumstances as to appear to have been abandoned, a constable may remove the vehicle (reg. 4).

PEDESTRIAN CROSSINGS – Sections 21–23, R.T.R. Act 1967, allow the establishment of road crossings for pedestrians and the making of regulations respecting their use.

The "Zebra" Pedestrian Crossings Regs. 1971 replace the Pedestrian Crossings Regs. 1954 and provide: Part I of Sched. 2

of the Regulations regulate the manner in which the presence and limits of a zebra crossing are to be indicated by marks or studs (they constitute two lines of studs across the carriageway, and black and white stripes between the studs). Part II of Sched. 2 indicate the size, colour and type of the traffic sign to be placed near a zebra crossing (at or near the end of such a crossing there shall be a yellow globe with flashing or constant light on a black and white banded post, and where necessary a lamp may be provided to illuminate foot passengers during the hours of darkness). Provision is also made for a new traffic sign to be placed on the carriageway in the vicinity of a zebra crossing for the purpose of making that carriageway a "zebra controlled area" in relation to that crossing (such an area will be indicated by white zig-zag broken lines extending from a "give way line" near the zebra crossing to a "terminal line") (reg. **5** and Sched. 3). Every foot passenger in an uncontrolled zebra crossing has precedence over any vehicle, and its driver shall afford such precedence. If a street refuge or central reservation interrupts such crossing, each side will be deemed a separate crossing (reg. **8**). "Uncontrolled zebra crossing" means a zebra crossing at which traffic is not for the time being controlled by a police constable in uniform or by a traffic warden (reg. **3**).

The driver of a vehicle shall not cause the vehicle or any part thereof to stop within the limits of a zebra crossing unless either he is prevented from proceeding by circumstances beyond his control or it is necessary for him to stop in order to avoid an accident. No foot passenger shall remain on the carriageway within the limits of a zebra crossing longer than is necessary for the purpose of passing over the crossing with reasonable despatch (reg. **9**).

Drivers of vehicles proceeding towards a zebra crossing are prohibited from overtaking a moving or stationary vehicle in a zebra controlled area (reg. **10**). Vehicles (other than a pedal cycle not having a sidecar attached) are prohibited from stopping in zebra controlled areas (reg. **12**)—but there are exceptions permitted by regs. **14** and **15**, e.g. vehicles used for fire brigade, ambulance or police purposes, or in connection with any building operation, demolition or excavation, or the removal of any obstruction, etc.; or if a vehicle has stopped for making a left or right turn; or a public service vehicle which is waiting, after having proceeded past the zebra crossing, for the purpose of enabling persons to board or alight from the vehicle.

The pattern of studs which by virtue of the **1954** Regs. marks the approach to a zebra crossing will cease to be of effect as from November **30**, **1973**. Until then (as also provided in reg. **14**), the driver of a vehicle shall not cause the vehicle or any part thereof to stop on the carriageway between an uncontrolled zebra crossing, the approach to which is indicated by a pattern of studs, and the line studs in that pattern (reg. **13**).

SCHOOL CROSSING PATROLS – Sections 24–25, R.T.R. Act 1967 allow county councils to appoint persons as school crossing patrols to patrol at places where children are crossing or seeking to cross roads on their way to or from school (or on their way from one part of the school to another (R.T. Act 1974, Sched. 6)) between 8 a.m. and 5.30 p.m. Any such patrol must be trained and wear uniform. When such a patrol exhibits the prescribed sign "Stop Children", which may be illuminated, the driver of a vehicle must stop and allow the children to cross the road. If the driver does not stop he commits a summary offence. See Traffic Signs (School Crossing Patrols) Regs. 1968.

STREET PLAYGROUNDS – Sections 26–27, R.T.R. Act 1967 give power to local authorities to prohibit traffic on roads to be used as playgrounds, and to make byelaws with respect to their use.

PARKING PLACES – Under ss. 28–51, R.T.R. Act 1967 and ss. 127, 130, Transport Act 1968, local authorities have powers to provide parking places for the purpose of relieving or preventing congestion of traffic. Parking places on roads must not unreasonably prevent access to any premises adjoining the road and must not be a nuisance. In certain streets local authorities have installed parking meters for the collection of charges for parking on highways. The Highways Act 1971, s. 30, gives highway authorities powers to provide areas on or near highways for the overnight parking of goods vehicles having an unladen weight of 2 tons or more or trailers, and for the transfer of loads, vehicle servicing, goods storage and handling facilities, and accommodation, refreshment and toilet facilities.

TRAFFIC SIGNS – Sections 54–68, R.T.R. Act 1967 deal with traffic signs which may be erected on or near roads. "Traffic sign" means any object or device (whether fixed or portable) for conveying warnings, information, requirements, restrictions, or prohibitions of any description prescribed or authorised by law to traffic on roads, or any specified description of traffic, and any line or mark on a road for conveying such warnings. No other traffic signs are permissible except those *re* bridges and those placed by any tramway, trolley vehicle, light railway, dock or harbour undertaking (s. 54).

A highway authority may cause or permit traffic signs to be placed on or near any road in conformity with the directions of the appropriate Minister (s. 55).

A constable, or a person acting under the instructions of the chief officer of police may place on a highway, or on any structure on a highway, traffic signs for giving effect to local traffic regulations (s. 57).

A constable, or a person acting under the instructions of the chief officer of police, may place on a highway, or on any structure on a highway, traffic signs of any size, colour and type authorised, indicating prohibitions, restrictions or requirements relating to vehicular traffic, as may be necessary or expedient to prevent or mitigate congestion or obstruction of traffic, or danger to or from traffic, in consequence of extraordinary circumstances. The continuous use of such signs is restricted to 7 days, and s. 14 of the R.T. Act 1960 applies to them (s. 58).

The highway authority may give written notice to the owner or occupier of land to remove any unauthorised traffic sign and has power to remove it (s. 61).

TRAFFIC SIGNS REGS. AND GENERAL DIRECTIONS 1975 give the traffic signs which may be placed on or near roads and directions as to their use. Many of these signs are merely of a warning or informative character and disregard of them, while not punishable as a specific offence under s. 22, R.T. Act 1972, may increase any liability for careless or dangerous driving.

As regards light signals, "green" indicates that a vehicle may proceed with due regard to the safety of other users of the road and subject to the directions of any police officer regulating traffic; "red" and "red with amber" prohibit movement beyond the stop line until "green" shows. "Amber" shown alone also prohibits movement beyond the stop line except in a case where the vehicle is so close to the stop line that it cannot safely be stopped before crossing the line. A new traffic sign comprising flashing red light signals is prescribed for stopping traffic. Vehicular traffic shall not proceed beyond the signals except in the case of any vehicle which is so close to the signal when the lights first begin to flash that it cannot safely be stopped before passing the signals. These flashing red light signals may be surmounted by a cross (regs. 31–34).

The carriageway marking called "the double white line" is prescribed by reg. 23. Subject to certain exceptions, vehicles must not stop on the road where this marking has been placed, and vehicles must travel on the left of a continuous line where it is placed on the left of a dotted line or a continuous line. A vehicle may stop as long as may be necessary on a road where this marking has been placed: (1) to enable a person to board or alight; (2) for loading or unloading goods; (3) for building or demolition work, to remove obstructions, etc. (However, if it is possible to perform the necessary operation by leaving the vehicle on a lay-by or road verge, this should be done.) The requirement that a vehicle must not stop where this marking has been placed does not apply to (a) fire brigade, ambulance and police vehicles; (b) pedal cycles without sidecars; (c) a vehicle prevented from proceeding by circumstances beyond the driver's control or to avoid an accident; (d) to anything done with the permission of a police constable in uniform or a traffic warden. It is permissible to cross a continuous white line to obtain access to another road, or to land or premises adjacent to the road, or, if necessary, (a) to pass a stationary vehicle; (b) owing to circumstances beyond the driver's control; (c) to avoid an accident, or (d) to comply with any direction of a police constable in uniform or a traffic warden. No vehicle shall cross or straddle a "broken white line" which is on the left of a "continuous white line" unless the driver can see that it is safe to do so.

The Regulations introduce symbols to replace words wherever possible in traffic signs for use on roads generally. Regulation 7 applies s. 22, R.T. Act 1972 (which makes it an offence for drivers to fail to conform to the indication given by certain traffic signs lawfully placed on roads) to certain types of signs. Regulation 11 provides that drivers of large or slow vehicles must telephone and get permission to cross a railway level crossing equipped with automatic barriers. "Large" means over 55 ft. long or 9 ft. 6 ins. wide or 32 tons total weight. "Slow" means 5 m.p.h. or less.

SPEED LIMITS ON RESTRICTED ROADS – It shall not be lawful for a person to drive a motor vehicle on a restricted road at a speed exceeding 30 m.p.h. but an order by Statutory Instrument may be made as respects any specified restricted road that the limit of speed be increased or reduced (R.T.R. Act 1967, s. 71). The offender must be warned of intended prosecution (see s. 179, R.T. Act 1972).

A "restricted road" means a road in which there is a system of street lighting by lamps placed not more than 200 yds. apart and which, if a trunk or classified road, had been provided before July 1, 1957. A direction may be given that a road shall cease to be a restricted road or that a specified road shall become a restricted road (R.T.R. Act 1967, s. 72).

Traffic signs shall be erected so as to give adequate guidance to drivers as to whether any, and if so what, limit of speed is to be observed on a road. A person shall not be convicted of exceeding a speed limit on a road which has no system of street lighting by lamps placed not more than 200 yds. apart unless the limit is indicated by traffic signs (s. 75).

SPEED LIMITS ON ROADS OTHER THAN RESTRICTED ROADS – Other than on restricted roads the Minister of Transport or the local authority may make an order prohibiting, either generally or during specified periods, the driving of motor vehicles at a speed exceeding the limit given in the order. Before making such an order a local authority shall consult the chief officer of police (s. 74).

TEMPORARY OR EXPERIMENTAL SPEED LIMITS – In the interest of safety and for facilitating the movement of traffic the Minister of Transport may impose temporary or experimental speed limits. There is power to impose both maximum and minimum speed limits, but minimum speed limits may be imposed only on specified roads. Exceeding a maximum speed limit fixed by an experimental order will be an offence under R.T.R. Act 1967,

s. 78A. Contravention of a minimum speed limit will be an offence under s. 77 (7), R.T.R. Act 1967 (an offender must be warned of intended prosecution). There is no power to order disqualification or endorsement for this offence, and no person shall be convicted of this offence on the opinion of one witness as to the speed at which the defendant was driving.

TRAFFIC SIGNS (SPEED LIMITS) REGS. AND GENERAL DIRECTIONS 1969 – These prescribe the signs which indicate to drivers where a speed limit begins and ceases. The figures (e.g. 30 or 40) in black on a white circle surrounded by a red ring will indicate that a speed limit is in force, and a transverse black bar in a white circle will indicate that this speed limit is not in force on the road.

These signs will be fitted with reflectors or will be illuminated.

SPEED LIMITS FOR CERTAIN CLASSES OF VEHICLES – It shall not be lawful for a person to drive a motor vehicle of any class or description on a road at a speed greater than the speed specified as the maximum speed for a vehicle of that class or description. (For Schedule, see Appendix I (R.T.R. Act 1967, s. 78)). The offender must be warned of intended prosecution.

SPEEDING OFFENCES GENERALLY – A person convicted of an offence of driving a motor vehicle on a road at a speed exceeding a limit imposed by or under any enactment mentioned in sub-s. (3) below shall be liable on summary conviction to a fine not exceeding £50 (s. 78A (1)).

A person prosecuted for such an offence as aforesaid shall not be liable to be convicted solely on the evidence of one witness to the effect that in the opinion of the witness the person prosecuted was driving the vehicle at a speed exceeding a specified limit (s. 78A (2)).

The enactments referred to in sub-s. (1) above are—(a) any enactment contained in this Act; (b) s. 2 of the Parks Regulation (Amendment) Act 1926; (c) any enactment passed after the commencement of the Road Traffic Act 1960 (s. 78A (3)).

If a person who employs other persons to drive motor vehicles on roads publishes or issues any time-table or schedule, or gives any directions, under which any journey or any stage or part of any journey is to be completed within some specified time, and it is not practicable in the circumstances of the case for that journey of that stage or part of the journey to be completed in specified time without the commission of such an offence as is mentioned in sub-s. (1) above, the publication or issue of the said time-table or schedule or the giving of the directions may be produced as prima facie evidence that the employer, as the case may be, procured or incited the persons employed by him to drive the vehicles to commit such offence as aforesaid" (s. 78A (4)).

The above s. 78A was added by R.T. Act 1972, s. 203.

SPEED LIMIT EXEMPTIONS – Any vehicle used for police, ambulance or fire brigade purposes is exempt from any speed limits if their observance would be likely to hinder the use of the vehicle for the purpose for which it is being used on that occasion (s. 79).

ENFORCEMENT AND ADMINISTRATION OF TRAFFIC LAWS – Section 80, R.T.R. Act 1967, deals with a "ticket" system involving a fixed penalty for dealing with certain offences punishable on summary conviction. These include parking a vehicle on a road during the hours of darkness without lights; or waiting or being left or parked, or being loaded or unloaded; failing to display a valid excise licence; and non-payment of a parking meter charge. The section is applicable throughout England and Wales. Although the usual processes of prosecution and fine remain, if a "ticket" is issued and the penalty duly paid, the offender is not liable to conviction. Section 81 authorises the employment of traffic wardens under the control of the police to perform duties prescribed, including the operation of the "ticket" system.

LIABILITY OF VEHICLE OWNER IN RESPECT OF CERTAIN FIXED PENALTY OFFENCES – Where a fixed penalty notice has been issued and the penalty has not been paid, the police may within 6 months serve a notice on the apparent owner informing him of the alleged offence and the fixed penalty. The notice requires the apparent owner to furnish the police with a "statutory statement of ownership" unless the penalty is paid within 14 days and invites him to furnish a "statutory statement of facts" concerning the driver at the relevant time (R.T. Act 1974, s. 1 and Sched. 1).

Where such a notice has been served and the fixed penalty has not been paid, and the person so served fails without reasonable excuse to comply with the notice, he commits an offence. If in compliance with or in response to a notice, any person furnishes a statement which is false in a material particular and does so recklessly or knowing it to be so false, he commits an offence (s. 1). A similar procedure for dealing with the liability of a vehicle owner in respect of excess parking charges is contained in s. 2. Local Authorities as well as the police are responsible for enforcement.

The law in respect of hired vehicles is contained in s. 3.

Proceedings for furnishing false information may be brought within six months from the date on which evidence to warrant the proceedings was known, but no proceedings can be brought more than 3 years after the offence was committed (s. 4).

DRIVING INSTRUCTION – Section 126 of the R.T. Act 1972 provides that it is an offence for any person to give paid tuition in driving a motor car unless his name is included in the register of approved instructors or he is licensed under this Act to give such instruction. Section 127 exempts police instructors from the provisions of s. 126. Section 128 provides for the maintenance of the register of approved instructors. Section 130 deals with the removal of names from the register. Section 131 deals with the issue of licences to trainee instructors; s. 132 with appeals to the Secretary of State from the decisions of the Registrar; s. 133 with examinations and tests of ability to teach driving; s. 134 with power to alter conditions for entry or retention in, and removal from, register and grant or revocation of licences under the Act; s. 135 with power to prescribe form of certificate of registration, etc.; s. 136 with the surrender of certificates and licences. Section 137 deals with the production of certificates and licences to the police and authorised persons and is as follows:

A person to whom a certificate prescribed under s. 135 is issued, or to whom a licence under Part V of this Act is granted, shall, on being so required by a police constable or any person authorised in writing by the Secretary of State in that behalf, produce the certificate or licence for examination (s. 137 (1)).

Where the name of a person is removed from the register or a licence granted under Part V of this Act to a person expires or is revoked, then, if that person fails to satisfy an obligation imposed on him by s. 136, a police constable or a person authorised as aforesaid may require him to produce any such certificate issued to him or the licence, and upon its being produced may seize it and deliver it to the Registrar (s. 137 (2)).

If a person who is required under sub-ss. (1) or (2) above to produce a document fails to do so, then, unless within 5 days beginning with the day next after that on which the production of the document was so required, it is produced – (a) where the requirement was made by a police constable, at such police station as, at the time the production was required, may have been specified by the person required to produce the document; (b) where the requirement was made by a person other than a police constable, at such place as the person by whom the requirement was made may, at the time aforesaid, have specified; he shall be guilty of an offence (s. 137 (3)).

The Secretary of State in exercise of his powers under the Act has made the Motor Cars (Driving Instruction). Regs. 1969 (as amended by 1970 and 1971 Regs.). These regulations are in four parts. Part I provides for certificates of approval as prescribed for display by persons whose names are in the register. Part II relates to the examination of ability to give instruction in the driving of motor cars, and contains an exemption from the written part of the examination for instructors who were registered with either the Motor Schools Association of Great Britain Limited or the Royal Automobile Club on May 10, 1967. Part III sets out provisions relating to the test of continued ability and fitness to give instruction, which Approved Driving Instructors may be required to take at intervals. Part IV states that the official title for use by persons whose names are in the register shall be "Ministry of Transport Approved Driving Instructor".

The Secretary of State has also made the Motor Cars (Driving Instruction) (Appeals) Rules 1969 and 1970, which lay down the procedure to be followed on an appeal to the Secretary of State by persons aggrieved by certain decisions of the Registrar who maintains the Register of Approved Driving Instructors.

Police Powers: R.T. Act 1972 and Theft Act 1968 – When a motor vehicle is on a road, these Acts give a constable certain powers regarding it, its driver, its owner, and the person in charge of it. These powers may be summarised as follows:

(1) Stop the vehicle—a constable in uniform can so require at any time (R.T. Act 1972, s. 159).

(2) Traffic signals—the driver of any vehicle must obey a constable regulating traffic (s. 22).

(3) Name and address of driver and of owner—must be given by driver on request (s. 162).

(4) Driving licence—driver, on request, must produce it for examination, either then or within 5 days at a specified police station and in certain cases give a statement of date of birth (s. 161).

(5) Insurance "certificate"—driver, on request, must produce it at the time or cause it to be produced within 5 days at a specified police station (s. 162).

If personal injury has happened and if it is not produced at the scene, the driver within 24 hours must report the accident at a police station or to a constable, and also produce his "certificate", either then or within 5 days at a specified police station (s. 166).

(6) False documents, seizure—on reasonable cause to believe a licence, "certificate", etc., is forged, false, altered, or used with intent to deceive it may be seized (s. 173).

(7) Arrest without warrant—when person driving, attempting to drive or in charge of a motor vehicle or riding a cycle is unfit to drive, or ride a cycle through drink or drugs (ss. 5 and 19).

When driving a motor vehicle recklessly, dangerously or carelessly, unless driver gives name and address or produces licence, or when riding a cycle recklessly, dangerously or carelessly, unless rider gives name and address (s. 164). (The power of arrest is subject to these offences being committed within the view of the constable.)

A person who, without lawful authority, takes a motor vehicle for his own or another's use, or knowing that any motor vehicle has been so taken, drives it or allows himself to be carried in or on it, or attempts to commit any of the foregoing offences, commits an arrestable offence (Theft Act 1968, s. 12).

If it appears to a constable in consequence of a breath test carried out by him on any person under s. 8 (1) or 8 (2) of the R.T. Act 1972, that the device by which the test is carried out indicates that the proportion of alcohol in that person's blood exceeds the prescribed limit, the constable may arrest that person without warrant, except while that person is at a hospital as a patient (s. 8 (4)).

If a person required by a constable under ss. 8 (1) or 8 (2) of the R.T. Act 1972, to provide a specimen of breath for a breath test fails to do so and the constable has reasonable cause to suspect him of having alcohol in his body, the constable may arrest him without warrant, except while he is at a hospital as a patient (s. 8 (5)).

A constable in uniform may arrest without warrant any person driving or attempting to drive a motor vehicle on a road whom he has reasonable cause to suspect of being disqualified (s. 100).

(8) Information—person keeping must give information as to the identity of driver alleged to be guilty of an offence to which R.T. Act 1972, s. 168 applies, also any other person must give any information in his power to give which may lead to such identification.

Owner must give information as to driver, insurance, etc., of vehicle on any occasion on which driver was bound to produce his insurance "certificate" (R.T. Act 1972, s. 167).

Police shall supply information to enable recovery of payment for emergency treatment (s. 156).

(9) Weighing—when a constable, authorised on behalf of the highway authority by his Police Authority or Chief Officer produces his authority he can require the person in charge of a motor vehicle to allow it to be weighed (s. 160).

(10) Eyesight—A constable having reason to suspect a motor driver to be driving with uncorrected defective eyesight may require him to submit to a test (R.T. Act 1972, s. 91).

CHAPTER 25

ROAD VEHICLES

	Page
Vehicles	336
Pedal Cycles	337
Hackney Carriages and Stage Coaches . .	339
Public Service Vehicles .	341
Goods Vehicles . .	352
Drivers' Hours . .	353
Mechanically Propelled Vehicles . . .	359
Registration and Licensing of Vehicles . . .	359
Exhibition of Licences and Registration Marks .	362
Vehicles Exempt from Licence Duty . .	365
Trade Licences . .	367
Hackney Carriages . .	372
Foreign-owned Motor Vehicles . . .	373
Road Traffic (Foreign Vehicles) Act 1972 . . .	374
Construction and Use of Motor Vehicles and Trailers . . .	375

Vehicles – The word "vehicle" may be used as a comprehensive term to include every conveyance the movement of which upon the highway goes to make up the expression "traffic", or more particularly "vehicular traffic". In this sense the Oxford English Dictionary defines "vehicle" as meaning any means of carriage, conveyance, or transport; a means of conveyance provided with wheels or runners and used for the carriage of persons or goods. Passenger vehicle means a vehicle constructed solely for the carriage of passengers and their effects (M.V. (C. & U.) Regs. 1973).

The Highway Act 1835, and the Town Police Clauses Act 1847 dealt with highways and streets and used the word "carriage" to include the vehicles of the period, such as carriages, wagons, carts and other animal-drawn vehicles, sledges, trucks, and barrows.

The Local Government Act 1888, s. 85, declares that bicycles, tricycles, and other similar machines are "carriages" within the meaning of the Highway Acts.

The Road Traffic Act 1972, s. 195, enacts that any motor vehicle or trailer shall be deemed to be a carriage within the meaning of any Act and of any rule, regulation or byelaw made under any Act, and if used as a carriage of any particular class, shall, for the purpose of any enactment relating to carriages of that class, be deemed to be a carriage of that class.

Thus, generally speaking, all road vehicles are "carriages", and owners and drivers have to comply with the law dealing with carriages, as well as to obey the particular rules affecting the class of vehicle they own or drive.

Road vehicles, irrespective of the power by which they are drawn or propelled, are either:

(1) Private vehicles, that is to say, vehicles which are not licensed by any authority to convey members of the public or goods for hire or reward, or

(2) Public vehicles, meaning vehicles which, under licence of the proper authority, carry on the roads passengers or goods for payment. Such vehicles are of various types, but all should have been passed by some authority as suitable for the purpose of carrying persons or goods on the highway for hire.

Public vehicles consist of:

(1) Tramcars and trolley vehicles. These vehicles are allowed on the roads under statutory authority. For the purposes of the Road Traffic Acts 1960 and 1972 "tramcar" includes any carriage used on any road by virtue of an Order made under the Light Railways Act 1896, and "trolley vehicle" means a mechanically propelled vehicle adapted for use upon roads without rails and moved by power transmitted thereto from some external source. See also R.T. Act 1972, s. 196.

(2) Hackney carriages and stage coaches. These are vehicles which are licensed by the Local Authority for standing or plying for hire in the streets of its district. They are dealt with later under "Hackney Carriages and Stage Coaches".

(3) Public service vehicles. These are certain classes of motor vehicles which are licensed for the carrying of passengers for hire or reward. They are regulated by Part III of the R.T. Act 1960, and particulars are given later under "Public Service Vehicles".

(4) Licensed goods vehicles, see later.

Special regulations apply to the nature and (or) use of a vehicle and are given under the following headings:

Pedal Cycles.
Hackney Carriages and Stage Coaches.
Public Service Vehicles.
Goods Vehicles.
Mechanically Propelled Vehicles.

Pedal Cycles – Bicycles, tricycles and other similar machines are carriages within the Highways Acts (Local Government Act 1888, s. 85).

Pedal cycles must display front white and rear red lights and reflectors during the hours of darkness. See "Lights on Vehicles", Chap. 24.

Only one person may travel on a pedal cycle unless it is prepared for the carriage of more than one person (R.T. Act 1972, s. 21).

It is an offence for a pedal cyclist to hold on to a motor vehicle for the purpose of being drawn (R.T. Act 1972, s. 30).

R.T. Act 1972, s. 66, allows the Secretary of State to make regulations governing the construction, equipment and use of cycles not being motor vehicles, including brakes, fitting of appliances for giving warning of approach and the testing and inspection by authorised persons of any equipment prescribed, and of lighting equipment and reflectors. Regs. may also be made to prohibit the sale of cycles which do not comply with the requirements. It will be an offence to sell or supply, or offer to sell or supply a cycle which does not comply with the Regs. It will be a defence to prove that it was sold, supplied or offered for export from Great Britain, or that there was reasonable cause to believe that it would not be used on a road in Great Britain, or would not be so used until it had been put into a condition in which it might be lawfully so used.

BRAKES ON PEDAL CYCLES REGS. **1954** apply to pedal bicycles and pedal tricycles.

Every cycle having any wheel with outside diameter exceeding 18 ins. shall:

(1) if it is "freewheeled" have two independent braking systems, one acting on the front wheel or wheels and the other acting on a rear wheel;

(2) if it is "fixedwheeled" have a braking system acting on the front wheel or wheels.

If it is a tricycle not constructed or adapted for the carriage of goods it will be sufficient to have two independent braking systems acting on the front wheel if it has two rear wheels or on the rear wheel if it has two front wheels.

Every other cycle shall have at least one braking system (reg. 4). All braking systems shall be efficient and kept in proper working order and should not act directly on tyres (reg. 5). No person shall ride or cause or permit a cycle to be ridden on a road unless it complies with these Regs. (reg. 3). Above Regs. do not apply to a cycle with pedals acting directly upon any wheel or to a cycle brought temporarily into the country by a person resident abroad (reg. 6). A police officer in uniform may test and inspect the brakes of any cycle on a road. He may do so on premises where the cycle is, within 48 hours of any accident in which the cycle was involved, if the owner of the premises consents (reg. 8).

Note.—"Owner" in this regulation may include the occupier.

The following sections of the R.T. 1972 Act apply to persons riding cycles:

S. 17 (reckless and dangerous cycling).

S. 18 (careless cycling).

S. 19 (cycling under the influence of drink or a drug) but not the attempting to so ride.

S. 159 (power of police to stop vehicles).

S. 164 (power to obtain names and addresses and to arrest in certain cases).

S. 179 (giving warning of intended prosecution) in cases under ss. 17 and 18 above (unless there has been an accident (R.T. Act 1974, Sched. 6)).

And s. 18 (which enables charge of careless cycling to be substituted for reckless or dangerous cycling).

Section 20 deals with a race or trial of speed on a public highway between cycles not being motor vehicles. It must be authorised and conducted under regulations made by the Minister. See Cycle Racing on Highways Regs. 1960.

Hackney Carriages and Stage Coaches – A hackney carriage, for traffic purposes, is a vehicle which stands or plies for hire in the streets, the driver putting the whole carriage at the disposal of the hirer, and the vehicle, if a motor vehicle, being adapted to carry less than 8 passengers.

These hackney carriages, when they stand or ply for hire in a district to which the Town Police Clauses Act 1847 applies, require to be licensed by the Local Authority (s. 37), and if mechanically propelled they are usually called taxicabs or taxis.

A stage coach or stage carriage is a vehicle which proceeds from stage to stage and which stands or plies for hire for passengers at separate fares in the streets.

A tramcar is a stage carriage for the purposes of the Stage Carriages Act 1832 (*Chapman* v. *Kirke* (1948)).

Such stage coaches when they stand or ply for hire in the districts mentioned below should be licensed for the purpose by the Local Authority.

Above vehicles are regulated by the Town Police Clauses Acts where applicable. The provisions of these Acts as to hackney carriages and stage coaches are incorporated with the Public Health Act 1875 (see ss. 171, 276).

Town Police Clauses Act 1847, s. 38, declares that every wheeled carriage, whatever may be its form or construction, used in standing or plying for hire in any street within the district shall be deemed to be a hackney carriage, but that the term shall not include any stage coach standing or plying for passengers to be carried for hire at separate fares. (However, certain offences are common to hackney carriages and stage coaches. See later.)

Town Police Clauses Act 1889, s. 3, defines the term "omnibus" as including every char-a-banc, wagonette, stage coach and other carriage plying or standing for hire for passengers at separate fares within the district (tramcars and omnibuses used for certain specified purposes being excepted).

However, the Road Traffic Act 1960 has restricted the extent of these definitions, as under s. 117 any motor vehicle which either carries passengers at separate fares or which is adapted to carry 8 or more passengers is now a "public service vehicle", and as such it must be licensed by the Licensing Authority and not by the Local Authority (see "Public Service Vehicles"). Accordingly a motor vehicle to be a "hackney carriage" must be a vehicle adapted to carry less than 8 passengers, and the term "stage coach" is used as applying to animal-drawn vehicles carrying passengers at separate fares.

The Town Police Clauses Acts 1847 and 1889 apply only to hackney carriages (as now defined) and to horse-drawn and other non-mechanically propelled "omnibuses" which are here termed stage coaches.

Under these Town Police Clauses Acts (where they apply) it is necessary that the proprietors, the drivers and conductors, and the hackney carriages and stage coaches shall be licensed by the local council. The local council at its discretion may license such passengers and persons, and the proprietors, drivers and conductors must comply with the provisions of the Acts and of any byelaws made by the council for the regulation of such vehicles.

Such local byelaws usually prescribe rules for the conduct of the drivers and conductors, for the safety and comfort of the passengers, for the standing places allotted for the vehicles, and for the fares which may be charged. They also provide that property left in the vehicles by passengers should be brought to an office so that same may be regained by the owners and the authorised rewards recovered for the finders.

The Town Police Clauses Act 1847 creates certain offences as regards hackney carriages, and the Town Police Clauses Act 1889 directs that certain of the sections of the 1847 Act shall apply to "omnibuses", a term which covers stage coaches as defined above.

Therefore hackney carriage and stage coach offences under the Town Police Clauses Act 1847, include the following:

S. 45: Plying for hire with an unlicensed vehicle.

S. 46: Driver plying for hire without licence.

Ss. 51, 52: Number of persons to be carried must be displayed outside; no more need be carried and that number must be carried if required.

S. 54: Demanding more than the previously agreed fare.

S. 58: Taking more than the authorised fare.

S. 61: Driver being intoxicated while driving, or driver injuring or endangering any person or property by furious driving or any other wilful misconduct. See also Stage Carriage Act 1832, s. 48.

S. 62: Leaving vehicle unattended in street.

S. 64: Obstruction of the street or of any other carriage, or of the hiring of any other hackney carriage (or stage coach).

S. 66: Hirer refusing to pay the authorised fare.

The offences under the Town Police Clauses Act 1847 which are peculiar to hackney carriages include:

S. 53: Refusing, without reasonable excuse, to take a hirer or would-be hirer to any place within the district.

S. 55: Agreement to pay more than the legal fare is not binding, and any excess paid may be recovered and the driver punished.

S. 57: If driven to a place there to wait, the driver is entitled to his fare and a deposit for waiting, but if he then goes away or refuses to account for the deposit he commits an offence.

S. 59: No person may be carried without the express consent of the hirer.

Public Health Act 1936, ss. 159, 160. The person in charge of a public conveyance must have it disinfected after it has conveyed any person suffering from a notifiable disease.

Such person must not enter or be conveyed in a public conveyance carrying passengers at separate fares and need not be taken in any other public conveyance until the cost of disinfection is paid.

Vehicles (Excise) Act 1971, s. 38, defines hackney carriage as a mechanically propelled vehicle standing or plying for hire.

As no place is mentioned this definition covers a carriage standing or plying for hire in any yard, premises or other private place, as well as in any street. This definition is an excise definition for revenue purposes only. If such an excise "hackney carriage" is mechanically propelled and a less rate of duty has been paid on it because it is used for hire work, then, in addition to its registration marks it must carry a hackney carriage plate, as set out in Sched. 4, showing its seating capacity (Road Vehicles (R. & L. Regs. 1971 (41 and 42)). The fact that a vehicle has this excise "hackney carriage" licence and plate does not render it a hackney carriage competent to stand or ply for hire in a street in a district to which the Town Police Clauses Act 1847 applies. Standing or plying for hire in a street of such district is allowable only when the vehicle is specially licensed for the purpose by the local Council, and such a locally licensed vehicle should carry a plate, bearing its licence number, and its driver should carry a numbered badge, both provided by the Council. In such case the additional "hackney carriage" plate is not necessary. See also "Hackney Carriages—(Excise)", later in this Chapter.

Public Service Vehicles - R.T. Act 1960, Part III, deals with certain motor vehicles used in the service of the public in carrying passengers for hire, and such vehicles are termed public service vehicles.

CLASSIFICATION OF PUBLIC SERVICE VEHICLES – A public service vehicle is a motor vehicle used for carrying passengers for hire or reward which either (a) is carrying passengers at separate fares, or (b) is not carrying passengers at separate fares but is adapted to carry 8 or more passengers. "Motor vehicle" here does not include a tramcar or trolley vehicle.

A stage carriage is a public service vehicle carrying passengers at separate fares not being an express carriage.

An express carriage is a public service vehicle carrying passengers at separate fares none of which is less than [5p] or such greater sum as may be prescribed. For this purpose (a) a composite fare for more than one journey shall not be regarded as representing the aggregate of fares for any less amount, and (b) no account shall be taken of any fare which is charged in the case of passengers of particular descriptions if a fare of not less than [5p] or such greater sum as may for the time being be prescribed, is charged for the like service in the case of all passengers not falling within any of those descriptions. See also Transport Act 1968, s. 145.

A contract carriage is a public service vehicle not carrying passengers at separate fares (s. 117). The holder of the licence must keep a record and the driver carry a work ticket (Contract Carriage Records Regs. 1960).

CIRCUMSTANCES AFFECTING CLASSIFICATION OF PUBLIC SERVICE VEHICLES – By s. 118 and Sched. 12 a vehicle adapted to carry less than 8 passengers and carrying passengers at separate fares for race meetings, public gatherings, etc. (Part I), for certain journeys with 4 passengers or less (Part II), for overseas visitors (Part III) and under certain conditions (Part IV, all Parts of Sched. 12) shall not be treated as a public service vehicle. Also a public service vehicle carrying passengers at separate fares shall be treated as a "contract carriage" when used for overseas visitors (Part III) or under certain conditions (Part IV of Sched. 12). See also the provisions of the rest of s. 118 and the supplementary provisions of Part V of Sched. 12.

A vehicle carrying for hire or reward agricultural workers to or from work during the 6 months from June 1, shall be deemed not to be a public service vehicle (s. 118).

TRAFFIC AREAS AND TRAFFIC COMMISSIONERS – England, Wales and Scotland are divided into 11 traffic areas. Each traffic area has Traffic Commissioners who issue licences. These traffic areas (and their headquarters) are as follows: Northern (Newcastle-on-Tyne), Yorkshire (Leeds), North Western (Manchester), West Midland (Birmingham), East Midland (Nottingham), Eastern (Cambridge), South Wales (Cardiff), Western (Bristol),

South Eastern (London), Metropolitan (London), and Scotland (Edinburgh) (ss. 119 and 120).

PUBLIC SERVICE VEHICLE LICENCES – It is an offence for any person to cause or permit a motor vehicle to be used on any road as a stage carriage, express carriage or contract carriage unless he holds the appropriate public service licence for the vehicle.

A stage carriage licence authorises the holder to use the vehicle as an express or as a contract carriage.

An express carriage licence authorises the holder to use the vehicle as a contract carriage.

In the case of a service of stage carriages, an express carriage licence shall authorise the holder to use the vehicle on the service if the Traffic Commissioners for each of the traffic areas in which the vehicle is to be used consent in writing thereto.

Applications for these licences shall be made to the Traffic Commissioners for the traffic area within or from which the vehicle is intended to be ordinarily operated.

A public service vehicle licence may be refused, suspended or revoked if the Traffic Commissioners consider from the conduct of the person or the manner in which the vehicle is being used, that he is not a fit person to hold the licence. A public service vehicle licence will last one year from the date on which it takes effect, unless previously revoked, and if suspended it will be of no effect during the time of suspension. Such a licence is valid in every other traffic area (s. 127). See also Transport Act 1968, s. 35.

CERTIFYING OFFICERS AND P.S.V. EXAMINERS – For the certification of fitness of public service vehicles "certifying officers" may be appointed to examine vehicles and issue certificates of fitness. For the purpose of the inspection of public service vehicles examiners may be appointed. Arrangements may be made with any police authority for policemen to be appointed examiners, if the Secretary of State agrees. Any certifying officer or examiner, on production, if so required, of his authority may enter and inspect any public service vehicle, and for that purpose may require a public service vehicle to be stopped or may enter premises. Obstructing him or failing to so stop a vehicle is an offence (s. 128).

CERTIFICATES OF FITNESS AND THEIR EFFECT – A public service vehicle licence for a motor vehicle adapted to carry 8 or more passengers shall not be granted unless a "certificate of fitness" has been issued and is in force in respect to the vehicle.

The Minister of Transport and a certifying officer have power to revoke a certificate of fitness. If the certificate is revoked or if the vehicle ceases to be a vehicle in respect of which such a certificate is in force, its licence ceases to be of effect (s. 129).

P.S.V. (CONDITIONS OF FITNESS, EQUIPMENT AND USE) REGS. 1972 – A certificate of fitness shall not be issued unless the vehicle complies with the conditions prescribed in these Regulations. The conditions deal with the stability, suspension, turning circle, guard rails, side overhang, brakes, steering, hub projection, fuel tanks, carburettors, exhaust pipes, locking of nuts, electrical equipment, body, steps, platforms, stairs, entrances, exits, doors, gangways, seats, windows, markings, ventilation, driver's accommodation, windscreens and wipers, passengers' communication with driver, wireless apparatus, luggage racks, general construction, etc.

Name and address of licence holder shall be displayed on the near side of the vehicle (reg. 40).

Every P.S.V. shall carry suitable and efficient fire extinguishing apparatus which must be maintained in good working order (reg 41).

Every vehicle used as an express or contract carriage shall carry a suitable receptacle, easily accessible and properly marked, containing the prescribed first aid dressings which must be maintained in good condition (reg 42).

No person shall cause or permit any unnecessary obstruction to any entrance or exit, or gangway of the vehicle (reg. 43).

No person shall cause or permit any unnecessary obstruction of the driver (reg. 44).

The body etc. shall be kept clean and in good condition (reg. 5). The internal lamps shall be alight during the hours of darkness when passengers are carried (reg. 46).

Petrol tanks shall not be opened or filled while the engine is running (reg. 48). A conductor is neccessary on a stage carriage with a seating capacity for more than 20 passengers; but is not necessary on a single decked vehicle with a seating capacity for not more than 32, nor on any other vehicle if the traffic commissioner has certified that one is not necessary (reg. 49). No highly inflammable or dangerous substance shall be carried unless safely packed (reg. 50).

NOTICE OF FAILURE IN, DAMAGE OR ALTERATION TO P.S.V.'S – The holder of a public service vehicle licence must report to the Traffic Commissioners:

(a) of the area where it occurs, any failure of or damage to the vehicle calculated to affect the safety of the public;

(b) of the area in which licence was issued, any alteration of the vehicle (s. 132).

Failure to do so is an offence (s. 132).

SUSPENSION OF P.S.V. LICENCES FOR DEFECTS – If a certifying officer or examiner finds that a public service vehicle is or is likely to become unfit for service unless its defects are remedied, he may suspend the licence, and shall so notify the licensee and the

Traffic Commissioners which granted the licence. Suspension lasts until removed (s. 133).

ROAD SERVICE LICENCES – This is a licence allowing a person to provide such a road service as may be specified therein. A vehicle shall not be used as a stage carriage or an express carriage except under such a licence or under a permit granted under s. 30, Transport Act 1968 which deals with permits for certain bus services in lieu of road service licences.

It is an offence for any person to use or cause or permit to be used a vehicle in contravention of this section, or for the holder of a road service licence to wilfully or negligently fail to comply with any condition attached to his licence. A road service licence will be necessary in respect of any route (s. 134).

A road service licence is granted by the Traffic Commissioners for the area which embraces the proposed route, but it will not authorise the use of a vehicle as a stage carriage or express carriage in any other Traffic Commissioners' area unless it has been "backed". The Traffic Commissioners may attach to a road service licence such conditions as they may think fit, and may vary them from time to time. When a road service licence or permit is granted, the Commissioners shall send particulars to every chief officer of police and every local authority in whose district or area any such service is to be provided (s. 135).

The Traffic Commissioners may revoke or suspend a road service licence or permit for non-compliance with its conditions and if so shall notify the police and local authorities of the places concerned (s. 136).

BACKING OF ROAD SERVICE LICENCE – A road service licence granted for one traffic area may be backed by the Traffic Commissioners for another traffic area, and if so backed shall have effect as if it were a road licence granted by them. On backing a road service licence the Traffic Commissioners may impose any condition they might have imposed on granting the licence (s. 137). However, licences for "corridor areas" (where passengers are merely carried through another traffic area) need not be so backed (s. 138).

DURATION OF ROAD SERVICE LICENCE – Under s. 139, R.T. Act 1960, the Public Service Vehicles (Duration of Road Service Licences) Regs. 1937 and 1938 prescribe that the licence may be for one or more periods or occasions, or the date of its expiry may be fixed. It is usually 3 years.

PARTICULARS TO BE PROVIDED BY APPLICANTS FOR ROAD SERVICE LICENCES – Section 140 sets out the particulars which an applicant for and a holder of a road service licence must submit to the Traffic Commissioners. These include time-tables, fare-tables, agreements with other operators etc.

APPEALS IN CONNECTION WITH LICENCES AND CERTIFICATES FOR PUBLIC SERVICE VEHICLES – Section 143 gives a right of appeal to the Minister of Transport in connection with the refusal, granting, etc., of public service vehicle licences, road service licences and certificates of fitness.

PUBLIC SERVICE VEHICLES (LICENCES AND CERTIFICATES) REGS. 1952, 1957, 1960, 1961, 1962 AND 1969 – The holder of a road service licence, or backing or certificate is bound to produce it for examination at his principal place of business on request of any police officer, certifying officer, P.S.V. examiner or person authorised by the Commissioners (reg. 9).

The fee for a public service vehicle licence is [£12·50] (reg. 17). The licence shall be carried in a container on the left side of the vehicle or on the windscreen adjacent to the excise licence so as to be clearly legible (reg. 19). If the vehicle is let on hire and used as a stage or express carriage, there shall be a notice on the front or on the near side of the vehicle bearing the words "On hire to" and the name of the holder of the road service licence under which it is used (reg. 20).

The fee for a certificate of fitness is [£6·50] (reg. 24). Change of ownership does not render the certificate invalid (reg. 26).

An application for a road service licence or backing (to allow running in another traffic area) shall be accompanied by a notice giving the prescribed particulars of the service (reg. 39). This notice will be published in the "Notices and Proceedings" periodically issued by the Commissioners of the area, which also contains the dates and places of their public sittings to hear applications, and their decisions (reg. 41).

Objections to applications will be in writing, giving the grounds (reg. 43). The fee for the licence is £1 for each year or part of a year. If not for more than 3 days the fee is [10p] per day (reg. 44). The dates prescribed for the expiry of licences and backings are the last days of February, June and November (reg. 45). The Commissioners may vary conditions already imposed, on giving notice to persons affected (reg. 46). A special occasion service may be licensed (fee [25p]) (reg. 47). If the licensee ceases to operate the service he shall notify the Commissioners forthwith and return the licence (reg. 48).

DRIVERS' AND CONDUCTORS' LICENCES – R.T. Act 1960. A person shall not drive or act as conductor of a public service vehicle on a road unless he is duly licensed by the Traffic Commissioners. A person shall not employ any unlicensed person to drive or act as conductor of a public service vehicle on a road.

A person is disqualified for such a driver's licence until he is 21, and for such a conductor's licence until he is 18.

A driver's licence may be limited to such types of vehicles as may be specified in the licence.

A licence as driver or conductor may be suspended or revoked by the Authority who granted it if the holder is considered unfit to hold it by reason of his conduct or physical disability.

Any contravention of this section will be an offence.

Application for licence shall be made to the Authority of the area in which the applicant resides. It may last 3 years from the date on which it takes effect, unless previously revoked, and if suspended shall be of no effect during the time of suspension. It will be valid in every traffic area (s. 144).

DRIVERS' AND CONDUCTORS' LICENCES REGS. 1934, 1962 AND 1972 – An applicant shall supply the prescribed information, which includes a certificate of character and a medical certificate (reg. 5). The fee is [5p] per year (reg. 7). He shall immediately sign his licence with his ordinary signature (reg. 8), but shall write nothing else on it (reg. 9). A licensee shall notify any change of address within 7 days (reg. 10). He shall produce his licence, or give the address at which it will be available for the next 5 days, on request of any constable, certifying officer, public service vehicle or goods vehicle examiner or person duly authorised by the Licensing Authority (reg. 11).

He shall be issued a badge (the property of the Minister) bearing a distinguishing letter and number and shall wear it in a conspicuous position when acting as driver or conductor (reg. 14). If his licence is suspended or revoked he shall return the licence and badge (regs. 13, 15). He shall report any loss, defacement, etc., of his licence or badge (regs. 12, 17). He shall keep the badge in his possession and shall not cause or permit it to be worn by any other person (reg. 19).

An appeal to summary courts in connection with the refusal, revocation, suspension, etc., of drivers' and conductors' licences is permitted by s. 145.

REGULATION OF CONDUCT OF DRIVERS, CONDUCTORS AND PASSENGERS – Regulations as to the conduct of drivers and conductors may be made, and failure to comply with any of the provisions of the regulations is an offence. A court can order endorsement of the licence. The person who has custody of the licence, if required by the court, shall produce the licence within a reasonable time for endorsement, and failure to do so is an offence (s. 146).

Regulations may be made to provide generally as to the conduct of passengers in public service vehicles and a breach of these regulations is an offence (s. 147).

By the Public Service Vehicles (Arrest of Offenders) Act 1975, if a constable suspects with reasonable cause that a person has contravened or failed to comply with a provision of the regs. made under s. 147 R.T. Act 1960 (which relates to the conduct of passengers in P.S.V.s.), the constable may require the person to give his name and address to the constable; and if the person (a) refuses to do so, or (b) gives a name and address but does not answer to the satisfaction of the constable questions put to him by the constable for the purpose of ascertaining whether the name and address are correct, the constable may arrest him without a warrant.

CONDUCT OF DRIVERS, CONDUCTORS AND PASSENGERS REGS. 1936 to 1975 – A driver or conductor of a public service vehicle when acting as such, shall be civil, ensure the safety of passengers, correctly give the route, fare and destination, give his name and name and address of employer, and particulars of his licence to any constable or person having reasonable cause to ask for it, help any person having authority to examine the vehicles and shall not smoke in the vehicle on the journey or when passengers are on board (reg. 4).

A driver when driving shall not talk with the conductor or other persons unless for safety reasons. This shall not apply to any communication by the driver with an authorised person on operational matters or in an emergency by means of wireless telegraphy apparatus (reg. 5). A conductor shall enforce the regulations relating to the conduct of passengers, see that the route, fare and destination notices are properly displayed, and shall not talk to the driver, except to stop the vehicle (reg. 6).

A driver of a stage or express carriage shall, when he stops, stop the vehicle close to the left of the road and must not stop there unreasonably long (reg. 7). A conductor of a stage or express carriage shall not delay unreasonably in signalling to the driver to start (reg. 8).

Public Service Vehicles: A passenger or intending passenger shall not be disorderly, enter or alight save by the doors provided, impede passengers wilfully and unreasonably, enter or remain when told not to do so because the vehicle is full or not allowed to pick up there, travel on the upper deck unless occupying a seat, travel in any part which is not for passengers, wilfully interfere with the vehicle or with any person, distract the driver's attention save to stop the vehicle, signal the vehicle to start, damage or soil the vehicle, distribute in the vehicle any printed, etc., matter or advertising articles, wilfully interfere with any notice on the vehicle, use any noisy instrument in the vehicle or make excessive noise, throw money, bottles, litter, etc., out of the vehicle, throw out any article, flag, streamer, etc., overhanging the road, or obstruct any person in the course of his duty (reg. 9).

Stage and Express Carriages: A passenger or intending passenger shall not smoke where smoking is prohibited or sell any article in the vehicle (reg. 9). If his condition or clothing is offensive he shall not enter or remain in the vehicle after an authorised person has requested him to leave and tendered his fare if previously paid.

He shall not have loaded firearms or any dangerous or offensive article, and requires the consent of an authorised person to have any bulky or cumbersome article. He shall not bring in any animal without the consent of an authorised person, or retain it after request to remove it (reg. 10).

(a) No passenger on a stage or express carriage shall use or attempt to use in relation to the journey which he is taking or intending to take—

(i) any ticket which has been altered or defaced; or

(ii) any ticket which has been issued to another person if such ticket bears thereon an indication that it is not transferable; or

(iii) without reasonable excuse, any period or season ticket which has expired.

(b) Every passenger on a stage or express carriage shall—

(i) declare, if so requested by the driver or the conductor, the journey he has taken or intends to take;

(ii) where the vehicle is being operated by a driver without a conductor, immediately on boarding the vehicle, unless otherwise directed by an authorised person or by notice displayed on the vehicle, pay to the driver the fare for the journey he intends to take, or insert in any fare collection equipment provided on the vehicle coins of such denominations as may be required to pay that fare, and where the vehicle is not being so operated, if so requested by the conductor, pay the fare for the journey he intends to take or has taken, and in either case accept any ticket provided therefor:

Provided that this sub-paragraph shall not apply if the passenger is already the holder of a ticket in respect of the journey he intends to take or has taken and he complies with any directions on the ticket or by notice on the vehicle or given by an authorised person, as to the inspection, perforation, endorsement or cancellation of the ticket by such person;

(iii) produce his ticket, if any, when required to do so by an authorised person or, if he fails to produce his ticket, pay, by whichever of the means specified in sub-paragraph (ii) of this paragraph is appropriate, the fare for the journey he intends to take or has taken;

(iv) on completion of the journey for which he has paid the fare leave the vehicle if so requested by the driver or the conductor or pay, by whichever of the means specified in sub-paragraph (ii) of this paragraph is appropriate, the fare for any journey which he takes or intends to take on the vehicle by way of continuation of that journey, or, where so directed by an authorised person or by a notice on the vehicle, pay the fare for that further journey on leaving the vehicle;

(v) on demand by an authorised person surrender on completion of the journey any ticket issued to him in respect of the journey;

(vi) on demand by an authorised person surrender any period or season ticket held by him at the expiry of the period for which it was issued to him.

(c) No passenger shall without reasonable excuse leave or attempt to leave a stage or express carriage without having paid the fare for the journey he has taken. (reg. 11).

An employee of the licensee is an "authorised person" (reg. 2).

GENERAL POWERS – Any passenger reasonably suspected of contravening these regulations shall give his name and address to the driver or conductor or to a constable, on demand. Any passenger contravening these regulations may be removed from the vehicle by the driver or conductor, or on request of the driver or conductor by any constable (reg. 12).

CONTROL OF NUMBER OF PASSENGERS – The Public Service Vehicles and Trolley Vehicles (Carrying Capacity) Regs. 1954, direct that the seating capacity of such vehicles shall be clearly marked either inside and visible from outside or on the rear or near side of the vehicle (reg. 8).

The number of seated passengers shall not exceed the fixed carrying capacity (but if only children up to 15 and their attendants up to 6 persons are carried 3 children will count as 2 passengers except in certain 12-seater vehicles where only up to 9 children may be so counted) and no standing passengers may be carried, except where it is allowed by the following Regulations (reg. 3).

During peak traffic or to avoid hardship a stage carriage or trolley vehicle may carry standing passengers on the lower deck of a double decker or on a single decker, up to one third of the seating capacity on the deck, or 8, whichever number is the less (reg. 4).

The Licensing Authority may authorise an express carriage to carry some standing passengers (reg. 5).

No standing passengers shall be carried on a half decked vehicle or on the upper deck of a double decker or if there is any vacant seat or unless a conductor is carried, or on a public service vehicle with a seating capacity not exceeding 12 in respect of which the first certificate of fitness was issued on or after April 11, 1958.

However the Licensing Authority may certify that a conductor is not required on a particular service (reg. 7 as amended by 1958 and 1966 Regs.).

If a person contravenes, or fails to comply with a provision of the above regulations, he shall be guilty of an offence (s. 148).

RECORDS OF LICENCES OF PUBLIC SERVICE VEHICLES – The police and local authority are authorised to inspect, without payment, the record of all licences which shall be kept by the Public Service Vehicles (Records of Licences) Regs. 1933, and to take copies or extracts therefrom. Certified copies of entries made in this record are admissible in evidence (s. 156). This also applies to permits issued under Transport Act 1968, s. 30.

RETURNS TO BE PROVIDED BY OPERATORS OF PUBLIC SERVICE VEHICLES – It shall be the duty of a person carrying on the business of operating public service vehicles to keep such accounts and records as the Minister may require, and failure to comply is an offence (s. 157).

FURTHER PUBLIC SERVICE VEHICLE REGULATIONS – The following further Public Service Vehicle Regs. deal with the matters indicated by their descriptive titles, and prescribe the fine for contraventions:

LOST PROPERTY REGS. 1934, 1958, 1960 – Any person who finds property accidentally left in a public service vehicle shall immediately hand it to the conductor (or driver if no conductor) (reg. 4). The conductor shall search his vehicle for left property before or at the end of any journey. Within 24 hours he shall hand any such property to the operator of the service, or if he is going off duty, to his relief conductor, who has the like responsibility. However, if claimed by a person who satisfies the conductor that he is the owner, it shall be returned to such person forthwith without fee or reward and the conductor shall report the facts to the operator (reg. 5).

Particulars of any found property shall reach the operator within 2 days and he shall keep a record of same, available at all reasonable times for inspection by the police and Licensing Authority (reg. 6). The operator is responsible for safe custody of such property, and if the name and address of the owner is readily ascertainable he should be notified by the operator (reg. 7).

Unclaimed property, after 3 months, vests in the operator, who may give it to the conductor or sell it (reg. 8). If such property is returned to the owner he shall pay the operator a fee of 5p, and if the value exceeds 10p, an additional sum ($\frac{1}{12}$ of the value and not exceeding £4) as a reward to be paid to the conductor (reg. 9) into whose possession the property first came (reg. 11).

The operator, after 48 hours, may destroy or sell perishable unclaimed property, and may at any time dispose of objectionable property (reg. 10). The operator has the right to open bags, packages, etc., so as to trace the identity of owners or to ascertain the contents (reg. 13). If property is claimed the operator may require the claimant to open the package, etc., and submit the contents for examination (reg. 14). Contravention of or failure to comply with the regulations is a summary offence, fine not exceeding £5 (reg. 15).

RESTRICTION OF INSTITUTION OF PROCEEDINGS – Except in the case of a breach of the Regulations as to the Conduct of Passengers in public service vehicles (s. 147) and the regulations for the control of the number of passengers (s. 148) proceedings for an offence under ss. 117 to 163 shall not in England and Wales be instituted except (a) by or on behalf of the Director of Public Prosecutions, or (b) by a person authorised in that behalf by the Traffic Commissioners, a chief officer of police or the council of a county, county borough or county district. But proceedings for an offence, by or on behalf of the Minister, may be taken for an offence under s. 157 (accounts, records and returns) (s. 161).

Goods Vehicles – The law relating to the regulation of the carriage of goods by road is contained in the Transport Act 1968, Part V. No person shall use a goods vehicle on a road for the carriage of goods: (a) for hire or reward; or (b) for or in connection with any trade or business carried on by him, except under an "operator's licence" (s. 60 (1)). The above does not apply (a) to the use of a small goods vehicle, or (b) to the use of a vehicle of any class scheduled in Regs. (s. 60 (2)). The performance by a local or public authority of their functions constitutes the carrying on of a business (s. 60 (3)).

A "small goods vehicle" is a goods vehicle which (a) does not form part of a vehicle combination and has a plated weight not exceeding 3½ tons or (not having a relevant plated weight) has an unladen weight not exceeding 30 cwts; or (b) forms part of a vehicle combination (not being an articulated combination) which is such that (i) the aggregate of the relevant plated weights of the vehicles comprised in the combination (exclusive of any small trailers) does not exceed 3½ tons; (ii) or the aggregate of the unladen weights (exclusive of any small trailer) does not exceed 30 cwts; or (c) forms part of an articulated combination which is such that (i) the aggregate of the unladen weight of the motor vehicle in the combination and the relevant plated weight of the trailer does not exceed 3½ tons; or (ii) the aggregate of the unladen weights of the motor vehicle and the trailer does not exceed 30 cwts (s. 60 (4)).

The "relevant plated weight" of a vehicle for the purpose of this section is the "gross weight" shown on a ministry plate (if one has been issued) or the maximum gross weight of the vehicle as shown on a plate affixed to the vehicle by virtue of reg. 30, C. & U. Regs. 1969.

A "small trailer" means a trailer having an unladen weight not exceeding 1 ton.

THE GOODS VEHICLES (OPERATORS' LICENCES) REGS. 1969 – These provide that s. 60 (1) above shall not apply to the following vehicles:

(1) tractors, ploughing machines and other agricultural engines used for agricultural and similar purposes;
(2) dual purpose vehicles;
(3) those used between neighbouring premises;

(4) P.S.V.s and any trailer drawn thereby;
(5) those used solely for carriage of not more than 15 passengers when drawing a trailer;
(6) a hackney carriage when used as such;
(7) a vehicle used for funerals;
(8) a vehicle used for police, fire brigade or ambulance purposes;
(9) a vehicle used for miners' rescue operations;
(10) vehicles without permanent bodies and on test, etc.;
(11) or used under a trade licence,
(12) or hired for armed or visiting forces;
(13) trailers used for road works;
(14) a road roller and its trailer;
(15) a vehicle used for lifeboat purposes;
(16) a vehicle with plant;
(17) a vehicle used by a local authority for road cleansing, watering, snow clearing, disposal of refuse, weights and measures or sale of food and drugs purposes, or distributing grit, salt, etc. on roads;
(18) a vehicle used for civil defence purposes;
(19) or one used by highway authorities for weighing vehicles;
(20) tower wagons and their trailers;
(21) vehicles carrying goods within an aerodrome;
(22) an electrically propelled vehicle;
(23) a showman's vehicle and its trailer (reg. 3 and Sched. 1).

These Regs. also govern the procedure for applying for licences; the publication of a periodical statement called "Applications and Decisions" (reg. 7); the identification of authorised vehicles (reg. 11), and the production of licences (reg. 14). There shall be an identity disc issued in respect of each vehicle authorised under an "operator's licence". The holder of the licence shall cause the "identity disc" to be affixed to the vehicle in a waterproof container, in a conspicuous place on the left or near side of the vehicle. The identity disc must at all times be readily legible (reg. 11).

The holder of a licence shall produce it for examination, if required to do so, by any police constable, any certifying officer or examiner, or by any person authorised by the licensing authority, and may elect to do so at his operating centre, head office or principal place of business (reg. 14).

The Goods Vehicles (Operator's Licences) (Temporary Use in Great Britain) Regs. 1975, exempt operators of foreign goods vehicles brought temporarily to Great Britain from the need to obtain an operator's licence under Part V of the Transport Act 1968.

Drivers' Hours – Part VI of the Transport Act 1968 is designed to secure the observance of proper hours of work by persons engaged in the carriage of passengers or goods by road, thus protecting the public from the risks of drivers suffering from fatigue (s. 95 (1)). The above applies to (a) passenger vehicles, i.e. (i) P.S.V.s; and (ii) motor vehicles (other than P.S.V.s) constructed or adapted to carry more than 12 passengers; (b) goods vehicles, i.e. (i) heavy and light locomotives, motor tractors and any articulated motor vehicle; and (ii) motor vehicles (other than those mentioned in para. (a) of this subsection) constructed or adapted to carry goods other than the effects of passengers (s. 90 (2)). References to a "driver" includes both an "employee-driver" and an "owner-driver" (s. 96 (2)).

The permitted driving time and periods of duty of drivers are provided for in s. 96, but subject to the Drivers' Hours (Goods Vehicles) (Modifications) Order 1970 (S.I. 1970 No. 257) and the Drivers' Hours (Passenger Vehicles) (Modifications) Order 1970 (S.I. 1970 No. 356), and the Drivers' Hours (Passenger and Goods Vehicles) (International Rules) Regs. 1973 (S.I. 1973, 379). For the purpose of enabling drivers to deal with cases of emergency or otherwise to meet a special need, the Secretary of State has made the Drivers' Hours (Goods Vehicles) (Exemption) Regs. 1972 (S.I. 1972 No. 574); and also the Drivers' Hours (Passenger Vehicles) (Exemptions) Regs. 1970 (S.I. 1970 No. 145) and (Amendment) Regs. 1970 (S.I. 1970 No. 649).

RECORDS OF HOURS OF WORK, ETC – The Secretary of State under powers given by the Transport Act 1968, s. 98, has made the Drivers' Hours (Goods Vehicles) (Keeping of Records) Regs. 1970 (S.I.1970 No. 123) and the Drivers' Hours (Passenger and Goods Vehicles) (Keeping of Records) (International Rules) Regs. 1973 (S.I. 1973 No. 380). These provide that drivers of goods vehicles must keep a current record of the prescribed information in their drivers' record books, and employers are required to cause drivers to keep such a record. The employer must keep a record of record books issued to drivers. The Regs. prescribe the form of drivers' record books and the manner of keeping them, and require a completed record book to be returned to the employer. Drivers must have their record books with them while on duty.

Completed record books and registers must be preserved for 6 months or longer if the Chief Officer of Police or licensing authority so directs. Drivers of certain vehicles are exempted from keeping a current record, e.g. drivers of Crown vehicles.

It is an offence to contravene any regulations which require drivers to keep, and employers to cause to be kept, in such books as may be specified in regulations relevant to the enforcement of Part VI (Drivers' Hours) of the Transport Act 1968 (s. 98). An officer (including a police officer) may require any person to produce and permit him to inspect and copy any such document, book, or record. Any person who makes or causes to be made, any entry in any such book, etc., which he knows to be false or, with intent to deceive alters or causes to be altered any such record or entry, commits an offence, and if an officer has reason to believe that any such offence has been committed he may seize that record or book (s. 99). This part of the Act does not apply in the case of motor vehicles while being used for police or fire brigade purposes (s. 102).

MAINTENANCE OF GOODS VEHICLES – "Examiners" shall be appointed to see that goods vehicles are maintained in a fit and serviceable condition and to secure the observance of the provisions of Part II of R.T. Act 1972, except s. 59, and Part V of the Transport Act 1968. An examiner may enter and inspect any goods vehicle and for that purpose may detain the vehicle, and he may at any time which is reasonable, enter any premises on which he has reason to believe that a goods vehicle is kept. It will be an offence to obstruct him in the performance of his duty (R.T. Act 1972, s. 56).

DEFINITIONS – "Authorised vehicle" means, in relation to an operator's licence, a vehicle authorised to be used thereunder, whether or not it is for the time being in use for a purpose for which a carrier's licence is required and whether it is specified therein as so authorised, or being of a type so authorised subject to a maximum number, is in the possession of the holder of the licence under an agreement for hire or loan, or, if a trailer, belongs to him or is in his possession under an agreement for hire purchase, hire or loan.

"Carriage of goods" includes the haulage of goods. Therefore, the Act applies to locomotives and tractors.

"goods" includes goods or burden of any description.

"goods vehicle" means a motor vehicle constructed or adapted for use for the carriage of goods, or a trailer so constructed or adapted (s. 196).

"tramcar" includes any carriage used on any road by virtue of an order made under the Light Railways Act 1896.

"trolley vehicle" means a mechanically propelled vehicle adapted for use upon roads without rails and moved by power transmitted thereto from some external source (R.T. Act 1972, s. 196).

Motor vehicle is a carriage.—A motor vehicle or trailer shall be deemed to be a carriage within the meaning of any Act, and of any rule, regulation or byelaw made under any Act, and if used as a carriage of any particular class shall for the purpose of any enactment relating to carriages of any particular class be deemed to be a carriage of that class (R.T. Act 1972, s. 195).

Thus generally speaking, all road vehicles are carriages and owners and drivers have to comply with the law dealing with carriages, as well as to obey the particular rules affecting the class of vehicle they own or drive.

LICENSING OF DRIVERS OF HEAVY GOODS VEHICLES – A person shall not drive a heavy goods vehicle of any class on a road unless he holds a licence (which remains in force for 3 years) for that purpose, and a person shall not employ another person to drive a heavy goods vehicle of any class on a road unless that other person is the holder of a licence for that purpose (R.T. Act 1972, s. 112).

"Heavy goods vehicle" means a vehicle of any of the following classes which is constructed or adapted for hauling or carrying goods or burden of any description, that is to say, a heavy locomotive, a light locomotive, a motor tractor, a heavy motor car and a motor car so constructed that a trailer may by partial superimposition be attached thereto in such a manner as to cause a substantial part of the weight of the trailer to be borne thereby (s. 124).

The licensing authority shall not grant a full licence to drive a heavy goods vehicle of any class unless he is satisfied that the applicant for the licence (a) has at some time during the period of five years ending on the date of the coming into force of the licence passed the prescribed test of competence to drive vehicles of that class; or (b) has within that period held a full licence authorising the driving of vehicles of that class (s. 114 (1)).

For the purpose of enabling an applicant to learn to drive a heavy goods vehicle with a view to passing the prescribed test of competence to drive, the licensing authority may issue to him a heavy goods vehicle driver's licence as a provisional licence (s. 114 (2)).

A licence issued by virtue of sub-s. (2) above or a full licence granted to an applicant who is under 21 on the date of the application shall be subject to the prescribed conditions, and if the person to whom it is issued fails to comply with any of the conditions he shall be guilty of an offence (s. 114 (3)).

It shall be an offence for a person to employ another person who is under 21 to drive a h.g.v. of any class in contravention of any prescribed conditions subject to which that other person's licence is issued (s.114 (4) added by R.T. Act 1974, s. 15).

Proceedings for an offence under s. 112 or 114 (3) of this Act shall not, in England or Wales, be instituted except by or on behalf of the Director of Public Prosecutions or by a person authorised in that behalf by the traffic commissioners, a chief officer of police or the council of a county or county district (s. 123).

THE HEAVY GOODS VEHICLES (DRIVERS' LICENCES) REGS. 1975, – Every person to whom a heavy goods vehicles driver's licence is granted shall forthwith sign it in ink with his usual signature (reg. 7). Failure to comply is an offence (reg. 27).

A full standard licence to drive any class of heavy goods vehicles shall also be treated for the purposes of Part IV of R.T.

Act of 1972 as a provisional standard licence to drive heavy goods vehicles of any other class which the holder is not prohibited under s. 4 of the Act of 1972 by reason of his age from driving (reg.9 (1)). In applying the provisions of paragraph (1) above the effect of the Motor Vehicles (Minimum Age for Driving (Amendment) Regulations 1975 shall be disregarded (reg. 9 (1A)).

Subject to para. (3) of this regulation, a provisional standard licence, including a full standard licence which is treated as a provisional standard licence under the foregoing paragraph, shall be subject to the following conditions, that is to say the holder shall not drive a heavy goods vehicle of any class which he may drive by virtue of the provisional standard licence: (a) otherwise than under the supervision of a person who is present with him in the vehicle and who holds a full standard licence to drive that class of vehicle; (b) unless there is clearly displayed in a conspicuous manner on the front and on the back of the vehicle a distinguishing mark in the form of a red "L" on white ground surmounted by letters HGV in red on white ground; (c) which is being used to draw a trailer, except where the trailer is part of an articulated vehicle being driven by the holder (reg. 9 (2)). Failure to comply is an offence (reg. 27).

The condition specified in para. 2 (a) of this regulation shall not apply whilst the holder of a provisional standard licence is undergoing a test and none of the conditions specified in para. 2 shall apply in relation to the driving of a h.g.v. of any class where the holder of the licence has passed a test for a vehicle of that class (reg. 9 (3)).

The new Regulation 9A (H.G.V. Trainee Drivers' Licences) sets out the conditions to which all h.g.v. trainee drivers' licences are subject make provision for h.g.v. drivers' provisional licences and for the further conditions applicable to such licences and enables a h.g.v. trainee drivers' full licence for one class of heavy goods vehicle to be treated as a provisional licence for another class of such vehicles.

Subject to para. (6) of this regulation, any such person as follows, that is to say: (a) the driver of a heavy goods vehicle on a road, or (b) a person who supervises the holder of a provisional licence, while the holder is driving a heavy goods vehicle on a road, shall, on being so required by a police constable or an examiner appointed under R.T. Act 1972, s. 56, produce his h.g.v. driver's licence for examination, so as to enable the constable or examiner to ascertain the name and address of the holder of the h.g.v. driver's licence, the date of issue, and the authority by which it was issued, and shall, on being so required by an examiner as aforesaid, give his name and address and acknowledge that such information as recorded by the examiner on the examiner's record sheet is correct by signing the said record sheet (reg. 14 (1)).

Subject to para. (6) of this regulation, any such person as follows, that is say:

(a) a person whom a police constable has reasonable cause to believe to have been the driver of a heavy goods vehicle at a time when an accident occurred owing to its presence on a road, or

(b) a person whom a police constable has reasonable cause to believe to have committed an offence in relation to the use of a heavy goods vehicle on a road, or

(c) a person whom a constable has reasonable cause to believe was supervising the holder of a provisional licence while driving a h.g.v. at a time when an accident occurred owing to the presence of the vehicle on a road, or at a time when an offence is suspected of having been committed by the said holder in relation to the use of the vehicle on a road,

shall, on being so required by a police constable, produce his h.g.v. driver's licence for examination so as to enable the constable to ascertain the name and address of the holder of the h.g.v. driver's licence, the date of issue, and the authority by whom it was issued (reg. 14 (2)).

Subject to para. (6) of this regulation, where a h.g.v. driver's licence has been suspended or revoked by a licensing authority, then if the holder of the h.g.v. driver's licence fails to deliver it to that authority for endorsement or cancellation as required by reg. 10 (1) of these Regulations, a police constable or an examiner appointed under R.T. Act 1972, s. 56 may require him to produce it, and upon its being produced may seize it and deliver it for endorsement or cancellation to that authority (reg. 14 (3)).

Subject to para. (6) below, where a Northern Ireland h.g.v. driver's licence has been suspended or revoked by a licensing authority, then if the holder of the licence fails to deliver it to that authority as required by reg. 10 (3) a constable or an examiner may require him to produce it, and upon its being produced may seize it and deliver it to that authority (reg. 14 (4)).

Subject to para. (6) of this regulation, where a police constable or an examiner appointed under s. R.T. Act 1972, s. 56 has resonable cause to believe that the person to whom a licence has been granted, or any other person, has knowingly made a false statement for the purpose of obtaining the grant of the h.g.v. driver's licence, the police constable or examiner may require the holder of the h.g.v. driver's licence to produce it to him (reg. 14 (5)).

If any person is unable to produce his h.g.v. driver's licence when required to do so in accordance with any of the foregoing paragraphs of this regulation, it shall be a sufficient compliance with that paragraph if: (a) in a case where the h.g.v. driver's licence was required by a police constable to be produced, within five days after the production of his h.g.v. driver's licence was so required he produces the h.g.v. driver's licence in person for examination for the same purposes at such police station as may have been specified by him at the time its production was required, or (b) in a case where the h.g.v. driver's licence was required by an examiner appointed under R.T. Act 1972, s. 56, to be produced, within 10 days after the production of his h.g.v. driver's licence was so required it is produced for examination for the same purposes at the office of such examiner or such licensing authority as may have been specified by him at the time its production was required (reg. 14 (6)).

The holder of a h.g.v. driver's licence shall, upon being required to do so by a licensing authority cause his h.g.v. driver's licence or his licence granted under Part III of the Act of 1972 to be produced to that authority within 10 days after the day on which the requirement was made (reg. 14 (7)). Failure to comply is an offence (reg. 27).

Mechanically Propelled Vehicles – The Road Vehicles (Registration and Licensing) Regs. 1971, contain the following definitions of mechanically propelled vehicles:

"Bicycle" means a mechanically propelled bicycle (including a motor scooter, a bicycle with attachment for propelling it mechanically and a motor bicycle used for drawing a trailer or sidecar) not exceeding 8 cwts. unladen.

"Invalid vehicle" means a mechanically propelled vehicle (including a cycle with attachment for propelling it mechanically) not exceeding 8 cwts unladen, and adapted and used for an invalid or invalids.

"Owner" as regards a vehicle means the person by whom the vehicle is kept.

"Pedestrian controlled vehicle" means a mechanically propelled vehicle with 3 or more wheels, not exceeding 8 cwts. unladen and neither made nor adapted for use nor used for the carriage of a driver or passenger.

"Tricycle" means a mechanically propelled tricycle (including a motor scooter and a tricycle with attachment for mechanical propulsion) not exceeding 8 cwts. unladen and not being a pedestrian controlled vehicle.

"Works truck" means a mechanically propelled vehicle designed for use in private premises and used on a road only in delivering goods from or to such premises to or from a vehicle on a road in the immediate neighbourhood, or in passing from one part of any such premises to another or to other private premises in the immediate neighbourhood or in connection with road works while at or in the immediate neighbourhood of the site of such works (reg. 3).

1. Registration and Licensing of Vehicles – Under the Vehicles (Excise) Act 1971, all mechanically propelled vehicles used or kept on a public road (that is a road repairable at the public expense—s. 38) except those vehicles specially exempted, must pay excise duties. These duties are to be paid on licences to be taken out by the persons keeping them (s. 1). A person keeps such a vehicle on a public road if he causes it to be on such a road for any period, however short, when it is not in use there (s. 38 (2)). A licence may be taken out for any period of 12 months, or 4 months if rate of duty exceeds £8 per annum. Authorised trade goods vehicles exceeding 11 tons weight unladen may have "seven day" road fund licences (s. 2). Vehicle excise duties are to be levied by the Secretary of State (s. 3). It is an excise offence for any person to use or keep on a public road any such vehicle for which a licence is not in force (s. 8). Every person applying for such licence must make a declaration and furnish the prescribed particulars. The licence is issued for the vehicle specified in the application and does not entitle the licensee to use any other vehicle (s. 12). The holder of a licence can surrender it and claim a refund of duty (s. 17).

When a licence has been taken out for a vehicle, and the vehicle is used in an altered condition or in a manner or for a purpose which renders it chargeable for a higher rate of duty the person so using such vehicle is liable to an excise penalty (s. 18). On the first issue of such a licence the Secretary of State must register the vehicle and assign it a registration mark (s. 19).

It is a summary offence to supply false or misleading particulars in any declaration for a vehicle licence or a trade licence or in any notification relating to it or to the keeper of a vehicle. It is also a summary offence to forge, fraudulently alter or use, or fraudulently lend or allow to be used by any other person any identification mark, trade plates or licence or registration document under the Act (s. 26). An "expired licence" is still a licence for the purposes of this section (*Taylor* v. *Emerson* (1962)).

Where it is alleged that a motor vehicle has been used or kept on a public road contrary to the provisions of ss. 8, 16 (7) and 18 (4), the person keeping shall give any information required by police or the Secretary of State as to the driver and any person using or keeping the vehicle, and any other person if so required shall give any information he can give as to the identity of any person using or keeping the vehicle. Failure to comply with the above will be a summary offence (s. 27).

THE ROAD VEHICLES (REGISTRATION AND LICENSING) REGULATIONS 1971, 1972 AND 1973 further provide:

A person who keeps a mechanically propelled vehicle and desires to obtain a licence for it shall apply to the Secretary of State not more than 14 days before the licence is to have effect.

Such person shall send with his application (comprising the prescribed declaration and prescribed particulars) any other document which he may be required to produce, (e.g. test certificate, evidence of insurance or security) the registration book, where one has been issued, and the amount of duty payable (reg. 4).

If a licence or registration book is lost, destroyed, mutilated, defaced or becomes illegible, or the colour of the licence has faded, the owner must apply to the Secretary of State for a duplicate. Where a duplicate has been issued to replace a lost registration book, and the book is found later on, the owner must take all reasonable steps to regain it and return it to the Secretary of State (reg. 6).

No person shall alter, deface, mutilate or add anything to a licence, or exhibit such a licence or a licence upon which the figures or particulars have become illegible or the colour has faded. No person shall exhibit anything which is intended to be or could be mistaken for a licence (reg. 7).

Before issuing a registration book or a duplicate, the Secretary of State may require proof that the vehicle accords with the declaration made. The book must be produced at any reasonable time for inspection by a police officer or a person acting on behalf of the Secretary of State. The Secretary of State may require the surrender of a registration book for correction if it contains incorrect particulars. No person, other than a person acting on behalf of the Secretary of State shall deface or mutilate any registration book or alter or obliterate any entry (reg. 8).

The registration mark assigned to a vehicle shall remain the registration mark of that vehicle until the vehicle is broken up, destroyed or sent permanently out of Great Britain (reg. 9).

If any alteration, other than an alteration mentioned in reg. 11 is made to a vehicle which affects the registration particulars, the owner shall notify the Secretary of State and send his registration book for amendment. If it affects the licence, the licence should be sent to the Secretary of State for an amended licence (reg. 10).

If the character or use of a vehicle is altered so as to render a higher rate of duty payable, the owner must make a fresh declaration and send it with the licence and registration book to the Secretary of State (reg. 11).

On a change of ownership of a vehicle, the previous owner must give the registration book to the new owner and may deliver to him any current licence. He must notify in writing the change of ownership to the Secretary of State. Upon acquiring the vehicle the new owner shall: (a) if he intends to use or keep the vehicle upon public roads, (other than under a trade licence) forthwith insert his name and address in the registration book and deliver it to the Secretary of State; (b) if he does not intend to use or keep the vehicle upon public roads, forthwith notify in writing the Secretary of State of the change of ownership; (c) if he intends to use the vehicle upon public roads solely under a trade licence, notify in writing the change of ownership to the Secretary of State at the expiration of 3 months unless in the meantime there has been a further change of ownership when notification must be made on that date (reg. 12).

On a change of address the owner must enter his new address in the registration book and send the book to the Secretary of State (reg. 13).

Where a vehicle is broken up, destroyed, or sent permanently out of Great Britain the owner must notify the Secretary of State and send him the registration book (reg. 14).

The Secretary of State on request by a local authority for any purpose connected with the investigation of an offence, or by or on behalf of a chief officer of police, shall supply full particulars of any vehicle registered with the Secretary of State free of charge, and shall supply to any person showing reasonable cause the name and address of the owner and the particulars of the last licence—25p fee (reg. 15).

2. Exhibition of Licences and Registration Marks – Under the Vehicles Excise Act 1971, any person who uses or keeps on a public road any mechanically propelled vehicle on which duty under this Act is chargeable, without there being fixed to and exhibited on that vehicle in the prescribed manner the vehicle Licence (formerly called the Road Fund Licence), commits an offence (s. 12).

The registration mark assigned to a vehicle shall be fixed in the prescribed manner on the vehicle, or on any other vehicle drawn by that vehicle, or on both (s. 19). If this mark is not so fixed, or if, being so fixed it is in any way obscured or rendered or allowed to become not easily distinguishable, the driver or where the vehicle is not being driven, the person keeping the vehicle is liable to summary fine. However, the person charged with obscuring, etc., such mark is not liable to conviction if he proves he has taken all reasonable steps to prevent it being obscured. Also, a driver is not liable to the penalty if he proves he had no reasonable opportunity of registering the vehicle and was driving it on a public road for the purpose of registering it (s. 22).

THE ROAD VEHICLES (REGISTRATION AND LICENSING) REGULATIONS 1971–1973 provide that every licence issued and in force for a mechanically propelled vehicle (except a tramcar) shall be fixed to and exhibited on the vehicle at all times while the vehicle is being used or kept on a public road. However, when a licence is delivered to a post office with an application for a new licence, no licence shall be displayed on the vehicle until the new licence is obtained.

Each such licence shall be fixed to the vehicle in a holder sufficient to protect the licence from the weather.

Position of licence:

(1) Invalid vehicle, tricycle or bicycle, other than those mentioned in (2) and (3) below—on near side in front of driving seat.
(2) Bicycle drawing a side-car or to which a side-car is attached when kept on a public road—on near side of handlebars or on nearside of side-car in front of the driving seat.
(3) Any vehicle with glass windscreen in front of the driver extending across the vehicle to its nearside—on or adjacent to nearside lower corner of the windscreen.
(4) Any other vehicle, if the vehicle is fitted with a driver's cab with a nearside window, on such window, or on nearside in front of the driver's seat or towards the front of a pedestrian controlled vehicle and between 2 ft. 6 ins. and 6 ft. above the road.

It must be clearly visible by daylight from the nearside of the road (reg. 16).

The size, shape and character of any registration mark shall be in accordance with the provisions of Sched. 2 of the Regs. (reg. 17).

Part I contains diagrams showing arrangement of registration marks, viz., the index letters followed or preceded by registration figures, or followed or preceded by registration figures and a letter to indicate the year of registration. The registration mark may be so constructed that it can be illuminated from behind by the translucency of the letters and figures. If so, it shall be formed of white letters and figures upon a black surface, and when illuminated they must appear white against a black background.

If the registration mark is not so constructed, it shall be formed of white, silver or light grey letters and figures on a black surface and indelibly inscribed on or so attached as not to be readily detachable. A flat plate of cast or pressed metal having raised letters and figures may be used.

Reflex-reflecting number plates as an alternative to the other types are permissible. A front plate shall be of black letters and figures against a white background of reflex-reflecting material, and a rear plate shall be of black letters or figures against a yellow background of reflex-reflecting material. If the vehicle is first registered on or after January 1, 1973 these plates shall be permanently and legibly marked with the British Standard specification number B.S.A.U. 145a. If the vehicle had been first registered before that date the plate may be marked with the specification number B.S.A.U. 145.

SIZE AND SHAPE – Except for bicycles, invalid vehicles and pedestrian controlled vehicles the registration mark should be on a flat rectangular plate or on a rectangular, flat and unbroken area on the surface of the vehicle. A registration mark must conform with one of two alternative groups of provisions.

Under the first group each letter and figure shall be 3½ in. high, ⅝ in. broad and take up (except the figure 1) 2½ in. width. There shall be a ½ in. space between each adjoining letter or figure, and an upper and lower margin of ½ in. and side margin of 1 in. However, there are slight variations for embossed or pressed registration marks. In the case of bicycles, invalid vehicles or pedestrian controlled vehicles, as regards the front registration mark, each letter and figure shall be 1¾ in. high, 5/16 in. broad and take up (except the figure 1) 1¼ in. width. There shall be a ¼ in. space between each adjoining letter or figure, and an upper and lower margin of ¼ in. and side margin of ½ in. As regards the rear registration mark each letter and figure shall be 2½ in. high, ⅜ in. broad and take up (except the figure 1) 1¾ in. width. There shall be ½ in. space between each adjoining letter or figure and an upper, lower and side margin of ½ in.

Under the second group of provisions each letter and figure shall be 3⅛ in. high, 9/16 in. broad and take up (except the figure 1) 2¼ in. width. There shall be a space of 7/16 in. between each adjoining letter or figure and an upper, lower and side margin of 7/16 in. However, there are slight variations for embossed or pressed registration marks.

In the case of bicycles, invalid vehicles or pedestrian controlled vehicles, as regards the front registration mark each letter and figure shall be 1¾ in. high, 5/16 in. broad, and take up (except the figure 1) 1¼ in. width. There shall be a space of 3/16 in. between each adjoining letter or figure, and an upper, lower and side margin of at least ¼ in. As regards the rear registration mark, each letter shall be 2½ in. high, ⅜ in. broad and take up (except the figure 1) 1¾ in. width. There shall be a space of ⅜ in. between each adjoining letter or figure, and an upper, lower and side margin of ⅜ in.

In the case of vehicles registered for the first time on or after October 1, 1938, not being works trucks or agricultural machines:

(a) The registration mark shall be fixed and displayed in the case of a bicycle, on the back of the vehicle, and in the case of any other vehicle, on both the front and back of the vehicle, so that in normal daylight it is easily legible 75 ft. to the front or rear.

(b) The front registration mark on an invalid vehicle or pedestrian controlled vehicle may be on a plate with duplicate faces facing sideways, or on both sides of the front mudguard, so as to be clearly legible from both sides. The rear registration mark shall be fixed and displayed so that in normal daylight it is easily legible 60 ft. to the rear (reg. 18).

The exhibition of registration marks of vehicles (other than works trucks) and agricultural machines first registered before October 1, 1938, shall be in accordance with the provisions of Sched. 3 of the Regs. (reg. 20).

The registration mark shall be exhibited (a) in the case of a bicycle, on the back of the vehicle, (b) in the case of any other vehicle, on both the front and back of the vehicle, and in either case, in a vertical position, so that the letter and figures are vertical and easily distinguishable. An invalid vehicle not being a bicycle or pedestrian controlled vehicle may have the front registration mark on a flat plate with duplicate faces (see Sched. 2) fixed on the vehicle in a vertical position, or may have it on both sides of the vehicle on the flat surface of the front mudguard.

WORKS TRUCKS – The owner of a works truck, or an agricultural machine shall ensure that the registration mark of the vehicle is displayed on both sides of the vehicle so that it is clearly legible from either side, or on the back of the vehicle so that it is clearly legible from behind, and in either case the letters and figures must be vertical (reg. 21).

TRAILERS – Except in the case of restricted vehicles, where one or more trailers are attached to a mechanically propelled vehicle, the owner shall ensure that the registration mark of the drawing vehicle is displayed on the trailer or rearmost trailer. In such case the drawing vehicle does not need a rear identification mark. However in the case of a vehicle drawn by a "restricted" vehicle (an agricultural machine, 1971 Act, Sched. 3, or a vehicle passing for short distances from land to land owned by the same owner, 1971 Act, s. 7) the registration mark fixed to and displayed on the trailer may, instead of being that of the drawing vehicle, be that of any other restricted vehicle owned by the same owner (reg. 22).

3. Vehicles Exempt from Licence Duty – Under the Vehicles (Excise) Act 1971, the following mechanically propelled vehicles are exempt from excise duty:

(a) Fire engines;
(b) Vehicles kept by Local Authority while being used or kept for the purposes of their fire brigade service;
(c) Ambulances;
(d) Road rollers;
(e) Vehicles used on tram lines not being tramcars used for passengers;
(f) Vehicles used or kept on a road solely for haulage of lifeboats and their gear;
(g) Vehicles not exceeding 8 cwt. used or kept on a road for invalids;
(h) Road construction vehicles used or kept on a road solely for such machinery on public roads;

(i) Vehicles constructed or adapted, and used, solely for the conveyance of machinery for spreading material on roads to deal with frost, ice or snow;
(j) Local Authority's watering vehicles;
(k) Tower wagons used solely for installing or maintaining street lighting (s. 4 (1)).

A mechanically propelled vehicle shall not be chargeable with excise duty by reason of its use for clearing snow from public roads by means of a snow plough or similar contrivance, whether forming part of the vehicle or not, or by reason of its being kept for such use or by reason of its use for the purpose of going to or from the place where it is to be used (s. 7 (3)). Exemption from vehicle excise duty is made permissible in respect of vehicles purchased by overseas residents (s. 6).

A mechanically propelled vehicle shall not be chargeable with any duty by reason of its sole use on public roads on its way to or from a previously arranged compulsory test, or when taking it to or from a place where work is to be or has been done on it to remedy the defects for which a test certificate was refused, or during the test, by an examiner or a person acting under his personal direction (s. 5 (1)).

A mechanically propelled vehicle intended to be used on public roads (a) only in passing from land occupied by the owner to other land also occupied by him, and (b) for distances not exceeding a total of 6 miles in any week, may be exempt from licence duty if authorised by the Secretary of State (s. 7 (1)).

Vehicles modified for invalids are also exempt and also a vehicle fitted with controls enabling it to be driven by a person having a particular disability or a vehicle specifically and extensively adapted for use by a person having a particular disability (Finance Act 1971, s. 7).

The Road Vehicles (Registration and Licensing) Regs. 1971 contain these further provisions regarding exemptions:

VEHICLES BELONGING TO THE CROWN – In the case of vehicles belonging to the Crown (except those used or appropriated for use for naval, military or air force purposes) declaration must be made, the vehicle is registered and given a registration mark. Registration books are not issued nor are licences. Every such vehicle shall carry a Certificate of Crown ownership (reg. 24).

VEHICLES USED FOR SPECIAL PURPOSES – In the case of mechanically propelled vehicles, other than Crown owned vehicles, which are used exclusively on roads not repairable at public expense or which are exempt from duty under paragraphs (a), (c), (d) or (e) of s. 4 (1) or s. 7 (1) of the Act, a declaration must be made and a registration book issued but no licence (reg. 25).

OTHER EXEMPT VEHICLES – In the case of mechanically propelled vehicles which are exempt from duty by ss. 4 or 6 or 7 of the Act, other than those to which reg. 25 applies and other than invalid carriages complying with s. 20, Chronically Sick and Disabled Persons Act 1970, and to vehicles exempted from duty under s. 7 (2) of the Act or s. 7, Finance Act 1971, application must be made and a registration book and licence marked "NIL" will be issued (reg. 26).

CIVIL DEFENCE VEHICLES – A mechanically propelled vehicle shall not be chargeable with duty under the Act by reason only of any use made of it for the purpose of a local or police authority's functions in connection with Civil Defence (reg. 27).

4. Trade Licences – The Secretary of State may issue special licences called "trade licences" to motor traders and vehicle traders to be used in connection with their trade or business (Vehicles (Excise) Act 1971, s. 16).

"Motor trader" means a manufacturer or repairer of, or dealer in mechanically propelled vehicles; and a person shall be treated as a dealer in such vehicles if he carries on a business consisting wholly or mainly of collecting and delivering mechanically propelled vehicles, and not including any other activities except activities as a manufacturer, or repairer of, or dealer in, such vehicles. "Vehicle tester" means a person, other than a motor trader, who regularly in the course of his business engages in the testing on roads of mechanically propelled vehicles belonging to other persons (s. 16 (8)).

The holder of a trade licence shall not be entitled by virtue of that licence: (a) to use more than one mechanically propelled vehicle at any one time, except in the case of a recovery vehicle drawing a disabled vehicle, or (b) to use any vehicle for any purpose other than such purposes as may be prescribed, or (c) to keep any vehicle on a road if it is not being used thereon (s. 16 (1)).

The holder of a trade licence shall not use a vehicle under the licence for the conveyance of goods or burden of any description other than: (a) a load which is carried solely for the purpose of testing or demonstrating the vehicle or any of its accessories or equipment and which is returned to the place of loading without having been removed from the vehicle except for such purpose or in the case of accident; or (b) in the case of a recovery vehicle, any such load as is referred to in the definition of such vehicle, or a load consisting of a disabled vehicle, or (c) any load built in as part of the vehicle or permanently attached thereto, or (d) a load consisting of parts, accessories or equipment designed to be fitted to the vehicle and of tools for so fitting them, or (e) a load consisting of a trailer.

Any person holding a trade licence who uses on a public road —(1) a greater number of vehicles at any one time than he is authorised to use, or (2) any vehicle for any purpose other than those authorised by regulations, is liable to an excise penalty (s. 16 (7)).

The Road Vehicles (Registration and Licensing) Regulations 1971, provide:

The holder of a trade licence must notify the Secretary of State of any change of address or change of name of his business (reg. 30).

The Secretary of State shall issue to every holder of a trade licence two trade plates; one of the plates shall contain means whereby the licence may be fixed thereto. The trade plates remain the property of the Secretary of State and shall be returned forthwith if the person to whom they are issued no longer holds a trade licence or if that person ceases to be a motor trader or vehicle tester. If a trade plate is lost, destroyed, mutilated or defaced, or the details thereon become illegible, or the colour fades, the holder must notify the Secretary of State, who will issue a replacement (reg. 31).

No person shall alter, deface, mutilate or add anything to any trade plate or exhibit upon any mechanically propelled vehicle any trade plate which has been altered, defaced, mutilated or added to as aforesaid or upon which the figures or particulars have become illegible or the colour has become altered by fading or otherwise.

No person shall exhibit on any mechanically propelled vehicle anything which could be mistaken for a trade plate (reg. 32).

No person shall use a vehicle on a public road by virtue of a trade licence except in accordance with the following provisions:

(a) there shall be fixed to and displayed on the vehicle the trade plates issued by the Secretary of State in such a manner that, if the trade plates contained a registration mark assigned to the vehicle, the provisions of regs. 18 and 19 would be complied with, notwithstanding the vehicle may not have been first registered on or after October 1, 1938, or it is a works truck or an agricultural machine;

(b) where in accordance with the provisions of the preceding paragraph a trade plate is required to be fixed to the front of a vehicle, the trade plate so fixed shall be that containing means for fixing the licence thereto, and the trade licence shall be fixed to the vehicle by means of that plate and exhibited on that plate so as to be at all times clearly visible by daylight (reg. 33).

No person, not being the holder of a trade licence, shall use on a public road a vehicle carrying trade plates and a trade licence unless with the consent of the holder of the trade licence (reg. 34).

In this regulation, "business purpose", in relation to a motor trader means:

(a) a purpose connected with his business as a manufacturer or repairer of or dealer in mechanically propelled vehicles, or

(b) a purpose connected with his business as a manufacturer or repairer of or dealer in trailers carried on in conjunction with his business as a motor trader (reg. 35 (1)).

For the purposes of sub-paragraphs (a) to (k) of para. (4) of this regulation, where a mechanically propelled vehicle is used on a public road by virtue of a trade licence and that vehicle is drawing a trailer, the vehicle and trailer shall be deemed to constitute a single vehicle (reg. 35 (2)).

Save as provided in reg. 36, no person, being a motor trader and the holder of a trade licence, shall use any mechanically propelled vehicle on a public road by virtue of that licence unless it is a vehicle which is temporarily in his possession in the course of his business as a motor trader or a recovery vehicle kept by him for the purpose of dealing with disabled vehicles in the course of that business (reg. 35 (3)).

Save as provided in reg. 36 and without derogation from the provisions of the last preceding paragraph of this regulation, no person, being a motor trader and the holder of a trade licence, shall use any mechanically propelled vehicle on a public road by virtue of that licence for a purpose other than a business purpose and other than one of the following purposes:

(a) for its test or trial or the test or trial of its accessories or equipment in the ordinary course of construction or repair or after completion in either such case;

(b) for proceeding to or from a public weighbridge for ascertaining its unladen weight or to or from any place for its registration or inspection by a person acting on behalf of the Secretary of State;

(c) for its test or trial for the benefit of a prospective purchaser, for proceeding at the instance of a prospective purchaser to any place for the purpose of such test or trial, or for returning after such test or trial;

(d) for its test or trial for the benefit of a person interested in promoting publicity in regard to it, for proceeding at the instance of such a person to any place for the purpose of such test or trial, or for returning after such test or trial;

(e) for delivering it to the place where the purchaser intends to keep it;

(f) for demonstrating its operation or the operation of its accessories or equipment when being handed over to the purchaser;

(g) for delivering it from one part of his premises to another part of his premises, or for delivering it from his premises to the premises of, or between parts of premises of, another manufacturer or repairer of or dealer in mechanically propelled vehicles or removing it from the premises of another manufacturer or repairer of or dealer in mechanically propelled vehicles direct to his own premises;

(h) for proceeding to or returning from a workshop in which a body or a special type of equipment or accessory is to be or has been fitted to it or in which it is to be or has been painted or repaired;

(i) for proceeding from the premises of a manufacturer or repairer of or dealer in mechanically propelled vehicles to a place from which it is to be transported by train, ship or aircraft or for proceeding to the premises of such a manufacturer, repairer or dealer from a place to which it has been so transported;

(j) for proceeding to or returning from any garage, auction room or other place at which vehicles are usually stored or usually or periodically offered for sale and at which the vehicle is to be or has been stored or is to be or has been offered for sale as the case may be;

(k) for proceeding to or returning from a place where it is to be or has been tested, or for proceeding to a place where it is to be broken up or otherwise dismantled; or

(l) in the case of a recovery vehicle:

(i) for proceeding to or returning from a place where assistance is to be, or has been, rendered to a disabled vehicle; or

(ii) for proceeding to or returning from a place where it is to be, or has been, held available for rendering assistance to a disabled vehicle; or

(iii) for carrying a disabled vehicle, or for towing such a vehicle (whether with the assistance of a trailer or not), from the place where it has broken down or from such other place where it is subsequently for the time being situated to a place for repair or storage or breaking up (reg. 35 (4)).

No person, being a motor trader and who is a manufacturer of mechanically propelled vehicles and the holder of a trade licence, shall use any mechanically propelled vehicle, kept by him solely for the purposes of conducting research and development in the course of his business as such a manufacturer, on a public road by virtue of that licence except for such a purpose (reg. 36).

No person, being a vehicle tester and the holder of a trade licence, shall use any mechanically propelled vehicle on a public road by virtue of that licence for any purpose other than testing it or any trailer drawn thereby or any of the accessories or equipment on such vehicle or trailer in the course of his business as a vehicle tester (reg. 37).

No person, being a motor trader and the holder of a trade licence, shall use a mechanically propelled vehicle on a public road by virtue of that licence for the conveyance of goods or burden of any description other than:

(a) a load which is carried by a vehicle being used for a

relevant purpose and is carried solely for the purpose of testing or demonstrating the vehicle or any of its accessories or equipment and which is returned to the place of loading without having been removed from the vehicle except for such last mentioned purpose or in the case of accident:

In this sub-paragraph, "relevant purpose" means a purpose mentioned in regulation 35 (4) (a), (c), (d) and (f) of these Regs.; or

(b) in the case of a recovery vehicle, being used for a relevant purpose, any such load as is referred to in the definition of such a vehicle contained in s. 16 (8) of the Act or a load consisting of a disabled vehicle;

In this sub-paragraph, "relevant purpose" means a purpose mentioned in reg. 35 (4) of these Regs.; or

(c) any load built in as part of the vehicle or permanently attached thereto; or

(d) a load consisting of parts, accessories or equipment designed to be fitted to the vehicle and of tools for so fitting them, the vehicle being used for a relevant purpose.

In this sub-paragraph, "relevant purpose" means a purpose mentioned in reg. 35 (4) (g) or (h) or (i) of these Regs.; or

(e) a load consisting of a trailer, the vehicle carrying the trailer being used for a relevant purpose.

In this sub-paragraph, "relevant purpose" means a purpose mentioned in reg. 35 (4) (e), (h) or (i) of these Regs. (reg. 38 (1)).

No person, being a motor trader and who is a manufacturer of mechanically propelled vehicles and the holder of a trade licence, shall use any mechanically propelled vehicle, kept by him solely for the purposes of conducting research and development in the course of his business as such a manufacturer on a public road by virtue of that licence for the conveyance of goods or burden of any description other than (a) a load which is carried for the purpose of testing the vehicle or any of its accessories or equipment, and which is returned to the place of loading without having been removed from the vehicle except for such purpose or in the case of accident; or (b) any load built in as part of the vehicle or permanently attached thereto, and nothing in the last preceding paragraph of this reg. shall be taken as applying to a mechanically propelled vehicle the use of which is restricted by this paragraph (reg. 38 (2)).

For the purposes of this regulation and the next succeeding regulation, where a vehicle is so constructed that a trailer may by partial superimposition be attached to the vehicle in such a manner as to cause a substantial part of the weight of the trailer to be borne by the vehicle, the vehicle and the trailer shall be deemed to constitute a single vehicle (reg. 38 (3)).

No person, being a vehicle tester and the holder of a trade licence, shall use a mechanically propelled vehicle on a public road by virtue of that licence for the conveyance of goods or burden of any description other than:

(a) a load which is carried solely for the purpose of testing or demonstrating the vehicle or any of its accessories or equipment and which is returned to the place of loading without having been removed from the vehicle except for such purpose or in the case of accident;

(b) any load built in as part of the vehicle or permanently attached thereto (reg. 39).

No person, being the holder of a trade licence, shall use a mechanically propelled vehicle on a public road by virtue of that licence for carrying any person on the vehicle or on any trailer drawn thereby other than:

(a) the driver of the vehicle, being the holder of the licence, an employee of the holder, or any person driving with the consent of the holder while (except in the case of a vehicle which is constructed to carry only one person) accompanied by the holder or an employee of his;

(b) any person required to be on the vehicle or trailer by, or by virtue of, the Road Traffic Act 1960;

(c) any person carried for the purpose of fulfilling his statutory duties in connection with an inspection of the vehicle or trailer;

(d) any person in a disabled vehicle being towed;

(e) the holder of the trade licence or an employee of his, if in either case his presence is necessary for the purpose for which the vehicle is being used;

(f) an employee of the holder of the trade licence proceeding to a place for the purpose of driving vehicles on behalf of the holder of the trade licence in the course of his business as a motor trader;

(g) a prospective purchaser or his servant or agent or any person requested to accompany the said prospective purchaser, or in the case of a vehicle being used for the purpose mentioned in reg. 35 (4) (f) of these Regulations, the purchaser or his servant or agent or any person requested to accompany the said purchaser;

(h) a person mentioned in reg. 35 (4) (d) of these Regulations (reg. 40 (1)).

Where a person coming within sub-para. (g) or (h) of the preceding paragraph is carried he shall be accompanied (except in the case of a vehicle which is constructed to carry only one person) by the holder of the trade licence or an employee of his (reg. 40 (2)).

5. Hackney Carriages – Under the Vehicles (Excise) Act 1971, a mechanically propelled hackney carriage (used for carrying passengers for hire), must, in addition to the registration mark, carry a distinctive sign indicating that it is a hackney carriage and the number of persons it seats (s. 21).

By the Road Vehicles (Registration and Licensing) Regulations 1964, the distinctive sign for hackney carriages (subject to the exceptions given below) shall comply with the diagram and specification in Sched. 4, and shall be exhibited on the back of the vehicle in an upright position so as at all times to be clearly visible in daylight from behind the vehicle. The sign consists of a semi-circular black mark, having a white, silver or light grey border and the words "Hackney Carriage . . . Seats" in white, silver or light grey, non-detachable letters. It shall be on a flat plate or upon a flat surface forming part of the vehicle. It must bear a number indicating the seating capacity of the vehicle

The exceptions are as follows:

(a) tramcars;

(b) vehicles in respect of which the rate of duty as a hackney carriage is not less than it would have been if it were licensed as a private vehicle;

(c) vehicles licensed to ply for hire which carry outside marks prescribed by the local authority indicating that they are hackney carriages so licensed; and

(d) hackney carriages temporarily adapted for and being used solely for the conveyance of goods in the course of trade. (See also Hackney Carriages and Stage Coaches, *ante*).

(e) vehicles with a seating capacity for 20 persons or more (reg. 41).

6. Foreign-owned Motor Vehicles – The Motor Vehicles (International Circulation) Order of 1975 contains provisions affecting motor vehicles and drivers from abroad, and the issue of International Permits to persons going abroad and documents for use outside the U.K. with vehicles. Persons resident outside the United Kingdom who hold a Convention Driving Permit or a British Forces (BFG) Driving Licence or a Domestic Driving Permit, may for one year drive in Great Britain motor vehicles of the class they are authorised by their permits or licence to drive without holding driving licences issued under the R.T. Act 1972. Such persons holding permits (but not holders of BFG licences) may for one year drive public service or heavy goods vehicles brought temporarily in to Great Britain which they are authorised by their permits to drive without holding public service or heavy goods vehicle driving licences, and, if over 18, may drive heavy motor vehicles temporarily brought into Great Britain, even though they may be under 21 (art. 2).

Under the Motor Vehicles (International Circulation) Regulations 1971, a registration authority shall assign to an exempted vehicle a registration mark which shall be:

(a) the registration mark recorded in the visitor's registration document in the case of a vehicle in respect of which there is produced a visitor's registration document recording a registration mark which consists of no letters or numerals other than Roman letters or ordinary European numerals or both, and

(b) in any other case either (i) the registration mark assigned to the vehicle under provisions applying in Northern Ireland; or (ii) a registration mark consisting of the letters QA, QB, etc., and of a registered number (reg. 5).

A registration mark need not be exhibited at the front of a vehicle if that is not required by the law under which or the authority by whom, the registration mark was issued (reg. 8 (1)).

A nationality sign shall be exhibited on the back of the vehicle, except vehicles registered by the British Authorities in Germany or the United States Authorities in Germany or France (reg. 8 (2)).

Where a registration authority assigns to the owner an identification mark of the Q series under reg. 5, he will also be given a registration card. The registration card must be produced for inspection at any reasonable time on request by a police or local taxation officer. It must not be altered, defaced, etc., and if it is lost, destroyed, mutilated, defaced, or becomes illegible the owner must apply for a duplicate (reg. 6).

Excise licences may be granted for vehicles brought temporarily into Great Britain (reg. 7).

Contraventions of these Regulations are punishable summarily.

The use of a foreign-owned motor vehicle in this country must be duly insured in respect of third party risks in this country. The owner should have an "International Motor Insurance Card" which is to be regarded as an insurance policy covering third party risks (M.V. (International Motor Insurance Card) Regs. 1971). See "Insurance Certificates", Chap. 24.

These vehicles are exempt from the Lighting Regulations if they have two front white lights and a red rear light and comply with the Geneva Convention 1949. See "Lights on Vehicles", Chap. 24.

They are also exempt from many of the Construction and Use Regulations. See Appendix II.

7. Road Traffic (Foreign Vehicles) Act 1972 – This Act is designed to secure the enforcement of certain road traffic laws relating to goods vehicles, public service vehicles and their drivers temporarily visiting Britain. The main police interest lies in sections 1–3. Most spot checks on foreign vehicles will be conducted at the ports.

Section 1 empowers the Department of the Environment's Examiners to prohibit the driving on a road of a foreign commercial vehicle when certain statutory provisions have been contravened. These provisions, which are listed in Sched. 2, relates to the mechanical fitness of the vehicle, the licensing or permit requirements of operators, and vehicle lighting requirements. The prohibition will be embodied in a written notice and may also be issued for obstruction of the Examiner by the driver. This notice may include a direction to remove the vehicle to a place where it will not cause an obstruction. Specially authorised police constables and weights and measures inspectors may also issue prohibition notices, but only in respect of overweight vehicles.

Section 2 provides that a person authorised to issue a prohibition notice may also grant an exemption notice. This could authorise the vehicle to be moved under specific conditions to a place for the purpose of having the defects remedied. The "specific conditions" may include restrictions on the route and speed of the vehicle. When the defects have been remedied, an authorised person may remove the prohibition by a written notice. Only an Examiner can remove a prohibition imposed by another Examiner, but a weights and measures inspector or a police constable can remove a prohibition imposed by such an inspector or police constable.

Section 3 makes it an offence to drive a vehicle in contravention of a prohibition or direction notice and empowers a uniformed police constable to detain and impound any such vehicle so driven, and to arrest the driver without warrant. He may also direct that the vehicle be removed to a suitable secure area and for this purpose may direct a qualified person to drive the vehicle. Provided reasonable steps have been taken for the security of the vehicle and its load, no liability can be accepted by the police for damage or loss. The power of detention will terminate when the prohibition notice has been removed.

8. Construction and Use of Motor Vehicles and Trailers - The Motor Vehicles (Construction and Use) Regs. 1973 contain the provision that every motor vehicle first registered before the expiration of one year from the making of any of these regulations by which the requirements as regards the construction or weight of any class or description of vehicles are varied, shall be exempt from the requirements of that regulation for a period of 5 years from the making thereof, provided it complies with any prior regulations affecting it (reg. 4).

Breaches of the Motor Vehicles (Construction and Use) Regs., involving the use of a vehicle are punishable under R.T. Act 1972, s. 40, and other contraventions under R.T. Act 1972, Sched. 4 Part I.

Details of the subjects of the above-mentioned regulations have been arranged alphabetically and are given in Appendix II.

CHAPTER 26

COMMUNICATIONS

	Page		Page
Post Office	376	Merchant Shipping Acts .	380
Telegraphs	378	Air Navigation . .	380
Wireless	378	Smuggling . . .	385
Railways	379		

Post Office – The Post Office Act 1953 deals with many offences in connection with the postal service.

The postal service is a monopoly, and it is unlawful for any unauthorised person to carry on a letter service (ss. 3, 4 as amended by the Post Office Act 1969).

INTERFERENCE WITH THE POSTAL SERVICE – Stealing mail bags, whether in transit or not, is an offence against the Theft Act 1968 (see Chap. 14).

It is an offence to unlawfully take away or open a mail bag or unlawfully take a postal packet in course of transmission by post out of a mail bag, in transmission in any vehicle, ship or aircraft on behalf of the Post Office (s. 53).

It is an offence for any person to fraudulently or wilfully detain or refuse to deliver up any postal packet or mailbag which is in course of transmission by post and ought to have been delivered to any other person, or which has been found by him or any other person (s. 55).

The wilful and malicious (with intent to injure any other person) opening or interfering with the due delivery of any postal packet which ought to have been delivered to that other person, is an offence when committed by a person not engaged in the business of the Post Office and who is not the parent or guardian of the person to whom the letter is addressed (s. 56).

Placing in or against any post office letter-box or telephone kiosk any dangerous, noxious or deleterious substance, or committing any injury or nuisance to same may be punished summarily or on indictment (s. 60).

Without authority affixing any notice or other thing, or painting or disfiguring any Post Office property, is a summary offence (s. 61).

Any wilful obstruction or molestation of a postal official in the execution of his duty, or of the course of business in a post office, is a summary offence and the offender can be removed by any constable on demand (s. 65).

Any imitations without due authority of post office stamps, envelopes, forms and marks, also fictitious stamps are prohibited, and are summary offences (ss. 62, 63).

Without authority displaying marks on any house, box or place implying that same is an official post office, letter-box, telephone box, etc., is a summary offence (s. 64).

Dishonestly using a public telephone or telex system with intent to avoid payment is an offence (s. 65A).

The forgery of money orders (or postal orders) is an offence (s. 23). See "Forgery", Chap. 17.

PROHIBITED POSTAL PACKETS – Sending any postal packet containing any dangerous, noxious or deleterious substance or anything likely to injure other postal packets or any officer of the Post Office, or any indecent or obscene picture book, writing or article, or having on the outside any marks of an indecent, obscene or grossly offensive character, is an offence punishable. summarily or on indictment (s. 11).

OFFENCES BY POSTAL OFFICIALS – Secreting any postal packet in course of transmission by post is an offence (s. 57).

Opening contrary to his duty any postal packet in course of transmission by post or wilfully delaying or detaining same is an offence, but the Secretary of State by warrant may direct the opening, delaying or detention of postal packets (s. 58).

Any carelessness, negligence or misconduct when in charge of a mail bag or postal packet in course of transmission by post is punishable summarily (s. 59).

DEFINITION – "Postal packet" means a letter, post card, newspaper and every packet or article transmissible by post and includes a telegram (s. 87).

"In transmission by post" covers the period from the time of its being delivered to the post office to the time of its being delivered to the person to whom it is addressed (s. 87).

For "Accommodation Addresses" see "Official Secrets Acts", Chap. 20. Also see "Evidence by Certificate", Chap. 7.

It is a summary offence to use the words "Royal Mail" or "Royal Air Mail" on any premises, vehicle, etc., without authority (s. 64).

A person who (a) sends, by means of a public telecommunication service, a message or other matter that is grossly offensive or of an indecent, obscene or menacing character, or (b) for the purpose of causing annoyance, inconvenience or needless anxiety to another, sends by those means a message that he knows to be false or persistently makes use for that purpose of public telecommunication services, commits an offence (Post Office Act 1969, s. 78).

Telegraphs – Several Telegraph Acts have dealt with the telegraph service since 1863. The Post Office is now responsible for the public telegraph and telephone services, and a telegram is a "postal packet" under the Post Office Act.

Telegrams must be promptly and accurately transmitted, their contents must not be improperly disclosed, and there must be no misuse of the service.

These statutes make it an offence for:

(1) Any person in the employment of the Post Office— to wilfully or negligently omit or delay to transmit or deliver any message (1863 Act, s. 45), or
to improperly divulge to any person the purport of any telegram (1863 Act, s. 45, and Post Office Protection Act 1884, s. 11). It shall be a defence if the act constituting the offence was done in obedience to a warrant under the hand of a Secretary of State (Post Office Act 1969, Sched. 5).

(2) Any person connected with the Post Office to disclose, contrary to his duty, the contents of any message entrusted to the Post Office for transmission (1868 Act, s. 20). (The defence mentioned in (1) above applies in this case also). This offence may be dealt with summarily by consent (M.C. Act 1952, s. 19 and Sched. 1).

(3) Any person to forge or wilfully and without due authority alter a telegram, or to utter a telegram knowing same to be forged, or to transmit by telegraph as a telegram or utter as a telegram any message which he knows to be not a telegram, is an offence (punishable summarily or on indictment), whether he had or had not an intent to defraud (Post Office Protection Act 1884, s. 11).

In such cases it is necessary to prove that the false telegram was sent with intent to deceive the person to whom it was sent. See also "Forgery", Chap. 17.

Wireless – Wireless telegraphy means any system of communication by telegraph without the aid of any wire connecting the points from and at which the messages or other communications are sent and received.

Under the Wireless Telegraphy Act 1949, it is an offence for any person to establish any wireless telegraphy station or install or use any apparatus for wireless telegraphy without a licence granted by the Post Office (s. 1). Any person using an apparatus for interfering with any wireless telegraphy (s. 13) or using wireless for sending false messages or for listening in without authority to other messages (s. 5) will commit an offence. The offence may be dealt with summarily, and in addition to punishment the apparatus may be forfeited (s. 14).

A justice on sworn information may issue a search warrant authorising entry and inspection of any premises, vehicle, vessel or aircraft specified and test of apparatus (s. 15).

The Marine and Broadcasting (Offences) Act 1967, was passed to suppress broadcasting from ships, aircraft and certain marine structures. Under s. 6 of the Act, a member of a police force shall have in external waters all the powers, protection and privileges which he has in the area for which he acts as constable.

Railways – Several Railway Regulation Acts provide for the protection of railway property against malicious injury and for the proper carrying out of railway traffic.

Any wilful obstruction of a railway servant in the execution of his duty or wilful trespass on railway premises is punishable summarily, and offenders may be arrested by railway officials (1840 and 1842 Acts). Any malicious act with intent to obstruct, upset or damage any engine, carriage or truck using a railway is an offence, and any unlawful act or wilful neglect which obstructs such engine, etc., is an offence (Malicious Damage Act 1861, ss. 35 and 36).

Any malicious act with intent to endanger the safety of any person travelling on a railway is an offence, and any unlawful act or wilful neglect which endangers the safety of any person so travelling is an offence (Offences against the Person Act 1861, ss. 32, 33 and 34).

Offences under the Railways Acts are as a rule dealt with by the railway police and officials of the railways concerned.

Intoxicating liquor may be sold for consumption on railway passenger vehicles without a licence from the justices.

The railways were nationalised by the Transport Act 1947, and the powers of the old companies were given to the British Transport Commission, which has now been replaced by the British Railways Board, the London Transport Executive and the Docks Board.

As well as the general law dealt with above there is also the following special railway Act—The British Transport Commission Act 1949.

In addition to other matters this Act allows stone throwing, etc., and trespass to be dealt with summarily without the necessity of proving deliberate malice, as follows:

(1) Unlawfully throwing or causing to fall or strike at, against, into or upon any engine, tender, motor, carriage or truck, or any works or apparatus on any railway, any wood, stone or other matter or thing likely to cause damage or injury to persons or property (s. 56).

(2) Trespassing upon any of the railway lines or upon any

railway embankment or cutting or upon any other lands of the Commission in dangerous proximity to any such lines of railway or other works or to any electrical apparatus used for or in connection with the railway. But no person shall be subject to a penalty unless notices warning persons not to tresspass have been placed and renewed as necessary (s. 55).

Merchant Shipping Acts – Every passenger steamer which carries more than 12 passengers shall be surveyed once at least in each year as provided in the Act; and no ship (other than a steam ferry boat working in chains) shall proceed to sea or on any voyage or excursion with more than 12 passengers on board, unless there is in force in respect of the ship a certificate as to survey, applicable to the voyage or excursion on which the ship is about to proceed, or that voyage or excursion is one in respect of which the Minister of Transport has exempted the ship from the requirements of this subsection (ss. 271 (as substituted by 1964 Act, s. 17) and 283).

The expression "passenger" means any person carried in a ship (whether or not for a fare) except (a) the master, officers and crew, (b) children under one year of age, and (c) certain other persons referred to in s. 26 (1) of the Merchant Shipping (Safety Convention) Act 1949 (e.g. shipwrecked persons).

Persons in passenger steamers who are guilty of misconduct in connection with the payment of their fares or their behaviour on board may be detained by the captain and his assistants and conveyed before a justice to be dealt with summarily (1894 Act, s. 287). See "Drunkenness", Chap. 38.

Under s. 31 Merchant Shipping Act 1970, if a seaman employed in a ship registered in the U.K. (other than a fishing vessel (s. 95)) is absent without leave and the ship is thereby delayed or goes to sea without him, and if his absence is deliberate and without reasonable cause or due to recklessness, he commits a summary offence.

Air Navigation – The Civil Aviation Act 1949 and the Civil Aviation (Licensing) Act 1960 deal with this subject. If an aircraft is so flown as to be the cause of unnecessary danger to any person or property, the pilot and the owner or hirer may be convicted summarily (s. 11). Any offence under the Act or Regulations thereunder shall be deemed to have been committed in any place where the offender may for the time being be (s. 60).

Trespassing on the land of a licensed aerodrome, if warning notices had been posted, is a summary offence (s. 38). A person shall not fly or cause or permit any other person to fly an aircraft unless there is in force a policy of insurance or a security against third party risks in relation to such flying. This will not apply if the owner is a local authority or a police authority or if the aircraft is being used for police purposes or if the presented amount has been deposited with the High Court (s. 43). The hirer of an aircraft for more than 14 days will be regarded as the owner (s. 49). This insurance is on the same lines as motor insurance and there must be certificates of insurance or security (s. 44).

Section 8 of the Act confers power to make Orders in Council regulating air navigation and for carrying out the Chicago Convention of December 7, 1944, regarding international civil aviation.

Public Health (Aircraft) Regs. 1952, 1954, 1961 and 1963 prescribe measures to prevent the spread of infectious diseases by aircraft.

Section 7 of the Civil Aviation (Licensing) Act 1960 prohibits aerial advertising and propaganda by aircraft while in the air over any part of the United Kingdom or its territorial waters. Any person who uses an aircraft for such purpose commits an offence if the advertisement or communication is audible or visible from the ground. However, under the Civil Aviation (Aerial Advertising) Regs. 1961, aircraft may be so used for civil defence, military or police purposes, emergencies and the identification of aircraft.

The Air Navigation Order 1974 regulates the use of aircraft.

An aircraft shall not fly over the United Kingdom unless it is registered; however, the following are exempt: Kites or captive balloons, gliders in certain circumstances and aircraft flown for experimental purposes, etc. (art. 3). The Civil Aviation Authority registers aircraft in the United Kingdom, and may cancel registration (art. 4).

No aircraft shall fly unless it bears the nationality and registration marks required by the law of the country in which it is registered. Aircraft registered in the United Kingdom shall bear the capital letter "G" and the four capital Roman letters assigned to it by the Authority (art. 5).

No aircraft shall fly unless there is in force in respect thereof a certificate of airworthiness, except

(a) a glider not used for public transport of passengers or aerial work,

(b) a balloon not used for public transport of passengers,

(c) a kite,

(d) an aircraft flying in accordance with the conditions stated in Sched. 2,

(e) an aircraft flying by special permission of the Authority (art. 7).

An aircraft shall not fly for the purpose of public transport or dropping or projecting any material for agricultural, public health or similar purposes unless (a) the aircraft and its engines, equipment and radio station are properly maintained, (b) there is in force a "Certificate of Maintenance" (art. 9).

No person under 17 shall have sole control of an aircraft in motion (art. 20 and Sched. 9) except in the case of a glider of which no person under 16 may have sole control when in motion (art. 24).

A person shall not wilfully or negligently act in a manner likely to endanger an aircraft or any person therein (art. 43).

A person shall not enter or be in any aircraft while drunk. A member of the crew of an aircraft must not be under the influence of drink or a drug to such an extent as to impair his capacity to act (art. 45).

An aircraft shall not fly unless it carries the documents it is required to carry. However, the documents may be kept at an aerodrome from which the aircraft takes off if it is intended to return to the same aerodrome without leaving the United Kingdom (art. 57).

The documents to be carried by aircraft registered in the United Kingdom are as follows:

On a flight for the purpose of public transport:

Documents A, B, C, D, E, F, H and, if the flight is international air navigation, Document G.

On a flight for the purpose of the public transport of passengers: Document J.

On a flight for the purpose of aerial work:

Documents A, B, C, E, F and, if the flight is international air navigation Document G.

On a flight, being international air navigation, for a purpose other than public transport or aerial work:

Documents A, B, C and G.

For the purposes of this Schedule:

"A" means the licence in force under the Wireless Telegraphy Act 1949 in respect of the aircraft radio station installed in the aircraft, and the current telecommunication log book required by this Order;

"B" means the certificate of airworthiness in force in respect of the aircraft;

"C" means the licences of the members of the flight crew of the aircraft;

"D" means one copy of the load sheet, if any, required by Article 27 of this Order in respect of the flight;

"E" means one copy of each certificate of maintenance, if any, in force in respect of the aircraft;

"F" means the technical log, if any, in which entries are required to be made under Article 9 (6) and the log book, if any, in which entries are required to be made under Article 10 (5) of this Order;

"G" means the certificate of registration in force in respect of the aircraft;

"H" means the operations manual, if any, required by Article 25 (2) (*a*) (iii) of this Order to be carried on the flight;

"J" means one copy of the certificate of release, if any, in force in respect of the aircraft.

For the purposes of this Schedule:

"International air navigation" means any flight which includes passage over the territory of any country other than the United Kingdom, except any of the Channel Islands, the Isle of Man, any country to which there is power to extend the Civil Aviation Act 1949 under section 66 (1) thereof or any British Protected State (Sched. 12).

The Commander of an aircraft shall within a reasonable time after being requested to do so by an authorised person (this includes a constable) cause to be produced (a) the certificates of registration and airworthiness, (b) the licences of its flight crew and (c) such other documents which must be carried under art. 57 and Sched. 12. The holder of any licence under the Order shall on demand by an authorised person, produce the licence—however in some cases he may have 5 days within which to produce it at a specified police station (art. 58).

No person shall with intent to deceive, forge, alter, etc., any document necessary under this Order, or use any such forged, etc., document or use one to which he is not entitled or lend any such document to another person or make false representation to procure any such document or alter, etc., any entry in any log-book or make wilfully or negligently any materially incorrect entry in a load sheet (art. 61).

Within the United Kingdom a captive balloon or a kite shall not be flown at a height of more than 60 metres above ground level nor within 5 kilometres of an aerodrome or within 60 metres of any vessel, vehicle or structure (art. 67).

The Authority may license an aerodrome on conditions (art 70) and aeronautical lights must be approved by the Authority (art. 76)who may take action to have extinguished or properly screened any light which is near an aerodrome or may be mistaken for an aerodrome light and which is dangerous to air navigation (art. 77).

Any person authorised by the Authority and any officer of police has the right of access at all reasonable times by day or night to any aerodrome or place where an aircraft has landed for the purpose of inspecting the aerodrome or aircraft or any document he has power to demand under the Order and for detaining the aircraft under the provisions of the Order (art. 82). No person shall obstruct or impede any person acting in the exercise of his powers or the performance of his duties under the provisions of the Order (art. 83).

LOW FLYING – Under the authority of art. 62, the Authority

has made the Rules of the Air and Air Traffic Control Regs. 1974. Rule 5 deals with low flying as follows:

(1) (a) An aircraft other than a helicopter shall not fly over any congested area below (i) such height as would enable the aircraft to alight clear of the area and without danger to persons or property on the surface, in the event of failure of a power unit, or (ii) a height of 1,500 ft. above the highest fixed object within 2,000 ft. of the aircraft, whichever is the higher.

(b) A helicopter shall not fly below such height as would enable it to alight without danger to persons or property on the surface, in the event of failure of a power unit.

(c) Except with the written permission of the Authority a helicopter shall not fly (i) over a congested area below a height of 1,500 ft. above the highest fixed object within 2,000 ft. of the helicopter; (ii) over an area prescribed for the purposes of this paragraph below such height as would enable it to alight clear of the area in the event of failure of a power unit.

(d) An aircraft shall not fly over or within 3,000 ft. of, any assembly in the open air of more than 1,000 persons, except with the written permission of the Authority and the written consent of the organisers nor below such height as would enable it to alight clear of the assembly in the event of failure of a power unit. Provided that where a person is charged with a contravention of this paragraph, it shall be a good defence to prove that the flight of the aircraft over, or within 3,000 ft. of, the assembly was made at a reasonable height and for a reason not connected with the assembly or with the event which was the occasion for the assembly. A procession is an assembly (*D.P.P.* v. *Roffey* (1959)).

(e) An aircraft shall not fly closer than 500 ft. to any person, vessel, vehicle or structure.

(2) (a) Paragraphs (1) (a) (ii) and (1) (c) (i) shall not apply to an aircraft flying on a notified route or on a special V.F.R. flight.

(b) Paragraphs (1) (d) and (e) shall not apply to an aircraft in the service of a police authority.

(c) Paragraphs (1) (d) and (e) shall not apply to the flight of an aircraft over or within 3,000 ft. of an assembly of persons witnessing an aircraft race or contest or exhibition of flying, if the aircraft is taking part in such race, etc., or is engaged in a flight arranged by or made with the written consent of the organisers.

(d) Paragraph (1) (e) shall not apply to (i) any aircraft while it is landing or taking off in accordance with normal aviation practice, (ii) any glider while it is hill-soaring.

(3) Nothing in this rule shall prohibit any aircraft from flying for the purpose of saving life.

(4) Nothing in this rule shall prohibit any aircraft from

taking off, landing or practicing approaches to landing at or checking navigational aides or procedures at a government or licensed aerodrome.

(5) Nothing in this rule shall apply to any captive balloon or kite.

Aerobatic flights over towns or populous areas are prohibited (rule 18).

AIR ACCIDENTS – The Civil Aviation (Investigation of Accidents) Regs. 1951, direct that when an accident occurs to a civil aircraft involving death or serious injury to any person, or serious damage to an aircraft, particulars should be notified to the local police and to the Minister of Aviation by the pilot or owner or operator (regs. 3 and 4). "Aircraft" includes all balloons (captive or free), gliders, airships and flying machines (reg. 1).

Such an aircraft should not be removed or interfered with for 3 days unless by authority, except when necessary to save life or to prevent danger or obstruction, etc. (reg. 5).

An Inspector of Accidents will investigate the accident (regs. 6-8), and if necessary, a special court will be appointed to hold a public inquiry (regs. 9 and 10).

Special provisions are made in respect of combined Military and Civil air accidents by the Air Navigation (Investigation of Combined Military and Civil Air Accidents) Regs. 1959 and 1960.

Customs and Excise Act 1952 requires aircraft flying to or from abroad to depart from or land at a Customs Airport (for customs clearance). If such an aircraft lands at a place other than a customs airport the commander should notify a customs officer or a constable. He should not allow goods to be unloaded without the officer's consent and no crew or passenger shall depart without the consent of an officer or constable save when necessary for safety (s. 15). Any customs officer or constable may prevent departure of an aircraft for abroad which is leaving from a place not a customs airport or from a customs airport before clearance is given (s. 25).

By the Tokyo Convention Act 1967, any act or omission taking place on board a British-controlled aircraft while in flight elsewhere than in or over the U.K. which would constitute an offence if taking place in the U.K. shall constitute that offence. If the offence takes place on board an aircraft in flight elsewhere than in or over the U.K. the consent of the D.P.P. is necessary for prosecution, but this shall not prevent the arrest, or the issue of a warrant for the arrest of any person in respect of an offence, or the remanding in custody, or on bail, of any person charged with any offence. Any offence committed on board an aircraft in flight shall be deemed to have been committed in any place in the U.K. where the offender may for the time being be (s. 1).

For details of the offence of Hijacking, see Chap. 8.

Smuggling – Acts of Parliament deal with the importation of goods into the country in three ways:

(1) The bringing in of some articles is absolutely forbidden; for example, indecent publications. See Chap. 11.

(2) Certain goods may not be imported unless the prescribed customs duties are paid thereon; for example, wine, spirits, tobacco, saccharine, and various manufactured articles.

(3) Some articles may not be brought into this country except under official licence or permission; for example, certain dangerous drugs. See "Dangerous Drugs", Chap. 39.

The importation of any article contrary to the law on the subject is termed "smuggling", and articles so imported illegally are called "contraband goods".

The Customs and Excise Service keep watch at seaports to prevent and detect breaches of the law.

The Customs and Excise Act 1952 deals with the prevention of smuggling in ss. 68–74. Customs officers, coastguards and police may search vehicles and vessels (s. 297). An excise or customs officer may search persons (s. 298) and obtain search warrants for premises (s. 296).

A constable, customs officer, etc., who suspects on reasonable grounds that signalling to smugglers is going on, may enter ships, aircraft, vehicles, houses and places and prevent same. Such signalling is an offence (s. 71). A person offering goods for sale as smuggled goods is liable to heavy penalty and may be detained (s. 74) by a constable, customs officer, etc. (s. 274) and dealt with by a court (s. 281).

It shall be the duty of every constable and every member of H.M. armed forces or coastguard to assist in the enforcement of the law as set out in the Act (Customs and Excise Act 1952, s. 5).

Any contravention or attempted evasion of the laws on the importation of goods is an offence, and the offender may be arrested or summoned.

PART VI – OTHER STATUTORY OFFENCES AND REGULATIONS

CHAPTER 27

VAGRANCY AND CHARITY

	Page
Vagrancy Acts	389
Idle and Disorderly Persons	389
Rogues and Vagabonds	389
Incorrigible Rogue	390
Begging	390
Vagrancy Frauds	391
Fraudulent Mediums	392
Charities	392
Street Collections	392
War Charities Act 1940	393
House to House Collections Act 1939	393
Regulations 1947	396
Common Lodging-houses	397

Vagrancy Acts – The Vagrancy Act 1824 was intended to prevent wasters and sturdy beggars from wandering about the country and committing sundry questionable acts by which an easy livelihood might be gained.

Offenders under the Act are arranged in three classes:

(1) Idle and Disorderly Persons (s. 3) – This term is applied to person committing any of the following offences:

(1) Begging in any public place (s. 3). See "Begging", later.

(2) Common prostitutes wandering in public places and behaving in an indecent or riotous manner (s. 3). See "Prostitution", Chap. 10.

(3) Pedlars wandering abroad and trading without licence (s. 3). See "Pedlars", Chap. 31.

Above offenders may be committed by one justice for 14 days or by two justices in Petty Sessions for one month, or may be fined.

(2) Rogues and Vagabonds (s. 4) – This term is applied to persons committing any of the following offences:

(1) Persons convicted a second time of being an idle and disorderly person.

(2) Persons arrested as "idle and disorderly" who violently resist arrest.

(3) Fortune-tellers and suchlike. See "Vagrancy Frauds", *post*.

(4) Begging by exposing wounds or deformities. See "Vagrancy Frauds".

(5) Collecting alms or charitable contributions under false pretences. See "Vagrancy Frauds".

(6) Sleeping out. See "Vagrancy Frauds".

(7) Exposing to public view obscene or indecent exhibitions. See "Indecent Publications", Chap. 11.

(8) Exposing the person with intent to insult any female. See "Indecent Exposure", Chap. 11.

(9) Being armed with any offensive weapon with intent to commit any arrestable offence.

(10) Found in or upon any premises or enclosed yard, garden or area for any unlawful purpose.

(11) Suspected persons or reputed thieves found frequenting or loitering with intent to commit an arrestable offence,

For full description of above three offences (9–11), see "Loiterers and Suspected Persons", Chap. 28.

Above offenders may be committed by one justice for 14 days, or by two justices in Petty Sessions for 3 months, or may be fined.

(3) Incorrigible Rogue (s. 5) – This term is applied to any person convicted as follows:

(1) For committing any offence for which he may be dealt with as a rogue and a vagabond (see the 11 offences above), having been previously convicted as a rogue and a vagabond.

(2) For violently resisting arrest as a rogue and vagabond.

(3) For escaping from a place of confinement before the expiration of the term for which committed or confined under the Vagrancy Act.

Persons convicted by the justices as incorrigible rogues shall be committed (either in custody or on bail – C.J. Act 1967, s. 20) to the next Crown Court, at which the circumstances are to be examined and they may be sentenced to up to 12 months' imprisonment. There is no appeal against such a conviction by justices, but the prisoner, if given leave, may appeal to the criminal division of the Court of Appeal against the sentence of the Crown Court (Criminal Appeal Act 1968, s. 10).

POWER OF ARREST – Any person may arrest without warrant anyone found committing an offence against the Act and bring him before a justice or hand him over to the police (but in the case of fortune tellers only the police can so arrest (s. 6)). See "Vagrancy Frauds", later.

Begging – As every person really in need of subsistence is entitled to supplementary benefit the law makes it a summary offence to beg or to try and obtain contributions from the public in any fraudulent manner.

Vagrancy Act **1824**, s. **3**: Every person wandering abroad or placing himself or herself in any public place, street, highway, court, or passage, to beg or gather alms, or causing or procuring or encouraging any child or children so to do, may be punished summarily as an idle and disorderly person.

Children and Young Persons Act **1933**, s. **4**: Causing or procuring or allowing any child or young person (under **16**) to be in any street, premises or place for the purpose of begging or receiving or inducing alms is a summary offence, and the child or young person may be dealt with as needing care, protection or control. See Chap. **12**.

Pedlars Act **1871**, s. **16**: If a pedlar is convicted of begging, the court must deprive him of his pedlar's certificate. See Chap. **31**.

Vagrancy Frauds – Persons convicted of the following offences under s. 4 of the Vagrancy Act 1824 may be punished summarily as rogues and vagabonds.

(1) FORTUNE TELLING – Every person pretending or professing to tell fortunes, or using any subtle craft, means or device by palmistry or otherwise, to deceive or impose on any of Her Majesty's subjects.

(2) FRAUDULENT COLLECTIONS – Every person going about as a gatherer or collector of alms, or endeavouring to procure charitable contributions of any nature or kind, under any false or fraudulent pretence.

(3) EXPOSING WOUNDS – Every person wandering abroad and endeavouring by the exposure of wounds or deformities to obtain or gather alms.

(4) SLEEPING OUT – Every person wandering abroad and lodging in any barn or outhouse or in any deserted or unoccupied dwelling or in the open air or under a tent or in any cart or waggon (with or in which he does not travel (1935 Act)) and not giving a good account of himself or herself (1824 Act, s. 4), provided that he declines any reasonably accessible free place of shelter or that he is a person who persistently wanders abroad and sleeps out or that by so sleeping out he causes or appears likely to cause damage, infection with vermin or other offensive consequences to property (Vagrancy Act 1935).

The police have power to arrest without warrant any persons found committing any of the above offences (s. 6), but in the case of "fortune telling" a constable must not arrest unless he has reason to believe that the offender will abscond or he is not satisfied as to the identity or place of residence of the offender (C.J. Act 1948, s. 68).

Fraudulent Mediums – The Fraudulent Mediums Act 1951 repealed the Witchcraft Act 1735 and s. 4 of the Vagrancy Act 1824 so far as it extends to spiritualistic mediums or persons using telepathy; clairvoyance or other similar powers or to persons using fraudulent devices in exercising such powers (s. 2).

However, s. 1 of the Act creates the offence of acting as a spiritualistic medium or using telepathy, clairvoyance or other similar powers with intent to deceive or when so acting using any fraudulent device when it is proved that the person so acted for reward. Proceedings require the consent of the Director of Public Prosecutions and they may be summary (with right to claim trial by jury) or on indictment.

However this section does not apply to anything done solely for the purpose of entertainment.

Charities – The law places no obstacles in the way of exercising charity, but it has taken some steps to check persons from obtaining undeserved assistance and to regulate the raising of money from the public for charitable purposes. Under the Charities Act 1960 charities must be registered with the Charity Commissioners who have powers to check abuses. There are exemptions from registration for "small and transient" charities.

The Vagrancy Act 1824 makes begging, obtaining alms by the exposure of wounds and deformities, and fraudulent alms collecting, summary offences, for which see above.

Street Collections – The Police, Factories, &c. (Miscellaneous Provisions) Act 1916, s. 5 as amended by Local Govt. Act 1972, Sch. 29, authorises the Common Council of the City of London, the police authority for the Metropolitan Police District or a district council to make regulations dealing with the collection of money or the sale of articles (e.g. flags or other tokens) in streets and public places for the benefit of charitable or other purposes. Any such regulations must be confirmed by the Secretary of State and shall not apply to the sale of articles in public places in the ordinary course of trade where no representation is made that any part of the proceeds will be devoted to charity.

Such regulations, when made, usually provide:

(1) that a permit must be obtained from the licensing authority for any such street collection or flag day;

(2) that every collector must have in possession a written authority to collect;

(3) that collectors must not cause annoyance or obstruction;

(4) that all money received must at once be placed in a closed receptacle;

(5) that no person must be rewarded for his services out of the proceeds of the collection, and

(6) that a proper account of the money collected and of the expenses incurred must be submitted to the licensing authority

War Charities Act 1940 – This Act makes it a summary offence to make any public appeal for assistance for any war charity, or to attempt to raise money for any such charity by promoting any bazaar, entertainment or similar means, unless the charity is exempted or registered under the Act and the governing body of the charity has in writing approved of such appeal or bazaar, etc. However, this does not apply to a collection at Divine service in a place of public worship, or to any war charity exempted by the Registration Authority from registration under the Act (s. 1).

A "war charity" is defined as any fund, association or undertaking having amongst its principal objects the relief of suffering or distress, caused by, or any other charitable purpose connected with war (i.e. any war, War Charities (Definition) Order 1943).

It does not apply to the Royal Patriotic Fund Corporation nor to any "war charity" administered by a government department (s. 11), but it does to any charity for disabled persons (National Assistance Act 1948, ss. 29, 41).

Accordingly every "war charity" must make application for registration or exemption to the Registration Authority (the local Council, s. 10), which must keep a Register of War Charities and supply the Charity Commissioners with particulars of same (s. 2). Registered war charities should be properly organised and should keep proper accounts which must be audited and copies sent to the Registration Authority at least once in every 12 months (s. 3).

Under s. 4 the Charity Commissioners may make regulations (see the War Charities Regs. 1940) and failure to comply with them or with the conditions laid down in s. 3 will be a summary offence.

In case of default a war charity may be removed from the register and the Charity Commissioners may take control (s. 5).

A licence under the House to House Collections Act 1939 may be refused if the collection is for a "war charity" which is not registered or exempted.

The chief officer of police may grant a certificate for a house to house collection to a "war charity" which is exempted from registration under this Act (s. 7).

It is a summary offence to make false statements or representations under this Act or for any person to falsely represent himself to be an officer or agent of a war charity (s. 8).

An offence under s. 4 can be dealt with summarily with fine. Proceedings for any other offence against the Act cannot be taken unless by or with the consent of the Charity Commissioners (Ryder Street, St. James's, London, S.W.1).

House to House Collections Act 1939 – This Act directs that no collection for a charitable purpose shall be made unless authorised under the Act (s. 1 (1)). "Collection" means an appeal to the public made by means of visits from house to house (including a place of business) to give, whether for consideration or not, money or other property, and "collector" means a person who makes such an appeal. "Charitable purpose" means any charitable, benevolent or philanthropic purpose whether or not the purpose is charitable within the meaning of any rule of law (s. 11).

If a person promotes such a collection and a collection thereunder is made in any locality, then unless he has a licence in force authorising him so to do, he shall be guilty of an offence (s. 1 (2)). A "promoter" of a collection means a person who causes others to act, whether for remuneration or otherwise, as collectors for the collection (s. 11).

If a person acts as collector in any locality for such a collection, then unless there is a licence in force for the collection, he shall be guilty of an offence (s. 1 (3)).

A police constable may require any person whom he believes to be acting as a collector for a charitable purpose to declare to him immediately his name and address and to sign his name. Failure to comply shall be an offence (s. 6).

A person may apply in the prescribed manner to the licensing authority (the Common Council of the City of London, the Metropolitan Commissioner or the district council) of the area for a licence authorising him to promote such a collection in any locality within the area. A licence may be granted for a definite period not longer than 12 months, but it may be for 18 months if the licensing authority wish to provide for the simultaneous expiration of such licences (s. 2).

A licence may be refused or revoked on any of the following grounds:

(a) The total amount likely to be applied for charitable purposes is inadequate in proportion to the likely amount of the collection.

(b) Remuneration excessive in relation to the amount likely to be applied for charitable purposes is likely to be or has been retained or received out of the proceeds by any person.

(c) The licence would be likely to facilitate begging or causing a child to beg, or that such an offence has been committed in connection with the collection.

(d) The applicant or licensee has been convicted of assault, rape, carnal knowledge, indecent assault, abduction, robbery, burglary, blackmail, offence in connection with street collections or any offence involving fraud or dishonesty (see Schedule to the Act) and is therefore not a fit and proper person to hold a licence.

(e) The applicant or licensee, in promoting a collection, has failed to exercise due diligence to secure fit and proper collectors or to secure compliance with the Regulations under the Act.

(f) The applicant or licensee has refused or neglected to furnish to the licensing authority such information as they may have reasonably required regarding any of the above matters.

If a licence is refused or revoked, the grounds shall be given and there may be an appeal to the Secretary of State (s. 2).

A licence may be refused if the collection is for a war charity which is not registered or exempted under the Act (s. 7, War Charities Act 1940), and any contravention of a regulation will be an offence (s. 4).

If a person, in connection with any appeal made by him to the public representing that it is for a charitable purpose, displays or uses:

(a) a prescribed badge or certificate of authority not being such as is held by him for the appeal pursuant to regulations made under the Act, or

(b) any badge or device or certificate or other document so nearly resembling a prescribed badge or authority as to be calculated to deceive – he shall be guilty of an offence (s. 5).

A punishment may be imposed on a person guilty of the offence of knowingly or recklessly making a statement false in a material particular, in furnishing any information for the purposes of this Act (s. 8).

Licence from the licensing authority is not necessary in two cases, viz.:

1. The Secretary of State may, by order, exempt from licence and authorise a collection in the localities described in the Order, by a person (or organisation) who pursues a charitable purpose throughout the whole of England or a substantial part thereof.

Such an Order has the effect of a licence in the localities named (s. 3).

2. A chief officer of police may grant a certificate to a person to collect for a charitable purpose which is local in character and is likely to be completed within a short period of time. A person holding such a certificate may authorise other persons to act as collectors. The holder of such a certificate is exempt from the requirements of the Act (and Regulations) except sections 5 (unauthorised use of badges, etc.) and 6 (liability to give name, etc., to police) and the penalties for contravention of these two sections (s. 1 (4)).

Any functions conferred on the chief officer of police by the Act or Regulations may be delegated by him to any police officer not below the rank of Inspector (s. 7 (2)).

The chief officer of police may grant a certificate for a house to house collection to a war charity which is exempted from registration under the Act (s. 7, War Charities Act 1940).

House to House Collections Regulations 1947 – These Regulations prescribe the form of certificates, applications for licence or order, collectors' certificates of authority, badges, and accounts to be rendered (7 Schedules).

The "chief promoter" of a collection is the person to whom a licence or order is granted, but there may also be promoters taking part in the work.

A "collecting box" means a box or other receptacle for money, securely closed and sealed so that it may not be opened without breaking the seal.

A "receipt book" means a book of detachable receipts consecutively numbered with counterfoils or duplicates correspondingly numbered (reg. 2).

Every promoter shall exercise all due diligence to secure that collectors are fit and proper persons and that they comply with the Regulations (reg. 5).

A promoter shall not permit any person to act as a collector unless the person is supplied with:

(a) a certificate of authority, as prescribed;

(b) a badge, as prescribed, showing the purpose of the collection, and

(c) if money is to be collected, a collecting box or a receipt book.

The purpose of the collection and a distinguishing number shall be marked on every collecting box or wrapper gummed on it (reg. 2 (3)) and on every receipt (reg. 6 (1)).

Every promoter shall secure that no certificate of authority, badge, etc., is issued unless the name and address of the collector with distinguishing number of box or receipt book is entered on a list, and shall secure that same are returned when the collection is finished or when the collector ceases to act as such (reg. 6 (2)).

Every collector shall:

(a) sign his name on his certificate of authority and produce it on demand to any police constable or person at a house visited for collecting;

(b) sign his name on his badge and wear it prominently when collecting, and

(c) keep his certificate and badge in his possession and return them to his promoter on demand or when the collection is completed (reg. 7).

No person under the age of 16 shall act or be authorised to act as a collector of money (reg. 8).

No collector shall importune any person to the annoyance of such person or remain in or at the door of any house if requested to leave by any occupant thereof (reg. 9).

When collecting money by a collecting box, a collector shall not receive money save by permitting the giver to place it in the collecting box issued to him. When collecting money by any other means the collector shall enter in the receipt book issued to him, in the presence of the contributor, the name of the contributor with amount given, and give him a signed receipt. All entries shall be in ink or indelible pencil (reg. 10).

Every collector shall return to a promoter his collecting box or receipt book, with the total amount collected, when the box is full or the receipt book is exhausted or on demand of a promoter or on ceasing to act as collector or when the collection is completed (reg. 11).

Every returned collecting box shall be examined, and if it contains money shall be opened in the presence of a promoter and another responsible person, contents counted and recorded on a list to be certified by the persons making the examination. Receipt books shall be similarly examined and amounts listed (reg. 12).

A licence or order may expressly allow collections in which instead of collecting boxes or receipt books, envelopes may be used; the givers to put their contributions therein and gum down the flaps (reg. 13).

The chief promoter shall furnish accounts of the collection, as prescribed by Regs. 14, 15 and 16. He shall also ensure that all certificates of authority and badges are destroyed when no longer required for the purpose (reg. 17).

Any contravention of a regulation will be a summary offence (s. 4) punishable by a fine (s. 8).

Common Lodging-houses – Public Health Act 1936. Part IX, ss. 235–248, regulates such premises.

A common lodging-house means a house (other than a re-establishment centre or a reception centre) provided for the purpose of accommodating by night poor persons, not being members of the same family, who resort thereto and are allowed to occupy one common room for the purpose of sleeping, or eating, and includes, where part only of a house is so used, the part so used (s. 235).

Letting on weekly tenancies does not prevent premises from coming within this definition (*People's Hostels, Ltd.* v. *Turley* (1938)).

No person shall keep a common lodging-house unless he is registered under this Act (s. 236) with the Local Authority, and the deputies of such a keeper shall also be registered (s. 237). Registration may be refused if keepers or deputies are not fit persons; if premises are not suitable and suitably equipped; or if such use is likely to cause annoyance or inconvenience to the neighbours (s. 238).

"Registered Common Lodging-House" shall be displayed on the outside of the house; the keeper or deputy shall be therein from 9 p.m. to 6 a.m.; lists of lodgers shall be sent to the Local Authority if beggars or vagrants are received; and free access shall be given at all times to authorised officers (s. 241). Infectious disease shall be notified and a magistrates' court may order closing if there is notifiable disease (ss. 242–245).

Contravention of the Act will be a summary offence (s. 246), and registration may be cancelled and the keeper disqualified (s. 247).

CHAPTER 28

PREVENTION OF CRIME

	Page		Page
Penalties . . .	399	Loiterers and Suspected Persons . . .	406
Discharge of Offenders .	400	Prisons . . .	408
Probation of Offenders .	401	Restriction of Offensive Weapons . . .	409
Borstal Institution . .	403		
Persistent Offenders .	404		

Penalties – The main preventive of crime is most probably the fear of incurring some penalty. Punishment for crime has been briefly dealt with in Chapter 1, but the Criminal Justice Acts 1948, 1961, 1967, 1972 and P. of C.C. Act 1973, have made many changes in and additions to the methods of punishing offences.

P. of C.C. Act 1973, s. 19: Neither the Crown Court nor a magistrates' court shall impose imprisonment on a person under 17. No court (or justice) shall impose imprisonment on a person under 21 unless no other method of dealing with him is appropriate.

1961 Act, s. 4: Where a court has power, or would have power but for the statutory restrictions upon the imprisonment of young offenders, to pass sentence of imprisonment on an offender not less than 14 but under 21, the court may order him to be detained in a detention centre. See Chap. 12.

1948 Act, s. 19: Instead of imposing imprisonment or punishing for breach of probation order, a magistrates' court may order an offender who is under 21, to attend at an attendance centre. See "Attendance Centre", Chap. 12.

S. 20: An offender not less than 15 but under 21, who is liable to imprisonment, may be sentenced by the Crown Court to Borstal training. See later.

Where a summary court is satisfied on medical evidence that an offender liable to imprisonment is suffering from mental illness, psychopathic disorder, or subnormality, it may make an order authorising the detention of the offender at a hospital or place him under guardianship (Mental Health Act 1959, s. 60). See Chap. 39.

Where a summary court convicts a person not less than 17 under the provisions of the Act of an indictable offence and considers he deserves greater punishment than the court can inflict, he can be committed in custody or on bail to the Crown Court for sentence (M.C. Act 1952, s. 29).

P. of C.C. Act 1973, s. 2: "Impose imprisonment" means pass a sentence of imprisonment or commit to prison in default of payment of money or for failing to do or abstain from doing anything required to be done or left undone. See also s. 126, M.C. Act 1952.

"Offence for which the sentence is fixed by law" means an offence for which the court is required to sentence the offender to death or imprisonment for life or to detention during H.M. pleasure.

C.J. Act 1948, s. 80 (6): Where the Act empowers a court, on convicting, to pass a sentence or make an order in lieu of dealing with the offender in any other manner, it does not take away any power of the court to order the offender to pay costs or compensation.

See also "Punishment for Crime", Chap. 1.

Discharge of Offenders - P. of C.C. Act 1973, s. 7: Where a court convicts a person of an offence (for which the sentence is not fixed by law) and is of opinion, having regard to the circumstances including the nature of the offence and the character of the offender, that it is inexpedient to inflict punishment and that probation is not appropriate, the court, by order, may discharge him absolutely, or may discharge him conditionally on condition that he commits no offence during a specified period not exceeding 3 years. In the latter case the court shall explain to the offender that if he commits another offence during the period he will be liable to be sentenced for the original offence.

S. 8: If a person conditionally discharged is convicted anywhere in Great Britain for an offence committed during the specified period, a judge or justice, as authorised by this section, may issue summons or warrant to bring him before the court which conditionally discharged him. If that court was a summary court it can deal with him for the original offence. If that court was the Crown Court and is not being held, the offender shall be committed in custody or on bail, by the summary court of the place where arrested, to the Crown Court concerned, to be dealt with for the original offence. Where a person conditionally discharged by a magistrates' court is convicted for an offence during the specified period by another magistrates' court, that court, if the first court consents, may also deal with him for the original offence.

S. 13: An absolute or conditional discharge shall not be deemed to be a conviction (imposing any disqualification or disability) for any purpose other than the purposes of this Act, except where an offender not less than 17 who is conditionally discharged commits another offence and is sentenced for his original offence. However, this section will not affect the right of an offender to appeal against his conviction or to plead autrefois convict, nor will it affect the revesting or restoration of any property in consequence of the conviction.

This "discharge" of a convicted offender should not be confused with the discharge of an accused person by examining justices who are not satisfied that there is sufficient evidence to put him on trial for any indictable offence.

Probation of Offenders - The P. of C.C. Act 1973 provides:

S. 2: Where a court convicts a person of an offence (for which the sentence is not fixed by law), the court, having regard to the circumstances including the nature of the offence and the character of the offender, may, instead of sentencing him, make a probation order, that is an order requiring him to be under the supervision of a probation officer for a specified period not less than one year nor more than 3 years. The order may in addition require the offender to comply with such requirements as the court considers necessary for securing his good conduct or for preventing future offences. Such an order may include requirements as to the residence of the offender after the court has considered his home surroundings. On the application of a probationer or probation officer, a court may discharge a probation order and substitute an order of conditional discharge (P. of C.C. Act 1973, s. 11). An application for such an order shall be by complaint (M.C. Rules 1968, r. 86).

Before a probation order is made, the court shall explain to the offender the effect of the order (and requirements) and that, if he fails to comply or commits another offence, he will be liable to be sentenced for the original offence. The order shall not be made unless he expresses his willingness (consent) to comply with the requirements thereof.

S. 3: Where a court is satisfied, on medical evidence, that the mental condition of an offender is such as requires and may be susceptible to treatment but is not such as to warrant his detention in pursuance of a hospital order under Part V of the Mental Health Act 1959 the court may, if a probation order is made, include a requirement that the offender shall submit to medical treatment as specified in the section.

S. 4: Where a court makes a probation order, it may include a requirement that the offender shall during the probation period attend at a day training centre.

S. 5 and Sched. 1: A court which makes a probation order may, on the application of the probationer or probation officer, discharge it. A supervising court (which means a magistrates' court or juvenile court for the place named in the order, s. 80) may amend a probation order. It may cancel or add requirements within the limits laid down in the Schedule but cannot reduce the period of probation or extend it beyond the 3 years. If the order is to be amended on the application of the probation officer the court shall summon the probationer to appear and if he is not less than 14, the court cannot amend unless he agrees to comply with the amendment. This is not necessary if the amendment amounts to a reduction of the requirements.

S. 6: If during the period of probation a probationer fails to comply with any of the requirements of the order, a justice of the supervising court (see above) may issue summons or warrant to bring him before the court.

That court may fine him [or make a community service order] or order him to attend at an attendance centre if he is so liable under the conditions of s. 19 of the C.J. Act 1948 (see "Attendance Centres", Chap. 12) or, if probation had been ordered by a summary court, may deal with him for the original offence (if so probation would end, s. 5 (4)) or, if the probation order had been made by the Crown Court, commit him in custody or on bail to appear before that court which may deal with him for the original offence. However a probationer required to submit to mental treatment (under s. 3) who refuses to undergo any surgical or other treatment, shall not be regarded as failing to comply with the requirement if the court considers his refusal was reasonable.

S. 8: If a probationer has been convicted in any part of Great Britain for an offence committed during his period of probation, a judge or justice, authorised under this section, may issue a summons or warrant to bring him before the court which made the probation order. If that court was a magistrates' court the summons or warrant should direct his appearance before the supervising court (see above).

If the probation order had been made by the Crown Court and the subsequent offence had been dealt with by a magistrates' court, that court can commit him in custody or on bail to the Crown Court which made the order. If the Crown Court convicts a person of an offence committed during the period of probation ordered by a court, the Crown Court can deal with him for the original offence. If a magistrates' court convicts a person of an offence committed during a period of probation ordered by another magistrates' court, that court, with the consent of the supervising court of the other place, may deal with him for the original offence.

S. 12 (1): A court which makes a probation order may allow any person to give security for the good behaviour of the offender.

S. 13: A conviction on which a probation order is made shall be deemed not to be a conviction for any purpose other than the purposes of the proceedings in which the order was made and of any subsequent proceedings against the offender under the foregoing provisions of the Act, provided that this shall not apply to the conviction where an offender, not less than 17 when put on probation, is subsequently sentenced for his original offence. Probation after conviction shall not be regarded as a disqualification or disability imposed by law on convicted persons. Probation does not prevent the offender from appealing against his conviction or relying on it in bar of any subsequent proceedings for the same offences nor does it affect the revesting or restoration of any property in consequence of the conviction.

S. 46: Where a probation officer makes a report to a court (other than a juvenile court) to assist the court in dealing with an offender, a copy of the report shall be given to the offender or his Counsel or Solicitor. However, if the offender is under 17 and is not represented, a copy need not be given to him, but shall be given to his parent or guardian if present in court.

S. 47 and Sched. 3: make arrangements for probation areas, probation committees, case committees for petty sessional divisions, probation officers and expenses. Schedule 5 directs that it shall be the duty of probation officers to supervise probationers and other persons placed under their supervision, and to advise, assist and befriend them, to enquire, as directed by the court, into the circumstances or home surroundings of any person so as to assist the court in dealing with his case, to advise, assist and befriend as prescribed, persons who have been released from custody and to perform such duties as may be prescribed or imposed by any enactment. See also the Probation Rules 1965–1974.

S. 49: The Secretary of State may approve and make rules for premises for persons required to reside therein by a probation order and such premises shall be known as "approved probation hostels" if the residents are employed outside the premises and in any other case as "approved probation homes".

S. 50: Any institution which is not an approved probation hostel or home, in which a probationer is required to reside otherwise than for mental treatment shall be subject to government inspection and a person appointed by the Secretary of State shall have power to enter and investigate the treatment of residents, and anyone who obstructs him will commit a summary offence.

M.C. Act 1952, s. 71, allows a court to order a person adjudged to pay a sum by summary conviction, to be placed under the supervision of a named person until the fine is paid. Such a person should befriend and advise the offender so as to induce him to pay and avoid committal to custody and should inform the court as to the offender's circumstances (M.C. Rules 1968, r. 46).

Borstal Institution – When a person not less than 15 but under 21 is convicted on indictment of an offence punishable with imprisonment, and having regard to the circumstances of the offence and after taking into account the offender's character and previous conduct, the court may pass a sentence of borstal training if it is of opinion that it is expedient that he should be detained for not less than 6 months. However, such sentence shall not be passed on a person under 17 on the day of his conviction unless no other method of dealing with him is appropriate.

Before passing such a sentence, the court must consider any report by or on behalf of the Secretary of State, and a copy of the report must be given to the offender, or his counsel or solicitor.

The foregoing provisions apply also to a committal for sentence of borstal training under s. 28, M.C. Act 1952 (C.J. Act 1948, s. 20 (1) and C.J. Act 1961, s. 1).

A magistrates' court which convicts such an offender may, if it considers it appropriate, commit him in custody or on bail (C.J. Act 1967, s. 20) to the Crown Court for sentence to Borstal training (s. 28, M.C. Act 1952). The Crown Court may do so or deal with him in any manner in which the magistrates' court might have dealt with him (C.J. Act 1948, s. 20 (5)).

Prison Act 1952, s. 43: The Secretary of State may provide Borstal Institutions and the Prison Act shall apply to them and to the persons detained therein, and the regulations as to measurement and photographing of prisoners shall also apply.

S. 49: A Borstal trainee who is unlawfully at large may be arrested by a constable without warrant and taken back to the Institution.

S. 45 (as amended by s. 11, C.J. Act 1961): A person sentenced to Borstal training shall be detained in a Borstal Institution for at least 6 months unless otherwise directed by the Secretary of State but not longer than 2 years. After release such a person, for 2 years from the date of his release, shall be under the supervision (with any specified requirements) of a society or person named by the Secretary of State, who may at any time modify or cancel the requirements or cancel the supervision. If such a supervisee fails to comply with any of the requirements he may be recalled, by order made by the Secretary of State, to a Borstal Institution and is liable to be detained there until the 2 years end or for 6 months after his arrest under the order. If he does not come back voluntarily he will be unlawfully at large and under s. 49 may be arrested by a constable without warrant and taken back to the Borstal Institution. Section 12, C.J. Act 1961 authorises a magistrates' court to return to Borstal an offender convicted of another offence while he is an absconder or on release under supervision.

For offence of harbouring escapees, see "Prison Breach", Chap. 21.

Persistent Offenders – No person shall be sentenced by a court to preventive detention or corrective training.

Where an offender is convicted on indictment of an offence punishable with imprisonment for a term of 2 years or more and the conditions specified below are satisfied, then, if the court is satisfied, by reason of his previous conduct and of the likelihood of his committing further offences, that it is expedient to protect the public from him for a substantial time, the court may impose an extended term of imprisonment.

The conditions referred to in the previous paragraph are (a) the offence was committed before the expiration of 3 years from a previous conviction of an offence punishable on indictment with imprisonment for a term of 2 years or more or from his final release from prison after serving a sentence of imprisonment, corrective training or preventive detention passed on such a conviction; and (b) the offender has been convicted on indictment on at least three previous occasions since he attained the age of 21 of offences punishable on indictment with imprisonment for a term of 2 years or more; and (c) the total length of the sentences of imprisonment, corrective training or preventive detention to which he was sentenced on those occasions was not less than 5 years and (i) on at least one of those occasions a sentence of preventive detention was passed on him; or (ii) on at least two of those occasions a sentence of imprisonment (other than a suspended sentence which has not taken effect) or of corrective training was so passed and of those sentences one was a sentence of imprisonment for a term of 3 years or more in respect of one offence or two were sentences of imprisonment each for a term of 2 years or more in respect of one offence.

Where an extended term of imprisonment is imposed on an offender under this section, the court shall issue a certificate (hereafter in this Act referred to as "an extended sentence certificate") stating that the term was so imposed (P. of C.C. Act 1973, s. 28).

For the purposes of condition (a) above, a certificate purporting to be signed by the governor of a prison to the effect (1) that a prisoner was finally released from that prison on a date specified in the certificate after serving a sentence so specified; or (2) that a prisoner had not been finally released from that prison on a date so specified after serving a sentence so specified; shall be evidence of the matter so certified.

For the purposes of condition (b) above, a person who has been convicted by a magistrates' court of an indictable offence and sentenced for that offence by a court of quarter sessions, or on appeal from such a court, to imprisonment, corrective training or preventive detention shall be treated as if he had been convicted of that offence on indictment.

For the purpose of determining whether conditions (a), (b) and (c) above are satisfied in relation to an offender no account shall be taken of any previous conviction or sentence unless notice has been given to the offender at least 3 days before the later sentence is passed on him that it is intended to prove the previous conviction or sentence to the court.

For the purposes of the last foregoing paragraph a certificate purporting to be signed by a constable or a prison officer that a copy of a notice annexed to the certificate was given to an offender shall be evidence that it was so given and of the contents of the notice (P. of C.C. Act 1973, s. 29).

Loiterers and Suspected Persons – The police have by law great powers for the arrest and prosecution of persons who by their actions appear likely to commit crime. A person may use reasonable force in the prevention of crime, or in effecting or assisting in the lawful arrest of offenders or suspected offenders, or of persons unlawfully at large. (This replaces the common law rules on the question when force is justified (C.L. Act 1967, s. 3)).

FREQUENTING AND LOITERING – Any person may arrest without warrant every suspected person or reputed thief frequenting or loitering about or in any river, canal or navigable stream, dock or basin, or any quay, wharf or warehouse near or adjoining thereto, or any street, highway or avenue leading thereto, or any place of public resort or any avenue leading thereto, or any street, highway or any place adjacent to a street or highway, with intent to commit an arrestable offence (Vagrancy Act 1824, s. 4, amended by Penal Servitude Act 1891, s. 7 and C.L. Act 1967, Sched. 2).

The prisoner may be convicted of this offence if from the circumstances of the case and from his known character as proved to the justices, it appears that his intent was to commit an arrestable offence. It shall not be necessary to show that the prisoner was guilty of any particular act or acts tending to show his purpose or intent (Prevention of Crimes Act 1871, s. 15). See also "Extent of Evidence", Chap. 7.

On conviction, prisoner will be treated as a rogue and a vagabond and is liable to 3 months imprisonment from two justices (Vagrancy Act 1824).

A "suspected person" under this section would appear to be a person who has acquired the character of a suspect by reason of his previous conduct.

His previous convictions, etc., need not be known by the police who arrested him (*R.* v. *Clarke* (1950)).

In *Hartley* v. *Ellnor* (1917), it was held that there need not be evidence of a previous conviction or of previous bad character, but that the conduct of the accused on the day in question might be sufficient to render him a suspected person.

In *Ledwith* v. *Roberts* (1937), it was held that there must be some previous act occasioning suspicion prior to the final act indicating the intent to commit an arrestable offence; in other words, one transaction by itself is not sufficient to justify arrest under the section.

The conduct or character of the person must be such as to show he is a "suspected person".

In *Rawlings* v. *Smith* (1938), it was held that *Ledwith* v. *Roberts* did not overrule *Hartley* v. *Ellnor* and that "frequenting" or "loitering" involves something which is continuous or repeated and does not depend on one single act.

Therefore to justify arrest as a suspected person one single suspicious act is not sufficient, and the prisoner's previous conduct should have been such as would make him a suspected person before his actual behaviour indicating intent to commit an arrestable offence which occasioned his arrest.

The driver of a motor vehicle may be a "loiterer" and also a "suspected person". See *Bridge* v. *Campbell* (1947).

A "reputed thief" would appear to be a person who from his associates, conduct, and general mode of living has previously come under notice as a person probably engaged in thieving.

Where the prisoner has been previously convicted as a rogue and a vagabond, or where he on arrest as a rogue and a vagebond (as above) violently resists arrest, he shall, on being convicted of the offence for which he was arrested, be deemed an incorrigible rogue, and the court should commit him (either in custody or on bail – C.J. Act 1967, s. 20) to the next Crown Court, which can order imprisonment not exceeding 1 year (Vagrancy Act 1824, ss. 5, 10).

FOUND ON PREMISES – Any person may arrest any person found in or upon any dwelling-house, warehouse, coach-house, stable or outhouse, or in any inclosed yard, garden or area for any unlawful purpose. The unlawful purpose must be the commission of some criminal offence. Prisoner will be dealt with as a rogue and a vagabond, and is liable to 3 months imprisonment (Vagrancy Act 1824, s. 4).

FOUND ARMED, ETC., WITH INTENT – Any person may arrest any person armed with any gun, pistol, hanger, cutlass, bludgeon or other offensive weapon or having upon him or her any instrument with intent to commit any arrestable offence. Prisoner will be dealt with as a rogue and a vagabond, and is liable to 3 months imprisonment (Vagrancy Act 1824, s. 4).

A county borough constable while on duty may arrest any idle and disorderly person whom he finds disturbing the public peace (Municipal Corporations Act 1882, s. 193).

FOUND WANDERING AND SLEEPING OUT – Any person may arrest any person found wandering about and lodging in any barn or outhouse, or in any deserted or unoccupied building, or in the open air, etc., as more fully described under "Vagrancy Frauds", Chap. 27, and not giving a good account of himself or herself. Prisoner will be treated as rogue and a vagabond and is liable to 3 months imprisonment (Vagrancy Act 1824, s. 4, and Vagrancy Act 1935).

The Prevention of Crime Act 1953 makes it an offence, punishable summarily or on indictment, for any person to have with him in any public place any offensive weapon without lawful authority or reasonable excuse, the proof thereof to lie on him.

In this connection "public place" means any highway and any premises or place to which the public have access, and "offensive weapon" means any article made or adapted for use for causing injury to the person or intended by its carrier for such use by him (*Woodward* v. *Koessler* (1958)). If an article (possessed lawfully or for good reason) is used offensively to cause injury this does not necessarily prove the intent required (that is to use for causing injury) which the prosecution must show in respect of articles which are not offensive weapons per se (*R.* v. *Dayle* (1973)). Where a weapon which is not offensive per se is carried, a conviction for an offence under s. 1 (1) of the Prevention of Crime Act 1953, must be supported by proof of intent to use it offensively before any occasion for its actual use has arisen (*Hylton* v. *Ohlson* (1975)). A constable may arrest without warrant any person whom he has reasonable cause to believe to be committing this offence if he is not satisfied as to that person's identity or place of residence, or has reasonable cause to believe that arrest is necessary in order to prevent the commission by him of any other offence in which an offensive weapon might be used.

Prisons – The Prison Act 1952 provides:

S. 8: Every prison officer while acting as such has all the powers, etc., of a constable. See "Arrest", Chap. 3.

S. 13: A person is deemed to be in legal custody while he is confined in or is being taken to or from any prison and while he is working or is otherwise outside the prison in the custody or control of a prison officer.

S. 22 deals with the removal of prisoners for judicial or other purposes. See "Habeas Corpus", Chap. 5.

S. 23: For taking a person to or from any prison (or place of detention, s. 43) under competent and proper order a constable or other officer may act outside the area of his jurisdiction, having all the powers, etc., of his office.

S. 39: Any person who aids any prisoner in escaping or attempting to escape from a prison or who, to help an escape, conveys anything into a prison or to a prisoner or places anything outside a prison for a prisoner, shall be guilty of an arrestable offence. See "Prison Breach", Chap. 21.

S. 40: The unlawful conveyance of spirits or tobacco into a prison or to or for a prisoner, or an officer allowing same.

S. 41: The unlawful conveyance of any letter or any other thing into or out of a prison or to or for a prisoner.

S. 49: A constable may arrest without warrant any prisoner unlawfully at large. See "Arrest", Chap. 3.

S. 53: "Prison" does not include a naval, military or air force prison.

The Prison Rules 1964 and 1974 deal with the treatment of prisoners.

Restriction of Offensive Weapons – Any person who manufactures, sells or hires or offers for sale or hire, or exposes or has in his possession for the purposes of sale or hire or lends or gives to any other person (a) any knife which has a blade which opens automatically by hand pressure applied to a button, spring or other device in or attached to the handle of the knife, sometimes known as a "flick knife" or "flick gun", or (b) any knife which has a blade which is released from the handle or sheath thereof by the force of gravity or the application of centrifugal force and which, when released, is locked in place by means of a button, spring, lever, or other device, sometimes known as a "gravity knife", shall be guilty of an offence.

The importation of any such knife is prohibited (Restriction of Offensive Weapons Acts 1959, 1961).

CHAPTER 29

PERSONS

	Page		Page
Aliens	410	Veterinary Surgeons .	417
Immigration Act 1971 .	412	Farriers	417
Husband and Wife . .	414	Pharmaceutical Chemists .	417
Landlord and Tenant .	414	Opticians . . .	417
Clergymen . . .	414	Nurses	417
Constables . . .	414	Midwives . . .	418
Lawyers, etc. . . .	416	Master and Servant .	418
Doctors	416	Architects . . .	418
Dentists	416	Personation . . .	418

Aliens – An alien is a foreigner, a subject or citizen of a foreign country. An alien, while in this country, is subject to its laws just as if he were a British subject.

The British Nationality Act 1948 defines the status of a British subject, a status derived by virtue of citizenship. Every person who is a citizen of the U.K. and colonies or is a commonwealth citizen under any enactment in force in Canada, Australia, New Zealand, India, Rhodesia, Ceylon, Ghana, Fiji, Malaysia, Cyprus, Nigeria, Sierra Leone, Tanzania, Jamaica, Trinidad and Tobago, Uganda, Kenya, Zanzibar, Malawi, Malta, Zambia, The Gambia, Guyana, Botswana, Lesotho, Singapore, Mauritius, Tonga and Barbados, shall by virtue of that citizenship have the status of a British subject.

REGISTRATION – The Immigration (Registration with Police) Regs. 1972 make provision as to the effect of a condition imposed under the Immigration Act 1971, requiring an alien to register with the police. Each police area is a registration district with a local register of aliens. The registration officer is the Chief Constable (reg. 4). An alien is required to attend the registration office and furnish such information, documents and other particulars (including a recent photograph) as may be required (reg. 5). In certain circumstances an alien is exempt from registration (reg. 6). An alien must notify any changes in the particulars required at registration, including change of address, within 7 days. When he is absent from his residence for over 2 months he must report his address and any later address, and his return to his registration officer. If the alien has no residence and travels about, after 7 days in any registration district he must report forthwith, and if he changes his address in any district, he must report his new address within 7 days. If an alien has no address he may have a resident referee to whom he shall report changes of address and who will keep the registration officer informed (reg. 7). Every alien, on demand by an immigration officer or constable, shall produce his registration certificate or else give a satisfactory reason for his failure to produce it. Where an alien has failed to produce his registration certificate he may be required within the following 48 hours to produce his certificate at a Police Station specified by the officer or constable (reg. 11).

The Immigration (Hotel Records) Order 1974 makes provision as respects the records to be kept of persons staying at hotels and similar premises. The keeper of any premises furnished or unfurnished where lodging or sleeping accommodation is provided for reward (except premises exempted by the Chief Constable such as schools, hospitals, clubs, etc.), shall keep a register (open to inspection by any constable or authorised person) of all persons over 16 staying there for one night or more. Every such person, on arrival, shall give his name and nationality. If he is an alien, he shall also give particulars of his passport or registration certificate, and on departure give his next destination. The keeper of the premises shall ask for all this and keep a record of same for at least 12 months (art. 19).

The Immigration (Control of Entry through Republic of Ireland) Order 1972. This Order excludes from the operation of s. 1 (3) of the Immigration Act 1971 (which exempts from control passengers travelling on local journeys within the common travel area, that is to say the area comprising the United Kingdom, Channel Islands, Isle of Man and the Republic of Ireland) certain persons who enter the United Kingdom through the Republic of Ireland (art. 3). The main classes of persons are those who merely passed through the Republic of Ireland, persons requiring visas, persons who entered the Republic of Ireland unlawfully and persons who are subject to directions given by the Secretary of State for their exclusion from the United Kingdom on the ground that such exclusion is conducive to the public good.

The Order also imposes restrictions on persons who are not patrial (other than those excluded from the operation of s. 1 (3)) and who enter the United Kingdom from the Republic after coming from a place outside the common travel area or after leaving the United Kingdom while having a limited leave to enter or remain there which has since expired (art. 4). These restrictions impose a limit on the period of their stay in the United Kingdom; except in relation to nationals of states who are members of the European Economic Community, a prohibition on taking up employment or any occupation for reward; and, in the case of certain persons over 16 years who require a visa to enter the United Kingdom, a requirement to register with the police.

The Immigration (Exemption from Control) Order 1972, exempts certain classes of persons from some or all of the provisions of the Immigration Act 1971 relating to those who are not patrial.

The Immigration (Places of Detention) Direction 1972, specifies places in which persons may be detained under the provisions of the Immigration Act 1971. When a person is detained pending examination and decision as to entry or pending removal, he may be detained at—

1. Any place used by an immigration officer for the purpose of his functions at a port or airport.
2. Any place specially provided for the purpose of detention at any port or at Government buildings.
3. Any place at which appeals under Part II of the Act are heard or any place specially provided for detention in the vicinity of such premises.
4. Any police station, prison or remand centre or, in the case of a person under the age of 17, any place of safety. (A place of safety has the same meaning as in the Children and Young Persons Act 1933.)

A person shall not continue to be detained in accordance with the provisions of the Direction elsewhere than in a place of safety, prison or remand centre if five days have elapsed since the day on which he was first detained.

Immigration Act 1971 – All those who are in this Act expressed to have the right of abode in the U.K. shall be free to live in, and to come and go into and from, the U.K. without let or hindrance except such as may be required under and in accordance with this Act to enable their right to be established or as may be otherwise lawfully imposed on any person (s. 1 (1)).

Section 2 of the Act indicates the persons who have a right of abode in the U.K. and these are called "patrial".

Section 3 contains general provisions for regulation and control of persons who are not patrial, and gives power to the Secretary of State to make rules for regulating entry and stay in the U.K. of such persons.

A person who is not patrial shall be guilty of an offence punishable on summary conviction in any of the following cases:

(a) if contrary to this Act he knowingly enters the United Kingdom in breach of a deportation order or without leave:

(b) if, having only a limited leave to enter or remain in the United Kingdom, he knowingly either—

  (i) remains beyond the time limited by the leave; or

  (ii) fails to observe a condition of the leave;

(c) if, having lawfully entered the United Kingdom without leave, he remains without leave beyond the time allowed;
(d) if, without reasonable excuse, he fails to comply with any requirement imposed on him to report to a medical officer of health, or to attend, or submit to a test or examination, as required by such an officer;
(e) if, without reasonable excuse, he fails to observe any restriction imposed on him as to residence or as to reporting to the police or to an immigration officer;
(f) if he disembarks in the United Kingdom from a ship or aircraft after being placed on board with a view to his removal from the United Kingdom;
(g) if he embarks in contravention of a restriction imposed by or under an Order in Council (s. 24 (1)).

A constable or immigration officer may arrest without warrant anyone who has, or whom he, with reasonable cause, suspects to have, committed or attempted to commit an offence under this section other than an offence under sub-s. (1) (d) above (s. 24 (2)).

Any person knowingly concerned in making or carrying out arrangements for securing or facilitating the entry into the United Kingdom of anyone whom he knows or has reasonable cause for believing to be an illegal entrant shall be guilty of an offence (s. 25 (1)).

Without prejudice to sub-s. (1) above a person knowingly harbouring anyone whom he knows or has reasonable cause for believing to be either an illegal entrant or a person who has committed an offence under s. 24 (1) (b) or (c) above, shall be guilty of an offence (s. 25 (2)).

A constable or immigration officer may arrest without warrant anyone who has, or whom he, with reasonable cause, suspects to have, committed an offence under sub-s. (1) above (s. 25 (3)).

Subsection (1) above shall apply to things done outside as well as to things done in the United Kingdom where they are done (a) by a citizen of the United Kingdom and Colonies; (b) by a British subject by virtue of s. 2 of the British Nationality Act 1948 (continuance of certain subjects of the Republic of Ireland as British subjects); (c) by a British subject without citizenship by virtue of s. 13 or 16 of that Act (which relate respectively to British subjects whose citizenship had not been ascertained at the commencement of that Act and to persons who had ceased to be British on loss of British nationality by a parent); (d) by a British subject by virtue of the British Nationality Act 1965; or (e) by a British protected person (within the meaning of the British Nationality Act 1948) (s. 25 (5)).

Where a person convicted on indictment of an offence under sub-s. (1) above is at the time of the offence (a) the owner or one of the owners of a ship, aircraft or vehicle **used** or intended to be used in carrying out the arrangements in respect of which the offence is committed; or (b) a director or manager of a company which is the owner or one of the owners of any such ship, aircraft or vehicle; or (c) captain of any such ship or aircraft then subject to sub-s. (7) and (8) below the court before which he is convicted may order the forfeiture of the ship, aircraft or vehicle.

In this subsection "owner" in relation to a ship, aircraft or vehicle which is the subject of a hire-purchase agreement, includes the person in possession of it under that agreement and, in relation to a ship or aircraft, includes a charterer (s. 25 (6)).

Husband and Wife – As regards any defence of coercion or compulsion, see "Excuses for Crime" (Chap. 1). As regards conspiracy, see Chap. 23.

As regards the giving of evidence by a wife against her husband, or vice versa, see "Accused Persons and their Husbands or Wives", Chap. 7.

The Married Women's Property Act 1964 provides that money and property derived from a housekeeping allowance shall, in the absence of agreement to the contrary, be treated as belonging to husband and wife in equal shares.

Landlord and Tenant – A landlord of a house may be held responsible if the house is conducted as a brothel. See "Brothels", Chap. 10.

Clergymen – Ministers of religion are by law specially protected when engaged in carrying out their duties in a place of Divine worship or in a burial ground, as follows:

Offences against the Person Act 1861, s. 36: This section makes it an offence to obstruct, prevent or endeavour to obstruct or prevent any clergyman or other minister in or from celebrating Divine service or officiating in any place of Divine service or in the performance of the burial service. It is also a misdemeanour to strike or offer any violence to any clergyman or other minister engaged in the discharge of his duties as above.

Ecclesiastical Courts Jurisdiction Act 1860, s. 2: It is a summary offence to molest, disturb or by any unlawful means disquiet or misuse any authorised preacher or clergyman celebrating any Divine service or office in any church, chapel or burial ground, and under s. 3 the offender may be arrested by any churchwarden or constable. See "Disturbing Public Worship", Chap. 20.

Constables – By the Police Act 1964, every member of a police force maintained for a police area, and every special constable, shall on appointment, be attested as a constable by making a declaration, ((a) in the case of the Metropolitan police district before the Commissioner or an Assistant Commissioner,

(b) in any other case before a justice of the peace) in the following form:

> I, of do solemnly and sincerely declare and affirm that I will well and truly serve Our Sovereign Lady the Queen in the office of constable, without favour or affection, malice or ill will; and that I will to the best of my power cause the peace to be kept and preserved, and prevent all offences against the persons and properties of Her Majesty's subjects; and that while I continue to hold the said office I will to the best of my skill and knowledge discharge all the duties thereof faithfully according to law (s. 18 and Sched. 2).

A member of a police force shall have all the powers and privileges of a constable throughout England and Wales, and a special constable shall have all the powers and privileges of a constable in the police area for which he is appointed (s. 19).

It is an offence to assault, or resist or wilfully obstruct a constable in the execution of his duty, or to assault, resist or wilfully obstruct a person assisting a constable in the execution of his duty (s. 51) and see Chap. 8.

Any person who with intent to deceive impersonates a member of a police force or special constable, or makes any statement or does any act calculated falsely to suggest that he is such a member or constable, shall be guilty of an offence and liable on summary conviction to imprisonment for a term not exceeding 6 months or to a fine not exceeding £100, or to both.

Any person, who, not being a constable, wears any article of police uniform in circumstances where it gives him an appearance so nearly resembling that of a member of a police force as to be calculated to deceive shall be guilty of an offence and liable on summary conviction to a fine not exceeding £100.

Any person who, not being a member of a police force or special constable, has in his possession any article of police uniform shall, unless he proves that he obtained possession of that article lawfully and has possession of it for a lawful purpose, be guilty of an offence and liable on summary conviction to a fine not exceeding £20.

In this section, "article of police uniform" means any article of uniform or any distinctive badge or mark or document of identification usually issued to members of police forces or special constables, or anything having the appearance of such an article, badge, mark or document; and "special constable" means a special constable appointed for a police area (s. 52).

Any person who causes, or attempts to cause, or does any act calculated to cause, disaffection amongst the members of any police force, or induces or attempts to induce, or does any act calculated to induce, any member of a police force to withhold his services or to commit breaches of discipline, shall be guilty of an offence and liable—(a) on summary conviction to imprisonment for a term not exceeding 6 months or to a fine not exceeding £100, or to both; (b) on conviction on indictment to imprisonment for a term not exceeding 2 years or to a fine or to both. This applies to a special constable (s. 53).

Lawyers, etc. – It is not lawful for a person who is not a barrister, solicitor or other qualified member of the legal profession to act as such.

It is a summary offence for any unqualified person wilfully to pretend to be a qualified solicitor (Solicitors Act 1974).

Various statutes allow certain authorised persons, who may not be lawyers and usually are not, to conduct court proceedings before magistrates: for example, inland revenue officers, factory inspectors, school inspectors, etc.

Various Acts authorise legal proceedings by a local authority for breaches of the Acts. Under s. 223, Local Government Act 1972, a local authority can authorise any member or officer of the authority to institute and carry on (or defend) summary proceedings. However a police officer is not a servant or agent or officer of a local authority (*Fisher* v. *Oldham Corporation* (1930)).

Doctors – It is an offence for any person to represent himself to be a registered medical practitioner when in fact he is not one.

A person who is duly qualified to practise any branch of the medical profession may register himself with the Medical Council, and his name will appear on the yearly "Medical Register".

The Medical Act 1956, s. 31, makes it a summary offence for any person to wilfully and falsely pretend that he is a physician, doctor of medicine, surgeon, general practitioner, apothecary, etc., duly registered under the Act, or that he is recognised in law as a physician, etc.

The Professions Supplementary to Medicine Act 1960 provides for the registration of chiropodists, dietitians, medical laboratory technicians, occupational therapists, physiotherapists, radiographers, and remedial gymnasts. The Act also establishes a Council for such professions and a Board (known as the Chiropodists Board, the Dietitians Board, etc.) for each of these professions under the general supervision of the Council (s. 1). A register of the members of each profession is maintained by the Board and is open to public inspection (s. 2). The use of the term "state registered chiropodist", etc., is restricted to persons who appear on the register (s. 6). Wilfully making false representations to obtain registration is an offence (s. 7).

Dentists – It is a summary offence for any person to practise or hold himself out as practising dentistry unless he is registered in the Dentists' Register. However, a registered medical practitioner may practise dentistry, and a registered chemist may extract teeth in urgent cases.

A company may carry on the business of dentistry if its business is confined to dentistry and the majority of its directors and all the operating staff are registered dentists.

Hospitals and approved dental schools may also carry on the business of dentistry. See the Dentists Acts 1956 and 1957.

Veterinary Surgeons – The Veterinary Surgeons Act 1966 makes provision for the management of the veterinary profession, the registration of veterinary surgeons and for regulating their professional education and professional conduct etc. It is an offence for an unqualified person to take or use the title of veterinary surgeon (s. 20).

Farriers – The Farriers (Registration) Act 1975 makes provision for the prevention and avoidance of suffering by, and cruelty to horses arising from the shoeing of horses by unskilled persons. The Act promotes the training of Farriers and Shoeing Smiths, provides for the establishment of a Farriers' Registration Council to register persons engaged in farriery and the shoeing of horses and prohibits the shoeing of horses by unqualified persons. The Act came into force on 1st Jan. 1976 with the exception of s. 16 (governing offences committed by unregistered persons) which was not in force at the date of going to press.

Pharmaceutical Chemists – Under the Medicines Act 1968, a person who sells goods by retail as a chemist or describes himself as a chemist and druggist or pharmaceutical chemist shall be registered with the Pharmaceutical Society as a pharmacist, and the Statutory Committee of the Pharmaceutical Society may remove his name from the register for misconduct. If he sells poisons he should exhibit his certificate of registration in his premises and have his premises registered.

Inspectors are appointed by the Society to enforce this Act (s. 25). See also "Poisons", Chap. 39.

Opticians – The Opticians Act 1958 established a General Optical Council to regulate the practice of opticians, etc. Under ss. 20–22 it is an offence (subject to certain exceptions) for a person who is not a registered ophthalmic optician to test the sight of another person; restrictions are placed on the sale and supply of appliances to correct, remedy, or relieve a defect of sight; and penalties are provided for persons pretending to be registered, etc.

Nurses – The Nurses Act 1957 authorised a General Nursing Council for England and Wales and this Council keeps a register of nurses for the sick and a roll of nurses. Before any person may be registered as a nurse and use the title "nurse", he or she must have undergone the prescribed training and have the prescribed experience in the nursing of the sick. The Council may issue certificates of registration and have power to cancel such registration.

Private agencies for the supply of nurses must be licensed by the relevant local authority (Nurses Agencies Act 1957).

It is a summary offence for any person except a registered nurse, an enrolled nurse or a children's nurse to unlawfully assume the name or title of nurse (Nurses Act 1957, s. 27). See also "Nursing Homes", Chap. 39.

Midwives – Under the Midwives Act 1951, a woman may not carry on the occupation of a midwife unless she is duly certified and has her name on the roll of midwives kept by the Central Midwives Board. It is a summary offence for any woman who is not certified under the Act to use the title of midwife or any description implying that she is a qualified or authorised midwife (s. 8). It is also an offence for any person not certified under the Act to attend a woman in childbirth unless under the supervision of a medical practitioner or unless in a case of sudden or urgent necessity (s. 9).

Local Health Authorities are required to provide certified midwives adequate for the needs of their areas (Health Services and Public Health Act 1968, s. 10), and when this is done it will be a summary offence for an unqualified person to act as a midwife for gain (s. 11).

Master and Servant – It is a summary offence to falsely personate a master and give a false servant's character, or to give false particulars of service regarding a servant, or for a person when offering himself as a servant to use a false character or give false particulars of his services (Servants' Characters Act 1792).

Architects – The Architects (Registration) Act 1931 established an Architects Registration Council, which keeps a register of architects. The name of a registered person may be struck off the register if he is convicted of a criminal offence or is found guilty of disgraceful conduct as an architect.

Under a similar Act of 1938, a person shall not practise or carry on business as an "architect" unless he is registered, on penalty of fine on summary conviction. This will not apply to the use of the title "naval architect", "landscape architect" or "golf course architect".

Personation – Personation is the passing of oneself off as another. False personation is a cheat punishable on indictment at common law, but apparently only if the cheat is of such a nature as affects or is likely to affect the public at large.

The wearing of or masquerading in the clothing of the opposite sex is not in itself an offence. The attendant circumstances, however, may justify prosecution for some specific offence.

Personating a woman's husband, and thereby having connection with her is rape. See Chap. 10.

Personation of a voter at an election is an offence. See Chap. 21.

Falsely pretending to act under the authority of a County Court is an offence (County Courts Act 1959, s. 188).

Personating bail, viz. without lawful authority or excuse (the proof of which is on the party accused) acknowledging in the name of any other person any recognizance or bail before any court, is an offence (Forgery Act 1861, s. 34).

False personation for any purpose prejudicial to the safety or interests of the State is an offence. See "Official Secrets Acts", Chap. 20.

Personation of a customs and excise officer for any unlawful purpose is punishable summarily or on indictment and the offender may be detained (s. 7) by a constable, etc. (s. 274) (Customs and Excise Act 1952).

It is an offence for any person, with intent to deceive, to impersonate a member of a police force or special constable (Police Act 1964, s. 52). See "Constables", *ante*.

It is a summary offence for any person with intent to deceive falsely to represent himself to be a person authorised by the Minister of Social Security or the Supplementary Benefits Commission to act in any capacity (Ministry of Social Security Act 1966, s. 31).

A person commits an offence if, with a view to purchasing or acquiring, or procuring the repair, test or proof of, any firearm or ammunition to which s. 1 of the Firearms Act 1968 applies, or a shot gut, he personates a person to whom a certificate has been granted (Firearms Act 1968, s. 3 (5)).

It is an offence for any person to personate another for the purpose of providing a blood sample for a test required to give effect to a direction under s. 20 of the Act (power of court to require use of blood tests) or to proffer a child knowing that it is not the child named in the direction (Family Law Reform Act 1969, s. 24).

CHAPTER 30

HER MAJESTY'S FORCES

	Page
Interference with Military	420
False Characters . .	420
False Discharges . .	420
Deserters and Absentees .	421
Property of H.M. Forces .	421
Pensioners . . .	422
Uniforms . . .	422
Decorations . . .	423
Billeting . . .	423
Requisitioning of Vehicles	424
Incitement to Disaffection Act 1934 . . .	425

Interference with Military – It is a summary offence for any person wilfully to obstruct or otherwise interfere with any officer, soldier or airman in the execution of his duties. To injure, drug, etc., any soldier so as to enable him to avoid military service is also a summary offence (Army and Air Force Acts 1955, s. 42). Under the Manœuvres Act 1958 it is a summary offence wilfully and unlawfully to obstruct or interfere with the execution of duly authorised military manœuvres, or, without due authority, to enter or remain in any camp (such trespasser may be removed by any constable or by order of any commissioned officer).

False Characters – It is a summary offence for any person joining or offering to join H.M. Naval, Military or Marine Forces, to make use of any forged statements as to his character or employment or of any statement as to his character or employment which to his knowledge is false. It is also a summary offence for any person to make a false written statement as to the character or employment of any man, to be used for the purpose of joining H.M. Forces (Seamen's and Soldiers' False Characters Act 1906).

False Discharges – It is a summary offence to forge the certificate of service or discharge of any person who has served in H.M. Forces, or to forge any certificate purporting to be one of service or discharge, or to knowingly make use of any such forged certificate, or to personate the holder of any such certificate (Seamen's and Soldiers' False Characters Act 1906).

Deserters and Absentees – The general rule is that on reasonable suspicion a constable may arrest without warrant any deserter or absentee without leave from H.M. regular forces (Navy, Army, Air Force and Marines). See Army and Air Force Acts 1955, s. 186, and Naval Discipline Act 1957, s. 105.

Such a person may be arrested with or without warrant and should be brought before a magistrates' court. The court may order him to be handed over to an escort or may remand him to prison or police custody to await an escort. His own authorities will subsequently deal with him.

Where the deserter or absentee has surrendered to or has been arrested by the police, a certificate from the officer in charge of the police station concerned giving the facts will be evidence of the matters so stated.

An absentee who has merely overstayed his leave and is willing to rejoin his unit, when an escort is considered unnecessary, may be put on the train for his unit, having been given a railway warrant if necessary.

Any person who denies he is a deserter or absentee or who asks to be taken before a magistrate should be taken before a magistrates' court (Army and Air Force Acts 1955, s. 186, and the Naval Discipline Act 1957, s. 105). If he claims that he is not an absentee or deserter and therefore is not subject to military law, the court should take depositions under the M.C. Act 1952 and Rules 1968. If the court decides that he is, he can appeal to the divisional court on a case stated and the magistrates' court should admit him to bail pending the decision. If no such appeal the court will commit him to military custody.

Reservists called out for annual training or on permanent service, who without reasonable excuse fail to join the colours, are liable to arrest, also members of the Territorial Army who fail, without reasonable excuse, to report on embodiment; but the police should not take action in such cases except on instructions from the military authorities.

Men of the Territorial Army who absent themselves from drills or training are not liable to arrest by the police.

It is a summary offence falsely to represent oneself to be a deserter (Army and Air Force Acts 1955, s. 191, and Naval Discipline Act 1957, s. 96).

It is a summary offence to procure or attempt to procure a soldier, sailor or airman to desert or absent himself without leave, or knowingly to aid a deserter or absentee without leave (Army and Air Force Acts 1955, s. 192, and Naval Discipline Act 1957, s. 97).

Property of Her Majesty's Forces – Under s. 195, Army and Air Force Acts 1955 and s. 98 of the Naval Discipline Act 1957, it is a summary offence to have any illicit dealings with any property of H.M. Forces. See also "Public Stores", Chap. 18.

Such illicit dealings include any

(1) Buying, exchanging, taking in pawn, detaining or receiving same from any person on any pretence whatever;

(2) Soliciting or enticing any person to sell, exchange, pawn or give away same; and

(3) Assisting or acting for any person in selling, exchanging, pawning or making away with same.

It will be a good defence for accused to prove that he acted in ignorance of the same being such property as described above, or that same was duly sold by the authorities, or that same was the personal property of an ex-member of the Forces.

If such property as above described is found in the possession of any person, he may be brought before a magistrates' court, and if the court has reasonable ground to believe that the property was illegally obtained as above he may be convicted unless he satisfies the court that he came by the property lawfully.

A magistrates' court may issue a warrant to search for such property as in the case of stolen goods.

Any person found committing the above offence may be arrested without warrant, and any person to whom any such army property is offered may, and should, arrest the person offering same for sale, pawn or delivery (Army and Air Force Acts 1955, s. 195 and Naval Discipline Act 1957, ss. 98 and 106).

An offence by a serving soldier in connection with government property at his barracks or camp should be dealt with by his commanding officer under military law (*R.* v. *Kirkup* (1950)).

Pensioners – In general, the making of any false statement or the supplying of any false information in connection with pensions, allowances, etc., is a summary offence.

It is a summary offence for any person to receive, detain or have in possession, as a pledge or security for a debt, any official document or certificate issued in connection with the right of any person to pension, pay, allowances, etc., in connection with service in Her Majesty's Forces (for a similar provision as regards pensions for civil non-effective services, see C.J. Act 1925, s. 37). It is also a summary offence for any person, without lawful authority or excuse (the proof of which shall lie on such person), to have in his possession any such official document or certificate or any certificate of discharge or any other official document issued in connection with the mobilisation or demobilisation of any of Her Majesty's Forces or its members (Army and Air Force Acts 1955, s. 196, and Naval Discipline Act 1957, s. 99).

Uniforms – Under the Uniforms Act 1894 it is a summary offence for any person not serving in the Military (or Air) Forces to wear without Her Majesty's permission the uniform of any of these Forces, or any dress having the appearance of or bearing any of the regimental or other distinctive marks of such uniform.

However, this prohibition of the unauthorised use of military uniform is not to prevent any person wearing any uniform in a stage play, music hall, circus, or *bona fide* military representation.

It is also a summary offence for any person not serving in Her Majesty's Naval or Military (or Air) Forces to wear any such uniform or dress resembling same, in such a manner and under such circumstances as to be likely to bring contempt on that uniform. It is a similar offence for any person to employ another to so wear that uniform or dress.

Using any official uniform without lawful authority for the purpose of gaining admission to a prohibited place or for purposes prejudicial to the safety or interests of the State is a misdemeanour (Official Secrets Act 1920, s. 1). See "Official Secrets Acts", Chap. 20.

Decorations – The rule is that any of the Sovereign's decorations or medals may only be worn by persons to whom they have been awarded, or by persons entitled to wear them.

The unauthorised use of any military decoration or medal or medal ribbon or any badge supplied or authorised by the Army or Air Council is prohibited, and it is a summary offence for –

(1) Any unauthorised person to use or wear same or anything as nearly resembling the same as to be calculated to deceive;

(2) Any person falsely to represent that he is or has been entitled to use or wear same;

(3) Any person, without lawful authority or excuse, to supply or offer to supply same to a person not authorised to use or wear same.

This section does not prohibit the wearing or supply of ordinary regimental badges or ornaments representing the same (Army and Air Force Acts 1955, s. 197).

Any illegal dealing in Naval, Military or Air Force decorations and medals, such as buying, taking in pawn, detaining, etc. (as given under "Property of Her Majesty's Forces") is a summary offence unless same are the personal property of an ex-member of the service or of the legal personal representatives of an officer or soldier who has died.

Billeting – Power is given by the Army and Air Force Acts 1955, for the compulsory provision by the police of accommodation for members of Her Majesty's Forces when proceeding on duty from place to place, and this is termed billeting.

Where a billeting requisition has been produced to the chief officer of police for the area specified in the requisition he must, on the demand of the commanding officer or any officer, soldier or airman authorised by him in writing, billet such number of persons or vehicles as may be required by the officer or soldier making the demand, not exceeding the number specified in the requisition. A chief officer of police may delegate these duties to a constable of any class (s. 156).

Billets may be provided in any inn, hotel or other premises providing sleeping accommodation for reward, in any building to which the public habitually have access, or which is wholly or partly maintained out of rates, or in any dwelling, outhouse, warehouse, barn or stables, but not in any other premises (s. 155).

A local authority may make a scheme for provision of billets and where such scheme is in force the chief officer of police must act in accordance with it (s. 157).

The occupiers of premises on which persons or vehicles have been billeted must furnish such accommodation, including meals, as the officer, soldier or airman demanding the billets may require, at the rates prescribed by law (s. 158).

Any person aggrieved by having an undue number of persons billeted upon him, or claiming exemption, may apply to a person or persons appointed on behalf of the local authority by the Minister of Housing and Local Government (s. 159).

Where any damage is caused by the billeting of persons or vehicles the occupier of the premises may recover damages from the Army or Air Council (s. 160).

Any person who refuses to receive and accommodate any person or vehicle billeted on him, or tries to pay off any person billeted on him instead of furnishing the accommodation is liable to summary prosecution (s. 161).

The above provisions apply to civilians employed with the forces (s. 162).

The prices payable for the accommodation provided are prescribed by regulations of the Army or Air Council made with the consent of the Treasury (s. 158).

Requisitioning of Vehicles – The Army and Air Force Acts 1955 provide for the compulsory requisitioning of vehicles, aircraft, horses, food, forage and stores for the purposes of Her Majesty's Forces.

A requisitioning order may be issued to a commanding officer who may give directions for the provision of all or any of the vehicles, specified in the order. A chief officer of police for any area specified in a requisitioning order must, whenever practicable, arrange for constables to be available for accompanying officers or soldiers requisitioning vehicles (s. 166).

Payment will be made for the use of, and any damage to such vehicles (s. 168).

Any persons failing to furnish any vehicle required by a requisitioning order, or obstructing any officer or other person in the exercise of his duties as to the requisitioning of vehicles is liable to summary prosecution (s. 171).

The above provisions apply to horses, aircraft, food, forage and stores as they apply to vehicles (s. 172).

Incitement to Disaffection Act 1934 – The offences under this Act are as follows:

(1) Maliciously and advisedly to endeavour to seduce any member of H.M. Forces from his duty or allegiance to Her Majesty (s. 1).

(2) With intent to commit or to aid, abet, counsel or procure the commission of any offence under s. 1, to have in possession or under control any document of such a nature that the dissemination of copies thereof among members of H.M. Forces would constitute such an offence (s. 2).

No prosecution under the Act shall take place without the consent of the Director of Public Prosecutions, to whom any case must be reported. See Appendix III.

If a judge of the High Court is satisfied by information on oath that there is reasonable ground for suspecting that an offence under the Act has been committed and that evidence of the commission thereof is to be found at any premises or place specified, he may grant a search warrant authorising entry, search and seizure in accordance with the section.

Anything seized may be retained for a month or until conclusion of proceedings commenced within that period, and the Police Property Act 1897 shall apply to such property (s. 2).

CHAPTER 31

DEALERS

	Page
Scrap Metal Dealers .	426
Pedlars	430
Hawkers . . .	431
Game Dealers. . .	431
Police Prosecutions. .	432
Domestic Servants' Registries	432
Dealers in Securities .	432
Mock Auctions Act 1961 .	434
Protection of Depositors Act 1963 . . .	435
Ministry of Social Security Act 1966 . . .	435

Scrap Metal Dealers – Scrap Metal Dealers Act 1964. Every local authority shall maintain a register of scrap metal dealers, and it is an offence for any person to carry on business as a scrap metal dealer unless he is registered with the local authority (s. 1 (1) and (7)).

A person shall be treated as carrying on business as a scrap metal dealer in the area of a local authority if, and only if, (a) a place (including any land, whether consisting of enclosed premises or not (s. 9)) in that area is occupied by him as a scrap metal store; (b) no place is occupied by him as a scrap metal store, whether in that area or elsewhere, but he has his usual place of residence in that area, or (c) no place is occupied by him as a scrap metal store whether in that area or elsewhere, but a place in that area is occupied by him wholly or partly for that business (s. 1 (2)).

On receipt of an application by any person carrying on or proposing to carry on business as a scrap metal dealer, the local authority shall enter the following particulars in the register: (a) full name; (b) address—if an individual, his usual place of residence; if a body corporate, of its registered or principal office; (c) the address of each place in the area (if any) occupied as a scrap metal store; (d) if the business is carried on in the circumstances mentioned in s. 1 (2) (b) above, the fact that the business is so carried on; (e) if the business is carried on in the circumstances mentioned in s. 1 (2) (c) above, the fact that the business is so carried on, and the address of the place (s. 1 (3) and (4)).

If any event occurs involving an alteration of particulars, the dealer must give notice to the local authority within 28 days. If the dealer ceases to carry on business he must give notice to the local authority within 28 days (s. 1 (5)). Failure to comply is an offence (s. 1 (7) or (8)).

Registration with a local authority lasts for 3 years and may be renewed for periods of 3 years (s. 1 (6)).

It shall be the duty of every local authority to enforce the provisions of this section (s. 1 (9)).

Special provisions are made for local authorities carrying on business as scrap metal dealers (s. 1 (10)).

Every scrap metal dealer shall, at each scrap metal store, keep a book and enter particulars with respect to (a) all scrap metal received at that place, and (b) all scrap metal either processed at, or despatched from, that place. He may keep two books, one for metal falling within (a) and the other for metal falling within (b) (s. 2 (1)).

The particulars required under s. 2 (1) (a) above are: (a) the description and weight of the scrap metal; (b) the date and time of the receipt of the scrap metal; (c) if the scrap metal is received from another person, the full name and address of that person; (d) the price, if any, payable in respect of the receipt of the scrap metal, if that price has been ascertained at the time when the entry in the book relating to that scrap metal is to be made; (e) where the requirements under "(d)" do not apply, the value of the scrap metal at the time when the entry is to be made as estimated by the dealer; (f) in the case of scrap metal delivered at the place in question by means of a mechanically propelled vehicle bearing a registration mark (whether the vehicle belongs to the dealer or not), the registration mark borne by the vehicle.

These particulars must be entered immediately after the receipt of the scrap metal (s. 2 (2) and (4)).

The particulars required under s. 2 (1) (b) above are: (a) the description and weight of the scrap metal; (b) the date of processing or, as the case may be, despatch of the scrap metal, and, if processed, the process applied; (c) in the case of scrap metal despatched on sale or exchange, the full name and address of the person to whom the scrap metal is sold or with whom it is exchanged, and the consideration for which it is sold or exchanged; (d) in the case of scrap metal processed or despatched otherwise than on sale or exchange, the value of the scrap metal immediately before its processing or despatch as estimated by the dealer.

These particulars must be entered immediately after the processing or despatch (s. 2 (3) and (4)).

Any book recording the above must be a bound book kept exclusively for the purpose and shall be retained for 2 years after the last entry was made (s. 2 (5)).

Any person who fails to comply with any of the requirements imposed on him by s. 2 commits an offence (s. 2 (6)).

"Processing", in relation to scrap metal includes melting down and any other process whereby the material ceases to be scrap metal, but does not include dismantling or breaking up (s. 2 (7)).

Where a registered scrap metal dealer satisfies a local authority that he carries on or proposes to carry on the business of a scrap metal dealer as part of the business of an itinerant collector (a person regularly engaged in collecting waste material and old, broken, worn out or defaced articles by means of visits from house to house (s. 9), the authority may make an order exempting him from the requirements of s. 2. Instead he will be subject to the following requirements: (a) on the sale by him of any scrap metal, he must obtain from the purchaser a receipt showing the weight of the scrap metal and aggregate price of sale; and (b) he must keep every such receipt for 2 years in such a way as to be able to produce it on demand to any authorised person (s. 3 (1)). Failure to comply is an offence, (s. 3 (4)).

Such an order shall not be made except after consultation with the chief officer of police, and may be revoked at any time (s. 3 (2) and (3)).

Where a scrap metal dealer does not occupy a scrap metal store, but no exemption order under s. 3 (1) has been made, he must keep a book either at his usual place of residence or at any other place occupied by him wholly or partly as a scrap metal dealer, and record as soon as practicable the receipt and disposal of scrap metal (s. 3 (5)).

Where a scrap metal dealer occupies a scrap metal store but no exemption order under s. 3 (1) has been made, and any scrap metal is received otherwise than at such store and is disposed of without being received at such store, (a) he must enter, as soon as practicable, particulars (see s. 2 (2) and (3)) in a book or books of the receipt and disposal of scrap metal, and (b) if he occupies more than one scrap metal store, the particulars shall be entered in a book or books kept at the place nearest to the place at which the scrap metal is received (s. 3 (6)).

Where a person is convicted of an offence under s. 1 (1) or s. 2, or of any offence which in the opinion of the court involves dishonesty, the court may, if it thinks fit, make an order directing that, while the order is in force, he shall be subject to the following additional requirements—that at any scrap metal store occupied by him (a) no scrap metal shall be received between 6 p.m. and 8 a.m., and (b) all scrap metal received at that place shall be kept in the form in which it is received there, for not less than 72 hours. Such an order shall specify a period, not exceeding 2 years, for which it is in force; it may be revoked by the court. Contravention of any requirement contained in the order is an offence (s. 4).

It is an offence for a scrap metal dealer to acquire any scrap metal from a person apparently under 16 years whether the scrap metal is offered by that person on his own behalf or on behalf of another person. It is a defence to prove that the person from whom he acquired the scrap metal was in fact 16 or over.

It is an offence for a person, on selling scrap metal to a scrap metal dealer, to give a false name or address to the dealer (s. 5).

Any constable has a right at all reasonable times: (a) to enter and inspect any place registered under s. 1 as a place which is occupied by a scrap metal dealer as a scrap metal store, or as a place occupied by a scrap metal dealer wholly or partly for his business; (b) to require production of and to inspect any scrap metal kept at that place, and any book required to be kept at that place, or any receipt, and to take copies of or extracts from any such book or receipt (s. 6 (1)).

If any officer of a local authority, authorised in writing, has reasonable grounds for believing that a place is being used as a scrap metal store and that place is not for the time being registered under s. 1, the officer has a right at any reasonable time, on producing (if required to do so) evidence of his authority, to enter that place for the purpose of ascertaining whether it is being used as a scrap metal store (s. 6 (2)).

If a justice of the peace is satisfied by information on oath that admission to a specific place is required in order to secure compliance with the Act, or to ascertain whether the Act is being complied with, he may issue a warrant authorising a person having a right of entry to that place to enter it at any time within 1 month if need be by force, (s. 6 (3)).

Except under a warrant granted under this section, no person is entitled by virtue of this section to enter any place by force (s. 6 (4)).

Any person who obstructs the exercise of any right of entry or inspection, or who fails to produce any book or any other document liable to inspection, commits an offence (s. 6 (5)).

A "scrap metal dealer" is a person who carries on a business which consists wholly or partly of buying and selling scrap metal, whether the scrap metal sold is in the form in which it was bought or otherwise, other than a business in the course of which scrap metal is not bought except as materials for the manufacture of other articles and is not sold except as a by-product of such manufacture or as surplus materials bought but not required for such manufacture (s. 9 (1)).

"Scrap metal" includes any old metal, any broken, worn out, defaced or partly manufactured articles made wholly or partly of metal and any metallic wastes, and also includes old, broken, worn out or defaced tooltips or dies made of "hard metal" or of cemented or sintered "metallic carbides" (s. 9 (2)).

"Scrap metal store" means a place where scrap metal is received or kept in the course of the business of a scrap metal dealer (s. 9 (2)).

"Local Authority" means the council of a district, the Common Council of the City of London or the council of a London borough (s. 9 (2)).

Pedlars – Under the Pedlars Act 1871 a pedlar is any hawker, pedlar, petty chapman, tinker, caster of metals, mender of chairs or other person who, without any horse or other beast bearing or drawing burden, travels and trades on foot and goes from town to town or to other men's houses, carrying to sell or exposing for sale any goods, wares or merchandise immediately to be delivered or offering for sale his skill in handicraft (s. 3).

It is an offence to act as a pedlar without a certificate (1871 Act, s. 4).

Such a certificate is granted by a chief officer of police when he is satisfied that the applicant—

(1) Has resided in his district during one month previous to his application;
(2) Is over 17 years of age;
(3) Is a person of good character; and
(4) In good faith intends to carry on the trade of a pedlar.

The certificate remains in force for one year from date of issue, and authorises the person to whom granted to act as a pedlar within any part of the United Kingdom (1871 Act, ss. 5, 6 and Pedlars Act 1881).

It is a summary offence to make false representations to obtain a certificate or to forge or use any counterfeit certificate (1871 Act, s. 12). It is also an offence to lend, transfer or borrow a pedlar's certificate (1871 Act, ss. 10 and 11).

Any convictions under the Pedlars Acts are to be endorsed on the certificate, and a court has power, when satisfied a holder is not in good faith carrying on the business of a pedlar or when he is convicted of any offence, to deprive him of his certificate.

If he is convicted of begging the court must take away his certificate (1871 Act, s. 16).

The following need not have a pedlar's certificate:

(1) Commercial travellers;
(2) Book agents authorised in writing by the publishers of such books;
(3) Sellers of vegetables, fish, fruit or victuals; and
(4) Sellers in legally established public fairs or markets (1871 Act, s. 23).

A pedlar is bound at all times, on demand, to produce and show his certificate to:

(1) Any justice,
(2) Any constable or officer of police,
(3) Any person to whom he offers his goods for sale,
(4) Any person in whose private grounds or premises he is found.

Refusal or failure to do so is a summary offence (1871 Act, s. 17).

Any person acting as a pedlar, who has no certificate or who refuses to show his certificate, may be arrested by any person to whom he is bound to produce his licence, and brought before a justice (1871 Act, s. 18).

Any constable or officer of police is empowered at any time to open and inspect any pack, box, bag, trunk or case in which a pedlar carries his goods. If a pedlar refuses to allow such inspection or prevents or attempts to prevent it, he may be arrested (s. 18) and fined (s. 19, 1871 Act).

Under s. 3 of the Vagrancy Act 1824 every petty chapman or pedlar wandering abroad and trading without being duly licensed or otherwise authorised by law, may be arrested and dealt with as an idle and disorderly person (see Chap. 27); but the holding of a certificate does not help if his conduct brings him within ss. 3, 4, 5, of the Vagrancy Act 1824 (1871 Act, s. 13).

Hawkers - Customs and Excise Act 1952, s. 161: Hawking spirits or selling same otherwise than in premises licensed for the sale of spirits is an offence and the offender may be arrested.

Explosives Act 1875, s. 30: It is an offence to hawk, sell or expose for sale gunpowder upon any highway or public place.

The hawking of petroleum must be conducted in accordance with the regulations as to its safe conveyance. See Chap. 33.

The conduct and location of street hawkers may be governed by local byelaws and regulations.

It is an offence (Highways Act 1959, s. 127) for any hawker to pitch any tent, booth, stall or stand on any part of the highway.

Game Dealers - Before a person may deal in game he must procure-

(1) A licence from the local District Council and then

(2) An excise licence (which expires on July 1) taken out at the Post Office.

A Council may not grant a game dealer's licence to an innkeeper, a retail beer-seller, a carrier or higgler, an owner, driver or conductor of a public conveyance or mail letter vehicle, or any person in the employ of any of these persons (Game Act 1831, s. 18, and Game Licences Act 1860).

Game under the Game Act 1831 includes hares, pheasants, partridges, grouse, heath or moor game and black game and a game dealer's licence is necessary to deal in such game imported from foreign countries.

A licence is not necessary to deal in snipe, woodcock, quail, landrail, rabbits or deer.

Under the Game Act 1831 a game dealer's licence is granted

for specified premises, outside of which a board must be fixed indicating that the person named is a licensed dealer, and he must not sell game elsewhere than at such premises (s. 28). He must not buy or sell any bird of game (except live birds for rearing or exhibition purposes or for sale alive) after the expiration of 10 days after the end of the open season for such bird. Any other person must not buy or sell such a bird after the same period (except live birds for rearing or exhibition purposes or for sale alive) (s. 4 as amended by Game Act 1970, s. 1). See Chap. 19.

Police Prosecutions – A Local Authority may authorise the bringing by any constable of proceedings for an offence under the Excise Acts relating to any duty of excise the levying of which has been transferred to the Authority with respect to licences for dealing in game, killing game, guns, and refreshment houses (Finance Act 1961, s. 11).

Domestic Servants' Registries – In every district in which s. 85 of the Public Health Acts Amendment Act 1907 has been adopted by the Local Authority, every person who carries on for the purpose of private gain the business of keeper of a female domestic servants' registry, must register his name, address and premises where such business is carried on, with the Local Authority.

The Local Authority may make byelaws prescribing the books to be kept and regulating the conduct of such business.

Any person duly authorised in writing by the Local Authority must at all reasonable times be afforded full and free power of entry into such registered premises to inspect such premises and the books required to be kept by byelaw.

It is a summary offence to carry on such business without being registered under this section, to refuse entry as above authorised, to contravene any byelaws made under this section, or to neglect to have a copy of such byelaws hung up in a conspicuous place in the registered premises, and in addition to or in lieu of any pecuniary penalty, the court may suspend or cancel the registration.

Dealers in Securities – The business of dealing in securities is regulated by a licensing system under the Prevention of Fraud (Investments) Act 1958.

By s. 26 of the 1958 Act, "Dealing in securities" means making or offering to make with any person or inducing or attempting to induce any person to enter into or offer to enter into (a) any agreement for or with a view to acquiring, disposing of, subscribing for or underwriting securities, or lending or depositing money to or with any industrial and provident society or building society, or (b) any agreement the purpose or pretended purpose of which is to secure a profit to any of the parties from the yield of securities or by reference to fluctuations in the value of securities.

"Securities" means: (a) shares or debentures or rights or interests in same; (b) securities of the Government of any part of H.M. Dominions or the Government of any foreign state; (c) rights in respect of money lent to or deposited with any industrial and provident society or building society, including those under any unit trust scheme (s. 26).

S. 1: No person shall carry on the business of dealing in securities except if he has a *principal's licence*, or act as a servant or agent in such business unless he has a *representative's licence*. Any contravention is punishable summarily or on indictment, but proceedings (except arrest, warrant or remand) require the consent of the Dept. of Trade or of the Director of Public Prosecutions. See Appendix III.

S. 2: There are many exceptions to this necessity for licences, including members of Stock Exchanges or of associations of dealers in securities (which are recognised by the Dept. of Trade: see s. 15); the Bank of England; any statutory or municipal corporation; any dealer exempted by the Dept. of Trade (see s. 16); any industrial and provident society (s. 10—now replaced by the Industrial and Provident Societies Act 1965); any building society (see s. 11); any manager or trustee under a unit trust scheme authorised by the Dept. of Trade (see s. 17), and the section also exempts certain actions by persons under certain given circumstances.

These licences are grantable by the Dept. of Trade, who have power to refuse and revoke them (ss. 3–6), and to make rules for regulating the conduct of business by holders of licences (s. 7). Licence holders have to supply information (s. 8) and the names and addresses of holders of licences have to be published (s. 9).

S. 13: as amended by the Protection of Depositors Act 1963. It is an indictable offence for any person to induce or attempt to induce another person to invest money, by any statement, promise or forecast which he knows to be misleading, false or deceptive, or by any dishonest concealment of material facts, or by the reckless making, dishonestly or otherwise, of any statement, promise or forecast which is misleading, false or deceptive.

Any person guilty of conspiracy to commit this offence shall be similarly punishable.

S. 14: It is an offence punishable summarily or on indictment, for any person to distribute, cause to be distributed or have in possession for distribution, any documents which to his knowledge are circulars inviting or inducing persons to invest money in securities. This does not apply to a proper prospectus complying with the Companies Act 1948 or to circulars sent by licensees or persons exempted from licence by the Act.

Proceedings (apart from arrest or remand) require the consent of the Dept. of Trade or the Director of Public Prosecutions.

A justice has power to grant a search warrant for such documents, to which the Police (Property) Act 1897 applies, subject to orders of a court.

S. 18: It is an offence punishable summarily or on indictment to knowingly furnish information, as required under the Act, which is false in a material particular.

S. 19: Corporations and their officers may be liable for offences against the Act.

S. 20: Summary proceedings under the Act may be taken in the place where the alleged offender is for the time being.

Under the Prevention of Fraud (Investments) Act Licensing Regulations of 1944 (continued in force under the 1958 Act), applications for principals' and representatives' licences must be made to the Dept. of Trade on the prescribed forms accompanied by the prescribed statutory declarations. Any change in the particulars which are required must be notified to the Dept. of Trade.

The Licensed Dealers (Conduct of Business) Rules 1960 regulate the conduct of business of licensed dealers, that is the holders of principals' licences, who are described as "licensed dealers in securities".

If a licensed dealer in writing offers to acquire or dispose of securities he must give the information prescribed, and he must issue a contract note giving the prescribed particulars in case of a sale or purchase of securities.

He must keep books of account, and a record of every transfer of securities.

He must not deal on terms involving payment by instalments unless the prescribed conditions are fulfilled.

Mock Auctions Act 1961 – It is an offence to promote or conduct, or to assist in the conduct of, a mock auction at which one or more lots prescribed in the Act are offered for sale (s. 1 (1)).

The prescribed articles are: plate, plated articles, linen, china, glass, books, pictures, prints, furniture, jewellery, articles of household or personal use or ornament or any musical or scientific instrument or apparatus (s. 3 (2)).

A sale of goods by way of competitive bidding is a mock auction if, but only if, during the course of the sale—(a) any lot is sold to a bidder, either at a price lower than his highest bid, or part of the price at which it is sold to him is repaid, or credited to him, or is stated to be so repaid or credited; or (b) the right to bid is restricted, or stated to be restricted to persons who have bought, or agreed to buy one or more articles, or (c) any articles are given away or offered as gifts (s. 1 (3)).

A sale of goods is not a mock auction if it is proved that the reduction in price, or the repayment or credit—(a) was on account of a defect discovered after the highest bid in question had been made, being a defect of which the auctioneer was unaware when the bid was made, or (b) was on account of damage sustained after that bid was made (s. 1 (4)).

Protection of Depositors Act 1963 – Any person who, by any statement, promise or forecast which he knows to be misleading, false or deceptive, or by any dishonest concealment of material facts, or by the reckless making (dishonestly or otherwise) of any statement, promise or forecast, which is misleading, false or deceptive, induces or attempts to induce another person —(a) to invest money on deposit with any person, or (b) to enter into or offer to enter into any agreement for that purpose, shall be guilty of an indictable offence (s. 1).

No proceedings for an offence under this Act shall be instituted in England and Wales except by or with the consent of the Director of Public Prosecutions or the Dept. of Trade.

Ministry of Social Security Act 1966 – It is a summary offence for any person who—(a) as a pledge or a security for a debt, or (b) with a view to obtaining payment from the person entitled thereto of a debt due either to himself or to any other person; receives, detains or has in his possession any document issued by or on behalf of the Minister of Social Security in connection with any benefit, pension or allowance. It is also a summary offence for any person to have such a document in his possession without lawful authority or excuse (the proof whereof shall lie on him) (s. 32).

CHAPTER 32

TRADE

	Page
Business Names . .	436
Printing and Publishing .	437
Trade Marks . . .	437
Trade Description . .	438
Hall-marks . . .	438
Weights and Measures .	440
Food and Drugs . .	440
Shops	441
Trading Representations (Disabled Persons) Act 1958	444
Trading Stamps Act 1964	444
Consumer Credit Act 1974	445

Business Names – The Registration of Business Names Act 1916 directs that every person or firm having a place of business in this country and carrying on any business or profession (s. 22) under a business name which does not consist of the true surnames of such person or partners or the corporate name of the corporation, must register under this Act (s. 1).

Registration is effected by sending the prescribed particulars to the Register Office of the Dept. of Trade, and this should be done within 14 days after the firm or person commences business. Any change in the particulars of registration should also be reported to the Register Office within 14 days after such change. The Registrar supplies a Certificate of Registration which must be exhibited in a conspicuous position at the principal place of business. He can refuse registration (Companies Act 1947, s. 116).

Every person or firm required under this Act to be so registered must mention in business letters, catalogues, circulars, and show-cards, on which the business name appears and which are sent to any person, the present surname (with Christian name or initials), any former Christian name or surname and the nationality if not British, of the person or persons carrying on such business or profession (s. 18).

It is an offence punishable by fine (summarily, s. 442) for anyone to trade under any title of which "Limited" or any contraction of that word is the last word, unless duly incorporated (as a company) with limited liability (Companies Act 1948, s. 439). The Companies Act 1948 gives a number of offences which might be committed by officers of companies and allows proceedings for any offence under the Act to be taken by the Director of Public Prosecutions or by the Dept. of Trade at any time within 12 months of discovery of the offence and not exceeding 3 years from the commission of the offence.

Printing and Publishing – It is a summary offence for any person to print any paper or book meant to be published or dispersed, without putting his name and address thereon, or to publish or disperse copies of same. Certain works are excepted, including address and business cards, price lists, sale catalogues of goods or estates, law proceedings, papers printed by authority of any public board or public office in the discharge of their duties.

An information for this offence must be in the name of the Attorney-General or Solicitor-General (Newspapers, Printers, and Reading Rooms Repeal Act 1869). Provision for relaxing certain requirements of the Act of 1869 is made by the Printer's Imprint Act 1961. See Stone, under title "Printers".

Trade Marks – A trade mark means a mark to be applied to goods which are the subject of trade, manufacture, or merchandise, and which is duly registered in the Register of Trade Marks. It is the property of its owner, and the Trade Marks Acts protect owners and the public against any fraudulent or improper use of trade marks.

Subject to the provisions of s. 6 of the Geneva Conventions Act 1957, it shall be a summary offence to use for any purpose whatever,

(1) Without the authority of the Army Council:

(a) the emblem of a red cross with vertical and horizontal arms of the same length, on and surrounded by a white ground, or the designation "Red Cross" or "Geneva Cross".

(b) the emblem of a red crescent moon on and surrounded by a white ground, or the designation "Red Crescent".

(c) the emblem in red surrounded by a white ground of a lion passing from right to left of the observer, holding a scimitar in its right forepaw, with the upper half of the sun shooting forth rays above the lion's back, or the designation "Red Lion and Sun".

(2) Without the authority of the Dept. of Trade: Any design of a white or silver cross with vertical and horizontal arms of the same length, on and surrounded by a red ground, being the heraldic emblem of the Swiss Confederation, or any other design so nearly resembling it which might be mistaken for it.

In such cases the consent of the Director of Public Prosecutions must be obtained before prosecution.

Medical units of H.M. Forces use the Red Cross. The British Red Cross Society is the only voluntary organisation which has been authorised by the Army Council to use the Red Cross emblem and the words "Red Cross" in the United Kingdom in time of peace.

Trade Description – A trade description is an indication direct, or indirect, and by whatever means given, of the following matters with respect to any goods or parts of goods: (a) quantity, size or gauge, (b) method of manufacture, etc., (c) composition, (d) fitness for purpose, etc., (e) other physical characteristics, (f) testing and results thereof, (g) approval by any person, (h) place or date of manufacture, etc., (i) name of manufacturer, etc., (j) and other history (Trade Descriptions Act 1968, s. 2). Any person who, in the course of trade or business, (d) applies a false description to any goods or (b) supplies or offers to supply any goods to which a false trade description is applied, commits an offence (Trade Descriptions Act 1968, s. 1). The duty of enforcing this Act has been laid on the consumer protection departments of local authorities (s. 26). The Trade Descriptions Act 1972, s. 1, sets out the offence of failing to indicate the country in which goods were manufactured or produced.

Hall-marks – Hall-marks are the marks on gold, silver and platinum wares which indicate that the metal therein is of the requisite standard of purity, also the date and place of testing. The principal statute on the subject is the Hallmarking Act 1973, which generally took effect on 1st Jan. 1975.

For unlawfully dealing with hall-marks see "Forgery", Chap. 17.

Pure or fine gold or silver is rather soft and does not wear well, and an alloy or small quantity of baser metal is added to render it harder and more durable. To check fraud, the law makes it compulsory that objects of gold, silver or platinum should be assayed (or tested) and hall-marked. Such articles must be sent to an Assay Office, where they are tested to ascertain the proportion of precious metal therein and duly stamped with the hall-marks.

There are four Assay Offices, viz. London, Birmingham, Sheffield and Edinburgh.

The hall-marks for gold and silver articles are as follows:

(1) The **standard mark,** showing the amount of pure metal in the article.

(2) The **hall-mark proper,** which is the local town or city mark, showing where the article was assayed and stamped. The following hall-marks are now in use: London—a leopard's head; Edinburgh—a castle; Birmingham—an anchor; Sheffield—a rose. Formerly there were assay offices at Chester and Glasgow. Their hall-marks were: Chester—a dagger between three wheat sheaves; Glasgow—a tree, fish, bell and bird.

(3) The **date mark,** which consists of one letter of the

alphabet. Each Assay Office had its own set of letters and can tell the date of stamping an article by the letter on it, although from 1975 all the Offices have the same date mark.

(4) The **maker's mark,** which consists of two or more letters, being the initials of the firm, the proprietor or the partners of the firm.

Formerly there was also a "duty mark", the King's head, but the duty on plate and the duty mark were abolished in 1890.

It is an offence in the course of trade or business to describe an unhallmarked article as being wholly or partly made of gold, silver or platinum, or to supply an article so described (s. 1). It is triable summarily or on indictment (Sched. 3), and local weights and measures authorities are charged with enforcement (s. 9).

GOLD ARTICLES – Standard or sovereign gold consists of 22 carats (or parts) fine or pure gold and 2 carats alloy, in every 24 carats. The term "carat" is not a real weight for gold; it is used merely to denote the quality.

The present legal standards of purity are as follows:

22 carat	916.6	parts per 1,000
18 carat	750	parts per 1,000
14 carat	585	parts per 1,000
9 carat	375	parts per 1,000

and the standard mark is a crown followed by the figures 916, 750, 585 or 375, as appropriate. Formerly, the crown only appeared on 22 and 18 carat gold, and the standard was indicated by the numbers 22, 18, 14, or 9. Objects assayed in Scotland carried a thistle in place of the crown.

As an example, an 18 carat gold article assayed in Birmingham since 1975 should bear the following marks: the maker's or sponsor's mark, a crown, the figures 750, an anchor and a date mark.

Plated articles are not marked, and may only be described as gold if the description is qualified by the words "plated" or "rolled". Certain articles are exempted from marking, notably coinage, raw materials and articles for export. Different marks apply to imported goods.

It should be noted that a lion passant (or walking) was the 22 carat gold standard mark up to the year 1844, but in that year it was replaced by the crown and 22. For 18 carat gold the standard mark between 1798 and 1974 was the crown and 18.

SILVER ARTICLES – There are two standards for silver articles: Sterling and Britannia.

Sterling silver contains 925 parts of silver per 1,000, and its standard mark is a lion passant. In the case of the Edinburgh Assay Office the mark is a lion rampant (standing on its hind legs), which replaces the thistle which applied prior to 1975.

Britannia silver is of a higher standard, containing 958.4 parts per 1,000, and its standard mark is a figure of Britannia. This higher standard was compulsory from 1697 to 1720, and silver plate of that time is known as Queen Anne silver.

Silver articles should also bear local hall-marks, date marks and makers' marks similar to those on gold articles, and similar exemptions apply.

A sterling silver article assayed in Birmingham should therefore bear the following hall-marks: Lion passant, anchor, date letter and initials of maker.

PLATINUM ARTICLES – Hallmarking for platinum was introduced for the first time by the Hallmarking Act 1973. Its standard of purity is 950 parts of platinum per 1,000, and, in addition to the maker's, office and date marks, a platinum article bears an orb surmounted by a cross.

Weights and Measures – The Weights and Measures Act 1963 prescribes a uniform system of weights and measures which must be used for trade purposes throughout the country.

It is a summary offence to sell by any weight or measure which is not authorised by the Act.

Inspectors are appointed by Local Authorities to enforce this Act. The Inspectors keep the local standard weights and measures, verify and stamp weights and measures, and inspect trade premises to examine the weights and measures therein.

Food and Drugs – The law designed to ensure that articles consumed by the people shall be wholesome and shall not be sold to the prejudice of the purchasers has been consolidated by the Food and Drugs Act 1955 followed by the Food Hygiene Regs. 1955. "Food" includes every article used for food or drink by man other than drugs and water, and includes articles used in the preparation of human food (1955 Act, s. 135).

"Food" includes drink, chewing gum, and other products of the like nature and use, and substances used as ingredients in the preparation of food or drink or of such products but does not include (a) water, live animals or birds (b) fodder feeding stuffs for animals, birds or fish (c) articles or substances used only as drugs (1955 Act, s. 135).

It is a summary offence to mix, with a view to sale, anything with any article of food so as to render it injurious to health, or anything with any drug or medicine (except by way of compounding) so as to injuriously affect its quality or potency or to sell or have for sale any such article (1955 Act, s. 1). It is also an offence, generally speaking, to sell to the prejudice of the purchaser any article of food or any drug, which is not of the nature, substance or quality of the article demanded by the purchaser (1955 Act, s. 2).

These are the main offences regarding the adulteration of food and drugs.

This Act also deals with unsound food, prevention of contamination of food, false warranty, false labels, hygiene in sale of food, etc., etc.

The Act is enforced by Local Authorities who appoint inspectors for the purpose. Public analysts are also employed to deal with samples of food and drugs submitted to them for test to detect whether there has been any adulteration.

Unsound or bad food may be dealt with under s. 9 of the Food and Drugs Act 1955. See "Food", Chap. 39.

Shops - The Shops Act 1950 repealed previous Acts dealing with shops and consolidates the previous law thereon.

It has been amended by the Shops (Revocation of Winter Closing Hours Provisions) Order 1952 which revoked all the provisions of the Act which related to special closing hours during winter.

"Shop" includes any premises where any retail trade or business is carried on. "Retail trade or business" includes barbers or hairdressers, sale of refreshments or intoxicants, lending books or periodicals for gain and retail sales by auction but not sale of programmes or catalogues at places of amusement (s. 74). Part I includes ss. 1-16.

S. 1 directs that every shop shall be closed for serving of customers not later than 1 p.m. on one weekday in every week. This day may be fixed by the occupier (Shops (Early Closing Days) Act 1965). This shall not prevent the serving of a customer already in the shop before closing or supply in a case of illness or supply of necessaries for a ship on arrival or departure.

This early closing day does not apply (unless extended to any of them by the Local Authority) to shops whose only trade or business is the sale of intoxicants, refreshments, aircraft, cycle and motor accessories, newspapers, etc., meat and other perishable articles, tobacco, etc., medicines, etc., also railway bookstalls and retail trade at exhibitions or shows (Sched. 1). Section 2 directs the closing of shops for serving of customers not later than 9 p.m. on the late day and 8 p.m. on any other day of the week (the late day shall be Saturday unless some other day is fixed by the Local Authority, s. 3). Such general closing shall not prevent serving a customer already in the shop or supply in case of illness.

Also Sched. 2 allows the sale of meals or refreshments for consumption on the premises or in trains, newly cooked food for consumption off the premises, intoxicants, tobacco, etc., on licensed premises during permitted hours; tobacco, sweets, etc., in theatres, etc., to the audience; medicines; sales from railway bookstalls; motor, cycle or aircraft accessories; stores for H.M. Forces or for ships on arrival or departure; also business at post offices, all these during closing hours.

S. 4: A Local Authority may fix 10 p.m. on the late day or 9.30 p.m. on any other week day for closing hours for sale of tobacco, etc.

S. 6: For sale of table waters, confectionery or ice cream the late day hour may be 10 p.m. and 9.30 p.m. on any other day of the week.

"Local Authority" in the Act means the Common Council of the City of London, the council of any London borough, and elsewhere the council of the district (s. 73).

Part II (ss. 17–39) of the Act deals with the conditions of employment in shops, including such subjects as half holidays (ss. 17, 18); meal times (ss. 19, 20); special arrangements *re* shop assistants in premises for the sale of refreshments (s. 21); Sunday employment (ss. 22, 23); hours of employment of young persons 16 to 18 (ss. 24–26) and of persons under 16 (s. 27); night employment (s. 31) and health and comfort of shop workers (ss. 37, 38).

Part III deals with modifications in special cases such as the suspension of the weekly half holiday and alteration of closing hours in holiday resorts, the alteration of closing hours and closing orders for exhibitions or shows or on special occasions such as Christmas (ss. 40–43).

S. 44 exempts premises where post office business is transacted from Part I and ss. 17–20 of the Act.

S. 45 exempts lending libraries not for private profit; clubs or institutions not for gain and fairs or bazaars or sales of work for charitable or non-private profit purposes from Part I and ss. 17–21 and 37 of the Act.

S. 46 exempts libraries for educational or recreation purposes from Part I and II of the Act on given conditions.

Part IV (ss. 47–67) deals with Sunday trading.

S. 47: Every shop shall be closed for the serving of customers on Sunday save as otherwise provided in the Act, and except when open for serving of customers for the purpose of the transactions given in Sched. 5—viz. for the sale of: intoxicants; meals or refreshments (except fried fish and chips at a fried fish and chips shop); newly cooked provisions; sweets, confectionery and ice cream; flowers, fruit and vegetables (not tinned or bottled); milk and cream (not tinned); medicines, etc., at duly registered premises; motor, cycle or aircraft accessories; tobacco and smokers' requisites; newspapers and magazines; books and stationery at main railway and omnibus book stalls; guide books, postcards, etc., at museums, parks and in vessels; photos for passports; sports requisites at sports places; fodder for horses, etc., at any farm, inn, etc. Also for post office business and funeral undertaker's business.

S. 48: The local authority may make partial exemption orders for limited opening of shops for the sale of bread and flour, confectionery, fish, groceries and other provisions (Sched. 6) on Sunday.

S. 49: The local authority has power to order the closing on Sunday of shops open for the purpose of sale of meals or refreshments for consumption off the premises.

S. 51: The local authority may provide, by order, for the opening of shops selling bathing or fishing requisites, photo requisites, toys, etc., books, etc., food (Sched. 7) at holiday resorts on Sunday.

S. 53: Jewish shops, if duly registered, may be open, on conditions, up to 2 p.m. on Sunday, if they are closed on Saturday.

S. 54: In London a Local Authority may, by order, allow the opening on Sunday up to 2 p.m., on conditions, of certain street markets and district shops.

S. 55: Goods sold retail shall not be delivered from a shop at any time when it would not be lawful to serve the customer in the shop, but this will not apply on a Sunday which is Christmas Day or is followed by Christmas Day on the Monday.

S. 56: This Sunday trading prohibition shall not prevent the supply of necessaries to a ship or aircraft on arrival or departure; the supply of goods to a club for the club; the cooking on Sunday before 1.30 p.m. of food for a customer; the supply of goods required in the case of illness.

A barber or hairdresser may at any time attend infirm persons or persons resident in a hotel or club, for the purposes of his business. Home handicraft workers may get certificates of exemptions from this prohibition which also does not apply to sea-going ships.

S. 58: This Part IV applies to any place where any retail trade or business is carried on as if that place were a shop, but this does not affect the sale by fishermen of freshly caught fish and the sale of produce at a farm, allotment or similar place.

S. 60: Nothing in the above provisions of Part IV as to Sunday trading shall apply to retail dealers in butcher's meat carrying on their business on Sunday, but unless allowed under the following provisions of the Act, it shall not be lawful for any person to carry on the business of a retail dealer in butcher's meat on Sunday and such a shop shall be closed to customers on Sunday (s. 61).

S. 62: Jewish retail dealers in Kosher meat may open shop on Sunday and serve customers with such meat provided that they are licensed by the local Jewish Committee, close their shops on Saturday, and notify the Local Authority (Kosher meat means butcher's meat killed and prepared by the Jewish ritual method (s. 74)).

S. 63: Butcher's meat must not be delivered except when the shop is lawfully open for customers, but this does not apply when Sunday is Christmas Day or the day before Christmas Day.

S. 65: Butcher's meat may be sold and delivered at any time for a ship or aircraft on its arrival or departure.

"Butcher's meat" means beef, mutton, veal, lamb or pork (including livers, etc.) whether fresh, chilled, frozen or salted and includes Kosher meat (s. 74).

Part V (ss. 68–77) contains general provisions.

S. 71: It shall be the duty of the local authority to enforce the Act and to take any necessary proceedings through its appointed inspector.

Trading Representations (Disabled Persons) Act 1958 – This Act provides for the registration of persons who sell or solicit orders for their goods by representations that disabled persons are employed in making or packaging the goods or benefit from their sale.

It is an offence in selling or soliciting orders for goods, for any representation that blind or otherwise disabled persons, (a) are employed in the production, preparation or packing of the goods or (b) benefit (other than as users) from the sale of the goods, to be made during visits from house to house, or by post, unless the person carrying on the business is registered (s. 1).

Trading Stamps Act 1964 – It is an offence for any person other than a company or an industrial provident society to carry on business as the promotor of a trading stamp scheme (s. 1).

It is an offence for a person to issue any trading stamp, or cause any trading stamp to be issued, or deliver any trading stamp to any person in connection with the sale of any goods or the performance of any services, unless such stamp bears on its face in clear and legible characters a value expressed in or by reference to current coin.

Where a company carries on such a scheme, the stamps must bear on their face in clear and legible characters either the name of the company or a business name registered under the Registration of Business Names Act 1916. In the case of an industrial provident society, the stamps must bear the name of the society (s. 2).

If the holder of any number of redeemable trading stamps to the value of [25p] so requests, the promoter must redeem them by paying their cash value. The holder may present the stamps at any reasonable time at the promoter's registered office, or send them by post to that office; or the stamps may be redeemed in any other manner afforded by the promoter. "Redeemable trading stamps" means trading stamps delivered in accordance with a trading stamp scheme (s. 3) as amended by Consumer Credit Act 1974, Sched. 4 (when in force).

Every catalogue and stamp book published by the promoter of such a scheme must contain a prominent statement of the name and the address of his registered office (s. 5).

It is an offence for the promoter of a trading stamp scheme, or for any person carrying on a trade or business in which such a scheme is operated, to issue or publish, or cause to be issued or published, an advertisement which conveys or purports to convey, the cash value of any trading stamps (a) by means of a statement which associates the worth of any trading stamps with what the holder pays or may pay to obtain them, or (b) in terms which are misleading or deceptive (s. 6).

In every shop in which a trading stamp scheme is operated there must be kept posted a notice stating the cash value of the stamps issued and giving such particulars as will enable customers readily to ascertain the number of stamps to which they are entitled, and if any current catalogue has been published a copy must be kept where it can be conveniently consulted by customers. The notice must be posted in such characters and in such a position as to be conveniently read by customers. Non-compliance, without reasonable excuse, is an offence.

It is an offence for any person to pull down any such notice (s. 7).

Where any offence committed by a corporation is proved to have been committed with the consent or connivance of any director, manager, secretary or other officer of the corporation, he, as well as the corporation, shall be deemed to be guilty of that offence and shall be liable to be proceeded against and punished accordingly (s. 8).

Consumer Credit Act 1974 – This Act establishes for the protection of consumers a new system administered by the Director General of Fair Trading of licensing and other control of traders concerned with the provision of credit, or the supply of goods on hire or hire-purchase, and their transactions. The enforcement of this Act is the responsibility of the Director General of Fair Trading and the local weights and measures authority. The Act was not generally in force at the date of going to press.

CHAPTER 33

EXPLOSIVES

	Page		Page
Explosives Offences .	446	Tank Wagons and Tank Trailers . . .	453
Petroleum . . .	448	Carbide of Calcium . .	454
Petroleum Spirit (Motor Vehicles, etc.) Regulations 1929 . . .	450	Acetylene . . .	454
Petrol Pumps . . .	451	Celluloid and Cinematograph Film . . .	454
Petroleum Spirit (Conveyance) Regulations .	452	Carbon Disulphide . .	456
		Gas Cylinders' Conveyance	456

Explosives Offences – The manufacture and keeping of gunpowder and other explosives is governed by the Explosives Acts 1875, 1923, and Emergency Laws (Misc. Provisions) Act 1953. See also Control of Explosives Orders 1953 and 1954, under which to obtain possession of gunpowder or safety fuse requires a licence from the chief officer of police, except in some exempted cases.

"Explosive" includes every substance used or made to produce a practical effect by explosion or a pyrotechnic effect; for example, gunpowder, dynamite, fulminate, fog signals, fireworks, cartridges, etc., etc.

These Acts and the Orders in Council made thereunder deal with the licences, supervision and safety requirements necessary for such dangerous substances. See the official "Guide to the Explosives Acts" on sale by H.M. Stationery Office.

The following statutes deal with offences in connection with explosives.

EXPLOSIVE SUBSTANCES ACT 1883 – This statute gives power to deal with persons using, making or having in possession explosives to use for unlawful objects, and creates the following 5 offences:

(1) Unlawfully and maliciously causing by an explosive substance an explosion of a nature likely to endanger life or cause serious injury to property whether such injury is caused or not (s. 2).

(2) Unlawfully and maliciously doing any act with intent to

cause, or conspiring to cause, such an explosion in the United Kingdom, whether such explosion takes place or not (s. 3 (a)).

(3) Unlawfully and maliciously making or having in possession or under control any explosive substance with intent by means thereof to endanger life or cause serious injury to property in the United Kingdom or enable others by means thereof to do so, whether an explosion takes place or not (s. 3 (b)).

(4) Making or knowingly having in possession or under control any explosive substance under such circumstances as to give rise to a reasonable suspicion that it is not for a lawful object, unless the contrary is proved (s. 4).

(5) Being accessory to the commission of any crime under this Act by in any manner whatsoever procuring, aiding, abetting or counselling its commission (s. 5).

Any person within or (being a subject of Her Majesty) without H.M. dominions may be liable under this Act.

A person may be arrested for an offence against the Act and brought before a justice and remanded, but no further proceedings may be taken without the consent of the Attorney-General (s. 7).

On reasonable ground for believing that such a crime has been committed the Attorney-General may order a special inquiry by a justice, who can examine witnesses on oath although no person is charged with the commission of the crime. Such witnesses must answer all questions put to them, but they are protected against the consequences of incriminating replies.

"Maliciously" under this Act means wilfully and not by accident, and "explosive substance" includes any materials for making any explosive, also any apparatus or part of apparatus used or intended to be used or adapted for causing any explosion.

A search warrant may be obtained in the same manner as a search warrant under the Explosives Act 1875 (s. 73). See "Search Warrant", Chap. 5.

OFFENCES AGAINST THE PERSON ACT 1861:

(1) Causing grievous bodily harm, disfiguring, etc., by unlawful and malicious explosion of any explosive substance (s. 28).

(2) Using explosives, corrosives, etc., in any manner with intent to cause grievous bodily harm, disfigurement, etc., whether bodily injury be effected or not (s. 29).

(3) Placing explosives near buildings or ships with intent to do bodily injury to any person, whether explosion or bodily injury be effected or not (s. 30).

(4) Knowingly having in possession or making any gunpowder, explosive substance, machine, etc., with intent by

means thereof to commit any of the indictable offences in the Act (s. 64).

A justice, on reasonable cause on oath, may issue his warrant to search in the day-time any house, carriage, vessel, place, etc., in which it is suspected any explosive substance is made, kept or carried for the purpose of committing any of these indictable offences (s. 65). See "Search Warrant, 1861 Act", Chap. 9.

EXPLOSIVES ACT 1875: (offences under):

(1) Gunpowder is not to be made or kept except on licensed (or registered) premises (ss. 4, 5).
(2) Exposure or sale of gunpowder upon any street or public place (s. 30).
(3) Sale of gunpowder to a child under thirteen years of age (s. 31).
(4) Exposure for sale, of gunpowder over 1 lb. in weight, without it being contained in a substantial receptacle and labelled "gunpowder" (s. 32).
(5) Throwing or firing fireworks on a street or public place (s. 80). See also "Highway Act" and "Town Police Clauses Act", Chap. 24.
(6) Subject to various modifications given in the Act, the provisions as to gunpowder are to apply to every other explosive (s. 39).

THE FIREWORKS ACT 1951 allows the destruction of fireworks which may be dangerous when in the possession of the public (s. 1). Fireworks must bear the address of the factory where made and the name of its occupier, except those weighing less than one-eighth of an ounce, sparklers, jumping crackers and throwdowns and any prescribed in regulations (s. 5). These requirements as to the making of fireworks and their containers shall not apply to fireworks consigned from a factory for transmission to a place outside the U.K., the Channel Islands and the Isle of Man (Fireworks Act 1964).

THE KEEPING OF FIREWORKS ORDER 1959 provides that the weights of fireworks which may be kept on registered premises shall not exceed: 2,000 lb., if kept in a specially constructed storage place or 500 lb. elsewhere in a closed receptacle. The quantity which may be kept in the part of premises to which the public have access is 100 lb.

Petroleum – The Petroleum (Consolidation) Act 1928 regulates the safe keeping of petroleum spirit (commonly known as petrol), and offences against it may be dealt with summarily.

The term "petroleum" includes crude petroleum, oil made from petroleum, or from coal, shale, peat or other bituminous substances, and other products of petroleum. The term "petroleum spirit" means such petroleum as when tested in the manner set forth in the Act gives off an inflammable vapour at a temperature of less than 73 degrees Fahrenheit (s. 23).

Thus "petroleum spirit" will include petrol, naphtha, benzine and such like highly inflammable bituminous liquids, and certain mixtures of petroleum with other substances, such as quick-drying varnishes.

Where any petroleum spirit is kept at any place, or is being sent or conveyed between any two places in Great Britain, or is sold or exposed or offered for sale, there shall be attached to, or where that is impracticable, displayed near, the vessel containing it, a label showing in conspicuous characters the words "Petroleum Spirit" and the words "Highly Inflammable", and the name and address of the owner, sender, or vendor.

However, petroleum spirit need not be so labelled during the seven days after its importation into this country, nor when carried on any motor vehicle, ship, aircraft or hovercraft and intended to be used only for the purposes thereof.

Petroleum spirit shall not be kept except under a petroleum spirit licence granted by the Local Authority, save only in the following cases:

(1) Petroleum spirit kept for private use or sale, which is kept in separate glass, earthenware or metal vessels, securely stopped and containing not more than one pint each, the total amount so kept not exceeding 3 gallons.

(2) Petroleum spirit kept for use in motor vehicles, motor boats, aircraft or specified engines, in accordance with any regulations made by the Secretary of State (see later).

The occupier of any premises in which petroleum spirit is kept in contravention of this section is liable to fine. Any holder of a petroleum spirit licence who contravenes any condition of his licence is liable to fine (s. 1).

The Local Authority for the granting of licences is the county, council or the harbour authority, and they may attach to any licence such conditions as they may consider expedient as to the safe keeping of petroleum spirit. Such licences may be transferred.

The occupier of a licensed premises must keep posted on the premises a notice setting out the conditions of his licence which have to be observed by his employees, viz. those conditions directing the precautions to be observed against the risk of fire or explosion. It is an offence not to have such a notice posted up, or to pull down any such notice, or to contravene any of the conditions set out in such notice (s. 2).

Ships carrying petroleum spirit as cargo, on entering a harbour must give notice of such cargo to the harbour authority (ss. 7 and 8).

Any of the provisions of this Act may be applied, by Order in

Council, to any substance (s. 19). The Act, with slight modifications, is applied by the Petroleum (Mixtures) Order 1929, to all mixtures (whether liquid, viscous or solid) of petroleum with any other substances, except mixtures which when tested do not give off an inflammable vapour at a temperature below 73 degrees Fahrenheit.

When loss of life or personal injury occurs by explosion or fire in which petroleum spirit is involved and in or about or in connection with any premises licensed under these Acts, the occupier must forthwith send notice of the matter to the Secretary of State, Home Office, London. If such notice is sent, the inspector of factories need not be notified. If a similar accident occurs in connection with any carriage, ship or boat conveying petroleum spirit or on or from which petroleum spirit is being loaded or unloaded, the owner or master of the carriage, ship or boat must send notice to the Secretary of State, except in cases where the petroleum spirit was for use only on that carriage, ship or boat, or in cases where notice has by law to be sent to some other Government department (s. 13).

The Secretary of State may direct an inquiry to be made by a Government inspector into the cause of any such accident, and if death has been caused the coroner's inquest shall be adjourned to allow of the presence of a Government inspector to watch the proceedings. A Government inspector has full power of entry, examination, etc., when engaged in carrying out any duty under this Act (ss. 14 and 15).

A Government inspector under the Explosives Acts has power to enter, inspect and examine premises licensed under this Act and premises in which petroleum spirit is or may be kept in contravention of the Act or Regulations (s. 16).

Any officer authorised in writing by the Local Authority may require any person who deals in petroleum or who keeps petroleum for the purposes of any trade or industry, to show him every place and vessel in which his petroleum is kept and to give him samples of such petroleum on payment. He may also test such samples on giving such person due notice in writing. Any refusal or wilful obstruction is a summary offence (s. 17).

A magistrates' court may give a warrant authorising entry and search for petroleum spirit kept, sent, conveyed, or exposed for sale in contravention of the Act (s. 18).

Petroleum Spirit (Motor Vehicles, etc.) Regulations 1929 – A licence from the Local Authority is necessary before petroleum spirit (petrol, etc.) may be kept for sale, but petrol for use in motor vehicles, motor boats, aircraft, engines used for propelling agricultural implements, stationary engines kept for domestic or agricultural purposes and generating power, heat or light, or engines used for canal or harbour works or in connection with the making or repair of roads, and which is not kept either wholly or partly for sale, may be kept without licence provided these regulations are observed. These regulations are to the following effect:

(1) Every storage place for keeping petroleum spirit must be ventilated and have an entrance to the open air. Means of extinguishing fire must be kept there. If attached to a dwelling house or a building where persons assemble it must be separated therefrom by a substantial and not readily inflammable floor or partition. If the spirit is kept in not more than 2 vessels of capacity not exceeding 2 gallons each, there may be an opening in such partition (not in a floor) if it is fitted with a self-closing and fire-resisting door (reg. 5).

(2) The spirit must be kept in strong and sound metal vessels, indelibly marked "Petroleum Spirit—Highly Inflammable" (regs. 2 to 4). Any fire, etc., must not be near it and it must not be exposed near any fire, etc. (regs. 9 and 10).

It must not be allowed to run into any sewer or sewer drain (reg. 12 and s. 27, Public Health Act 1936). It must not be used in a storage place except as fuel for any such engine kept therein. However, one gill may be used for cleaning or repair work, and it may be used as fuel for any properly constructed lighting or heating apparatus therein (reg. 11).

(3) Not more than 60 gallons may be kept in any one storage place (reg. 6).

(4) The spirit must not be kept in any vessel holding more than 2 gallons unless:

(i) the storage place is over 20 ft. from any building or highway;

(ii) provision is made to prevent the spirit flowing out of the storage place; and

(iii) notice is given in writing to the local Authority previously and every January following (reg. 7).

(5) The spirit shall not be kept in any place within 20 ft. of a building or inflammable substance otherwise than in the fuel tank of a motor vehicle, engine or aircraft and in not more than 2 vessels of capacity not exceeding 2 gallons each, unless notice is given each January to the local authority (reg. 8).

(6) Additional restrictions apply as regards engines used for making or repairing roads, such as notice to Local Authority, 30 gallons limit, vessels must not exceed 2 gallons capacity and must be kept in an iron locker which must be safely situated (reg. 13).

Petrol Pumps – Any instrument used in trade for measuring liquid fuel or lubricating oil for sale in individual quantities not exceeding 20 gallons, other than a simple independent measure to which the Weights and Measures Acts apply, must be stamped and regularly tested.

Any flexible discharge hose should not exceed 12 ft. in length (Measuring Instruments (Liquid Fuel and Lubricating Oil) Regs. 1929).

Petroleum Spirit (Conveyance by Road) Regulations 1957 and 1966, provide for the safe conveyance of petroleum spirit by road, but do not apply to its conveyance on any vehicle for use in the propulsion of that vehicle. Regulation 19 prohibits the carrying of vessels containing petroleum spirit on tank wagons or tank trailers, but not in composite vehicles.

They also do not apply to the conveyance on a vehicle of petroleum spirit not exceeding 32 gallons in closed containers holding not more than 2 gallons or in closed metal drums holding not more than 10 gallons, or not exceeding 50 gallons in a single closed steel barrel, but this exception does not apply to tank wagons, tank trailers, public service vehicles and vehicles hawking petroleum spirit (reg. 12).

Any vehicle used for conveying petroleum spirit shall be strongly constructed and in compliance with the directions of the Regulations (reg. 22 and Schedule).

A trailer carrying petroleum spirit shall not be drawn by—

(1) Any vehicle other than a motor tractor or a petroleum conveying vehicle, and only one such trailer may be drawn.

(2) A motor tractor unless the exhaust system is in front of the prescribed fire-resisting shield and unless any electric lighting is as prescribed.

(3) A vehicle conveying petroleum other than petroleum spirit unless the vehicle complies with the provisions applying to petroleum spirit conveying vehicles and unless the total amount of petroleum and petroleum spirit conveyed does not exceed 2,500 gallons (reg. 8).

Every vehicle conveying petroleum spirit by road shall be constantly attended by at least one person over 18 years of age, except when halted in an approved place. The driver may be regarded as a person whilst in, or in close proximity to, the vehicle (reg. 7).

Persons engaged in loading, unloading or conveying petroleum spirit shall observe all precautions necessary for preventing fire or explosion (reg. 2).

A person on or attending a vehicle conveying petroleum spirit shall not smoke nor carry matches or lighters (reg. 4).

No fire or artificial light capable of igniting inflammable vapour nor explosive substance nor anything capable of causing fire or explosion shall be allowed or carried on any vehicle conveying petroleum spirit (reg. 5), and an efficient extinguisher shall be carried on every such vehicle (reg. 6). Care must be taken to prevent the escape of petroleum spirit into any drain or sewer (reg. 3).

Petroleum spirit shall not be supplied direct from a vehicle carrying it in bulk to any mechanically propelled vehicle (reg. 9).

The owner of a vehicle used for conveyance of petroleum spirit is responsible for providing a copy of these Regulations for his employees and shall ensure they know and carry out their provisions (reg. 26).

Tank Wagons and Tank Trailers – The filling pipe shall be kept securely closed except when filling the tank (reg. 13) and the dipping pipe shall be kept securely closed except when filling or emptying the tank or testing the petroleum spirit contained in the tank on premises licensed for the purpose (reg. 14). When filling or emptying the tank, a competent person not under 18 years of age shall be in constant attendance, the engine of the vehicle shall be stopped until all tanks are closed (if horse drawn, the horses shall be removed and the wheels scotched), a dangerous static charge of electricity shall be prevented, the delivery piping or hose shall be sound, and it must be ascertained that the tank will hold the quantity to be delivered (reg. 15). For delivery into a storage tank, see reg. 16.

Such a vehicle shall not draw a trailer unless it is a tank trailer, and if its capacity exceeds 1,500 gallons, it shall not draw a trailer (reg. 18).

If the conveying vehicle is not a tank wagon or tank trailer, the petroleum spirit shall be in a vessel either of metal, or of glass, earthenware or material of such a nature that it will not permit leakage. If of metal it must be in good condition and not exceeding 50 gallons capacity, or 90 gallons if it contains a mixture with a content of not more than 75 per cent. of petroleum (1958 Regs.). In the case of glass, etc., containers each vessel shall contain not more than one pint of petroleum spirit and shall be packed in sawdust or other suitable material to prevent movement in an outer container of metal, wood or fibre which must be kept securely closed during conveyance, and the outer container must not contain in the aggregate more than 3 gallons of petroleum spirit. No vessel shall be filled or emptied while on the vehicle, and if empty shall be securely closed (reg. 23).

The load shall be protected from fire by a fire resisting cover and no part of the load shall project beyond the sides or back of the vehicle nor above the level of the top of the fire resisting shield which is necessary between the engine and the load (reg. 24).

Any vehicle conveying petroleum spirit shall not draw a trailer which is not used or intended to be used exclusively for conveying petroleum spirit (reg. 25). If a trailer forms part of an articulated vehicle it is deemed to be one vehicle for the purpose of these Regulations (reg. 28).

Any contravention of these Regulations is a summary offence (s. 6, Petroleum Consolidation Act 1928).

Carbide of Calcium – Under the Petroleum (Carbide of Calcium) Orders 1929, 1947, a vessel containing carbide of calcium (which is a solid giving off acetylene gas when water or even moisture is added) must bear in conspicuous letters "Carbide of Calcium", "Dangerous if not kept dry", "The contents of this package are liable if brought into contact with moisture to give off a highly inflammable gas", and the name and address of the owner, vendor or sender (art. 3).

The quantity which may be kept without licence is as follows:

1. 5 lb. if kept in hermetically closed metal vessels, each containing not more than 1 lb.
2. 28 lb. provided the following conditions are observed:
   (1) Kept in hermetically closed metal vessels;
   (2) Kept in a dry and well-ventilated place;
   (3) Due precautions to keep away unauthorised persons;
   (4) Notice given to Local Authority;
   (5) If a fixed generator is used, instructions as to its care and use must be posted up close by.

In all other cases a licence from the Local Authority is necessary before calcium carbide may be kept (art. 2).

The Petroleum (Consolidation) Act 1928, applies to carbide of calcium.

It must not be passed into a public drain or sewer (s. 27 Public Health Act 1936).

Acetylene – Acetylene is a highly inflammable and explosive gas, and is, when liquid or compressed or mixed with air or oxygen, deemed to be an explosive under the Explosives Act 1875, s. 104.

Orders in Council 1937, 1947, direct that such acetylene should not be manufactured, imported, kept, conveyed or sold, but do not interfere with acetylene mixed with air in a burner for burning or lighting purposes. The Compressed Acetylene Order 1919 declares that acetylene contained in a suitable porous substance and in metal cylinders properly made, tested and labelled will not be deemed an explosive.

Celluloid and Cinematograph Film – The Celluloid and Cinematograph Film Act 1922 is intended to lessen the risk incurred by the storing of such an inflammable substance as celluloid.

The Act applies to the keeping or storing of:

(1) Raw Celluloid in quantities of over 1 cwt. or in smaller quantities unless kept in a properly closed metal case.

"Celluloid" includes xylonite and other similar substances containing nitrated cellulose or other nitrated products, but does not include explosives under the Explosives Act 1875, and "raw celluloid" means celluloid which has not been subjected to any process of manufacture, and celluloid scrap or waste.

(2) Cinematograph Film, in quantities over twenty reels or 80 lb. in weight or in smaller quantities unless each reel is kept in a properly closed metal case.

"Cinematograph film" means any film containing celluloid and intended for use in a cinematograph or similar apparatus.

A temporary deposit in premises of cinematograph film for the purposes of examination, repair, etc., is a "keeping", but a temporary deposit of celluloid or cinematograph film in premises during the course of delivery, conveyance, or transport, will not be a "keeping" under the Act (ss. 2 and 9).

The following must not be used for such keeping or storing:

(1) Premises situated underneath premises used for residential purposes.

(2) Premises so situated that a fire occurring therein might interfere with the means of escape from the building or any adjoining building.

(3) Premises forming part of a building, unless separated from the building by fire-resisting partitions, or so situated and constructed that a fire therein is not likely to spread to the building and the Local Authority has given its sanction (s. 1),

Before any premises may be used for such keeping or storing, the occupier must furnish the Local Authority (the council of the county or London Borough, or the Common Council of the City of London) with a written statement of his name, the address of the premises and the nature of the business there carried on (s. 1 (a)), and must pay the prescribed annual fee (s. 4).

Conditions which must be observed in respect to such premises:

(1) Such means of escape in the case of fire as the Local Authority may reasonably require must be provided and properly maintained.

(2) The safety regulations in Sched. 1 to the Act must be duly observed (such as, no open fire or light, no smoking or matches, fire extinguishers, etc.).

(3) Any regulations made by the Secretary of State must be duly observed (s. 1).

Any contravention of the Act is a summary offence. An employee who contravenes any of the safety and other regulations made under the Act will also be guilty of a summary offence (s. 3).

The Act does not apply to:

(1) Premises licensed under the Cinematograph Act 1909.

(2) Premises to which the Factories Act 1961 applies except in the cases mentioned in s. 1 (as given above) in which certain premises must not be used for such keeping and storing (s. 2).

The Cinematograph Film Stripping Regulations 1939 apply to premises in which the stripping (removal of emulsion from) and drying of cinematograph film is done and which are supervised by the Inspectors of Factories.

Carbon Disulphide – This is a highly inflammable liquid. It must be conveyed in steel or iron containers each holding not more than 50 gallons, or in bottles each holding not more than 5 pints packed separately in wooden cases, each case containing not more than 3 gallons of it, or in mechanically driven tank wagons securely closed and without trailers. All must be marked "Carbon Disulphide—Highly Inflammable". No fire, etc., is allowable on the vehicle and attendants thereon must not smoke. Means of extinguishing fire must be carried. These rules will not apply when less than 28 lb. of the liquid is carried on a vehicle and if the weight of the liquid in any single container other than a metal one does not exceed 7 lb. (ss. 6, 19, Petroleum Consolidation Act 1928 and Carbon Disulphide (Conveyance by Road) Regs. 1958 and 1962).

Gas Cylinders' Conveyance – The Gas Cylinders (Conveyance) Regulations, 1931, 1947 and 1959, direct that, when conveyed by road, vessels containing any of the following gases in a compressed state—air, argon, carbon monoxide, coal gas, hydrogen, methane, neon, nitrogen and oxygen—shall have been constructed and tested in the manner prescribed by the Regulations.

Such vessels shall also have been tested in the prescribed manner within the preceding five years, and they shall be marked with the date of the last test, the name and address of the firm by whom compressed and the name of the gas contained.

They shall be painted (near the valve) with the identification colour prescribed for each gas (e.g. oxygen, black).

They shall be properly secured so as not to project beyond the sides or ends of the vehicle, unless they are securely attached to a cradle.

The Regulations do not apply to cylinders whose capacity does not exceed 12 lb. of water.

The Compressed Gas Cylinders (Fuel for Motor Vehicles) Conveyance Regulations 1940, provide for the conveyance by road of cylinders containing compressed coal gas, carbon monoxide, hydrogen or methane, and which are fitted to motor vehicles solely for the storage of gaseous fuel under pressure for the propulsion of the vehicle.

Such cylinders shall be made of forged steel or brass or bronze, constructed and tested as prescribed in the Regulations. They shall also have been tested within the preceding two years, and shall bear the date of the test. They shall be marked with the words "For gas propulsion only, working pressure —— lbs. per square inch", and with the water capacity in cubic feet.

A table shall be affixed to the vehicle giving the date of last test, the date of manufacture, the water capacity and the manufacturer's mark and number, of each cylinder.

The Gas Cylinders (Conveyance) Regulations (as above) do not apply to such cylinders.

See also "Gas Propelled Vehicles", Appendix II.

CHAPTER 34

FIREARMS

	Page
Firearms Act 1968	458
Firearm Certificate	458
Shot Gun Certificate	459
Firearms Dealers	459
Conversion of Weapons	460
Prohibitions and Exemptions	460
Criminal Use of Firearms	464
Possession of Firearms by Minors	467
Supplying Firearms to Minors, Person Drunk or Insane	468
Grant, Renewal, Variation and Revocation of Firearm and Shot Gun Certificates	468
Police Register	471
Gun Barrel Proof Acts 1868 and 1950	478

Firearms Act 1968 – This Act consolidates previous enactments dealing with Firearms, Air Guns and Shot Guns. The Act is in four Parts: Part I deals with possession, handling and distribution of weapons and ammunition; prevention of crime and measures to protect public safety. Part II deals with firearm and shot gun certificates and the registration of firearms dealers. Part III contains provisions for law enforcement and punishment. Part IV deals with miscellaneous matters, including the power of the Secretary of State to make rules for implementing the Act and the exercise of police functions.

Requirement of Firearm Certificate – Subject to any exemption under this Act, it is an offence for a person—(a) to have in his possession, or to purchase or acquire, a firearm to which this section applies without holding a firearm certificate in force at the time, or otherwise than as authorised by such a certificate; (b) to have in his possession, or to purchase or acquire, any ammunition to which this section applies without holding a firearm certificate in force at the time, or otherwise than as authorised by such a certificate, or in quantities in excess of those so authorised (s. **1** (1)).

It is an offence for a person to fail to comply with a condition subject to which a firearm certificate is held by him (s. **1** (2)).

This section applies to every firearm except—(a) a shot gun

(that is to say a smooth-bore gun with a barrel not less than 24 ins. in length, not being an air gun); and (b) an air weapon (that is to say, an air rifle, air gun or air pistol not of a type declared by rules made by the Secretary of State under s. 53 of this Act to be specially dangerous) (s. 1 (3)).

By the Firearms (Dangerous Air Weapons) Rules 1969, an air weapon (viz. an air rifle, air gun or air pistol) capable of discharging a missile so that the missile has, on being discharged from the muzzle of the weapon, kinetic energy in excess, in the case of an air pistol, of 6 ft. lb. or, in the case of an air weapon other than an air pistol, of 12 ft. lb., is declared to be specially dangerous. However, it does not extend to weapons designed for use only under water.

This section applies to any ammunition for a firearm, except the following articles, namely: (a) cartridges containing 5 or more shot, none of which exceeds ·36 inch in diameter; (b) ammunition for an air gun, air rifle or air pistol; and (c) blank cartridges not more than one inch in diameter measured immediately in front of the rim or cannelure of the base of the cartridge (s. 1 (4)).

Requirement of Certificate for Possession of Shot Guns – Subject to any exemption under this Act, it is an offence for a person to have in his possession, or to purchase or acquire, a shot gun without holding a certificate under this Act authorising him to possess shot guns (s. 2 (1)).

It is an offence for a person to fail to comply with a condition subject to which a shot gun certificate is held by him (s. 2 (2)).

Business and Other Transactions with Firearms and Ammunition – A person commits an offence if, by way of trade or business, he—(a) manufactures, sells, transfers, repairs, tests or proves any firearm or ammunition to which s. 1 of this Act applies, or a shot gun; or (b) exposes for sale or transfer, or has in his possession for sale, transfer, repair, test or proof any such firearm or ammunition, or a shot gun, without being registered under this Act as a firearms dealer (s. 3 (1)).

It is an offence for a person to sell or transfer to any other person in the United Kingdom, other than a registered firearms dealer, any firearm or ammunition to which s. 1 of this Act applies, or a shot gun, unless that other produces a firearm certificate authorising him to purchase or acquire it or, as the case may be, his shot gun certificate, or shows that he is by virtue of this Act entitled to purchase or acquire it without holding a certificate (s. 3 (2)).

It is an offence for a person to undertake the repair, test or proof of a firearm or ammunition to which s. 1 of this Act applies, or of a shot gun, for any other person in the United Kingdom other than a registered firearms dealer as such, unless that other produces or causes to be produced a firearm certificate authorising him to have possession of the firearm or ammunition or, as the case may be, his shot gun certificate, or shows that he is by virtue of this Act entitled to have possession of it without holding a certificate (s. 3 (3)).

Subsections (1) to (3) above have effect subject to any exemption under subsequent provisions of this Part of this Act (s. 3 (4)).

A person commits an offence if, with a view to purchasing or acquiring, or procuring the repair, test or proof of, any firearm or ammunition to which s. 1 of this Act applies, or a shot gun, he produces a false certificate or a certificate in which any false entry has been made, or personates a person to whom a certificate has been granted, or makes any false statement (s. 3 (5)).

It is an offence for a pawnbroker to take in pawn any firearm or ammunition to which s. 1 of this Act applies, or a shot gun (s. 3 (6)).

Conversion of Weapons – Subject to this section, it is an offence to shorten the barrel of a shot gun to a length less than 24 ins. (s. 4 (1)).

It is not an offence under sub-s. (1) above for a registered firearms dealer to shorten the barrel of a shot gun for the sole purpose of replacing a defective part of the barrel so as to produce a barrel not less than 24 ins. in length (s. 4 (2)).

It is an offence for a person other than a registered firearms dealer to convert into a firearm anything which, though having the appearance of being a firearm, is so constructed as to be incapable of discharging any missile through its barrel (s. 4 (3)).

A person who commits an offence under s. 1 of this Act by having in his possession, or purchasing or acquiring, a shot gun which has been shortened contrary to sub-s. (1) above or a firearm which has been converted contrary to sub-s. (3) above (whether by a registered firearms dealer or not), without holding a firearm certificate authorising him to have it in his possession, or to purchase or acquire it, shall be treated for the purposes of provisions of this Act relating to the punishment of offences as committing that offence in an aggravated form (s. 4 (4)).

Weapons Subject to General Prohibition – A person commits an offence if, without the authority of the Secretary of State, he has in his possession, or purchases or acquires, or manufactures, sells or transfers—(a) any firearm which is so designed or adapted that, if pressure is applied to the trigger, missiles continue to be discharged until pressure is removed from the trigger or the magazine containing the missiles is empty; (b) any weapon of whatever description designed or adapted for the discharge of any noxious liquid, gas or other thing; and (c) any ammunition containing, or designed or adapted to contain, any such noxious thing (s. 5 (1)).

The weapons and ammunition specified in sub-s. (1) of this section are referred to in this Act as "prohibited weapons" and "prohibited ammunition" respectively (s. 5 (2)).

An authority given to a person by the Secretary of State under this section shall be in writing and be subject to conditions specified therein (s. 5 (3)).

The conditions of the authority shall include such as the Secretary of State, having regard to the circumstances of each particular case, thinks fit to impose for the purpose of securing that the prohibited weapon or ammunition to which the authority relates will not endanger the public safety or the peace (s. 5 (4)).

It is an offence for a person to whom an authority is given under this section to fail to comply with any condition of the authority (s. 5 (5)).

The Secretary of State may at any time, if he thinks fit, revoke an authority given to a person under this section by notice in writing requiring him to deliver up the authority to such person as may be specified in the notice within 21 days from the date of the notice; and it is an offence for him to fail to comply with that requirement (s. 5 (6)).

Power to Prohibit Movement of Arms and Ammunition – The Secretary of State may by order prohibit the removal of firearms or ammunition—(a) from one place to another in Great Britain; or (b) from Great Britain to Northern Ireland; or (c) for export from Great Britain, unless the removal is authorised by the chief officer of police for the area from which they are to be removed, and unless such other conditions as may be specified in the order are complied with (s. 6 (1)).

An order under this section may apply—(a) either generally to all such removals, or to removals from and to particular localities specified in the order; and (b) either to all firearms and ammunition or to firearms and ammunition of such classes and descriptions as may be so specified; and (c) either to all modes of conveyance or to such modes of conveyance as may be so specified; but no such order shall prohibit the holder of a firearm certificate from carrying with him any firearm or ammunition authorised by the certificate to be so carried (s. 6 (2)).

It is an offence to contravene any provision of—(a) an order made under this section; or (b) an order made under s. 9 of the Firearms Act 1920 (the former enactment corresponding to s. 18 of the Firearms Act 1937 and this section); or (c) any corresponding Northern Irish order, prohibiting the removal of firearms or ammunition from Northern Ireland to Great Britain (s. 6(3)).

An order under this section shall be made by Statutory Instrument and may be varied or revoked by a subsequent order made thereunder by the Secretary of State (s. 6 (4)).

POLICE PERMIT – A person who has obtained from the chief officer of police for the area in which he resides a permit for the purpose in the prescribed form may, without holding a certificate under this Act, have in his possession a firearm and ammunition in accordance with the terms of the permit (s. 7 (1)).

It is an offence for a person to make any statement which he knows to be false for the purpose of procuring, whether for himself or for another person, the grant of a permit under this section (s. 7 (2)).

AUTHORISED DEALING WITH FIREARMS – A person carrying on the business of a firearms dealer and registered as such under this Act, or a servant of such a person may, without holding a certificate, have in his possession, or purchase or acquire a firearm or ammunition in the ordinary course of that business (s. 8 (1)).

It is not an offence under s. 3 (2) of this Act for a person-- (a) to part with the possession of any firearm or ammunition, otherwise than in pursuance of a contract of sale or hire or by way of gift or loan, to a person who shows that he is by virtue of this Act entitled to have possession of the firearm or ammunition without holding a certificate; or (b) to return to another person a shot gun which he has lawfully undertaken to repair, test or prove for the other (s. 8 (2)).

CARRIERS, AUCTIONEERS, ETC. – A person carrying on the business of an auctioneer, carrier or warehouseman, or a servant of such a person, may, without holding a certificate, have in his possession a firearm or ammunition in the ordinary course of that business (s. 9 (1)).

It is not an offence under s. 3 (1) of this Act for an auctioneer to sell by auction, expose for sale by auction or have in his possession for sale by auction a firearm or ammunition without being registered as a firearms dealer, if he has obtained from the chief officer of police for the area in which the auction is held a permit for that purpose in the prescribed form and complies with the terms of the permit (s. 9 (2)).

It is an offence for a person to make any statement which he knows to be false for the purpose of procuring, either for himself or for another person, the grant of a permit under sub-s. (2) of this section (s. 9 (3)).

It is not an offence under s. 3 (2) of this Act for a carrier or warehouseman, or a servant of a carrier or warehouseman, to deliver any firearm or ammunition in the ordinary course of his business or employment as such (s. 9 (4)).

SLAUGHTER OF ANIMALS – A person licenced under s. 39 of the Slaughterhouses Act 1974, may, without holding a certificate, have in his possession a slaughtering instrument and ammunition therefor in any slaughter-house or knacker's yard in which he is employed (s. 10 (1)).

The proprietor of a slaughter-house or knacker's yard or a person appointed by him to take charge of slaughtering instruments and ammunition therefor for the purpose of storing them in safe custody at that slaughter-house or knacker's yard may, without holding a certificate, have in his possession a slaughtering instrument or ammunition therefor for that purpose (s. 10 (2)).

SPORTS, ATHLETICS AND OTHER APPROVED ACTIVITIES – A person carrying a firearm or ammunition belonging to another person holding a certificate under this Act may, without himself holding such a certificate, have in his possession that firearm or ammunition under instructions from, and for the use of, that other person for sporting purposes only (s. 11 (1)).

A person may, without holding a certificate, have a firearm in his possession at an athletic meeting for the purpose of starting races at that meeting (s. 11 (2)).

A member of a rifle club or miniature rifle club or cadet corps approved by the Secretary of State may, without holding a certificate, have in his possession a firearm and ammunition when engaged as a member of the club or corps in, or in connection with, drill or target practice (s. 11 (3)).

A person conducting or carrying on a miniature rifle range (whether for a rifle club or otherwise) or shooting gallery at which no firearms are used other than air weapons or miniature rifles not exceeding ·23 inch calibre may, without holding a certificate, have in his possession, or purchase or acquire, such miniature rifles and ammunition suitable therefor; and any person may, without holding a certificate, use any such rifle and ammunition at such a range or gallery (s. 11 (4)).

A person may, without holding a shot gun certificate, borrow a shot gun from the occupier of private premises and use it on those premises in the occupier's presence (s. 11 (5)).

A person may, without holding a shot gun certificate, use a shot gun at a time and place approved for shooting at artificial targets by the chief officer of police for the area in which that place is situated (s. 11 (6)).

THEATRE AND CINEMA – A person taking part in a theatrical performance or a rehearsal thereof, or in the production of a cinematograph film, may, without holding a certificate, have a firearm in his possession during and for the purpose of the performance, rehearsal or production (s. 12 (1)).

Where the Secretary of State is satisfied, on the application of a person in charge of a theatrical performance, a rehearsal of such a performance or the production of a cinematograph film, that such a firearm as is described in s. 5 (1) (a) of this Act is required for the purpose of the performance, rehearsal or production, he may under s. 5 of this Act, not only authorise that person to have possession of the firearm but also authorise such other persons as he may select to have possession of it while taking part in the performance, rehearsal or production (s. 12 (2)).

EQUIPMENT FOR SHIPS AND AIRCRAFT – A person may, without holding a certificate—(a) have in his possession a firearm or ammunition on board a ship, or a signalling apparatus or ammunition therefor on board an aircraft or at an aerodrome, as part of the equipment of the ship, aircraft or aerodrome; (b) remove a signalling apparatus or ammunition therefor, being part of the equipment of an aircraft, from one aircraft to another at an aerodrome, or from or to an aircraft at an aerodrome to or from a place appointed for the storage thereof in safe custody at that aerodrome, and keep any such apparatus or ammunition at such a place; and (c) if he has obtained from an officer of police a permit for the purpose in the prescribed form, remove a firearm from or to a ship, or a signalling apparatus from or to an aircraft or aerodrome, to or from such place and for such purpose as may be specified in the permit (s. 13 (1)).

It is an offence for a person to make any statement which he knows to be false for the purpose of procuring, either for himself or for another person, the grant of a permit under sub-s. (1) (c) of this section (s. 13 (2)).

PERSONS TEMPORARILY IN GREAT BRITAIN – A person who has been in Great Britain for not more than 30 days in all in the preceding 12 months may have in his possession, or purchase or acquire, a shot gun without holding a shot gun certificate (s. 14).

HOLDER OF NORTHERN IRISH CERTIFICATE – Section 2 (1) of this Act does not apply to a person holding a firearm certificate issued in Northern Ireland authorising him to possess a shot gun (s. 15).

Possession of Firearm with Intent to Injure – It is an offence for a person to have in his possession any firearm or ammunition with intent by means thereof to endanger life, or to enable another person by means thereof to endanger life, whether any injury has been caused or not (s. 16).

Use of Firearm to Resist Arrest – It is an offence for a person to make or attempt to make any use whatsoever of a firearm or imitation firearm with intent to resist or prevent the lawful arrest or detention of himself or another person (s. 17 (1)).

If a person, at the time of his committing or being arrested for an offence specified in Sched. 1 to this Act, has in his possession a firearm or imitation firearm, he shall be guilty of an offence under this subsection unless he shows that he had it in his possession for a lawful object (s. 17 (2)).

For purposes of this section, the definition of "firearm" in s. 57 (1) of this Act shall apply without paragraphs (b) and (c) of that subsection, and "imitation firearm" shall be construed accordingly (s. 17 (4)).

The offences to which s. 17 (2) applies are:

1. Offences under the Criminal Damage Act 1971, s.1 (destroying or damaging property).

2. Offences under any of the following provisions of the Offences Against the Person Act 1861:

sections 20 to 22 (inflicting bodily injury; garrotting; criminal use of stupefying drugs);
section 30 (laying explosive to building, etc.);
section 23 (endangering railway passengers by tampering with track);
section 38 (assault with intent to commit felony or resist arrest);
section 47 (criminal assaults);
section 56 (child-stealing and abduction).

3. Offences under such of the provisions of s. 4 of the Vagrancy Act 1824, as are referred to in and amended by s. 15 of the Prevention of Crimes Act 1871 and s. 7 of the Penal Servitude Act 1891 (suspected persons and reputed thieves being abroad with criminal intent).

4. Theft, burglary, blackmail and any offence under s. 12 (1) (taking of motor vehicle or other conveyance without owner's consent) of the Theft Act 1968.

5. Offences under s. 51 (1) of the Police Act 1964 (assaulting constable in execution of his duty).

6. Offences under any of the following provisions of the Sexual Offences Act 1956:

section 1 (rape);
sections 17 and 20 (abduction of women).

7. Aiding or abetting the commission of any offence specified in paras. 1 to 6.

8. Attempting to commit any offence so specified.

Carrying Firearm with Criminal Intent – It is an offence for a person to have with him a firearm or imitation firearm with intent to commit an indictable offence, or to resist arrest or prevent the arrest of another, in either case while he has the firearm or imitation firearm with him (s. 18 (1)).

In proceedings for an offence under this section proof that the accused had a firearm or imitation firearm with him and intended to commit an offence, or to resist or prevent arrest, is evidence that he intended to have it with him while doing so (s. 18 (2)).

Carrying Firearm in a Public Place – A person commits an offence if, without lawful authority or reasonable excuse (the proof whereof lies on him) he has with him in a public place a loaded shot gun or loaded air weapon, or any other firearm (whether loaded or not) together with ammunition suitable for use in that firearm (s. 19).

Trespassing with Firearm – A person commits an offence if, while he has a firearm with him, he enters or is in any building or part of a building as a trespasser and without reasonable excuse (the proof whereof lies on him) (s. 20 (1)).

A person commits an offence if, while he has a firearm with him, he enters or is on any land as a trespasser and without reasonable excuse (the proof whereof lies on him) (s. 20 (2)).

In sub-s. (2) of this section the expression "land" includes land covered with water (s. 20 (3)).

Possession of Firearms by Persons previously Convicted of Crime – A person who has been sentenced to preventive detention, or to imprisonment or to corrective training for a term of 3 years or more, shall not at any time have a firearm or ammunition in his possession (s. 21 (1)).

A person who has been sentenced to Borstal training, to corrective training for less than 3 years or to imprisonment for a term of 3 months or more but less than 3 years, shall not at any time before the expiration of the period of 5 years from the date of his release have a firearm or ammunition in his possession (s. 21 (2)).

A person who—(a) is the holder of a licence issued under s. 53 of the Children and Young Persons Act 1933 (which provides for the detention of children and young persons convicted of serious crime, but enables them to be discharged on licence by the Secretary of State); or (b) is subject to a recognizance to keep the peace or to be of good behaviour, a condition of which is that he shall not possess, use or carry a firearm, or is subject to a probation order containing a requirement that he shall not possess, use or carry a firearm; shall not, at any time during which he holds the licence or is so subject, have a firearm or ammunition in his possession (s. 21 (3)).

Where by s. 19 of the Firearms Act (Northern Ireland) 1969, or by any other enactment for the time being in force in Northern Ireland and corresponding to this section, a person is prohibited in Northern Ireland from having a firearm or ammunition in his possession, he shall also be so prohibited in Great Britain at any time when to have it in his possession in Northern Ireland would be a contravention of the said s. 19 or corresponding enactment (s. 21 (3 A)).

It is an offence for a person to contravene any of the foregoing provisions of this section (s. 21 (4)).

It is an offence for a person to sell or transfer a firearm or ammunition to, or to repair, test or prove a firearm or ammunition for, a person whom he knows or has reasonable ground for believing to be prohibited by this section from having a firearm or ammunition in his possession (s. 21 (5)).

A person prohibited under sub-ss. (1), (2), (3) or (3A) of this section from having in his possession a firearm or ammunition may apply to the Crown Court for a removal of the prohibition; and if the application is granted that prohibition shall not then apply to him (s. 21 (6)).

Acquisition and Possession of Firearms by Minors – It is an offence for a person under the age of 17 to purchase or hire any firearm or ammunition (s. 22 (1)).

It is an offence for a person under the age of 14 to have in his possession any firearm or ammunition to which s. 1 of this Act applies, except in circumstances where under s. 11 (1), (3) or (4) of this Act he is entitled to have possession of it without holding a firearm certificate (s. 22 (2)).

It is an offence for a person under the age of 15 to have with him an assembled shot gun except while under the supervision of a person of or over the age of 21, or while the shot gun is so covered with a securely fastened gun cover that it cannot be fired (s. 22 (3)).

Subject to s. 23 below, it is an offence for a person under the age of 14 to have with him an air weapon or ammunition for an air weapon (s. 22 (4)).

Subject to s. 23 below, it is an offence for a person under the age of 17 to have an air weapon with him in a public place, except an air gun or air rifle which is so covered with a securely fastened gun cover that it cannot be fired (s. 22 (5)).

Exceptions from s. 22 (4) and (5) – It is not an offence under s. 22 (4) of this Act for a person to have with him an air weapon or ammunition while he is under the supervision of a person of or over the age of 21; but where a person has with him an air weapon on any premises in circumstances where he would be prohibited from having it with him but for this subsection, it is an offence—(a) for him to use it for firing any missile beyond those premises; or (b) for the person under whose supervision he is to allow him so to use it (s. 23 (1)).

It is not an offence under s. 22 (4) or (5) of this Act for a person to have with him an air weapon or ammunition at a time when—(a) being a member of a rifle club or miniature rifle club for the time being approved by the Secretary of State for the purposes of this section or s. 11 (3) of this Act, he is engaged as such a member in or in connection with target practice; or (b) he is using the weapon or ammunition at a shooting gallery where the only firearms used are either air weapons or miniature rifles not exceeding ·23 inch calibre (s. 23 (2)).

Supplying Firearms to Minors – It is an offence to sell or let on hire any firearm or ammunition to a person under the age of 17 (s. 24 (1)).

It is an offence—(a) to make a gift of or lend any firearm or ammunition to which s. 1 of this Act applies to a person under the age of 14; or (b) to part with the possession of any such firearm or ammunition to a person under that age, except in circumstances where that person is entitled under s. 11 (1), (3) or (4) of this Act to have possession thereof without holding a firearm certificate (s. 24 (2)).

It is an offence to make a gift of a shot gun or ammunition for a shot gun to a person under the age of 15 (s. 24 (3)).

It is an offence—(a) to make a gift of an air weapon or ammunition for an air weapon to a person under the age of 14; or (b) to part with the possession of an air weapon or ammunition for an air weapon to a person under that age except where by virtue of s. 23 of this Act the person is not prohibited from having it with him (s. 24 (4)).

In proceedings for an offence under any provision of this section it is a defence to prove that the person charged with the offence believed the other person to be of or over the age mentioned in that provision and had reasonable ground for the belief (s. 24 (5)).

Supplying Firearm to Person Drunk or Insane – It is an offence for a person to sell or transfer any firearm or ammunition to, or to repair, prove or test any firearm or ammunition for, another person whom he knows or has reasonable cause for believing to be drunk or of unsound mind (s. 25).

Application for, and Grant of, Certificates – An application for the grant of a firearm or shot gun certificate shall be made in the prescribed form to the chief officer of police for the area in which the applicant resides and shall state such particulars as may be required by the form (s. 26 (1)).

The certificate, unless revoked or cancelled, lasts for 3 years and is renewable for a further 3 years by the chief officer of police for the area in which the holder resides, and so from time to time (s. 26 (3)).

There is an appeal to the Crown Court if a chief officer of police refuses to grant or renew a certificate or has revoked it (ss. 26 (4) and 44).

It is an offence for a person to make any statement which he knows to be false for the purpose of procuring, whether for himself or any other person, the grant or renewal of a certificate under this Act (s. 26 (5)).

SPECIAL PROVISIONS ABOUT FIREARM CERTIFICATES – A firearm certificate shall be granted by the chief officer of police if he is satisfied that the applicant has a good reason for having in his possession, or for purchasing or acquiring, the firearm or ammunition in respect of which the application is made, and can be permitted to have it in his possession without danger to the public safety or to the peace:

Provided that a firearm certificate shall not be granted to a person whom the chief officer of police has reason to believe to be prohibited by this Act from possessing a firearm to which s. 1 of this Act applies, or to be of intemperate habits or unsound mind, or to be for any reason unfitted to be entrusted with such a firearm (s. 27 (1)).

SPECIAL PROVISIONS ABOUT SHOT GUN CERTIFICATES – A shot gun certificate shall be granted or, as the case may be, renewed by the chief officer of police unless he has reason to believe that the applicant—

(a) is prohibited by this Act from possessing a shot gun; or

(b) cannot be permitted to possess a shot gun without danger to the public safety or to the peace (s. 28 (1)).

VARIATION OF FIREARM CERTIFICATES – The chief officer of police for the area in which the holder of a firearm certificate resides may at any time by notice in writing vary the conditions subject to which the certificate is held, except such of them as may be prescribed, and may by the notice require the holder to deliver up the certificate to him within 21 days from the date of the notice for the purpose of amending the conditions specified therein (s. 29 (1)).

A firearm certificate may also, on the application of the holder, be varied from time to time by the chief officer of police for the area in which the holder for the time being resides; and a person aggrieved by the refusal of a chief officer of police to vary a firearm certificate may in accordance with s. 44 of this Act appeal against the refusal (s. 29 (2)).

It is an offence for a person to make any statement which he knows to be false for the purpose of procuring, whether for himself or another person, the variation of a firearm certificate (s. 29 (3)).

REVOCATION OF CERTIFICATES – A firearm certificate may be revoked by the chief officer of police for the area in which the holder resides if—

(a) the chief officer is satisfied that the holder is prohibited by this Act from possessing a firearm to which s. 1 of this Act applies or is of intemperate habits or unsound mind, or is otherwise unfitted to be entrusted with such a firearm; or

(b) the holder fails to comply with a notice under s. 29 (1) of this Act requiring him to deliver up the certificate (s. 30 (1)).

A shot gun certificate may be revoked by the chief officer of police if he is satisfied that the holder is prohibited by this Act from possessing a shot gun or cannot be permitted to possess a shot gun without danger to the public safety or to the peace (s. 30 (2)).

A person aggrieved by the revocation of a certificate under sub-ss. (1) (a) or (2) of this section may in accordance with s. 44 of this Act appeal to the Crown Court against the refusal (s. 30 (3)).

Where a certificate is revoked by a chief officer of police under this section, he shall by notice in writing require the holder to surrender the certificate; and it is an offence for the holder to fail to do so within 21 days from the date of the notice, or from dismissal or abandonment of any appeal (s. 30 (4)).

Fee for Certificate and Exemption from Paying it in Certain Cases – Subject to this Act, there shall be payable:

(a) on the grant of a firearm certificate, a fee of £2·50;

(b) on the renewal of a firearm certificate or on the replacement of such a certificate which has been lost or destroyed, a fee of £1·25;

(c) on any variation of a firearm certificate (otherwise than when it is renewed or replaced at the same time) so as to increase the number of firearms to which the certificate relates, a fee of £1·25;

(d) on the grant or renewal of a shot gun certificate, a fee of 75p; and

(e) on the replacement of a shot gun certificate which has been lost or destroyed, a fee of 37½p (s. 32 (1)).

No fee shall be payable on the grant to a responsible officer of a rifle club, miniature rifle club, or cadet corps approved for the purpose by the Secretary of State, of a firearm certificate in respect of firearms or ammunition to be used solely for target practice or drill by the members of the club or corps, or on the variation or renewal of a certificate so granted (s. 32 (2)).

No fee shall be payable on the grant, variation or renewal of a firearm certificate if the chief officer of police is satisfied that the certificate relates solely to and, in the case of a variation, will continue when varied to relate solely to:

(a) a firearm or ammunition which the applicant requires as part of the equipment of a ship; or

(b) a signalling apparatus, or ammunition therefor, which the applicant requires as part of the equipment of an aircraft or aerodrome; or

(c) a slaughtering instrument, or ammunition therefor, which the applicant requires for the purpose of the slaughter of animals (s. 33 (3)).

No fee shall be payable on the grant, variation or renewal of a firearm certificate which relates solely to and, in the case of a variation, will continue when varied to relate solely to a signalling device which, when assembled and ready to fire, is not more than 6 ins. long and which is designed to discharge a flare, or to ammunition for such a device (s. 32 (3A)).

No fee shall be payable:

(a) on the grant or renewal of a firearm certificate relating solely to a firearm which is shown to the satisfaction of the chief officer of police to be kept by the applicant as a trophy of war; or

(b) on any variation of a certificate the sole effect of which is to add such a firearm as aforesaid to the firearms to which the certificate relates,

if the certificate is granted, renewed or varied subject to the condition that the applicant shall not use the firearm (s. 32 (4)).

Police Register – For purposes of this Act, the chief officer of police for every area shall keep in the prescribed form a register of firearms dealers (s. 33 (1)).

Except as provided by s. 34 of this Act, the chief officer of police shall enter in the register the name of any person who, having or proposing to have a place of business in the area, applies to be registered as a firearms dealer (s. 33 (2)).

In order to be registered, the applicant must furnish the chief officer of police with the prescribed particulars, which shall include particulars of every place of business at which he proposes to carry on business in the area as a firearms dealer and, except as provided by this Act, the chief officer of police shall enter every such place of business in the register (s. 33 (3)).

When a person is registered, the chief officer of police shall grant or cause to be granted to him a certificate of registration (s. 33 (4)).

A person for the time being registered shall, on or before June 1 in each year:

(a) surrender his certificate to the chief officer of police; and

(b) apply in the prescribed form for a new certificate (s. 33 (5)).

GROUNDS FOR REFUSAL OF REGISTRATION – The chief officer of police shall not register an applicant as a firearms dealer if he is prohibited to be so registered by order of a court (s. 34 (1)).

The chief officer of police may refuse to register an applicant, if he is satisfied that the applicant cannot be permitted to carry on business as a firearms dealer without danger to the public safety or to the peace (s. 34 (2)).

A person aggrieved by the refusal of a chief officer of police to register him as a firearms dealer, or to enter in the register a place of business of his, may in accordance with s. 44 of this Act appeal against the refusal (s. 34 (5)).

FEE FOR REGISTRATION AND RENEWAL THEREOF – Subject to this Act, on the registration of a person as a firearms dealer there shall be payable by him a fee of £20 (s. 35 (1)).

Before a person for the time being registered as a firearms dealer can be granted a new certificate of registration under s. 33 (5) of this Act, he shall pay a fee of £4 (s. 35 (3)).

CONDITIONS OF REGISTRATION – The chief officer of police may at any time impose conditions subject to which the registration of a person as a firearms dealer is to have effect and may at any time, of his own motion or on the application of the dealer, vary or revoke any such condition (s. 36 (1)).

A person aggrieved by the imposition or variation of, or refusal to vary or revoke, any condition of a firearms dealer's registration may in accordance with s. 44 of this Act appeal against the imposition, variation or refusal (s. 36 (3)).

Sections 37 and 38 deal with the registration of new places of business of firearms dealers and the removal from the police register of a dealer's name or place of business.

Offences in Connection with Registration – A person commits an offence if, for the purpose: (a) of procuring the registration of himself or another person as a firearms dealer; or (b) of procuring, whether for himself or another person, the entry of any place of business in a register of firearms dealers, he makes any statement which he knows to be false (s. 39 (1)).

A person commits an offence if, being a registered firearms dealer, he has a place of business which is not entered in the register for the area in which the place of business is situated and carries on business as a firearms dealer at that place (s. 39 (2)).

A person commits an offence if he fails to comply with any of the conditions of registration imposed on him by the chief officer of police under s. 36 of this Act (s. 39 (3)).

Compulsory Register of Transactions in Firearms – Subject to s. 41 of this Act, every person who by way of trade or business manufactures, sells or transfers firearms or ammunition shall provide and keep a register of transactions and shall enter or cause to be entered therein the particulars specified in Sched. 4 to this Act (s. 40 (1)).

In sub-s. (1) above and in the said Sched. 4, any reference to firearms is to be construed as not including a reference to air weapons or component parts of, or accessories to, air weapons; and any reference therein to ammunition is to be construed as not including: (a) cartridges containing 5 or more shot, none of which exceeds ·36 inch in diameter; (b) ammunition for an air gun, air rifle or air pistol; or (c) blank cartridges not more than one inch in diameter measured immediately in front of the rim or cannelure of the base of the cartridge (s. 40 (2)).

Every entry shall be made within 24 hours after each transaction (s. 40 (3)). Any police officer, duly authorised in writing by the chief officer of police, shall be allowed on demand to enter the premises of such a person and inspect all stock in hand. Such person on request shall produce his register of transactions for inspection by any police officer duly authorised or by an officer of customs and excise (s. 40 (4)).

It is an offence for a person to fail to comply with any provision of this section or knowingly to make any false entry in the register required to be kept thereunder (s. 40 (5)).

Nothing in this section applies to the sale of firearms or ammunition by auction in accordance with the terms of a permit issued under s. 9 (2) of this Act (s. 40 (6)).

The particulars to be entered by firearms dealer in register of transactions are:

1. The quantities and description of firearms and ammunition manufactured and the dates thereof.

2. The quantities and description of firearms and ammunition purchased or acquired with the names and addresses of the sellers or transferors and the dates of the several transactions.

3. The quantities and description of firearms and ammunition accepted for sale, repair, test, proof, cleaning, storage, destruction or other purpose, with the names and addresses of the transferors and the dates of the several transactions.

4. The quantities and description of firearms and ammunition sold or transferred with the names and addresses of the purchasers or transferees and (except in cases where the purchaser or transferee is a registered dealer) the areas in which the firearm certificates were issued, and the dates of the several transactions.

5. The quantities and description of firearms and ammunition in possession for sale or transfer at the date of the last stocktaking or such other date in each year as may be specified in the register (Sched. 4).

Under s. 41, chief officers of police are given discretion to exempt from all or any of the provisions about keeping of records by persons who process components for manufacturers but who do not handle complete shot guns.

Transactions with Persons not Registered Dealers – A person who sells, lets on hire, gives or lends a firearm or ammunition to which s. 1 of this Act applies to another person in the United Kingdom, not being a registered firearms dealer shall, unless the other person shows that he is by virtue of this Act entitled to purchase or acquire the firearm or ammunition without holding a firearm certificate, comply with any instructions contained in the certificate produced; and in the case of a fire-arm he shall, within 48 hours from the transaction, send by registered post or the recorded delivery service notice of the transaction to the chief officer of police by whom the certicate was issued (s. 42 (1)).

It is an offence for a person to fail to comply with this section (s. 42 (2)).

There is a right of appeal to the Crown Court against police decisions under Part II of the Act (s. 44).

Consequences where Registered Dealer Convicted of Offence – If a registered firearms dealer is convicted of an offence relevant for the purposes of this section the court may order his name to be removed from the register, and that he (and any employee concerned) shall not be registered as a firearms dealer, and that any person who may knowingly employ such convicted person shall not be (or remain) registered as a firearms dealer, and that the stock of business shall be disposed of (s. 45 (1)).

The relevant offences for the purpose of this section are (a) all offences under this Act except those under ss. 2, 22 (3) or 24 (3), or an offence relating specifically to air weapons; and (b) offences against the enactments relating to customs in respect of import or export of firearms, ammunition or of shot guns (s. 45 (2)). There may be an appeal to the Crown Court against such an order (s. 45 (3)).

Power of Search with Warrant – If a justice of the peace is satisfied by information on oath that there is reasonable ground for suspecting that an offence relevant for the purposes of this section has been, is being, or is about to be committed, he may grant a search warrant authorising a constable named therein: (a) to enter at any time any premises or place named in the warrant, if necessary by force, and to search the premises or place and every person found there; (b) to seize and detain any firearm or ammunition which he may find on the premises or place, or on any such person, in respect of which or in connection with which he has reasonable ground for suspecting that an offence relevant for the purposes of this section has been, is being or is about to be committed; and (c) if the premises are those of a registered firearms dealer, to examine any books relating to the business (s. 46 (1)).

The offences relevant for the purposes of this section are all offences under this Act except an offence under s. 22 (3) or on offence relating specifically to air weapons (s. 46 (2)).

Powers of Constables to Stop and Search – A constable may require any person whom he has reasonable cause to suspect: (a) of having a firearm, with or without ammunition, with him in a public place; or (b) to be committing or about to commit, elsewhere than in a public place, an offence relevant for the purposes of this section, to hand over the firearm or any ammunition for examination by the constable (s. 47 (1)).

It is an offence for a person having a firearm or ammunition with him to fail to hand it over when required to do so by a constable under sub-s. (1) of this section (s. 47 (2)).

If a constable has reasonable cause to suspect a person of having a firearm with him in a public place, or to be committing or about to commit, elsewhere than in a public place, an offence relevant for the purposes of this section, the constable may search that person and may detain him for the purpose of doing so (s. 47 (3)).

If a constable has reasonable cause to suspect that there is a firearm in a vehicle in a public place, or that a vehicle is being or is about to be used in connection with the commission of an offence relevant for the purposes of this section elsewhere than in a public place, he may search the vehicle and for that purpose require the person driving or in control of it to stop it (s. 47 (4)).

For the purpose of exercising the powers conferred by this section a constable may enter any place (s. 47 (5)).

The offences relevant for the purpose of this section are those under ss. 18 (1) and (2) and 20 of this Act (s. 47 (6)).

(The Secretary of State has emphasised in Parliament that the exercise of the powers conferred by the Act would be closely supervised. Care should be taken that these powers are used properly and with discretion.)

Production of Certificates – A constable may demand, from any person whom he believes to be in possession of a firearm or ammunition to which s. 1 of this Act applies, or of a shot gun, the production of his firearm certificate or, as the case may be, his shot gun certificate (s. 48 (1)).

If a person upon whom a demand is made under this section fails to produce the certificate or to permit the constable to read it, or to show that he is entitled by virtue of this Act to have the firearm, ammunition or shot gun in his possession without holding a certificate, the constable may seize and detain the firearm, ammunition or shot gun and may require the person to declare to him immediately his name and address (s. 48 (2)).

If under this section a person is required to declare to a constable his name and address, it is an offence for him to refuse to declare it or to fail to give his true name and address (s. 48 (3)).

Police Powers in Relation to Arms Traffic – An officer of police may search for and seize any firearms or ammunition which he has reason to believe are being removed, or to have been removed, in contravention of an order made by the Secretary of State under s. 6 (s. 49 (1)).

A person having the control or custody of any firearms or ammunition in course of transit, shall on demand by a constable, allow him all reasonable facilities for the examination and inspection thereof and shall produce any documents in his possession relating thereto (s. 49 (2)). Failing to comply is an offence (s. 49 (3)).

Special Powers of Arrest – A constable making a search of premises under the authority of a warrant under s. 46 of this Act may arrest without warrant any person found on the premises whom he has reason to believe to be guilty of an offence relevant for the purposes of that section (s. 50 (1)).

A constable may arrest without warrant any person whom he has reasonable cause to suspect to be committing an offence under ss. 19 (carrying firearm in a public place), 20 (trespassing with firearms by persons previously convicted of crime) or 47 (2) (failing to hand over firearm or ammunition when required to do so by constable), and, for the purpose of exercising the power conferred by this subsection, may enter any place (s. 50 (2)).

A constable may arrest without warrant a person who refuses to declare his name and address when required to do so under s. 48 (2) of this Act, or whom he in such a case suspects of giving a false name and address or of intending to abscond (s. 50 (3)).

Forfeiture and Disposal of Firearms; Cancellation of Certificate by Convicting Court – Where a person is convicted of an offence under this Act (other than an offence under s. 22 (3) or an offence relating specifically to air weapons) or is convicted of a crime and sentenced to imprisonment, preventive detention, corrective training, borstal training, or detention in a detention centre, or is bound over or put on probation with a requirement not to have a firearm, the court may forfeit or dispose of any firearm or ammunition found in his possession and cancel his firearm or shot gun certificate (s. 52 (1)).

Where the court cancels a certificate under this section: (a) the court shall cause notice to be sent to the chief officer of police by whom the certificate was granted; and (b) the chief officer of police shall by notice in writing require the holder of the certificate to surrender it; and (c) it is an offence for the holder to fail to surrender the certificate within 21 days from the date of the notice given him by the chief officer of police (s. 52 (2)).

A constable may seize and detain any firearm or ammunition which may be the subject of an order for forfeiture under this section (s. 52 (3)).

A court of summary jurisdiction may, on the application of the chief officer of police, order any firearm or ammunition seized and detained by a constable under this Act to be destroyed or otherwise disposed of (s. 52 (4)).

Rules for Implementing the Act – The Secretary of State has made the Firearms Rules 1969, under the powers granted to him by s. 53. These prescribe the forms to be used in connection with the grant of certificates and permits for the purpose of the Firearms Act 1968, and the registration of firearms dealers and also the form of the register of transactions to be kept by such dealers (s. 53).

Application of Parts I and II to Crown Servants – Persons in the service of Her Majesty (including police) in their capacity as such need not have a certificate to enable them to have possession of firearms and ammunition, but must have one to purchase and acquire same, unless duly authorised in writing to acquire same for the public service.

A person in the naval, military or air service of Her Majesty, on application on the prescribed form, satisfying the police that he is required to acquire a firearm and ammunition for his own use in his capacity as such, is entitled to a free firearm certificate authorising him to purchase or acquire same, or, as the case may be, to the grant of a shot gun certificate (s. 54).

Services of Notices – Notices under the Act may be served by registered post or by the recorded delivery service (s. 56).

Definitions – In this Act, the expression "firearm" means a lethal barrelled weapon of any description from which any shot, bullet or other missile can be discharged and includes: (a) any prohibited weapon, whether it is such a lethal weapon as aforesaid or not; and (b) any component part of such a lethal or prohibited weapon; and (c) any accessory to any such weapon designed or adapted to diminish the noise or flash caused by firing the weapon; and so much of s. 1 of this Act as excludes any description of firearm from the category of firearms to which that section applies shall be construed as also excluding component parts of, and accessories to, firearms of that description (s. 57 (1)).

In this Act, the expression "ammunition" means ammunition for any firearm and includes grenades, bombs and other like missiles, whether capable of use with a firearm or not, and also includes prohibited ammunition (s. 57 (2)).

"firearms dealer" means a person who, by way of trade or business, manufactures, sells, transfers, repairs, tests or proves firearms or ammunition to which s. 1 of this Act applies, or shot guns;

"imitation firearm" means any thing which has the appearance of being a firearm (other than such a weapon as is mentioned in s. 5 (1) (b) of this Act) whether or not it is capable of discharging any shot, bullet or other missile;

"public place" includes any highway and any other premises or place to which at the material time the public have or are permitted to have access, whether on payment or otherwise (s. 57 (4)).

For purposes of this Act; (a) the length of the barrel of a fire-arm shall be measured from the muzzle to the point at which the charge is exploded on firing; and (b) a shot gun or an air weapon shall be deemed to be loaded if there is ammunition in the chamber or barrel or in any magazine or other device which is in such a position that the ammunition can be fed into the chamber or barrel by the manual or automatic operation of some part of the gun or weapon (s. 57 (6)).

The Act does not interfere with the operations of the London and Birmingham proof houses and it does not apply to an antique firearm sold, transferred or possessed as a curiosity or ornament (s. 58 (1) (2)).

Nothing in the Act relieves any person using or carrying a firearm from his obligation to take out a licence to kill game under the enactments requiring such a licence (s. 58 (5)).

Gun Barrel Proof Acts 1868 and 1950 – Proof is the compulsory testing of new shotguns or other small arms before sale to ensure their safety when in use. The law contained in the above Acts and in various Rules of Proof, especially those of 1925 and 1954, prescribe that no small arm may be sold, exchanged or exported, exposed or kept for sale or exchanged or pawned unless it has been duly proved as shown by the authorised proof marks thereon. Information on proof matters may be obtained from the Proof Master of either The Proof House, 48 Commercial Road, London, E.1. or The Gun Barrel Proof House, Banbury Street, Birmingham, 5.

CHAPTER 35

ANIMALS

	Page
Diseases of Animals .	479
Cruelty to Animals .	482
Prevention of Unnecessary Pain	484
Operations on Animals .	484
Injured Animals . .	485
Performing Animals .	485
Horses	486
Dogs	488
Birds	492
Destructive Imported Animals Act 1932 . .	496
Slaughter of Animals .	496
Riding Establishments .	497
Pet Animals . . .	499
Animal Boarding Establishments . . .	500
Conservation of Seals Act 1970	500
Animals Act 1971 . .	502
Badgers Act 1973 . .	502

Diseases of Animals – The Act now dealing with this subject is the Diseases of Animals Act 1950, which has repealed the 1894 Act and several other similar Acts and consolidated the law on the matter. The Act empowers the Minister of Agriculture, Fisheries and Food to make Orders, and s. 89 continues in effect all previous Orders and Regulations made under the repealed Acts respecting the various diseases to which animals are liable.

"Animals", unless the context otherwise requires, means cattle, sheep and goats and all other ruminating (cud chewing) animals and swine.

This definition has by Order of 1952, been extended to horses, asses, mules and jennets.

"Cattle" means bulls, cows, oxen, heifers and calves.

"Carcase" means the carcase of an animal and includes part of a carcase.

"Poultry" unless the context otherwise requires, means domestic fowls, turkeys, geese, ducks, guinea fowls, pigeons also pheasants and partridges and this definition by Order of 1953, has been extended to parrots.

"Disease" as regards "animals" means cattle plague (rinder pest), pleuro-pneumonia, foot and mouth disease, sheep pox, sheep scab or swine fever and this definition, by Order of 1952, has been extended to glanders and farcy.

"Disease" as regards "poultry" means fowl pest, fowl cholera, fowl pox, etc., and the definition has been extended to psittacosis, by Order of **1953**.

"Horse" includes ass and mule (s. **84**).

Ss. **3–7** give the Minister power to deal with diseases of horses and animals. He can order eradication areas and attested (free from disease) areas and can authorise inspection of animals and horses. Obstruction of an authorised inspector will be a summary offence. (There are similar provisions in s. **23** of the Agriculture Act 1967).

S. **8**: Every person having in his possession or under his charge an animal affected with disease shall keep that animal separate from animals not so affected and notify with all practicable speed the fact to the local police who shall pass on the information as directed by the Minister's Order. See Tuberculosis Order 1938.

S. **8** (1A) Any person who knows or suspects that an animal is affected with Rabies shall give notice of that fact to a constable unless (a) he believes on reasonable grounds that another person has given such notice, or (b) is exempted from doing so by an order under s. 1 of this Act, and if the animal is in his possession or under his charge, shall as far as practicable keep the animal separate from other animals. (Added by Rabies Act 1974, s. 4).

S. **10**: Places and Areas may be declared to be infected with disease and under s. **11**. Orders may deal with the movement, isolation, destruction, etc., of animals and the disinfection of persons and places. Section **12** allows the putting up at an infected place, notice forbidding persons to enter without permission.

Ss. **13–18**: Empower the slaughter of animals in cases of cattle plague, pleuro-pneumonia, foot and mouth disease and swine fever, and of animals and horses in cases of other diseases prescribed by Order; the disposal of the carcases and compensation to the owners.

Ss. **20–23** allow the Minister to make orders regulating the movement and carriage of animals.

Ss. **24–35** deal with the import of animals, also Scheds. 1 and 2 to the Act.

Ss. **36–41** prescribe the conditions for the export of animals and horses (see later).

Ss. **42, 43** allow the Minister to make Orders for periodical sheepdipping or some other remedy for sheep scab, and the examination of sheep.

S. **44**: The Minister may make Orders as to dogs—such as muzzling, collars, stray dogs and the seizure and disposal of unmuzzled and stray dogs and dogs not kept under control.

Ss. **45–51** relate to poultry, the eradication of their diseases, their slaughter in case of disease, their import, their protection in transit and the power of an inspector to enter premises where poultry are kept. See also Live Poultry (Restrictions) Order 1957, Live Poultry (Movement Records) Orders 1958, the Disinfection Order 1956, and Agriculture Act 1967.

S. 59: "Local Authority" means as respects a London borough, the borough council and as respects each county, the county council; any "body" appointed by the Minister as such for a port, and a local authority shall enforce the Act.

S. 71: The police shall execute and enforce this Act and every Order of the Minister. When a person is seen or found committing or is reasonably suspected of being engaged in committing an offence against this Act, a constable without warrant may stop and detain him and if his name and address are not known to the constable and the person fails to give them to the satisfaction of the constable, the constable may, without warrant, apprehend him. The constable may whether stopping or apprehending or not, stop, detain and examine any animal, vehicle, boat or thing to which the suspected offence relates and require same to be forthwith taken back to the place whence unlawfully removed and execute and enforce that requisition. If any person obstructs or impedes or assists in so doing a constable or other officer in the execution of this Act or Order under it, he may be arrested without warrant.

A person arrested under this section shall be taken with all practicable speed before a justice and shall not be detained without a warrant longer than is necessary for the purpose. The law as to release of persons on recognizances by police shall apply in such cases.

The foregoing provisions of this section respecting a constable extend and apply to any person called by the constable to his assistance.

A constable shall forthwith report in writing to his Superior Officer every case in which he stops any person, animal, vehicle, boat or thing under this section and of his proceedings consequent thereon.

S. 73: An inspector appointed by the Ministry or by the local authority has all the powers which a constable has under this Act. He can enter land, premises, vehicles, etc., on reasonable grounds of suspicion.

Ss. 78–81: Offences under this Act, or Orders or local regulations are punishable summarily with fine and the more serious offences, such as doing prohibited acts without licence or using false licences or digging up buried carcases, etc., may be punished summarily by imprisonment.

S. 83: Where the owner or person in charge of an animal is charged with an offence against this Act, relative to disease or illness of the animal, the presumption is that he knew of the existence of the disease or illness, unless he shows to the satisfaction of the court that he had not knowledge thereof and could not with reasonable diligence have obtained that knowledge.

See also Diseases of Animals Act 1975, when in force.

Cruelty to Animals – Protection of Animals Act 1911, s. 1: This section declares that it is an offence of cruelty punishable summarily by imprisonment or fine or both, for:

(1) Any person to do any of the following acts or to cause or procure or being the owner, to permit same to be done:

(a) Cruelly beat, kick, ill-treat, over-ride, over-drive, over load, torture, infuriate or terrify any animal;

(b) Cause any unnecessary suffering to any animal either by doing or omitting to do some act;

(c) Convey or carry any animal in such a manner of position as to cause that animal any unnecessary suffering (Diseases of Animals Act 1950, s. 22, provides for the supply of food and water for animals carried by railway companies, and s. 50 of the Act deals with the conveyance of live poultry).

(d) Subject any animal to any operation which is performed without due care and humanity. See later.

Note—Under the Abandonment of Animals Act 1960, if any person being the owner or having charge or control of any animal shall without reasonable cause or excuse abandon it, whether permanently or not, in circumstances likely to cause the animal any unnecessary suffering, or cause or procure or, being the owner permit it to be so abandoned, he shall be guilty of an offence of cruelty, as above.

(2) Any person to cause, procure or assist at the fighting or baiting of any animal ("animal" includes fowl, s. 15) or to use or permit any premises to be used for such purpose. Cock-fighting Act 1952 makes it a summary offence to have possession of appliances for use in the fighting of domestic fowl for the purpose of using or permitting its use for such purpose. (The Town Police Clauses Act 1847, where it applies, makes it a summary offence by s. 28 for any person in any street to the obstruction, danger or annoyance of residents or passengers to set on or urge any dog or other animal to attack, worry or put in fear any person or animal, and by s. 36, for any person to conduct any place for the fighting, baiting or worrying of any animals).

(3) Any person, wilfully or without reasonable excuse, to administer or cause or procure or being the owner to permit the administration of any poisonous or injurious drug or substance to any animal (see also s. 8, later).

An owner will be deemed to have permitted cruelty if he has failed to exercise reasonable care and supervision in respect to the protection of the animal therefrom.

However, this section will not apply:

(1) To the destruction of an animal as food for mankind unless it was accompanied by unnecessary suffering, or

(2) To the coursing or hunting of any captive animal, unless it is set free in an injured, mutilated or exhausted condition, or unless (Protection of Animals Act (1911) Amendment Act 1921) it is hunted in an enclosed space from which it has no reasonable chance of escape.

(3) To vivisection carried out under licence.

S. 15: "Animal" means any domestic or captive animal. "Domestic animal" includes any animal or fowl of whatsoever kind or species which is tame or which has been or is being sufficiently tamed to serve some purpose for the use of man.

"Captive animal" includes any animal (not being a domestic animal), of whatsoever kind or species, including bird, fish and reptile, which is in captivity or confinement or which is maimed, pinioned or subjected to any contrivance to prevent its escape.

Ss. 2 and 3: On conviction of the owner for cruelty to an animal, the court may direct that the animal be destroyed, if satisfied it would be cruel to keep it alive, or may deprive the owner of the ownership and make an order as to the disposal of the animal. The court may disqualify him from having custody of any animal or animals (Protection of Animals (Amendment) Act 1954).

S. 7: The person impounding or causing to be impounded any animal in any pound must supply it with food and water on penalty of summary fine. See "Impounding Animals", Chap. 24.

S. 8: It is a summary offence, punishable by fine, to sell or dispose of any grain or seed which has been rendered poisonous except for *bona fide* use in agriculture, or to lay down or cause to be laid down on any land or building any poison or poisonous matter. It will be a defence to prove that such poison was laid down for the destruction of rats or mice or other small vermin, and that reasonable precautions were taken to prevent injury thereby to dogs, cats, fowls, other domestic animals or wild birds (Protection of Animals (Amendment) Act 1927, s. 1).

S. 10: When a person sets or causes to be set any spring trap likely to catch a hare or rabbit, it is a summary offence punishable by fine, if he does not inspect or cause to be inspected such trap at reasonable intervals and at least once a day.

Rabbit clearance areas may be ordered. Spring traps for animals must, after July 31, 1958 (or otherwise by Order), be of the approved type. Spring traps for hares or rabbits must not be used elsewhere than in rabbit holes, unless permitted by licence. The knowingly spreading of myxomatosis is illegal (Pests Act 1954). See also Prevention of Damage by Pests (Threshing and Dismantling of Ricks) Regs. 1950 as to the fencing of ricks before they are dismantled.

S. 12: A police constable may arrest without warrant any

person whom he has reason to believe is guilty of an offence under the Act which is punishable by imprisonment without the option of a fine (see s. 1) whether on his own view thereof or on complaint of any other person who shall give his name and address.

When a constable, under this Act, arrests a person in charge of a vehicle or animal, he is empowered to take charge of such vehicle or animal and deposit it in some place of safe custody.

S. 13: Where proceedings under this Act are taken against the driver or conductor of a vehicle, his employer may be summoned to produce such driver or conductor at the hearing. The owner of the animal may be summoned to produce the animal for the inspection of the court.

The Transit of Animals Orders 1927, 1930, 1931, 1939, 1947, and the Animals (Sea-Transport) Orders 1930, 1952, provide for the conveyance of animals without unnecessary suffering between home ports and between home and foreign ports.

The Animals (Cruel Poisons) Act 1962, prohibits the killing of animals by cruel poisons and gives power for Regulations to be made prohibiting or restricting the use of any poison for destroying animals. The Animals (Cruel Poisons) Regs. 1963, prohibit the putting or placing of phosphorus and red squill in or upon any land or building for the purpose of destroying animals of any description, and strychnine for destroying mammals of any description except moles. Contravention of the Regulations is an offence and where a poison is used contrary to the Regulations the defence afforded in the proviso to s. 8 of the Protection of Animals Act 1911 will not be available.

Prevention of Unnecessary Pain and Distress for Livestock – By the Agriculture (Miscellaneous Provisions) Act 1968, any person who causes unnecessary pain or unnecessary distress to any livestock for the time being situated on agricultural land and under his control or permits any such livestock to suffer any such pain or distress of which he knows or may reasonably be expected to know shall be guilty of an offence (s. 1 (1)).

The above shall not apply to any act lawfully done under the Cruelty to Animals Act 1876, or to any thing done or omitted by or under the direction of any person in accordance with the terms of a licence issued by the Minister for the purpose of enabling that person to undertake scientific research (s. 1 (2)).

Operations on Animals – Cruelty to Animals Act 1876, makes it an offence to perform on any living animal any experiment calculated to give pain, except on licence and subject to the restrictions prescribed in the Act. Any public exhibition of experiments on living animals calculated to give them pain is illegal. The Act enables a search warrant to be granted to a constable on sworn information that such experiments are being unlawfully carried out. The carrying out of such experiments is termed "vivisection", meaning the cutting up when alive. This Act does not apply to invertebrate animals.

Protection of Animals (Anaesthetics) Act 1954 repealed the Animals (Anaesthetics) Act 1919, and declares that any operation on the sensitive tissues or bone structures of an animal (not a bird, fish or reptile) without an anaesthetic to prevent pain shall be deemed an operation performed without due care and humanity under s. 1, Protection of Animals Act 1911.

However this Act does not apply to injections, etc., by hollow needle or operations as specified in Sched. 1 such as first aid in an emergency, quick or minor operations, tail docking or castration before certain ages.

The classes of operations in which anaesthetics must be used have been enlarged by the Protection of Animals (Anaesthetics) Act 1964.

Injured Animals – Protection of Animals Act 1911, s. 11: If a police constable finds any animal (meaning any horse, mule, ass, bull, sheep, goat or pig) so diseased or so severely injured or in such a physical condition that in his opinion it cannot be removed without cruelty, he shall, if the owner is absent or refuses to consent to the destruction of the animal, summon a veterinary surgeon residing within a reasonable distance. If such veterinary surgeon certifies that the animal is mortally injured or so severely injured or so diseased or in such physical condition that it is cruel to keep it alive, it will be lawful for the constable, without the consent of the owner, to have the animal slaughtered with as little suffering as practicable and to have the carcase removed from the highway if it is thereon.

If the veterinary surgeon certifies that the animal can without cruelty be removed, the person in charge of the animal should have it removed, and if he fails to do so the constable may cause it to be so removed.

Any expenses incurred by the constable under this section may be recovered from the owner summarily as a civil debt.

If the owner by his cruelty is responsible for the condition of an injured animal, a court has power to order the destruction of the animal. See "Cruelty to Animals".

Where injury to an animal is the result of cruelty, see "Cruelty to Animals", and where the injury has been malicious and affects the owner, see "Malicious Damage", Chap. 15.

Performing Animals – Performing Animals (Regulation) Act 1925, ss. 1 and 5: No person shall exhibit any performing animal at any entertainment to which the public are admitted whether on payment or otherwise, or train any animal for the purpose of any such exhibition, unless he is registered with the County or Borough Council of the place where he resides.

S. 7: This Act does not apply to training or exhibition for *bona fide* military, police, agricultural, or sporting purposes.

S. 3: Any constable or any person authorised by the Local Authority, may enter at all reasonable times and inspect any premises on which any performing animals are trained, exhibited or kept. He can inspect any animals found therein and require the production of the certificate of registration under the Act. However, he is not entitled to go on or behind the stage during any public performance.

S. 2: On proof of cruelty, a court may make an order prohibiting such training or exhibition or imposing conditions.

S. 4: It is a summary offence for—

(1) Any unregistered person to exhibit or train any performing animal;

(2) Any registered person to exhibit or train any performing animal with respect to which or in a manner with respect to which he is not registered;

(3) Any person to obstruct any constable or authorised officer acting under this Act;

(4) Any person to conceal any animal to avoid inspection;

(5) Any registered person without reasonable excuse to fail to produce his certificate;

(6) Any person to fail to comply with any order of a court made under this Act;

(7) Any person to apply for registration when prohibited from being so registered.

When a person is convicted under this Act or under the Protection of Animals Acts, the court may cancel his registration or disqualify him from registration.

Protection of Animals Act 1934 prohibits any public performance ("rodeo") in which unbroken horses or untrained bulls are thrown, untrained bulls are struggled with, or horses or bulls are stimulated by any cruelty to buck. The promoters and operators are liable to £100 fine and (or) 3 months' imprisonment and the onus of proof that an animal was broken or trained rests on them.

Cinematograph Films (Animals) Act 1937 prohibits the public exhibition of film scenes in connection with the production of which, suffering may have been caused to animals.

Horses – Horse Breeding Act 1958: A person who keeps a stallion which has attained the age of 2 years without a licence or permit commits a summary offence, unless it was 4 years old before January 1, 1949, or unless it is a thoroughbred or a pony of a prescribed breed. If a person travels for service a stallion exempted under one of these two categories, or exhibits it on any premises not in his occupation with a view to its use for service or permits same to be done, unless the stallion is licensed by the Ministry of Agriculture, Fisheries and Food he commits a summary offence (s. 1 and the Horse Breeding Rules 1948, 1974 and 1975).

Under s. 10, the person in charge of the stallion must produce the licence or a certified copy thereof, to any person engaging the service of the stallion or to any police officer or other authorised person.

It is a summary offence to forge or fraudulently alter or use or to permit to be fraudulently altered or used any such licence or certified copy thereof (s. 11).

Diseases of Animals Act 1950. No horse, ass or mule may be shipped from any port in Great Britain to any port outside the United Kingdom unless—

(1) A veterinary surgeon appointed by the Minister for such purpose has certified in writing that it is capable of being conveyed to such port and disembarked without cruelty and is capable of being worked without suffering (s. 37) (the Ponies Act 1969, improves the conditions under which ponies may be exported and restricts the export of certain ponies); or

(2) A thoroughbred horse accompanied by a written certificate from a steward or the secretary of the Jockey Club, that it is travelling for racing or breeding purposes or has arrived in Great Britain not more than one month previous for racing purposes (s. 40).

Any such certificate shall be given to the Master of the vessel who, on demand, shall produce it to any constable or officer of the Ministry and allow a copy of it to be taken (ss. 37, 40).

If any horse examined or inspected under s. 37 is found to be in such a physical condition that it is cruel to keep it alive or to be permanently incapable of being worked without suffering the inspector shall forthwith slaughter it or cause it to be slaughtered (s. 37).

If a horse being exported under a veterinary inspector's certificate has a limb broken or is otherwise seriously injured while on board the ship so as to be incapable of being disembarked without cruelty the Master shall cause it to be slaughtered with a proper killing instrument which must be carried on the ship (s. 39).

Transit of Horses Order 1951 provides for the proper conveyance of horses in rail and road vehicles and Horses (Sea-Transport) Orders 1952 and 1958 with their conveyance by sea. The Exported Cattle Protection Order 1957, as amended, requires that any cattle exported from Great Britain to any place outside the United Kingdom, the Channel Islands, the Isle of Man or the Republic of Ireland, whether by sea or air, shall be rested for 10 hours before they are loaded. They must be given adequate food, water and shelter, and an animal may be removed from the ship or aircraft if it is likely to be exposed to unnecessary suffering during transit.

The Exported Ponies Protection Order 1958 provides that no pony shall be shipped by sea or by air from Great Britain to any place outside Europe, unless it has been inspected by a veterinary inspector and certified to be capable of being conveyed without unnecessary suffering. "Pony" means any horse not more than 14 hands in height, except a foal travelling with its dam if the dam is over 14 hands.

Docking and Nicking of Horses Act 1949 prohibits the docking (removal of any bone from the tail) or nicking (severing of any tendon or muscle in the tail) of horses (including ponies and mules) unless a veterinary surgeon certifies it is necessary for their health.

No docked horse shall be imported except on licence or for export as soon as practicable.

Dogs – The law makes an owner responsible for the licensing and custody of his dogs.

Diseases of Animals Act 1950, s. 44, allows the Minister of Agriculture, Fisheries and Food to make Orders regarding dogs—dealing with their muzzling and control; collars with name and address of owner; stray dogs; seizure and disposal of stray dogs, unmuzzled dogs and dogs not under control.

LICENSING OF DOGS – Dog Licences Act 1959: It is an offence for any person to keep a dog above the age of 6 months without having in force a licence to keep such dog, or to keep a greater number of dogs than he is licensed to keep. The onus of proving the age of a dog rests on the accused (s. 12). A dog licence lasts for 12 months from the first day of the month in which it is taken out (s. 9). They are personal licences and are not transferable. They cost [37½p] each (s. 1). They are procurable at local district offices, or at premises of appointed agents (e.g. post offices) (Post Office Act 1969, s. 134).

It is also an offence for a licensed person not to produce his licence to be examined and read by a constable or authorised officer within a reasonable time after request for its production (s. 13).

Every person in whose custody, charge or possession or in whose house or premises any dog shall be found or seen, shall be deemed to be the person keeping the same unless the contrary be proved (s. 12).

Dogs used as guides by blind persons are exempt from licence (s. 3), also hounds under the age of 12 months belonging to masters of hounds and never entered in or used with any pack of hounds (s. 2). No duty shall be chargeable in respect of a dog kept and used solely for tending sheep or cattle on a farm or in the exercise of the occupation of a shepherd (s. 4).

Local Government Act 1966, s. 36, allows the Minister of Agriculture, Fisheries and Food to amend the provisions of the Dog Licences Act 1959.

DANGEROUS DOGS – Town Police Clauses Act 1847, s. 28 (as amended by Rabies Act 1974): It is an offence for any person in any street in any district where the Act applies, to the obstruction, annoyance or danger of the residents or passengers—

(1) To suffer to be at large any unmuzzled ferocious dog;

(2) To set on or urge any dog or other animal to attack, worry or put in fear any person or animal.

Dogs Act 1871, s. 2: A magistrates' court may hear any complaint that a dog is dangerous and not kept under proper control, and, if it appears that the dog is dangerous, may order it to be kept by the owner under proper control or destroyed. The complaint may be preferred by a police officer (*Smith* v. *Baker* (1960)).

Dogs (Amendment) Act 1938, as amended by Sched. 9, C.J. Act 1948 and C.J. Act 1972, Sched. 5: If an order to destroy is made the owner can appeal to the Crown Court. If the owner intends to appeal he must give notice accordingly within the period within which notice of appeal to the Crown Court may be given against the order, and the dog must be kept under proper control until any appeal is decided. If the owner gives notice that he does not intend to appeal the order for destruction takes effect.

Dogs Act 1906, s. 1 (as amended): If a dog is proved to have injured cattle or poultry or chased sheep it may be dealt with as a dangerous dog under s. 2 of the Dogs Act 1871. The word "cattle" includes horses, mules, asses, sheep, goats and swine. The word "poultry" includes domestic fowls, turkeys, geese, ducks, guinea-fowls and pigeons (Diseases of Animals Act 1950). See also Public Health Acts Amendment Act 1907, s. 81. See *Goodway* v. *Becher* (1951) where it was held that the owner acted reasonably in respect of his shooting a dog in defence of his poultry.

DOGS AND LIVESTOCK – Animals Act 1971, s. 9: It is a defence to a claim for damages for killing or injuring a dog that it was done for the protection of livestock, that the police were informed within 48 hrs., and that it was done by someone entitled to act to protect the livestock. Killing a marauding dog is permissible under this provision if there are reasonable grounds for believing that an attack is imminent and no other reasonable means of averting it is available, or where an attack has already occurred. "Livestock" means cattle, horses, asses, mules, hinnies, sheep, pigs, goats, poultry, deer not in the wild state, and, while in captivity, pheasants, partridges and grouse.

"Poultry" means domestic varieties of fowls, turkeys, geese, ducks, guinea-fowls, pigeons, peacocks and quails (s. 11).

Dogs (Protection of Livestock) Act 1953: The owner or person in charge of a dog which worries livestock on any agricultural land (which is not excluded by Order) will be guilty of a summary offence liable to fine up to £10, on second conviction with same dog, fine up to £50.

"Worrying" means attacking or chasing in such a way as may reasonably be expected to cause injury or suffering. However, the owner or person authorised by him may use a dog to drive off trespassing livestock but not to attack them (s. 1).

"Agricultural land" means arable, meadow or grazing land, or land used for poultry or pig farming, market gardens, allotments, nursery grounds or orchards.

"Livestock" means cattle, sheep, goats, swine, horses, asses, mules or poultry. "Poultry" means domestic fowls, turkeys, geese or ducks (s. 3).

For an offence under the Act no proceedings shall be brought except: (a) by or with consent of the local chief officer of police, or (b) by the occupier of the land, or (c) by the owner of the livestock in question.

If a dog is found on any land and no person is present who admits he is the owner or in charge of it, and a police officer has reasonable cause to believe that the dog has been worrying livestock on that land which appears to him as "agricultural" he may seize the dog and detain it until the owner has claimed it and paid all expenses. If not claimed within 7 days the dog may be treated as a stray dog under s. 3, Dogs Act 1906 (s. 2).

STRAY DOGS – Dogs Act 1906, s. 3: Where a police officer has reason to believe that any dog found in a highway or place of public resort is a stray dog, he may seize the dog and detain it until the owner has claimed it and paid all expenses incurred. Where the owner is known, the police shall serve on him notice in writing that the dog has been seized and may be sold or destroyed if not claimed within 7 clear days after service of the notice.

Where any dog so seized has been kept for 7 clear days, or, if such notice has been served, for seven days after service of notice, and the owner has not claimed the dog and paid all expenses incurred, the police may cause the dog to be sold or destroyed. Such notice may be served personally or by leaving it at, or by sending it by post to, the owner's address. A register of all dogs seized must be kept by the police and be open for inspection at all reasonable times by the public on payment of [5p] fee. The police must properly feed and maintain all seized dogs.

S. 4 (and Dogs (Amendment) Act 1928): Any person who takes possession of a stray dog shall forthwith either return the dog to its owner or take the dog to the police station nearest to the place where the dog was found and give particulars of the finding. If the finder wishes to keep the dog he will be given a certificate in the form prescribed and may take the dog, but is bound to keep it for not less than one month. If he does not want it, it will be treated as a seized stray dog. Failure to comply with above is a summary offence. Penalty, £2.

S. 6 (and Dogs (Amendment) Act 1928): It is an offence for any person knowingly and without reasonable excuse, to permit the carcase of any head of cattle (including horses, mules, asses, sheep, goats and swine) belonging to him or under his control, to remain unburied in a field or other place to which dogs can gain access.

CONTROL OF DOGS – The Control of Dogs Orders 1930, 1931 direct that every dog while in a highway or in a place of public resort shall wear a collar with name and address of the owner inscribed thereon or on a plate or badge attached thereto.

Provided that this requirement shall not apply to any pack of hounds, or to any dog while being used for sporting purposes or for the capture or destruction of vermin or for driving or tending of cattle or sheep.

Any dog not so complying with the order may be seized and treated as a stray dog, and any person committing or aiding, abetting, counselling or procuring the commission of any breach of the Order is liable to fine, or to imprisonment if a second or subsequent similar offence occurs within 12 months.

An Amendment Order of 1930 declares that where a dog is found in such a place not wearing a collar as prescribed, the owner, the person in charge, and any person allowing the dog to be so there, shall each be guilty of an offence.

A Local Authority may, under this Order, make regulations for requiring that dogs shall be kept under control between sunset and sunrise for the prevention of worrying of cattle (including horses, mules, asses, sheep, goats and swine).

Road Traffic Act 1972, s. 31: A local authority may by Order made after consultation with the police and confirmation by the Secretary of State, designate a road. Then any person who causes or permits a dog to be on a designated road without the dog being held on a lead will commit a summary offence. This shall not apply to dogs for driving sheep or cattle or sporting dogs under proper control.

GUARD DOGS – The Guard Dogs Act 1975 prohibits the use of unattended guard dogs at premises which are defined to exclude agricultural land and dwelling houses. A guard dog may not be used at such premises unless it is at all times under the control of a handler or properly secured in his absence, and the handler is required to ensure that the dog is so controlled or secured. Where a guard dog is on premises, notices to that effect must be displayed at all entrances (s. 1). The dog must not be at liberty to go freely about the premises. Breach of these requirements is a summary offence punishable by a fine not exceeding £400 (s. 5). These provisions came into force on 1st Feb. 1976.

INJURY OR CRUELTY TO DOGS – Protection of Animals Act 1911, s. 9: It is an offence to use, cause, procure, or being the owner to permit to be used, any dog for the purpose of drawing or helping to draw any cart or truck on any public highway.

Protection of Animals (Cruelty to Dogs) Act 1933: If a person is convicted of cruelty to a dog the court may disqualify him for keeping a dog and for having a dog licence, for such period as the court thinks fit. If such person during the period of disqualification keeps a dog or applies for or obtains a dog licence he is liable to £25 fine and 3 months' imprisonment. After 6 months he may apply to the court to remove the disqualification. Under the Protection of Animals Act 1911, ss. 2 and 3, the court may also direct the dog to be destroyed if necessary and may deprive the owner of the ownership.

For general cruelty, see "Cruelty to Animals".

BREEDING OF DOGS ACT 1973 – By this Act a person who keeps a breeding establishment for dogs except under the authority of a licence granted by a local Authority, commits an offence. A licence may not be granted to a person disqualified under this Act, the Pet Animals Act 1951, the Protection of Animals (Cruelty to Dogs) Act 1933, the Protection of Animals (Amendment) Act 1954 or the Animal Boarding Establishment Act 1963.

RABIES – The Rabies (Importation of Dogs, Cats and other Mammals) Order 1974 prohibits the landing in Gt. Britain of an animal brought from a place outside Gt. Britain (Art. 4 (1)). The prohibition does not apply to an animal brought to Gt. Britain from a place in Northern Ireland, Republic of Ireland, Channel Islands or the Isle of Man, provided such animals have not been outside the British Isles within the preceding 6 months. No person shall land or attempt to land an animal in Gt. Britain, the landing of which is prohibited under Art. 4 (1), or cause or permit the landing or attempted landing of any such animal. (Arts. 16 and 17).

Under the Rabies (Control) Order 1974 a person who knows or suspects that an animal (whether in captivity or not) is affected with rabies, or was at the time of its death so affected, shall with all practicable speed give notice of that fact to an Inspector or to a Police Constable unless he believes on reasonable grounds that another person has done so. The Divisional Veterinary Officer must be informed immediately.

Birds – The Protection of Birds Act 1954 repeals and replaces all the previous Wild Bird Protection Acts, which ranged from 1880 to 1939 (it has been amended by the Protection of Birds Act 1967).

Under s. 1 it is an offence to wilfully kill, injure or take or attempt to do so any wild bird or its nest while in use or its eggs, or to have in possession or control any wild bird recently killed or taken (unless allowed under the Act), but there are many exceptions to this comprehensive section.

"Wild Bird" means any wild bird but in the Act does not include pheasant, partridge, grouse, or moor game, black or heath game or, in Scotland, ptarmigan, except as regards s. 5 (which prohibits certain methods of killing or taking birds), s. 10 (which gives power to grant licences to kill or take birds) and s. 12 (which deals with enforcement of penalties) (s. 14).

The Act deals with 5 classes of wild birds as follows:

(1) *Sched. 1, Part I.* This schedule protects certain birds and their eggs at all times. This list of 58 birds (as amended) includes corncrake, eagle, quail, swan, hawks and the barn owl. An offence in respect of them is punishable by a special penalty (s. 1).

(2) *Sched. 1, Part II.* This protects certain birds during the close season. This list (as amended) includes greylag goose, whimbrel and 6 species of wild duck.
An offence in respect of them is punishable by special penalty (s. 1).

(3) *Sched. 2.* This allows certain birds to be killed or taken at any time by authorised persons. This list includes crow, gull, jackdaw, magpie, rook, sparrow, starling, wood pigeon.
An authorised person may kill or take or attempt to do so any of the birds in this Sched. 2 or take or destroy their eggs and nests or take the eggs of wild geese, ducks or swans for hatching (s. 2).
"Authorised person" means the owner or occupier (or any person authorised by him) of land on which the action authorised is taken; any person authorised in writing by the local authority of the area; any person authorised in writing by certain bodies such as water or fishery authorities, but such authority does not give any right of entry upon any land.
"Local authority" means the council of a county, district or London borough, and the Common Council of the City of London.
"Occupier" includes any person having the right of hunting, shooting or fishing (s. 14).

(4) *Sched. 3.* This allows certain birds to be killed or taken outside the close season (except on Sundays in certain areas. Wild Birds (Sundays) Orders 1955, 1956 and 1957). This list includes the greylag goose and 4 other kinds of

wild geese, mallard, teal, wigeon and 11 other kinds of wild duck, curlew, plover, snipe, woodcock.

The close season for snipe is February 1 to August 11, for wild duck and wild geese February 21 to August 31, for capercaille and (except in Scotland) woodcock February 1 to September 30, and in any other case February 1 to August 31 (s. 2).

(5) *Sched. 4.* This covers birds which may not be sold alive unless close ringed and bred in captivity. The list includes blackbird, bullfinch, goldfinch, greenfinch, lark, robin, sparrow, starling, thrush, yellow hammer.

RESTRICTIONS ON SALE, ETC. – Unless authorised by licence under s. 10, it will be an offence to sell, offer for sale or have in possession for sale any live bird of Sched. 4 other than a close ringed bird bred in captivity, any dead wild bird of Sched. 3 during the period February 28 to August 31, or any dead wild bird or the skin or plumage of a wild bird of some other species unless it was lawfully imported or lawfully killed, or the egg of a wild bird (if such species has nested in this country) except the eggs of gulls for food or feeding purposes and the eggs of wild duck, wild geese and swans for hatching. A justice on sworn information may grant a warrant to any constable to enter and search premises for evidence of an offence under this section (s. 6). (The prohibition of sale of dead wild geese applies throughout the year. Protection of Birds Act 1967, s. 3).

The Secretary of State and other authorities may grant licences authorising the killing or taking etc. of wild birds for various purposes (s. 10).

PROHIBITIONS OF METHODS OF KILLING OR TAKING BIRDS – It will be an offence (with special penalty), unless on licence under s. 10, to set in position without reasonable precautions, traps, snares etc. likely to injure wild birds (except those for other purposes); to use nets, birdlime etc. to catch birds; to use a live bird, tethered etc., as a decoy; to use a very large bore etc. gun for killing birds; to use artificial light to attract birds other than those in Sched. 2; to use aircraft or motor vehicle or boat to pursue and kill or take a wild bird.

However a net or cage trap may be used by an authorised person for taking Sched. 2 birds or for taking for ringing or marking and a net duck decoy used before this Act is still allowable (s. 5).

RESTRICTIONS ON IMPORTATION – Unless authorised by licence under s. 10, the importation is prohibited of any common quail, alive or dead, of any dead lapwing or the eggs of any lapwing, and during period from February 1 to August 31 of any dead Sched. 3 bird or wild duck or wild goose.

The Secretary of State may expand such restrictions (s. 7).

CAPTIVE BIRDS – It will be an offence with special penalty to keep or confine any bird in a cage or receptacle in which the bird cannot stretch its wings freely, but this will not apply to domestic poultry or birds in course of conveyance or so kept for exhibition (under 72 hours) or while getting veterinary treatment.

It will be a special penalty offence (s. 8).

BIRD SANCTUARIES – The Secretary of State, may by order allow the establishment of bird sanctuaries within the area of a Local Authority, within which interference with wild birds and their nests and eggs is prohibited (s. 3). The Local Authority may institute proceedings for any offence under the order (s. 12).

ENFORCEMENT – A constable may without warrant stop and search any person found committing an offence against the Act and any vehicle, boat or animal which that person may then be using, and may arrest that person if he fails to give his name and address to the constable's satisfaction, and seize and detain any wild bird nest or egg or any weapon or other article capable of being used to kill or take wild birds which may be in the person's possession.

The council of a non-metropolitan county, metropolitan district or London borough or the Common Council of the City of London may institute proceedings (s. 12).

Under s. 74 of the Public Health Act 1961, a local authority may take any steps for the purpose of abating or mitigating any nuisance, annoyance or damage caused by the congregation in any built-up area of house doves, pigeons, starlings or sparrows. This includes taking reasonable steps to seize, destroy or otherwise dispose of any house doves or pigeons which are believed to have no owner. Such seizure and destruction must be carried out humanely and must not be in contravention of the Protection of Birds Act 1954.

The Protection of Birds Act 1967 provides for a special penalty for the offence of disturbing nesting birds (s. 4); restrictions respecting the ringing and marking of wild birds (s. 5); the use of poisonous substances, electrical devices, etc. (s. 6); and special protection in severe weather (s. 7).

Where a constable has reasonable grounds for suspecting that any person has, in contravention of s. 1, Protection of Birds Act 1954, taken or destroyed an egg of a bird included in Sched. 1 to that Act and that evidence of the commission of the offence is to be found on that person or any vehicle, boat or animal which that person may be using, the constable may without warrant stop and search that person and any such vehicle, boat or animal and may (a) arrest that person if he fails to give his name and address to the constable's satisfaction; and (b) seize and detain for the purposes of proceedings under that Act anything which may be in that person's possession which is evidence of the commission of the offence (Protection of Birds Act 1967, s. 11).

Destructive Imported Animals Act 1932 – This Act gives power to prohibit and control the importation or keeping of destructive animals which are not native to the country. The musk rat or musquash damages river banks, crops, etc., and the Musk Rats Order 1932 prohibited their importation or keeping except under licence.

The Musk Rats Order 1933 prohibits their importation and licences to keep them have been revoked. It is therefore an offence to import or keep or turn loose these pests and the police may seize them. The public are asked to kill any such rats found at large and to notify the Ministry of Agriculture and Fisheries, London, of their existence in any place.

The Grey Squirrels Order 1937 similarly prohibits the importation into, or the keeping within, Great Britain, of grey squirrels.

Slaughter of Animals – The law on this subject includes the Slaughter of Animals (Prevention of Cruelty) Regs. 1958, the Slaughter of Poultry Act 1967 and the Slaughterhouses Act 1974. Slaughter-houses and knackers' yards must be licensed. It is an offence (a) for the occupier of any premises to use them as a slaughter-house or knacker's yard, or (b) for any other person to so use the premises unless the occupier is licensed (1974 Act, s. 1). The licensed occupier of a slaughter-house or knacker's yard shall display in a conspicuous position on the premises a legible notice with the words, "Licensed Slaughter-house" or "Licensed Knacker's Yard". Failure to do so is an offence (1974 Act, s. 13). It is an offence to wilfully obstruct any person acting in the execution of Part I of the Act, or of any bye-law or warrant made or issued under it (1974 Act, s. 21). No animal to which the 1974 Act applies (i.e. horses, cattle, sheep, swine and goats) shall be slaughtered in a slaughter-house or knacker's yard unless such animal is instantaneously killed or stunned so as to be insensible to pain until it dies. Such killing or stunning shall be by a mechanically operated instrument. However no person shall be liable for any contravention of above, for killing by the approved Jewish method for food or for killing by the approved Mahommedan method for food (s. 36, 1974 Act).

"Slaughter-house" means any premises or place used for the killing of animals the flesh of which is intended for human consumption (s. 45, 1974 Act).

"Knacker's yard" means any building, premises or place used in connection with the business of killing animals whose flesh is not intended for sale for human consumption (s. 45, 1974 Act).

No animal shall be slaughtered or stunned in a slaughter-house or knacker's yard by any person except a person (18 years or over) duly licensed by the local authority (s. 39, 1974 Act).

No swine over 12 weeks old shall be slaughtered in any place other than a slaughter-house or knacker's yard unless it is instantaneously slaughtered or stunned so as to be insensible to pain, in either case by a mechanically operated instrument. However this will not apply to the slaughter of swine at a laboratory or research station, etc. if done for diagnosis of disease or research for veterinary or medical purposes (1974 Act, s. 37).

Contraventions of the Act are punishable summarily but it would be a good defence to prove that by reason of an accident or other emergency the contravention was necessary for preventing physical injury or suffering to any person or animal (1974 Act, s. 36).

The Regulations of 1958 deal with lairages (premises in which animals awaiting slaughter are confined), slaughter-houses and knacker's yards. They detail the conditions which must be observed to prevent unnecessary pain and suffering to animals therein.

Animals should be killed with as little suffering as possible (s. 1, 1958 Act), and if in pain must be slaughtered without delay (reg. 18). No horse shall be worked after it has been delivered to a knacker's yard (reg. 21). Every animal delivered to a knacker's yard shall be kept on the premises until killed and must be slaughtered within 48 hours from the time of delivery (reg. 22). A person under 15 should not be in a knacker's yard while slaughtering or cutting up of carcases is taking place (reg. 23).

The occupier of a knacker's yard must keep accurate records of all animals received. The record must be made in ink or indelible pencil within 24 hours of the slaughter of the animal or of its receipt (reg. 32). The record shall be produced for inspection at all reasonable times on request by an authorised officer of the local authority or the Minister (reg. 35).

Contravention of the regulations is punishable summarily but a person shall not be guilty if he proves that by reason of accident or other emergency, the contravention was necessary for preventing physical injury or suffering to any person or animal (reg. 36).

A constable has the right to enter a knacker's yard by day or when business is carried on, to see if any contravention of the Act has occurred. Any person refusing such entry or obstructing him can be punished summarily (Protection of Animals Act 1911, s. 5).

Riding Establishments Acts 1964 and 1970 – It is an offence for a person to keep a riding establishment except under the authority of a licence (which may be a provisional licence for not more than 6 months) granted by a local authority, fee not exceeding £10. A licence may be granted to a person over 18 years or a body corporate, who is not disqualified under this Act, the Protection of Animals (Cruelty to Dogs) Act 1933; the Pet Animals Act 1951; the Protection of Animals (Amendment) Act 1954, or the Animal Boarding Establishments Act 1963.

On receipt of an application for such a licence, the local authority will consider the report of a veterinary surgeon or practitioner on the suitability of the premises, etc., and also have regard to whether the applicant is a suitable person to hold a licence and to the need for securing suitable accommodation for the horses; adequate food and drink; control of diseases, etc. Appropriate steps should be taken for the protection and extrication of horses in case of fire and, in particular, that the name, address and telephone number of the licence holder or some other responsible person will be kept displayed in a prominent position on the outside of the premises and that instructions as to action to be taken in the event of fire will be kept displayed in a prominent position on the outside of the premises.

Any person aggrieved by the refusal of a local authority to grant a licence or by a condition in the licence may appeal to a magistrates' Court. A licence will remain in force for a year from the day on which it comes into force. Contravention or non-compliance with a condition of the licence is an offence (s. 1).

A local authority may authorise an inspection to be made of any premises where they have reason to believe a person is keeping a riding establishment; any premises for which a licence is in force; and any premises for which application for a licence has been made.

Any authorised person may, on producing his authority if required, enter at all reasonable times any such premises and inspect them and any horses found thereon and anything therein for the purpose of making his inspection reports or for ascertaining whether any offence has been or is being committed.

Any person who wilfully obstructs or delays any person in the exercise of his powers of entry or inspection commits an offence (s. 2).

If any person—

(a) at a time when a horse is in such a condition that its riding would be likely to cause suffering to the horse, lets out the horse on hire or uses it for the purpose of providing, in return for payment, instruction in riding or for the purpose of demonstrating riding;

(aa) lets out on hire for riding or uses for the purposes of providing, in return for payment, instruction in riding or for the purpose of demonstrating riding any horse aged 3 years or under or any mare heavy with foal or any mare within 3 months after foaling;

(b) supplies for a horse which is let out on hire by him for riding equipment which is used in the course of the hiring and suffers, at the time when it is supplied, from a defect of such a nature as to be apparent on inspection and as to be likely to cause suffering to the horse or an accident to the rider;

(c) fails to provide such curative care as may be suitable, if any, for a sick or injured horse which is kept by him with a view to its being let out on hire or used for a purpose mentioned in paragraph (a) of this subsection;

(d) in keeping a riding establishment knowingly permits any person, who is for the time being disqualified under this Act from keeping a riding establishment, to have control or management of the keeping of the establishment; or

(e) with intent to avoid inspection under s. 2 of this Act, conceals, or causes to be concealed, any horse maintained by the riding establishment;

he shall be guilty of an offence under this Act (s. 3, (1) as amended by Riding Establishments Act 1970, s. 3).

A person who gives false information for the purpose of obtaining a licence commits an offence (s. 3 (2)).

A local authority may take proceedings for any offence under the Act (s. 5).

The keeping of a riding establishment means the carrying on of a business of keeping horses for the purpose of their being let out on hire for riding and/or the purpose of their being used in providing, in return for payment, instruction in riding. It does not include any such premises conducted solely for military or police purposes or by the London Zoological Society.

"Horse" includes any mare, gelding, pony, foal, colt, filly or stallion, or any ass, mule or jennet (s. 6).

Pet Animals – The Pet Animals Act 1951 deals with the keeping of a pet shop, that is the carrying on at premises of any nature including a private dwelling (and any stall or barrow in a market) of a business of selling animals (any vertebrate animals) as pets or keeping same with a view to their sale. This includes selling or keeping for sale cats and dogs for domestic purposes and any animal for ornamental purposes. However keeping or selling pedigree animals bred by a person or the offspring of his pet animals are excluded, and the local authority may exempt the breeder of pedigree animals who also sells animals as pets (s. 7).

No person shall keep a pet shop except on licence granted by the Local Authority (council of county district or borough or City of London (s. 7)), which can specify conditions and which expires at the end of the year. If the licence is refused there can be an appeal to the local summary court (s. 1). It will be an offence to sell animals as pets in any part of a street or public place, except at a stall or barrow in a market (s. 2) or to sell an animal as a pet to a person under 12 (s. 3).

The Local Authority may authorise in writing inspection of licensed pet shops and any wilful obstruction or delay of the "inspector" will be an offence (s. 4). Offences may be prosecuted summarily (s. 5) by the Local Authority (s. 6).

Animal Boarding Establishments – Under the Animal Boarding Establishments Act 1963, no person shall keep a boarding establishment for dogs or cats except under the authority of a licence granted by a Local Authority. A licence may not be granted to a person disqualified under this Act, the Pet Animals Act 1951, the Protection of Animals (Cruelty to Dogs) Act 1933, or the Protection of Animals (Amendment) Act 1954.

A register must be kept containing a description of the animal, date of arrival and departure, name and address of owner, and it must be available for inspection at all times by an officer of the local authority or authorised veterinary officer (s. 1).

A Local Authority may authorise in writing any of its officers or any veterinary officer to inspect any premises, and who, on production of the authority if so required, may enter any such premises at all reasonable times to ascertain whether an offence has been or is being committed. Obstruction of such a person is an offence (s. 2).

Contravention of any provision of the Act is an offence. A person convicted of any offence under this Act, the Protection of Animals Act 1911, or the Pet Animals Act 1951, may have his licence under this Act cancelled and may be disqualified from keeping a boarding establishment (s. 3).

The keeping of such an establishment means the carrying on by a person at premises of any nature (including a private dwelling) of a business of providing accommodation for other people's animals. However, it shall not apply where a person provides such accommodation in connection with a business of which the provision of that accommodation is not the main activity (s. 5).

Guard Dogs Act 1975, s. 2, provides that a person carrying out the business of hiring out guard dogs must hold a licence in respect of his kennels from the local authority. This provision had not been brought into force at the date of going to press.

Conservation of Seals Act 1970 – This Act provides for the protection and conservation of seals in Great Britain and in the adjacent territorial waters. If any person (a) uses for the purpose of killing or taking any seal, any poisonous substance, or (b) uses for the purpose of killing, injuring or taking any seal, any fire-arm other than a rifle using ammunition, having a muzzle energy of not less than 600 footpounds and a bullet weighing not less than 45 grains, he shall be guilty of an offence (s. 1 (1)). (However, there are exceptions—see ss. 9 and 10 below).

The Secretary of State may by Order vary the description of firearms and ammunition prohibited for use against seals (s. 1 (2)). There is an annual close season for seals, as follows: grey seals (*Halichoerus grypus*) September 1 to December 31 (inclusive), and common seals (*Phoca vitulina*) June 1 to August 31 (inclusive). It is an offence to wilfully kill, injure or take a seal during the close seasons, but, for exceptions, see ss. 9 and 10 below.

A constable may stop any person he suspects with reasonable cause of committing an offence under this Act and may—(a) without warrant arrest that person if he fails to give his name and address to the constable's satisfaction; (b) without warrant search any vehicle or boat which that person may be using at that time; and (c) seize any seal, seal skin, firearm, ammunition or poisonous substance which is liable to be forfeited under s. 6 of this Act (s. 4 (1)).

A constable may sell or otherwise dispose of any seal seized under this section and the net proceeds of any sale shall be liable to forfeiture in the same manner as the seal sold: Provided that no constable shall be subject to any liability on account of his neglect or failure in the exercise of the powers conferred on him by this subsection (s. 4 (2)).

The court by which a person is convicted of an offence under this Act may order the forfeiture of any seal or seal skin in respect of which that offence was committed or of any seal, seal skin, firearm, ammunition or poisonous substance in his possession at the time of the offence (s. 6).

Where any offence under this Act is committed at some place on the sea coast or at sea outside the area of any commission of the peace, the place of the commission of the offence shall, for the purposes of the jurisdiction of any court, be deemed to be any place where the offender is found or to which he is first brought after the commission of the offence (s. 7).

Any person who attempts to commit an offence under this Act shall be guilty of an offence (s. 8 (1)). Any person who, for the purpose of committing an offence under this Act, has in his possession any poisonous substance or any firearm or ammunition the use of which is prohibited by s. 1 (1) (b) of this Act shall be guilty of an offence (s. 8 (2)).

A person shall not be guilty of an offence under ss. 2 or 3 of this Act by reason only of:

(a) the taking or attempted taking of any seal which had been disabled otherwise than by his act and was taken or to be taken solely for the purpose of tending it and releasing it when no longer disabled;

(b) the unavoidable killing or injuring of any seal as an incidental result of a lawful action;

(c) the killing or attempted killing of any seal to prevent it from causing damage to a fishing net or fishing tackle in his possession or in the possession of a person at whose request he killed or attempted to kill the seal, or to any fish for the time being in such fishing net, provided that at the time the seal was in the vicinity of such net or tackle (s. 9 (1)).

A person shall not be guilty of an offence under ss. 1, 2 or 3 of this Act by reason only of the killing of any seal which had been so seriously disabled otherwise than by his act that there was no reasonable chance of its recovering (s. 9 (2)).

The Secretary of State may issue a licence to any person authorising that person for certain purposes (e.g. scientific or educational purposes or the prevention of damage to fisheries) to kill or take seals during the close season or outside the close season by means which are otherwise prohibited (s. 10). The Secretary of State may authorise in writing entry onto any land for the purpose of obtaining information relating to seals or for protection of fisheries to any person. Wilfully obstructing such an authorised person is an offence (s. 11).

Animals Act 1971 – This Act makes provision with respect to civil liability for damage done by animals and with respect to the protection of livestock from dogs. Where any livestock strays on to any land and is not then under the control of any person, the occupier of the land may detain it, but the right to do so ceases (a) after 48 hours, unless notice of the detention has been given to the officer in charge of a police station and to the owner, if known; or (b) when such amount is tendered to the person detaining the livestock and is sufficient to satisfy any claim he may have for damage and expenses in respect of the livestock; or (c) if he has no such claim, when the livestock is claimed by a person entitled to its possession (s. 7 (2) and (3)).

Where the livestock has been so detained for less than 14 days, it may be sold at a market or public auction, unless proceedings are then pending for its return (s. 7 (4)).

In any civil proceedings for killing or causing injury to a dog, it shall be a defence to prove: (a) that the defendant acted for the protection of any livestock and was entitled to do so; and (b) within 48 hours of the killing or injury notice thereof was given by the defendant to the officer in charge of a police station (s. 9).

Badgers – The Badgers Act 1973 provides that if any person wilfully kills, injures or takes, or attempts to kill, injure or take any badger (save as permitted by the Act) he commits an offence. If any person has in his possession or under his control (a) a recently killed badger, or (b) a pelt from a freshly skinned badger (save as permitted by the Act) he commits an offence (s. 1).

CHAPTER 36

BETTING AND GAMING

	Page
Betting, Gaming and Lotteries Act 1963	503
Betting	504
Lotteries and Prize Competitions	511
Amusements with Prizes	514
Gaming Act 1968	517

Betting – According to the Oxford Dictionary betting is the staking of money or other value on the event of a doubtful issue.

Betting, Gaming and Lotteries Act 1963 consolidated the law relating to betting, gaming, lotteries and connected matters. The Act is in 5 parts as follows:

Part I (ss. 1 to 31) deals with Betting.

Ss. 1–8	General restrictions on betting.
Ss. 9–10	Licensed betting offices.
S. 11	Special provisions with respect to bookmakers and betting agency permits.
Ss. 12–15	The Totalisator Board and pool betting on horse races.
Ss. 16–20	Special provisions with respect to licensed tracks.
Ss. 21–22	Special provisions with respect to young persons.
S. 23	Power of entry on tracks.
Ss. 24–30	Contributions for benefit of horse racing by bookmakers and Totalisator Board.
S. 31	Accounts and reports of Levy Board and Totalisator Board.

Part II (ss. 32 to 40) dealt with Gaming (ss. 32–39 were repealed by the Gaming Act 1968—see later).

Part III (ss. 41 to 47) deals with Lotteries and Prize Competitions. Amendments to this Part of the Act are made by the Lotteries Act 1975.

Part IV (ss. 48 to 50) deals with Amusements with prizes, but ss. 49 (4) and 50 were repealed by the Gaming Act 1968.

Part V (ss. 51 to 58) deals with general matters.

There are 8 Schedules to the Act which are concerned with the following matters:

Sched. 1	Bookmaker's permits, betting agency permits and betting office licences.
Sched. 2	Registered pool promoters.
Sched. 3	Licensing of tracks for betting.
Sched. 4	Rules for licensed betting offices.
Sched. 5	Totalisators on dog racecourses.
Sched. 6	Permits for provision of amusement with prizes.
Sched. 7	Promotion of small lotteries by registered societies.
Part I	Registration of societies.
Part II	Returns to be made by promoters.
Sched. 8	Repeals.

Part I.—Betting – *Restriction on the use of premises for betting transactions with persons resorting thereto.*

It is an offence for a person to use any premises, or cause or knowingly permit any premises to be used, as a place where persons resorting thereto may effect pool betting transactions. (s. 1 (1) (a)), except—

(1) on an approved racecourse on a day on which only horse races take place with the authority of the Totalisator Board (s. 4 (1) (a));

(2) on a licensed dog racecourse and then only in accordance with the provisions of the Act (s. 4 (1) (b));

(3) in a licensed betting office (s. 9 (1)).

It is also an offence for a person to use, or cause or knowingly permit any other person to use, any premises for effecting any other betting transactions by that person or that other person with persons resorting thereto. This does not apply:

(1) where the user of the premises and all the persons with whom the betting transactions are effected (a) either reside or work on those premises, or (b) are holders of bookmaker's permits or are acting on behalf of such holders (s. 1 (1) (b));

(2) to anything done on an approved horse racecourse on a day on which horse races but no other races take place (s. 1 (5) (a));

(3) to anything done on any track on any day on which bookmaking may lawfully be carried on. This exemption will not apply to the use on a track which is not an approved horse racecourse by a bookmaker for the purposes of his business—(a) of any permanent structure other than a structure used by him in common with members of the public, or (b) of any position on the track specially reserved for his use by the occupier of the track (s. 1 (5) (b) and s. 1 (6)).

(4) The above does not apply to a licensed betting office (s. 1 (1) and s. 9 (1)).

Any person who, for any purpose connected with the effecting of a betting transaction, resorts to any premises which are being used in contravention of the above commits an offence (s. 1 (2)).

Proof that any person was on any premises used for unlawful betting shall be evidence that he resorted thereto for that purpose unless he proves that he was there for *bona fide* purposes not connected with effecting a betting transaction (s. 1 (3)).

"Premises" includes any place and any vessel (s. 55).

RESTRICTION ON BOOKMAKING EXCEPT UNDER BOOKMAKER'S PERMIT – A person who acts as a bookmaker on his own account and does not hold a valid bookmaker's permit commits an offence. This does not apply to a registered pool promoter who receives or negotiates bets by way of pool betting. If the holder of a bookmaker's permit, on being required by a constable to produce his permit for examination refuses or without reasonable cause fails to do so, he commits an offence (s. 2).

AUTHORISATION AND REGISTRATION OF BOOKMAKER'S AGENTS – No person shall by way of business receive or negotiate bets as servant or agent to another bookmaker or to the Totalisator Board unless—(a) he has attained the age of 21 years; (b) he is authorised in writing by that other bookmaker or by the Board; (c) in the case of a person acting as servant or agent to another bookmaker, that other bookmaker is the holder of a bookmaker's permit or betting agency permit.

Provided that this shall not apply to any person who is the holder of such a permit or who receives or negotiates bets on premises occupied by the holder of such a permit or by the Board (s. 3 (1)).

If any bet is received or negotiated by any person as servant or agent to another bookmaker or to the Board in contravention of the above, both that person and the other bookmaker or the Board commit an offence (s. 3 (2)).

The Board and the holder of a bookmaker's permit or betting agency permit shall keep a register of persons who are authorised to act as their servants or agents, and shall not grant any such authorisation without making the appropriate entry in the register. Contravention of these provisions is an offence (s. 3 (3)).

A constable may require the production of any authority in writing or register which must be kept or issued by virtue of this section. Failure to comply is an offence (s. 3 (4)).

Section 3 does not apply to bets made by way of pool betting (s. 3 (6)).

RESTRICTION OF POOL BETTING – No pool betting (see Betting and Gaming Duties Act 1972, s. 10) shall be carried on on any track except—

(a) on an approved horse racecourse when only horse races take place, by the Totalisator Board, or with the authority of that Board, by the persons having the management of the racecourse, or

(b) on a dog racecourse which is a licensed track, by means of a totalisator operated under s. 16 of the Act by the occupier of the track or a person authorised in writing.

Contravention of the above is an offence. However, this does not prohibit a person from receiving or negotiating bets on an approved horse racecourse by way of sponsored pool betting.

No person shall carry on any pool betting business otherwise than on a track unless he is a registered pool promotor (see Sched. 2); any contravention is an offence. This does not apply to sponsored pool betting business (s. 4).

"Pool betting business" means business involving the receiving or negotiating of bets made by way of pool betting (s. 55).

RESTRICTION OF BETTING ON TRACKS – Betting by bookmaking or by totalisator shall not take place on any track on more than 104 days (130 days on a licensed track dog racecourse) in any year beginning with July 1, nor on Good Friday, Christmas Day or Sunday or on more than 14 days in any one month except on an approved horse racecourse (s. 5 as amended by B.G. & L. (Amendment) Act 1971, s. 1).

RESTRICTION OF BOOKMAKING ON TRACKS – Except on an approved horse racecourse on a day on which it is used only for horse races, bookmaking shall not be carried on on any track unless the occupier holds a track betting licence. This does not apply to anything done on any track on any day if (a) during the 12 months beginning with 1st July, bookmaking has not been carried on on that track on more than 7 previous days, and (b) 7 days notice by post of the intended bookmaking has been given to the chief officer of police by the occupier.

Bookmaking shall not be carried on on any licensed track on any day which is not one of the betting days notified to the licensing authority under s. 2 of the B.G. & L. (Amendment) Act 1971 (s. 6).

RESTRICTION OF BETTING ON DOG RACECOURSES – On any day on which a track is being used as a dog racecourse, betting by bookmaking or totalisator shall not take place (a) in connection with more than 8 races, or (b) otherwise than during one continuous period not exceeding 4 hours. However 4 "special betting days" are permissible in any year, but not more than 4, on any of which there may be 16 dog races and betting for 8 hours in the aggregate (s. 7 as amended by B.G. & L. (Amendment) Act 1971, s. 2).

The occupier of a track may plead in defence to charges under ss. 5, 6 and 7 that the contravention occurred without his consent or connivance and that he exercised all due diligence to prevent it.

PROHIBITION OF BETTING IN STREETS AND PUBLIC PLACES – Any person frequenting or loitering in a street or public place, on behalf either of himself or of any other person, for the purposes of bookmaking, betting, agreeing to bet, or paying, receiving or settling bets commits an offence, and shall be liable to forfeit all books, cards, papers, and other articles relating to betting found in his possession. This shall not apply to anything done on any ground used, or adjacent to ground used, for the purpose of a racecourse for racing with horses on a day on which horse races take place on that racecourse.

A constable may take into custody without warrant any person found committing this offence, and may seize and detain any article liable to be forfeited under the Act.

"Street" includes any bridge, road, lane, footway, subway, square, court, alley or passage, whether a thoroughfare or not, which is for the time being open to the public, and the doorways and entrances of premises abutting upon, and any ground adjoining and open to a street (s. 8).

Being in a public place long enough to effect the purpose is "frequenting" (*Airton* v. *Scott* (1909) and *Clark* v. *Taylor* (1948)

BETTING OFFICE LICENCES AND BETTING AGENCY PERMITS – Where in the case of any premises there is for the time being in force a licence authorising the holder to use those premises as a betting office (betting office licence), s. 1 (1) shall not apply to the use of those premises for effecting betting transactions with or through the licence holder or any servant or agent of his. However, the licence does not authorise the use of those premises for any pool betting transaction made otherwise than by way of sponsored pool betting.

It is an offence for the holder of a betting agency permit to refuse, or unreasonably fail, to produce his permit for examination on being required to do so by a constable (s. 9).

CONDUCT OF LICENSED BETTING OFFICES – A licensed betting office must be managed in accordance with the rules set out in Sched. 4 (see below), and in the case of any contravention of any of the rules, the licensee and any servant or agent of his by whom the contravention was committed, commits an offence.

However, it shall be a defence for the licensee if he can prove that the contravention took place without his consent or connivance and that he exercised all due diligence to prevent it (s. 10 (1)).

The licensee or his servant or agent may refuse to admit to, or may expel from, the licensed premises any person who is drunken, violent, quarrelsome or disorderly or whose presence might cause a contravention of the rules for the conduct of betting offices. Any person who is liable to be expelled from the licensed premises and who fails to leave on being requested to do so by the licensee, his servant or agent, or any constable commits an offence (s. 10 (2)).

Any constable may, on the request of the licensee or his servant or agent, help to expel from a licensed betting office any person whom the constable has reasonable cause to believe to be liable to be expelled and may use such force as may be required for that purpose (s. 10 (3)).

Any constable may enter any licensed betting office to see whether the rules set out in Sched. 4 for the conduct of licensed betting offices are being complied with. Obstructing the constable will be an offence (s. 10 (4)).

If, save in a licensed betting office or in such manner as may be prescribed on premises giving access to such an office, any advertisement is published (a) indicating that any particular premises are a licensed betting office, or (b) indicating where any such office may be found, or (c) drawing attention to the availability of, or to the facilities afforded to persons resorting to, such offices, then in the case of an advertisement in connection with the office of a particular licensee, that licensee and in every case any person who published the advertisement or caused or permitted it to be published, commits an offence.

However, it will be a defence for a person charged to prove—

(1) that he did not know and had no reasonable cause to suspect that the advertisement was, and that he had taken all reasonable steps to ascertain that it was not, such an advertisement, or

(2) if he is a licensee, that the advertisement was published without his consent or connivance and that he exercised all due diligence to prevent the publishing of the advertisement (s. 10 (5)).

Sched. 4—Rules for Licensed Betting Offices—

(1) The premises shall be closed on Good Friday, Christmas Day and every Sunday, and shall not be used for any purpose other than the effecting of betting transactions.

(2) Persons apparently under 18, or known by the licensee or his staff to be under 18, must not be admitted to the premises.

(3) The licensee must (a) display his betting office licence on the premises, (b) exhibit on the premises such notices as may be prescribed, (c) must comply with any prescribed restrictions respecting the exhibiting of signs or written matter on the premises.

(4) Neither the licensee nor any servant or agent of his shall, while any other person is on the licensed premises, encourage him to bet.

(5) No facilities must be provided or allowed to be used for seeing any television broadcast or hearing any sound broadcast intended for public reception; and no music, dancing or other entertainment must be provided or allowed and no refreshment of any kind shall be served on the premises.

(6) Persons resorting to licensed betting offices must not have access thereto through any premises used for any other business.

THE BETTING (LICENSED OFFICE) REGULATIONS 1960 – Regulation 1. Licensed betting offices shall be closed between 6.30 p.m. and 7 a.m. the following morning.

Regulation 2. The holder of a betting office licence may exhibit on premises giving access to a licensed betting office — (a) inside a building comprising the licensed premises (i) a notice capable of being enclosed by a rectangle 3 sq. ft. in area consisting in addition to his name, only of the words "licensed betting office" and words or signs to direct persons resorting thereto; (ii) on or beside a door giving immediate access to the licensed betting office a notice giving the times the office is open; (b) elsewhere than inside a building comprising the licensed premises, a notice, in addition to his name, in not more than one place in characters not exceeding 3 in. in height, and consisting only of the words "licensed betting office" and the times when the office is open.

Regulation 3. (1) A conspicuous notice stating that persons under 18 are not admitted must be displayed in a conspicuous place inside the licensed premises. (2) No written matter or sign of any description other than the betting office licence and the notice required forbidding admittance to persons under 18, shall be exhibited inside the licensed premises except (a) in such a manner that the matter exhibited cannot be read from outside those premises, the rules subject to which betting transactions are effected on those premises, and information relating to events in connection with which betting transactions may be or have been effected thereon, and a page containing such information taken from a newspaper may be exhibited although it does not consist solely of such information; (b) such notices as may be requisite for securing the orderly conduct of the betting office and compliance with the provisions of Sched. 4 to the Act, and (c) such advertisements relating to other licensed betting offices as are mentioned in s. 10 (5).

CANCELLATION OF AND DISQUALIFICATION FOR BOOKMAKER'S OR BETTING AGENCY PERMIT – If the holder of a bookmaker's permit or of a betting agency permit is convicted (a) of an offence under ss. 1 (1), 4 (1) 5, 6, 8, (which deal with general restrictions on betting) or s. 21 (betting with young persons), or (b) of any offence involving fraud or dishonesty; or if the holder of a betting agency permit is convicted under s. 2 (1) (acting as a bookmaker on his own account without a bookmaker's permit), the court may order his permit to be forfeited and cancelled.

It is an offence for the holder of a bookmaker's permit or betting agency permit to employ any person known to him to be disqualified because of a conviction for any of these offences (s. 11).

Sections 12–15 deal with the constitution, functions and powers of the Horse Race Totalisator Board.

TOTALISATORS ON LICENSED TRACKS – On any licensed track being a dog racecourse, a totalisator may be set up and operated only on any betting day, while the public are admitted and no other sporting events are taking place on the track, and for betting with persons resorting to the track on dog races run on that track on that day. The totalisator must be operated in accordance with Sched. 5 to the Act.

While it is being thus lawfully operated bookmakers as such shall not be excluded from the track and space for bookmaking shall be afforded them (s. 16).

SPECIAL RIGHTS OF OCCUPIER OF LICENSED TRACK WHERE TOTALISATOR IS OPERATED – The occupier of the track shall have the exclusive right to authorise any person to carry on pool betting business on a dog race or to take bets at "totalisator" odds on dog races (s. 17).

CHARGES TO BOOKMAKERS ON LICENSED TRACKS – Limits are prescribed to the charges which may be made to bookmakers and their assistants for admission to tracks to carry on their business s. 18).

OCCUPIERS OF LICENSED TRACKS NOT TO HAVE AN INTEREST IN BOOKMAKING THEREON – The occupier of a licensed track or his servant or agent or any person holding an interest in the track shall not directly or indirectly engage in bookmaking on that track (s. 19).

The occupier of a licensed track is not required to permit betting thereon at any time at which no totalisator is being operated on that track (s. 20).

BETTING WITH YOUNG PERSONS – It is an offence for any person (a) to have a betting transaction with a young person under the age of 18; (b) to employ a person under 18 in the effecting of any betting transaction or in a licensed betting office; or (c) to receive or negotiate any bet through a person under 18. However, it will not be an offence under the above by reason of (1) the employment of a person under 18 in betting transactions by post, or (2) the carriage by a person under 18 of a communication relating to a betting transaction for the purposes of its conveyance by post. It shall be a defence to prove that at the time of the alleged offence the person alleged to be under 18 had in fact attained that age (s. 21).

BETTING CIRCULARS NOT TO BE SENT TO YOUNG PERSONS – It is an offence for any person for the purpose of earning commission, reward or profit, to send or cause to be sent to a person he knows to be under 18 years of age, any circular, notice, advertisement, letter, telegram or other document inviting the person receiving it to make any bet, or to take any share in any betting transaction or to apply to any person or place for information or advice for the purpose of any bets or for information as to any race, fight, game, sport or other contingency upon which betting is generally carried on. If such document names any person to whom payment may be made or from whom information may be obtained, such person will be deemed to have been the sender unless he proves the contrary.

If such document is sent to any person under 18 years of age at any university, school or other place of education, the sender will be deemed to have known such a person was an infant unless he proves he has reasonable ground for believing such person was of full age (s. 22, as amended by Family Law Reform Act 1969, Sched. 1).

POWER OF ENTRY ON TRACKS - Any person authorised in writing by the licensing authority and any constable may at all reasonable times enter upon any track to see whether the Act is being complied with. It is an offence to obstruct him (s. 23).

The remaining sections (24-31) of Part I of the Act deal with contributions for the benefit of horse racing by bookmakers and the Totalisator Board.

Part III.—Lotteries and Prize Competitions - A lottery is a distribution of prizes by lot or chance.

Subject to the provisions of this Act and the Lotteries Act 1975, all lotteries are unlawful (s. 41) but the following shall be deemed not to be unlawful provided the prescribed conditions are observed:

1. Small lotteries incidental to certain entertainments (s. 43, as amended by Lotteries Act 1975, Sched. 4).
2. Private lotteries (s. 44).
3. Small lotteries for charitable, sporting or other purposes (s. 45, as amended by Lotteries Act 1975, s. 13).
4. Lotteries of Art Unions (Betting and Lotteries Act 1934, s. 25 (1) and (2), and 1963 Act, s. 46).

OFFENCES IN CONNECTION WITH LOTTERIES - It is an offence for any person in connection with any lottery in Great Britain or elsewhere, to print tickets; to sell or distribute tickets or to offer or advertise or have them in possession for this purpose; to print, publish, distribute or have for publication or distribution any advertisement or list of prize winners or descriptive matter relating to the lottery calculated to act as an inducement to persons to participate in the lottery or other lotteries; to bring or invite to send into Great Britain for sale or distribution any ticket or advertisement; to send or attempt to send out of Great

Britain the proceeds or records of such tickets; to use or knowingly permit the use of any premises for lottery purposes; to cause or procure or attempt to procure any person to do any of the above acts.

It shall be an offence for which proceedings can be directed only by the Director of Public Prosecutions, to publish in a newspaper (or other periodical publication) any such matter descriptive of a lottery as is calculated to act as an inducement to persons to participate in a lottery. It shall be a defence in a prosecution to prove that the lottery in question was one declared by this Act not to be unlawful and that the defendant reasonably believed that none of the prescribed conditions had been broken, or that it was a game of chance and the defendant reasonably believed it was being conducted in such circumstances that no offence was committed (s. 42).

EXEMPTIONS OF SMALL LOTTERIES INCIDENTAL TO CERTAIN ENTERTAINMENTS – Small lotteries promoted as part of bazaars, sales of work, fêtes, dinners, dances, sporting or athletic events and other entertainments of a similar character shall not be unlawful lotteries, provided the following conditions are observed:

(a) The whole proceeds of the entertainment and lottery, after deducting the expenses of the entertainment (excluding the expenses of the lottery), the printing of the lottery tickets, and not more than £50 or such greater sum as may be specified by order (Lotteries Act 1975, s. 14) expended on lottery prizes, shall be devoted to purposes other than private gain.

(b) None of the lottery prizes shall be money prizes.

(c) Tickets shall not be sold or issued and the result shall not be declared, except on the premises and during the progress of the entertainment.

(d) The lottery shall not be the only or the only substantial inducement to persons to attend the entertainment.

If any of these conditions are broken every person concerned in the promotion or conduct of the lottery shall be guilty of an offence unless he proves the offence was committed without his consent or connivance and that he exercised all due diligence to prevent it (s. 43).

EXEMPTION OF PRIVATE LOTTERIES – Private lottery means a lottery in Great Britain which is promoted for, and in which the sale of tickets is confined to, either (a) members of one society club or other association established and conducted for purposes not connected with gaming, wagering or lotteries (each local branch of a society to be reckoned as a separate and distinct "society"), or (b) persons who work on the same premises, or (c) persons who reside on the same premises; and which is promoted by persons to whom, under the terms of the section, tickets may be sold. In the case of a "society" the lottery must be authorised in writing by the governing body of the society. Such a society under the Act means a small local society and not one extending over a large area (*Keehan* v. *Walters* (1948)).

Such a private lottery shall not be unlawful, provided the following conditions are observed:

(a) The whole proceeds less printing expenses shall be devoted to prizes, or in the case of a society, to prizes or to purposes of the society, or to both.

(b) No notice or advertisement of the lottery shall be given except a notice on the premises and particulars on the tickets.

(c) The price of every ticket shall be the same and shall be stated on the ticket.

(d) Every ticket shall bear the name and address of each of the promoters, a statement of the persons to whom sale is restricted, and a statement that any prize won shall be given only to the person to whom the winning ticket was sold by the promoters. No prize shall be delivered except in accordance with that statement.

(e) No tickets shall be issued except by way of sale and on receipt of the full price, and no money, etc., so received by a promoter shall be returned.

(f) No tickets shall be sent through the post.

If any of the above conditions are broken, each promoter and each person breaking a condition, shall be guilty of an offence, but it will be a defence for a promoter to prove that the offence was committed without his consent or connivance and that he exercised all due diligence to prevent it (s. 44).

EXEMPTION OF CERTAIN SMALL LOTTERIES CONDUCTED FOR CHARITABLE, SPORTING OR OTHER PURPOSES – Certain small lotteries will not be unlawful if:

(1) they are promoted on behalf of a society registered by the local authority (that is, the council of the county district or county borough, etc.: Sched. 7, para. 1), the society being one established and conducted wholly or mainly for one or more of the following purposes (a) charitable, (b) athletic games or sports, (c) other purposes which are not for private gain or commercial undertakings, and the lotteries are to raise money for such a society. Any purpose for which any society is established or conducted which is calculated to benefit the society as a whole shall not be held to be a purpose of private gain by reason only that action taken in its fulfilment would result in benefit to any person as an individual. "Society" includes club, organisation or association of persons and any separate branch or section of it.

(2) the prescribed conditions are complied with (non-compliance is an offence). They number 13 and include: no prize to exceed £1,000 and no ticket to cost more than 25p; total value of tickets sold not to exceed £5,000; no public advertising; proceeds less expenses (not to exceed 25 per cent.) to go to the society.

Full return of the proceeds, etc. shall be made by the promoters to the Local Authority (s. 45 and Sched. 7, as amended by Lotteries Act 1975, s. 13).

Lotteries of Art Unions, promoted and conducted in accordance with the Art Unions Act 1846, shall be deemed not to be unlawful lotteries (s. 46, see also Betting and Lotteries Act 1934, s. 25 (1) and (2)).

Prize Competitions are restricted to the extent that it shall be unlawful to conduct in or through any newspaper (or other periodical publication, s. 55), or in connection with any trade or business (except pool betting or sponsored pool betting), or the sale of any article to the public:

(a) Any competition offering prizes for forecasts of the result either of a future event or of a past event the result of which is not yet ascertained or not yet generally known.

(b) Any other competition success in which does not depend to a substantial degree upon the exercise of skill.

Contravention of above is an offence, without prejudice or liability to prosecution under s. 42 (s. 47).

The sale of football pool competition coupons by a newspaper and tobacconist shop was held not unlawful as the sale was not in connection with the trade or business (*I.T.P. London, Ltd.* v. *Winstanley* (1947)).

Part IV.—Amusements with Prizes – *Amusements with prizes at non-commercial entertainments.* Section 48 applies to the provision, at any entertainment to which s. 43 of the Act applies, of any amusement with prizes which constitutes a lottery or gaming or both but does not constitute—(a) gaming to which Part II of the Gaming Act 1968 applies, or (b) gaming by means of a machine to which Part III of that Act applies.

Where any such amusement constitutes a lottery, nothing in ss. 41 or 42 of this Act shall apply to it.

In relation to any such amusement (whether it constitutes a lottery or not) the conditions set out in s. 48 (4) shall be observed, and if either of those conditions is contravened every person concerned in the provision or conduct of that amusement shall be guilty of an offence unless he proves that the contravention occurred without his consent or connivance and that he exercised all due diligence to prevent it.

The conditions referred to above are (a) that the whole proceeds of the entertainment, after deducting the expenses of the entertainment, shall be devoted to purposes other than private gain; and (b) that the facilities for winning prizes at amusements to which this section applies, or those facilities together with any other facilities for participating in lotteries or gaming, shall not be the only, or the only substantial, inducement to persons to attend the entertainment (s. 48, substituted by Lotteries Act 1975, Sched. 4).

AMUSEMENTS WITH PRIZES AT COMMERCIAL ENTERTAINMENTS – Notwithstanding the provisions of ss. 41 and 42, this section permits the provision of amusements with prizes—(a) on any premises if a permit is granted by the local authority under Sched. 6, and (b) at occasional fairs of short duration provided by travelling showmen on premises not previously used in that year on more than 27 days for the holding of such a fair, subject to the following conditions: (a) that the amount paid for any one chance to win does not exceed 10p; (b) that the aggregate amount taken by way of the sale of chances in any one determination of winners of prizes does not exceed £5 and that the sale of those chances and the declaration of the result take place on the same day and on the premises on which and during the time when, the amusement is provided; (c) that no money prize exceeds 10p; (d) that the winning of, or the purchase of a chance to win, a prize does not entitle any person whether or not subject to a further payment by him, to any further opportunity to win money or money's worth, by taking part in any amusement with prizes or in any gaming or lottery; (e) in the case of a pleasure fair that the opportunity to win prizes is not the only, or the only substantial, inducement to persons to attend the fair (s. 49, as amended).

Part V.—General – *Search warrants.*—If a justice of the peace is satisfied on information on oath that there is reasonable ground for suspecting that an offence under this Act is being, has been, or is about to be committed on any premises, he may issue a warrant authorising any constable to enter those premises, if necessary by force, at any time within 14 days, from the issue of the warrant and search them.

Any constable executing the search warrant may: (a) seize and remove any document, money or valuable thing, instrument or other thing whatsoever found on the premises which he has reasonable cause to believe may be required as evidence, and (b) arrest and search any person found on the premises whom he has reasonable cause to believe to be committing or to have committed any such offence (s. 51).

The court which convicts any person of any offence under this Act may order anything produced to the court and shown to its satisfaction to relate to the offence to be forfeited and either destroyed or dealt with in such other manner as the court may order (s. 52).

Where an offence under this Act committed by a body corporate is proved to have been committed with the consent or connivance of, or to be attributable to any neglect on the part of, any director, manager, secretary or similar officer, he as well as the body corporate shall be guilty of that offence (s. 53).

PRIVATE GAIN – In construing ss. 43 or 48 proceeds of any entertainment, lottery, gaming or amusement promoted on behalf of a society to which this subsection extends, which are applied for any purpose calculated to benefit the society as a whole shall not be held to be applied for purposes of private gain by reason only that their application for that purpose results in benefit to any person as an individual (s. 54 (1)).

For the purposes of s. 48, where any payment falls to be made by way of a hiring, maintenance or other charge in respect of a gaming machine within the meaning of s. 33, or in respect of any equipment for holding a lottery or gaming at any entertainment, then, if, but only if, the amount of that charge falls to be determined wholly or partly by reference to the extent to which that or some other such machine or equipment is used for the purposes of lotteries or gaming, that payment shall be held to be an application of the stakes hazarded or proceeds of the entertainment, as the case may require, for purposes of private gain, and accordingly any reference in those provisions to expenses shall not include a reference to any such charge falling to be so determined (s. 54 (2)).

Subsection (1) above extends to any society which is established and conducted either—(a) wholly for purposes other than purposes of any commercial undertaking, or (b) wholly or mainly for the purposes of participation in or support of athletic sports, or athletic games; and the expression "society" includes any club, or association of persons by whatever name called and any separate branch or section thereof (s. 54 (3)).

DEFINITIONS – "Bookmaker" means any person other than the Totalisator Board who (a) whether on his own account or as servant or agent to any other person, carries on, whether occasionally or regularly, the business of receiving or negotiating bets or conducting pool betting operations; or (b) by way of business in any manner holds himself out, or permits himself to be held out, as a person who receives or negotiates bets or conducts such operations, so, however, that a person shall not be deemed to be a bookmaker by reason only of the fact (i) that he carries on, or is employed in, sponsored pool betting business; or (ii) that he operates, or is employed in operating, a totalisator.

"Dog race" means a race in which an object propelled by mechanical means is pursued by dogs.

"Totalisator" means the contrivance for betting known as the totalisator or parimutuel, or any other machine or instrument of betting of a like nature, whether mechanically operated or not.

"Track" means premises on which races of any description, athletic sports or other sporting events take place.

Miscellaneous – The importation for publication in the United Kingdom of any advertisement or notice relating to a lottery is prohibited (Revenue Act 1898, s. 1 as amended by Customs & Excise Act 1952, Sched. 10). Any such material is forfeited and may be disposed of by the Customs Authorities.

GAMING IN LICENSED PREMISES AND REFRESHMENT HOUSES – Licensing Act 1964, s. 177: the holder of a justices' licence must not suffer any game to be played in the premises which would be an offence under the Gaming Act 1968 or allow a requirement or restriction under s. 6 of that Act to be contravened. Summary offence punishable by fine.

The Late Night Refreshment Houses Act 1969, s. 9, makes it a summary offence for any person licensed to keep a refreshment house under the Act, to knowingly suffer gaming which is unlawful.

CHEATING AT PLAY – Gaming Act 1845, s. 17, declares that every person who, by any fraud or cheating, in playing with cards, dice, or other game, or in taking part in the stakes or wagers, or betting on the players, or in wagering on the event of any game, sport, pastime, or exercise, wins from any other person any money or valuable thing, commits an offence.

Gaming Act 1968 – "Gaming" is defined as "the playing of a game of chance for winnings in money, or money's worth, whether any person playing the game is at risk of losing any money or money's worth or not" (s. 52). The above definition is subject to the provisions of s. 52 (3) to (5) which provides: (a) that a lottery permitted by ss. 43 to 45 of the 1963 Act is not prohibited by the law of gaming, in cases where the lottery is also a game, and, therefore "gaming", and each winner of a prize is ascertained by reference to not more than three determining factors, each of those factors being either the result of a draw or other determination or the outcome of an event; (b) that "gaming" does not include the making of bets by way of pool betting; and (c) that a machine is not used for gaming if it offers a successful player no more than another free turn or the return of his stake, or a part of it.

The Act is arranged in 4 parts:

Part I (ss. 1–8).	Gaming elsewhere than on premises licensed or registered under Part II.
Part II (ss. 9–25).	Gaming on premises licensed or registered under Part II.
Part III (ss. 26–39).	Gaming by means of machines.
Part IV (ss. 40–54).	Miscellaneous and supplementary provisions.

In addition there are 12 Schedules.

GAMING TO WHICH PART I APPLIES – It does not apply to gaming with slot machines, nor to certain minor entertainments and amusements, but it does apply to all gaming other than gaming in premises licensed or registered under Part II (s. 1).

NATURE OF GAME – No gaming to which Part I applies shall take place where any one or more of the following conditions are fulfilled—

(a) the game involves playing or staking against a bank, whether the bank is held by one of the players or not;
(b) the nature of the game is such that the chances in the game are not equally favourable to all the players;
(c) the nature of the game is such that the chances in it lie between the player and some other person, or (if there are two or more players) lie wholly or partly between the players and some other person, and those chances are not as favourable to the player or players as they are to that other person.

The above shall not have effect in relation to gaming which takes place on a domestic occasion in a private dwelling, and shall not have effect in relation to any gaming where the gaming takes place in a hostel, hall of residence or similar establishment which is not carried on by way of a trade or business and the players consist exclusively or mainly of persons who are residents or inmates in that establishment (s. 2).

NO CHARGE FOR TAKING PART IN GAMING – No gaming to which Part I applies shall take place in circumstances where (apart from any stakes hazarded) a charge, in money or money's worth, is made in respect of that gaming (s. **3** (1)).

Subject to the next following subsection, any admission charge shall, unless the contrary is proved, be taken to be a charge made as mentioned in sub-s. (1) of this section (s. **3** (2)).

For the purposes of this section a payment which constitutes payment of, or of a quarterly or half-yearly instalment of, an annual subscription to a club, or which constitutes payment of an entrance subscription for membership of a club, shall not be taken to be a charge made as mentioned in sub-s. (1) above, provided that this subsection shall not apply to a club unless it is shown that the club is so constituted and conducted, in respect of membership and otherwise, as not to be of a temporary character, and, in relation to an entrance subscription, shall not apply unless it is shown that the payment is not made in respect of temporary membership of the club (s. **3** (3)).

The provisions above are subject to s. 40 (s. **3** (4)).

NO LEVY ON STAKES OR WINNINGS – No gaming to which this Part of this Act applies shall take place where a levy is charged on any of the stakes or on the winnings of any of the players, whether by way of direct payment or deduction, or by the exchange of tokens at a lower rate than the rate at which they were issued, or by any other means (s. 4).

GAMING IN PUBLIC PLACES – No person shall take part in gaming to which Part I applies (a) in any street, or (b) (subject to s. 6) in any other place to which, whether on payment or otherwise, the public have access (s. 5 (1)).

A constable may arrest without warrant anyone whom he finds in a street, or in any such place as is mentioned in para. (b) of the preceding subsection, and whom he suspects, with reasonable cause, to be taking part in gaming there in contravention of that subsection (s. 5 (2)).

"Street" has the meaning given in s. 8 of the 1963 Act (s. 5 (3)).

GENERAL PROVISIONS AS TO GAMING ON PREMISES LICENSED FOR RETAIL SALE OF LIQUOR – Section 6 provides an exception to the rule that gaming is not permitted in places where the public have access. On premises in respect of which there is a justices' on-licence, other than a restaurant or residential licence, dominoes, cribbage and other equal chance games authorised by the licensing justices may be played (s. 6).

SPECIAL PROVISIONS AS TO PERSONS UNDER 18 – Gaming by persons under 18 years of age in public houses and hotels is absolutely forbidden (s. 7).

OFFENCES – If any gaming takes place in contravention of the provisions of ss. 2 to 4 of the Act, every person concerned in the organisation or management of the gaming shall be guilty of an offence (s. 8 (1)).

For the purposes of the preceding subsection any person who takes part in procuring the assembly of the players shall be taken to be concerned in the organisation of the gaming (s. 8 (2).

Without prejudice to the preceding provisions of this section, where any gaming takes place on any premises, or in any vessel or vehicle, in contravention of any of the provisions of ss. 2 to 4 of this Act, any person who, knowing or having reasonable cause to suspect that the premises, vessel or vehicle would be used for gaming in contravention of any of those provisions,

(a) allowed the premises, vessel or vehicle to be used for the purposes of gaming to which this Part of this Act applies, or

(b) let, or let on hire, the premises, vessel or vehicle, or otherwise made the premises, vessel or vehicle available, to any person by whom an offence under sub-s. (1) of this section is committed in connection with the gaming,

shall be guilty of an offence (s. 8 (3)).

GAMING TO WHICH PART II APPLIES – This Part of the Act applies to all gaming which takes place on premises in respect of which either (a) a licence under the Act is for the time being in force, or (b) a club or a miners' welfare institute is for the time being registered under this Part of the Act, and which is not gaming by means of any machine to which Part III of the Act applies (s. 9).

GAMING BOARD FOR GREAT BRITAIN – The Act authorises the establishment of a Gaming Board for Great Britain. The Board is required to keep under review the extent and character of gaming, and the location of gaming facilities, with particular reference to premises licensed or registered under the Act (s. 10).

PARTICIPATION IN GAMING – Gaming in licensed and registered premises is confined to persons actually present at the time on the premises where the gaming takes place and forbids anyone to game on behalf of another who is not present (s. 12 (1)).

Where gaming to which Part II applies takes place on premises in respect of which a licence is in force, then, subject to the following provisions of this section, no person shall participate in the gaming unless either—

(a) he is a member of the club specified in the licence who, at the time when he begins to take part in the gaming, is eligible to take part in it; or
(b) he is a *bona fide* guest of a person who is a member of that club and who, at the time when the guest begins to take part in the gaming, is eligible to take part in it,

and neither the holder of the licence nor any person acting on his behalf or employed on the premises in question shall participate in the gaming (s. 12 (2)).

For the purposes of sub-s. (2) of this section a member of the club specified in the licence is eligible to take part in the gaming at any particular time if either—

(a) he was admitted to membership of the club in pursuance of an application in writing made by him in person on the premises in question, and at that time at least 48 hours have elapsed since he applied for membership of the club; or
(b) since becoming a member of the club he has given notice in writing in person on those premises to the holder of the licence, or to a person acting on behalf of the holder of the licence, of his intention to take part in gaming on those premises, and at that time at least 48 hours have elapsed since he gave that notice (s. 12 (3)).

Where gaming takes place on premises in respect of which a licence under the Act is in force, and consists of a game which involves playing or staking against a bank, nothing in sub-s. (1) or sub-s. (2) of this section shall prevent the holder of the licence or a person acting on his behalf from holding the bank or having a share or interest in it (s. 12 (4)).

For the purposes of sub-s. (2) of this section a person shall not be precluded from being a *bona fide* guest as mentioned in paragraph (b) of that subsection by reason only that he makes a payment which is lawfully required in accordance with s. 14 of the Act (s. 12 (5)).

Where gaming to which Part II applies takes place on premises in respect of which a club or miners' welfare institute is for the time being registered under this Part of the Act, no person shall participate in the gaming unless either—

(a) he is a member of the club or institute and there has been an interval of at least 48 hours between the time when he applied or was nominated for membership of the club or institute and the time when he begins to take part in the gaming; or

(b) he is a *bona fide* guest of a person who is a member of the club or institute and there has been an interval of at least 48 hours between the time when that person applied or was nominated for membership of the club or institute and the time when the guest begins to take part in the gaming;

and for the purposes of paragraph (b) of this subsection a person shall be taken not to be a *bona fide* guest if he himself makes any payment required for enabling him to obtain access to the premises, or to a part of them which is a part in which the gaming takes place, or if (apart from any stakes hazarded and the payment of any losses incurred by him in the gaming) he makes any payment in money or money's worth in respect of the gaming (s. 12 (6)).

For the purposes of this section a person participates in the gaming if (a) he takes part in the gaming as a player; or (b) where the game involves playing or staking against a bank, he holds the bank or has a share or interest in it (s. 12 (7)).

The preceding provisions of this section shall have effect subject to s. 20 of the Act (which contains special provisions as to Bingo Clubs: s. 12 (8)).

RESTRICTIONS ON GAMES TO BE PLAYED – Playing in any licensed or registered club of any banker's game or game of unequal chance is prohibited, unless permitted by Regulations made under the section (s. 13). The Gaming Clubs (Bankers' Games) Regs. 1970 (S.I. No. 800) regulate the manner in which the games of roulette, crap, baccarat and blackjack are to be played.

CHARGES FOR TAKING PART IN GAMING – Gaming to which Part II of the Act applies is prohibited if any charge for gaming (apart from stakes) is made, except as permitted by Regulations (s. 14). The Gaming Clubs (Hours and Charges) Regs. 1970 (S.I. No. 799) and 1975 (S.I. No. 604) regulate the hours and charges permissible.

LEVY ON STAKES OR WINNINGS – Except in licensed premises where permitted by Regulations, any levy on stakes or winnings is prohibited. By s. 52 (7), this prohibition applies whether a charge or levy is compulsory, customary or voluntary (s. 15).

PROVISION OF CREDIT FOR GAMING – Allowing any form of credit for gaming in a licensed club is prohibited. But cashing a cheque to provide means for gaming which has not yet taken place is allowed, provided the cheque is not post-dated and any tokens given in exchange are at the normal rate. Where the holder of a licence under this Act, or a person acting on behalf of or under any arrangement with the holder of such a licence, accepts a cheque in exchange for cash or tokens to be used by a player in gaming to which this Part of the Act applies, he shall, not more than two banking days later, cause the cheque to be delivered to a bank for payment or collection. This section annuls any other statutory provisions which would invalidate such cheques (s. 16).

EXCLUSION OF PERSONS UNDER 18 – Except as provided by ss. 20 and 21, no person under 18 shall be present in any room while gaming, to which Part II applies, takes place in that room (s. 17).

GAMING ON SUNDAYS – No gaming shall take place on any Sunday on any premises licensed under the Act (a) between 3 a.m. and 2 p.m. in the Inner London area or (b) between 2 a.m. and 2 p.m. elsewhere (s. 18).

APPROVAL BY BOARD OF PERSONS CONNECTED WITH GAMING – Gaming operatives employed in licensed premises must obtain certificates of approval from the Gaming Board (s. 19).

SPECIAL PROVISIONS AS TO BINGO CLUBS – The Act makes special provisions for "bingo club premises." "Linked bingo", that is, games of bingo played in common with people on other premises and offering common prizes, is permissible. The play must conform to conditions which make it, for practical purposes, simultaneous throughout all the premises concerned. The aggregate prize money of all the "linked bingo games" must not exceed £1,000 in any one week. A member is eligible to play in bingo club premises if there is an interval of at least 24 hours between his application for membership and his taking part in the gaming. Persons under 18 may be present in rooms where bingo is being played, but they must not take part. Prizes in bingo club premises may not be subsidised beyond an aggregate of £400 in any one week, but this sum may be varied by an order of the Secretary of State (s. 20, as amended).

SPECIAL PROVISIONS AS TO GAMING FOR PRIZES – Section 21 applies to any gaming which (being gaming to which Part II of the Act applies) is gaming for prizes in respect of which the following conditions are fulfilled: (a) the amount paid by any person for any one chance shall not exceed 10p; (b) the aggregate amount taken by way of the sale of chances in any one determination of winners of prizes does not exceed £5, and the sale of those chances and the declaration of the result take place on the same day and on the premises on which, and at the time when, the game is played; (c) no money prize exceeding 10p is distributed or offered; (d) the winning of or the purchase of a chance to win a prize does not entitle any person (whether subject to a further payment by him or not) to any further opportunity to win money or money's worth by taking part in any other gaming or in any lottery, and (e) the aggregate amount or value of the prizes on any one determination of winners does not exceed £5.

Section 13 of this Act shall not have effect in relation to any gaming to which this section applies which takes place on premises in respect of which a licence under this Act is for the time being in force and, in relation to any such gaming, s. 3 of this Act, as applied by s. 14 of this Act, shall not be taken to be contravened by reason only that a person pays for a chance to win a prize.

In bingo club premises, young people may be present if they do not take part as players (s. 21, as amended).

FURTHER POWERS TO REGULATE LICENSED CLUBS – The Secretary of State is empowered to make regulations prescribing the manner in which rules of games are to be displayed, for preventing unfair play, to add to the grounds upon which licences must or may be refused, etc. (s. 22); the Secretary of State has made the Gaming Clubs (Licensing) Regs. 1969, the Gaming Clubs (Hours and Charges) Regs. 1970, the Gaming Clubs (Prohibition of Gratuities) Regs. 1970, and the Gaming Clubs (Permitted Areas) Regs. 1971.

OFFENCES UNDER PART II – Subject to the following provisions of this section, if any of the provisions of ss. 12 to 20 of this Act, or of any regulations made under sub-s. (1), sub-s. (2) or sub-s. (4) of s. 22 of this Act are contravened in relation to any premises,

(a) the holder of the licence, if they are premises in respect of which a licence under this Act is for the time being in force, or

(b) every officer of the club or institute, if they are premises in respect of which a club or a miners' welfare institute is for the time being registered under this Part of this Act,

shall be guilty of an offence (s. 23 (1)).

Without prejudice to the preceding subsection, but subject to sub-s. (3) of this section, if any such provisions as are mentioned in the preceding subsection are contravened in relation to any gaming (or, in the case of the provisions of s. 16 (3) of this Act, are contravened in relation to a cheque accepted in exchange for cash or tokens to be used by a player in any gaming), every person concerned in the organisation or management of the gaming shall be guilty of an offence (s. 23 (2)).

Where a person is charged with an offence under either of the preceding subsections in respect of a contravention of any such provisions as are mentioned in sub-s. (1) of this section, it shall be a defence for him to prove—(a) that the contravention occurred without his knowledge; and (b) that he exercised all such care as was reasonable in the circumstances to secure that the provisions in question would not be contravened (s. 23 (3)).

Any person guilty of an offence under sub-s. (1) or sub-s. (2) of this section shall be liable—(a) on summary conviction to a fine not exceeding £400; (b) on conviction on indictment, to a fine or to imprisonment for a term not exceeding two years or to both (s. 23 (4)).

Where, on the grant or renewal of a licence under this Act in respect of any premises, or on registering or renewing the registration of a club or a miners' welfare institute under this Part of this Act, the licensing authority or sheriff imposed any restrictions under para. 24 or para. 25 of Sched. 2, under para. 11 of Sched. 3 or under para. 13 of Sched. 4 to this Act, sub-ss. (1) to (3) of this section shall have effect in relation to any contravention of those restrictions as they have effect in relation to any contravention of the provisions of ss. 12 to 20 of this Act (s. 23 (5)).

If any person, for the purpose of obtaining, for himself or for any other person, a certificate of approval under s. 19 of this Act, or the reinstatement of such a certificate after it has been revoked by the Board, makes a statement which he knows to be false in a material particular; or recklessly makes a statement which is false in a material particular, he shall be guilty of an offence and liable on summary conviction to a fine not exceeding £200 (s. 23 (6)).

DISQUALIFICATION OF PREMISES – A court by which a person is convicted of a breach of the conditions of a licence, or of any restrictions attached to it, may disqualify the premises concerned for a period up to 5 years, which thereby cancels the licence (s. 24).

SCOPE OF PART III – Part III of the Act deals with gaming by means of any machine (which includes any apparatus) which (a) is constructed or adapted for playing a game of chance, and (b) has a slot or other aperture for the insertion of cash or tokens (s. 26 (1)).

In the preceding subsection, the reference to playing a game of chance by means of a machine includes playing a game of chance partly by means of a machine and partly by other means if (but only if) the element of chance in the game is provided by means of the machine (s. 26 (2)).

In this Part of this Act, "charge for play" means an amount paid in money or money's worth by or on behalf of a player in order to play one or more games by means of a machine to which this Part of this Act applies (s. 26 (3)).

Sections 27 to 29 deal with the sale, supply and maintenance of machines.

REGISTRATION UNDER PART III – The use of machines for gaming on premises licensed or registered under the Act is governed by s. 30 (which applies the provisions of Sched. 7), s. 31 (which deals with the use of machines by virtue of licence or registration), and s. 32 (which empowers the licensing authority to allow more than two machines).

USE OF MACHINES FOR GAMING BY WAY OF AMUSEMENT WITH PRIZES AT NON-COMMERCIAL ENTERTAINMENTS – Section 33 applies to the following kinds of entertainment, elsewhere than on premises licensed or registered under the Act, that is to say, bazaars, sales of work, fêtes, dinners, dances, sporting or athletic events and other entertainments of a similar character, provided the proceeds after deducting expenses are devoted to purposes other than private gain. Where a machine to which this Part of this Act applies is used for gaming as an incident of an entertainment to which this section applies, the opportunity to win prizes by means of the machine, or that opportunity together with any other facilities for participating in lotteries or gaming shall not be the only, or the only substantial, inducement to persons to attend the entertainment (s. 33).

OTHER USES OF MACHINES FOR AMUSEMENT PURPOSES – The conditions specified in the following provisions of this section shall be observed where a machine to which this Part of this Act applies is used for gaming—

(a) on any premises in respect of which a permit granted for the purposes of this section is for the time being in force; or
(b) on any premises in respect of which a licence under this Act and a direction given under s. 32 of this Act are for the time being in force, where, by virtue of that direction, the provisions of this section have effect in relation to the premises; or
(c) on any premises used wholly or mainly for the purpose of a pleasure fair consisting wholly or mainly of amusements provided otherwise than by means of machines to which this Part of this Act applies, being premises in respect of which a permit granted under s. 49 of the Act of 1963 is for the time being in force; or
(d) at a travelling showmen's pleasure fair (s. 34 (1)).

The charge for play for playing a game once by means of the machine shall be one or more coins or tokens inserted in the machine of an amount or value not exceeding (or, if more than one, not in the aggregate exceeding) 5p (s. 34 (2)).

Except as provided by sub-ss. (4) and (9) of this section, in respect of any one game played by means of the machine no player or person claiming under a player shall receive, or shall be entitled to receive, any article, benefit or advantage other than one (and only one) of the following, that is to say:

(a) a money prize not exceeding 15p or a token which is, or two or more tokens which in the aggregate are, exchangeable only for such a money prize;
(b) a non-monetary prize or prizes of a value or aggregate value not exceeding 40p or a token exchangeable only for such a non-monetary prize or such non-monetary prizes;
(c) a money prize not exceeding 15p together with a non-monetary prize of a value which does not exceed 40p less the amount of the money prize, or a token exchangeable only for such a combination of a money prize and a non-monetary prize;
(d) one or more tokens which can be used for playing one or more further games by means of the machine and, in so far as they are not so used, can be exchanged for a non-monetary prize or non-monetary prizes at the appropriate rate (s. 34 (3), as amended).

The condition specified in sub-s. (3) above shall not be taken to be contravened by reason only that a player, after inserting in the machine an amount permitted in accordance with sub-s. (2) and playing a game successfully, is afforded by the automatic action of the machine an opportunity to play one or more further games without inserting any further coin or token in the machine, if in respect of all those games:

(a) he does not receive, and is not entitled to receive, any article other than a money prize or money prizes of an amount or aggregate amount not exceeding 15p; and
(b) he does not receive, and is not entitled to receive, any other benefit or advantage apart from the opportunity to play the further game or games (s. 34 (4), as amended).

In the case of a travelling showmen's pleasure fair the opportunity to win prizes by means of amusements which constitute gaming, shall not constitute the only, or the only substantial, inducement to persons to attend the fair (s. 34 (5)).

The Secretary of State may by order direct that any provision of this section which is specified in the order and which specifies a sum shall have effect as if, for that sum, there were substituted such other sum as may be specified in the order (s. 34 (9)).

RESTRICTION ON OTHER GAMING BY MEANS OF MACHINES – The use of slot machines for gaming is prohibited (s. 35) except in licensed or registered premises (ss. 31 and 32); at non-commercial entertainments (s. 33); or for amusement with prizes (s. 34).

REMOVAL OF MONEY FROM MACHINES – The emptying of machines on licensed or registered premises by persons other than the licence holder or a club employee, or, on registered premises an officer, member or employee of the club or institute is prohibited (s. 36).

ENTERTAINMENT NOT HELD FOR PRIVATE GAIN – Gaming carried on at entertainments promoted to raise money otherwise than for private gain is lawful provided: (a) not more than one payment (not exceeding 75p) is made for entrance fee or stake; (b) not more than one distribution of prizes (total not exceeding £75) is made; (c) the whole proceeds (less expenses including the provision of prizes) are not applied for private gain, and (d) the expenses must not exceed reasonable cost of the facilities provided.

If two or more such entertainments are given by the same persons in the same place on any day, this section applies as if they were one entertainment.

If several such entertainments in the series take place on several days the prizes may total up to £150.

Such gaming may take place on premises to which the public have access other than in a street, and payment may be required to obtain access thereto. However these entertainments may not be held on premises licensed or registered under Part II (s. 41, as amended).

PROVISION FOR INSPECTORS AND RIGHTS OF ENTRY AND RELATED RIGHTS (s. 43) – The Gaming Board may appoint inspectors for the purposes of the Act (sub-s. (1)). Gaming Inspectors and constables are empowered to enter and inspect licensed premises, but not registered premises (sub-s. (2)). The holder of a licence under the Act commits an offence if (a) he fails without reasonable excuse to admit an inspector or constable; (b) fails without reasonable excuse to permit an inspector or constable to inspect the premises or any machine or other equipment on the premises; (c) fails, without reasonable excuse, to produce any book or document which the inspector or constable reasonably requires to inspect, and to allow copies to be taken (sub-s. (3)). A justice of the peace who receives information on oath and is satisfied that there are reasonable grounds for suspecting that an offence under this Act has been or is about to be committed, may issue a search warrant authorising any constable, with or without one or more inspectors, to enter premises, if necessary by force, at any time up to 14 days (sub-s. (4)). A constable executing a search warrant may (a) seize and remove anything found on the premises which may be required as evidence, and (b) arrest and search any person found on the premises whom he has reasonable cause to believe to be committing or to have committed any such offence (sub-s. (5)). The Gaming Board and Chief Officers of police are empowered to demand information from licensed and registered clubs and failure to comply will be an offence (sub-ss. (6) (7) and (8)). Fire authorities have rights of entry to licensed premises (sub-s. 9).

"Game of chance" does not include any athletic game or sport, but, with that exception, includes a game of chance and skill combined, and a pretended game of chance or of chance and skill combined. In determining whether a game, which is played otherwise than against one or more other players, is a game of chance and skill combined, the possibility of superlative skill eliminating the element of chance shall be disregarded.

"Gaming" means the playing of a game of chance for winnings in money or money's worth, whether any person playing the game is at risk of losing any money or money's worth or not. Section 52 (3) prevents a lottery permitted by ss. 43 to 45 of the 1963 Act from being prohibited by the law of gaming, in cases where the lottery (a distribution of prizes according to chance) is also a game, and therefore "gaming". Section 52 (4) excludes pool betting from the scope of the gaming law, and s. 52 (5) provides that a machine is not used for gaming if it offers a successful player no more than another turn free or the return of his stake, or a part of it.

CHAPTER 37

PUBLIC ENTERTAINMENTS

	Page
Theatres	529
Sunday Theatre Act	532
Theatrical Employers Registration Act 1925	533
Cinematograph Acts	534
Music, Singing, and Dancing	537
Billiards	539
Ingress and Egress	539
Sunday Entertainments Act 1932	540
Hypnotism Act 1952	541
Safety of Sports Grounds	541

Theatres – The Theatres Act 1968 repealed the Theatres Act 1843, and abolished censorship of the theatre (s. 1).

PROHIBITION OF PRESENTATION OF OBSCENE PERFORMANCES OF PLAYS – For the purposes of this section, a performance of a play shall be deemed to be obscene if, taken as a whole, its effect was such as to tend to deprave and corrupt persons who were likely, having regard to all relevant circumstances, to attend it (s. 2 (1)).

Subject to ss. 3 and 7 of this Act, if an obscene performance of a play is given, whether in public or private, any person who (whether for gain or not) presented or directed that performance will be committing an offence (s. 2 (2)).

No person shall be proceeded against in respect of a performance of a play or anything said or done in the course of such a performance: (a) for an offence at common law where it is of the essence of the offence that the performance or, as the case may be, what was said or done was obscene, indecent, offensive, disgusting or injurious to morality; or (b) for an offence under s. 4 of the Vagrancy Act 1824 consisting of wilfully exposing to public view an indecent exhibition, and no person shall be proceeded against for an offence at common law of conspiring to corrupt public morals, or to do any act contrary to public morals or decency, in respect of an agreement to present or give a performance of a play, or to cause anything to be said or done in the course of such a performance (s. 2 (4)).

DEFENCE OF PUBLIC GOOD – A person shall not be convicted of an offence under s. 2 of this Act if it is proved that the giving of the performance in question was justified as being for the public good on the ground that it was in the interests of drama, opera, ballet or any other art, or of literature or learning (s. 3 (1)).

Section 3 (2) allows expert evidence to be admitted.

INCITEMENT TO RACIAL HATRED BY MEANS OF PUBLIC PERFORMANCE OF A PLAY – Subject to s. 7 of this Act, if there is given a public performance of a play involving the use of threatening, abusive or insulting words, any person who (whether for gain or not) presented or directed that performance shall be guilty of an offence under this section if: (a) he did so with intent to stir up hatred against any section of the public in Great Britain distinguished by colour, race or ethnic or national origins; and (b) that performance, taken as a whole, is likely to stir up hatred against that section on grounds of colour, race or ethnic or national origins (s. 5 (1)).

PROVOCATION OF BREACH OF PEACE BY MEANS OF PUBLIC PERFORMANCE OF A PLAY – Subject to s. 7 of this Act, if there is given a public performance of a play involving the use of threatening, abusive or insulting words or behaviour, any person who (whether for gain or not) presented or directed that performance shall be guilty of an offence under this section if: (a) he did so with intent to provoke a breach of the peace; or (b) the performance, taken as a whole, was likely to occasion a breach of the peace (s. 6 (1)).

Exceptions for performances given in certain circumstances are provided for (s. 7).

RESTRICTION OF INSTITUTION OF PROCEEDINGS – Proceedings for an offence under ss. 2, 5 or 6 of this Act or an offence at common law committed by the publication of defamatory matter in the course of a performance of a play shall not be instituted in England and Wales except by or with the consent of the Attorney-General (s. 8).

The script (if any, including stage directions) on which a performance is based, shall be *prima facie* evidence of what happened in the course of a performance (s. 9).

POWER TO MAKE COPIES OF SCRIPTS – If a police officer of or above the rank of superintendent has reasonable grounds for suspecting: (a) that an offence under ss. 2, 5 or 6 of this Act has been committed by any person in respect of a performance of a play; or (b) that a performance of a play is to be given and that an offence under the said ss. 2, 5, or 6 is likely to be committed by any person in respect of that performance, he may make an order in writing under this section relating to that person and that performance (s. 10 (1)).

Every order made under this section shall be signed by the police officer by whom it is made, shall name the person to whom it relates, and shall describe the performance to which it relates in a manner sufficient to enable that performance to be identified (s. 10 (2)).

Where an order under this section has been made, any police officer, on production if so required of the order: (a) may require the person named in the order to produce, if such a thing exists, an actual script on which the performance was or, as the case may be, will be based; and (b) if such a script is produced to him, may require the person so named to afford him an opportunity of causing a copy thereof to be made (s. 10 (3)).

Any person who without reasonable excuse fails to comply with a requirement under sub-s. (3) above will commit an offence (s. 10 (4)).

Where, in the case of a performance of a play based on a script, a copy of an actual script on which that performance was based has been made by or on behalf of a police officer by virtue of an order under this section relating to that performance; s. 9 (1) of this Act shall apply in relation to that copy as it applies in relation to an actual script on which the performance was based (s. 10 (5)).

LICENSING OF PREMISES FOR PUBLIC PERFORMANCE OF PLAYS – Subject to the following provisions of this Act, no premises, whether or not licensed for the sale of intoxicating or exciseable liquor, shall be used for the public performance of any play except under and in accordance with the terms of a licence granted under this Act by the licensing authority (s. 12 (1)).

A licence shall not be required for any premises under any enactment other than this Act by reason only of the public performance at those premises of a play (s. 12 (2)).

For the purposes of sub-s. (2) above, any music played at any premises by way of introduction to, in any interval between parts of, or by way of conclusion of a performance of a play or in the interval between two such performances shall be treated as forming part of the performance or performances, as the case may be, if the total time taken by music so played on any day amounts to less than one quarter of the time taken by the performance or performances of the play or plays given at the premises on that day (s. 12 (3)).

Schedule 1 to this Act shall have effect with respect to licences under this Act (s. 12 (4)).

Schedule 1 to the Act contains provisions for the grant, renewal and transfer of licences by the licensing authority—in London the Greater London Council and in a district in England and Wales, the district council. An applicant for the grant or transfer of a licence under this Act shall give 21 days' notice of his intention to the licensing authority and the chief officer of police.

ENFORCEMENT – An offence is committed if a public performance of a play is given at premises in respect of which a licence is not in force. Any person concerned in the organisation or management of such a performance, and any other person who knowingly or who had reasonable cause to suspect that the offence would be committed allowed the premises to be used, would be liable (s. 13 (1)).

If performances are held in licensed premises in contravention of the conditions of a licence the licensee, and any other person who knowingly or having a reasonable cause to suspect that the offence would be committed allowed the premises to be used, commit an offence (s. 13 (2))

REVOCATION OF LICENCE – The licensing authority may revoke a licence held by a person convicted of an offence under s. 13 (2) (s. 13 (5)). The appeal procedure is governed by s. 14.

POWERS OF ENTRY AND INSPECTION – If a justice of the peace is satisfied by information on oath that there are reasonable grounds for suspecting, as regards any premises specified in the information: (a) that a performance of a play is to be given at those premises, and that an offence under ss. 2, 5 or 6 of this Act is likely to be committed in respect of that performance; or (b) that an offence under s. 13 (1) of this Act is being or will be committed in respect of those premises, the justice may issue a warrant under his hand empowering any police officer or, in a case falling within para. (b) above, any police officer or authorised officer of the licensing authority at any time within 14 days from the date of the warrant to enter the premises and: (i) in a case falling within para. (a) above, to attend any performance of a play which may be given there; (ii) in a case falling within para. (b) above, to inspect the premises (s. 15 (1)).

For the purpose of enforcing the licensing provisions of s. 13 (2) and Sched. 1, an authorised officer of the licensing authority, or a police officer, is empowered at all reasonable times to enter premises at which he has reason to believe that a performance of a play is being or is about to be given, to check whether the licensing conditions are being complied with (s. 15 (2) and (3)).

OFFENCES BY BODIES CORPORATE – Where an offence has been committed by a body corporate with the consent or connivance or through the neglect of any director, manager, secretary or similar officer these individuals can be prosecuted for the offence, as well as the body corporate (s. 16).

Licensing Act 1964, s. 199 (as amended by Theatres Act 1968, Sched. 2) allows the proprietor of a duly licensed theatre to sell by retail beer, spirits and wine, subject to the local permitted hours, without the necessity of having a justices' licence. However, the proprietor must give notice to the Clerk to the Licensing Justices of his intention to sell intoxicants by retail.

Sunday Theatre Act 1972 – No person shall be guilty of an offence or subject to any penalty under the Sunday Observance

Act 1780 by reason of his having managed conducted, assisted at, or otherwise taken part in or attended or advertised the performance of any play on a Sunday at premises (a) licensed under the Theatres Act 1968; or (b) in respect of which a licensing authority may impose requirements by notice in writing under s. 17 (2) of the Theatre Act 1968 (which relates to plays performed at premises under the authority of letters patent) nor shall the said Act of 1780 apply to those premises by reason of the performance therein of any play on a Sunday (s. 1).

No premises in respect of which a licence under the Theatres Act 1968 is for the time being in force or in respect of which a licensing authority have power to impose conditions in writing under s. 17 (2) of the Theatres Act 1968 shall be used for the public performance of any play on Sunday (a) between the hours of three in the morning and two in the afternoon if the premises are in any part of the inner London area which is designated by an order made for the purposes of this paragraph by the Secretary of State; or (b) between the hours of two in the morning and two in the afternoon if the premises are in any part of England or Wales other than a part of the inner London area so designated (s. 2(1)).

For the purposes of this section premises shall be deemed to be used for the public performance of a play at any time during which members of the public are present in the auditorium of the premises in connection with such a public performance (s. 2 (3)).

Contravention of the provisions of s. 2 is an offence (s. 3).

Theatrical Employers Registration Act 1925 – This Act renders it necessary for every theatrical employer to register with the council of the district in which he resides, and if he has no fixed place of residence he may register with any such council (s. 13).

Every such Registration Authority keeps a register, open to the public inspection on payment of a fee, and every registered theatrical employer is supplied with a certificate of registration (ss. 1 and 4).

"*Theatrical Employer*" means any person who by himself or any agent engages or employs at any one time three or more theatrical performers (s. 13). However, this Act does not apply to:

(1) Any person who has in force a theatre licence or a licence for music and dancing, and

(2) Any person who, not for gain or in the way of business, employs or engages theatrical performers for charitable objects or other similar purposes (s. 11).

"*Theatrical Performer*" includes any actor, singer, dancer, acrobat, or performer employed in any place of public entertainment, or to rehearse with a view to so acting, etc., or to take part in anything being photographed or otherwise recorded as a picture suitable or intended for exhibition by means of a cinematograph or other similar apparatus. It also includes all persons employed or engaged as a chorus or crowd, but does not include stage hands and members of an orchestra (s. 13).

OFFENCES BY A THEATRICAL EMPLOYER UNDER S. 10 OF THE ACT:

(1) To abandon the theatrical performers during the course of their engagement. He will be deemed to have abandoned them if he absents himself without paying all wages and expenses due to them, unless he proves his absence was not with that intent (see s. 5 (2)).

(2) To act as a theatrical employer without being registered.

(3) To supply false, misleading or incorrect particulars to the Registration Authority, or fail to inform that authority of any change of circumstances.

(4) To apply for registration while his registration is suspended or cancelled, but under s. 9 he may apply 3 years after cancellation.

(5) To fail to produce a certificate (if any) or to produce a false certificate, to any court dealing with a charge under this Act.

(6) To apply for registration on behalf of a company or firm of which any person whose registration has been suspended or cancelled is a director, manager, partner, etc. (see s. 5 (1)).

(7) After his registration has been cancelled and has not been renewed, to act as agent for any other theatrical employer

A magistrates' court may fine and imprison for any of the above offences and may also suspend for a period or cancel the registration (s. 6).

A magistrates' court may also cancel or suspend registration when it is satisfied that a theatrical employer has deliberately failed to pay money due to theatrical performers (s. 7).

The Theatrical Employers Registration (Amendment) Act 1928, allows a registration authority to take proceedings for any offence under the 1925 Act, to apply for the suspension or cancellation of a registration, and to oppose the renewal of any cancelled registration. Where an applicant for registration or a registered person has been convicted of any offence involving dishonesty and has been sentenced to prison, the registration authority may refuse his application or cancel or suspend his registration, but if so such person may appeal to a magistrates' court.

Cinematograph Acts – The 1909 Act, as amended and supplemented by the 1952 Act deals with the licensing and safety of cinemas.

Subject to the exceptions in s. 7 of the 1909 Act and to those provided in the 1952 Act, the Acts and Regulations thereunder apply as respects all cinematograph exhibitions whether given by means involving the use of inflammable or non-inflammable films or by means not involving the use of films (s. 1, 1952 Act).

"Cinematograph exhibition" means an exhibition of moving pictures produced on a screen by means which include the projection of light (s. 9, 1952 Act).

No cinematograph exhibition shall be given unless the Safety Regulations are complied with, or, save as otherwise provided by the Act, elsewhere than in premises licensed for the purpose under the Act (s. 1, 1909 Act as amended by Schedule to the 1952 Act).

LICENCES – A district council may grant such licences or their transfers. A licence may be for a year or for a shorter period, and may be subject to any conditions or restrictions as may be prescribed. For a licence or transfer 7 days' written notice to the licensing authority and to the chief officer of police is necessary, but notice for a renewal is not necessary (s. 2, 1909 Act amended by Schedule to the 1952 Act).

Any Act which restricts or regulates premises for public entertainment or amusement shall not apply to premises or ships used, by authority of a Secretary of State or the Admiralty, for officially controlled entertainments and this includes music, etc., plays and cinematograph exhibitions (Revision of the Army and Air Force Acts (Transitional Provisions) Act 1955, s. 4 and Sched. 3).

Music and dancing licences are not required for cinematograph exhibitions which include representations of persons dancing, etc., with accompanying music. Music played on the premises in the introduction or in intervals of such an exhibition shall be treated as music accompanying the exhibition if the time taken is less than one quarter of the total time of the exhibition on that day (s. 7, 1952 Act).

CHILDREN – The licensing authority in granting a licence shall impose conditions or restrictions prohibiting the admission of children (persons under 16, 1952 Act, s. 9) to exhibitions designated as unsuitable for children. The authority should also consider what conditions or restrictions might be imposed on the admission of children to other cinematograph exhibitions showing works designated as of some other description (s. 3, 1952 Act).

Subject to the provisions of this Act no premises shall be used, except with the *consent* of the licensing authority for a cinematograph exhibition organised wholly or mainly as an exhibition for children. The authority may impose special conditions or restrictions on the grant of the consent (s. 4, 1952 Act).

The "consent" is a sort of licence; 7 days' notice is necessary; there are powers of entry; penalties may be incurred, see s. 4, 1952 Act.

At such an exhibition a prescribed number of attendants (aged 16 and over) must be present. At any cinematograph exhibition no child under 5 shall be admitted unless in charge of a person aged 16 or over and no child under 12 shall be admitted after 7 p.m. unless in charge of a person aged 16 or over (Cinematograph (Children) (No. 2) Regs. 1955 which apply to exhibitions other than those in private dwelling houses to which the public are not admitted and exempted exhibitions. See reg. 1).

EXEMPTIONS FROM LICENCE – When such an exhibition is proposed on premises used occasionally and exceptionally only and not more than on 6 days in a year for such purpose a licence will not be necessary if the occupier gives 7 days' notice to the licensing authority and to the chief officer of police and complies with the Safety Regulations and any conditions imposed by the licensing authority (s. 7 (2), 1909 Act). However see Safety Regs. 28 (necessity for licence), and 29 to 34. Also regs. 35 to 42, where inflammable films are used.

Where such an exhibition is proposed in a moveable structure a licence will not be necessary if the owner has a licence for the structure, granted by his own licensing authority and he gives 2 days' written notice to the licensing authority and to the chief officer of police and complies with the Safety Regulations and any conditions imposed by the licensing authority (s. 7 (3), 1909 Act).

However if inflammable films are used the Safety Regs. 1 to 34 will apply and also the requirements in Safety Regs. 35 to 42, if no inflammable films are used.

If such an exhibition is given in a private dwelling house to which the public are not admitted whether on payment or otherwise the 1909 Act (requiring licence) shall not apply (s. 7 (3), 1909 Act). However see Safety Reg. 28 (necessity for licence) and regs. 29 to 34 if inflammable films are used.

"Exempted exhibitions" are those to which the public are not admitted or to which the public are admitted without payment (s. 5, 1952 Act). Several exemptions are allowed by this s. 5, including exemption from licence if the films are non-inflammable, but under Safety Reg. 28, a licence will be necessary if inflammable films are used. This s. 5 should be studied in full.

Also an "exempted organisation", which is one certified as not conducted or established for profit may have an exempted exhibition under the s. 5 of the 1952 Act.

POWERS – A constable or any person appointed by the licensing authority may at all reasonable times enter any premises whether licensed or not, in which he has reason to believe that a cinematograph exhibition is being or is about to be given so as to see that the Acts or Regulations or the conditions of any licence have been complied with.

Any person preventing or obstructing the entry of such constable or person will commit a summary offence (s. 4, 1909 Act).

The owner of apparatus using it or allowing it to be used or the owner of premises allowing premises to be used in contravention of the Acts or Regulations or of the conditions or restrictions of any licence granted, will commit a summary offence punishable by fine (s. 3, 1909 Act). Any person aggrieved by the refusal or revocation of a licence or consent or by any terms, conditions or restrictions imposed may appeal to the Crown Court (s. 6, 1952 Act).

REGULATIONS – The Cinematograph (Safety) Regs. 1955, 1958 and 1965 contain requirements—in Part I (regs. 1 to 27), generally in connection with such exhibitions, *re* seats, exits, attendants, fire, lighting, etc.; in Part II (regs. 28 to 34), additional where inflammable films are used; in Part III (regs. 35 to 42) where premises are so used only occasionally; in Part IV (regs. 43 to 47), in connection with television exhibitions; in Part V (regs. 48 to 51), miscellaneous.

The Cinematograph Films (Animals) Act 1937, prohibits the public exhibition of film scenes involving cruelty to animals.

Music, Singing and Dancing – The general rule is that it is necessary for any person who habitually keeps or uses any house, room, garden or other place, for public dancing, singing, music or other entertainment of the like kind, to have a licence for music and dancing.

The requirements of the law vary according to the locality, as follows:

(1) London and the surrounding area within 20 miles, including Surrey. Within this area licences are necessary and are issued by the Local Councils concerned.

(2) The rest of England and Wales over 20 miles distant from London and outside Surrey. In areas where Part IV of the Public Health Acts Amendment Act 1890, has been adopted, or in areas where local Acts or Orders on the subject are in force, licences are required. In other parts of the country licences are not necessary. See Paterson's Licensing Acts, Chap. 15.

Public Health Acts Amendment Act 1890, Part IV, s. 51, requires that any house, room, garden, or other place, whether licensed or not for the sale of intoxicants, shall not be kept or used for public dancing, singing, music or other public entertainment of the like kind, without a licence for the purpose from the justices. The justices, sitting in licensing sessions, may grant, transfer or renew licences for a year or less period, under such terms and conditions and subject to such restrictions as they may determine. Premises licensed for the sale of liquor will not need a music and dancing licence for recorded music, or wireless or television broadcasts, or for music or singing by not more than two performers (Licensing Act 1964, s. 182).

Applicants for new licences or for transfers must give 14 days notice to the Clerk of the Justices and to the chief of police. No notice need be given of an application for renewal of a licence. Justices in petty sessions may grant without notice a temporary licence for a period not exceeding 14 days. A notice showing the purpose for which it is licensed must be kept posted on the door or entrance of every place so licensed, and such premises must not be opened for such purpose except on the days and during the hours stated in the licence.

Any house or place kept or used for any of these purposes without a licence shall be deemed a disorderly house and the occupier is liable to a fine of £5 per day. As regards the right to prosecute, see "Public Health Acts", Chap. 39. If a licence holder breaks or disregards any of the terms or conditions on which his licence was granted, he is liable to a fine of £20 and a daily penalty of £5, and his licence may be revoked.

Under the Sunday Observance Act 1780, any house, room, or other place opened or used for public entertainment or amusement on Sunday, and to which persons are admitted on payment, may be deemed a disorderly house or place. (But the performance of plays in licensed theatres on a Sunday is no longer an offence—Sunday Theatres Act 1972.) The persons responsible may be liable to summary prosecution under s. 51 of the Public Health Acts Amendment Act 1890, if the section is in force in the locality. But see "Sunday Entertainments", later.

A licence is not required for public singing, dancing, music, stage plays or cinema exhibitions in authorised naval, military and air force recreation rooms, which may be so used on any day (Revision of Army and Air Force Acts (Transitional Provisions) Act 1955, s. 4 and Sched. 3). If a public swimming bath is used for public music, dancing, stage plays, cinematograph exhibition or other public entertainment of the like kind, the necessary licence must be obtained (Public Health Act 1936, s. 226).

The Private Places of Entertainment (Licensing) Act 1967, provides for the licensing of certain private places of entertainment promoted for gain. It is an adoptive Act, and the areas in which it can be adopted are those in which various public and general or local Acts are in force, regulating the provision of public music, dancing or entertainment of the like kind. The licensing authority may make it a condition of the licence that the police shall have a right of entry into the premises.

Billiards – A billiard licence under the Gaming Act 1845, is necessary for every house, room, or place, kept for public billiard playing or where a public billiard table or bagatelle board or instrument of like kind is kept at which persons are admitted to play, except in the case of a fully licensed public house, which under this Act is not required to have a billiard licence.

Gaming Act 1845, s. 10: The justices may grant billiard licences at the usual general annual licensing meeting. Notice similar to that given in liquor licensing applications is necessary in the case of a grant or transfer. The licence is for a year, and no notice is required for a renewal.

S. 11: Any person keeping a public billiard table or bagatelle board or like instrument without being duly licensed so to do and not holding a public house licence for the premises shall be liable to the penalties provided by paragraphs (a) and (b) of sub-s. (1) of s. 56 of the Betting, Gaming and Lotteries Act 1963, or any person so licensed for billiards who does not keep the words "licensed for billiards" near the door and on the outside of his premises, is liable to a fine of £10.

S. 12: A licensee is liable to summary punishment for any breach of the conditions of his licence. The conditions include the prevention of drunkenness or other disorderly conduct on the premises.

S. 13: A licensee (who is not the holder of an on-licence) having a public billiard table must not allow any person to play at such table or instrument between 1 a.m. and 8 a.m. or at any time on Sundays, Christmas Day, Good Friday, or any days of public fast or thanksgiving. However, a publican having a public billiard table may allow play on such table on the days mentioned, but not between 1 a.m. and 8 a.m. on any day (Licensing Act 1964, s. 182).

S. 14 authorises the police to enter at any time any house, room, or place, where any public billiard table or instrument of the like kind is kept for play, and it is a summary offence to refuse admittance. See "Billiards", Chap. 38.

Ingress and Egress – Under the Public Health Act 1936, s. 59, certain public and other buildings shall have such means of ingress and egress and passages or gangways as the Local Authority deem satisfactory, regard being had by them to the purposes for which the building is intended to be, or is, used, and the number of persons likely to resort thereto at any one time.

These buildings include—any theatre and any hall, etc., used as a place of public resort; any restaurant, shop, store or warehouse to which the public are admitted and in which more than twenty persons are employed; any club which should be registered under the Licensing Act 1961; any school not exempted;

any church or place of public worship dating before 1890, or exempt before this Act.

(The section does not apply to a private house to which the public are admitted occasionally or exceptionally).

For reasons of safety a magistrates' court may order the closing of any such building. The person having control of any such building must secure that the means of ingress and egress and the passages and gangways are kept free and unobstructed while persons are assembled in the building.

Children and Young Persons Act 1933, s. 12: Where an entertainment for children or at which the majority of the audience are children, is given in any building not a private dwelling-house, and over one hundred children attend, there must be a sufficient number of adult attendants so as to take sufficient precautions for the safety of the children. A constable may enter any building in which he has reason to believe such an entertainment is being or is about to be held, so as to see that this section is complied with, and an officer so authorised by the authority which licenses entertainments has the like power of entering premises so licensed.

This section applies to the whole country.

Sunday Entertainments Act 1932 as amended by the Sunday Cinema Act 1972 – The licensing authority for cinemas may permit licensed cinemas to be opened and used on Sundays, subject to conditions that the employees have not been employed on each of the previous 6 days either by the employer in any occupation or by any other employer in connection with similar entertainments, and to any other conditions that the authority think fit to impose. Breach of any condition is punishable summarily (s. 1).

This section also applies s. 4 of the Cinematograph Act 1909 (given previously), and therefore a constable has power of entry.

A licensing authority is empowered to grant licences in respect of musical entertainments (that is, concerts of music with or without singing or recitation, s. 5), on Sundays and to attach special conditions thereto (s. 3).

No person shall be guilty of an offence or subject to any penalty under the Sunday Observance Act 1780, by reason of his connection with the holding of any cinema entertainment allowed under this Act; any musical entertainment licensed under this Act or otherwise authorised; any museum, picture gallery, zoological or botanical garden or aquarium; or any lecture or debate (s. 4).

NOTE ON SUNDAY OBSERVANCE ACTS – The 1625 Act ordered fines on persons attending plays or other unlawful pastimes on Sundays. The 1667 Act prohibited tradesmen, etc., from working at their ordinary callings (except from charity or necessity), or publicly selling goods on Sundays (but see "Shops", Chap. 32).

The 1780 Act prescribed penalties for the Sunday opening or using for public entertainment or amusement or for debating, of any house, room or other place to which persons are admitted for payment. Such a house or place is to be deemed a disorderly house. The advertising of same is also an offence. By s. 1 of the Sunday Theatre Act 1972 the performance of plays in licensed Theatres on a Sunday is no longer an offence. But s. 2 of the Act restricts the hours on which plays can take place on Sundays.

Hypnotism Act 1952 – Where an authority has power to grant licences for public music, singing and dancing (see previously) it has power to attach to the licence conditions regulating or prohibiting hypnotism on any person at the licensed place (s. 1).

No person shall perform hypnotism on any living person at any public entertainment at any unlicensed place unless authorised by the authority to grant music, etc., licences in the area, or by the council of the district in a place where there is no authority having power to grant music, etc., licences (s. 2). This does not apply to an exhibition, demonstration or performance of hypnotism that takes place in the course of the performance of a play within the meaning of the Theatres Act 1968 (s. 2 (1A), added by Theatres Act 1968, Sched. 2).

It will be a summary offence to hypnotise any person under 18 at any public entertainment (s. 3 as amended by Sched. 1, Family Law Reform Act 1969).

"Hypnotism" includes mesmerism and any similar process to produce induced sleep or trance in any person but does not include self induced hypnotism (s. 6).

Any police constable may enter any premises where any entertainment is held on reasonable cause to believe that a breach of the Act is being or may be done (s. 4).

Safety of Sports Grounds Act 1975 – The Secretary of State may by order designate as a stadium requiring a "safety certificate" any sports stadium which in his opinion has accommodation for more than 10,000 spectators (s. 1). A person authorised by (a) the local authority, (b) the Chief Officer of Police, (c) the building authority, or (d) the Secretary of State may, on production of his authority, enter a sports ground at any reasonable time, and make such inspection of it and such enquiries relating to it as he considers necessary for the purposes of this Act, and in particular may examine records of attendance at the ground and records relating to the maintenance of safety at the ground and take copies of such record (s. 11).

CHAPTER 38

LIQUOR LICENSING LAWS

	Page
Licensed Premises and Intoxicating Liquor	542
Justices' Licences	543
Excise Licences and Law	543
Occasional Licence	545
Hotel	545
Restaurants and Guest Houses	546
Billiards	547
Sale of Tobacco	548
Billeting	548
Music, etc.	548
The Licensing Justices	548
Grant of Licences	548
Renewal of Licences	549
Transfer of Licences	550
Removal of a Licence	551
Appeal	551
Register of Licences	551
Disqualified Persons and Premises	552
Permitted Hours	552
Extended Hours	555
Seasonal Licences	556
Exemption Order	556
Compulsory Closing	556
The Licensed Premises	556
Conduct of Licensed Premises	557
Sale of Intoxicants	558
Offences, not of Drunkenness, by non-licensed Persons	560
Prosecution	561
Police Powers of Entry	562
Drunkenness	562
Clubs	565
Seamen's Canteens	568
Late Night Refreshment Houses	568
Licensing, New Towns	570
Methylated Spirits	570

Licensed Premises and Intoxicating Liquor – A person must not sell intoxicating liquor, by retail, unless he holds a justices' licence, an occasional licence or canteen licence authorising him to do so, and he must not so sell or expose for sale except at the place authorised by the justices' licence or canteen licence (Licensing Act 1964, s. 160).

It is the duty of the police to enforce the provisions of the Licensing Acts, which provide for the licensing of premises by the justices, for the regulation of such licensed premises, and for the orderly conduct of persons in connection with licensed premises and intoxicants.

The most important of these Acts are the Licensing Acts of 1872, 1902 and 1964.

In this chapter, "1964" indicates the Licensing Act 1964, and "club" means registered club.

"Intoxicating Liquor" means spirits, wine, beer, cider, and any other fermented, distilled or spirituous liquor, but (apart from cider) does not include any liquor for the sale of which by wholesale no excise licence is required.

"Cider" includes perry.

"Wine" means any liquor obtained from the alcoholic fermentation of fresh grapes or the must of fresh grapes, whether or not fortified or flavoured, and includes "made-wine", defined as any liquor obtained from the fermentation of any substance or by mixing such a liquor with any other liquor, but not including beer, black beer, spirits or non-excisable cider (1964, s. 201, as amended by Finance (No. 2) Act 1975, Sched. 3).

"Licensed Premises" under these Acts are regarded as premises in respect of which a justices' licence or an occasional licence is in force, and as including a reference to any premises in respect of which a notice under s. 199 (c) is in force (1964, s. 200, as amended by Finance Act 1967, Sched. 7 and Theatres Act 1968, Sched. 2).

The justices may grant a licence for premises within the area of their jurisdiction authorising the sale thereon by retail of some specified kind or kinds of intoxicating liquor. Such premises will then be "licensed premises".

Justices' Licences – Section 1 (3) of the Licensing Act 1964, as amended by the Finance Act 1967, limits the kinds of justices' licences to: (a) on-licences authorising the sale of (1) intoxicating liquor of all descriptions, (2) beer, cider and wine only, (3) beer and cider only, (4) cider only and (5) wine only; and (b) off-licences authorising the sale of (1) intoxicating liquor of all descriptions, and (2) beer, cider and wine only.

Any of the licences mentioned above and also justices' licences for clubs may be granted as a 7-day licence, or as a 6-day licence (viz. to be kept closed on Sundays) or as an early closing licence (viz. to close at night one hour earlier than the usual closing hour), or as a 6-day and early closing licence (1964, s. 65).

Forgery of a justices' licence or knowingly tendering a forged licence is a serious offence (1964, s. 36).

Excise Licences and Law – The Customs and Excise Act 1952, has consolidated with amendments much of the law relating to customs and excise.

Section 5: It will be the duty of every constable and every member of H.M. Armed Forces or coastguard to assist in the enforcement of the law relating to any assigned matter (that is every duty which by law has to be performed by the Customs and Excise, s. 307).

Obstruction of or interference with any person acting under the Act is a serious offence and the offender may be detained (s. 10).

The Finance Act 1967, abolished retail excise licences for the sale or supply of intoxicants. However excise licences are required in the following cases:

(1) A distiller's excise licence for the manufacture of spirits (s. 93). The unlawful making of spirits incurs a heavy penalty and any person found in the premises or place may be detained (s. 106) by a constable, etc. (s. 274). On reasonable grounds of suspicion that a still, spirits, etc., are unlawfully in any building or place a constable may obtain a justices' search warrant and remove same (s. 296).

(2) An excise licence for the brewing of beer (ss. 125 to 138).

(3) No person shall make made wine (as defined above) for sale unless he holds an excise licence for that purpose (ss. 139 to 142).

(4) No person shall deal wholesale in spirits, beer, wine or British wine without an excise licence in respect of any such liquor.

Dealing wholesale means the sale at any one time to any one person of quantities not less than:

(a) spirits, wine or made wine—2 gallons or one case;
(b) beer—4½ gallons or 2 cases (s. 146 as amended by Weights and Measures Act 1963, s. 59).

"Case" means one dozen units each not less than 23 nor more than 28 fluid ounces, or the equivalent of that number of such units made up wholly or partly of containers of a larger or smaller size.

(5) An excise wholesale dealer's licence (s. 146), authorises sale by retail if the premises are exclusively used for the sale of intoxicating liquor and mineral waters and there is no internal communication with any other business premises and the sale by retail is to a person lawfully carrying on a business of selling intoxicants by retail, or to a mess or registered club or for delivery outside Great Britain or to a person engaged in any business carried on by the retailer (Licensing Act 1964, s. 181 as amended by Finance Act 1967, Sched. 7).

An excise licence is not necessary for the sale wholesale of black beer; perfumes; flavouring essences not for intoxicants; spirits, wine or sweets so medicated as to be medicines; any liquor under specified gravity or proof limits (s. 157); or liqueur chocolates (1964, s. 167).

Selling by retail means the sale at any one time to any one person of quantities not exceeding:

(a) spirits, wines or made wine—2 gallons or one case;
(b) beer or cider—4½ gallons or 2 cases.

Section 296: A customs and excise officer who has a writ of assistance or a justices' search warrant may enter a place and if necessary break into it, search and remove anything liable to forfeiture under the Act, but entry shall not be made by night (between 11 p.m. and 5 a.m., s. 307) except in the company of a constable.

Section 297: On reasonable suspicion that any vehicle or vessel is carrying any goods which are chargeable with any duty not paid or which are being unlawfully removed or which are liable to forfeiture under the Acts, a customs and excise officer or constable or member of H.M. armed forces or coastguard may stop and search such vehicle or vessel.

Occasional Licence – On giving 24 hours' notice or more to the chief officer of police, the holder of a justices' on-licence (other than the holder of a residential licence) may apply to the local court of petty sessions for two justices' consent to the grant of an occasional licence for a place other than his licensed premises.

The justices may consent to the licence for a period not exceeding 3 weeks at one time, and between such hours as may be specified in the occasional licence. The licence shall not authorise the sale of intoxicants on Christmas Day or Good Friday or any day of public fast or thanksgiving. It may be granted on Sundays (except in parts of Wales where there are no permitted hours for licensed premises on Sundays).

The justices may grant a licence without a hearing if written application is made at least a month before the occasion for which a licence is required, and provided there is no objection by the police. An occasional licence may not be granted to the holder of a residential licence, but may be granted to the holder of a restaurant licence or "combined licence" if the justices are satisfied that the sale of liquor will be ancillary to the provision of substantial refreshment.

An occasional licence ceases to have effect if the parent justices' licence itself lapses (Licensing Act 1964, s. 180, as amended by Finance Act 1967, Sched. 7).

The Licensing Act 1964, ss. 179 and 200 apply the following sections to occasional licences: ss. 172–178, and s. 12, Licensing Act 1872.

Hotel – Under s. 1, Hotel Proprietors Act 1956, an hotel is an establishment which offers food, drink and if so required sleeping accommodation, without special contract, to any traveller who appears able and willing to pay a reasonable sum for what is provided and who is in a fit state to be received.

Under s. 2, the proprietor of an hotel will not be liable for loss or damage to property brought to the hotel except where at the time of the loss or damage sleeping accommodation had been engaged for the traveller and if occurred during the period for which the traveller was a guest (midnight to midnight). Such liability does not extend to vehicles or property therein or to animals.

Such liability will not exceed £50 for one article or £100 in the aggregate except where it was due to the default, etc., of the proprietor or where it was expressly deposited for safe custody or where such deposit was refused, etc. However the prescribed notice (in Schedule to the Act) limiting the liability of the proprietor should be conspicuously displayed in the hotel.

Such an hotel within the meaning of the Act shall be deemed to be an inn (s. 1).

An inn is a house of entertainment for travellers.

Restaurants and Guest Houses – *Restaurant Licence.*— This is a licence which is granted for premises structurally adapted and *bona fide* used, or intended to be used, for habitually providing the customary main meal at mid-day or in the evening, or both, for the accommodation of persons frequenting the premises. Intoxicating liquor shall not be sold or supplied on the premises otherwise than to persons taking table meals there and for consumption by such a person as an ancillary to his meal (1964, s. 94 (1)).

"Table meal" means a meal eaten by a person seated at a table, or at a counter or other structure which serves the purpose of a table and is not used for the service of refreshments for consumption by persons not seated at a table or structure serving the purpose of a table (1964, s. 201).

RESIDENTIAL LICENCE – This is a licence granted for premises *bona fide* used, or intended to be used, for the purpose of habitually providing for reward board and lodging, including breakfast and one other of the customary main meals. Intoxicating liquor shall not be sold or supplied on the premises otherwise than to persons residing there or their private friends *bona fide* entertained by them at their own expense, and for consumption by such a person or his private friend either on the premises or with a meal supplied at, but to be consumed off the premises (e.g. a picnic-lunch) (1964, s. 94 (2)).

A person shall be treated as residing in the premises although he sleeps in a separate building, provided it is an annex occupied and managed with the premises (1964, s. 201).

RESTAURANT AND RESIDENTIAL LICENCE – (In this chapter this is called a "combined licence"): This is a licence granted for premises which satisfy the conditions for a residential and a restaurant licence, as above. Intoxicating liquor shall not be sold or supplied otherwise than as permitted by the conditions of a restaurant licence or of a residential licence (1964, s. 94 (3)).

It is an implied condition of any restaurant, residential or "combined" licence that suitable beverages other than intoxicating liquor (including drinking water) shall be equally available for consumption with or otherwise as an ancillary to meals served therein (1964, s. 94 (5)).

Licensing justices when granting a new residential or "combined" licence, unless it appears to them that there is a good reason for not doing so, must attach a condition that there shall be afforded in the premises an adequate sitting room for the use of paying guests. This room must not be used for sleeping accommodation, for the service of meals or the supply or consumption of intoxicating liquor (1964, s. 96).

Licensing justices may refuse an application for the grant or renewal of a restaurant, residential or "combined" licence on any of the following grounds: (a) that the applicant is under 21 or is not a fit and proper person, (b) that the premises are not qualified, or are not suitable and convenient for the use contemplated, (c) that within 12 months preceding the application (i) a justices' on-licence for the premises has been forfeited, or (ii) the premises have been ill-conducted while a justices' on-licence or a refreshment house licence was in force, or (iii) the required condition as to sitting accommodation has been habitually broken, or (iv) the condition as to the availability of beverages other than intoxicating liquor has been habitually broken (1964, s. 98 (1)).

The licensing justices may also refuse an application for the grant of a restaurant or "combined" licence if the trade done in the premises in providing refreshment to persons resorting there (excluding residents) does not habitually consist to a substantial extent in providing table meals of a kind to which the consumption of intoxicating liquor might be ancillary (1964, s. 98 (2)).

Licensing justices may also refuse an application for the grant of a restaurant, residential, or "combined" licence on the ground that the sale or supply of intoxicating liquor on the premises is undesirable—(a) in the case either of a residential or "combined" licence because a large proportion of the paying guests or diners is habitually made up of young persons unaccompanied, or (b) in the case either of a restaurant or "combined" licence because a large proportion of the persons resorting to the premises, but not provided with board and lodging, is habitually made up of young persons unaccompanied, or (c) because the contemplated provision of intoxicants would be by "self-service" methods, i.e. any method allowing a customer to help himself on payment or before payment. "Young person unaccompanied" means a person under 18 years who is not accompanied and paid for by his parent or by a person of full age (1964, s. 98(3)).

Billiards – A person who holds a publican's licence (i.e. who is fully licensed) may have public billiard tables in his licensed premises without having to take out a billiard licence. He must not allow play thereat between 1 a.m. and 8 a.m. (Gaming Act 1845, s. 13, Licensing Act 1964, s. 182 (2)). See "Billiards" Chap. 37.

Sale of Tobacco – A licensee may take out an excise licence for the sale of tobacco (Customs and Excise Act 1952, ss. 173 to 194). The Shops Act 1950, prescribes closing hours and closing times for shops, but exemption is allowed for shops whose business is the sale of tobacco and smokers' requisites and which may be open for customers during "closing hours" and on Sundays. Also tobacco may be sold to the audience in theatres, etc., and in liquor licensed premises during permitted hours. See "Shops", Chap. 32.

Billeting – Licensed premises are liable, under s. 155 of the Army Act 1955, to have soldiers billeted (or lodged) in them. See "Billeting", Chap. 30.

Music, etc. – In urban districts where Part IV of the Public Health Acts Amendment Act 1890, is in force, any place used for public music, singing, etc., must be licensed by the justices. This applies to premises licensed under the Licensing Acts, and public music, etc., must not be given on such premises unless the necessary additional licence has been obtained. See "Music, Singing and Dancing", Chap. 37.

However, the licensee may have a piano to be used by his customers, etc., but if the room or place is used for the regular musical entertainment, etc., of the public, he should procure a licence allowing such use but such a licence is not required for wireless or television or recorded music or musical performance by one or two performers (Licensing Act 1964, s. 182 (1)).

The Licensing Justices (a committee of the justices of the district) deal with the licensing of houses for the sale of intoxicants, but any offence against the Licensing Laws is brought before justices sitting in an ordinary magistrates' court, as the licensing justices are not a summary court (*Boulter* v. *Kent JJ.* (1897)). At one time it was considered that licensing justices had no power to state a case, but in *Jeffrey* v. *Evans* (1964) the divisional court held that they could. This decision was approved by the Court of Appeal in *R.* v. *East Riding Quarter Sessions* (1967).

Grant of Licences – Under the Licensing Act 1964, new licences may be granted at any licensing sessions (s. 2). Licences normally last for 12 months from 5 April unless forfeited for misconduct (s. 26). A provisional new on-licence may be granted for premises about to be constructed or in course of construction, but when the building is completed a final order must be obtained (1964, s. 6).

An applicant for a new licence must—

(1) Give 21 days' written notice to the Clerk to the Justices; the Chief Officer of Police; the Local Authority (in an urban parish, the clerk to the rating authority; in a borough included in a rural district, the town clerk as well as the clerk to the rating authority; and in a rural parish, the clerk of the parish council or chairman of the parish meeting), and to the fire authority. This notice should give applicant's name, address and occupation during the 6 months preceding (1964, Sched. 2).

(2) Not more than 28 days before the licensing sessions, display notice of his application for a period of 7 days in a place on or near the place to be licensed, where it can conveniently be read, or if the application is for a provisional grant, on or near the proposed site;

(3) Advertise his application in a local newspaper between 2 and 4 weeks of the hearing.

(4) Deposit a plan of the premises with the Clerk to the Licensing Justices if an on-licence is sought.

The applicant shall attend the hearing in person if so required by the licensing justices, who may compel the attendance of witnesses or the production of documents. The application may be opposed by any person. Evidence will be given and the licensing justices will give their decision, granting it with or without conditions or refusing it (1964, Sched. 2). A person aggrieved by a decision or order of the licensing justices may appeal to the Crown Court (1964, s. 21).

A licence lasts from the time of grant to the end of the licensing year (i.e. April 4), or if granted during the last 3 months of the licensing year, until the end of the following licensing year (1964, s. 26).

Renewal of Licences – An annual justices' licence expires annually, and its holder, if he wishes to remain licensed, should apply for its renewal. Licences may be renewed at any licensing meeting, but the holders need not attend unless objection is made to the renewal. Notice of intention to oppose the renewal of a licence may be given by any person. Such notice should be in writing and should contain the grounds of opposition. It should be served on the holder of the licence not less than 7 days previous to the licensing sessions (1964, s. 7).

Even if no written notice of objection has been served, verbal objection may be made at the licensing sessions and the justices may adjourn the consideration of the matter to another day (1964, s. 7). Usually opposition to renewal comes from the police on the ground of misconduct or from the licensing justices on the ground of redundancy (viz. too many licensed premises in the locality). Before renewing an on-licence the justices may require plans of the premises and may, on renewal, order structural alterations necessary for the proper conduct of the business (1964, s. 19) and there may be appeal to the Crown Court against such an order (1964, s. 21).

The renewal of an "old" justices on-licence which existed on August 15, 1904, and of an old beerhouse licence in force on May 1, 1869, cannot be refused except on the grounds specified in the Act, viz. misconduct, etc., of the applicant, or the disorderly, etc., character of the premises (1964, s. 12).

All evidence with respect to the renewal of a licence must be given on oath (1964, s. 7). Evidence regarding the grant or transfer of a licence may not be on oath if the justices so decide.

A "term" licence for a period up to 7 years did not need annual renewal, but when it expires a new licence has to be applied for if required (1964, Sched. 14). Existing "term" licences will run their course but no new ones may be granted.

Transfer of Licences – A transfer means the substitution of one person for another, as holder of the justices' licence for a certain premises. The licensing justices—sitting in transfer sessions (viz. from 4 to 8 special meetings for the purpose each year) or in a General Annual Licensing Meeting—may authorise the transfer of a justices' licence in respect to certain premises to one person in substitution for another person who holds or has held the licence.

Transfer may be granted only in the following cases:

(1) Death of licence holder.

(2) Where the licence holder becomes incapable through illness or other infirmity.

(3) Bankruptcy of licence holder.

(4) Where licence holder has given up or is about to give up his occupation of the premises.

(5) Wilful neglect or omission of occupier of premises (who is about to quit the premises) to apply for a renewal.

(6) Where the licence has been forfeited or its holder disqualified and the owner of the premises has obtained a protection order to carry on the business.

(7) Where the licence is in suspense.

The new licensee must be a fit and proper person to hold a licence (1964, s. 3).

A person desirous of obtaining the transfer of a licence must give 21 days' written notice to the clerk to the justices, the chief officer of police, the Local Authority (in an urban parish, the clerk of the rating authority; in a borough included in a rural district, the town clerk as well as the clerk to the rating authority; and in a rural parish, the clerk of the parish council or chairman of the parish meeting).

This notice should give applicant's name, address and occupation during the 6 months preceding (1964, Sched. 2).

This notice is usually accompanied by a character paper signed by 5 ratepayers, and the police should verify these signatures and report to the justices regarding applicant's character.

On death or bankruptcy of the licensee or appointment of a trustee, his personal representative or trustee may carry on the business until the next licensing sessions but one (1964, s. 10).

If the transfer of a licence becomes necessary, owing to death, forfeiture, etc., the justices in petty sessions may grant **a protection order** (or temporary transfer) enabling the applicant to carry on business pending the grant of a transfer at the usual licensing sessions. Such an order would enable the owner of the premises or his agent to preserve the licence if the licence holder has forfeited his licence. For such an order a week's written notice to the police (or shorter notice or no notice in case of emergency) will be sufficient. This protection order is made by endorsement on the existing licence (1964, ss. 10 and 11).

Removal of a Licence – This means the removal of a justices' licence from the premises in respect of which it was granted, to other premises. Such a removal may be either special or ordinary. A "special removal" may be applied for when licensed premises are to be pulled down or occupied for any public purpose, or are rendered unfit for licensed purposes by fire, tempest or other unavoidable calamity. The procedure resembles a renewal (1964, s. 15).

An ordinary removal may be applied for when the licensee wishes to carry on his licensed business in other premises, and the procedure is similar to that to be observed when a person applies for a new licence (1964, s. 5 and Sched. 2).

There may be a provisional grant of an ordinary removal to premises about to be constructed (1964, s. 6).

No licence shall be granted by way of removal of a restaurant, residential or "combined" licence. (1964, s. 93).

Appeal – Any person aggrieved by the refusal or grant of a renewal, transfer, or special removal of a justices' licence or by an order for structural alterations on renewal of licence may appeal to the Crown Court (1964, s. 21).

If a licensee appeals against forfeiture of his licence on conviction, the convicting court may grant a temporary licence until the appeal ends (1964, s. 189).

Register of Licences – The Clerk of the Licensing Justices (who is the clerk of petty sessions) keeps a register of all justices' licences granted in the district. This register contains particulars of each licence, convictions of the holders for licensing offences and other matters relating to the licence. The police may inspect this register without payment (1964, ss. 28 to 35).

Disqualified Persons and Premises – The following are disqualified from holding a justices' licence:

(1) Any Sheriff's officer or officer executing the legal process of any court.

(2) Any person convicted of forging a justices' licence or of knowingly using a forged justices' licence, or of permitting his licensed premises to be used as a brothel (1964, s. 9).

(3) Any person during the period he was ordered to be disqualified on conviction for selling intoxicating liquor without a justices' licence (1964, s. 160).

(4) Any person disqualified under any other Act—for example, a licensed pilot, a person convicted of harbouring thieves.

(5) Premises on land acquired for the provision of facilities in connection with a "special" road (1964, s. 9).

The court has power to disqualify for restaurant, etc., licences on conviction of certain offences (1964, s. 100; as amended by the Refreshment Houses Act 1964).

Permitted Hours – The Licensing Act 1964 provides that intoxicants may be sold or supplied in any licensed premises or club for consumption on or off the premises, during certain hours, which are called the "permitted hours."

During the other hours of the day it is an offence to supply or sell or consume or take away any intoxicant (1964, s. 59). This provision applies to licensed premises and registered clubs but it does not prohibit or restrict:

(a) sale or supply to or consumption by, residents in the premises;

(b) ordering or dispatching intoxicants for consumption off the premises;

(c) sale to a trader for his trade or to a registered club for the club;

(d) sale or supply to any canteen (Government or Naval authorised, s. 201) or mess (authorised Naval, Military or Air Force, s. 201) (1964, s. 63);

(e) sale in international airports (1964, s. 87);

(f) during the first 10 minutes after the end of any period forming part of the permitted hours—

(i) the consumption on the premises of intoxicating liquor supplied during those hours,
or,

(ii) the taking from the premises of intoxicating liquor so supplied, and not supplied or taken away in an open vessel (1964, s. 63);

(g) during the first half hour after the end of any such period the consumption on the premises by persons taking meals if intoxicating liquor was supplied during those hours for consumption as an ancillary to their meals (1964, s. 63);

(h) where there is a "special hours certificate" for music and dancing, consumption on the premises during the first half hour after the end of those hours of intoxicating liquor supplied during those hours (1964, s. 76);

(i) the taking of intoxicating liquor from the premises by a resident;

(j) the supply of intoxicating liquor for consumption on the premises to any private friends of a resident who are *bona fide* entertained by him at his own expense, or the consumption of intoxicating liquor by persons so supplied;

(k) the supply of intoxicating liquor for consumption on the premises to persons employed there or the consumption of liquor so supplied if it is supplied at the expense of the employer or manager (1964, s. 63);

(l) in licensed premises with an extended hours order the consumption of intoxicants during the first half hour after the entertainment ends of intoxicants supplied before it ends (1964, s. 70).

The permitted hours in licensed premises on weekdays shall be 11 a.m. to 3 p.m. and 5.30 p.m. to 10.30 p.m. On Sundays, Christmas Day and Good Friday, the permitted hours are 12 noon to 2 p.m. and 7 p.m. to 10.30 p.m. In the metropolis and in any other licensing district where the justices decide, permitted hours may continue till 11 p.m. The licensing justices may modify the permitted hours so that the total number of hours on any weekday shall be 9 ending at 10.30 p.m., or 9½ ending at 11 p.m., but the hours shall not begin before 10 a.m. and there must be a single break of 2 hours in the afternoon (1964, s. 60).

The justices have power to grant variations in the permitted hours during periods of the year, or even on different days of the week (1964, s. 61).

In off-licensed premises the permitted hours on weekdays may begin at 8.30 a.m. and continue without any break until 10.30 p.m. (or 11 p.m. if on-licensed premises in the area are permitted to remain open till that time). On Sundays, Christmas Day and Good Friday, the permitted hours for off-licensed premises will be the same as the permitted hours for on-licensed premises in the area (1964, s. 60).

On the application of the holder of an on-licence, the justices may insert a condition in the licence (if they are satisfied that the premises are structurally adapted for the purpose) that a specified separate part of the premises shall be used exclusively for off-licence sales. Sales of intoxicants for consumption off the premises may take place in this separate part during the hours permitted for off-licensed premises so long as the off-sales department is not connected by any internal communication open to customers with a part of the premises used for on-sales (1964, s. 86).

As a result of a poll held under 1964 Act, s. 66, there are no permitted hours for licensed premises on Sundays in some districts in Wales).

Licensed premises need not be open for the sale of intoxicating liquor or for any other purpose during the permitted hours, unless they are obliged to do so by a condition attached to the licence (1964, s. 90).

For premises similarly qualified the permitted hours for luncheon guests may be extended to 3 p.m. where the permitted hours fall short of 3 p.m. (e.g. Sundays, Christmas Day and Good Friday when the morning period ends at 2 p.m.). A notice of such extensions shall be conspicuously posted in the premises (1964, s. 89).

The permitted hours in registered clubs are given later under "Clubs".

Where the licensing justices are satisfied that the licensed premises are structurally adapted and *bona fide* used or intended to be used for habitually providing substantial refreshment for persons frequenting the premises, the permitted hours may have an added hour at the end of the evening (supper hour extension) during the time the licensee applies the section to his premises after he has given 14 days' notice to the chief of police and until April 4 in any year. During the said hour intoxicants are to be supplied only for consumption at a meal in a part of the premises usually set apart for the service of persons taking such meals. For other parts of the premises the normal permitted hours apply (1964, ss. 68 and 69).

The licensing justices may grant a "special hours certificate" to an hotel or restaurant which has a music and dancing licence and is structurally adapted and *bona fide* used or intended to be used for music and dancing and substantial refreshment is supplied to which intoxicants are ancillary (1964, s. 77).

In such case the permitted hours will be 12.30 p.m. to 3 p.m. and 6. 30 p.m. to 2 a.m. next morning or 3 a.m. in the metropolis. On any day on which music and dancing is not provided after midnight the permitted hours must stop at midnight. On any day that music and dancing ends between midnight and 2 a.m. (or 3 a.m. as the case may be) the permitted hours must end when the music and dancing end. The permitted hours must end at midnight on Maundy Thursday and Easter Eve (1964, s. 76).

A special hours certificate may be revoked on the application of the chief officer of police showing cause (1964, s. 81).

It shall be unlawful outside the permitted hours to supply or consume intoxicants at any party organised for gain on premises kept or habitually used for such organised parties. However, this shall not apply to parties on licensed premises or at a canteen, mess or registered club as part of its activities or for which an occasional licence has been granted.

The suppliers, permitters, deliverers and consumers of intoxicants in contravention of this section are punishable on summary conviction (1964, s. 84).

A search warrant may be granted by a justice to a constable to enter at any time or times within one month, to search any such premises (as above) and to seize and remove intoxicants, and after seizure to demand name and address of any person found on the premises. Failure to give name and address or giving false name and address shall be a summary offence (1964, s. 85).

Licensed premises may be open at any time for the sale of food and non-intoxicants.

Under 1964 Act, s. 65, a licensee may hold a licence with a condition that he has no permitted hours on Sundays (6-day licence) or that his permitted hours cease one hour earlier than usual at night (early closing licence).

Extended Hours – In any licensed premises which hold a "supper hour" certificate and which are structurally adapted and *bona fide* used for the purpose of habitually providing musical or other entertainment in addition to substantial refreshment (the sale and supply of intoxicants being ancillary thereto) the licensing justices may extend permitted hours on week-days until 1 a.m. During the extended hours the sale, supply and consumption of intoxicants is not limited to persons taking substantial refreshment. However, this does not apply to any part of the premises not habitually set apart for refreshment and entertainment, and does not authorise the sale or supply of intoxicants in any such part of the premises or for consumption off the premises, nor on a day on which no entertainment is provided, or after the entertainment or the provision of substantial refreshment has ended. Intoxicants may not be sold or supplied, except as an ancillary to a meal, to a person admitted either after midnight or less than half an hour before the entertainment is due to end.

Extended hours do not apply on Good Friday or extend beyond midnight on Maundy Thursday or Easter Eve. Except for Easter Saturday an order may allow the sale or supply of intoxicants after midnight on a Saturday and up to 1 a.m. on a Sunday.

"Entertainment" must be by persons actually present and performing.

Application may be made by a chief of police for the revocation of an order. Where an order is made the holder of the licence must notify the police within 14 days and send a copy of the order (1964, ss. 70 to 73). The licensee must keep posted in a conspicuous place a notice stating the effect of the order (1964, s. 89).

Seasonal Licences – At the request of the holder the justices may insert in the licence a condition that during a part or parts of the year there shall be no permitted hours. Such a licence is called a seasonal licence, and a "special hours" certificate granted in respect of such premises will only operate while the premises are open (1964, ss. 64 and 80).

Exemption Order – The holder of a justices' on-licence or the secretary of a club may obtain from the justices in petty sessions an exemption order authorising him to sell and supply intoxicants during non-permitted hours, as specified in the order.

A general order of exemption may be granted where the justices are satisfied it will be for the accommodation of numbers of persons attending any public market or following any trade or calling. The order must give the hours of exemption and the days on which same are allowed.

A special order of exemption may similarly be granted for licensed premises or clubs for any special occasion or occasions, usually for a ball, dinner or entertainment (1964, s. 74).

Compulsory Closing – Any two justices may order the closing of licensed premises in case of riot or tumult, actual or expected and any person acting by the order of any justice may use any necessary force to close such premises (1964, s. 188).

The Licensed Premises – The licensee must keep fixed on the premises conspicuously, as directed by the justices, his name with the word "licensed" followed by a description of his licence and must not indicate that he is authorised to sell any intoxicant he is not authorised to sell. This does not apply to the holder of a residential licence. In the case of a restaurant or "combined" licence, a notice is required that intoxicating liquor may be sold for consumption on the premises with meals (1964, s. 183).

The holder of a justices' licence, occasional licence, canteen licence, or a general or special order of exemption must produce his licence or order of exemption on demand, to a justice, or constable (1964, s. 185, as amended by Finance Act 1967, Sched. 7).

A constable may at any time enter licensed premises, a licensed canteen or premises having a "special hours certificate" for the purpose of preventing or detecting the commission of any offence against the Act. If any person, himself or by any person in his employ or acting with his consent fails to admit a constable demanding entry under this section he commits a summary offence (1964, s. 186).

There must be no internal communication between any licensed premises and any non-licensed premises used for public resort or as a refreshment house. It will be an offence if any person makes or allows to be made or uses any such communication. If the licence holder be convicted of this offence, his licence is forfeited (1964, s. 184).

Structural alterations affecting the area used for drinking must not be made without the licensing justices' consent and a Magistrates' Court, on proof, may declare the licence forfeited or order that the premises be restored to their original condition. The consent of the licensing justices is not required to certain alterations (1964, s. 20). When renewing a licence the justices may direct structural alterations to be carried out (1964, s. 19).

Licensed premises shall not be used for a magistrates' court or for licensing sessions or for a coroner's inquest if any other suitable place is provided (1964, s. 190).

Conduct of Licensed Premises

(1) A licensee must exclude children under 14 years from the bars (parts used exclusively or mainly for sale and consumption of intoxicants (1964, s. 201) but not when it is set apart for the service of table meals and the supply of intoxicants is confined to persons having table meals there (1964, s. 171)) of licensed premises during the permitted hours. Children of the licensee, or resident but not employed there or merely passing through a bar to some other part of the premises to which there is no other convenient access, or in railway refreshment rooms, or other premises made to be used *bona fide* for any purpose to which the holding of a justices' licence is merely ancillary are excepted (1964, s. 168).

(2) A licensee must not knowingly suffer to remain on his premises any constable on duty, unless he is there in the execution of his duty; he must not supply any liquor or refreshment by gift or sale to any constable on duty except by authority of his superior officer, and he must not bribe or attempt to bribe any constable (1964, s. 178).

(3) He must not knowingly allow his premises to be the habitual resort or place of meeting of reputed prostitutes. Such persons may remain only the necessary time for the purpose of obtaining reasonable refreshment (1964, s. 175). See also T.P.C. Act 1847, s. 35.

(4) He must not permit his premises to be a brothel. If convicted his licence is forfeited (1964, s. 176).

(5) He must not suffer any game to be played in the premises

which would be an offence under the Gaming Act 1968, or allow a requirement or restriction under s. 6 of that Act to be contravened (1964, s. 177).

(6) He must not allow the payment of wages on his premises to workmen not his own employees (Payment of Wages Act 1883).

(7) Without prejudice to any other right to refuse admission or expel he may refuse to admit to, or may expel from his premises, any person who is drunken, violent, quarrelsome or disorderly or whose presence thereon would subject him to a penalty under this Act. Any such person who fails to leave when requested commits an offence and any constable when requested shall help to expel any such person using any necessary force (1964, s. 174). See also "Drunkenness", later.

(8) He must not allow children and young persons to sing, play, perform etc., in his licensed premises, unless within the rules set out under "Employment of Juveniles", Chap. 12.

(9) He must not permit drunkenness or any violent, quarrelsome or riotous conduct to take place on his premises (1964, s. 172).

(10) He must not employ any person under 18 in the bar of his licensed premises while the bar is open for sale or consumption of intoxicants even if such person gets no wages for his work. (This applies to occasional licences and to theatre bars (1964, s. 170)).

(11) He must not without reasonable excuse have in his possession on the licensed premises any intoxicant that he is not authorised to sell (1964, s. 162).

Sale of Intoxicants

(1) He must not sell any intoxicating liquor to a drunken person (1964, s. 172).

(2) He must not sell or supply any intoxicants to any person who is on the "black list" as a habitual drunkard (see 1902 Act, s. 6).

(3) In licensed premises the licensee or his servant must not knowingly sell intoxicants to a person under 18, or knowingly allow a person under 18 to consume intoxicating liquor in a bar, nor shall the licensee knowingly allow any person to sell intoxicants to a person under 18 (1964, s. 169). However, the sale to or purchase by a person over 16 of beer, porter, cider or perry for consumption at a meal in a part of the premises (not a bar) usually set apart for the service of meals is permissible.

(4) The licensee or his servant must not knowingly deliver, nor must the licensee knowingly allow any person to deliver, to a person under 18 intoxicants sold in licensed premises for consumption off the premises, except where the delivery is made at the residence or place of work of the purchaser (provided that this will not apply where the person under 18 is

a member of the licensee's family or his servant or apprentice and is employed as a messenger to deliver intoxicants) (1964, s. 169).

(5) He must not sell or supply any liquor or refreshment to any constable on duty, unless by the authority of his superior officer (1964, s. 178).

(6) A person, in pursuance of a sale by him of intoxicants shall not deliver himself or by his servant or agent any such liquor from any van, vehicle, basket, etc., unless before despatch it has been ordered, and particulars are entered in a delivery book or invoice carried by the person delivering, and in a day book kept on his premises. Intoxicants must not be delivered at any address not specified in such document and day book. No other intoxicants, not recorded in such document and day book, may be carried in any vehicle or receptacle used for delivery. Any constable has power to examine any such vehicle or document. These rules do not restrict the supply to a trader for his trade, or to a club for the club purposes (1964, s. 163).

(7) Intoxicants must not be supplied on credit in licensed premises, licensed canteens or clubs. No person shall sell or supply intoxicants or consume intoxicants in such premises unless same is paid for before or at the time sold or supplied, but where consumed with a meal they may be paid for at the same time as the meal is paid for. In the case of licensed premises, if liquor is sold or supplied for consumption by a resident or his guests it may be paid for with his accommodation (1964, s. 166).

(8) No person in licensed premises, licensed canteens or clubs shall sell or supply an amount of intoxicants exceeding the measure asked for. Giving excess measure is known as the "long pull" and this is forbidden (1964, s. 165).

(9) The Measuring Instruments (Intoxicating Liquor) Regs. 1965, relate to measuring instruments, other than capacity measures, for use in measuring intoxicating liquors in public houses and on other premises where such liquor is sold by retail.

(10) A person must not sell or expose for sale by retail any intoxicating liquor unless he holds a justices' licence, an occasional licence or a canteen licence for the sale of that intoxicating liquor, nor at any place except that place for which he is authorised by the licence (1964, s. 160).

It is an offence for a person to knowingly sell or deliver or cause to be sold or delivered, any spirits, in order that they may be unlawfully retailed, consumed or brought into home use. It is also an offence for any person to receive, buy or procure any spirits from a person not authorised to sell or deliver them (Customs and Excise Act 1952, s. 161).

However, a *bona fide* commercial traveller may at any place take orders for the intoxicants which his employer is duly licensed to sell. A person in unlicensed premises may order intoxicants which are *bona fide* purchased outside and brought in for his use, he then paying.

(11) A person shall not hawk, or save as permitted by the Act, sell or expose for sale any spirits otherwise than on premises for which he holds a licence to sell spirits (Customs and Excise Act 1952, s. 161).

(12) A licensee must not allow drinking in contravention of the terms of his licence. If the holder of a justices' licence which does not allow the sale of a particular intoxicant for consumption on the premises knows or consents to its being drunk on the road or adjoining his premises or on premises near or adjoining which belong to him, etc., or in the licensed premises, he commits an offence. It is also an offence if an "off-licensee" arranges for intoxicants to be taken to be sold for his profit and consumed in some place belonging to him or sells any spirits or wine in an open vessel (1964, s. 164, as amended by Finance Act 1967, Sched. 7).

Nothing in the Act shall apply to the sale or consumption of intoxicants in canteens (authorised by the Secretary of State, s. 201) (1964, s. 199).

(13) An on-licensed holder must not knowingly sell or supply intoxicating liquor to persons to whom he is not permitted by the conditions of the licence to sell or supply it; and the holder of a restaurant, residential or "combined" licence must not knowingly permit intoxicating liquor sold in pursuance of the licence to be consumed on the licensed premises by persons for whose consumption of it there he is not permitted by the conditions of the licence to sell it (1964, s. 161).

Offences, not of Drunkenness, by non-licensed Persons –

(1) Selling or exposing for sale intoxicating liquor by retail without a justices' licence, occasional licence or canteen licence (1964, s. 160).

(2) Making, dealing in or selling intoxicants without an excise licence (Customs and Excise Act 1952, ss. 93, 125, 139, 146.)

(3) Consuming in or taking from licensed premises or clubs any intoxicants except during permitted hours and ten minutes afterwards. However, consumption on such premises during non-permitted hours is permissible in the case of a resident, a private friend, and a person at a meal (1964, ss. 59 and 63; see "Permitted Hours").

It is not an offence in itself to be on licensed premises during non-permitted hours.

(4) Consuming in licensed premises or clubs any intoxicants which were supplied for a meal during the one hour extension of permitted hours, except at such meal (1964, s. 68).

(5) Consuming in licensed premises or clubs any intoxicant

not paid for before or at the time (viz. supplied on credit) except where consumed at a meal or when supplied to a resident or his guests and paid for with his accommodation (1964, s. 166).

(6) Being in licensed premises and procuring or attempting to procure intoxicating liquor for consumption by any drunken person, or aiding any drunken person in obtaining or consuming any intoxicating liquor in any licensed premises (1964, s. 173).

(7) A person under 18 shall not in licensed premises buy or attempt to buy any intoxicating liquor nor consume intoxicating liquor in a bar (1964, s. 169).

(8) No person shall buy or attempt to buy intoxicating liquor for consumption in a bar in licensed premises, by a person under 18 (1964, s. 169).

(9) Causing, etc., a non-resident child under 14 to be in the bar of licensed premises during the permitted hours (1964, s. 168).

(10) Sending a person under 18 to licensed premises, etc., to obtain any intoxicating liquor (1964, s. 169).

(11) Giving intoxicants to a child under 5 years except on a doctor's order or in case of sickness or other emergency (Children and Young Persons Act 1933, s. 5).

(12) Paying wages on licensed premises (Payment of Wages Act 1883).

(13) Failing to quit licensed premises, being a person whose presence thereon would subject the licensee to a penalty under the Licensing Acts (see "Conduct of Licensed Premises" above), upon being requested to quit the premises by the licensee or his servant or any constable (1964, s. 174). See also "Drunkenness", later.

Prosecution – Breaches of the Acts are punishable on summary conviction (1964, s. 194). Any person aggrieved by an order or conviction made by a magistrates' court may appeal to the Crown Court as allowed in summary cases. For appeal against a decision of the licensing justices see "Appeal" on a previous page.

Evidence that any person, not the licensee or his employee (or the occupier of a licensed canteen or his employee), consumed or intended to consume intoxicants in the premises (or canteen) shall be evidence that the liquor was sold on behalf of the holder of a justices' licence (occasional licence or canteen licence) to that person.

Evidence that a transaction in the nature of a sale took place shall be evidence of a sale without proof that money passed.

Evidence that consumption of intoxicants was about to take place shall be evidence of consumption without proof of actual consumption (1964, s. 196, as amended by Finance Act 1967, Sched. 7).

Police Powers of Entry – A constable may at any time enter licensed premises, a licensed canteen or premises having a special hours certificate for the purpose of preventing or detecting the commission of any offence against this Act. Any failure to admit him will be an offence (1964, s. 186).

A justice, on sworn information that there is reasonable ground to believe that any intoxicating liquor is sold by retail or exposed or kept for sale by retail at any place where its sale by retail is not authorised, may grant a search warrant to a constable, authorising him to enter, if need be by force, at any time or times, within a month the place named and search for, seize and remove any intoxicating liquor found which the constable has reasonable grounds for supposing to be there for unlawful sale.

When the constable has seized the liquor and its vessels he may demand the name and address of any person found on the premises. It is an offence to fail to comply or to give a false name or address. If such person fails to answer satisfactorily, he may be arrested.

Persons so found on the premises, unless they prove they were there for lawful purpose, are liable to fine (1964, s. 187).

Drunkenness – Drunkenness in itself is not an offence against the law. There is no legal definition of drunkenness; it is a state or condition of a person which is the result of his consumption of an intoxicant and which is shown by the loss of control of his faculties. Drunkenness becomes a summary offence when it occurs in a public place or licensed premises or is accompanied by the particular circumstances laid down in certain statutes.

A habitual drunkard is a person who, while not a mentally disordered person, is at times dangerous to himself or to others or incapable of managing himself or his affairs, by reason of habitual intemperate drinking of intoxicants, or the habitual taking, except upon medical advice, of opium or other dangerous drugs.

Habitual drunkards may be dealt with under the Inebriates Acts. See Stone, under title "Drunkenness".

The statutes creating the offences in connection with drunkenness in some cases give the constable the power to arrest the offender without warrant. If arrested the offender should be brought to a police station, where he will either be released in due course on bail to be summoned, or detained for prosecution in court.

These drunkenness offences are as follows:

(1) Every person found drunk in any highway or other public place whether a building or not, or on any licensed

premises (which includes any place where intoxicating liquor is sold under an occasional licence) (1872 Act, s. 12 as supplemented by 1964, s. 200). Unless such person is incapable of taking care of himself he should not be arrested, as he may only be summoned for this 1872 Act offence. This offence is known as simple drunkenness, and is punishable by fine. Every person found drunk on licensed premises when such premises are open to the public is liable under this section. One justice, sitting alone, may deal with this offence (C.J.A. Act 1914, s. 38).

A person found drunk in any highway or other public place whether a building or not or on any licensed premises, and apparently incapable of taking care of himself may be arrested (1902 Act, s. 1).

This offence is commonly known as "drunk and incapable", and is punishable under s. 12, 1872 Act, or by other Acts dealing with drunkenness, but the offence is "simple drunkenness."

(2) Being guilty, while drunk, of riotous or disorderly behaviour in any highway or other public place whether a building or not. Such person may be arrested (1872 Act, s. 12).

(3) Drunk while in charge on any highway or other public place of any carriage, horse, cattle (including pigs and sheep), or steam engine. A bicycle is such a carriage (*Corkery* v. *Carpenter* (1950)). Such person may be arrested (1872 Act, s. 12).

(4) Drunk when in possession of any loaded firearms. Such person may be arrested (1872 Act, s. 12). This offence may be committed anywhere, and no person need have been endangered.

(5) Found drunk in any highway or other public place whether a building or not, or on any licensed premises, while having the charge of a child apparently under the age of 7 years. Such person may be arrested (1902 Act. s. 2).

"Public place," for the purposes of the above 5 offences, includes any place to which the public have access, whether on payment or otherwise (1902 Act, s. 8).

(6) Driving or attempting to drive a motor vehicle on a road or other public place while unfit to drive through drink or drugs (R.T. Act 1972, s. 5(1)).

(7) Being in charge of a motor vehicle on a road or other public place while unfit to drive through drink or drugs (R.T. Act 1972, s. 5 (2)). (For the offence of driving, etc., a motor vehicle with a blood alcohol concentration above the prescribed limit, see under "Road Traffic Acts, etc". Chap. 24.)

(8) Riding cycle, not being a motor vehicle, on a road or other place while unfit to ride through drink or drugs (R.T. Act 1972, s. 19).

A person committing one of these 3 offences (Nos. 6, 7 and 8) may be arrested without warrant by a constable. He is not liable to prosecution under s. 12, Licensing Act 1872 (see No. 3 above).

Being in charge of a motor vehicle depends on the facts of the case. See *Jowett-Shooter* v. *Franklin* (1949) and *Jones* v. *English* (1951). If a person leaves a motor vehicle on a road or public place he is still in charge of it unless he puts some other person in charge of it (*Haines* v. *Roberts* (1953)).

It has been held that any place to which the public in fact have access is a "public place" under this section *R.* v. *Collinson* (1931) and *Elkins* v. *Cartlidge* (1947).

(9) Being drunk, violent, quarrelsome or disorderly on licensed premises, and failing to quit on request by the licensee, his servant or any constable. A constable is required, on demand of the licensee or his servants, to help to expel every such person from the premises and may use such force as may be required for the purpose (1964, s. 174).

(10) Being drunk, riotous, quarrelsome or disorderly in any licensed refreshment house and refusing or neglecting to quit on request from the manager or his servant or any constable. Constables are required to assist in expelling such offenders (Late Night Refreshment Houses Act 1969, s. 9 (4)).

(11) Being drunk in any street (of any urban district) and guilty of riotous or indecent behaviour therein, or being guilty of any violent or indecent behaviour in any police office or police station house (in any urban district) (Town Police Clauses Act 1847, s. 29, where the Act is in force). Where s. 81 of the Public Health Acts Amendment Act 1907, is in force by order, "street" includes any unfenced ground adjoining a street and any place of public resort or recreation ground under the control of the Local Authority. The Metropolitan Police Act 1839, s. 58, provides a similar penalty for similar conduct in the London Metropolitan Police area.

(12) The driver of any hackney carriage (in any urban district) who is intoxicated while driving commits an offence (Town Police Clauses Act 1847, s. 61, where in force).

The London Hackney Carriages Act 1843, s. 28, deals with a driver of a hackney carriage or a driver or conductor of a stage carriage in the Metropolitan Police district who is drunk during his employment as such.

(13) Being drunk on board a passenger steamer and refusing to leave same when requested, or being drunk and persisting in attempting to enter a passenger steamer after having been refused admission (Merchant Shipping Act 1894, s. 287). See "Merchant Shipping Acts", Chap. 26.

The penalties that may be imposed for the offences mentioned in paras. 1–5, 10, 11 and 13 above were increased by the Penalties for Drunkenness Act 1962.

Clubs – A club may be defined as a voluntary association of a number of persons who meet together for purposes mainly social but perhaps including other purposes such as sport, politics, literature, each member contributing a certain sum, and the association being conducted under rules. A club is not defined in law, and the court in any particular case may have to decide on the facts whether an association is or is not a club.

SALE AND SUPPLY OF INTOXICATING LIQUOR IN CLUB PREMISES – Intoxicating liquor may not be supplied on any club premises by or on behalf of the club to a member or guest unless the club is registered or licensed. A person supplying or authorising the supply of intoxicating liquor in contravention of the above commits an offence.

In any registered club, intoxicating liquor may only be supplied for consumption off the premises to a member in person.

Intoxicating liquor shall not be supplied by or on behalf of a registered club to a member or guest except at club premises in respect of which a club is registered or at any premises or place which the club is using on a special occasion, when only members and their guests are admitted, and the liquor is supplied only for consumption in the premises or place.

If intoxicating liquor is kept in any premises or place by or on behalf of a club for supply to members or their guests in contravention of this section every officer of the club commits an offence unless he shows that it was so kept without his knowledge or consent (1964, s. 39).

PERMITTED HOURS IN CLUBS – The permitted hours in registered clubs shall be fixed by the rules of the club, as follows: (a) the hours shall not on any day be longer nor begin earlier or end later than the general licensing hours, (b) there shall be a break in the afternoon of not less than 2 hours, and (c) on Sundays, Christmas Day and Good Friday, the break shall include the hours from 3 p.m. to 5 p.m. and there shall not be more than 3½ hours after 5 p.m.

Written notice (signed by the Chairman or Secretary) of the hours fixed as the permitted hours shall be given to the Clerk to the Justices (1964, s. 62).

QUALIFICATIONS FOR REGISTRATION OF CLUBS – To be registered a club must hold a "registration certificate" issued by a magistrates' court. A "registration certificate" lasts for 12 months and may be renewed or surrendered. On the second or subsequent renewal the certificate may be renewed for such number of years (not exceeding 10) as may be requested or for any less number of years. The rules of the club must provide for an interval of at least 2 days between a person being nominated or his application for membership and his admission. Persons becoming members without prior nomination or application may not be admitted to the privileges of membership without an interval of at least 2 days between their becoming members and their admission.

A club shall be qualified for registration, if (a) it is established and conducted in good faith and has not less than 25 members, and (b) intoxicating liquor is not supplied otherwise than by or on behalf of the club, and (c) the purchase and supply of intoxicants are managed by the general body of members or by an elective committee of that body, and (d) there are no arrangements for any person to receive at the expense of the club any commission or percentage or similar payment with reference to purchases of intoxicants, and (e) there are no arrangements for any person directly or indirectly to derive any pecuniary benefit from the supply of intoxicants by or on behalf of the club (1964, ss. 40 and 41).

OBJECTION TO AND CANCELLATION OF REGISTRATION OF CLUBS, AND DISQUALIFICATION OF PREMISES – Objection to the issue or renewal of a registration certificate may be made by the chief officer of police, the local authority or by any person affected by reason of his occupation of or interest in other premises. The grounds for objection are—(a) that the application does not give information required, or the information is incomplete or inaccurate, or the application is otherwise not in conformity with Part II of the Act; (b) that the premises are not suitable and convenient for the purpose in view of their character and condition, and of the size and nature of the club; (c) that the club does not satisfy the conditions as to qualification for registration given in s. 41 of the Act (see above); (d) that the club is conducted in a disorderly manner or for an unlawful purpose, or that the rules of the club are habitually disregarded as respects the admission of persons to membership or to the privileges of membership or in any other material respect, and (e) that the club premises or any of them (including premises in respect of which the club is not registered or seeking registration) are habitually used for an unlawful purpose or for indecent displays, or as a resort of criminals or prostitutes, or that in any such premises there is frequent drunkenness, or there have within the preceding 12 months been illegal sales of intoxicating liquor or persons not qualified to be supplied with intoxicating liquor there are habitually admitted for the purposes of obtaining it.

A magistrates' court, if satisfied that the ground of objection is made out, may refuse the application. They must refuse the application if any of grounds (a) to (c) are substantiated, but with regard to ground (b) having regard to any steps taken or proposed to be taken to remove the ground of objection, the court may, if it thinks it reasonable to do so, grant the application.

A complaint for the cancellation of a registration certificate may be made to a magistrates' court by a chief officer of police or the local authority on grounds (c) to (e).

If satisfied that the matter of complaint is substantiated the court must cancel the certificate and may order that the premises shall not be occupied and used for the purposes of any registered club for a specified period (1964, ss. 44 and 47).

SALE OF INTOXICATING LIQUOR BY REGISTERED CLUBS – The rules of a registered club may provide admission to the club of persons other than members and their guests, and for the sale of intoxicants to them for consumption on the premises, without a licence.

A magistrates' court may refuse to issue or renew a registration certificate if it considers that the club is not established and conducted in good faith as a club. On the issue or renewal of a registration certificate, the court may attach to the certificate such conditions restricting sales of intoxicants as it thinks reasonable but must not prevent sale to a member of another club, if (a) the other club is registered in the locality and is temporarily closed, (b) both clubs exist for learned, educational or political objects of a similar nature, or (c) both clubs are primarily for ex-members of Her Majesty's Forces who are members of an organisation established by Royal Charter or (d) each of the clubs is a working men's club. Conditions made may later be varied or revoked on renewal or on application by the club, or on complaint in writing made against the club by the police or Local Authority (1964, s. 49).

MAINTENANCE OF REGISTER – The Clerk to the Justices has to keep a register of clubs holding registration certificates in the area. The register shows the permitted hours of the club and (a) the object of the club, (b) the name of the secretary, (c) the date of issue, renewal or variation of the certificate and the period for which it is in force, and (d) the address of any premises to which the certificate relates. The register is open to inspection at all reasonable times on payment of 5p by any person, and without payment by any officer of police, and officer of customs or excise or of a local authority. A single registration certificate may relate to any number of premises of the same club (1964, ss. 51 and 52).

APPEAL TO THE CROWN COURT – A club may appeal to the Crown Court against any decision of a magistrates' court refusing to issue or renew a registration certificate, or cancelling a registration certificate, or against any decision of a magistrates' court as to the conditions of a registration certificate relating to sales of intoxicants (1964, s. 50).

INSPECTION OF PREMISES BEFORE FIRST REGISTRATION – Where a new club registration certificate is applied for an appointed officer of the local authority on giving 48 hours' notice, may inspect the premises. The police also have the right of inspection but only if special reasons exist for so doing. Similar rights arise where a renewal application relates to different, additional or enlarged premises (1964, s. 45).

The provisions for "supper-hour" extension, the special hours certificate and the extended hours certificate in relation to restaurants, etc., providing entertainment apply also (with modifications) to a registered club on a certificate or order of a magistrates' court.

SEARCH WARRANTS – The police have no legal right to enter and inspect clubs unless they have a search warrant. If a justice of the peace is satisfied by information on oath that there is reasonable ground for believing (a) that there is ground for cancelling (in whole or in part) a registration certificate held by a club, and that evidence of it is to be obtained at the club premises, or (b) that intoxicating liquor is sold or supplied by or on behalf of the club in club premises for which the club does not hold a registration certificate or a justices' licence, or is kept in any club premises for sale or supply in contravention of Part II of the Act (which relates to the sale and supply of intoxicating liquor in club premises); he may issue a search warrant to a constable authorising him at any time within one month to enter the club premises by force if necessary and search them and seize any documents relating to the business of the club (1964, s. 54).

LICENSING OF CLUB PREMISES – A club may apply for a justices' licence which if granted will include authority to supply intoxicating liquor to members. Such a licence must be in the name of an officer of the club, nominated for the purpose, and the rights and obligations of a licensee will apply to him (1964, s. 55). As the premises of a licensed club are licensed premises the police will have a general right of entry, and the club will not be able to fix its permitted hours but will be subject to those applying to other licensed premises in the area, and the restrictions on the sale or supply of intoxicating liquor to persons under 18 will apply.

Seamen's Canteens – The licensing justices may grant licences to these canteens. Food and non-intoxicants must be provided when intoxicants are on sale. The local permitted hours must be observed and the premises must be conducted as directed by the Licensing Acts (1964, Part X and s. 179).

Late Night Refreshment Houses – The Late Night Refreshment Houses Act 1969 consolidates the Refreshment Houses Acts 1860–1967, but does not change the substance of the law.

For the purposes of this Act, a "late night refreshment house" is a house, room, shop or building kept open for public refreshment, resort and entertainment at any time between the hours of 10 p.m. and 5 a.m. the following morning, other than a house, room, shop or building which is licensed for the sale of beer, cider, wine and spirits (s. 1).

A person who keeps a late night refreshment house must be licensed to do so. The licensing authorities are district councils and the councils of London boroughs and the Common Council of City of London.

It is an offence for a person to keep a late night refreshment house without having a licence in force (s. 2).

Every licensing authority shall keep a list or register of licences granted by them for late night refreshment houses in their area, showing in respect of each licence the name and place of abode of the licensee and the name and description of the premises which are the subject of the licence (s. 6).

The licensing authority has power to impose conditions as to opening after 11 p.m., and may prohibit opening between 11 p.m. and 5 a.m. In the event of a contravention of a condition imposed by the licensing authority, the licensee shall be guilty of an offence. A person aggrieved by a condition imposed may appeal to a magistrates' court (s. 7).

Where s. 8 (1) applies to a late night refreshment house, it shall not be lawful to make any charge for or in connection with the entertainment of persons in the refreshment house during the hours of late opening, whether for the supply of food or drink, for admission, for service of any description or for any other matter, except any reasonable charge for the use of cloakroom or toilet facilities, unless: (a) a tariff of charges made in the refreshment house is during those hours kept displayed in such position and in such manner that it can be conveniently read by persons frequenting the refreshment house and, if so required by s. 8 (4), can be so read by any such person before entering; and (b) the charge is specified for the matter in question in the tariff or is less than a charge so specified (s. 8 (1)).

Where s. 8 (2) applies to a late night refreshment house it shall not be lawful to seek to obtain custom for the refreshment house by means of personal solicitation outside or in the vicinity of the refreshment house (s. 8 (2)).

Section 8 ((1) or (2) or both) shall apply to a late night refreshment house if, but only if, the licensing authority have made that a condition of the grant or renewal of a licence for the refreshment house, and have not revoked the condition; and a licensing authority may impose such a condition in any case where it appears to them desirable in order to ensure that persons frequenting the refreshment house are not misled as to the nature or cost of the entertainment provided (s. 8 (3)).

Where s. 8 (1) applies, the tariff of charges must be able to be read before entering by any person frequenting the refreshment house, if it is so stated by the condition applying the subsection, and on any renewal of the licence the condition may be varied so as to include or omit any such statement (s. 8 (4)).

In the event of a contravention of s. 8 ((1) or (2)) the keeper of the refreshment house and any person responsible for the contravention (other than a person who did not know of the condition applying the subsection) shall be guilty of an offence; and where a person is charged with such an offence, it shall be for him to show that he did not know of the condition (s. 8 (5)).

In this section "the hours of late opening" means any period between the hours of 10 p.m. and 5 a.m. the following morning during which the refreshment house is open (s. 8 (6)).

If the licensee of a late night refreshment house knowingly permits unlawful gaming therein or knowingly permits prostitutes, thieves, or drunken and disorderly persons to assemble at, or continue in or upon, his premises, he shall be guilty of an offence.

The reference to unlawful gaming is to the playing of any game in such circumstances that an offence is committed under Part II of the Betting, Gaming and Lotteries Act 1963.

If a person who is drunk, riotous, quarrelsome or disorderly in a late night refreshment house licensed under this Act refuses or neglects to leave it on being requested to do so by the manager or occupier, or his agent or servant, or by any constable he shall be guilty of an offence (s. 9).

A constable may, at any time when he thinks fit, enter a late night refreshment house licensed under this Act and go upon any premises belonging thereto; and the licensee or any other person being his employee or acting by his direction shall be guilty of an offence if he fails or refuses to admit a constable demanding admittance under this subsection (s. 10 (1)).

Every constable is hereby authorised and required, on the demand of the manager or occupier of a late night refreshment house licensed under this Act, or of any servant or agent of the manager or occupier, to assist in expelling from the refreshment house drunken, riotous, quarrelsome and disorderly persons (s. 10 (2)).

Licensing, New Towns – The Licensing Act 1964, ss. 108 to 117 deals with liquor licensing matters in new towns on the following lines.

A new town shall have a committee to arrange for licensed premises (s. 108) and which shall make proposals as to the establishment and distribution of such premises and submit them to the Minister of Housing and Local Government for his confirmation (s. 109). The licensing justices will deal with the grant of new licences and removals (s. 111).

Methylated Spirits – Under the Customs and Excise Act 1952, methylated spirits means spirits mixed in Great Britain or

Northern Ireland with some other substance in accordance with Regulations made under the Act (s. 307). No person shall make or deal wholesale in same unless he holds an excise licence as an authorised methylator (s. 116) nor shall a person sell same without an excise licence (s. 117).

No person shall prepare or sell as a beverage or mixed with a beverage any methylated spirits or methylalcohol or their mixtures (s. 121).

The sale of methylated spirits is not affected by the Licensing Act 1964: see s. 199 of that Act.

CHAPTER 39

PUBLIC HEALTH

	Page
Public Health Acts . .	572
Poisons	574
Misuse of Drugs Act 1971	576
Mental Health . .	579
Nursing Homes . .	581
Births, Deaths and Marriages	581
Burials	582
Fires	582
Coroners and Inquests .	584
Fumigation . . .	587
Unauthorised Dumping .	587
Poisonous Waste . .	587
Abatement of Litter .	587
Noise Abatement . .	588

Public Health Acts – The Public Health Acts form a code of regulations designed to promote the good health of the community. They create many offences which, strictly speaking, are not within the sphere of police work, but it is advisable that police should have some knowledge of these Acts. Offences against these laws are dealt with by the Local Authorities, and as a rule the duty of the police is confined to reporting such breaches of the Acts as may come under their notice.

Portions of these Acts are consolidated in the Public Health Act 1936. Only a few of its provisions are applicable to London.

Section 298 of the Public Health Act 1936 states that proceedings for an offence under the Act, shall not, without the consent of the Attorney-General, be taken by anyone other than a party aggrieved or a Council or body whose function it is to enforce the Act or byelaws.

FOOD – Any place in which food for human consumption is prepared, stored or kept for sale must be kept clean, etc., so as to prevent the risk of contamination to food in the place. See Food and Drugs Act 1955, s. 13, and Food Hygiene Regs. 1955.

A collector of or dealer in rags, old clothes or similar articles must not sell or deliver from premises used for the business or when collecting same, any article of food or drink to any person or any article whatsoever including any animal, fish, bird or other living thing to anyone under 14 (Public Health Act, 1936 s. 154 as amended by Public Health Act 1961, s. 42).

An authorised officer of a Local Authority may examine any

food intended for human consumption which has been sold or is exposed or offered for sale or is kept for sale, and if it appears unfit for human consumption, may seize it and take it to be dealt with by a justice (Food and Drugs Act 1955, s. 9).

HORSEFLESH – The flesh of horses, asses or mules may not be sold, exposed or kept for sale for human food elsewhere than in a place on which a notice is displayed stating that horseflesh is sold there (Food and Drugs Act 1955, s. 24). See "Knackers", Chap. 35.

INFECTIOUS (NOTIFIABLE) DISEASES – The exposure in public places, shops, public conveyances, etc., of persons or articles liable to convey notifiable disease will be an offence. Infected articles, conveyances, premises, etc., must be disinfected.

Relatives, attendants or occupiers and doctors must notify certain infectious diseases to the medical officer of health of the district.

The notifiable diseases include smallpox, cholera, plague, typhus, relapsing fever. See 1936 Act, s. 343, as amended.

NUISANCES – The Local Authority has power to deal with refuse, scavenging, noxious matter, keeping of animals, etc. (1936 Act, Part II, ss. 72–82). Also nuisances of ponds, rivers, etc., and it is an offence to deposit ashes, stones, dust, etc., in rivers, streams, etc. (s. 259).

If the following are in such a state as to be a nuisance or prejudicial to health, viz, any premises, any animal so kept, any accumulation or deposit, any dust or effluvia from any trade, etc., any factory, workshop or workplace, the Local Authority may serve notice on the person responsible requiring him to abate same, which is termed a statutory nuisance. If the nuisance is not abated the person responsible may be summarily prosecuted, fined and ordered to abate the nuisance (1936 Act, Part III, ss. 91–100).

OFFENSIVE TRADES – Certain noxious or offensive trades, businesses or manufactures, are not to be established without the consent of the Local Authority. Nuisance caused by the effluvia from the products used in trades may be dealt with summarily on proof that same is a nuisance or prejudicial to health (1936 Act, ss. 92, 107–109).

SANITARY CONVENIENCES USED IN COMMON – It is a summary offence for any person to injure or improperly foul same (1936 Act, s. 52).

SMOKEY CHIMNEYS – The Clean Air Acts 1956 and 1968 make provision for abating the pollution of the air, by prohibiting the issue of dark smoke from chimneys, by requiring that new furnaces shall be as far as practicable smokeless and by requiring that grit and dust from furnaces shall be minimised. The duty of enforcing the provisions of the Act is laid on the Local Authority.

UNFIT DWELLINGS – When any premises used for human habitation appear to be in a condition prejudicial to health the Local Authority may take action (Public Health Act **1936**, s. **83**).

Canal boats used as dwellings shall be registered with a Local Authority (**1936** Act, Part X).

Tents, vans, sheds, movable dwellings, etc., used for human habitation come under ss. **268**, **269** of the **1936** Act.

VERMINOUS ARTICLES – No dealer shall (a) prepare for sale, or (b) sell or offer or expose for sale, or (c) deposit with any person for sale, any household article (furniture, bedding or clothing, or any similar article) that he knows to be verminous (Public Health Act **1961**, s. **37**).

Poisons – The Pharmacy and Poisons Act **1933** as amended by the Pharmacy and Medicines Act **1941** and the Pharmacy Act **1954** deals with the registration of chemists and pharmacists (see "Pharmaceutical Chemists", Chap. 29), and together with the Poisons Rules 1972, made under the Pharmacy and Poisons Act **1933**, regulates the sale and supply of poisons.

The subject will be governed by the Poisons Act **1972** when brought into force.

AUTHORISED SELLER OF POISONS – This term is applied to

(1) a registered pharmacist who sells drugs by retail;

(2) a body corporate (or company) which sells drugs by retail, and

(3) a representative continuing the business of a registered pharmacist who is an authorised seller of poisons, but has died or become of unsound mind or bankrupt.

Provided that in all these cases a registered pharmacist is in personal control and his certificate of registration is exhibited on the premises, and provided also that the premises are registered with the Pharmaceutical Society for the purpose.

POISONS LIST – A list of the substances which are to be treated as "poisons" has been prepared by an Advisory Committee (called the Poisons Board) and approved by the Secretary of State.

The list is given in Sched. 2 of the Poisons List Order **1972**. This poisons list is in two parts, viz.:

Part I, containing poisons which may be sold only by an authorised seller of poisons; and

Part II, containing poisons which may be sold by an authorised seller of poisons or by a person whose name is on a list kept by the Local Authority of persons entitled to sell poisons named in Part II of the list, and who is known as a "listed seller of Part II poisons".

LOCAL AUTHORITY – This is the council of a county, or London borough and the Common Council of the City of London.

The Local Authority shall keep a list of persons entitled to sell the poisons in Part II of the Poisons List, and a person having premises in the area may apply to have his name put in the list as a person authorised to sell such poisons in such premises. He must pay a fee and may be refused if he or his premises are not considered fit. If on the list and if he is convicted of an offence the court may order his name to be removed from the list. To supervise such persons local inspectors shall be appointed who may enter premises, examine, inquire and take samples, and they may prosecute offenders and conduct the proceedings.

The Pharmaceutical Society also has inspectors with similar powers as regards sellers of poisons.

SALE OF POISONS – It shall not be lawful for a person to sell—

(1) Part I poisons—unless he is an authorised seller of poisons, selling on duly registered premises under supervision of a registered pharmacist.

(2) Part II poisons—unless either he is an authorised seller of poisons selling on duly registered premises or his name is in the "Local Authority's list", and he sells in the premises so authorised.

(3) Any poison—unless the container of the poison is duly labelled with the name and proportion of the poison, the word "poison" and the name and address of seller.

Poison shall not be sold or offered for sale by means of an automatic machine.

SALE OF PART I POISONS – As stated above only an authorised seller of poisons may sell such poisons, and it shall not be lawful—

(a) To sell same to any person unless that person is certified in writing (as prescribed) or is known by the seller, to be a person to whom the poison may properly be sold.

(b) To deliver same until the sale is recorded (as prescribed) in a book and the purchaser has signed the entry.

Exemption from the above restrictions is allowed in the case of—

(1) Medicines provided or ordered by a doctor, dentist or veterinary surgeon, or by an authorised seller of poisons, but same must be labelled with name and address of the provider and a record (as prescribed) shall be kept.

(2) Wholesale sales, and sales for export to doctors, etc., hospitals, etc., public services, etc.

Proceedings may be taken within 12 months after the offence.

Misuse of Drugs Act 1971 – This Act deals with dangerous or otherwise harmful drugs. Schedule 2 lists the drugs which are termed "controlled drugs". These drugs are arranged as Class "A", "B", or "C" drugs. Class "A" includes: cocaine, morphine, opium (whether raw, prepared or medicinal) and pethedine; Class "B" includes amphetamine, cannabis and cannabis resin, codeine and ethylmorphine; Class "C" includes amphetamine-like drugs which are considered to present lesser dangers (s. 2). The importation and exportation of controlled drugs are prohibited except under licence issued by the Secretary of State or authorised by Regs. made under s. 7 of the Act (s. 3). The production and supply of controlled drugs is restricted, subject to Regulations under s. 7 (s. 4 (1)). The Secretary of State has issued the Misuse of Drugs Regulations 1973 and 1975. It is an offence, subject to the statutory defence contained in s. 28 (see later): (a) to produce a controlled drug in contravention of sub-s. (1) above; or (b) to be concerned in the production of such a drug in contravention of sub-s. (1) by another (s. 4 (2)). It is also an offence, subject to s. 28, (a) to supply or offer to supply a controlled drug to another in contravention of sub-s. (1), or (b) to be concerned in the supplying of such a drug to another in contravention of that subsection, or (c) to be concerend in the making to another in contravention of that subsection of an offer to supply such a drug (s. 4 (3)). Subject to any Regs. under s. 7, it shall not be lawful for a person to have possession of a controlled drug (s. 5 (1)). Subject to s. 28 and the statutory defence under s. 5 (4) it is an offence for a person to have a controlled drug in his possession in contravention of s. (1) 5 (s. 5 (2)).

Subject to s. 28 it is an offence for a person to have a controlled drug in his possession, whether lawfully or not, with intent to supply it to another in contravention of s. 4 (1) (s. 5 (3)). Unless properly authorised it shall be unlawful for any person to cultivate any plant of the genus *cannabis* (s. 6 (1)). Subject to s. 28, it is an offence to cultivate any such plant in contravention of sub-s. (1) of this section (s. 6 (2)).

The Secretary of State is empowered to make regulations authorising activities, which would otherwise be unlawful, by persons who normally are authorised to supply and possess controlled drugs, e.g. doctors, dentists, pharmacists, etc. (s. 7).

The occupier or person concerned in the management of any premises who knowingly permits or suffers any of the following activities to take place on the premises, commits an offence: (a) producing or attempting to produce a controlled drug; (b) supplying or attempting to supply a controlled drug to another, or offering to supply a controlled drug to another; (c) preparing opium for smoking; (d) smoking cannabis, cannabis resin or prepared opium (s. 8).

Subject to s. 28, it is an offence for a person: (a) to smoke or otherwise use prepared opium; or (b) to frequent a place used for a purpose of opium smoking; or (c) to have in his possession—(i) any pipes or other utensils made or adapted for use in connection with the smoking of opium, being pipes or utensils which have been used by him or with his knowledge and permission in that connection or which he intends to use or permit others to use in that connection; or (ii) any utensils which have been used by him or with his knowledge and permission in connection with the preparation of opium for smoking (s. 9).

The Secretary of State is empowered to make regulations for preventing misuse of controlled drugs (s. 10) and may direct special precautions for the safe custody of controlled drugs to be taken at certain premises (s. 11). It is an offence to contravene a direction given by the Secretary of State prohibiting prescribing, supplying, etc., of controlled drugs by practitioners who have been convicted of offences in connection with drugs (s. 12). To contravene a direction by the Secretary of State prohibiting prescribing, supply, etc., of controlled drugs by practitioners is an offence (s. 13).

In certain circumstances the Secretary of State is empowered to obtain information from doctors, pharmacists, etc., e.g. where there exists a social problem caused by the extensive misuse of dangerous or otherwise harmful drugs in their area. Failure to comply with a notice requiring information or giving false information in purported compliance with the request is an offence (s. 17).

It is an offence for a person to contravene certain regulations made under the Act; or to contravene a condition of some licences issued under the Act; or to give false information in purported compliance with an obligation to give information under or by virtue of Regs.; or to give false information for purposes of obtaining issue or renewal of a licence or other authority (s. 18).

It is an offence for a person to attempt to commit an offence under any other provision of this Act or to incite or attempt to incite to commit such an offence (s. 19).

A person commits an offence if in the U.K. he assists in or induces the commission in any place outside the U.K. of an offence punishable under the provisions of a corresponding law in force in that place (s. 20).

SEARCH – A constable or other person authorised by the Secretary of State shall, for the purposes of the execution of this Act, have power to enter the premises of a person carrying on business as a producer or supplier of any controlled drugs and to demand the production of, and to inspect any books or documents relating to dealings in any such drugs and to inspect any stocks of any such drugs (s. 23 (1)). If a constable has reasonable grounds to suspect that any person is in possession of a controlled drug in contravention of this Act or of any regulations made thereunder, the constable may (a) search that person, and detain him for the purpose of searching him; (b) search any vehicle or vessel in which the constable suspects that the drug may be found, and for that purpose require the person in control of the vehicle or vessel to stop it; (c) seize and detain, for the purposes of proceedings under this Act, anything found in the course of the search which appears to the constable to be evidence of an offence under this Act. "Vessel" includes a hovercraft, and this subsection does not prejudice any power of search or any power to seize or detain property which a constable otherwise has (s. **23** (2)). A justice of the peace is authorised to grant a warrant to a constable to search premises if there is reasonable ground for suspecting that an offence under the Act is being committed there (s. **23** (3)).

A person commits an offence if he: (a) intentionally obstructs a person in the exercise of his powers under this section; or (b) conceals from a person acting in the exercise of his powers under sub-s. (1) above any such books, documents, stocks or drugs as are mentioned in that subsection; or (c) without reasonable excuse (proof of which shall lie on him) fails to produce any such books or documents as are so mentioned where their production is demanded by a person in the exercise of his powers under that subsection (s. **23** (4)).

A constable may arrest without warrant a person who has committed, or whom the constable, with reasonable cause, suspects to have committed, an offence under this Act, if: (a) he, with reasonable cause, believes that the person will abscond unless arrested; or (b) the name and address of that person are unknown to, and cannot be ascertained by him; or (c) he is not satisfied that a name and address furnished by that person as his name and address are true (s. **24** (1)).

This section shall not prejudice any power of arrest conferred by law apart from this section (s. **24** (2)). Where a person is convicted of an offence under the Act, the convicting court may forfeit anything shown to the satisfaction of the court to relate to the offence (s. 27).

Where a person is charged with offences under s. 4 (2) and (3), s. 5 (2) and (3), s. 6 (2) and s. 9, it shall be a defence for the accused to prove that he neither knew of nor suspected nor had reason to suspect the existence of some fact alleged by the prosecution which it is necessary for the prosecution to prove if he is to be convicted of the offence charged (s. 28).

References to misusing a drug are references to misusing it by taking it, and the reference to the taking of a drug is a reference to the taking of it by a human being by way of any form of self-administration, whether or not involving assistance by another (s. **37** (2)). For the purposes of this Act the things which a person has in his possession shall be taken to include anything subject to his control which is in the custody of another (s. **37** (3)).

Mental Health – The Mental Health Act 1959 makes provision with respect to the treatment and care of mentally disordered persons.

Definition and classification of mental disorder—

"Mental disorder" means mental illness, arrested or incomplete development of mind, psychopathic disorder, and any other disorder or disability of mind.

"Severe subnormality" means a state of arrested or incomplete development of mind which includes subnormality of intelligence, and is of such a nature or degree that the patient is incapable of living an independent life or of guarding himself against serious exploitation, or will be so incapable when of an age to do so.

"Subnormality" means a state of arrested or incomplete development of mind (not amounting to severe subnormality) which includes subnormality of intelligence and which requires or is susceptible to medical treatment or other special care or training of the patient;

"Psychopathic disorder" means a persistent disorder or disability of mind (whether or not including subnormality or intelligence) which results in abnormally aggressive or seriously irresponsible conduct, and requires or is susceptible to medical treatment (s. 4).

RETURN AND RE-ADMISSION OF PATIENTS ABSENT WITHOUT LEAVE – Where a mentally disordered patient absents himself from hospital without leave, or fails to return to the hospital at the expiration of a period of leave, or absents himself without permission from any place where he is required to reside in accordance with conditions imposed on the grant of leave of absence, he may be taken into custody and returned to the hospital or place by any mental welfare officer, any officer on the hospital staff, any constable or any person authorised in writing by the managers of the hospital.

Where a mental patient subject to guardianship absents himself without leave, he may be taken into custody and returned by an officer of a local social services authority, any constable, or any person authorised in writing by the guardian or a local social services authority, subject to the limitation that in the case of a psychopathic or sub-normal patient he may not be taken into custody after 6 months, and in any other case after 28 days (s. 40).

POWERS OF COURTS TO ORDER HOSPITAL ADMISSION OR GUARDIANSHIP – Where a person is convicted before the Crown Court of an offence other than an offence the sentence for which is fixed by law, or is convicted by a magistrates' court of an offence punishable on summary conviction with imprisonment, and the court is satisfied on medical evidence that the offender is mentally disordered, it may by order authorise his admission to and detention in a specified hospital or place him under the guardianship of a local social services authority or of a person approved by such authority (s. 60).

WARRANT TO SEARCH FOR AND REMOVE PATIENTS (s. 135) – If it appears to a justice of the peace, on information on oath laid by a mental welfare officer that there is reasonable cause to suspect that a person believed to be suffering from mental disorder – (a) has been, or is being, ill treated, neglected or kept otherwise than under proper control, or (b) being unable to care for himself, is living alone, the justice may issue a warrant authorising any constable named therein to enter, if need be by force, any premises specified in the warrant in which that person is believed to be, and, if thought fit, to remove him to a place of safety with a view to arranging for his admission to hospital, or for other treatment or care (s. 135 (1)).

If it appears to a justice of the peace, on information on oath laid by any constable or other person who is authorised by or under the Act to take a patient to any place, or to take into custody or retake a patient (a) that there is reasonable cause to believe that the patient is to be found on premises within the jurisdiction of the justice, and (b) that admission to the premises has been refused or that a refusal of such admission is apprehended, the justice may issue a warrant authorising any constable named therein to enter the premises, if need be by force, and remove the patient (s. 135 (2)).

A patient who is removed to a place of safety under this section may be detained there for not more than 72 hours (s. 135 (3)).

When executing a warrant under s. 135 (1) above, the constable shall be accompanied by a mental welfare officer and a doctor. When executing a warrant under s. 135 (2) above, he may be accompanied (a) by a doctor, (b) by any person authorised by or under the Act to take or retake the patient (s. 135 (4)).

It shall not be necessary in any information or warrant under s. 135 (1) above to name the patient concerned (s. 135 (5)).

"Place of safety" includes a police station, a mental nursing home or residential home for mentally disordered persons or any other suitable place the occupier of which is willing temporarily to receive the patient (s. 135 (6)).

MENTALLY DISORDERED PERSONS FOUND IN PUBLIC PLACES – If a constable finds in a place to which the public have access a person who appears to him to be suffering from mental disorder and to be in immediate need of care or control, the constable may, if he thinks it necessary to do so in the interests of that person or for the protection of other persons, remove that person to a place of safety.

A person removed to a place of safety may be detained there for not more than 72 hours for the purpose of enabling him to be examined by a medical practitioner and to be interviewed by a mental welfare officer and of making any necessary arrangements for his treatment or care (s. 136).

RETAKING OF PATIENTS ESCAPING FROM CUSTODY – If any person being in legal custody by virtue of the provisions of the Act escapes (e.g. while being conveyed from one place to another or while being detained in a place of safety, etc.), he may be retaken —(a) in any case, by the person who had his custody immediately before the escape, or by any constable or mental welfare officer, and (b) in the case of persons liable to be detained in hospital or subject to guardianship, by any other person authorised under s. 40, provided that the retaking under (b) must be within 6 months if the patient is over 21 years of age and is psychopathic or subnormal, and within 28 days in any other case (s. 140 (1), (2)).

Nursing Homes – The Nursing Homes Act 1975 provides for the registration and inspection of nursing homes, that is, premises for the nursing of persons suffering from any sickness, injury or infirmity, including maternity homes, but not including approved hospitals and any mental nursing homes within the meaning of the Mental Health Act 1959.

It is a summary offence for any person to carry on a nursing home or a mental nursing home without being duly registered in respect thereof by the Secretary of State. Any certificate of registration must be kept affixed in a conspicuous place in the home.

Births, Deaths and Marriages – Under s. 203, Public Health Act 1936, every birth should be notified within 36 hours to the Medical Officer of Health of the district, by the father (if he is residing in the house at the time) and by the person in attendance on the mother.

Under the Births and Deaths Registration Acts 1874, 1926 and 1953, the birth of every living or stillborn child (except a foetus under 28 weeks gestation) must be reported to the Registrar of Births, Deaths and Marriages within 42 days. Every death must be reported to the registrar within 5 days. The body of a deceased person (or of a still-born child) must not be disposed of until the person effecting the disposal has received a certificate from the registrar who has registered the death or an order from the coroner. The person effecting the disposal of the body must within 4 days notify the registrar as to the date, place, and means of disposal of the body. A dead body is not to be removed out of England without notice to the coroner. Contraventions of these Acts are summary offences.

The Marriage Acts 1949 to 1962 deal with marriage questions and repeal much previous law on the subject.

It is an offence for any person to solemnise matrimony falsely pretending that he is in holy orders (s. 75).

A marriage between persons either of whom is under the age of 16 shall be void (s. 2). It may be a defence to a charge of defiling a girl under 16 or of indecent assault (Sexual Offences Act 1956, ss. 6 and 14).

Only the bare facts of any judicial proceeding to secure divorce or restitution of conjugal rights may be published. See Chap. 11.

The making of false declarations, statements, etc., in connection with the registration of births and deaths and the celebration of marriage is also an offence under the Perjury Act (see Chap. 21) and the falsifying, etc., of official records of same is an arrestable offence under the Forgery Act (see Chap. 17).

Burials – Under the Burial Laws Amendment Act 1880, it is an offence to interfere in any manner with the decent and orderly conducting of any burial, whether it is being carried out with or without a religious service.

Under the Cemeteries Clauses Act 1847, it is a summary offence to play games or sports, or discharge firearms (save at a military funeral), or commit any nuisance in a cemetery, or to wilfully and unlawfully disturb persons assembled in a cemetery for the purpose of burying any body therein.

The Burial Act 1857 makes it a summary offence to remove any body or remains of a body from a burial ground without licence.

It is a summary offence to knowingly bury any body in a burial ground which has been closed as such by order (Burial Act 1855).

It is an offence at common law to remove without lawful authority a dead body from the grave.

The cremation in proper manner (Cremation Acts 1902 and 1952) of a body is permissible, but if there is reasonable ground for holding an inquest it is an offence to prevent it by destruction of the body.

Councils districts shall cause to be buried or cremated the body of any person who has died or been found dead in their area in any case where no suitable arrangements for the disposal of the body have been or are being made otherwise than by the council (National Assistance Act 1948, s. 50, as amended by Local Govt. Act 1972, Sch. 29).

A justice on medical evidence may order a dead body in a building to be removed by the local authority to a mortuary or buried forthwith (Public Health Act 1936, s. 162).

Fires – The Fire Services Acts 1947 to 1959 direct as follows:

Every county council shall be the fire authority for its area (s. 4) and two or more may combine for fire-fighting purposes (ss. 5–12). Every fire authority shall make provision for fire-fighting purposes (s. 1) and shall make arrangements for mutual assistance (s. 2). It will have power to provide and maintain fire alarms and to employ its fire brigade for purposes other than fire-fighting purposes (s. 3) and shall ensure the provision of an adequate available supply of water (ss. 13–16).

"Fire-fighting purposes" means the purposes of the extinction of fire and the protection of life and property in case of fire (s. 38).

Any member of a fire brigade on duty or any constable may enter, and if necessary break into, any premises or place in which a fire has or is reasonably believed to have broken out or any premises or place which it is necessary to enter for the purpose of extinguishing a fire or of protecting from acts done for fire-fighting purposes without the consent of the owner or occupier; and may do all such acts and things as he may deem necessary for extinguishing fire or for protecting from fire any such premises or place or rescuing any person or property therein (s. 30 (1)).

Any wilful obstruction or interference with a member of a fire brigade engaged in operations for fire-fighting purposes will be a summary offence (s. 30 (2)).

The senior officer present of such fire brigade shall have sole charge and control of all the operations for the extinction of a fire and may require the water supply in an area to be shut off so as to give a greater supply for the extinction of the fire (s. 30 (3), (4)).

The senior police officer or in the absence of any police the senior fire brigade officer present at a fire may close to traffic any street or stop or regulate traffic in any street (including any alley, passage, etc., whether a thoroughfare or not (s. 38)) when he considers it is necessary or desirable to do so for fire-fighting purposes (s. 30 (5)).

It is a summary offence to knowingly give or cause to be given a false alarm of fire to any fire brigade or to any member thereof (s. 31).

Any person who uses a fire hydrant unauthorisedly or who damages or obstructs a fire hydrant otherwise than in consequence of its lawful use will commit a summary offence (s. 14 (5)).

In urban districts it is a summary offence to wilfully set or cause to be set on fire any chimney, and if any chimney accidentally goes on fire the person occupying or using the premises is liable to a fine, unless he satisfies the court that such fire was not due to any omission, neglect or carelessness of himself or his servant (Town Police Clauses Act 1847, ss. 30, 31 where the Act applies).

Making a fire on a highway is a summary offence (Highways Act 1959, ss. 117 and 140).

The Children's Nightdresses Regs. 1964 impose requirements in relation to children's nightdresses, so that no person may sell or have in his possession for sale a children's nightdress not complying with the Regs. (breach of the Regs. is an offence under the Consumer Protection Act 1961).

For the law on "fireguards", see Chap. 12.

Coroners and Inquests – The office of Coroner is of ancient origin, having been instituted in England in the twelfth century as a Crown office by the Norman Kings.

The Coroner was the King's officer in a county or borough charged to keep a record of all sudden (that is unnatural or against the course of nature) deaths, forfeitures and other occurrences by which money or property might fall to the Crown.

The Coroner with the aid of a jury investigated such matters and his inquiry was called an inquisition, hence the term "inquest".

A Coroner's inquest is a court of law although no person is accused before him. The Coroner examines witnesses on oath, and while usually following the ordinary rules of evidence, he may admit any evidence he thinks fit, especially hearsay evidence. His duty is to ascertain how the deceased came by his death, and he is not bound to follow the usual procedure of law courts.

The duties of Coroners are now regulated by the Coroners Acts 1887 to 1954, and the Coroners Rules 1953.

It is the duty of the Coroner to investigate the death of any person, when informed that such death has been sudden, violent or unnatural. Cases of sudden death under any circumstances of suspicion should be reported to the Coroner.

On reasonable grounds of suspicion a Coroner may institute inquiries into any case of death.

A Coroner may also institute inquiries and hold an inquest regarding the finding of gold or silver hidden in any private place. See "Treasure Trove", Chap. 18.

A Coroner must hold an inquest in the following cases:

(1) When there is reasonable cause to suspect that a person has died either a violent or an unnatural death, or has died a sudden death of which the cause is unknown; or

(2) When a person has died in prison; or

(3) When a person has died under such circumstances as to require an inquest in accordance with any Act of Parliament, e.g. when a person confined in a mental or inebriate institution dies without satisfactory medical evidence as to the cause of death (1887 Act, s. 3).

He must have reasonable cause to suspect that death may have been due to other causes than common illness before he is entitled to hold an inquest. The question whether an inquest ought to be held is one for the Coroner to decide on the circumstances of each individual case.

The body should be lying within his jurisdiction before the Coroner may hold an inquest. It is an offence at common law to dispose of a body in order to prevent an inquest being held or to obstruct the Coroner or his jury in their inquiry.

Even if the body has been destroyed or is not recoverable, an inquest may be held if the Secretary of State so directs (1926 Act, s. 18).

A Coroner may allow a body to be moved into the jurisdiction of another Coroner so that an inquest may be held there (1926 Act, s. 16).

A Coroner's inquest may be held anywhere, but it must not be held in premises licensed for the sale of intoxicants if other suitable premises are available (Licensing Act 1964, s. 190). It should be held within a reasonable time after death.

The Coroner should summon a jury if there is reason to suspect that the death was due to—

(1) Murder, manslaughter or infanticide; or

(2) Any accident, poisoning or disease which must be notified to any Government department or official, e.g. mining, factory, explosives, railway and petroleum accidents, and certain industrial poisonings and diseases; or

(3) An accident arising out of the use of a vehicle in a street or public highway; or

(4) Circumstances prejudicial to the health or safety of the public, e.g. food poisoning cases, epidemics, deaths under anaesthetics; or has

(5) Occurred in prison or under such circumstances as to require an inquest under some Statute other than the Coroners Act 1887.

Apart from this requirement a Coroner may hold an inquest either with or without a jury as he thinks fit (1926 Act, s. 13).

If the Coroner considers it necessary he may order a post mortem examination of the body by a qualified medical man (1926 Act, ss. 22 to 24, and Coroners Rules 1953, rr. 2 to 10). If the chief officer of police informs the Coroner that a person may be charged with the murder etc. of the deceased, the Coroner should consult him as to the pathologist who is to make the post mortem examination (r. 3). If the chief officer of police desires to be represented at this examination he may be represented by a member of his force (r. 4).

A Coroner's jury consists of not less than 7 or more than 11 persons. Any person exempted from ordinary jury service is exempt from service on a Coroner's jury. The Coroner must view the body but the jury need not do so unless they so desire or unless the Coroner so directs (1926 Act, s. 14).

Under the Coroners Rules 1953, an inquest should be carried on in a formal manner (r. 13) and should be held in public but the Coroner may exclude the public in the interest of national security (r. 14). It should not be held on a Sunday (r. 15). A properly interested person may be allowed by the Coroner to examine any witness either in person or by counsel or solicitor, but the police cannot examine witnesses except through counsel or solicitor (r. 16). The Coroner may examine a witness first and the witness may be examined lastly by his representative (r. 17).

The proceedings shall be directed *solely* to ascertain:

(1) Who the deceased was.

(2) How, when and where he came by his death.

(3) The persons, if any, to be charged should the jury find that death was caused by murder, manslaughter or infanticide.

(4) The particulars required for the registration of his death (r. 26).

The Coroner shall make notes of the evidence at every inquest other than the ones at which he takes depositions (r. 30).

No person shall be allowed to address the court as to the facts (r. 31).

The Coroner shall sum up the evidence to the jury and direct them as to the law before they consider their verdict (r. 32).

The jury are sworn. The Coroner may accept the verdict of the majority of the jury provided the minority is not more than two (1926 Act, s. 15). There may be an appeal to the Queen's Bench.

If a juror or witness duly summoned to attend an inquest does not attend he may be fined (1887 Act, s. 19). No juror shall be liable to be punished for non-attendance on a Coroner's jury unless he had been served with a summons no later than 6 days before the day he was required to attend (s. 19 (3A) as added by the Juries Act 1974, Sched. 2). Such an absent witness may also be arrested and brought there on the Coroner's warrant.

A person shall not be summoned to attend as a juror at inquests held in the same Coroner's area on more than 3 days (adjournments excepted) in any year (r. 35).

Any prisoner concerned should always be given the opportunity of attending an inquest, and giving evidence, which he may do after caution from the Coroner. An order may be obtained from the Secretary of State to bring a prisoner to an inquest (C.J. Act 1961, s. 29).

The inquisition or finding of a Coroner's jury (viz. their verdict) is to be in writing signed by the jurors and by the Coroner. If it charges any person with murder, manslaughter or infanticide, the Coroner may commit such person for trial (1926 Act, s. 25).

If the chief officer of police requests the Coroner to adjourn an inquest on the ground that a person may be charged with the murder, manslaughter or causing death by reckless or dangerous driving, s. 1, Road Traffic Act 1972, or infanticide of the deceased, the Coroner shall adjourn the inquest for 14 days or longer and on police application he may grant a further adjournment (Coroners Rules 1953, r. 22).

If the Coroner is informed before the jury have given their verdict that some person has been charged before examining justices with the murder, manslaughter, infanticide, causing death by reckless or dangerous driving, or aiding, abetting, counselling or procuring the suicide of the deceased, he shall, in the absence of reason to the contrary, adjourn the inquest until after the conclusion of the criminal proceedings, and then, if he thinks fit, he may resume the inquest as a fresh inquest (1926 Act s. 1, R.T. Act 1972, s. 1 and Suicide Act 1961, Sched. 1).

Fumigation – When premises and articles not in the open air are to be fumigated with hydrogen cyanide or any substance added by Order in Council, notification has to be given to the nearest police station and elaborate precautions have to be taken and observed. See the Hydrogen Cyanide (Fumigation) Act 1937, and the Regulations of 1951 thereunder.

Unauthorised Dumping – Under the Civic Amenities Act 1967, any person who, without lawful authority,—(a) abandons on any land in the open air, or on any other land forming part of a highway, a motor vehicle or anything which formed part of a motor vehicle and was removed from it in the course of dismantling the vehicle on the land; or (b) abandons on any such land any thing other than a motor vehicle, being a thing which he has brought to the land for the purpose of abandoning it there, shall be guilty of an offence (s. 19 (1)).

A person who leaves any thing on any land in such circumstances or for such a period that he may reasonably be assumed to have abandoned it or to have brought it to the land for the purpose of abandoning it there shall be deemed to have abandoned it there or, as the case may be, to have brought it to the land for that purpose unless the contrary is shown (s. 19 (2)).

Poisonous Waste – Under the Deposit of Poisonous Waste Act 1972 it is an offence to deposit on land waste which is poisonous, noxious or polluting when its presence on the land is liable to give rise to an environmental hazard. Waste constitutes an environmental hazard if it subjects persons or animals to a material risk of death, injury or impairment of health, or if it threatens to pollute a water supply. The offence is triable summarily or on indictment (s. 1).

The Act also creates a duty to notify the local and river authorities of the respective areas when waste to which the Act applies is to be moved from one area and deposited in another. Failure to notify is a summary offence (s. 3).

The Act will be repealed when the Control of Pollution Act 1974, containing more elaborate provisions as to pollution generally, is brought into force.

Abatement of Litter – If any person without proper authority throws down, drops or otherwise deposits in, into or from any place in the open air to which the public are entitled or permitted to have access without payment, and leaves anything whatsoever in such circumstances as to cause, contribute to, or tend to lead to, the defacement by litter of any place in the open air, he shall be guilty of a summary offence.

Any covered place, open to the air on at least one side, and available for public use shall be treated as being a place in the open air.

Power to institute proceedings for an offence under this Act is given to many local authorities, without prejudice to the powers of any other person (Litter Act 1958, s. 1). The court in sentencing a person convicted of an offence against the Litter Act 1958 shall have regard to the nature of the litter and any resulting risk of injury to persons or animals or of damage to property (Dangerous Litter Act 1971).

Noise Abatement – The Noise Abatement Act 1960 (which will be repealed and replaced by the Control of Pollution Act 1974, when in force) makes new provisions in respect of the control of noise and vibration. A noise or vibration which is a nuisance shall be a statutory nuisance (s. 1). See Public Health Acts, *ante*.

A loudspeaker in a street shall not be operated (a) between 9 p.m. and 8 a.m. for any purpose, and (b) at any other time for advertising any entertainment, trade or business. Any contravention of the above is a summary offence. "Street" includes a highway, and any other road, footway, square, or court which is for the time being open to the public.

However, the above does not apply to the operation of a loudspeaker—(a) used for police, fire brigade or ambulance purposes, or by a local authority within their area; (b) used for communicating with persons on a vessel for the purpose of directing the movement of a vessel; (c) if the loudspeaker forms part of a public telephone system; (d) used on a vehicle to entertain or communicate with the driver or passenger, or is part of an instrument for giving warning to other traffic, and is used so as not to give cause for annoyance to persons in the vicinity; (e) used by transport undertakings to make announcements to passengers or employees; (f) by a travelling showman on land used for a pleasure fair; (g) in case of emergency.

Provision is made for the use of a loudspeaker between 12 noon and 7 p.m. to advertise the sale of perishable commodities for human consumption if the advertising is by means other than words and the loudspeaker is operated so as not to give reasonable cause for annoyance to persons in the vicinity.

"Loudspeaker" includes a megaphone or any other device for amplifying sound.

Proceedings for an offence under this section may, without prejudice to the powers of any other person to take such proceedings, be taken by the Local Authority (s. 2).

APPENDIX I

SPEED LIMITS FOR MOTOR VEHICLES

(See Chapter 24, TRAFFIC)

Maximum speed limits in miles per hour on public roads are prescribed by Sched. 5 to the Road Traffic Regulation Act 1967 as follows:

SCHEDULE

LIMITS OF SPEED FOR VEHICLES OF CERTAIN CLASSES

Class of Vehicle (See also paragraph 13)	*Maximum speed, miles per hour*
VEHICLES OTHER THAN TRACK LAYING VEHICLES	
1. *Passenger Vehicles*, that is to say, vehicles constructed solely for the carriage of passengers and their effects, and *dual purpose vehicles:*	
1) a passenger vehicle having an unladen weight exceeding 3 tons, or adapted to carry more than 7 passengers exclusive of the driver, in respect of which a public service vehicle licence granted under s. 127 of the Road Traffic Act 1960 is in force	50
(2) a passenger vehicle having an unladen weight not exceeding 30 hundredweight, adapted to carry more than 7 passengers exclusive of the driver and in respect of which a public service vehicle licence granted under s. 127 of the Road Traffic Act 1960 is not in force	50
(3) a vehicle having an unladen weight exceeding 3 tons, or adapted to carry more than 7 passengers exclusive of the driver, not being a vehicle which falls within sub-paragraph (1) or (2) above	40
(4) a vehicle drawing one trailer when the drawing vehicle is either a motor car adapted to carry not more than 7 passengers exclusive of the driver or a passenger vehicle	

which has an unladen weight not exceeding 30 hundredweight and is adapted to carry more than 7 passengers exclusive of the driver—

(*a*) in a case where the relevant conditions specified in paragraph 25 below are satisfied, or the drawing vehicle is a foreign vehicle 50

(*b*) in any other case 40

(5) a vehicle drawing one trailer in circumstances not falling within sub-paragraph (4) above–

(*a*) in the case of a passenger vehicle having an unladen weight exceeding 3 tons, or adapted to carry more than 7 passengers exclusive of the driver, in respect of which a public service vehicle licence granted under s. 127 of the Road Traffic Act 1960 is in force 40

(*b*) in the case of a vehicle not falling within sub-paragraph (a) above 30

(6) a vehicle drawing more than one trailer . . . 20

(7) a vehicle not fitted with pneumatic tyres and a vehicle drawing a trailer not so fitted 20

(8) an invalid carriage 20

2. *Goods vehicles*, that is to say, vehicles constructed or adapted for use for the conveyance of goods or burden of any description, but not including dual-purpose vehicles—

(1) generally, except for vehicles falling within sub-paragraph (2) or (3) (*a*) below · 40

(2) vehicles having an unladen weight not exceeding 30 hundredweight, when not drawing a trailer . . 50

(3) vehicles drawing a trailer, not being articulated vehicles— . . . .

(*a*) in the case of a trailer drawn by a motor car having an unladen weight not exceeding 30 hundredweight when the relevant conditions specified in paragraph 25 below are satisfied or the drawing vehicle is a foreign vehicle 50

(*b*) in the case of a trailer drawn by a heavy motor car or by a motor cycle 30

(*c*) in the case of a trailer drawn by a motor car having an unladen weight exceeding 30 hundredweight if the trailer—

(i) being a load-carrying trailer, has an unladen weight exceeding 5 hundredweight, or

(ii) being neither a living van nor a load-carrying trailer, has an unladen weight exceeding 15 hundredweight 30

(4) vehicles drawing more than one trailer . . . 20

(5) vehicles not fitted with pneumatic tyres, if drawing trailers or having an unladen weight exceeding 1 ton, and vehicles drawing trailers not fitted with pneumatic tyres 20

(6) vehicles not fitted with resilient tyres and vehicles drawing trailers not so fitted 5

3. *Motor tractors:*

(1) generally except for vehicles falling within the following sub-paragraph 20

(2) vehicles fitted with pneumatic tyres, equipped with springs and wings and which satisfy the conditions as to brakes specified in paragraph 20(*a*) below or such vehicles drawing a trailer so fitted and equipped and which satisfies the conditions as to brakes specified in paragraph 20 (*b*) below 30

(3) if drawing two or more trailers 12

(4) If not fitted with resilient tyres or drawing trailers not so fitted 5

4. *Heavy locomotives and light locomotives:*

(1) generally, except for vehicles falling within the following sub-paragraph 12

(2) vehicles fitted with pneumatic tyres, equipped with springs and wings and which satisfy the conditions as to brakes and weight specified in paragraph 20 (*a*), (*c*) and (*d*) below or such vehicles drawing a trailer so fitted and equipped and which satisfies the conditions as to brakes specified in paragraph 20 (*b*) below if the further conditions as to the weight of a vehicle and trailer specified in paragraph 20 (*e*) below are complied with . . 20

(3) if drawing two or more trailers 12

(4) if not fitted with resilient tyres or drawing trailers not so fitted 5

TRACK-LAYING VEHICLES

5. *Motor cars and heavy motor cars* 20

6. *Motor tractors:*

(1) generally 20

(2) if drawing two or more trailers 5

7. *Light locomotives:*

(1) generally 12

(2) if drawing more than two trailers 5

8. *Heavy locomotives* 5

9. Track-laying vehicles which do not satisfy both of the following conditions—

(*a*) that the vehicle is fitted with springs between its frame and the weight-carrying rollers, and

(*b*) that the vehicle is fitted with resilient material between the rims of the weight-carrying rollers and the road surface,

and vehicles drawing track-laying trailers which do not satisfy both of those conditions 12

10. Track-laying vehicles satisfying neither of the said conditions, and vehicles drawing track-laying trailers satisfying neither of those conditions 5

11. Combined track-and-wheel vehicles not fitted with resilient tyres, and vehicles drawing trailers which are combined track-and-wheel vehicles not fitted with resilient tyres . 5

12. Vehicles drawing trailers, where the drawing or any of the drawn vehicles, not being a track-laying vehicle, is not fitted with resilient tyres 5

Interpretation and Application

13. A vehicle falling within two or more classes specified in this Schedule shall be treated as falling within that class for which the lowest limit of speed is specified.

14. (1) In this Schedule "dual-purpose vehicle" means a vehicle constructed or adapted for the carriage both of passengers and of goods or burden of any description being a vehicle of which the unladen weight does not exceed 2 tons and which either—

(*a*) satisfies the conditions as to construction specified in the following sub-paragraph; or

(*b*) is so constructed or adapted that the driving power of the engine is, or by the appropriate use of the controls of the vehicle can be, transmitted to all the wheels of the vehicle.

(2) The conditions as to construction referred to in sub-paragraph (1) above are the following—

(*a*) the vehicle must be permanently fitted with a rigid roof, with or without a sliding panel:

(*b*) the area of the vehicle to the rear of the driver's seat must—

(i) be permanently fitted with at least one row of transverse seats (fixed or folding) for two or more passengers and those seats must be properly sprung or cushioned and provided with upholstered back-rests, attached either to the seats or to a side or the floor of the vehicle, and

(ii) be lit on each side and at the rear by a window or windows of glass or other transparent material having an area or aggregate area of not less than 2 square feet on each side and not less than 120 square inches at the rear;

(*c*) the distance between the rearmost part of the steering wheel and the backrests of the row of transverse seats satisfying the requirements specified in head (*b*) (i) of this sub-paragraph (or, if there is more than one such row of seats, the distance between the rearmost part of the steering wheel and the backrests of the rearmost such row) must, when the seats are ready for use, be not less than one-third of the distance between the rearmost part of the steering wheel and the rearmost part of the floor of the vehicle.

15. In this Schedule "load-carrying trailer" means a trailer, not being a living van, which is constructed or adapted for use for the conveyance of goods or burden of any description.

16. Deleted by the Motor Vehicles (Variation of Speed Limits) Regs. 1973.

17. In this Schedule "articulated vehicle" means a vehicle which consists of a motor vehicle drawing a trailer where the trailer is so attached to the drawing vehicle that part of the trailer is superimposed upon the drawing vehicle, and when the trailer is uniformly loaded not less than 20 per cent of the weight of its load is borne by the drawing vehicle.

18. In this Schedule, in relation to a vehicle (including a trailer)—

(*a*) "fitted with pneumatic tyres" means that every wheel of the vehicle is fitted with pneumatic tyres:

(*b*) "fitted with resilient tyres" means that every wheel of the vehicle is fitted either with pneumatic tyres or with other soft or elastic tyres; and

(*c*) "equipped with springs and wings" means that the vehicle—

(i) is equipped with suitable and sufficient springs between each wheel and the frame of the vehicle, and

(ii) unless adequate protection is afforded by the body of the vehicle, is provided with wings or other similar fittings to catch, so far as practicable, mud or water thrown up by the rotation of the wheels.

19. In this Schedule "track-laying" means so designed and constructed that the weight is transmitted to the road surface either by means of continuous tracks or by a combination of wheels and continuous tracks, and "combined track-and-wheel vehicle" means a vehicle so designed and constructed that its weight is transmitted to the road surface by a combination of wheels and continuous tracks.

20. The conditions referred to in paragraphs 3 (2) and 4 (2) above are as follows:

(*a*) the motor tractor, or, as the case may be, the locomotive, shall be equipped with an efficient braking system having two means of operation or with two efficient braking systems each having a separate means of operation, the system or systems being so designed and constructed that, notwithstanding the failure of any part (other than a fixed member or a brake shoe anchor pin) through or by means of which the force necessary to apply the brakes is transmitted, there is still available for application by the driver to not less than half the number of the wheels of the vehicle brakes sufficient under the most adverse conditions to bring it to rest within a reasonable distance:

(*b*) the trailer shall be equipped with an efficient braking system so constructed—

(i) that when the trailer is being drawn the brakes are capable of being applied by the driver of the drawing vehicle to at least two of the wheels of a trailer having not more than four wheels and to at least four, but not less than half, of the wheels of a trailer having more than four wheels, and

(ii) that it is not rendered ineffective by the non-rotation of the engine of the drawing vehicle;

(*c*) the weight transmitted to the road surface by any one wheel of the locomotive, where no other wheel is in the same line transversely, shall not exceed 4½ tons, the total weight so transmitted by any two wheels in line transversely shall not exceed 9 tons and the sum of the weights so transmitted by all the wheels shall not exceed—

(i) in the case of a vehicle having not more than four wheels, 14 tons,

(ii) in the case of a vehicle having more than four but not more than six wheels, 20 tons, and

(iii) in the case of a vehicle having more than six wheels, 24 tons;

(*d*) the weight transmitted by the locomotive (whether laden or unladen) to any strip of the surface of a road on which it rests contained between any two parallel lines drawn 2 feet apart on that surface at right angles to the longitudinal axis of the vehicle shall not exceed 11 tons; and

(*e*) the maximum laden weight of the locomotive and trailer shall not exceed 22 tons or, if the trailer is fitted with power-assisted brakes which can be operated by the driver of the drawing vehicle and are not rendered ineffective by the non-rotation of its engine, and if that vehicle is equipped with a warning device so placed as to be readily visible to the driver when in the driving seat of the vehicle in order to indicate an impending failure or deficiency in the vacuum or pressure system, 32 tons.

21. For the purposes of this Schedule measuring or testing apparatus, and any ballast necessary in connection, therewith, drawn upon one wheel by a vehicle, when used solely for or in connection with testing or measurement purposes, shall not, ifthe wheel is fitted with a pneumatic tyre and does not transmit to the road surface a weight exceeding 2 hundredweight, be treated as a trailer.

22. For the purposes of paragraphs 20 and 21 above, two wheels of a vehicle shall be regarded as one wheel if the distance between the centres of their respective areas of contact with the road is less than 18 inches.

23. A heavy motor car or motor car drawing a trailer and being used as a public service vehicle or as a goods vehicle shall be treated as not drawing a trailer if the trailer is used solely for the carriage of a container or containers for holding, or plant and materials for producing, for the purpose of the propulsion of the drawing vehicle, any fuel that is wholly gaseous at 60 degrees Fahrenheit under pressure of 30 inches of mercury.

24. (1) Paragraphs 1 to 4 above do not apply to, and paragraphs 5 to 12 above apply only to, track-laying vehicles and vehicles drawing track-laying trailers or trailers some of which are track-laying.

(2) Paragraphs 1 to 12 above do not apply to vehicles for the time being used in the conduct of experiments or trials under section 6 of the Roads Improvement Act 1925 or section 249 of the Highways Act 1959.

25. The relevant conditions referred to in paragraphs 1 (4) and 2 (3) above in relation to a vehicle drawing a trailer and the trailer so drawn are as follows:

(*a*) appropriate weights shall be displayed as follows:—

(i) in the case of the drawing vehicle, its kerbside weight shall be legibly marked in a conspicuous and readily accessible position—

(A) inside the vehicle, or

(B) outside the vehicle and on its left or near side, and

(ii) in the case of the trailer being a living van, or being neither a living van nor a load-carrying trailer, its maximum gross weight shall be legibly marked in a conspicuous and readily accessible position on the left or near side of, and on the outside of, the trailer;

(*b*) the appropriate weights referred to in (*a*) above may be stated in imperial units or in metric units but the same units shall be employed for both the drawing vehicle and the trailer, and if metric units are employed the weights shall be stated in kilograms.

(*c*) there shall be exhibited in a conspicuous position at the rear of the trailer a plate which complies in all respects with the following requirements—

(i) the plate shall be circular or elliptical, shall be fixed in a vertical position facing squarely to the rear of the trailer, shall, if elliptical, be placed so that the major axis is in the horizontal position, and shall be kept clean and unobscured so as to be plainly visible from behind the trailer,

(ii) the surface facing to the rear shall be black and shall display thereon the number "50" in white or silver or light grey figures,

(iii) the plate, if circular, shall be not less than 4 inches in diameter, and, if elliptical, shall be not less than 3 inches in height and $4\frac{1}{4}$ inches in width,

(iv) each figure of the said number shall be not less than $1\frac{3}{4}$ inches in height and $1\frac{1}{4}$ inches in total width, the width of every part of each figure shall be not less than $\frac{5}{16}$ inch, and the space between the nearest parts of the two figures shall not be less than $\frac{1}{4}$ inch, and

(v) no part of any such figure shall project from the surface of the said plate by more than $\frac{3}{16}$ inch;

(*d*) the following weight ratios shall be observed—

(i) where the trailer drawn is a living van, its maximum gross weight shall not exceed the kerbside weight of the drawing vehicle,

(ii) where the trailer drawn is a braked load-carrying trailer, its laden weight shall not exceed the kerbside weight of the drawing vehicle,

(iii) where the trailer drawn is an unbraked load-carrying trailer, its laden weight shall not exceed 60 per cent of the kerbside weight of the drawing vehicle,

(iv) where the trailer drawn is a braked trailer, being neither a living van nor a load-carrying trailer, its maximum gross weight shall not exceed the kerbside weight of the drawing vehicle, and

(v) where the trailer drawn is an unbraked trailer, being neither a living van nor a load-carrying trailer, its maximum gross weight shall not exceed 60 per cent of the kerbside weight of the drawing vehicle.

26. In this Schedule—

"braked trailer" means a trailer which is equipped with a braking system in accordance with Regulation 70 of the Motor Vehicles (Construction and Use) Regulations 1973, whether or not that Regulation applies to it;

"unbraked trailer" means a trailer which is not so equipped;

"foreign vehicle" means—

(*a*) a motor vehicle brought into Great Britain and displaying a registration mark mentioned in Regulation 5 of the Motor Vehicles (International Circulation) Regulations 1971, a period of twelve months not having elapsed since the vehicle in question was last brought into Great Britain; or

(*b*) a vehicle in the service of a visiting force or of a headquarters.

"kerbside weight" means, in relation to a motor vehicle, the weight of the vehicle (inclusive of any towing bracket with which it is normally equipped) when it carries—

(i) no person thereon, and

(ii) a full supply of fuel in its tank, an adequate supply of other liquids incidental to its propulsion and no load other than the loose tools and equipment with which the vehicle is normally equipped;

"maximum gross weight" means, in relation to a trailer, the weight which it is designed or adapted not to exceed when in normal use and travelling on a road laden;

"vehicle in the service of a visiting force or of a headquarters" has the same meaning as in Article 8 (6) of the Visiting Forces and International Headquarters (Application of Law) Order 1965."

The maximum speed limit for motor vehicles on all roads in

England and Wales is 70 m.p.h. (70 miles per hour Speed Limit (England) Order 1967 and Motorways Traffic (Speed Limit) (England) Regs. 1967). There are similar provisions for Wales.

APPENDIX II

REGULATIONS AS TO THE CONSTRUCTION AND USE OF MOTOR VEHICLES AND TRAILERS

(See Chapter 25, ROAD VEHICLES)

The Motor Vehicles (Construction and Use) Regulations 1973 apply, except where the context otherwise requires, to wheeled vehicles only (reg. 4). Every motor vehicle and trailer must be wheeled or a tracklaying vehicle except motor cycles and invalid carriages which must be wheeled (reg. 8). Each of these regulations when referred to herein will be indicated by the letters "Reg". and the number of the regulation. The regulations are in this Appendix dealt with under alphabetical headings.

Exemptions – Road rollers are not subject to regs. 11, 12, 23, 27, 44, 45, and 51. (reg 4).

Vehicles proceeding to a port for export are not subject to regs. 9 to 12, 14 to 21, 23, 24, 28 to 74, and 91. Regulations 11, 12, 20, 45, 51, 55, 60, 71, 72, 74 and 76 to 88, apply only to motor vehicles and trailers used upon highways. Regulations 12, 49, 58, 60, 61 and 64 do not apply to pedestrian controlled vehicle.

A motor vehicle registered before the end of one year from the making of any regulation (other than regs. 89 and 138 to 146) affecting construction or weight is exempt from its requirements for 5 years providing it complies with any previous similar regulations (reg. 4).

Motor vehicles or trailers brought into Great Britain temporarily by a person resident abroad are not subject to many of the Construction Rules of Part II of the regulations, and only regs. 9, 42 to 44, 48, 52, 57, 65, 68 and 69 will apply, provided that such vehicles comply with the requirements of the International Convention 1926 or of the Road Traffic Convention, Geneva, 1949 (reg. 4). Certain vehicles are exempted from the requirements relating to brakes, strength of side door latches and hinges, constructionof petrol tanks, mirrors, audible warning instruments, noise, radio interference suppression, and emission of smoke or vapour. The vehicles concerned are those in respect of which a type approval certificate or a certificate of conformity has been issued under the M.V. (Type Approval) Regs. 1973, and 1975 and the exemptions apply in so far as the vehicles in question conform to the Directives of the E.E.C. (reg. 4A).

Part II (regs. 8 to 73 inclusive) except regs. 9, 42 to 44, 48, 52, 57 and 65, shall not apply to any motor vehicle manufactured in Great Britain which (1) has been purchased by a person who is temporarily in Great Britain and is or is about to be resident abroad and in respect of which—(a) relief from purchase tax has been afforded, or (b) there is no liability to pay purchase tax, for a period—(i) in the case of (a) not exceeding one year during which relief from purchase tax continues, and (ii) in the case of (b) not exceeding one year from the date it was purchased by such a person as a new vehicle from a manufacturer or dealer, provided the vehicle complies in every respect with the requirements specified in the last preceding paragraph as if the vehicle had been brought temporarily into Great Britain; or (2) has been zero rated under regs. 44 or 45 Value Added Tax (General) Regs. 1972 (reg. 4).

Also regs. 9 to 12, 14 to 20, 22 to 30, 33A, 34, 36 to 88, and 130 shall not apply to any vehicle in the service of a visiting force (reg. 4).

Regulations 8 to 73, 74 to 106 and 132 shall not apply to (a) a motor vehicle submitted for a test under R.T. Act 1972, s. 43, while it is being used on a road in connection with that test by a person empowered to carry out that test or by a person acting under his direction or (b) to a motor vehicle or trailer submitted for examination under R.T. Act 1972, s. 45, while it is being used on a road in connection with that examination by a person empowered to carry out that examination or by a person acting under his direction.

Regulations 18, 20, 27 (4), 61, 64 and 110 (2) of these regulations shall not apply to any motor car or motor cycle in respect of which a certificate has been issued by the Officer in Charge of the National Collections of Road Transport, the Science Museum, London, S.W.7, that it was designed before January 1, 1905, and constructed before December 31, 1905, and paragraphs (1) to (3), (5) to (7), (9) to (11) and (13) to (15) of regulation 59 of these regulations shall not apply to any such motor car if it complies with the provisions of paragraph (8) of the said regulation 59 as though it were a vehicle first registered under the Motor Car Act 1903 before January 1, 1915, and paragraphs (1), (2), (5) and (6) of regulation 62 shall not apply to any such motor cycle if it complies with the provisions of paragraph (4) of the said regulation 62 as though it were a motor cycle first registered under the Motor Car Act 1903 or the Roads Act 1920 before January 1, 1927 (reg. 4).

The provisions of regs. 8 to 73 (except reg. 8 (2)) applicable to trailers and regs. 75 and 118 shall not apply (a) to any towing implement drawn by a motor vehicle while it is not attached to any vehicle except the one drawing it if (i) the towing implement is not being drawn during the hours of darkness, and (ii) the drawing vehicle does not exceed 20 m.p.h., or (b) to any vehicle drawn by a motor vehicle in the exercise of a statutory power of removal (reg. 4).

Any reference in the regulations to a vehicle which is being drawn by a motor vehicle in the exercise of a statutory power of removal or to a broken down vehicle shall include a reference to any towing implement used for drawing any such vehicle (reg. 4).

In relation to a land tractor which complies with the conditions mentioned below (a) regs. 12, 18, 27 and 52 to 61 shall not apply; (b) reg. 74 shall not apply if its unladen weight does not exceed 3,050 kilograms. Regs. 48 to 51 shall apply in relation to a land tractor which is a heavy motor car or motor car as they apply in relation to a land tractor which is a motor tractor. The conditions are that while a land tractor is used on a road (a) it does not haul any object except (i) a land implement or a land implement conveyor which is being hauled to or from the site of agricultural, grass cutting, forestry, land levelling, dredging or similar operations or from one part of a farm or forestry estate to another part; or (ii) an agricultural trailer; (b) it does not carry any load except any such load as it is constructed or adapted to carry; (c) if it is a three-wheeled vehicle fitted with a removable appliance, it does not carry any load; (d) if it is a land tractor fitted with a removable appliance in or on which any such load as aforesaid could be carried, it does not carry any load in or on such appliance unless there is at least 1.22 metres between the centre of the area of contact with the road surface of (i) a rear wheel, where only one appliance is being used for the carriage of a load and is fitted to the back of the vehicle; (ii) any wheel on one side of the vehicle, in any other case; and that of the nearest wheel on the other side; (e) if it is a land tractor carrying a load in or on a removable appliance inconformity with the foregoing conditions, it does not draw a trailer and not more than one such appliance is fitted to it at any one time or, where one such appliance is a specified appliance for the purposes of the Vehicles (Excise) Act 1971, Sched. 4, Para. 8 (2), not more than two of such appliances fitted at opposite ends of the tractor; (f) if it is not driven at a speed exceeding 20 m.p.h. (reg. 5).

Special application of certain Regulations – The Secretary of State is satisfied (a) that it is requisite that the provisions of regs. 34 (1), 40 (1) and 41 (1) (being provisions which vary the requirements as regards the construction of the vehicles specified in each of those regulations) shall apply at April 1, 1973 to such of the vehicles respectively so specified as are registered under the Vehicles (Excise) Act 1971 before the expiration of one year from the making of these regulations; and (b) that notwithstanding that the said provisions will then apply to those vehicles no undue hardship or inconvenience will be caused thereby (reg. 6 (1)).

Nothing in reg. 4 (6) shall be taken to affect the application of the said regs. 34 (1), 40 (1) and 41 (1) (reg. 6 (2)).

Provision as respects Trade Descriptions Act 1968 – Where by a provision of any regulation hereof any vehicle or any of its parts or equipment is required to be marked with a specification number or the registered certification trade mark of the British Standards Institution or with an approval mark, nothing in that provision shall be taken to authorise any person to apply any such number or mark to the vehicle, part or equipment in contravention of the Trade Descriptions Act 1968 (reg. 7).

Abnormal Indivisible Load – Means a load which cannot without undue expense or risk of damage be divided into two or more loads for conveyance on a road (reg. 3) and owing to its dimensions or weight can only be carried by motor vehicles or trailers the use of which on roads is lawful only by reason of an Order of the Minister of Transport made under s. 42 of the Road Traffic Act 1972. See "Special Types", later.

Agricultural Trailer – Means a trailer the property of a person engaged in agriculture which is not used on a road for the conveyance of goods or burden other than agricultural produce or articles required for the purposes of agriculture (reg. 3).

It need not have springs (reg. 12) nor trailer plate (reg. 75), nor soft, or pneumatic tyres when on a highway (regs. 71, 72). If it is merely an agricultural vehicle not constructed to carry a load, it does not count as a "trailer" for the purpose of additional attendants (s. 34) or as regards the number of trailers permissible to be drawn (reg. 136).

A trailer made before January 15, 1931, for the conveyance of horses and cattle and used for that purpose or for some other purpose connected with agriculture need not have soft, elastic or pneumatic tyres (reg. 71). An agricultural trailer constructed before July 1, 1947, and drawn by a motor tractor or a land tractor which is not a motor tractor need not have a braking system if laden weight does not exceed 4,070 kilograms and is the only trailer drawn and speed does not exceed 10 m.p.h. (reg. 70).

Ambulances – They may carry gongs, bells, sirens, or two-tone horn (reg. 27), and use them if necessary at any time (reg. 110). The speed limits do not apply if their observance would hinder the use of any vehicle for ambulance purposes (s. 79,

R.T.R. Act 1967). The engine need not be stopped while vehicle is used for ambulance purposes (reg. 116).

The overhang limit does not apply to a motor car used as an ambulance by a local authority (reg. 58).

Articulated Vehicle – Means a heavy motor car or motor car with trailer so attached to the drawing vehicle that part is superimposed thereon and when trailer is uniformly loaded not less than 20 per cent. of the weight of the load is borne by the drawing vehicle (reg. 3). In such a case the vehicle itself is deemed to be constructed to carry a load (R.T. Act 1972, s. 191).

A vehicle so constructed that it can be divided into two parts, both of which are vehicles and one of which is a motor vehicle shall (when not so divided) be treated for the purposes of R.T. Act 1972 as that motor vehicle with the other part attached as a trailer (R.T. Act 1972, s. 191). There is a similar provision with respect to the R.T.R. Act 1967, in s. 100 of that Act.

ATTENDANT additional to driver is not necessary (reg. 135).

BRAKES – See "Brakes" later.

LENGTH – See "Length" later.

The total laden weight shall not exceed 20,330 kilograms if the trailer part has less than four wheels. If it has four or more wheels the limit is 24,390 kilograms (reg. 82).

Trailer plate is not necessary (reg. 75).

Wings are not necessary for the rear wheels of a heavy motor car forming part of an articulated vehicle used only for carriage of round timber (reg. 56).

Attendants – Two persons shall be employed in driving or attending a heavy or light locomotive on a highway, and if it draws a trailer or trailers, one or more persons in addition to the two aforesaid shall be employed for attending to the trailer or trailers at the rate of one such additional person for each trailer in excess of one. This does not apply to a road roller while rolling a road. If a motor vehicle other than a locomotive draws a trailer or trailers on a highway one person in addition to the driver must be carried to attend to the trailer or trailers. As regards "attendants", the term "trailer" does not include a vehicle used solely for carrying water for the motor vehicle or any agricultural vehicle not made to carry a load. Any person causing or permitting a breach of this section commits an offence (R.T. Act 1972, s. 34). By reg. 135 the above requirements as to attendants do not apply to:

(1) An articulated vehicle.

(2) A land locomotive or land tractor drawing a land implement or land implement conveyor or a land tractor drawing an agricultural trailer.

(3) A motor car or motor cycle drawing a trailer with not

more than two wheels or a motor car drawing a 4-wheeled trailer with two close coupled wheels on each side.

(4) A motor tractor drawing a closed meat van between docks, railway stations and wholesale markets.

(5) A motor tractor drawing a machine or implement used for maintenance, repair or cleansing of roads.

(6) A motor tractor drawing a trailer designed and used for street cleansing or the collection or disposal of refuse, etc.

(7) A works truck drawing any works trailer, weight unladen of each vehicle not exceeding 1,525 kilograms.

(8) A heavy motor vehicle or motor car drawing a "gas" trailer.

(9) Where a motor vehicle is drawing a trailer which has no other brakes, other than a parking brake, and brakes which automatically come into operation on the overrun of the trailer.

(10) In the case of a road roller.

(11) A motor vehicle belonging to the Secretary of State for Defence drawing a trailer with brakes which can be applied by the driver of the motor vehicle.

(12) A motor vehicle drawing a broken down vehicle unable to steer.

(13) A vehicle which is being drawn by a motor vehicle in the exercise of a statutory power of removal in such manner that the drawn vehicle cannot be steered by its own steering gear.

(14) A towing implement which is being drawn by a motor vehicle while it is not attached to any vehicle except the one drawing it.

(15) A motor vehicle drawing a trailer or trailers and every such trailer is fitted with power-assisted or power-operated brakes which can be operated by the driver and are not rendered ineffective by the non-rotation of the engine of the drawing vehicle—(i) where one such trailer is drawn; or (ii) where two or more such trailers are drawn, if one attendant is carried either on the drawing vehicle or a trailer for the purpose of attending to the trailers.

(16) Any locomotive propelled by the combustion of liquid fuel or by electrical power whether or not it is drawing a trailer or trailers (reg. 135).

Audible warning instrument – (1) Subject to the provisions of this regulation, every motor vehicle shall be fitted with an instrument capable of giving audible and sufficient warning of its approach or position.

(2) The sound emitted by any instrument of the kind described in (1) above, fitted to a motor vehicle, being a motor vehicle first used on or after August 1, 1973, shall be continuous and uniform and not strident.

(3) Paragraph (1) of this regulation shall not apply to a works truck or a pedestrian controlled vehicle.

(4) Except as provided in paragraphs (5) and (6) of this regulation, no motor vehicle shall be fitted with a gong, bell, siren or two-tone horn.

(5) The following vehicles may be fitted with a gong, bell, siren or two-tone horn:

(*a*) motor vehicles used for fire brigade, ambulance or police purposes;
(*b*) motor vehicles owned by a body formed primarily for the purposes of fire salvage and used for those or similar purposes;
(*c*) motor vehicles owned by the Forestry Commission or by local authorities and used from time to time for the purposes of fighting fires;
(*d*) motor vehicles owned by the Secretary of State for Defence and used for the purposes of the disposal of bombs or explosives;
(*e*) motor vehicles used for the purposes of the Blood Transfusion Service under Part II of the National Health Service Act 1946 or under Part II of the National Health Service (Scotland) Act 1947;
(*f*) motor vehicles used by Her Majesty's Coastguard or the Coastguard Auxiliary Service to aid persons in danger or vessels in distress on or near the coast; and
(*g*) motor vehicles owned by the National Coal Board and used for the purposes of rescue operations at mines.

(6) A motor vehicle used for the conveyance of goods for sale from the vehicle may, if it is also fitted with an instrument or apparatus for the purpose of complying with paragraph (1) of this regulation, be fitted with an instrument or apparatus other than a two-tone horn designed to emit a sound for the purpose of informing members of the public that goods are on the vehicle for sale.

(7) References in paragraphs (4) and (5) of this regulation to a gong, bell or siren include references to any instrument or apparatus capable of emitting a sound similar to that emitted by a gong, bell or siren (reg. 27).

USE OF AUDIBLE WARNING INSTRUMENTS

(1) Subject to the provisions of this regulation, no person shall—

(*a*) in the case of a vehicle which is stationary on a road, at any time other than at times of danger due to another moving vehicle on or near the road; or
(*b*) in the case of a vehicle which is in motion on a restricted road, between the hours of 11.30 in the evening and 7 in the following morning,

sound or cause or permit to be sounded any instrument or apparatus fitted to or otherwise carried on the vehicle, being an instrument or apparatus capable of giving audible and sufficient warning of its approach or position.

(2) Subject to the provisions of this regulation and without prejudice to the provisions of the foregoing paragraph, no person shall sound or cause or permit to be sounded a gong, bell, siren, any instrument or apparatus capable of making a sound similar to that emitted by a gong, bell or siren, or a two-tone horn, fitted to or otherwise carried on a vehicle (whether it is stationary or not).

(3) Nothing in paragraph (1) or (2) of this regulation shall have effect to prevent the sounding of an instrument or apparatus fitted to, or otherwise carried on, a vehicle at a time when the vehicle is being used for one of the relevant purposes specified in regulation 27(5) and it is necessary or desirable to do so either to indicate to other road users the urgency of the purposes for which the vehicle is being used, or to warn other road users of the presence of the vehicle on the road.

(4) Nothing in paragraph (1) of this regulation shall have effect to prevent the driver of a vehicle or some other authorised person sounding or causing or permitting to be sounded an instrument or apparatus fitted to or otherwise carried on the vehicle (a) if it is sounded for the purpose of raising an alarm as to the theft or attempted theft of the vehicle or its contents (b) if the vehicle is a P.S.V. and the instrument or apparatus is sounded for the purpose of summoning assistance for the driver, the conductor or an inspector.

(5) Subject to the provisions of s. 2 (1) and (3) of the Noise Abatement Act 1960 and notwithstanding the provisions of paragraph (2) of this regulation, a person may sound or cause or permit to be sounded an instrument or apparatus other than a two-tone horn fitted to or otherwise carried on a vehicle, being an instrument or apparatus designed to emit a sound for the purpose of informing members of the public that the vehicle is conveying goods for sale, if—

(*a*) when the instrument is sounded, it is sounded only for that purpose; and

(*b*) in a case where a vehicle is on a restricted road, the instrument is sounded otherwise than between the hours of 11.30 in the evening and 7 in the following morning.

(6) In this regulation:

"restricted road" means a length of road—

(*a*) on which there is provided a system of street lighting furnished by means of lamps placed not more than 200 metres apart, or

(*b*) as respects which there is in force a direction under section 72 (3) of the R.T.R. Act 1967 that the said length shall become a restricted road for the purposes of section 71 of that Act or a direction under section 1 (4) of the Road Traffic Act 1934 which, by virtue of paragraphs 1 and 10 of Schedule 8 to the 1967 Act, has effect under that Act as such a direction as aforesaid (reg. 110).

Brakes – "Braking efficiency", in relation to the application of brakes to a motor vehicle at any time, means the maximum braking force capable of being developed by the application of those brakes, expressed as a percentage of the weight of the vehicle including any persons (not being fare paying or other travelling passengers) or load carried in the vehicle at that time.

"Multi-pull means of operation", in relation to a braking system means a device which causes the muscular energy of the driver to apply the brakes of that system progressively as a result of successive applications of that device by the driver.

"Split braking system", in relation to a motor vehicle, means a braking system so designed and constructed that—

(*a*) it comprises two independent sections of mechanism capable of developing braking force such that, excluding the means of operation, a failure of any part (other than a fixed member or a brake shoe anchor pin) of one of the said sections shall not cause a decrease in the braking force capable of being developed by the other section;

(*b*) the said two sections are operated by a means of operation which is common to both sections;

(*c*) the braking efficiency of either of the said two sections can be readily checked;

"Stored energy", in relation to a braking system of a vehicle, means energy (other than the muscular energy of the driver or the mechanical energy of a spring) stored in a reservoir for the purpose of applying the brakes under the control of the driver, either directly or as a supplement to his muscular energy.

For the purpose of these regulations a brake drum shall be deemed to form part of the wheel and not of the braking system (reg. 3).

PARKING BRAKE – (1) Save as provided in paragraph (3) of this regulation, every motor vehicle registered before January 1, 1968 shall be equipped with a braking system (which may be one of the braking systems prescribed in regulations 46, 47, 50, 54 (other than paragraph 2), and 59 (other than paragraph 2)) so designed and constructed that it can at all times be set so as effectually to prevent two at least, or in the case of vehicle with only three wheels one, of the wheels from revolving when the vehicle is not being driven or is left unattended.

(2) Save as provided in paragraph (3) of this regulation, every motor vehicle first used on or after January 1, 1968 shall be

equipped with a braking system so designed and constructed that—

(*a*) its means of operation, whether being a multi-pull means of operation or not, is independent of the means of operation of any braking system required by regulation 54 (5) or, as the case may be, regulation 59 (5) to have a total braking efficiency of not less than 50 per cent.;

(*b*) its braking force, when the vehicle is not being driven or is left unattended—

(i) can at all times be maintained in operation by direct mechanical action without the intervention of any hydraulic, electric or pneumatic device; and

(ii) when so maintained in operation by direct mechanical action is capable of holding the vehicle stationary on a gradient of at least 1 in 6·25 without the assistance of stored energy.

(3) Nothing in paragraphs (1) and (2) of this regulation shall apply to—

(*a*) a two-wheeled motor cycle with or without a sidecar attached;

(*b*) an invalid carriage; or

(*c*) a land locomotive first used on or before January 1, 1932 (reg. 13).

VACUUM OR PRESSURE BRAKING SYSTEMS – Every motor vehicle first used on or after October 1, 1937 which is equipped with a braking system which embodies a vacuum or pressure reservoir or reservoirs shall be provided with a warning device so placed as to be readily visible to the driver of the vehicle when in the driving seat in order to indicate any impending failure or deficiency in the vacuum or pressure system:

Provided that in the case of a vehicle the unladen weight of which does not exceed 3,050 kilograms and which is propelled by an internal combustion engine and equipped with a braking system embodying a vacuum reservoir or reservoirs, the vacuum therein being derived directly from the induction system of the engine, it shall not be necessary to provide such a warning device if, in the event of a failure or deficiency in the vacuum system, the brakes of that braking system are sufficient under the most adverse conditions to bring the vehicle to rest within a reasonable distance (reg. 14).

LOCOMOTIVES – Every locomotive first used before June 1, 1955 shall be equipped with an efficient braking system, the brakes of which act upon all the wheels of the vehicle other than the steering wheels, and so designed and constructed that the application of the brakes will bring the vehicle to rest within a reasonable distance:

Provided that this regulation shall not apply to a locomotive first used on or before January 2, 1933 if the locomotive is propelled by steam and the engine thereof is capable of being reversed (reg. 46).

(1) This regulation (reg. 47) shall apply to every locomotive first used on or after June 1, 1955.

(2) Every locomotive to which this regulation applies shall be equipped with an efficient braking system or efficient braking systems in either case having two means of operation, so designed and constructed that notwithstanding the failure of any part (other than a fixed member or a brake shoe anchor pin) through or by means of which the force necessary to apply the brakes is transmitted, there shall still be available for application by the driver to not less than half the number of the wheels of the vehicle brakes sufficient under the most adverse conditions to bring the vehicle to rest within a reasonable distance:

Provided that this paragraph shall not apply in the case of a road roller if the vehicle is equipped with one braking system with one means of operation.

(3) The application of one means of operation shall not affect or operate the pedal or hand lever of the other means of operation.

(4) No braking system shall be rendered ineffective by the non-rotation of the engine.

(5) All the brakes which are operated by one of the means of operation shall be capable of being applied by direct mechanical action without the intervention of any hydraulic, electric or pneumatic device.

(6) Where any brake shoe is capable of being applied by more than one means of operation, all the wheels of a locomotive to which this regulation applies shall be fitted with brakes all of which are operated by one of the means of operation:

Provided that—

(*a*) where a vehicle has more than six wheels, at least four of which are steering wheels, it shall be a sufficient compliance with this paragraph if brakes are fitted to all the wheels, other than two steering wheels which are situated on opposite sides of the vehicle, and if all such brakes are operated by one of the means of operation;

(*b*) where a vehicle has more than four wheels and the drive is transmitted to all wheels other than the steering wheels without the interposition of a differential driving gear or similar mechanism between the axles carrying the driving wheels, it shall be deemed to be a sufficient compliance with this paragraph if one means of operation operates the brakes on two driving wheels situated on opposite sides of the vehicle and the other means of operation operates brakes on all the other wheels required to be fitted with brakes by this paragraph; and

(*c*) where means of operation are provided in addition to

those prescribed by this regulation such additional means of operation may be disregarded for the purposes of this paragraph.

(7) One at least of the means of operation shall be capable of causing brakes to be applied directly, and not through the transmission gear, to not less than half the number of the wheels of the vehicle:

Provided that where a locomotive to which this regulation applies has more than four wheels and the drive is transmitted to all wheels other than the steering wheels without the interposition of a differential driving gear or similar mechanism between the axles carrying the driving wheels, it shall be deemed to be a sufficient compliance with this paragraph if the brakes applied by one means of operation act directly on two driving wheels on opposite sides of the vehicle and the brakes applied by the other means of operation act directly on all other driving wheels.

(8) For the purpose of this regulation—

(*a*) not more than one front wheel shall be included in half the number of the wheels of the vehicle for the purposes aforesaid except that this provision shall not apply to a locomotive with more than three wheels, whether or not any brake shoe is capable of being applied by more than one means of operation, if as respects the fitting of its wheels with brakes and the operation of those brakes the provisions of paragraph (6) of this regulation relating to such matters are complied with; and

(*b*) every moving shaft to which any part of a braking system or any means of operation thereof is connected or by which it is supported shall be deemed to be part of that system (reg. 47).

TRACTORS – (1) Every motor tractor shall be equipped with an efficient braking system or efficient braking systems in either case having two means of operation, so designed and constructed that, notwithstanding the failure of any part (other than a fixed member or a brake shoe anchor pin) through or by means of which the force necessary to apply the brakes is transmitted, there shall still be available for application by the driver to not less than half the number of the wheels of the vehicle brakes sufficient under the most adverse conditions to bring the vehicle to rest within a reasonable distance:

Provided that this paragraph shall not apply in the case of a road roller or a land tractor, not propelled by steam, if the vehicle is equipped with one braking system with one means of operation.

(2) The application of one means of operation shall not affect or operate the pedal or hand lever of the other means of operation.

(3) In the case of vehicles first used on or after April 1, 1938 no braking system shall be rendered ineffective by the non-rotation of the engine:

Provided that this paragraph shall not apply in the case of any vehicle referred to in sub-paragraph (*b*) of paragraph (7) of this regulation.

(4) In the case of a motor tractor first used on or after April 1, 1938 all the brakes which are operated by one of the means of operation shall be capable of being applied by direct mechanical action without the intervention of any hydraulic, electric or pneumatic device.

(5) Where any brake shoe is capable of being applied by more than one means of operation, all the wheels of the motor tractor shall be fitted with brakes all of which are operated by one of the means of operation:

Provided that where means of operation are provided in addition to those prescribed by this regulation such additional means of operation may be disregarded for the purposes of this paragraph.

(6) In the case of a motor tractor first used after January 14, 1931, other than a land tractor, one at least of the means of operation shall be capable of causing brakes to be applied directly, and not through the transmission gear, to not less than half the number of the wheels of the vehicle:

Provided that where a motor tractor has more than four wheels and the drive is transmitted to all wheels other than the steering wheels without the interposition of a differential driving gear or similar mechanism between the axles carrying the driving wheels, it shall be deemed to be a sufficient compliance with this paragraph if the brakes applied by one means of operation act directly on two driving wheels on opposite sides of the vehicle and the brakes applied by the other means of operation act directly on all other driving wheels.

(7) For the purpose of this regulation—

(*a*) in the case of a motor tractor first used on or after October 1, 1938—

(i) not more than one front wheel shall be included in half the number of the wheels of the vehicle for the purposes aforesaid except that this provision shall not apply to a motor tractor with more than three wheels, whether or not any brake shoe is capable of being applied by more than one means of operation, if as respects the fitting of its wheels with brakes and the operation of those brakes the provisions of paragraph (5) of this regulation relating to such matters are complied with, and

(ii) every moving shaft to which any part of a braking system or any means of operation thereof is connected or by which it is supported shall be deemed to be part of that system; and

(*b*) in the case of a motor tractor propelled by steam the

engine shall be deemed to be an efficient braking system with one means of operation if the engine is capable of being reversed and, in the case of a motor tractor first used on or after October 1, 1943, is incapable of being disconnected from any of the driving wheels of the vehicle except by the sustained effort of the driver (reg. 50).

HEAVY MOTOR CARS – (1) Save as provided in paragraph (2) of this regulation, every heavy motor car shall be equipped either with an efficient braking system having two means of operation or with two efficient braking systems each having a separate means of operation:

Provided that for the purpose of this paragraph no account shall be taken in the case of a heavy motor car first used on or after January 1, 1968 of a multi-pull means of operation, unless that means, at the first application, operates an hydraulic, electric or pneumatic device which causes brakes to be applied sufficient to have a total braking efficiency of not less than the total braking efficiency required by paragraph (5) (*b*) of this regulation in relation to brakes as applied by a second independent means of operation.

(2) Nothing in the paragraph (1) or (3) of this regulation shall apply in the case of a heavy motor car, if the said vehicle is equipped with one efficient braking system with one means of operation and the said system is a split braking system.

(3) Save as provided in paragraph (2) of this regulation, the braking system or braking systems of every heavy motor car first used after August 15, 1928, shall be so designed and constructed that, notwithstanding the failure of any part (other than a fixed member or a brake shoe anchor pin) through or by means of which the force necessary to apply the brakes is transmitted, there shall still be available for application by the driver to not less than half the number of the wheels of the vehicle brakes sufficient under the most adverse conditions to bring the vehicle to rest within a reasonable distance.

(4) The braking system or braking systems of every heavy motor car to which Schedule 4 applies and first used before January 1, 1968 shall comply with the requirements of that Schedule relating to the efficiency of the brakes of such heavy motor cars.

(5) The braking system or braking systems of every heavy motor car first used on or after January 1, 1968, which is not a works truck or a pedestrian controlled vehicle shall—

(*a*) have brakes acting on all the wheels of the vehicle which as applied by one means of operation have a total braking efficiency of not less than 50 per cent.;

(*b*) except in the case mentioned in the following sub-paragraph (*c*), have brakes which as applied by a second independent means of operation have a total braking efficiency of not less than 25 per cent.;

(*c*) in the case of a heavy motor car equipped with a split braking system in accordance with paragraph (2) of this regulation, have brakes which in the event of a failure of any part (other than a fixed member of a brake shoe anchor pin) of one of the independent sections comprised in the split braking system are such that there remain brakes applied by the other section sufficient to have a total braking efficiency of not less than 25 per cent.

(6) The braking system or braking systems of every heavy motor car first used after August 15, 1928 and before January 1, 1968 and which is a goods vehicle other than a pedestrian controlled vehicle or a works truck and is a rigid vehicle with two axles shall—

(*a*) have brakes which as applied by one means of operation have a total braking efficiency of not less than 45 per cent.;

(*b*) except in the case mentioned in the following sub-paragraph (*c*), have brakes which as applied by a second independent means of operation have a total braking efficiency of not less than 20 per cent.;

(*c*) in the case of a heavy motor car equipped with a split braking system in accordance with paragraph (2) of this regulation, have brakes which in the event of a failure of any part (other than a fixed member or a brake shoe anchor pin) of one of the independent sections comprised in the split braking system are such that there remain brakes applied by the other section sufficient to have a total braking efficiency of not less than 20 per cent.

(7) The braking system or braking systems of every heavy motor car first used after August 15, 1928 and before January 1, 1968, and which is a goods vehicle other than a pedestrian controlled vehicle or a works truck and is a rigid vehicle with more than two axles or is constructed or adapted to form part of an articulated vehicle shall—

(*a*) have brakes which as applied by one means of operation have a total braking efficiency of not less than 40 per cent.;

(*b*) except in the case mentioned in the following sub-paragraph (*c*), have brakes which as applied by a second independent means of operation have a total braking efficiency of not less than 15 per cent.;

(*c*) in the case of a heavy motor car equipped with a split braking system in accordance with paragraph (2) of this regulation, have brakes which in the event of a failure of any part (other than a fixed member or a brake shoe anchor pin) of one of the independent sections comprised in the split braking system are such that there remain brakes applied by the other section sufficient to have a total braking efficiency of not less than 15 per cent.

(8) The braking system or braking systems of every heavy motor car first used on or before August 15, 1928, not being a heavy motor car to which the said Schedule 4 applies shall be sufficient under the most adverse conditions to bring the vehicle to rest within a reasonable distance.

(9) Paragraphs (1) and (3) of this regulation shall not apply in the case of a works truck if it is equipped with one braking system having one means of operation.

(10) The application of one means of operation shall not affect or operate the pedal or hand lever of the other means of operation.

(11) In the case of vehicles first used on or after April 1, 1938 no braking system shall be rendered ineffective by the non-rotation of the engine:

Provided that this paragraph shall not apply in the case of any vehicle referred to in paragraph (16) (*b*) of this regulation.

(12) All the brakes of a heavy motor car which are operated by one means of operation shall be capable of being applied by direct mechanical action without the intervention of any hydraulic, electric or pneumatic device:

Provided that this paragraph shall not apply to a heavy motor car which satisfies the requirements of regulation 13 (2) of these Regulations.

(13) In the case of a heavy motor car first used before January 1, 1968, where any brake shoe is capable of being applied by more than one means of operation all the wheels of the heavy motor car shall be fitted with brakes all of which are operated by one of the means of operation:

Provided that—

(*a*) where a heavy motor car has more than six wheels, at least four of which are steering wheels, it shall be a sufficient compliance with this paragraph if brakes are fitted to all the wheels, other than two steering wheels which are situated on opposite sides of the vehicle, and all such brakes are operated by one of the means of operation;

(*b*) where a heavy motor car has more than four wheels and the drive is transmitted to all wheels other than the steering wheels without the interposition of a differential driving gear or similar mechanism between the axles carrying the driving wheels, it shall be deemed to be a sufficient compliance with this paragraph if one means of operation operates the brakes on two driving wheels situated on opposite sides of the vehicle and the other means of operation operates brakes on all the other wheels required to be fitted with brakes by this paragraph; and

(c) where means of operation are provided in addition to those prescribed by this regulation such additional means of operation may be disregarded for the purposes of this paragraph.

(14) One at least of the means of operation shall be capable of causing brakes to be applied directly, and not through the transmission gear, to not less than half the number of the wheels of the vehicle:

Provided that—

(a) in the case of a heavy motor car having brakes acting on all the wheels of the vehicle and capable of being applied by one means of operation, any shaft leading from any differential driving gear of an axle to a driving wheel shall be deemed not to form part of the transmission gear;

(b) where in the case of any other heavy motor car it has more than four wheels and the drive is transmitted to all wheels other than the steering wheels without the interposition of a differential driving gear or similar mechanism between the axles carrying the driving wheels, it shall be deemed to be a sufficient compliance with this paragraph if the brakes applied by one means of operation act directly on two driving wheels on opposite sides of the vehicle and the brakes applied by the other means of operation act directly on all other driving wheels.

(15) Paragraphs (10) to (14) inclusive of this regulation shall not apply to a heavy motor car first used on or before August 15, 1928.

(16) For the purpose of this regulation—

(a) in the case of any motor vehicle—

(i) not more than one front wheel shall be included in half the number of the wheels of the vehicle for the purposes aforesaid except that this provision shall not apply either to a heavy motor car with more than three wheels, whether or not any brake shoe is capable of being applied by more than one means of operation, if as respects the fitting of its wheels with brakes and the operation of those brakes the provisions of paragraph (13) of this regulation relating to such matters are complied with, or to a works truck, and

(ii) every moving shaft to which any part of a braking system or any means of operation thereof is connected or by which it is supported shall be deemed to be part of that system; and (*b*) in the case of a heavy motor car propelled by steam and not used as a public service vehicle the engine shall be deemed to be an efficient braking system with one means of operation if the engine is capable of being reversed and, in the case of a heavy motor car first used on or after January 1, 1927, is incapable of being disconnected from any of the driving wheels of the vehicle except by the sustained effort of the driver (reg. 54).

MOTOR CARS (reg. 59) – as reg. 54 (1) except "motor car" for "heavy motor car".

(2) as reg. 54 (2) except "motor car" for "heavy motor car".

(3) Save as provided in paragraph (2) of this regulation, the braking system or braking systems of every motor car shall be so designed and constructed that notwithstanding the failure of any part (other than a fixed member or a brake shoe anchor pin) through or by means of which the force necessary to apply the brakes is transmitted there shall still be available for application by the driver to not less than half the number of the wheels of the vehicle brakes sufficient under the most adverse conditions to bring the vehicle to rest within a reasonable distance:

Provided that in the event of such failure as aforesaid it shall not be necessary for brakes to be available for application by the driver—

(*a*) in the case of a motor car first used before October 1, 1938, to more than two wheels;

(*b*) in the case of a vehicle having less than four wheels, to more than one wheel.

(4) as reg. 54 (4) except "motor car" for "heavy motor car".

(5) as reg. 54 (5) except "motor car" for "heavy motor car".

(6) The braking system or braking systems of every motor car first used after January 1, 1915 and before January 1, 1968 and which is a goods vehicle exceeding 1,525 kilograms in unladen weight other than a dual-purpose vehicle, a pedestrian controlled vehicle or a works truck and is a rigid vehicle with two axles shall—

"*a*", "*b*" and "*c*" as "*a*", "*b*" and "*c*" in reg. 54 (6) except "motor car" for "heavy motor car".

(7) The braking system or braking systems of every motor car first used after January 1, 1915 and before January 1, 1968 and which is a goods vehicle exceeding 1,525 kilograms in unladen weight other than a dual-purpose vehicle, a pedestrian controlled vehicle or a works truck and is a rigid vehicle with more than two axles or is constructed or adapted to form part of an articulated vehicle shall—

"*a*", "*b*" and "*c*" as "*a*", "*b*" and "*c*" in reg. 54 (7) except "motor car" for "heavy motor car".

(8) Paragraphs (1) and (3) of this regulation shall not apply in the case of a motor car first registered under the Motor Car Act 1903 before January 1, 1915 but—

(*a*) such a motor car shall be equipped with an efficient braking system;

(*b*) that system shall be so designed and constructed that brakes shall be available for application by the driver, in the case of a vehicle with not less than four wheels, to two wheels of the vehicle, and in the case of a vehicle with less than four wheels, to one wheel of the vehicle; and

(*c*) if such a motor car is not one to which the said Schedule 4 applies, the brakes required by the foregoing sub-paragraph to be available for application shall be brakes sufficient under the most adverse conditions to bring the vehicle to rest within a reasonable distance.

(9) The foregoing paragraphs of this regulation shall not apply in the case of a works truck if it is equipped with one braking system with one means of operation.

(10) The application of one means of operation shall not affect or operate the pedal or hand lever of the other means of operation.

(11) In the case of vehicles first used on or after April 1, 1938, no braking system shall be rendered ineffective by the non-rotation of the engine:

Provided that this paragraph shall not apply in the case of any vehicle referred to in paragraph (15) (*b*) of this regulation.

(12) All the brakes of a motor car which are operated by one of the means of operation shall be capable of being applied by direct mechanical action without the intervention of any hydraulic, electric or pneumatic device:

Provided that this paragraph shall not apply to a motor car which satisfies the requirements of regulation 13 (2).

(13) in the case of a motor car first used before January 1, 1968 with more than three wheels where any brake shoe is capable of being applied by more than one means of operation all the wheels shall be fitted with brakes all of which are operated by one of the means of operation:

Provided that—

"*a*", "*b*", and "*c*" as "*a*", "*b*" and "*c*" in reg. 54 (13) except "motor car" for "heavy motor car".

(*d*) this paragraph shall not apply to a pedestrian controlled vehicle not exceeding 410 kilograms in weight unladen; and

(*e*) in the case of a motor car the unladen weight of which does not exceed 2,040 kilograms or which is constructed solely for the carriage of passengers and their effects and adapted to carry not more than seven passengers exclusive of the driver, it shall be deemed to be a sufficient compliance with this paragraph if one means of operation operates brakes fitted to all but two of the wheels and, as respects each of those two wheels, operates a brake on the shaft leading thereto and no gearing is interposed between the brake and the wheel.

(14) One at least of the means of operation shall be capable of causing brakes to be applied directly and not through the transmission gear to not less than half the number of the wheels of the vehicle:

Provided that—

(*a*) in the case of a motor car having brakes acting on all the wheels of the vehicle and capable of being applied by one means of operation, any shaft leading from any differential driving gear of an axle to a driving wheel shall be deemed not to form part of the transmission gear;

(*b*) in the case of a motor car having more than four wheels and first used before October 1, 1938, it shall be deemed to be sufficient compliance with this paragraph if one of the means of operation applies brakes directly and not through the transmission gear to not less than two of the wheels of the vehicle; and

(*c*) where a motor car has more than four wheels and the drive is transmitted to all wheels other than the steering wheels without the interposition of a differential driving gear or similar mechanism between the axles carrying the driving wheels, it shall be deemed to be a sufficient compliance with this paragraph if the brakes applied by one means of operation act directly on two driving wheels on opposite sides of the vehicle and the brakes applied by the other means of operation act directly on all other driving wheels.

(15) For the purpose of this regulation—

(*a*) in the case of a motor car first used on or after October 1, 1938—

(i) not more than one front wheel shall be included in half the number of the wheels of the vehicle for the purposes aforesaid:

Provided that this provision shall not apply—

(1) to a motor car the unladen weight of which does not exceed 1,020 kilograms,

(2) to a motor car which is a passenger vehicle constructed or adapted to carry not more than seven passengers exclusive of the driver,

(3) to a works truck, or

(4) to a motor car with more than three wheels, whether or not any brake shoe is capable of being

applied by more than one means of operation, if as respects the fitting of its wheels with brakes and the operation of those brakes the provisions of paragraph (13) of this regulation relating to such matters are complied with, and

(ii) every moving shaft to which any part of a braking system or any means of operation thereof is connected or by which it is supported shall be deemed to be part of that system; and

(*b*) in the case of a motor car propelled by steam and not used as a public service vehicle, the engine shall be deemed to be an efficient braking system with one means of operation if the engine is capable of being reversed and is incapable of being disconnected from any of the driving wheels of the vehicle except by the sustained effort of the driver (reg. 59).

MOTOR CYCLES – (1) Every motor cycle shall be equipped either with an efficient braking system having two means of operation or with two efficient braking systems each having a separate means of operation.

(2) The braking system or braking systems with which a motor cycle is required to be equipped shall be so designed and constructed that notwithstanding the failure of any part (other than a fixed member or a brake shoe anchor pin) through or by means of which the force necessary to apply the brakes is transmitted there shall still be available for application by the driver to at least one wheel of the vehicle brakes sufficient under the most adverse conditions to bring the vehicle to rest within a reasonable distance.

(3) The braking system or braking systems of every motor cycle to which Schedule 4 applies shall comply with the requirements of that Schedule relating to the efficiency of the brakes of such motor cycles.

(4) Paragraphs (1) and (2) of this regulation shall not apply in the case of a motor cycle first registered under the Motor Car Act 1903 or the Roads Act 1920 before January 1, 1927 but—

(*a*) such a motor cycle shall be equipped with an efficient braking system, and

(*b*) that system shall be so designed and constructed that brakes shall be available for application by the driver to at least one wheel of the vehicle.

(5) The foregoing paragraphs of this regulation shall not apply in the case of a works truck if it is equipped with one braking system having one means of operation.

(6) In the case of a motor cycle required to have two means of operating brakes, the application of one means of operation shall not affect or operate the pedal or hand lever of the other means of operation (reg. 62).

INVALID CARRIAGES – Every invalid carriage shall be equipped with an efficient braking system, the brakes of which act on at least two wheels of the vehicle, so designed and constructed that the application of the brakes shall bring the vehicle to rest within a reasonable distance (reg. 66).

TRAILERS – (1) Save as provided in paragraph (3) of this regulation, every trailer manufactured before January 1 1968 and every agricultural trailer whenever manufactured which in either case exceeds 102 kilograms in weight unladen shall be equipped with an efficient braking system the brakes of which are capable of being applied when it is being drawn—

(*a*) to at least two wheels in the case of a trailer having not more than four wheels;
(*b*) to at least four wheels in the case of a trailer having more than four wheels; and
(*c*) in the case of trailers manufactured after April 1, 1938, to at least half the number of wheels of the trailer,

and so constructed that—

(i) the brakes can be applied either by the driver of the drawing vehicle or by some other person on such vehicle or the trailer,
(ii) in the case of a trailer forming part of an articulated vehicle and being permanently attached to the drawing vehicle, the brakes are capable of being set so as effectively to prevent two at least of the wheels from revolving when the trailer is not being drawn, and
(iii) in the case of any other trailer, the brakes are capable of being set so as effectively to prevent two at least of the wheels from revolving when the trailer, whether it is attached to the drawing vehicle or not, is not being drawn:

Provided that the provisions of item (i) of this paragraph shall not apply in the case of a trailer if the brakes of the trailer automatically come into operation on the overrun of the trailer.

In this paragraph the expression "permanently attached" means that the trailer can only be detached from the drawing vehicle by an operation involving the use of facilities which are normally found only in a workshop.

(2) Save as provided in paragraph (3) of this regulation, every trailer manufactured on or after January 1, 1968, except an agriculture trailer, and which exceeds 102 kilograms in weight unladen shall be equipped with an efficient braking system so designed and constructed that—

(*a*) when the trailer is being drawn, the brakes of that braking system are capable of being applied to all the wheels of the trailer by the driver of the drawing vehicle using the means of operation applying those of the brakes of the drawing vehicle which were designed and constructed to have the highest braking efficiency of any of the brakes of any braking system with which the drawing vehicle is equipped;

(*b*) when the trailer is being drawn, in the event of a failure of any part (other than a fixed member or a brake shoe anchor pin) of the braking system with which the drawing vehicle is equipped (excluding the means of operation of a split braking system) or of any part (other than as aforesaid) of the braking system with which the trailer is equipped, brakes shall still be capable of being applied to at least two wheels of the trailer or, in the case of a two-wheeled trailer, to one wheel in the manner indicated in the last preceding sub-paragraph or by the driver using any other means of operation of a braking system with which the drawing vehicle is by these regulations required to be equipped;

(*c*) when the trailer is stationary—

(i) the brakes of that system can also be applied to at least two wheels of the trailer and released by a person standing on the ground by a means of operation fitted to the trailer;

(ii) the braking force of that system can, when applied in the manner indicated in sub-paragraph (*a*) or (*c*) (i) of this paragraph, at all times be maintained in operation by direct mechanical action without the intervention of any hydraulic, electric or pneumatic device; and

(iii) such braking force, when so applied and so maintained in operation by direct mechanical action, is capable of holding the trailer stationary on a gradient of at least 1 in 6·25 without the assistance of stored energy:

Provided that the provisions of sub-paragraphs (*a*) and (*b*) of this paragraph shall not apply in the case of a trailer if the brakes of the trailer automatically come into operation on the overrun of the trailer.

(3) Paragraphs (1) and (2) of this regulation shall not apply—

(*a*) to any land implement or land implement conveyor drawn by a motor vehicle;

(*b*) to any trailer designed for use and used for street cleansing which does not carry any load other than its necessary gear and equipment;

(*c*) to any broken down vehicle which is being drawn by a motor vehicle in consequence of the breakdown;

(*d*) to any agricultural trailer manufactured before July 1,

1947 when drawn by a motor tractor or a land tractor which is not a motor tractor if—

(i) its laden weight does not exceed 4,070 kilograms,
(ii) it is the only trailer so drawn, and
(iii) it is not drawn at a speed exceeding 10 miles per hour; or

(*e*) to any trailer used only for the carriage of plant and materials for producing gas for the propulsion of the drawing vehicle if the drawing vehicle is either a goods vehicle weighing not less than 2,030 kilograms in weight unladen or a public service vehicle.

(4) In the case of trailers manufactured on or after April 1, 1938, the braking system shall be so constructed that it is not rendered ineffective by the non-rotation of the engine of the drawing vehicle (reg. 70).

MAINTENANCE OF BRAKES – (1) Every part of every braking system and of the means of operation thereof fitted to a motor vehicle or trailer shall at all times while the vehicle or trailer is used on a road—

(*a*) be maintained in good and efficient working order and be properly adjusted;

(*b*) in the case of motor vehicles to which Schedule 4 applies and first used before January 1, 1968 be so maintained that the brakes forming part of the system comply with the requirements as to the efficiency of brakes which are applicable to such a vehicle by virtue of the provisions contained in regulation 54 (4), regulation 59 (4) and regulation 62 (3);

(*c*) in the case of motor vehicles to which paragraph (5) of either regulation 54 or regulation 59 applies, where such a vehicle is not being used while drawing a trailer, be so maintained that the brakes forming part of the system comply with the requirements as to the efficiency of brakes which are applicable to such a vehicle by virtue of the provisions contained in either of such paragraphs;

(*d*) in the case of motor vehicles to which paragraph (6) or (7) of either regulation 54 or regulation 59 applies, where such a vehicle is not being used while drawing a trailer, be so maintained that the brakes forming part of the system comply with the requirements as to the efficiency of brakes which are applicable to such a vehicle by virtue of the provisions contained in any of such paragraphs; and

(*e*) in the case of motor vehicles or trailers to which paragraph (2) of regulation 13, or as the case may be, paragraph (2) of regulation 70 applies, be so maintained that the system complies with the requirements as to its braking force which are applicable to such a vehicle by virtue of sub-paragraph (*b*) (ii) of regulation 13 (2) or by virtue of sub-paragraph (*c*) (iii) of regulation 70 (2).

(*f*) in the case of motor vehicles or trailers to which reg. 4A applies, be so maintained that the braking devices conform to the requirements of the relevant E.E.C. Council Directive.

(2) Where a motor vehicle to which paragraph (5) of either regulation 54 or regulation 59 applies is being used while drawing a trailer manufactured on or after January 1, 1968 (other than a trailer not required by these Regulations to be equipped with a braking system), whether or not that motor vehicle and trailer together form an articulated vehicle, then every part of every braking system with which that motor vehicle is equipped and every part of every braking system with which the trailer is equipped shall be so maintained that, when the brakes of any braking system of that motor vehicle (being a system to which the said paragraph (5) applies) are applied by their means of operation and the brakes of any braking system of that trailer applied by that same means of operation are applied, those brakes together produce the same total braking efficiencies as would be required of the brakes of such a motor vehicle when applied by that means of operation if that motor vehicle were not drawing a trailer.

(3) Where a motor vehicle to which paragraph (5) of either regulation 54 or regulation 59 applies being a goods vehicle, is being used while drawing a trailer manufactured before January 1, 1968 (other than a trailer not required by these Regulations to be equipped with a braking system), whether or not that motor vehicle and trailer together form an articulated vehicle, then every part of every braking system with which that motor vehicle is equipped and every part of every braking system with which the trailer is equipped shall be so maintained that, when the brakes of any braking system of the motor vehicle (being a system to which the said paragraph (5) applies) are applied by their means of operation they produce (whether assisted by the brakes on the trailer or not) the same total braking efficiencies as would be required of the brakes of such a motor vehicle when applied by that means of operation if that motor vehicle were not drawing a trailer and if it were treated as being a motor vehicle first used before January 1, 1968 and as having to comply with paragraph (7) of either regulation 54 or regulation 59 notwithstanding that the said paragraph does not apply to that motor vehicle.

(4) Where a motor vehicle to which paragraphs (6) or (7) of either regulation 54 or regulation 59 applies is being used while drawing a trailer (whenever manufactured) other than a trailer

not required by these Regulations to be equipped with a braking system, whether or not that motor vehicle and trailer together form an articulated vehicle, then every part of every braking system with which that motor vehicle is equipped and every part of every braking system with which the trailer is equipped shall be so maintained that, when the brakes of any braking system with which the motor vehicle is equipped are applied by their means of operation, they produce (whether assisted by the brakes on the trailer or not) the same total braking efficiencies as would be required of the brakes of such a motor vehicle when applied by that means of operation if that motor vehicle were not drawing a trailer, and if, in the case of a motor vehicle to which the said paragraph (6) applies, it were treated as being a motor vehicle having to comply with paragraph (7) of either regulation 54 or regulation 59.

(5) Where a motor vehicle to which regulation 13 (2) applies is attached to a trailer manufactured on or after January 1, 1968 (other than a trailer not required by these Regulations to be equipped with a braking system), whether or not that motor vehicle and trailer together form an articulated vehicle, and the combination of those vehicles is stationary, then every part of every braking system with which that motor vehicle is equipped and every part of every braking system with which the trailer is equipped shall be so maintained that the brakes of those systems as applied by the means of operation specified in the said paragraph (2) can together produce a braking force sufficient to hold the combination of vehicles stationary on a gradient of at least 1 in 6·25 without the assistance of stored energy (reg. 94).

APPLICATION OF BRAKES OF TRAILERS – Where a trailer is drawn by a motor vehicle whether wheeled or track laying the driver (or in the case of a locomotive one of the persons employed in driving or tending the locomotive) shall be in a position readily to operate any brakes required by these Regulations to be fitted to the trailer as well as the brakes of the motor vehicle unless a person other than the driver is in a position and competent efficiently to apply the brakes of the trailer:

Provided that this regulation shall not apply in the case of trailers which in compliance with these Regulations, are fitted with brakes which automatically come into operation on the overrun of the trailer or where a motor vehicle is drawing a broken down vehicle, whether or not in consequence of a breakdown, in such a manner that the broken down vehicle cannot be steered by its own steering gear (reg. 118).

No person in charge of a motor vehicle, whether wheeled or track laying, or trailer drawn thereby shall cause or permit such trailer to stand when detached from the drawing vehicle unless one at least of the wheels of the trailer is prevented from revolving by the setting of the brake or the use of a chain (reg. 119).

Brakes may be tested (reg. 137). See "Testing and Inspection" and "Quitting Vehicle".

SCHEDULE 4

(see Regulations 54, 59, 62, and 94)

REQUIREMENTS WITH RESPECT TO THE EFFICIENCY OF THE BRAKES OF CERTAIN MOTOR VEHICLES

1. This Schedule applies to a motor vehicle which is a heavy motor car, a motor car or a motor cycle and is not—

- (*a*) a goods vehicle the unladen weight of which exceeds 1,525 kilograms;
- (*b*) a public service vehicle adapted to carry 8 or more passengers;
- (*c*) an articulated vehicle or a vehicle constructed or adapted for the purpose of forming part of an articulated vehicle;
- (*d*) a works truck; or
- (*e*) a pedestrian controlled vehicle;

and references to a motor vehicle in the following provisions of this Schedule shall be construed accordingly.

In this paragraph "goods vehicle" does not include a dual-purpose vehicle.

2. For the purposes of this Schedule a two-wheeled motor cycle shall not, by reason that a sidecar is attached thereto, be treated as three-wheeled.

3. In the case of a motor vehicle having at least four wheels and required to have two means of operating brakes—

- (*a*) if each means of operation applies brakes to at least four wheels, the brakes as applied by one of the means shall have a total braking efficiency of not less than 50 per cent. and the brakes as applied bythe other means shall have a total braking efficiency of not less than 25 per cent.;
- (*b*) if only one of the means of operation applies brakes to at least four wheels, the brakes as applied by that means shall have a total braking efficiency of not less than 50 per cent. and the brakes as applied by the other means shall have a total braking efficiency of not less than 25 per cent.; and
- (*c*) if neither means of operation applies brakes to at least four wheels, the brakes as applied by one of the means shall have a total braking efficiency of not less than 30 per cent. and the brakes as applied by the other means shall have a total braking efficiency of not less than 25 per cent.

4. In the case of a three-wheeled motor vehicle required to have two means of operating brakes—

(*a*) if each means of operation applies brakes to all three wheels, the brakes as applied by one of the means shall have a total braking efficiency of not less than 40 per cent. and the brakes as applied by the other means shall have a total braking efficiency of not less than 25 per cent.;

(*b*) if only one of the means of operation applies brakes to all three wheels, the brakes as applied by that means shall have a total braking efficiency of not less than 40 per cent. and the brakes as applied by the other means shall have a total braking efficiency of not less than 25 per cent.; and

(*c*) if neither means of operation applies brakes to all three wheels, the brakes as applied by one of the means shall have a total braking efficiency of not less than 30 per cent. and the brakes as applied by the other means shall have a total braking efficiency of not less than 25 per cent.

5. In the case of a motor vehicle, being a two-wheeled motor cycle, required to have more than one means of operating brakes, the brakes as applied by one of the means shall have a total braking efficiency of not less than 30 per cent. and the brakes as applied by the other means shall have a total braking efficiency of not less than 25 per cent.

6. In the case of a motor vehicle not required to have two means of operating brakes—

(*a*) if the vehicle has at least four wheels and one or more means of operation applying brakes to at least four wheels, the brakes as applied by that means or one of those means shall have a total braking efficiency of not less than 50 per cent.;

(*b*) if the vehicle has at least four wheels and no means of operation applying brakes to at least four wheels, the brakes as applied by the means or one of the means of operation shall have a total braking efficiency of not less than 30 per cent.;

(*c*) if the vehicle is three-wheeled and has one or more means of operation applying brakes to all three wheels, the brakes as applied by that means or one of those means shall have a total braking efficiency of not less than 40 per cent.;

(*d*) if the vehicle is three-wheeled and has no means of operation applying brakes to all three wheels, the brakes as applied by the means or one of the means of operation shall have a total braking efficiency of not less than 30 per cent.; and

(e) if the vehicle is two-wheeled, the brakes as applied by the means or one of the means of operation shall have a total braking efficiency of not less than 30 per cent.

Broken Down Vehicles – When such are being towed in consequence of the breakdown, the following regulations do not apply: reg. 12 (springs); reg. 20 (diameter of wheels); reg. 68 (length); reg. 69 (width); reg. 70 (brakes); reg. 71 and 72 (tyres); reg. 73 (wings); reg. 75 (trailer plate). See also "Obstruction" and "Tow Rope" in this Appendix and "Towed Vehicles", under "Lights on Vehicles", Chap. 24.

The towed vehicle, for the time a "trailer", is still a motor vehicle and its steersman is the person in charge though not driving it.

Control – No person actually driving a motor vehicle shall be in such a position that he cannot have proper control over the same or that he cannot retain a full view of the road and traffic ahead (reg. 111). See "View".

Crane – If a crane or other special apparatus is more or less permanently fixed on a motor vehicle it is part of the vehicle and is not a "load" (s. 253, R.T. Act 1960).

There is no restriction on the size of the wheels of a mobile crane (reg. 20), which also need not have springs (reg. 12). A mobile crane may be an "engineering plant". See "Special Types of Motor Vehicles".

Dangerous Vehicle – A motor vehicle, its trailers, and all parts and accessories shall at all times be in such condition and the number of passengers, the manner in which any passengers are carried and the conditions of loading shall be such that no danger is caused or is likely to be caused to any person on the vehicle or trailer or on a road.

The load shall at all times be so secured or in such a position as not likely to cause danger to any person by its falling wholly or in part or by any other movement of the load . The vehicle or trailer shall not be used for any purpose for which it is so unsuitable as to cause or be likely to cause danger to any person on the vehicle or trailer or on a road.

The number of passengers on a public service vehicle must not exceed that prescribed by Regulations (reg. 90).

For any contravention of above see "Penalty".

Deck – This means a floor or platform upon which seats are provided for passengers. "Gangway" means a space provided for access to or exit from passengers' seats but does not include a staircase or any space in front of a seat required only for passengers.

"Single decked vehicle" means a vehicle upon which no part of a deck or gangway is vertically above another deck or gangway.

"Double decked vehicle" means one having two decks, one wholly or partially above the other, each deck having a gangway.

"Half decked vehicle" means one which is not single or double decked (reg. 3).

Driver's Duties – The driver of a motor vehicle must not unnecessarily drive backwards (see "Reversing"); must not cause obstruction (see "Obstruction"); must when driving be in position for control (see "Control") and full view (see "View"); must stop engine and put on brakes when leaving the vehicle (see "Quitting Vehicle") if driving alone a steam vehicle must stop when attending to the furnace (see "Steam Vehicles") and should not stand his vehicle on his right side of the road facing on-coming traffic during the hours of darkness (reg. 115; but see "Obstruction" later) (regs. 111 to 116).

Dual Purpose Vehicle – This is a vehicle constructed or adapted for the carriage both of passengers and of goods or burden of any description being a vehicle whose unladen weight does not exceed 2,040 kilograms and which either:

(i) is so constructed or adapted that the driving power of the engine is, or by the appropriate use of the controls of the vehicle can be, transmitted to all the wheels of the vehicle, or

(ii) satisfies the following conditions as to construction, namely:

(*a*) the vehicle must be permanently fitted with a rigid roof, with or without a sliding panel;

(*b*) the area of the vehicle to the rear of the driver's seat must—

(i) be permanently fitted with at least one row of transverse seats (fixed or folding) for two or more passengers and those seats must be properly sprung or cushioned and provided with upholstered back-rests, attached either to the seats or to a side or the floor of the vehicle; and

(ii) be lit on each side and at the rear by a window or windows of glass or other transparent material having an area or aggregate area of not less than 1,850 sq. cms. on each side and not less than 770 sq. cms. at the rear;

(*c*) the distance between the rearmost part of the steering wheel and the backrests of the row of transverse seats satisfying the requirements specified in head (i) of the foregoing sub-paragraph (*b*) (or, if there is more than one such row of seats, the distance between the rearmost part of the steering wheel and the back-rests of the rearmost such row) must, when the seats are ready for use, be not less than one-third of the distance between the rearmost part of the steering wheel and the rearmost part of the floor of the vehicle;

Such a vehicle, as regards speed limits, is regarded as a passenger vehicle (Sched. 5, R.T.R. Act 1967, and reg. 3).

Fire Vehicles – If a turntable fire escape is a heavy motor car (over 4,070 kilograms) and does not have pneumatic tyres, it should have soft or elastic tyres (reg. 55). Fire Brigade wheeled vehicles may use gongs, bells, sirens or two-tone horns (reg. 27) at all times when necessary (reg. 110). The speed limits do not apply if their observance would hinder the use of any vehicle for fire purposes. See "Exemptions from Speed Limit", Chap. 24. Any expanding or extensible contrivance forming part of a turntable fire escape fixed to a vehicle does not count for length, nor does a fire escape ladder count for overhang (reg. 3).

They need not stop engines, etc., when fire fighting (reg. 116).

Forestry Commission – Vehicles owned by the Forestry Commission and used from time to time for fire fighting purposes may be fitted with a gong, bell, siren or two-tone horn (reg. 27), and such instrument may be used when the vehicles are used for fire fighting (reg. 110).

Furniture Vans – Wheeled trailers specially designed and used for the conveyance of furniture and other similar household effects, if constructed before January 15, 1931, need not have soft elastic or pneumatic tyres (reg. 71).

Gas-propelled Vehicles – "Gas" is any fuel that is wholly gaseous at 16·7° centigrade under 760 mms. of mercury (reg. 3). "Gas equipment" is a container for holding or materials for producing gas. "Gas trailer" is one used solely for gas equipment for propulsion of the drawing vehicle (reg. 3).

Regulation 42 directs that the provisions of Sched. 3 to the regs. shall be complied with in the case of every motor vehicle or trailer which has a container for storage of gas for propulsion of the vehicle. These requirements shall be in addition to any requirements of Regulations for the conveyance of gas.

It is not necessary to stop the engine of a stationary gas propelled vehicle (reg. 116).

Attendants for such trailers are not necessary (reg. 135).

Glass – In the case of wheeled motor vehicles first used on or after January 1, 1959—(a) being passenger vehicles or dual-purpose vehicles, the glass of windscreens and all windows on the outside (b) being goods vehicles, other than dual-purpose vehicles, the glass of windscreens and all windows in front and on either side of the driver's seat shall be safety glass. The glass of windscreens and windows facing to the front on the outside of any motor vehicle registered before January 1, 1959 (except glass fitted to the upper deck of a double-decked vehicle) shall be safety glass (reg. 24).

Safety glass is glass that if fractured does not fly into fragments likely to cause severe cuts (reg. 3). All glass or transparency fitted to motor vehicles shall be maintained in such condition that it does not obscure the vision of the driver while driving on a road (reg. 93). See also "Mirror".

Heavy Motor Car – Means a motor vehicle constructed itself to carry a load or passengers, the weight of which unladen exceeds $2\frac{1}{2}$ tons and which is not a "motor car" (R.T. Act 1972, s. 190).

ATTENDANTS – If a trailer is drawn on the highway a person additional to the driver shall be carried to attend it (s. 34). See "Attendants".

BRAKES – See "Brakes".

DRIVERS' HOURS OF DUTY – See Transport Act 1968, s. 96; Chap. 24.

MARKINGS – The owner shall cause the unladen weight to be marked on the left or near side. This does not apply to a vehicle not registered under the Roads Act 1920 or the Vehicles (Excise) Acts 1949 and 1971 (reg. 74).

Overhang (approximately) shall not exceed 60 per cent. of the distance between the front and rear axles. This does not apply to heavy motor cars first used before August 15, 1928, nor to works trucks or street cleansers or refuse vehicles nor to a load tipping vehicle if overhang does not exceed 1·15 metres. In road heating vehicles no part of the heating plant shall be taken into account (reg. 53).

TRAILER – Only one may be drawn on the highway but this shall have effect as if for the word "one" there were substituted the word "two" in relation to a case where one of the trailers being drawn is a towing implement and the other is a vehicle part of which is secured to and either rests on or is suspended from the towing implement (reg. 136). See "Trailers".

TYRES – Every wheel of a heavy motor car must have pneumatic tyres except the following which must have pneumatic, soft or elastic tyres: heavy motor cars first used on or before January 2, 1933: heavy motor cars over 4,070 kilograms weight unladen mainly used on rough ground or unmade roads: street cleansers: refuse collectors: turntable fire escapes: tower wagons: works trucks (reg. 55).

WEIGHT – The total laden weight on a road shall not exceed for a 4-wheeler 14,230 kilograms, for a 6-wheeler 20,330 kilograms and for over 6 wheels 24,390 kilograms. There are special provisions with respect to "a prior 1968 vehicle", "a post 1968 vehicle" and "a temporarily imported vehicle" (see reg. 79).

The total laden weight on a highway of the vehicle and its trailer shall not exceed 22,360 kilograms (reg. 81), provided that in the case of a wheeled trailer drawn by a wheeled heavy motor car the total laden weight may be 24,390 kilograms (reg. 81). See "Weight".

WIDTH shall not exceed 2·5 metres (reg. 52).

WINGS or mudguards are necessary unless the body gives adequate protection, but this does not apply to the rear wheels when part of an articulated vehicle for conveyance of round timber, nor to an unfinished vehicle going to works for completion nor to a works trucks (reg. 56).

Indivisible Loads – No limit is prescribed for the length of a trailer constructed and normally used for the conveyance of indivisible loads of exceptional length (reg. 68). An indivisible load means one which cannot without undue expense or risk of damage be divided into two or more loads for road conveyance (reg. 3). See "Special Types of Motor Vehicles".

Industrial Tractor – Means a tractor, not being a land tractor, which—(a) has unladen weight not exceeding 7,370 kilograms, (b) is designed and used primarily for work off roads, or for maintenance (including any such tractor when fitted with an implement or implements designed primarily for use in connection with such work, whether or not any such implement is of itself designed to carry a load), and (c) if so constructed as to be incapable of exceeding a speed of 20 miles per hour on the level under its own power (reg. 3).

Inspection – See "Testing and Inspection".

Invalid Carriage – Means a motor vehicle not exceeding 5 hundredweight unladen and specially made for and used solely by a person suffering from some physical defect or disability (R.T. Act 1972, s. 190). For the purposes of Part III of the Act and all Regs. thereunder (which relate to the minimum age for driving motor vehicles and the licensing of drivers thereof) the maximum weight of an "invalid carriage" is 8 hundredweight (M.V. (Driving Licences) Regs. 1971), It must be a wheeled vehicle (reg. 8).

It shall not be more than 2.2 metres wide (reg. 65), and it shall not draw a trailer (reg. 124). It need not have parking brakes (reg. 13), nor speed indicator (reg. 18). It shall have an efficient braking system acting on two wheels (reg. 66) and wings or other similar fittings to catch mud or water thrown up by the wheels (reg. 67).

Part VI of the R.T. Act 1972, *re* insurance, does not apply to invalid carriages (s. 143).

Land Implement – Means any implement or machinery used with a land locomotive or land tractor for agriculture, grass cutting, forestry, land levelling, dredging or similar operations, and includes a living van and a trailer carrying only the necessary gear and equipment of the land locomotive or tractor which draws it (reg. 3).

An attendant additional to the driver is not necessary when drawn by a land locomotive or land tractor (R.T. Act 1972, s. 34 reg. 135). Brakes (reg. 70), wings (reg. 73), trailer plate (except living vans) (reg. 75) and springs or resilient material (reg. 12) are not required. There are no limits to its length (reg. 68), the diameter of its wheels (reg. 20) and to its width (reg. 69). Its tyres need not be soft (regs, 71, 72).

Land Implement Conveyor – Means a trailer (not exceeding 510 kilograms, unladen weight), which is specially designed and constructed for the conveyance of one land implement; marked with its unladen weight; fitted with pneumatic tyres, and drawn by a land locomotive or a land tractor (reg. 3).

It need not have springs (reg. 12), brakes (reg. 70), wings (reg. 73), trailer plate (reg. 75). An attendant additional to the driver is not necessary when drawn by a land locomotive or land tractor (R.T. Act 1972, s. 34, reg. 135).

Land Locomotive – Means a locomotive (over $7\frac{1}{4}$ tons) designed and used primarily for work on the land for agriculture, forestry, land levelling, dredging and similar operations, which is on a road only when going to and from its land work and which on a road hauls nothing other than land implements or land implement conveyors (reg. 3).

If it draws a land implement or land implement conveyor the requirement as to attendants does not apply (reg. 135).

If first used before January 1, 1932, it need not have parking brakes (reg. 13). It need not have springs (reg. 12) nor a mirror (reg. 23). It need not have soft tyres if its smooth soled steering wheels have 125 mms. tyres (reg. 45) and its driving wheels 305 mms. wide tyres, all smooth soled or with diagonal iron bars (reg. 45).

Land Tractor – Means a motor tractor (under 7,370 kilograms designed and used primarily for work on the land in connection with agriculture, grass cutting, forestry, land levelling, dredging and similar operations, which belongs to a person engaged in agriculture or forestry or to a contractor for such operations and is not constructed or adapted for the conveyance of a load other than (a) water, fuel, accumulators and other equipment for propulsion, loose tools and equipment; (b) a load in or on any appliance which satisfies the conditions whereby the vehicle to which the appliance is fitted does not become chargeable with duty as a goods vehicle, and (c) an implement fitted to the tractor and used on farms or forestry estates in connection with any of the above operations (reg. 3).

If it draws a land implement the requirement as to attendants does not apply (reg. 135).

If it is a road roller or if it is not driven by steam one braking system with one means of operation is sufficient (reg. 50), and it need not have soft tyres if the steering wheels have 60 mms. smooth soled tyres and the driving wheels have smooth soled or diagonal crossbar tyres 150 mms. wide for over 3,050 kilograms land tractors and 76 mms. wide for land tractors not exceeding 3,050 kilograms weight unladen (reg. 51).

If it is a land tractor which complies with the conditions set out in reg. 5 (see "Exemptions") it need not have springs (reg. 12); speedometer (reg. 18); warning instrument (reg. 27); or markings, if unladen weight does not exceed 3,050 kilograms (reg. 74), and regs. 17, and 53 to 61 do not apply to such vehicle.

If a land tractor is a heavy motor car or a motor car the regulations as to overall width, overhang, brakes and tyres will apply as they apply to a land tractor which is a motor tractor (reg. 5).

Every land tractor shall be equipped with a mirror fitted externally on the off-side and so constructed and fitted as to assist the driver, if he so desires, to become aware of traffic on that side rearwards, unless he can easily obtain a clear view of traffic to the rear (including traffic to the rear of any trailer being drawn) without having any mirror fitted to the tractor (reg. 23).

Lavatory – If a motor vehicle first used on or after January 15, 1931, or trailer has a urinal, closet, lavatory basin or sink, it shall empty every closet or urinal pan into a tank on the vehicle, properly ventilated and deodorised and no basin or sink shall drain into this tank (reg. 36), and nothing from such closet, urinal, basin or sink shall be discharged or allowed to leak on to a road (reg. 105).

Length – Overall length is exclusive of driving mirror, starting handle, hood when down, turntable fire escape ladder (or expanding or extensible contrivance forming part thereof), telescopic fog lamp, snowplough, 305 mms. post office letter box, any container for customs clearance seal, and front corner marker lamp (reg. 3).

The overall length of an articulated vehicle shall not exceed 15 metres, provided that this paragraph shall not apply in the case of an articulated vehicle constructed and normally used for the conveyance of indivisible loads of exceptional length (i) if each wheel of the vehicle is fitted with a pneumatic tyre, or (ii) if each wheel of the vehicle is not so fitted but the vehicle is not driven at a speed exceeding 12 miles per hour. The overall length of a public service vehicle which is constructed or adapted for use as such a vehicle or a chassis which is constructed for such a vehicle shall not exceed 12 metres.

The overall length of a motor vehicle other than one falling within either of the two foregoing paragraphs shall not exceed 11 metres (reg. 9).

A trailer shall not exceed 7 metres in length, provided that the maximum length may be 12 metres in the case of a trailer which (a) has not less than 4 wheels and where the distance between the centres of the respective areas of contact with the road of the foremost and rearmost wheels on the same side is not less than $\frac{3}{5}$ of its length, and (b) is drawn by a motor vehicle of 2,030 kilograms or more unladen weight, but this does not apply to a trailer constructed and used for indivisible loads of exceptional length, to a land implement, to the trailer part of an articulated vehicle, to a broken-down vehicle being towed in consequence of the break down, to a trailer which is a trolley vehicle in course of construction or delivery, to a road tar mixing plant or a road planing machine provided that the total length of such vehicle and trailer shall not exceed 18.3 metres (reg. 68).

Lifting Appliances – Implements suspended from lifting appliances fitted to a vehicle shall be secured so as to avoid danger to other persons on the vehicle or on the road (reg. 134).

Locomotive – Means a motor vehicle exceeding 7¼ tons weight unladen and not constructed itself to carry a load. It is a drawing vehicle. If over 11½ tons it is termed a "heavy locomotive" and if under 11½ tons it is a "light locomotive" (R.T. Act 1972, s. 190). The regulations apply equally to both types of locomotive save where otherwise indicated (reg. 3).

ATTENDANTS – When on a highway two persons shall drive or attend it, with one additional attendant for each trailer drawn (s. 34). See "Attendants".

DRIVERS' HOURS OF DUTY – See Transport Act 1968, s. 96: Chap. 24.

MARKINGS – The owner shall have the unladen weight marked on the left or near side (reg. 74).

TRAILERS – Three may be drawn on a highway (s. 65) and they need not have wings if drawn by a vehicle restricted to 12 miles per hour (reg. 73).

TYRES – see "Tyres".

WARNING INSTRUMENT or horn is necessary on a locomotive (reg. 27).

Not more than ¾ of the total weight of a locomotive having not more than 4 wheels and first used before June 1, 1955, shall be transmitted to the road by any two wheels (reg. 44).

The laden weight of a locomotive shall not exceed 20,830 kilograms but more is allowable if proper springs, soft tyres and more wheels (reg. 76). The total weight on a road by any 2 wheels in line transversely shall not exceed 11,180 kilograms but this does not apply to a road roller or to a vehicle with not more than 4 wheels first used before June 1, 1955 (reg. 76).

The total weight of all its trailers laden or unladen, shall not exceed 40,650 kilograms (reg. 77).

WIDTH shall not exceed 2·75 metres (reg. 43).

Markings – The owner shall cause the following to be plainly marked on some conspicuous place on the left or near side of:

(1) A locomotive—the unladen weight (reg. 74).

(2) A motor tractor (other than a land tractor exempted by reg. 5)—the unladen weight (reg. 74).

(3) A heavy motor car—the unladen weight. This does not apply to a vehicle not registered under the Roads Act 1920 or the Vehicles (Excise) Acts 1949 and 1971 (reg.74). See "Mechanically propelled Vehicles", Chap. 25.

Mascots – A motor vehicle first used on or after October 1, 1937, shall not carry a mascot in any position where it is likely to strike any person with whom the vehicle may collide unless the mascot is not liable to cause injury to such person through any projection thereon (reg. 132).

Meat Vans – When a motor tractor draws a closed wheeled trailer specially constructed and used for the conveyance of meat between docks and railway stations and wholesale markets it need not have an additional attendant (reg. 135).

Mirror – (1) Save as provided in paragraph (2) of this regulation:

(*a*) the following motor vehicles, that is to say, every passenger vehicle adapted to carry more than seven passengers exclusive of the driver and every goods vehicle, including every dual-purpose vehicle, but excluding locomotives and motor tractors, shall be equipped with at least two mirrors one of which shall be fitted externally on the off-side of the vehicle and the other either internally or on the nearside externally and the mirrors shall be so constructed and fitted to the motor vehicle as to assist the driver, if he so desires, to become aware of traffic to the rear and on both sides rearwards; and

(*b*) every land tractor shall be equipped with a mirror fitted externally on the off-side of the tractor and so constructed and fitted to the tractor as to assist the driver, if he so desires, to become aware of traffic on that side rearwards, unless he can easily obtain a clear view of traffic to the rear (including traffic to the rear of any trailer being drawn) without having any mirror fitted to the tractor; and

(*c*) subject to the provisions of the foregoing sub-paragraphs every motor vehicle shall be equipped either internally or externally with a mirror so constructed and fitted to the motor vehicle as to assist the driver, if he so desires, to become aware of traffic to the rear of the vehicle.

(2) Paragraph (1) of this regulation shall not apply:

(*a*) to a two-wheeled motor cycle with or without a sidecar attached;

(*b*) to a land locomotive;

(*c*) to a motor vehicle when drawing a trailer if a person is carried on the trailer in a position which affords an uninterrupted view to the rear and such a person is provided with efficient means of communicating to the driver the effect of signals given by the drivers of other vehicles to the rear thereof;

(*d*) to a works truck if the driver can easily obtain a clear view of traffic to the rear; or

(*e*) to a pedestrian controlled vehicle.

(3) In the case of a motor vehicle first used on or after April 1, 1969, the edges of any mirror fitted internally to the vehicle to assist any person, if he so desires, to become aware of traffic to the rear of the vehicle shall be surrounded by some material such as will render those edges and that material unlikely to cause severe cuts in the event of the mirror or that material being struck by any occupant of the vehicle (reg. 23).

Motor Car – Means a motor vehicle constructed itself to carry a load or passengers, which is not a "motor cycle" or "invalid carriage", and the unladen weight of which does not exceed 2½ tons, or 3 tons if made solely to carry not more than seven passengers (R.T. Act 1972, s. 190). "Motor car" also includes a motor vehicle constructed or adapted for the conveyance of goods or burden of any description:

(*a*) which carries a container for gas fuel for the propulsion of the vehicle whose weight does not exceed 3½ tons.

(*b*) which does not carry such container, etc., the weight of the vehicle not exceeding 3 tons (R.T. Act 1972, s. 190).

ATTENDANTS – If it is wheeled and draws a trailer with not more than two wheels on the highway a person additional to the driver need not be carried to attend it (reg. 135).

BRAKES – See "Brakes".

DRIVERS' HOURS OF DUTY (goods) – See Transport Act 1968, s. 96: Chap. 24.

OVERHANG – It shall not exceed 60 per cent. of the wheelbase. The regulation does not apply to a car first used on or before January 2, 1933, nor to street cleansing vehicles, refuse vehicles, ambulances and works trucks (reg. 58).

TRAILER – See "Trailers".

TYRES – See "Tyres".

WEIGHTS – The maximum weights allowable in the case of a motor car on the road are 9,150 kilograms on 2 transverse wheels 14,230 kilograms on 4 wheels, 20,330 kilograms on 6 wheels and 24,390 kilograms if more than 6 wheels. There are special provisions with respect to a "prior 1968 vehicle", a "post 1968 vehicle", and a "temporarily imported vehicle" (reg. 79).

WINGS or mudguards are necessary unless the car body affords adequate protection, but this does not apply to the rear wheels of the motor vehicle part of an articulated vehicle for carriage of round timber nor to an unfinished vehicle going to works for completion nor to a works truck (reg. 61).

WIDTH – The overall width of a motor car shall not exceed 2·5 metres (reg. 57).

Motor Cycle – Means a motor vehicle with less than four wheels and not exceeding 8 hundredweight unladen, which is not an "invalid carriage" (R.T. Act 1972, s. 190). It must be a wheeled vehicle (reg. 8). It need not have a reflecting mirror it if is two wheeled with or without a sidecar (reg. 23), or springs (reg. 12). It shall have wings or mudguards except in the case of a works truck (reg. 64).

ATTENDANT extra to driver for a trailer is not necessary where the trailer has not more than two wheels or has brakes which can be applied by the driver of a motor cycle which belongs to H.M. Services (reg. 135).

BRAKES – See "Brakes".

PASSENGERS – If any person in addition to the driver is carried astride on a two-wheeled motor cycle (whether it has a sidecar or not) suitable supports or rests for the feet of such passenger must be available (reg. 129). See also R.T. Act 1972, s. 16, which allows only one such pillion rider.

SIDECAR wheel shall not be wholly outside the length extremities of the motor cycle (reg. 121). See "Sidecar".

TRAILER – See "Trailers".

TYRES – See "Tyres".

Motor Tractor – Means a motor vehicle not constructed itself to carry a load and of weight unladen not exceeding 7¼ tons (R.T. Act 1972, s. 190).

ATTENDANTS – When it draws a trailer on the highway an attendant additional to driver shall be carried (R.T. Act 1972, s. 34), except when it draws a road repair or cleansing machine (reg. 135), or a meat trailer, a street cleanser or a refuse collector or is a motor vehicle drawing an unsteerable broken down vehicle or a trailer with brakes applicable by the driver of the drawing vehicle belonging to H.M. Forces (reg. 135).

BRAKES – See "Brakes".

MARKINGS – When on a highway the owner shall have the unladen weight marked on the left side (reg. 74).

OVERHANG shall not exceed 1·83 metres (reg. 49).

SPRINGS – see "Springs".

TRAILER – See "Trailers".

TYRES – See "Tyres".

WEIGHT – The total weight of the tractor and its trailer on a highway shall not exceed 22,360 kilograms but in some cases may be up to 32,520 kilograms (reg. 81). See "Weight".

WIDTH shall not exceed 2·5 metres (reg. 48).

Noise – No motor vehicle shall be used on a road in such manner as to cause any excessive noise which could have been avoided by the exercise of reasonable care on the part of the driver (reg. 107).

No person shall use or cause or permit to be used on a road any motor vehicle or trailer which causes any excessive noise.

However, it will be a good defence to proceedings under this regulation to prove that the noise was due to some temporary or accidental cause and could not have been prevented by due diligence and care on the part of the owner or driver.

Also, if the driver or person in charge who is not the owner is prosecuted under this regulation, it will be a good defence to prove that the noise arose through a defect in design or construction, or through the negligence or fault of some other person whose duty was to keep the vehicle in proper condition or to properly pack the load, and could not have been prevented by reasonable diligence and care on the part of such driver or person in charge (reg. 106).

The driver shall, when the vehicle is stationary otherwise than through enforced stoppage due to traffic necessities, stop the action of the machinery of the vehicle, so far as may be necessary for the prevention of noise. However, this does not apply so as to prevent the working of the machinery when it is necessary to do so on account of any derangement of it, or when its working is required for some ancillary purpose nor does it apply to a gas-propelled vehicle (reg. 109). See also "Silencer" and "Audible warning instrument".

Except as provided by the regulation every motor vehicle first used after April 1, 1970, shall be so constructed that the noise emitted by it does not exceed the sound level in decibels indicated in Sched. 9 (reg. 29).

Subject to the provisions set out in the regulation, no person shall use or cause or permit to be used on a road any vehicle at a time when the noise emitted by that vehicle exceeds the maximum sound level permitted (reg. 108).

Obstruction – No person in charge of a motor vehicle or trailer shall cause or permit the motor vehicle or trailer to stand on a road so as to cause any unnecessary obstruction thereof (reg. 114). The highway is not a parking place unless specially designated as such. The use of a highway must be reasonable.

During the hours of darkness (see Chap. 24) no person shall, except with the permission of a police officer in uniform, cause or permit any motor vehicle to stand on any road otherwise than with the left or near side of the vehicle as close as may be to the edge of the carriageway. This shall not apply to:

(*a*) Any motor vehicle used for fire brigade, ambulance, police or defence purposes if compliance would hinder the use of the vehicle for such purpose;

(*b*) any motor vehicle standing on a part of a road specially set aside for parking or for hackney carriages or for public service vehicles or for taking up or setting down passengers if compliance would conflict with the "law" allowing such standing;

(*c*) any motor vehicle waiting to set down or pick up passengers under Regulations or directions by the chief officer of police;

(*d*) any motor vehicle in a "one way" road;

(*e*) any motor vehicle used in connection with building operations, repair of another vehicle, removal of obstruction, maintenance of any road or laying, etc., of a sewer, pipe, wire, cable, post, etc., for gas, water or electricity, if compliance would hinder such use of the vehicle (reg. 115).

Opening of Doors – No person shall open or cause or permit to be opened any door of a motor vehicle or trailer on a road so as to cause injury or danger to any person (reg. 117).

Overhang – This is the distance from the rear of the vehicle excluding hood when down, post office box up to 305 mms., turntable fire escape ladder, luggage carrier fitted to a seven-passenger motor car, and an attachment not exceeding 305 mms. for drawing a trailer by a public service vehicle, to the non-steering axle of a vehicle having not more than 3 axles only one of which is a non-steering axle, or to a point 110 mms. in rear of the foremost non-steering axle of a vehicle with 3 or 4 axles of which the two rear are non-steering (see reg. 3). It shall not exceed 1·83 metres in a motor tractor or a land tractor which is a heavy motor car or a motor car (reg. 49) nor 60 per cent of the wheelbase in a heavy motor car with some exceptions given in the regulation (reg. 53) and in a motor car with some exceptions, including ambulances, works trucks and refuse and street cleansing vehicles (reg. 58). For side overhang, see "Width".

Pedestrian Controlled Vehicle – This is a motor vehicle which is controlled by a pedestrian and not constructed or adapted for use or used for the carriage of a driver or passenger (reg. 3). The following requirements do not apply to such vehicles—springs if all wheels have pneumatic tyres (reg. 12); minimum diameter wheels (reg. 20); mirror (reg. 23); certain requirements as to brakes if the vehicle does not exceed 8 hundredweight unladen (reg. 59); pneumatic tyres if all tyres are soft or elastic (reg. 63); warning instrument (reg. 27).

For registration and licensing purposes such a vehicle means a mechanically propelled vehicle with 3 or more wheels which does not exceed 8 hundredweight unladen and which is neither constructed nor adapted for use nor used for the carriage of a driver or passenger (Road Vehicles (Reg. and Lic.) Regs. 1971, reg. 3).

Plates—certain vehicles to be equipped with – (1) This regulation applies to:

(*a*) every heavy motor car and motor car first used on or after January 1, 1968, not being a passenger vehicle, a dual-purpose vehicle, a land tractor, a works truck, or a pedestrian controlled vehicle; and

(*b*) every locomotive and motor tractor first used on or after April 1, 1973, not being a land locomotive, land tractor, industrial tractor, works truck, engineering plant, pedestrian controlled vehicle, or a vehicle manufactured before October 1, 1972, and

(*c*) every trailer manufactured on or after January 1, 1968 which exceeds 1,020 kilograms in weight unladen and is other than:

(i) a trailer not constructed or adapted to carry any load, other than plant or special appliance or apparatus which is a permanent or essentially permanent fixture, and not exceeding 2,290 kilograms in total weight;

(ii) a living van not exceeding 2,040 kilograms in weight unladen and fitted with pneumatic tyres;

(iii) a works trailer;

(iv) a trailer mentioned in regulation 70 (3);

(v) a trailer which was manufactured and used outside Great Britain before it was first used in Great Britain.

(2) Every vehicle to which this regulation applies shall be equipped with a plate securely affixed to the vehicle in a conspicuous and readily accessible position and the said plate shall contain in the case of a heavy motor car or motor car the particulars required by Part I of Sched. 2 and in the case of a trailer the particulars required by Part II of that Schedule, the said particulars being completed in accordance with Part III of that Schedule and the plate otherwise complying with the provisions contained in that Part (reg. 39).

Police Vehicles – They can carry gongs, bells, sirens and two-tone horns (reg. 27) and may use them when necessary at all times (reg. 110).

Public Service Vehicles – Regulation 79 deals with the laden weight of a heavy motor car and of a motor car, but it does not apply to public service vehicles. Such vehicles, if heavy motor cars or motor cars are limited to 9,150 kilograms weight on 2 transverse wheels, and to a total of 14,230 kilograms on all the wheels, when fully equipped for service with weights for the full number of seated passengers, 63·5 kilograms for each person. If registered after December 31, 1954, and more than 8 standing passengers may be carried another 63·5 kilograms for each passenger in excess of 8, must be included (reg. 78). There are special provisions with respect to a "prior 1968 vehicle", a "post 1968 vehicle" and a "temporarily imported vehicle".

A public service vehicle which is a motor car or a heavy motor car shall not exceed 2·5 metres in width (regs. 52 and 57). Overall length of a public service vehicle shall not exceed 12 metres (reg. 9). Overall height shall not exceed 4·57 metres (reg. 10).

A public service vehicle shall not draw a trailer but it may draw another empty public service vehicle in an emergency or a gas trailer for its propulsion. It may also draw a trailer if its use has been approved by the traffic commissioners and the trailer and means of attachment have been approved by a certifying officer (reg. 127).

Quitting Vehicle – No person shall cause or permit to be on a road any motor vehicle which is not attended by a person duly licensed to drive it unless the engine is stopped and the relevant parking brake is effectively set. "Relevant parking brake" means: (*a*) in the case of a motor vehicle to which reg. 4A applies, the parking brake provided in accordance with the relevant EEC Council Directive; and (*b*) in the case of any other motor vehicle the parking brake provided in accordance with Reg. 13.

The stopping of the engine shall not apply to a fire brigade vehicle fighting fire; to a gas propelled vehicle or to a vehicle when it is being used for police or ambulance purposes or motor vehicles, the engines of which are used to drive special machinery (reg. 116).

Railway Vehicles – Wheeled motor tractors not exceeding 4,070 kilograms weight unladen used for railway shunting and used on a road only for passing to and from such work need not have springs (reg. 12).

Refuse Vehicles – These are vehicles and trailers designed and used for the collection or disposal of refuse or of contents of gullies or cesspools. An attendant for such a wheeled trailer drawn by a motor tractor need not be carried (reg. 135). Pneumatic tyres are not necessary on such wheeled trailers (reg. 72), or on such vehicles (reg. 55), but they must have pneumatic, soft or elastic tyres (reg. 60).

There is no limit to the size of their wheels (reg. 20), nor to the overhang if they are heavy motor cars (reg. 53).

Reversing – Every motor vehicle exceeding in weight unladen 410 kilograms shall be capable of being so worked that it may travel forwards or backwards (reg. 21).

Except in the case of a road roller or other road plant at work no person shall cause a motor vehicle to travel backwards for a greater distance or time than may be requisite for the safety or reasonable convenience of the occupants of the vehicle or of other traffic on the road (reg. 112).

Road Cleansing Vehicles – These are vehicles and trailers designed and used for street cleansing. If a motor tractor draws any machine or implement for this purpose an attendant for the trailer need not be carried (reg. 135). Pneumatic tyres need not be on the wheels of such wheeled trailers (reg. 72), or of such heavy motor cars (reg. 55), or of such motor cars over 1,020 kilograms weight unladen (reg. 60), but both types of motor cars must have, at least soft or elastic tyres. There is no limit to the size of their wheels (reg. 20), nor to overhang (regs. 53 and 58). If such a trailer does not carry any load other than its necessary gear and equipment it need not have a braking system (reg. 70).

Road Repair Vehicles – When a motor tractor draws any machine or implement used for the maintenance or repair of roads an additional attendant need not be carried (reg. 135). A heavy motor car exceeding 4,070 kilograms weight unladen mainly used in operations on rough ground or unmade roads need not have pneumatic tyres, but should have soft or elastic tyres (reg. 55), and if it has pneumatic tyres and does not proceed at more than 20 miles per hour and does not exceed 4,070 kilograms in weight it need not have springs (reg. 12).

Road plant at work may travel backwards (reg. 112).

Road Rollers – These vehicles must be registered and carry identification marks. The requirements as to the variation of wheel load and the distribution of weight (regs. 11 and 44), springs (reg. 12), reflecting mirrors (reg. 23), warning instrument or horn (reg. 27), and soft or elastic tyres (regs. 45 and 51), do not apply (reg. 4). One braking system with one means of operation will be sufficient if a wheeled vehicle not propelled by steam (reg. 50).

The prohibition against travelling backwards for an unnecessary distance does not apply if engaged on road work (reg. 112). Attendants are not necessary (reg. 135 and R.T. Act 1972, s. 34). Its water cart need not have a trailer plate (reg. 75), its water trailer need not have pneumatic soft, or elastic tyres (regs. 71 and 72). Regulation 29 (noise) does not apply.

Roads Experiments – Vehicles used under s. 249, Highways Act 1959, for experiments or trials on roads, are not subject to the Regulations, see "Special Types", nor are they subject to the ordinary speed limits (R.T.R. Act 1967, Sched. 5).

Salvage Corps – Such wheeled vehicles may carry gongs, bells, sirens or two-tone horns (reg. 27) and may use them when necessary at all times (reg. 110).

Seat Belts and Anchorage Points – (1) Except as provided by paragraph (2) of this regulation, this regulation applies to (*a*) every motor car registered on or after January 1, 1965 and (*b*) every three-wheeled motor cycle, the unladen weight of which exceeds 255 kilograms first used on or after September 1, 1970.

(2) This Regulation does not apply:

(*a*) to a goods vehicle unless it was constructed on or after September 1, 1966, is registered on or after April 1, 1967, and has an unladen weight not exceeding 1,525 kilograms;

(*b*) to a three-wheeled motor cycle manufactured before March 1, 1970, or a two-wheeled motor cycle with side-car;

(*c*) to a passenger vehicle or a dual-purpose vehicle being in either case a vehicle adapted to carry more than twelve passengers exclusive of the driver;

(*d*) to a land tractor;

(*e*) to a works truck;

(*f*) to an electrically propelled goods vehicle;

(*g*) to a pedestrian controlled vehicle;

(*h*) to a vehicle in respect of which, under section 23 of the Purchase Tax Act 1963, any tax has been remitted and has not subsequently becone payable, or which has been zero rated under regs. 44 or 45 of The Value Added Tax (General) Regs. 1972;

(*i*) to a vehicle constructed before June 30, 1964; or

(*j*) to a vehicle which has been used on roads outside Great Britain and has been imported into Great Britain, whilst it is being driven after its importation into Great Britain on the journey from the place where it has arrived in Great Britain to a place of residence of the owner or driver of the vehicle, and on the journey from any such place to a place where, by previous arrangement, the vehicle will be provided with such anchorage points and seat belts as will comply with the requirements of this regulation.

(3) Every vehicle to which this regulation applies shall be provided with anchorage points designed to hold body-restraining seat belts securely in position on the vehicle for:

(*a*) the driver's seat; and

(*b*) the specified passenger's seat:

Provided that this paragraph shall not apply so as to require anchorage points to be provided for any seat which is a seat with integral seat belt anchorages.

(4) Every vehicle to which this regulation applies shall be provided with:

(*a*) a body-restraining seat belt designed for use by an adult for the driver's seat; and

(*b*) a body-restraining seat belt for the specified passenger's seat:

Provided that this paragraph shall not apply to a vehicle:

(*a*) while it is being used under a trade licence within the meaning of the Vehicles (Excise) Act 1971; or

(*b*) while it is being driven from premises of the manufacturer by whom it was made, or of a distributor of vehicles or dealer in vehicles:

(i) to premises of a distributor of vehicles, dealer in vehicles or purchaser thereof, or

(ii) to premises of a person obtaining possession thereof under a hiring agreement or hire-purchase agreement.

(5) Every seat belt provided in pursuance of this regulation shall, if the seat for which it is provided is a seat with integral seat belt anchorages, be properly secured to the integral seat belt anchorage points forming part thereof, or, if the seat for which it is provided is not such a seat, be properly secured to the structure of the vehicle by the anchorage points provided for it under paragraph (3) of this regulation and to any other anchorage points provided on the seat for it.

(6) Subject to the next succeeding paragraph, where a seat belt, other than a restraining device for a young person or a seat belt comprising a lap belt and shoulder straps, is provided in pursuance of this regulation for a motor car or a motor cycle first used on or after April 1, 1973, and in either case manufactured on or after October 1, 1972, the following additional conditions shall apply as respects that seat belt—

(*a*) the belt shall be so arranged that a person can, when sitting in the seat for which the belt is provided and with the belt previously adjusted to fit him, remove the belt from the device required by sub-paragraph (*c*) of this paragraph and by using one hand, or by taking the belt with one hand and transferring it from one hand to the other, put the belt on;

(*b*) the fastenings by means of which the belt is secured on secured on the wearer shall be so designed that they can be engaged with a single movement of one hand in one direction and released with such a movement in one direction;

(*c*) an efficient device, unlikely to become dislodged in normal use, for retaining the belt in position when stowed away shall be provided and the centre of this device shall be located not more than 75 mms. behind a point which is in the same horizontal plane and is positioned on the rear side of the door aperture provided for access to the front seat:

For the purpose of determining the position of the aforesaid point the door and any rubber, felt or other soft trimming or sealing material around the door aperture shall be disregarded;

(*d*) the said device shall be at a sufficient height from the floor of the vehicle to ensure that, so far as is practicable, any part of the belt that would come in contact with the clothing of a person wearing the belt in normal circumstances does not lie on the floor when the belt is in the stowed position;

(*e*) it shall be possible to stow away the belt for retention on the device mentioned in sub-paragraph (*c*) of this paragraph without employing any manual device for adjusting the belt to fit the wearer; and (*f*) the belt after being put on the wearer, shall either adjust automatically to fit him or be such that the said manual device shall be convenient to use and capable of being operated with one hand.

(7) The last preceding paragraph shall not apply to:—

(*a*) a seat belt fitted to the specified passenger's seat which is treated as such by virtue of sub-paragraph (*b*) of paragraph (9) of this regulation; or

(*b*) a seat belt fitted to the specified passenger's seat of a goods vehicle which has an unladen weight of more than 915 kilograms and has more than one forward facing front seat for a passenger alongside the driver's seat, any such seats for passengers being joined together in a single structure.

(8) (*a*) Every motor car manufactured on or after September 1, 1966, and registered on or after April 1, 1967, and every three-wheeled motor cycle manufactured on or after April 1, 1972, and first used on or after October 1, 1972, which is provided with seat belt anchorage points in pursuance of paragraph (3) of this regulation shall be legibly and permanently marked with the specification number of the British Standard for seat belt anchorage points, namely, either B.S. AU 48: 1965 or B.S. AU 48a.

(*b*) Where in the case of any motor car to which this regulation applies and which was registered on or after April 1, 1967, or in the case of any motor cycle to which this regulation applies and which was first used on or after October 1, 1972, the driver's seat or the specified passenger's seat is a seat with integral seat belt anchorages, such seat shall be legibly and permanently marked with the specification number of the British Standard for Seats with Integral Seat Belt Anchorages followed by the suffix "1", namely, either B.S. AU 140/1: 1967 or B.S. AU A140a/1.

(*c*) If any seat with integral seat belt anchorages is provided on or after January 1, 1969, for a motor car to sign which this regulation applies and which was manufactured on or after September 1, 1966 and registered on or after April 1, 1967, or is provided on or after July 1, 1971, for a motor cycle to which this regulation applies and which was manufactured on or after January 1, 1971, and first used on or after July 1, 1971, the vehicle for which it is so provided shall be legibly and permanently marked with the specification number, namely, either B.S. AU 140: 1967 or B.S. AU 140a.

(*d*) Each seat belt provided for any person in any vehicle to which this regulation applies shall be legibly and permanently marked with the specification number of the British Standard for Seat Belt Assemblies for Motor Vehicles, namely, either B.S. 3245: 1960 or, except in the case of a restraining device for a young person, B.S. AU 160a, and with the registered certification trade mark of the British Standards Institution.

(9) In this regulation—

"body restraining seat belt" means a seat belt designed to provide restraint for both the upper and lower parts of the trunk of the wearer in the event of an accident to the vehicle;

"seat belt" means a belt intended to be worn by a person in a vehicle and designed to prevent or lessen injury to its wearer in the event of an accident to the vehicle and includes, in the case of a restraining device for a young person, any special chair to which the belt is attached;

"seat with integral seat belt anchorages" means a seat which is fitted with all the anchorage points required for use in connection with the seat belt provided for that seat, and

"specified passenger's seat" means—

(*a*) in the case of a vehicle which has one forward-facing front seat alongside the driver's seat, such seat, and in in the case of a vehicle which has more than one such seat, the one furthest from the driver's seat; or

(*b*) if the vehicle normally has no seat which is the specified passenger's seat under the last preceding sub-paragraph, the forward-facing front seat for a passenger which is foremost in the vehicle and furthest from the driver's seat unless there is a fixed partition separating such seat from the space in front of it alongside the driver's seat.

Showmen's Trailers – The overall width of a wheeled trailer in use before January 15, 1931, by a travelling showman in connection with his business may be 2·88 metres (reg. 69).

Sidecar – A sidecar shall be so attached to its motor cycle that the wheel thereof is not wholly outside planes perpendicular to the longitudinal axis of the motor cycle passing through the extreme projecting points in the front and in the rear of the motor cycle (reg. 121). If so attached, and if it complies with the prescribed conditions (e.g. tyres, wings, wheels, glass), the sidecar is regarded as forming part of the motor cycle, and not as being a trailer (Road Traffic Act 1972, s. 190).

If a sidecar does not so comply it is a trailer, and for drawing of trailers by motor cycles, see "Trailers".

Side-door Latches and Hinges (Strength of) – Private cars first used on or after July 1, 1972, shall be marked with an approval mark to indicate that the vehicles are fitted with anti-burst latches and hinges to reduce the risk of the side doors opening in a collision. Exemptions are allowed for certain models (reg 15).

Silencer – Every vehicle propelled by an internal combustion engine shall be fitted with a silencer, expansion chamber or other contrivance suitable and sufficient for reducing as far as may be reasonable the noise caused by the escape of the exhaust gases from the engine (reg. 28).

No person shall use or cause or permit to be used on a road any such vehicle so that the exhaust gases pass into the air without first passing through the silencer, which shall be kept in efficient working order and shall not be altered so that the noise of the exhaust gases is made greater (reg. 98). Silencers may be tested (reg. 137). See "Testing", "Noise".

Smoke, Ashes, etc. – Every motor vehicle shall be so constructed that no avoidable smoke or visible vapour is emitted therefrom (reg. 31).

If solid fuel is used, there shall be an efficient appliance to prevent the emission of sparks or grit, and also a tray or shield to prevent ashes and cinders from falling on the road (reg. 35).

No person shall use, cause or permit to be used on a road any motor vehicle from which any smoke, visible vapour, grit, sparks, ashes, cinders or oily substance is emitted if the emission thereof causes or is likely to cause damage to any property or injury to any person who is actually at the time or who reasonably may be expected on the road or is likely to cause danger to any such person as aforesaid (reg. 101).

Where a motor vehicle (other than a works truck) propelled by a compression ignition engine is fitted with a device for starting the engine by supplying it with excess fuel, the device, and any apparatus for operating it, shall be so fitted that the device cannot readily be used by any person on the vehicle. This regulation does not apply if the device is so designed that it cannot cause the engine to be supplied with excess fuel after the engine has been started or does not cause any increase in the smoke or visible vapour emitted from the vehicle (reg. 32). Such a device must be maintained and it must not be used while the vehicle is in motion on a road (reg. 103).

Speedometer – Every motor vehicle first used on or after October 1, 1937, except invalid carriages, works trucks, motor cycles with engine capacity not exceeding 100 c.c., motor cycles neither made nor used for the carriage of a driver or passenger, vehicles not allowed by law to do more than 12 miles per hour and vehicles incapable of exceeding 12 miles per hour, shall be fitted with an instrument so constructed and in such a position as at all times readily to indicate to the driver within a margin of accuracy of plus or minus 10 per cent., if and when he is driving at a speed greater than 10 miles per hour (reg. 18).

The speedometer shall at all material times be kept in good working order but it will be a defence to prove any defect occurred during the journey in question or that at the time steps had already been taken to remedy the defect. The speedometer must be kept free from any obstruction which might prevent it being easily read (reg. 91).

Springs – Every motor vehicle and every trailer drawn thereby shall be equipped with suitable and sufficient springs between each wheel and the frame of the vehicle:

Provided that this regulation shall not apply—

(*a*) to any vehicle first used on or before January 1, 1932;
(*b*) to any motor tractor not exceeding 4,070 kilograms in weight unladen if each unsprung wheel of the vehicle is fitted with a pneumatic tyre;
(*c*) to any land locomotive, land implement, land implement conveyor, agricultural trailer or trailer used solely for the haulage of felled trees;
(*d*) to any tractor not exceeding 4,070 kilograms in weight unladen used in connection with railway shunting operations which is only used on a road when passing from one portion of the railway track to another for the purpose of such operations;
(*e*) to motor cycles;
(*f*) to mobile cranes;
(*g*) to works trucks and works trailers;
(*h*) to any vehicle not exceeding 4,070 kilograms in weight unladen specially designed for and mainly used in operations which necessitate working on rough ground or unmade roads if each wheel of the vehicle is fitted with a pneumatic tyre and if the vehicle is not driven or drawn at a speed exceeding 20 miles per hour;
(*i*) to any vehicle not exceeding 4.070 kilograms in weight unladen constructed or adapted for use and used solely for road sweeping if each wheel of the vehicle is fitted with a pneumatic tyre or a tyre of soft or elastic material and if the vehicle is not driven or drawn at a speed exceeding 20 miles per hour;
(*j*) to any pedestrian controlled vehicle, all the wheels of which are equipped with pneumatic tyres; or
(*k*) to any broken down vehicle which is being drawn by a motor vehicle in consequence of the breakdown (reg. 12).

Steam Vehicles – A wheeled steam locomotive with engine capable of being reversed, and first used on or before January 2, 1933, need not have brakes (reg. 46). If the engine is capable of being reversed, it will be deemed an efficient braking system for a wheeled steam tractor (reg. 50) and for a wheeled steam heavy motor car or motor car not used as a public service vehicle (regs. 54 and 59). The total weight on the road of a wheeled steam heavy motor car or motor car which is not a public service vehicle may be 14,230 kilograms (4-wheeler) and 20,330 kilograms (6-wheeler). Also the weight on any two transverse wheels of such a vehicle may be 9,150 kilograms (see reg. 79). No smoke, visible vapour, sparks, grit, ashes, cinders or oily substance shall be emitted on a road (reg. 101). See "Smoke, Ashes, etc.".

The driver of a steam vehicle other than a motor car shall stop the vehicle whenever it is necessary to attend to the furnace except where two persons are carried to drive or attend the vehicle (reg. 113).

Steering Gear – All steering gear when the vehicle is on the road shall be maintained in good and efficient working order and properly adjusted (reg. 95). It may be tested (reg. 137).

Steering Mechanism – Private cars and their derivatives first used on or after July 1, 1972, shall be marked with an approval mark to indicate that the vehicles are fitted with a protective type of steering mechanism. Exemptions are allowed for certain models. (reg. 16).

Straddle Carrier – Means a motor vehicle constructed to straddle and lift its load for transportation (reg. 3). It is not a works truck (reg. 3) and must not draw a trailer (reg. 124). See "Special Types", later.

Television Sets – Not to be used in a motor vehicle if the screen is visible to the driver or if it might distract the driver of any other vehicle on the road (reg. 133).

Testing and Inspection – (1) Any police constable in uniform and any person for the time being appointed by the Minister of Transport as a certifying officer or public service vehicle examiner under Part III of the 1960 Act or under any enactment repealed by that Act or as an examiner appointed under Part IV of that Act or under s. 56 (1) of the 1972 Act or appointed by the commissioner of police of the metropolis to examine and inspect public carriages for the purposes of the Metropolitan Public Carriage Act 1869, or appointed by the police authority to act under the direction of the Chief Officer of Police for the purposes of s. 53 of the 1972 Act, who shall produce his authority if required, is hereby empowered to test and inspect the brakes, silencers, steering gear, tyres, lighting equipment and reflectors of any motor vehicle or trailer on any premises where that motor vehicle or trailer is, subject however to the consent of the owners of the premises.

(2) The power conferred by this regulation to test and inspect the brakes, silencers, steering gear, tyres, lighting equipment and reflectors of a vehicle on any premises where the vehicle is shall not be exercised unless either the owner of the vehicle consents or notice of the date and time at which it is proposed to carry out the test and inspection has been given to him in accordance with the provisions of the following paragraph.

(3) The said notice shall be given to the owner of the vehicle personally or left at his address not less than 48 hours before the time of the proposed test and inspection or shall be sent to him not less than 72 hours before that time by recorded delivery service at his address.

(4) The provisions of paragraph (2) of this regulation shall not apply in the case of a test and inspection made within 48 hours of an accident to which section 25 of the 1972 act applies and in which the vehicle has been involved.

(5) For the purposes of this regulation, the owner of the vehicle shall be deemed to be:

(*a*) in the case of a vehicle which is for the time being registered under the Vehicles (Excise) Act 1971 and is not being used under a trade licence under that Act the person appearing as the owner of the vehicle in the register kept by the Secretary of State under that Act;

(*b*) in the case of a vehicle used under a trade licence, the holder of the licence; and

(*c*) in the case of a vehicle exempt from excise duty by virtue of the Motor Vehicles (International Circulation) Order 1975, the person resident outside the United Kingdom who has brought the vehicle into Great Britain,

and in cases (*a*) and (*b*) the address of the owner as shown on the register or, as the case may be, on the licence may be treated as his address (reg. 137).

Tow Rope – Where a motor vehicle draws a trailer by means of a rope or chain, or when one trailer draws another by such means, the rope or chain must not exceed 4·5 metres in length, Where a motor vehicle draws a trailer or trailers, if the distance between the vehicles exceeds 1·5 metres then the connections must be clearly visible from either side (reg. 120).

Tower Wagon – If it is a heavy motor car (over 2½ tons) it need not have pneumatic tyres, but tyres shall at least be soft or elastic (reg. 55).

"Tower wagon" means a goods vehicle (*a*) into which there is built as part of the vehicle any expanding or extensible contrivance designed for facilitating the erection, inspection, repair or maintenance of overhead structures or equipment, and (*b*) which is neither constructed nor adapted for use nor used for the conveyance of any load, except such a contrivance and articles used in connection therewith (Vehicles (Excise) Act 1971, Sched. 4).

Towing Implement – Means any device on wheels designed to enable a motor vehicle to draw another vehicle by attaching the device in such a manner that part of the other vehicle is secured to and either rests on or is suspended from the device, so that some but not all of its wheels are raised off the ground (reg. 3).

See reg. 4 (12) and (13) under "Exemptions".

An attendant additional to the driver is not necessary when a towing implement is being drawn by a motor vehicle if it is not attached to any vehicle except the one drawing it (reg. 135).

Trailers – The R.T. Act 1972, s. 190 defines a "trailer" as a vehicle drawn by a motor vehicle. A sidecar attached to a motor cycle shall be regarded as part of the vehicle, and not as being a trailer.

Every trailer shall be either a wheeled vehicle or a tracklaying vehicle (reg. 8).

A gas trailer is a trailer used solely for gas equipment for propelling the drawing vehicle (reg. 3).

ATTENDANTS – If one or more trailers are drawn on a highway the general rule is that additional help to the driver shall be provided. See "Attendants", for the exceptions.

BRAKES – See "Brakes".

LENGTH – The maximum length of a trailer should not exceed 7 metres (reg. 68), but for exceptions, see "Length".

MINISTRY TEST DATE DISC – Trailers for which goods vehicle test certificates have been issued must carry a current test date disc in a conspicuous position (reg. 141).

NUMBER – (1) Subject to paragraph (2) below, the number of trailers which may be drawn by a motor vehicle on a road shall not exceed—

(*a*) in the case of a locomotive, three;

(*b*) in the case of a motor tractor, one, if laden, or two, if unladen;

(*c*) in the case of a motor car or heavy motor car, one.

(2) A motor car or a heavy motor car may draw two trailers on a road in a case where one of the trailers being drawn is a towing implement and the other is a vehicle, part of which is secured to and either rests on, or is suspended from, the towing implement.

(3) For the purposes of this Regulation—

(*a*) the expression "trailer" does not include a vehicle used solely for carrying water for the purposes of the drawing vehicle or an agricultural vehicle not constructed to carry a load; and

(*b*) an articulated vehicle, when being drawn by another motor vehicle because the articulated vehicle has broken down, shall, if the articulated vehicle is unladen, be treated in relation to the drawing vehicle as a single trailer (reg. 136).

These restrictions on the number of trailers do not apply to vehicles in the service of the armed forces of the Crown (R.T. Act 1972, s. 188).

OBSTRUCTION – No person in charge of a trailer shall cause or permit it to stand on a road so as to cause any unnecessary obstruction (reg. 114).

PROHIBITIONS ON TRAILERS – No trailer shall be used for conveyance of passengers for hire or reward (reg. 125). An invalid carriage and a straddle carrier shall not draw a trailer (reg. 124). A motor cycle shall not draw a trailer exceeding 254 kilograms unladen or 1·5 metres in width (reg. 123).

A public service vehicle must not draw a trailer but may draw a gas trailer. An empty public service vehicle may tow another empty public service vehicle in case of emergency. It may also draw a trailer if its use has been approved by the traffic commissioners and the trailer and means of attachment have been approved by a certifying officer (reg. 127).

A motor cycle with not more than two wheels and without a sidecar shall not draw a trailer, but it may tow a broken-down motor cycle in consequence of the breakdown (reg. 122).

Where a motor vehicle is drawing only one trailer the overall length of the combination of vehicles shall not exceed 18 metres. (There is an exception in the case of indivisible loads and broken down vehicles.) Where a motor vehicle is drawing two or more trailers or only one trailer constructed and normally used for the conveyance of indivisible loads of exceptional length, the overall length of the motor vehicle shall not exceed 9·2 metres and unless the conditions specified in Schedule 8 (including 48 hours' notice to the police) have been complied with the overall length of the combination of vehicles shall not exceed 29·5 metres.

Where a motor vehicle is drawing two trailers only one such trailer may exceed 7 metres in overall length, and, where a motor vehicle is drawing three trailers, no trailer in the combination of vehicles shall exceed 7 metres in overall length (reg. 128).

SPEED – If a trailer is drawn the rate of speed is limited. See Appendix I.

TRAILER PLATE – One is necessary (reg. 75), but for exceptions, see "Trailer Plate".

TYRES – The tyres on any wheels should be pneumatic, soft or elastic (reg. 71): when on a highway, reg. 4), but for exceptions, see "Tyres".

WEIGHT – The total weight transmitted to the road by any two transverse wheels of a wheeled trailer shall not exceed 9,150 kilograms. The total laden weight of a trailer with less than 6 wheels and not forming part of an articulated vehicle shall not exceed 14,230 kilograms. The total laden weight of a trailer which has no other brakes than a parking brake, and brakes which automatically come into operation on the overrun of the trailer, shall not exceed 3,560 kilograms.

The maximum total weight of all the trailers, laden or unladen, drawn by a locomotive (on a highway, reg. 4) shall not exceed 40,650 kilograms (reg. 77).

The total laden weight of a trailer together with that of any motor tractor, heavy motor car or motor car drawing it shall not exceed 22,360 kilograms (reg. 81). However, it may be 24,390 kilograms in the case of a trailer drawn by a motor tractor or heavy motor car or motor car, if both are wheeled and it may be exceed 22,360 kilograms (reg. 81). However, it may be 22,360 kilograms in the case of a trailer drawn by a motor tractor or heavy motor car or motor car, if both are wheeled and it may be up to 32,520 kilograms if with special brakes and warning device for them (reg. 81).

Reg. 89 A requires the display of appropriate weights on motor vehicles and on trailers drawn by them where the speed limit under Sched. 5 of R.T.R. Act 1967 (as amended) for the motor vehicle, when drawing the trailer, is 50 m.p.h. This regulation also prohibits the display on a trailer of a "50" plate when the speed limit prescribed is less than 50 m.p.h.

WIDTH – The maximum width should not exceed 2·3 metres (reg. 69), but for exceptions, see "Width".

WINGS – These are necessary (reg. 73), but for exceptions, see "Wings".

For other provisions affecting trailers, see "Dangerous Vehicle", "Lavatory", "Noise", "Obstruction", "Springs", "Tow-rope", and "Wheels".

Trailer Plate – The back of the rearmost trailer drawn by a motor vehicle on a road shall display a trailer plate. This is a plate consisting of a white triangle bearing 9 red reflex lenses. It shall be clean and unobscured, vertical, in the centre or offside, and not more than 1·22 metres from the ground. This will not apply to articulated vehicles, broken-down vehicles being towed in consequence of the break-down, trailers drawn by motor cycles, being passenger vehicles or by motor cars that are either passenger vehicles or dual purpose vehicles made for not more than seven passengers, trailers for carrying round timber, land implements (except living vans), land implement conveyors, agricultural trailers and road rollers' water carts, and any trailer carrying two obligatory reflectors complying with the R.V.L. Regs. 1971 (reg. 75).

Trees and Round Timber – When these are being hauled on trailers the following regulations as to trailers will not apply: 12 (springs), 73 (wings), and 75 (trailer plate).

Rear wheels of a heavy motor car forming part of an articulated vehicle used for carrying round timber need not have wings (reg. 56).

Tyres – A pneumatic tyre is a collapsible continuous air-filled chamber round a wheel. It should comply with the following conditions:

(1) A continuous closed chamber containing air at a pressure substantially exceeding atmospheric pressure when normally used but not subject to a load.

(2) Capable of being inflated and deflated without removal from the wheel or vehicle.

(3) When deflated and subject to a normal load the sides of the tyre collapse (reg. 3).

"Recut pneumatic tyre" means any pneumatic tyre in which an existing tread pattern has been cut or burnt deeper or a new tread pattern has been cut or burnt except where the pattern is cut entirely in additional material added to the tyre for the purpose (reg. 3).

A soft or elastic tyre is one of soft or elastic material which is continuous or in close-fitting sections round the circumference of the wheel and is of such thickness and design as to minimise so far as is possible vibration when the vehicle is in motion and is so constructed as to be free from any defect which might cause damage to the surface of a road (reg. 3).

"Wide tyre" means a pneumatic tyre as respects which its area of contact with the road surface is not less than 300 mms in width (reg. 3).

Locomotives should have (when used on a highway, Reg. 4) pneumatic, soft or elastic tyres on their wheels, except in the case of land locomotives which have smooth-soled tyres not less than 125 mms. wide on their steering wheels (reg. 45), and in the case of a wheeled vehicle tyres (smooth soled or with diagonal cross bars) not less than 300 mms. wide on their driving wheels (reg. 45). This does not apply to road rollers (reg. 4).

Motor Tractors (when used on a highway, reg. 4) should have pneumatic, soft or elastic tyres on their wheels. This does not apply to steering wheels of land tractors which have smooth-soled tyres not less than 60 mms. wide on their steering wheels (reg. 51) nor to land tractors with every driving wheel 150 mms. wide if weight unladen exceeds 3,050 kilograms or 76 mms. wide if weight unladen does not exceed 3,050 kilograms providing the tyres are either smooth soled or have diagonal crossbars not more than 76 mms. apart (reg. 51). Recut pneumatic tyres shall not be fitted to any wheel of a motor tractor the weight of which unladen is less than 2,540 kilograms unless the rim diameter of the wheel is 405 mms. or more. This does not apply to road rollers (reg. 4). See also "Land Tractor" and reg. 5.

Heavy Motor Cars (when used on highways, reg. 4) should have pneumatic tyres on their wheels, but this does not apply to heavy motor cars over 4,070 kilograms weight unladen mainly used on rough ground or unmade roads; or to vehicles of Local Authorities used for street cleansing or refuse disposal; or to turntable fire escapes; or to tower wagons or works trucks if in each such case the vehicle, has soft or elastic tyres (reg. 55).

This also does not apply to a heavy motor car first used on or before January 2, 1933, if it has soft or elastic tyres (reg. 55). If a land tractor is a heavy motor car it will need similar tyres to those it must have if it were a motor tractor (reg. 5).

MOTOR CARS – (1) Save as provided in paragraph (3) of this regulation, every wheel of a motor car shall be fitted with a pneumatic tyre.

(2) Recut pneumatic tyres shall not be fitted to any wheel of a motor car except—

(*a*) where the motor car is a goods vehicle the weight of which unladen is 2,540 kilograms or more and the rim diameter of the wheel is 405 mms. or more; or

(*b*) in the case of an electrically propelled goods vehicle.

(3) In the case of any of the following descriptions of vehicles every wheel may, subject to the provisions of paragraph (2) of this regulation, be fitted with a pneumatic tyre, or a tyre of soft or elastic material:

(*a*) motor cars the weight of which unladen does not exceed 1,020 kilograms;

(*b*) works trucks;

(*c*) motor cars registered on or before January 2, 1933;

(*d*) motor cars designed for use and used solely in connection with street cleansing, the collection or disposal of refuse or the collection or the disposal of the contents of gullies or cesspools; and

(*e*) electrically propelled goods vehicles the weight of which unladen does not exceed 1,270 kilograms (reg. 60).

Motor Cycles shall have pneumatic tyres, other than recut pneumatic tyres, but this does not apply to works trucks or pedestrian controlled vehicles if all the wheels have soft or elastic tyres (reg. 63).

Trailers (when used on a highway, reg. 4) should have pneumatic tyres or soft or elastic tyres on their wheels (reg. 71). However, this does not apply:

(1) to any land implement or agricultural trailer;

(2) to any wheeled trailer made before January 15, 1931; and specially designed for the conveyance of horses and cattle and used for that purpose or for agricultural purposes;

(3) to any wheeled trailer made before January 15, 1931, and specially designed and used for the conveyance of furniture;

(4) to any trailer for the purpose of carrying water for a road roller used for roads (reg. 71).

(1) Save as provided in paragraph (3) below, every wheel of a trailer manufactured after January 1, 1933, when drawn by a heavy motor car or a motor car shall be fitted with a pneumatic tyre.

(2) Save as provided in paragraph (3) of this Regulation, where trailers of the following descriptions manufactured after January 1, 1933, are drawn by a heavy motor car or motor car every wheel of such trailers shall be fitted with a pneumatic tyre, other than a recut pneumatic tyre:

(*a*) a trailer which does not exceed 1.020 kilograms in weight unladen;
(*b*) a trailer which is not constructed or adapted to carry any load other than plant or other special appliance or apparatus which is a permanent or essentially permanent fixtures and which does not exceed 2,290 kilograms in total weight; or
(*c*) a trailer which is a living van which does not exceed 2,040 kilograms in weight unladen.

(3) Paragraphs (1) and (2) of this regulation shall not apply to any trailer:

(*a*) which is a works trailer;
(*b*) which is designed for use and used solely in connection with street cleansing, the collection or disposal of refuse or the collection or disposal of the contents of gullies or cesspools;
(*c*) when drawn by a heavy motor car every wheel of which is not required to be fitted with a pneumatic tyre;
(*d*) when used for the purpose of carrying water for a road roller which is being used in connection with the construction, maintenance or repair of roads;
(*e*) which is a land implement or an agricultural trailer drawn by a land tractor; or
(*f*) which is a broken down vehicle and is being drawn by a motor vehicle in consequence of the breakdown (reg. 72).

CONDITION AND MAINTENANCE OF TYRES – (1) Save as provided in paragraphs (1A) and (2) of this regulation, no person shall use or cause or permit to be used on a road any motor vehicle or trailer a wheel of which is fitted with a pneumatic tyre, if:

(*a*) the tyre is unsuitable having regard to the use to which the motor vehicle or trailer is being put or to the types of tyres fitted to its other wheels;
(*b*) the tyre is not so inflated as to make it fit for the use to which the motor vehicle or trailer is being put;
(*c*) the tyre has a break in its fabric, or has a cut in excess of 25 mms. or 10 per cent. of the section width of the tyre,

whichever is the greater, measured in any direction on the outside of the tyre and deep enough to reach the body cords;

(*d*) the tyre has any lump or bulge caused by separation or partial failure of its structure;

(*e*) the tyre has any portion of the ply or cord structure exposed; or

(*f*) where the tyre is fitted to a wheel of a motor vehicle, being a motor cycle whereof the cylinder capacity of the engine does not exceed 50 cubic centimetres, the tread of the tyre does not show throughout at least three quarters of the breadth of the tread and round the entire outer circumference of the tyre a pattern the relief of which is clearly visible, or where the tyre is fitted to the wheel of any other motor vehicle or any trailer, the tread pattern (excluding any tie-bar) of the tyre does not have a depth of at least 1 mm. throughout at least three quarters of the breadth of the tread and round the entire outer circumference of the tyre:

Provided that this sub-paragraph shall not apply in the case of a motor cycle having three wheels, the unladen weight of which does not exceed 102 kilograms and which is incapable of exceeding a speed of 12 miles per hour on the level under its own power or in the case of a pedestrian controlled vehicle being a works truck;

(1A) Paragraph (1) of this regulation shall not prohibit the use on a road of a motor vehicle or trailer by reason only of the fact that a wheel of the vehicle or trailer is fitted with a tyre which is deflated or not fully inflated and which has any of the defects described in sub-paragraph (*c*), (*d*) or (*e*) of paragraph (1) of this regulation, if the tyre and the wheel to which it is fitted are so constructed as to make the tyre in that condition fit for the use to which the motor vehicle or trailer is being put and the outer sides of the wall of the tyre are so marked as to enable the tyre to be identified as having been constructed to comply with the requirements of this paragraph; and

(2) Nothing in paragraph (1) of this regulation shall apply to a land locomotive, and tractor, land implement or land implement conveyor, or to an agricultural trailer when the trailer is being drawn by a land tractor and nothing in that paragraph or in the next succeeding paragraph shall apply to a broken down vehicle or to a vehicle proceeding to a place where it is to be broken up, in either case being drawn by a motor vehicle at a speed not exceeding 20 miles per hour.

(3) No person shall use or cause or permit to be used on a road any motor vehicle or trailer a wheel of which is fitted with a recut pneumatic tyre the fabric of which has been cut or exposed by the recutting process.

(4) Without prejudice to paragraphs (1) and (3) of this regulation, all the tyres of a motor vehicle or trailer shall at all times while the vehicle or trailer is used on a road be maintained in such condition as to be fit for the use to which the vehicle or trailer is being put, and as to be free from any defect which might in any way cause damage to the surface of the road or danger to persons on or in the vehicle or to other persons using the road (reg. 99).

View – Every motor vehicle shall be so constructed that the driver, while controlling it, can at all times have a full view of the road and traffic ahead (reg. 22). No person actually driving a motor vehicle shall be in such a position that he cannot have proper control over the vehicle or that he cannot retain a full view of the road and traffic ahead (reg. 111).

Weight – *Locomotive.*—The laden weight of a wheeled locomotive on a road shall not exceed 20,830 kilograms. If it has springs and pneumatic, soft or elastic tyres, it may be 22,360 kilograms if less than 6 wheels, 26,420 kilograms if 6 wheels, 30,490 kilograms if more than 6 wheels. The total weight on 2 transverse wheels shall not exceed 11,180 kilograms but this does not apply to a road roller or to a vehicle with not more than 4 wheels registered before June 1, 1955 (reg. 76). The total weight of all its trailers shall not exceed 40,650 kilograms (reg. 77).

Except in the case of a road roller (reg. 4), not more than three-fourths of the total weight of a wheeled locomotive having not more than 4 wheels and registered before June 1, 1955, shall be transmitted to the road by any two wheels (reg. 44).

MOTOR TRACTOR – The unladen weight shall not exceed 7¼ tons (R.T. Act 1972, s. 190). Wheeled trailers may be 24,390 kilograms and may be up to 32,520 kilograms if the trailer has power assisted brakes operable by the driver with warning to driver device. This regulation does not apply to a trailer forming part of an articulated vehicle (reg. 81).

HEAVY MOTOR CAR AND MOTOR CAR – The total weight transmitted by a wheeled heavy motor car or motor car not a public service vehicle to the road (when on a highway, reg. 4) shall not exceed:

14,230 kilograms—if not more than 4 wheels.
20,330 kilograms—if over 4 but not more than 6 wheels.
24,390 kilograms—if more than 6 wheels.

so, however, that in relation to a vehicle first used on or after June 1, 1973, not being a vehicle to which regulation 83 applies and in so far as it is a vehicle to which either of sub-paragraphs (*b*) and (*c*) of this paragraph applies, for the weight limits of 20,330 kilograms and 24,390 kilograms specified in those sub-paragraphs there shall be substituted respectively weight limits of 16,260 kilograms and 18,290 kilograms.

Weight on road by one wheel where no other wheel is in the same line transversely shall not exceed 4,580 kilograms, weight on two transverse wheels shall not exceed 9,150 kilograms. There are special provisions with respect to a "prior 1968 vehicle", a "post 1968 vehicle", and a "temporarily imported vehicle" (reg. 79).

In the case of a wheeled vehicle, whether laden or unladen, the weight transmitted by more than 2 wheels to any strip of road upon which the vehicle rests contained between any two parallel lines drawn on that surface at right angles to the longitudinal axis of the vehicle—(a) less than 1·02 metres apart shall not exceed 11,180 kilograms, (b) less than 1·22 metres but 1·02 metres or more apart shall not exceed 16,260 kilograms, and (c) less than 2·13 meters apart, but 1·22 metres or more apart shall not exceed 18,290 kilograms (reg. 88). This also applies to trailers. The total laden weight on the highway of a trailer wheeled or track-laying and its heavy motor car or motor car shall not exceed 22,360 kilograms (reg. 81) but if a wheeled trailer is drawn by a wheeled heavy motor car or wheeled motot tractor or motor car the weight may be 24,390 kilograms and it may be 32,520 kilograms if special brakes with warning device for them (reg. 81).

TRAILER – The permissible weights of trailers depending on the types of vehicles drawing, are given under "Trailers".

OTHER MOTOR VEHICLES – The maximum unladen weights of motor cars, motor cycles and invalid carriages are given under "Classes or descriptions of Vehicles", Chap. 24.

Wheels – The "wheel" of a motor vehicle or trailer means a wheel the tyre or rim of which when the vehicle is in motion on a road is in contact with the ground (reg. 3). "Wheeled" means that the whole weight of the vehicle is transmitted to the road surface by means of wheels (reg. 3).

All the wheels of a motor vehicle or of a trailer which have not got pneumatic tyres (used on a highway, reg. 4) shall have a rim diameter of not less than 670 mms. This does not apply to works trucks or works trailers; pedestrian controlled vehicles: vehicles for street cleansing or refuse collection; mobile cranes; land implements; any broken down vehicle drawn by a motor vehicle as a result of the breakdown and any electrically propelled goods vehicle not exceeding 1270 kilograms unladen weight. It does not apply to a wheel fitted to a motor car first used on or before July 1, 1936, if the diameter inclusive of tyre is not less than 670 mms. Motor vehicles first used or or before January 2, 1933, and trailers made before January 1, 1933, do not come under this regulation (reg. 20).

A wheeled motor vehicle or trailer with more than 4 wheels

and a trailer with more than 2 wheels which is part of an articulated vehicle and a tracklaying vehicle or trailer with more than 2 wheels shall be made so as to ensure that all wheels will remain in contact with the road and will not be subjected to abnormal variations of load, but this will not apply to any steerable wheel if the load on it does not exceed 3,560 kilograms (reg. 11). This does not apply to road rollers (reg. 4).

Any 2 wheels shall be regarded as one wheel if the distance between the centres of the wheel tracks is less than 460 mms. (reg. 3).

Width – The maximum allowable widths are:

2·75 metres for a locomotive (reg. 43).

2·5 metres for a motor tractor including a land tractor (reg. 5 and 48), a heavy motor car (reg. 52), a motor car (reg. 57).

2·2 metres for an invalid carriage (reg. 65).

2·3 metres for a trailer (reg. 69).

The width may be up to 2·5 metres if (a) every wheel of the trailer is fitted with pneumatic tyres, (b) the trailer is drawn by a locomotive, motor tractor, or a heavy motor car, or, where the trailer forms part of an articulated vehicle the other part of which is a motor car, the motor car exceeds 2,030 kilograms in weight unladen, (c) every wheel of the drawing vehicle (except a locomotive) is fitted with pneumatic tyres, (d) the width of the trailer does not extend more than 305 mms. on either side of the drawing vehicle.

A travelling showman's trailer in use before January 15, 1931, may be up to 2·68 metres wide, and a trailer made before January 1, 1933, and converted from solid to pneumatic tyres, may be 2·3 metres wide at the wheels (reg. 69). "Width" does not include mirror, direction indicator, snowplough, tyre distortion due to weight of vehicle and if vehicle was registered before January 2, 1939, a 105 mms. projection of a swivelling window to allow hand signals, any container for custom's clearance seal, and front corner or side marker lamp (reg. 3), and the trailer width limits do not apply to a land implement or to a trailer which is a trolley vehicle in the course of construction or delivery or to a broken-down vehicle being towed in consequence of breakdown (reg. 69).

No load shall be carried on a vehicle where the overall width of the vehicle and its load exceeds 4·3 metres (but see "Special Types of Motor Vehicles", later) (reg. 131).

No load shall be carried on a motor vehicle or trailer if it projects more than 305 mms. beyond the overall width or if the total width of the load exceeds 2·9 metres, but this will not apply to:

(a) an indivisible load if the prescribed notice is given to the chief officer of police of every district through which the load will pass (see "Special Types of Motor Vehicles", later), and

(b) the carriage of loose agricultural produce not baled or crated (reg. 131).

Windscreen wipers – (1) In the case of a vehicle which is fitted with a windscreen, the vehicle shall be fitted with one or more efficient automatic windscreen wipers, unless the driver can obtain an adequate view to the front of the vehicle without looking through windscreen, for example by opening the windscreen or looking over it.

(2) The windscreen wipers required by the last preceding paragraph shall be capable of clearing the windscreen so that the driver has an adequate view of the road in front of the near and off sides of the vehicle in addition to an adequate view to the front of the vehicle (reg. 25).

Windscreen washers – (1) Subject to the following paragraph every motor vehicle, which is required to be fitted with one or more efficient automatic windscreen wipers by virtue of the last preceding regulation, shall be fitted with a windscreen washer capable of clearing, in conjunction with those windscreen wipers, the area of the windscreen swept by those windscreen wipers of mud or other similar deposit.

(2) This regulation shall not apply to land tractors, vehicles which are incapable by reason of their construction of exceeding 20 miles per hour on the level under their own power or vehicles being used for the time being as stage carriages or on any journey incidental to such use (reg. 26).

Wings – Wings or other similar fittings to catch, so far as practicable, mud or water thrown up by the wheels or tracks, shall be provided for motor cycles which are not works trucks (reg. 64), invalid carriages (reg. 67), heavy motor cars, and motor cars except rear wheels of articulated vehicles used for carrying round timber, works trucks, and unfinished vehicles proceeding to a works for completion (regs. 56, 61).

Such fittings are necessary also for rear wheels of trailers unless adequate protection is afforded by the body (reg. 73), except land implements, land implement conveyors, living vans, water carts, trailers for round timber, fire brigade pumps, trailers drawn by a vehicle restricted to 12 miles per hour or less and unfinished trailers proceeding to a works for completion or any broken down vehicle drawn as a result of a breakdown (reg. 73).

Works Trucks and Trailers – A works truck is a vehicle (not a straddle carrier) designed for use in private premises and used on a road only in delivering goods from or to such premises, to or from a vehicle on a road in the immediate neighbourhood, or in passing from one part of any such premises to another or to other private premises in the immediate neighbourhood or in connection with road works while at or in the immediate neighbourhood of the site of such works (reg. 3).

A works trailer is a trailer designed for similar use and used on a road for similar purposes (reg. 3).

The following regulations do not apply to works trucks—regs. 12 (springs): 18 (speedometer): 20 (diameter of wheels): 23 (mirror if driver has view to the rear): 27 (warning instrument): 32 (excess fuel): 55 (tyres if soft or elastic): 61 (wings): 63 (tyres if soft or elastic): 64 (wings).

The following regulations do not apply to works trailers—regs. 12 (springs): 20 (diameter of wheels): 72 (tyres): 135 (attendants if weight of works truck and trailer does not exceed 1,525 kilograms.

Special Types of Motor Vehicles – The R.T. Act 1972, s. 42, allows the Secretary of State to authorise the use of special types of motor vehicles on roads and he has made the Motor Vehicles (Authorisation of Special Types) General Order 1973 which authorises the use on roads of the following vehicles which do not comply in all respects with the requirements of the Construction and Use Regulations.

Part I: Nothing in this Order relating to speed shall authorise any speed in excess of any other speed limit imposed by any other enactment (art. 4).

Part II deals with miscellaneous vehicles not fully complying with the Regulations and authorises their use on roads as follows:

Art. 5: Tracklaying vehicles and tracklaying trailers used on roads only for demonstration or for proceeding to railway stations for shipment and not carrying burden for hire and reward provided that the written consent of the highway authorities concerned is first obtained.

Art. 6: Naval, Military, Air Force and Aviation vehicles (which are for combative or training purposes, guns, stores, tanks, searchlights, aircraft, flying operations, drawing aircraft or constructed before January 1, 1949. See Sched. 1).

Art. 7: Lifeboat vehicles, viz. tracklayers also trailers used for drawing or launching lifeboats.

Art. 8: Motor tractors for use as grasscutters or hedge trimmers. They must not exceed 2·5 metres wide except when in operation and when not engaged in operations all cutting or trimming blades must be effectively guarded so that no danger is likely to be caused to any person. (*Note.* – a pedestrian controlled grasscutter is not a motor vehicle, R.T. Act 1972, s. 193).

Art. 9: Hedge trimmers controlled by a pedestrian, of unladen weight not exceeding 410 kilograms, the overall width not exceeding 2·29 metres, and when not actually engaged in operations all trimming blades must be guarded so that no danger is likely to be caused to any person.

Art 10: Trailers used as grasscutters or hedge trimmers. The unladen weight must not exceed 1,020 kilograms if drawn by a locomotive, a motor tractor or a heavy motor car, and 815 kilograms in any other case. The overall width must not exceed 2·6 metres. When not in operation the cutting blades must be guarded. The machine must not be drawn at a speed exceeding 20 miles per hour.

Art. 11: Pedestrian-controlled road maintenance vehicles—the Secretary of State has authorised the use on roads of motor vehicles constructed or adapted for road maintenance, which are pedestrian controlled, notwithstanding that they do not comply in all respects with the requirements of regs. 11, 13, 34, 50 and 62 the C. & U. Regs., subject to the condition that all other relevant conditions of those regs. are complied with, and subject to the following restrictions (a) the weight shall not exceed 410 kilograms and (b) the vehicle shall have an efficient braking system. Road maintenance means: gritting of roads; the laying of road markings; the clearance of frost, snow or ice; or any other work of maintaining roads.

Art. 12: Vehicles for experiments or trials under s. 249, Highways Act 1959.

Art. 13: Straddle carrier, provided it is used only for demonstration or on sale or for passing from premises to another premises in the immediate neighbourhood or for repair: speed not to exceed 12 miles per hour: length of vehicle and load or of vehicle or its load not to exceed 9·2 metres except with the consent (on 2 days' notice) of the police: width not to exceed 2·9 metres.

Art. 14: Harvesting land tractors—provided any trailer drawn is two wheeled and used solely for necessary equipment; width limit 4.3 metres; one attendant necessary if width exceeds 3.5 metres: if over 2.9 metres wide and it is to travel more than 5 miles, 24 hours' notice to be given to police who can prescribe route: all these land tractors are subject to a speed limit of 12 miles per hour. All cutting blades must be effectively guarded.

Art. 15: Hay and straw balers (motor tractors) provided width does not exceed 2·44 metres; overhang does not exceed 2·44 metres speed limit 10 miles per hour.

Art. 16: Excavations carriers—viz. heavy motor car or trailer or articulated vehicle specially made for use in private premises for moving excavated material and fitted with tipping body or moving platform for discharging load. Provided that vehicle is used only for proceeding to and from private premises or between private premises and a port: no heavy motor car not part of an articulated vehicle shall draw a trailer: if a trailer is drawn by a motor vehicle no other trailer allowed: length of trailer not to exceed 8·54 metres and length of articulated vehicle not to exceed 13·4 metres: speed limit 12 miles per hour: all wheels must have pneumatic tyres: if width is over 3·5 metres one attendant in addition to the driver must be in attendance. Heavy motor cars and articulated vehicles may not transmit more than 22,860 kilograms weight by any two wheels in line transversely or 50,800 kilograms overall.

Before using such vehicle over 2·44 metres wide on a tramcar road or such a vehicle over 2·9 metres wide on any road the owner shall give 2 days' notice to the police who may prescribe the time or route. Highway and bridge authorities must also be similarly notified.

Art. 17 authorises, subject to specified conditions, the use on roads of motor vehicles and trailers or types of motor vehicles and trailers constructed for use outside the United Kingdom, of new or improved types of motor vehicles and trailers constructed for tests or trials, and of motor vehicles and trailers equipped with new or improved equipment or types of equipment.

Art. 18 permits the use on roads of vehicles fitted with "moveable platforms".

Part III deals with abnormal indivisible loads and engineering plant.

Art. 19: Abnormal indivisible load means a load (a) which cannot without undue expense or risk of damage be divided into two or more loads for the purpose of carriage on roads, and (b) which, (i) owing to its dimensions, cannot be carried by a heavy motor car or trailer or a combination of a heavy motor car and trailer complying in all respects with the requirements of the Construction and Use Regs. or (ii) owing to its weight cannot be carried by a heavy motor car or trailer or a combination of a heavy motor car and trailer having a total laden weight of less than 24,390 kilograms and complying in all respects with the requirements of the Construction and Use Regs.

Art. 20: Heavy motor cars and trailers specially made for the carriage of such loads and locomotives and tractors specially made to draw such trailers are allowed by this Order to travel on roads, under the following conditions—

> Every such vehicle shall be wheeled: overall width of such heavy motor car, trailer or locomotive shall not exceed 2·9 metres and of a trailer 2·9 metres except where a greater width (20 feet limit) is necessary for the safe carriage of the load on the trailer, overall width of such a load or of the vehicle and load shall not exceed 6·1 metres and overall length shall not exceed 27·4 metres: all wheels shall have tyres pneumatic, soft or elastic: total weight on road shall not exceed 152,400 kilograms: a heavy motor car or trailer shall be used only for the carriage of such a load and a locomotive or tractor shall be used only for the drawing of trailers authorised by this article, in both cases subject to the condition that no vehicle or combination of vehicles shall carry more than one such load at

any one time provided that subject to the requirements of the Construction and Use Regs. as to the laden weights on road it shall be permissible for a vehicle and any vehicles used in combination to carry more than one such load of the same character and where such a load is carried articles of a similar character may be carried.

Art. 19: Engineering plant means moveable plant or equipment: being a motor vehicle or trailer specially made for the special purposes of engineering operations or a mobile crane, both of which cannot comply in all respects with the requirements of the Construction and Use Regs.

Art. 21: This plant is allowed to be on roads provided that: such a plant other than a mobile crane, is used on a road only in proceeding to and from the site of engineering operations or when actually engaged in such operations and carrying no load other than necessary equipment or necessary materials: no engineering plant other than a mobile crane shall draw a trailer other than one which is an engineering plant or a living van or office; no mobile crane shall draw a trailer: a mobile crane is to be used on a road only on journeys and not for lifting or carrying burden otherwise than when actually engaged in engineering operations: such a "plant" must be either wheeled or tracklaying: all wheels not having pneumatic soft or elastic tyres shall have smooth tyres with rounded edges (provided that gritting machines for use on ice-bound roads may have tyres shod with diagonal cross-bars): it should have an efficient brake or if steam-driven a reversing engine: a trailer should have an efficient brake or suitable scotches: no such motor vehicle over 7·93 metres long shall draw a trailer but may draw a broken-down vehicle. The total weight on the road shall not exceed 152,400 kilograms; the overall length must not exceed 27·4 metres, and overall width must not exceed 6·1 metres.

Art. 22: The Secretary of State may authorise, subject to conditions, the use on roads of other vehicles and trailer) i.e. not "special types") carrying loads exceeding 4·3 metres wide but not exceeding 6.1 metres.

Art. 23: The speed limit for a motor vehicle and trailer authorised under (a) art. 20 is 12 miles per hour, unless they are empty, not more than 2.9 metres wide and comply with certain requirements of the C. & U. Regs. with respect to springs etc., when it shall be 20 miles per hour; (b) art. 21 is 12 miles per hour, and (c) art. 22 is 20 miles per hour. These speed limits do not apply on special roads.

Art. 24. Attendants: This article applies in the case of a vehicle authorised by art. 22, and in the case where: (a) the overall width of a vehicle authorised by arts. 20 or 21, and its load, exceeds 3·5 metres; or (b) the overall length of a vehicle authorised by arts. 20 or 21, and its load, exceeds 18·3 metres;

or (c) a motor vehicle and trailer with its load exceeds 18·3 metres in length, or (d) a motor vehicle and trailer or trailers, the use of which is so authorised, which together with its load exceed 25·9 metres in length; or (e) a vehicle authorised by arts. 20 or 21 carrying a load having a forward projection exceeding 1·83 metres in length or a rearward projection exceeding 3·05 metres in length. In all these cases it is necessary to have one attendant in addition to the driver.

Art. 25. Marking of projecting loads. Where a load projects between 1·07 metres and 3·05 metres to the rear of the vehicle it must be made clearly visible. Where a load projects more than 1·83 metres to the front or 3·05 metres to the rear of the vehicle it must be fitted with marker boards (see Sched. 8 of C. & U. Regs.). At night the marker boards must be indirectly illuminated.

Art. 26. A vehicle more than 4·3 metres wide may not be used without the written approval of the Secretary of State. The notice giving the Secretary of State's approval must be carried on the vehicle

Art. 27. Notice to Police: The police must be given 2 clear days' notice of movement when (a) the width of the vehicle or its load is more than 2·9 metres, (b) the length of the vehicle is more than 18·3 metres, (c) the length of any combination of vehicles is more than 25·9 metres, (d) the load projects more than 3·05 metres to the front or rear, and (e) the total laden weight exceeds 76,200 kilograms.

Art. 28: gives directions as to the notice (Part II of Sched. 2) to be given to the highway and bridge authorities but this article does not apply to the vehicles owned or under the control of the Admiralty, War Office or Air Force.

Art. 29. The driver of a vehicle carrying an abnormal indivisible load shall not cause or permit that vehicle to enter on any bridge whilst there is on that bridge another vehicle carrying an abnormal indivisible load. Except under circumstances beyond his control, such a driver must not allow the vehicle to remain stationary on any bridge.

Art. 30. Where a vehicle, laden or unladen, which has a gross weight of more than 32,250 kilograms, becomes stationary on any bridge, then the person in charge must move it clear of the bridge as soon as practicable without applying a concentrated load to the surface; but if such movement is not practicable without applying a concentrated load to the surface by means of jacks, rollers or similar devices, the advice of the bridge authority shall be sought.

APPENDIX III

REGULATIONS AS TO THE PROSECUTION OF OFFENCES

The Prosecution of Offences Regulations 1946, dated August 23, 1946, made by the Attorney-General with the approval of the Lord Chancellor and the Secretary of State under the Prosecution of Offences Acts 1879 to 1908, are as follows (summarised and with notes in brackets):

1. It shall be the duty of the Director of Public Prosecutions to institute, undertake or carry on criminal proceedings in the following cases:

(*a*) Any offence punishable with death (these include treason, and piracy with violence).

(*b*) Any case referred to him by a Government department in which he considers criminal proceedings should be instituted.

(*c*) Any case which appears to him to be of importance or difficulty or which for any other reason requires his intervention.

2. The Director shall, on application or on his own initiative, give advice to Government departments, Clerks to Justices, chief officers of police and such other persons as he may think right in any criminal matter which appears to him to be of importance or difficulty.

3. The Director may assist prosecutors by authorising special expenses.

4. The Director may employ a solicitor to act as his agent in a prosecution.

5. The Director shall in all matters be subject to the directions of the Attorney-General.

6. (1) The chief officer of every police district shall, as respects offences alleged to have been committed in his district, report to the Director:

(*a*) Every offence punishable with death (see above).

(*b*) Every offence in respect of which the prosecution has

by statute to be undertaken by or with the consent of the Director. These offences include:

(1) Incitement to Disaffection Act 1934, s. 3; consent necessary.

(2) Prevention of Fraud (Investments) Act 1958, s. 1: unlicensed dealer in securities, and s. 14 (distributing circulars inviting persons to invest in securities); consent of Dept. of Trade or Director necessary.

(3) Firearms Act 1968, s. 51; summary proceedings for an offence under the Act after six months and within four years after the commission of the offence can be instituted by or by direction of the Director.

(5) Betting, Gaming and Lotteries Act 1963, s. 42. The Director only can prosecute or direct prosecution of a newspaper, etc., for publishing inducement to take part in a lottery.

(*c*) Every indictable case in which the prosecution is wholly withdrawn or is not proceeded with within a reasonable time.

(*d*) Every case in which a request for information is made by the Director.

(*e*) Every case in which it appears to the chief officer of police that the advice or assistance of the Director is desirable.

(2) The chief officer of police shall also report, as respects offences alleged to have been committed within his district, to the Director:

(*a*) Offences under the following Acts:

(1) Sexual Offences Act 1956 (incest).

(2) Official Secrets Acts 1911 to 1939.

(3) Forgery Act 1913, s. 2 (forgery, with intent to defraud, of many specified valuable documents) and s. 3 (forgery with intent to defraud or deceive, of certain documents, mainly official).

(4) Coinage Offences Act 1936.

(*b*) Offences of sedition (including seditious libel), conspiracies to pervert or defeat the course of justice, libel on persons occupying judicial or public offices, bribery and corruption of or by a public official.

(*c*) Offences of manslaughter, attempted murder, rape, abortion, carnal knowledge of mental defectives, defilement of girls under thirteen years of age, indecent offences upon a number of children or young persons, sexual offences against a child or young person involving the communication of a venereal disease, and cases in which there has been a previous conviction for the same or a similar sexual offence and the offence charged is one that can be dealt with summarily.

(*d*) Cases of obscene or indecent libels, exhibitions or publications in which it appears to the chief officer of police that there is a *prima facie* case for prosecution; and

(*e*) Cases under the Extradition Acts 1870 to 1932, and the Fugitive Offenders Act 1967.

7. When reporting an offence punishable with death the chief officer of police shall supply the Director with

(*a*) A full report on the circumstances;

(*b*) copies of the statements of any witnesses; and

(*c*) A report of any proceedings taken before a Coroner or justice in connection with the offence.

8. A justice or Coroner to whom the Director has sent notice that he is carrying on any criminal proceedings, shall, within three days of receipt of the notice, transmit to the Director all the documents and things connected with the case (see s. 5 of the Prosecution of Offences Act 1879).

9. In any case in which the prosecution for an offence instituted before examining justices or a court of summary jurisdiction is wholly withdrawn or is not proceeded with within a reasonable time, the clerk to the justices or to the court shall send to the Director a report of the case and shall supply the Director with any further information or documents he may require (1879 Act, s. 5).

10. The Regulations dated January 25, 1886, are revoked.

Note. – As regards the offences given above which are to be reported to the Director, it would seem that "undetected crime" need not be so reported, and that it would not be necessary to report any such offence unless there is a *prima facie* case against an alleged offender. Similarly it would not seem necessary to report when the police apply for the withdrawal of a summons or warrant.

Criminal Justice Act 1925, s. 34, directs that any document purporting to be the consent, fiat or order for or to the institution of any criminal proceedings and to be signed by the Attorney-General, the Solicitor-General, the Director or an Assistant Director of Public Prosecutions shall be admissible as *prima facie* evidence without further proof.

Suicide Act 1961, s. 2, directs that no proceedings under this section (which deals with criminal liability for complicity in another's suicide) shall be instituted except by or with the consent of the D.P.P.

PROSECUTION AND PUNISHMENT OF ROAD TRAFFIC OFFENCES

ROAD TRAFFIC ACT 1972, SCHEDULE 4

PROSECUTION AND PUNISHMENT OF OFFENCES

PART I

Offences under this Act

1 Provision creating offence	2 General nature of offence	3 Mode of prosecution	4 Disqualification	5 Endorsement	6 Additional provisions
1	Causing death by reckless or dangerous driving.	On indictment.	Obligatory.	Obligatory.	Section 181 and paragraph 3 of Part IV of this Schedule apply.
2	Reckless, and dangerous, driving generally.	(*a*) Summarily. (*b*) on indictment.	(*a*) Obligatory, if committed within 3 years after a previous conviction of an offence under section 1 or 2. (*b*) Dicretionary if committed otherwise than as mentioned in paragraph (*a*) above.	Obligatory.	Sections 179, 181 and 183 and paragraphs 1, 2, 3, 5 and 6 of Part IV of this Schedule apply.

1 Provision creating offence	2 General nature of offence	3 Mode of prosecution	4 Disqualification	5 Endorsement	6 Additional provisions
3	Careless, and inconsiderate, driving.	Summarily.	Discretionary.	Obligatory.	Sections 179, 181 and 183 and paragraphs 4 and 7 of Part IV of this Schedule apply.
4 (4)	Driving under age.	Summarily.	Discretionary.	Obligatory.	Sections 181 and 183 apply.
5 (1)	Driving or attempting to drive when unfit to drive through drink or drugs.	(*a*) Summarily. (*b*) On indictment.	Obligatory.	Obligatory.	Sections 181 and 183 and paragraph 3 of Part IV of this Schedule apply.
5 (2)	Being in charge of a motor vehicle when unfit to drive through drink or drugs.	(*a*) Summarily. (*b*) On indictment.	Discretionary.	Obligatory.	Sections 181 and 183 and paragraph 3 of Part IV of this Schedule apply.
6 (1)	Driving or attempting to drive with blood-alcohol concentration above the prescribed limit.	(*a*) Summarily. (*b*) On indictment.	Obligatory.	Obligatory.	Sections 181 and 183 and paragraph 3 of Part IV of this Schedule apply.

6 (2)	Being in charge of a motor vehicle with blood-alcohol concentration above the prescribed limit.	(*a*) Summarily. (*b*) On indictment.	Discretionary.	Obligatory.	Sections 181 and 183 and paragraph 3 of Part IV of this Schedule apply.
8 (3)	Failing to provide a specimen of breath for a breath test.	Summarily.	—	—	Sections 181 and 183 apply.
9 (3)	Failing to provide a specimen of blood or urine for a laboratory test.	(*a*) Summarily. (*b*) On indictment.	(*a*) Obligatory if it is shown as mentioned in paragraph (i) of column 4 of R.T. Act 1972, Sched. 4. (*b*) Discretionary if it is not so shown.	Obligatory.	Sections 181 and 183 and paragraph 3 of Part IV of this Schedule apply.
14	Motor racing and speed trials on highways.	Summarily.	Obligatory.	Obligatory.	Sections 181 and 183 apply.
15	Other unauthorised or irregular competitions or trials on highways.	Summarily.	—	—	—
16	Carrying passenger on motor cycle contrary to section 16.	Summarily.	Discretionary.	Obligatory.	Sections 181 and 183 apply.
17	Reckless, and dangerous, cycling.	Summarily.	—	—	Sections 179, 181 and 183 apply.

1 Provision creating offence	2 General nature of offence	3 Mode of prosecution	4 Disqualification	5 Endorsement	6 Additional provisions
18	Careless, and inconsiderate, cycling.	Summarily.	—	—	Sections 179, 181 and 183 and paragraphs 4 and 7 of Part IV of this Schedule apply.
19	Cycling when unfit through drink or drugs.	Summarily.	—	—	Sections 181 and 183 apply.
20	Unauthorised or irregular cycle racing or trials of speed on highways.	Summarily.	—	—	Sections 181 and 183 apply.
21	Carrying passenger on bicycle contrary to section 21.	Summarily.	—	—	Sections 181 and 183 apply.
22	Failing to comply with traffic directions.	Summarily.	Discretionary, if committed in respect of a motor vehicle by a failure to comply with a direction of a constable or an indication given by a sign specified for the pur-	Obligatory, if committed as described in the entry in column 4 relating to this offence.	Sections 179, 181 and 183 apply.

				poses of this paragraph in regulations made by the Secretary of State for the Environment and the Secretary of State Scotland acting jointly.		
23	Pedestrian failing to stop when directed by constable regulating traffic.	Summarily.		—	—	—
24	Leaving vehicles in dangerous positions.	Summarily.		Discretionary, if committed in respect of a motor vehicle.	Obligatory, if committed in respect of a motor vehicle.	Sections 179, 181 and 183 apply.
25 (4)	Failing to stop after accident and give particulars or report accident.	Summarily.		Discretionary.	Obligatory.	Sections 181 and 183 apply.
26 (2)	Obstructing inspection of vehicles after accident.	Summarily.		—	—	—
29	Tampering with motor vehicles.	Summarily.		—	—	Section 181 applies.
30 (1)	Holding or getting on to vehicle in order to be carried.	Summarily.		—	—	Section 181 applies.

1 Provision creating offence	2 General nature of offence	3 Mode of prosecution	4 Disqualification	5 Endorsement	6 Additional provisions
30 (2)	Holding on to vehicle in order to be towed.	Summarily.	—	—	Sections 181 and 183 apply.
31 (1)	Dogs on designated roads without being held on lead.	Summarily.	—	—	—
32 (3)	Driving or riding motor cycles in contravention of regulations requiring wearing of protective headgear.	Summarily.	—	—	—
33	Selling, etc., helmet not of prescribed type as helmet for affording protection for motor cyclists.	Summarily.	—	—	—
34 (4)	Causing, etc. heavy motor vehicles to be driven or to haul without proper crew.	Summarily.	—	—	Section 181 applies.
35 (3)	Unauthorised motor vehicle trial on footpaths or bridleways.	Summarily.	—	—	Sections 181 and 183 apply.

36	Driving motor vehicles elsewhere than on roads.	Summarily.	—	—	Sections 181 and 183 apply.
40 (5)	Contravention of construction and use regulations.	Summarily.	Discretionary if committed by using, or causing or permitting the use of, any motor vehicle or trailer— (*a*) as described in paragraph (*a*) in the entry in column 4 of R.T. Act 1972, Sched. 4 relating to this offence; or (*b*) in breach of a construction and use requirement as to brakes, steering-gear, or tyres; except where the offender proves that he did not know and had no reasonable cause to suspect that the facts of the case were such that the offence would be committed.	Obligatory if committed as described in the entry in column 4 relating to this offence, but subject to the exception there mentioned.	Sections 181 and 183 apply.
44 (1)	Using, etc., vehicle without required test certificate being in force.	Summarily.	—	—	Sections 181 and 183 apply.

1 Provision creating offence	2 General nature of offence	3 Mode of prosecution	4 Disqualification	5 Endorsement	6 Additional provisions
Regulations under 45 (7)	Contravention of requirement of regulations that driver of goods vehicle being tested be present throughout test or drive vehicle, etc., which is declared by regulations to be an offence.	Summarily.	—	—	—
46 (1)	Using, etc., goods vehicle without required plating certificate being in force.	Summarily.	—	—	Sections 181 and 183 apply.
46 (2)	Using, etc., goods vehicle without required goods vehicle test certificate being in force.	Summarily.	—	—	Sections 181 and 183 apply.
46 (3)	Using, etc., goods vehicle with alteration thereto required to be but not notified to Secretary of State under regulations under section 45	Summarily.	—	—	Sections 181 and 183 apply.

Regulations under 50 (5)	Contravention of requirement of regulations that driver of goods vehicle being tested after notifiable alteration be present throughout test and drive vehicle, etc., which is declared by regulations to be an offence.	Summarily.	—	—	—
51 (1)	Using, etc., goods vehicle without required certificate being in force showing that it complies with type approval requirements applicable to it.	Summarily.	—	—	Sections 181 and 183 apply.
51 (2)	Using, etc., certain goods vehicles for drawing trailer when plating certificate does not specify maximum laden weight for vehicle and trailer.	Summarily.	—	—	Sections 181 and 183 apply.

1 Provision creating offence	2 General nature of offence	3 Mode of prosecution	4 Disqualification	5 Endorsement	6 Additional provisions
51 (3)	Using, etc., goods vehicle with alteration thereto required to be but not notified to Secretary of State under regulations under section 48.	Summarily.	—	—	Sections 181 and 183 apply.
53 (4)	Obstructing testing of vehicle by examiner on road or failing to comply with requirements of section 53 or Schedule 3.	Summarily.	—	—	—
54 (5) (including application by 55 (3))	Failure of owner of vehicle discovered to be defective on roadside test or further test to give required certificate or declaration.	Summarily.	—	—	—
54 (6) (including application by	Failure of person in charge of vehicle on roadside test or	Summarily.	—	—	—

55 (5)	Obstructing further testing of vehicle by Secretary of State's officer or failing to comply with requirements of section 55 or paragraph 3 or 4 of Schedule 3.	Summarily.	—	—	—
56 (3)	Obstructing goods vehicle examiner inspecting goods vehicle or entering premises where such vehicle believed to be.	Summarily.	—	—	—
56 (5)	Person in charge of stationary goods vehicle refusing etc., to proceed to nearby place of inspection.	Summarily.	—	—	—
57 (9)	Driving, etc., goods vehicle in contravention of prohibition on driving it as being unfit for service.	Summarily.	—	—	Sections 181 and 183 apply.

1 Provision creating offence	2 General nature of offence	3 Mode of prosecution	4 Disqualification	5 Endorsement	6 Additional provisions
59 (3)	Contravention of regulations requiring goods vehicle operator to inspect, and keep records of inspections of, goods vehicles.	Summarily.	—	—	—
60 (3)	Selling, etc., unroadworthy vehicle or trailer or altering vehicle or trailer so as to make it unroadworthy.	Summarily.	—	—	—
61 (2)	Obstructing examiner testing condition of used vehicles at sale rooms, etc.	Summarily.	—	—	—
62	Selling, etc., goods vehicle without required certificate being in force showing that it complies with type approval requirements applicable to it.	Summarily.	—	—	—

65 (5)	Drawing more than prescribed number of trailers.	Summarily.	—	—	Sections 181 and 183 apply.
66 (5)	Selling, etc., pedal cycle in contravention of regulations as to brakes, bells, etc.	Summarily.	—	—	—
81 (1)	Causing, etc., vehicle to be on road in contravention of provisions as to lighting, etc., of vehicles.	Summarily.	—	—	Sections 181 and 183 apply.
81 (2)	Selling, etc., wrongly made tail lamps or reflectors.	Summarily.	—	—	—
84 (1)	Driving without a licence.	Summarily.	Discretionary, if the offence is committed by driving a motor vehicle in a case where either no licence authorising the driving of that vehicle could have been granted to the offender or, if a provisional (but no other) licence to drive it could have been granted to him, the driving would not have complied with the conditions thereof.	Obligatory, if committed as described in the entry in column 4 relating to this offence.	Sections 181 and 183 apply.

1 Provision creating offence	2 General nature of offence	3 Mode of prosecution	4 Disqualification	5 Endorsement	6 Additional provisions
84 (2)	Employing a person to drive without a licence.	Summarily.	—	—	Section 181 applies.
88 (6)	Failing to comply with any conditions prescribed for driving under provisional licence or full licence treated as provisional licence.	Summarily.	Discretionary.	Obligatory.	Sections 181 and 183 apply.
89 (3)	Driving licence holder failing, when his particulars become incorrect, to surrender licence and give particulars.	Summarily.	—	—	—
91 (1)	Driving with uncorrected defective eyesight.	Summarily.	Discretionary.	Obligatory.	—
91 (2)	Refusing to submit to test of eyesight.	Summarily.	Discretionary.	Obligatory.	—

99 (*a*)	Obtaining driving licence while disqualified.	Summarily.	—	—	Section 180 applies.
99 (*b*)	Driving while disqualified.	(*a*) Summarily. (*b*) On indictment.	Discretionary.	Obligatory.	Sections 180, 181 and 183 apply.
101 (4) (including application by 103 (4))	Failing to produce licence to court for endorsement on conviction of offence involving obligatory endorsement or on committal for sentence, etc., for offence involving obligatory or discretionary disqualification when no interim disqualification ordered.	Summarily.	—	—	—
101 (6)	Applying for or obtaining licence without giving particulars of current endorsement.	Summarily.	—	—	—
103 (2)	Failing to produce driving licence to court making order for interim disqualification on committal for sentence, etc.	Summarily.	—	—	—

1 Provision creating offence	2 General nature of offence	3 Mode of prosecution	4 Disqualification	5 Endorsement	6 Additional provisions
104 (4)	Failing to state to court or give information as to date of birth or sex.	Summarily.	—	—	—
104 (5)	Failing to furnish Secretary of State with evidence of date of birth, etc.	Summarily.	—	—	—
111 (2)	Failing to produce to court Northern Ireland driving licence.	Summarily.	—	—	—
112 (1)	Driving heavy goods vehicle without heavy goods vehicle driver's licence.	Summarily.	—	—	Sections 181 and 183 apply.
112 (2)	Employing a person to drive heavy goods vehicle without heavy goods vehicle driver's licence.	Summarily.	—	—	Section 181 applies.

114 (3)	Failing to comply with conditions of heavy goods vehicle driver's licence.	Summarily.		—	—	Sections 181 and 183 apply.
Regulations under 119 (2)	Contravention of regulations about heavy goods vehicle drivers' licences which is declared by regulation to be an offence.	Summarily.		—	—	—
126 (3)	Giving of paid driving instruction by unregistered and unlicensed persons or their employers.	Summarily.		—	—	—
135 (2)	Unregistered instructor using title or displaying badge, etc., prescribed for registered instructor, and employers using such title, etc., in relation to his unregistered instructor or issuing misleading advertisement, etc.	Summarily.		—	—	—
136	Failure of instructor to surrender to Registrar certificate or licence.	Summarily.		—	—	—

1 Provision creating offence	2 General nature of offence	3 Mode of prosecution	4 Disqualification	5 Endorsement	6 Additional provisions
137 (3)	Failing to produce certificate of registration or licence as driving instructor.	Summarily.	—	—	—
143	Using motor vehicle while uninsured or unsecured against third-party risks.	Summarily.	Discretionary.	Obligatory.	Sections 180, 181 and 183 apply.
147 (4)	Failing to surrender certificate of insurance or security to insurer on cancellation or make statutory declaration of loss or destruction.	Summarily.	—	—	—
151 (2)	Failing to give information, or wilfully making false statement, as to insurance or security when claim made.	Summarily.	—	—	—
159	Failing to stop vehicle when required by constable.	Summarily.	—	—	Sections 181 and 183 apply.

160 (1)	Refusing or neglecting to allow motor vehicle or trailer to be weighed, etc.	Summarily.	—	—	Sections 181 and 183 apply.
161 (4)	Failing to produce driving licence to constable or to state date of birth.	Summarily.	—	—	Sections 181 and 183 apply.
161 (5)	Failing to furnish Secretary of State with evidence of date of birth, etc.	Summarily.	—	—	—
162 (1)	Failing to give constable certain names and addresses or to produce certificate of insurance or certain test and other like certificates.	Summarily.	—	—	Sections 181 and 183 apply.
162 (3)	Supervisor of learner-driver failing to give constable certain names and addresses.	Summarily.	—	—	Section 181 applies.
164 (1)	Refusing to give, or giving false, name and address in case of reckless, dangerous, careless or inconsiderate driving or cycling.	Summarily.	—	—	Sections 181 and 183 apply.

1 Provision creating offence	2 General nature of offence	3 Mode of prosecution	4 Disqualification	5 Endorsement	6 Additional provisions
165	Pedestrian failing to give constable his name and address after failing to stop when directed by constable controlling traffic.	Summarily.	—	—	—
166 (1)	Failure by driver, in case of accident involving injury to another, to produce evidence of insurance or security or to report accident.	Summarily.	—	—	Sections 181 and 183 apply.
167	Failure by owner of motor vehicle to give police information for verifying compliance with requirement of compulsory insurance or security.	Summarily.	—	—	Sections 181 and 183 apply.

168 (3)	Failure of person keeping vehicle and others to give police information as to identity of driver, etc., in the case of certain offences.	Summarily.	—	—	—
169 (1)	Forgery, etc., of licences, test certificates, certificates of insurance and other documents and things.	(*a*) Summarily. (*b*) On indictment	—	—	Section 180 applies.
170 (1)	Making false statements in connection with licences under this Act and with registration as an approved driving instructor.	Summarily.	—	—	Section 180 applies.
170 (2)	Making, or making use of, false statements relating to goods vehicles.	Summarily.	—	—	—
170 (3)	Producing false evidence or making false declaration in connection with applications for vehicle excise licences for vehicles required to have test certificates.	Summarily.	—	—	—

1 Provision creating offence	2 General nature of offence	3 Mode of prosecution	4 Disqualification	5 Endorsement	6 Additional provisions
170 (4)	Making false statements as to the remedying of defects discovered in vehicles on roadside tests.	Summarily.	—	—	—
170 (5)	Making, or making use of, false entry in records required to be kept of condition of goods vehicles.	Summarily.	—	—	—
170 (6)	Making false statement or withholding material information in order to obtain the issue of insurance certificates, etc.	Summarily.	—	—	Section 180 applies.
171	Issuing false insurance certificates, etc., or false test certificates.	Summarily.	—	—	Section 180 applies.

172	Using goods vehicle with unauthorised weights as well as authorised weights marked thereon.	Summarily.	—	—	—
174	Personation of, or of person employed by, authorised examiner.	Summarily.	—	—	—
175	Taking, etc., in Scotland a motor vehicle without authority or, knowing that it has been so taken, driving it or allowing oneself to be carried in it without authority.	(*a*) Summarily. (*b*) On indictment.	Discretionary.	Obligatory.	Sections 181 and 183 and paragraph 8 of Part IV of this Schedule apply.
187 (2)	Failing to attend, give evidence or produce documents to, inquiry held by Secretary of State, etc.	Summarily.	—	—	—
Schedule1 para. 5 (1)	Applying warranty to protective helmet in defending proceedings under section 33 where no warranty given.	Summarily.	—	—	—

1 Provision creating offence	2 General nature of offence	3 Mode of prosecution	4 Disqualification	5 Endorsement	6 Additional provisions
para. 5 (2)	Giving to purchaser of protective helmet a false warranty in case where warranty might be defence in proceedings under section 33.	Summarily.	—	—	—

Col. 4 (Punishment) of R.T. Act 1972, Sched. 4 has been omitted from this Appendix.

PART II

Other Offence Involving Obligatory Disqualification and Endorsement

Manslaughter, by the driver of a motor vehicle.

PART III

Other Offences Involving Discretionary Disqualification and Obligatory Endorsement

1. Stealing or attempting to steal a motor vehicle.

2. An offence, or attempt to commit an offence, in respect of a motor vehicle under section 12 of the Theft Act 1968 (taking conveyance without consent of owner, etc., or, knowing it has been so taken, driving it or allowing oneself to be carried in it).

3. An offence under section 25 of the Theft Act 1968 (going equipped for stealing, etc.) committed with reference to the theft or taking of motor vehicles.

4. An offence under section 13 (4) of the Road Traffic Regulation Act 1967 (contravention of traffic regulations on special roads) committed in respect of a motor vehicle otherwise than by unlawfully stopping or allowing the vehicle to remain at rest on a part of a special road on which vehicles are in certain circumstances permitted to remain at rest.

5. An offence under section 23 (5) of the Road Traffic Regulation Act 1967 (contravention of pedestrian crossing regulations) committed in respect of a motor vehicle.

6. An offence under section 25 (2) of the Road Traffic Regulation Act 1967 (failure to obey sign exhibited by school crossing patrol) committed in respect of a motor vehicle.

7. An offence under section 26 (6) or 26A (5) of the Road Traffic Regulation Act 1967 (contravention of order prohibiting or restricting use of street playground by vehicles) committed in respect of a motor vehicle.

8. An offence punishable by virtue of section 78A of the Road Traffic Regulation Act 1967 (speeding offences under that and other Acts).

PART IV

Supplementary provisions as to prosecution, trial and punishmen of offences

4. Where a person is charged in England or Wales before a magistrates' court with an offence under section 2 or with an offence under section 17, and the court is of opinion that the offence is not proved, then, at any time during the hearing or immediately thereafter the court may, without prejudice to any

other powers possessed by the court, direct or allow a charge for an offence under section 3 or, as the case may be, section 18 to be preferred forthwith against the defendant and may thereupon proceed with that charge, so however that he or his solicitor or counsel shall be informed of the new charge and be given an opportunity, whether by way of cross-examining any witness whose evidence has already been given against the defendant or otherwise, of answering the new charge, and the court shall, if it considers that the defendant is prejudiced in his defence by reason of the new charge's being so preferred, adjourn the hearing.

5. Where a person is prosecuted on indictment in England or Wales for an offence to which section 179 does not apply, section 179 (2) shall not be taken to prejudice any power of the jury on the charge for that offence, if they find him not guilty of it, to find him guilty of an offence against section 2.

7. A person may be convicted of an offence against section 3 or 18 notwithstanding that the requirement of section 179 (2) has not been satisfied as respects that offence where—

(*a*) the charge for the offence has been preferred against him by virtue of paragraph 4 above, and
(*b*) the said requirement has been satisfied, or does not apply, as respects the alleged offence against section 2 or, as the case may be, section 17.

PART V

Interpretation

1. For the purposes of the entries in Part I of this Schedule relating to an offence under section 5 (1), 6 (1) or 9 (3) "the relevant time" means—

(*a*) in relation to a person required under section 8 (1) to provide a specimen of breath for a breath test, the time when he was so required;
(*b*) in relation to a person required under section 8 (2) to provide such a specimen, the time of the accident;
(*c*) in relation to a person arrested under section 5 (5), the time of his arrest.

APPENDIX V

PRINCIPAL ARRESTABLE OFFENCES

Offence	*Act and Section*
ABDUCTION	
of child under 14	O.A.P. Act 1861, s. 56
of woman by force or for her property	Sexual Offences Act 1956, s. 17
of heiress	. . . . . . s. 18
ABORTION	
using poison or instruments to procure	O.A.P. Act 1861, s. 58
supplying poison, etc., to procure .	. . . . s. 59
ABSTRACTING OF ELECTRICITY .	Theft Act 1968, s. 13
AIRCRAFT	
destroying or damaging . .	Protection of Aircraft Act 1973.
ARSON	Criminal Damage Act 1971.
ASSAULT	
on gamekeeper by poachers . .	Night Poaching Act 1828, s. 2
on authorised person saving wreck .	O.A.P. Act 1861, s. 37
occasioning actual bodily harm .	. . . . s. 47
with intent to rob . . .	Theft Act 1968, s. 8
with intent to commit buggery .	Sexual Offences Act 1956, s. 16
BIGAMY	O.A.P. Act 1861, s. 57
BIOLOGICAL WEAPONS	
development etc.	Biological Weapons Act 1974, s. 1.
BLACKMAIL	Theft Act 1968, s. 21
BUGGERY	Sexual Offences Act 1956, s. 12
BURGLARY	Theft Act 1968, s. 9
aggravated	. . . . s. 10
CHEATING AT PLAY . . .	Gaming Act 1845, s. 17
CHILD DESTRUCTION . . .	Infant Life (Preservation) Act 1929
CHILDREN	
abandoning	O.A.P. Act 1861, s. 27
sexual intercourse with girl under 13	Sexual Offences Act 1956, s. 5
CONSPIRACY	
to cause explosion	Explosives Substances Act 1883, s. 3
to murder	O.A.P. Act 1861, s. 4
CORRUPTION	
when H.M. Government is concerned	Public Bodies Corrupt Practices Act 1889; Prevention of Corruption Act 1906, s. 1

Attempts to commit any of the above offences are also "arrestable offences"

Offence	*Act and Section*
COUNTERFEIT COIN	
making counterfeit current coin	Coinage Offences Act 1936, s. 1
gilding any coin	s. 2
impairing gold or silver coin	s. 3
possessing three or more counterfeit coin resembling gold or silver coin	s. 5
buying or selling counterfeit coin at a lower rate or value than same purports to be	s. 6
importing and exporting	s. 7
making, etc., coining implements	s. 9
conveying coining tools out of Mint	s. 10
CRIMINAL DAMAGE	
destroying or damaging property	Criminal Damage Act 1971, s. 1
threats to destroy or damage property	s. 2
possessing anything with intent to destroy or damage property	s. 3
DANGEROUS DRUGS	
offences against Act	Misuse of Drugs Act 1971, s. 24
DECEPTION	
obtaining property by	Theft Act 1968, s. 15
obtaining pecuniary advantage by	s. 16
DRILLING, ILLEGAL	Unlawful Drilling Act 1819, s. 1
DRUGS Administering—	
with intent to commit offence	O.A.P. Act 1861, s. 22
with intent to endanger life	s. 23
with intent to injure	s. 24
with intent to procure abortion	s. 58
ESCAPE	
assisting prisoners to	Criminal Justice Act 1961, s. 22
EXPLOSIVES	
causing bodily injury by	O.A.P. Act 1861, s. 28
using, with intent to do grievous bodily injury	s. 29
placing near building or ship with intent to do bodily injury	s. 30
causing explosion likely to endanger life	Explosive Substances Act 1883, s. 2
attempting to cause explosions or making or possessing with intent to endanger life	s. 3
making or possessing under suspicious circumstances	s. 4
FALSE ACCOUNTING	Theft Act 1968, s. 17
FALSE STATEMENTS	
by company directors	s. 19
FIREARMS	
possession with intent to endanger life or injure property	Firearms Act 1968, s. 16
use of firearms to resist arrest	s. 17 (1)
possessing while committing an offence specified in Sched. 1	s. 17 (2)
carrying firearms or imitation firearms with intent to commit indictable offence or to resist arrest	s. 18 (1)

Attempts to commit any of the above offences are also "arrestable offences"

Offence	*Act and Section*
FORGERY	
destruction of official records of births, baptisms, etc.	Forgery Act 1861, ss. 36, 37
wills, bonds, deeds or bank notes, valuable securities, documents of title	Forgery Act 1913, s. 2
documents, stamped with Great Seal, registers of births, baptisms, marriages and deaths and official documents	s. 3
seals and dies	s. 5
uttering forged document, seal or die	s. 6
demanding money on forged document	s. 7
possession of forged bank note, forged stamp, die or label	s. 8
making or possessing certain paper or implements	s. 9
FRAUDS BY DIRECTORS, etc.	Prevention of Fraud (Investments) Acts 1958
HANDLING STOLEN GOODS	Theft Act 1968, s. 22
HIJACKING	Hijacking Act 1971
INCEST	Sexual Offences Act 1956, s. 10
INDECENT ASSAULT	
female under 13	Sexual Offences Act 1956, s. 14 Indecency with Children Act 1960, s. 2
on male	Sexual Offences Act 1956, s. 15
INFANTICIDE	Infanticide Act 1938, s. 1
MALICIOUS DAMAGE	
to ships by false signals	Malicious Damage Act 1861 s. 47
to buoys	s. 48
causing explosion likely to endanger life or injure property	Explosive Substances Act 1883, s. 2
conspiring to cause explosions	s. 3
MANSLAUGHTER	O.A.P. Act 1861, s. 5
MARRIAGE	
to solemnise, falsely pretending to be in Holy Orders	Marriage Act 1949, s. 75
MOTOR VEHICLE	
causing death by reckless or dangerous driving	Road Traffic Act 1960, s. 1
MURDER	Murder (Abolition of Death Penalty) Act 1965
conspiracy to	O.A.P. Act 1861, s. 4
MUTINY, INCITING TO	Incitement to Mutiny Act 1797, s. 1
OFFICIAL SECRETS—spying	Official Secrets Act 1920 s. 1
PERJURY	
in judicial proceedings	Perjury Act 1911, s. 1
not in judicial proceedings	s. 2
as to marriages	s. 3
as to births and deaths	s. 4
subornation	s. 7
PERSONATION	
of bail	Forgery Act 1861, s. 34
PIRACY	Piracy Acts 1698–1844
POACHING by 3 or more, armed	Night Poaching Act 1828, s. 9

Attempts to commit any of the above offences are also "arrestable offences"

Offence	*Act and Section*
POISON	
administering so as to endanger life, etc.	O.A.P. Act 1861, s. 23
administering with intent to injure	. . . s. 24
PROSTITUTION	
living on earnings of . . .	Sexual Offences Act 1956, s. 30
woman exercising control over a prostitute	. . . . . . s. 31
living on earnings of male prostitution	. . . . . 1967, s. 5
RAILWAYS	
endangering safety of passengers .	O.A.P. Act 1861, ss. 32, 33
maliciously obstructing . .	Malicious Damage Act 1861, s. 35
RAPE	Sexual Offences Act 1956, s. 1
REMOVAL OF ARTICLES	
from places open to the public .	Theft Act 1968, s. 11
ROBBERY	Theft Act 1968, s. 8
SEXUAL INTERCOURSE	
with girl under 13 . . .	Sexual Offences Act 1956, s. 5
permitting girl under 13 to use premises for	. . . . . . s. 25
SPRING GUNS	
setting with intent to inflict grievous bodily harm	O.A.P. Act 1861, s. 31
SUICIDE aiding and abetting . .	Suicide Act 1961, s. 2 (but see p. 115 and note on p. 668)
SUPPRESSION OF DOCUMENTS	
dishonestly destroying, defacing or concealing valuable security, will, etc.	Theft Act 1968, s. 20 (1)
dishonestly procuring execution of valuable security . . .	. . . . s. 20 (2)
TAKING MOTOR VEHICLE	
or other conveyance without authority (pedal cycles excepted) .	. . . . s. 12
THEFT	. . . . s. 7
THREATS	
to destroy or damage property .	Criminal Damage Act 1971, s. 2
to murder	O.A.P. Act 1861, s. 16
TREASON	Treason Acts
TREASON FELONY . . .	Treason Felony Act 1848
WOUNDING	
with intent to do grievous bodily harm or resist arrest . . .	O.A.P. Act 1861, s. 18
unlawful (grievous bodily harm) .	. . . . s. 20
throwing corrosives . . .	. . . . s. 29

Attempts to commit any of the above offences are also "arrestable offences"

APPENDIX VI

THE JUSTICES' CLERKS RULES 1970

These rules provide that the things specified in the Schedule below, which are authorised to be done by, to or before a single justice of the peace, may be done by, to or before a Justices' Clerk.

SCHEDULE

1. The laying of an information or the making of a complaint, other than an information or complaint substantiated on oath.

2. The issue of any summons, including a witness summons.

3. The adjournment of the hearing of a complaint if the parties to the complaint consent to the complaint being adjourned.

4.—(1) The further adjournment of criminal proceedings with the consent of the prosecutor and the accused if, but only if,

(*a*) the accused, not having been remanded on the previous adjournment, is not remanded on the further adjournment; or

(*b*) the accused, having been remanded on bail on the previous adjournment, is remanded on bail on the like terms and conditions.

(2) The remand of the accused on bail at the time of further adjourning the proceedings in pursuance of sub-paragraph (1) (*b*) above.

5. The determination that a complaint for the revocation, discharge, revival, alteration, variation or enforcement of an affiliation order or an order enforceable as an affiliation order be dealt with by a magistrates' court acting for another petty sessions area in accordance with the provisions of Rule 34 or 49 of the Magistrates' Courts Rules 1968.

6. The allowing of further time for payment of a sum enforceable by a magistrates' court.

7. The making of a transfer of fine order, that is to say, an order making payment by a person of a sum adjudged to be paid by a conviction enforceable in the petty sessions area in which he is residing.

8. The making of an order before an inquiry into the means of a person under section 44 of the Criminal Justice Act 1967 that that person shall furnish to the court a statement of his means in accordance with section 44 (8).

9. (Repealed.)

10. The giving of consent for another magistrates' court to deal with an offender for an earlier offence in respect of which, after the offender had attained the age of 17 years, a court had made a probation order or an order for conditional discharge, where the Justices' Clerk is the Clerk of the Court which made the order or, in the case of a probation order, of that court or of the supervising court.

11. The amending, in accordance with paragraph 2 (1) of Schedule 1 to the Criminal Justice Act 1948, now (P. of C.C. Act 1973) of a probation order made after the probationer had attained the age of 17 years by substituting for the petty sessions area named in the order the area in which the probationer proposes to reside or is residing.

TABLE OF REFERENCES TO STATUTES

PAGE

Statute of Treasons 1351 179
Justices of the Peace Act 1361 . . . . . . 65, 226
Sunday Observance Act 1625 540
Sunday Observance Act 1667 540
Witchcraft Act 1735 392
Constables Protection Act 1750 28
Sunday Observance Act 1780 . . . . . 533, 538, 540
Servants' Characters Act 1792 418
Incitement to Mutiny Act 1797, s. 1 12
Unlawful Drilling Act 1819 206
s. 1 22
Vagrancy Act 1824 . . . . 392, 406
s. 3 . . . . 124, 389, 391, 431
s. 4 . 94, 128, 201, 389, 391, 392, 406, 407, 431, 465, 529
s. 5 . . . . 407, 431
s. 6 . . . . 26, 128, 390, 391
s. 10 407
Night Poaching Act 1828 195
s. 1 . . . . 23, 196, 197
s. 2 . . . . 24, 196, 197
s. 9 . . . . 23, 196, 197
s. 12 196
Game Act 1831 . . . . 196, 197, 431
s. 2 197
s. 3 197
s. 4 . . . . 197, 432
s. 5 197
s. 18 431
s. 23 197
s. 28 432
s. 30 . . . . 196, 197
s. 31 . . . . 23, 196, 197
ss. 32, 34 196
s. 35 196
s. 41 196
Stage Carriage Act 1832 339
s. 48 341
Highway Act 1835 336
s. 72 248
s. 78 . . . . 245, 251, 253
Vagrancy Act 1838, s. 2 125

PAGE

Metropolitan Police Act 1839 . . . 253
s. 54 . . . 25
s. 58 . . . 564
s. 66 . . . 188
City of London Police Act 1839, s. 48 . . . 188
Railway Regulation Act 1840 . . . 379
Railway Regulation Act 1842 . . . 379
Pound Breach Act 1843 . . . 218
Theatres Act 1843 . . . 529
Evidence Act 1843 . . . 85
London Hackney Carriages Act 1843, s. 28 . . . 564
Libel Act 1843, ss. 4, 5 . . . 238
Night Poaching Act 1844 . . . 195, 196
Gaming Act 1845 . . . 539
ss. 10, 11 . . . 539
s. 12 . . . 539
s. 13 . . . 539, 548
s. 14 . . . 539
s. 17 . . . 517
Art Unions Act 1846 . . . 514
Cemeteries Clauses Act 1847 . . . 582
Town Police Clauses Act 1847 . . . 326, 339, 340, 341
s. 3 . . . 245
ss. 21, 22 . . . 252
ss. 24, 25 . . . 250
s. 26 . . . 218
s. 28 26, 127, 128, 129, 245, 247, 251, 253, 482, 489
s. 29 . . . 364
ss. 30, 31 . . . 583
s. 35 . . . 125, 557
s. 36 . . . 482
s. 37 . . . 339
s. 38 . . . 339
ss. 45, 46 . . . 340
ss. 51, 52 . . . 340
s. 53 . . . 341
s. 54 . . . 340
ss. 55, 57 . . . 341
s. 58 . . . 340
s. 59 . . . 340
s. 61 . . . 340, 564
ss. 62, 64, 66 . . . 341
Treason Felony Act 1848 . . . 205
Indictable Offences Act 1848, s. 13 . . . 53
Prevention of Offences Act 1851, s. 11 . . . 24
Evidence Act 1851, s. 13 . . . 15
Evidence Amendment Act 1853 . . . 95
Burial Act 1855 . . . 582
Summary Jurisdiction Act 1857, s. 6 . . . 66
Burial Act 1857 . . . 582
Remission of Penalties Act 1859 . . . 11
Refreshment Houses Act 1860 . . . 568
Ecclesiastical Courts Jurisdiction Act 1860—
s. 2 . . . 22, 214, 414
s. 3 . . . 22, 214, 414
Game Licences Act 1860 . . . 197, 431
Accessories and Abettors Act 1861 . . . 13
s. 8 . . . 13
Malicious Damage Act 1861 . . . 24
s. 35 . . . 24, 379
s. 36 . . . 379
ss. 47, 48 . . . 24, 194
Forgery Act 1861 . . . 184
ss. 27, 28 . . . 185

PAGE

Forgery Act 1861—(*cont.*)
s. 34 . . . . 185, 419
ss. 36, 37 185
Offences against the Person Act 1861 . . 56, 106, 108, 115, 135
s. 1 115
s. 4 . . . 12, 115
s. 5 . . . 115, 143
s. 9 115
s. 16 . . . 106, 115
s. 17 194
s. 18 . . . 108, 110
s. 20 . 39, 106, 108, 110, 465
ss. 21–23 . 108, 110, 465
s. 24 109
s. 27 . 39, 137, 143, 153
s. 28 110
s. 29 . . 109, 110, 447
s. 30 447
ss. 32–34 . . . 379
s. 35 253
s. 36 414
s. 37 194
s. 38 . . . 107, 465
ss. 42, 43 . . 106, 143
ss. 44, 45 . . 64, 106
s. 46 107
s. 47 . . 39, 106, 465
s. 56 . 142, 143, 155, 465
s. 57 . . . 214, 215
s. 58 . . . 12, 135
s. 59 136
s. 60 39
s. 64 . . . 116, 448
s. 65 . . . 116, 448
Poaching Prevention Act 1862 195
Town Gardens Protection Act 1863 26
Telegraph Act 1863, s. 45 378
Criminal Procedure Act 1865—
s. 3 97
ss. 4, 6 99
Criminal Law Amendment Act 1867—
s. 6 79
s. 7 79
Telegraph Act 1868, s. 20 . . . . 39, 378
Gun Barrel Proof Act 1868 478
Newspapers, Printers and Reading Rooms Repeal Act 1869 . 437
Debtors Act 1869 174
Metropolitan Public Carriage Act 1869 650
Extradition Act 1870 . . . . 116, 670
Foreign Enlistment Act 1870 214
Dogs Act 1871 s. 2 489
Pedlars Act 1871 . . . . 157, 430
ss. 3, 4 430
ss. 5, 6 430
ss. 10–12 430
s. 13 431
s. 16 . . . . 391, 430
s. 17 431
s. 18 . . . . 24, 431
s. 19 431
s. 23 430
Prevention of Crimes Act 1871—
s. 15 . . . . 94, 406, 465
s. 18 . . . . 16, 99
Licensing Act 1872 542
s. 12 . . . . 23, 262, 263, 545, 562, 563, 564
Births and Deaths Registration Act 1874 581
Explosives Act 1875 . . . . 56, 446, 455
ss. 4, 5 448

PAGE

Explosives Act 1875—(*cont*).
s. 30 . . . . 431, 448
s. 31 . . . . 154, 448
ss. 32, 39 448
s. 73 . . . . 57, 447
s. 78 22
s. 80 448
Public Stores Act 1875 193
ss. 4–7, 9, 10 193
Public Health Act 1875—
s. 4 243
ss. 171, 276 . . . . 247, 339
Conspiracy and Protection of Property Act 1875—
s. 3 229
ss. 4, 5 230
s. 7 230
Customs Consolidation Act 1876—
s. 42 131
Cruelty to Animals Act 1876 . . . . . . 56, 484
Sched. I 485
Bills of Sale Act 1878 219
Prosecution of Offences Act 1879 668
s. 5 670
Burial Laws Amendment Act 1880 582
Ground Game Act 1880 197
Pedlars Act 1881 . . . . 157, 430
Summary Jurisdiction (Process) Act 1881 49
Newspaper Libel and Registration Act 1881 238
Municipal Corporations Act 1882, s. 193 . . . . 24, 62, 407
Explosive Substance Act 1883 446
s. 2 . . . . 110, 446
s. 3 446
ss. 4, 5, 7 447
Payment of Wages in Public Houses Prohibition Act 1883 . 558, 561
Post Office (Protection) Act 1884, s. 11 378
Riot (Damages) Act 1886 228
Coroners Act 1887 . . . . 584, 585
s. 3 584
s. 19 586
Oaths Act 1888 82
Local Government Act 1888, s. 85 . . . . 245, 253, 336, 337
Law of Libel Amendment Act 1888 238
Town Police Clauses Act 1889 . . . . . . 339, 340
s. 3 339
Indecent Advertisements Act 1889 129
ss. 3–5 129
s. 6 23
Revenue Act 1889, s. 2 182
Interpretation Act 1889—
s. 27 58
s. 33 16

PAGE

Public Bodies Corrupt Practices Act 1889—
s. 1 . . . . . 221, 222
s. 4 221
Public Health Acts Amendment Act 1890 . . . 537, 548
s. 51 . . . . . 537, 538
Stamp Duties Management Act 1891 . . . 39, 184
s. 13 185
Penal Servitude Act 1891, s. 7 . . . 27, 94, 406, 465
Hares Preservation Act 1892 . . . 198
Uniforms Act 1894 . . . 422
Merchant Shipping Act 1894 . . . 193, 194, 305
ss. 271, 283 380
s. 287 . . . . . 380, 564
Light Railways Act 1896 . . . 324, 337, 355
Police (Property) Act 1897 . . 57, 178, 188, 190, 192, 425, 434
s. 1 . . . . . 188, 190
s. 2 . . . . . 188, 190
Criminal Evidence Act 1898—
s. 1 . . . . . 84, 96, 118, 134
s. 4 84
Sched. 84
Revenue Act 1898, s. 1 . . . 517
Cremation Act 1902 . . . 582
Licensing Act 1902 . . . 542
s. 1 . . . . . 23, 563
s. 2 . . . . . 23, 153, 563
s. 6 558
s. 8 563
Motor Car Act 1903 . . . 299, 600, 617, 619
Seamen's and Soldiers' False Characters Act 1906 . . . 420
Dogs Act 1906 . . . 489
s. 1 489
s. 3 490
s. 4 490
s. 6 491
Prevention of Corruption Act 1906 . . . 221, 222
Ground Game (Amendment) Act 1906 . . . 197
Public Health Acts (Amendment) Act 1907—
s. 81 . . . . . 127, 489, 564
s. 85 432
Prosecution of Offences Act 1908 . . . 69, 668
s. 3 69
Public Meeting Act 1908, s. 1 . . . 25, 233
Cinematograph Act 1909 . . . 456
s. 1 535
s. 2 535
s. 3 537
s. 4 . . . . . 537, 540
s. 7 . . . . . 534, 535, 536
Oaths Act 1909 . . . 82
Perjury Act 1911 . . . 36, 45, 88, 218, 219, 221
s. 1 219
ss. 2–4 219
s. 5 . . . . . 39, 220

PAGE

Perjury Act 1911—(*cont.*)
s. 6 219
s. 7 220
s. 9 . . . . 37, 220
s. 13 220
s. 15 219
Protection of Animals Act 1911 . . . . . . 19, 500
s. 1 . . . . 482, 484, 485
s. 2 . . . . 64, 483, 492
s. 3 . . . . 483, 492
s. 4 486
s. 5 497
s. 7 . . . . 250, 483
s. 8 . . . . 482, 483, 484
s. 9 492
s. 10 483
s. 11 485
s. 12 . . . . 19, 483
s. 13 484
s. 15 . . . . 482, 483
Official Secrets Act 1911 . . . . . . 56, 209, 669
s. 1 . . . . 210, 211
s. 2 210
s. 3 210
s. 6 . . . . 24, 211
s. 7 210
s. 8 212
s. 9 . . . . 57, 212
Forgery Act 1913 . . . . . . 45, 56, 113, 182, 184
s. 1 . . . . 183, 186
s. 2 . . . . 39, 184, 185, 186, 669
s. 3 . . . . 184, 667
s. 4 . . . . 39, 184, 186
s. 5 184
s. 6 . . . . 183, 184, 185
s. 7 . . . . 39, 184
s. 8 . . . . 185, 186
s. 9 185
ss. 16, 17 184
s. 18 185
Criminal Justice Administration Act 1914—
s. 24 59
s. 28 . . . . 16, 215
s. 38 . . . . 30, 563
Bankruptcy Act 1914 174
s. 154 174
ss. 155, 156, 159, 164 174
Police, Factories, &c. (Miscellaneous Provisions) Act 1916, s. 5 392
Registration of Business Names Act 1916 . . . . 436, 444
s. 1 436
s. 18 436
s. 22 436
Prevention of Corruption Act 1916 222
Venereal Disease Act 1917 129

PAGE

Animals (Anaesthetics) Act 1919 485
Aliens Restriction (Amendment) Act 1919—
s. 3 206
Firearms Act 1920—
s. 9 461
s. 16 207
Emergency Powers Act 1920 235
Roads Act 1920 . . . . 600, 619, 630, 635
Official Secrets Act 1920 209
s. 1 . . . . 211, 423
ss. 3, 4 211
s. 5 212
s. 7 . . . . 12, 211
s. 8 42
Protection of Animals Act (1911) Amendment Act 1921 . 483
Celluloid and Cinematograph Film Act 1922 454
ss. 1, 2 . . . . 455, 456
s. 3 456
ss. 4–9 455
Sched. I 455
Explosives Act 1923 446
Law of Property Act 1925, s. 193 201
Performing Animals (Regulation) Act 1925—
s. 1 485
s. 2 486
s. 3 486
s. 4 486
s. 5 485
s. 7 486
Theatrical Employers Registration Act 1925—
ss. 1, 3, 4 533
ss. 5–7, 9, 10 534
s. 11 533
s. 13 . . . . 533, 534
Roads Improvement Act 1925, s. 6 595
Public Health Act 1925, s. 74 . . . . . . 24, 253
Criminal Justices Act 1925—
s. 12 . . . . . 35 s. 37 422
s. 13 . . . . . 79 s. 38 186
s. 28 . . . . . 219 s. 39 226
s. 34 . . . . . 670 s. 41 217
s. 35 . . . . . 183 s. 47 9
s. 36 . . . . 39, 185 s. 49 . . . . 32, 52
Parks Regulation (Amendment) Act 1926, s. 2 331
Births and Deaths Registration Act 1926 581
Coroners (Amendment) Act 1926—
s. 1 587
ss. 13, 14 585
s. 15 586
ss. 16, 18 585
s. 20 252
ss. 22–24 586
s. 25 586
Judicial Proceedings (Regulation of Reports) Act 1926 . . . 131

PAGE

Protection of Animals (Amendment) Act 1927, s. 1 . . . 483
Currency and Bank Notes Act 1928 186
s. 12 186
Dogs (Amendment) Act 1928 . . . . . . 490, 491
Petroleum (Consolidation) Act 1928 . . . . 56, 448, 454
ss. 1, 2 449
s. 6 . . . . 454, 456
ss. 7, 8 449
s. 19 . . . . 449, 456
s. 23 449
Agricultural Credits Act 1928, s. 11 39
Theatrical Employers Registration (Amendment) Act 1928 . 534
Infant Life (Preservation) Act 1929 . . . . . 136, 137
Road Traffic Act 1930—
s. 5 296
s. 45 267
Sentence of Death (Expectant Mothers) Act 1931 . . . 115
Architects (Registration) Act 1931 418
Destructive Imported Animals Act 1932 496
Sunday Entertainment Act 1932, s. 1 540
s. 2 540
ss. 3–5 540
Extradition Act 1932 670
Children and Young Persons Act 1933 . 4, 31, 56, 131, 137, 138, 140, 145, 146, 147, 412
s. 1 106, 140, 141, 143, 153, 156
s. 3 . 126, 141, 143, 156
s. 4 . 141, 143, 156, 391
s. 5 . . 141, 153, 561
s. 7 . 4, 141, 144, 156, 157
s. 10 153
s. 11 154
s. 12 . . . 142, 540
s. 13 . 20, 62, 114, 120, 126, 142, 143
s. 14 143
s. 15 143
s. 17 142
s. 18 . . 145, 146, 155
s. 19 . . . 145, 158
s. 20 . 145, 146, 157, 158
s. 21 . . . 145, 146
s. 22 145
s. 23 . . 143, 145, 147
s. 24 . . 145, 147, 154
s. 25 . . 145, 148, 158
s. 26 . . . 145, 146
s. 27 145
s. 28 . . . 145, 148
s. 29 145
s. 30 . . 145, 146, 147
s. 31 . . . 150, 157
s. 34 150
s. 36 . . . . 42, 154
s. 37 42
s. 38 . . 82, 85, 144, 154
s. 39 . . . 131, 150
s. 40 . 115, 118, 122, 126, 139, 143
ss. 41–43 144
s. 45 31
s. 46 . . 31, 33, 150, 151, 154, 157
s. 47 . . . . 31, 42
s. 48 . . . . 31, 151
s. 49 . . . . 131, 150
s. 50 . . . . 10, 154
s. 53 . . . . 115, 466
s. 56 151
s. 99 143
s. 107 . 138, 144, 154, 155, 157
Sched. I . 20, 126, 142, 143, 144
Protection of Animals (Cruelty to Dogs) Act 1933 . 492, 497, 500
Pharmacy and Poisons Act 1933 574
Administration of Justice (Miscellaneous Provisions) Act 1933, s. 2 37

PAGE

Protection of Animals Act 1934 486
Road Traffic Act 1934, s. 1 607
Incitement to Disaffection Act 1934—
s. 1 425
s. 2 425
s. 3 669
Betting and Lotteries Act 1934, s. 25 . . . . . 511, 514
Vagrancy Act 1935 . . . . 381, 407
Extradition Act 1935 116
Counterfeit Currency (Convention) Act 1935 . . . . 182, 186
ss. 1, 3, 4 182
Coinage Offence Act 1936 . . . . 39, 56, 179, 181, 182, 669
s. 1 . . . . 179, 182
s. 2 180
s. 3 . . . . 39, 180, 181, 182
s. 4 39
s. 5 181
s. 6 . . . . 180, 182
s. 7 . . . . 39, 180, 181, 182
s. 8 . . . . 20, 39, 180, 181, 182
ss. 9, 10 . . . . 180, 182
s. 11 . . . . 20, 180, 181
s. 13 182
s. 14 179
s. 17 . . . . 179, 182
Public Health Act 1936 . . . . 243, 572
s. 13 247
s. 27 . . . . 451, 454
s. 52 573
s. 59 539
ss. 72–82 573
s. 83 574
ss. 91–100, 107–109 . 573
s. 154 . . . 155, 572
ss. 159, 160 . . . 341
s. 162 582
s. 203 581
s. 224 128
s. 226 538
ss. 235–237 . . . 397
ss. 238–240 . . . 397
ss. 241–247 . . 397, 398
s. 248 397
s. 259 573
ss. 268, 269 . . . 574
s. 298 572
s. 343 573
Public Order Act 1936 . . . . 225, 230
s. 1 . . . . 25, 230, 231
s. 2 . . . . 231, 232
s. 3 232
s. 4 . . . . 25, 232
s. 5 . . . . 25, 232
s. 6 25
s. 7 . . . . 25, 231, 232, 233
s. 9 . . . . 230, 231, 232
Firearms Act 1937, s. 18 461
Cinematograph Films (Animals) Act 1937 . . . . 486, 537
Hydrogen Cyanide (Fumigation) Act 1937 587
Dogs Amendment Act 1938 489
Evidence Act 1938, ss. 3, 4 89
Infanticide Act 1938 . . . . 115, 137, 153
Architects Registration Act 1938 418

PAGE

House to House Collections Act 1939 . . . 393
s. 1 . . . 394, 395
s. 2 . . . 394, 395
s. 3 . . . 395
s. 4 . . . 393, 395, 397
s. 5 . . . 395
s. 6 . . . 394, 395
s. 7 . . . 395
s. 8 . . . 395, 397
s. 11 . . . 394
Official Secrets Act 1939 . . . 210, 211, 669
War Charities Act 1940 . . . 393
ss. 1–5 . . . 393
s. 7 . . . 393, 395
ss. **8**, 10, 11 . . . 393
Pharmacy and Medicines Act 1941 . . . 574
ss. 9, 10 . . . 136
Education Act 1944 . . . 137, 145
s. 35 . . . 145, 153, 155
ss. 36, 37 . . . 145
s. 39 . . . 145
s. 40 . . . 145, 155
s. 44 . . . 155
s. 58 . . . 146, 154
s. 114 . . . 145
s. 120 . . . 145
Sched. VIII . . . 154, 158
Statutory Instruments Act 1946 . . . 4
National Health Service Act 1946 . . . 605
Fire Services Act 1947 . . . 583
s. 2 . . . 582
s. 3 . . . 583
ss. 4–12 . . . 582
ss. 13–16, 30, 31, 38 . . . 583
Agriculture Act 1947, ss. 98, 100 . . . 197
Crown Proceedings Act 1947 . . . 222
Companies Act 1947, s. 116 . . . 436
Transport Act 1947 . . . 379
National Assistance Act 1948 . . . 140
s. 29 . . . 393
s. 41 . . . 393
s. 50 . . . 582
Companies Act 1948 . . . 433
s. 438 . . . 220
s. 439 . . . 436
s. 442 . . . 436
Sched. XV . . . 220
Children Act 1948 . . . 137, 139, 140, 159
s. 1 . . . 139, 158, 159
s. 2 . . . 139, 159
s. 3 . . . 140
s. 4 . . . 139
s. 5 . . . 155
ss. 10, 13 . . . 140
s. 19 . . . 140, 156
s. 38 . . . 139
ss. 39–41, 51 . . . 140
s. 59 . . . 140, 159
Nurseries and Child-Minders Regulations Act 1948 . . . 139
s. 1 . . . 139, 153
ss. 2, 3 . . . 139
s. 4 . . . 139, 153
ss. 5, 7, 8, 11 . . . 139
British Nationality Act 1948 . . . 410, 413

PAGE

British Nationality Act 1948—(*cont.*)
- s. 2 . . . . 110, 413
- s. 13 . . . . 110, 413
- s. 16 . . . . 110, 413

Criminal Justice Act 1948 . . . . . . 8, 137, 399
- ss. 1, 2 8
- s. 3 8
- s. 4 399
- s. 7 8
- s. 17 34
- s. 19 . . 152, 159, 402
- s. 20 . . 159, 399, 404
- s. 31 15
- s. 37 66
- s. 39 16
- s. 41 89
- s. 48 152
- s. 52 152
- s. 66 . . . . 20, 217
- s. 68 . . . . 27, 391
- s. 80 . . . . 400, 401
- Sched. I 702
- Sched. VIII . . . 489
- Sched. IX 31

Marriage Act 1949 581
- s. 2 . . . . 156, 582
- s. 75 581

Wireless Telegraphy Act 1949 . . . . 378, 382
- s. 1 378
- ss. 5, 13 378
- ss. 14, 15 379

Civil Aviation Act 1949 380
- s. 8 381
- s. 11 380
- s. 38 380
- ss. 43, 44, 49 381
- s. 60 380
- s. 66 383
- Sched. XII 383

Representation of the People Act 1949 222
- s. 84 . . . . 25, 323
- s. 87 223
- ss. 99, 100 223
- s. 101 223
- s. 146 223
- ss. 147, 159 223
- Sched. II 25, 223

Justices of the Peace Act 1949 32
- s. 3 32
- s. 15 319
- s. 44 30

Vehicles (Excise) Act 1949 . . . . 630, 635

Docking and Nicking of Horses Act 1949 488

British Transport Commission Act 1949 379
- s. 55 380
- s. 56 379

Merchant Shipping (Safety Convention) Act 1949, s. 26 . 380

Diseases of Animals Act 1950 . . . . . 479, 487, 489
- ss. 3–7 480
- ss. 8, 10–18 480
- ss. 20, 21 480
- s. 22 . . . . 480, 482
- ss. 23–36 480
- s. 37 . . . . . 480, 487
- s. 38 480
- s. 39 . . . . . 480, 487
- s. 40 . . . . . 480, 487
- ss. 41–43 480

PAGE

Diseases of Animals Act 1950—(*cont.*)
s. 44 . . . 480
ss. 45–49 . . . 480
s. 50 . . . 482, 488
s. 51 . . . 480
s. 59 . . . 481
s. 71 . . . 19, 481
ss. 73, 78–81, 83 . . 481
s. 84 . . . 480
s. 89 . . . 479
Scheds. I, II . . 480
Shops Act 1950 . . . 441, 548
ss. 1–12 . . . 441
s. 13 . . . 441
ss. 14–16 . . . 441
ss. 17–39 . . . 442
ss. 40–50 . . . 442
s. 51 . . . 442, 443
s. 52 . . . 442
ss. 53–56 . . . 442, 443
s. 57 . . . 442
s. 58 . . . 146, 443
s. 59 . . . 442
ss. 60–63 . . . 442, 443
s. 64 . . . 442
s. 65 . . . 442, 443
s. 66 . . . 442
s. 67 . . . 442
ss. 68–70 . . . 444
s. 71 . . . 444
s. 73 . . . 442
s. 74 . . 441, 443, 444
ss. 75–77 . . . 444
Scheds. I, II . . 441, 480
Scheds. V, VI . . 442
Sched. VII . . . 443
Gun Barrel Proof Act 1950 . . . 478
Pet Animals Act 1951 . . . 492, 497, 499, 500
ss. 1, 2 . . . 499
s. 3 . . . 154, 499
ss. 4–6 . . . 499
s. 7 . . . 499
Fraudulent Mediums Act 1951 . . . 392
ss. 1, 2 . . . 392
Midwives Act 1951 . . . 418
ss. 8, 9, 11 . . . 418
Fireworks Act 1951, ss. 1, 5 . . . 448
Cinematograph Act 1952—
s. 1 . . . 535
s. 3 . . . 535
s. 4 . . . 536
s. 5 . . . 536
s. 6 . . . 537
ss. 7, 9 . . . 535
Sched. . . . 535
Hypnotism Act 1952—
ss. 1, 2 . . . 541
s. 3 . . . 541
ss. 4, 6 . . . 541
Heating Appliances (Fire Guards) Act 1952 . . . 142
Defamation Act 1952 . . . 239
Cockfighting Act 1952 . . . 482
Children and Young Persons (Amendment) Act 1952 . . . 137
s. 8 . . . 142, 143, 154
s. 11 . . . 142, 143
Cremation Act 1952 . . . 582
Prison Act 1952 . . . 408
s. 8 . . . 25, 408
s. 13 . . . 408
s. 22 . . . 66, 408
s. 23 . . . 408
s. 25 . . . 11
s. 39 . . . 217, 408
ss. 40, 41 . . . 408
s. 43 . . . 151, 404, 408

PAGE

Prison Act 1952—(*cont.*)
s. 49 . . 25, 217, 408
Customs and Excise Act 1952
s. 5 . . . 386, 543
s. 7 419
s. 9 222
s. 10 543
ss. 15, 25 . . . 385
ss. 68–74 . . . 386
s. 93 . . . 544, 560
s. 106 . . . 544
ss. 116, 117, 121 . . 571
s. 125 . . 544, 560
ss. 126–138 . . 544
s. 139 . . 544, 560
ss. 140–142 . . . 544
s. 146 . . 544, 560
Magistrates' Courts Act 1952
s. 1 . 44, 45, 46, 50, 51, 52
s. 2 . . . 30, 31, 50
s. 3 . . . 46, 50
s. 4 . . . 32, 34
s. 6 . . . 35, 62
s. 7 . . . 35, 64
s. 8 . . . 60, 205
s. 13 . . . 33, 42, 51
s. 14 . . 33, 51, 62, 63
s. 15 33
ss. 16, 17 . . . 34
s. 18 . 31, 39, 40, 41, 50
s. 19 6, 13, 14, 31, 33, 38, 39, 40, 50, 68, 106, 108, 120, 138, 184, 185, 220, 378
s. 22 64
s. 23 40
s. 24 40
s. 25 7, 31, 39, 41, 107, 124, 133
s. 26 63
s. 28 64, 66, 149, 151, 159, 404
s. 29 40, 41, 64, 66, 101, 158, 300, 400
s. 35 13
s. 36 10
s. 37 48
s. 38 . . 27, 61, 149
s. 39 189
s. 40 . . 51, 149, 150
s. 41 79
s. 42 . . . 45, 64
s. 43 . . . 47, 51, 64
s. 44 47
s. 45 . . . 43, 47, 51
s. 46 . . . 47, 51, 63
s. 53 409
. 56, 182, 184, 385, 543, 570
s. 157 . . . 544
s. 161 . 431, 559, 560
ss. 173–188 . . . 548
s. 189 . . . 548
ss. 190–194 . . . 548
s. 274 . 386, 419, 544
s. 281 . . . 386
s. 283 . . . 65
s. 296 . . 386, 544
s. 297 . . 386, 545
s. 298 . . . 386
s. 307 . 543, 545, 570
Sched. X . . . 517
. 6, 30, 31, 33, 58, 62, 64, 421
s. 47 . . . 47, 63
ss. 48–55 . . . 47
s. 56 31
s. 57 . . . 31, 42, 85
ss. 58–62 . . . 31
s. 64 54
s. 66 55
s. 67 54
s. 68 55
s. 71 403
s. 77 . . 47, 49, 50, 97
s. 78 . . . 34, 82
s. 81 51
s. 82 . . . 49, 220
s. 83 . . . 64, 65
s. 87 . . . 65, 66
s. 88 65
s. 89 . . . 64, 65, 66
s. 90 . . . 65, 66
s. 91 225
s. 92 59
s. 93 62
s. 94 226
s. 95 59
s. 96 . . . 59, 61
s. 97 61
s. 98 . . . 30, 41, 63
s. 99 . . . 34, 42
s. 100 . . . 45, 47
s. 101 . . . 46, 52
s. 102 . 52, 53, 55, 56
s. 103 53
s. 104 . . . 45, 68
s. 105 . . . 58, 61, 63
s. 107 34
s. 108 34

PAGE

Magistrates' Courts Act 1952—(*cont.*)
s. 109 . . 34, 58
s. 110 . . 34, 58
s. 111 . . 34, 58
s. 121 . . 30, 32
ss. 123, 124 . . . 30
s. 125 . . . 6, 31
s. 126 . 30, 63, 138, 400
s. 130 31
Sched. I 7, 13, 14, 38, 39, 40, 106, 108, 120, 163, 184, 185, 220, 378
Sched. II 10
Sched. V 35
Prevention of Crime Act 1953 . . . . . . 24, 408
s. 1 408
Emergency Laws (Misc. Provisions) Act 1953 446
Dogs (Protection of Livestock) Act 1953 490
s. 1 490
s. 2 490
s. 3 490
Births and Deaths Registration Act 1953 581
Post Office Act 1953 . . . . 184, 376
ss. 3, 4 376
s. 11 . . . . 11, 377
s. 23 . . . . 185, 377
s. 53 . . . . 39, 53
ss. 55, 56 . . . 39, 376
s. 57 . . . . 39, 377
s. 58 . . . . 39, 377
s. 59 377
ss. 60, 61 376
ss. 62–65 377
s. 65A 377
s. 68 12
s. 87 377
Currency and Bank Notes Act 1954 186
Protection of Birds Act 1954 . . . . . . 492, 495
s. 1 . . . . 492, 495
s. 2 . . . . 493, 494
s. 3 495
s. 5 . . . . 493, 494
s. 6 494
s. 7 494
s. 8 495
s. 10 . . . . 493, 494
s. 12 . . . . 493, 495
s. 14 493
Sched. I . . . 493, 495
Sched. II . . . 493, 494
Sched. III . . . 493, 494
Sched. IV 494
Coroners Act 1954 584
Pharmacy Act 1954 574
Protection of Animals (Amendment) Act 1954 483, 492, 497, 500
Protection of Animals (Anaesthetics) Act 1954 485
Pests Act 1954 483
s. 2 197
Children and Young Persons (Harmful Publications) Act 1955 153
Army Act 1955 . . . . 423, 424
s. 42 420
s. 155 548
s. 156 424
ss. 157–162 424
s. 166 305
s. 168 424
ss. 171, 172 . . . 425
s. 186 . . . 19, 421
ss. 191, 192 . . . 421
s. 195 . . 20, 421, 422
s. 196 422
s. 197 423
Air Force Act 1955 . . . . 423, 424
s. 42 420
s. 156 424
ss. 157–162 424
s. 166 305
s. 168 424
ss. 171, 172 425
s. 186 420
ss. 191, 192 . . . 421
s. 195 . . . 421, 422
s. 196 422
s. 197 423

PAGE

Revision of the Army and Air Force Acts (Transitional Provisions) Act 1955—
- s. 4 . . . 535, 538
- Sched. III . . . 535, 538

Food and Drugs Act 1955 . . . 440
- ss. 1, 2 . . . 440
- s. 9 . . . 440, 441, 573
- s. 13 . . . 572
- s. 24 . . . 573
- s. 89 . . . 261
- s. 135 . . . 440

Food and Drugs (Scotland) Act 1956, s. 27 . . . 261

Dentists Act 1956 . . . 416

Magistrates' Courts (Appeals from Binding Over Orders) Act 1956 . . . 226

Clean Air Act 1956 . . . 573

Hotel Proprietors Act 1956—
- s. 1 . . . 545, 546
- s. 2 . . . 545
- Sched. . . . 546

Sexual Offences Act 1956 . . . 35, 56, 117, 126, 669
- s. 1 . . . 119, 465
- s. 2 . . . 109, 119, 143
- ss. 3, 4 . . . 119, 143
- s. 5 . . . 119, 143, 154
- s. 6 119, 143, 156, 160, 582
- s. 7 . . . 119, 143
- s. 9 . . . 120
- s. 10 . . . 120, 143
- s. 11 . . . 121, 143, 157
- s. 12 . . . 118, 132, 143
- s. 13 . . . 132, 143
- s. 14 . 120, 143, 156, 582
- s. 15 106, 118, 132, 143, 156
- s. 16 . . . 118, 132, 143
- s. 17 . . . 122, 465
- s. 19 . . . 122, 143, 158
- s. 20 . 122, 143, 156, 465
- s. 21 . . . 123
- s. 22 . . . 118, 121, 143
- s. 23 . 118, 121, 143, 159
- s. 24 . . . 122, 143
- s. 25 . . . 122, 143
- s. 26 . . . 122, 143, 156
- s. 27 . . . 122
- s. 28 . 120, 123, 143, 156
- s. 29 . . . 123
- ss. 30, 31 . 7, 39, 41, 123
- s. 32 7, 39, 41, 118, 123, 132
- ss. 33–35 . . . 125
- s. 36 . . . 123
- s. 38 . . . 121
- s. 39 . . . 118, 132
- s. 40 . . . 26, 118, 126
- s. 41 . 26, 118, 123, 126
- ss. 42–44 . . . 118
- s. 45 . . . 118, 120, 122
- s. 46 . . . 118
- Sched. I . . . 125
- Sched. II 118, 119, 123, 125, 132

Medical Act 1956, s. 31 . . . 416

Homicide Act 1957—
- s. 2 . . . 113
- ss. 3, 4 . . . 114

Nurses Act 1957 . . . 417
- s. 27 . . . 418

Nurses Agencies Act 1957 . . . 418

Solicitors Act 1957 . . . 416

Dentists Act 1957 . . . 416

Magistrates' Courts Act 1957 . . . 33
- s. 1 . . . 33, 150, 302
- s. 3 . . . 101
- s. 4 . . . 33

PAGE
Geneva Conventions Act 1957, s. 6 437
Naval Discipline Act 1957 321
ss. 96, 97 421
s. 98 . . . . 421, 422
s. 99 422
s. 105 421
Slaughter of Animals Act 1958—
s. 1 497
Opticians Act 1958 417
ss. 20–22 417
Litter Act 1958 588
s. 1 588
Horse-Breeding Act 1958 486
ss. 1, 10 487
s. 11 487
Prevention of Fraud (Investments) Act 1958 . . . 432
s. 1 . . . . 433, 669
s. 2 433
ss. 3–9 433
ss. 10, 11 433
s. 13 433
s. 14 . . . . 433, 669
ss. 15–17 433
ss. 18–20 434
s. 26 . . . . 432, 433
Trading Representations (Disabled Persons) Act 1958 . . 432
s. 1 444
Children Act 1958 . . . . 137, 138
ss. 1, 2 138
s. 3 . . . . 138, 155
ss. 4, 5 138
s. 6 . . . . 138, 139
s. 7 . . . . 138, 139
s. 8 . . . . 138, 139
ss. 9–13 138
s. 14 . . . . 138, 139
ss. 15, 16 138
s. 17 . . . . 138, 159
Manœuvres Act 1958 420
County Courts Act 1959 218
ss. 30, 127 218
s. 188 418
Highways Act 1959 . . . . 247, 293
s. 117 . . . 247, 583
s. 121 . . . 23, 243
s. 127 . . . 248, 431
s. 135 . . . 218, 250
s. 140 . . . 248, 583
s. 141 248
ss. 143, 146, 152 . . 249
s. 249 . . . . 595, 643
ss. 262, 271 . . . 249
s. 295 248
Restriction of Offensive Weapons Act 1959 409
Fire Services Act 1959 582
Dog Licences Act 1959 . . . . 488, 489
s. 1 488
ss. 2, 3 488
s. 4 489
s. 9 488
s. 12 488
s. 13 488

PAGE

Street Offences Act 1959 124
s. 1 . . . . 26, 124 s. 2 124
Obscene Publications Act 1959 . . . . . 56, 92, 129
s. 1 130
s. 2 . . . . 130, 131
s. 3 130
s. 4 131
Mental Health Act 1959 . . 120, 133, 185, 399, 401, 579, 581
s. 4 . . . . . 579 s. 135 580
s. 40 . . . 579, 581 s. 136 . . . 24, 581
s. 60 . . 8, 352, 399, 579 s. 140 581
ss. 127, 128 . . . 120 Sched. VII 63
Road Traffic Act 1960 259, 299, 314, 320, 325, 337, 340, 341, 346, 372
s. 14 . . . . . 329 s. 144 . 159, 347, 352
s. 74 . . . . . 267 s. 145 . . 347, 352
s. 100 . . . 296 s. 147 . 25, 351, 352
s. 117 . 340, 342, 352 s. 148 . . 350, 352
s. 118 . . 342, 352 ss. 149–155 . . . 352
ss. 119, 120 . . 343, 352 s. 156 . . . 352
ss. 121–126 . . . 352 s. 157 . . 351, 352
s. 127 343, 352, 589, 590 ss. 158–163 . . . 352
ss. 128, 129 . . 343, 352 s. 232 . . . 312
s. 132 . . 343, 352 s. 233 . . 185, 313
s. 133 . . 345, 352 s. 239 . . . 315
ss. 134–140 . . 345, 352 s. 253 . . . 627
ss. 141, 142 . . 352 s. 269 . . . 325
s. 143 . . 346, 352 Sched. XII 342
Indecency with Children Act 1960 35, 118, 126, 134, 137, 143, 154
ss. 1, 2 134
Game Laws (Amendment) Act 1960 . . 24, 195, 196, 197
s. 1 23
Civil Aviation (Licensing) Act 1960 380
s. 7 381
Abandonment of Animals Act 1960 . . . . 19, 482
Charities Act 1960 392
Administration of Justice Act 1960 66
s. 11 216
ss. 14, 15 67
s. 16 67
Professions Supplementary to Medicines Act 1960 . . . 416
ss. 1, 2 416
ss. 6, 7 416
Noise Abatement Act 1960 588
s. 1 588
s. 2 . . . . 588, 606
Oaths Act 1961 82
Restriction of Offensive Weapons Act 1961 409
Printers' Imprint Act 1961 437
Factories Act 1961 456
Finance Act 1961, s. 11 . . . . 197, 432
Criminal Justice Act 1961—
s. 1 . . . . 156, 399, 404
s. 4 . . . . 151, 152, 155, 399
s. 8 157

PAGE

Criminal Justice Act 1961—(*cont.*)
ss. 11, 12 404
s. 13 152
s. 22 218
s. 29 . . . . 67, 586
s. 30 25
s. 35 . . . . 21, 217
Sched. I. 152
Consumer Protection Act 1961 583
Mock Auctions Act 1961, s. 1 . . . . . . 434, 435
s. 3 434
Suicide Act 1961 . . . . 114, 143
s. 1 114
s. 2 . . . . 115, 670
Sched. I 587
Licensing Act 1961 539
s. 6 554
Highways (Miscellaneous Provisions) Act 1961 247
s. 7 247
Public Health Act 1961—
s. 37 574
s. 42 . . . . 155, 572
s. 74 495
Criminal Justice Administration Act 1962 106
s. 13 . . . . 40, 41
Sched. III 137
Animals (Cruel Poisons) Act 1962 484
Marriage (Wales and Monmouthshire) Act 1962 . . . 581
Acts of Parliament Numbering and Citation Act 1962 . . 4
Penalties for Drunkenness Act 1962 564
Road Traffic Act 1962—
s. 5 299
Betting, Gaming and Lotteries Act 1963 . . . 4, 20, 56, 570
s. 1 . . . . 504, 505, 507, 509
s. 2 . . . . 505, 509
s. 3 505
s. 4 . . . . 504, 506, 509
ss. 5, 6 . . . . 506, 509
s. 7 506
s. 8 . . . . 20, 507, 509, 519
s. 9 . . . . 503, 504, 507
s. 10 . . . . 508, 509, 510
ss. 11–15 510
s. 16 506
ss. 17–20 510
s. 21 . . . . 158, 505, 510
s. 22 . . . . 158, 511
ss. 23–31 511
s. 33 516
s. 41 . . . . 512, 515
s. 42 . . . . 511, 514, 515, 669
s. 43 . . . . 511, 512, 514, 516, 517, 528
s. 44 . . . . 511, 513, 517

PAGE

Betting, Gaming and Lotteries Act 1963—(*cont.*)
s. 45 . . . . 511, 514, 517, 528
s. 46 511
s. 47 514
s. 48 . . . . 514, 515, 516
s. 49 . . . . 515, 525
ss. 51–53 515
s. 54 516
s. 55 . . . . 505, 506, 514
s. 56 539
Sched. II 504
Sched. IV 504, 507, 508, 509
Sched. V 510
Sched. VI 504, 515
Sched. VII 513, 514
Purchase Tax Act 1963, s. 23 644
Nursing Homes Act 1963 579
Protection of Depositors Act 1963 433
s. 1 435
Weights and Measures Act 1963 440
s. 59 544
Deer Act 1963—
ss. 1–3 198
s. 4 198
s. 5 . . . . 22, 198
s. 6 198
s. 7 199
Scheds. I, II 198
Children and Young Persons Act 1963 137
s. 3 145
s. 9 20
s. 10 20
s. 16 . . . . 10, 102, 154
s. 17 31
s. 18 . . . . 151, 157
s. 23 156
s. 25 150
s. 27 . . . . 35, 154
s. 28 82
s. 34 146
s. 35 146
s. 37 . . . . 146, 147, 148, 156
s. 41 147
s. 43 148
s. 48 139
s. 57 150
Sched. II 31
Sched. III 31, 140, 146, 148
Sched. V 150
Criminal Justice (Scotland) Act 1963—
s. 39 53
s. 40 33
Animal Boarding Establishments Act 1963 . . 492, 497, 500
s. 1 500

PAGE

Animal Boarding Establishments Act 1963—(*cont.*)
ss. 2, 3, 5 500
Public Order Act 1963. 233
s. 6 233
Married Women's Property Act 1964 414
Fireworks Act 1964 448
Licensing Act 1964 . . . 56, 147, 542, 548, 552, 565
s. 1 543
s. 2 548
s. 3 550
s. 5 550
s. 6 . . . . 548, 550
s. 7 . . . . 549, 550
s. 9 . . . . 125, 552
s. 10 551
s. 11 551
s. 12 550
s. 15 550
s. 19 550
s. 20 557
s. 21 . . . . 549, 550, 551
s. 26 . . . . 548, 549
ss. 28–35. 552
ss. 36, 39, 40, 41 543
ss. 44, 45, 47, 49 565
ss. 50–52, 54, 55 565
s. 59 . . . . 552, 560
ss. 60, 61 553
s. 62 565
s. 63 . . . . 552, 553, 560
s. 64 556
s. 65 . . . . 543, 555
s. 66 554
s. 68 . . . . 554, 560
s. 69 554
s. 70 . . . . 553, 555
ss. 71–73. 555
s. 74 556
s. 76 . . . . 553, 554
s. 77 554
s. 80 556
ss. 81, 84 555
s. 85 555
s. 86 554
s. 87 552
s. 89 . . . . 554, 556
s. 90 654
s. 93 551
s. 94 . . . . 546, 547
s. 96 547
s. 98 547
s. 100 . . . . 125, 126, 552
ss. 108–117 570
s. 160 . . . . 542, 552, 559, 560

PAGE

Licensing Act 1964—(*cont.*)
s. 161 560
s. 162 558
s. 163 559
s. 164 560
s. 165 559
s. 166 . . . . 559, 561
s. 167 . . . . 156, 544
s. 168 . . . . 142, 155, 557, 561
s. 169 . . . . . . 142, 157, 159, 558, 559, 561
s. 170 . . . . 142, 558
s. 171 557
s. 172 . . . . 545, 558
s. 173 . . . . 545, 561
s. 174 . . . . 545, 558, 561, 564
s. 175 . . . . 125, 545, 557
s. 176 . . . . 125, 545, 557
s. 177 . . . . 517, 545, 558
s. 178 . . . . 222, 545, 557, 559
s. 179 . . . . 125, 126, 545, 565
s. 180 545
s. 181 544
s. 182 . . . . 538, 539, 548
s. 183 556
s. 184 557
s. 185 556
s. 186 . . . . 556, 562
s. 187 . . . . 23, 562
s. 188 . . . . 228, 556
s. 189 551
s. 190 . . . . 557, 585
s. 194 561
s. 196 562
s. 199 . . . . 532, 543, 560, 571
s. 200 . . . . 543, 563
s. 201 . . . . . . 543, 545, 546, 552, 557, 560
Sched. II 549, 550, 551
Sched. XIV 550
Emergency Powers Act 1964 234
Merchant Shipping Act 1964, s. 17 380
Protection of Animals (Anaesthetics) Act 1964 . . . 485
Police Act 1964 . . . . 228, 414
s. 17 222
s. 18 415
s. 19 415
s. 47 229
s. 51 . . . . 107, 415, 465
s. 52 . . . . 415, 419
s. 53 . . . . 222, 416
Sched. II 415
Scrap Metal Dealers Act 1964 426
s. 1 . . . . 426, 427, 428
s. 2 . . . . 427, 428
ss. 3, 4 428

PAGE

Scrap Metal Dealers Act 1964—(*cont.*)
s. 5 . . . . 141, 156, 429
s. 6 429
s. 9 . . . . 426, 428, 429, 430
Riding Establishments Act 1964 . . . . . 159, 497
s. 1 498
s. 2 . . . . 498, 499
s. 3 499
ss. 5, 6 499
Trading Stamps Act 1964—
ss. 1–3, 5 444
ss. 6–8 445
Obscene Publications Act 1964 . . . . . 56, 92, 129
s. 1 . . . . 130, 131
s. 2 131
Diplomatic Privileges Act 1964, s. 4 90
Refreshment Houses Act 1964 552
Industrial and Provident Societies Act 1965 433
Criminal Evidence Act 1965. 92
British Nationality Act 1965 . . . . . . 110, 413
Shops (Early Closing Days) Act 1965 441
Backing of Warrants (Republic of Ireland) Act 1965 . . 53
Redundancy Payments Act 1965 220
Criminal Procedure (Attendance of Witnesses) Act 1965 . . 78
s. 1 36
s. 2 . . . . 49, 79
s. 3 217
s. 4 49
s. 8 50
Murder (Abolition of Death Penalty) Act 1965 . . . 115
s. 1 115
Race Relations Act 1965—
s. 6 233
s. 7 232
Rent Act 1965—
s. 30 . . . . 233, 234
s. 32 234
Irish Extradition Act 1965 53
Supplementary Benefit Act 1966 85
See Ministry of Social Security Act 1966
s. 29 219
s. 31 419
s. 32 435
s. 33 85
Veterinary Surgeons Act 1966 416
s. 20 416
Local Government Act 1966, s. 36 489
General Rate Act 1967—
s. 99 . . . . 52, 55
s. 102 54
Private Places of Entertainment (Licensing) Act 1967 . . 538
Agriculture Act 1967 480
s. 23 480
Slaughter of Poultry Act 1967 496

PAGE

Refreshment Houses Act 1967 568
Marine &c., Broadcasting (Offences) Act 1967 . . . 379
s. 6 379
Protection of Birds Act 1967 . . . . . . 493, 495
s. 3 494
s. 4 495
ss. 5–7 495
s. 11 495
Tokyo Convention Act 1967—
s. 1 . . . . 110, 385
s. 2 110
s. 4 213
s. 5 110
Sched. 213
Finance Act 1967 . . . . 543, 544
Sched. VII 543, 544, 545, 556, 560, 562
Criminal Law Act 1967 . . . . . 6, 7, 14, 21, 107, 399
s. 1 7
s. 2 . . . . 22, 53, 79, 168
s. 3 406
s. 4 . . . . 14, 39
s. 5 14
s. 12 205
Sched. II 406
Sched. III 123, 137
Sexual Offences Act 1967 132
s. 1 . . . . 120, 133, 160
s. 2 133
s. 4 . . . . 39, 132, 133
s. 5 . . . . . . 7, 26, 39, 41, 124, 125, 133
s. 7 133
s. 8 134
Fugitive Offenders Act 1967 . . . . . . 15, 670
Civic Amenities Act 1967 587
s. 19 587
Road Traffic Regulation Act 1967 . . . . . 293, 313
s. 1 325
s. 5 325
ss. 6, 7 325
s. 8 259
s. 9 325
s. 10 325
ss. 11, 12 325
s. 13 695
ss. 15, 16 325
s. 17 326
ss. 18–22 326
s. 23 . . . . 326, 695
s. 24 328
ss. 25, 26 . . . 328, 695
s. 26A 695
ss. 27–32 328
ss. 33–37 328
ss. 38, 39 328
s. 40 328
s. 41 328
s. 42 . . . . 324, 328
s. 43 328
s. 44 328
ss. 45, 46 328
ss. 47–51 328
s. 53 326
ss. 54, 55 328
s. 56 328
s. 57 328
s. 58 . . . . 328, 329
ss. 59, 60 328
s. 61 . . . . 328, 329
ss. 62–68 328
s. 71 607
s. 72 . . . . 330, 606
ss. 74, 75 330

PAGE

Road Traffic Regulation Act 1967—(*cont.*)
s. 77 . . 317, 330, 331
s. 78 . . 294, 317, 331
s. 78A . 317, 331, 695
s. 79 . . . 332, 602
s. 80 332
s. 81 332
s. 85 312
s. 86 . . . 313, 314
s. 87 326
s. 99 322
s. 100 603
s. 103 323
s. 112 325
Sched. III 325
Sched. V 587, 629, 643, 654
Sched. VIII 607

Criminal Justice Act 1967 33
s. 1 35
s. 2 . . 36, 40, 78, 229
s. 3 36
s. 4 36
s. 5 238
s. 6 36
s. 8 5
s. 9 . . . 68, 88, 221
s. 10 89
s. 11 100
s. 18 . . . 60, 138
s. 20 . . 390, 404, 407
s. 23 . . . 21, 61
s. 24 . . 33, 46, 52, 138
s. 25 130
s. 27 . . . 39, 184
s. 28 30
s. 29 10
s. 30 . . . 62, 63
s. 33 . 16, 51, 138, 149, 155
s. 44 702
s. 65 8
s. 89 . . . 36, 88, 221

Sea Fish (Conservation) Act 1967, ss. 1, 16, 22 200

Abortion Act 1967 136
ss. 1, 5 136

Criminal Appeal Act 1968—
s. 1 65
s. 7 65
s. 10 . . . . 65, 390
s. 30 191
s. 33 65
s. 42 191

Firearms Act 1968 154
s. 1 419, 458, 459, 460, 469, 473, 475, 477
s. 2 . . 459, 464, 474
s. 3 . 419, 459, 460, 462
s. 4 460
s. 5 . 460, 461, 463, 477
s. 6 . . . 461, 475
s. 7 462
s. 8 462
s. 9 . . . 462, 473
s. 10 463
s. 11 . . 463, 467, 468
s. 12 . . . 463, 464
ss. 13–16 464
s. 17 . . 107, 464, 465
s. 18 . . . 465, 475
s. 19 . . 23, 466, 476
s. 20 . 23, 419, 466, 475, 476
s. 21 . . 23, 466, 467
s. 22 155, 157, 467, 468, 475
s. 23 . . 157, 467, 468
s. 24 . 154, 156, 468
ss. 25, 26 . . . 468
ss. 27–29 . . . 409
s. 30 . . . 465, 470
s. 32 . . . 470, 471
s. 33 . . 470, 471, 472
s. 34 . . . 471, 472
s. 35 472
s. 36 472
s. 37 472
ss. 38, 39 . . . 472
ss. 40, 41 . . 472, 473
s. 42 474
s. 44 468, 469, 470, 472, 474
s. 45 474
s. 46 474

PAGE

Firearms Act 1968—(*cont.*)
s. 47 . . 23, 475, 476
s. 48 . . . 23, 476
s. 49 . . . 475, 476
s. 50 . . 22, 475, 476
s. 51 669
s. 52 475
s. 53 . . . 459, 477
ss. 54, 56 . . . 477
s. 57 . . 465, 477, 478
s. 58 478
Sched. I . . . 464
Sched. IV . . 472, 473
Trade Descriptions Act 1968 602
ss. 1, 2, 26 438
Agriculture (Miscellaneous Provisions) Act 1968 . . . 484
s. 1 484
Health Services and Public Health Act 1968—
s. 10 418
s. 47 571
s. 60 139
Theatres Act 1968 . . . . 529, 533
s. 1 529
s. 2 . . . . 529, 530, 532
s. 3 . . . . 529, 530
ss. 5, 6 . . . . 530, 532
s. 7 . . . . 529, 530
s. 8 530
ss. 9, 10 . . . . 530, 531
s. 12 531
s. 13 532
ss. 14–16 532
s. 17 533
Sched. I 531
Sched. II 532, 543
Hovercraft Act 1969 323
Theft Act 1968 . . . . . 39, 56, 84, 163, 174, 376
s. 1 . . 164, 169, 173
s. 2 . . 164, 165, 169
s. 3 165
s. 4 164, 165, 166, 173, 187
s. 5 . . 164, 166, 173
s. 6 . . 164, 166, 167
s. 8 167
ss. 9, 10 . . . 163
s. 11 167
s. 12 26, 167, 168, 173, 334, 465, 695
ss. 13, 14 . . . 168
s. 15 167, 169, 170, 171, 172
ss. 16, 17 . . 169, 170
ss. 18, 19 . . . 170
s. 20 . . . 170, 171
s. 21 . . . 109, 171
s. 22 171
s. 23 . . . 26, 172
s. 24 . . . 171, 172
s. 25 . 26, 172, 173, 695
s. 26 . . . 56, 188
s. 27 . . . 89, 94, 171
s. 28 . . . 191, 192
s. 29 163, 164, 167, 169, 170, 171, 173
s. 30 . . . 84, 85
s. 32 . . . 171, 200
s. 34 109, 165, 166, 171, 173
Sched. I . 26, 173, 174, 200
Clean Air Act 1968 573
Civil Evidence Act 1968, s. 10 319
Gaming Act 1968 . . . . 56, 503, 514, 517, 558
s. 1 517
ss. 2–4 . . . . 518, 519
s. 5 . . . . 20, 519
s. 6 . . . . 517, 519, 558
s. 7 . . . . 158, 519
s. 8 519

PAGE

Gaming Act 1968—(*cont.*)
s. 9 519
s. 10 519
s. 12 . . . . 519, 521, 523, 524
s. 13 . . . . 521, 523, 524
s. 14 . . . . 521, 523, 524
s. 15 . . . . 522, 523, 524
ss. 16–19 . . . . 522, 523, 524
s. 20 . . . . 521, 522, 523, 524
s. 21 . . . . 522, 523
s. 22 523
s. 23 . . . . 523, 524
s. 24 524
s. 26 . . . . 524, 525
s. 27 525
ss. 28–30 525
ss. 31–33 . . . . 525, 527
s. 34 . . . . 525, 526, 527
s. 35 527
s. 36 527
s. 40 518
s. 41 527
s. 43 527
s. 52 . . . . 517, 522, 528
Scheds. II–IV 524
Medicines Act 1968 417
s. 25 417
Transport Act 1968 . . . . . . 324, 326, 352, 353, 355
s. 30 . . . . 185, 345, 351
s. 35 343
s. 90 354
s. 95 354
s. 96 . . . . 354, 630, 634, 637
s. 98 354
s. 99 355
s. 102 355
s. 126 325
s. 127 . . . . 313, 328
s. 128 325
s. 130 328
s. 145 342
Genocide Act 1969 . . . . 115, 116
s. 1 116
Representation of the People Act 1969 . . . . . 159, 222
Tattooing of Minors Act 1969 159
ss. 1, 3 153
Ponies Act 1969 487
Family Law Reform Act 1969—
s. 1 . . . . 138, 158
s. 2 159
s. 9 160
s. 12 158
s. 20 419
s. 24 419

PAGE

Family Law Reform Act 1969—(*cont.*)
Sched. I 121, 158, 511, 541
Post Office Act 1969 376
s. 78 378
s. 134 488
Sched. IV 185, 210
Sched. V. 378
Late Night Refreshment Houses Act 1969 . . 125, 126, 565
ss. 1, 2, 6, 7 569
s. 8 . . . . 569, 570
s. 9 . . . . 125, 517, 564, 570
s. 10 570
Children and Young Persons Act 1969 . . . 137, 144, 157
s. 1 145
s. 6 39
s. 10 150
s. 29 149
s. 49 140
s. 50 . . . . 140, 156
Sched. V. . . . 33, 36, 88, 138, 140, 141, 149, 150, 158, 159
Firearms Act (Northern Ireland) 1968, s. 19 466
Game Act 1970 197
s. 1 432
Conservation of Seals Act 1970—
s. 1 . . . . 500, 501, 502
ss. 2, 3 . . . . 501, 502
s. 4 . . . . 20, 501
s. 6 501
ss. 7, 8 501
ss. 9, 10 . . . . 500, 502
s. 11 502
Administration of Justice Act 1970 234
s. 40 . . . . 234, 235
s. 50 138
Riding (Establishments Act 1970 497
s. 3 499
Merchant Shipping Act 1970—
ss. 31, 95 380
Chronically Sick and Disabled Persons Act 1970—
s. 20 . . . . 293, 367
s. 21 293
Indecent Advertisements (Amendment) Act 1970, s. 1 . . . 129
Vehicles (Excise) Act 1971 . 308, 320, 359, 365, 372, 602, 630, 635, 644, 651
ss. 1–3 360
s. 4 366
s. 5 366
s. 6 366
s. 7 . . . . 365, 366, 367
s. 8 360
s. 12 . . . . 360, 362
s. 16 . . . . 360, 367, 368
ss. 17, 18 360
s. 19 . . . . 360, 362

PAGE

Vehicles (Excise) Act 1971—(*cont.*)
s. 21 373
s. 22 362
s. 26 . . . . 185, 360
s. 27 360
s. 38 . . . . 341, 360
Sched. III 365
Sched. IV 341, 601, 651
Animals Act 1971, s. 9 . . . . 489, 502
s. 7 502
s. 11 490
Courts Act 1971 29
Sched. VIII 66
Coinage Act 1971—
ss. 9, 10 180
s. 12 181
Betting, Gaming and Lotteries (Amendment) Act 1971, ss. 1, 2 506
Dangerous Litter Act 1971 588
Misuse of Drugs Act 1971—
ss. 2, 3 576
ss. 4–6 . . . . 576, 578
s. 7 576
s. 8 577
s. 9 577
ss. 10–13 577
ss. 17–20 576
s. 23 . . . . 577, 578
s. 24 . . . . 24, 578
s. 27 578
s. 28 . . . . 576, 578
s. 37 578
Sched. II 576
Highways Act 1971 249
s. 30 328
s. 31 249
ss. 32, 33 250
Criminal Damage Act 1971 . . . . 20, 56, 176
s. 1 . . . . 39, 176, 177, 465
s. 2 . . . . 39, 109, 176, 177
s. 3 . . . . 39, 177
s. 5 177
ss. 6, 9 178
s. 10 178
Finance Act 1971, s. 7 . . . . 366, 367
Hijacking Act 1971 111
s. 1 110
Immigration Act 1971 . . . . 23, 410, 412
s. 1 . . . . 411, 412
ss. 2, 3 412
ss. 24, 25 . . . 23, 413, 414
Sunday Cinema Act 1972, s. 1 540
Road Traffic Act 1972 . . . 25, 243, 251, 293, 297, 300, 305, 308, 323, 325, 337, 338, 355, 357, 359, 373, 603

PAGE

Road Traffic Act 1972—(*cont.*)
s. 1 . 319, 324, 586, 587
s. 2 252, 254, 311, 319, 324, 695, 696
s. 3 253, 254, 311, 319, 324, 696
s. 4 156, 157, 158, 159, 254, 255, 300, 319, 320, 324, 257
s. 5 26, 256, 257, 258, 259, 260, 261, 262, 298, 302, 314, 319, 324, 334, 563, 696
s. 6 256, 257, 260, 261, 262, 298, 302, 319, 321, 696
s. 7 257, 259, 261, 319, 321
s. 8 257, 258, 259, 261, 262, 319, 321, 335, 696
s. 9 256, 259, 260, 261, 262, 298, 302, 319, 321, 696
s. 10 90, 257, 260, 261, 319, 321
s. 11 . 261, 262, 319, 321
s. 12 . . . 261, 262
s. 13 262
s. 14 . . 262, 319, 324
s. 15 . . 262, 312, 319
s. 16 . . 262, 319, 637
s. 17 262, 263, 311, 317, 319, 338, 695, 696
s. 18 263, 311, 317, 319, 339
s. 19 26, 263, 319, 334, 339, 563
s. 20 . . . 263, 319
s. 21 . . 263, 319, 338
s. 22 250, 251, 264, 308, 319, 329, 330, 334
s. 22A . . . 264
ss. 23, 24 . . 264, 319
s. 25 . . 264, 265, 319
s. 26 . . 265, 319, 326
ss. 27, 28 . . . 319
s. 29 . . 265, 319, 324
s. 30 . 265, 319, 324, 338
s. 31 . . 266, 319, 491
s. 32 . . 266, 312, 319
s. 33 266
s. 34 266, 319, 324, 603, 630, 632, 634, 638, 643
s. 35 . . . 267, 319
s. 36 . 201, 267, 319, 324
s. 36A
s. 36B. . . 267, 312
s. 37 . . . 267, 319
s. 40 268, 314, 319, 324, 375
s. 41 . . . 268, 319
s. 42 268, 291, 319, 602, 663
s. 43 268, 269, 315, 319, 600
s. 44 269, 310, 319, 320, 324
s. 45 268, 269, 312, 314, 319, 320, 600
s. 46 . 269, 310, 319, 320
s. 47 312, 314, 315, 319, 320
ss. 48, 49 . . 319, 320
s. 50 . . 312, 319, 320
s. 51 319
s. 52 . . . 319, 324
s. 53 . 270, 312, 319, 650
s. 54 319
s. 55 . . . 312, 319
s. 56 257, 258, 259, 312, 314, 315, 319, 320, 355, 650
ss. 57, 58 . . 315, 319
s. 59 . 312, 315, 319, 355
s. 60 . . 270, 319, 324
s. 60A . . . 270
s. 61 319
s. 62 319
ss. 63, 64 . . . 319
s. 65 . . . 319, 634
s. 66 . . . 319, 388
s. 67 319
s. 68 270, 272, 273, 274, 275, 276, 277, 278, 279, 293, 319, 321, 324
s. 69 270, 272, 273, 274, 275, 276, 277, 278, 279, 288, 293, 319, 321, 324
s. 70 270, 272, 273, 274, 275, 276, 277, 278, 279, 288, 293, 319, 321, 324
s. 71 270, 272, 273, 274, 275, 276, 277, 278, 279, 280, 293, 319, 321, 324
s. 72 270, 272, 273, 274, 275, 276, 277, 278, 279, 293, 319, 321, 324
s. 73 270, 272, 273, 274, 275, 276, 277, 278, 279, 293, 319, 321, 324
s. 74 270, 272, 273, 274, 275, 276, 277, 278, 279, 293, 319, 321, 324
s. 75 270, 272, 273, 274, 275, 276, 277, 278, 279, 293, 319, 321, 324
s. 76 270, 272, 273, 274, 275,

PAGE

Road Traffic Act 1972—(*cont.*)
s. 76 276, 277, 278, 279, 288, 293, 319, 321, 324
s. 77 270, 272, 273, 274, 275, 276, 277, 278, 279, 289, 293, 319, 321, 324
s. 78 270, 272, 273, 274, 277, 278, 279, 293, 319, 321, 324
s. 79 270, 271, 272, 278, 279, 293, 319, 321, 324
s. 80 270, 293, 319, 321, 324
s. 81 279, 287, 293, 319, 321, 324
s. 82 . . . 279, 319
s. 83 319
s. 84 . 294, 295, 219, 324
s. 85 . 296, 313, 319, 324
s. 86 . . 313, 319, 324
s. 87 295, 296, 297, 304, 309, 319, 324
s. 87A . . . 314
s. 88 294, 302, 319, 320, 324
s. 89 294, 297, 309, 319, 324
s. 90 . . 297, 319, 324
s. 91 297, 312, 319, 324, 335
s. 93 298, 299, 303, 316, 319, 324
ss. 94, 95 . 299, 319, 324
ss. 96–99 . . 300, 319
s. 100 26, 300, 319, 324, 335
s. 101 298, 301, 302, 303, 316, 319, 324
s. 102 . . 319, 324
s. 103 . . 319, 324
s. 104 302, 303, 319, 324
s. 105 . 303, 319, 324
s. 107 . 299, 319, 324
ss. 108–110 . . 319, 324
s. 111 . 303, 319, 324
s. 112 . . 319, 356
ss. 113, 114 . 319, 356
ss. 115–118 . . . 319
s. 119 . 312, 313, 319
ss. 120–122 . . . 319
ss. 123, 124 . 319, 356
s. 125 . . . 319
ss. 126, 127 . . . 323
s. 128 . . . 333
ss. 130–134 . . . 333
s. 135 . . 313, 333
s. 136 . . . 333
s. 137 . . 314, 333
s. 143 306, 310, 324, 632
s. 144 . . 305, 324
s. 145 . . . 306
ss. 146, 147 . 306, 324
s. 148 . 306, 307, 324
ss. 149, 150 . . 324
s. 151 . . 307, 324
ss. 152, 153 . . 324
ss. 154, 155 . 307, 324
s. 156 . 307, 324, 335
s. 158 . . . 324
s. 159 308, 319, 324, 334, 339
s. 160 309, 319, 324, 335
s. 161 309, 311, 319, 324, 334
s. 162 310, 311, 313, 320, 324, 334
s. 163 . . . 311
s. 164 26, 253, 262, 263, 311, 319, 324, 334, 339
s. 165 . . 264, 319
s. 166 . 311, 324, 334
s. 167 . 312, 324, 335
s. 168 . 312, 319, 335
s. 169 185, 312, 314, 315
ss. 170, 171 . 314, 315
s. 172 . . . 314
s. 173 . 173, 315, 334
s. 174 . . 315, 319
s. 175 . . 319, 324
s. 177 . 315, 316, 317
s. 178 . 89, 318, 319
s. 179 253, 254, 262, 263, 264, 317, 318, 319, 324, 330, 339, 696
s. 180 . . . 318
s. 181 . . 89, 318
s. 182 . 90, 318, 319
s. 183 . . . 319
s. 188 310, 320, 321, 653
s. 189 . . . 321
s. 190 255, 322, 323, 630, 631, 634, 636, 637, 638, 647, 652, 659
s. 191 . . 323, 603
s. 192 . . . 323
s. 193 . . 323, 663
s. 194 . . 323, 324
s. 195 . 324, 336, 355
s. 196 243, 245, 324, 337, 355
s. 198 . 253, 254, 271
s. 203 . . . 331
s. 207 . . . 325
Sched. I . . . 266
Sched. III . . 270, 300

PAGE

Road Traffic Act 1972—(*cont.*)
Sched. IV . . 89, 253, 254, 263, 298, 301, 315, 317, 318, 319, 375
Deposit of Poisonous Waste Act 1972 587
ss. 1, 3 587
Betting and Gaming Duties Act 1972, s. 10 505
Sunday Theatre Act 1972 538
s. 1 . . . . 532, 541
ss. 2, 3 533
Road Traffic (Foreign Vehicles) Act 1972—
s. 1 374
ss. 2, 3 . . . . 374, 375
Sched. II 375
Trade Descriptions Act 1972, s. 1 438
Children Act 1972 154
Poisons Act 1972 574
Criminal Justice Act 1972 399
s. 1 149
s. 6 192
s. 24 303
s. 33 230
s. 43 149
s. 45 34
s. 48 134
s. 51 49
s. 58 188
Sched. V 489
Sched. VI 138
Local Government Act 1972—
s. 223 416
Sched. 29 . . . . 392, 582
Protection of Wrecks Act 1973 194
Administration of Justice Act 1973, s. 1 32
Costs in Criminal Cases Act 1973—
s. 1 68
s. 2 69
ss. 3, 4 68
Hallmarking Act 1973 . . . . 438, 439
ss. 1, 9 439
Sched. III 439
Sched. VII 185
Protection of Aircraft Act 1973—
s. 1 . . . . 110, 111
ss. 2–5 111
s. 6 110
ss. 10, 16, 19 111
Badgers Act 1973 502
s. 1 502
Breeding of Dogs Act 1973 492
Powers of Criminal Courts Act 1973 . . . . . . 8, 399, 702
s. 2 . . . . 400, 401
s. 3 . . . . 401, 402
s. 4 401
s. 5 . . . . . 401, 402
s. 6 402
s. 7 400

PAGE

Powers of Criminal Courts Act 1973—(*cont.*)
s. 8 . . . 400, 402
s. 11 401
s. 12 402
s. 13 . . 15, 400, 402
ss. 14–17 . . . 153
s. 19 . 8, 158, 159, 399
s. 22 8
s. 28 405
s. 29 406
s. 35 . 34, 174, 175, 193
s. 42 40
s. 43 . . . 188, 190
s. 44 . . 300, 301, 303
s. 45 404
ss. 46, 47 . . . 403
s. 49 . . . 403, 404
s. 50 403
s. 53 49
Sched. I . . . 401
Sched. III . . . 403
Sched. V . . . 403
Slaughterhouse Act 1974 496
ss. 1, 13, 21 496
s. 36 . . . . 496, 497
s. 37 497
s. 39 . . . . 462, 496
s. 45 496
Biological Weapons Act 1974—
ss. 1, 2, 4 207
Rabies Act 1974 489
s. 4 480
Juries Act 1974—
s. 12 38
s. 16 37
s. 17 38
Sched. II 586
Consumer Credit Act 1974 445
Sched. IV 444
Control of Pollution Act 1974 . . . . 587, 588
Solicitors Act 1974 416
Road Traffic Act 1974 317
ss. 1–4 332
s. 6 264
s. 7 267
s. 9 . . . . 268, 270, 279
s. 12 270
s. 13 . . . . 314, 319
s. 15 356
s. 18 251
s. 20 305
s. 24 270
Sched. I 332
Sched. III 302
Sched. VI 253, 254, 263, 264, 328, 339
Sched. VII 270
Trade Union and Labour Relations Act 1974—
ss. 15, 29 230
Rehabilitation of Offenders Act 1974 . . . . . 15, 101
s. 9 . . . . 212, 213
Prevention of Terrorism (Temporary Provisions) Act 1974 . 25
s. 1 . . . . 25, 207
s. 2 . . . . 25, 208
ss. 3, 7 . . . . 25, 208, 209

PAGE

Prevention of Terrorism (Temporary Provisions) Act 1974—(*cont.*)
Sched. III 208, 209, 303
Farriers (Registration) Act 1975 417
s. 16 417
Nursing Homes Act 1975 581
Diseases of Animals Act 1975 481
Finance (No. 2) Act 1975—
Sched. III 542
Guard Dogs Act 1975 491
s. 1 492
s. 2 500
s. 5 492
Salmon and Freshwater Fisheries Act 1975 199
ss. 1–6 199
ss. 19, 20, 22 200
ss. 25, 27 199
ss. 31, 34 200
s. 35 199
Safety of Sports Grounds Act 1975—
ss. 1, 11 541
Public Service Vehicles (Arrest of Offenders) Act 1975 . 25, 347
Lotteries Act 1975 511
s. 11 511
s. 13 514
s. 14 512
Sched. IV 511, 515

TABLE OF REFERENCES TO CASES

PAGE

Adair *v.* Fleming, 1932 S.L.T. 263 265
Airton *v.* Scott (1909), 100 L.T. 393; 73 J.P. 148 . . . 507
Ames *v.* McLeod, 1969 S.C.(J) 1 258
Andrews *v.* Director of Public Prosecutions, [1937] A.C. 576 (H.L.); [1937] 2 All E.R. 552; 101 J.P. 386 . . . 114
Boulter *v.* Kent Justices, [1897] A.C. 556 (H.L.); 61 J.P. 532 . 548
Bracegirdle *v.* Oxley, [1947] K.B. 349; [1947] 1 All E.R. 126; 11 J.P. 131 253
Bridge *v.* Campbell (1947), 177 L.T. 444; 63 T.L.R. 470 . . 407
Bryant *v.* Marx (1932), 96 J.P. 383; [1932] All E.R. Rep. 518 243, 324
Bugge *v.* Taylor, [1941] 1 K.B. 198; 104 J.P. 467 . . . 243
Button and Swain *v.* Director of Public Prosecutions. *See* R. *v.* Button and Swain.
Chandler *v.* Director of Public Prosecutions, [1964] A.C. at p. 777 (H.L.); [1962] 3 All E.R. 142; [1962] 3 W.L.R. at p. 702; 106 Sol. Jo. 588 210
Chapman *v.* Kirke, [1948] 2 K.B. 450; [1948] 2 All E.R. 556; 112 J.P. 399 339
Chic Fashions (West Wales), Ltd *v.* Jones, [1968] 2 Q.B. 299 (C.A.); [1968] 1 All E.R. 229; [1968] 2 W.L.R. 201; 132 J.P. 175 57
Christie *v.* Leachinsky, [1947] A.C. 573 (H.L.); [1947] 1 All E.R. 567; 111 J.P. 224 . . . . 17, 28
Clark *v.* Taylor (1948), 112 J.P. 439; 92 Sol. Jo. 634 . . 507
Corkery *v.* Carpenter, [1951] 1 K.B. 102; [1950] 2 All E.R. 745; 114 J.P. 481 563
Cruickshank *v.* Devlin, 1974 S.L.T. (Sh. Ct.) 81 . . . 258
Dawson *v.* Winter (1932), 149 L.T. 18; 49 T.L.R. 128 . . 265
Director of Public Prosecutions *v.* Morgan, [1976] A. C. at p. 192; [1975] 2 All E.R. 347; [1975] 2 W.L.R. at p. 923; 139 J.P. 476 119
Director of Public Prosecutions *v.* Roffey (1959), 123 J.P. 241 . 384
Duncan *v.* Jones, [1936] 1 K.B. 218; [1935] All E.R. Rep. 710; 99 J.P. 399 235
Duncan *v.* Toms (1887), 56 L.J.M.C. 81; 51 J.P. 631 . . 45
Elias *v.* Pasmore, [1934] 2 K.B. 164; [1934] All E.R. Rep. 380; 98 J.P. 92 17
Elkins *v.* Cartlidge, [1947] 1 All E.R. 829; 177 L.T. 519 . . 564
Ellis *v.* Nott-Bower (1896), 60 J.P. 760; 13 T.L.R. 35 . . 265
Evans *v.* Ewels, [1972] 2 All E.R. 22; [1972] 1 W.L.R. 671; 136 J.P. 394 128
Fagan *v.* Metropolitan Police Commissioner, [1969] 1 Q.B. 439; [1968] 3 All E.R. 442; 133 J.P. 16 105

PAGE

Fisher *v.* Oldham Corporation, [1930] 2 K.B. 364; [1930] All E.R. Rep. 96; 94 J.P. 132 . . . . 210, 416

Fisher *v.* Raven, [1964] A.C. 210 (H.L.); [1963] 2 All E.R. 389, [1963] 2 W.L.R. at p. 1146; 127 J.P. 382 . . . 174

Flockhart *v.* Robertson, [1950] 2 K.B. 498; [1950] 1 All E.R. 1091; 114 J.P. 304 232

Gill *v.* Carson, [1917] 2 K.B. 674; 81 J.P. 250 244

Goodway *v.* Becher, [1951] 2 All E.R. 349; 115 J.P. 435 . . 489

Gough *v.* Rees (1929), 142 L.T. 424; 94 J.P. 53 14

Green *v.* Dunn, [1953] 1 All E.R. 550 265

Haines *v.* Roberts, [1953] 1 All E.R. 344; [1953] 1 W.L.R. 309; 117 J.P. 123 564

Harding *v.* Price, [1948] 1 K.B. 695; [1948] 1 All E.R. 283; 112 J.P. 189 265

Harman *v.* Wardrop (1971) 135 J.P. 255; 115 Sol. Jo. 146 . 258

Hartley *v.* Ellnor (1917), 86 L.J.K.B. 938; [1916–17] All E.R. Rep. 260; 81 J.P. 201 . . . . 406, 407

Hastings and Folkestone Glassworks, Ltd. *v.* Kalsan, [1949] 1 K.B. 214 (C.A.); [1948] 2 All E.R. 1013; 113 J.P. 31 . . . 7

Holman *v.* Ward. *See* Ward *v.* Holman.

Hylton *v.* Ohlson (1975), 125 N.L. Jo. 261 408

I.T.P. (London), Ltd. *v.* Winstanley, [1947] K.B. 422; [1947] 1 All E.R. 177; 111 J.P. 68 514

Jeffrey *v.* Evans, [1964] 1 All E.R. 536; [1964] 1 W.L.R. 505; 128 J.P. 252 . . . . 66, 548

John Lewis & Co. *v.* Tims. *See* Lewis (John) & Co. *v.* Tims

Johnson *v.* Phillips, [1975] 3 All E.R. 682; [1976] 1 W.L.R. 65; 140 J.P. 37 107

Jones *v.* English, [1951] 2 All E.R. 853; 115 J.P. 609 . . . 564

Jordan *v.* Burgoyne, [1963] 2 Q.B. 744; [1963] 2 All E.R. 225; [1963] 2 W.L.R. 1045; 127 J.P. 368 233

Jowett-Shooter *v.* Franklin, [1949] 2 All E.R. 730; 113 J.P. 525 . . . . 303, 564

Kay *v.* Butterworth (1945), 173 L.T. 191; 110 J.P. 75 . . 254

Keehan *v.* Walters, [1948] 1 K.B. 19; 177 L.T. 552 . . . 513

Kingman *v.* Seager, [1938] 1 K.B. 397; 101 J.P. 543 . . . 253

Knowler *v.* Rennison, [1947] K.B. 488; *sub nom.* Rennison *v.* Knowler, [1947] 1 All E.R. 302; 111 J.P. 171 303

Leach *v.* R., [1912] A.C. 305 (H.L.); *sub nom.* Leach *v.* Director of Public Prosecutions, 76 J.P. 203 84

Ledwith *v.* Roberts, [1937] 1 K.B. 232 (C.A.); [1936] 3 All E.R. 570; 101 J.P. 23 . . . . 406, 407

Lewis *v.* Cattle, [1938] 2 K.B. 454; [1938] 2 All E.R. 368; 102 J.P. 239 210

Lewis (John) & Co. *v.* Tims, [1952] A.C. 676 (H.L.); [1952] 1 All E.R. 1203; 116 J.P. 275 27

Lines *v.* Hersom, [1951] 2 K.B. 682; [1951] 2 All E.R. 650; 115 J.P. 494 303

McCrone *v.* Riding, [1938] 1 All E.R. 157; 102 J.P. 109 . . 254

Mancini *v.* Director of Public Prosecutions, [1942] A.C.1 (H.L.); [1941] 3 All E.R. 272; 28 Cr. App. Rep. 65 . . . 114

Moran *v.* Director of Public Prosecutions (1974) Times, 12th December 231

North *v.* Gerrish (1959), 123 J.P. 313 265

PAGE

North *v.* Pullen (1961), 126 J.P. 88; 106 Sol. Jo. 77 . . 18
Peek *v.* Towle, [1945] K.B. 458; [1945] 2 All E.R. 611; 109 J.P. 160 265
People's Hostels, Ltd. *v.* Turley, [1939] 1 K.B. 149; [1938] 4 All E.R. 72; 102 J.P. 509 397
R. *v.* Baker (1883), 47 J.P.N. 666 106
R. *v.* Baskerville, [1916] 2 K.B. 658 (C.C.A.); [1916–17] All E.R. Rep. 38; 80 J.P. 446 . . . . . . 13, 83
R. *v.* Blamires Transport Services, Ltd., [1964] 1 Q.B. 278 (C.C.A.); [1963] 3 All E.R. 170; [1963] 3 W.L.R. 496; 127 J.P. 519 237
R. *v.* Bodmin Justices, *Ex parte* McEwen, [1947] K.B. 321; [1947] 1 All E.R. 109; 111 J.P. 47 42
R. *v.* Bove, [1970] 2 All E.R. 20: [1970] 1 W.L.R. 949; 134 J.P. 418 258
R. *v.* Boyle, [1954] 2 Q.B. 292 (C.C.A.); [1954] 2 All E.R. 721; [1954] 3 W.L.R. 364; 118 J.P. 481 50
R. *v.* Burton (1875), 32 L.T. 539; 39 J.P. 532 . . . 14
R. *v.* Button and Swain, [1966] A.C. 591 (H.L.); [1965] 3 W.L.R. 1131; *sub nom.* Button and Swain *v.* Director of Public Prosecutions, [1965] 3 All E.R. 587; 130 J.P. 48 . . . 227
R. *v.* Camelleri, [1922] 2 K.B. 122 (C.C.A.); 86 J.P. 135 . . 91
R. *v.* Campbell, *Ex parte* Hoy, [1953] 1 Q.B. 585 (C.C.A.); [1953] 1 All E.R. 684; [1953] 2 W.L.R. 576 16
R. *v.* Chapman, [1959] 1 Q.B. 100 (C.C.A.); [1958] 3 All E.R. 143; [1958] 3 W.L.R. 401; 122 J.P. 462 122
R. *v.* Clark, [1955] 2 Q.B. 469 (C.C.A.); [1955] 3 All E.R. 29; [1955] 3 W.L.R. 313 83
R. *v.* Clarke, [1949] 2 All E.R. 448; 33 Cr. App. Rep. 216 . 119
R. *v.* Clarke, [1950] 1 K.B. 523 (C.C.A.); [1950] 1 All E.R. 546; 114 J.P. 192 406
R. *v.* Collinson (1931), 75 Sol. Jo. 491 (C.C.A.); 23 Cr. App. R. 49 564
R. *v.* Cooper (1974), 138 J.P. Jo. 707 258
R. *v.* Crossan, [1939] N.I. 106 303
R. *v.* Cummings, [1948] 1 All E.R. 551 (C.C.A.); 92 Sol. Jo. 284 91
R. *v.* Dayle, [1973] 3 All E.R. 1151 (C.A.); [1974] 1 W.L.R. 181; 138 J.P. 65 408
R. *v.* De Munck, [1918] 1 K.B. 635 (C.C.A.); [1918–19] All E.R. Rep. 499; 82 J.P. 160 124
R. *v.* Donovan, [1934] 2 K.B. 498 (C.C.A.); [1934] All E.R. Rep. 207, 98 J.P. 409 105
R. *v.* Durham Justices, *Ex parte* Laurent, [1945] K.B. 33; [1944] 2 All E.R. 530; 109 J.P. 21 59
R. *v.* East Riding Quarter Sessions, *Ex parte* Newton, [1968] 1 Q.B. 32; [1967] 3 All E.R. 118; [1967] 3 W.L.R. 1098 66, 548
R. *v.* Essex Justices, *Ex parte* Final, [1963] 2 Q.B. 816; [1962] 3 All E.R. 924; [1962] 2 W.L.R. 38; 127 J.P. 39 . . 16
R. *v.* Fletcher (1949), 113 J.P. 365 (C.C.A.) 101
R. *v.* Freebody (1935), 25 Cr. App. Rep. 69 (C.C.A.) . . 83
R. *v.* Fussell, [1951] 2 All E.R. 761 (C.C.A.); 115 J.P. 562 . 7
R. *v.* Garforth (1970), 114 Sol. Jo. 770 (C.A.) . . . 258
R. *v.* Hall, [1964] 1 Q.B. 273 (C.C.A.); [1963] 2 All E.R. 1075; [1963] 3 W.L.R. 482; 127 J.P. 489 132
R. *v.* Highgate Justices, *Ex parte* Petrou, [1954] 1 All E.R. 406; [1954] 1 W.L.R. 485; 113 J.P. 151 68

PAGE

R. *v.* Holland, Lincolnshire Justices (1882), 46 J.P. 312 . . 126

R. *v.* E. J. M. Jones, [1970] 1 All E.R. 209 (C.A.); [1970] 1 W.L.R. 211; 134 J.P. 215 258

R. *v.* King, [1964] 1 Q.B. 285 (C.C.A.); [1963] 3 All E.R. 561; [1963] 3 W.L.R. 892; 107 Sol. Jo. 832 215

R. *v.* Kirkup (1950), 34 Cr. App. R. 150 (C.C.A.) . . . 422

R. *v.* Lapworth, [1931] 1 K.B. 117 (C.C.A.); [1930] All E.R. Rep. 340; 95 J.P. 2 84

R. *v.* Lillyman, [1896] 2 Q.B. 167; [1895–9] All E.R. Rep. 586; 60 J.P. 536 91

R. *v.* MacDonagh, [1974] Q.B. 448 (C.A.); [1974] 2 All E.R. 257; [1974] 2 W.L.R. 529; 138 J.P. 488 258

R. *v.* Mills, [1963] 1 Q.B. 522 (C.C.A.); [1963] 1 All E.R. 202; [1963] 2 W.L.R. 137; 127 J.P. 176 136

R. *v.* Morris, [1951] 1 K.B. 394 (C.C.A); [1950] 2 All E.R. 965; 115 J.P. 5 8

R. *v* Neal, [1949] 2 K.B. 590 (C.C.A.); [1949] All E.R. 438; 113 J.P. 468 16

R. *v.* Osborne, [1905] 1 K.B. 551; [1904–7] All E.R. Rep. 54; 69 J.P. 189 91

R. *v.* Parrott (1913), 8 Cr. App. Rep. 186 (C.C.A.) . . . 210

R. *v.* Rumping, [1962] 2 All E.R. 233 (C.C.A.); [1962] 3 W.L.R. 763; 106 Sol. Jo. 330; affirmed *sub nom.* Rumping *v.* Director of Public Prosecutions, [1964] A.C. 814 (H.L.); [1962] 3 All E.R. 256; [1962] 3 W.L.R. at p. 770; 106 Sol. Jo. 668 . 65

R. *v.* Sandbach, *Ex parte* Williams, [1935] 2 K.B. 192; [1935] All E.R. Rep. 680; 99 J.P. 251 227

R. *v.* Sharpe and Stringer, [1938] 1 All E.R. 48 (C.C.A.); 102 J.P. 113 224

R. *v.* Sheridan, [1937] 1 K.B. 223 (C.C.A.); [1937] 2 All E.R. 883; 100 J.P. 319 16

R. *v.* Thomson (1966), 110 Sol. Jo. 788 (C.A.) 237

R. *v.* Tolson (1889), 23 Q.B.D. 168; [1886–90] All E.R. Rep. 26; 54 J.P. 4, 20 215

R. *v.* Van Pelz, [1943] 1 K.B. 157 (C.C.A.); [1943] 1 All E.R. 36; 107 J.P. 24 101

R. *v.* Warn, [1937] 4 All E.R. 327 (C.C.A.); 102 J.P. 46 . . 16

R. *v.* Webb [1964] 1 Q.B. 357 (C.C.A.); [1963] 3 All E.R. 177; [1963] 3 W.L.R. 638; 127 J.P. 516 124

R. *v.* Wickins (1958), 42 Cr. App. Rep. 236 (C.C.A.) . . 303

R. *v.* Woolwich Justices, *Ex parte* Toohey, [1965] 3 All E.R. 825; [1966] 2 W.L.R. 402; 130 J.P. 90; affirmed, [1967] 2 A.C. 1 (H.L.); [1966] 2 W.L.R. 1442; *sub nom.* Toohey *v.* Woolwich Justices, [1966] 2 All E.R. 429; 130 J.P. 326 107

Rawlings *v.* Smith, [1938] 1 K.B. 675; [1938] 1 All E.R. 11; 102 J.P. 181 407

Rumping *v.* Director of Public Prosecutions. *See* R. *v.* Rumping.

Sakhiya *v.* Allen, [1973] A.C. 152 (H.L.); [1972] 2 All E.R. 311; [1972] 2 W.L.R. 1116; 136 J.P. 414 258

Saycell *v.* Bool, [1948] 2 All E.R. 83; 112 J.P. 341 . . . 324

Seekings *v.* Clarke (1961), 105 Sol. Jo. 181; 59 L.G.R. 268 . 245

Sheffield Corporation *v.* Kitson, [1929] 2 K.B. 322; 93 J.P. 135 . 247

Smith *v.* Baker, [1960] 3 All E.R. 653; [1961] 1 W.L.R. 38; 125 J.P. 53 489

PAGE

Solomon *v.* Durbridge (1956), 120 J.P. 231 244
Stirland *v.* Director of Public Prosecutions, [1944] A.C. 315 (H.L.) [1944] 2 All E.R. 13; 109 J.P. 1 84
Taylor *v.* Emerson (1962), 106 Sol. Jo. 552; 60 L.G.R. 311 . 360
Taylor *v.* Goodwin (1879), 4 Q.B.D. 228; [1874–80] All E.R. Rep. 873; 43 J.P. 653 253
Thomas *v.* Dando, [1951] 2 K.B. 620; [1951] 1 All E.R. 1010; 115, J.P. 344 243
Thomas *v.* Lindop, [1950] 1 All E.R. 966; 114 J.P. 290 . . 14
Thomas *v.* Sawkins, [1935] 2 K.B. 249; [1935] All E.R. Rep. 655; 99 J.P. 295 235
Toohey *v.* Woolwich Justices. *See* R. *v.* Woolwich Justices, *Ex parte* Toohey.
Wallace *v.* Major, [1946] K.B. 473; [1946] 2 All E.R. 87; 110 J.P. 231 324
Ward *v.* Holman [1964] 2 Q.B. 580; [1964] 2 All E.R. 729; *sub nom.* Holman *v.* Ward, 128 J.P. 397 233
Whittall *v.* Kirby, [1947] K.B. 194; [1946] 2 All E.R. 552; 111 J.P. 1 303
Woodward *v.* Koessler, [1958] 3 All E.R. 557; [1958] 1 W.L.R. 1255; 123 J.P. 14 408
Woolmington *v.* Director of Public Prosecutions, [1935] A.C. 462 (H.L.); [1935] All E.R. Rep. 1; 25 Cr. App. R. 72 . 81, 97, 113

TABLE OF ORDERS, REGULATIONS AND RULES

Arranged by subjects alphabetically

PAGE

Acetylene—Compressed Acetylene Order 1919 (S.R.O. 809) . 454
Acetylene Orders 1937 (S.R. & O. 349), 1947 (S.R.O. 805) . 454
Air Navigation (Investigation of Combined Military and Civil Air Accidents) Regs. 1959 (S.I. 1388), 1960 (S.I. 1526) . . 385
Air Navigation Order 1974 (S.I. 1114) . . . 158, 381 to 383
Aircraft—Public Health (Aircraft) Regs. 1952 (S.I. 1410), 1954, 1961, 1963 (S.I. 1257) 381
Aliens Orders 1953 (S.I. 167), 1957, 1960, 1964, 1969, 1970 (S.I. 151) 19, 156, 157
Animals (Cruel Poisons) Regs. 1963 (S.I. 1278) . . . 484
Animals—Diseases of Animals Orders 1952 (S.I. 1236), 1963 (S.I. 37) 479, 480
Animals (Sea Transport) Orders 1930 (S.R.O. 923), 1952 (S.I. 1291) 484
Animals—Transit of Animals Orders 1927 (S.R.O. 289), 1930, 1931, 1939, 1947 (S.R.O. 2915) 484
Attendance Centre Rules 1958 (S.I. 1990) 152
Aviation—Civil Aviation (Investigation of Accidents) Regs. 1951 (S.I. 1653) 385
Betting (Licensed Offices) Regs. 1960 (S.I. 2333) 509
Brakes on Pedal Cycles Regs. 1954 (S.I. 966) 338
Carbon Disulphide (Conveyance by Road) Regs. 1958 (S.I. 318) 1962 (S.I. 2527) 456
Carbide of Calcium (Petroleum) Orders 1929 (S.R.O. 992), 1947 (S.R.O. 1426) 454
Children—Juvenile Courts (Constitution) Rules 1954 (S.I. 1711) 31
Children (Performances) Regs. 1968 (S.I. 1728) 147
Children's Nightdresses Regs. 1964 (S.I. 1153) 583
Cinematograph (Children) (No. 2) Regs. 1955 (S.I. 1909) . 536
Cinematograph Film Stripping Regs. 1939 (S.R.O. 571) . . 456
Cinematograph (Safety) Regs. 1955 (S.I. 1129), 1958, 1965 (S.I. 282) 536, 537
Civil Aviation (Aerial Advertising) Regs. 1961 (S.I. 2102) . 381
Civil Aviation (Investigation of Accidents) Regs. 1951 (S.I. 1653) 385
Collections—House to House Collections Regs. 1947 (S.R.O. 2662) 396, 397
Compressed Acetylene Order 1919 (S.R.O. 809) 454
Compressed Gas Cylinders (Fuel for Motor Vehicles) Conveyance Regs. 1940 (S.R.O. 2009) 456

PAGE
Control of Dogs Orders 1930 (S.R.O. 379), 1931 (S.R.O. 80) . 491
Control of Explosives Orders 1953 (S.I. 1598), 1954 (S.I. 757) . 446
Convention. Road Traffic. Geneva 1949 . 281, 290, 374, 599
Coroners Rules 1953 (S.I. 205) . . . . . . 584 to 589
Cycle Racing on Highways Regs. 1960 (S.I. 250), 1963 (S.I. 929) 263, 339
Detention Centre Rules 1952 (S.I. 1432), 1968 (S.I. 1014) . 152
Diseases of Animals Orders 1952 (S.I. 1236), 1953 (S.I. 37) 479, 480
Dogs—Control of Dogs Orders 1930 (S.R.O. 379), 1931 (S.R.O. 80) 491
Drivers' Hours (Goods Vehicles) (Exemption) Regs. 1972 (S.I. 574) 354
Drivers' Hours (Goods Vehicles) (Keeping of Records) Regs. 1970 S.I. 123), 1973 (S.I. 380) 354
Drivers' Hours (Goods Vehicles) (Modifications) Order 1970 (S.I. 257) 354
Drivers' Hours (Passenger and Goods Vehicles) (International Rules) Regs. 1973 (S.I. 379) 354
Drivers' Hours (Passenger Vehicles) (Exemptions) Regs. 1970 (S.I. 145, 649) 354
Drivers' Hours (Passenger Vehicles) (Modifications) Order 1970 (S.I. 356) 354
Evidence by Certificate Rules 1961 (S.I. 248), 1962 (S.I. 2319) 90
Explosives, Control of, Orders 1953 (S.I. 1598), 1954 (S.I. 757) 446
Exported Cattle Protection Order 1957 (S.I. 170) . . . 487
Exported Ponies Protection Order 1958 (S.I. 1271) . . 488
Extradition (Genocide) Order 1970 (S.I. 147) 116
Firearms (Dangerous Air Weapons) Rules 1969 (S.I. 47) . . 459
Firearms Rules 1969 (S.I. 1219) 477
Fish—Immature Sea Fish Order 1968 (S.I. 1618) . . . 200
Food Hygiene Regs. 1955 (S.I. 1906) 440, 572
Functions of Traffic Wardens Order 1970 (S.I. 1958) . . 251
Gaming Clubs (Bankers' Games) Regs. 1970 (S.I. 800) . . 521
Gaming Clubs (Hours and Charges) Regs. 1970 (S.I. 799) 521, 523
Gaming Clubs (Licensing) Regs. 1969 (S.I. 1110), 1975 (S.I. 604) 523
Gaming Clubs (Permitted Areas) Regs. 1971 (S.I. 1538) . . 523
Gaming Clubs (Prohibition of Gratuities) Regs. 1970 (S.I. 1644) 523
Gas—Compressed Gas Cylinders (Fuel for Motor Vehicles) Conveyance Regs. 1940 (S.R.O. 2009) 456
Gas Cylinders (Conveyance) Regs. 1931 (S.R.O. 679), 1947, 1959 (S.I. 1919) 456
Geneva. Road Traffic Convention 1949 . . 281, 290, 374, 599
Goods Vehicles (Operators' Licences) Regs. 1969 (S.I. 1636) 352, 353
Goods Vehicles (Operators' Licences) (Temporary Use in Great Britain) Regs. 1975 (S.I. 1046) 353
Goods Vehicles (Plating and Testing) Regs. 1971 (S.I. 352) . 269
Grey Squirrels Order 1937 (S.R.O. 478) 496
Heavy Goods Vehicles (Drivers' Licences) Regs. 1975 (S.I. 36), 1975 (S.I. 739) . . . . 356 to 359
Horse Breeding Rules 1948 (S.I. 2667), 1974 (S.I. 1962), 1975 (S.I. 1777) 487
Horses (Sea Transport) Orders 1952 (S.I. 1291), 1958 (S.I. 1272) 487
Horses—Transit of Horses Order 1951 (S.I. 335) . . . 487
House to House Collections Regs. 1947 (S.R.O. 2662) . 396, 397

PAGE

Hydrogen Cyanide (Fumigation) Regs. 1951 (S.I. 1759) . . 587
Immature Sea Fish Order 1958 (S.I. 1618) 200
Immigration (Control of Entry through Republic of Ireland) Order 1972 (S.I. 1610) 411
Immigration (Exemption from Control) Order 1972 (S.I. 1613) 411
Immigration (Hotel Records) Order 1972 (S.I. 1689) . . 412
Immigration (Places of Detention) Directions 1972 . . 412
Immigration (Registration with Police) Regs. 1972 (S.I. 1758) 410, 411
Imprisonment and Detention (Air Force) (Amendment) Rules 1961 (S.I. 2397) 218
Imprisonment and Detention (Army) (Amendment) Rules 1961 (S.I. 2395) 218
Indictments (Procedure) Rules 1933 (S.R.O. 745) . . . 37
Investments—Prevention of Fraud (Investments) Act Licensing Regs. 1944 (S.R.O. 119) 434
Justices' Clerks Rules 1970 (S.I. 231) 69, 701, 702
Juvenile Courts (Constitution) Rules 1954 (S.I. 1711) . . 31
Keeping of Fireworks Order 1959 (S.I. 1311) 448
Licensed Dealers (Conduct of Business) Rules 1960 (S.I. 1216) 434
Live Poultry (Movement Records) Order 1958 (S.I. 1344) . 480
Live Poultry (Restrictions) Order 1957 (S.I. 787) . . . 480
Magistrates' Court (Children and Young Persons) Rules 1970 (S.I. 1792) 31, 138, 150, 151
Magistrates' Courts (Amendment) Rules 1975 (S.I. 126) . 30, 33
Magistrates' Courts (Amendment) (No. 2) Rules 1975 (S.I. 518) . 66
Magistrates' Courts (Backing of Warrants) Rules 1965 (S.I. 1602) 53
Magistrates' Courts Rules 1968 (S.I. 1920) . . 30, 33, 101, 421
Rule 1 . . . . 43, 44
Rule 4 . . . . 34, 43, 78
Rule 5 35
Rule 12 45
Rule 13 43
Rule 14 43
Rule 18 46
Rule 19 . . . . 40, 99
Rule 21 41
Rule 29 79
Rule 34 701
Rule 44 . . . . 54, 55
Rule 45 . . . . 54, 55, 58
Rule 46 403
Rule 49 701
Rule 55 49
Rule 56 90
Rule 61 33
Rules 65–68. 66
Rule 72 59
Rule 77 . . . . 58, 63
Rule 80 57
Rule 81 . . . . 45, 46
Rule 82 . . . . 47, 48
Rule 83 . . . . 45, 52

PAGE

Magistrates' Courts Rules 1968 (S.I. 1920)—(*cont.*)
Rule 84 298
Rule 86 401
Rule 88 47
Rule 92 49
Rule 93 51
Measuring Instruments (Intoxicating Liquor) Regs. 1965 (S.I. 1815) 559
Measuring Instruments (Liquid Fuel and Lubricating Oil) Regs. 1929 (S.R.O. 183) 452
Menai Suspension Bridge (Traffic Regulation) Order 1955 (S.I. 1282) 326
Misuse of Drugs Regs. 1973 (S.I. 797), 1975 576
Motor Cars (Driving Instruction) (Appeals) Rules 1969 (S.I. 86), 1970 (S.I. 86) 334
Motor Cars (Driving Instruction) Regs. 1969 (S.I. 85), 1970 (S.I. 966), 1971 (S.I. 351) 333
Motor Cycles (Protective Helmets) Regs. 1974 (S.I. 2000) . 266
Motor Cycles (Wearing of Helmets) Regs. 1973 (S.I. 180) . 266
Motor Vehicles (Authorisation of Special Types) General Order 1973 (S.I. 1101) . . . . 663 to 667
Motor Vehicles (Competitions and Trials) (England) Regs. 1969 (S.I. 414) 262
Motor Vehicles (Compulsory Insurance) Regs. 1973 (S.I. 2143), 1974 (S.I. 791, 2186) 308, 313
Motor Vehicles (Construction and Use) Regs. 1969 (S.I. 321), 1970 S.I. 49), 1973 (S.I. 24) 245, 269, 336, 352, 375, 597, 599 to 663, 667
Motor Vehicles (Construction and Use) (Track Laying Vehicles) Regs. 1955 (S.I. 990) 245
Motor Vehicles (Driving Licences) Regs. 1971 (S.I. 451), 1975 (S.I. 521) . . . . . 296, 303 to 305, 310, 322, 631
Motor Vehicles (International Circulation) Order 1975 (S.I. 1208) 373, 651
Motor Vehicles (International Circulation) Regs. 1971 (S.I. 937) 373, 374, 597
Motor Vehicles (International Motor Insurance Card) Regs. 1971 (S.I. 792) 311, 374
Motor Vehicles (Minimum Age of Driving) Regs. 1963 (S.I. 1025), 1975 (S.I. 1730) 160, 255, 256, 357
Motor Vehicles (Rear Markings) Regs. 1970 (S.I. 1700), 1972 (S.I. 842), 1975 (S.I. 297) 292
Motor Vehicles (Tests) (Exemptions) Regs. 1969 (S.I. 1171), 1971 (S.I. 165), 1974 (S.I. 1023) 289
Motor Vehicles (Tests) Regs. 1968 (S.I. 1714), 1969 (S.I. 1171), 1971 (S.I. 165), 1972 (S.I. 898), 1975 (S.I. 1130) . 268, 269
Motor Vehicles (Third Party Risks) Regs. 1972 (S.I. 1217) 307, 308, 310
Motor Vehicles (Type Approval) Regs. 1973 (S.I. 1199), 1975 (S.I. 642) 600
Motor Vehicles (Variation of Speed Limit) Regs. 1973 (S.I. 747) 593
Motorways Traffic (Speed Limit) (England) Regs. 1967 (S.I. 1041) 598
Musk Rats Orders 1932 (S.R.O. 154) 1933 (S.R.O. 106) . . 496

PAGE

Naval Detention Quarters (Amendment) Rules 1962 (S.I. 1242) 218
Pests—Prevention of Damage by Pests (Threshing and Dismantling of Ricks) Regs. 1950 (S.I. 1172) 483
Petroleum (Carbide of Calcium) Orders 1929 (S.R.O. 992) 1947 (S.R.O. 1426) 454
Petroleum (Mixtures) Order, 1929 (S.R.O. 993) 450
Petroleum-Spirit (Motor Vehicles &c.) Regs. 1929 (S.R.O. 952) 450, 451
Petroleum-Spirit (Conveyance by Road) Regs. 1957 (S.I. 191), 1966 (S.I. 1199) . . . . 452 to 454
Poisons List Order 1972 (S.I. 1938) 574
Poisons Rules 1972 (S.I. 1939) 574
Police (Disposal of Property) Regs. 1975 (1975 No. 1474) 188, 189
Poultry, Live (Movement Records) Order 1958 (S.I. 1344) . 480
Poultry, Live (Restrictions) Order 1957 (S.I. 787) . . . 480
Poultry Premises and Vehicles (Disinfection) Order 1956 (S.I.11) 480
Prevention of Damage by Pests (Threshing and Dismantling) Regs. 1950 (S.I. 1172) 483
Prevention of Fraud (Investments) Act Licensing Regs. 1944 (S.R.O. 119) 434
Prevention of Terrorism (Supplemental Temporary Provisions) Order 1974 (S.I. 1974 No. 1975) 209
Prisons Rules 1964 (S.I. 388), 1974 (S.I. 713) 409
Probation Rules 1965–74 (S.I. 723), 1974 (S.I. 1064) . . 403
Prosecution of Offences Regs. 1946 (S.R.O. 1467) . 69, 131, 668
Public Health (Aircraft) Regs. 1952 (S.I. 1410), 1954, 1961, 1963 (S.I. 1257) 381
Public Service Vehicles and Trolley Vehicles (Carrying Capacity) Regs. 1954 (S.I. 160), 1958, 1966 (S.I. 674) 350
Public Service Vehicles (Conditions of Fitness, Equipment and Use) Regs. 1972 (S.I. 751) 344
Public Service Vehicles (Conduct of Drivers, Conductors and Passengers) Regs. 1936 (S.R.O. 619), 1975 (S.I. 461) 348 to 350
Public Service Vehicles (Contract Carriage Records) Regs. 1960 (S.I. 1503) 342
Public Service Vehicles (Drivers' and Conductors' Licences) Regs. 1934 (S.R.O. 1321), 1962 (S.I. 920), 1972 (S.I. 1061) 347
Public Service Vehicles (Duration of Road Service Licences) Regs. 1937 (S.R.O. 414) 1938 (S.R.O. 747) . . . 345
Public Service Vehicles (Licences and Certificates) Regs. 1952 (S.I. 900), 1957, 1960, 1961, 1962, 1969 (S.I. 32) . . 344
Public Service Vehicles (Lost Property) Regs. 1934 (S.R.O. 1268), 1958, 1960 (S.I. 2197) 351
Public Service Vehicles (Records of Licences) Regs. 1933 (S.R.O. 653) 350
Rabies (Control) Order 1974 (S.I. 2212) 492
Rabies (Importation of Dogs, Cats and other Mammals) Order 1974 (S.I. 211) 492
Raising of the School Leaving Age Order 1972 (S.I. 444) . 145
Removal and Disposal of Vehicles (Alteration of Enactments) Order 1967 (S.I. 1900) 326
Removal and Disposal of Vehicles Regs. 1958 (S.I. 43) . . 326
Representation of the People Regs. 1950 (S.I. 1254) and 1954 (S.I. 498) 224

PAGE

Riot Damages Regs. 1921 (S.R.O. 1536) 228
Road Vehicles Lighting Regs. 1971 (S.I. 694), 1973 (S.I. 1006) 271, 279 to 292, 654
Road Vehicles Lighting (Standing Vehicles) (Exemption) (General) Regs., 1975 (S.I. 1495) 271, 293
Road Vehicles (Registration and Licensing) Regs. 1971 (S.I. 450), 1972 (S.I. 1535), 1973 (S.I. 870) 292, 293, 341, 359 to 373, 640
Road Vehicles (Use of Lights during Daytime) Regs. 1975 (S.I. 245) 287
Rules of the Air and Air Traffic Control Regs. 1974 (S.I. 1401) 384, 385
70 miles per hour (Speed Limit) (England) Order 1967 (S.I. 1040) 598
Shops (Revocation of Winter Closing Hours Provisions) Order 1952 (S.I. 1862) 441
Slaughter of Animals (Prevention of Cruelty) Regs. 1958 (S.I. 2166) 155, 496, 497
Summary Jurisdiction Process (Isle of Man) Order 1928 (S.R.O. 377) 48
Traffic Regulation Orders (Procedure) (England and Wales) Regs. 1961 (S.I. 485) 325
Traffic Signs and General Directions 1975 (S.I. 1536) . 329, 330
Traffic Signs (School Crossing Patrols) Regs. 1968 (S.I. 1826) . 328
Traffic Signs (Speed Limits) Regulations and General Directions 1969 (S.I. 1487) 331
Traffic Signs (Temporary Obstructions) Regs. 1966 (S.I. 1474), 1975 (S.I. 49) 267
Traffic Wardens Functions Order 1970 (S.I. 1958) . . . 251
Transit of Animals Orders 1927 (S.R.O. 289), 1930, 1931, 1939, 1947 (S.R.O. 2915) 484
Transit of Horses Order 1951 (S.I. 335) 487
Tuberculosis Order 1938 (S.I. 165) 480
Use of Invalid Carriages on Highways Regs. 1970 (S.I. 1391) . 293
Value Added Tax (General) Regs. 1972 (S.I. 1147) . . 600, 644
Vehicles and Driving Licences Records (Evidence) Regs. 1970 (S.I. 1997) 91
Visiting Forces and International Headquarters (Application of Law) Order 1965 (S.I. 1536) 597
War Charities (Definition) Order 1943 (S.R.O. 1147) . . 393
War Charities Regs. 1940 (S.R.O. 1533) 393
Wild Birds (Sunday) Orders 1955 (S.I. 1286), 1956, 1957 (S.I. 429) 493
"Zebra" Pedestrian Crossing Regs. 1971 (S.I. 1524) . 326, 327

INDEX

The figures in heavy type indicate the main references to the subject matter.

PAGE

Abandoning, Child **137,** 139, 153
——, Theatrical performers 534
——, Vehicle . . 326, 587
Abatement of Litter . 587
——, Noise . . . 588
Abduction . **122,** 156, 158
——, Arrestable offences . 697
——, Children . . 155
——, Evidence . . 84
Abetting . 13, 14, 299
——, Suicide **115,** 143, 587, 670
Abnormal indivisible load 602, 665
Abode, Summons . 47, 48
Abortion . . 135, 136
——, Arrestable offences . 697
Abroad, Juveniles employed . **148,** 158
——, Vehicles from . 290
Absconder, Borstal . . 404
Absentees, Army . 19, **421**
——, Merchant sailors . 380
Absolute discharge . . 400
Accessories . . 13, 14
Accident, Aircraft . . 385
——, Excuse for crime . 9
——, Homicide . 112, 113
——, Inquests . 584, 585
——, Motor . . . 264
——, ——, Breath Test . 258
——, Petroleum . . 450
Accommodation Address . 211
Accomplice . . . 13
——, Evidence . 13, 83
Accounting, False . 169, 698
Accused . . . 50
——, Charge . . 50, 75

PAGE

Accused, Defence facilities 76
——, Evidence . . 83
——, Interrogation 70 *et seq.*
——, Solicitor . 73, 76
Acetylene . . . 454
Acquittal . . . 63
Acrobat, Child . . 147
Act of Parliament . . 4
Actors . . . 529 *et seq.*
Acts of Terrorism . 25, 209
Address, Accommodation. 211
Addresses to Court . . 42
Adjournment . . . 62
Admissions . . . 76
——, Evidence . . 87
——, Formal . . . 88
Adult 138
Adulteration, Food . . 440
Advertisements, Abortion 136
——, Aerial . . . 381
——, Betting . 508, 510, 511
——, Indecent . 23, **128**
——, Lost property . 171
——, Stolen property . 171
——, Trading stamps . 444
Aerodrome . 111, 380, 383
Affidavit . . . 45
——, False . . . 219
——, Forgery . . 183
Affirmation . . . 82
——, Perjury . . 219
Affray 227
——, Arrest . . 18, 227
Age, in court . . . 138
Agents, Bookmakers' . 505
——, Books . . . 430
——, Bribery . . 221

PAGE

Agents, Theatrical employers 533
Ages fixed by Law . 153 *et seq.*
——, Firearms . 467, 468
——, Marriage . 156, 582
——, Motors . 157, 158, 159, 160, **254,** 320
Aggravated Assault . . 106
Agricultural Land, dogs . 490
Agricultural vehicles
——, Age for Driving 254, 255, 256
——, Lights . . . 274
——, Petrol . . . 450
——,Trailers . 603, 604, 621
Aiding and abetting 13, 14, 299
Aiding and Abetting Suicide **115,** 143, 587, 670
Air Force
(*see also* Army)
——, Army and Air Force Act . . 420 *et seq.*
——, Vehicles **299,** 320, 321, 663
——, Lights . 276, 277, 289
Air Guns . 154, 157, 467
Air Navigation . 380 *et seq.*
Aircraft . . 380 *et seq.*
——, Accidents . . 385
——, Aerial advertising . 381
——, Aerobatics . . 385
——, Arrest . . . 111
——, Customs . . 385
——, Damage . . 110
——, Destruction . . 110
——, Firearms . 111, 464
——, hijacking . 110, 699
——, Low Flying . . 383
——, ——, Exhibition . 384
——, ——, Helicopter . 384
——, ——, Race . . 384
——, offences . . 110
——, Petrol . . . 450
——, Protection . . 110
——, Requisitioning . 424
——, Roads . . . 663
——, Search . . . 209
——, Tokyo Convention 213, 385
Airport, Permitted hours 552
Alcohol, Blood, Level in Driver's 256 *et seq.*, 321, 563
——, Evidence . . 90
Alibi, Evidence . . 100

PAGE

Alibi, Notice of . . 100
Aliens . . 156, 157, **410**
——, Arrest . . 19, 413
——, Business names . 436
——, Change of address . 410
——, Children 156, 157, 412
——, Common travel area, 411
——, Detention . . 412
——, Disaffection . . 206
——, English Law . . 10
——, Exemptions . . 412
——, Hotel records . 411
——, Juries . . . 7
——, Non-patrials . 411, 412
——, Registration . 410, 412
——, Republic of Ireland 411
Ambassadors . . 10
Amber Lamp . . 281, 291
Ambulances . . . 602
——, Blue Light . 281, 290
——, Lighting 277, 281, 290
——, Speed . . . 332
——, Warning Instruments 605
Ammunition 458, 464, 466 *et seq.*
——, Auction . . 462
——, Auctioneers carrying 462
——, Business transactions 459
——, Carriers carrying . 462
——, Certificate . . 459
——, Children 154, 157, 458 *et seq.*, 467, 468
——, Definition . . 477
——, Export . . . 461
——, Forfeiture . . 476
——, Movement, prohibited 461
——, Northern Ireland . 466
——, Personation . . 419
——, Police permit . 462
——, Possession . 466, 467
——, ——, Minors . 467, 468
——, Previous convictions 466
——, Prohibited . . 459
——, Sale . . . 458
——, ——, Drunk or insane persons . . 468
——, ——, Minors . 467, 468
——, Search . . . 474
——, Test or proof . . 459
——, Transfer . . 462
Amphetamine . . . 576
Amusements with Prizes . 514, 515
Anaesthetics, Animals . 485

PAGE
Anaesthetics, Inquests . 585
Analysts 441
——, Certificate of 90, 260
Angling . . 26, 173, 199
Animals 479
——, Abandonment 482
——, Arrest—diseases 19, 481
——, ——, Protection 19, 483
——, Badgers . . . 502
——, Boarding establishments . 500
——, Captive . . 483
——, Carcases, theft . 166
——, ——, unburied . 491
——, Conveyance 482, 484, 487
——, Cruel poisons . . 484
——, Cruelty . . . 482
——, Damage by . . 502
——, Destructive . . 496
——, Diseases . . . 479
——, Domestic . . . 483
——, Footway offences 245, 246
——, Highways 245, 246, 247, 250, 251, 252
——, Imported . . 496
——, Impounding . 250, 483
——, Injured . . . 485
——, Knackers' yards 496, 497
——, Nuisances 245, 246, 247, 250, 573
——, Operations . . 484
——, Pain or distress, preventing . . 484
——, Performing . . 485
——, Pet 499
——, Pound breach 218
——, Rabies . . 480, 482
——, Requisitioning . 424
——, Riding Establishments 497
——, Road offences 245, 246, 247, 252
——, Rodeo . . . 486
——, Seals, protection . 500
——, Slaughter 463, 485, 487, 496
——, ——, Firearms . 463
——, ——, Knackers . 497
——, Theft . . . 165
——, Wild, criminal damage . . 178
——, ——, theft . . 165
Anti-dazzle . . . 280
Antiques, Firearms . . 478
Appeal . . . 38, **64**

PAGE
Appeal, Binding over . 226
——, Case Stated . . 65
——, Cinematograph . 537
——, Clubs . . . 567
——, Courts . . . 9
——, Crown Court . 64, 65
——, Deserter . . 421
——, Disqualification (driving) . . 299
——, Firearms . 468, 469
——, ——, Dealers 471, 474
——, Fresh evidence . 65
——, House of Lords . 65
——, House to House Collections . . 395
——, Incorrigible Rogue . 390
——, Leave . . . 65
——, Liquor licensing 551, 561
——, Pet Shop . . 499
——, Probation . . 403
——, Recognizance . 59
——, Riding establishments 498
Apprehension (*see* Arrest)
Appropriates, meaning . 165
Architects . . . 418
Areas, prohibited . . 210
Armed Forces, Vehicles 289, **320,** 321, 424, 663
——, Lights . . 277, 289
Armed with intent . **407,** 464, 465
Army and Air Force Act 422 *et seq.*
Army, Absentees . 19, **421**
——, Arrest . 19, 20, **421**
——, Billeting . . 423
——, Characters, False . 423
——, Decorations . . 420
——, Deserters . . 421
——, Harbouring escapees 218
——, Interference with Military . . 420
——, Lights . . 277, 289
——, Pensioners . . 422
——, Property . . 421
——, Recreation rooms . 538
——, Requisitioning of vehicles . . 424
——, Uniforms . . 422
——, Vehicles **320,** 321, 424, 663
Arrest . . . 7, 17
——, Absentees . 19, **421**
——, Affray . . 18, 227
——, Aircraft . . 111

PAGE
Arrest, Aliens . . 19, **413**
——, Assault . 18, 106, 107, 108
——, Bail
(*see also* Bail) 21, 61, 62
——, Betting, street 20, **507**
——, Biological Weapons 207
——, Birds Protection . 495
——, Borstal Institution . 404
——, Brawling 22, 214, 414
——, Breach of peace 18, 108
225
——, Children 10, 20, 75, **142,**
148
——, Coinage offences 20, **181**
——, Criminal damage, 20, 23
——, Cruelty to animals
19, 483
——, Customs Acts . 386
——, Cyclist . . . 26
——, Damage, public
grounds . . 26
——, Dangerous driving 25, 253,
311
——, Dangerous drugs 24, 578
——, Deer . 22, 173, 198
——, Deserters . 19, 421
——, Diseases of animals
19, **481**
——, Disorderly conduct 25
——, Drilling 22, **206**
——, Driver, Breath Test 335
——, ——, Disqualified . 300
——, Drugs, misuse . 24
——, Drunkenness . 23, 258
562-563
——, Election offences 25, **224**
——, Escape . . . 217
——, Explosives . 22, **447**
——, Firearms 22, 23, 464, 476
——, Fishery laws . 173, 199
——, Force . . 17, 406
——, Fortune Telling
27, 390, 391
——, Going equipped for
stealing . . 172
——, Hawkers . . 431
——, Hawking spirits . 431
——, Highways, obstructing
23, 253
——, Idle and Disorderly
Persons . 62, 407
——, Illegal immigrants 23, 413
——, Indecent advertisements
23, **129**

PAGE
Arrest, Indecent assault . 120
——, Indecent exposure . 128
——, Infants . . . 10
——, Inquest witness . 586
——, Loiterers . 27, **406**
——, Meetings . 25, 233
——, Mentally Disordered
Person 24, 580, 581
——, Motor cars 25, 26, 334, 335
——, Night time . . 24
——, Offensive, Conduct . 233
——, ——, Weapons 24, 407
——, Official Secrets Act
24, **212**
——, Pedlars . . 24, 431
——, Poaching, night 23, 24, 196
——, Political uniforms . 231
——, Power to . . 7
——, Privilege from . 86
——, Procuration . . 118
——, Prohibited immigrant 23
413
——, Property, Army, etc.
20, 422
——, Prostitution 26, 118, 123
et seq., 133
——, Public Order 25, 231–233
——, Public stores . . 193
——, Railways . 24, 379
——, Re-arrest . . 28
——, Rescue . . . 218
——, Resisting . . 464
——, Riot . . . 18
——, R.T. Act 25, 262, 263
335
——, Seals . . 20, 501
——, Smuggling . . 386
——, Soliciting . . 118
——, Streets, T.P.C. Act . 247
——, Suspected persons 25, 26,
27, 406 *et seq.*
——, Suspended sentence 390
——, Suspicion . . 18
——, Taking motor vehicle 167
——, Terrorism . 25, 208
——, Town Gardens . 26
——, Town Police Clauses
Act . . 26, 247
——, Trespass . 200, 201
——, Unlawful assembly . 227
——, Unnecessary . . 27
——, Vagrancy 27, **390,** 391
——, Warrant 27, 51–53, 61, 62
——, Wrecks . . . 194

PAGE
Arrestable offence 6, 7, **697** *et seq.*
——, Arrest . . 18, 21, 22
——, Assisting offenders . 14
——, Attempt 22, **697** *et seq.*
——, Concealment . . 14
——, List of . . 697 *et seq.*
——, Warrant . . 53
Arson, Abolition . . 176
——, Arrestable Offence . 697
Art Unions . . 511, 514
Articulated Vehicle 322, 593, **603**
——, Brakes . . 623, 624
——, Driver, Age . . 256
——, ——, Hours . . 354
——, Learner Driver . 304
——, Length . . 633
——, Wings . . 603, 662
Ashes, Motors. . . 648
Assault . . 105 *et seq.*
——, Affray . . . 227
——, Aggravated . . 106
——, Aircraft . . 110
——, Arrest . 18, 106, 107
——, Arrestable offences . 697
——, Binding to keep peace 225
——, Burning . . 109
——, Children 106, 139, 140, 143
——, Choking . . 108
——, Clergymen . . 414
——, Constable . . 415
——, County Court bailiff 218
——, Dismissal certificate 64
——, Drugging . . 108
——, Explosives . . 109
——, Indecent 106, **120**, 132, 154
——, Justification . . 9
——, Menaces . . 109
——, Poisoning . . 108
——, Police, on . 18, 107
——, Punishing child 106, 141
——, Statutory . . 106
——, Threats . . 109
——, Wounding . . 108
——, Wrecks . . . 194
Assay Office . . . 438
Assisting Offenders . . 14
Athletics, Firearms . . 463
Attempt . . . 13
——, Armed . . . 465
——, Arrestable offence 697 *et seq.*
——, Driving . . 257
——, Rescue . . 107, 218

PAGE
Attendance Centres **152**, 159, 399, 402
Attendants, Motors . 603
——, ——, Special types 664, 666
——, Trailers . . 652
Attorney-General, Abortion 136
——, Aircraft . . 111
——, Appeal . . . 66
——, Biological Weapons 207
——, Bribery . . 221
——, Coinage . . 181
——, Corrupt Practices . 221
——, Crown Proceedings . 222
——, Domestic Proceedings 31
——, Explosives . . 446
——, Harmful Publications 153
——, Hijacking . . 110
——, Indecent Reports . 131
——, Official secrets . 212
——, Printing, etc. . . 437
——, Public Health Act . 572
——, Public Order Act . 231
——, Terrorism . . 208
Auction, Firearms . . 462
——, Mock 434
Auctioneers, Carrying firearms . . . 462
Audible Warning Instrument . . . 604
Authorised examiner, personation . . 315
——, vehicle . . . 355
Automatic machines, Gaming . . 524 *et seq.*
——, Juvenile smoking . 144
——, Poisons . . . 575
Autrefois Acquit . . 63
——, *Convict* . . . 16
Aviation, Civil . . 380

Backing, Licence, P.S.V. . 345
Badge, Collector's 395, 396, 397
——, Hackney carriage 341, 373
——, Public service vehicle 347
Badgers . . . 502
Bagatelle . . . 539
Bail 59
——, Breach, arrest . 21
——, Children 62, 143, 157
——, Personating . . 419
——, Police—by . 61, 143
——, Refusal of . . 60
——, Remand . . 62

PAGE
Balers 664
Balloon . . 381, 383
Ballot papers 223
Bank note 182, 184, **185**–**186**
Bankruptcy offences . 174
Bar, Licensed premises 557 *et seq.*
Barbed wire 248
Barbers 442
Bastardy, Appeal . . . 65
Baths, Public . 128, 538
Battery 105
Bawdy house (*see* Brothels)
B.B.C, Children . . . 147
Begging . . . 389, **390**
——, Children **141,** 143, 156, 391
——, Pedlars . . 391, 430
Behaviour, Insulting, etc. 232, 233
——, Sureties . 225, 226
Bell, Motor vehicle **605,** 629, 641, 643
Besetting 230
Betting . . . 503 *et seq.*
——, Advertising 508, 510–511
——, Agency permit 505, 507, 509
——, Bookmakers', agents 505
——, Bookmakers', permits 505, 509
——, Cheating . . . 517
——, Definitions . . . 516
——, Juveniles . 158, 510
——, Licensed Office Regulations . . . 509
——, Office licences . . 507
——, ——, Conduct of 507–509
——, ——, Rules . . . 508
——, Pool . . 505, 506
——, Search warrants . 515
——, Street . . 20, **507**
——, Totalisators . 510, 516
——, Track (*see* Track)
Bicycle 337
——, Brakes 338
——, Carriage . 336, 337
——, Cycling offences 262, 263 311, 563
——, Drunkenness . 263, 563
——, Footways . . . 245
——, Licence . . . 363
——, Lights and Reflectors **274,** 337

PAGE
Bicycle, Motor (*see* Motor cycle)
——, Persons carried . 263
——, Registration mark 363, 364
——, Theft 168
——, Vehicle 265
Bigamy 214
——, Arrestable offence . 697
Bill, Indictment . . . 37
——, Parliamentary . . 4
Billeting 423
——, Licensed premises . 548
Billiards 539
——, Licensed premises . 547
Binding over . 8, 59, **225**–**226**
Bingo Clubs . . . 522
Biological weapons . . 207
Birds . . . . 492 *et seq.*
——, Fighting . . . 482
——, Nuisance . . . 495
Births 581
——, Concealment of . 137
——, Date of 302
——, Perjury . . . 219
Blackmail 109
——, Arrestable offence . 697
——, Obtaining goods by 171
Blasphemy 214
——, Libel 238
Blind, Dogs 488
——, Goods, pretendedly made by . . . 444
Blood test 256
——, Driver, Alcohol limit 256 *et seq.*, 563
——, Off road . . . 258
——, Personation . . . 419
Blood transfusion vehicle 290, 605
Board of Trade, Business names . . . 436
——, Depositors . . . 435
——, Securities . 433, 434
Bodies, Dead . 582, 584, 585
Bomb disposal vehicle 290, 605
Bookmakers, Agents . . 505
——, Definition . . . 516
——, Permits . 505, 509
Books, Bankruptcy . . 174
——, Dangerous drugs . 578
——, Domestic servants . 432
——, Falsification . . 174
——, Indecent . 128–131
——, ——, Post office . . 377

PAGE
Books, Indecent, Smuggling 386
——, Knackers . . 497
——, Printing . . 437
——, Registration, Motor 361 *et seq.*
——, Sale of intoxicants . 559
——, Scrap metal dealers 427
——, Sunday sale . . 442
Boroughs, Arrest . . 24
——, Bail by Police . 61
Borstal Institution 399, **403**
——, Committal . . 156
——, Harbouring escapee 218
——, Relevant age . 156, 159
——, Trainee, Arrest . 404
Brakes, Cycles – – 338
——, Efficiency . . 625
——, Heavy motor cars 612–616, 625
——, Inspection . . 650
——, Invalid carriages . 619
——, Locomotives . . 608
——, Maintenance . . 622
——, Motor cars 616–619, 625
——, ——, Cycles . 619, 625
——, ——, Tractors 610–612
——, ——, Vehicles 607 *et seq.*
——, Parking . . 607
——, Testing . . 270, 650
——, Trailers 620, 622, 623, 624
Braking Systems, Multi-pull 607
——, Pressure . . 608
——, Split 607, 612, 613, 621
——, Stored energy . 607
——, Vacuum . . 608
Brawling . 22, 214, 414
Breach of Peace . 225, 226
——, Arrest . 18, 108, **225**
——, Sureties 22, 225, 226
——, Threats . . 109
Bread 442
Break-down vehicles . 290
Breath test . . 257, 696
——, Definition . . 261
——, Driver . . 257 *et seq.*
——, Off road . . 258
Bribery . . . 221, 222
——, Billeting . . 424
——, Elections . . 222
——, Police, Licensed person 557
Bridges . 243, **325,** 666, 667
——, Menai 326
Bridleways, Motor vehicles 267

PAGE
British Protected Person 413
British Transport Commission . . 379
British Wine . . . 544
Broadcast music, etc. 538, 548
Broken Down Vehicles 326, 621, **627**
Brothels . . . 125
——, Children 126, 141, 143, 156
——, Homosexual practices 125
——, Licensed premises . 557
——, Procuration . . 121
Buggery . 120, **133,** 134
——, Arrestable offence . 697
——, Consent . . 132
Builders' Skips, Control of 249
Buildings, Burglary. . 163
——, Explosives . 447, 448
——, Ingress and egress . 539
——, Meaning . . 163
——, Open to public . 167
——, ——, Theft . . 167
——, Trespass, armed . 466
Built-up Area, Speed . 330
Burden of proof . **97,** 481
Burglary . . . 163
——, Aggravated . . 163
——, Arrestable offence . 697
——, Going equipped for stealing . . 172
Burials 582
——, Brawling . 214, 414
Burning, Assault . . 109
Business Names Registration . . 436, 444

Cadet Corps, Firearms . 470
Canal boats . . . 574
Cannabis . . . 576
Cannabis Resin . . 576
Canteen, Licence 542, 559 560, 561
——, Permitted hours . 552
——, Sale on credit. . 559
——, Seamen's . . 568
Captive Animals . . 483
——, Birds . . . 495
Caravan, Plates . 596, 641
——, Weight . . . 596
Carbide of Calcium . . 454
Carbon Disulphide . . 456
Carcase, Criminal damage 178
——, Theft . . . 166

PAGE
Carcase, Unburied . . 491
Care, Children and young person . 142, 144
——, Order . . . 145
——, Proceedings, . . 144
Careless driving . 253, 311
Carnal knowledge . . 119
Carriages . . 323, 336
——, Driver's offences 247, 253 *et seq.*
——, Drunkenness . . 563
——, Hackney . 339 *et seq.*
——, Offences . . 253
——, Petrol conveying . 453
——, Requisitioning . 424
——, Stage . . 339, 342
Carriageway, Annoyance . 248
——, Danger . . . 248
——, Definition . . 248
Carriers, Firearms . . 462
Carts, Dog drawn . . 492
——, Driver's offences 247, 253 *et seq.*
——, Lights . . . 290
Case, Progress . . 38
——, Stated . 41, **65,** 548
Casuals (*see* Supplementary Benefit)
Cats, Boarding Establishment . . . 500
Cattle, Diseases . . 479
——, Dogs worrying . 490
——, Drunkenness in charge 563
——, Export . . . 487
——, Highways and streets 250
——, Impounding . . 250
——, Injured . . 485
——, Knackers . . 497
——, Pound breach . 218
——, Straying . . 250
——, Unburied . . 491
Caution . . . 70 *et seq.*
Celluloid and Cinematograph Film . . . 455
Cemeteries . . . 582
——, Brawling . 214, 414
Censorship, Theatrical, abolition . . . 529
Centre, Attendance **152,** 159, 399, 402
——, Detention **151,** 218
——, Remand (*see* Remand Centre)

PAGE
Certificates, Air 381, 382, 383
——, Alcohol . . 90, 260
——, Aliens . . . 411
——, Ammunition . . 459
——, Analyst 90, 260, 261
——, Business names . 436
——, Chemists . . 417
——, Collections 394, 395, 396
——, Court register . 90
——, Deposit . . 307
——, Diplomatic privilege 90
——, Dismissal, assault 64, 106
——, Dogs, exemption . 488
——, Drink, etc. 90, 260
——, Driving instructors 333
——, Evidence by **89,** 318, 406, 421
——, Extended hours 555, 568
——, ——, Sentence . 405
——, False motor . . 334
——, Firearm. . . 459
——, Fitness, PS.V. 343, 344
——, Game . . . 197
——, Goods vehicle 346, 347
——, H.M. Forces . 420, 422
——, Insurance 306, 307, 334, 381
——, ——, Forgery . 185
——, Midwives . . 418
——, Motor vehicle . 89
——, Nurses . . . 418
——, Ownership . . 307
——, Passenger steamer . 380
——, Pedlars . . 158, 430
——, Performing animals 485
——, Perjury . . 219
——, Persistent Offenders, 405
——, Posting (of) . . 48
——, Security . **307,** 380
——, ——, Forgery 185, 186
——, Service (of) . . 48
——, Shot gun . . 459
——, Special Hours 553, 554, 556, 568
——, Statement to police 72
——, Test . . . 269
——, Theatrical employers 534
Certifying Officers, P.S.V. 343, 347
Certiorari . . . 66
Challenges, Fight . . 105
——, Jury . . . 38
Channel Is., Arrests 20, 25

PAGE
Channel Is., Embarkation cards . . 209
——, Harbouring escapee 218
——, Landing cards . 209
——, Theft from mails . 168
——, Warrants . . 52
Chapel (*see* Church)
Charabanc 340
Character, Accused's 41, 81
——, after conviction . 100
——, Evidence 92, 93, 94
——, False . . 418, 420
——, H.M. Forces . . 420
——, Liquor Licences . 550
——, Pedlars . . . 430
——, Servants . . 418
Charge, Procedure . . 75
Charities . . 392 *et seq.*
——, Gaming . . 527
——, War . . . 393
Charity and Vagrancy 389 *et seq.*
Cheating 517
——, Arrestable offence . 697
Chemists 417
——, Dangerous Drugs . 576
——, Poisons . . . 574
Child, Definition, C. & Y.P. Act 1933 138, 145, 154
——, C. Act 1948 . 140, 159
——, Destruction . 136, 697
——, Education Act 1944 145
——, Foster . . 138, 155
——, Protection . . 138
Children and Young Persons Acts . . . 137
Children and Persons under 18 . . 135 *et seq.*
(*see also* Juvenile)
——, Abandoning **137,** 139, 153
——, Ages . . 153 *et seq.*
(*see also* Ages)
——, Air Guns 154, 157, **467**
——, Aliens . . 156, 157
——, Arrest . . 10, 75
——, Arrest, Power 20, **143,** 148
——, Arrestable offences . 697
——, Assaulting 106, 140, 141, 143
——, Bail . 61, 62, 143, 157
——, Begging 140, 143, 156, 391
——, Betting . . 158, 510
——, Beyond control . 145

PAGE
Children, Brothels **125,** 140, 143, 156
——, Capital punishment 155
——, Care proceedings . 144
——, Cinemas . . 535
——, Collectors . . 396
——, Committee . . 140
——, Concealment of birth 137
——, Conditional discharge 400, 401
——, Conviction . . 102
——, Court **31,** 40, 41, 138, 150, 151, 152, 400, 401
——, Cruelty to . 140 *et seq.*
——, Damages or compensation . 410, 403
——, Dangerous performances **147,** 154, 156
——, Driving, minimum age 157, 158, 159, 160, **254,** 320
——, Education **145,** 153, 155
(*see also* Education)
——, Employment **145,** 155, 158
——, Employment, Abroad **148,** 158
——, Entertainments by . 147
——, ——, safety 142, 540
——, Evidence 35, 36, 82, 83, 144, 154
——, Explosives . . 448
——, Fire, unprotected 141, 154
——, Firearms 154, 157, 158, **467, 468**
——, Foster . . 138, 155
——, Gaming . . 519
——, Guardianship 138 *et seq.*
——, ——, Order . . 145
——, Harmful publications 153
——, Homes . . . 140
——, Homosexual acts 132, 133
——, Hospital order . 145
——, Indecency with 119, 120, 132, **133,** 154
——, Indictable offence . 37
——, Infanticide . 113, 137
——, Interrogation . **74**
——, Intoxicants 141, 153, 155, 157, 159, 555 *et seq.*
——, Invalid Carriage . 157
——, Kidnapping . 143, 155
——, Knackers . 155, 497

PAGE

Children, Liability for Crime **10**
——, Licensed premises 155, 157, 158, 557 *et seq.*
——, ——, Restaurants, etc. 547
——, Magistrates' Court . 150
——, Marriage . . 159
——, Minders . **139,** 153
——, Moral danger . . 145
——, Motor Cycle . . 157
——, Motors . 156, 157, 158, 159, 160, 254, 320
——, Neglect of 140, 143, 145
——, Nightdresses . . 592
——, Oath . . 82, 154
——, Offenders . 148 *et seq.*
——, Officer . . . 140
——, Pedlar's certificate . 157
——, Previous convictions 101
——, Prostitution . 123, 156
——, Protection . . 138
——, Public Service Vehicle 159
——, Punishment . 106, 140
——, Rags Dealer . . 155
——, Restaurants, etc. . 547
——, School crossing patrols 328
——, Scrap Metal Dealers 141, 156, **428**
——, Search warrant 118, 126, 143
——, Shot Gun 155, 465, 468
——, Smoking 141, **144,** 156
——, Statement as evidence 35
——, Street playgrounds . 328
——, Suffocation . 140, 153
——, Supervision order . 145
——, Tattooing . 153, 159
——, Traffic sign . . 328
——, Vagrants . . 141
Chimneys . . 573, 583
Chiropodists . . . 416
Chocolates, Liqueur – 544
Choking, Assault . . 108
Chorister . . . 146
Christmas Day, Betting . 506
——, Billiards . . 539
——, Game laws . . 198
——, Occasional Licence . 545
——, Permitted hours . 553
——, Shops . . . 443
Church, Brawling, . 214, 414
Church, Ingress and egress 540
Cider . . . 543, 544

PAGE

Cigarettes, children 141, **144,** 156
Cinema . 534 *et seq.*, 540
Cinematograph Act . 534
——, Film . . . 455
——, ——, Firearms . 463
——, Fund . . . 540
Circumstantial evidence . 95
——, Coinage offences . 182
——, Murder . . . 113
Citation of Acts . . 4
Citizen . . . 410, 413
Civil injury . . . 5
Clairvoyance . . . 392
Classification of Crime . 6
——, of Motor vehicles . 321
Clear Days . . . 63
Clergymen . . . 414
Close seasons, Birds, wild 493, 494
——, Deer . . . 198
——, Fishery laws . . 200
——, Game dealers . 432
——, ——, Laws . . 198
——, Seals . . . 500
Closing Hours
——, Licensed premises 552 *et seq.*
——, Refreshment Houses 570
——, Shops . . 441 *et seq.*
Clubs . . . 443, **565**
——, Appeal . . . 567
——, Bingo . . . 522
——, Excise licence . 543
——, Gaming . 519 *et seq.*
——, Justices Licence . 543
——, Permitted Hours . 565
Coastguard rescue vehicle 290, 605
Cocaine 576
Coercion 9
Coinage offences . . 179
——, Arrest . . . 20
——, Burden of proof . 97
Collars on dogs . . 491
Collections, Fraudulent . 391
——, House to House 393 *et seq.*
——, Street . . . 392
——, Theft from . . 167
Commercial travellers . 430
Commitment . . **57,** 63
——, Incorrigible rogue 390, 407
——, Rogue and vagabond 40

PAGE
Commitment, Sentence 41, 101
——, Trial . . . 35
——, Warrant . 53, 54
——, Written Statement 35, 40
——, Youthful offender . 151
Common Danger driving 25, 253
Common land . . 201
Common Law, Arrest . 18
Commonwealth citizen . 410
Communications . 376 *et seq.*
——, Air . . 380 *et seq.*
——, Post . . . 376
——, Rail . . . 379
——, Ships . . . 380
——, Smuggling . . 386
——, Telegraph . . 378
——, Wireless . . 378
Community Service . 153
Company, Business names 436
——, Directors, False statements . . 170
——, ——, Liability for theft 170
——, False accounting . 169
——, False statements . 170
——, Falsification . . 169
——, Liability for Crime 10, 170
——, Limited . . 436
——, Poisons . . 574
——, Property . . 166
——, Summons . . 47
——, Theft, liability . 170
Compensation 34, **174**, 193, 401, 403
——, Criminal damage . 174
——, Order . . 174, 193
——, Probation . . 403
Competent Evidence . 82
——, Witnesses . . 85
Competitions, Prize . 514
Complaint . 45, 47, 51
Compounding offences 14, 15
Compulsion, offence . 9
Concealing offences . 14, 15
Concealment of birth . 137
Conditional discharge . 400
Conduct, Admissions . 76
——, Indecent . . 127
——, Offensive . 232, 233
Conductors . . 346 *et seq.*
Confessions . . . 76
——, Evidence . 83, 87
——, Privilege . . 96

PAGE
Consent, Assault . . 106
——, Belief in, rape . 119
——, Homosexual acts, private . . . 133
——, Indecency 120, 132, 133
——, Rape, etc. . . 119
(*see also* Attorney-General, and Director of Public Prosecutions)
Consideration, Previous offences . . 16
Conspiracy and Defamation 237
Conspiracy . . . 237
——, Arrestable offence . 697
——, Husband and wife . 9
——, Incitement . . 12
——, Indictment . . 50
——, Labour disputes . 229
——, Murder . . . 115
Constable . . . 414
(*see also* Police)
——, Assault . . . 415
——, Bribery . 221, 557
——, Dangerous drugs . 577
——, Dogs . . . 490
——, Drivers, Tests for Alcohol . 256 *et seq.*
——, Examining officer . 209
——, Game Laws . . 197
——, Licensed Premises 556, 557
——, Office . . . 210
——, Personation . 415, 419
——, Prosecution by . 432
——, Protection Act . 28
——, Refusal to assist . 228
——, Scrap metal . . 429
——, Voting . . . 224
Construction and use 245, 375 599 *et seq.*
Consumer credit . . 445
Contempt of Court . 216
Continuing offence . . 68
Continuous bail . . 61
Contraband . . . 386
Contract carriages . . 343
(*see also* Public service vehicles)
Contract of service, breaking 230
Control, Motors . . 627
Conveyance
(*see also* Vehicle)
——, Meaning . . 168
——, Theft . . . 167

PAGE

Convicted persons . . 51
Convictions, Character . 100
——, Children . . 102
——, Previous 15, 33, 93, **101,** 319, 405
——, Record and proof . 15
Coroners 584
——, Court . . 31, 584
——, Director P. P. . 670
Corporal punishment, Prison 8
Corporations (*see* Company, and Municipal Corporations)
Corrective Training. . 405
——, Harbouring escapee 218
Corroboration . 83
——, Accomplice . **13**, 83
——, Perjury . . 220
——, Procuration . 83, 121
——, Sexual offences 83, 117, 119, 121, 122
——, Speeding . . 83
Corrosives, Assault . 109, 447
Corrupt Practices, Elections 222
Costs in Criminal Cases . 68
Count, Indictment . . 50
Counterfeit, Coinage 179 *et seq.*, 698
——, Currency . 181, 698
——, Official Secrets Acts 211
County Court, Personation 419
——, Rescue 218
Coursing, Cruelty . . 483
——, Poaching . . 197
Courts 29
——, Air Accidents . 385
——, Clearing . . 42
——, Contempt . . 216
——, Coroners . 31, 584
——, Crown . . 29, 64, 65
——, Appeal, Criminal Division . . 29, 65
——, Domestic Proceedings 31
——, High 29
——, Juvenile 31, 42, 150, 151, 154,
——, Magistrates . 30 *et seq.*
——, Occasional . . 30
——, Open . . . 36, 41
——, Powers, mental patients . . 579–580
——, Q.B.D. 29
——, Speeches . . 41
——, Summary 30, 31, 32, 33

PAGE

Courts, Supreme Court . **29**
——, Witnesses out of 42, **85**
Crane, Motor . . **627**, 660
Credibility, Females . 117
——, Witnesses . 82, 98
Credit, Bankrupt . . 174
——, Sale of intoxicants . 547
Cremation . . . 582
Crime 5
——, Accessories . . 13
——, and offence . . 6
——, Attempt . . 13
——, Classification . . 6
——, Definition of (1871). 5
——, Excuses. . . 8
——, Exemptions . . 10
——, Incitement . . 12
——, Judges' rules . . 70
——, Prevention . . 399
——, Vehicle used for . 300
Criminal damage . 176 *et seq.*
——, Arrestable offence 176, 698
——, Compensation . 174
——, Damaging property 176, 698
——, Destroying property 176, 698
——, Evidence . . 178
——, Intent, possessing anything with 177, 698
——, Police Property . 178
——, Search Warrant . 177
——, Threats . 177, 698
Criminal Firearms . . 464
Criminal Justice Act 1967
——, Bail . . 21, 60
——, ——, Breach arrest. 21
Criminal Law Act 1967 6, 14
——, Arrest . . 21, 22
——, Arrestable offence . 5, 7
——, Offence . . . 6, 7
——, Persistent Offenders 405
Criminals . . . 12
Cross-examination . 82, **98**
——, Defendant . . 83
——, Hostile witness . 97
Crossings, Road . 326 *et seq.*
——, School children . 328
Crown, Court . . . 29
——, Appeal . . . 65
——, Firearms . . 477
——, Proceedings against 222
——, Vehicles . 289, 319

PAGE

Crown Court, Licensing . 366
——, ——, Lighting 277, 289
Cruelty, Animals . . 482
——, Birds . . . 494
——, Children . 140 *et seq.*
——, Dogs . . . 492
——, Riding establishments 497
Cul de sac . . . 243
Currency notes, Forgery 184, 186
Current coin . . . 180
Custody . . 58, 67, 71
——, Child . . . 142
——, Legal . . 21, 408
Customs, Law . . 3
Customs Officers, Air navigation . . 385
——, ——, Smuggling . 386
Cycling, Arrest 26, 262, 263
——, Careless . 263, 311
——, Dangerous . 264, 311
——, Drunk, etc. . . 263
——, Racing on highway 263
——, Reckless, etc. 262, 263
Cylinders, Gas . . 456

Damage, Animals, by . 502
——, Compensation 34, **174,** 193, 401, 403
——, Driving, by . . 253
——, Highway . . 247
——, Parent or Guardian 401, 403
——, Riot 228
(*see also* Criminal Damage; Malicious Damage)
Dancing licence . . 537
——, Licensed premises . 548
Dangerous Dogs . . 489
——, Motors . . . 62c
Dangerous driving 25, 114, **252,** 311, 671
—— ——, Arrest 25, 253, 311
—— ——, Death by 252, 671
Dangerous drugs 476 *et seq.*, 698
—— ——, Arrest . 24, 578
—— ——, Arrestable offence . . 576, 698
—— ——, Controlled 576 *et seq.*
—— ——, Exportation . 576
—— ——, Importation . 576
—— ——, Licence . . 576
—— ——, Misuse . 576 *et seq.*
—— ——, Regulations . 577

PAGE

Dangerous drugs, Search . 577
Dangerous performances **147,** 154, 156
Darkness, Hours of . 279
Days, Clear . . . 63
Daytime, Lights on Vehicles 287
Dead Bodies . 582, 584, 585
Dealers 426
——, Firearms 462, 471, 473, 477
——, Game . . . 197
——, Intoxicants, wholesale 544
——, Scrap metals . . 426
——, Verminous articles 574
Death Penalty . 115, 205 668
——, Abolition . . 115
Deaths 581
——, Inquests . . 584
——, Perjury . . 219
——, Registration . . 581
Debtors, Unlawful harassment . . . 234
Deception, Cheating at play 517
——, Conspiracy . . 237
——, Food and drugs . 440
——, Goods obtained by . 168
——, Meaning . . 171
——, Pecuniary advantage obtained by . 169
——, Property obtained by 167, 168
——, Securities obtained by 170
——, War charity . . 393
Deck, Motors . . . 627
Declarations, Dying **77,** 91
——, False . . . 220
——, Licensing vehicle . 220
——, Police Constable 414, 415
Decorations . . . 423
Decoy birds . . . 492
Deer, Arrest . . . 22
——, Offences . 24, 198
——, Taking or killing 22, 173, 198
Defamation . . 232 *et seq.*
Defective Female 120, 122, 123
—— ——, Consent . . 132
—— Male, Consent . 133
Defence, Costs . . 68
Defendant . . . 50
——, Summons . 45 *et seq.*

PAGE
Defilement . 154, 156, 160
Defraud, Conspiracy . 237
——, Forgery . . 183
Dentists. 416
——, Dangerous drugs . 576
Depositions . . 34, 38, **78**
——, Children . . 143
——, Ill persons . . 79
Depositors, Protection . 435
Deserters 421
——, Merchant sailors . 380
Destructive imported animals 496
Detainer 228
Detention, Brothels 121, 122
——, Centres . **151,** 154, 155, 218
——, Females . 121, 122
——, Police Station 58, 261
——, Preventive 218, 404, 405
Die, Forgery . 184, 185, 186
Dietitians 416
Diminished Responsibility 113
Direct Evidence . . 86
——, Examination . . 98
Direction Indicator . 291
Director of Fair Trading . 445
Director of Public Prosecutions . . **69,** 668
——, Abortion . . 135
——, Arrestable offence, concealment . 14
——, Assisting offenders . 14
——, Bribery, Public Officials . . . 222
——, Coinage offences . 182
——, Companies offences 437
——, Concealing offences 14
——, Conspiracy against justice . . 224
——, Disaffection . 425, 669
——, Election offences . 223
——, Extradition . . 15
——, False Information . 14
——, Forgery . . 184
——, Fraudulent Mediums etc. 392
——, Heavy goods vehicles 356
——, Incest . . . 669
——, Indecent and sexual offences . . 120
——, Indictable offences . 7
——, Libel on officials . 238
——, Lotteries . 512

PAGE
Director of Public Prosecutions, Obscene or indecent matter . 129, 130
——, Official secrets . 212
——, Piracy . . . 213
——, Prosecution withdrawn, etc. . 7
——, Protection of Depositors . . . 435
——, Public service vehicles 352
——, Rape, etc. . . 120
——, Red Cross, etc. . 437
——, Regulations, App. III 668
——, Securities . 433, 434
——, Sedition, seditious libel . . . 206
——, Suicide . . 114, 670
Directors, False statements 170
——, Liability for theft . 170
Disabled, etc. person, Goods pretendedly made by . . . 444
——, Invalid carriages . 293 321, 322, 359, 631
——, Motor vehicles 295, 296
Disaffection, Aliens . 206
——, Incitement . . 425
——, Libel . . . 238
——, Police . 222, 415
——, Prosecution . 425, 669
——, Sedition . . 206
Discharge, Absolute **8,** 400
——, Conditional . **8,** 400
——, H.M. Forces . . 420
Diseases (*see* Animals)
Dismissal, Certificate of 64, 106
Disorderly and Idle Persons 389, 391
Disqualification, Animals 500
——, Dogs . . . 492
——, Gaming clubs . 524
——, Motors 298 *et seq.*, 302, 303 316, 695
——, Liquor licences . 552
——, Riding establishment 499
——, Speed limit . . 330
Distraint . . . 54
Distress Warrant . . 54
Disturbing Meetings . 235
——, Public Worship 22, 214
Divorce reports . . 140
Doctors 416
——, Dangerous drugs 576, 577

PAGE
Doctors, Poisons . . 575
——, Privilege . . 96
Documentary evidence **86,** 88, 91
Documents, Air navigation 382
——, Aliens . . . 411
——, Army, etc. . . 422
——, Bankruptcy . . 174
——, Business, evidence . 91
——, Concealing . . 170
——, Defacing . . 170
——, Destroying . . 170
——, Falsification . 169, 174
——, Forgery . . 183
——, Meaning . . 170
——, Motor, false . . 334
——, Official Secrets Acts 210–212
——, Pensioners . 422, 435
——, Privilege . . 96
——, Suppression . . 170
Dogs . . . 488 *et seq.*
——, Boarding establishments . . 500
——, Breeding establishments . . 492
——, Collars . . . 491
——, Control . . 266, 491
——, Cruelty . . . 492
——, Dangerous . . 489
——, Fighting . . 482
——, Guard . . . 491
——, Licensing . . 488
——, Livestock . . 489
——, ——, Protection . 502
——, Rabies . . 491, **492**
——, Races . . 504 *et seq.*
——, Stray . . . 490
——, Unattended guard . 491
Domestic
—— Animals, Cruelty 479 *et seq*
—— Proceedings, Court . 31
—— Servants Registries . 432
Door, Motor Vehicle . 640
Doves 495
Drilling 206
——, Arrest . . . 22
——, Arrestable offence . 698
Driver, Alcohol in blood 90, 256 *et seq.*, 321, 563
——, Conduct P.S.V. . 347
——, Cruelty to animals . 482
——, Disability . 295, 296
——, Duties, motor . 628

PAGE
Driver, Eyesight . 297, 335
——, Foreign 295, 305, 373
——, Hackney carriage 340, 341
——, Hours . . 353, 354
——, Identity . 312, 319
——, Licence (*see* Driving Licence)
——, Lights . . 270 *et seq.*
——, Minimum age . 254
——, Physical fitness . 295
——, P.S.V. . . 346 *et seq.*
——, Rules . . . 251
——, Steam vehicles . 650
——, Traffic Regulations 250
——, View . . . 659
Driving . . . 257, 258
——, Attempting . . 257
——, Careless. . 253, 311
——, Dangerous 25, 114, **252,** 311, 671
——, ——, Death by 311, 671
——, Documents, forgery 312
——, Hours of Duty 353, 354
——, Instructors, registration . . 332
Driving Licence . 294 *et seq.*
——, Appeal . . 296, 299
——, Disability . . 295
——, Disqualification 298 *et seq.*, 303, 316, 695
——, Driving without . 294
——, Duration . . 297
——, Endorsement . 301, 331 695
——, Foreigner . 295, 305
——, Hackney Carriage . 340
——, Heavy Goods Vehicle 303, **356**
——, International Permit 305, 373
——, Invalid Vehicle 293, 295
——, Motor Cycle . 304
——, Mowing Machine . 304
——, Northern Ireland . 303
——, Offences . . 294
——, Persons from abroad 295, 305, 373
——, Physical fitness . 295
——, Production . . 309
——, Provisional 254, 255, 304, 309, 356
——, Public Service Vehicle 346

PAGE
Driving Licence, Records, evidence . . 90
——, Stage Coach . . 339
——, Test, Competence 296, 299, 304
—— ——, Fitness 295, 297, 304
Drugging, Animals . . 482
——, Assault . . . 108
——, Rape, etc. . . 119
——, Soldiers . . 420
Drugs (*see* Dangerous Drugs, and Food and Drugs)
Drunkenness . . . **562**
——, Aircraft . . 382
——, Arrest . . . 23
——, Bicycle . 26, 263
——, Billiards . . 539
——, Child, in charge of . 154
——, ——, Suffocation 140, 153
——, Excuse . . . 9
——, Firearms . 468, 563
——, Hackney carriages 340, 564
——, Motors . 26, 256 *et seq.* 563, 564
——, Permitting . . 558
——, Refreshment Houses 570
——, Vehicle, in charge of 256, 563, 564
Dual Purpose Lamps . 280
——, ——, Vehicle 352, 589, 592, **628**
Duel 105
Dumping, Unauthorised . 587
Duress 9
Duties, Customs . . 385
Dwelling-house,
——, Burglary . . 163
——, Celluloid, etc. . 455
——, Cinematograph . 536
——, Found in . . 407
——, Trespass . . 201
——, Unfit . . . 574
Dying declaration **71,** 80, 91
Dynamite 446

Early closing of shops . 441
Education Act 1944 . 145
Education, Compulsory **145,** 153, 155
——, Wandering child 141, 153
Eels 199

PAGE
Eggs, Birds' . . 493–495
Egress and Ingress . 539
Eire (*see* Ireland)
Elections, Offences . 222
——, Personation . 222, 418
Electricity, Theft . . 168
Embarkation card . . 209
Embracery . . . 38
Emergency Powers . . 235
Employment, Children **145,** 155, 158
——, ——, Abroad **148,** 159
——, ——, Power of Entry 148
——, Labour Disputes . 229
Enclosed Premises (*see* Inclosed Premises)
Endorsement, Licence 301, 331

Engineering plant . . 666
Entertainments, Public . 529
——, Billiards . . 539
——, Children's 142, **147,** 540
——, Cinemas . 534, 540
——, Dancing . . 537
——, Ingress and egress . 539
——, Music . . 537, 548
——, Sundays . 532, 540
——, Theatres . . 529
Entry, Forcible . . 228
——, Gaming clubs . 527
——, Illegal . 23, 412, 413
——, ——, Non-patrials 23, 412, 413
Equipment and use, public services vehicles 344
Escape . . 217, 698
——, Arrest . . . 217
——, Borstal . . . 404
——, From fit person . 157
——, Harbouring . . 217
——, Mental patients . 581
Estreat, Recognizance . 61
Eviction, Unlawful . . 233
Evidence 70 *et seq.*, 81 *et seq.*
——, Accomplice . **13,** 83
——, Accused persons . 83
——, Admissions **76,** 83, 86, 87, 88
——, ——, Formal . 88
——, Alcohol in Blood . 257
——, Armed trespass . 466
——, Bigamy . 214, 215
——, Blood test . 256, 260
——, Certificate **89,** 260, 318, 421

PAGE
Evidence, Character 83, 93, 94, 100
——, Children 82, 83, 84, 143, 154
——, Circumstantial . 95
——, Coinage offences . 182
——, Confessions **77,** 83, 86
——, Corroboration . 83
(*see also* Corroboration)
——, Criminal damage . 178
——, Deposition 34, 38, **78**
(*see also* Depositions)
——, Diseases of animals 481
——, Document, business 91
——, Driving licences . 90
——, Drunken driving . 257
——, Dying declaration **76,** 80, 91
——, Endorsement on licence . . 301
——, Examination, witness 98
——, Expert . 90, 92, 93
——, Extent of . . 93
——, Firearms, Trespass 466
——, Frequenting . . 406
——, Fresh . . . 65
——, Handling stolen goods 94
——, Handwriting . 92
——, Hearsay . . 91
——, Husband and wife 83, 118, 132, 215
——, Identity . . 319
——, Inquests . 584 *et seq.*
——, Judges' Rules . 70
——, Leading questions . 96
——, Loitering . . 406
——, Nature of . . 86
——, Oath . . . 82
——, Official secrets . 210
——, Opinion . . 92
——, Privilege . . 95
——, Procuration . . 121
——, Proof, Onus of . 97
——, Prosecution . . 83
——, Rebutting . . 100
——, Records. . . 318
——, Speeding . . 330
——, Statements, Written 35, 36, 40, 86, **87,** 220
——, Vehicle licences . 90
——, Voluntary statement 73
——, Witness (*see* Witness)
——, Written statements **35, 36, 40, 86, 87,** 220

PAGE
Examination-in-chief 82, **98**
Examiners, Authorised, personation . . 315
——, Bicycles . . 338
——, Goods vehicles . 355
——, P.S.V. . 343, 344
Examining Justices .32, 34
Examining officer, Constable 209
Excavation carriers . 664
Excise Duty, Vehicles 359, 360
——, Exemptions . 365–367
——, Foreign . . 373
Excise Licence, Liquor . 543
——, Motor . . 359 *et seq.*
——, Prosecutions . . 432
——, Retail . . . 543
(*see also* Licences)
Exclusion order . 25, 208
Excuse, Crime . . 9
——, Homicide . . 112
Execution, Warrant . 52
Exemption from liability for Crime . . 10
Exemption order (Liqour) 556
Exhibitions, Indecent . 127
Exits 539
Expert evidence . 90, 92, 93
——, obscenity . . 92
Expired motor licence . 360
Explosives . . 163, 446
——, Arrest . . . 22
——, Arrestable offences . 698
——, Assault by . . 109
——, Fishery laws . . 199
——, Hawking . . 431
——, P.S.V. . . 348
——, Search Warrant . 56
Export, Cattle . . 487
——, Horses . . . 487
——, Ponies . . . 488
Exposure, Child . . 140
——, Indecent . **128,** 390
——, Wounds . 390, 397
Express carriages . 342 *et seq.*
(*see also* Public Service vehicles)
Extended Hours Certificate 555, 568
——, Sentence . . 405
Extent of evidence . . 93
Extortion . . . 222
——, Threats . . 109
Extradition . . 15, 670
——, Assisting Offenders 14

PAGE
Eyesight, Driver's . 297, 335

Factories 186
False Accounting . 169, 698
——, Alarm, Fire . . 583
——, Characters, H.M. Forces . . 420
——, Description of goods 438 439
—— Discharges . . 420
——, Discharges . . 420
——, Information . 14
——, Motor licences, etc, 334, 360
——, Perjury . . 218
——, Pretences (*see* Deception)
——, Registration, Births, etc. . . . 582
——, Statements 170, 219, 220, 313, 420, 435, 460, 462, 698
—— ——, Company directors . . 170
——, Trade Marks . 438
——, Vehicle or trade licences . . 360
——, Weights and measures 440
——, Written statements 220
Falsification of accounts 169, 698
Fares, P.S.V. . . . 342
Farriers 417
Felony, Former law . 7
Females, Abduction **122,** 156, 158
——, Assault . . . 106
——, Clearing Court . 42
——, Clothing, Personation 418
——, Credibility . . 117
——, Detention . . 121
——, Offences against . 117
——, Search warrant 118, 122, 126
Fences, Barbed wire . 248
Fighting, Animals . 482
Film, Cinematograph . 455
——, Inflammable . . 535
Finger Prints 15, **51,** 149, 155
Fire Guards . . 141, 142
——, Nightdresses . . 584
Fire Vehicles . . 629
—— ——, Blue light 281, 290

PAGE
Fire Vehicles, Licences . 365
—— ——, Lights . . 281
—— ——, Speed . . 332
—— ——, Warning instrument . . 605, 627
Firearms 163, **458** *et seq.*, 698
——, Air guns and shot guns 154, 157, 458, 466, 467, 468
——, Aircraft, on . . 464
——, Arms traffic . . 476
——, Arrest . 22, 23, 464, 476
——, ——, Resisting . 464
——, Arrestable offences 698
——, Athletics . . 463
——, Auction . . 462
——, Auctioneers carrying 462
——, Burglary . . 163
——, Cadet corps . . 470
——, Carriers . . 462
——, Cemeteries . . 582
——, Certificates 458, 464, 468, 469, 470, 475, 476
——, ——, false . . 460
——, Children 154, 157, 467, 468
——, Cinematograph films 463
——, Conversion . . 490
——, Criminal intent 464, 465
——, Crown servants . 477
——, Dealers 462, 471, 473, 477
——, Deer . . 198, 199
——, Definition . 163, 477
——, Disposal . . 476
——, Drunkenness 468, 562
——, Export . . 461
——, Fees . . . 470
——, Fish . . . 199
——, Forfeiture . . 476
——, Imitation 464, 465, 477
——, Insane persons . 468
——, Intent to injure 464, 465
——, Movement, prohibited 491
——, Northern Ireland . 466
——, Notices . . . 477
——, Pawnbrokers . . 460
——, Permits . . 462
——, Personation . . 419
——, Possession 107, 464, 466, 467
——, Previously convicted persons . . 466
——, Prohibited . . 460

PAGE

Firearms, Prosecutions . 669
——, Public Place . 466, 478
——, Register . 471, 472
——, Registration . 471, 472
——, Repair, test or proof 489
——, Rifle Clubs . . 470
——, Road Offences 246, 248
——, Rules . . . 477
——, Sale 459, 467, 468, 472
——, Seals . . . 500
——, Search . . 474, 475
——, Ships, on . . 464
——, Slaughter of animals 462
——, Temporary residents 464
——, Testing . . . 478
——, Theatrical performances . . 463
——, Transfer . 472, 473
——, Transactions 472, 473
——, Trespass . . 466
Fires 583
——, Carbide of calcium . 454
——, Carbon disulphide 456
——, Celluloid . 454, 455
——, Children 141, 154, 584
——, Petroleum . 450–454
——, Roads . . 246, 248
Fireworks, Explosives 446, 448
——, Roads . 246, 248, 448
Fish, Sea 200
——, Taking or destroying 26, **173**
——, Weapons . . 199
Fishing boats . . . 380
Fitness, Certificate P.S.V. 343
Fixed penalty offences . 332
Flag days 392
Flotsam 194
Flowers, Theft . . . 165
Food 440, 572
——, Early closing, shops 441 *et seq.*
——, Requisitioning . 424
Food and Drugs . . . 440
Footpath . 244, 245, 267
(*see also* Footway)
Footway, Invalid carriage on 293
——, Motor vehicles . 267
——, Offences . 243 *et seq.*
——, Parking . . . 267
Force, Arrest . . 17, 406
Forcible Entry and detainer 228

PAGE

Foreign, Enlistment . 214
——, Goods Vehicle 373, 374, 375
——, Motor Vehicles 373, 374, 375
——, Offenders, fugitive **15,** 670
Foreigner, Driving Licence 373
——, Interrogation . 75
Forestry Commission Vehicles 290, 605, **629**
Forfeiture, Firearms . 476
Forgery 183
——, Affidavit . . 45
——, Air Navigation . 383
——, Arrestable offences . 699
——, Characters, H.M. Forces . . 420
——, Driving Documents 312, 313
——, Factories Act 1961 186
——, Motor Documents, etc 185, 312, 313, 314, 360
——, Official Secrets Acts 211
——, Parking meter ticket 313
——, Pedlars . . . 430
——. Post office . . 377
——, Registration, birth, etc. 581
——, Stallion licence . 486
——, Telegrams . . 378
Fortune telling 26, 390, 391
Foster Child . **138,** 155
Found Committing . . 24
Fraud, Company . 170, 699
——, Conspiracy . . 237
——, Investments . . 435
——, Play (Cheating) . 517
——, Restitution . . 190
——, Vagrancy . . 391
Fraudulent Mediums . 392
Frequenting . . . 406
Fruits, Theft . . 165
Fuel, Excess, Starting Device . . 648
Fugitive offenders **15,** 670
Fumes 270
Fumigation . . . 587
Funerals . . . 582
Furious driving . . 253
Furniture Vans . . 629

Game Dealers 197, 198, **431**
——, Laws . . . 197
——, Poaching . 195–197

PAGE
Game, Prosecutions . 432
Games, Cemeteries . 582
——, Highways . . 248
Gaming . . . 517 *et seq.*
(*see also* Betting)
——, Amusements . 525
——, Automatic machines 524 *et seq.*
——, Bingo clubs . . 522
——, Board . . . 520
——, Charge prohibited . 518
——, Charges . . 521
——, Charities . . 527
——, Cheating at play . 517
——, Cheques . . 522
——, Clubs, . 519 *et seq.*
——, Definition . 517, 528
——, Disqualification . 524
——, Domestic . . 518
——, Inspection . . 527
——, Levy on stakes 518, 521
——, Licence . 519 *et seq.*
——, Licenced Premises 517, 519 *et seq.*, 557
——, Machines . 524 *et seq.*
——, Miners' Welfare institute . 519 *et seq.*
——, Offences . 519, 523
——, Participation . . 520
——, Permitted . 518, 521
——, Prizes . . . 522
——, Public places, in . 519
——, Refreshment houses 517, 570
——, Regulations . . 523
——, Restrictions . 518, 521
——, Sundays . . 522
——, Young persons 519, 522
Garrotting . . . 108
Gas, Acetylene . . 454
——, Compressed cylinders 456
——, Conveyance . . 456
——, Motor vehicles . 629
——, Noxious, Gun. . 460
——, Strikes . . . 230
Geneva Cross . . . 347
Genocide . . . 115
Glass, Motors . . 629
Glider Trailer . . 593
Gliders . 381, 382, 384, 385
Gold 438
——, False trade description 439
——, Hall-marks . 438, 439
Gongs, Motor **605**, 629, 641, 643

PAGE
Good behaviour . 225, 226
Good Friday (*see* Christmas Day)
Goods, False description 438
——, Meaning . . 171
——, Obtained by deception 171
——, Stolen (*see* Stolen Goods)
Goods Vehicles 320, 337, 352 *et seq.*
——, Brakes . 612, 613, 623
——, Crown . 320, 513
——, Drivers' licences 356–359
——, Glass windows . 629
——, Heavy, . . 356 *et seq.*
——, Hours of work 353, 354
——, Identity Disc . 353
——, Learner Driver 303, 304, 356
——, Licensing . 91, 352
——, Plates . . 269, 314
——, Relative plated weight 352
——, Test certificate . 269
——, Weight . . . 314
Grass-cutting machines 323, 663
——, Provisional licence 304
Grievous bodily harm, Burglary . . . 163
Grayhounds, Poaching . 197
Gross Indecency . 132, 133
——, Private, Consent . 133
Guard dogs, Unattended . 491
Guardian . . 138 *et seq.*
——, Child beyond control 145
Guardianship order . 145
Guilty, plea . . . 33
Guilty, knowledge, Coinage 182
——, Evidence . . 93
——, Handling stolen goods 171
Gun, Air . 154, 157, 467
——, Barrel proof . . 478
——, Firearms Act 458 *et seq.*
——, Found Armed . 407
——, Poaching . 195 *et seq.*
——, Road Offences 246, 248
Gunpowder, Hawking . 431
——, Possession . . 446
——, Sale . . 154, 448
Gymnasts . . . 416

Habeas Corpus . . 67

PAGE
Habitual Criminal . 404, 405
—— Drunkard . 558, 562
Hackney carriages 339–341, 372
——, Drunkenness 340, 564
——, Excise . . . 341
——, Lighting . . 277
——, Offences . . 340
——, Plates . 341, 372, 373
Hairdressers . . 443
Hall-marks . . . 438
——, Forgery . . 185
——, Gold . . 438, 439
——, Platinum . 438, 440
——, Silver . . . 439
Handcarts, Lights . . 290
Handling stolen goods (*see* Stolen goods)
Handwriting, Evidence . 92
Harassment, Tenants . 233
Harbouring, Escape . 218
——, Prohibited immigrant 413
—— Prostitutes . . 124
—— Spies, etc . . 210
Hares, Game dealers . 431
——, Game laws . 197, 198
——, Poaching . 195, 196
——, Traps . . . 483
Harmful Publications . 153
Harvesting machines . 664
Hawkers 431
——, Arrest . . . 431
—— Licence, prosecution 432
——, Tent, etc. . 248, 431
Headlamps, Vehicles on 271, 279, 281 *et seq.*
——, Dipped beam 272, 281, 282, 283, 284, 285
——, Horse-drawn agricultural vehicles . 274
——, Moped . 274, 282, 283
——, Motor bicycle 282, 283, 285
——, Multi-purpose . 272
——, Public service vehicles 284
——, Regulations . . 273
——, Sidecar 282, 283, 284
——, Single unit . 273, 285
——, Temporary residents 282
——, Three-wheeled vehicles 282, 283
——, Two-wheeled vehicles 282
——, Use . . . 286
——, Visitors from abroad 282
Hearsay evidence . 91, 584

PAGE
Heavy goods vehicles **356** *et seq.*
——, Parking on footway 267
Heavy locomotives . 320, 322
——, Brakes . . 608 *et seq.*
——, Construction and use 608, **634**
——, Driver, age . . 254
Heavy motor car . 320, 322
——, Brakes . . 612 *et seq.*
——, Construction and use 612, **630**, 659
——, Drivers (*see* Drivers)
——, Plates . . . 640
——, Rear markings . 292
——, Tyres . . . 655
Hedgecutting machines . 663
Helicopter, low flying . 384
Helmets, M/Cyclists . 266
Her Majesty's Forces . 420
Highways . . 243 *et seq.* (*see also* Road; Street)
——, Act, 1959 . . 247
——, Arrest . . 23, 245
——, Booths . . 248
——, Builders' skips . 249
——, Cattle grids . . 248
——, Code . . . 267
——, Cycle racing . . 263
——, Damage . . 247
——, Embarkments . 248
——, Fences . . . 249
——, Fires . 246, 248, 584
——, Meetings . . 235
——, Obstruction 243, 245, 249
——, Proceedings . . 249
——, Rails and beams . 249
——, Rope . . 246, 248
——, Rubbish . . 249
——, Traffic signs . 248
Highways Act, 1835 . 245
Hijacking . . . 110
——, Arrestable offence . 699
Hire, Consumer credit . 445
Hire-purchase, Consumer credit 245
Hired vehicle, owner 310, 312
Holding on to Motors . 265
Homes, Children's . . 140
——, Probation . . 403
Homicide . . 112 *et seq.*
——, Aircraft, on . . 110
——, Inquests . 584 *et seq.*
——, Legal consequences 115
Homosexual acts . 132–134

PAGE
Homosexual acts, Limitation of proceedings 123, 132
——, Private, consent . 133
Horn, Motors . . 605
—— ——, Two-Tone **605**, 629, 640, 643
Horseflesh 573
Horserace Totalisator Board 504, 505, 510, 511
Horse Vehicles, Licensing 339
——, Lighting . . 274
Horses 479, 486
——, Farriers . . 417
——, Knackers . . 497
——, Requisitioning . 419
——, Riding establishment 497
——, Shoeing . . 417
——, Slaughter . 487, 497
Hospital order . . 145
Hostels, Probation . 403
Hostile Witness . . 97
Hotel 545
——, Aliens . . . 411
Hours, Darkness . . 279
——, Driving . 353, 354
——, Extended . . 555
——, Permitted . 552 *et seq.*
——, Refreshment houses 570
——, Shop, closing . 441 *et seq.*
House of Lords . . 29
House to House Collections 393 *et seq.*
Housekeeping allowance . 414
Hovercraft . . . 323
Husband and wife . . 414
——, Accessory . . 13
——, Bigamy . . 214
——, Coercion and Crime 9
——, Conspiracy . . 9
——, Evidence 84, 85, 118, 134
——, Privilege . . 95
——, Rape . . . **119**
——, Theft . . . 84
Hydrogen, Cyanide . 587
Hypnotism . . . 541

Identification, Aircraft . 381
——, Bigamy . . 215
——, Conviction record . 15
——, Evidence . . 92
——, Foreign motors . 373
——, Hackney carriages 341, 372, 373

PAGE
Idle and disorderly persons 389, 391
——, Arrest . . 62, 406
——, Pedlars . . 389, **431**
Ignorance of Law . . 9
Illegal practices, Elections 222
Imitation Firearm . 464, 465
Immigration, Illegal . 412
——, Illegal entrant 23, 402, 412, 413
——, ——, Harbouring . 413
——, Non-patrials . 411, 412
Impounding animals . 250
——, Rescue . . 218
Imprisonment 8, 150, 399 *et seq.*
——, First offender . 33
——, Release 404, 405, 406
Incest . . 120, 669, 699
Inchoate crime . . 12
Incitement to crime . 12
——, Principal . . 12
—— to disaffection . 425
Inclosed premises yard or area . . . 407
——, Found on . . 407
——, Trespass . . 201
Incorrigible rogues . 390
——, Appeal . . 390
Indecency . . 127 *et seq.*
——, Advertisements 23, **128**
——, ——, Arrest . . 23
——, Assault 106, 119, **120,** 132, 155
——, Child, with 119, 120, **132,** 155
——, Clearing court . 42
——, Complaint, evidence 91
——, Exhibitions . . 128
——, Exposure . . 128
——, Language . . 127
——, Males . . 132, 133
——, ——, Private . 133
——, Plays . . . 529
——, Post Office . . 377
——, Publications . 128 *et seq.*
——, Smuggling . . 386
——, Theatre . . 529
Indicators, Direction . 291
Indictable offences . . 6, 50
——, Limitation of proceedings . . . 67
——, Night, arrest . 24
——, Progress of case . 38
Indictment . . 37, 50

PAGE
Indictment, Crime . . 6
——, Progress of case . 38
Indivisible loads **629,** 667, 665
Industrial tractor . . 631
Infant, Betting . . 509
——, Gaming . . 519
——, Liability for offence 10
——, Life protection . 136
(*see also* Children)
Infanticide . . 113, 137
——, Arrestable offence . 699
Infectious diseases . . 573
——, Aircraft . . 381
——, Public conveyances. 341
Informant, Privilege . 96
Information . . . 44
——, False . . . 14
——, Justices' Clerks Rules 701
——, Motor vehicles . 335
——, Official Secrets Acts 210, 211
——, Warrant . . 51
Ingress and egress . . 359
Injured animals . . 485
Injury, Civil . . . 5
——, Conspiracy . . 237
——, Intimidation . 230
Inn 546
Inquests . . 584 *et seq.*
——, Coroner's court 31, 584
——, Petroleum . . 450
——, Treasure trove . 584
Insanity 8
(*see also* Mental disorder)
Inspection, Chemists . 417
——, Vehicles . . 650
Inspectors, Cinematograph Film . . 455
——, Factory . . 450
——, Factory . . 450
——, Food and Drugs . 441
——, Gaming . . 527
——, Pet shops . . 499
——, Poisons . . 575
——, Shops . . . 441
——, Weights and Measures 440
Insurance
——, Aircraft . . 380
——, Certificates, Motor **307,** 311, 334
—— ——, Forgery . 184
——, Foreign Motors . 374
——, Motor 305 *et seq.*, 311
——, Passenger . 306, 307

PAGE
Intent . . . 5, 13
——, Assault . . . 105
——, Attempted crime . 13
——, Coinage . . 181
——, Criminal damage 177, 698
——, Evidence . . 93
——, Firearms, to injure, etc. . . 464, 465
——, Forgery . . 184
——, Theft . . . 166
Internal communication . 557
International Circulation 373, 374
Interpreter . . . 75
Interrogation, Directions 75, 76
——, Judges' Rules 70 *et seq.*
Intimidation . . . 230
Intoxicants . . 542 *et seq.*
——, Aircraft . . 382
——, Children 140, 153, 154, 157, 158, 557 *et seq.*
——, Licences . 542 *et seq.*
——, Measures . 544, 559
——, Railways . . 379
——, Refreshment houses . . 569
——, Sale . . . 558
——, ——, Club 544, 565, 567
——, ——, From Vehicles 559
——, ——, Offences 557 *et seq.*
——, Theatres . . 531
——, Unregistered clubs 565
Invalid vehicle 293, 322, 359, **631**
——, Brakes . . . 619
——, Driving licence 295, 296
——, Exemptions . . 293
——, Licensing . 363, 367
——, Lights . . 274
——, Registration mark 363, 364
Involuntary act . . 5
Ireland (Northern) Ammunition . 466
——, Driving Licence . 303
——, Embarkation cards 209
——, Firearms . 464, 466
——, Landing cards . 209
——, Shotgun certificates . . 464
——, Theft from mails . 168
——, Warrants . . 52
Ireland (Republic) . . 411
——, Embarkation cards 209

PAGE

Ireland (Republic), Immigrants . 411
——, Landing cards . 209
——, Warrants . . 53
Irish Republican Army, Proscribed organisation 208
——, Uniform . . 231
Isle of Man, Arrest . 20, 25
——, Embarkation cards 209
——, Harbouring escapee 218
——, Landing cards . 209
——, Theft from mails . 168
——, Warrants . 49, 52
Italy, Vehicle Lights . 287

Jetsam . . . 193, 194
Jewish shops . . 443
Jostling (obstruction) . 244
Judges' rules . 70 *et seq.*
—— Statement, 1955 . 101
Judicial notice . . 98
——, proceedings, Reports 131
Juries . . . 36 *et seq.*
——, Challenges . . 37
——, Coroners . 582 *et seq.*
——, Number . . 37
——, Trial by . 36 *et seq.*
Jurisdiction, Ouster of . 107
Jury trial right 7, 31, 39, 40
Justice, Obstructing . 224
Justices' Clerks Rules 1970 701
Justices of the Peace . 32
——, Binding over . 225, 226
——, Examining 32, 34, 38, 40
——, Licensing . . 548
——, Liquor licences 542 *et seq.*
——, Proceedings . . 33
Justifiable Homicide 9, **112**
Justification . . 9
Juvenile (*see also* Children and persons under 21)
——, Beyond control . 145
——, Court (*see* Juvenile Court)
——, Offenders . . 148
——, Press . . 131, 150
——, Smoking . . 144
Juvenile Court . 31, 151
——, Appeal . . 151
——, Breach of Order . 401
——, Care proceedings 144, 145
——, Child beyond control 145

PAGE

Juvenile Court, Oath . 82
——, Reports . . 150

Kidnapping . . . 155
Kites . . 246, 381, 383
Knackers . . 496, 497
——, Licence . . 496
——, Yard . . . 496
Knowledge (*see* Guilty knowledge)
Kosher meat . . . 443

Laboratory Technicians 416
Labour disputes . . 229
Lagan 194
Lamps, Agriculture . 274
——, Amber . . . 292
——, Bicycles . 272, 274
——, Blue . . . 290
——, Combined with reflectors . . 272
——, Daytime . . 287
——, Distinctive . . 290
——, Exemptions . . 277
——, Extinguishing . 246
——, Front 271, 273, 275, 276, **279**
——, Headlamps (*see* Headlamps)
——, Invalid Carriages . 274
——, Movement . . 272
——, Multi-purpose . 272
——, Overhanging Loads. 275
——, Position . . 273
——, Projecting loads . 275
——, Rear 271, 272, 273, 275, 276, 277, **287**
——, Restriction . . 272
——, Towing vehicles . 276
——, Trailers . 276, 278
——, Tricycles . . 274
——, Variations . . 277
——, Vehicles . 270 *et seq.*
Land implement 621, **632,** 662
—— ——, Conveyor 621, 632, 662
——, Locomotive . 608, 632
——, Theft . . . 165
——, Things attached to 165
—— ——, Theft . . 165
—— Tractor . 601, 610, **632**
Landing cards . . 209
Landlord . . . 414
——, Brothels . 125, 414

PAGE
Language, Indecent . 127
Larceny (*see* Theft)
Late Night Refreshment House . 568–570
——, Definition . . 568
——, Drunkenness . 570
——, Gaming . 517, 570
——, Licence . . 569
——, Prostitutes . . 570
——, Register . . 569
——, Tariff . . . 569
Lavatory, Common . 572
——, Motors . . . 633
Law, Common . . 3
——, ——, Definition . 3
——, Statute . . . 4
Lawyers 416
——, Privilege . . 96
Leading questions 96, 97, 98
Legal Custody . 21, 217
Length, Motors . . 633
Letters (*see* Postal pactets)
Libel 238
——, Seditious . 206, 238
Licences, Aircraft . 380 *et seq.*
——, Animal boarding establishment . 499
——, Betting Office 504, 507 *et seq.*
——, Billiards . . 539
——, Birds . . . 494
——, Canteen 542, 559, 560, 561
——, Carbide of calcium . 454
——, Celluloid and cinematograph film . 456
——, Cinematograph . 535
——, Coinage . . 180
——, Conductors 340, 346, 347
——, Contract Carriage . 343
——, Dangerous drugs 575, 576
——, Dangerous performances (children) . 148
——, Disinterment . . 582
——, Disqualification, Motor 298 *et seq.*, 303, 316 331, 695
——, Dog racecourse 504, 506, 510
——, Dogs . . 488, 492
——, Driving (*see* Driving Licence)
——, Employment abroad 148
——, Explosives . . 446

PAGE
Licences, Express Carriage 343
——, False . . 185, 334
——, —— statements . 313
——, Fishing . . . 199
——, Foreign drivers . 373
——, Forged . . 185
——, Game . . . 197
——, Game dealers 197, 198, 431
——, Gaming . 519 *et seq.*
——, Goods vehicles . 352
——, Gun . . 197, 432
——, Hackney carriage . 339
——, Hawkers . . 431
——, Heavy goods, drivers 356–359
——, Horse, docked, import 488
——, House to House collections . 394 *et seq.*
——, Hypnotism . . 541
——, Intoxicating liquors 542 *et seq.*
——, Knackers . . 496
——, Motor vehicles 359 *et seq.*
——, Music singing, dancing 537, 548
——, Occasional **545,** 558, 559, 560, 561
——, Pet Animals . . 499
——, Petroleum spirit 449 *et seq.*
——, Provisional, Driving 255, 304
——, Public service vehicles 343 *et seq.*
——, Refreshment house 432, 569
——, Release on . . 406
——, Residential (*see* Residential and Restaurant Licences)
——, Riding Establishments 497
——, Road Fund . . 362
——, Road service . 345
——, Seals . . . 502
——, Seasonal . . 556
——, Securities, dealers in 432
——, Slaughterhouse . 496
——, Stage carriages . 343
——, Stallions . . 486
——, Sunday entertainments 540
——, Theatre . 531, 532
——, Track . 506, 510, 511

PAGE

Licences, Trade, motor . 367 *et seq.*
——, Treasury (coinage) 180
Licensed premises . 542 *et seq.*
——, Billeting . 424, 548
——, Children 154, 157, 158, 557 *et seq.*
——, Conduct of . . 557
——, Gaming 517, 519, 557
——, Inquests . . 585
——, Residentail (*see* Residential and Restaurant Licences)
——, Television, etc. 538, 548
Licensing, Liquor Laws 542 *et seq.*
——, Airports . . 552
——, Arrest . 23, 562, 563
——, Bribery . 222, 557
——, Brothels . 125, 557
——, Canteen 542, 552, 559, 560, 561
——, Clubs . 552, 548, **565**
——, Drunkenness 562 *et seq.*
——, Justices . 543, **548**
——, Licences . 542 *et seq.*
——, ——, Disqualifications 552
——, ——, Excise . . 543
——, ——, Grant . . 548
——, ——, Removal . 542
——, ——, Renewal . 549
——, ——, Transfer . 550
——, Mess . . 544, 552
——, New Towns . . 570
——, Occasional **545,** 558, 559, 560, 561
——, Offences . 557 *et seq.*
——, Permitted hours . 552
——, Prostitutes 125, 126, 557
——, Railways . . 379
——, Refreshment houses 569
——, Register . . 551
——, Riot . . . 228
——, Theatres . 531, 532
Lifeboats . . 354, 663
Lifting appliances . . 634
Light locomotives . 254, 320, 322, 595, 634
Light Signals, Road . 329
Lighthouses . . . 194
Lights on vehicles 270 *et seq.* (*see also* Lamps)
——, Daytime . . 287

PAGE

Lights on vehicles, Exemption 277, 290
——, Headlamps (*see* Headlamps)
——, Long Vehicles 278, 289
——, Offences . . 278
——, Parking . . 293
——, Poor visibility . 287
——, P.S.V. . . 272
——, Registration mark 272, 292
——, Regulations . . 273
——, Sale of defective . 279
——, Testing . . . 270
——, Trailers 276, 278, 289
——, Vehicles from abroad 281
Limitation of Proceedings 67
——, Companies Act . 436
——, Game Act . . 196
——, Homosexual acts 123, 132, 133
——, Information . 45
——, Motor licences, etc . 317
——, Perjury . . 219
——, Poisons . . . 575
Limited Company . . 436
Liqueur Chocolates . . 544
Liquor laws (*see* Licensing)
Listed Seller, poisons . 574
Litter, Abatement . . 587
Livestock, Dogs . . 489
——, Pain or distress, preventing . . 484
——, Protection from dogs 502
——, Straying on land . 502
Load-carrying trailer . 593
Loads, Indivisible **631,** 665, 667
——, Overhanging . 275
——, Projecting . . 275
Local Authority, Animals 499
——, Bird Sanctuaries . 495
——, Destruction of birds 495
——, Game Laws . . 197
——, Justices' Licences 549, 550
——, Nursing Homes . 581
——, Poisons . . . 575
——, Prosecutions . . 432
——, Riding establishments 497
——, Scrap metal dealers 426 *et seq.*
——, Speed limit . . 330
Locomotives . . . 254
——, Brakes . . 608 *et seq.*

PAGE
Locomotives, Construction and use . . 608, **634**
——, Definition . . 322
——, Driver, age . . 254
——, Drivers' hours . 354
——, Plates . . . 640
——, Land . . 608, 632
——, Tyres . . . 655
Lodging-houses, Aliens . 411
——, Common . . 397
Loiterers . . 390, 406
——, Arrest . . **406,** 407
——, Evidence . . 94
——, Prostitution . . 26
London Traffic Area . 325
London Transport Executive vehicles . 305
Long pull . . . 559
Long vehicle, Lights . 278
Lords, House of . . 29
Lost property . 171, 187
——, P.S.V . . . 351
——, Rewards . 26, 171
Lotteries . . 511 *et seq.*

Machinery, Noise, motors 638
Magistrates . . . 32
Magistrates' Court 30, 150, 390
Mail bag, Theft . . 168
Mails (*see* Post Office)
Maim 108
Malice, Evidence . . 95
——, Murder . . . 113
Malicious damage (*see also* Criminal Damage)
——, Arrestable offences . 699
——, Explosives . 446–448
——, Railways . . 379
——, Telegraphs . . 378
——, Wrecks . . . 194
Man (*see* Isle of Man)
Mandamus . . . 67
Manœuvres . . . 420
Manslaughter . 114, 699
——, Aircraft, on . . 110
Mantraps . . . 201
Mark (*see* Registration mark, Trade marks and Hall-marks)
Markings, Motors . . 635
Marriages . 156, 159, **582**
——, Age . . 156, 159
——, Bigamy . . 214
——, Perjury . . 219

PAGE
Marriages, Solemnisation 582, 699
Married woman (*see* Husband and wife)
Mascots, Motor . . 635
Masquerading . . 418
Master and servant . 418
Maternity Homes . . 581
Mats, Shaking . . 246
Measures (*see* Weights and Measures)
Meat vans . . . 635
Mechanically propelled vehicles . . 359
——, Trade licence . . 367
——, Registration and licensing . 359 *et seq.*
Medals 423
——, Counterfeit coin 180, 181
Medical (*see* Doctors)
Medicine, etc., Early closing 441
Mediums, fraudulent . 392
Meetings 230, 231, 232, 235
——, Disorderly 223, 232, 233, 235
——, Election . . 223
——, Public . 207, 230–233, 235
Memory, Refreshing . 97
Menaces. . . . 109
Menai Bridge . . . 326
Mens rea . . . 5
Mental Disorder . 579 *et seq.*
——, Arrest . . 24, 580
——, Excuse for crime 9, 113
——, Firearms . . 468
——, Forgery of documents . . 185
——, Homosexual practices . 133
——, Murder . . . 113
——, Sexual intercourse 120, 122, 123
——, Unnatural crimes 120, 133
Mental Patients . . **579**
——, Escape . . . 581
——, Warrant . . 580
Merchant Shipping Acts . 380
——, Wrecks . . . 193
Merchant Ships, Homosexual Acts on . 133
Metals (*see* Scrap metal dealer) . 426 *et seq.*
Methylated Spirits . . 571

PAGE

Metropolitan Traffic Area . 325
Midwives 418
Military (*see* Army)
Miners' Welfare Institute, Gaming . 519 *et seq.*
Min. of Social Security Act 1966 . . 85, 435
——, Documents . . 435
——, Evidence, spouses, . 85
Minor, Meaning . . 158
(*see also* Children and Persons under 21)
Mirror, Motors . . 635
——, Tractors . . 633
Miscarriage . . . 135
Misconduct by Public Officers . . . 222
Misprision, Treason . . 205
Mistake 9
——, Property acquired by 166
Mock Auctions . . 434
Money Order Forgery . 185
Money (paper) offences 185–186
Moneylenders . . 428
Moped, Headlamps . 282, 283
Morphine . . . 576
Motive 5
——, Evidence . . 93
Motor Car . . . 321
——, Age for driving . 254
——, Brakes 616 *et seq.*, 625
——, Construction and use 616, **636**
——, Obstruction . . 244
——, Plates . . . 640
——, Seat belts . . 643
——, Tyres . . . 656
Motor Cycle . . . 322
——, Brakes . . 619, 625
——, Construction and use 619, **635**
——, Crown . . . 320
——, Driver, age . . 254
——, Helmets . . 266
——, Identity of driver . 312
——, Learner driver 303, 304
——, Lights 274, 282, 283, 285
——, Pillion riding . . 262
——, Pre-1905 . . 600
——, Provisional driving licence . . 254
——, Registration mark 363 *et seq.*
——, Sidecar . . . 647

PAGE

Motor Cycle, Towing . 653
——, Tyres . . . 656
Motor Mower . 304, 323, 663
Motor Tractor 610, **638**, 659
——, Driver, age . . 254
——, ——, Licence . . 255
——, Drivers' hours . 354
——, Plates . . . 640
——, Provisional driving licence . . 255
——, Tyres . . . 655
Motor Trade Licences 367 *et seq.*
Motor Vehicles (*see also* Vehicles) . . 321
——, Abandoned . 326, 587
——, Accidents . 258, **264**
——, Ages, Driving 156, 158, 159, **254**
——, Army, etc. 289, 320, 663
——, Arrest . . . 25
——, Audible Warning Instrument . . 604
——, Brakes . . 607 *et seq.*
——, Bridges . . . 325
——, Bridleways . . 267
——, Broken down 326, 627
——, Carriages . 336, 339
——, Certificate, Evidence 90, 260
——, Charge of, Unfit in . 563
——, Classification . . 321
——, Common land 201, 267
——, Construction and use 375, 599 *et seq.*
——, Crime, Used for . 300
——, Crown . . 319 *et seq.*
——, Dangerous driving 252, 311
——, Direction indicators . . 291
——, Door, opening . 640
——, Drivers' duties . 628
——, Driving instruction 332
——, Driving licence (*see* Driving licence)
——, Drunkenness 25, 256 *et seq.*, 563, 564
——, Dual Purpose 352, 589, 592, **628**
——, Excise Duty . . 359
—— ——, Exemptions . 365
—— ——, Foreign . . 374
——, Excise Licence 359 *et seq.*
——, Footway, on . . 267
——, Foreign owned 373, 374

PAGE

Motor Vehicles, Forgery . 185
——, Gas . . . 456
——, Gas Propelled . 629
——, Getting on moving . 265
——, Holding on to . 265
——, Horn, etc. . . 604
——, Hovercraft . . 323
——, Index Marks, forgery 185
——, Indicators . . 291
——, Insurance 305 *et seq.*, 311
——, Licensing . 359 *et seq.*
——, ——, Forgery . 185
——, ——, Keeping without 255
——, Lights . . 270 *et seq.*
——, Loads, Overhanging 275
——, Loads, Projecting . 275
——, Manslaughter . . 114
——, Meaning . . 321
——, Mirrors . . . 635
——, Motor Mowers 304, 323 663
——, Noise . . . 638
——, Obstruction 244, 326, 639
——, Owner . . 311, 332
——, Parking (*see* Parking)
——, Petrol . . . 450
——, Pre-1905 . . 600
——, Rear markings . 292
——, Registration . 359 *et seq.*
——, ——, Forgery . 185
——, Removal . . 326
——, Requisitioning . 424
——, Road Fund licence . 362
——, Road racing . . 262
——, Special types . . 663
——, Speed Limits . 589 *et seq.*
——, Speedometers . 648
——, Springs . . . 649
——, Starting device . 648
——, Stop lamp . . 291
——, Stopping by Police . 299
——, Taking of . 167, 334
——, Tampering with . 265
——, Television . . 650
——, Testing . . . 650
——. Theft . . 167, 334
——, Tower Wagon . 651
——, Towing Implement 651
——, Towrope . . 651
——, Tractors . . 322
——, Trade descriptions 602
——, ——, licences . 367

PAGE

Motor Vehicles, Trailers (*see* Trailers)
——, Trespass . 201, 267
——, Trials . . . 267
——, Used for crime . 300
——, Visiting Forces . 289
——, Warning instrument 604
——, Weight 308, 323, 325, 335, 596, 597, **659**
——, Windscreen washers 662
——, —— Wipers . . 662
Mowing machines . 304, 323, 663
——, Provisional licence . 304
Multi-purpose lamps . 272
Murder . . . 7, 113
——, Abroad . . . 115
——, Aircraft, in . . 111
——, Conspiracy . . 697
——, Diminished Responsibility . 113
——, Incitement . 12, 113
——, Inquest . 4, 585
——, Penalty . . . 113
——, Threats, Written 110, 113
Mushrooms, Theft . . 165
Music, Cinemas . . 535
——, Licensed premises . 548
——, Singing and dancing 537, 538, 554
Musk rats . . . 496
Mutiny, Incitement 12, 699
Myxomatosis . . . 483

Name and address . 310, 311
——, Aliens . . 410, 411
——, Business 436
——, Dangerous drugs . 24
——, Licensed premises . 556
——, Printing . . 437
——, Scrap metal dealers 426, 429
——, Seals . . . 20
——, Trading stamps . 446
National Assistance Act 1948 . . . 140
(*see also* Min. of S.S. Act 1966)
——, Coal Board rescue vehicle . 290, 605
Nature of evidence . . 86
Navy (*see also* Army—as to Desertion, Property, etc.)
——, Forgery . . 185

PAGE

Navy, Lights . . 277, 289
——, Vehicles **321,** 424, 663
Neglect, Children . 140, 143
——, Escape . . . 217
——, Manslaughter . 114
——, Railways . . 379
Nets 199
New Towns . . . 570
Newspapers (*see* Press)
Night, Arrest . . . 24
——, Billiards . . 539
——, Deer, killing . . 198
——, Dogs 491
——, Fish, taking or destroying . . 26
——, Lights on vehicles 270 *et seq.*
——, Poaching . . 195
——, Refreshment house 568
——, Scrap metal dealers 428
——, Spring Guns, etc. . 201
Nightdresses, Children's 583
Noise Abatement . . 588
——, Motor vehicles . 638
Non-patrial . 411, 412, 413
Northern Ireland (*see* Ireland)
Note-book, Evidence 91 97, 102
Notice of prosecution . 317
Notices and Proceedings, P.S.V. . . . 346
Notifiable diseases (*see* Infectious diseases)
Nuclear Accident Vehicle 290
Nuisances, Arrest in town 26
——, Barbed wire . . 248
——, Birds . . . 495
——, Highways . 243 *et seq.*
——, Meetings . . 235
——, Obstructions . . 244
——, Public health . . 573
——, Smoke . . . 573
Nurseries . . 139, 153
Nurses 411
Nursing homes . . 581

Oath 82
——, Perjury . . 218
Obscene 127
(*see also* Indecency)
——, Books, etc. . . 129
——, Libel . . . 238
——, Plays . . . 529
——, Post Office . . 377
——, Telephone calls . 377

PAGE

Obstruction
——, Builders' skips . 249
——, Carriages . . 252
——, Cinematograph Act 537
——, Clergymen . . 414
——, Constable . . 415
——, Coroners . . 584
——, Customs and Excise 543
——, Dangerous drugs . 578
——, Diseases of animals 481
——, Fire . . . 583
——, Footways . 245, 252
——, Hackney carriages 341
——, Highways and streets . 244 *et seq.*
——, Knackers . . 497
——, Meetings . . 235
——, Metal dealers . . 429
——, Military. . . 420
——, Motor vehicles 244, 245, 326, **639**
——, Passengers, P.S.V. 348
——, Performing animals 486
——, Petroleum . . 450
——, Police, of 18, **107,** 108
——, Post Office . . 376
——, Public Justice . 224
——, Railways . . 379
——, Riding establishments 498
——, Requisitioning of Vehicles . . 424
——, Road . 244, 267, 639
——, Vehicles . . 244
——, Wrecks . . . 194
Occasional Court-House . 30
Occasional licence . **545,** 558, 559, 560, 561
Off-licensed Premises . 553
Offence 6, 7
——, Arrestable 6, 697 *et seq.*
(*see also* Arrestable Offence)
——, Common Law . 4
——, Compounding. . 14
——, Concealing . . 14
——, Indictable . . 6, 7
——, Judges' Rules . 70
——, Limitation of proceedings . . . 67
——, Prevention of Crimes Act, 1871 . . 406
——, Prosecution Regs. . 668
——, Road Traffic 315 *et seq.*, 671 *et seq.*
——, Sentence fixed by law 400

PAGE
Offence, Statutory . . 4
Offenders, Assisting . 14
——, Community Service . 153
——, Discharge . . 400
——, Persistent . . 404
——, Probation . . 401
——, Rehabilitation 15, 101
——, ——, Period . 15, 101
Offensive Conduct . . 232
——, Arrest . . . 25
——, Meetings 25, 232–233
——, Public Place 225, 232, 233
——, Trades . . . 573
——, Weapons 25, 163, 232, 390, 407, **409,** 460, 466
——, —— Restriction . 409
Official documents, Forgery 183 *et seq.*
——, Misuse . . . 210
——, Privilege . . 96
Official Secrets Act . . 209
——, Arrest . . . 24
——, Incitement . . 12
——, Personation . . 419
——, Post Office Officials . 210
——, Search . . . 57
——, Trial . . . 42
Oil Pumps 451
Omnibus 340
Onus of proof . . 97
Open Court . . . 41
——, Coroners . . 584
Operation on animals . 484
——, Cruelty, animals . 482
Opinion 92
——, Speed . . . 331
Opium 576
Opticians . . . 417
Oral evidence . . 87
Orders, Statutory . . 5
——, Witness . 34, 78
Organisations, Quasi-Military . . . 231
Ouster of jurisdiction . 107
Outstanding charges . 16
Overcrowding P.S.V. 340, 350
Overhanging, Loads . 275
——, Motors . . . 640
Overt Act 13
Owner, Hired Vehicle 310, 312
——, Motor vehicle 311, 332

Palm prints . 16, **51,** 149, 155
Palmist, Arrest 27, 381

PAGE
Panel, Jury . . . 37
Paper money offences 185, 186
Pardon 11
Parent 140
——, Child beyond control 145
——, Compensation
Parking, Brakes . . 607
——, Fixed penalty . 332
——, Footways . . 267
——, Lights . . 293
——, Meter, forgery . 313
——, Places . . . 328
——, Removal . . 326
——, Vehicles 267, 326, 639
——, Verges, . . . 267
Parol evidence . . 87
Parrots 478
Passage on roads . 244, 250
Passenger, Vehicle . 336, 629
——, Vessels . . . 380
Passengers, Conduct 347, 348, 380
——, Cycle . . . 263
——, Insurance . . 306
——, Motor Cycle . . 262
——, Number 340, 342, 350
——, Regs. P.S.V. . 347, 348
Passport, Forgery . . 185
Patients, Mental 579 *et seq.*
Patrials 412
Patrol, School Crossing . 328
Pawnbrokers, Decorations 423
——, Firearms . . 460
——, Property, H. M. Forces 422
——, Public Stores . 193
Peace,
(*see also* Breach of Peace)
——, Keeping of . . 18
——, ——, Recognizance 59
Peaceful picketing . . 229
Pecuniary advantage, Obtaining by deception 169
Pedal cycles . . . 337
——, Brakes . . . 338
——, Drunkenness . 263, 563
——, Footways . . 245
——, Learner driver . 304
——, Lights and reflectors **274,** 337
——, Offences . 262, 263
——, Persons carried . 263
——, Theft . . . 167

PAGE

Pedestrian Controlled vehicles 304, 359, 363, **640**
——, Provisional licence . 304
——, Registration mark . 363
Pedestrian Crossings . 326
Pedlars 430
——, Arrest . . . 24
——, Begging . . 391
Penal servitude . . 8
Penalties . . 8, **399**
——, Road Traffic Offences 315 *et seq.*, 315 *et seq.*
Pensioners 422
Perambulators, lights . 290
Performing animals . 485
Perjury 218, 582
——, Affidavit . . 45
——, Arrestable offences . 699
——, Evidence . . 36
Permit, Betting Agency 505, 507
——, Bookmakers . 505, 507
——, Driving . . 373
——, Firearms . . 462
——, Sunday cinemas . 540
Permitted hours (Liquor) 552
——, Clubs . . . 565
——, Off-licence . . 553
——, Wales . . 545, 554
Persistent offender . . 404
——, Certificates . . 405
Personation 418
——, Ammunition . . 419
——, Arrestable offences 699
——, Authorised Examiners 315
——, Bail . . . 419
——, Blood test . . 419
——, Child . . . 419
——, Elections . . 222
——, Evidence . . 82
——, Firearms . . 419
——, Juror . . . 38
——, Master . . . 418
——, Official Secrets Act 211
——, Rape . . **119**, 418
——, Shot gun . . 419
Pet animals . . . 499
Pethedine 576
Petrol . . . 448 *et seq.*
——, Hawking . . 431
Petrol pumps . . . 451
Pharmacists . . 417, 576
Phosphorus . . . 484

PAGE

Photograph, Aliens . . 410
——, Contempt of court . 210
Physiotherapists . . 416
Picketing . . . 131
——, Peaceful . . 229
Picture houses . . 534
Pictures, indecent 128 *et seq.*
Pigeon . . . 493, 495
(*see also* Poultry)
Pigs, slaughter . . 496
Pillion riding . . 262
Piracy . . . 8, 213, 699
Pirate Radio Stations . 379
Place Betting, Street . 506
——, of Safety . 138, 143
——, Prohibited . . 210
——, Public, Drunkenness, 562, 563
——, ——, meaning . 230
Plan or drawing, evidence 89
Plants, Theft . . . 165
Plate, Good vehicle 269, 314
——, Hackney carriage 341, 373
——, Hall-marks . . 438
——, Motor Registration 363, 364
——, Trade . . . 367
——, Trailer . . 596, 640
——, Vehicle 269, 314, 363, 364, 596, 640
Platinum, False Trade description . . 439
——, Hallmarking . . 440
Playgrounds, street . 328
Plays, Stage . . 529 *et seq.*
——, ——, Censorship, abolition . . . 529
Poaching 24, 195 *et seq.*, 699
Poisoning, Animals . 483, 484
——, Arrestable offence . 700
——, Evidence . . 91
——, Fishery laws . . 199
——, Inquest . . 585
——, Malicious . . 109
——, Seals . . 500, 501
Poisonous Waste . . 587
Poisons 574
Police, Actions against . 27
——, Assaulting, etc. 107, 108
——, Authority, collections 392
——, Bail . . 61, 143
——, Billeting, etc. . 423
——, Bribery . 221, 557
——, Canvassing at elections 223

PAGE

Police, Constable (*see* Constable)
——, Detention by . . 58
——, Disaffection, etc. . 222
——, Elections . . 223
——, Fires . . . 583
——, Game Laws . . 197
——, Informant . . 96
——, Intoxicants . . 557
——, Law . . . 3
——, Licensed premises **556, 562**
——, Meetings . . 235
——, Mental disorder 579, 580
——, Misconduct . . 222
——, Name and Addresses 310
——, Note book . . 74
——, Obstructing 18, **107,** 108
——, Official Secrets Act 210
——, Personating . 415, 419
——, Powers, R.T. Act 308 *et seq.*, 334 *et seq.*
——, Property, Crime, used for . . . 190
——, ——, Criminal damage 178
——, ——, Disposal . 190
——, ——, Police Property Act . **188,** 192, 434
——, Property Act, **188,** 192, 434
——, ——, Fund . . 189
——, Prosecutions by . 432
——, Questioning by 70 *et seq.*
——, Reports, Evidence . 91
——, Special vehicles . 666
——, Trade Unions . 229
——, Traffic . . 250, 328
Uniform . . . 415
——, Vehicle . 334, 605, **641**
——, ——, Blue light . 290
——, Voting, elections . 223
Ponies, Export . . 488
PoolBetting . . 504, 505
Poor Relief (*see* Min. of S.S. Act 1966)
Positive evidence . . 86
Possession . . . 166
——, Coinage offences 181, 182
——, Explosives . 446 *et seq.*
——, Firearms 107, 465, 466
——, Fishery laws . . 200
——, Forcible entry . 228
——, Obscene article . 130

PAGE

Possession, Pensioners' papers . . 422
——, Police uniform . 415
——, Property, H.M. Forces 422
——, Public stores . . 193
——, Wreck . . . 194
Post Office . . . 376
——, Closing . . 442
——, Incitement . . 12
——, Indecent packets . 131
——, Motor licence . 362
Postal Packet . . 371
——, Indecent . . 131
——, Prohibited . . 377
——, Recorded delivery 47, 49, 90
——, Theft . . . 168
Poultry . . . 479, 480
——, Damage by dogs . 489
——, Diseases . 479, 480
Pound, Breach . . 218
——, Feeding animals 250, 483
——, Impounding . . 250
Power of Entry (employment) . . 148
Premises, Found on . 407
Press in Court . . 42
——, Children Acts. 131, 150
——, Domestic Proceedings 35
——, Indecent reports . 131
Presumptions . . 91
Prevention of crime (dealing with Probation, Borstal, etc.) . 399 *et seq.*
Preventive detention 8, 213, 404, 405
Previous Convictions 15, 33, 90, 94, 98, 101, 405
——, Evidence 15, 90, 101
——, Inadmissibility . 15
——, Proof . . . 15
Priest, Privilege . . 96
Primary evidence . . 86
Principal, Incitement . 12
——, Offence . . . 13
——, Recognizance . 59
Printing and publishing . 437
Prison breach . **217,** 408
Prisoner. . . . 50, 51
——, Attendance required 67
——, Bail . . . 59
(*see also* Bail)
——, Caution . 70 *et seq.*

PAGE
Prisoner, Commitment . **57,** 63
——, Escape . . **217,** 408
——, Evidence . . 83
——, Habeas Corpus . 67
——, Inquests . . 584
——, Judges' Rules . 70
——, Questions to . 70 *et seq.*
——, Rescue . . . 218
——, Search . . . 17
——, Witness . . 83
——, Youthful offender 148, 149, 158
Prisons 408
——, Certificate . . 405
——, Corporal punishment 8
——, Offences . . 408
——, Offenders . . 8
Private Vehicles . . 337
Privilege 95
——, Cross-examination . 99
——, Reports . . 238
——, Witness . . 86
Prize Competitions . . 514
—— fight . . . 105
—— for Amusements 514, 515
Probation of offenders **8, 401**
——, Appeal . . . 64
——, Community Service. 153
——, Order, amendment . 702
Procedure (dealing with Summons, Warrants, Bail, etc.) . 44
Processions 232
Proclamation of Emergency 236
Procuration . . 121, 159
——, Arrest . . . 26
——, Buggery . 133, 134
——, Corroboration 83, 121
——, Threats . . 109
Procure, meaning . . 136
Profane 127
Progress of a case . . 38
Prohibited Place . . 210
—— Uniform 230, 231, 415, 423
—— Weapons . . . 460
Projecting loads, Marking 275, 667
Promise, Bribery . . 221
Proof, Burden of . . 97
——, Convictions . . 15
——, Gun barrel . . 478
Property . . 165, 187
——, Belonging to another 166

PAGE
Property, Corporation . 166
——, Crime, Used for . 190
——, Criminal damage 176 *et seq.*, 698
——, Definition . . 178
——, H.M. Forces . . 421
——, Lost 26, 171, 187, 351
——, Meaning . . 165
——, Mistake, acquired by 166
——, Obtaining by deception . . . 168
——, Police, Criminal damage 178
——, ——, Police Property Act **188,** 192, 434
——, Possession . . 166
——, P.S.V., Lost . . 351
——, Restitution **188** *et seq.*, 403
——, Sale or transfer . 192
(*see also* Stolen property)
——, Trust . . . 166
——, ——, Criminal damage 178
Proscribed organisation 25, 207, 208
——, Arrest . . . 25
——, Support. . . 207
——, Uniforms . . 208
Prosecution, Costs . . 68
——, Evidence . 81 *et seq.*
——, Lawyer, etc. . . 416
——, Licensing Acts . 561
——, of Offences Regs. 69, 668
——, Restriction . . 317
——, Road Traffic Offences 315 *et seq.*, 671 *et seq.*
——, Time Limitation . 67
——, Warning 253, 254, 331
Prosecutor . . . 43
Prostitution . . 118, 123
——, Arrestable offences . 700
——, Children . 120, 156
——, Male . . 26, 133
——, ——, Limitation . 123
——, Licensed Premises 125, 557
——, Procuration . 121, 159
——, Refreshment houses 570
Protection, Child . . 138
——, Constable's . . 27
—— Order (liquor) . . 550
Provocation, Assault 106, 114
Provisional Driving Licences 254, 255, 304, 309, 356

PAGE

Public Body, Definition 222
Public entertainments 529 *et seq.* (*see also* Entertainments)
Public health . . 572 *et seq.*
Public Justice Offences, including Perjury, Bribery, etc. 216 *et seq.*
Public meetings 230–233, 235
Public Mischief . 15, 237
Public official, Bribery . **221**
——, Forgery . . 184
——, Misconduct . . 222
——, Official Secrets Acts 210
——, Public Stores . . 193
Public Order, including Riot, etc. . . . 225 *et seq.*
Public place, Children Acts 138
——, Drunkenness . 562, 563
——, Firearm . **466,** 478
——, Gaming . . 518
——, Meaning 230, 408, 478
——, Meetings 207, 230–233, 235
——, Mentally disordered person . . 580
——, Offensive weapon . 577
——, Public Order . 225 *et seq.*
——, Uniforms, Prohibited 208
Public policy, Privilege . 96
Public service vehicles 337, 341 *et seq.*, 641
——, Classification . . 342
——, Drivers and Conductors . . 346 *et seq.*
——, ——, conduct 347, 348
——, ——, hours . 353, 354
——, ——, minors . . 159
——, Equipment and use 344
——, Fitness . . . 344
——, Foreign . 373, 374
——, Licences . 343, 345
——, ——, Appeals . 346
——, ——, Records . 350
——, Lights . . . 284
——, Lost property . 351
——, Passengers . 347, 348
——, Returns. . . 351
——, Tickets . . . 349
Public stores . . **193,** 421
Public vehicle . . 337
Publications, Indecent 128 *et seq.*
Publishing 437
Pumps, petrol and oil . 451
Punishment, Child, etc. 106, 141

PAGE

Punishment, For Crime . 8
——, Road traffic offences 315 *et seq.*, 671 *et seq.*

Queen's Bench Division 29, 66
——, Evidence . . 13
——, Peace . . . 225
Questioning, Explosives Substances Act 1883 447
——, Official Secrets Acts 211
——, Persons . 70 *et seq.*
Questions, Leading . **96,** 97
Quitting motor vehicle . 642

Rabbits, Game dealers . 431
——, Myxomatosis . . 483
——, Poaching . . 195
——, Traps . . . 483
Rabies . . . 480, **492**
Race relations . . 115
Racecourse (*see also* Betting) 503 *et seq.*
Racing, Air . . . 384
——, Road . . . 262
Radio-activity, Vehicle . 290
Radiographers . . 416
Rags, Dealers . 155, 561
Railway vehicles . . 642
Railways 379
——, Arrestable offences . 700
Rape . . **119,** 155, 692
——, Burglary . . 163
——, Consent . . 119
——, ——, Belief in . 119
——, Defence. . . 119
——, Evidence . 84, 91
Rates, Warrants . . 55
Real evidence . . 86
Reaping machines . . 664
Rear Markings, Vehicles . 292
Rear registration mark, Lighting . . 292
——, Position, etc. . 364, 365
Re-arrest . . . 28
Rebutting evidence . 100
Recalled witness . 82, **99**
Receiver of wreck . . 194
Reckless cycle riding . 262
Recognizance . . . 58
——, Bail, breach . . 21
——, Forgery . . 185
——, Peace . . . 225
——, Prisoner, Bail 59, 60
——, Probation . . 393

PAGE

Recorded Delivery 47, 49, 89
Recorded Music . 538, 548
Recorder . . . 30
Recut Tyres . 656, 657, 658
Red, Crescent . . 437
——, Cross . . 437, 438
——, Lion and Sun . 437
Red Squill . . . 484
Re-examination . 82, **99**
Reflector, Additional 278, 289
——, Amber . . . 289
——, Bicycles . . 274
——, Combined with light 272
——, Obligatory . . 271
——, Red 272, 273, 274, 276
——, Sale of defective . 279
——, Testing . . . 269
Refreshing memory . 97
Refreshment during interrogation . . 74
Refreshment houses 568 *et seq.*
——, Definition . . 568
——, Drunkenness . . 570
——, Gaming . 517, 570
——, Licence . . . 569
——, Prostitutes . 125, 570
——, Register . . 569
——, Tariff . . . 569
Refuse vehicles . . 642
Registered Post summons 47
Registers, Aliens . . 410
——, Animal boarding establishments . 500
——, Architects . . 418
——, Births, deaths and marriages . . 571
——, Bookmakers' agents 505
——, Business names . 436
——, Charities . . 392
——, Chemists . . 417
——, Clubs 565, 566, 567
——, Common lodging-houses . . 397
——, Dentists . . 416
——, Doctors . . 416
——, Dogs, Stray . . 490
——, Domestic servants . 432
——, Driving instructors 332
——, Firearms . 471, 472
——, Hotel, Aliens . . 411
——, Late night refresh-
——, Late night refreshment houses . 569
——, Liquor licences . 551

PAGE

Registers, Lodgings, etc., aliens . . 411
——, Medical . . . 416
——, Midwives . . 418
——, Motors . . 359 *et seq.*
——, ——, foreign-owned 373
——, Nurses . . . 417
——, Nursing Homes . 579
——, Opticians . . 417
——, Performing animals 485
——, Perjury . . 219
——, Refreshment houses 569
——, Scrap metal dealers 426
——, Theatrical Employers 533
——, Trade marks . . 437
——, Various professions 416 *et seq.*
——, Vehicles . 359 *et seq.*
——, Veterinary surgeons 417
——, War charities . 393
Registration, Vehicles 348 *et seq.*
——, ——, Forgery . 185
——, Book . . 361, 362
——, Mark . 292, 362 *et seq.*
——, ——, Foreign . 373
Regulation of vehicular traffic . . 250
Regulations, Statutory . 5
Rehabilitation of offenders 15, 101
——, Period . . 15, 101
Relevant evidence . . 93
——, Questions . . 98
Remand . . 53, 62
Remand Centre . . 151
——, Age for . . . 159
——, Alien . . . 412
——, Detention . . 151
——, Escape . . . 218
——, Harbouring Escapee 218
Remission of penalty . 11
Removal of liquor licence 543
Removal of vehicles . 326
Renewal of liquor licence 549
Rent Act 1965 . . 233
Reports, Indecent . . 131
Reputed thief, Definition. 407
——, Loitering, etc. 390, 406
Requisitions, Army, etc . 424
Res gestae . . . 91
Rescue 218
——, Attempted . . 107
Reservists . . . 421

PAGE

Residential and Restaurant Licences . . 546
——, Brothel . . 126
——, Name . . . 556
——, Occasional licence . 545
——, Prostitutes . . 125
——, Removal . . 551
——, Unauthorised consumption . . 560
Resilient Tyres . . 593
Resisting police . . 107
Restitution of stolen property . . . **188**
Reversing Lights . 272, **288**
——, Motors . . . 642
Rewards, Stolen Property 26, 171
Riding, Establishments 159, **497**
——, Footway . . 245
——, Furiously . . 253
Rifle Clubs . . . 470
Riot 228
——, Arrest . . . 18
——, Damage . . 228
Road 243
(*see also* Highways; Street)
——, Cleansing Vehicles 290, **642,** 660
——, Clearance Vehicles 281, 290
——, Damage . 248, 325
——, Experiments . . 647
——, Racing . . 253, 262
——, Repair Vehicles . 643
——, Sweeper. 290, 642, 660
——, Works . . . 325
Road Fund Licence . 362
Road Rollers . . . 643
——, Driver, Age . . 255
——, Learner driver . 304
Road Service Licence . 345
Road Traffic Acts . . 252
——, Arrest 25, 262, 263, 334
——, Cycles . . . 338
——, Experiments . . 643
——, Hackney carriages . 340
——, Offences 315 *et seq.* 671 *et seq.*
——, ——, Fixed penalties 332
——, ——, Previous convictions . . 319
——, Police powers 308 *et seq.*, 334 *et seq.*
——, Prosecution and punishments 315 *et seq.*, 671 *et seq.*

PAGE

Road Traffic, Traffic regulation . 250 *et seq.*
Robbery . . 167, 700
——, Mails . . 168, 377
Rodeo 486
Rogue and Vagabond . 389
——, Indecency . . 128
——, Loiterers, etc. 389, 390, 406, 407
Ropes, Road . . . 248
Rout 228
Rubbish, Road . . 246
Rules, Judges' . . 70

Sabotage . . . 210
Safety, Place of . 138, 143
Sailors 380
(*see also* Merchant Shipping Acts and Seamen)
Sale, Firearms 459, 468, 473
——, Intoxicants . 558, 565
——, Mock Auction . 434
Salmon 199
Salvage Corps . . 643
Satisfactory evidence . 82
Schools,
——, Attendance . . 145
——, Crossing Patrols . 328
——, Interviewing child . 74
Scooter, Motor . . 359
Scotland,
——, Theft from mails . 168
——, Warrants . 49, 53
Scrap Metal, Children 141, 156, **428**
——, Dealers . . 426 *et seq.*
Sea Fishing industry . 200
Seals, Close season . . 500
——, Conservation . 20, 500
——, Firearms . 500, 501
——, Forfeiture . . 501
——, Licences . . 501
——, Offences . . 500
——, ——, Arrest . 20, 501
——, ——, Attempts . 501
——, Poisoning . 500, 501
——, Protection . . 500
Sealskin, Forfeiture . 501
——, Seizure . . . 500
Seamen, Canteens . . 568
——, Merchant shipping . 380
——, Uniforms . . 423
Search, Accused . . 17
——, Birds, protection . 495

PAGE
Search, Drugs . . 576
——, Firearms . . 474
——, Poaching . . 195
——, Prevention of terrorism 208, 209
——, Prisoner . . 17
——, Public stores . . 193
——, Ship . . . 209
——, Woman . . . 209
Search warrant **55,** 118, 126
——, Aerodrome . . 111
——, Aircraft . . 111
——, Betting and Gaming 515
——, Biological weapons . 207
——, Birds . . . 494
——, Children, for 118, 126, 143
——, Clubs . . . 568
——, Coinage offences . 184
——, Criminal damage . 177
——, Disaffection . . 425
——, Excise . . 374, 544
——, Explosive 56, 57, 116, 448
——, Females, for . . 118
——, Firearms . . 474
——, Forgery . . 184
——, Harmful Publications 153
——, Licensing Acts 555, 562
——, Obscene articles . 130
——, Offences, 1861 Act . 116
——, Official Secrets Acts **56, 212**
——, Operations on animals 484
——, Organisations . 231
——, Petroleum . . 450
——, Prevention of terrorism 208, 299
——, Property, H.M. Forces 422
——, Prostitution . . 118
——, Public Order Act . 231
——, Scrap metal dealers 429
——, Securities . . 434
——, Sexual offences 118, 126
——, Smuggling . . 386
——, Vivisection . . 484
——, Wireless . . 379
——, Wrecks . . . 194
Searchlights . . . 281
Seasonal licence . . 556
Seat belts (Motors) . 643 *et seq.*
——, Anchorage points . 645
Seating capacity . 340, 350
Secondary evidence . 86

PAGE
Securities, dealers in . 432
——, Execution, deception 170
——, Suppression, etc. . 170
Security certificate . 307, 381
Sedition . . . 206
——, Libel . . 206, 238
Sentence, Appeal against . 64
——, Committal for (*see* Commitment)
——, Extended . . 405
——, Fixed by law . . 400
Servant, Domestic registries 432
——, Master and . . 418
Service, by post . 47, 49
——, Recorded delivery 47, 49, 90
Sessions, Licensing . 548 *et seq.*
Sexual intercourse 118 *et seq.*, 700
Sexual Offences Act 1967 39, 40, 133
Sexual offences . . 117
——, Character . . 94
——, Child's evidence . 35
——, Corroboration 83, 117, 119, 121
——, Hearsay evidence . 91
——, Homosexual acts, private . . . 133
Ship (*see* Vessel)
Shoeing smiths . . 417
Shops . . . 441 *et seq.*
——, Trading stamps . 444
Shot Gun 155, 459, 464, 466, 468, 478
——, Certificate . **459,** 464, 468
——, Child . 155, 467, 468
——, Conversion . . 460
——, Dealers . 462, 471, 473, 477
——, Personation . . 419
——, Public place . . 466
——, Testing . . . 478
Showmen's Trailers . **647,** 661
Sidecar, Construction and use . . . 647
——, Licence . . . 363
——, Lights . 282, 283, 284
Signs, Traffic . 267, 328–330
Silencers, Motors . **647,** 650
Silver, False trade description 439
——, Hall-marks . 438, 439
Similar offences, Evidence 94

PAGE

Singing licence . . . 537
——, Licenced premises 537, 548
Sirens . **605,** 629, 641, 643
Slander 238
Slaughter, Animals 462, 485, 488, 496
—— ——, Knackers . 497
Sleeping out . . . 391, 407
Smoke, Chimneys . . . 573
——, Motor Vehicles 270, **648** 650
Smoking, Carbon Disulphide 456
——, Celluloid, etc. . 455
——, Juveniles 141, **144,** 156
——, Opium . . . 576
——, Petrol conveyance . 452
——, P.S. vehicles . . 348
Smuggling 386
Snow Clearance . . . 366
Social Security Offences, Documents . . 435
——, Evidence . 85, 435
Soliciting . 117 *et seq.*, 132
Solicitor 416
——, Communicating with 73, 76
Sovereign, The . . . 10
——, Foreign . . . 10
——, Treason . . . 205
Sparrows 495
Special Constable . . . 415
——, Aviation . . . 380
——, Disaffection, etc. . 222
——, Personating . . 415
Special Hours Certificate 553, 554, 556, 568
Special Reasons (motors) 301, **303**
Special Type of Motor Vehicles . . . 663
Speeches in court . . . 42
Speed limits 330–332, 589 *et seq.*
——, Exemptions . . . 332
——, Indicator, Motors . 666
——, Offences . . . 331
——, Special types . . 666
——, Time-tables . . . 331
Speedometer 648
Spirits, Hawking . 431, 560
——, Methylated . . . 570
Spiritualism 392

PAGE

Sports, Firearms . . 463
Spring guns, etc, . 201, 700
Springs, Motors . . 649
Spying . . . 209, 210
Squirrels, Grey . . 496
Stage Carriages . . 339
(*see also* Public service vehicles)
Stage Coaches . 329 *et seq.*
Stage Plays . . 527 *et seq.*
Stallion horses . . 486
Stamps, Forgery . . 185
——, Post Office . . 376
——, Trading . . 444
Starlings 495
Starting Device, Vehicle . 648
Statement, Administrative directions . 74–76
——, Child's . . 35, 74
——, False . . 218–221
—— ——, Company directors . . . 170
——, Foreigner . . . 75
——, Incriminating, copy 72, 73
——, Injured persons 77, 80
——, Judges' Rules 70 *et seq.*
——, Material . . 219
——, Perjury . . 219
——, Voluntary . . 73
——, Written, evidence 35, 40, 86, **87,** 220
Statute 4
—— Law 4
Statutory assaults . . 106
Statutory Instruments . 5
Stealing (*see also* Theft)
——, Going equipped for 172
Steam vehicles . . 649
Steering gear, Motors 270, 650
Stipendiary Magistrate . 32
Stolen Goods, Blackmail, obtained by . . 171
——, Deception, Obtained by . . . 171
——, Evidence . . 94
——, Guilty knowledge . 171
——, Handling 89, 171, 699
——, ——, Evidence . 94
——, H.M. Forces . 421, 422
——, Police Property Act 188
——, Public stores . . 193
——, Restitution . . 190

PAGE

Stolen Goods, Rewards for . 26, 171
——, Scope of offences . 171
Stones, Throwing, Street . 246
Stop lamp . . . 291
Stores, Public . **193,** 421
——, Requisitioning . 424
Straddle carrier . **650,** 664
Stray Animals . . 250
—— Dogs . . . 490
Street
(*see also* Highways, Road)
——, Betting . . 20, 507
——, Children Acts . 138
——, Collections . . 392
——, Definition . . 243
——, Indecency . 127 *et seq.*
——, Nuisances and obstruction . . 244 *et seq.*
——, Playgrounds . . 328
——, Refuge . . . 327
——, Trading . . 146
——, Traffic regulation . 250
Strikes 229
Strychnine . . . 484
Stupefying (*see* Drugging)
Subornation of perjury . 220
Subpoena 49
Suffocating, Assault . 108
——, Child . . 140, 153
Suicide . . . **114,** 143
——, Aiding and Abetting **115,** 143, 587, 670
——, Prosecutions . . 670
Summary, Case procedure 41
——, Court . . 30, 32, 33
——, Offences 6, 7, **30,** 136, 163, 167–171
——, ——, Conspiracy to commit . . 237
——, Limitation . . 67
——, Trial . . 39–41
——, Uttering Offences 184, 185
Summons . . . 45
——, Ignorance of . . 46
——, Information . . 45
——, Justices' clerks, by . 701
——, Service . . . 47
——, Witness . . 49
Sunday, Billiards . . 539
——, Child employment . 146
——, Entertainments 532, 540
——, Game laws . . 198
——, Gaming . . 522

PAGE

Sunday, Inquests . . 585
——, Observance 442, 443, 532 539, 540
——, Occasional licence . 545
——, Permitted hours 552–555
——, Shops . . 442, 443
——, Theatre . . 532
——, Wales . . 545, 554
——, Warrant, execution 52, 55
Supervision . . 401 *et seq.*
——, Borstal . . . 404
——, Detention Centre . 151
——, Released prisoner . 152
Supervision order, Care proceedings . 145
Supplementary Benefit . 390
Sureties, Bail . . . 60
——, Contempt of court . 217
——, Good behaviour 225, 226
——, Peace . . 225, 226
——, Recognizance . 58
Suspected persons . 390, **406**
——, Arrest . 27, 406, 407
——, Statements . . 70
Sweets (*see* British Wine)
Swine, Slaughter . . 496
Sworn, Lawfully . . 219
System, Evidence . . 94

Table Meal . . . 546
Taking motors . 167, 334
Tampering with motors . 265
Tank Wagons and Tank Trailers . . 453
Tanks 663
Tattooing, Minors . 153, 159
Taxicabs . . 339 *et seq.*
Telegraph . . . 378
——, Accused's right to . 76
——, Official Secrets Act 211
Telepathy . . . 392
Telephone . . 376, 377
——, Accused's right to . 76
——, Obscene matter . 377
Television, Licensed premises . 537, 548
——, Motor Vehicle . 650
Tenant 414
——, Brothels . 125, 414
——, Harassment . 233–234
Tents 574
——, Hawkers . . 431
——, Highways . . 248
Territorial Army . . 421

PAGE

Terrorism, Acts of . 25, 209
——, Arrest . . . 208
——, Documents . . 209
——, Exclusion order 25, 208
——, Prevention . 25, 208
——, Suspicion . . 25
Testing Bicycles . . 338
——, Eyesight . 297, 335
——, Vehicles 268, 269, 270, 650
——, ——, Certificates 269
Theatres . . . 529
——, Censorship, abolition 529
——, Entry and inspection 532
——, Firearms . . 463
——, Ingress and egress . 539
——, Intoxicating liquor . 532
——, Licensing . 530, 532
——, Sunday Observance 532
——, Young Person in bar 558
Theatrical Employers . 533
Theft . . . 164 *et seq.*
——, Animals . 26, 165
——, Appropriates, meaning 165
——, Arrest . . . 26
——, Bankruptcy offences 174
——, Belonging to another, meaning . . 167
——, Carcase . . . 166
——, Collection, from . 167
——, Company, False statements . . 170
——, Compensation for damage . . 174
——, ——, Liability . 170
——, Deception . . 168
(*see also* Deception)
——, Deer . . 26, 173
——, Dishonestly, meaning 164
——, Documents, suppression, etc. . . 170
——, Electricity . . 168
——, False accounting . 169
——, ——, statements . 170
——, Fish . . 26, 173
——, Flowers . . 165
——, Fruit . . . 165
——, Going equipped for stealing . 26, 172
——, Goods in transit . 89
——, Husband and wife . 84
——, Intention . . 166
——, Land . . . 165
——, Motor vehicles 167, 334

PAGE

Theft, Mushrooms . . 165
——, Pecuniary advantage, obtaining by deception . . . 169
——, Places open to public 167
——, Property, Meaning . 165
——, ——, Obtaining by deception . . 168
——, Robbery . . 167
——, Things growing wild 165
——, Wild creatures . 165
Therapists . . . 416
Third Party motor insurances 305 *et seq.*
Threats and menaces 109, 700
——, Arrest . . . 18
——, Criminal damage 176, 698
——, Forcible entry . 229
——, Letters . . . 109
——, Sureties . . 226
Threshing machines . 664
Title to land, Assault . 107
Tobacco, Children 141, 144, 157
——, Hawking . . 431
——, Licensed premises . 548
Tokyo Convention . 213, 385
Totalisator . . . 510
(*see also* Betting)
——, Board 504, 505, 510, 511
——, Meaning . . 516
Tower wagon . . 366, **651**
Towing vehicles 276, 326, **651**
——, Broken-down **627,** 653, 657
——, Speed limits 589 *et seq.*, 596, 597
——, Weight . . 596, 597
Towrope, Motors . . 651
Town Police Clauses Act 1847, Arrest . 26
——, Driver's offences . 251
——, Hackney carriages 337
——, Nuisances . 245–247
Tracklaying vehicles 592, 594, 663
Tracks, Betting . 503 *et seq.*
——, Bookmakers . . 510
——, Meaning . . 510
——, Occupier . . 510
——, Pool Betting . . 505
——, Restriction 504, 505, 506
——, Totalisators . 510, 516
Tractor 322
——, Age for driving . 254

PAGE
Tractor, Brakes . . 610
——, Construction and use 610, **638**
——, Drivers . 254, 255, 304
——, ——, Hours . 353, 354
——, Industrial . . 631
——, Land . 601, 610, **632**
——, Plates . . . 640
Trade 436
——, Descriptions . . 438
——, ——, Vehicles . 608
——, Disputes . . 229
——, Licences, Motor 360, 367 *et seq.*
—— Marks . . . 437
—— ——, Forgery . . 185
——, Offensive . . 573
——, Plates . . 368, 369
——, Stamps . . . 444
——, Unions . . . 229
Trading Representation . 444
Trading Stamps . . 444
Traffic Areas . . . 342
——, Commissioners . 342
——, Dangerous driving . 252
——, Definition . . 336
——, Directions . . 329
——, Drivers' rules 251 *et seq.*
——, Highway Code . 267
——, Indicators . . 291
——, Laws, enforcement . 334
——, Licensing Authority P.S.V. . 343 *et seq.*
——, Lights . . . 320
——, Regulation . 250, 325
——, ——, Special cases . 325
——, Restriction . . 325
——, Signs . . 267, 328
——, Survey . . . 250
——, Ticket system . 332
——, Wardens . 251, 332
Trailers 267, 278, 352, 353, 620, **652**
——, Additional reflectors 289
——, Age for driving 159, 160, 255, 256
——, Agricultural . . 602
——, Attendants . 266, 652
——, Braked . . . 597
——, Brakes . . 620 *et seq.*
——, Gas . . 629, 653
——, Glider . . . 593
——, Learner driver . 304
——, Length . . 634, 652

PAGE
Trailers, Lights 276, 278, 289
——, Load carrying . 593
——, Number . . 652
——, Obstruction . . 653
——, Opening door . 640
——, Plate . 596, 640, **654**
——, Petroleum . . 453
——, Prohibitions . . 652
——, Rear markings . 292
——, Registration mark . 365
——, Showmen's . 647, 671
——, Speed Limits 589 *et seq.*, 596, 597
——, Straddle carrier . 650
——, Trade Licences . 370
——, Tyres . . 653, 656
——, Unbraked . . 597
——, Weight . 596, 597, 653
——, Width . . . 653
Tramcars . 324, 337, 355
——, Accidents . . 265
——, Driving offences . 254
——, Lights . . . 271
Transport Commission . 379
Traps, Animals . . 483
——, Birds . . . 494
——, Man . . . 201
Treason . . 8, **205,** 700
——, Bail . . . 60
——, Compounding. . 14
——, Indictable offence . 7
Treasure trove . 187, 584
——, Coroner's Court . 31
——, Inquest . . 584
Treating at elections . 223
Trees, Carriage . . 654
Trespass . . . 200
——, Aerodrome . . 380
——, Armed . . . 466
——, Burglary . . 163
——, Firearms . . 466
——, Forcible entry . 229
——, Meetings . . 235
——, Military camp . 420
——, Poaching . 195, 196
——, Railways . . 379
Trial by Jury . 36 *et seq.*
——, Committal . . 58
——, Indictable offence . 37
——, Jury claim . 7, 31, 40, 41
——, Progress . . 38
——, Summary . 39–41
(*see also* Summary)

PAGE

Wild animals, Criminal damage . . . 178
——, Theft 165
Wild birds 492
(*see also* Birds)
Wilful act 5
Will, Forgery 184
——, Suppression, etc. . 170
Windscreen, Licence . 363
——, Washers . . . 662
——, Wiper 662
Wings, Motors . . . 662
Wireless 378
——, Extra-territorial . 379
——, Official Secrets Acts 211
Witness . . . 81 *et seq.*
——, Accomplice . 13, 83
——, Allowances . . 69
——, Arrest privilege . 86
——, Child 35
——, Competency . 82, 84, **85**
——, Corrupt practice . 223
——, Credibility . . 82
——, Cross-examination . 98
——, Dangerously ill . 79
——, Deposition . 78, 79
——, Examination . 82, 96
——, Explosives offences 447
——, Hostile 97
——, Husband and wife 83–86, 118, 132, 134, 214
——, Insane . . 79, 85
——, Interference with 86, 216
——, In prison . . 86
——, Inquests . 585, 586
——, Number of . . 83
——, Order . . 34, 78, 79
——, Out of court . 42, **85**
——, Perfect . . . 102

PAGE

Witness, Perjury . 83, 218
——, Personation case . 83, 222
——, Privilege . 86, **95**
——, Re-examination . 99
——, Recalling . 82, **99**
——, Refreshing memory 97
——, Subpoena . . 49
——, Summons . 46, 48, 49
——, Unwilling . . 97
——, Warrant . 46, 49
Witness, Order, Attend trial 34, 78
——, Conditional . 34, 78, 79
——, Contempt . . 217
——, Deposition . 78, 79
Witness Summons 46, 48, 49
——, Contempt . . 217
Woman, Search . . 209
Work Ticket, P.S.V. . 342
Works Trucks . 359, **662**
——, Registration mark . 365
Wounding . . . 108
——, Arrest . . . 18
Wrecks 184
Written Statements, Evidence 35, 40, 86, **87**, 220

Young person . 135 *et seq.*
(*see also* Children)
——, Betting . . . 510
——, Finger prints . . 149
——, Indictable offence 39, 40
Youthful Offenders, Punishment . . . 151
——, Treatment . . 148

Zebra Crossings . 326, 327

Printed in Great Britain by
Butler & Tanner Ltd, Frome and London

PAGE

Vehicles, Owner . 310, 311
——, Parking (*see* Parking)
——, Passenger . 336, 630
——, Petrol conveying . 452
——, Plates . . . 640
——, Police . 290, 334, 605, **641**
——, Public service (*see* Public service vehicles)
——, Railway . . 642
——, Rear markings . 292
——, Refuse . . . 642
——, Registration . 359 *et seq.*
——, Regulation of traffic 250 *et seq.*
——, Removal . . 326
——, Requisitioning . 424
——, Road cleansing 290, 291, **642,** 660
——, —— repair . 290, 643
——, ——, Rollers . . 643
——, Special types . . 663
——, Speed limits 330–332, 589
——, Standing . 252, 264
——, Steering gear . . 650
——, Testing . . 268–270
——, Theft . . . 167
——, Towing . 276, 326, **651**
——, Tracklaying 592, 594, 663
——, Unroadworthy . 270
——, Works . . . 662
Venue 50
Verdict . . . 38, 63
——, Coroner's Jury 585–587
Verge, Parking on . . 267
Verminous Articles . . 574
Vessels, Burglary . . 163
——, Drugs, search for . 578
——, Drunkenness . . 564
——, Explosives . . 448
——, Firearms . . 464
——, Foreign enlistment . 214
——, Gaming on . . 519
——, Merchant Shipping . 380
——, ——, Passengers . 380
——, Petrol . . . 449
——, Piracy . . . 212
Veterinary surgeons . 417
——, Animal boarding establishments . 500
——, Riding establishments 498
View from motors . . 659
Visting Forces
——, Lights, Vehicles . 289

PAGE

Vivisection, Animals . 484
Voters (*see* Election offences)

Wagers (*see* Betting)
Wagons . . . 251
(*see also* Carts)
Wales, Permitted Hours 545, 554
——, Theft from mails . 168
Wandering, Found . . 407
——, with Child . . 141
War Charities . . 585
Warning Instrument 338, **604** *et seq.*
Warning, of Prosecution . 253, 254, 331
Warrants . . . 51
(*see also* Search warrants)
——, Arrest with . 27, 53
——, Arrest without 18 *et seq.*
——, Arrestable offence . 53
——, Bail . . . 61
——, Commitment . 53, 54, 57
——, Detention . 58, 118
——, Distress . . 54
——, Information . . 44
——, Letter, etc. . . 377
——, Mental Patients . 581
——, Probation . . 402
——, Prostitution, trading 118
——, Sexual Offences . 126
Waste, Poisonous . . 587
Waste land . . . 201
Water Bailiffs. . . 199
——, Strikes . . . 230
Weapons, Biological . 207
——, Offensive 25, 163, 232, 390, 407, **409,** 460, 466
——, ——, Meaning . 409
——, ——, Prohibited . 460
——, ——, Public meeting 232
——, ——, Restriction . 409
Weight, motor vehicles 308, 323, 325, 335, 596, 597, **659**
——, Invalid carriage . 631
——, Unladen . 322, 659
Weights and measures . 440
——, Intoxicants . 544, **599**
Wheelbarrow, Lights . 290
Wheels, Motors . . 660
Whipping . . . 8
White slave traffic . . 121
Width, Motors . . 661
Wife (*see* Husband and wife)

PAGE

Tricycle (*see also* Bicycle)
——, Licence, position . 363
——, Lighting . . 274
——, Motor . . . 359
Trolley vehicles 324, 350, 355
——, Passengers . . 350
Trout 199
Trust property, Criminal damage . . 178
Two-Tone Horn **604,** 629, 641, 643
Tyres, Motor 590, 591, 592, 593, **655**
——, ——, Condition and maintenance 657
——, ——, Recut 656, 657, 658
——, ——, Testing . 270
——, Trailer . . 653, 656

Unburied carcases . . 491
Undue influence, Elections 223
Uniforms . . . 422
——, Irish Republican Army 231
——, Official Secrets Acts 211
——, Police . . . 415
——, Political 209, 230, 231
——, Proscribed organisation . . 208, 231
United Kingdom . 410, 411
Unlawful assembly . . 227
——, Drilling . . 206
Unlawful possession, Pensioner's Papers . 422
——, Property, H.M. Forces 422
(*see also* Possession)
Unnatural crimes . . 132
——, Limitation of proceedings . . 132
——, Mental patient 120, 133
——, Private, consent . 133
Unsound mind 8, 579 *et seq.*
Unwilling witness . . 97
Urinals . . . 129, 171
Urine test 90, 257, 259, 260, 261
——, Driver, Alcohol limit 90, 257, 259, 260, 261
Uttering, Coin . 179, 180
——, Forgery . . 184
——, Summary trial . 185
——, Threatening letter . 109

Vagabonds . . . 389

PAGE

Vagrancy . . . 389
——, Arrest . . 27, 380
——, Begging . . 390
——, Children . . 141
——, Frauds . . 391
——, Idle and disorderly 389
——, Incorrigible rogues . 390
——, Loiterers . 390, 406
——, Rogues and vagabonds 389
Vapour 270
Vehicles . . 336 *et seq.*
(*see also* Motor Vehicles)
——, Abandoned . . 326
——, Abroad, from . 290
——, Alteration . . 361
——, Authorised . . 355
——, Bicycle (*see* Bicycle)
——, Brakes **605** *et seq.*, 650
——, Break-down . . 290
——, Broken down 317, **627,** 653, 657
——, Carriages (*see* Carriages)
——, Construction and use 268, **599** *et seq.*
——, Crown . . 319–321
——, Dangerous . . 637
——, Dangerous driving . 252
——, Destruction, etc. . 362
——, Drugs, search for . 578
——, Drunkenness 256 *et seq.*, 563, 564
——, Dual Purpose 352, 589, 592, **628**
——, Fire . . . 629
——, Firearms, search for 475
——, Foreign . 373, 374
——, Forestry Commission 290, 605, 629
——, Gaming on . . 519
——, Gas propelled . 629
——, Goods **341** *et seq.*, 613, 629
——, ——, Brakes . . 623
——, ——, Identity discs 353
——, Hackney carriage . 339
——, Heavy Goods . 356
——, Licensing, Motors 359 *et seq.*
——, Lifting appliances . 634
——, Lighting . 270 *et seq.*
——, Mechanically propelled . . 359
——, Obstruction . 244 *et seq.*, 326, **639**